Fodor's 98

Italy

[handwritten notes:]
Venice
CIPRIANI
outdoor casual
dining
Homemade Pasta &
ch. gelato
by garden on Road
CIPS

The complete guide, thoroughly up-to-date

Packed with details that will make your trip

The must-see sights, off and on the beaten path

What to see, what to skip

Mix-and-match vacation itineraries

City strolls, countryside adventures

Smart lodging and dining options

Essential local do's and taboos

Transportation tips, distances and directions

Key contacts, savvy travel tips

When to go, what to pack

Clear, accurate, easy-to-use maps

Books to read, videos to watch, background essays

Fodor's Travel Publications, Inc.
New York • Toronto • London • Sydney • Auckland
www.fodors.com/

Fodor's Italy

EDITOR: Caragh Rockwood

Editorial Contributors: Robert Andrews, Barbara Walsh Angelillo, Barbara Lazear Ascher, David Brown, Sheila Brownlee, Nancy Coons, Giuliano Davenport, Laura M. Kidder, Jennifer Paull, Heida Sarna, Helayne Schiff, M. T. Schwartzman (Gold Guide editor), Dinah A. Spritzer

Editorial Production: Tracy Patruno

Maps: David Lindroth, *cartographer;* Steven K. Amsterdam, *map editor*

Design: Fabrizio La Rocca, *art director;* Guido Caroti, *associate art director;* Jolie Novak, *photo editor*

Production/Manufacturing: Mike Costa

Cover Photograph: Angelo Lomeo

Copyright

Special Sales

CONTENTS

ON THE ROAD WITH FODOR'S

WE'RE ALWAYS THRILLED to get letters from readers, especially one like this:

It took us an hour to decide what book to buy and we now know we picked the best one. Your book was wonderful, easy to follow, very accurate, and good on pointing out eating places, informal as well as formal. When we saw other people using your book, we would look at each other and smile.

Our editors and writers are deeply committed to making every Fodor's guide "the best one"—not only accurate but always charming, brimming with sound recommendations and solid ideas, right on the mark in describing restaurants and hotels, and full of fascinating facts that make you view what you've traveled to see in a rich new light.

About Our Writers

Our success in achieving our goals—and in helping to make your trip the best of all possible vacations—is a credit to the hard work of our extraordinary writers. Amid the shops along Rome's Via Condotti, inside the *trattorie* of Trieste, and at the latest art exhibitions in Venice, you'll find Barbara Walsh Angelillo, Robert Andrews, and Giuliano Davenport studying the sights and sleuthing like undercover agents.

The first time that **Barbara Walsh Angelillo** arrived in Rome, she was traveling on a tight schedule; still, she had time to fall in love with both the city and a dark-eyed Italian—simultaneously. Well aware that this was one of the hazards of touring Italy, she kept to her schedule and left Rome after only three days. Within a year, however, Barbara said *arrivederci* to her native New York City to settle, marry, and raise three children in Italy. As a freelance travel writer and editor, she loves to share her expertise about Italy with readers, and she has been doing so—mostly covering the regions of Rome, Florence, Tuscany, Liguria, and Piedmont—for Fodor's for more than 30 years. She also is associate editor of the glossy, bimonthly, English-language magazine, *Italy Italy,* which is published in Rome and distributed in the United States and elsewhere. To unwind, Barbara vacations in what she calls "two of Italy's most special places," Umbria and the Amalfi Coast.

Robert Andrews has familial roots in Sicily and has been wedded to Italy (the south of the country in particular) for most of his life. Though based in Bristol, England, where he pursues a parallel career as an anthologist of quotations, Robert visits the old boot annually and leaves ever more enlightened and exhilarated. In addition to covering Emilia-Romagna, Umbria, Campania, Apulia, Sicily, and Sardinia for us, he has written for many publications and coauthored books on Sardinia and Sicily.

Although born in Ireland, **Giuliano Davenport** gives away his Italian roots at the mere mention of his name. From his base in Dublin—where he works as a tour guide and is training to be an architect—he has covered Venice, the Venetian Arc, the Dolomites, and Milan, Lombardy, and the Lakes—all the while visiting friends and family scattered throughout the peninsula.

After testing her palate as a restaurant reviewer for *Chicago Magazine,* **Nancy Coons** moved to Europe in 1987; based in her 300-year-old farmhouse in Lorraine, she has written about European culture and food for the *Wall Street Journal, European Travel & Life, Opera News,* and *National Geographic Traveler.* In addition to her new essay, "The Artless Art of Italian Cooking," she has critiqued Swiss fondue, Luxembourg ham, Belgian *frites,* and quiche of northeastern France for Fodor's. Her travels in Italy have always been equally divided among churches, museums, and the kitchens of native friends.

New This Year

Barbara Walsh Angelillo has mapped out two new foodie- and garden-friendly Great Itineraries in Chapter 1. A Gourmet Tour starts with sumptuous *gianduiotti* chocolates in Piedmont and winds down with the robust reds of Chianti. The Italian Gardens Tour explores luxurious gardens in the Lake District and former Medici villas around Florence, some of which are detailed in our new Side Trip from Florence in Chapter 3. And Nancy Coons recalls savoring Italy's earthy *cucina* and *vino* in her new Portraits of Italy essay, "The Artless Art of Cooking."

Also this year, Fodor's joins Rand McNally, the world's largest commercial mapmaker, to bring you a detailed color map of Italy. Just detach it along the perforation, and drop it in your tote bag.

We're also proud to announce that the American Society of Travel Agents has endorsed Fodor's as its guidebook of choice. ASTA is the world's largest and most influential travel trade association, operating in more than 170 countries, with 27,000 members pledged to adhere to a strict code of ethics reflecting the Society's motto, "Integrity in Travel." ASTA shares Fodor's devotion to providing smart, honest travel information and advice to travelers, and we've long recommended that our readers consult ASTA member agents for the experience and professionalism they bring to the table.

On the Web, check out Fodor's site (www.fodors.com/) for information on major destinations around the world and travel-savvy interactive features. The Web site also lists the 80-plus radio stations nationwide that carry the Fodor's Travel Show, a live radio call-in program that airs every weekend. Tune in to hear guests discuss their wonderful adventures—or call in to get answers for your most pressing travel questions.

How to Use This Book

Organization

Up front is the **Gold Guide,** an easy-to-use section divided alphabetically by topic. Under each listing you'll find tips and information that will help you accomplish what you need to in Italy. You'll also find addresses and telephone numbers of organizations and companies that offer destination-related services and detailed information and publications.

The first chapter in the guide, **Destination: Italy,** helps get you in the mood for your trip. New and Noteworthy cues you in to trends and happenings, What's Where gets you oriented, Pleasures and Pastimes describes activities and sights that really

make Italy unique, Great Itineraries suggests some stellar tours, Fodor's Choice showcases our top picks, and Festivals and Seasonal Events alerts you to special events you'll want to seek out.

Chapters in *Italy '98* are arranged in order of tourist interest, cities first. Each **city chapter** begins with an Exploring section, which is subdivided by neighborhood; each subsection recommends a walking or driving tour and lists sights in alphabetical order. Each **regional chapter** is divided by geographical area; within each area, towns are covered in logical geographical order, and attractive stretches of road and minor points of interest between them are indicated by the designation *En Route*. Throughout, Off the Beaten Path sights appear after the places from which they are most easily accessible. And within town sections, all restaurants and lodging are grouped together.

To help you decide what to visit in the time you have, all chapters begin with **recommended itineraries;** you can mix and match those from several chapters to create a complete vacation. The **A-to-Z section** that ends all chapters covers getting there and getting around. It also provides helpful contacts and resources.

At the end of the book you'll find **Portraits,** with a chronology, wonderful essays about the food and art/architecture in Italy, a helpful art glossary, and recommended reading and videos with Italy as a backdrop. The **Italian Vocabulary** will also come in handy.

Icons and Symbols

★	Our special recommendations
✕	Restaurant
🏠	Lodging establishment
✕🏠	Lodging establishment whose restaurant warrants a detour
☺	Good for kids (rubber duckie)
☞	Sends you to another section of the guide for more information
✉	Address
☎	Telephone number
☉	Opening and closing times
💲	Admission prices (those we give apply only to adults; substantially reduced fees are almost always available for children, students, and senior citizens)

Numbers in white and black circles that appear on the maps, in the margins, and within the tours correspond to one another.

Dining and Lodging

The restaurants and lodgings we list are the cream of the crop in each price range. Price charts appear in the Pleasures and Pastimes section that follows each chapter introduction.

Hotel Facilities

We always list the facilities that are available—but we don't specify whether they cost extra: when pricing accommodations, always ask what's included. In addition, assume that all rooms have private baths unless otherwise noted.

Assume that hotels operate on the **European Plan** (EP, with no meals) unless we note that they use the **Full American Plan** (FAP, with all meals), the **Modified American Plan** (MAP, with breakfast and dinner daily), or the **Continental Plan** (CP, with a Continental breakfast daily).

Restaurant Reservations and Dress Codes

Reservations are always a good idea; we note only when they're essential or when they are not accepted. Book as far ahead as you can, and reconfirm when you get to town. Unless otherwise noted, the restaurants listed are open daily for lunch and dinner. We mention dress only when men are required to wear a jacket or a jacket and tie. Look for an overview of local habits in the Pleasures and Pastimes section that follows each chapter introduction.

Credit Cards

The following abbreviations are used: **AE,** American Express; **DC,** Diners Club; **MC,** MasterCard; and **V,** Visa.

Don't Forget to Write

You can use this book in the confidence that all prices and opening times are based on information supplied to us at press time; Fodor's cannot accept responsibility for any errors. Time inevitably brings changes, so always confirm information when it matters—especially if you're making a detour to visit a specific place. In addition, when making reservations be sure to mention if you have a disability or are traveling with children, if you prefer a private bath or a certain type of bed, or if you have specific dietary needs or any other concerns.

Were the restaurants we recommended as described? Did our hotel picks exceed your expectations? Did you find a museum we recommended a waste of time? If you have complaints, we'll look into them and revise our entries when the facts warrant it. If you've discovered a special place that we haven't included, we'll pass the information along to our correspondents and have them check it out. So send us your feedback, positive *and* negative: email us at editors@fodors.com (specifying the name of the book on the subject line), or write to the Italy editor at Fodor's, 201 East 50th Street, New York, New York 10022. Have a wonderful trip!

Karen Cure
Editorial Director

Italy

Europe

SMART TRAVEL TIPS A TO Z

Basic Information on Traveling in Italy, Savvy Tips to Make Your Trip a Breeze, and Companies and Organizations to Contact

A
AIR TRAVEL

MAJOR AIRLINE OR LOW-COST CARRIER?

Most people choose a flight based on price. Yet there are other issues to consider. Major airlines offer the greatest number of departures; smaller airlines—including regional, low-cost and no-frill airlines—usually have a more limited number of flights daily. Major airlines have frequent-flyer partners, which allow you to credit mileage earned on one airline to your account with another. Low-cost airlines offer a definite price advantage and fewer restrictions, such as advance-purchase requirements. Safetywise, low-cost carriers as a group have a good history, but **check the safety record before booking** any low-cost carrier; call the Federal Aviation Administration's Consumer Hotline (☞ Airline Complaints, *below*).

➤ MAJOR AIRLINES: **Alitalia** (☎ 800/223–5730) to Rome, Milan, and Venice. **American Airlines** (☎ 800/433–7300) to Milan. **Continental Airlines** (☎ 800/231–0856) to Rome and Milan. **Delta Air Lines** (☎ 800/241–4141) to Rome and Milan. **Northwest Airlines** (☎ 800/225–2525) to Milan. **TWA** (☎ 800/892–4141) to Rome and Milan. **United Airlines** (☎ 800/538–2929) to Milan. **US Airways** (☎ 800/428–4322) to Rome.

➤ FROM THE U.K.: Direct service from Heathrow is provided by **Alitalia** (☎ 0171/602–7111 or 0990/448–259) and **British Airways** (☎ 0345/222–111). From Manchester there are one or two direct flights daily to Milan, and at least three weekly to Rome. Privately run **Meridiana** (☎ 0171/839–2222) has direct flights between London and Olbia on Sardinia on Tuesday and Saturday in summer, and daily flights to Cagliari via Florence throughout the year.

Lower-priced charter flights to a range of Italian destinations are available throughout the year.

GET THE LOWEST FARE

The least-expensive airfares to Italy are priced for round-trip travel. Major airlines usually require that you **book far in advance and stay at least seven days** and no more than 30 to get the lowest fares. Ask about "ultrasaver" fares, the cheapest; they must be booked 90 days in advance and are nonrefundable. A little more expensive are "supersaver" fares, which require only a 30-day advance purchase. Remember that penalties for refunds or scheduling changes are stiffer for international tickets, usually about $150. International flights are also sensitive to the season: **plan to fly in the off season** for the cheapest fares. If your destination or home city has more than one gateway, **compare prices to and from different airports.** Also price off-peak-hour flights, which may be significantly less expensive.

To save money on flights from the United Kingdom and back, **look into an APEX or Super-PEX ticket.** APEX tickets must be booked in advance and have certain restrictions. Super-PEX tickets can be purchased at the airport on the day of departure—subject to availability.

DON'T STOP UNLESS YOU MUST

When you book, **look for nonstop flights and remember that "direct" flights stop at least once.** International flights on a country's flag carrier are almost always nonstop; U.S. airlines often fly direct. Try to **avoid connecting flights,** which require a change of planes. Two airlines may jointly operate a connecting flight, so ask if your airline operates every segment—you may find that your preferred carrier flies you only part of the way.

USE AN AGENT

Travel agents, especially those who specialize in finding the lowest fares (☞ Discounts & Deals, *below*), can be especially helpful when booking a plane ticket. When you're quoted a price, **ask your agent if the price is likely to get any lower.** Good agents know the seasonal fluctuations of airfares and can usually anticipate a sale or fare war. However, waiting can be risky: the fare could go *up* as seats become scarce, and you may wait so long that your preferred flight sells out. A wait-and-see strategy works best if your plans are flexible, but if you must arrive and depart on certain dates, don't delay.

CHECK WITH CONSOLIDATORS

Consolidators buy tickets for scheduled flights at reduced rates from the airlines then sell them at prices that beat the best fare available directly from the airlines, usually without advance restrictions. Sometimes you can even get your money back if you need to return the ticket. Carefully read the fine print detailing penalties for changes and cancellations, and **confirm your consolidator reservation with the airline.**

➤ CONSOLIDATORS: United States Air Consolidators Association (✉ 925 L St., Suite 220, Sacramento, CA 95814, ☎ 916/441–4166, ℻ 916/441–3520).

AVOID GETTING BUMPED

Airlines routinely overbook planes, knowing that not everyone with a ticket will show up, but sometimes everyone does. When that happens, airlines ask for volunteers to give up their seats. In return these volunteers usually get a certificate for a free flight and are rebooked on the next flight out. If there are not enough volunteers the airline must choose who will be denied boarding. The first to get bumped are passengers who checked in late and those flying on discounted tickets, so **get to the gate and check in as early as possible,** especially during peak periods. Always **bring a photo ID to the airport.** You may be asked to show it before you are allowed to check in.

ENJOY THE FLIGHT

For more legroom, **request an emergency-aisle seat**; don't however, sit in the row in front of the emergency aisle or in front of a bulkhead, where seats may not recline. If you don't like airline food, **ask for special meals when booking.** These can be vegetarian, low-cholesterol, or kosher, for example.

To avoid jet lag try to maintain a normal routine while traveling. At night **get some sleep.** By day **eat light meals, drink water (not alcohol), and move about the cabin** to stretch your legs. Some carriers have prohibited smoking throughout their systems; others allow smoking only on certain routes or even certain departures from that route, so **contact your carrier regarding its smoking policy.**

COMPLAIN IF NECESSARY

If your baggage goes astray or your flight goes awry, **complain right away.** Most carriers require that you file a claim immediately.

➤ AIRLINE COMPLAINTS: U.S. Department of Transportation **Aviation Consumer Protection Division** (✉ C-75, Washington, DC 20590, ☎ 202/366–2220). **Federal Aviation Administration (FAA) Consumer Hotline** (☎ 800/322–7873).

WITHIN ITALY

Alitalia and its domestic affiliate ATI—in addition to smaller, privately run companies such as Meridiana and Air One—complete an extensive network of internal flights in Italy. Ask your domestic or Italian travel agent about discounts, which include a 50% family reduction and up to 30% off certain night flights.

➤ INFORMATION: **Alitalia** (☎ 06/65621 or 06/65643 for main Rome office; 02/62811 for main Milan office). **Meridiana** (☎ 0789/4745057 for main Olbia office). **Air One** (☎ 06/56386216 for main Rome office).

AIRPORTS & TRANSFERS

The major gateways to Italy include Rome's Leonardo da Vinci Airport, better known as Fiumicino, and Milan's Malpensa Airport. Flying time is 8½ hours from New York,

SMART TRAVEL TIPS / THE GOLD GUIDE

10–11 hours from Chicago, and 12–13 hours from Los Angeles. If you are going directly to Florence and landing at Rome's Fiumicino, you can make connections at the airport for a flight to Florence; you can also take the FS airport train to Rome's Termini Station, where fast trains for Florence are frequent during the day. Smaller, minor gateways (☞ *below*) are served by domestic and some international flights.

➤ MAJOR AIRPORT INFORMATION: Rome's **Leonardo da Vinci Airport or Fiumicino** (⊠ 30 km/19 mi southeast of Rome, ☎ 06/65953640). Milan's **Malpensa Airport** (☎ 02/38011172).

➤ MINOR AIRPORT INFORMATION: Milan's **Linate** (⊠ 10 km/6 mi east of Milan, ☎ 02/74852200). Venice's **Marco Polo** airport (⊠ Tessera, about 10 km [6 mi] north of Venice, ☎ 041/2609260). Florence's **A. Vespucci Airport,** called **Peretola** (⊠ 10 km [6 mi] northwest of Florence, ☎ 055/333498) and **Galileo Galilei Airport** (⊠ Pisa, 80 km [50 mi] west of Florence, ☎ 050/500707). Bologna's **Guglielmo Marconi** (⊠ Borgo Panigale, 7 km [4 mi] from Bologna, ☎ 051/6479615). Naples's **Capodichino Airport** (⊠ 8 km [5 mi] north of Naples, ☎ 081/7896111). Palermo's **Punta Raisi Airport** (⊠ 32 km [20 mi] west of Palermo, ☎ 091/591698).

B

BEACHES

Italy isn't the place for an exclusively beach holiday. With the exception of Sardinia, you'll find cleaner water and better beaches at lower prices in other parts of the world. The waters that are least polluted and best for swimming are in Sardinia (except around Cagliari, Arbatax, and Porto Torres); off portions of the coasts of Calabria and Apulia; and off the islands of Elba, Capri, Ischia, Ustica, the Aeolian group, and western Sicily. Topless bathing is widespread (though not always de rigueur), except for a few staid family-type beaches near large cities. Nudism is discreetly practiced on out-of-the-way beaches, mainly on the islands and on deserted stretches of the mainland coast. Singles will find the liveliest resorts on the Adriatic Coast and on the coasts of Tuscany and Calabria.

BOAT TRAVEL

Ferries connect the mainland with all major islands. There is frequent daily ferry and hydrofoil service between towns and lakes in the lake district. Car ferries operate to Sicily, Sardinia, Elba, Ponza, Capri, Ischia, the Lido near Venice, and other islands.

➤ FERRY LINES: **Tirrenia** (☎ 06/4814779 in Rome; 010/258041 in Genoa; 081/7613688 in Naples) operates ferries to Sicily and Sardinia. **Lauro** (☎ 081/5522838) has hydrofoils and car ferries to Capri and Ischia. **Adriatica** (☎ 06/4818341) connects Italy with Greece. **FS** ferries (☎ 0766/23273) sail from Civitavecchia to Golfo Aranci, near Olbia. **Navarma** (⊠ Piazzale Premuda, Elba, ☎ 0565/225211), **Elba Ferries** (⊠ Viale Regina Margherita, Elba, ☎ 0565/220956), and **Toremar** (⊠ Piazzale Premuda 13, Elba, ☎ 0565/31100) serve Elba from Piombino. For the lake district contact **Navigazione Laghi** (⊠ Via Ariosto 21, Milan, ☎ 02/4812086).

BUS TRAVEL

FROM THE U.K.

If you're traveling by bus from the United Kingdom, **bring a few French francs to spend en route.** And be sure to consider the train (☞ Train Travel, *below*), as bus fares are quite high, especially when you take the long and tiring overnight journey into account. Eurolines runs a weekly bus service to Rome that increases to three times a week between June and September.

➤ INFORMATION: **Eurolines** (⊠ 52 Grosvenor Gardens, London SW1W 0AU, ☎ 0171/730–8235 or 0171/730–3499; or contact any National Express agent).

WITHIN ITALY

Italy's bus network is extensive, although not as attractive as those in other European countries, partly because of the low cost of train travel. Schedules are often drawn up with commuters and students in mind and may be sketchy on weekends. Regional bus companies often provide the only means of getting to out-of-the-way places. Even when this is not the case, buses can be faster and more direct than local trains, so it's a good idea to **compare bus and train schedules.**

Local bus companies operate in many regions (☞ Getting Around by Bus *in* individual chapters). In the hillier parts of Italy, particularly in the Alpine north, they take over when the gradients become too steep for train travel. A village shop or café will sometimes double as the ticket office and bus stop. You should **buy your ticket before you board.**

Most of the major cities have urban bus services, usually operating on a system involving the purchase of tickets before you board (from a machine, newsstand, or tobacco store) and stamping the ticket in the machine on the bus. These buses are inexpensive, but they can become unbearably jammed at rush hours. Remember that there are also lunchtime rush hours in the hotter periods, particularly in the south, when people go home for a siesta.

➤ ITALIAN COMPANIES: **SITA** (⊠ Viale Cadorna 105, Florence, ☎ 055/278611) operates throughout the country. **Autostradale** (⊠ Piazzale Castello 1, Milan, ☎ 02/801161) serves much of northern Italy. **Lazzi** (⊠ Via Mercadante 2, Florence, ☎ 055/363041) operates in Tuscany and central Italy. Bus information is available at local tourist offices and travel agencies.

BUSINESS HOURS

Banks are open weekdays 8:30–1:30 and 2:45–3:45. Most churches are open from early morning until noon or 12:30, when they close for two hours or more; they open again in the afternoon, closing about 7 PM or later. Major cathedrals and basilicas, such as St. Peter's, are open all day. Note that sightseeing in churches during religious rites is usually discouraged.

Museum hours vary and may change with the seasons. Many important national museums are closed one day a week, often on Monday. Always check locally. Most shops are open from 9:30 to 1 and from 3:30 or 4 to 7 or 7:30. In all but resorts and small towns, shops close on Sunday and one half-day during the week. Some tourist-oriented shops in places such as Rome and Venice are open all day, also on Sunday, as are some department stores and supermarkets.

Post offices are open 8–2; central and main district post offices stay open until 8 or 9 PM for some operations. The main post office in major cities is open on Sunday 8:30–7. Barbers and hairdressers, with some exceptions, are closed Sunday and Monday.

C

CAMERAS, CAMCORDERS, & COMPUTERS

Always **keep your film, tape, or computer disks out of the sun.** Carry an extra supply of batteries, and **be prepared to turn on your camera, camcorder, or laptop** to prove to security personnel that the device is real. Always **ask for hand inspection of film,** which becomes clouded after successive exposure to airport x-ray machines, and **keep videotapes and computer disks away from metal detectors.**

➤ PHOTO HELP: **Kodak Information Center** (☎ 800/242–2424). *Kodak Guide to Shooting Great Travel Pictures,* available in bookstores or from Fodor's Travel Publications (☎ 800/533–6478); $16.50 plus $4 shipping.

CUSTOMS

Before departing, **register your foreign-made camera or laptop with U.S. Customs** (☞ Customs & Duties, *below*). If your equipment is U.S.-made, call the consulate of the country you'll be visiting to find out whether the device should be registered with local customs upon arrival.

CAR RENTAL

Rates in Rome begin at $49 a day and $167 a week for an economy car with air-conditioning, a manual transmission, and unlimited mileage. This does not include the 19% tax on car rentals. Note that recent Italian legislation now permits certain rental wholesalers, such as Auto Europe, to drop the VAT (☞ Taxes, *below*). Many companies impose mandatory theft insurance on all rentals; coverage costs $12–$18 a day.

➤ MAJOR AGENCIES: **Avis** (☎ 800/331–1212; 0990/900500 in the U.K.). **Budget** (☎ 800/527–0700, 0800/181181 in the U.K.). **Dollar** (☎ 800/800–4000, 0990/565656 in the

U.K., where it is known as Eurodollar). **Hertz** (☎ 800/654–3001, 800/263–0600 in Canada, 0345/555888 in the U.K.). **National InterRent** (☎ 800/227–3876; 0345/222525 in the U.K., where it is known as Europcar InterRent).

CUT COSTS

To get the best deal, **book through a travel agent who is willing to shop around.** Also **ask your travel agent about a company's customer-service record.** How has it responded to late plane arrivals and vehicle mishaps? Are there often lines at the rental counter, and, if you're traveling during a holiday period, does a confirmed reservation guarantee you a car?

Be sure to **look into wholesalers,** companies that do not own fleets but rent in bulk from those that do and often offer better rates than traditional car-rental operations. Prices are best during off-peak periods. Rentals booked through wholesalers must be paid for before you leave the United States.

➤ RENTAL WHOLESALERS: **Auto Europe** (☎ 207/842–2000 or 800/223–5555, FAX 800/235–6321). **Europe by Car** (☎ 212/581–3040 or 800/223–1516, FAX 212/246–1458) **DER Travel Services** (✉ 9501 W. Devon Ave., Rosemont, IL 60018, ☎ 800/782–2424, FAX 800/282–7474 for information, 800/860–9944 for brochures). **Kemwel Group** (☎ 914/835–5555 or 800/678–0678, FAX 914/835–5126).

NEED INSURANCE?

When driving a rented car you are generally responsible for any damage to or loss of the vehicle. Before you rent, **see what coverage you already have** under the terms of your personal auto-insurance policy and credit cards.

Collision policies that car-rental companies sell for European rentals typically do not cover stolen vehicles. Before you buy additional coverage for theft, find out if your credit card or personal auto insurance will cover the loss. All car-rental companies operating in Italy require that you buy theft-protection policies.

BEWARE SURCHARGES

Before you pick up a car in one city and leave it in another, **ask about drop-off charges or one-way service fees,** which can be substantial. Note, too, that some rental agencies charge extra if you return the car before the time specified on your contract. To avoid a hefty refueling fee, **fill the tank just before you turn in the car,** but be aware that gas stations near the rental outlet may overcharge.

MEET THE REQUIREMENTS

In Italy your own driver's license is acceptable. An International Driver's Permit is a good idea; it's available from the American or Canadian automobile associations, or, in the United Kingdom, from the Automobile Association or Royal Automobile Club.

CHILDREN & TRAVEL

CHILDREN IN ITALY

Although Italians love children and are generally very tolerant and patient with them, they provide few amenities for them. In restaurants and trattorias you may find a high chair or a cushion for the child to sit on, but rarely do they offer a children's menu. Order a *mezza porzione* (half-portion) of any dish, or ask the waiter for a *porzione da bambino* (child's portion).

Discounts do exist. Always ask about a *sconto bambino* (child's discount) before purchasing tickets. Children under six or under a certain height ride free on municipal buses and trams. Children under 18 who are EU citizens are admitted free to state-run museums and galleries, and there are similar privileges in many municipal or private museums.

Be sure to plan ahead and **involve your youngsters** as you outline your trip. When packing, include things to keep them busy en route. On sightseeing days try to schedule activities of special interest to your children (noted with a ☺). If you are renting a car don't forget to **arrange for a car seat** when you reserve.

HOTELS

Most hotels in Italy allow children under a certain age to stay in their parents' room at no extra charge, but others charge them as extra adults; be sure to **ask about the cutoff age for children's discounts.**

The Luxury Collection of ITT-Sheraton Hotels has more than 20 properties in Italy, all of which welcome families. Notable are the two on the Lido in Venice, which are right on the beach and have a parklike area for children to enjoy. Club Med has a "Mini Club" (for ages 4–9) and a "Kids Club" (for ages 10 and 11) at its ski village in Sestriere; there are also kids' programs at summer resort villages in Metaponto (Basilicata) and on the islands of Sicily and Sardinia, marketed mainly to Europeans. Some of the Valtur vacation villages also have special facilities and activities for children.

➤ BEST CHOICES: ITT-Sheraton Hotels (☎ 800/221–2340). Club Med (⊠ 40 W. 57th St., New York, NY 10019, ☎ 800/258–2633). Valtur (⊠ Via Milano 42, Roma, ☎ 06/4821000, FAX 06/4706334).

FLYING

As a general rule, infants under two not occupying a seat fly at greatly reduced fares and occasionally for free. If your children are two or older **ask about children's airfares.**

In general the adult baggage allowance applies to children paying half or more of the adult fare. When booking, **ask about carry-on allowances for those traveling with infants.** In general, for babies charged 10% of the adult fare you are allowed one carry-on bag and a collapsible stroller, which may have to be checked; you may be limited to less if the flight is full.

According to the FAA it's a good idea to use safety seats aloft for children weighing less than 40 pounds. Airlines, however, can set their own policies: U.S. carriers allow FAA-approved models but usually require that you buy a ticket, even if your child would otherwise ride free, since the seats must be strapped into regular seats. Airline rules vary regarding their use, so it's important to **check your airline's policy about using safety seats during takeoff and landing.** Safety seats cannot obstruct any of the other passengers in the row, so get an appropriate seat assignment as early as possible.

When making your reservation, **request children's meals or a free-standing bassinet** if you need them; the latter are available only to those seated at the bulkhead, where there's enough legroom. Remember, however, that bulkhead seats may not have their own overhead bins, and there's no storage space in front of you—a major inconvenience.

GROUP TRAVEL

If you're planning to take your kids on a tour, look for companies that specialize in family travel.

➤ FAMILY-FRIENDLY TOUR OPERATORS: **Grandtravel** (⊠ 6900 Wisconsin Ave., Suite 706, Chevy Chase, MD 20815, ☎ 301/986–0790 or 800/247–7651) for people traveling with grandchildren ages 7–17. **Families Welcome!** (⊠ 92 N. Main St., Ashland, OR 97520, ☎ 541/482–6121 or 800/326–0724, FAX 541/482–0660). **Rascals in Paradise** (⊠ 650 5th St., Suite 505, San Francisco, CA 94107, ☎ 415/978–9800 or 800/872–7225, FAX 415/442–0289).

CONSUMER PROTECTION

Whenever possible, **pay with a major credit card** so you can cancel payment if there's a problem, provided that you can provide documentation. This is a good practice whether you're buying travel arrangements before your trip or shopping at your destination.

If you're doing business with a particular company for the first time, **contact your local Better Business Bureau and the attorney general's offices** in your state and the company's home state, as well. Have any complaints been filed?

Finally, if you're buying a package or tour, always **consider travel insurance** that includes default coverage (☞ Insurance, *below*).

➤ LOCAL BBBs: **Council of Better Business Bureaus** (⊠ 4200 Wilson Blvd., Suite 800, Arlington, VA 22203, ☎ 703/276–0100, FAX 703/525–8277).

CUSTOMS & DUTIES

When shopping, **keep receipts** for all of your purchases. Upon reentering the country, **be ready to show customs officials what you've bought.** If you feel a duty is incorrect, appeal the assessment. If you object to the way your clearance was handled, get the inspector's badge number. In either case, first ask to see a supervisor, then write to the port director at the address listed on your receipt. Send a copy of the receipt and other appropriate documentation. If you still don't get satisfaction you can take your case to customs headquarters in Washington.

ENTERING ITALY

Of goods obtained anywhere outside the EU or goods purchased in a duty-free shop within an EU country, the allowances are: (1) 200 cigarettes or 100 cigarillos or 50 cigars or 250 grams of tobacco; (2) 2 liters of still table wine or 1 liter of spirits over 22% volume or 2 liters of spirits under 22% volume or 2 liters of fortified and sparkling wines; and (3) 50 milliliters of perfume and 250 milliliters of toilet water.

Of goods obtained (duty and tax paid) within another EU country, the allowances are: (1) 800 cigarettes or 400 cigarillos or 400 cigars or 1 kilogram of tobacco; (2) 90 liters of still table wine plus (3) 10 liters of spirits over 22% volume plus 20 liters of spirits under 22% volume plus 60 liters of sparkling wines plus 110 liters of beer.

ENTERING THE U.S.

You may bring home $400 worth of foreign goods duty-free if you've been out of the country for at least 48 hours and haven't already used the $400 allowance or any part of it in the past 30 days.

Travelers 21 and older may bring back 1 liter of alcohol duty-free. In addition, regardless of your age, you are allowed 200 cigarettes and 100 non-Cuban cigars. (At press time, a federal rule restricting tobacco access to persons 18 years and older did not apply to importation.) Antiques, which the U.S. Customs Service defines as objects more than 100 years old, enter duty-free, as do original works of art done entirely by hand, including paintings, drawings, and sculptures.

You may also send packages home duty-free: up to $200 worth of goods for personal use, with a limit of one parcel per addressee per day (and no alcohol or tobacco products or perfume worth more than $5); label the package PERSONAL USE, and attach a list of its contents and their retail value. Do not label the package UNSOLICITED GIFT, or your duty-free exemption will drop to $100. Mailed items do not affect your duty-free allowance on your return.

➤ INFORMATION: **U.S. Customs Service** (Inquiries: ⊠ Box 7407, Washington, DC 20044, ☎ 202/927–6724; complaints: ⊠ Commissioner's Office, 1301 Constitution Ave. NW, Washington, DC 20229; registration of equipment: ⊠ Resource Management, 1301 Constitution Ave. NW, Washington, DC 20229, ☎ 202/927–0540).

ENTERING CANADA

If you've been out of Canada for at least seven days you may bring in C$500 worth of goods duty-free. If you've been away for fewer than seven days but more than 48 hours, the duty-free allowance drops to C$200; if your trip lasts 24–48 hours, the allowance is C$50. You may not pool allowances with family members. Goods claimed under the C$500 exemption may follow you by mail; those claimed under the lesser exemptions must accompany you.

Alcohol and tobacco products may be included in the seven-day and 48-hour exemptions but not in the 24-hour exemption. If you meet the age requirements of the province or territory through which you reenter Canada you may bring in, duty-free, 1.14 liters (40 imperial ounces) of wine or liquor *or* 24 12-ounce cans or bottles of beer or ale. If you are 16 or older you may bring in, duty-free, 200 cigarettes and 50 cigars; these items must accompany you.

You may send an unlimited number of gifts worth up to C$60 each duty-free to Canada. Label the package UNSOLICITED GIFT—VALUE UNDER $60. Alcohol and tobacco are excluded.

➤ INFORMATION: **Revenue Canada** (⊠ 2265 St. Laurent Blvd. S, Ottawa, Ontario K1G 4K3, ☎ 613/993–0534, 800/461–9999 in Canada).

ENTERING THE U.K.

If your journey was wholly within European Union (EU) countries you needn't pass through customs when you return to the United Kingdom. If you plan to bring back large quantities of alcohol or tobacco, check on EU limits beforehand.

➤ INFORMATION: **HM Customs and Excise** (⊠ Dorset House, Stamford St., London SE1 9NG, ☎ 0171/202–4227).

D

DISABILITIES & ACCESSIBILITY

ACCESS IN ITALY

Italy has only recently begun to provide facilities such as ramps, telephones, and rest rooms for people with disabilities; such things are still the exception, not the rule. Travelers' wheelchairs must be transported free of charge, according to Italian law, but the logistics of getting a wheelchair on and off trains and buses can make this requirement irrelevant. Seats are reserved for people with disabilities on public transportation, but few buses have lifts for wheelchairs. High, narrow steps for boarding trains create additional problems. In many monuments and museums, even in some hotels and restaurants, architectural barriers make it difficult, if not impossible, for those with disabilities to gain access. In Rome, however, St. Peter's, the Sistine Chapel, and the Vatican Museums are all accessible by wheelchair, as is the Uffizi in Florence.

Contact the nearest Italian consulate regarding bringing a Seeing Eye dog into Italy; this requires an import license, a current certificate detailing the dog's inoculations, and a letter from your veterinarian certifying the dog's health.

➤ LOCAL RESOURCES: **The Italian Government Travel Office** (ENIT; ☞ Visitor Information, *below*) can provide a list of hotels that provide access and addresses of Italian associations for travelers with disabilities.

TIPS AND HINTS

When discussing accessibility with an operator or reservationist, **ask hard questions.** Are there any stairs, inside *or* out? Are there grab bars next to the toilet *and* in the shower/tub? How wide is the doorway to the room? To the bathroom? For the most extensive facilities meeting the latest legal specifications, **opt for newer accommodations,** which are more likely to have

been designed with access in mind. Older buildings or ships may offer more limited facilities. Be sure to **discuss your needs before booking.**

➤ COMPLAINTS: **Disability Rights Section** (⊠ U.S. Department of Justice, Box 66738, Washington, DC 20035-6738, ☎ 202/514–0301 or 800/514–0301, FAX 202/307–1198, TTY 202/514–0383 or 800/514–0383) for general complaints. **Aviation Consumer Protection Division** (☞ Air Travel, *above*) for airline-related problems. **Civil Rights Office** (⊠ U.S. Department of Transportation, Departmental Office of Civil Rights, S-30, 400 7th St. SW, Room 10215, Washington, DC 20590, ☎ 202/366–4648) for problems with surface transportation.

TRAVEL AGENCIES & TOUR OPERATORS

The Americans with Disabilities Act requires that travel firms serve the needs of all travelers. That said, you should note that some agencies and operators specialize in making travel arrangements for individuals and groups with disabilities.

➤ TRAVELERS WITH MOBILITY PROBLEMS: **Access Adventures** (⊠ 206 Chestnut Ridge Rd., Rochester, NY 14624, ☎ 716/889–9096) is run by a former physical-rehabilitation counselor. **Accessible Journeys** (⊠ 35 W. Sellers Ave., Ridley Park, PA 19078, ☎ 610/521–0339 or 800/846–4537, FAX 610/521–6959) runs escorted tours exclusively for travelers with mobility impairments. **Flying Wheels Travel** (⊠ 143 W. Bridge St., Box 382, Owatonna, MN 55060, ☎ 507/451–5005 or 800/535–6790) specializes in European cruises and tours. **Hinsdale Travel Service** (⊠ 201 E. Ogden Ave., Suite 100, Hinsdale, IL 60521, ☎ 630/325–1335) benefits from the advice of wheelchair traveler Janice Perkins. **Wheelchair Journeys** (⊠ 16979 Redmond Way, Redmond, WA 98052, ☎ 206/885–2210 or 800/313–4751) makes general travel arrangements.

➤ TRAVELERS WITH DEVELOPMENTAL DISABILITIES: **Sprout** (⊠ 893 Amsterdam Ave., New York, NY 10025, ☎ 212/222–9575 or 888/222–9575, FAX 212/222–9768).

DISCOUNTS & DEALS

Be a smart shopper and **compare all your options before making a choice.** A plane ticket bought with a promotional coupon may not be cheaper than the least expensive fare from a discount ticket agency. For high-price travel purchases, such as packages or tours, keep in mind that what you get is just as important as what you save. Just because something is cheap doesn't mean it's a bargain.

LOOK IN YOUR WALLET

When you use your credit card to make travel purchases you may get free travel-accident insurance, collision-damage insurance, and medical or legal assistance, depending on the card and the bank that issued it. American Express, MasterCard, and Visa provide one or more of these services, so **get a copy of your credit card's travel-benefits policy.** If you are a member of the American Automobile Association (AAA) or an oil-company-sponsored road-assistance plan, always **ask hotel or car-rental reservationists about auto-club discounts.** Some clubs offer additional discounts on tours, cruises, or admission to attractions. And don't forget that auto-club membership entitles you to free maps and trip-planning services.

DIAL FOR DOLLARS

To save money, **look into "1-800" discount reservations services,** which use their buying power to get a better price on hotels, airline tickets, even car rentals. When booking a room, always **call the hotel's local toll-free number** (if one is available) rather than the central reservations number—you'll often get a better price. Always ask about special packages or corporate rates.

When shopping for the best deal on hotels and car rentals **look for guaranteed exchange rates,** which protect you against a falling dollar. With your rate locked in you won't pay more even if the price goes up in the local currency.

➤ AIRLINE TICKETS: ☎ 800/FLY–4–LESS.

➤ HOTEL ROOMS: **Hotels Plus** (☎ 800/235–0909). **International Marketing & Travel Concepts** (IMTC; ☎ 800/790–4682).

SAVE ON COMBOS

Packages and guided tours can both save you money, but don't confuse the two. When you buy a package your travel remains independent, just as though you had planned and booked the trip yourself. Fly/drive packages, which combine airfare and car rental, are often a good deal. If you **buy a rail/drive pass** you'll save on train tickets and car rentals. All Eurail- and Europass holders get a discount on Eurostar fares through the Channel Tunnel.

JOIN A CLUB?

Many companies sell discounts in the form of travel clubs and coupon books, but these cost money. You must use participating advertisers to get a deal, and only after you recoup the initial membership cost or book price do you begin to save. If you plan to use the club or coupons frequently you may save considerably. Before signing up, find out what discounts you get for free.

➤ DISCOUNT CLUBS: **Entertainment Travel Editions** (✉ Box 1068, Trumbull, CT 06611, ☎ 800/445–4137); $28–$53. **Great American Traveler** (✉ Box 27965, Salt Lake City, UT 84127, ☎ 800/548–2812); $49.95 per year. **Moment's Notice Discount Travel Club** (✉ 7301 New Utrecht Ave., Brooklyn, NY 11204, ☎ 718/234–6295); $25 per year, single or family. **Privilege Card International** (✉ 201 E. Commerce St., Suite 198, Youngstown, OH 44503, ☎ 330/746–5211 or 800/236–9732); $74.95 per year. **Sears's Mature Outlook** (✉ Box 9390, Des Moines, IA 50306, ☎ 800/336–6330); $14.95 per year. **Travelers Advantage** (✉ CUC Travel Service, 3033 S. Parker Rd., Suite 1000, Aurora, CO 80014, ☎ 800/548–1116 or 800/648–4037); $49 per year, single or family. **Worldwide Discount Travel Club** (✉ 1674 Meridian Ave., Miami Beach, FL 33139, ☎ 305/534–2082); $50 per year family, $40 single.

DRIVING

There is an extensive network of *autostrade* (toll highways), complemented by equally well-maintained but free *superstrade* (expressways). All are clearly signposted and numbered. The ticket you are issued upon entering an autostrada must be returned when you exit and pay the toll; on some shorter autostrade, mainly connecting highways, the toll is paid upon entering. Viacard cards, on sale at many autostrada locations, make paying tolls easier and faster. A *raccordo* is a connecting expressway. *Strade statali* (state highways, denoted by *S* or *SS* numbers) may be single-lane roads, as are all secondary roads; directions and turnoffs are not always clearly marked.

FUEL AVAILABILITY & COST

Only a few gas stations are open on Sunday, and most close for a couple of hours at lunchtime and at 7 PM for the night. Self-service pumps may be few and far between outside major cities. Gas stations on autostrade are open 24 hours. Gas costs about 2,500 lire per liter.

PARKING

In most cities, parking space is at a premium; historic town centers are closed to most traffic, and peripheral parking areas are usually full. Parking in an area signposted ZONA DISCO is allowed for limited periods (from 30 minutes to 2 hours or more—the limit is posted); if you don't have the cardboard disk to show what time you parked, you can use a piece of paper. It's advisable to **leave your car only in guarded parking areas.** Unofficial parking attendants can help you find a space but offer no guarantees. In major cities your car may be towed away if illegally parked.

RULES OF THE ROAD

Driving is on the right, as in the United States. Regulations are largely as in Britain and the United States, except that the police have the power to levy on-the-spot fines. In most Italian towns the use of the horn is forbidden in certain, if not all, areas; a large sign, ZONA DI SILENZIO, indicates where. Speed limits are 130 kph (80 mph) on autostrade and 110 kph (70 mph) on state and provincial roads, unless otherwise marked. Fines for driving after drinking are heavy, with the additional possibility of six months' imprisonment.

➤ AUTO CLUBS: **Automobile Club of Italy** (ACI; ✉ Via Marsala 8, 00185 Roma, ☎ 06/49982389, FAX 06/4998234), with offices in cities throughout Italy. In the United States: **American Automobile Association** (☎ 800/564–6222). In the United Kingdom: **Automobile Association** (AA; ☎ 0990/500–600), **Royal Automobile Club** (RAC; ☎ 0990/722–722 for membership, 0345/121–345 for insurance).

➤ BREAKDOWNS: **ACI Emergency Service** (✉ Servizio Soccorso Stradale, Via Solferino 32, 00185 Roma, ☎ 06/44595) offers 24-hour road service. Dial 116 from any phone, 24 hours a day, to reach the nearest ACI service station.

E
ELECTRICITY

To use your U.S.-purchased electric-powered equipment, **bring a converter and adapter.** The electrical current in Italy is 220 volts, 50 cycles alternating current (AC); wall outlets take Continental-type plugs, with two round prongs.

If your appliances are dual-voltage, you'll need only an adapter. Don't use 110-volt outlets, marked FOR SHAVERS ONLY, for high-wattage appliances such as blow-dryers. Most laptops operate equally well on 110 and 220 volts and so require only an adapter.

EMERGENCIES

➤ IMPORTANT NUMBERS: **Carabinieri** (military police; ☎ 112). **Fire** (☎ 115). **Italian Automobile Club** (☎ 116). **Medical emergency and ambulance** (☎ 118; not yet operational in all areas; alternatively call 113). **Police** (☎ 113).

G
GAY & LESBIAN TRAVEL

➤ TOUR OPERATORS: **Olivia** (✉ 4400 Market St., Oakland, CA 94608, ☎ 510/655–0364 or 800/631–6277), for cruises and resort vacations for lesbians. **Hanns Ebensten Travel** (✉ 513 Fleming St., Key West, FL 33040, ☎ 305/294–8174), one of the oldest operators in the gay market.

➤ GAY- AND LESBIAN-FRIENDLY TRAVEL AGENCIES: **Advance Damron** (✉ 1 Greenway Plaza, Suite 800, Houston, TX 77046, ☎ 713/682–2002 or 800/695–0880, FAX 713/888–1010). **Club Travel** (✉ 8739 Santa Monica Blvd., West Hollywood, CA 90069, ☎ 310/

358–2200 or 800/429–8747, FAX 310/
358–2222). **Islanders/Kennedy Travel**
(⊠ 183 W. 10th St., New York, NY
10014, ☎ 212/242–3222 or 800/
988–1181, FAX 212/929–8530). **Now
Voyager** (⊠ 4406 18th St., San Francisco, CA 94114, ☎ 415/626–1169
or 800/255–6951, FAX 415/626–
8626). **Yellowbrick Road** (⊠ 1500
W. Balmoral Ave., Chicago, IL 60640,
☎ 773/561–1800 or 800/642–2488,
FAX 773/561–4497). **Skylink Women's
Travel** (⊠ 3577 Moorland Ave., Santa
Rosa, CA 95407, ☎ 707/585–8355
or 800/225–5759, FAX 707/584–5637),
serving lesbian travelers.

H

HEALTH

The Centers for Disease Control and
Prevention (CDC) in Atlanta caution
that most of Southern Europe is in the
"intermediate" range for risk of con-
tacting traveler's diarrhea. Part of this
risk may be attributed to an increased
consumption of olive oil and wine,
which can have a laxative effect on
stomachs used to a different diet. The
CDC also advises all international
travelers to swim only in chlorinated
swimming pools, unless they are
absolutely certain the local beaches
and freshwater lakes are not contaminated.

MEDICAL PLANS

No one plans to get sick while traveling, but it happens, so **consider signing up with a medical-assistance
company.** Members get doctor referrals, emergency evacuation or repatri-
ation, 24-hour telephone hot lines for
medical consultation, cash for emergencies, and other personal and legal
assistance. Coverage varies by plan,
so **review the benefits carefully.**

➤ MEDICAL-ASSISTANCE COMPANIES:
International SOS Assistance (⊠ Box
11568, Philadelphia, PA 19116,
☎ 215/244–1500 or 800/523–8930;
⊠ Box 466, pl. Bonaventure, Montréal, Québec H5A 1C1, ☎ 514/874–
7674 or 800/363–0263; ⊠ 7 Old
Lodge Pl., St. Margarets, Twickenham
TW1 1RQ, England, ☎ 0181/744–
0033). **MEDEX Assistance Corporation** (⊠ Box 5375, Timonium,
MD 21094, ☎ 410/453–6300 or
800/537–2029). **Traveler's Emergency Network** (⊠ 3100 Tower Blvd.,

Suite 1000B, Durham, NC 27707,
☎ 919/490–6055 or 800/275–4836,
FAX 919/493–8262). **TravMed** (⊠ Box
5375, Timonium, MD 21094, ☎ 410/
453–6380 or 800/732–5309). **Worldwide Assistance Services** (⊠ 1133
15th St. NW, Suite 400, Washington,
DC 20005, ☎ 202/331–1609 or 800/
821–2828, FAX 202/828–5896).

HOLIDAYS

National holidays include January 1
(New Year's Day); January 6 (Epi-
phany); April 12 and 13 (Easter
Sunday and Monday); April 25 (Lib-
eration Day); May 1 (Labor Day or
May Day); August 15 (Assumption of
Mary, also known as Ferragosto);
November 1 (All Saints' Day); De-
cember 8 (Immaculate Conception);
December 25 and 26 (Christmas Day
and Boxing Day).

The feast days of patron saints are
observed locally. Many businesses
and shops may be closed in Florence,
Genoa, and Turin on June 24 (St. John
the Baptist); in Rome on June 29 (Sts.
Peter and Paul); in Palermo on July 15
(Santa Rosalia); in Naples on Septem-
ber 19 (San Gennaro); in Bologna on
October 4 (San Petronio); in Trieste
on November 3 (San Giusto); and in
Milan on December 7 (St. Ambrose).
Venice's feast of St. Mark is April 25,
the same as Liberation Day. Also *see*
Festivals and Seasonal Events *in*
Chapter 1.

I

INSURANCE

Travel insurance is the best way to
protect yourself against financial loss.
The most useful policies are trip-
cancellation-and-interruption, default, medical, and comprehensive
insurance.

Without insurance you will lose all
or most of your money if you cancel
your trip, regardless of the reason. It's
essential that you **buy trip-cancella-
tion-and-interruption insurance,** particularly if your airline ticket, cruise, or
package tour is nonrefundable and
cannot be changed. When considering
how much coverage you need, look
for a policy that will cover the cost of
your trip plus the nondiscounted price
of a one-way airline ticket, should you
need to return home early. Also **consider default or bankruptcy insurance,**

which protects you against a supplier's failure to deliver.

Medicare generally does not cover health-care costs outside the United States, nor do many privately issued policies. If your own policy does not cover you outside the United States, **consider buying supplemental medical coverage.** Remember that travel health insurance is different from a medical-assistance plan (☞ Health, *above*).

Citizens of the United Kingdom can buy an annual travel-insurance policy valid for most vacations during the year in which it's purchased. If you are pregnant or have a preexisting medical condition, make sure you're covered.

If you have purchased an expensive vacation, particularly one that involves travel abroad, comprehensive insurance is a must. **Look for comprehensive policies that include trip-delay insurance,** which will protect you in the event that weather problems cause you to miss your flight, tour, or cruise. A few insurers sell waivers for preexisting medical conditions. Companies that offer both features include Access America, Carefree Travel, Travel Insured International, and Travel Guard.

Always **buy travel insurance directly from the insurance company**; if you buy it from a travel agency or tour operator that goes out of business you probably will not be covered for the agency or operator's default, a major risk. Before you make any purchase, **review your existing health and homeowner's policies** to find out whether they cover expenses incurred while traveling.

➤ TRAVEL INSURERS: In the U.S., **Access America** (✉ 6600 W. Broad St., Richmond, VA 23230, ☎ 804/285–3300 or 800/284–8300), **Carefree Travel Insurance** (✉ Box 9366, 100 Garden City Plaza, Garden City, NY 11530, ☎ 516/294–0220 or 800/323–3149), **Near Travel Services** (✉ Box 1339, Calumet City, IL 60409, ☎ 708/868–6700 or 800/654–6700), **Travel Guard International** (✉ 1145 Clark St., Stevens Point, WI 54481, ☎ 715/345–0505 or 800/826–1300), **Travel Insured International** (✉ Box 280568, East Hartford, CT 06128–0568, ☎ 860/528–7663 or 800/243–3174), **Travelex Insurance Services** (✉ 11717

Burt St., Suite 202, Omaha, NE 68154-1500, ☎ 402/445–8637 or 800/228–9792, FAX 800/867–9531), **Wallach & Company** (✉ 107 W. Federal St., Box 480, Middleburg, VA 20118, ☎ 540/687–3166 or 800/237–6615). In Canada, **Mutual of Omaha** (✉ Travel Division, 500 University Ave., Toronto, Ontario M5G 1V8, ☎ 416/598–4083, 800/268–8825). In the U.K., **Association of British Insurers** (✉ 51 Gresham St., London EC2V 7HQ, ☎ 0171/600–3333).

L

LANGUAGE

In the main tourist cities, language is not a big problem. You can always find someone who speaks at least a little English, albeit with a heavy accent; remember that the Italian language is pronounced exactly as it is written (many Italians try to speak English by enunciating every syllable, with disconcerting results). You may run into a language barrier in the countryside, but a phrase book and close attention to the Italians' astonishing use of pantomime and expressive gestures will go a long way.

Try to **master a few phrases for daily use** (*see* Italian Vocabulary, at the back of this book), and familiarize yourself with the terms you'll need to decipher signs and museum labels. To get the most out of museums, you'll need English-language guidebooks to exhibits; look for them in bookstores and on newsstands, as those sold at the museums are not necessarily the best.

LODGING

Options are numerous, from hotels to camping grounds to short-term rentals in city or country.

APARTMENT & VILLA RENTALS

If you want a home base that's roomy enough for a family and comes with cooking facilities, **consider a furnished rental.** These can save you money, however some rentals are luxury properties, economical only when your party is large. Home-exchange directories list rentals (often second homes owned by prospective house swappers), and some services search for a house or apartment for you (even a castle if that's your fancy) and handle the paperwork. Some send an illustrated catalog; others send photographs only of specific properties, sometimes at a charge. Up-front registration fees may apply.

➤ RENTAL AGENTS: **At Home Abroad** (⊠ 405 E. 56th St., Suite 6H, New York, NY 10022, ☎ 212/421–9165, 𝖥𝖠𝖷 212/752–1591). **Europa-Let/ Tropical Inn-Let** (⊠ 92 N. Main St., Ashland, OR 97520, ☎ 541/482–5806 or 800/462–4486, 𝖥𝖠𝖷 541/482–0660). **Hometours International** (⊠ Box 11503, Knoxville, TN 37939, ☎ 423/690–8484 or 800/367–4668). **Interhome** (⊠ 124 Little Falls Rd., Fairfield, NJ 07004, ☎ 201/882–6864, 𝖥𝖠𝖷 201/808–1742). **Property Rentals International** (⊠ 1008 Mansfield Crossing Rd., Richmond, VA 23236, ☎ 804/378–6054 or 800/220–3332, 𝖥𝖠𝖷 804/379–2073). **Rental Directories International** (⊠ 2044 Rittenhouse Sq., Philadelphia, PA 19103, ☎ 215/985–4001, 𝖥𝖠𝖷 215/985–0323). **Rent-a-Home International** (⊠ 7200 34th Ave. NW, Seattle, WA 98117, ☎ 206/789–9377 or 800/488–7368, 𝖥𝖠𝖷 206/789–9379). **Vacation Home Rentals Worldwide** (⊠ 235 Kensington Ave., Norwood, NJ 07648, ☎ 201/767–9393 or 800/633–3284, 𝖥𝖠𝖷 201/767–5510). **Villas and Apartments Abroad** (⊠ 420 Madison Ave., Suite 1003, New York, NY 10017, ☎ 212/759–1025 or 800/433–3020, 𝖥𝖠𝖷 212/755–8316). **Villas International** (⊠ 605 Market St., Suite 510, San Francisco, CA 94105, ☎ 415/281–0910 or 800/221–2260, 𝖥𝖠𝖷 415/281–0919). **Hideaways International** (⊠ 767 Islington St., Portsmouth, NH 03801, ☎ 603/430–4433 or 800/843–4433, 𝖥𝖠𝖷 603/430–4444) is a travel club whose members arrange rentals among themselves; yearly membership is $99.

➤ ITALY-ONLY AGENCIES: **Cuendet USA** (⊠ 165 Chestnut St., Allendale, NJ 07041, ☎ 201/327–2333; ⊠ Suzanne T. Pidduck, c/o Rentals in Italy, 1742 Calle Corva, Camarillo, CA 93010, ☎ 800/726–6702). **Vacanze in Italia** (⊠ 22 Railroad Ave., Great Barrington, MA 01230, ☎ 413/528–6610 or 800/533–5405).

➤ IN THE U.K.: **CV Travel** (⊠ 43 Cadogan St., London SW3 2PR, En-

gland, ☎ 0171/581–0851). **Magic of Italy** (⊠ 227 Shepherds Bush Rd., London W6 7AS, England, ☎ 0181/748–7575).

CAMPING

Camping is a good way to find accommodations in otherwise overcrowded resorts, and camper rental agencies operate throughout Italy; contact your travel agent for details. Make sure you **stay only on authorized campsites** (camping on private land is frowned upon), and **get an international camping *carnet* (permit)** from your local camping association before you leave home. The Touring Club Italiano publishes a multilingual *Guida Camping d'Italia* (Guide to the Camping in Italy), available in bookstores in Italy for about 30,000 lire, with more detailed information on sites. Camp rates for two people, with car and tent, average about 45,000 lire a day.

➤ DIRECTORY OF CAMPGROUNDS: Write to the **Federazione Italiana del Campeggio e del Caravanning** (⊠ Federcampeggio, Casella Postale 23, 50041 Calenzano, Firenze, 𝖥𝖠𝖷 055/8825918) and request *Campeggiare in Italia;* send three international reply coupons to cover mailing. It's also available through the **ENIT office** in the United States and at **tourist information offices** in Italy (☞ Visitor Information, *below* and *in* individual chapters).

FARM HOLIDAYS & AGRITOURISM

Rural accommodations in the Agritourism category are increasingly popular with both Italians and tourists.

➤ AGENCIES: **Italy Farm Holidays** (⊠ 547 Martling Ave., Tarrytown, NY 10591, ☎ 914/631–7880, 𝖥𝖠𝖷 914/631–8831). **Agriturismo** (⊠ Corso Vittorio 101, 00186 Roma, ☎ 06/68521), **Terra Nostra** (⊠ Via XXIV Maggio 43, 00187 Roma, ☎ 06/46821). **Turismo Verde** (⊠ Via degli Scialoja 6, 00196 Roma, ☎ 06/3611051).

HOME EXCHANGES

If you would like to exchange your home for someone else's, **join a home-exchange organization,** which will send you its updated listings of available exchanges for a year and will include your own listing in at least one of them. The arrangements are up to you.

➤ EXCHANGE CLUBS: **HomeLink International** (✉ Box 650, Key West, FL 33041, ☎ 305/294–7766 or 800/638–3841, FAX 305/294–1148) charges $83 per year.

HOTELS

Italian hotels are classified from five-star (deluxe) to one-star (very basic hotels and small inns). Stars are assigned according to standards set by regional boards (there are 20 in Italy), but rates are set by each hotel. During slack periods, or when a hotel is not full, it is often possible to negotiate a discounted rate. In the major cities, room rates are on a par with other European capitals: Deluxe and four-star rates can be downright extravagant. In those categories, **ask for one of the better rooms,** since less desirable rooms—and there usually are some—don't give you what you're paying for. Except in deluxe and some four-star hotels, rooms may be very small compared to U.S standards.

In all hotels there is a rate card inside the door of your room, or inside the closet door; it tells you exactly what you will pay for that particular room (rates in the same hotel may vary according to the location and type of room). On this card, breakfast and any other optionals must be listed separately. Any discrepancy between the basic room rate and that charged on your bill is cause for complaint to the manager and to the local tourist office.

Although, by law, breakfast is supposed to be optional, most hotels quote room rates including breakfast. When you book a room, specifically **ask whether the rate includes breakfast** (*colazione*). You are under no obligation to take breakfast at your hotel, but in practice most hotels expect you to do so. It is encouraging to note that many of the hotels we recommend are offering generous buffet breakfasts instead of simple, even skimpy "continental breakfasts." Remember, if the latter is the case, you can **eat for less at the nearest coffee bar.**

Hotels that we list as ($$) and ($)—moderate to inexpensively priced

accommodations—may charge extra for optional air-conditioning. In older hotels the quality of the rooms may be very uneven; if you don't like the room you're given, request another. This applies to noise, too. Front rooms may be larger and have a view, but they also may have a lot of street noise. If you're a light sleeper, **request a quiet room when making reservations.** Rooms in lodgings listed in this guide have a shower and/or bath, unless noted otherwise. Remember to **specify whether you care to have a bath or shower** since not all rooms, especially lodgings outside major cities, have both.

Major cities, such as Rome and Milan, have no official off-season as far as hotel rates go, though some hotels will reduce rates during the slack season upon request. Always **inquire about special rates.** You can save considerably on hotel rooms in Venice and Florence and in such resorts as Sorrento and Capri during their off-seasons. Major cities have hotel-reservation service booths in train stations.

➤ BEST-KNOWN CHAINS: **ITT-Sheraton/The Luxury Collection** (✉ 745 5th Ave., New York, NY 10151, ☎ 800/221–2340, 1678/835035 toll-free in Italy, FAX 212/421–5929), has more than 20 Italian properties, almost all five-star deluxe; **Jolly** (✉ 800/247–1277 in New York state, 800/221–2626 elsewhere, 800/237–0319 in Canada, 1670–7703 toll-free in Italy), with 32 four-star hotels in Italy; **Ata-hotels** (✉ Via Lampedusa 11/A, 20141 Milano, ☎ 02/895261, 1678/23013 toll-free in Italy, FAX 02/8465568; some bookable through E&M Associates, ☎ 212/599–8280 or 800/223–9832), with 20 mostly four- and five-star hotels; and **Starhotels** (✉ Via Belfiore 27, 50144 Firenze; ☎ 055/36921, 1678/60200 toll-free in Italy, 800/448–8355 for bookings, FAX 055/36924), with 14 mainly four-star hotels. **Space Hotels** (☎ 1678/13013 toll-free in Italy; or book through Supranational, ☎ 416/927–1133 or 800/843–3311) has about 50 independently owned four- and five-star (some three-star) hotels. **Italhotels** (☎ 1678/01004 toll-free in Italy) also has about 50 independently owned four- and five-star hotels.

AGIP Motels (☎ 06/4440183 reservations in Italy) is a chain of about 50, mostly four-star motels on main highways; the motels are commercial, functional digs for traveling salesmen and tourists needing forty winks, but they—and the Jolly hotels—can be the best choice in many out-of-the-way places. The Forte group has taken over some top-of-the-line AGIP properties throughout Italy. **Best Western** (☎ 800/528–1234 for reservations), an international association of independently owned hotels, has some 75 mainly three- and four-star hotels in Italy; call to request the *Europe and Middle East Atlas* that lists them.

Family Hotels (✉ Via Faenza 77, 50123 Firenze, ☎ 055/217975, FAX 055/2381905; for information, not booking), which groups about 75 independently owned, family-run two- and three-star hotels (some one-star), offers good value. A spin-off of this group, the **Sun Rays Pool** (☎ 055/4620080) comprises three- and four-star hotels.

M
MAIL

POSTAL RATES

Airmail letters (lightweight stationery) to the United States and Canada cost 1,300 lire for the first 19 grams and an additional 600 lire for every additional unit of 20 grams. Airmail postcards cost 1,100 lire if the message is limited to a few words and a signature; otherwise, you pay the letter rate. Airmail letters to the United Kingdom cost 800 lire; postcards, 650 lire. You can buy stamps at tobacconists.

RECEIVING MAIL

Mail service is generally slow; allow up to 10 days for mail from Britain, 15 days from North America. Correspondence can be addressed to you care of the Italian post office. Letters should be addressed to your name, "c/o Ufficio Postale Centrale," followed by "Fermo Posta" on the next line, and the name of the city (preceded by its postal code) on the next. You can **collect it at the central post office** by showing your passport or photo-bearing ID and paying a small fee. American Express also has a general-delivery service. There's no charge for cardholders, holders of American Express Traveler's checks,

or anyone who booked a vacation with American Express.

MONEY

The unit of currency in Italy is the lira. There are bills of 500,000, 100,000, 50,000, 10,000, 5,000, 2,000, and 1,000 lire. Coins are 500, 200, 100 and 50 lire. At press time, the exchange rate was about 1,595 lire to the U.S. dollar, 1,157 lire to the Canadian dollar, and 2,402 lire to the pound sterling.

ATMS

Before leaving home, **make sure your credit cards have been programmed for ATM use in Italy.** Note that Discover is accepted mostly in the United States. Local bank cards often do not work or may access only your checking account; **ask your bank about a MasterCard/Cirrus or Visa debit card,** which works like a bank card but can be used at any ATM displaying a MasterCard/Cirrus or Visa logo. These cards, too, may tap only your checking account; check with your bank about their policy. ATM machines in Italy accept 4-digit pin numbers only.

➤ ATM LOCATIONS: **Cirrus** (☎ 800/424–7787). A list of **Plus** locations is available at your local bank.

COSTS

Italy's prices are in line with those in the rest of Europe, with costs in its main cities comparable to those in other major capitals, such as Paris and London. The days when the country's high-quality attractions came with a comparatively low Mediterranean price tag are long gone. With the cost of labor and social benefits rising and an economy weighed down by the public debt, Italy is therefore not a bargain, but there is an effort to hold the line on hotel and restaurant prices that had become inordinately expensive by U.S. standards. Depending on season and occupancy, you may be able to obtain unadvertised lower rates in hotels; always inquire. Among major cities, Venice and Milan are the most expensive; resorts such as the Costa Smeralda, Portofino, and Cortina d'Ampezzo cater to the rich and famous and charge top prices. Though Capri is generally considered a millionaire's playground, it can accommodate the less affluent. Everywhere in Italy, if you want the luxury of four- and five-star hotels, be prepared to pay top rates.

As in most countries, prices vary from region to region and are a bit lower in the countryside than in the cities. Good value for the money can be had in the scenic Trentino–Alto Adige region and in the Dolomites, in Umbria and the Marches, and on the Amalfi Coast. With a few exceptions, southern Italy, Sicily, and Sardinia also offer good values, but hotels are not always up to par.

When you make hotel reservations, ask explicitly whether breakfast is included in the rate. By law, breakfast is optional, but some hotels pressure guests to eat breakfast on the premises—and then charge a whopping amount for it. Find out what breakfast will cost at the time you book, or at least when you check in, and if it seems high, avoid misunderstanding by clearly stating that you want a room without breakfast.

SAMPLE PRICES

Admission to the Vatican Museums is 15,000 lire; to the Uffizi Gallery, 12,000 lire. The cheapest seat at Rome's Opera House runs 25,000 lire; a movie ticket is 12,000 lire. Going to a Milan disco will set you back about 35,000 lire. A daily English-language newspaper is 2,400 lire.

A Rome taxi ride (1⅓ km, or 1 mi) costs 10,000 lire. An inexpensive hotel room for two, including breakfast, in Rome is about 190,000 lire; an inexpensive Rome dinner is 40,000 lire, and a ½ liter carafe of house wine, 6,000 lire. A simple pasta item on the menu runs about 13,000 lire, a cup of coffee 1,200–1,400 lire, and a rosticceria lunch, about 15,000 lire. A Coca-Cola (standing) at a café is 2,200 lire and a pint of beer is 7,000 lire.

CURRENCY EXCHANGE

For the most favorable rates, **change money at banks.** Although fees charged for ATM transactions may be higher abroad than at home, Cirrus and Plus exchange rates are excellent, because they are based on wholesale rates offered only by major banks. You won't do as well at exchange booths in airports or rail and bus stations, in hotels, in restaurants, or in stores, although you may find their hours more convenient. To avoid lines at airport exchange booths, **get a small amount of local currency before you leave home.**

➤ EXCHANGE SERVICES: **International Currency Express** (☎ 888/842–0880 on the East Coast or 888/278–6628 on the West Coast for telephone orders). **Thomas Cook Currency Services** (☎ 800/287–7362 for telephone orders and retail locations).

TRAVELER'S CHECKS

Whether or not to buy traveler's checks depends on where you are headed. **Take cash if your trip includes rural areas** and small towns, traveler's checks to cities. If your checks are lost or stolen, they can usually be replaced within 24 hours. To ensure a speedy refund, buy your checks yourself (don't ask someone else to make the purchase). When making a claim for stolen or lost checks, the person who bought the checks should make the call.

P
PACKING FOR ITALY

The weather is considerably milder in Italy than in the north and central United States or Great Britain. In summer, stick with clothing that is as light as possible, although a sweater may be necessary for cool evenings, especially in the mountains even during the hot months. Brief summer afternoon thunderstorms are common in Rome and inland cities, so an umbrella will come in handy. In winter bring a medium-weight coat and a raincoat for Rome and farther south; northern Italy calls for heavier clothes, gloves, hats, and boots. Even in Rome and other milder areas, central heating may not be up to your standards, and interiors can be cold and damp; take wools or flannel rather than sheer fabrics. Bring sturdy shoes for winter, and comfortable walking shoes in any season.

Italians dress exceptionally well. They do not usually wear shorts in the city, unless longish Bermudas happen to be in fashion. Men aren't required to wear ties or jackets anywhere, except in some of the grander hotel dining rooms and top-level restaurants, but are expected to look reasonably sharp—and they do. Formal wear is the exception rather than the rule at the opera nowadays, though people in expensive seats usually do get dressed up.

Dress codes are strict for visits to churches—especially St. Peter's in Rome and St. Mark's in Venice—and to the Vatican Museums. Women must cover bare shoulders and arms—a shawl will do—but no longer need cover their heads. Shorts are taboo for both men and women. For the huge general papal audiences, no rules of dress apply other than those of common sense. For other types of audience, the Vatican Information Office will give requirements.

For sightseeing, **pack a pair of binoculars**; they will help you get a good look at painted ceilings and domes. If you stay in budget hotels, **take your own soap**; many such hotels do not provide it or give guests only one tiny bar per room. To be safe, **bring an extra pair of eyeglasses or contact lenses** in your carry-on luggage, and if you have a health problem, **pack enough medication** to last the entire trip or have your doctor write you a prescription using the drug's generic name, because brand names vary from country to country. It's important that you **don't put prescription drugs or valuables in luggage to be checked**: it might go astray. To avoid problems with customs officials, carry medications in the original packaging. Also, **don't forget the addresses of offices that handle refunds of lost traveler's checks.**

LUGGAGE

In general, you are entitled to check two bags on flights within the United States and on international flights leaving the United States. A third piece may be brought on board, but it must fit easily under the seat in front of you or in the overhead compartment.

If you are flying between two foreign destinations, note that baggage allowances may be determined not by piece but by weight—generally 88 pounds (40 kilograms) in first class, 66 pounds (30 kilograms) in business class, and 44 pounds (20 kilograms) in economy. If your flight between two cities abroad *connects* with your transatlantic or transpacific flight, the piece method still applies.

Airline liability for baggage is limited to $1,250 per person on flights within the United States. On international flights it amounts to $9.07 per pound or $20 per kilogram for checked baggage (roughly $640 per 70-pound bag) and $400 per passenger for unchecked baggage. Insurance for losses exceeding these amounts can be bought from the airline at check-in for about $10 per $1,000 of coverage; note that this coverage excludes a rather extensive list of items, which is shown on your airline ticket.

Before departure, **itemize your bags' contents** and their worth, and label the bags with your name, address, and phone number. (If you use your home address, cover it so that potential thieves can't see it readily.) Inside each bag, **pack a copy of your itinerary.** At check-in, **make sure that each bag is correctly tagged** with the destination airport's three-letter code. If your bags arrive damaged or fail to arrive at all, file a written report with the airline before leaving the airport.

PASSPORTS & VISAS

Once your travel plans are confirmed, **check the expiration date of your passport.** It's also a good idea to **make photocopies of the data page**; leave one copy with someone at home and keep another with you, separate from your passport. If you lose your passport, promptly call the nearest embassy or consulate and the local police; having a copy of the data page can speed replacement.

U.S. CITIZENS

All U.S. citizens, even infants, need only a valid passport to enter Italy for stays of up to 90 days.

➤ INFORMATION: **Office of Passport Services** (☎ 202/647–0518).

CANADIANS

You need only a valid passport to enter Italy for stays of up to 90 days.

➤ INFORMATION: **Passport Office** (☎ 819/994–3500 or 800/567–6868).

U.K. CITIZENS

Citizens of the United Kingdom need only a valid passport to enter Italy for stays of up to 90 days.

➤ INFORMATION: **London Passport Office** (☎ 0990/210–10) for fees and documentation requirements and to request an emergency passport.

S

SAFETY

The best way to **protect yourself against purse snatchers and pickpockets** is to wear a money belt or a pouch on a string around your neck, both concealed. If you carry a bag or camera, be absolutely sure it has straps; you should sling it across your body bandolier-style. Always be astutely aware of stealthy pickpockets, especially when in jam-packed big-city buses and subways, when making your way through train corridors, and in busy piazzas.

SENIOR-CITIZEN TRAVEL

EU citizens over 60 are entitled to free admission to state museums, as well as to many other museums—always ask at the ticket office. Older travelers may be eligible for special fares on Alitalia. When renting a car, **ask about promotional car-rental discounts,** which can be cheaper than senior-citizen rates.

To qualify for age-related discounts, **mention your senior-citizen status up front** when booking hotel reservations (not when checking out) and before you're seated in restaurants (not when paying the bill). Note that discounts may be limited to certain menus, days, or hours.

➤ ADVENTURE TRAVEL: **Overseas Adventure Travel** (⊠ Grand Circle Corporation, 625 Mt. Auburn St., Cambridge, MA 02138, ☎ 617/876–0533 or 800/221–0814, FAX 617/876–0455).

➤ EDUCATIONAL TRAVEL PROGRAMS: **Elderhostel** (⊠ 75 Federal St., 3rd floor, Boston, MA 02110, ☎ 617/426–7788). **Interhostel** (⊠ University of New Hampshire, 6 Garrison Ave., Durham, NH 03824, ☎ 603/862–1147 or 800/733–9753, FAX 603/862–1113).

SHOPPING

The notice PREZZI FISSI (fixed prices) means just that; in shops displaying this sign it's a waste of time to bargain unless you're buying a sizable quantity of goods or a particularly costly object. Always bargain, however, at outdoor markets (except food markets) and when buying from street vendors. For a comprehensive introduction to the joys of shopping, Italian style, *see* Pleasures & Pastimes *in* Chapter 1. For information on VAT refunds, *see* Taxes, *below.*

SPORTS

Italians are sports lovers, and there are several daily newspapers devoted solely to sports. No trip to Italy is complete without witnessing the fiercely popular *calcio* (soccer) craze—from the ubiquitous big-league teams' paraphernalia to the raving fans at a match. The climate makes it almost impossible to resist the temptation to try a cannonball serve on the red-clay tennis courts, sink a birdie putt on a scenic green, or just hike up a hill to savor the fresh air and views. Winters, of course, see ski enthusiasts trying their luck on the slopes of the Apennines and the Alps (*see* regional chapters for recommended resorts).

PARTICIPANT

➤ CANOEING: **Federazione Italiana Canoa e Kayak** (⊠ Viale Tiziano 70, 00196 Roma, ☎ 06/36858525).

➤ GOLF: **Federazione Italiana Golf** (⊠ Viale Tiziano 74, 00196 Roma, ☎ 06/36851).

➤ HORSEBACK RIDING: **Associazione Nazionale per il Turismo Equestre** (⊠ Via A. Borelli 5, 00161 Roma, ☎ 06/4441179).

➤ SAILING: **Federazione Italiana Vela** (⊠ Viale Brigata Bisagno 2, 16129 Genoa, ☎ 010/589431).

SPECTATOR

➤ BASKETBALL: **Federazione Italiana Pallacanestro** (⊠ Via Fogliano 15, 00199 Roma, ☎ 06/8863071).

➤ SOCCER: **Federazione Italiana Giuoco Calcio** (⊠ Via Gregorio Allegri 14, 00198 Roma, ☎ 06/84911).

➤ TENNIS: **Italian Tennis Federation** (⊠ Viale Tiziano 74, 00196 Roma, ☎ 06/36858510).

STUDENTS

To save money, **look into deals available through student-oriented travel agencies.** To qualify you'll need a bona fide student ID card. Members of international student groups are also eligible.

LOCAL RESOURCES

The Centro Turistico Studentesco (CTS) is a student and youth travel agency with offices in major Italian cities; CTS helps its clients find low-cost accommodations and bargain fares for travel in Italy and elsewhere. CTS is also the Rome representative for EuroTrain International.

➤ STUDENT IDs AND SERVICES: **Centro Turistico Studentesco (CTS;** ✉ Via Genova 16, Roma, ☎ 06/4679271). **Council on International Educational Exchange (CIEE;** ✉ 205 E. 42nd St., 14th floor, New York, NY 10017, ☎ 212/822–2600 or 888/268–6245, FAX 212/822–2699), for mail orders only, in the United States. **Travel Cuts** (✉ 187 College St., Toronto, Ontario M5T 1P7, ☎ 416/979–2406 or 800/ 667–2887) in Canada.

➤ HOSTELING: **Hostelling International—American Youth Hostels** (✉ 733 15th St. NW, Suite 840, Washington, DC 20005, ☎ 202/783– 6161, FAX 202/783–6171). **Hostelling International—Canada** (✉ 400-205 Catherine St., Ottawa, Ontario K2P 1C3, ☎ 613/237–7884, FAX 613/ 237–7868). **Youth Hostel Association of England and Wales** (✉ Trevelyan House, 8 St. Stephen's Hill, St. Albans, Hertfordshire AL1 2DY, ☎ 01727/855–215 or 01727/845–047, FAX 01727/844–126). Membership in the U.S., $25; in Canada, C$26.75; in the U.K., £9.30).

➤ STUDENT TOURS: **Contiki Holidays** (✉ 300 Plaza Alicante, Suite 900, Garden Grove, CA 92840, ☎ 714/740– 0808 or 800/266–8454, FAX 714/740– 0818). **AESU Travel** (✉ 2 Hamill Rd., Suite 248, Baltimore, MD 21210- 1807, ☎ 410/323–4416 or 800/638– 7640, FAX 410/323–4498).

T

TAXES

HOTEL

The service charge and the 9% IVA, or VAT tax, are included in the rate except in five-star deluxe hotels, where the IVA (12% on luxury hotels) may be a separate item added to the bill at departure.

RESTAURANT

A service charge of approximately 15% is added to all restaurant bills; in some cases the menu may state that the service charge is already included in the menu prices.

VALUE-ADDED TAX (VAT)

Value-added tax (IVA) is 19% on clothing and luxury goods. On most consumer goods, it is already included in the amount shown on the price tag, whereas on services, it may not be.

To **get an IVA refund,** when you are leaving Italy take the goods and the invoice to the customs office at the airport or other point of departure and have the invoice stamped. (If you return to the United States or Canada directly from Italy, go through the procedure at Italian customs; if your return is, say, via Britain, take the Italian goods and invoice to British customs.) Under Italy's IVA-refund system, a non-EU resident can obtain a refund of tax paid after spending a total of 300,000 lire in one store (before tax—and note that price tags and prices quoted, unless otherwise stated, include IVA). Shop with your passport and ask the store for an invoice itemizing the article(s), price(s), and the amount of tax. Once back home—and within 90 days of the date of purchase—mail the stamped invoice to the store, which will send the IVA rebate to you. A growing number of stores in Italy (and Europe) are members of the Tax-Free Shopping System, which expedites things by providing an invoice that is actually a Tax-Free Cheque in the amount of the refund. Once stamped, it can be cashed at the Tax-Free Cash refund window at major airports and border crossings; you can also opt to have the refund credited to your credit card or bank account, or sent directly home. To save a step at the airport or border, you can send the Cheque to a Tax-Free Shopping address.

TELEPHONES

The country code for Italy is 39.

Here are area codes for major cities: Bologna, 051; Brindisi, 0831; Florence, 055; Genoa, 010; Milan, 02; Naples, 081; Palermo, 091; Perugia, 075; Pisa, 050; Rome, 06; Siena, 0577; Turin, 011; Venice, 041; Verona, 045. When calling from abroad, the initial 0 from the local area code should be left out. For example, a call from New

York City to Rome would be dialed as
011 + 39 + 6 + phone number.

CALLING HOME

Since hotels tend to overcharge,
sometimes exorbitantly, for long-
distance and international calls, it is
best to make such calls from Telefoni
offices, where operators will assign
you a booth, help you place your
call, and collect payment when you
have finished, at no extra charge.
There are Telefoni offices, designated
TELECOM, in all cities and towns,
usually in major train stations and in
the center business districts. You can
**make collect calls from any phone by
dialing 172-1011,** which will get you
an English-speaking operator. Rates
to the United States are lowest 'round
the clock on Sunday and 11 PM−8 AM
(Italian time) on weekdays.

From major Italian cities, you can
place a direct call to the United
States by reversing the charges or
using your phone credit card number. When calling from pay telephones, insert a 200-lire coin that
will be returned upon completion of
your call. You automatically reach
an operator in the country of destination and thereby avoid all language difficulties.

Before you go, **find out the local access
codes** for your destinations. AT&T,
MCI, and Sprint long-distance services
make calling home relatively convenient, but you may find the local
access number blocked in many hotel
rooms. First ask the hotel operator to
connect you. If the hotel operator
balks, ask for an international operator, or dial the international operator
yourself. One way to improve your
odds of getting connected to your
long-distance carrier is to **travel with
more than one company's calling card**
(a hotel may block Sprint, for example, but not MCI). If all else fails, call
your phone company collect in the
United States or call from a pay phone
in the hotel lobby.

➤ FOR ACCESS CODES: **AT&T US-
ADirect** (☎ 800/874−4000). **MCI
Call USA** (☎ 800/444−4444). **Sprint
Express** (☎ 800/793−1153).

OPERATORS & INFORMATION

For general information in English,
dial 176. To place calls from one

European country to another via
operator-assisted service, dial 15. To
place intercontinental telephone calls
via operator-assisted service (or for
intercontinental information), dial
170 or long-distance access numbers
(☞ Calling Home, *above*).

PAY PHONES

Pay phones accept a 200-lire coin,
two 100-lire coins, or a 500-lire coin,
but **consider buying a *carta telefonica*
(prepaid calling card).** Scheda phones
are becoming common everywhere.
You buy the card (values vary—5,000
lire, 10,000 lire, etc.) at Telefoni offices, post offices, and tobacconists.
Tear off the corner of the card, and
insert it in the slot. When you dial, its
value appears in the window. After
you hang up, the card is returned so
you can use it until its value runs out.

TIPPING

Tipping practices vary, depending on
where you are. The following guide-
lines apply in major cities, but Italians
tip smaller amounts in smaller cities
and towns. Tips may not be expected
in cafés and taxis north of Rome.

In restaurants a service charge of
about 15% usually appears as a
separate item on your check. A few
restaurants state on the menu that
cover and service charge are included.
Either way, it's customary to leave
an additional 5%–10% tip for the
waiter, depending on the service. Tip
checkroom attendants 500 lire per
person, rest room attendants 200 lire;
in both cases tip more in expensive
hotels and restaurants. Tip 100 lire
for whatever you drink standing up
at a coffee bar, 500 lire or more for
table service in a smart café, and less
in neighborhood cafés. At a hotel bar
tip 1,000 lire and up for a round or
two of cocktails.

Taxi drivers are usually happy with
5%–10% of the meter amount. Railway and airport porters charge a fixed
rate per bag. Tip an additional 500 lire
per person, but more if the porter is
very helpful. Theater ushers expect
500 lire per person, and more for very
expensive seats. Give a barber 2,000–
3,000 lire and a hairdresser's assistant
3,000–8,000 lire for a shampoo or
cut, depending on the type of establishment.

On sightseeing tours, tip guides about 2,000 lire per person for a half-day group tour, more if they are very good. In museums and other places of interest where admission is free, a contribution is expected; give anything from 500 to 1,000 lire for one or two persons, more if the guard or caretaker has been especially helpful. Service station attendants are tipped only for special services.

In hotels, give the *portiere* (concierge) about 15% of his bill for services, or 5,000–10,000 lire if he has been generally helpful. For two people in a double room, leave the chambermaid about 1,000 lire per day, or about 4,000–5,000 a week, in a moderately priced hotel; tip a minimum of 1,000 lire for valet or room service. Increase these amounts by one-half in an expensive hotel, and double them in a very expensive hotel. In very expensive hotels, tip doormen 1,000 lire for calling a cab and 2,000 lire for carrying bags to the check-in desk, bellhops 3,000–5,000 lire for carrying your bags to the room and 3,000–5,000 lire for room service. One-third to one-half of these amounts is acceptable in moderately priced hotels.

TOUR OPERATORS

Buying a prepackaged tour or independent vacation can make your trip to Italy less expensive and more hassle free. Because everything is prearranged you'll spend less time planning.

Operators that handle several hundred thousand travelers per year can use their purchasing power to give you a good price. Their high volume may also indicate financial stability. But some small companies provide more personalized service; because they tend to specialize, they may also be more knowledgeable about a given area.

A GOOD DEAL?

The more your package or tour includes, the better you can predict the ultimate cost of your vacation. Make sure you know exactly what is covered, and **beware of hidden costs.** Are taxes, tips, and service charges included? Transfers and baggage handling? Entertainment and excursions? These can add up.

If the package or tour you are considering is priced lower than in your wildest dreams, **be skeptical.** Also, **make sure your travel agent knows the accommodations** and other services. Ask about the hotel's location, room size, beds, and whether it has a pool, room service, or programs for children, if they matter. Has your agent been there in person or sent others you can contact?

BUYER BEWARE

Each year consumers are stranded or lose their money when tour operators—even very large ones with excellent reputations—go out of business. So **check out the operator.** Find out how long the company has been in business, and ask several agents about its reputation. **Don't book unless the firm has a consumer-protection program.**

Members of the National Tour Association and United States Tour Operators Association are required to set aside funds to cover your payments and travel arrangements in case the company defaults. Nonmembers may carry insurance instead. Look for the details, and for the name of an underwriter with a solid reputation, in the operator's brochure. Note: When it comes to tour operators, **don't trust escrow accounts.** Although there are laws governing charter-flight operators, no governmental body prevents tour operators from raiding the till. For more information, *see* Consumer Protection, *above.*

➤ TOUR-OPERATOR RECOMMENDATIONS: **National Tour Association** (NTA; ✉ 546 E. Main St., Lexington, KY 40508, ☎ 606/226–4444 or 800/755–8687). **United States Tour Operators Association** (USTOA; ✉ 342 Madison Ave., Suite 1522, New York, NY 10173, ☎ 212/599–6599, FAX 212/599–6744).

USING AN AGENT

Travel agents are excellent resources. When shopping for an agent, however, you should **collect brochures from several sources**; some agents' suggestions may be skewed by promotional relationships with tour and package firms that reward them for volume sales. If you have a special interest, **find an agent with expertise in that area** (☞ Travel Agencies, *below*). Don't rely solely on your agent, who may be unaware of small-niche operators. Note that some special-interest travel companies only sell directly to the public and that some large operators only accept bookings made through travel agents.

SINGLE TRAVELERS

Prices for packages and tours are usually quoted per person, based on two sharing a room. If traveling solo, you may be required to pay the full double-occupancy rate. Some operators eliminate this surcharge if you agree to be matched with a roommate of the same sex, even if one is not found by departure time.

GROUP TOURS

Among companies that sell tours to Italy, the following are nationally known, have a proven reputation, and offer plenty of options. The classifications used below represent different price categories, and you'll probably encounter these terms when talking to a travel agent or tour operator. The key difference is usually in accommodations, which run from budget to better, and better-yet to best.

➤ SUPER-DELUXE: **Abercrombie & Kent** (✉ 1520 Kensington Rd., Oak Brook, IL 60521-2141, ☎ 630/954–2944 or 800/323–7308, FAX 630/954–3324). **Travcoa** (✉ Box 2630, 2350 S.E. Bristol St., Newport Beach, CA 92660, ☎ 714/476–2800 or 800/992–2003, FAX 714/476–2538).

➤ DELUXE: **Central Holidays** (✉ 206 Central Ave., Jersey City, NJ 07307, ☎ 201/798–5777 or 800/935–5000). **Donna Franca Tours** (✉ 470 Commonwealth Ave., Boston, MA 02215, ☎ 617/375–9400 or 800/225–6290). **Globus** (✉ 5301 S. Federal Circle, Littleton, CO 80123-2980, ☎ 303/797–2800 or 800/221–0090, FAX 303/347–2080). **Maupintour** (✉ 1515 St. Andrews Dr., Lawrence, KS 66047, ☎ 913/843–1211 or 800/255–4266, FAX 913/843–8351). **Perillo Tours** (✉ 577 Chestnut Ridge Rd., Woodcliff Lake, NJ 07675, ☎ 201/307–1234 or 800/431–1515). **Tauck Tours** (✉ Box 5027, 276 Post Rd. W, Westport, CT 06881-5027, ☎ 203/226–6911 or 800/468–2825, FAX 203/221–6828).

➤ FIRST-CLASS: **Brendan Tours** (✉ 15137 Califa St., Van Nuys, CA 91411, ☎ 818/785–9696 or 800/421–8446, FAX 818/902–9876). **Caravan Tours** (✉ 401 N. Michigan Ave., Chicago, IL 60611, ☎ 312/321–9800 or 800/227–2826, FAX 312/321–9845). **Collette Tours** (✉ 162 Middle St., Pawtucket, RI 02860, ☎ 401/728–3805 or 800/832–4656, FAX 401/728–1380). **Delta Dream Vacations** (☎ 800/872–7786). **Gadabout Tours** (✉ 700 E. Tahquitz Canyon Way, Palm Springs, CA 92262-6767, ☎ 619/325–5556). **Trafalgar Tours** (✉ 11 E. 26th St., New York, NY 10010, ☎ 212/689–8977 or 800/854–0103, FAX 800/457–6644). **TWA Getaway Vacations** (☎ 800/438–2929). **United Vacations** (☎ 800/328–6877).

➤ BUDGET: **Cosmos** (☞ Globus, *above*). **Trafalgar** (☞ *above*).

PACKAGES

Like group tours, independent vacation packages are available from major tour operators and airlines. The companies listed below offer vacation packages in a broad price range.

➤ AIR/HOTEL: **American Airlines Fly AAway Vacations** (☎ 800/321–2121). **Delta Dream Vacations** (☎ 800/872–7786). **DER Tours** (✉ 11933 Wilshire Blvd., Los Angeles, CA 90025, ☎ 310/479–4140 or 800/937–1235). **4th Dimension Tours** (✉ 7101 S.W. 99th Ave., #105, Miami, FL 33173, ☎ 305/279–0014 or 800/644–0438, FAX 305/273—9777). **United Vacations** (☎ 800/328–6877).

➤ FLY/DRIVE: **American Airlines Fly AAway Vacations** (☎ 800/321–2121). **Delta Dream Vacations** (☎ 800/872–7786).

➤ FROM THE U.K.: **Italian Escapades** (✉ 227 Shepherds Bush Rd., London W6 7AS, ☎ 0181/748–2661). **Page and Moy Holidays** (✉ 136–140 London Rd., Leicester, LE2 1EN, ☎ 0116/250–7676). **Carefree Italy** (✉ Allied Dunbar House, East Park, Crawley, West Sussex RH10 6AJ, ☎ 01293/552277) offers accommodations in apartments, castles, and farmhouses.

THEME TRIPS

Travel Contacts (✉ Box 173, Camberley, GU15 1YE, England, ☎ 127667/7217, FAX 1/2766–3477) represents over 150 tour operators in Europe.

➤ ADVENTURE: **Adventure Center** (✉ 1311 63rd St., #200, Emeryville, CA 94608, ☎ 510/654–1879 or 800/227–8747, ℻ 510/654–4200). **Himalayan Travel** (✉ 110 Prospect St., Stamford, CT 06901, ☎ 203/359–3711 or 800/225–2380, ℻ 203/359–3669).

➤ ART AND ARCHITECTURE: **Amelia Tours International** (✉ 28 Old Country Rd., Hicksville, NY 11801, ☎ 516/433–0696 or 800/742–4591, ℻ 516/579–1562). **Archeological Tours** (✉ 271 Madison Ave., Ste. 904, New York, NY 10016, ☎ 212/986–3054, ℻ 212/370–1561). **Endless Beginnings Tours** (✉ 12650 Sabre Springs Pkwy., Ste. 207-105, San Diego, CA 92128, ☎ 619/679–5374 or 800/822–7855, ℻ 619/679–5376).

➤ BALLOONING: **Buddy Bombard European Balloon Adventures** (✉ 855 Donald Ross Rd., Juno Beach, FL 33408, ☎ 561/837–6610 or 800/862–8537, ℻ 561/837–6623).

➤ BICYCLING: **Backroads** (✉ 801 Cedar St., Berkeley, CA 94710-1800, ☎ 510/527–1555 or 800/462–2848, ℻ 510-527–1444). **Bike Riders** (✉ Box 254, Boston, MA 02113, ☎ 617/723–2354 or 800/473–7040, ℻ 617/723–2355). **Butterfield & Robinson** (✉ 70 Bond St., Toronto, Ontario, Canada M5B 1X3, ☎ 416/864–1354 or 800/678–1147, ℻ 416/864–0541). **Ciclismo Classico** (✉ 13 Marathon St., Arlington, MA 02174, ☎ 617/646–3377 or 800/866–7314, ℻ 617/641–1512). **Euro-Bike Tours** (✉ Box 990, De Kalb, IL 60115, ☎ 800/321–6060, ℻ 815/758–8851). **Europeds** (✉ 761 Lighthouse Ave., Monterey, CA 93940, ☎ 800/321–9552, ℻ 408/655–4501). **Progressive Travels** (✉ 224 W. Galer Ave., Ste. C, Seattle, WA 98119, ☎ 206/285–1987 or 800/245–2229, ℻ 206/285–1988). **Rocky Mountain Worldwide Cycle Tours** (✉ 333 Baker St., Nelson, BC, Canada V1L 4H6, ☎ 250/354–1241 or 800/661–2453, ℻ 250/354–2058). **Uniquely Europe** (✉ 2819 1st Ave., Ste. 280, Seattle, WA 98121-1113, ☎ 206/441–8682 or 800/426–3615, ℻ 206/441–8862).

➤ CRUISING: **EuroCruises** (✉ 303 W. 13th St., New York, NY 10014-1207, ☎ 800/688–3876, ℻ 212/366–4747).

➤ FOOD AND WINE: **Amelia Tours** (☞ Art and Architecture, *above*). **Annemarie Victory Organization** (✉ 136 E. 64th St., New York, NY 10021, ☎ 212/486–0353, ℻ 212/751–3149). **Cuisine International** (✉ Box 25228, Dallas, TX 75225, ☎ 214/373–1161 or ℻ 214/373–1162). **Donna Franca Tours** (☞ Group Tours, *above*). **Hazan Classic Enterprises** (✉ Box 285, Circleville, NY 10919, ☎ 914/692–7104, ℻ 914/692–2659).

➤ HISTORY: **Herodot Travel** (✉ 775 E. Blithedale, Box 234, Mill Valley, CA 94941, ☎ ℻ 415/381–4031).

➤ HOMES AND GARDENS: **Coopersmith's England** (✉ Box 900, Inverness, CA 94937, ☎ 415/669–1914, ℻ 415/669–1942). **Endless Beginnings Tours** (☞ Art and Architecture, *above*). **Esplanade Tours** (✉ 581 Boylston St., Boston, MA 02116, ☎ 617/266–7465 or 800/426–5492, ℻ 617/262–9829). **Expo Garden Tours** (✉ 70 Great Oak, Redding, CT 06896, ☎ 203/938–0410 or 800/448–2685, ℻ 203/938–0427).

➤ HORSEBACK RIDING: **Equitour FITS Equestrian** (✉ Box 807, Dubois, WY 82513, ☎ 307/455–3363 or 800/545–0019, ℻ 307/455–2354).

➤ LEARNING: **Earthwatch** (✉ Box 9104, 680 Mount Auburn St., Watertown, MA 02272, ☎ 617/926–8200 or 800/776–0188, ℻ 617/926–8532) organizes research expeditions. **Smithsonian Study Tours and Seminars** (✉ 1100 Jefferson Dr. SW, Room 3045, MRC 702, Washington, DC 20560, ☎ 202/357–4700, ℻ 202/633–9250).

➤ MOTORCYCLE: **Beach's Motorcycle Adventures** (✉ 2763 W. River Pkwy., Grand Island, NY 14072-2053, ☎ 716/773–4960, ℻ 716/773–5227).

➤ MUSIC: **Dailey-Thorp Travel** (✉ 330 W. 58th St., #610, New York, NY 10019-1817, ☎ 212/307–1555 or 800/998–4677, ℻ 212/974–1420).

➤ PILGRIMAGES: **Pilgrimage Tours and Travel** (✉ 39 Beechwood Ave., Manhasset, NY 11030, ☎ 516/627–2636 or 800/669–0757).

➤ Spas: **Great Spas of the World** (✉ 630 5th Ave., New York, NY 10111, ☎ 212/599–0382 or 800/772–8463, FAX 212/599–0380). **Spa-Finders** (✉ 91 5th Ave., #301, New York, NY 10003-3039, ☎ 212/924–6800 or 800/255–7727). **Spa Trek Travel** (✉ 475 Park Ave. S., New York, NY 10016, ☎ 212/779–3480 or 800/272–3480, FAX 212/779–3471).

➤ Tennis: **Championship Tennis Tours** (✉ 7350 E. Stetson Dr., #106, Scottsdale, AZ 85251, ☎ 602/990–8760 or 800/468–3664, FAX 602/990–8744).

➤ Villa Rentals: **Eurovillas** (✉ 1398 55th St., Emeryville, CA 94608, ☎ FAX 707/648–2066). **Rentals in Italy** (✉ 1742 Calle Corva, Camarillo, CA 93010-8428, ☎ 805/987–5278 or 800/726–6702, FAX 805/482–7976). **Villas International** (✉ 605 Market St., San Francisco, CA 94105, ☎ 415/281–0910 or 800/221–2260, FAX 415/281–0919).

➤ Walking/Hiking: **Abercrombie & Kent** (☞ Group Tours, *above*). **Above the Clouds Trekking** (✉ Box 398, Worcester, MA 01602-0398, ☎ 508/799–4499 or 800/233–4499, FAX 508/797–4779). **Backroads** (☞ Bicycling, *above*). **Butterfield & Robinson** (☞ Bicycling, *above*). **Ciclismo Classico** (☞ Bicycling, *above*). **Country Walkers** (✉ Box 180, Waterbury, VT 05676-0180, ☎ 802/244–1387 or 800/464–9255, FAX 802/244–5661). **Euro-Bike Tours** (☞ Bicycling, *above*). **Mountain Travel-Sobek** (✉ 6420 Fairmount Ave., El Cerrito, CA 94530, ☎ 510/527–8100 or 800/227–2384, FAX 510/525–7710). **Progressive Travels** (☞ Bicycling, *above*). **Uniquely Europe** (☞ Bicycling, *above*). **Wilderness Travel** (✉ 801 Allston Way, Berkeley, CA 94710, ☎ 510/548–0420 or 800/368–2794, FAX 510/548–0347).

➤ Yacht Charters: **Huntley Yacht Vacations** (✉ 210 Preston Rd., Wernersville, PA 19565, ☎ 610/678–2628 or 800/322–9224, FAX 610/670–1767). **Lynn Jachney Charters** (✉ Box 302, Marblehead, MA 01945, ☎ 617/639–0787 or 800/223–2050, FAX 617/639–0216). **Ocean Voyages** (✉ 1709 Bridgeway, Sausalito, CA 94965, ☎ 415/332–4681 or 800/299–4444, FAX 415/332–7460).

All Italian trains have first and second classes. On local trains the higher first-class fare gets you little more than a clean doily on the headrest of your seat, but on long-distance trains you get wider seats and more legroom and better ventilation and lighting. At peak travel times, first-class train travel is worth the difference. Remember to **always make seat reservations in advance,** for either class.

The fastest trains on the Ferrovie dello Stato (FS), the Italian State Railways, are the Pendolino Eurostar (ETR 460 trains), operating on several main lines, including Rome–Milan, via Florence and Bologna; seat reservations and supplement are included in the fare. Next-fastest trains are the Intercity (IC) trains, for which you pay a supplement and for which seat reservations may be required and are always advisable. *Interregionale* trains usually make more stops and are a little slower. *Regionale* and *locale* trains are the slowest; many serve commuters.

To avoid long lines at station windows, **buy tickets and make seat reservations up to two months in advance** at travel agencies displaying the FS emblem. Agencies cannot make same-day seat reservations, but can sell tickets for the same day. If you have to reserve at the last minute, reservation offices at the station accept reservations up to three hours before departure. You may be able to get a seat assignment just before boarding the train; look for the conductor on the platform. Trains can be very crowded on weekends and during holiday and vacation seasons; reserve seats in advance or, if the train originates where you get on, get to the station early to find a seat. A card just outside the compartment or over the seat indicates whether it has been reserved. Carry compact bags for easy overhead storage.

All tickets must be date-stamped in the small yellow or red machines near the tracks before you board. Once stamped, your ticket is valid for six hours if your destination is within 200 km, for 24 hours for destinations beyond that. You can get on and off at will at stops in between for the duration of the ticket's validity. If you don't stamp your ticket in the machine, you must actively seek out a conductor to validate the ticket on the train, paying 10,000 lire extra for the service. If you merely wait in your seat for him to collect your ticket, you must pay a 30,000 lire fine in addition. You also pay a hefty penalty if you purchase your ticket on board the train. You can buy train tickets for destinations within a 100-km (62-mi) range at tobacconists and at ticket machines in stations.

Note that in some Italian cities (including Milan, Turin, Genoa, Naples, and Rome) there are two or more main-line stations, although one is usually the principal terminal or through-station. Be sure of the name of the station at which your train will arrive, or from which it will depart.

There is refreshment service on all long-distance trains, with mobile carts and a cafeteria or dining car. Tap water on trains is not drinkable.

To save money, **look into rail passes** (☞ Discount Passes, *below*), but be aware that if you don't plan to cover many miles, you may come out ahead by buying individual tickets.

➤ FROM THE U.K.: **British Rail** (☎ 0171/834–2345). **French Railways** (☎ 0891/515–477); calls charged at 49p a minute peak rate, 39p all other times.

DISCOUNT PASSES

If Italy is your only destination in Europe, **consider purchasing an Italian Railpass,** which allows unlimited travel on the entire Italian Rail network. Prices begin at $132 for four days of travel in second class within a one-month period and $194 in first class. Passes that are good for longer periods of time are also available, as are Flexipasses, which allow a limited amount of train travel within a certain period.

Once in Italy, **inquire about the Carta Verde if you're under 26** (40,000 lire for one year), which entitles the holder to a 20% discount on all first- and second-class tickets. Those under 26 should also inquire about discount travel fares under the Billet International Jeune (BIJ) scheme. The special one-trip tickets are sold by EuroTrain

International at its offices in various European cities and by travel agents, mainline rail stations, and youth travel specialists.

You can **purchase the Carta d'Argento if you're over 60** (40,000 lire for one year), good for a 20% discount on all first- and second-class tickets, except for travel June 26–August 14 and December 18–28.

Italy is one of 17 countries in which you can **use EurailPasses,** which provide unlimited first-class rail travel, in all of the participating countries, for the duration of the pass. If you plan to rack up the miles, get a standard pass. These are available for 15 days ($522), 21 days ($678), one month ($838), two months ($1,188), and 3 months ($1,468). If your plans call for only limited train travel, **look into a EuroPass,** which costs less money than a EurailPass. Unlike EurailPasses, however, you get a limited number of travel days, in a limited number of countries, during a specified time period. For example, a two month pass ($316) allows five days of rail travel (additional days $42 each) and is good only in France, Germany, Italy, Spain, and Switzerland; rail travel to Austria, Hungary, Portugal, Greece, Holland, Luxembourg, and Belgium can be added to the pass for additional fees.

In addition to standard EurailPasses, **ask about special rail-pass plans.** Among these are the Eurail Youthpass (for those under age 26), the Eurail Saverpass (which gives a discount for two or more people traveling together), a Eurail Flexipass (which allows a certain number of travel days within a set period), the Eurail-drive Pass and the EuroPass Drive (which combines travel by train and rental car).

Whichever pass you choose, remember that you must **purchase your Eurail-Pass or EuroPass before you leave** for Europe.

Many travelers assume that rail passes guarantee them seats on the trains they wish to ride. Not so. You need to **book seats ahead even if you are using a rail pass;** seat reservations are required on some European trains, particularly high-speed trains, and are a good idea on trains that may be crowded—particularly in summer on popular routes. You will also need a reservation if you purchase sleeping accommodations.

➤ UNIQUE GUIDEBOOK: *Italy by Train* by Tim Jepson (Fodor's Travel Publications, ☎ 800/533–6478 or from bookstores); $16.

➤ DISCOUNT PASSES: Eurail- and EuroPasses are available through travel agents and **Rail Europe** (✉ 226-230 Westchester Ave., White Plains, NY 10604, ☎ 914/682–5172 or 800/438–7245; ✉ 2087 Dundas E., Suite 105, Mississauga, Ontario L4X 1M2, ☎ 416/602–4195), **DER Tours** (✉ Box 1606, Des Plaines, IL 60017, ☎ 800/782–2424, FAX 800/282–7474), or **CIT Tours Corp.** (✉ 342 Madison Ave., Suite 207, New York, NY 10173, ☎ 212/697–2100, 800/248–8687, 800/248–7245 in western U.S.). Italian rail passes can be purchased through DER Tours or CIT Tours as well.

TRANSPORTATION

Public transportation is the fastest mode of travel among Italy's cities. It is also relatively inexpensive in comparison to the costs of renting a car and paying for gas and tolls. Italy's cities are served by an extensive state railway system (☞ Train Travel, *above*), with fast service on main lines (Milan-Venice-Florence-Rome-Naples) that in some cases beats plane travel in time and cost. The state system and some private lines radiate to smaller towns, but service can be sporadic.

Buses (☞ Bus Travel, *above*), somewhat less comfortable than trains and slightly less expensive, offer more frequent service to certain smaller cities and towns that are served only by secondary train lines, Siena included. Buses are also better relied upon in more rugged areas: the Dolomites, Liguria, Tuscany, and the Amalfi Coast, for instance. Ferries and hydrofoils ply among the islands; some islands, such as Capri and Ischia, have helicopter service, a more expensive alternative.

Getting around in Italy by plane (☞ Air Travel, *above*) is an expensive but viable option, and it is the fastest means of traveling long distances, as in to Sicily and Sardinia. Look for special bargain rates that can defray costs. Train and bus connections between airports and city centers are usually smooth.

Italy has an intricate network of autostrade routes, good highways, and secondary roads, making renting a car (☞ Car Rental *and* Driving, *above*) for travel among most cities a feasible but expensive alternative to public transportation (not to mention complaints of white-knuckle driving by those inexperienced with autostrade speeds). A car can be a good investment if you are interested in carefree countryside rambles, offering time to explore more remote towns. Having a car in major cities, however, often leads to parking and traffic headaches, plus additional expense in the form of garage and parking fees.

TRAVEL AGENCIES

A good travel agent puts your needs first. **Look for an agency that specializes in your destination, has been in business at least five years, and emphasizes customer service.** If you're looking for an agency-organized package or tour, your best bet is to choose an agency that's a member of the National Tour Association or the United States Tour Operators Association (☞ Tour Operators, *above*).

➤ LOCAL AGENT REFERRALS: **American Society of Travel Agents** (ASTA; ☎ 800/965–2782 for 24-hr hot line, FAX 703/684–8319). **Alliance of Canadian Travel Associations** (✉ Suite 201, 1729 Bank St., Ottawa, Ontario K1V 7Z5, ☎ 613/521–0474, FAX 613/521–0805). **Association of British Travel Agents** (✉ 55–57 Newman St., London W1P 4AH, ☎ 0171/637–2444, FAX 0171/637–0713).

TRAVEL GEAR

Travel catalogs specialize in useful items, such as compact alarm clocks and travel irons, that can **save space when packing.** They also offer dual-voltage appliances, currency converters, and foreign-language phrase books.

➤ MAIL-ORDER CATALOGS: **Magellan's** (☎ 800/962–4943, FAX 805/568–5406). **Orvis Travel** (☎ 800/541–3541, FAX 540/343–7053). **TravelSmith** (☎ 800/950–1600, FAX 800/950–1656).

U

U.S. GOVERNMENT

The U.S. government can be an excellent source of inexpensive travel information. When planning your trip, **find out what government materials are available.**

➤ ADVISORIES: **U.S. Department of State American Citizens Services Office** (⊠ Room 4811, Washington, DC 20520); enclose a self-addressed, stamped envelope. **Interactive hot line** (☎ 202/647–5225, FAX 202/647–3000). **Computer bulletin board** (☎ 202/647–9225).

➤ PAMPHLETS: **Consumer Information Center** (⊠ Consumer Information Catalogue, Pueblo, CO 81009, ☎ 719/948–3334) for a free catalog that includes travel titles.

V

VISITOR INFORMATION

➤ AT HOME: **Italian Government Tourist Board** (ENIT; ⊠ 630 5th Ave., New York, NY 10111, ☎ 212/245–4822, FAX 212/586–9249; ⊠ 401 N. Michigan Ave., Chicago, IL 60611, ☎ 312/644–0990, FAX 312/644–3019; ⊠ 12400 Wilshire Blvd., Suite 550, Los Angeles, CA 90025, ☎ 310/820–0098, FAX 310/820–6357; ⊠ 1 Pl. Ville Marie, Ste 1914, Montréal, Québec H3B 3M9, ☎ 514/866–7667, FAX 514/392–1429; ⊠ 1 Princes St., London W1R 8AY, ☎ 0171/408–1254, FAX 0171/493–6695).

➤ TOURIST OFFICES ABROAD: **Rome** (⊠ Via Parigi 5, ☎ 06/48899253). **Florence** (⊠ Via Cavour 1/r, next to Palazzo Medici–Riccardi, ☎ 055/290832). **Venice** (⊠ Palazzetto Selva, off Piazza San Marco, ☎ 041/5226356). **Milan** (⊠ Via Marconi 1, ☎ 02/809662). **Naples** (⊠ Piazza dei Martiri 58, ☎ 081/405311). **Palermo** (⊠ Piazza Castelnuovo 35, ☎ 091/583847).

W

WHEN TO GO

The main tourist season runs from April to mid-October. For serious sightseers the best months are from fall to early spring. The so-called low season may be cooler and inevitably rainier, but it has its rewards: less time waiting on lines and closer-up, unhurried views of what you want to see.

Tourists crowd the major art cities at Easter, when Italians flock to resorts and to the country. From March through May, busloads of eager schoolchildren on excursions take cities of artistic and historical interest by storm.

CLIMATE

Weatherwise, the best months for sightseeing are April, May, June, September, and October—generally pleasant and not too hot. The hottest months are July and August, when brief afternoon thunderstorms are common in inland areas. Winters are relatively mild in most places on the main tourist circuit but always include some rainy spells. In general, the northern half of the peninsula and the entire Adriatic Coast, with the exception of Apulia, are rainier than the rest of Italy.

If you can avoid it, don't travel at all in Italy in August, when much of the population is on the move, especially around Ferragosto, the August 15 national holiday, when cities such as Rome and Milan are deserted Đand many restaurants and shops are closed. (Of course, with residents away on vacation, this makes crowds less of a bother for tourists.) Except for a few year-round resorts, such as Taormina and some towns on the Italian Riviera, coastal resorts usually close up tight from October or November to April; they're at their best in June and September, when everything is open but uncrowded.

➤ FORECASTS: **Weather Channel Connection** (☎ 900/932–8437), 95¢ per minute from a Touch-Tone phone.

Climate in Italy

The following are average daily maximum and minimum temperatures for major cities in Italy.

MILAN

Jan.	40F	5C	May	74F	23C	Sept.	75F	24C
	32	0		57	14		61	16
Feb.	46F	8C	June	80F	27C	Oct.	63F	17C
	35	2		63	17		52	11
Mar.	56F	13C	July	84F	29C	Nov.	51F	10C
	43	6		67	20		43	6
Apr.	65F	18C	Aug.	82F	28C	Dec.	43F	6C
	49	10		66	19		35	2

ROME

Jan.	52F	11C	May	74F	23C	Sept.	79F	26C
	40	5		56	13		62	17
Feb.	55F	13C	June	82F	28C	Oct.	71F	22C
	42	6		63	17		55	13
Mar.	59F	15C	July	87F	30C	Nov.	61F	16C
	45	7		67	20		49	10
Apr.	66F	19C	Aug.	86F	30C	Dec.	55F	13C
	50	10		67	20		44	6

VENICE

Jan.	42F	6C	May	70F	21C	Sept.	75F	24C
	33	1		56	13		61	16
Feb.	46F	8C	June	76F	25C	Oct.	65F	19C
	35	2		63	17		53	12
Mar.	53F	12C	July	81F	27C	Nov.	53F	12C
	41	5		66	19		44	7
Apr.	62F	17C	Aug.	80F	27C	Dec.	46F	8C
	49	10		65	19		37	3

1 Destination: Italy

UNDER THE SPELL OF ITALY

THEY CAME FOR THE LIGHT, they came for culture, they came for inspiration. Above all, they came to discover something that was missing in themselves. Passion, perhaps. A heightened sense of awareness. They came not simply to find themselves but to become their best selves.

Keats, Shelley, Byron, James, Goethe, Wagner, Prendergast, Renoir, Monet, and centuries of tourists who did not record their inspiration for the ages, but who, like Miss Lavish in E. M. Forster's *Room with a View,* knew that "one doesn't come to Italy for niceness . . . one comes for life."

And how is this life delivered unto one? If you ask the traveler of this decade, the answers will be various. For some it is the layers of history, physically present to walk upon, the reassuring sense of place and continuity that comes from a casual coexistence with antiquity. Twentieth-century businessmen and women stroll through the Roman Forum, swinging their briefcases and chatting of today's deals as they pass between the 5th-century-BC Corinthian columns of the Temple of Castor and Pollux.

It is as if one could hold out a hand and feel the touch of Pliny the Elder, Livy, or Catullus. A young woman, fresh from college Latin, made the mistake of visiting the Forum at high noon in August, suffered heat stroke, and was certain she heard Cicero speak before she fainted. There are those who would tell you that it wasn't the heat—Cicero *had* spoken.

Another woman, seven months pregnant when she and her husband traveled to Ravenna, swears that as she beheld the dazzling gold and lapis lazuli of San Vitale's 5th-century mosaics her unborn child leapt for joy. There is no guarding against it; life will fill you to brimming as Italy has its way with you.

For the sybarite, the palate is awakened by the clear, true flavors of wine and food that taste faintly of the earth and sea from which they came. Buckwheat pasta in Bormio; polenta, black with squid ink, in Venice; creamy gelato at Giolitti in Rome; or the perfectly comforting bowl of risotto in Siena, served by a family in their nameless restaurant. You will hear, on the other side of the Atlantic, the longings of travelers returned home, who, as the light begins to change in early September, yearn for *gamberetti,* Venetian shrimp the size of a baby's fingertip. Summer causes them to recall the simple delight of sitting beneath large shade trees on the banks of Lake Como, drinking cool wine from earthenware pitchers. Winter's winds bring memories of Alpine chills chased by a fiery draft of grappa.

It is the dream that takes you back, just as it was the dream that enveloped you while you were there. You will notice that those who travel in Italy seem to do so in a state of reverie. Perhaps it is the diaphanous gauze of light that softens physical outlines and blurs the distinction between past and present. A light conducive to daydreams. A light that both intensifies life and makes it gentler to the touch.

Of course, there are those who have been rudely awakened from the dream by a revved-up 1990s state-of-the-art motorcycle outside their 19th-century Roman hotel. They will grumpily tell of the shocking presence of 20th-century blight in a land that seemed impervious to such intrusion. In the heat of disillusion, they will complain of the "real" Italy, of Roman traffic jams, thefts in Naples, Venice as Disneyland, a highway system around Milan as attractive as the New Jersey Turnpike. They will warn that you, a woman, must not be persuaded by the charms of an Italian gentleman who commits his heart and future within a three-minute walk across a piazza.

There is truth in what they say, but the generosity of the Italians and the striking physical beauty of their land make it possible to live in the dream alongside the blight. You cannot arrive in Venice without driving through the gray air of Mestre, polluted by oil refineries. But once your water taxi is negotiating the Grand Canal, you lose yourself in time and space. And that is what Italy is about . . . losing and finding yourself in time and space. By morning, as the rudely awakened dreamer stands on the Palatine Hill and smells the wild fennel just as Horace did, all is forgiven.

It is the natural as well as the man-made wonders that entrance. In the Valtellina Valley you will sit in grottoes where the Caesars sat to soak in hot mineral springs, and you will feel the curing effects of waters that were said to ease the pain of gout, arthritis, and politics. You can indulge in the mindless delights of the Amalfi Coast exactly as 19th-century English travelers did when they came to rest their minds, weary from the obligatory acquisition of culture in the north. Here, where rocky cliffs are caught in a perpetual dive to the sea, nothing seems more important than tonight's dinner or lovemaking.

Italy may be the most sensual of countries. Perhaps it is the basic simplicity that returns one to the simplest human emotions: the organic nature of all that surrounds you, each century seeming to grow from the land. Or perhaps it is the heightened sense of romance that comes from the constant reminders of the very best of that of which people are capable—the serenity of Bellini's altarpiece in San Zaccaria, the compassion of Michelangelo's *Pietà* in St. Peter's, the symmetry of a Palladian villa rising from the earth of the Veneto. Or it could be living among people for whom life's pleasures are celebrated rather than guiltily indulged.

Whatever it is, to experience Italy one needs time, not necessarily in days but in solitude. It is in the silent times that Italy will be revealed to you. Early morning, watching the light shine on the Pantheon, while strong Italian coffee wakens your senses. Dawn on the Grand Canal as dark green water is sprayed with gold and the only sound is a gondolier's oar breaking the silent surface. Midnight in the Forum, Daisy Miller's undoing and Byron's inspiration. Sunrise in Stelvio National Park, where eagles soar overhead and you are knee-deep in wildflowers.

And one must believe in that elusive commodity, happiness. This is a country that, through the ages, in fact and fiction, has promised that possibility. Goethe, having fled the restrictive court life of Weimar, wrote from Rome in September 1788: "I can honestly say I have never been so happy in my life as now." And in *Room with a View,* Forster observed that when his young provincial heroine, Lucy, finally dared forfeit her Baedeker for experience, "then the pernicious charm of Italy worked on her, and, instead of acquiring information, she began to be happy."

You, too, should relinquish this book from time to time and observe with an uninstructed eye, drift into the dream, and allow yourself to be charmed.

—Barbara Lazear Ascher

NEW AND NOTEWORTHY

Italy is in the throes of planning for the **Jubilee Year of 2000,** when a record number of pilgrims is expected to flock to Rome and other tourist destinations along the peninsula. Some travelers, in fact, will carefully avoid Rome during the year of the millennium, fearing apocalyptic overcrowding and transportation snarls.

In Rome, the pace of public works and restorations has picked up in preparation for the Jubilee. The interior of the **Basilica di San Pietro** (St. Peter's Basilica) is being cleaned, and the exterior is undergoing a three-year face-lift. Only one-fifth of the facade will be hidden by scaffolding at any one time. Expect many other church facades, however, to be under wraps for restoration. Similar work on the **Colosseo** (Colosseum) continues.

One of the thornier aspects of Rome bracing itself for the exodus of visitors are the public works projects to eliminate traffic bottlenecks and provide speedier public transportation. Construction of an underpass in the Castel Sant'Angelo–St. Peter's Basilica area is sure to make traffic in the vicinity slower than ever for the next two years.

After 13 years of structural restorations that started from the building's very foundations, the **Galleria Borghese** has been reopened, its marvelous collections back in place. The gallery, where Canova's languid reclining marble portrait of barebreasted Paolina Borghese is a big draw, now has a bookshop, a café, and other amenities. By 1998, the three museums holding the archaeological collections of the **Museo Nazionale Romano** (National Museum of Rome) group—composed of the new museums in Palazzo Altemps and Palazzo Massimo alle Terme, plus the renovated Museo Terme di Diocleziano—should all be open. Try to see the **Via Appia Antica** (Ancient Appian Way) on Sunday, when the city has banned most automobile traffic, transforming the oldest of Roman roads into an archaeological park. In the heart of Rome's shopping district, the 19th-century **Galleria Colonna** has been transformed into a chic shopping arcade, with boutiques purveying Bulgari baubles and Armani collections.

In April 1997, on Rome's 2,750 birthday, Romans hailed the return of the **statue of Marcus Aurelius**—though only a copy—to its pedestal in Piazza del Campidoglio on the Colle Capitolino (Capitoline Hill), where it has always symbolized the city's timeless grandeur. The original remains inside the **Musei Capitolini** (Capitoline Museums).

Artful travelers no longer need be intimidated by long lines at Florence's **Galleria degli Uffizi** (Uffizi Gallery). Thanks to a ticket reservation service introduced in 1997, at Consorzio ITA in Florence, you can book ahead and sail past the lines at the ticket office. **Naples' Museo Capodimonte,** palatial treasure trove of Bourbon art and aristocratic artifacts including a fabulous porcelain collection, has been refurbished and reopened.

Opera fans have been reassured that the summer season of the **Rome Opera,** ousted from the Terme di Caracalla (Baths of Caracalla), will have a suitable site. The 1997–98 season at **Milan's La Scala** will be operagoers' last chance to attend performances in the splendid theater at the heart of the city before it is temporarily closed for restoration. La Scala will not move to a temporary theater, as originally announced, until a worthy venue has been built. In Palermo the grand old **Teatro Massimo** reopened after 23 years.

In Turin, 1998 offers a rare occasion to see the **Sacra Sindone** (Holy Shroud), believed by some to be the shroud in which Christ's body was wrapped. The shroud is displayed to the public only on rare occasions, the last of which was during the Holy Year 1975. Pope John Paul II has given permission to display the shroud in 1998 during the 500th anniversary of the founding of Turin's Duomo. The shroud was housed in the Cappella della Sacra Sindone (Chapel of the Holy Shroud) in the Duomo before the chapel suffered a severely damaging fire in April 1997; at press time (spring 1997) it was not yet determined where the Holy Shroud—reportedly unscathed by the fire—would be displayed, and the chapel was closed indefinitely. The public's next scheduled date with the shroud will be unusually soon—in 2000, the next Holy Year.

Anyone who is put off by the hairpin turns in the serpentine roads of the **Amalfi Coast** can now arrive with greater ease. Scheduled boat service from Naples and Salerno has been increased, with commuterlike timetables that allow you to make day trips or overnight circuits taking in Capri, Ischia, Sorrento, Positano, and Amalfi—all with killer views.

WHAT'S WHERE

Like a Santa Claus stocking, the boot of Italy overflows with unsurpassable sights—from top to toe. Here is a sampling of the infinite variety of the country's many regions and attractions.

Rome

Latium's holy claim to fame, Rome is split on its west side by the zigzagged Tiber River, which is a mere 25 km (16 mi) from its mouth at the Tyrrhenian Sea. Antique, Renaissance, Baroque—and always papal—the Eternal City allows you a walk around where Nero fiddled, a visit to the Forum in which the Romans crowded to hear Mark Antony's eulogy, and a lunch in the vicinity of Charlemagne's coronation site. Rome possesses a veritable Grand Canyon of culture, built up with stratified layers of pagan, medieval, and modern. But it's also about a walk through the cobblestone alleys of Trastevere—Rome's Greenwich Village; a *Campari* break in a timeless piazza; an hour stolen alongside a splashing fountain, blessed by the balm of Roman sunshine. From here you are a cool 190 km (117 mi) northwest of Naples, the gateway to the splendorous south.

Florence

Florence, the "Athens of Italy" and the key to the Renaissance, hugs the banks of the Arno River where it lies folded among the emerald cypress-studded hills of north-central Tuscany. Elegant and somewhat aloof, as if set apart by its past greatness, this historic center of European civilization still shares with Rome the honor of first place among Italian cities for the magnitude of its artistic works, among them Botticelli's siren and Michelangelo's powerful *David*. Down every street and *vicolo* (alley) and in every piazza you'll make new discoveries of Romanesque, Gothic, or Renaissance architecture; sheltered within these churches, cloisters, and towers are masterful painting and sculpture of the Quattrocento and Cinquecento periods. Equally as splendid are the magnificent chapels and palaces of the Medici—whose patronage rocketed Florence to the forefront of the Renaissance—which stand unabashed amid the city's vibrant modern pulse.

Tuscany

Without a doubt, Nature outdid herself in Tuscany, the region on the Ligurian and Tyrrhenian seas that beholds Florence. Punctuated by thickly wooded hills, snowcapped peaks, sun-warmed vineyards, olive groves, and dramatic hill towns, Tuscany's milk-and-honey vistas have changed little since Renaissance artists first beheld them. Not surprisingly, you'll find some of Italy's greatest art treasures here, including the 13th-century Leaning Tower of Pisa and Piero della Francesca's *Legend of the True Cross* frescoes in Arezzo. The time traveler will be entranced by medieval Siena, "the Pompeii of the Middle Ages," as it was called by the philosopher Taine. Perched dramatically above a fertile valley, San Gimignano—with its Manhattan-like skyline of medieval towers—may jettison you into a Who-turned-back-the-clock? sensation of Mark Twain's Connecticut Yankee when he arrived in King Arthur's court. With a glass of Vernaccia di San Gimignano in hand, you'll feel like lingering long.

Venice

Rising from the waters of the Venetian lagoons like a mirage, the city of canals is unlike any other. A romantic maze of alleys, waterways, and tiny squares and bridges playing hide-and-seek with each other, Venice is a magical world apart. In this city of Marco Polo, Titian, and Vivaldi, a *vaporetto* ride down the Grand Canal—Venice's own Fifth Avenue—is a fairy-tale-like journey past the city's shimmering, most sumptuous palaces, the Ca' Rezzonico, the Palazzo Pésaro, and the Ca' d'Oro. "Venice is like eating an entire box of chocolate liqueurs in one go," Truman Capote once remarked, and he's right: the city is stuffed with the most spectacular Bellini, Veronese, and Tiepolo paintings. During February's Carnival, you'll find even the pigeons are pressed for space in Piazza San Marco, the city's heart. The best time to catch Venice is during the Historic Regatta (the first week of September) when the 18th-century canvases of Canaletto seem to come to life.

Venetian Arc

The green plains of the mainland stretching beyond the Venetian lagoon harbor some of Italy's smaller art cities, individual artistic variations on the overall Venetian theme. Elegant Vicenza, which bears the signature of the great 16th-century architect Andrea Palladio, blends rustic beauty with a jigger of 18th-century Venetian chic. Here, the wealthy citizenry devised ways to make la vita all the more dolce at noble villas (many of which are now museums): Palladio's La Rotonda, the hauntingly beautiful La Malcontenta (along the idyllic Brenta Canal), and the Villa Barbaro in Maser. Farther west, Verona is famed for the Tombs of the Della Scala lords, the romantic settings associated with Shakespeare's *Romeo and Juliet,* and an ancient Roman arena (still packing in the crowds for thrilling opera performances). Art lovers head for Padua to catch Giotto's Scrovegni Chapel and Donatello's powerful statue of the *condottiere* (mercenary general) Gattamelata. To truly unwind, head for Asolo, the City with a Hundred Horizons: it's a magical hill town replete with villas and gardens, but there's not a single souvenir shop or espresso bar.

Italian Riviera

The Italians perfected *il dolce far niente*—the sweet art of idleness—and they must have done it right here in Liguria, site of the Italian rivieras. Called "the island," the province is enclosed by mountain ranges that create an ideal climate for the narrow coastal strip (you can sip coffee outdoors in winter and linger under palm trees at Christmastime). Here, in jet-set resorts and quaint fishing villages, tourists recover from vacation overload. The Riviera di Ponente (Western Riviera) runs from the French border to Genoa and is best known for San Remo, Monte Carlo's less expensive cousin. The eastern counterpart, the Riviera di Levante, is made up of Camogli, Rapallo, Levanto, Cinque Terre, Portovenere, San Fruttuoso, glowing like pearls on a string. Of these, Portofino—the Palm Beach of Italy—is the beauty-contest winner. The Crusaders, who once used Portofino for its refueling resources, have been replaced by today's top-of-the-heap who arrive in their yachts to sun and soak. When doing nothing becomes too exhausting, there is always Genoa—the region's thriving metropolis—for stimulation.

Piedmont/Valle d'Aosta

Piedmont and the grand Valle d'Aosta in the northwest corner of Italy come as delightful surprises in a land of continuous natural splendor. The characteristics of neighboring France and Switzerland blend harmoniously with the region's Italian heritage. Geographically, the area combines the lure of the highest Alpine peaks—such as Mont Blanc and Mont Cervino (the Matterhorn)—in ranges that fan out along the south, west, and north boundaries and the broad flatlands of the plain. Here, at Breuil-Cervinia, Courmayeur, and Sestriere, skiing is at its best. Alpine valleys harboring 14th- and 15th-century castles—witnesses to turbulent days of old—are anchored by Turin, the "Italian Detroit," home of the Fiat empire. The city's other well-known imports—Borsalino hats, vermouth, and Asti Spumante—mark it as a great cosmopolitan center.

Milan, Lombardy, and the Lakes

Lombardy stretches south from the Alps to the River Po, and not far from the modern metropolis of Milan are the dreamlike resort lakes of Como, Maggiore, and Garda, whose 19th-century summer palaces, exotic formal gardens, and Alpine vistas give them some of the most achingly beautiful settings in Italy. Milan's cultural identity is as diverse as its changeable weather: international fashion capital, industrial and banking center, crucible of modern design. The must-see's here include La Scala—the equivalent of paradise to opera performers and fans; the gigantic Gothic Duomo; the Brera and Poldi Pezzoli museums; Leonardo da Vinci's *Last Supper;* and, of course, stopping and shopping at Versace, Valentino, and Armani. Farther south, tour the great Renaissance cities of the plain: Pavia, Cremona, and Mantua, home to the palaces of the Gonzaga. On the edge of the Alps, Bergamo awaits with its hilltop *città alta,* a charming medieval center. For those who believe holidays are fantasies, the apricot-color villages, palaces, and gardens of the lakes region cannot be bettered. Lake Como has gorgeous villas, many around the beguiling town of Bellagio; along Lake Garda is the Brescian Riviera, and on Lake Maggiore you'll find the storybook Borromean Islands and glowing Stresa. Here you may not find great art treasures or encounter the long-lost pagan past, but, if you are in search of it, you will certainly find peace.

The Dolomites

Northwest Italy's Dolomite Mountains—Nature's skyscrapers—draw scenery-hungry tourists by the thousands. Many come in hot pursuit of the charming meadows and valleys; the crystal clear lakes; the stupefying cliffs, curiously shaped peaks, and splintered crags whose resplendent hues range from pale rose at dawn to declamatory purple at dusk. (Leonardo da Vinci depicted these peaks in the haunting background of his *Mona Lisa.*) For other visitors this region is the ultimate year-round sports playground—with the seeing just as important as the skiing in jet-set Cortina d'Ampezzo. Take the Strada del Vino (Wine Route) from Bolzano to Trento, where there is a famous cathedral and the moated Castello del Buonconsiglio; enjoy the "grape cure" at Merano; zip along the 48 hairpin turns of the Stelvio Pass; absorb the vistas of the Grande Strada delle Dolomiti (Great Dolomites Road); and top it all off with a skydiving stop at the historic town of Bressanone, where Gothic and Baroque art blend harmoniously.

Emilia-Romagna

Gourmets the world over argue that Emilia-Romagna's greatest contribution to mankind has been gastronomic. In the birthplace of fettucine, prosciutto, tortellini, and lasagna, you need never worry about any of the restaurants you walk into. The region on the Adriatic between Tuscany and Lombardy also contains an abundance of cultural riches—the legacies of the Farnese family in Piacenza and Parma, the Este family in Modena and Ferrara, the Malatesta in Rimini, and the Bentivoglio in Bologna. Bologna—*dotta e grassa* (learned and fat)—is home to Italy's oldest university as well as to the spirits of Copernicus, Galileo, and Dante. The area between Piacenza and Parma is opera country—Verdi's villa of Sant'Agata is in Busseto. The polished city of Parma nourished two of Italy's greatest painters, Parmigianino and Correggio. For a breather, head along the Adriatic coast to the principal summer resort of Rimini and the Byzantine beauty of mosaic-rich Ravenna, glittering as brightly as it did 1,500 years ago.

Umbria and the Marches

Legends linger here in the evergreen land of the saints, the birthplace of St. Francis and St. Claire (Assisi), St. Benedict (Norcia), and St. Rita (Cascia). The strange, bluish haze that tints the landscape has inspired writers to characterize the region as mystical and ethereal. Here, medieval enclaves wear their ancient histories lightly, and majestic valleys refuse to pose for tourists' cameras. Umbria, the region surrounded by Latium, Tuscany, and the Marches, bears a rich artistic inheritance that includes the frescoes of Giotto and Pietro Lorenzetti in Assisi's Basilica of St. Francis, the brooding Palazzo dei Consoli in Gubbio, and the Gothic glory of Orvieto's cathedral. For a "deep, delicious bath of medievalism," as Henry James wrote, a visit to Assisi is an imperative; the spirit of St. Francis gently permeates the hillside town. For more urbane pleasures, head for Spoleto's celebrated Festival of Two Worlds or Perugia's popular jazz concerts. Eastward, in the off-the-beaten-track region of the Marches on the Adriatic, is Urbino, where the Renaissance first came to full flower. It is full of treasures by such illustrious artists as Bramante, Raphael, and Piero della Francesca. A visit to its Ducal Palace reveals more about the wealth and artistic energy of the Renaissance than a shelf of history books.

Campania

Magnetic, magical, and magnificent, Campania is the Italy many travelers dream about. Emperors and kings, popes and artists, musicians and writers have made its sea-wreathed resorts and starlit isles their homes for more than 2,000 years—and well they might, for this is a compressed realm of undiluted beauty. Naples—the most operatic of cities—rules over the unequaled panorama of its bay. Once ancient Romans led the carefree life at nearby Pompeii; today, travelers soak up the 24-karat sun on Capri—a pint-size island paradise that is as intoxicating as its delicious wines. Down the shoreline along Amalfi Drive is shockingly beautiful Ravello, where just about the bluest view on tap takes in the Gulf of Salerno. From here, take a day trip to Paestum's ancient temples. Head back to Sorrento, Positano, and Amalfi, famed as places of play and pleasure.

Apulia

Misguided tourists think that after a visit to Naples and a drive around the Amalfi coast to Salerno (maybe as far afield as Paestum) they have seen Italy's south. The truth is they have barely entered the gate. Italy's far south is composed of the ancient provinces of Apulia (Puglia), Lucania (the Basilicata), and Calabria—the heel, instep, and arch, respectively, of Italy's boot. Often overlooked Apulia is steeped in ancient history and rich with tantalizing sights that are only now coming to the surface. The region invites aimless exploration: seek out its whitewashed ports, imposing castles, and strange igloo-shape dwellings called *trulli*. The cities of Brindisi, Bari, and Lecce hold many fascinations, and the coastline is full of seductions—unspoiled coves, bougainvillea-draped vistas, and seas that shimmer like sheets of turquoise.

Sicily

On this fabled island, you may ski down a snow-muffled volcano, walk through palm and orange groves, and swim within sight of flowering almond trees—all in the same day. Many visitors first head for Taormina, a town whose natural beauties are so great that even the overdevelopment of the past 50 years has not spoiled its grandeur. The city's views of the sea and Mt. Etna come close to panoramic perfection. In summer, Taormina hosts an arts festival, with many of its events held in its spectacular 3rd-century-BC Greek Theater. Sicily's main metropolis, Palermo, has always been at the crossroads of civilization: Phoenician colony, Carthaginian town, capital of an Arab emirate, commercial hub of Europe and Asia under Norman rule, center of learning under Frederick II. Nearby is Sicily's most important art treasure, the cathedral of Monreale, with its glorious medieval mosaics. On the southwestern coast lies Agrigento, with its stellar relic from antiquity, the Valley of the Temples. Among the ancient Greek buildings here, the Temple of Concord is the best preserved in the world after that of Theseus in Athens.

Sardinia

Too distant from imperial and papal Rome to be influenced by the character of the mainland, Sardinia is as unique as its weather-worn landscape. Visitors arrive at this diamond-in-the-rough landscape by air or sea at Cagliari in the south, Olbia in the northeast, or Alghero in the northwest. Although the indigenous culture is one of Italy's most interesting, many travelers opt to explore the high-profile Costa Smeralda. This chic resort was developed by the Aga Khan, who discovered its charms when his yacht took shelter from a storm. "Secret paradise" of tycoons and actresses in years past, the Costa is now an open, upscale vacationland. Sardinia's most expensive hotels are here, and the current scions of the House of Savoy—modern Italy's one royal dynasty—return annually in their yachts. Intrepid travelers head for the *nuraghi,* cyclopean stones that are among prehistory's enigmas. Severely beautiful Sardinia remains a prime destination for those in search of a vacation forgetaway.

PLEASURES AND PASTIMES

The Art of Enjoying Art

Travel veterans will tell you that the endless series of masterpieces in Italy's churches, palaces, and museums can cause first-time visitors—eyes glazed over from a heavy downpour of images, dates, and names—to lean, Pisa-like, on their companions for support. After a surfeit of Botticellis and Bronzinos and the 14th Raphael, even the

miracle of the High Renaissance may begin to pall. The secret, of course, is to act like a turtle—not a hare—and take your sweet time. Instead of trotting after briskly efficient tour guides, allow the splendors of the age to unfold—slowly. Get out and explore the actual settings—medieval chapels, Rococo palaces, and Romanesque town squares—for which these marvelous examples of Italy's art and sculpture were conceived centuries ago and where many of them may still be seen in situ.

Musems are only the most obvious places to view art; there are always the trompe l'oeil renderings of Assumptions that float across Baroque church ceilings and piazza scenes that might be Renaissance paintings brought to life. Instead of studying a Gothic statue in Florence's Bargello, spend an hour in the medieval cloisters of the nearby convent of San Marco; by all means, take in Michelangelo's *Slaves* in Florence's Accademia, but then meander down the 15th-century street, a short bus ride away, where he was born. You'll find that after three days traipsing through museums, a walk through a quiet neighborhood will act as a much-needed restorative of perspective.

Of course, there may be many art treasures that will not quicken your pulse, but one morning you may see a Caravaggio so perfect, so beautiful, that your knees will buckle.

Il Dolce Far Niente

The idea of vacation was probably invented by some hardworking Roman emperor and, ever since, the Italians have been fine-tuning what they call il dolce far niente—the sweet art of idleness. Today, even relaxing can feel like a chore, but thanks to Italy's opulent villas, picture-perfect coastal resorts, and dreamy hill towns, you can idle here more successfully than anywhere else. But it takes more than trading in a silk tie for a T-shirt; you have to adjust to the deeper, subtler rhythms of leisure, Italian style. Hours spent over a Campari in a sun-splashed café; days spent soaking up the sun on the Amalfi coast; an afternoon spent painting a watercolor on the shores of Lake Como: You may be pleasantly surprised to find that such pursuits prove more beneficial than forced marches through the obligatory sights. The luxury is often in the lingering.

Dining

In Italy, cookery is civilization. In the days of the Roman legions, pundits used to say, *"Ubi Roma ibi allium"* (Where there are Romans, there is garlic). Ever since the days of the Caesars—when emperors quickly learned the wisdom of *"Stomaco pieno, anima consolata"* (Full stomach, satisfied soul)—Italian chefs have taken one of life's sensory pleasures and made it into an art, and today travelers can feast on an incredible array of culinary delights. Of course, Italian food has come a long way since the days when Horace, the great poet of ancient Rome, feasted on lamprey boiled in five-year-old wine, the liver of a goose fattened on figs, and apples picked by the light of the waning moon. But you can still enter restaurants in Bologna, enjoy a dish of tortellini, and be told, *"Anche Dante le ha mangiate cósi"* (Dante also ate them this way). In fact, the newest trend in Italian cooking is to serve up the old—the simple, rustic, time-honored forms of cucina *simpatica, rustica,* and *trattoria*—with a nouvelle flair.

Among Italian chefs, there is concern that membership in the European Union will affect the country's unique regional cooking. The use of processed ingredients and nonorganically grown vegetables is taking its toll. Happily, food critics rejoice that much of Italian cooking remains *puro* and *sincero*—true to the country's culinary traditions.

Dining is a marvelous part of the total Italian experience, a chance to enjoy authentic specialties and ingredients. Visitors have a choice of eating places, ranging from a *ristorante* (restaurant) to a trattoria, *tavola calda,* or *rosticceria.* A trattoria is usually a family-run place, simpler in decor, menu, and service than a ristorante, and slightly less expensive. Some rustic-looking spots call themselves *osterie* but are really restaurants. (A true *osteria* is a wineshop—a basic, down-to-earth tavern.)

None of the above eateries serves breakfast; in the morning you go to a coffee bar, which is where you can also find sandwiches, pastries, and other snacks that are perfect for later in the day. Tell the cashier what you want, pay for it, and then take the stub to the counter, where you order. Remember that table service is extra; don't sit at a table unless you want to be served. On the other hand, if you do sit down, you'll be allowed to linger as long as you like.

In eating places of all kinds the menu is posted in the window or just inside the door so you can see what you're getting into (in a snack bar or tavola calda the price list is usually displayed near the cashier). In all but the simplest places there's a *coperto* (cover charge) and usually also a *servizio* (service charge) of 10%–15%, only part of which goes to the waiter. A *menù turistico* (tourist menu) includes taxes and service, but beverages are usually extra.

Generally, a typical meal in a restaurant or trattoria consists of at least two courses: a first course of pasta, risotto, or soup; and a second course of meat or fish. Side dishes such as vegetables and salads cost extra, as do desserts. There is no such thing as a side dish of pasta; pasta is a course in itself and Italians would never think of serving a salad with it; the salad comes later. Years ago, pasta dishes were inexpensive because restaurateurs made their profit on the total of the first and second courses. Now, tourists and even some diet-conscious Italians tend to order only one course—usually a pasta, perhaps followed by a salad or vegetables—so hosts have jacked up the price of first courses. Now, about antipasto: many a misunderstanding arises over a lavish offering of antipasto, which literally means "before the meal." No matter how generous and varied the antipasto, the host expects you to order at least one other course. Pizza is in a category by itself and is a one-dish meal, even for the Italians. But some replace the starter course of pasta with a small pizza.

Tap water is safe almost everywhere unless labeled *"non potabile."* Most people order bottled *acqua minerale* (mineral water), either *gassata* (carbonated), or *naturale,* or *non gassata* (without bubbles). In a restaurant you order it by the *litro* (liter) or *mezzo litro* (half-liter); often the waiter will bring it without being asked, so if you don't like it, or want to keep your check down, make a point of ordering *acqua semplice* (tap water). You can also order *un bicchiere di acqua minerale* (a glass of mineral water) at any bar. If you are on a low-sodium diet, ask for everything (within reason) *senza sale* (without salt).

Lunch is served in Rome from 1 to 3, dinner from 8 to 10, or later in some restaurants. Service begins and ends a half hour earlier in Florence and Venice, an hour earlier in smaller towns in the north, and a half hour to one hour later in the south. Almost all eating places close one day a week and for vacations in summer and/or winter. *Buon appetito!*

Shopping

"Made in Italy" has become synonymous with style, quality, and craftsmanship whether it refers to high fashion or Maserati automobiles. The best buys are leather goods of all kinds—from gloves to bags to jackets—silk goods, knitwear, gold jewelry, ceramics, and local handicrafts. The most important thing to keep in mind when shopping in Italy is that every region has its specialties. Venice is known for glassware, lace, and velvet; Milan and Como for silk; the Dolomites and the mountainous regions of Calabria and Sicily for hand-carved wooden objects; Florence for straw goods, gold jewelry, leather, and paper products; Naples for coral and cameos; Assisi for embroidery; and Deruta, Gubbio, Vietri, and many towns in Apulia and Sicily for ceramics.

In general, the idea that bargaining is the rule in Italy is mistaken. There is no universal policy, but for the most part prices are fixed in the better shops. Where you see the sign PREZZI FISSI (fixed prices) you can be sure that there is no bargaining to be done. However, you can bargain to your heart's delight at outdoor markets and when buying from street vendors.

Unless your purchases are too bulky, avoid having them shipped home; if the shop seems extremely reliable about shipping, get a written statement of what will be sent, when, and how.

GREAT ITINERARIES

Classical Highlights

Well colonized by the ancient Greeks, then epicenter of the Roman Empire, Italy has a wealth of classical sites, many of them quite well preserved, thanks in part to the Italian appreciation for history and heritage. Rome was, of course, the glorious capital of the Roman Empire, and a number of ancient sites remain there today, seemingly plunked down in the middle of the bustling modern metropolis. It is quite an experience to turn a corner and see a famous building, such as the Colosseum, across the street, with Fiats and Vespas buzzing blithely past its crumbling arches. Campania, too, has a number of important classical landmarks, from both the Roman and the Greek eras. Below the volcanic cone of Mt. Vesuvius, the buried ruins of Pompeii are the most famous, but even better-preserved relics are still being unearthed from the lava at nearby Herculaneum. Farther down the coast is Paestum, the remains of an ancient town with remarkably well-preserved Greek temples; some classicists enjoy uncrowded Paestum more than either Pompeii or Herculaneum.

Those with more time or a more intense interest in ancient times will want to follow this itinerary all the way to Sicily, the large island just off the toe of Italy's boot. Heavily colonized by the Greeks, Sicily was a center of trade and culture in the Hellenic world, and it still is richly endowed with remarkable sites, most notably Agrigento and Siracusa.

Duration

7–17 days

Getting Around

BY CAR➤ On the A2 autostrada, it takes about three hours to drive from Rome to Naples. Most of the classical sites in Campania can be seen on day trips from Naples; the farthest away is Paestum, 99 km (60 mi) down the coast on S18. If you choose to continue on to Sicily, take either the overnight car ferry from Naples to Palermo, Sicily, or drive down the A3 autostrada (488 km/302 mi) to Villa San Giovanni in Calabria, where frequent ferry service crosses the strait in a half hour to Messina, Sicily, 235 km (145 mi) east of Palermo. Sicily's main sites are spread out to every corner of the large island, so you will have to stop overnight near each site. It's a 128-km (80-mi) drive south from Palermo to Agrigento, on the island's southwest coast; Selinunte is up the coast from Agrigento, along S115 about 100 km (60 mi). Agrigento is 212 km (132 mi) from Siracusa.

PUBLIC TRANSPORTATION➤ Train service between Rome and Naples is fast and frequent, taking less than two hours on express trains. The Circumvesuviana train line can take you conveniently from Naples to Pompeii and Herculaneum. There is an FS train station right in Paestum. There is a ferry from Naples to Palermo, Sicily, and a main train line runs from Palermo to Siracusa. Other sites on Sicily are better reached by bus than by the unreliable local train service.

The Main Route

2–3 NIGHTS: ROME➤ Spend at least a day exploring Ancient Rome—the Capitoline Hill, the Roman Forum, the Circus Maximus, the Colosseum, the Pantheon—and on subsequent days, venture out to the Appian Way and the Catacombs, or study classical sculptures in the Vatican museums and antiquities in the Museo Nazionale.

3–5 NIGHTS: NAPLES➤ After arriving from Rome, spend the afternoon at the Museo Archeologico Nazionale. Herculaneum and Pompeii can be visited in one day from Naples, but it would be a very full day, and it is best to break it into two separate excursions. On another day, enjoy an excursion down the Amalfi coast or take the A3 autostrada to Paestum, with its well-preserved Greek temples. An optional day can be spent touring the area just west of Naples, taking in the Roman amphitheater at Pozzuoli, spooky Lake Avernus, the Roman resort town at Baia with its excavated baths, and the Sibyl's Cave at Cumae, perhaps the oldest Greek colony in Italy.

1 NIGHT: FERRY TO SICILY

1 NIGHT: PALERMO➤ Visit the National Archaeological Museum and nearby Segesta, with its fine Doric Greek temple.

1–2 NIGHTS: AGRIGENTO➤ Explore the Valley of the Temples, an extensive Greek site, and if you have time, make your way up the coast to see the Greek temple complex at Selinunte.

1–2 NIGHTS: SIRACUSA➤ Visit the Archaeological Park in town, the splendid Archaeological Museum, and, if there's time, take an excursion to see the mosaics at the Imperial Roman Villa at Casale, just north of Piazza Amerina.

1 NIGHT (OPTIONAL): TAORMINA➤ Get a fine view of Mt. Etna and see the town's Greek theater, still used for the summer arts festival.

1 NIGHT: FERRY TO NAPLES

1 NIGHT: RETURN TO ROME

Information
☞ Chapters 2, 13, and 15.

Italian Gardens

Using the living materials and elements of nature to achieve studied aesthetic effects, Italians have been masters at creating gardens, an art that flourished from the Renaissance and Baroque ages well into the 19th century. Usually framing country villas or grand city palaces, the most spectacular gardens are laid out with an artist's eye for perspective and color; many are studded with statuary and fanciful fountains. A tour of some of Italy's most beautiful gardens would begin in Milan, gateway to the lake district, ideally in spring, when azaleas and rhododendrons are in glorious bloom. The gardens of the Medici villas near Florence have a more austere feel, their beauty found in artful arrangements of evergreen shrubs. Note that some gardens are not open to the public during winter months and are subject to seasonal conditions; call ahead.

To plant the elaborately tiered gardens of Isola Bella and Isola Madre in the Borromean Islands off Stresa, on Lake Maggiore, a 16th-century count had laborers haul earth to the islands in boats. The effort was well worth it, as these gardens have become one of the Stresa's chief attractions. Within sight of the islands, between Intra and Pallanza on the promontory of Verbania, is the vast garden of Villa Taranto, laid out in the 20th century and one of Europe's finest. On Lake Como, only one stop on the lake ferry separates the gardens of Villa Carlotta in Tremezzo from those of Villa Melzi in Bellagio, which some regard as the most serendipitous site in the entire lake district. If you have time, you can take a leisurely ferry trip around the Maggiore or Como lake to get glimpses of many more villa gardens from the boat.

Make Florence your base for a series of visits to the gardens of the Medici villas on the city's outskirts. Before heading out of the city, spend a half day in the Giardini Boboli, laid out for Eleanor of Toledo, wife of Duke Cosimo I. You can peruse the garden of Villa Gamberaia, east of Florence, on a half-day excursion. It is also possible to explore the gardens of Villa di Castello and nearby Medici Villa La Pietraia, north of the city, in a half day, alternating these excursions with city sightseeing.

Duration

6–9 days

Getting Around

BY CAR➤ On A8 and A26, Stresa is about 95 km (59 mi) northwest of Milan. Make Stresa your base for ferry trips to the Borromean Islands and Verbania. From Stresa backtrack on the A8 to pick up A9 to Como, a distance of 75 km (47 mi). Follow the scenic lakeshore road northeast for 29 km (18 mi) from Como to Bellagio. Tremezzo and Villa Carlotta are only one stop away on the ferry. From Bellagio drive southeast 22 km (14 mi), enjoying the scenery along the Lecco branch of Lake Como, picking up S36 at Lecco. Just south of Monza pick up A1 for Florence, 344 km (213 mi) from Lecco. Villa Gamberaia, near Settignano, is 6½ km (4 mi) northeast of the center of Florence. Villa di Castello is 5 km (3 mi) northwest of downtown Florence, in the direction of Sesto Fiorentino. Villa La Pietraia is ⅛ mile east of Villa di Castello.

BY PUBLIC TRANSPORTATION➤ There is train service between Milan and Stresa (about 60 minutes) and between Milan and Como (about 30 minutes). Lake ferry service is frequent and makes it easy to explore lakeside villages on lakes Maggiore and Como. The bus from Como to Bellagio takes about 75 minutes, depending on traffic, and it takes about the same time to reach Lecco from Bellagio by bus. The train ride from Lecco to Milan takes about 30 minutes, and the train ride from Milan to Florence takes about 3–3½ hours. To reach Villa Gamberaia from Florence take Bus 10, marked Settignano. To reach Villa La Pietraia take Bus 28; Villa di Castello is within walking distance.

The Main Route

2–3 NIGHTS: STRESA➤ Spend the better part of one day exploring the Borromean Islands, from the decorative Baroque palace and terraced gardens on Isola Bella to the Renaissance-style villa on Isola Madre, surrounded by a lush park where peacocks strut their stuff amid banks of azaleas, rhododendrons, and camelias. The next day hop on a ferry to Verbania and get off at the Villa Taranto embarcadero. Some 20,000 species—many rare and exotic—grow in the gardens, adorned with terraces, cascades, and fountains.

2–3 NIGHTS: BELLAGIO➤ In this beauty spot on Lake Como romantic vistas are everywhere. At Villa Melzi a fabulous staircase abloom with spring azaleas and topped by a neoclassic palace is the centerpiece of a park studded with statues. Just across the lake in Tremezzo, Villa Carlotta was a wedding present to Charlotte of Russia in 1843; the luxuriant gardens and park are known for a spectacular flowering of rhododenrons and azaleas in April and May. From Tremezzo, take the ferry to Sala Comacina where there is regular ferry service to Villa del Balbaniello during visiting hours; check hours with Bellagio or Tremezzo tourist offices. This is perhaps one of the most romantic sites of all.

2–3 NIGHTS: FLORENCE➤ Roam through the Giardini Boboli, noting how the plan was ingeniously adapted to a very irregular site. Then, together with some city sightseeing to help you focus on the Medici influence in Florence, devote half days to excursions to the Medici villas. Villa Gamberaia's elegant Italian garden is set in olive groves on the hill of Settignano. Sculptures by Renaissance masters adorn the 16th-century Italian garden at Villa La Pietraia, where there is also a park landscaped in 19th-century style. More than 500 lemon trees stud the large Italian garden of Villa di Castello.

Information

☞ Chapters 3 and 9.

A Gourmet Tour

Sampling Italy's best food and wines in the very places they are produced will enlighten your understanding of the country and its people. In a country where good eating and drinking is the rule practically everywhere, this itinerary is necessarily selective. It starts in Piedmont, universally recognized as birthplace of some of the world's really great red wines.

The first stop is Turin, a gracious city renowned for exquisite chocolates called *gianduiotti* and for the equally delectable pastries to be enjoyed in grand, fin-de-siècle cafés. Southeast of Turin in the Monferrato and Langhe districts, rolling hills are blanketed with the vineyards that produce Barolo, "king of wines and wine of kings," in addition to Barbaresco and others. The provincial city of Asti has lent its name to Spumante, a sparkling white that brings bubbles of gaiety to every kind of celebration in Italy. Some like it sweet, especially as a dessert wine, but many choose the brut version, much like champagne and made by the same method. (Be sure to try some in Trento, where some of Italy's best Spumanti are produced.) Capital of the Langhe wine country is Alba, where the October wine and truffle fair features a rousing medieval-style tournament.

No Italian food aficionado shall pass up Emilia-Romagna's Parma, a gastronomically rewarding detour. As rich in history and art as in its culinary delights, Parma deserves at least an overnight, if possible.

Head east to the Veneto, another region of premium wines and tasty specialties. In Verona you can drink Valpolicella or Soave and dine on tender boiled meat. Due north of Verona, in the Dolomites, follow the Wine Road, the Strada del Vino, which starts near Bolzano. Cooking here is an irresistible blend of Italian and Austrian accents, for this used to be the South Tyrol. Charming Treviso is a base for an excursion on another wine road, the Strada del Vino Rosso (Red Wine Road), through Cabernet and Merlot country along the Piave River. A plate of hearty *pasta e fagioli*, the hearty pasta-and-bean-soup specialty of the Veneto region, will sustain you. Farther east, the Friuli-Venezia Giulia region is the realm of white wines and country cooking with a Mittel-European flavor.

Either Florence or Siena could be your base for a ramble through the Chianti district, where you can delve into the subtle differences in vintages and perhaps swerve out of the district's official confines into the realm of Brunello di Montalcino. To acquire an insider's way with Tuscan food, take a cooking course in Lorenza de' Medici's Renaissance villa, Badia a Coltibuono (✉ Gaiole in Chianti, ☎ 0577/749031).

Duration
6–14 days

Getting Around

BY CAR➤ Asti is 60 km (37 mi) east of Turin on A21. From Asti, S231 traces the course of the Tanaro River southwest to Alba, a drive of 30 km (18 mi). Return to Asti to head east on A21 and A4 to Verona, a distance of 270 km (167 mi). On your way you could make a gourmet's detour, leaving A21 at the Piacenza exit and driving southeast on A1 for 60 km (37 mi) to reach Parma. On A22 Trento is 135 km (84 mi) north of Verona. Continue north on the same autostrada to reach Bolzano, 60 km (37 mi) from Trento. The S47 through the Valsugana leads east and south to Bassano del Grappa and Treviso, a total distance of 135 km (84 mi). The wine country around Udine is about 115 km (71 mi) from Treviso, by way of the A4 and A23. A22 from Verona or A13 from Padua connect with A1 for Florence. The distance between Treviso and Siena is 360 km (223 mi).

PUBLIC TRANSPORTATION➤ Local trains and buses run from Turin to Asti and Alba. Return to Turin to get a train on the main east–west line to Verona, where there is frequent service on another main line to Trento and Bolzano. Return to Verona for a train to Padua. Treviso can be reached by train or bus from Padua. Udine is on a main line that passes through Padua. There is fast service on the same line to Florence, where you can get a local train or bus to Siena. Local buses serve the Chianti district.

The Main Route

1–2 NIGHTS: TURIN➤ Dine on as many as 30 antipasti followed by a creamy risotto, and top off your meal with a delectable dessert. Then head for one of the city's historic cafés to drink in the atmosphere along with your espresso. And don't forget to pick up some chocolates.

2 NIGHTS: ASTI➤ Spend a day exploring the wineries in the area. Spend another day in Alba, stopping at Castello di Barolo (Barolo Castle) to sample the wine and visit the wine museum. Let the aroma of white truffles titillate your senses, and treat your tastebuds to a range of culinary specialties that exalt this regal tuber. En route to Verona, make a detour to Parma for a quintessential Italian meal.

1–2 NIGHTS: VERONA➤ This could be your base for excursions north to Trento and Bolzano. Verona's ancient Roman Arena, medieval buildings, and characteristic restaurants deserve some attention, too.

1–2 NIGHTS: BOLZANO➤ An optional overnight stop, it allows time to enjoy local food and wines at your leisure and to follow the Wine Road that starts at Caldaro, 15 km (9 mi) south of Bolzano.

2 NIGHTS: TREVISO➤ Medieval buildings, swift-flowing water in canals, mill wheels and an abundance of inns where you can savor local dishes and wines make this a good base for exploring the area. You could spend a day on an excursion to Udine, or follow the Wine Road from Conegliano, where sparkling, fruity Prosecco is made.

1 NIGHT: UDINE➤ Another optional overnight, this attractive city was ruled by Venice and shows it, with stone Venetian lions rampant on graceful buildings and columns in pretty piazzas. The Collio wine district and some distinctive local food specialties are sure to be of interest.

2–3 NIGHTS: FLORENCE OR SIENA➤ Spend at least two days roaming through the Chianti district, which lies between Florence and Siena, stopping at villages harboring a precious art work or two by Tuscan masters and pausing to dine at country inns. Many wineries offer guided tours of their cellars, often part of historic estates belonging to families that can trace their origins back to the Middle Ages or the Renaissance era.

Information

☞ Chapters 3, 4, 6, 8, 10, 11.

FODOR'S CHOICE

No two people agree on what makes a perfect vacation, but it's fun and helpful to know what others think. Here's a compendium drawn from the must-see lists of hundreds of Italian tourists. For detailed information about these memories-in-the-making, refer to the appropriate chapters in this book.

Quintessential Italy

★ **Bellagio, Lake Como.** Once called "Italy's prettiest town," it still seems to be more of an operetta set than a resort. Surrounded by sumptuous villas and gardens, the town has long played host to honeymooners, kings, and celebrated visitors who love its faded millionaires' gentility.

★ **Piazza del Campo, Siena.** This shell-shaped piazza delimited by the austere Palazzo Civico symbolizes the grace and power of a proud medieval city where an age-old rivalry with Florence still fires the tongues and souls of the Senesi. During the Palio, the square explodes in a frenzy of medieval pageantry and passion with the dizzying horse race.

★ **Lecce, Apulia.** Extravagant Baroque churches—a flowering of golden stone—are the showpieces of this city in Italy's deep south, stomping ground of the ancient Greeks, bold Crusaders, and a landed aristocracy. All left their marks.

★ **San Gimignano, Tuscany.** In this quintessential Tuscan town, stand on the steps of the Collegiata church at sunset as the swallows swoop in and out of the famous medieval towers, twittering softly as they coast on the air.

Lodging and Dining Gems

★ **Gualtiero Marchesi, Erbusco, Lago d'Iseo.** Spectacular flights of fantasy grounded with classic Lombardian finesse are masterminded by the restaurant's namesake chef, the founder of *la cucina nuova*. No creative fancy is spared—from Far East touches to the whimsy of origami to caviar garnishes. $$$$

★ **La Scalinatella, Capri.** At breakfast, contemplate the blue of the sky from this hotel's terrace—then spend the rest of the morning gazing at the water below; it's full of kaleidoscopic hues of turquoise, lavender, and aquamarine. $$$

★ **Il Cibreo, Florence.** In one of Florence's best, chef Fabrio Picci reinterprets Tuscan classics, served in an Old World, truly Florentine atmosphere. It's off the beaten path, but its location next to a marketplace promises the freshest of ingredients—and imagination. $$

★ **Villa Las Tronas, Alghero, Sardinia.** Turn-of-century gentility pervades this royal mansion on a rocky bluff above the sea. Plush gardens shelter you regally, amid modern comforts and expansive views. *$$$–$$$$*

★ **Accademia, Venice.** Just beyond the hotel's iron gate, a secret garden awaits, complete with mini Palladian-style villa, canal parterre, and verdant trees. It's both enchanting and cheery, but no secret. *$$*

★ **La Tazza d'Oro, Rome.** Those who claim that the national coffee habit is the key to the Italian disposition find conclusive proof here in Italy's best cup of coffee. Do as the Romans do: order a glass of water as a chaser. *$*

Special Memories

★ **Spoleto, Umbria.** Descending the stairs toward Spoleto's medieval cathedral, the broad ramp, flanked by low medieval buildings, fans out as it spills down toward the pale stone sanctuary, studded with rose-colored windows and mosaics set against the verdant green backdrop of Umbria's hills.

★ ***Passeggiata*, Taormina.** For perfect people-watching in an unforgettable seaside setting, head for Corso Umberto at dusk and witness the pagentry. All turn out for the promenade, pausing for *gelato* or *caffè* and casting a vigilant eye toward hovering Mt. Etna.

★ **Procession of San Efisio, Caligari.** Tradition isn't just a cliché in Sardinia's tourist-trade lexicon, and none of the island's other time-honored festivals has the exuberance of Caligari's annual binge.

★ **Sunset Gondola Ride, Grand Canal, Venice.** For a truly magic moment, ply along the surrealistic waterway, lined with fairytale-like *palazzi*, veiled in silvery mists.

Where Art Comes First

★ **Cappelle Medicee, San Lorenzo, Florence.** This grandiose complex is a Michelangelan tour de force: the earthy marble slabs in the Cappella dei Principi resonate in architectural equilibrium; the allegorical sculptural figures in the New Sacristy have such an impact, his contemporaries invented a word for the phenomenon—*terribilità* (dreadfulness).

★ **Ducal Palace, Urbino.** If the Renaissance was, in ideal form, a celebration of the nobility of man and his works, of the light and purity of the soul, then in no other palace in Italy are these tenets better illustrated.

★ **Giotto Fresco Cycle, Cappella degli Scrovegni, Padua.** The realism depicted in these frescoes—executed from 1303 to 1305—which includes the first blue skies in Western painting, was revolutionary.

★ **I Frari, Venice.** In this great Venetian Gothic church, you'll find two of Titian's most spectacular altarpieces; their blazing colors and luminosity cast 20th-century electricity into shadow.

★ **La Rotonda, Vicenza.** Italy's most famous Palladian villa was the inspiration for Thomas Jefferson's Monticello. If you run into the delightfully friendly owner, Count Ludovico di Valmarana, he'll direct you to the unequaled Tiepolo frescoes at his family's Villa of the Dwarfs down the road.

★ **Valley of the Temples, Agrigento, Sicily.** More than 20 centuries of silence and solitude greet you at this famous archaeological site, where more than 100 evocative structures built before the year 1 AD have been preserved.

FESTIVALS AND SEASONAL EVENTS

Italy's top seasonal events are listed below, and any one of them could provide the stuff of lasting memories. Contact the **Italian Government Travel Office** for exact dates and further information.

EARLY DEC.➤ The **Feast of St. Ambrose,** in Milan, officially opens La Scala's opera season.

DEC.–JUNE➤ The **Opera Season** is in full swing at La Scala in Milan and elsewhere, notably in Turin, Rome, Naples, Parma, Venice, and Genoa.

DEC. 31➤ Rome stages a rousing **New Year's Eve** celebration, with fireworks, in Piazza del Popolo.

JAN. 5–6➤ **Epiphany Celebrations.** Roman Catholic Epiphany celebrations and decorations are evident throughout Italy. Notable is the Epiphany Fair at Piazza Navona in Rome.

EARLY FEB.➤ **Almond Blossom Festival** in Agrigento. A week of folk music and dancing, with groups from many countries, in the Valley of the Temples.

FEB. 2–12➤ **Carnival in Venice.** A big do in the 18th century, revived in the last half of the 20th century, this includes plays, masked balls, fireworks, and indoor and outdoor happenings of every sort. During **Carni-**

val in Viareggio, masked pageants, fireworks, a flower show, and parades are among the festivities on the Tuscan Riviera.

FEB.➤ The **Carnival in Ivrea,** near Turin, includes three days of folklore, costumes, and parades, culminating in the Battle of the Oranges, with real fruit flying through the air.

MAR. 28➤ In Rome, a torchlit nighttime **Good Friday Procession** led by the pope winds from the Colosseum past the Foro Romano and up the Colle Palatino.

MAR. 30➤ The Easter Sunday **Scoppio del Carro,** or "Explosion of the Cart," in Florence, is the eruption of a cartful of fireworks in the Piazza del Duomo, set off by a mechanical dove released from the altar during High Mass.

LATE APR.–EARLY JULY➤ The **Florence May Music Festival** is the oldest and most prestigious Italian festival of the performing arts.

MAY 1➤ The **Feast of Sant'Efisio** in Cagliari sees a procession of marchers and others in splendid Sardinian costume.

MID-MAY➤ During the **Race of the Candles,** the procession of bearers, in local costume, carrying towering wooden pillars, leads to the top of Mt. Ingino in Gubbio.

MAY 20➤ **Sardinian Cavalcade.** A traditional procession of more than 3,000 people in Sardinian costumes makes its way through Sassari.

LATE MAY➤ The **Palio of the Archers** is a medieval crossbow contest in Gubbio.

EARLY JUNE➤ The **Battle of the Bridge,** in Pisa, is a medieval parade and contest. The **Flower Festival,** in Genzano (Rome), is a religious procession along streets carpeted with flowers in splendid designs. The **Regatta of the Great Maritime Republics** sees keen competition among the four former maritime republics—Amalfi, Genoa, Pisa, and Venice.

LATE JUNE➤ **Soccer Games in 16th-Century Costume,** in Florence, commemorate a match played in 1530. Festivities include fireworks displays.

LATE JUNE–EARLY JULY➤ The **Festival of Two Worlds,** in Spoleto, is a famous performing-arts festival.

JUNE AND JULY➤ The **Summer Operetta Festival** is held in Trieste.

EARLY JULY AND MID-AUG.➤ The **Palio Horse Race,** in Siena, is a colorful bareback horse race with participants competing for the *palio* (banner).

MID-JULY➤ The **Feast of the Redeemer** is a procession of gondolas and other craft, commemorating the end of the epidemic of 1575 in Venice. The fireworks over the lagoon are spectacular.

EARLY JULY–LATE AUG.➤ The **Arena of Verona Outdoor Opera Season** heralds spectacular productions in the 22,000-seat Roman amphitheater of Verona.

EARLY AUG.➤ The **Joust of the Quintana** is a historical pageant in Ascoli Piceno.

LATE AUG.–EARLY SEPT.➤ The **Siena Music Week** features opera, concerts, and chamber music. The **Venice Film Festival,** oldest of the international film festivals, takes place mostly on the Lido.

LATE AUG.–MID-SEPT.➤ The **Stresa Musical Weeks** comprise a series of concerts and recitals in Stresa.

AUTUMN

EARLY SEPT.➤ The **Historic Regatta** includes a traditional competition between two-oar gondolas in Venice. The **Joust of the Saracen** is a tilting contest with knights in 13th-century armor in Arezzo.

MID-SEPT.➤ The **Joust of the Quintana** is a 17th-century-style joust and historical procession in Foligno.

EARLY OCT.➤ Alba's **100 Towers Tournament** features costumes and races and is held simultaneously with the **Truffle Fair,** a food fair centered on the white truffle.

OCT. 4➤ The **Feast of St. Francis** is celebrated in Assisi, his birthplace.

2 Rome

The Eternal City—of heavenly sculptural, pinnacled Renaissance, hedonistic Baroque masterpieces—is where Nero fiddled, Mark Anthony praised Caesar, and Charlemagne was crowned. Today you may marvel at the venerated treasures in the footsteps of these revered predecessors while sipping caffè, exploring swank boutiques, and dodging speeding Vespas. In no other city will you find such a heady mix of classical elegance, earthiness, and energy.

Updated by
Barbara Walsh
Angelillo

COMING OFF THE AUTOSTRADA at Roma Nord or Roma Sud, you can tell by the traffic that you are entering a grand nexus: all paths lead to Rome. As you enter the city proper, edifices, icons, and images to match your expectations take shape: a bridge with heroic statues along its parapets; a towering cake of ornate marble decorated with allegorical figures in extravagant poses; a piazza and an obelisk under an umbrella of pine trees. You then spot what looks like a multistory parking lot; with an awesome gasp, you realize it is the fabled Colosseo (Colosseum).

More than Florence, more than Venice, Rome is Italy's treasure trove, packed as it is with masterpieces from more than two millennia of artistic achievement. Here, the ancient Romans made us heirs-in-law to what we call Western civilization. At Cinecittà Studios, Federico Fellini filmed *La Dolce Vita* and *8½*. And Michelangelo Buonarroti painted the Sistine Ceiling here.

History is pervasive in Rome life; its formidable legacy is upheld by its people, knit into the fabric of their everyday life. Popes, Vandals, the Borgias and Napoléon, Gianlorenzo Bernini, Mussolini, and the ancient Romans themselves all left their physical and spiritual marks on the city. Students walk dogs in the park that was once the mausoleum of the family of the Emperor Augustus; Raphaelesque madonnas line up for buses on every corner. Modern Rome has one foot in the past, one in the present—a delightful stance that allows you to have an espresso in a square designed by Bernini, then take a subway home to a flat in a renovated Renaissance palace. "When you first come here you assume that you must burrow about in ruins and prowl in museums to get back to the days of Numa Pompilius or Mark Anthony," Maud Howe observes in her book, *Roma Beata*. "It is not necessary; you only have to live, and the common happenings of daily life—yes, even the trolley car and your bicycle—carry you back in turn to the Dark Ages, to the early Christians, even to prehistoric Rome."

Remember, *"Bisogna vivere a Roma coi costumi di Roma"* (When in Rome, do as Rome does). Rather than feel intimidated by the art and culture, contemplate the grandeur from a table at a sun-drenched café on Piazza Navona. There's just so much to take in that you will vow to return, and do so by throwing a coin in the Trevi Fountain—it works.

Pleasures and Pastimes

Dining

The ritual of gathering around the table is the Romans' main preoccupation, aside from their families and perhaps their cars. Dining out is all the nightlife most Romans need, and a summer evening's meal alfresco can be one of the city's most pleasant experiences. There was a time when you could predict the clientele and prices of a Roman eating establishment by whether it was called a *ristorante* (restaurant), trattoria, or *osteria* (tavern). These names have become interchangeable. A rustic-looking spot that calls itself an osteria may turn out to be chic and expensive. Generally speaking, however, a trattoria is a family-run place, simpler in decor, cuisine, and service—and slightly less expensive—than a ristorante. A true osteria is a wineshop, very basic and down to earth, where the only function of the food is to keep customers sober.

Lodging

Rome has the range of accommodations you would expect of any great city, from the squalid *alberghetti* (little hotels) around the railway sta-

tion to the grand monuments to luxury and elegance on Via Vittorio
Veneto. Appearances can be misleading here: many crumbling stucco
facades may promise little from the outside, but they often hide interiors of considerable elegance.

EXPLORING ROME

Rome presents a particular challenge for visitors: just as they begin to
feel hopelessly smitten by the spell of the city, they realize they don't
have the time—let alone the energy—to see more than a fraction of its
treasures. It's wise to start out knowing this, and to have a focused
and flexible itinerary. A ramble through a picturesque quarter of Old
Rome can be just as enlightening as a chapel redolent of incense or a
trek through marbled miles of museum corridors.

Though large, Rome invites walking; the bus system is also a sur-
mountable option for weary legs. Plan your day to take into account
the varying hours places are open—which usually means mixing classical and Baroque, museums and parks, the center and the environs.
Most churches are usually open from 8 or 9 until noon or 12:30, and
from 3 or 4 until about 7. Major basilicas are open all day in season.
You may take refuge in the age-old adage, Rome wasn't built in a day;
be Nero-esque in your rambles and fiddle while you roam with frequent *gelato* (ice cream) breaks. The Italian author Silvio Negro said
it best: *"Roma, non basta una vita"* (Rome, a lifetime is not enough).

*Numbers in the text correspond to numbers in the margin and on the Rome
and Old Rome maps.*

Great Itineraries

IF YOU HAVE 3 DAYS

Begin your first day at Piazza Venezia and survey Rome from atop the
Colle Capitolino (Capitoline Hill). Next, explore the Foro Romano
(Roman Forum) and see the Colle Palatino (Palatine Hill) and the
Colosseo (Colosseum). In the afternoon, combine sightseeing with
shopping and make your way through the neighborhood around the
Scalinata di Spagna (Spanish Steps) and the Fontana di Trevi (Trevi Fountain). The following morning, visit the Basilica di San Pietro (St. Peter's
Basilica) and the Cappella Sistina (Sistine Chapel; during weekdays in
certain months, the last admission into the Vatican Museums is 4, so
you have the option to hit the St. Peter's Basilica on the afternoon of
your first day during these times, stamina permitting; ☞ The Vatican:
Rome of the Popes, *below*). After lunch, walk through Baroque Rome,
exploring its splendor. Take it easy on your third morning: explore a
museum or site of interest and then relax at a café and watch the passing parade. Spend your final afternoon and evening exploring the picturesque Ghetto and Trastevere neighborhoods.

IF YOU HAVE 5 DAYS

If you have an extra couple of days, spend your first three exploring
the sights covered above, but in the morning of the fourth day wander through Villa Borghese and see the Canova and Bernini sculptures
in the Galleria Borghese (Borghese Gallery). On the fifth day, make an
excursion either to the Appian Way or to Ostia Antica, an ancient city
comparable to Pompeii for interest and atmosphere. After a sustain-
ing lunch, see some of Rome's most historic churches and Michelangelo's *Moses*.

IF YOU HAVE 7 DAYS

Devote more time to the museums and galleries mentioned above that
interest you most. Explore a kindred neighborhood, or one you liked

best, allowing plenty of time for poking into odd corners and courtyards and churches, and for café-sitting. Make a couple of excursions
outside Rome.

Ancient Rome: Glories of the Caesars

This walk takes you through the very core of Roman antiquity, through
what was once the epicenter of the known world—the Roman Forum—
and gives you a look at how Michelangelo transformed Capitoline Hill,
the seat of ancient Rome's government, into a Renaissance showcase.
The rubblescape of marble fragments scattered over the area of the Forum
makes all but students of archaeology ask: is this the grandeur that was
Rome? Just consider that much of the history fed to students the world
over happened right here. This square—occasionally an enormous
banquet hall where imperial Rome could be simultaneously enter-
tained (as our times have observed thanks to such Hollywood epics as
Quo Vadis, Ben-Hur, and *Cleopatra*)—was the birthplace of much of
Western civilization. Roman law and powerful armies were created here,
banishing the barbarian world for a millennium. Here, all Rome
shouted as one, "Caesar has been murdered," and crowded to hear Mark
Anthony's eulogy for the fallen leader. Legend has it that St. Paul tra-
versed the Forum en route to his audience with Nero. After a more
than 27-centuries-long parade of pageantry, it is not surprising that Shelley and Gibbon reflected on the sense of *sic transit gloria mundi* on
these same grounds.

*Numbers in the text correspond to numbers in the margin and on the
Rome map.*

A Good Walk

Rome, as everyone knows, was built on seven hills (Colle Capitolino,
Colle Palatino, Monte Esquilino, Monte Viminale, Monte Cello, Monte
Quirinale, and Colle Aventino). Begin your walk on the **Colle Capitolino** ①—the site of Michelangelo's spectacular piazza and Rome's City
Hall, Palazzo Senatorio, which was built over the Tabularium, the ancient hall of records. Flanking the palazzo are both halves of Rome's
most noteworthy museum complex, the **Musei Capitolini** ②, made up
of the Museo Capitolino and the Palazzo dei Conservatori, which contain works of art gathered by Pope Sixtus V, one of the earliest papal
patrons of the arts. Off to the side of the Colle Capitolino, at the head
of its formidable flight of steep steps, stands the ancient redbrick
church of **Santa Maria d'Aracoeli** ③. Below the gardens to the left of
the Palazzo Senatorio are the **Foro di Cesare** and the forum named after
the Emperor Trajan, separated by Via dei Fori Imperiali; the latter contains the **Colonna di Traiano** ④. Descend Via San Pietro in Carcere, actually a flight of stairs, to the gloomy **Carcere Mamertino** ⑤ and the
Foro Romano ⑥, continuing along the ancient Via Sacra where, on the
right, you will come across the **Colle Palatino** ⑦, site of Rome's earliest settlement. Leaving the Colle Palatino by way of the San Gregorio
exit, you'll come upon the imposing **Arco di Constantino** ⑧ and, beyond it, the **Colosseo** ⑨, one of antiquity's most famous monuments.
Don't forget to check out the view from the park laid out over the ruins
of Nero's **Domus Aurea** ⑩, his sumptuous palace, behind the Colosseo.

TIMING

It takes about 30 minutes to walk the route, plus two hours to visit
the Musei Capitolini, from two to three hours to explore the Foro Romano and the Colle Palatino, and from 20 minutes to an hour to see
the Colosseo.

Sights to See

❽ Arco di Constantino (Arch of Constantine). This imposing arch was erected in AD 315 to celebrate Constantine's victory over Maxentius. Not only is it the best preserved of Rome's triumphal arches, it is also the largest (69 ft high, 85 ft wide, and 23 ft deep) and one of the last great monuments of ancient Rome. It once stood at the head of the Via Sacra, but now stands in glorious isolation alongside the Colosseo (☞ *below*).

OFF THE BEATEN PATH

CIMITERO ACCATTOLICO (NON-CATHOLIC CEMETERY) – About a 20-minute walk south from the Arch of Constantine along Viale Aventino, behind the Piramide, a stone pyramid built in 12 BC at the order of the Roman *praetor* (senior magistrate) who was buried there, is a cemetery reminiscent of a country churchyard. Among the headstones you'll find Keats's tomb and the place where Shelley's heart was buried. ☒ *Via Caio Cestio 6,* ☎ *06/5741141 (ring bell for custodian).* ☒ *Offering of 500 lire–1,000 lire.* ☽ *Daily 8–11:30 and 3:20–5:30.*

❺ Carcere Mamertino (Mamertine Prison). This series of gloomy, subterranean cells is where Rome's vanquished enemies were finished off. Some historians believe that St. Peter was held prisoner here, and legend has it that he miraculously brought forth a spring of water with which to baptize his jailers. ☒ *Donation requested.* ☽ *Daily 9–12:30 and 2–7:30.*

★ **❶ Colle Capitolino** (Capitoline Hill). Though most of the buildings on Michelangelo's piazza date from the Renaissance, the hill was once the epicenter of the Roman Empire, the place where the city's first and holiest temples stood, including its most sacred, the Temple of Jupiter. The city's archives were kept in the Tabularium (hall of records), the tall, gray-stone structure that forms the foundation of today's city hall, **Palazzo Senatorio.** By the Middle Ages, the Campidoglio (the Capitol), as the hill was already called then, had fallen into ruin. In 1537, Pope Paul III decided to restore its grandeur for the triumphal entry into the city of Charles V, the Holy Roman Emperor, and called upon Michelangelo to create the staircase ramp; the buildings on three sides of the Campidoglio; the slightly convex pavement and its decoration; and the pedestal for the bronze equestrian statue of Marcus Aurelius. A work from the 2nd century AD, the statue stood here from the 16th century until 1981. The statue—the most celebrated equestrian bronze to survive from classical antiquity—was mistakenly believed to represent the Christian emperor Constantine rather than the pagan Marcus Aurelius, hence its survival through the centuries. A legend foretells that some day the statue's original gold patina will return, heralding the end of the world. To forestall destiny, the city fathers had it restored and placed in the Museo Capitolino (☞ *below*), saving not only what was left of the gold, but also the statue's bronze, once seriously menaced by air pollution. A copy was set up on the original pedestal in 1997. As Michelangelo's preeminent urban set piece, the piazza sums up all the majesty of High-Renaissance Rome.

❼ Colle Palatino (Palatine Hill). A lane known as the Clivus Palatinus, whose worn paving stones were once trod by emperors and their slaves, climbs from the Forum area to a site that historians identify with Rome's earliest settlement. About a century ago, Rome's greatest archaeologist, Rodolfo Lanciani, excavated a site on Palatine Hill and found evidence testifying to Romulus's historical presence, thereby contradicting early critics who deemed Romulus to be a myth. The story goes that the twins Romulus and Remus were abandoned as infants but were suckled by a she wolf on the banks of the Tiber and adopted by a shepherd. Encouraged by the gods to build a city, the twins chose a site in 735 BC, fortifying it with a wall that Lanciani identified by digging on Palatine Hill. During the building of the city, the brothers quarreled, and in a fit of anger Romulus killed Remus.

Despite its location overlooking the Forum with its extreme traffic congestion and attendant noise, Palatine Hill was the most coveted address for ancient Rome's rich and famous. More than a few of the 12 Caesars called Palatine Hill home—including Caligula, who met his premature end in the Cryptoporticus tunnel, which today still stands and remains unnerving. The palace of Tiberius was the first to be built here; others followed, most notably the gigantic extravaganza constructed for emperor Domitian.

In the **Circo Massimo** (Circus Maximus), the giant arena laid out between Palatine and Aventine hills, more than 300,000 spectators watched chariot races while the emperor surveyed the scene from his palace on Palatine Hill.

❹ Colonna di Traiano (Trajan's Column). Trajan's ashes were buried inside the base of this column, which stands in what was once **Foro di Traiano** (Trajan's Forum), with its huge semicircular market building, adjacent to the ruins of the **Foro di Augusto** (Forum of Augustus). ⊠ *Piazza Santa Maria di Loreto.*

★ ❾ Colosseo (Colosseum). Massive and majestic, ancient Rome's most famous monument was begun by the Flavian emperor Vespasian in AD 72, and inaugurated eight years later with a program of games and shows lasting 100 days. More than 50,000 spectators could sit within the arena's 573-yard circumference, which was faced with marble, accented with hundreds of statues, and had the velarium—an ingenious system of saillike awnings rigged on ropes manned by sailors culled from imperial warships—to protect the audience from the sun and rain. Before the imperial box, gladiators would salute the emperor and cry, *"Ave, imperator, morituri te salutant"* (Hail, emperor, men soon to die salute thee); it is said that when one day they heard the emperor Claudius respond, "or maybe not," they became so offended that they called a strike.

Originally known as the Anfiteatro Flavio (Flavian Amphitheater), it was called the Colosseum, as reported by the Venerable Bede in 730, after a truly colossal gilded bronze statue of Nero in the vicinity that stood until the end of the 6th century. The arena later served as a quarry from which materials were filched to build Renaissance-era churches and palaces. Finally, it was declared sacred by the Vatican in memory of the many Christians believed martyred there (scholars now maintain that no Christians met their death in the Colosseum, but rather in Rome's imperial circuses). During the 19th century, romantic poets lauded the glories of the amphitheater when viewed by moonlight. Now its arches glow at night with mellow golden spotlights—less romantic, perhaps, but still impressive. Portions of the arena will be closed during ongoing restoration. ⊠ *Piazza del Colosseo,* ☎ *06/7004261.* ▧ *General admission free, upper levels 8,000 lire.* ☉ *Apr.–Sept., Mon.–Tues. and Thurs.–Sat. 9–7, Wed. and Sun. 9–1; Oct.–Mar., Mon.–Tues. and Thurs.–Sat 9–3, Wed. and Sun. 9–1.*

NEED A BREAK?	About half a block from the Colosseum is **Pasqualino** (⊠ Via Santi Quattro 66), a reasonably priced neighborhood trattoria with a few sidewalk tables providing a view of the arena's marble arches. The trattoria is closed Monday. For delicious gelato try **Ristoro della Salute** (⊠ Piazza del Colosseo 2a), one of Rome's best *gelaterie* (ice-cream parlors).

⑩ Domus Aurea. On the Colle Oppio (Oppian Hill), a ridge of the Monte Esquilino (Esquiline Hill), are faint traces of Nero's sumptuous palace—later buried under Trajan's Baths—which was built after the great fire of AD 64 destroyed much of the city. (Incidentally, historians now believe Nero to be blameless in this event.) Also known as the Golden House, it was a structure so huge it evoked the complaint, "All Rome has become a villa."

Foro di Cesare (Caesar's Forum). This is the oldest of the Imperial Fora, those built by the emperors as opposed to those built during the earlier, Republican period (6th–1st centuries BC) as part of the original Roman Forum.

❻ Foro Romano (Roman Forum). In what was once a marshy valley between the Capitoline and Palatine hills, this was the civic heart of Republican Rome, the austere enclave that preceded the hedonistic society that grew up under the emperors in the 1st to the 4th century AD. Today it seems no more than a baffling series of ruins, marble fragments, isolated columns, a few worn arches, and occasional paving stones. Yet it once was filled with stately and extravagant buildings—temples, palaces, shops—and crowded with people from all corners of the world. What you see today are the ruins not of one period, but of almost 900 years, from about 500 BC to AD 400. Making sense of these scarred and pitted stones is not easy; you may want just to wander along, letting your imagination dwell on Cicero, Julius Caesar, and Mark Anthony, who delivered the funeral address in Caesar's honor from the rostrum just left of the **Arco di Settimio Severo** (Arch of Septimius Severus).

One of the grandest of all antiquity, this arch was built in AD 203 to celebrate the emperor Severus's victory over the Parthians, and was topped by a bronze equestrian statuary group with no fewer than six horses. Most visitors also explore the large brick senate hall, the **Curia,** which survives as it was in the era of Diocletian in the late 3rd century AD; the three Corinthian columns (a favorite of 19th-century poets)—all that remains of the **Tempio di Vespasiano** (Temple of Vespasian); the circular **Tempio di Vesta** (Temple of Vesta), where the highly privileged vestal virgins kept the sacred flame alive; and the **Arco di Tito** (Arch of Titus), which stands in a slightly elevated position on a spur of Palatine Hill. The view of the Colosseum from the arch is superb and reminds us that it was the emperor Titus who helped finish the vast amphitheater, begun earlier by his father, Vespasian. Now cleaned and restored, the arch was erected in AD 81 to celebrate the sack of Jerusalem 10 years earlier, after the great Jewish revolt. A famous relief shows the captured contents of Herod's Temple—including its huge seven-branched menorah—being carried in triumph down Rome's Via Sacra. ⊠ *Entrances on Via dei Fori Imperiali, Piazza Santa Maria Nova, and Via di San Gregorio,* ☎ *06/6990110.* ⌑ *12,000 lire.* ☉ *Apr.–Sept., Mon.–Sat. 9–6, Sun. 9–1; Oct.–Mar., Mon.–Sat. 9–3, Sun. 9–1.*

❷ Musei Capitolini (Capitoline Museums). The collections in the twin Museo Capitolino and Palazzo dei Conservatori were assembled in the 15th century by Pope Sixtus V, one of the earliest of the great papal patrons of the arts. Although parts of the collection may excite only archaeologists and art historians, others contain some of the most famous—and not to be missed—pieces of classical sculpture, such as the poignant *Dying Gaul,* the regal *Capitoline Venus* (recently identified as another Mediterranean beauty, Cleopatra herself), and the delicate *Marble Faun* that inspired 19th-century novelist Nathaniel Hawthorne's novel of the same name. Remember that many of the works here and in Rome's other museums were copied from Greek originals. For hundreds of years, craftsmen of ancient Rome prospered by producing copies of Greek statues, using a process called "pointing," by which exact replicas could be created to order.

Portraiture, however, was one area in which the Romans outstripped the Greeks. The hundreds of Roman portrait busts in the Sala degli Imperatori and Sala dei Filosofi of the **Museo Capitolino** constitute an ancient *Who's Who*. Within these serried ranks are 48 of the Roman emperors, ranging from Augustus (died AD 14) to Theodosius (died 395). Many of them were eminently forgettable, but some were men of genius; a few added nothing to the Roman way of life except new ways of dying. On one console, you'll see the handsomely austere Augustus, who "found Rome a city of brick and left it one of marble." On another rests Claudius "the stutterer," an indefatigable builder brought vividly to life in Robert Graves's *I, Claudius*. In this company is also Nero, most notorious of the emperors—though by no means the worst—who built for himself the fabled Domus Aurea (☞ *above*). And, of course, the baddies: cruel Caligula and Caracalla, and the dissolute, eerily modern boy-emperor, Heliogabalus.

Unlike the Greeks, whose portraits are idealized and usually beautiful, the Romans belonged to the "warts and all" school of representation. Many of the busts that have come down to us, seen clearly in that of Commodus, the emperor-gladiator (found in a gallery on the upper level of the museum), are nearly savage in the relentlessness of their portrayals. As you leave the museum, be sure to stop in the courtyard at the gigantic, reclining figure of Oceanus, found in the Roman Forum and later dubbed Marforio, one of Rome's famous "talking statues" to which citizens from the 1500s up to the 20th century affixed anonymous notes of political protest and satirical verses.

The **Palazzo dei Conservatori** is a trove of ancient and Baroque treasures. Lining the courtyard are the colossal fragments of a head, leg, foot, and hand—all that remains of the famous statue of the emperor Constantine the Great, who believed that Rome's future in the 3rd century AD lay with Christianity. These immense effigies were much in vogue in the later days of the Roman empire. The resplendent Salone dei Orazi e Curiazi on the first floor is a ceremonial hall with a magnificent gilt ceiling, carved wooden doors, and 16th-century frescoes. At either end of the hall reign statues of the Baroque Age's most charismatic popes, Bernini's marble effigy of Urban VIII and his rival Algardi's bronze statue of Innocent X. The world-renowned symbol of Rome, the *Capitoline Wolf,* a 6th-century-BC Etruscan bronze, holds a place of honor in the museum; the suckling twins were added during the Renaissance to adapt the statue to the legend of Romulus and Remus (☞ Palatine Hill, *above*). ⊠ *Museo Capitolino and Palazzo dei Conservatori, Piazza del Campidoglio,* ☎ *06/67102071.* ▣ *10,000 lire, free last Sun. of month.* ☉ *Tues.–Sat. 9–7, Sun. 9–1.*

❸ **Santa Maria d'Aracoeli.** This stark, redbrick church is one of the first Christian churches in Rome. Legend recounts that it was on this spot that the Sybil predicted to Augustus the coming of a Redeemer. The emperor responded by erecting the Ara Coeli—the Altar of Heaven. The Aracoeli is best known for Pinturicchio's 15th-century frescoes in the first chapel on the right and for the **Santo Bambino,** a much-revered wooden figure of the Christ Child (today a copy of the 15th-century original). During the Christmas season, children recite poems from a miniature pulpit here. ⊠ *Piazza d'Aracoeli.* ☉ *Oct.–May, daily 7–noon and 4–6; June–Sept., daily 7–noon and 4–6:30.*

The Vatican: Rome of the Popes

Some people go to the Vatican to behold a work of art—Michelangelo's frescoes, rare archaeological marbles, or Bernini's statues. Others make the pilgrimage to find their souls in the most overwhelming architectural achievement of the Renaissance, the Basilica di San Pietro. In between these two extremes lies an awe-inspiring landscape with a famous sight for every taste and inclination. Museum rooms decorated by Raphael, antique sculptures like the *Apollo Belvedere* and the *Laocoön,* walls daubed by Fra Angelico, famous paintings by Giotto and Leonardo, and chief among revered *non plus ultras,* the ceiling of the Sistine Chapel: for the lover of beauty, few places are as historically important as this epitome of faith and grandeur. What gave all this impetus was a new force that emerged as the emperors of ancient Rome presided over their declining empire: Christianity came to Rome, and the seat of the popes was established over the tomb of St. Peter, thereby making the Vatican the spiritual core of the Roman Catholic Church. Be aware that dress rules must be adhered to in St. Peter's and the Vatican (☞ St. Peter's Basilica, *below*).

A Good Walk

Start your walk at the **Castel Sant'Angelo** ⑪, the fortress that stands sentinel over the Vatican, and take in the beauty of the Ponte Sant'Angelo before turning right onto Via della Conciliazione (or taking the more picturesque route west along Borgo Pio) to the Vatican. Once inside **Piazza San Pietro** ⑫, sumptuous architectural detail awaits at **Basilica di San Pietro** ⑬, the largest church of Christendom. To the right as you enter is Michelangelo's stunning *Pietà,* of the many treasures to be seen, be sure not to miss the Museo Storico in the Sacristy, the excavations below the church. Also explore the Giardini Vaticani and the Grotte Vaticane, the last repose of the popes.

TIMING

Allow two hours for a visit to Castel Sant'Angelo. The walk from Castel Sant'Angelo to Piazza San Pietro takes about 30 minutes. You'll need an hour to see the Basilica di San Pietro, plus 30 minutes for the Museo Storico, 15 minutes for the Grotte Vaticane, 30 minutes to visit the roof, and an hour to climb to the lantern. To avoid the crowds, get to the Basilica di San Pietro early in the morning, at lunchtime, or in the late afternoon.

Sights to See

★ ⑬ **Basilica di San Pietro** (St. Peter's Basilica). The physical statistics of Rome's sublime sanctuary are staggering: it covers about 18,100 square yards, runs 212 yards in length, and carries a dome that rises 435 ft and measures 138 ft across its base. Its history is equally impressive: no fewer than five of Italy's greatest artists—Bramante, Raphael, Peruzzi, Antonio Sangallo the Younger, and Michelangelo—died while striving to erect this new St. Peter's. The history of the original St. Peter's goes back to the year AD 319, when the emperor Constantine built a basilica over the site of the tomb of St. Peter. This early church stood for more than 1,000 years, undergoing a number of restorations, until it was on the verge of collapse. Reconstruction began in 1452, but was abandoned due to a lack of funds. In 1506 Pope Julius II instructed the architect Donato Bramante (1444–1514) to raze the existing structure and build a new and greater basilica, but it wasn't until 1626 that the new church was completed and dedicated. In 1546 Pope Paul III persuaded the aging Michelangelo to take on the job of completing the building. Returning to Bramante's ground plan, Michelangelo designed the dome to cover the crossing, but his plans, too, were modified after his death. The cupola, one of the most beautiful in the world, was completed by Della Porta and Fontana. Under the portico, Filarete's 15th-century bronze doors, salvaged from the old basilica, are in the central portal. Off the entry portico, Bernini's famous *Scala Regia*, the ceremonial entryway to the Vatican Palace and one of the most magnificent staircases in the world, is graced with Bernini's dramatic statue of Constantine the Great.

The cherubs over the holy water fonts will give you an idea of just how huge St. Peter's is: the sole of the cherub's foot is as long as the distance from your fingers to your elbow. It is because the proportions of this giant building are in such perfect harmony that its vastness may escape you at first. But in its megascale—inspired by the spatial volumes of ancient Roman ruins—it reflects Roman *grandiosità* in all its majesty.

Over an altar in a side chapel is Michelangelo's **Pietà**. It is difficult to determine whether this moving work, sculpted when he was only 22, owes more to the man's art than to his faith. As we contemplate this masterpiece we are able to understand a little better that art and faith sometimes partake of the same impulse.

Four massive piers support the dome at the crossing, where the mighty Bernini **baldacchino** (canopy) rises high above the papal altar. "What the barbarians didn't do, the Barberini did," 17th-century wags quipped when Barberini Pope Urban VIII had the bronze stripped from the Pantheon's portico and melted down to make the baldacchino (using what was left over for cannonballs). The pope celebrates mass here, over the grottoes holding the tombs of many of his predecessors. Also here, deep in the excavations under the foundations of the original basilica, is what is believed to be the tomb of St. Peter. The bronze throne above the main altar in the apse, the Cathedra Petri, is Bernini's work (1656) and it covers a wooden and ivory chair that St. Peter himself is said to have used. However, scholars tell us that this throne probably dates only to the Middle Ages. We come to these contradictions often. Faith, in the end, outweighs authenticity when it is a question of sacred objects. See how the adoration of a million lips has completely worn down the bronze on the right foot of the statue of St. Peter near the crossing.

The scale of the aisles and decoration and the vast sweep of the dome over the ceremonial entrance to the crypt, which is surrounded by votive lamps, bring home the point that St. Peter's is much more than a church; it was intended to function as the glorious setting for all the pomp and panoply of ecclesiastical ceremony. Indeed, only when it serves as the brightly lit background for a great gathering do its vast dimensions find their full expression. *Note: Ushers at the entrance of St. Peter's Church will not allow entry to persons wearing shorts, miniskirts, sleeveless T-shirts, or other revealing clothing (it's advisable for women to carry a scarf to cover bare shoulders and upper arms). This dress code pertains to the entire Vatican, including the Sistine Chapel and the museums.*

A small but rich collection of Vatican treasures is housed in the **Museo Storico** (Historical Museum) in the Sacristy, among them precious antique chalices and the massive 15th-century sculptured bronze tomb of Pope Sixtus V by Antonio Pollaiuolo (1429–98). ▣ *8,000 lire.* ⊘ *Apr.–Sept., daily 9–6; Oct.–Mar., daily 9–5.*

The entrance to the **Grotte Vaticane** (Vatican Grottoes), which hold the tombs of many popes, is at the crossing. The only exit from the grottoes leads outside St. Peter's, to the courtyard that holds the entrance to the roof and dome. ▣ *Free.* ⊘ *Apr.–Sept., daily 7–6; Oct.–Mar., daily 7–5.*

The roof of the church, reached by elevator or stairs, is a landscape of domes and towers. A short interior staircase leads to the base of the dome for a dove's-eye view of the interior of St. Peter's Basilica. Only if you are stout of heart and sound of lung should you attempt the very taxing and claustrophobic climb up the narrow stairs—there's no turning back!—to the balcony of the lantern, where the view embraces the Vatican gardens as well as all of Rome. ⊠ *Elevator 6,000 lire, stairs 5,000 lire.* ⊙ *Apr.–Sept., daily 8–6; Oct.–Mar., daily 8–5.*

OFF THE BEATEN PATH	**EXCAVATIONS** – Visit these under St. Peter's for a fascinating glimpse of the underpinnings of the great basilica, which was built over the cemetery where archaeologists say they have found St. Peter's tomb. Apply a few days in advance (or try in the morning for the same day) to Ufficio Scavi (Excavations Office), on the right beyond the Arco delle Campane entrance to the Vatican, which is left of the basilica. Tell the Swiss guard you want the Ufficio Scavi, and he will let you by. ☎ 06/69885318. ⊠ *Guide 10,000 lire, audiotape tour 6,000 lire if available.* ⊙ *Ufficio Scavi Mon.–Sat. 9–5.*

🖐 ⓫ **Castel Sant'Angelo** (Sant'Angelo Castle). For hundreds of years this fortress guarded the Vatican, to which it is linked by the Passetto, an arcaded passageway. According to legend, Castel Sant'Angelo got its name during the plague of 590, when Pope Gregory the Great, passing by in a religious procession, had a vision of an angel sheathing its sword atop the stone ramparts. Though it may look like a stronghold, Castel Sant'Angelo was in fact built as a tomb for the emperor Hadrian in AD 135. By the 6th century, it had been transformed into a fortress, and it remained a refuge for the popes for almost 1,000 years. It has dungeons, battlements, cannons and cannonballs, and a collection of antique weaponry and armor.

The upper terrace, below the massive bronze angel commemorating Gregory's vision, evokes memories of Tosca, Puccini's poignant heroine in the opera of the same name, who threw herself off these ramparts with the cry, *"Scarpia, avanti a Dio!"* ("Scarpia, we meet before God!"). One of Rome's most beautiful bridges, **Ponte Sant'Angelo** spans the Tiber in front of the fortress and is studded with graceful angels designed by Gianlorenzo Bernini.

The lower levels formed the base of Hadrian's mausoleum; ancient ramps and narrow staircases climb through the castle's core to courtyards and frescoed halls and rooms holding a collection of antique arms and armor. Off the loggia is a café. ⊠ *Lungotevere Castello 50,* ☎ *06/6875036.* ⊠ *8,000 lire.* ⊙ *Mon.–Sat. 9–2, Sun. 9–noon; closed 2nd and 4th Tues. of month.*

Giardini Vaticani (Vatican Gardens). A tour offers a two-hour jaunt through the pope's backyard, half by bus and half on foot, with a guide. Tickets are available at the Vatican Information Office (⊠ Piazza San Pietro, ☎ 06/69884466). Make reservations two or three days in advance. ⊠ *18,000 lire.* ⊙ *Apr.–Oct., Mon., Tues., Thurs.–Sat. at 10; Nov.–Mar., Sat at 10., weekdays on request for groups.*

Papal Audience. John Paul II, 264th Pope of the Roman Catholic Church, holds mass audiences on Wednesday mornings at 11, in a large modern audience hall or in St. Peter's Square in summer, if it's not too hot. You must apply for tickets in advance; there are several sources (☞ *below*), but if you are pressed for time it may be easier to arrange for them through a travel agency. Of course, you can avoid the formalities by seeing the pope when he makes his weekly appearance at the window of the Vatican Palace, every Sunday at noon when he is in Rome, to address the crowd and give a blessing. On summer Sundays he may give the blessing at his summer residence at Castel Gandolfo. For audience tickets apply in writing well in advance to Prefettura della Casa Pontificia (✉ 00120 Vatican City), indicating the date you prefer, the language you speak, and the hotel where you will be staying. Or go to the prefecture (☎ 06/6982), through the bronze door in right-hand colonnade; the office is open Monday and Tuesday 9–1 for the Wednesday audience, although last-minute tickets may be available. You can also pick up free tickets at North American College (✉ Via dell'Umiltà 30, ☎ 06/6789184) and through Santa Susanna American Church (✉ Piazza San Bernardo, ☎ 06/4827510). For a fee, travel agencies make arrangements that include transportation (☞ Guided Tours *in* Rome A to Z, *below*).

⑫ **Piazza San Pietro** (St. Peter's Square). As you enter the square you are entering Vatican territory. This square (actually an oval) is one of Bernini's most spectacular masterpieces. Completed in 1667, after 11 years' work—a relatively short time in those days, considering the vastness of the task—the square can hold 400,000 people. It is surrounded by a curving pair of quadruple colonnades, which are topped by a balustrade and statues of 140 saints. Look for the two stone disks set into the pavement on each side of the obelisk. If you stand on one disk, a trick of perspective makes the colonnades seem to consist of a single row of columns. Bernini had an even grander visual effect in mind when he designed the square. By opening up this immense, airy, and luminous space in a neighborhood of narrow, shadowy streets, he created a contrast that would surprise and impress anyone who emerged from the darkness into the light, in a characteristically Baroque metaphor. But in the 1930s, Mussolini ruined it all. To celebrate the "conciliation" between the Vatican and the Italian government under the Lateran Pact of 1929, he conceived of Via della Conciliazione, the broad, rather soulless avenue that now forms the main approach to St. Peter's and gives the eye time to adjust to the enormous dimensions of the square and church, nullifying Bernini's grand Baroque effect.

NEED A
BREAK?

Borgo Pio, a street a block or two from St. Peter's Square, has several trattorias offering economical *menù turistico* (tourist menus). For about 20,000 lire you can have a simple meal at **Il Pozzetto** (✉ Borgo Pio 167), closed Monday. The tiny **Dolceborgo** pastry shop (✉ Borgo Pio 162) is the place to go for cookies and creamy concoctions.

Musei Vaticani: Beyond the Sistine Ceiling

The Vatican Palace has been the residence of popes since 1377. Actually, it represents a collection of buildings that cover more than 13 acres, containing an estimated (no one has bothered to count them) 1,400 rooms, chapels, and galleries. Other than the pope and his papal court, the occupants are some of the most famous art masterpieces in the world. The main entrance to the museums, on Viale Vaticano, is a long walk from Piazza San Pietro, but there is bus service between the Vatican Information Office (☞ Giardini Vaticani, *above*) and a secondary museum entrance. The bus goes through the Vatican gardens and costs 2,000 lire, and although it deposits you at a side entrance, it saves a lot of walking and allows a glimpse of some of Vatican City that would be off-limits otherwise. Some city buses stop near the museums' main entrance on Viale Vaticano: Bus 49 from Piazza Cavour stops right in front; Bus 80 and Tram 19 stop at Piazza Risorgimento, halfway between St. Peter's and the museums. The Ottaviano stop on Metro

A also is in the vicinity. Be aware that dress rules must be adhered to in St. Peter's and the Vatican (☞ Vatican Museums, *below*).

Beyond the **Cappella Sistina,** many sections of the **Musei Vaticani** ⑭ are not to be overlooked: the **Museo Egiziano;** the **Chiaramonti** and **Museo Pio Clementino,** which are given over to classical sculptures (among them some of the best-known statues in the world—the *Laocoön,* the *Belvedere Torso,* and the *Apollo Belvedere*—works that, with their vibrant humanism, had a tremendous impact on Renaissance art); and the **Museo Etrusco di Villa Giulia.** Finally, you should make sure to visit the **Galleria dei Candelabri** and the **Galleria degli Arazzi,** hung with marvelous tapestries executed from Raphael's designs.

TIMING

The shortest itinerary takes approximately 90 minutes; others range from three to four and a half hours. To avoid the crowds, get there before opening time, or go at lunchtime or in the last few hours before closing.

Sights to See

★ ⑭ **Musei Vaticani** (Vatican Museums). The immense collections housed here are so rich that unless you are an art history buff, you will probably want to just skim the surface, concentrating on pieces that strike your fancy. The Sistine Chapel is a must, of course, and that's why you may have to wait in line to see it; after all, every tourist in Rome has the same idea. Pick up a leaflet at the main entrance to the museums in order to see the overall layout. Special posters at the entrance and throughout the museums plot a choice of four color-coded itineraries. The Sistine Chapel is at the far end of the complex, and the leaflet charts two abbreviated itineraries through other collections to reach it. You can rent a taped commentary in English explaining the Sistine Chapel and the Raphael Rooms. Below, we give some of the highlights, whether or not you follow the itineraries suggested by the curators.

The **Galleria delle Carte Geografiche** (Gallery of Maps) is intriguing; the **Appartamento di S. Pio V,** a little less so. The **Stanze di Raffaello** (the Raphael Rooms), are second only to the Sistine Chapel in artistic interest. In 1508, Pope Julius II employed Raphael Sanzio, on the recommendation of Bramante, to decorate the rooms with biblical scenes. The result was a Renaissance tour de force. Of the four rooms, the second and third were decorated mainly by Raphael. The others were decorated by Giulio Romano and other assistants of Raphael; the first room is known as the Incendio Room, with frescoes painted by Romano.

It's hard to overstate the importance of the **Stanza della Segnatura** (Room of the Signature); here papal bulls were signed. When people talk about the High Renaissance—thought by many to be the pinnacle of Western art—these frescoes often come up. The theme of the room— which may broadly be said to be "enlightenment"—reflects the fact that this was Julius's private library. Theology triumphs in the fresco known as the *Disputa,* or *Debate on the Holy Sacrament.* The *School of Athens* glorifies some of philosophy's greatest exponents, including Plato and Socrates at the fresco's center. The pensive figure on the stairs is sometimes thought to be modeled on Michelangelo, who was painting the Sistine Ceiling at the same time Raphael was working here. All the revolutionary characteristics of High Renaissance paintings are here: naturalism (Raphael's figures lack the awkwardness that pictures painted only a few years earlier still contained); humanism (the idea that man is the most noble and admirable of God's creatures); and a profound interest in the ancient world, the result of the 15th-century rediscovery of archaeology and classical antiquity. There's a tendency to go into something of a stupor when confronted with "great art" of this kind. The fact remains that the frescoes in this room virtually dared its occupants to aspire to the highest ideas of law and learning—an amazing feat for an artist not yet 30.

The tiny **Cappella di Nicholas V** (Chapel of Nicholas V) is aglow with frescoes by Fra Angelico (1387–1455), the Florentine monk whose sensitive paintings were guiding lights for the Renaissance. The **Appartamento Borgia** is worth seeing for the elaborately painted ceilings, designed and partially executed by Pinturicchio (1454–1513), but the rooms have been given over to the Vatican's large, but not particularly impressive, collection of modern religious art.

In 1508, while Raphael was put to work on his series of rooms, the redoubtable Pope Julius II commissioned Michelangelo to fresco the more than 10,000 square ft of the **Cappella Sistina** (Sistine Chapel) ceiling singlehandedly. The task took four years of mental and physical anguish. It's said that for years afterward Michelangelo couldn't read anything without holding it up over his head. The result, however, was the masterpiece that you can now see, its colors cool and brilliant after restoration. Bring a pair of binoculars to get a better look at this incredible work (unfortunately, you're not allowed to lie down on the floor to study the frescoes above, the viewing position of choice in decades past; by the time you leave the chapel, your neck may feel like Michelangelo's, so you may also want to study it—to take a cue from 19th-century visitors—with the aid of a pocket mirror).

The ceiling is literally a painted Bible: Michelangelo's subject was the story of humanity before the coming of Christ, seen through Augustinian tenets of faith popular in early 16th-century theological circles. While some of the frescoed panels are veritable stews of figures, others—especially the depiction of God's outstretched hand giving Adam the spark of life in the *Creation of Adam*—are forcefully simple, revealing how much Michelangelo imparted on the school of painting from the discipline of sculpture. In 1541, some 30 years after completing the ceiling, Michelangelo was commissioned to paint the *Last Judgment* on the wall over the altar. If the artist's ceiling may be taken as an expression of the optimism of the High Renaissance, the *Last Judgment*, by contrast, is a veritable guided tour through Hell. Not surprisingly, since in the intervening years Rome had been sacked and pillaged by the French (who had used the Sistine Chapel to stable their horses).

In the interim, the grim Counter Reformation movement had been adopted by the Church, and the papal court was now so offended by the nakedness of Michelangelo's *Last Judgment* figures that they hired artist Daniele da Volterra—forever after known as *il braghettone* (the breeches-maker)—to paint loincloths over the offending parts. The aged and embittered artist painted his own face on the wrinkled human skin in the hand of St. Bartholomew, below and to the right of the figure of Christ, which he clearly modeled on the *Apollo Belvedere* (now on exhibit in the Vatican galleries). Like the ceiling, the *Last Judgment* has been cleaned, surprising viewers with its clarity and color after restorers unveiled their work in April 1994. Was Michelangelo a master of vibrant color? Or is the "new" Sistine a travesty of Michelangelo's intentions? Opinions remain divided, but most art historians believe the restoration is true to Michelangelo's original vision.

The exhibition halls of the **Biblioteca Vaticana** (Vatican Library) are bright with frescoes and contain a sampling of the library's rich collections of precious manuscripts. Room X, Room of the Aldobrandini

Marriage, holds a beautiful Roman fresco of a nuptial rite. More classical statues are on view in the new wing. At the Quattro Cancelli, a cafeteria offers a well-earned break. The **Pinacoteca** (Picture Gallery) displays mainly religious paintings by such artists as Giotto, Fra Angelico, and Filippo Lippi, and Raphael's exceptional *Transfiguration, Coronation,* and *Foligno Madonna.*

In the **Museo Profano** (Pagan Antiquities Museum), modern display techniques enhance another collection of Greek and Roman sculptures. The **Museo Pio Cristiano** (Christian Antiquities Museum) has early Christian and medieval art (its most famous piece is the 3rd-century AD statue, the *Good Shepherd*). The **Museo Missionario-Etnologico** (Ethnological Museum) exhibits art and artifacts from exotic places throughout the world (open Wednesday and Saturday only). The complete itinerary ends with the **Museo della Storia** (Historical Museum), whose collection of carriages, uniforms, and arms can be opened by a custodian on request.

In all, the Vatican Museums offer a staggering foray into the realms of art and history; it's foolhardy to try to see all the collections in one day. ⊠ *Viale Vaticano,* ☎ *06/69883860.* ▨ *15,000 lire; free last Sun. of month.* ⊘ *Easter wk and mid-Mar.–mid-June and Sept.–Oct., weekdays 8:45–4:45 (last admission at 4), Sat. 8:45–1:45 (last admission at 1); Oct.–mid-Mar. (except Easter) and mid-June–Aug., Mon.–Sat. 8:45–1:45 (last admission at 1); last Sun. of every month 9–1; closed religious holidays (Jan. 1 and 6, Feb. 11, Mar. 19, Easter Sun. and Mon., May 1, Ascension Thurs., Corpus Christi, June 29, Aug. 15 and 16, Nov. 1, Dec. 8, Dec. 25 and 26); Sun., excepting last Sun. of month. Visitors are expected to refrain from wearing shorts, miniskirts, sleeveless T-shirts, or other revealing clothing; it's advisable for women to carry a scarf to cover bare shoulders and upper arms.*

NEED A   Neighborhood trattorias that are far better and far less popular with
BREAK?   tourists than those opposite the Vatican Museum entrance include
              Hostaria Dino e Toni (⊠ Via Leone IV 60), where you can dine on typi-
              cal Roman fare at moderate, even inexpensive prices; **La Caravella** (⊠
              Via degli Scipioni 32 at Via Vespasiano, off Piazza Risorgimento),
              serves Roman specialties, including pizza during lunch, every day but
              Thursday, when it's closed.

Old Rome: Gold and Grandeur

The neighborhood known as Vecchia Roma (Old Rome) is one of Rome's most beautiful districts, thick with narrow streets with curious names, airy Baroque piazzas, and picturesque courtyards. Occupying the horn of land that pushes the Tiber westward toward the Vatican, it has been an integral part of the city since ancient times, and its position between the Vatican and the Lateran palaces, both seats of papal rule, puts it in the mainstream of Rome's development from the Middle Ages onward. It includes such world-famous sights as the Pantheon—ancient Rome's most perfectly preserved building—but it is mainly an excursion into the 16th and 17th centuries, when Baroque art triumphed in Rome. Today, it boasts some of Rome's most coveted residential addresses.

The most important clue to the Romans is their Baroque art—not its artistic technicalities, but its spirit. When you understand that, you will no longer be a stranger in Rome. Flagrantly emotional, heavily expressive, and sensuously visual, the 17th-century artistic movement known as the Baroque was born in Rome, the creation of three geniuses, the sculptor and architect Gianlorenzo Bernini and the painters Annibale Caracci and Caravaggio. Ranging from the austere drama found in Caravaggio's painted altarpieces to the jewel-laden, gold-on-gold detail of 17th-century Roman palaces, Baroque style was intended to both shock and delight by upsetting the placid, "correct" rules of the Renaissance masters. By appealing to the emotions, it became a powerful weapon in the hands of the Counter Reformation.

Numbers in the text correspond to numbers in the margin and on the Old Rome map.

A Good Walk

Start on Via del Plebiscito, near Piazza Venezia, at the huge church of **Il Gesù** ①, the grandmother of all Baroque churches. Walk north to Piazza della Minerva, where in the church of **Santa Maria sopra Minerva** ② you will find the tomb of Fra Angelico. Turn down Via della Minerva to reach the **Pantheon** ③. From Piazza della Rotonda in front of the Pantheon, take Via Giustiniani onto Via della Dogana Vecchia to the church of **San Luigi dei Francesi** ④, a pilgrimage spot for art lovers everywhere. Just north on Via della Dogana is the church of **Sant' Agostino** ⑤, in the eponymous piazza of the same name. Check out historic **Palazzo Altemps** ⑥, off Piazza Sant'Apollinare, before arriving at **Piazza Navona** ⑦, one of Rome's showpiece piazzas, home to Bernini's Fontana dei Quattro Fiumi and the church of Sant'Agnese in Agone, the quintessence of Baroque architecture. Take Via Tor Millina west to Via della Pace and follow it north to Piazza della Pace, where a semicircular portico stands in front of the 15th-century church of **Santa Maria della Pace** ⑧. Explore the byways on the north side of Corso Vittorio Emanuele II before crossing over one of Rome's great thoroughfares and take a side street south to aristocratic **Via Giulia** east to **Palazzo Falconieri** ⑨, and, just east, **Palazzo Farnese** ⑩, perhaps the most beautiful Renaissance palace in Rome. On your way back to Corso Vittorio Emanuele II along Via Farnese, go through **Campo dei Fiori** ⑪ before coming to the **Museo Baracco** ⑫. Across the way, note one of the outstanding architectural monuments of Renaissance Rome, the **Palazzo Massimo alle Colonne** ⑬, and, two blocks east along the bustling street, the huge, 17th-century church of **Sant'Andrea della Valle** ⑭. Finally, head down Corso del Rinascimento to No. 40, the church of **Sant'Ivo alla Sapienza** ⑮, with a golden lantern atop the dome in the shape of a spiral.

TIMING

Allow about three hours for this walk, plus 10 or 15 minutes to see each church along the way.

Sights to See

⑪ **Campo dei Fiori.** The best time to visit this square—whose name translates as the Field of Flowers—is on weekday and Saturday mornings, when the outdoor market fills the square with color and bustle. It was once the scene of public executions (including that of philosopher-monk Giordano Bruno, whose statue broods in the center). ☉ *Market Mon.–Sat. 7–1:30.*

① **Il Gesù.** Grandmother of all Baroque churches, this huge structure was designed by Vignola in about 1650. The church is the tangible symbol of the power of the Jesuits, who were a major force in the Counter Reformation in Europe. It remained undecorated for about 100 years, but when it finally was decorated, no expense was spared. Its interior drips with gold and lapis lazuli, gold and precious marbles, gold and more gold—all covered by a fantastically painted ceiling by Baciccia

Old Rome

that seems to swirl down to merge with the painted stucco figures at its base. ⊠ *Piazza del Gesù.*

⑫ Museo Baracco (Baracco Museum). Housed in a charming little Renaissance town house, this museum features a varied collection of sculptures from ancient Mediterranean civilizations. ⊠ *Via dei Baullari 1,* ☎ *06/68806848.* ◱ *3,750 lire.* ◷ *Tues.–Sat. 9–7, Sun. 9–1.*

⑥ Palazzo Altemps. Those interested in ancient sculpture should not miss one of Rome's greatest collections of classical antiquities, housed in this historic building. Opened in 1997, it houses the collections of ancient Roman (and Egyptian) sculpture of the **Museo Nazionale Romano.** Look for the *Galata,* a poignant work portraying a barbarian warrior who chooses death for himself and his wife rather than humiliation by the enemy, in the famed Ludovisi collection. The palace's stunning early 16th-century courtyard and gorgeously frescoed ceilings make an impressive setting for the sculptures. ⊠ *Via Sant'Apollinare 8,* ☎ *06/6833759.* ◱ *12,000 lire (includes admission to Museo Nazionale delle Terme).*

⑨ Palazzo Falconieri. Borromini's masterful work of architecture houses nothing of interest to the visitor, but the building itself makes one of Rome's most elegant attractions. In order to get a good look at this gracefully imposing building, go around the block and view it from along the Tiber embankment. ⊠ *Via Giulia 1.*

⑩ Palazzo Farnese. Michelangelo had a hand in building what is now the French Embassy and perhaps the most beautiful Renaissance palace in Rome. Within is the **Galleria** vault painted by Annibale Carracci between 1597 and 1604—the second-greatest ceiling in Rome; write in advance to the embassy (⊠ Ambassador, French Embassy, Piazza Farnese 64, 00186 Rome) for special permission to view it. The **Galleria Carracci** (Carracci Gallery) depicts the loves of the gods, a supremely pagan theme that the artist painted in a swirling style that announced the birth of Baroque. It's said that Carracci was so dismayed at the miserly fee he received—the Farnese family was extravagantly rich even by the standards of 15th- and 16th-century Rome's extravagantly rich—that he took to drink and died shortly thereafter. Those who sympathize with the poor man's fate will be further dismayed to learn that the French government pays one lira every 99 years as rent for their sumptuous embassy. ⊠ *Piazza Farnese.*

⑬ Palazzo Massimo alle Colonne. A graceful columned portico marks this inconspicuous but seminal architectural monument of Renaissance Rome, built by Baldassare Peruzzi in 1527. Via del Paradiso, across Corso Vittorio Emanuele II, affords a better view. ⊠ *Corso Vittorio Emanuele II 141.*

③ Pantheon. Paradoxically, this is one of Rome's most perfect, well-preserved, and perhaps least-appreciated ancient monuments. Built on the site of an earlier pantheon erected in 27 BC by Augustus's general Agrippa, it was entirely rebuilt by the emperor Hadrian around AD 120. It was actually designed by Hadrian himself. The most striking thing about the Pantheon is not its size, immense though it is (until 1960 the dome was the largest ever built); rather it is the remarkable unity of the building. You don't have to look far to find the reason for this harmony: the diameter of the dome is exactly equal to the height of the walls. The hole in the ceiling is intentional: the oculus at the apex of the dome signifies the "all-seeing eye of heaven." Note the original bronze doors: they have survived more than 1,800 years, centuries more than the interior's rich gold ornamentation, long since plundered by popes and emperors. ✉ *Piazza della Rotonda,* ☎ *06/68300230.* 🎟 *Free.* ☽ *Mon.–Sat. 9–4:30, Sun. 9–1.*

NEED A BREAK? The café scene in the square in front of the Pantheon rivals that of nearby Piazza Navona. Some of Rome's best gelaterie are here, within a few steps of one another. Romans consider nearby **Giolitti** (✉ Via Uffizi del Vicario 40) superlative and take its gelato and snack counters by storm. Remember to pay the cashier first and hand the stub to the man at the counter when you order your cone. You're out of luck Monday, when it's closed. If you're a cappuccino addict, head for the nearby **Tazza d'Oro** (✉ Via degli Orfani 84).

★ ☾ ❼ **Piazza Navona.** This famed 17th-century piazza, which mimics the oval form of Emperor Domitian's stadium, is one of Rome's showpiece attractions. It still has the carefree air of the days when it was the scene of Roman circus games, medieval jousts, and 17th-century carnivals. Today, this renowned spot often attracts fashion photographers and Romans out for their evening *passeggiata* (promenade). The Christmas fair held in the piazza from early December through January 6 is lively and fun for children, with rides, games, Santa Claus, and the Befana (the ugly but good witch who brings candy and toys to Italian children on the Epiphany). Bernini's splashing **Fontana dei Quattro Fiumi** (Fountain of the Four Rivers), with an enormous rock squared off by statues representing the four corners of the world, makes a fitting centerpiece. Behind the fountain stands the church of **Sant'Agnese in Agone,** the absolute quintessence of Baroque architecture, built by the Pamphili Pope Innocent X and still owned by his descendants, the Doria Pamphili. The facade—a wonderfully rich mélange of bell towers, concave spaces, and dovetailed stone and marble—is by Carlo Rainaldi and Francesco Borromini (1599–1667), a contemporary and sometime rival of Bernini. One story has it that the Bernini statue nearest the church is hiding its head because it can't bear to look upon the "inferior" Borromini facade; in fact, the facade was built after the fountain, and the statue hides its head because it represents the Nile River, whose source was unknown until relatively recently.

NEED A BREAK? **Tre Scalini** café (✉ Piazza Navona 30) actually invented the *tartufo,* a luscious chocolate-covered ice-cream specialty. Note that you'll pay twice as much if you eat outside and that it's closed Wednesday. For a casual *insalata* (salad) or a *panino* (small sandwich), go to **Cul de Sac** (✉ Piazza Pasquino 73 off Piazza Navona). **Insalata Ricca** (✉ Via del Paradiso next to church of Sant'Andrea della Valle) also has light fare at informal prices.

★ ❹ **San Luigi dei Francesi.** In the last chapel on the left are three stunningly dramatic works by Caravaggio (1571–1610), the master of the heightened approach to light and dark. The inevitable coin machine will light up his *Calling of St. Matthew, Matthew and the Angel,* and *Matthew's Martyrdom,* seen from left to right, and Caravaggio's mastery of light takes it from there. Time has fully vindicated the artist's patron, Cardinal Francesco del Monte, who commissioned these works and stoutly defended their worth from the consternation of the clergy of San Luigi, who didn't appreciate the artist's roistering and unruly lifestyle; they are now acknowledged as among the world's greatest paintings. ✉ *Piazza San Luigi dei Francesi.* ☽ *Fri.–Wed. 7:30–12:30 and 3:30–7, Thurs. 7:30–12:30.*

❺ **Sant'Agostino.** Caravaggio's celebrated *Madonna of the Pilgrims*—which scandalized all Rome because it pictured pilgrims with dirt on the soles of their feet—can be found in this small church, over the first altar on the left. ⊠ *Piazza di Sant'Agostino.*

⑭ Sant'Andrea della Valle. This huge, 17th-century church looms mightily over a busy intersection. Aficionados of Puccini, who set the first act of his opera *Tosca* here, have been known to hire a horse-drawn carriage at night for an evocative journey that traces the course of the opera (from Sant'Andrea up Via Giulia to Palazzo Farnese—Scarpia's headquarters—to the locale of the opera's climax, Castel Sant'Angelo). ⊠ *Piazza Vidoni 6.*

⑮ Sant'Ivo alla Sapienza. Borromini's inspirational church has what must surely be the most fascinating dome in all Rome—topped by a golden spiral said to have been inspired by a bee's stinger. ⊠ *Corso Rinascimento 40.*

❽ Santa Maria della Pace. Hidden away in a corner of Old Rome, gracing Piazza Santa Maria della Pace, are a semicircular portico and 15th-century church. In 1656, Pietro da Cortona was commissioned by Pope Alexander VII to enlarge its tiny piazza (to accommodate the carriages of the church's wealthy parishioners), and the result was one of Rome's most delightful little architectural stage sets, complete with bijou-size palaces. Within the church are two great Renaissance treasures: Raphael's frescoes of the Sibyls (above the first altar on the right near the front door) and the cloister designed by Bramante, the very first expression of High Renaissance style in Rome. Santa Maria della Pace is rarely open but if you take the alleylike Vicolo along the left-hand side of the church and ring the bell at the first entryway on the right, the nuns will usually permit you to enter. ⊠ *Piazza Santa Maria della Pace.*

❷ Santa Maria sopra Minerva. Practically the only Gothic-style church in Rome, the attractions are Michelangelo's *Risen Christ* and the tomb of the gentle 15th-century artist Fra Angelico. Have some coins handy for the *luce* (light) boxes that illuminate the **Cappella Carafa** (Carafa Chapel) in the right transept, where exquisite 15th-century frescoes by Filippo Lippi (circa 1457–1504) are well worth the small investment (Lippi's most famous student was Botticelli). In front of the church, Bernini's charming elephant bearing an Egyptian obelisk has an inscription on the base stating something to the effect that it takes a strong mind to sustain solid wisdom. ⊠ *Piazza della Minerva.*

Via Giulia was named after Pope Julius II and has functioned for more than four centuries as the "salon of Rome," address of choice for Roman aristocrats. It is lined with elegant palaces, including Palazzo Falconieri (☞ *above*), and old churches (one, San Eligio, reputedly designed by Raphael himself). The area around Via Giulia is a wonderful section to wander through and get the feel of daily life as carried on in a centuries-old setting; this experience is enhanced by the dozens of antiques shops in the neighborhood.

Vistas and Views: From the Scalinata di Spagna to the Fontana di Trevi

Though it has a bustling commercial air, this part of the city also holds some great visual allurements. The most extravagant of all is the elaborate marble confection that is the monument to Vittorio Emanuele II. Among the things to look for are stately palaces, Baroque ballrooms, and the greatest example of portraiture in Rome, Velazquez's incomparable *Innocent X*. Those with a taste for the sumptuous theatricality of Roman ecclesiastical architecture—heroic illusionistic ceiling painting in particular—will find this a rewarding area. The highlights are the Trevi Fountain and the Spanish Steps, 18th-century Rome's most famous example of city planning.

Numbers in the text correspond to numbers in the margin and on the Rome map.

A Good Walk

Start at the flamboyant **Monumento di Vittorio Emanuele II** ⑮ in Piazza Venezia, home of the Tomba del Milite Ignoto. As you look up Via del Corso, to your left is **Palazzo Venezia** ⑯, an art-filled Renaissance palace where Mussolini once addressed the crowds. On Saturday, you can visit the picture gallery known as Galleria Colonna, in the **Palazzo Colonna** ⑰, east of Piazza Venezia. From Piazza Venezia head north on Via del Corso, one of the city's busiest shopping streets, to the **Palazzo Doria Pamphili** ⑱. A quick detour west will bring you to the sumptuous 17th-century church of **Sant'Ignazio** ⑲. If you continue north on Via del Corso you will reach Piazza Colonna and the ancient **Colonna di Marcus Aurelius** ⑳. Continue north on Via del Corso and take a right onto chic Via Condotti, which gives you a head-on view of the Piazza di Spagna and the **Scalinata di Spagna** ㉑; to the right of the steps, at No. 26, is the **Fondazione Keats-Shelley Memorial** ㉒, in which the English Romantic poet Keats lived. If you climb the Spanish Steps you will get a good view of Rome's skyline from the top, and you can take a slight detour onto Via Gregoriana to discover the **Palazzetto Zuccari** ㉓. From the narrow (southern) end of Piazza di Spagna take Via Propaganda Fide to Sant'Andrea delle Fratte, and take a left onto Via del Nazareno, then crossing busy Via del Tritone to Via della Stamperia. This street leads to the **Fontana di Trevi** ㉔, one of Rome's most famous landmarks.

TIMING

The walk takes approximately two to three hours. In the morning the air is cleaner and car and pedestrian traffic is lighter.

Sights to See

⑳ **Colonna di Marcus Aurelius.** This ancient column is an extraordinary stone history book. Its detailed reliefs spiraling up to the top illustrate the emperor's victorious campaigns against the barbarians. ⊠ *Piazza Colonna.*

㉒ **Fondazione Keats-Shelley Memorial** (Keats and Shelley Memorial House). English Romantic poet John Keats lived in what is now a museum dedicated to him and his great contemporary and friend, Percy Bysshe Shelley. You can visit his tiny rooms, preserved as they were when he died here in 1821. ⊠ *Piazza di Spagna 26, next to the Spanish Steps,* ☏ *06/6784235.* ☞ *5,000 lire.* ☉ *June–Sept., weekdays 9–1 and 3–6; Oct.–May, weekdays 9–1 and 2:30–5:30.*

★ ㉔ **Fontana di Trevi** (Trevi Fountain). Tucked away off Via del Tritone in a minuscule piazza, the fountain is a spectacular fantasy of mythical sea creatures amidst cascades of splashing waters. It was featured in the 1954 film *Three Coins in the Fountain* and, of course, was the scene of Anita Ekberg's aquatic frolic in Fellini's *La Dolce Vita.* The fountain is the world's most spectacular wishing well: legend has it that you can ensure your return to Rome by tossing a coin into the fountain. At night, the spotlit piazza takes on the festive air of a crowded outdoor party.

⑮ **Monumento di Vittorio Emanuele II.** The huge bronze sculpture group atop this vast marble monument is visible from many parts of the city, making this modern Rome's most flamboyant landmark. It was erected in the late 19th century to honor Italy's first king, Vittorio Emanuele

II, and the unification of Italy. Sometimes said to resemble a typewriter in the Victorian style, it houses the **Tomba del Milite Ignoto** (Tomb of the Unknown Soldier), with its eternal flame. Although the monument has been closed to the public for many years, plans are in the works to reopen it. The views from the top of the steps are among Rome's best. Opposite the monument, note the enclosed wooden veranda fronting the palace on the corner of Via del Plebiscito and Via Corso. For the many years that she lived in Rome, Napoléon's mother had a fine view from here of the local goings-on. ⊠ *Piazza Venezia.*

🖐 ㉓ **Palazzetto Zuccari.** Near the top of the Spanish Steps (☞ *below*) stands what many consider the most amusing house in all of Italy, designed to look like a grimacing stone monster. The entrance is through the monster's mouth; the eyes are the house's windows. It was designed in 1591 by the Mannerist painter Federico Zuccari (1540–1609), whose home this was. Zuccari sank all his money into this bizarre creation, dying in debt before his curious memorial, as it turned out to be, was completed. It is now the property of the **Biblioteca Hertziana,** Rome's prestigious fine arts library. ⊠ *Via Gregoriana 30.*

⑰ **Palazzo Colonna.** Rome's most patrician family opens up its fabulous home to the public once a week. The entrance to the picture gallery, **Galleria Colonna,** which is open only on Saturday morning, is a secondary one, behind a plain, obscure-seeming door. The old masters are lackluster, but the gallery should be on your must-do list because the **Sala Grande** is truly the grandest 17th-century room in Rome. More than 300 ft long, and decorated with a bedazzlement of chandeliers, colored marble, and enormous paintings, it is best known today as the site where Audrey Hepburn met the press in *Roman Holiday.* ⊠ *Via della Pilotta 17,* ☎ *06/6794362.* 🎟 *10,000 lire.* ☉ *Sept.–July, Sat. 9–1.*

⑱ **Palazzo Doria Pamphili.** The 18th-century facade of this palazzo on Via del Corso is only a small part of a bona-fide patrician palace, still the residence of a princely family, who rent out many of the palazzo's 1,000 rooms. You shouldn't miss seeing the family's incredibly rich art collection in the frescoed gallery and the few salons opened in 1996. Pride of place is given to the famous (and pitiless) 17th-century Velazquez portrait of the Pamphili Pope *Innocent X,* but don't overlook Caravaggio's poignant *Rest on the Flight to Egypt*—and, time permitting, catch the guided tour of the state apartments, which gives a discreet glimpse of an aristocratic lifestyle. Pundits say most Roman palazzi consist of one bathroom, two bedrooms, and 40 ballrooms, and after this tour, you can understand why. ⊠ *Piazza del Collegio Romano 2,* ☎ *06/6797323.* 🎟 *Picture gallery 12,000 lire, private-apartments tour 5,000 lire.* ☉ *Fri.–Wed. 10–5.*

⑯ **Palazzo Venezia.** A blend of medieval solidity and genuine Renaissance grace, this building houses a good collection of paintings, sculptures, and objets d'art in its grand salons, some of which Mussolini used as his offices. Notice the balcony over the main portal, from which Il Duce addressed huge crowds in the eponymous **Piazza Venezia** below. Nowadays, the square's most imposing figure is the policeman directing traffic from his little podium in the middle, whose almost comical display of orchestration is a constant source of amusement to passersby. ⊠ *Via del Plebiscito 118,* ☎ *06/6798865.* 🎟 *10,000 lire.* ☉ *Tues.–Sat. 9–1:30, Sun. 9–12:30.*

⑲ **Sant'Ignazio.** The false interior dome in this sumptuous 17th-century church is a trompe l'oeil oddity among the lavishly frescoed domes of the Eternal City. To get the full effect of the illusionistic ceiling painted by Andrea del Pozzo, stand on the small disk set into the floor of the nave to view his *Glory of St. Ignatius Loyola*. The church contains some of Rome's most splendorous, jewel-encrusted altars. If you're lucky, you might be able to catch an evening concert performed here. The church is the focus of Raguzzini's 18th-century Rococo piazza, where the buildings are arranged almost as in a stage set, reminding us that theatricality was a key element of almost all the best Baroque and Rococo art. ⊠ *Piazza Sant'Ignazio.*

NEED A BREAK? The **Antico Caffè Greco** (⊠ Via Condotti 86), a 200-year-old institution, ever a haunt of artists and literati, has tiny, marble-top tables and velour settees; it's a beautifully preserved place to stop for a drink. Goethe, Byron, and Liszt were habitués; Buffalo Bill stopped in when his Wild West road show hit Rome. It's still a haven for writers and artists, and for ladies carrying Versace shopping bags. Note that it's closed Sunday and you pay a premium for table service.

★ ㉑ **Scalinata di Spagna** (Spanish Steps). Both the steps and the **Piazza di Spagna** get their names from the Spanish Embassy and the Holy See (the Vatican), opposite the American Express office, though the staircase was built with French funds in 1723. In an allusion to the Church of Trinità dei Monti at the top of the hill, the staircase is divided by three landings (beautifully banked with blooming azaleas from mid-April to mid-May). For centuries, the Scalinata (as natives refer to the steps) has been the place to see and be seen. This area has always welcomed tourists: 18th-century dukes and duchesses on their Grand Tour, 19th-century artists and writers in search of inspiration—among them, Stendhal, Balzac, Thackeray, and Byron—and today's enthusiastic hordes. Bernini's **Fontana della Barcaccia** (Fountain of the Old Boat) is near the center of the piazza. ⊠ *Piazza di Spagna.*

NEED A BREAK? Stop for a gelato or a panino at **Caffè Leonardo** (⊠ Piazza Mignanelli 21/a, near American Express office); it's open until 2 AM.

Historic Churches: Heavenly Monuments of Faith

It is hard not to be impressed by the historic and architectural grandeur of Rome's major churches. Three churches are the highlights of this walk, two of them major basilicas with roots in the early centuries of Christianity.

A Good Walk

Not far from Piazza Venezia and the Roman Forum is the church of **San Pietro in Vincoli** ㉕, off Via Cavour. Look for Via San Francesco da Paola, a street staircase that passes under the old Borgia palace and leads to the church. Return to Via Cavour, which veers northeast to **Santa Maria Maggiore** ㉖, and from there Via Merulana going south leads straight to **San Giovanni in Laterano** ㉗. The adjoining Palazzo Laterano houses the Museo Storico Vaticano; across the street, a small building houses the **Scala Santa** ㉘, or Holy Stairs, supposedly from Pilate's Jerusalem palace. Circle the palace to see the 6th-century octagonal Battistero di San Giovanni, forerunner of many such buildings throughout Italy.

TIMING

The walk alone takes approximately 90 minutes, plus 15–20 minutes in the churches. Allow at least an hour to explore San Clemente. A visit to the Museo Storico Vaticano will take you about 45 minutes.

Sights to See

㉗ **San Giovanni in Laterano.** Many are surprised when they discover that the cathedral of Rome is not St. Peter's but this church. Dominating the piazza whose name it shares, this immense building is where the present pope still officiates in his capacity as Rome's bishop. The towering facade and Borromini's cool baroque interior emphasize the majesty of its proportions.

The adjoining **Palazzo Laterano** (Lateran Palace), once the early popes' official residence and still technically part of the Vatican, now houses the offices of the Rome Diocese and the **Museo Storico Vaticano** (Vatican Historical Museum). ⊠ *Piazza San Giovanni in Laterano.* ▣ *6,000 lire.* ☉ *Museum Sat. and the 1st Sun. of each month 8:45–1.*

<table>
<tr><td>OFF THE
BEATEN PATH</td><td>

SAN CLEMENTE – The remains of ancient Roman dwellings and a 4th-century church below the upper church of San Clemente are among Rome's most intriguing subterranean sights. ⊠ *Via San Giovanni in Laterano,* ☎ *06/70451018.* ▣ *Donation requested.* ☉ *Mon.–Sat. 9–noon and 3:30–6, Sun. 10–noon.*

SANTI QUATTRO CORONATI – This 12th-century church, part of a fortified abbey that provided refuge to early popes and emperors, is in one of the most unusual corners of Rome, a quiet island that has resisted the tide of time and traffic flowing beneath its ramparts. Few places in Rome are as reminiscent of the Middle Ages. Don't miss the cloister with its well-tended gardens and 12th-century fountain. The entrance is the door in the left nave; ring if it's not open. You can also ring at the adjacent convent for the key to the Oratory of San Silvestro, with 13th-century frescoes. ⊠ *Largo Santi Quattro Coronati.*
</td></tr>
</table>

㉕ **San Pietro in Vincoli.** The church houses St. Peter's chains (under the altar) and Michelangelo's *Moses,* a powerful statue almost as famed as his frescoes in the Sistine Chapel. The *Moses* was destined for the tomb of Julius II, but Michelangelo was driven to distraction by the interference of Pope Julius and his successors, and the tomb was never finished. The statue is a remarkable sculpture but the church is usually jammed with tour groups, and the monument itself fronts a large, ugly souvenir shop. ⊠ *Piazza San Pietro in Vincoli off Via Cavour.*

㉖ **Santa Maria Maggiore.** One of the oldest and most spacious churches in Rome, it was built on the spot where a 3rd-century pope witnessed a miraculous midsummer snowfall. It is resplendent with gleaming mosaics—those on the arch in front of the main altar date from the 5th century. The apse mosaic dates from the 13th century—an opulently carved wood ceiling believed to have been gilded with the first gold brought from the New World. ⊠ *Piazza Santa Maria Maggiore off Via Cavour.*

㉘ **Scala Santa** (Sacred Stairs). A small building opposite the Lateran Palace (☞ *above*) houses the so-called Holy Stairs, claimed to be the staircase from Pilate's palace in Jerusalem. Behind the palace is the 6th-century octagonal **Battistero di San Giovanni** (St. John's Baptistery), forerunner of many similar buildings throughout Italy, and Rome's oldest and tallest obelisk, brought from Thebes and dating from the 15th century BC. ⊠ *Piazza San Giovanni in Laterano.*

From the Monte Quirinale to the Piazza della Repubblica: Princely Palaces and Romantic Fountains

On this tour you'll see ancient Roman sculptures and early Christian churches but concentrate on the 16th and 17th centuries, when Baroque art—and Bernini—triumphed in Rome.

A Good Walk

Begin on **Monte Quirinale** ㉙, the highest of Rome's seven hills. Here you'll find the Palazzo del Quirinale, official residence of the president of Italy. Also of note is the **Palazzo Pallavicini-Rospigliosi** ㉚, a 17th-century palace with some exquisite examples of Baroque art. Along Via del Quirinale (which becomes Via XX Settembre) is the church of **Sant'Andrea** ㉛, considered by many to be Bernini's finest work, and, at the Quattro Fontane (Four Fountains) crossroads, the church of **San Carlo alle Quattro Fontane** ㉜, designed by Bernini's rival Borromini. Take a left on Via delle Quattro Fontane to reach the imposing **Palazzo Barberini** ㉝, where the Galleria Nazionale d'Arte Antica is home to splendid masterpieces by Raphael and Caravaggio. Down the hill is Piazza Barberini and the **Fontana Tritone** ㉞, another Bernini design. Cross the piazza and begin your gradual climb up Via Vittorio Veneto, curving past the U.S. Embassy and turning off onto Via Bissolati. On the corner of Piazza San Bernardo is the church of **Santa Maria della Vittoria** ㊱, known for Bernini's Baroque decoration. It's not far down Via Orlando to **Piazza della Repubblica** ㊲, where you will find the pretty Fontana delle Naiadi. On one side of the square is an ancient Roman brick facade, which marks the church of Santa Maria degli Angeli. Beyond, on the near corner of Piazza del Cinquecento, the vast square in front of Termini Station, is the last stop on this walk, the **Museo Nazionale Romano** ㊳, where there are plentiful examples of the fine mosaics and masterful paintings that decorated ancient Rome's villas and palaces.

TIMING

The walk takes approximately 90 minutes, plus 10–15 minutes for each church visited, and two hours each for visits to the Galleria Nazionale in Palazzo Barberini and the Museo Nazionale Romano.

Sights to See

㉞ **Fontana Tritone** (Triton Fountain). Centerpiece of Piazza Barberini is Bernini's graceful fountain, designed in 1637 for the sculptor's munificent patron, Pope Urban VIII, whose Barberini coat of arms, featuring bees once again, is at the base of the large shell.

㉙ **Monte Quirinale** (Quirinal Hill). This is the highest of ancient Rome's seven hills and the one where ancient Romans and, later, the popes built their residences in order to escape the deadly miasmas and the malaria of the low-lying area around the Forum. Every day at 4 PM the ceremony of the changing of the guards at the portal includes a sprightly miniparade, complete with band. The fountain in the square boasts ancient statues of Castor and Pollux reining in their unruly steeds, and a basin salvaged from the Roman Forum. The **Palazzo del Quirinale**, the largest on Piazza Quirinale, belonged first to the popes, then to Italy's kings, and is now the official residence of the nation's president.

㊳ **Museo Nazionale Romano** (National Museum). Palazzo Massimo alle Terme holds a major part of the collections of the National Museum. Here you can see extraordinary examples of the fine mosaics and masterful paintings that decorated ancient Rome's palaces and villas, as well as some of antiquity's most fabled sculptures, including the *Ludovisi Throne, Lancellotti Discus Thrower,* and the *Castelporziano Discus Thrower.* On the second floor (scheduled to open in 1997) don't miss the fresco—depicting a lush garden in bloom—that came from the villa that Livia, wife of Emperor Augustus, owned outside Rome. ✉ *Largo Villa Peretti 2,* ☎ *06/48903501.* 🎟 *12,000 lire (includes Museo delle Terme di Diocleziano,* ☞ *below).* ⊙ *Tues.–Sat. 9–2, Sun. 9–1.*

㉝ Palazzo Barberini (Galleria Nazionale d'Arte Antica). Along with architect Carlo Maderno, Borromini helped make the splendid 17th-century Palazzo Barberini a residence worthy of Rome's leading art patron, Pope Urban VIII, who began this palazzo for his family in 1625. Inside, the gallery offers some fine works by Raphael (the *Fornarina*) and by Caravaggio. Rome's biggest ballroom is here; its ceiling, painted by Pietro da Cortona, depicts Immortality bestowing a crown upon Divine Providence escorted by—"a bomber squadron," to quote Sir Michael Levey—of mutant bees (bees featured prominently in the heraldic device of the Barberini). ✉ *Via delle Quattro Fontane 13,* ☎ *06/4814591.* 🎟 *8,000 lire.* ⊙ *Tues.–Sat. 9–7, Sun. 9–1.*

㉚ Palazzo Pallavicini-Rospigliosi. This palace was built in 1605 for Cardinal Scipione Borghese; on the first day of each month, visitors can view Guido Reni's fresco of *Aurora*—a landmark in Baroque painting—in the palace's park pavilion. ✉ *Via XXIV Maggio 43, just off Piazza del Quirinale* ☎ *06/4827224.* 🎟 *Free.* ⊙ *1st day of month 10–noon and 3–5.*

㊲ Piazza della Repubblica. This piazza has a typical 19th-century layout, but the curving porticoes echo the immense ancient **Terme di Diocleziano** (Baths of Diocletian), which once stood here. Built in the 4th century AD, they were the largest and most impressive of the baths of ancient Rome, and their vast halls, pools, and gardens could accommodate 3,000 people at a time. Also part of the great baths was an **Aula Ottagonale** (Octagonal Hall) that now holds a sampling of ancient sculptures found there, including two beautiful bronzes. ✉ *Via Romita.* 🎟 *Free.* ⊙ *Daily 10–1 and 3–6.*

Another part of the Baths of Diocletian was later transformed into a monastery and then into the **Museo Terme di Diocleziano.** The cloister holds the Museo Nazionale Romano's collection of ancient inscriptions on stone. Lining the **giardino** (garden) paths are bits and pieces of ancient Rome. ✉ *Viale E. De Nicola 79,* ☎ *06/4880530.* 🎟 *12,000 lire (includes Palazzo Massimo alle Terme).* ⊙ *Tues.–Sat. 9–2, Sun. 9–1.*

The pretty **Fontana delle Naiadi** (Fountain of the Naiads), a turn-of-the-century addition to the piazza, features voluptuous bronze ladies wrestling happily with marine monsters. The curving ancient Roman brick facade on one side of the piazza marks the church of **Santa Maria degli Angeli,** adapted by Michelangelo from the vast central chamber of the colossal baths. The scale of the church's interior gives you an idea of the grandeur of the ancient building.

㉜ San Carlo alle Quattro Fontane. Borromini's church at the Quattro Fontane (Four Fountains) crossroads is an architectural gem. In a space no larger than the base of one of the piers of St. Peter's, Borromini attained geometric perfection. Characteristically, the architect chose a subdued white stucco for the interior decoration, so as not to distract from the form. The exterior of the church is Borromini at his bizarre best, all curves and rippling movement. Outside, four charming fountains frame views in four directions. ✉ *Via del Quirinale 23.*

㉟ Santa Maria della Concezione. One of the most bizarre sights in Rome is the crypt of this Capuchin church, where you can see—if you like that sort of thing—the skeletons and assorted bones of 4,000 dead monks artistically arranged in four macabre chapels. ⊠ *Via Veneto 27,* ☎ *06/4871185.* ☞ *Donation requested.* ⊙ *Daily 9–noon and 3–6.*

㊱ Santa Maria della Vittoria. This church is known for Bernini's Baroque decoration of the Cornaro Chapel, an exceptional fusion of architecture, painting, and sculpture, in which the *Ecstasy of St. Teresa* is the focal point. Bernini's audacious conceit was to model the chapel as a theater: members of the Cornaro family—sculpted in white marble—watch from theater boxes as, center stage, St. Teresa, in the throes of mystical rapture, is pierced by a gilded arrow held by an angel. To quote one 18th-century observer, President de Brosses: "If that is divine love, I know what it is." ⊠ *Via XX Settembre.*

㊲ Sant'Andrea. This is a small but imposing Baroque church designed and decorated by Bernini, who considered it one of his finest works and liked to come here occasionally just to sit and enjoy it. ⊠ *Via del Quirinale.*

Amid Sylvan Glades: From the Villa Borghese to the Ara Pacis

Beautiful masterpieces are as common as bricks on this walk, which offers more visual excitement than most cities possess in their entire environs. Along the way, Villa Borghese, Rome's largest park, can alleviate gallery gout by offering an oasis in which to enjoy an espresso at the Casino Valadier or picnic under the ilex trees. Just be sure to pick up your foodstuffs in advance, whether ready-to-go from the snack bars or do-it-yourself from *alimentari* (grocery stores), as you'll find only fast-food carts within the park itself.

A Good Walk

Start at **Porta Pinciana** ㊴, one of the entrances to Villa Borghese. Follow Viale del Museo Borghese to the **Galleria Borghese** ㊵ and its fabulous sculpture collection. Head to the southwest corner of the park to enjoy the view of Rome from the **Pincio** ㊶ belvedere before descending the ramps to **Piazza del Popolo** ㊷. At the north end of the piazza, next to the 400-year-old city gate, the Porta del Popolo, is the church of **Santa Maria del Popolo** ㊸, with one of the richest art collections of any church in the city. Stroll south along Via Ripetta to the **Augusteum,** built by Caesar Augustus; next to it is the **Ara Pacis** ㊹, built in 13 BC.

TIMING

The walk takes approximately two hours; allow an additional hour for the Galleria Borghese, and another additional hour for the stroll past the Augusteum and to see the Ara Pacis.

Sights to See

㊹ Ara Pacis (Altar of Augustan Peace). This altar, sheltered in an unattractive modern edifice on the northwest corner of Piazza Augusto Imperatore, was erected in 13 BC to celebrate the era of peace ushered in by Augustus's military victories. The reliefs showing the procession of the Roman imperial family are magnificent and moving. Notice the poignant presence of several forlorn children; historians now believe they attest to the ambition of Augustus's wife, the Empress Livia, who succeeded in having her son, Tiberius, ascend to the throne by dispatching his family rivals with poison. Next to it is the imposing bulk of the marble-clad **Mausoleo di Augusto** (Mausoleum of Augustus) Augustus built for himself and his family. ⊠ *Via Ripetta,* ☎ *06/68806848.* ☞ *3,750 lire.* ⊙ *Tues.–Sat. 9–7, Sun. 9–1:30.*

㊵ Galleria Borghese (Borghese Gallery). Cardinal Scipione Borghese's 1613 palace—a place to flaunt his fabulous antiquities collection and elegant fetes—is today a monument to 18th-century Roman interior decoration at its most extravagant, dripping with porphyry and alabaster. Throughout the grand salons are statues of various deities, including one officially known as Venus Vincitrix, but there has never been any doubt as to its real subject: Pauline Bonaparte, Napoléon's sister, who married Prince Camillo Borghese in one of the storied matches of the 19th century. Sculpted by Canova, the princess reclines on a chaise lounge, bare-bosomed, her hips swathed in classical drapery, the very model of haughty detachment and sly come-hither. Pauline is known to have been shocked that her husband took pleasure in showing off the work to his guests. This coyness seems all the more curious given the reply she is supposed to have made to a lady who asked her how she could have posed for the work: "Oh, but the studio was heated." But then it was exactly the combination of aristocratic disdain and naïveté that is said to have made her irresistible in the first place.

Other rooms at the Galleria Borghese hold important sculptures by Bernini, including the *David* and *Apollo and Daphne*. The gallery's renowned picture collection includes splendid works by Titian, Caravaggio, and Raphael, among others. After extensive structural repairs and restoration, the Gallery was fully reopened in 1997. ⊠ *Piazza Scipione Borghese, off Via Pinciana,* ☎ *06/8548577.* 🎟 *8,000 lire.* ☉ *May–Sept., Tues.–Sat. 9–7, Sun. 9–1; Oct.–Apr., Tues.–Sun. 9–1.*

㊷ Piazza del Popolo. For many years this beautifully proportioned square functioned as an exceptionally attractive parking lot that happened to have a 3,000-year-old **obelisco** (obelisk) in the middle (now traffic and parking are limited). The often-photographed bookend **Baroque churches** at the southern end of the piazza are not, first appearances to the contrary, twins. At one end of the square is the 400-year-old **Porta del Popolo,** Rome's northern city gate.

NEED A
BREAK?

Rosati (⊠ Piazza del Popolo 4) is a café that has never gone out of style, forever a rendezvous of literati, artists, and actors. Its sidewalk tables, tearoom, and upstairs dining room can revive you with an espresso, snack, lunch, or dinner—all with a hefty price tag.

㊶ Pincio. The southwestern corner of **Villa Borghese,** Rome's peaceful 17th-century park built as the pleasure gardens of the powerful Borghese family, occupies the Pincian Hill, one of the seven hills of ancient Rome. The park and belvedere were laid out by the early 19th-century architect Valadier as part of his overall plan for Piazza del Popolo. Back then, counts and countesses liked to take their evening passeggiata here in the hopes of meeting Pius IX, the last pope to go about Rome on foot. Here you'll find the pricey Casina Valadier restaurant, where you can enjoy the views from the terrace café—the prettiest place in Rome to have a cappuccino.

㊴ Porta Pinciana (Pincian Gate). One of the historic city gates in the Aurelian Walls surrounding Rome, the Porta itself was built in the 6th century AD, about three centuries after the walls were built to keep out the barbarians. These days it is one of the entrances to Villa Borghese.

㊸ Santa Maria del Popolo. This church next to the Porta del Popolo (☞ *above*) goes almost unnoticed, but it has one of the richest collections of art of any church in Rome. Here you'll find Raphael's High Renaissance masterpiece, the **Cappella Chigi** (Chigi Chapel) as well as two stunning Caravaggios in the **Cappella Cerasi** (Cerasi Chapel), which definitively prove just how modern 17th-century art can be. Elsewhere in the church, the great names—Bramante, Bernini, Pinturicchio, Sansovino, Caracci—resound in the silence. ⊠ *Piazza del Popolo.*

Across the Tiber: The Ghetto, Tiber Island, and Trastevere

This walk takes you through separate communities, each staunchly resisting the tides of change, including the Jewish ghetto. In picturesque Trastevere you will find "the Romans of Rome": blunt, uninhibited, sharp-eyed, friendly, sincere, often beautiful, and seldom varnished. Despite rampant gentrification, Trastevere remains about the most tightly knit community in Rome, its inhabitants proudly proclaiming their descent—whether real or imagined—from the ancient Romans.

A Good Walk

Begin in the old ghetto, on Via del Teatro Marcello, which leads to Piazza Campitelli, just north; take Via dei Funari to Piazza Mattei, where one of Rome's loveliest fountains, the 16th-century **Fontana delle Tartarughe** ㊺, is tucked away. Take Via della Reginella into **Via Portico d'Ottavia,** heart of the Jewish ghetto. On the Tiber is a **synagogue.** The **Teatro di Marcello** ㊻, behind the **Portico d'Ottavia,** was originally a theater designed to hold 20,000 people. Follow Via di Teatro di Marcello south, passing the ruins of two small temples: the **Tempio della Fortuna Virilis** ㊼ and the circular **Tempio di Vesta** ㊽. Across Piazza Santa Maria in Cosmedin is the 12th-century church of Santa Maria in Cosmedin, in **Piazza Bocca della Verità** ㊾, with the marble Bocca Della Verità. Retracing your steps, walk upstream along the Tiber, cross Ponte Fabricio over **Isola Tiberina** ㊿, and then head into **Trastevere.**

Begin your exploration of Trastevere at **Piazza in Piscinula** (you will need a good street map to make your way around this intricate maze of winding side streets), take Via dell'Arco dei Tolomei, cross Via dei Salumi, and turn left onto Via dei Genovesi and then right to the piazza in front of **Santa Cecilia in Trastevere** �51. Aficionados of the Baroque will want to walk several blocks southwest down Via Anicia to **San Francesco a Ripa** �52 to see a famous Bernini sculpture. Follow Via San Francesco a Ripa to the very heart of the *rione,* or district, of Trastevere, to the lovely **Piazza di Santa Maria in Trastevere** �53, site of the lovely 12th-century church of Santa Maria in Trastevere. With a detailed map, find your way through the narrow byways to Piazza Sant' Egidio and Via della Scala, continuing on to Via della Lungara, where you'll find **Villa Farnesina** �54, which includes frescoes by Raphael. From Trastevere, climb Via Garibaldi to the Janiculum Hill, which offers views spanning the whole city, and where you'll find the church of **San Pietro in Montorio** �55, built in 1481.

TIMING

The walk takes approximately three hours, plus 10–15 minutes for each church visited, and about 30 minutes for a visit to Villa Farnesina.

Sights to See

㊺ **Fontana delle Tartarughe.** The 16th-century "Fountain of the Turtles" in Piazza Mattei is one of Rome's loveliest. Designed by Giacomo della Porta in 1581 and sculpted by Taddeo Landini, the piece revolves around four bronze boys, each grasping a dolphin that jets water into marble shells, and several bronze tortoises each held in the boys' hands and drinking from the fountain's upper basin. The tortoises are the fountain's most brilliant feature, a 17th-century addition by, inevitably, Bernini. The piazza is named for the Mattei family, which built **Palazzo Mattei** on Via Caetani, worth a peek for its sculpture-rich courtyard and staircase.

㊿ **Isola Tiberina.** Ancient Ponte Fabricio links the ghetto neighborhood of Trastevere (☞ *below*) to this island, where a city hospital stands on a site that has been dedicated to healing ever since a temple to Aesculapius was erected here in 291 BC. If you have time, and if the river's not too high, walk down the stairs for a different perspective on the island and the Tiber.

Palazzo Corsini. This elegant palace holds a collection of large, dark, and dull paintings, but stop in to climb the extraordinary 17th-century stone staircase, itself a drama of architectural shadows and sculptural voids. ⊠ *Via della Lungara 10.*

49 Piazza Bocca della Verità (Mouth of Truth Square). On the site of the Forum Boarium, ancient Rome's cattle market, this square was later used for public executions. Its sinister name is derived from the marble mouth—actually part of an ancient drain cover—set into the entry portico of the 12th-century church of **Santa Maria in Cosmedin.** In the Middle Ages anyone accused of lying would be forced to put his hand into the mouth and warned that if he didn't tell the truth the mouth would close and cut off his hand.

OFF THE
BEATEN PATH

COLLE AVENTINO (AVENTINE HILL) – One of the seven hills of ancient Rome, it is now a quiet residential neighborhood that most tourists don't see. It has several of the city's oldest and least-visited churches, and some surprises: the view from the keyhole in the gate to the garden of the Knights of Malta (⊠ Piazza Cavalieri di Malta) and another, unusual view of Rome from the walled park off Via Santa Sabina.

TERME DI CARACALLA (BATHS OF CARACALLA) – The scale of the towering ruins of ancient Rome's most beautiful and luxurious public baths hints at their past splendor. Inaugurated by Caracalla in 217, the baths were used until the 6th century. An ancient version of a swank athletic club, the baths were open to all, though men and women used them separately; citizens could bathe, socialize, and exercise in huge pools and richly decorated halls and libraries. ⊠ Via delle Terme di Caracalla. ☉ Apr.–Sept., Tues.–Sat. 9–6, Sun.–Mon. 9–1; Oct.–Mar., Tues.–Sat. 9–3, Sun.–Mon. 9–1.

53 Piazza di Santa Maria in Trastevere. The showpiece of this piazza is the 12th-century church of **Santa Maria in Trastevere.** The mosaics on the church's facade—which add light and color to the piazza, especially at night when they are spotlit—are believed to represent the Wise and Foolish Virgins. The interior often produces involuntary gasps from unsuspecting viewers: an enormous nave bathed in a mellow glow from medieval mosaics and overhead gilding, the whole framed by a processional of two rows of gigantic columns. There are larger naves in Rome, but none quite so majestic.

52 San Francesco a Ripa. This church in Piazza San Francesco d'Assisi is a must for fans of the Baroque. It holds one of Bernini's most hallucinatory sculptures, a dramatically lighted statue of the Blessed Ludovica Albertoni, ecstatic at the prospect of entering heaven as she expires on her deathbed. ⊠ *Piazza San Francesco d'Assisi.*

55 San Pietro in Montorio. One of the key Renaissance buildings in Rome stands in the cloister of this church, built by order of Ferdinand and Isabella of Spain in 1481 over the spot where St. Peter is said to have been crucified. The **Tempietto,** Bramante's little temple, is an architectural gem and was one of the earliest and most successful attempts to produce an entirely classical building. ⊠ *Via Garibaldi, Gianicolo.* ☉ *Daily 9–noon and 4–6.*

51 Santa Cecilia in Trastevere. Mothers and children love to dally in the delightful little garden in front of this church in Piazza Santa Cecilia, and there's no reason why you shouldn't join them for a bit before you duck inside for a look at the very grand 18th-century interior and the languid statue of St. Cecilia under the altar.

Sinagoga (Synagogue). The large, bronze-roofed synagogue on the Tiber is a Roman landmark. It contains a museum of precious ritual objects and fabrics and other exhibits documenting the history of the Jewish community in Rome. ⊠ *Lungotevere Cenci,* ☎ *06/6864648.* 🎫 *8,000 lire.* ☉ *Mon.–Thurs. 9:30–1:30 and 2–5, Fri. 9:30–2, Sun. 9:30–12:30.*

㊻ Teatro di Marcello. The Teatro, hardly recognizable as a theater today, was originally designed to hold 20,000 spectators. It was begun by Julius Caesar; today, the apartments carved out in its remains have become one of Rome's most prestigious residential addresses. ⊠ *Via del Teatro di Marcello.* ☉ *Concerts only.*

㊼ Tempio della Fortuna Virilis (Temple of Manly Fortune). This rectangular temple dates from the 2nd century BC and is built in the Greek style, as was the norm in the early years of Rome. For its age, it is remarkably well preserved, in part due to its subsequent consecration as a Christian church. ⊠ *Piazza Bocca della Verità.*

㊽ Tempio di Vesta. All but one of the 20 original Corinthian columns in Rome's most evocative small ruin remain intact. Like the Temple of Manly Fortune (☞ *above*), it was built in the 2nd century BC, considerably earlier than the ruins in the Roman Forum. ⊠ *Piazza Bocca dell Verità.*

Trastevere. This area consists of a maze of narrow streets that is still, despite evident gentrification, one of the city's most authentically Roman neighborhoods. Literally translated, Trastevere means "across the Tiber," and indeed the Trasteverini, a breed apart, have always been proud and combative, chagrined at the reputation their quarter has acquired for purse snatching (but it happens; don't carry a purse and keep your camera out of sight). Among self-consciously picturesque trattorias and trendy tearooms, you also find old shops and dusty artisans' workshops in alleys festooned with laundry hung out to dry. One of the most unaffected parts of Trastevere lies around **Piazza in Piscinula,** where the tiny **San Benedetto,** the smallest medieval church in the city, is opposite the restored medieval Casa dei Mattei. Take a stroll along Via dell'Arco dei Tolomei and Via dei Salumi, shadowy streets showing the patina of the ages.

Via Portico d'Ottavia. Along this street in the heart of the Jewish ghetto are buildings where medieval inscriptions, ancient friezes, and half-buried classical monuments attest to the venerable history of this neighborhood. The old **Chiesa di Sant'Angelo in Pescheria** was built right into the ruins of the Portico d'Ottavia, which served as a kind of foyer for the Teatro di Marcello (☞ *above*).

㊾ Villa Farnesina. Money was no object to extravagant host Agostino Chigi, a banker from Siena who financed many a papal project. His munificence is evident in this elegant villa, built for him about 1511. When Raphael could steal some precious time from his work on the Vatican Stanze and from his wooing of the Fornarina, he came over to execute some of the frescoes, notably a luminous *Galatea.* Chigi delighted in impressing guests by having his servants clear the table by casting precious dinnerware into the Tiber. Naturally, the guests did not know of the nets he had stretched under the waterline to catch everything. ⊠ *Via della Lungara 230,* ☎ *06/6540565.* 🎫 *Free.* ☉ *Mon.–Sat. 9–1.*

Quo Vadis? The Catacombs and the Appian Way

An exploration of the beginnings of Christianity in Rome on this tour offers a respite from museums, but requires a long time on your feet. Do it on a sunny day and take along a picnic or have lunch at one of the pleasant restaurants near the catacombs. The Rome EPT office offers a free, informative pamphlet on this itinerary.

A Good Tour

Resist any temptation to undertake the 1½ km (1 mi) walk between Porta San Sebastiano and the catacombs; it is a dull and tiring hike on a heavily trafficked, cobblestone road, with stone walls the only scenery. Instead, hop on Bus 218 from San Giovanni in Laterano or Bus 660 from the Colli Albani Metro stop on Line A to the **Via Appia Antica** ㊹ Stay on the bus until you reach the catacombs; the most scenic walk along the ancient road lies beyond them.

TIMING

Allow one hour for this walk, plus one hour for catacombs.

Sights to See

㊹ **Via Appia Antica.** This is "the Queen of Roads," completed in 312 BC by Appius Claudius, who also built Rome's first aqueduct. One of the two important catacombs on Via Appia Antica is that of **San Callisto,** one of the best preserved of these underground cemeteries. A friar will guide you through its crypts and galleries. ⊠ *Via Appia Antica 110,* ☎ *06/5136725.* 🎟 *8,000 lire.* ☾ *Apr.–Sept., Thurs.–Tues. 8:30–noon and 2:30–5:30; Oct.–Jan. and Mar., Thurs.–Tues. 8:30–noon and 2:30–5.*

The other important example, the 4th-century **San Sebastiano** catacomb was named for the saint who was buried here. It burrows underground on four levels. The only one of the catacombs to remain accessible during the Middle Ages, it is the origin of the term "catacomb," for it was in a spot where the road dips into a hollow, a place the Romans called *catacumbas* (near the hollow). Eventually, the Christian cemetery that had existed here since the 2nd century came to be known by the same name, which was applied to all underground cemeteries discovered in Rome in later centuries. ⊠ *Via Appia Antica 136,* ☎ *06/7887035.* 🎟 *8,000 lire.* ☾ *Apr.–Sept., Fri.–Wed. 8:30–noon and 2:30–5:30; Oct. and Dec.–Mar., Fri.–Wed. 8:30–noon and 2:30–5.*

On the east side of Via Appia Antica are the ruins of the **Circo di Massenzio** (Circus of Maxentius), where the obelisk now in Piazza Navona once stood.

The circular **Tomba di Cecilia Metella** (Tomb of Cecilia Metella), mausoleum of a Roman noblewoman who lived at the time of Julius Caesar, was transformed into a fortress in the 14th century. It marks the beginning of the most evocative stretch of Via Appia Antica, lined with tombs and fragments of statuary. Cypresses and umbrella pines stand guard over the ruined sepulchers, and the occasional tracts of ancient paving stones are the same ones trod by triumphant Roman legions.

DINING

As the pace of Roman life quickens, more fast-food joints are opening, offering a wider choice of light meals. There are variations of the older Italian institutions of the *tavola calda* (hot table) and the *rosticceria* (rotisserie), both of which offer hot and cold dishes to be taken out or eaten on the premises, some sold by the portion, others by weight. You usually select your food, get a check at the counter and pay for it at the cashier, who gives you a stub to give to the counter person when you pick up the food. Newer snack bars are cropping up, and all-day pizza places selling various kinds of pizza by the slice seem to have sprouted on every block. Quick meals are also available in a spate of so-called pubs opening up around town.

Despite these changes, many Romans stick to the tradition of having their main meal at lunch, from 1 to 3, though you won't be turned away if hunger strikes shortly after noon. Dinner is served from 8 or 8:30 until about 10:30 or 11. Some restaurants stay open much later, especially in summer, when patrons linger at sidewalk tables to enjoy the *ponentino* (evening breeze). Almost all restaurants close one day a week (it's usually safest to call ahead to reserve) and for at least two weeks in August, when it can sometimes seem impossible to find sustenance in the deserted city. This is not a bad time to picnic. You can buy provisions in neighborhood *alimentari* (food stores) that aren't closed for vacation.

Local cheeses are mild *caciotta* and sharp Pecorino. Fresh ricotta is also used in a number of dishes. Typical wines of Rome are those of the Castelli Romani: Frascati, Colli Albani, Marino, and Velletri. *Acqua semplice* (tap water) is safe everywhere in Rome, so if you're on a budget, order it instead of *acqua minerale*, which comes *gassata* (sparkling) or *liscia* (not sparkling).

The typical Roman pasta is fettuccine, golden egg noodles that are at their classic best when freshly made and laced with *ragù*, a thick, rich tomato and meat sauce. Carbonara-style pasta is usually made with spaghetti or thicker, spaghetti-like *bucatini;* the cooked pasta is tossed with a sauce of egg yolk, chunks of fried *guanciale* (unsmoked bacon), Parmesan cheese, and lots of freshly ground black pepper. Spaghetti *all'amatriciana* has a piquant sauce of tomato, guanciale, and *peperoncini* (small, hot red chiles). Tiny potato or flour gnocchi, served with a tomato sauce and a sprinkling of Parmesan or Pecorino, are a Roman favorite for Thursday dinner.

Abbacchio, baby lamb, is at its best in the spring; a summer favorite is *pollo coi peperoni,* stewed chicken with peppers. *Fritto misto* usually includes zucchini, *carciofi* (artichokes), and *baccalà* (codfish) fried in batter. Artichokes are served *alla romana* (sautéed whole with garlic and mint), or *alla giudia* (fried whole, with each petal crisp and light enough to melt in your mouth). Tender peas are sautéed with prosciutto to make *piselli al* prosciutto.

The automatically applied *pane e coperto* (bread and cover charge) has been eliminated in many restaurants but you may be charged extra for bread, anyway. And a *servizio* (service charge) of 10%–12% still appears on many checks; remember that in the end your waiter will see only a small part of that sum, so another 5% is welcome. A fixed-price *menù turistico* (tourist menu) includes taxes and services, but usually not drinks.

Italians have exquisite taste in clothing—even seen on toddlers. Though seemingly rare, even dressing down for an Italian is an elegant affair, especially in cities. Dress up accordingly, especially in the more posh restaurants that require jacket and tie.

CATEGORY	COST*
$$$$	over 120,000 lire
$$$	70,000–120,000 lire
$$	40,000–70,000 lire
$	under 40,000 lire

Prices are per person, for a three-course meal, including house wine and taxes.

Central Rome

$$$$ ✕ **El Toulà.** Rome's prestigious El Toulà—one of the many spin-offs of the former namesake in Treviso—has the warm, welcoming comforts of a 19th-century country house, with white walls, antique furniture in dark wood, heavy silver serving dishes, and spectacular fruit and flower arrangements. There's a cozy bar off the entrance, where you can sip a *prosecco* (Venetian semisparkling white wine), the aperitif best suited to the chef's Venetian specialties, which include risotto with artichokes and *fegato alla veneziana* (liver with onions). ✉ *Via della Lupa 29/b,* ☎ *06/6873750. Reservations essential. Jacket and tie. AE, DC, MC, V. No lunch Sat. Closed Sun., Aug., and Dec. 24–26.*

$$$$ ✕ **La Pergola.** From this elegant rooftop restaurant in the Cavalieri
★ Hilton—built on Monte Mario, one of the highest of the hills overlooking the city—a fabulous view of Rome, via wraparound windows, whets your appetite for the imaginative cuisine. Frescoes and Tuscan garden images with latticework and potted lemon trees denote a decidedly Italian theme. The menu changes with the seasons and might include artichoke ravioli with tomatoes or breast of guinea fowl served on a parsley purée. You may dine outdoors in good weather. ✉ *Via Cadlolo 101,* ☎ *06/35091. Reservations essential. Jacket and tie. AE, DC, MC, V. No lunch. Closed Sun.–Mon.*

$$$$ ✕ **La Terrazza dell'Eden.** An empyrean of culinary art, La Terrazza un-
★ furls an unparalleled view of Rome's seven hills before your eyes, unfairly distracting you from the dilemma of choosing from one of several menus designed to please diverging tastes. It has been hailed internationally as one of the city's best restaurants (many consider it *the* best). La Terrazza's seamless fusion of superlative cuisine and service, elegant but comfortable atmosphere, and that panorama—with a piano bar á la carte—make dining there a definitive Roman experience. ✉ *Hotel Eden, Via Ludovisi 49,* ☎ *06/47812552. Dinner reservations essential. Jacket and tie. AE, DC, MC, V.*

$$$$ ✕ **Les Etoiles.** Ask for a view of St. Peter's when you reserve a table at the rooftop restaurant of the Atlante Star hotel; the cupola is especially magical at night, when illuminated. The menu varies, depending on what tempts the chef at the market. Dishes range from pasta with porcini mushrooms or seasonal vegetables and classic or creative risotto (for two) to fresh seafood and choice grilled meats. ✉ *Hotel Atlante Star, Via dei Bastioni 1, in the Prati section,* ☎ *06/6893434. Reservations essential. Jacket and tie. AE, DC, MC, V.*

$$$$ ✕ **Relais Le Jardin.** In the Parioli residential district, this restaurant is famous for its chichi crowd. It's in the exclusive Lord Byron hotel, itself a triumph of studied interior decoration. The menu is a tempting compendium of seasonal, newer-than-now nouvelle specialties. If on the menu, try the duck breast in citrus marinade with Gorgonzola walnut sauce or the sea bass in potato crust. ✉ *Hotel Lord Byron, Via Giuseppe de Notaris 5,* ☎ *06/3220404. Reservations essential. Jacket and tie. AE, DC, MC, V. Closed Sun. and 3 wks in Aug.*

$$$$ ✕ **Sans Souci.** All the glitz and glamour of the dolce vita days of Rome in the 1950s lives on in this overdecorated but superb subterranean sanctuary of gourmet delights. Service is literally fit for a king—and the Sans Souci has had a few among its customers, along with Hollywood bigwigs and business magnates. It is the only restaurant in Rome with a doorman, but don't let that intimidate you, for the staff is courteous and attentive. The menu presents both French and Italian dishes, among them truffled terrine de foie gras and *agnello al timo* (roast lamb with thyme). ✉ *Via Sicilia 20,* ☎ *06/4821814. Reservations essential. Jacket and tie. AE, DC, MC, V. No lunch. Closed Mon. and mid-Aug.–Sept. 6.*

$$$ ✕ **Coriolano.** The only tourists who find their way to this classic restaurant near Porta Pia are likely to be gourmets looking for quintessential Italian *cucina*—and that means market-fresh ingredients, especially seafood, light homemade pastas, and choice olive oil. The tables in the antique-filled small dining room are set with immaculate white linen, sparkling crystal, and silver. Seafood dishes vary, but *tagliolini all'aragosta* (thin noodles with lobster sauce) is usually on the menu; also order the seasonal porcini mushrooms (prepared with a secret recipe). The wine list is predominantly Italian, but includes some French and California choices. ✉ *Via Ancona 14,* ☎ *06/44249863. Jacket and tie. AE, DC, MC, V. Closed Sun., Sat. in July, and Aug.*

$$$ ✕ **Corsetti–Il Galeone.** On a market square in Trastevere, this spot is decorated like an old galleon, lined with well-seasoned wood and laden with nautical accessories. Seafood is the specialty, but you will also find an ample selection of typical Roman pastas and meat dishes, as well as the famous carciofi alla romana. ✉ *Piazza San Cosimato 27,* ☎ *06/5809009. AE, DC, MC, V.*

$$$ ✕ **Da Checco er Carrettiere.** You'll find Da Checco tucked away behind Piazza Trilussa in Trastevere. It has the look of a country inn, with hanging garlic braids and an antipasto table that features some unusual specialties, such as a well-seasoned mashed potato-and-tomato mixture. Among the hearty pasta offerings are spaghetti *alla carrettiera* (with black pepper, sharp cheese, and olive oil), and linguine with scampi. Seafood (which can be expensive) is the main feature on the menu, but traditional Roman meat dishes are offered, too. This is a great place to soak up genuine Trastevere color and hospitality. ✉ *Via Benedetta 10,* ☎ *06/5817018. Reservations essential. AE, DC, MC, V. No dinner Sun. Closed Mon. and Aug. 10–Sept. 10.*

$$$ ✕ **Il Convivio.** Don't be intimidated by the opaque glass, closed door, and doorbell at the entrance. This, as its name suggests, is a convivial little restaurant, and it is earning a reputation as one of Rome's best. Reservations are essential, for it accommodates only 30 diners. The food is what it's all about: classic Italian (and Roman) dishes prepared with flair and a brilliant use of herbs, as in shellfish with tarragon and lamb with thyme. The *menù degustazione* (tasting menu) is good value. ✉ *Via dell'Orso 44,* ☎ *06/6869432. Reservations essential. AE, DC, MC, V. Closed Sun.*

$$$ ✕ **Passetto.** Benefiting from a choice location near Piazza Navona, Passetto has been a favorite with Italians and tourists for many years: it's a place you can rely on for classic Italian food and gracious service. If you can, eat on the terrace—it's especially memorable at night; the mirrored dining room is more staid. Roman specialties, such as cannelloni and abbacchio, are featured. ✉ *Via Zanardelli 14,* ☎ *06/6540569. Jacket and tie. AE, DC, MC, V. No lunch Mon. Closed Sun.*

$$$ ✕ **Piperno.** A favorite, in the old Jewish ghetto next to historic Palazzo Cenci, Piperno has been in business for more than a century. It is *the* place to go for Rome's extraordinary carciofi alla giudia. You eat in three small wood-paneled dining rooms or at one of a handful of tables outdoors. Try *filetti di* baccalà (fillet of cod), pasta *e ceci* (a thick soup of pasta tubes and chickpeas), *fiori di zucca* (stuffed zucchini flowers), and artichokes. ✉ *Monte dei Cenci 9,* ☎ *06/6542772. AE, DC, MC, V. No dinner Sun. Closed Mon. and Aug.*

$$$ ✕ **Ranieri.** Walk down a quiet street off fashionable Via Condotti to
★ find this historic restaurant, founded by a one-time chef of Queen Victoria. Ranieri remains a favorite with travelers for its traditional atmosphere and decor, with damask-covered walls, velvet banquettes, crystal chandeliers, and old paintings. The Italian-French cuisine is excellent: portions are abundant, and checks remain comfortably in the low end of this price category. Among the many specialties on the vast menu

56

Rome Dining

are *gnocchetti alla parigina* (feather-light dumplings with cheese sauce) and *mignonettes alla Regina Vittoria* (veal with pâté and an eight-cheese sauce). ⊠ *Via Mario dei Fiori 26*, ☎ *06/6786505. Reservations essential. AE, DC, MC, V. Closed Sun.*

$$$ ✕ Vecchia Roma. Two decades ago, discerning American travelers re-
★ alized that Vecchia Roma was too special to be left to the Romans—so they've made it their own. Tucked away on a frozen-in-time piazza near the Campidoglio, Vecchia Roma has frescoed accents and quintessential Roman decor. It features classic Roman specialties and main-course salads in summer and a wide choice of sauces served with polenta in the winter. Romans in the know always choose the seasonal specialties—such as porcini that taste just like filet mignon—that can be extraordinary. Dining outside in good weather is recommended. ⊠ *Piazza Campitelli 18*, ☎ *06/6864604. Reservations essential. AE, DC. Closed Wed. and mid-Aug.*

$$ ✕ Cannavota. On the square next to San Giovanni in Laterano, Cannavota has a large and faithful following and has fed generations of neighborhood families over the years. Seafood dominates, but carnivores are satisfied also. Try one of the pastas with seafood sauce—fettuccine with scampi is a good choice—and then go on to grilled fish or meat. The cheerful atmosphere and rustic decor make for an authentically Roman experience. ⊠ *Piazza San Giovanni in Laterano 20*, ☎ *06/77205007. AE, DC, MC, V. Closed Wed. and Aug. 1–20.*

$$ ✕ Colline Emiliane. Not far from Piazza Barberini, this unassuming trattoria offers exceptionally good *cibo* (food). Behind an opaque glass facade are a couple of plain dining rooms, where you are served light homemade pastas, a special chicken broth, and meats ranging from boiled beef to *giambonetto di vitella* (roast veal) and *cotoletta alla bolognese* (veal cutlet with cheese and prosciutto). Family-run, it's quiet and soothing—a good place to rest after a sightseeing stint. Service is cordial and discreet. ⊠ *Via degli Avignonesi 22*, ☎ *06/4817538. MC, V. Closed Fri. and Aug.*

$$ ✕ Costanza. In Rome, one man's archaeological site can be another man's eatery. As its ancient Roman brickwork reveals, this fashionable trattoria occupies a small part of the Theater of Pompey, where Julius Caesar met his end. Serious gourmands rave about this spot, which has become a meeting place for artists, actors, and politicos. The mixed hot and cold antipasto is a specialty, as are crepes with mushrooms and risotto with zucchini flowers. ⊠ *Piazza del Paradiso 65*, ☎ *06/6861717. AE, DC, MC, V. Closed Sun. and Aug.*

$$ ✕ Dal Bolognese. Long a haunt of the art crowd, this classic restaurant on Piazza del Popolo is a trendy choice for a leisurely lunch between sightseeing and shopping. While dining, feast your eyes on an extensive array of contemporary paintings or on the view of the piazza from the new upstairs dining rooms. As the name of the restaurant promises, the cooking here adheres to the hearty tradition of Bologna, with homemade pastas in creamy sauces and steaming trays of boiled meats. For dessert, there's *dolce della mamma* (a concoction of gelato, zabaglione, and chocolate sauce). ⊠ *Piazza del Popolo 1*, ☎ *06/3611426. AE, MC, V. Closed Mon. and Aug. 7–22.*

$$ ✕ La Campana. This inconspicuous trattoria off Via della Scrofa has a venerable history: there has been an inn on this spot since the 15th century, and the two plain dining rooms occupy what were once stables. It's a homey place, with friendly waiters, snowy white linens on close-set tables, and good Roman food at reasonable prices. The menu offers such specialties as *vignarola* (sautéed fava beans, peas, and artichokes), rigatoni with prosciutto and tomato sauce, and *olivette di vitello con purée* (tiny veal rolls with mashed potatoes). ⊠ *Vicolo della Campana 18*, ☎ *06/6867820. AE, DC, MC, V. Closed Mon. and Aug.*

$$ ✕ Le Maschere. For a taste of southern Italian (Calabrian) fare, this informal cellar restaurant is hidden away between Largo Argentina and Piazza Campo dei Fiori—in summer look for the planters and the few outdoor tables. Dark rustic walls are hung with everything from paper garlands to old utensils; there are pottery wine jugs and rush-bottom chairs. To start, order spicy Calabria salami or hit the expansive antipasto table, and then go on to pizza or pasta with broccoli or with tomato and eggplant sauce. Grilled meat and seafood make up the list of second courses. Music on weekends and efficient service make for a pleasant evening. ✉ *Via Monte della Farina 29,* ☎ *06/6879444. AE, DC, MC, V. No lunch. Closed Mon. and mid-Aug.–mid-Sept.*

$$ ✕ Mariano. Near Via Veneto, Mariano (who is actually Tonino, Mariano's son-in-law and successor) is an exponent of quality and tradition. Since he leaves flights of culinary fancy to others, you can be sure of finding authentic Roman and central-Italian cuisine here, including delicate egg pastas, game, and abbacchio in season. ✉ *Via Piemonte 79,* ☎ *06/4745256. AE, DC, MC, V. No lunch Sat. Closed Sun.*

$$ ✕ Orso 80. This bright and bustling trattoria in Old Rome, has both a Roman and an international following and is known, above all, for a fabulous antipasto table. Try the homemade egg pasta or the bucatini all'amatriciana; there's plenty of seafood on the menu, too. For dessert, the ricotta cake, a genuine Roman specialty, is always good. ✉ *Via dell'Orso 33,* ☎ *06/6864904. AE, DC, MC, V. Closed Mon. and Aug.*

$$ ✕ Osteria da Nerone. Between the Colosseum and the church of San Pietro in Vincoli, this family-run trattoria features a tempting antipasto table and fresh pastas. The specialty is fettuccine *al Nerone* (with peas, salami, and mushrooms), but the homemade ravioli are good, too. In fair weather you eat outdoors with a view of the Colosseum. ✉ *Via Terme di Tito 96,* ☎ *06/4745207. DC, MC, V. Closed Sun. and Aug.*

$$ ✕ Otello alla Concordia. The clientele in this popular spot—it's off a shopping street near Piazza di Spagna—is about evenly divided between tourists and workers from shops and offices in the area. The former like to sit outdoors in the courtyard in any weather; the latter have their regular tables in one of the inside dining rooms. The menu offers classic Roman and Italian dishes, and service is friendly and efficient. Since every tourist in Rome knows about it, and since the regulars won't relinquish their niches, you may have to wait for a table; go early. ✉ *Via della Croce 81,* ☎ *06/6781454. Reservations not accepted. AE, DC. Closed Sun.*

$$ ✕ Paris. On a small square just off Piazza Santa Maria in Trastevere, Paris (named after a former owner, not the city) has a reassuring, understated ambience, without the hokey flamboyance of so many eating places in this gentrified neighborhood. It also has a menu featuring the best of classic Roman cuisine: homemade fettuccine, delicate fritto misto and, of course, baccalà. In fair weather opt for tables on the little piazza. ✉ *Piazza San Callisto 7/a,* ☎ *06/5815378. AE, DC, MC, V. No dinner Sun. Closed Mon. and 3 wks in Aug.*

$$ ✕ Pierluigi. In the heart of Old Rome, Pierluigi is a longtime favorite with foreign residents of Rome and Italians in the entertainment field. On busy evenings it's almost impossible to get a table, so make sure you reserve well in advance. Seafood dominates (if you're in the mood to splurge, try the lobster), but traditional Roman dishes are offered, too, including fried zucchini blossoms and simple spaghetti. Eat in the pretty piazza in summer. ✉ *Piazza dei Ricci 144,* ☎ *06/6868717. AE, V. Closed Mon. and 2 wks in Aug.*

$$ ✕ Romolo. Nowhere else do the lingering rays of the setting Roman ★ sun seem more inviting than from the tavern garden of this charming Trastevere haunt—reputedly the onetime home of Raphael's lady love, the Fornarina. Generations of Romans and tourists have enjoyed its romantic courtyard and historic dining room, where, in the evening, strolling musicians serenade diners. The cuisine is appropriately Roman; specialties include mozzarella *alla fornarina* (deep-fried, with ham and anchovies) and *braciolette d'abbacchio scottadito* (grilled baby lamb chops). Alternatively, try one of the new vegetarian pastas featuring carciofi or radicchio. Meats are charcoal grilled; there's also a wood-burning oven. ⊠ *Via di Porta Settimiana 8,* ☎ *06/5818284. AE, DC, V. Closed Mon. and Aug. 2–23.*

$$ ✕ **Sora Lella.** What was once a simple trattoria ensconced on the Tiberina Island is now a monument to the late founder herself, a beloved example of true Roman warmth and personality. And although prices are much higher than when Sora Lella presided over the cash desk, the cooking is still 100% Roman. Rigatoni all'amatriciana and *maialino all'antica roma* (suckling pig with prunes and baby onions) are usually on the menu, but leave room for *the* quintessential Roman ricotta cake. ⊠ *Via Ponte Quattro Capi 16,* ☎ *06/6861601. AE, DC, MC. Closed Sun. and Aug.*

$$ ✕ **Tana del Grillo.** Near Santa Maria Maggiore, this family-run restaurant features the specialties of one of Italy's least-known regional cuisines—that of Ferrara. Sausages and salami of various types, gnocchi and lasagna or *pasticcio di maccheroni* (pasta casserole) are typical dishes, but the pièce de résistance is the *bollito,* a steaming cart laded with several types of boiled meat, which the waiter will carve to your order. ⊠ *Via Alfieri 4,* ☎ *06/70453517. AE, DC, MC, V. No lunch Mon. Closed Sun.*

$$ ✕ **Tullio.** This Tuscan trattoria off Via Veneto and Piazza Barberini opened in the dolce vita days of the 1950s, when this area was the center of Roman chic and bohemian life. It soon acquired a faithful clientele of politicians, journalists, and artists, and it has changed little over the years. Decor and menu are simple. The latter offers typically Tuscan *pasta e fagioli* (thick soup of pasta and beans), grilled steaks and chops, and fagioli *all'uccelletto* (with tomato and sage). ⊠ *Via San Nicolò da Tolentino 26,* ☎ *06/4818564. Reservations essential. AE, DC, MC, V. Closed Sun. and Aug.*

$ ✕ **Baffetto.** The emphasis here is on good old-fashioned value: Baffetto is Rome's best-known inexpensive pizza restaurant, plainly decorated and very popular. You'll probably have to wait in line outside on the cobblestones and then share your table once inside. The interior is mostly given over to the ovens, the tiny cash desk, and the simple, paper-covered tables. *Bruschetta* (grilled bread, usually topped with chopped fresh tomato, basil, garlic, and olive oil) and *crostini* (mozzarella toast) are the only variations on the pizza theme. Turnover is fast: this is not the place to linger over your pie. ⊠ *Via del Governo Vecchio 114,* ☎ *06/6861617. Reservations not accepted. No credit cards. No lunch. Closed Sun. and Aug.*

$ ✕ **Birreria Tempera.** This old-fashioned beer hall is very busy at
★ lunchtime, when it's invaded by businesspeople and students from the Piazza Venezia area. There's a good selection of salads and cold cuts, as well as pasta and daily specials. Bavarian-style specialties such as goulash and wurst and sauerkraut prevail in the evening, when light and dark Italian beers flow freely. ⊠ *Via San Marcello 19,* ☎ *06/6786203. Reservations not accepted. No credit cards. Closed Sun. and Aug.*

$ ✕ **Cottini.** For lunch or dinner, this cafeteria on the corner of Piazza Santa Maria Maggiore is reliable. The food counter and tables are in the back, beyond the large coffee bar and pastry counters. Salads, hot pastas, and main courses are always fresh, and they are served with a smile. The in-house bakery concocts such tempting desserts as crème caramel and chocolate cake. ✉ *Via Merulana 287,* ☎ *06/4740768. Reservations not accepted. AE, DC, MC, V.*

$ ✕ **Fagianetto.** Massive wooden beams on high are as solid as the reputation of this family-run trattoria near Termini Station. It has a regular neighborhood clientele, but also satisfies tourists' appetites with a special menu for about 20,000 lire. But you may well be tempted by à la carte offerings such as rigatoni *alla norcina* (with a sauce of crumbled sausage and cream) or osso buco *con funghi* (with mushrooms). Service is swift and courteous. ✉ *Via Filippo Turati 21,* ☎ *06/4467306. AE, DC, MC, V. Closed Mon.*

$ ✕ **Fratelli Menghi.** Neighborhood regulars frequent this trattoria that has been in the same family for as long as anyone can remember (a portrait of Pop is on the wall in one dining room) and serves typical Roman fare. There's usually a thick hearty soup such as minestrone, and other standbys, including *involtini* (meat roulades). ✉ *Via Flaminia 57,* ☎ *06/3200803. AE, DC, MC, V. Closed Sun.*

$ ✕ **Grappolo d'Oro.** This centrally located trattoria off Campo dei
★ Fiori has been a favorite for decades with locals and foreign residents, one of whom wrote it up in the *New Yorker* some years ago. This measure of notoriety has not induced the graying, courteous owners to change their two half-paneled dining rooms or menu, which features pasta all'amatriciana and scaloppine any way you want them. Inquire about the day's special. ✉ *Piazza della Cancelleria 80,* ☎ *06/6897080. AE, DC, MC, V. Closed Sun. and Aug.*

$ ✕ **Perilli.** A bastion of authentic Roman cooking and trattoria atmosphere since 1913, this is the place to go to try rigatoni *con pagliata* (with baby veal intestines)—if you're into that sort of thing. Otherwise the all'amatriciana and carbonara sauces are classics. The house wine is a golden nectar from the Castelli Romani. ✉ *Via Marmorata 39,* ☎ *06/5742415. No credit cards. Closed Wed.*

$ ✕ **Polese.** It's best to come here in good weather, when you can sit outdoors under trees and look out on the charming square off Corso Vittorio Emanuele II in Old Rome. Like most centrally located inexpensive eateries in Rome, it is crowded on weekends and weekday evenings in the summer. Straightforward Roman specialties include fettuccine *alla Polese* (with cream and mushrooms) and *vitello alla fornara* (roast brisket of veal with potatoes). ✉ *Piazza Sforza Cesarini 40,* ☎ *06/6861709. AE, DC, MC, V. Closed Tues., 15 days in Aug., and 15 days in Dec.*

$ ✕ **Pollarola.** This typical Roman trattoria, near Piazza Navona and Campo dei Fiori, has artificial flowers on the tables but—as a special feature—it also has an ancient, authentic Roman column embedded in the rear wall. Try a pasta specialty such as cannelloni with meat sauce, or pollo *in porchetta* (with bacon and herbs). The house wines, white or red, are good. You can eat outdoors in nice weather. ✉ *Piazza della Pollarola 24 (Campo dei Fiori),* ☎ *06/68801654. AE, DC, V. Closed Sun.*

$ ✕ **Tavernetta.** The central location—between the Trevi Fountain and the Spanish Steps—and the good-value tourist menu make this a reliable bet for a simple, filling meal. The menu features Sicilian and Abruzzese specialties; try the pasta with eggplant or the porchetta (in this case, roast suckling pig). Both the red and the white house wines are good. ✉ *Via del Nazareno 3,* ☎ *06/6793124. Reservations essential. AE, DC, MC, V. Closed Mon. and Aug.*

$ ✕ **Tre Pupazzi.** The "three puppets" after which the trattoria is named are the worn stone figures on a fragment of an ancient sarcophagus that embellishes a building on this byway near the Vatican. The tavern, founded in 1625, wears its centuries lightly, upholding a tradition of good food, courteous service, and reasonable prices. The menu offers classic Roman and Abruzzese trattoria fare, including fettuccine and abbacchio, plus pizzas at lunchtime (a rarity in Rome) and well past midnight. ✉ *Via dei Tre Pupazzi at Borgo Pio,* ☎ *06/6868371. AE, MC, V. Closed Sun.*

Along Via Appia Antica

$$ ✗ **Cecilia Metella.** From the entrance on Via Appia Antica, practically opposite the catacombs, you walk uphill to a low-lying but sprawling construction designed for wedding feasts and banquets. There's a large terrace shaded by vines for outdoor dining. Although obviously geared to larger groups, Cecilia Metella also gives couples and small groups full attention, good service, and traditional Roman cuisine. The specialties are the searing-hot *crespelle* (crepes), served in individual casseroles, and pollo *al Nerone* (à la Nero; flambéed, of course). ✉ *Via Appia Antica 125,* ☎ *06/5136743. AE, MC, V. Closed Mon. and last 2 wks in Aug.*

$$ ✗ **L'Archeologia.** In this farmhouse just beyond the catacombs, you dine indoors beside the fireplace in cool weather or in the garden under age-old vines in the summer. The atmosphere is friendly and intimate, and specialties include homemade pastas, abbacchio scottadito, seafood, and some Greek dishes. ✉ *Via Appia Antica 139,* ☎ *06/7880494. AE, MC, V. Closed Thurs.*

LODGING

Palatial surroundings, luxurious comfort, and high standards of service can be taken for granted in the city's five-star ($$$$) establishments, but in other categories, especially $$ and $, standards vary considerably. Fortunately for tourists, many Rome hotels have upgraded their facilities, readjusting their rates only slightly. In general, Fodor's hotel choices for Rome have been made with an eye to good value and convenient location.

The old-fashioned Roman pensione no longer exists as an official category, but, although now graded as inexpensive hotels, some preserve the homey atmosphere that makes visitors prefer them, especially for longer stays.

There are distinct advantages to staying in a hotel within easy walking distance of the main sights, particularly now that so much of downtown Rome is closed to daytime traffic. You can leave your car at a garage and explore on foot. One disadvantage, however, is noise, because Romans are voluble—with or without cars to add to the din. Ask for an inside room if you are a light sleeper, but don't be disappointed if it faces a dark courtyard.

Because Rome's religious importance makes it a year-round tourist destination, there is never a period when hotels are predictably empty, so you should always try to make reservations, even if only a few days in advance, by phone or fax. Always inquire about special low rates, often available in both winter and summer if occupancy is low. If you do arrive without reservations, try **HR,** Hotel Reservation service (☎ 06/6991000), with desks at Leonardo da Vinci Airport (more commonly referred to as Fiumicino Airport) and Termini Station (an English-speaking operator is available daily 7 AM–10 PM). **EPT** information offices (✉ Via Parigi 5, ☎ 06/48899253; ✉ Termini Station, ☎ 06/4871270; ✉ Leonardo da Vinci Airport, ☎ 06/65956074) can also help. **Municipal tourist information booths** (✉ Largo Goldoni/Via del Corso; Via dei Fori Imperiali; Via Nazionale) can help with accommodations at no charge. Avoid official-looking men who approach tourists at Termini

Station: they tout for the less desirable hotels around the train station. **CTS** (⊠ Via Genova 16, a 10-minute walk from the station, ☎ 06/46791), a student travel agency, can help find rooms.

Room rates in Rome are on a par with, or even higher than, those in most other European capitals, but a favorable exchange rate can make them more attractive. Ask whether the room rate includes breakfast. An extra charge, anything from 7,000 to 27,000 lire depending on the category of hotel, may be added for this, but remember that you're not obliged to take breakfast in the hotel. If you don't want to, make this clear when you check in. Air-conditioning in lower-priced hotels may cost extra; in more expensive hotels it will be included in the price. All hotels have rate cards on the room doors or inside the closet. These specify exactly what you have to pay and detail any extras. If business is slack, hotels in all categories may give you a discount rate. Ask for *la tariffa scontata* (the discount rate).

CATEGORY	COST*
$$$$	over 600,000 lire
$$$	350,000–450,000 lire
$$	250,000–350,000 lire
$	under 250,000 lire

*Prices are for a standard double room for two, including tax and service.

$$$$ 🏨 **Cavalieri Hilton.** Though the Cavalieri is outside the imaginary confines of the city's center, distance has its advantages, one of them being the magnificent view from the hotel's hilltop site (ask for a room facing the city). This hotel is a stylish oasis of quiet and comfort, with good taste and a distinctive Italian flair. If you can tear yourself away from your balcony, the terraces, gardens, and swimming pool, you will find a courtesy shuttle bus leaving for the center of Rome every hour. Don't miss the rooftop La Pergola (☞ Dining, *above*). ⊠ *Via Cadlolo 101, 00136,* ☎ *06/35091,* ℻ *06/35092241. 376 rooms and suites. 2 restaurants, bar, indoor and outdoor pools, beauty salon, health club. AE, DC, MC, V.*

$$$$ 🏨 **De La Ville Inter-Continental.** For the well-heeled, this is a finely honed option just a stone's throw from the top of the Spanish Steps. Guests often ask for the rooms their great-grandparents favored; regulars are treated like family here—one reason the place is usually booked solid. Other lures include a lobby replete with marble and gilt furnishings; tastefully subdued guest rooms; and a staff high on initiative. Don't miss the morning meal served in the La Piazzetta restaurant: adorned with twinkling chandeliers, silky bergères, and taffeta-draped French doors, it has to be the prettiest breakfast in Rome. ⊠ *Via Sistina 69, 00187,* ☎ *06/67331,* ℻ *06/6784213. 192 rooms, 23 suites. Bar, free parking. AE, DC, MC, V.*

$$$$ 🏨 **Eden.** A hotel for whispered superlatives in praise of its dashing el-
★ egance and stunning vistas of Rome, the Eden was once the preferred haunt of Hemingway, Ingrid Bergman, and Fellini, and of many celebrities before them. Precious antiques, sumptuous Italian fabrics, linen sheets, and marble baths exude understated elegance. The views from the rooftop bar and restaurant will take your breath away, and La Terrazza dell'Eden (☞ Dining, *above*) merits raves, too. ⊠ *Via Ludovisi 49, 00187,* ☎ *06/478121,* ℻ *06/4821584. 112 rooms and suites. Restaurant, bar, exercise room, free parking. AE, DC, MC, V.*

$$$$ 🏨 **Excelsior.** To Romans and many others, the white Victorian cupola of the Excelsior is a symbol of Rome at its most cosmopolitan. The hotel's porte cochere has long sheltered Europe's aristocrats and Hollywood's royalty as they alighted from their Rollses and Ferraris. They entered the polished doors that still open onto a world of luxury lav-

Rome Lodging

Albergo del Sole al
Pantheon, **11**
Alimandi, **2**
Amalia, **3**
Arenula, **16**
Art Deco, **30**
Britannia, **33**
Campo dei Fiori, **13**
Cardinal, **15**
Carriage, **17**
Cavalieri Hilton, **1**

De La Ville
Inter-Continental, **21**
D'Este, **36**
Duca d'Alba, **37**
Eden, **22**
Excelsior, **25**
Farnese, **5**
Giulio Cesare, **6**
Grand, **29**
Hassler, **19**

Internazionale, **20**
La Residenza, **24**
Locarno, **7**
Majestic, **23**
Marcella, **27**
Marcus, **9**
Margutta, **8**
Miami, **32**
Minerva, **12**
Montreal, **35**

Morgana, **34**
Portoghesi, **10**
Romae, **28**
Sant'Anna, **4**
Scalinata di
Spagna, **18**
Siviglia, **31**
Teatro di Pompeo, **14**
Victoria, **26**

ished with mirrors, carved moldings, Oriental rugs, crystal chandeliers, and huge, baroque floral arrangements. The theme of gracious living prevails throughout the hotel in splendidly appointed rooms and marble baths. ⊠ *Via Veneto 125, 00187,* ☎ *06/4708,* ℻ *06/4826205. 377 rooms and suites. Restaurant, bar, barbershop, beauty salon, free parking. AE, DC, MC, V.*

$$$$　🏨 **Grand.** A 100-year-old establishment of class and style, this hotel caters to an elite international clientele. It's only a few minutes from Via Veneto. Off the richly decorated, split-level main salon—where afternoon tea is served every day—is an intimate bar, a chic rendezvous. The spacious bedrooms are decorated in gracious Empire style, with smooth fabrics and thick carpets in tones of blue and pale gold. Crystal chandeliers and marble baths add a luxurious note. The Grand also offers one of Italy's most beautiful dining rooms, called simply Le Restaurant. ⊠ *Via Vittorio Emanuele Orlando 3, 00185,* ☎ *06/4709,* ℻ *06/4747307. 170 rooms and suites. Restaurant, bar, free parking. AE, DC, MC, V.*

$$$$　🏨 **Hassler.** Located at the top of the Spanish Steps, the Hassler boasts
★　　sweeping views of Rome from its front rooms and rooftop restaurant; other rooms overlook the gardens of Villa Medici. The hotel is run by the distinguished Wirth family of hoteliers, which assures a cordial atmosphere and imperial service from the well-trained staff. The public rooms have an extravagant 1950s elegance—especially the clubby winter bar, summer garden bar and the glass-roofed lounge, with gold marble walls and a hand-painted tile floor. The comfortable guest rooms are decorated in a variety of classic styles, some with frescoed walls. The penthouse suite is resplendent with antiques and has a huge terrace. ⊠ *Piazza Trinità dei Monti 6, 00187,* ☎ *06/699340,* ℻ *06/6789991. 100 rooms and suites. Restaurant, bar, beauty salon. AE, DC, MC, V.*

$$$$　🏨 **Majestic.** In the 19th-century tradition of grand hotels, this establishment on Via Veneto offers sumptuous furnishings and spacious rooms, with up-to-date accessories such as CNN, minibars, strongboxes, and white marble bathrooms. There are authentic antiques in the public rooms, and the excellent restaurant looks like a Victorian conservatory. The Ninfa grill-café on street level is an intimate venue for light meals and drinks. Many suites have whirlpool baths. ⊠ *Via Veneto 50, 00187,* ☎ *06/486841,* ℻ *06/4880984. 95 rooms and suites. Restaurant, bar. AE, DC, MC, V.*

$$$$　🏨 **Minerva.** The Holiday Inn Crowne Plaza Minerva is the very stylish reincarnation of the hostelry that occupied this 17th-century palazzo for centuries, hosting literati from Stendhal to Sartre and de Beauvoir. Entirely redone, with a stunning new stained-glass lobby ceiling designed by renowned architect Paolo Portoghesi, the Minerva has everything a guest could want in the way of comfort, all in an absolutely central location. And from the roof terrace you can almost touch the immense, flattened dome of Hadrian's Pantheon. ⊠ *Piazza della Minerva 69, 00186,* ☎ *06/69941888,* ℻ *06/6794165. 134 rooms. Restaurant, bar. AE, DC, MC, V.*

$$$　🏨 **Albergo del Sole al Pantheon.** This small hotel has been in its central location opposite the Pantheon since the 15th century. It has been tastefully decorated with a blend of modern and antique furnishings. Ceilings are high, floors are tiled in terra-cotta, and there is a charming courtyard for alfresco breakfast in good weather. ⊠ *Piazza della Rotonda 63, 00186,* ☎ *06/6780441,* ℻ *06/69940689. 25 rooms. Bar. AE, DC, MC, V.*

$$$　🏨 **Cardinal.** Staying at this hotel is like stepping inside a Renaissance
★　　painting—it was built by Bramante, first architect of St. Peter's, and is set on magnificent Via Giulia, whose immutable vistas have scarcely

changed since the 15th century. Cardinals would feel right at home: the lobby is a riot of red, while the rooms upstairs are almost ascetic. Serene, severe, and subdued, many of the rooms feature antique engravings and Olympian-high ceilings. Of course, the interiors don't matter much when Via Giulia—lined with beautiful *palazzi* and opulent antique stores—is right out your doorstep. ⊠ *Via Giulia 62, 00186,* ☎ *06/68802719,* FAX *06/6786376. 73 rooms. Bar. AE, DC, MC, V.*

$$$ 🏨 **Farnese.** A turn-of-the-century mansion, totally renovated in 1991,
★   the Farnese is near the Metro and within walking distance of St. Peter's. Furnished with great attention to detail in art deco style, it has an intimate atmosphere, dazzling modern baths, charming fresco decorations, and a roof garden. ⊠ *Via Alessandro Farnese 30, 00192,* ☎ *06/3212553,* FAX *06/3215129. 24 rooms. Bar, free parking. AE, DC, MC, V.*

$$$ 🏨 **Giulio Cesare.** An aristocratic town house in the residential, but central, Prati district, the Giulio Cesare is a 10-minute walk across the Tiber from Piazza del Popolo. It's beautifully run, with a friendly staff and a quietly luxurious air. The rooms are elegantly furnished, with chandeliers, thick rugs, floor-length drapes, and rich damasks in soft colors. Public rooms have Oriental carpets, old prints and paintings, marble fireplaces, and a grand piano. The buffet breakfast is a veritable banquet. ⊠ *Via degli Scipioni 287, 00192,* ☎ *06/3210751,* FAX *06/3211736. 90 rooms. Bar, garden. AE, DC, MC, V.*

$$$ 🏨 **Victoria.** A 1950s luxury in the public rooms, solid comfort throughout, and impeccable management are the main features of this hotel near Via Veneto. Oriental rugs, oil paintings, welcoming armchairs, and fresh flowers add charm to the public spaces, and the rooms are well furnished with armchairs and other amenities ignored by many modern decorators. American businesspeople, who prize the hotel's personalized service and restful atmosphere, are frequent guests. Some upper rooms and the roof terrace overlook the majestic pines of Villa Borghese. ⊠ *Via Campania 41, 00187,* ☎ *06/473931,* FAX *06/4871890. 110 rooms. Restaurant, bar. AE, DC, MC, V.*

$$ 🏨 **Art Deco.** This hotel's name tells all about its glamorous decor, attuned to the elegance and fancy of the 1920s, with whimsical accents in Deco paintings and antiques. Underlying the style is reassuring technology: a fail-safe electrical system, air-conditioning, and whirlpool baths. The hotel is in a residential neighborhood 10 minutes from Termini Station and handy to public transport. Book through Best Western or directly for the best rates. ⊠ *Via Palestro 19, 00185,* ☎ *06/4457588,* FAX *06/4441483. 49 rooms. Restaurant, bar. AE, DC, MC, V.*

$$ 🏨 **Britannia.** This fine small hotel is a very special place, offering su-
★   perior quality at moderate rates. Its quiet but central location is one attraction; a caring management is another. Guests are coddled with English-language dailies and local weather reports delivered to their rooms each morning, and with sybaritic marble bathrooms and well-furnished rooms. ⊠ *Via Napoli 64, 00184,* ☎ *06/4883153,* FAX *06/4882343. 32 rooms. Breakfast room. AE, DC, MC, V.*

$$ 🏨 **Carriage.** The Carriage's location is what makes it special: it's just two blocks away from the Spanish Steps, in the heart of Rome. The stylish decor uses subdued Baroque accents and antique reproductions to give the hotel a touch of elegance. Though some of the rooms are pint-size, and a couple open onto an air shaft, several have little terraces, and all guests can avail of the roof garden. ⊠ *Via delle Carrozze 36, 00187,* ☎ *06/6793312,* FAX *06/6788279. 27 rooms and suites. AE, DC, MC, V.*

$$ 🏨 **D'Este.** The fresh-looking decor in this distinguished 19th-century hotel evokes turn-of-the-century comfort, with brass bedsteads and lamps and dark wood period furniture. Rooms are quiet, light, and spacious;

many can accommodate family groups. The attentive owner-manager likes to have fresh flowers in the halls and sees that everything works. He encourages inquiries about special rates, particularly during the slack summer months. It's within hailing distance of Santa Maria Maggiore and close to Termini Station (you can arrange to be picked up there by the hotel car). ⊠ *Via Carlo Alberto 4/b, 00185,* ☎ *06/4465607,* FAX *06/4465601. 37 rooms. Bar. AE, DC, MC, V.*

$$ ⊞ **Duca d'Alba.** This elegant hotel has made a stylish contribution to the ongoing gentrification of the Suburra, the neighborhood near the Colosseum and the Roman Forum. The tasteful neoclassic decor is in character with ancient Roman motifs, custom-designed furnishings, and marble bathrooms. All rooms are entirely soundproofed; a few have tiny terraces. The four-bed suite with kitchenette is an excellent money-saving option for a family or a group of friends. This well-run establishment offers exceptionally good value: rates are at the lowest rung in the category. The attentive staff is another plus. ⊠ *Via Leonina 14, 00184,* ☎ *06/484471,* FAX *06/4884840. 28 rooms. AE, DC, MC, V.*

$$ ⊞ **Internazionale.** Near the top of the Spanish Steps and in a swank building on desirable Via Sistina, this hotel has double-glazed windows to ensure peace and quiet. Rooms on the fourth floor have terraces; the fourth-floor suite has a private terrace and a frescoed ceiling. The decor throughout is in soothing pastel tones, with some antique pieces, mirrors, and chandeliers. The location commands rates slightly over the maximum for the category. ⊠ *Via Sistina 79, 00187,* ☎ *06/69941823,* FAX *06/6784764. 42 rooms. AE, MC, V.*

$$ ⊞ **La Residenza.** Americans mostly frequent this hotel in a converted
★ town house near Via Veneto, with first-class comfort and a great atmosphere. The canopied entrance, spacious well-furnished lounges, and the bar and terrace are of the type you would expect to find in a deluxe lodging. Rooms, done out in aquamarine and beige with bentwood furniture, have large closets, color TVs, refrigerator-bars, air-conditioning, and heated towel racks. Rates include a generous American-style buffet breakfast. ⊠ *Via Emilia 22, 00187,* ☎ *06/4880789,* FAX *06/485721. 27 rooms. Bar, free parking. MC, V.*

$$ ⊞ **Locarno.** Art aficionados have long appreciated this hotel's preserved fin-de-siècle charm, intimate feel, and its central location off Piazza del Popolo. Rooms feature coordinated wallpaper and fabric prints, lacquered wrought-iron beds, and some antiques juxtaposed with modern gadgets: electronic safes and air-conditioning. Amenities include an ample buffet breakfast, bar service on the panoramic roof garden, and complimentary bicycles. ⊠ *Via della Penna 22, 00186,* ☎ *06/3610841,* FAX *06/3215249. 45 rooms. Bar, lobby lounge, bicycles. AE, DC, MC, V.*

$$ ⊞ **Marcella.** Known to connoisseurs as one of Rome's best midsize ho-
★ tels, with the feel of a smaller, more intimate establishment, this is 10 minutes from Via Veneto or Termini Station. Here you can do your sightseeing from the roof terrace, taking in the view while you breakfast. Many rooms also have good views, and they are all furnished with flair, showing a tasteful use of color, floral prints, and mirrored walls, echoing the elegant winter-garden decor of the lounges and bar. The spacious and flexible suites are ideal for families. ⊠ *Via Flavia 106, 00187,* ☎ *06/4746451,* FAX *06/4815832. 75 rooms. Bar, free parking. AE, DC, MC, V.*

$$ ⊞ **Morgana.** After enjoying the dashingly marbled lobby, the antique
★ accents in fully carpeted halls, and soundproofed rooms decorated with fine fabrics, you'll agree this is an elegantly conceived hotel. The Morgana offers excellent value and shows the management's attention to comfort and detail. The atmosphere is cordial and the rates are low in this category. It's also convenient to Termini Station. ⊠ *Via Filippo*

Turati 33, 00185, ☎ 06/4467230, FAX 06/4469142. 90 rooms. Bar, airport shuttle. AE, DC, MC, V.

$$ 🏨 **Portoghesi.** In the heart of Old Rome, the Portoghesi is a small hotel with big atmosphere. From a tiny lobby, an equally tiny elevator takes you to the quiet bedrooms, all decorated with floral prints and reproduction antique furniture. ⊠ *Via dei Portoghesi 1, 00186, ☎ 06/6864231, FAX 06/6876976. 28 rooms. Breakfast room. MC, V.*

$$ 🏨 **Sant'Anna.** An example of the gentrification of the picturesque old Borgo neighborhood in the shadow of St. Peter's, this fashionable small hotel has ample, air-conditioned bedrooms in art deco style. The frescoes in the breakfast room and fountain in the courtyard are typical Roman touches. There is no elevator to take you up to the top floors, but it's worth the climb to stay in one of the spacious attic rooms, each with a little terrace. ⊠ *Borgo Pio 134, 00193, ☎ 06/68801602, FAX 06/68308717. 20 rooms. Breakfast room. AE, DC, MC, V.*

$$ 🏨 **Scalinata di Spagna.** An old-fashioned pensione loved by generations of romantics, this tiny hotel is booked solid for months—even years—ahead. Its location at the top of the Spanish Steps, inconspicuous little entrance, quaint hodgepodge of old furniture, and view from the terrace where you breakfast make it seem like your own special, exclusive inn. And that's why rates for some rooms go over the top of this category. ⊠ *Piazza Trinità dei Monti 17, 00187, ☎ 06/6793006, FAX 06/69940598. 15 rooms. MC, V.*

$$ 🏨 **Siviglia.** You are transported back to a more opulent era in this freshly renovated 19th-century mansion in the quieter residential fringe of the Termini Station area. Like the several embassies in the neighborhood, it, too, has bright flags flying at the entrance. Inside, Venetian glass chandeliers and antique reproduction furniture give the lounges considerable character; rooms are simpler, with a light, airy touch. ⊠ *Via Gaeta 12, 00185, ☎ 06/4441196, FAX 06/4441195. 42 rooms. Bar. AE, MC, V.*

$$ 🏨 **Teatro di Pompeo.** Where else can you breakfast under the ancient stone vaults of Pompey's Theater, historic site of Julius Caesar's assassination? At this intimate and refined little hotel in the heart of Old Rome you are part of that history; at night, guests sleep under restored beamed ceilings that date from the days of Michelangelo. The tastefully furnished rooms offer comfort as well as charm. Book well in advance. ⊠ *Largo del Pallaro 8, 00186, ☎ 06/68300170, FAX 06/68805531. 13 rooms. AE, DC, MC, V.*

$ 🏨 **Alimandi.** On a side street only a block from the Vatican Museums,
★ this family-operated hotel offers excellent value in a neighborhood with moderately priced shops and restaurants. A spiffy lobby and ample lounges, a tavern for night owls, terraces, and roof gardens are some of the perks here. Rooms are spacious, airy, and well furnished; many can accommodate extra beds. The few rooms without bath are real bargains. ⊠ *Via Tunisi 8, 00192, ☎ 06/39723948, FAX 06/39723943. 35 rooms, 26 with bath. Parking (fee). AE, DC, MC, V.*

$ 🏨 **Amalia.** Handy to the Vatican and the Cola di Rienzo shopping district, this small former pensione is owned and operated by the Consoli family—Amalia and her brothers. On several floors of a 19th-century building, it has large rooms with functional furnishings, TV sets, direct-dial telephones, pictures of angels on the walls, and gleaming marble bathrooms (hair dryers included). The Ottaviano stop of Metro A is a block away. ⊠ *Via Germanico 66, 00192, ☎ 06/39723356, FAX 06/39723365. 30 rooms, 25 with bath or shower. Bar. AE, MC, V.*

$ 🏨 **Arenula.** This hotel—with a luminous and cheerful all-white interior—is one of Rome's best values for the price. Rooms have pale wood furnishings and gleaming bathrooms, as well as double-glazed windows and air-conditioning. Several have space for extra beds. The buffet breakfast—and extra fee—is optional. But nobody is perfect, and the catch at the four-story Arenula is that the graceful oval staircase of white marble and wrought iron is the only way up—there is no elevator. It's found on an age-worn byway off central Via Arenula, on the edge of the picturesque Ghetto neighborhood. ⊠ *Via Santa Maria dei Calderari 47 (Via Arenula), 00186,* ☎ *06/6879454,* ℻ *06/6896188. 50 rooms, 38 with bath. DC, MC, V.*

$ 🏨 **Campo dei Fiori.** Frescoes, exposed brickwork, and picturesque effects throughout this little hotel in Old Rome could well be the work of a set designer. There's an aura of fantasy and romanticism in the decoration, with the layout cleverly designed to make the most of limited space. A few rooms are so compact they're almost claustrophobic; other rooms are larger, and all have an unusual decorative feature of some kind to remind you that you are in the heart of Rome. The hotel has no elevator, but the climb to the roof terrace rewards you with a marvelous view and a great area to relax. Rates for the best rooms exceed parameters in this price category. ⊠ *Via del Biscione 6, 00186,* ☎ *06/68806865,* ℻ *06/6876003. 27 rooms, 14 with bath. MC, V.*

$ 🏨 **Marcus.** The location, down the street from the Spanish Steps, is the premier feature of this small, homelike hotel occupying a large apartment on one floor of an 18th-century cardinal's palazzo. Many rooms have antique fireplaces; otherwise they are furnished in a rather dowdy, old-fashioned style, as seen in the main living room, which has comfortable armchairs and a crystal chandelier. Double-glazed windows keep out most of the noise of central Rome. ⊠ *Via Clementina 94, 00184,* ☎ *06/68300320,* ℻ *06/68300312. 15 rooms. AE, MC, V.*

$ 🏨 **Margutta.** The lobby and halls in this small hotel are unassuming, ★ but rooms are a pleasant surprise, with a clean and airy look, attractive wrought-iron bedsteads, and modern baths. Though it's in an old building, there is an elevator. It's centrally located on a quiet side street between the Spanish Steps and Piazza del Popolo. ⊠ *Via Laurina 34, 00187,* ☎ *06/3223674,* ℻ *06/3200395. 21 rooms. AE, DC, MC, V.*

$ 🏨 **Miami.** Its location in a dignified 19th-century building on Rome's important Via Nazionale puts this hotel in a strategic spot for sightseeing, shopping, and getting around in general; it is on main bus lines and near Termini Station and the Metro. The marble floors, chrome trim, and dark colors are brightened by the friendly family-style management. Rooms on the courtyard are quieter. ⊠ *Via Nazionale 230, 00184,* ☎ *06/4817180,* ℻ *06/484562. 34 rooms. AE, DC, MC, V.*

$ 🏨 **Montreal.** This is a compact hotel on a central avenue across the square from Santa Maria Maggiore, only three blocks from Termini Station, with bus and subway lines close by. On two floors of an older building, it has been totally renovated and offers fresh-looking rooms. The owner-managers are pleasant and helpful, and the neighborhood has plenty of reasonably priced eating places, plus one of Rome's largest outdoor markets. ⊠ *Via Carlo Alberto 4, 00185,* ☎ *06/4457797,* ℻ *06/4465522. 20 rooms. AE, DC, MC, V.*

$ 🏨 **Romae.** In the better part of the Termini Station neighborhood, the Romae has the advantages of a strategic location (within walking distance of many sights, and handy to bus and subway lines), a very friendly and helpful management, and good-size rooms that are clean and airy. The pictures of Rome in the small lobby and breakfast room, the luminous white walls and light wood furniture in the rooms, and the bright little baths all have a fresh look. Amenities such as satellite TV, a hair dryer in every room, and breakfast included in the room rate make this hotel a very good value. Families benefit from special rates and services. ⊠ *Via Palestro 49, 00185,* ☎ *06/4463554,* ℻ *06/4463914. 20 rooms. Breakfast room. AE, DC, MC, V.*

NIGHTLIFE AND THE ARTS

The Arts

A vast array of music, dance, opera, and film is offered in Rome. Schedules of events are published in daily newspapers: pick up *Trovaroma,* the weekly entertainment guide published every Thursday as a supplement to the daily *La Repubblica;* the *Guest in Rome* booklet distributed free at hotel desks; and flyers available at EPT and city tourist information offices. An English-language periodical, *Wanted in Rome,* is available at centrally located newsstands and has good listings of events. There are listings in English in the back of the weekly *Romac'è* booklet, with handy bus information for each listing.

Concerts

CLASSICAL

Rome has long hosted a wide variety of classical music concerts, although it is a common complaint that the city does not have adequate concert halls; a new concert hall is currently under construction. Depending on the venue, concert tickets can cost from 15,000 to 50,000 lire. A principal concert series is performed at **Accademia di Santa Cecilia** (✉ Concert hall and box office: Via della Conciliazione 4, ☎ 06/68801044. The **Accademia Filarmonica Romana** (✉ Teatro Olimpico, Via Gentile da Fabriano 17, ☎ 06/3234890) is another venue. The **Istituzione Universitaria dei Concerti** (✉ San Leone Magno auditorium, Via Bolzano 38, ☎ 06/3610051) hosts concerts. **RAI** at Foro Italico (☎ 06/36865625) is another principal series. The internationally respected **Gonfalone** series concentrates on Baroque music (✉ Via del Gonfalone 32, ☎ 06/6875952). The **Associazione Musicale Romana** (☎ 06/6568441) organizes a yearlong schedule of music festivals and concerts. **Il Tempietto** (☎ 06/4814800) also organizes music festivals and concerts throughout the year.

There are also many small concert groups. Many concerts are free, including all those performed in Catholic churches, where a special ruling permits only concerts of religious music. Look for posters outside churches announcing free concerts. **The Church of Sant'Ignazio** (✉ Piazza Sant'Ignazio) often hosts concerts in a spectacularly frescoed setting.

ROCK, POP, AND JAZZ

Rock, pop, and jazz concerts are frequent, especially in summer, although even performances by big-name stars may not be well advertised. Tickets for these performances are usually handled by **Orbis** (✉ Piazza Esquilino 37, ☎ 06/4744776). **Ricordi** music store (✉ Via del Corso 506, ☎ 06/3612331; ✉ Viale Giulio Cesare 88, ☎ 06/3720216) also sells tickets.

Dance

The **Rome Opera Ballet** gives regular performances at the Teatro dell'Opera (☞ Opera, *below*), often with leading international guest stars. Rome is regularly visited by classical ballet companies from Russia, the United States, and Europe; performances are at the Teatro dell'Opera, Teatro Olimpico, or at one of the open-air venues in summer. Small classical and modern dance companies from Italy and abroad give performances in various places; check concert listings.

Film

Rome has dozens of movie houses, but the only one to show exclusively English-language films is the **Pasquino** (✉ Vicolo del Piede off Piazza Santa Maria in Trastevere, ☎ 06/5803622). Films here are not dubbed, but are shown in English, sometimes with Italian subtitles. Several movie theaters show films in the original language on certain days of the week; the listings in *Romac'è* are reliable. Pick up a weekly schedule at the theater or consult the daily papers.

Opera

The opera season runs from November or December to May, and performances are staged in the **Teatro dell'Opera** (⊠ Piazza Beniamino Gigli, ☎ 06/4817003). Tickets go on sale two days before a performance, and the box office is open 10–5. Prices range from about 30,000 to 150,000 lire for regular performances; they can go much higher for an opening night or an appearance by an internationally acclaimed guest singer. Standards may not always measure up to those set by Milan's fabled La Scala, but, despite strikes and shortages of funds, most performances are respectable.

After the summer opera season was evicted from the ruins of the ancient **Terme di Caracalla** (Baths of Caracalla; ☞ Across the Tiber *in* Exploring Rome *above*) and a temporary venue was created in **Villa Borghese,** the debate over a permanent open-air venue continues. The most likely choice is **Villa Pepoli,** a parklike area adjacent to the ruins of the Baths.

Nightlife

Although Rome is not one of the world's most exciting cities for nightlife (despite the popular image of the city as the birthplace of *La Dolce Vita*), discos, live-music spots, and quiet late-night bars have proliferated in recent years. This has been true in the streets of the old city and in far-flung parts of town. The "flavor of the month" factor works here, too, and many places fade into oblivion after their five minutes of fame. The best sources for an up-to-date list of late-night spots are the "Night Scene" section of *Romac'è* and *Metropolitan,* an English-language biweekly sold at many newsstands.

Bars

Rome has a range of bars offering drinks and background music. Jacket and tie are in order in the elegant **Blue Bar** of the Hostaria dell'Orso (⊠ Via dei Soldati 25, ☎ 06/6864250) and in **Le Bar** of the Grand hotel (⊠ Via Vittorio Emanuele Orlando 3, ☎ 06/482931). **Jazz Club** (⊠ Via Zanardelli 12, ☎ 06/6861990), near Piazza Navona, is a classic wateringhole with seating at the bar or in leather-upholstered booths. Light meals are available, and there's live music a few nights a week. It's open from 9:30 PM to 2:30 AM and on Sunday from noon to 4 for brunch. **Flann O'Brien** (⊠ Via Napoli 29, ☎ 06/4480418) has the look and atmosphere of a good Irish pub but also serves decent cappuccino.

Attendance at **Antico Caffè della Pace** (⊠ Via della Pace 3, ☎ 06/6861216), near Piazza Navona, ranges from coffeehouse intellectuals to chichi types. **Bar del Fico** (⊠ Piazza del Fico 26, ☎ 06/6865205), is a down-to-earth, authentically Roman alternative to the more sophisticated bars in the Piazza Navona area. **Le Cornacchie** (⊠ Piazza Rondanini 53, ☎ 06/6864485), near the Pantheon, has an oversize (for Rome) bar, serves meals, and is open until 2 AM.

The cafés on **Via Veneto** and big-hotel bars draw mainly tourists and are good places to meet other travelers in the over-30 age group.

BEER HALLS AND PUBS

Beer halls and a plethora of new English, Scottish, and Irish pubs are popular with young Italians and foreigners. **Birreria Marconi** (⊠ Via di Santa Prassede 9/c, ☎ 06/486636), near Santa Maria Maggiore, is also a pizzeria. It is closed Sunday. **Birreria Santi Apostoli** (⌑ Piazza Santi Apostoli 52, ☎ 06/6788285) is open every day until 2 AM. Among the pubs, **Fiddler's Elbow** (⌑ Via dell'Olmata 43, ☎ 06/4872110) has a Hiberian feel and encourages singing; it's open 5 PM–midnight. **Four Green Fields** (⌑ Via Costantino Morin 42, off Via della Giuliana, ☎ 06/3595091) features live music and is open daily from 8:30 PM to 2 AM. **Trinity College** (⌑ Via del Collegio Romano 6, ☎ 06/678647272) has a classic Dublin look and a young Roman clientele. Pubby **Fonclea** (⌑ Via Crescenzio 82/a, ☎ 06/6896302), near Castel Sant'Angelo, has live music ranging from jazz to Latin American to rhythm-and-blues, depending on who's in town. The kitchen whips up Mexican and Italian food.

CAFÉS

Locals and foreigners of all nations and ages gather at Rome's cafés on Piazza della Rotonda, in front of the Pantheon, and in the vicinity of Piazza Navona or in Piazza Santa Maria in Trastevere.

WINE BARS

Informal wine bars are popular with Romans who like to burn the midnight oil but don't dig disco music. Near the Pantheon is **Spiriti** (⌑ Via Sant'Eustachio 5, ☎ 06/6892499), which serves light lunches at midday and is open until 1:30 AM. **Enoteca Roffi** (⌑ Via della Croce 76/a, ☎ 06/6790896) is near the Spanish Steps. **Cavour 313** (⌑ Via Cavour 313, ☎ 06/6785496), near the Roman Forum, offers snacks and cheese plates to accompany the wine of your choice. **Trimani Wine Bar,** between Piazza della Repubblica and Porta Pia (⌑ Via Cernaia 37/b, ☎ 06/4469630), is the family-run annex of one of Rome's most esteemed wine shops. You can sample some great wines at the counter or with a light, fixed-price meal at an upstairs table. The bar is open Monday–Saturday noon–3:30 and 6–midnight. At **Cul de Sac** (⌑ Piazza Pasquino 73, ☎ 06/68801094), near Piazza Navona, you find good wines and snacks in tight quarters.

Discos and Nightclubs

Most discos open about 10:30 PM and charge an entrance fee of around 30,000–35,000 lire, which may include the first drink. Subsequent drinks cost about 10,000–15,000 lire. Some discos also open on Saturday and Sunday afternoons for patrons under 16.

Two disco dance floors and another for dancing to live music keep everyone rocking at **Smile** (⌑ Via Schiaparelli 29–30, entrance at Via Luciani 52, ☎ 06-3221251), where an under-30 crowd sometimes includes young actors. Special events such as beauty pageants, fashion shows, and theme parties are featured. It is closed from Sunday to Tuesday. An annex is around the corner; currently called **Tatum** (⌑ Via Luciani 52), it has deafening disco music for the underage and is open Thursday–Saturday. The **Stellarium** (⌑ Via Lidia 44, ☎ 06-7809885), a.k.a. Palacio della Salsa, has popular prices (entrance about 15,000 lire) and is one of the hottest spots for Latin American beats and the latest disco dances. **Deco** (⌑ Via Cesare Beccaria 22, ☎ 06/3611240) is big, with decor reminiscent of the 1930s but disco music that is off the charts.

Jackie O' (⌑ Via Boncompagni 11, ☎ 06/4885754) is an upscale favorite with the rich and famous for dinner and disco dancing. **Gilda** (⌑ Via Mario dei Fiori 97, near Piazza di Spagna, ☎ 06/6784838) is the place to spot famous Italian actors and politicians. This sophisticated nightspot has a piano bar, as well as a restaurant, dance floors, and live music. Jackets are required. It's closed Monday. The **New Open**

Gate (⊠ Via San Nicola da Tolentino 4, ☎ 06/4824464) is one of the trendiest discos in town.

One of Rome's first discos, **The Piper** (⊠ Via Tagliamento 9, ☎ 06/8414459) is still hot and a magnet for young movers and shakers. It has disco music, live groups, and pop videos. Occasionally, there's ballroom dancing for an older crowd, and Sunday afternoon is for teenagers. It is open from 10 PM until 5 AM and is closed Monday and Tuesday. The under-25 crowd lets loose at **Gossip Café** (⊠ Via Romagnosi 11, ☎ 06/3611348). **Follia** (⊠ Via Ovidio 17, ☎ 06/68308435) lures celebrities and a tony young crowd with disco music and a piano bar.

Music Clubs

Jazz, folk, pop, and Latin music clubs are flourishing in Rome, particularly in the picturesque Trastevere and Testaccio neighborhoods. Jazz clubs are especially popular, and talented local groups may be joined by visiting musicians from other countries. As admission, many clubs require that you buy a membership card for about 10,000–20,000 lire.

In the Trionfale district near the Vatican, **Alexanderplatz** (⊠ Via Ostia 9, ☎ 06/39742171) has both a bar and a restaurant, and features nightly live programs of jazz and blues played by Italian and foreign musicians. For the best live music, including jazz, blues, rhythm and blues, African, and rock, go to **Big Mama** (⊠ Vicolo San Francesco a Ripa 18, ☎ 06/5812551). There is also a bar and snack food. Latin rhythms are the specialty at **Berimbau** (⊠ Via dei Fienaroli 30/b, ☎ 06/5813249), a live music club with a Brazilian accent and disco dancing after the show.

In the trendy Testaccio neighborhood, **Akab–Cave** (⊠ Via di Monte Testaccio 68, ☎ 06/5744485) is a big, bare, casual venue for live rock and jazz groups, with dancing. **Music Inn** (⊠ Largo dei Fiorentini 3, ☎ 06/68802220) is Rome's top jazz club and features some of the biggest names on the international scene. It also has a restaurant, which is closed Monday.

Live performances of jazz, soul, and funk by leading musicians draw celebrities to **St. Louis Music City** (⊠ Via del Cardello 13/a, ☎ 06/4745076). There is also a restaurant; it's closed Sunday.

OUTDOOR ACTIVITIES AND SPORTS

Beaches

The beaches nearest Rome are at **Ostia,** a busy urban center in its own right. You can reach it by train from Ostiense Station. **Castelfusano** is nearby; you can take a bus there from Ostia. **Fregene** is a villa colony reached by COTRAL bus from Via Lepanto stop of Metro A in Rome. **Castelporziano** is a public beach area maintained by the city, and you can also reach it by bus from Ostia. Some establishments, such as **Kursaal** (⊠ Lungomare Catullo 36, at Castelfusano, ☎ 06/5621303) have swimming pools, strongly recommended as alternatives to the notoriously polluted waters of this part of the Mediterranean.

For cleaner water and more of a resort atmosphere, you have to go farther afield. To the north of Rome, **Santa Marinella** offers shoals, sand, and attractive surroundings. **Santa Severa** is also north of Rome, and a nice beach. To the south, **Sabaudia** is known for miles of sandy beaches. **San Felice Circeo** is a classy resort. **Sperlonga** is a picturesque old town flanked by beaches and pretty coves.

Participant Sports

Biking

You can rent a bike at **I Bike Rome** (⊠ Underground parking lot at Villa Borghese, ☎ 06/3225240). Also try **St. Peter Motor Rent** (⊠ Via di Porta Castello 43, ☎ 06/6875714; ⊠ Piazza Navona 69). There are **rental concessions** at the Piazza di Spagna and Piazza del Popolo metro stops, at Largo San Silvestro, Largo Argentina, Viale della Pineta in Villa Borghese, and at **Viale del Bambino** on the Pincio.

Bowling

There's a large American-style bowling center at **Bowling Brunswick** (⊠ Lungotevere Acqua Acetosa, ☎ 06/8086147). A smaller one is **Bowling Roma** (⊠ Viale Regina Margherita 181, ☎ 06/8551184).

Fitness Facilities

The **Cavalieri Hilton** (⊠ Via Cadlolo 101, ☎ 06/35091) has a running path on its grounds as well as outdoor and indoor pools, two clay tennis courts, an exercise area, a sauna, and a steam room. The **Sheraton Roma** (⊠ Viale del Pattinaggio, ☎ 06/5453) has a heated outdoor pool, tennis court, two squash courts, and a sauna, but no gym. The **Sheraton Golf** (⊠ Viale Parco de' Medici 22, ☎ 06/659788) has a fitness center and 18-hole golf course. Two tennis courts and a 25-meter pool are at the **St. Peter's Holiday Inn** (⊠ Via Aurelia Antica 415, ☎ 06/6642).

The **Roman Sport Center** (⊠ Via del Galoppatoio 33, ☎ 06/3201667) is a full-fledged sports center occupying vast premises next to the underground parking lot in Villa Borghese; it has two swimming pools, a gym, aerobic workout areas, squash courts, and saunas. It is affiliated with the **American Health Club** (⊠ Largo Somalia 60, ☎ 06/86212411).

Golf

Nonmembers are welcome in these clubs, all with 18 holes, but must show the membership cards of their home golf or country clubs. The oldest and most prestigious golf club in Rome is the **Circolo del Golf Roma** (⊠ Via Appia Nuova 716/a, ☎ 06/7803407). Among the newest is **Golf Club Parco de' Medici** (⊠ Viale Parco de' Medici 22, ☎ 06/6553477). The **Country Club Castel Gandolfo** (⊠ Via Santo Spirito 13, Castel Gandolfo, ☎ 06/9312301) is also one of the newest. The **Golf Club Fioranello** (⊠ Viale della Repubblica, ☎ 06/7138080) is at Santa Maria delle Mole, off Via Appia Antica. There is a course at the **Olgiata Golf Club** (⊠ Largo Olgiata 15, Via Cassia, ☎ 06/30889141).

Horseback Riding

There are several riding clubs in Rome. The most central is the **Associazione Sportiva Villa Borghese** (⊠ Via del Galoppatoio 23, ☎ 06/3606797). You can also ride at the **Società Ippica Romana** (⊠ Via Monti della Farnesina 18, ☎ 06/3240592) and at the **Circolo Ippico Olgiata** (⊠ Largo Olgiata 15, ☎ 06/30888792), outside the city on Via Cassia.

Running

The best bet for running in the inner city is the **Villa Borghese,** which offers the approximate ⅔-km (½-mi) circuit of the Pincio, among the marble statuary. A longer run in the park itself might include a loop around **Piazza di Siena,** a grass horse track. Although most traffic is barred from Villa Borghese, government and police cars sometimes speed through. Be careful to stick to the sides of the roads. For a long run away from all traffic, try **Villa Ada** and **Villa Doria Pamphili** on the Janiculum. On the other hand, if you really love history, run at the old

Circus Maximus, or along **Via delle Terme di Caracalla,** which is flanked by a park. There is also a path at **Cavalieri Hilton** (☞ Fitness Facilities, *above*).

Swimming

The outdoor pools of the **Cavalieri Hilton** (☞ Fitness Facilities, *above*) and the **Hotel Aldovrandi** (✉ Via Ulisse Aldovrandi 15, ☎ 06/3223993) are lush summer oases open to nonguests. The **Roman Sport Center** (✉ Via del Galoppatoio 33, ☎ 06/3201667) has two swimming pools, and there's another one at the **American Health Club** (✉ Largo Somalia 60, ☎ 06/86212411).

Tennis

Increasingly popular with Italians, tennis is played in private clubs and on many public courts that can be rented by the hour. Your hotel *portiere* (concierge) will direct you to the nearest courts and can book for you. A prominent Roman club is the **Tennis Club Parioli** (✉ Largo de Morpurgo 2, Via Salaria, ☎ 06/86200882).

Spectator Sports

Basketball

Basketball continues to grow in Italy, with many American pros now playing on Italian teams. In Rome, games are played at the **Palazzo dello Sport** in the EUR district (✉ Piazzale dello Sport, ☎ 06/5925107).

Horse Racing

There's flat racing at the lovely century-old **Capannelle** track (✉ Via Appia Nuova 1255, ☎ 06/7183143), frequented by a chic crowd on big race days. The trotters meet at the **Tor di Valle** track (✉ Via del Mare, ☎ 06/5290269).

Horseback Riding

The **International Riding Show,** held in May, draws a stylish crowd to the amphitheater of Piazza di Siena in Villa Borghese. The competition is stiff, and the program features a cavalry charge staged by the dashing mounted corps of the carabinieri. For information, call the **Italian Federation of Equestrian Sports** (✉ Viale Tiziano 74, ☎ 06/36858528).

Soccer

Italy's favorite spectator sport stirs passionate enthusiasm among partisans. Games are usually held on Saturday afternoons and Wednesday evenings throughout the fall–spring season. Two teams—Roma and Lazio—play their home games in the Olympic Stadium at the extensive **Foro Italico** sports complex (✉ Viale dei Gladiatori, ☎ 06/3336316), built by Mussolini on the banks of the Tiber. Tickets are on sale at the box office before the games; your hotel portiere may be able to help you get tickets in advance.

Tennis

A top-level international tournament is held at the Tennis Stadium at **Foro Italico** in May. For information, call the **Italian Tennis Federation** (✉ Viale Tiziano 70, ☎ 06/36858510).

SHOPPING

Shopping in Rome is a must, no matter what your budget. You're sure to find something that suits your fancy *and* your pocketbook, but don't expect to get bargains on Italian brands, such as Benetton, that are exported to the United States; prices are about the same on both sides of the Atlantic.

Shops are open from 9 or 9:30 to 1 and from 3:30 or 4 to 7 or 7:30. There's a tendency in Rome for shops in central districts to stay open all day, and hours are generally becoming more flexible throughout the city. Department stores and centrally located UPIM and Standa stores are open all day. Remember that most stores are closed Sunday, though this is changing, too. Generally, with the exception of food and technical-supply stores, most stores also close on Monday mornings from September to June and Saturday afternoons in July and August.

Most Italian sizes are not uniform, so always try on clothing before you buy, or measure gift items. Glove sizes are universal. Remember that Italian stores generally will *not* refund your purchases and that they often cannot exchange goods because of limited stock. *Always* take your purchases with you; having them shipped home from the shop can cause hassles. If circumstances are such that you can't take your goods with you, and if the shop seems reliable about shipping, get a firm written statement of *when* and *how* your purchase will be sent.

Prezzi fissi means that prices are fixed, and it's a waste of time bargaining unless you're buying a sizable quantity of goods or a particularly costly object. Most stores have a fixed-price policy, and most honor a variety of credit cards. They will also accept foreign money at the current exchange rate, give or take a few lire. Ask for a receipt for your purchases; you may need it at customs on your return home.

It's possible to obtain a refund on the VAT tax, which is included in the selling price. To be eligible, you must spend at least 300,000 lire in one store (☞ The Gold Guide).

Bargains

You can often find good buys in knitwear and silk scarves at stands on the fringes of outdoor food markets. These vendors move to another market each day, so finding one is a question of luck. Bargaining is still an art at **Porta Portese** flea market (☞ Food and Flea Markets, *below*) and is routine when purchasing anything from a street vendor. On **Via Cola di Rienzo** there is usually a stand with a range of blown-glass items. The market at **Via Sannio** (San Giovanni in Laterano) features job lots of designer shoes and ranks of stalls selling new and used clothing at bargain prices. It is open weekdays 10–1, Saturday 10–6. The morning market in the piazza at the center of the **Testaccio** neighborhood is also known for stands selling designer shoes. For boutique fashions at discount prices, go to **Labels-for-Less** (⌧ Via dei Serviti 27, near Trevi Fountain). Bargain hunters will also love **Vesti a Stock** (⌧ Via Germanico 170).

Department Stores

Rinascente (⌧ Near Piazza Colonna) sells clothing and accessories only. Another Rinascente (⌧ Piazza Fiume) has the same stock, plus furniture and housewares. **Coin** (⌧ Piazzale Appio, near San Giovanni in Laterano) has fashions for men and women and housewares. There is another Coin in the U.S.-style shopping mall at Cinecittà Due (☞ Shopping Malls, *below*). The **UPIM** and **Standa** chains offer low to moderately priced goods. They're the place to go for a pair of slippers, a sweater, a bathing suit, or such to see you through until you get home. In addition, they carry all kinds of toiletries and first-aid needs. Most Standa and UPIM stores have invaluable while-you-wait shoe-repair service counters.

Food and Flea Markets

Rome's biggest and most colorful outdoor food market is at **Campo dei Fiori** (⌧ South of Piazza Navona). **Via Andrea Doria** (⌧ About a five-minute walk north of the entrance to the Vatican Museums) is equally

Rome Shopping

Ai Monasteri, **16**
Albanesi, **23**
Albertina, **22**
Aston, **27**
Campo dei Fiori, **8**
Ceresa, **21**
Cinecittà Due, **34**
Coin, **35**
Di Cori, **32**
Fratelli Bassetti, **13**
Frugoni, **11**

Jesurum, **29**
Labels–for–Less, **33**
Lavori Artigianali
Femminili, **20**
Le Tartarughe, **14**
Luisa Spagnoli, **24**
Magli, **26**
Myricae, **17**
Nardecchia, **15**
Nickol's, **28**

Porta Portese, **9**
Rinascente, **18**
Tanca, **12**
Testaccio, **10**
Vesti a Stock, **2**
Via Andrea Doria, **1**
Via Cola di Rienzo, **3**
Via della
Conciliazione, **5**

Via del Tritone, **19**
Via di Porta
Angelica, **4**
Via Giulia, **6**
Via Monserrato, **7**
Via Nazionale, **31**
Via Sannio, **36**
Via Veneto, **25**
Volterra, **30**

big and bustling. Smaller markets can be found throughout the city. There's room for bargaining at the flea market on Sunday morning at **Porta Portese** (⊠ Take Via Ippolito Nievo, off Viale Trastevere); it now offers mainly new or secondhand clothing, but there are still a few dealers in old furniture and intriguing junk. Beware of pickpockets and don't go if you can't stand crowds. All outdoor markets are open from early morning to about 2, except Saturday, when they may stay open all day.

Shopping Districts

The most elegant and expensive shops are concentrated in the Piazza di Spagna area, especially along **Via Condotti. Via Borgognona** is also a fashionable street. Art galleries are concentrated on **Via Margutta**. **Via del Babuino** is the place to go for antiques. There are several high-fashion designer establishments on **Via Gregoriana.** Well-heeled clotheshorses also head to **Via Sistina.** Bordering the top-price Via Sistina shopping district is **Via del Corso,** lined with shops and boutiques of all kinds where prices and goods are competitive. Tony **Via Frattina** is also on the cusp of the Via Sistina district. **Via del Gambero** is also a good bet for competitively priced, high-end boutiques.

Via del Tritone, leading up from Piazza Colonna off Via del Corso, has some medium-priced, and a few expensive, shops selling everything from fashion fabrics to trendy furniture. On **Via Veneto** you'll find more high-priced boutiques and shoe stores, as well as newsstands selling English-language newspapers, magazines, and paperback books. **Via Nazionale** features shoe stores, moderately priced boutiques, and shops selling men's and women's fashions. **Via Cola di Rienzo** offers high-quality wares of all types; it's a good alternative to the Piazza di Spagna area.

In Old Rome, **Via dei Coronari** has antiques and designer home accessories. **Via Monserrato** also features antiques dealers galore, plus a few art galleries. **Via Giulia** is also a decorative arts bonanza. In the **Pantheon** area there are many shops selling liturgical objects and vestments. But the place to go for religious souvenirs is, obviously, the area around **St. Peter's,** especially **Via della Conciliazione** and **Via di Porta Angelica.**

Shopping Malls

The **Cinecittà Due** mall was the first of several megamalls now catering to Roman consumers, and it is the handiest—just take Metro A to the Subaugusta stop. The mall has 100 shops, including a **Coin** department store branch, a big supermarket, snack bars, and cafés (⊠ Piazza di Cinecittà, Viale Palmiro Togliatti, ☎ 06/7220902).

Specialty Stores

ANTIQUES AND PRINTS

For old prints and antiques, the **Tanca** shop (⊠ Salita dei Crescenzi 10, near Pantheon) is a good hunting ground. Early photographs of Rome and views of Italy from the archives at **Alinari** (⊠ Via Aliberti 16/a) make memorable souvenirs. **Nardecchia** (⊠ Piazza Navona 25) is reliable for prints. Stands in **Piazza della Fontanella Borghese** sell prints and old books.

CLOTHING BOUTIQUES

All the big names in Italian fashion—Versace, Ferre, Valentino, Armani, Missoni—are represented in the Piazza di Spagna area. **Sorelle Fontane** (⊠ Salita San Sebastianello 6), one of the first houses to put Italy on the fashion map, has a large boutique with an extensive line of ready-to-wear clothing and accessories. **Carlo Palazzi** (⊠ Via Borgognona 7) has elegant men's styles and accessories. **Mariselaine** (⊠ Via Condotti 70) is a top-quality women's fashion boutique. **Le Tartarughe** (⊠ Via Piè di Marmo 17) has understated, versatile, and easy-to-wear garments,

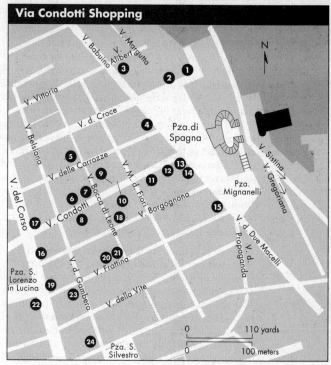

Via Condotti Shopping

including packable knits and jerseys. **Camomilla** (⊠ Piazza di Spagna 58) has trendy styles for women.

EMBROIDERY AND LINENS

Frette (⊠ Piazza di Spagna 11) is a Roman institution for fabulous trousseaux. **Marisa Padovan** (⊠ Via Bocca di Leone 28) shows exclusive and expensive lingerie. **Lavori Artigianali Femminili** (⊠ Via Capo le Case 6) offers exquisitely embroidered household linens, infants' and children's clothing, and blouses.

HANDICRAFTS

For pottery, handwoven textiles, and other handicrafts, **Myricae** (⊠ Piazza del Parlamento 38) has a good selection. A bottle of liqueur, jar of marmalade, or bar of chocolate handmade by Cistercian monks in several monasteries in Italy makes an unusual, tasty gift to take home; they are all for sale at **Ai Monasteri** (⊠ Piazza Cinque Lune 2).

JEWELRY

What Cartier is to Paris **Bulgari** (⊠ Via Condotti 10) is to Rome; the shop's elegant display windows hint at what's beyond the guard at the door. **Buccellati** (⊠ Via Condotti 31) is a tradition-rich Florentine jewelry house renowned for its silver work; it ranks with Bulgari for quality and reliability. You'll find tempting selections of small silver objects at **Fornari** (⊠ Via Frattina 71) and **Frugoni** (⊠ Via Arenula 83). **Bozart** (⊠ Via Bocca di Leone 4) features dazzling costume jewelry in keeping with the latest fashions.

KNITWEAR

Luisa Spagnoli (⊠ Largo Goldoni 43; Via Frattina 116; Via Veneto 130) is always reliable for good quality at the right price and styles to suit American tastes. **Albertina** (⊠ Via Lazio 20) elevates knitwear to the level of high fashion, imparting line and substance to creations that never go out of style.

LEATHER GOODS

The most famous of Rome's leather shops is **Gucci** (⊠ Via Condotti 8). It has a full assortment of accessories on the first floor, a fashion boutique for men and women and a scarf department on the second floor, and many Japanese customers, who line up to get in on busy days. **Roland's** (⊠ Piazza di Spagna 74) has an extensive stock of good-quality leather fashions and accessories, as well as stylish casual wear in wool and silk. More reasonably priced fine-leather goods, including many handbags, can be found at **Ceresa** (⊠ Via del Tritone 118). **Volterra** (⊠ Via Barberini 102) is well stocked and offers a wide selection of handbags at moderate prices. For gloves as pretty as Holly Golightly's, head to **Sermoneta** (⊠ Piazza di Spagna 61). **Di Cori,** a few steps away, also has a good selection of gloves; there's another Di Cori store at Via Nazionale 183. **Merola** (⊠ Via del Corso 143) carries a line of expensive top-quality gloves and scarves.

For timeless elegance in splendid silk scarves and ties, leather accessories, and fine shoes **Ferragamo** (⊠ Via Condotti 73; Via Condotti 66) is one of Rome's best; you pay for quality here, but you can get great buys during the periodic sales. **Nickol's** (⊠ Via Barberini 21) is in the moderate price range and is one of the few stores in Rome that stocks shoes in American widths. **Mario Valentino** (⊠ Via Frattina 58) is a top name for stylish shoes and leather fashions. In the dolce vita days, Hollywood stars bought their shoes at **Albanesi** (⊠ Via Lazio 21), still a mecca of fashion in footwear. **Bruno Magli** (⊠ Via del Gambero 1; Via Veneto 70) is known for well-made shoes and matching handbags at high to moderate prices. **Campanile** (⊠ Via Condotti 58) has four floors of shoes in the latest, as well as classic, styles and other leather goods.

SILKS AND FABRICS

Fratelli Bassetti (⊠ Corso Vittorio Emanuele II 73) has a vast selection of world-famous Italian silks and fashion fabrics in a rambling palazzo. **Aston** (⊠ Via Buoncompagni 27) stocks couture-level fabrics for men and women. You can find some real bargains when *scampoli* (remnants) are on sale.

SIDE TRIPS

One of the easiest excursions from the capital takes you 25 km (15½ mi) west to the sea, where tall pines stand among the well-preserved ruins of Ostia Antica, the main port of ancient Rome. East of Rome lie some of the region's star sites, which could be combined along a route that loops through the hills where ancient Romans built their summer resorts. The biggest attraction is Tivoli, which could be seen on a half-day excursion from Rome. But if you continue eastward to Palestrina, you can see a vast sanctuary famous in ancient times. And you could also fit in a visit to the site on which St. Benedict founded the hermitage that gave rise to Western monasticism. The monastery of St. Benedict is in Subiaco—not easy to get to unless you have a car, but you may want to make the effort to gain an insight into medieval mysticism.

Ostia Antica

Founded around the 4th century BC, Ostia Antica is reminiscent of Pompeii, but on a smaller scale and in a prettier, parklike setting. It makes for a fascinating visit and a welcome change from museums and churches. Fair weather and good walking shoes are requisites. On hot days, be there when the gates open or go late in the afternoon.

A visit to the excavations takes two to three hours, including 15–20 minutes for the museum.

Numbers in the margin correspond to numbers on the Rome Environs map.

① **Ostia Antica** was inhabited by a cosmopolitan population of rich businessmen, wily merchants, sailors, and slaves. The great *horrea* (warehouses) were built in the 2nd century AD to handle huge shipments of grain from Africa; the *insulae* (forerunners of the modern apartment building) provided housing for the growing population. Under the combined assaults of the barbarians and the Anopheles mosquito, and after the Tiber changed course, the port was eventually abandoned. Tidal mud and windblown sand covered the city, which lay buried until the beginning of this century. Now it has been extensively excavated and is well maintained. **Porta Romana,** one of the city's three gates, opens onto the **Decumanus Maximus,** the main thoroughfare crossing the city from end to end.

Black-and-white mosaic pavements representing Neptune and Amphitrite decorate the **Terme di Nettuno** (Baths of Neptune). Directly behind the baths is the barracks of the fire department, which played an important role in a town with warehouses full of valuable goods and foodstuffs.

On one side of the Decumanus Maximus is the beautiful **theater,** built by Augustus and completely restored by Septimius Severus in the 2nd century AD. In the vast Piazzale delle Corporazioni, where trade organizations similar to guilds had their offices, is the **Temple of Ceres:** this is appropriate for a town dealing in grain imports, since Ceres, who gave her name to cereal, was the goddess of agriculture. You can visit the **House of Apuleius,** built in Pompeiian style—containing fewer windows then, and built lower than those in Ostia. Next to it is the **Mithraeum,** with balconies and a hall decorated with symbols of the cult of Mithras. This men-only religion, imported from Persia, was especially popular with legionnaires.

On Via dei Molini you can see a **mill,** where grain for the warehouses next door was ground with the stones that are still there. Along Via di Diana you come upon a *thermopolium* (bar) with a marble counter and a fresco depicting the fruit and foodstuffs that were sold here. At the end of Via dei Dipinti is the **Museo Ostiense,** which displays some of the ancient sculptures and mosaics found among the ruins.

The **Forum** holds the monumental remains of the city's most important temple, dedicated to Jupiter, Juno, and Minerva; other ruins of baths; a basilica (in Roman times a basilica served as a secular hall of justice); and smaller temples.

Via Epagathiana leads toward the Tiber, where there are large warehouses, erected in the 2nd century AD to deal with the enormous amounts of grain imported into Rome during that period, the height of the Empire.

The **House of Cupid and Psyche,** a residential house, was named for a statue found there; you can see what remains of a large pool in an enclosed garden decorated with marble and mosaic motifs. It takes little imagination to notice that even in ancient times a premium was placed on water views: the house faces the shore, which would have been only about ⅓ km (¼ mi) away. On Via della Foce are the **House of Serapis,**

Rome Environs

Orvieto

Lago di Bolsena

Terni

S71

S2

Tiber

Bomarzo

Narni

S3

S209

S3

Marta

Viterbo

Villa Lante

Orte

S313

Rieti

S1 bis

Caprarola

Lago di Vico

S4

Tarquinia

Civita Castellana

V. Solaria

S493

S2

Monterosi

S3

A1

Tiber

Cassia

Civitavecchia

Lago di Bracciano

Autostrada Rome-L'Aquila

Bracciano

V. Flaminia

Autostrada del Sole

Mandela

Cerveteri

Vicovaro

A24

S1

A12

Bagni di Tivoli

3

5 Subiaco

V. Aurelia

2 Tivoli

Rome

V. Tiburtina

S5

Hadrian's Villa

Fiumicino

V. Prenestina

V. Casilina

S155

4 Palestrina

Ostia Antica 1

S8

V. del Mare

A2

Frascati

S. Cesareo

Lido di Ostia

Appia

Autostrada del Sole

S601

S148

S7

Lago di Albano

Velletri

Tyrrhenian Sea

S207

Latina

ITALY

Anzio

0   10 miles

0   15 km

a 2nd-century multilevel dwelling, and the **Baths of the Seven Wise Men,** named for a fresco found there. There is another apartment building on Cardo degli Aurighi.

The **Porta Marina** leads to what used to be the seashore. In the vicinity are the ruins of the **synagogue,** one of the oldest in the Western world. On Via Semita dei Cippi you can see the **House of Fortuna Annonaria,** the richly decorated house of a wealthy Ostian. This is another place to marvel at the skill of the mosaic artists and, at the same time, to realize that this really was someone's home. One of the rooms opens onto a secluded garden.

The admission charge to the **Ostia Antica excavations** includes entrance to the **Museo Ostiense** (Ostiense Museum), which is on the grounds. ⊠ *Via dei Romagnoli,* ☎ *06/5650022.* ⊡ *8,000 lire.* ☉ *Excavations daily 9 AM–1 hr before sunset, museum daily 9–1:30.*

Dining

$$ ✕ **Monumento.** Handily located near the entrance to the excavations, this appealing trattoria serves Roman specialties and seafood. ⊠ *Piazza Umberto I,* ☎ *06/5650021. AE, DC, MC, V. Closed Mon. and Aug. 20–Sept. 7.*

$$ ✕ **Sbarco di Enea.** Also near the excavations, this restaurant is heavy on ancient-Roman atmosphere, with Pompeiian-style frescoes and chariots in the garden. On summer evenings you dine outdoors by torchlight, served by waiters in Roman costume. You'll probably come for lunch, when you can enjoy *farfalle con granchio* (bow-tie pasta with crab sauce) or linguine with lobster sauce and other seafood specialties, without all the hoopla. ⊠ *Via dei Romagnoli 675,* ☎ *06/5650034. AE, MC. Closed Mon. and Feb.*

Arriving and Departing

By car, follow **Via del Mare** southwest, which leads directly from Rome to Ostia (a 30- to 40-minute trip).

There is regular **train service** to the Ostia Antica station from Ostiense train station, near Porta San Paolo; the ride takes about 30 minutes. A long walkway links Ostiense station with the Piramide stop on Metro B; save steps by making connections with the train from Ostiense at the Magliana stop on Metro B. Trains from Ostiense run every half hour.

Tivoli, Palestrina, and Subiaco

You will explore two of the Rome area's most attractive sights: Villa Adriana (Hadrian's Villa) and the Villa d'Este in Tivoli, though the road east from Rome to Tivoli passes through some uninspiring industrial areas and burgeoning suburbs. You'll know you're close when you see vast quarries of travertine marble and smell the sulfurous vapors of the little spa, Bagni di Tivoli. Both sites are outdoor and entail a lot of walking.

Only 27 km (17 mi) south of Tivoli on S636 and 37 km (23 mi) east of Rome along Via Prenestina, Palestrina is set on the slopes of Mt. Ginestro, from which it commands a sweeping view of the green plain and distant mountains.

You could continue on to Subiaco, tucked away in the mountains above Tivoli and Palestrina. This excursion is best made by car because it's nearly a 3-km (2-mi) walk from Subiaco to Santa Scolastica, and another half hour by footpath up to San Benedetto.

Tivoli

② **Hadrian's Villa,** 3 km (2 mi) south of Tivoli, should be visited first, especially in summer, to take advantage of cool mornings. Hadrian's Villa was an emperor's theme park, an exclusive retreat where the marvels of the classical world were reproduced for a ruler's pleasure. Hadrian, who succeeded Trajan as emperor in AD 117, was a man of genius and intellectual curiosity. Fascinated by the accomplishments of the Hellenistic world, he decided to re-create it for his own enjoyment by building this villa over a vast tract of land below the ancient settlement of Tibur. From AD 118 to 130, architects, laborers, and artists worked on the villa, periodically spurred on by the emperor himself, as he returned from another voyage full of ideas for even more daring constructions. After his death in AD 138, the fortunes of his villa declined. It was sacked by barbarians and Romans alike; by the Renaissance, many of his statues and decorations had ended up in the Villa d'Este. Still, it is an impressive complex.

The exhibits in the visitors' center at the entrance and the scale model in the building adjacent to the bar will increase your enjoyment of the villa by helping you make sense out of what can otherwise be a maze of ruins. It's not the single elements, but the peaceful and harmonious effect of the whole, that makes Hadrian's Villa such a treat. Oleanders, pines, and cypresses growing among the ruins heighten the visual impact. A visit here should take about 90 minutes. ⊠ *Villa Adriana.* 🎫 *8,000 lire.* ☉ *Daily 9 AM–90 min before sunset.*

③ **Villa d'Este** is Tivoli's main attraction. Ippolito d'Este was an active figure in the political intrigues of mid-16th-century Italy. He was also a cardinal, thanks to his grandfather, Alexander VI, the infamous Borgia pope. To console himself at a time when he saw his political star in decline, Ippolito tore down part of a Franciscan monastery that occupied the site he had chosen for his villa. Then the determined prelate diverted the Aniene River into a channel to run under the town and provide water for the Villa d'Este's fountains. Big, small, noisy, quiet, rushing, and running, the fountains create a late Renaissance playground. Though time is beginning to take its toll, and the fountains and gardens aren't as well kept as in the cardinal's day, it is easy to see why many travelers of the past considered Villa d'Este one of the most beautiful spots in Italy. Villa d'Este requires a lot of stair walking and takes about an hour. ⊠ *Villa d'Este, Tivoli.* 🎫 *5,000 lire.* ☉ *Daily 9 AM–90 min before sunset.*

DINING

$$$ ✗ **Adriano.** At the entrance to Hadrian's Villa this restaurant is a handy but pricey place to have lunch and to rest before heading up the hill to the Villa d'Este. The food is very good and the atmosphere relaxing. ⊠ *Via di Villa Adriana 194,* ☎ *0774/382235. AE, DC, MC, V. No dinner Sun.*

$ ✗ **Del Falcone.** A central location—on the main street leading off Largo Garibaldi—means that this restaurant is popular and often crowded. In the ample and rustic dining rooms, you can try homemade fettuccine and cannelloni. Country-style grilled meats are excellent. ⊠ *Via Trevio 34,* ☎ *0774/22358. No credit cards. Closed Mon.*

Palestrina

④ Palestrina is surprisingly little known outside Italy, except to students of ancient history and music lovers. Its most famous native son, Giovanni Pierluigi da Palestrina, born here in 1525, was the renowned composer of 105 masses, as well as madrigals, magnificats, and motets. But the town was celebrated long before the composer's lifetime.

Ancient Praeneste, modern Palestrina, was founded much earlier than Rome. It was the site of the Temple of Fortuna Primigenia, which dates from the beginning of the 2nd century BC. This was one of the biggest, richest, and most frequented temple complexes in all antiquity. People came from far and wide to consult its famous oracle, yet in modern times, no one had any idea of the extent of the complex until World War II bombings exposed ancient foundations that stretched way out into the plain below the town. It has since become clear that the temple area was larger than the town of Palestrina is today. Now you can make out the four superimposed terraces that formed the main part of the temple; they were built up on great arches and were linked by broad flights of stairs. The whole town sits on top of what was once the main part of the temple.

Large arches and terraces scale the hillside up to the **Palazzo Barberini,** built in the 17th century along the semicircular lines of the original temple. It's now a museum containing material found on the site, some dating back to the 4th century BC. The collection of splendid engraved bronze urns, plundered by thieves in 1991 and later recovered, takes second place to the chief attraction, a 1st-century-BC mosaic representing the Nile in flood. This delightful work—a large-scale composition in which form, color, and innumerable details captivate the eye—is alone worth the trip to Palestrina. But there's more: a model of the temple as it was in ancient times, which will help you appreciate the immensity of the original construction. ⊠ *Museo Nazionale Archeologico, Palazzo Barberini, Palestrina,* ☎ *06/9538100.* ⌨ *6,000 lire.* ☉ *Spring and fall, Tues.–Sun. 9–6; summer, Tues.–Sun. 9–7:30; winter, Tues.–Sun. 9–4.*

DINING

$$ ✕ **Stella Coccia.** In this dining room of a small, centrally located hotel
★ in Palestrina's public garden, you'll find simple decor, a cordial welcome, local dishes, such as light and freshly made fettuccine served with a choice of sauces, and more unusual items, such as pasta e fagioli *con frutti di mare* (with shellfish). ⊠ *Hotel Stella, Piazzale Liberazione,* ☎ *06/9538172. AE, DC, MC, V.*

Subiaco

❺ What draws travelers to Subiaco is the 6th-century **Monastery of St. Benedict,** a landmark of Western monasticism. Between the town and St. Benedict's hermitage on the mountainside is the **Convento di Santa Scolastica** (Convent of Saint Scholastic), the only one of the hermitages founded by St. Benedict to have survived the Lombard invasion of Italy in the 9th century. It has three cloisters; the oldest dates from the 13th century. The library, which is not open to visitors, contains some precious volumes; this was the site of the first print shop in Italy, set up in 1474. ⌨ *Free.* ☉ *Daily 9–12:30 and 4–7.*

The Monastery of St. Benedict was built over the grotto where the saint lived and meditated. Clinging to the cliff on nine great arches, it has resisted the assaults of humans for almost 800 years. Over the little wooden veranda at the entrance, a Latin inscription augurs PEACE TO THOSE WHO ENTER. Every inch of the upper church is covered with frescoes by Umbrian and Sienese artists of the 14th century. In front of the main altar, a stairway leads down to the lower church, carved out of the rock, with yet another stairway down to the grotto where Benedict lived as a hermit for three years. The frescoes here are even earlier than those above; look for the portrait of St. Francis of Assisi, painted from life in 1210, in the Chapel of St. Gregory, and for the oldest fresco in the monastery, in the Shepherd's Grotto. ⌨ *Free.* ☉ *Daily 9–12:30 and 3–6.*

In the town of Subiaco, the 14th-century **church of San Francesco** is decorated with frescoes by Il Sodoma. Ring the bell for admission.

DINING

$ ✕ **Belvedere.** This small hotel on the road between the town and the monasteries is equipped to feed crowds of skiers from the slopes of nearby Mt. Livata, as well as pilgrims on their way to St. Benedict's hermitage. The atmosphere is homey and cordial. Specialties include homemade fettuccine with a tasty ragù sauce and grilled meats and sausages. ⊠ *Via dei Monasteri 33,* ☎ *0774/85531. Reservations not accepted. No credit cards.*

$ ✕ **Mariuccia.** This modern barnlike restaurant, close to the monasteries, caters to wedding parties and other groups but is calm enough on weekdays. There's a large garden and a good view from the picture windows. House specialties are homemade fettuccine with porcini mushrooms and *scaloppe al* tartufo (truffled veal scallops). In the summer you dine outdoors under bright umbrellas. ⊠ *Via Sublacense,* ☎ *0774/84851. No credit cards. Closed Mon. and Nov.*

Tivoli, Palestrina, and Subiaco A to Z

ARRIVING AND DEPARTING

By Bus. COTRAL buses leave for **Tivoli** every 15 minutes from the terminal at the Rebbibia stop on Metro B, but not all take the route that passes near Hadrian's Villa. Inquire which bus passes closest to Villa Adriana and tell the driver to let you off there. The ride takes about 60 minutes. For **Palestrina,** take the COTRAL bus from the Anagnina stop on Metro A. From Rome to **Subiaco,** take the COTRAL bus from the Rebbibia stop on Metro B; buses leave every 40 minutes; the circuitous trip takes one hour and 45 minutes.

By Car. For Tivoli, take Via Tiburtina or the Rome–L'Aquila autostrada (**A24**). To get to **Palestrina** directly from Rome, take either Via Prenestina or Via Casilina or take the Autostrada del Sole (**A2**) to the San Cesareo exit and follow signs for Palestrina; this trip takes about one hour. It's best to drive from Rome to **Subiaco.** Take **S155** east for about 40 km (25 mi) before turning left onto **S411** for the remaining 25 km (15 mi) to Subiaco; the trip takes about 70 minutes.

By Train. FS trains connect Rome's Termini and Tiburtina stations with **Tivoli** in about 30 minutes; Villa d'Este is about a 20-minute walk from the station in Tivoli. The FS train from Termini Station to **Palestrina** takes about 40 minutes; you can then board a bus from the train station to the center of town.

GETTING AROUND

By Bus. There is local bus service between **Tivoli** and **Palestrina,** but check schedules locally.

By Car. From **Tivoli** to **Palestrina,** follow signs for Via Prenestina and Palestrina. To get to **Subiaco** from either Tivoli or Palestrina, take the autostrada for L'Aquila (**A24**) to the Vicovaro–Mandela exit, then follow the local road to Subiaco.

GUIDED TOURS

CIT (☎ 06/47941) has half-day excursions to Villa d'Este in Tivoli. **American Express** (☎ 06/67641), **Appian Line** (☎ 06/4884151), and **Carrani Tours** (☎ 06/4824194) have tours that include Hadrian's Villa.

VISITOR INFORMATION

Tivoli (⊠ Largo Garibaldi, ☎ 0774/21249). **Subiaco** (⊠ Via Cadorna 59, ☎ 0774/822013).

ROME A TO Z

Arriving and Departing

By Bus

There is no central bus terminal in Rome. **COTRAL** (☎ 06/5915551) is the suburban bus company that connects Rome with outlying areas and other cities in the Lazio region. Long-distance and suburban buses terminate either near Tiburtina Station or near outlying Metro stops such as Rebbibia and Anagnina. The COTRAL terminal at the Lepanto Metro station, for buses to Civitavecchia and towns along the coast northwest of Rome, will be relocated when the new leg of Metro A is completed. For COTRAL bus information call weekdays 7:45 AM–4:40 PM, Saturday 7:45 AM–2 PM.

By Car

The main access routes from the north are **A1** (Autostrada del Sole) from Milan and Florence or the **A12/E80** highway from Genoa. The principal route to or from points south, including Naples, is the **A2**. All highways connect with the **GRA**, which channels traffic into the center. Markings on the GRA are confusing: take time to study the route you need.

By Plane

Most international flights and all domestic flights arrive at **Leonardo da Vinci Airport,** also known as **Fiumicino,** 30 km (19 mi) outside the city. Some international and charter flights land at **Ciampino,** a civil and military airport on Via Appia Nuova, 15 km (9 mi) from the center of Rome. For airport and flight information for Fiumicino (☎ 06/65953640); for Ciampino (☎ 06/794941).

BETWEEN THE AIRPORT AND DOWNTOWN

By Car. Follow the signs for Rome on the expressway from the airport, which links with the Grande Raccordo Anulare (**GRA**), the beltway around Rome. The direction you take on the GRA depends on where your hotel is, so get directions from the car-rental people at the airport.

By Taxi. A taxi from the airport to the center of town costs about 70,000–80,000 lire, including supplements for airport service and luggage, and the ride takes 30–40 minutes, depending on traffic. Private limousines can be hired at booths in the arrivals hall; they charge a little more than taxis but can take more passengers. Ignore gypsy drivers; stick to yellow or white cabs. A booth inside the arrivals hall provides taxi information.

By Train. To get to downtown Rome from Fiumicino Airport, you have a choice of two trains. Inquire at the airport (at EPT or train information counters) as to which takes you closest to your hotel. The non-stop **Airport-Termini express** (marked FS and run by the state railway) takes you directly to Track 22 at Termini station, Rome's main train station, well served by taxis and the hub of Metro and bus lines. The ride to Termini takes 30 minutes; departures are hourly, beginning at 7:50 AM from the airport, with a final departure at 10:05 PM. Tickets cost 13,000 lire. **FM1,** the other airport train, runs from the airport to Rome and beyond, with its terminal in Monterotondo, a suburban town to the east. The main stops in Rome are at Trastevere, Ostiense, and Tiburtina stations; at each you can find taxis and bus and/or metro connections to other parts of Rome. This train runs from Fiumicino from 6:15 AM to 12:15 AM, with departures every 20 minutes, a little less frequent in off-hours. The ride to Tiburtina takes 40 minutes. Tickets cost 7,000 lire. For either train you buy your ticket at automatic vending machines (you need Italian currency). There are ticket counters at some stations (⊠ Termini Track 22, Trastevere, Tiburtina). Date-stamp the ticket at the gate before you board.

By Train

Termini Station is Rome's main train terminal; the **Tiburtina** and **Ostiense** stations serve some long-distance trains, many commuter trains, and the FM1 line to Fiumicino Airport. Some trains for Pisa and Genoa leave Rome from, or pass through, the **Trastevere** Station. For train information, call ☎ 06/4775, 7 AM–10:30 PM. You can find English-speaking staff at the information office at Termini Station, or ask for information at travel agencies. You can purchase tickets up to two months in advance either at the main stations or at travel agencies bearing the FS (Ferrovie dello Stato) emblem (☞ Train Travel *in* The Gold Guide). Lines at station ticket windows may be very long, and electronic ticket machines are complex, though they have instructions in English; you can save time by buying your ticket at a travel agency. Remember that you can reserve a seat up to one day in advance at a travel agency, or up to three hours in advance at a train station. Tickets for train rides within a radius of 100 km (62 mi) of Rome can be purchased at tobacco shops as well as at ticket machines on the main concourse. Like all train tickets, they must be date-stamped before you board, at the machine near the track.

Getting Around

Although most of Rome's sights are in a relatively circumscribed area, the city is too large to be seen solely on foot. Take the Metro (subway), a bus, or a taxi to the area you plan to visit, and expect to do a lot of walking once you're there. Wear a pair of comfortable, sturdy shoes, preferably with rubber or crepe soles to cushion the impact of the *sampietrini* (cobblestones). Heed our advice on security and get away from the noise and polluted air of heavily trafficked streets by taking parallel streets whenever possible. You can buy transportation-route maps at newsstands, and ATAC (Rome's public transit authority) information and ticket booths may have free maps, which can also be obtained from the municipal information booths. The free city map distributed by Rome EPT offices is good; it also shows Metro and bus routes, although bus routes are not always marked clearly.

Rome's integrated **Metrebus** transportation system includes buses and trams (ATAC), Metro and suburban trains and buses (COTRAL), and some other suburban trains (FS) run by the state railways. A ticket valid for 75 minutes on any combination of buses and trams and one entrance to the Metro costs 1,500 lire. You are supposed to date-stamp your ticket when you board the first vehicle, stamping it again when boarding for the last time within 75 minutes. Tickets are sold at tobacconists, newsstands, some coffee bars, automatic ticket machines positioned in Metro stations and some bus stops, and at ATAC and COTRAL ticket booths (in some Metro stations, on the lower concourse at Termini station, and at a few main bus terminals). A BIG tourist ticket, valid for one day on all public transport, costs 6,000 lire. A weekly ticket (Settimanale, also known as CIS) costs 24,000 lire and can be purchased only at ATAC booths. Try to avoid the rush hours (8–9, 1–2:30, 7–8), and beware of pickpockets, especially when boarding and getting off vehicles, particularly on the Metro and on Buses 64 (Termini–Vatican) and 218 and 660 (Catacombs). When purchasing tickets for excursions outside Rome on COTRAL buses or trains, buy a return ticket, too, to save time at the other end.

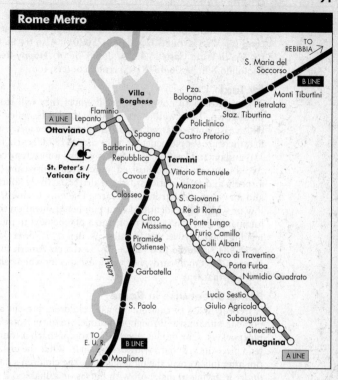

By Bicycle

Pedaling through Villa Borghese, along the Tiber, and through the center of the city when traffic is light is a pleasant way to see the sights, but remember: Rome is hilly. (For information on bicycle rentals, ☞ Outdoor Activities and Sports, *above*.) **Secret Walks** (✉ Viale Medaglie d'Oro 127, 00136 Rome, ☎ 06/39728728) organizes all-day bike tours of Rome covering major sights and some hidden ones; summer tours include a stop for a swim. The same tours are available by moped.

By Bus

Orange **ATAC** (☎ 06/46954444 information) city buses and tram lines run from about 6 AM to about midnight, with night buses (indicated N) on some lines. *Remember to board at the back and exit at the middle.* The compact electric buses of lines 117 and 119 take handy routes through the center of Rome that can save lots of steps.

By Horse-Drawn Carriage

A ride in a horse-drawn carriage can be fun when traffic is light, especially on a Sunday or holiday or during the summer. Come to terms with the driver before starting out. City-regulated rates are about 50,000 lire for a 30-minute ride, and about 85,000 for an hour. Refuse to pay more. You can find carriages at Piazza di Spagna, Piazza Venezia, and on Via del Corso near the Hotel Plaza.

By Metro

This is the easiest and fastest way to get around and there are stops near most of the main tourist attractions. The Metro opens at 5:30 AM, and the last trains leave the farthest station at 11:30 PM (on Saturday night trains run until 12:30 AM). There are two lines—A and B—which intersect at Termini Station.

By Scooter

You can rent a moped or scooter and mandatory helmet at **Scoot-a-Long** (✉ Via Cavour 302, ☎ 06/6780206). Also try **St. Peter's Moto** (✉ Via di Porta Castello 43, ☎ 06/6875714). **Happy Rent** (✉ Piazza Esquilino 8/h, ☎ 06/4818185) rents scooters, too.

By Taxi

Taxis in Rome do not cruise, but if empty they will stop if you flag them down. Taxis wait at stands and can also be called by phone, in which case you're charged a small supplement. The meter starts at 4,500 lire; there are supplements for night service (5,000 extra from 10 PM–7 AM) and on Sunday and holidays, as well as for each piece of baggage. Avoid unmarked, unauthorized, unmetered gypsy cabs (numerous at airports and train stations), whose drivers actively solicit your trade and may demand astronomical fares. Use only licensed, metered yellow or white cabs, identified by a numbered shield on the side, an illuminated taxi sign on the roof, and a plaque next to the license plate reading SERVIZIO PUBBLICO. To call a cab, dial ☎ 3875, ☎ 3570, ☎ 4994, or ☎ 88177. **Radio Taxi** (☎ 06/3875) accepts American Express and Diners Club credit cards, but you must specify when calling that you will pay that way.

Being Streetwise in Rome

A (repeat) word of caution: "gypsy" children, present around sights popular with tourists throughout Europe, are rife in Rome and are adept pickpockets. One modus operandi is to approach a tourist and proffer a piece of cardboard with writing on it. While the unsuspecting victim attempts to read the message *on* it, the children's hands are busy *under* it, trying to make off with purses or valuables. If you see such a group (recognizable by their unkempt appearance), do not even allow them near you—they are quick and know more tricks than you do. Also be aware of persons, usually young men, who ride by on motorbikes, grab the shoulder strap of your bag or camera, and step on the gas. Wear or carry your bag on the side away from the street edge of the sidewalk, or, best of all, wear a money belt. Don't carry more money than you need, and don't carry your passport unless you need it to exchange money. A useful expression to ward off panhandlers is *"Vai via!"* (Go away!).

Contacts and Resources

Car Rental

Avis (☎ 06/42824728). **Budget** (☎ 06/4820966). **Eurodollar** (☎ 06/167018668). **Hertz** (☎ 06/167808016). **Maggiore** (☎ 06/167867067).

Consulates

U.S. Consulate (✉ Via Veneto 121, ☎ 06/46741). **Canadian Consulate** (✉ Via Zara 30, ☎ 06/445981). **U.K. Consulate** (✉ Via Venti Settembre 80A, ☎ 06/4825441).

Doctors and Dentists

Salvator Mundi Hospital (☎ 06/588961). **Rome American Hospital** (☎ 06/22551).

Emergencies

Police (☎ 06/4686). **Ambulance** (Red Cross) (☎ 06/5510).

English-Language Bookstores

Economy Book and Video Center (✉ Via Torino 136, ☎ 06/4746877). **Anglo-American Bookstore** (✉ Via della Vite 102, ☎ 06/6784347). **Lion Bookshop** (✉ Via dei Greci, 33/36, ☎ 06/32654007). **Open Door** (✉

Via della Lungaretta 25 Trastevere, ☎ 06/5896478,). **Corner Bookstore** (⊠ Via del Moro 48, Trastevere, ☎ 06/5836942).

Guided Tours

ORIENTATION TOURS

American Express (⊠ Piazza di Spagna 38, ☎ 06/67641), **CIT** (⊠ Piazza della Repubblica 64, ☎ 06/47941), **Appian Line** (☎ 06/4884151), and other operators offer three-hour tours in air-conditioned 60-passenger buses with English-speaking guides. There are four standard itineraries: "Ancient Rome" (including the Roman Forum and Colosseum), "Classic Rome" (including St. Peter's Basilica, Trevi Fountain, and the Janiculum Hill), "Christian Rome" (some major churches and the Catacombs), and "The Vatican Museums and Sistine Chapel." Most cost about 53,000 lire, but the Vatican Museums tour costs about 60,000 lire. American Express tours depart from Piazza di Spagna, and CIT from Piazza della Repubblica, both with some hotel pickups; Appian Line picks you up at your hotel.

American Express and other operators can provide a luxury car for up to three people, a limousine for up to seven, and a minibus for up to nine—all with English-speaking driver—but guide service is extra. Almost all operators offer "Rome by Night" tours, with or without pizza or dinner and entertainment. You can book tours through travel agents.

Though operators and names change, there is usually some kind of bus tour following a continuous circle route through the center of town, stopping at important sites where you can get on and off at will. Check with the Rome tourist information offices for the name of the current operator and schedules.

The least-expensive organized sightseeing tour of Rome is run by **ATAC** (☎ 06/46954444 information), the municipal bus company. Bus 110 tours leave from Piazza dei Cinquecento, in front of Termini Station, last about three hours, and cost about 15,000 lire. The driver provides a commentary, and you're given an illustrated guide with additional information. Buy tickets at the ATAC information booth in front of Termini Station; there is at least one tour daily, departing at 2:30 (3:30 in summer).

The least-expensive sightseeing "tours" of Rome are the routes of certain buses and trams that pass major sights. Time your ride to avoid rush hours. The small electric Bus 119 scoots through the heart of Old Rome, with stops near the Pantheon, the Spanish Steps, and Piazza del Popolo, among other sights. Several buses have long routes crossing Piazza Venezia, heart of the city. They are Bus 56 from Via Po and Via Veneto to Trastevere; Bus 62 from Porta Pia to the Vatican walls; Bus 81 from San Giovanni in Laterano to the Vatican walls; Bus 492 from Tiburtina station to the Vatican walls; Bus 90 from the Baths of Caracalla to Foro Italico. Trams 13 and 19 offer views of many neighborhoods. The fare for 75 minutes of sightseeing is a bargain 1,500 lire.

PERSONAL GUIDES

American Express (⊠ Piazza di Spagna 38, ☎ 06/67641). **CIT** (⊠ Piazza della Repubblica 64, ☎ 06/47941). Main **EPT** (⊠ Via Parigi 5, ☎ 06/48899253).

SPECIAL-INTEREST TOURS

You can make your own arrangements (at no cost) to attend a public papal audience in the Vatican or at the pope's summer residence at Castel Gandolfo (☞ The Vatican *in* Exploring Rome, *above*). You can also book through agencies, which take you by bus to the Vatican for the audience, show you some sights along the way, and return you to or near your hotel, for about 40,000 lire. The excursion for the pope's noon blessing on summer Sundays at Castel Gandolfo costs about 45,000 lire. Agencies that arrange these tours include **CIT**, **Appian Line**, and **Carrani Tours** (☞ Travel Agencies, *below*).

WALKING TOURS

Secret Walks (⊠ Viale Medaglie d'Oro 127, 00136 Rome, ☎ 06/39728728) has repertories of theme walks for small groups conducted in English by connoisseurs of the city who give an insider's view of Rome's major sights as well as its hidden corners. **Scala Reale** (⊠ Via Varese 46, 00185 Rome, ☎ 06/44700898, in US 800–732–2863, ext. 4052) is similar to Secret Walks. These agencies also offer full-day walks, evening strolls, bike or scooter tours, a tour for the physically disabled, and excursions outside the city.

If you have a reasonable knowledge of Italian, you can take advantage of the free guided visits and walking tours organized by Rome's cultural associations and the city council for museums and monuments. These usually take place on Sunday mornings. Check the daily newspapers.

Late-Night Pharmacies

The pharmacies below have some English-speaking staff. **Farmacia Internazionale Capranica** (⊠ Piazza Capranica 96, ☎ 06/6794680). **Farmacia Internazionale Barberini** (⊠ Piazza Barberini 49, ☎ 06/4825456). **Farmacia Cola di Rienzo** (⊠ Via Cola di Rienzo 213, ☎ 06/3243130). Most are open 8:30–1 and 4–8; some are open all night. Pharmacies take turns opening on Sunday. A schedule is posted in each pharmacy.

Travel Agencies

American Express (⊠ Piazza di Spagna 38, ☎ 06/67641). **CIT** (⊠ Piazza della Repubblica 64, ☎ 06/47941). **CTS** (⊠ Via Genova 16, ☎ 06/46791 or 06/4679271) specializes in youth and budget travel and discount fares. **Appian Line** (⊠ Via Barberini 109, ☎ 06/4884151) arranges trips to the Vatican. Also try **Carrani Tours** (⊠ Via Vittorio Emanuele Orlando 95, ☎ 06/4880510).

Visitor Information

EPT (⊠ Via Parigi 5, ☎ 06/48899255; ⊠ Termini Station, near Track 4; ⊠ Leonardo da Vinci Airport). Municipal tourist-information booths are at Largo Goldoni (⊠ At the corner of Via Condotti and Via del Corso in the Spanish Steps area), Via dei Fori Imperiali (⊠ At the corner of Via Cavour and across the street from the entrance to the Roman Forum), and Via Nazionale (⊠ in front of the Palazzo delle Esposizioni). All will help you find a hotel room (☞ Lodging, *above*).

You can find helpful information, including museum hours and listings of what's going on in Rome in the English language biweekly *Wanted in Rome* and in the English pages of the weekly *Romac'è,* both available on newsstands. Many hotels distribute the free booklet *Un Ospite a Roma (A Guest in Rome)*, with selected listings.

3 Florence

Birthplace of the Renaissance, Florence has been a mecca for travelers since the 19th century, when English ladies flocked here to stay in charming pensiones and paint watercolors. They were captivated by a wistful Botticelli smile, impressed by the graceful dignity of Donatello's bronze David, *and moved by Michelangelo's provocative* Slaves *twisting restlessly in their marble prisons. Since then, millions have followed in their footsteps.*

Updated by
Barbara Walsh
Angelillo

FLORENCE IS ONE OF THE PREEMINENT TREASURES of Europe, and it is a time-honored mecca for sightseers from all over the world. But as a city, Florence (Firenze to Italians) can be surprisingly forbidding—at first glance. Its architecture is predominantly Early Renaissance and retains many of the implacable, fortresslike features of pre-Renaissance palazzi, whose facades were mostly meant to keep intruders out rather than to invite sightseers in. With the exception of a very few buildings, the classical dignity of the High Renaissance and the exuberant invention of the Baroque are not to be found here. The typical Florentine exterior gives nothing away, as if obsessively guarding secret treasures within.

The treasures, of course, are very real. And far from being a secret, they are famous the world over. The city is an artistic treasure trove of unique and incomparable proportions. A single historical fact explains the phenomenon: Florence gave birth to the Renaissance. In the early 15th century the study of antiquity—of the glory that was Greece and the grandeur that was Rome—became a Florentine passion, and with it came a new respect for learning and a new creativity in art and architecture. In Florence, that remarkable creativity is everywhere in evidence.

Though there had been a town here since Roman times, it wasn't until the 11th and 12th centuries that Florence started to make its mark. At this time Florentine cloth began to do particularly well in foreign markets, the various trades organized themselves in powerful unions (or *arti*), and the Florentines took over as the most important bankers in Europe thanks to their florin-based currency. They were perpetually at loggerheads with other Tuscan towns, such as Pisa and Siena, and this is why Florence has such a defensive air, and why its cathedral—the town's symbol—is so huge: it had to be bigger and more splendid than anyone else's. They kept expanding, despite periodic devastating plagues, and equally destructive civil strife. (One of the victims of the internal rift was the great poet Dante, author of the *Divine Comedy,* who happened to be on the losing side; he died in exile, cursing his native town.)

Meanwhile the banking families became more and more powerful, and in the early 15th century one of them, the Medici, began to outstrip all others. The most famous of them, Lorenzo de' Medici, was not only an astute politician, he was also a highly educated man and a great patron of the arts. He gathered around him, in the late 15th century, a court of poets, artists, philosophers, architects, and musicians, and organized all kinds of cultural events, festivals, and tournaments. It was Florence's golden period of creativity, when art made great leaps toward a new naturalism through the study of perspective and anatomy, when architects forged a new style based on the techniques used by the ancient Romans. The Renaissance man was born, a man who, like Leonardo da Vinci, could design a canal, paint a fresco, or solve a mathematical problem with equal ease.

Things changed with Lorenzo's death in 1492. First, his successor handed over most of Florence's key territories to the invading French king, Charles VIII, and then the city was sacked by the French army. A "republic" was set up, and one of its most vocal citizens was a charismatic, hellfire-preaching Dominican monk, Savonarola, who activated a moral cleanup operation to which the Florentines took with fanatical enthusiasm. He himself was accused of heresy and executed, or hanged (his corpse was burned on a pyre in Piazza della Signoria). After a decade or so of internal unrest, the republic fell and the Medici were recalled to power. But even with the Medici back, Florence never regained its former prestige. By the 1530s all the major artistic talent had left the city—Michelangelo, for one, had settled in Rome. The now ineffectual Medici, calling themselves grand dukes, remained nominally in power until the line died out in 1737, and thereafter Florence passed from the Austrians to the French and back again, until the mid-19th-century unification of Italy, when for seven years it became the capital of Italy under King Vittorio Emanuele II.

Florence was "discovered" in the 19th century by the first art historians. It became a mecca for travelers, particularly the Romantics, including Keats and Shelley, who were inspired by the grandeur of its classicism and the elegance of its child, the Renaissance. It was also the favorite city of those English ladies of the *Room-with-a-View* type, who flocked here to stay in charming pensiones and paint romantic watercolors of the surrounding countryside. For them, the allure of Florence lay in its artistic treasures: they were captivated by a wistful Botticelli smile, impressed by the graceful dignity of Donatello's bronze *David*, and moved by Michelangelo's provocative *Slaves* twisting restlessly in their marble prisons. Today, millions of modern visitors follow in their footsteps. As the sun sets over the Arno and, as Mark Twain described it, "overwhelms Florence with tides of color that make all the sharp lines dim and faint and turn the solid city to a city of dreams," it's hard not to fall under the city's magic spell.

Pleasures and Pastimes

Art
No city in Italy can match Florence's astounding artistic wealth. Important paintings and sculptures are everywhere, and art scholars and connoisseurs have been investigating the subtleties and complexities of these works for hundreds of years. But what makes the art of Florence a revelation to the ordinary sightseer is a simple fact that scholarship often ignores: an astounding percentage of Florence's art is just plain beautiful. Nowhere in Italy—perhaps in all of Europe—is the act of looking at art more rewarding.

Dining
Florentines are justifiably proud of their robust food, claiming that it became the basis for French cuisine when Catherine de' Medici took a battery of Florentine chefs with her when she reluctantly relocated to become Queen of France in the 16th century. You can sample such specialties as creamy *fagioli al fiasco* (slow-cooked beans) and *ribollita* (a thick soup of white beans, bread, cabbage, and onions) in bustling trattorias where you share long wooden tables set with paper place mats. The casual, convivial atmosphere in these places puts you in the Florentine mode. Like the Florentines, take a break at a wineshop during the day and discover some little-known but excellent types of Chianti.

Lodging
Whether you are in a five-star hotel or a more modest establishment you may have one of the greatest pleasures of all: a room with a view. Florence has so many famous landmarks that it's not hard to find lodgings with a vista to remember. And the equivalent of the genteel pensiones of yesteryear still exist, though they are now officially classified as hotels. Usually small and intimate, they often have a quaint appeal that fortunately does not preclude modern plumbing.

Shopping
Since the days of the medieval guilds, Florence has been synonymous with fine craftsmanship and good business. Such time-honored Florentine

specialties as antiques (and reproductions), bookbinding, jewelry, lace, leather goods, silk, and straw attest to that. More recently, the Pitti fashion shows and the burgeoning textile industry in nearby Prato have added fine clothing to the long list of merchandise available in the shops of Florence. Another medieval feature is the distinct feel of the different shopping areas, a throwback to the days when each district supplied a different product.

EXPLORING FLORENCE

Sightseeing in Florence is space intensive. Everything that you probably want to see is concentrated in a relatively small district in the historic core of the city. But there is so much packed into the area that you may find yourself slogging from one mind-boggling sight to another and feeling overwhelmed. If you are not an inveterate museum enthusiast, take it easy. Don't try to absorb every painting or fresco that comes into view. There is second-rate art even in the Galleria degli Uffizi and the Palazzo Pitti (*especially* the Pitti), so find some favorites and enjoy them at your leisure.

Walking through the streets and alleyways in Florence is a discovery in itself, but to save time and energy (especially on your third or so day in the city), make use of the efficient bus system. Buses also provide the least-fatiguing way to reach Piazzale Michelangelo, San Miniato, and the Fortezza Belvedere. It is easy to make excursions to, say, Fiesole or the Medici villas by city bus. Most churches are usually open from 8 or 9 until noon or 12:30, and from 3 or 4 until about 7. Usually the Duomo in larger towns and cities is open all day throughout the year.

In between your blitzes into the Renaissance and beyond, stop to breathe in the city, the marvelous synergy between history and modern Florentine life. Firenze is a living, bustling metropolis that has managed to preserve its predominantly medieval street plan and predominantly Renaissance infrastructure while successfully adapting to the insistent demands of 20th-century life. Do not miss the forest for the trees. And, speaking of forests, during the Guelph–Ghibelline conflict of the 13th and 14th centuries, Florence was a forest of towers—more than 200 of them, if the smaller three- and four-story towers are included. Today only a handful survive, but if you look closely you'll find them as you explore the city's core.

Numbers in the text correspond to numbers in the margin and on the Florence map.

Great Itineraries

You can see most of Florence's outstanding sights in three days. Plan your day around the opening hours of museums and churches; to gain a length on the tour groups in high season, go very early in the morning or around closing time. If you can, allow a day to explore each neighborhood.

IF YOU HAVE 3 DAYS

Spend day one exploring the historic core of Florence, which will give you an eyeful of such masterpieces as Ghiberti's renowned bronze doors at the Battistero (Baptistery), Giotto's Campanile, Brunelleschi's cupola hovering atop the Duomo, Botticelli's mystical spring muse at the Galleria degli Uffizi (Uffizi Gallery). On day two, wander north of the Duomo and take in the superb treasure trove of works ranging from Michelangelo's *David* at the Galleria dell'Accademia (Accademia Gallery) to the lavish frescos at the Cappella dei Magi and the Museo di San Marco. On this afternoon (or on the afternoon of day three) head southeast to Santa Croce or west to Santa Maria Novella. On the third day, cross the Ponte Vecchio to the Arno's southern bank and explore the Oltrarno district, being sure not miss the Brunelleschi-designed church of Santo Spirito, Masaccio's frescoes in the church of Santa Maria del Carmine, and the effusion of local color.

IF YOU HAVE 5 DAYS

Break down the above itinerary into shorter ones, adding a few optional sites, such as Piazzale Michelangelo, halfway up a hill on the Arno's southern bank—where the expansive view of the city is yours to savor—and San Miniato, farther up the same hill, or the Cenacolo di Sant'Apollonia, on the northern part of the city center, near the Museo di San Marco. At the Duomo, climb Giotto's Campanile, which also affords breathtaking views of the city. Take Bus 7 from the station or Piazza del Duomo to enchanting Fiesole. Spend more time in the Galleria degli Uffizi and Bargello or one of the smaller museums such as the Museo dell'Opificio delle Pietre Dure, southeast of and just around the corner from the Galleria dell'Accademia, or the excellent Museo di Storia della Scienza, on the Arno, immediately east of the Galleria degli Uffizi, and the Museo di Santa Maria Novella.

IF YOU HAVE 8 DAYS

Refer to the itineraries above, but add an all-day excursion to Siena or a couple of half-day trips to the Medici villas around Florence (☞ Side Trips, *below*). Visit more of Florence's interesting smaller churches, including Santa Maria Maddalena dei Pazzi, about four blocks east of the Galleria dell'Accademia; in the chapter hall is Perugino's masterful *Crucifixion*. On the trail of additional and little known artistic gems, see Andrea del Castagno's fresco of The Last Supper in the Cenacolo di Sant'Apollonia, northwest of the Museo di San Marco. There are similar treasures in the Chiostro dello Scalzo, just north of the Museo di San Marco, and the Cenacolo di Santo Spirito, west of Piazza Pitti.

The Historic Heart of Florence: From the Duomo to the Giardini Boboli

To say that Florence's historic center, stretching from the Piazza del Duomo in the north to the Giardini Boboli across the Arno to the south, is beautiful could be misconstrued as an understatement. Indeed, this relatively small area is home to some of the most important artistic treasures in the world. This smorgasbord of churches, medieval towers, Renaissance *palazzi* (palaces), and world-class museums and galleries is not a static testimony to the artistic and architectural genius of the past millennium, but a shrine to some of the most outstanding aesthetic achievements of Western history.

A Good Walk

Start at the **Duomo** ① and **Battistero** ②, climbing the **Campanile** ③ if you wish, then visit the **Museo dell'Opera del Duomo** ④, behind the Duomo. You can go directly south from in front of the Duomo to the Piazza della Signoria by way of Via Calzaiuoli, passing **Orsanmichele** ⑤, or go instead directly south from the Museo dell'Opera del Duomo along Via del Proconsolo to the **Bargello** ⑥ (opposite the ancient Badia Fiorentina, built in 1285). From the Bargello head west to Via Calzaiuoli, then south to discover the architectural splendors of the **Piazza della Signoria** ⑦, including the Loggia dei Lanzi and the **Palazzo Vecchio** ⑧. The **Palazzo degli Uffizi** ⑨, Italy's most important art gallery, is off the south side of the piazza. Leave the piazza from the southwest corner along Via Vacchereccia. To the left, at the corner with Via Por Santa Maria (which is lined with stores), is the **Mercato Nuovo** ⑩, whose stalls

are packed with typical Florentine wares. Follow Via Por Santa Maria
to the river and Florence's most famous bridge, the **Ponte Vecchio** ⑪.

TIMING

Before much of the historic heart of Florence was closed to traffic, you
had to keep dodging passing cars and mopeds as you walked the narrow streets. Now you have to elbow your way through moving masses
of fellow tourists, especially in the neighborhood delimited by the
Duomo, Piazza Signoria, Uffizi, and Ponte Vecchio. It takes about 40
minutes to walk the route, with 45 minutes to one hour each for the
Museo dell'Opera del Duomo and for Palazzo della Signoria; one to
1½ hours for the Bargello and a minimum of two hours for the Uffizi.
To avoid the crowds, you may want to make this walk in the afternoon, when all the sights and museums (except the Bargello) are open.

A special museum ticket valid for six months at seven city museums,
including the Palazzo Vecchio, the Museum of Firenze Com'Era (Museum of Florentine History), and the Museum of Santa Maria Novella,
costs 15,000 lire and is a good buy if you're planning to do some of
these museums. Inquire at any city museum.

Sights to See

Badia Fiorentina. This ancient church was built in 1285; its graceful
bell tower (best seen from the interior courtyard) is one of the most
beautiful in Florence. The interior of the church proper was half-
heartedly remodeled in the Baroque style during the 17th century; its
best-known work of art is Filippino Lippi's delicate *Apparition of the
Virgin to St. Bernard* (1486), on the left as you enter. The painting—
one of Lippi's finest—is in superb condition and is worth exploring in
detail. The Virgin's hands are perhaps the most beautiful in the city.
(To illuminate, drop a coin in the box near the floor to the painting's
right). ⊠ *Via del Proconsolo*.

★ ❻ **Bargello.** During the Renaissance this building was used as a prison,
and the exterior served as a "most-wanted" billboard: effigies of notorious criminals and Medici enemies were painted on its walls. Today,
it houses the **Museo Nazionale**, home to what is probably the finest
collection of Renaissance sculpture in Italy. Michelangelo, Donatello,
and Benvenuto Cellini are the preeminent masters here, and the concentration of masterworks is remarkable, though they stand among an
eclectic array of arms, ceramics, and enamels. For Renaissance art lovers,
the Bargello is to sculpture what the Uffizi is to painting.

One particular display—easily overlooked—should not be missed. In
1402 Filippo Brunelleschi and Lorenzo Ghiberti competed to earn the
most prestigious commission of the day: the decoration of the north
doors of the baptistery in Piazza del Duomo. For the competition, each
designed a bronze bas-relief panel on the theme of the Sacrifice of Isaac;
both panels are on display, side by side, in the room devoted to the
sculpture of Donatello on the upper floor. The judges chose Ghiberti
for the commission; you can decide for yourself whether or not they
were right. ⊠ *Via del Proconsolo 4,* ☎ *055/2388606.* ▭ *8,000 lire.*
⊙ *Daily 8:30–2. Closed 1st, 3rd, 5th Sun. and 2nd, 4th Mon. of
month.*

★ ❷ **Battistero** (Baptistery). The octagonal baptistery is one of the supreme
monuments of the Italian Romanesque and one of Florence's oldest.
Local legend has that it was once a Roman temple of Mars; modern
excavations, however, suggest its foundation was laid in the 6th or 7th
century AD, well after the collapse of the Roman Empire. The round-
arched Romanesque decoration on the exterior probably dates from
the 11th or 12th century. The interior ceiling mosaics (finished in

1297) are justly famous, but—glitteringly beautiful as they are—they could never outshine the building's most renowned feature: its bronze Renaissance doors decorated with panels crafted by Lorenzo Ghiberti (1378–1455). The doors, on which Ghiberti spent most of his adult life (1403–52), are on the north and east sides of the baptistery—at least copies are—and the Gothic south door panels were designed by Andrea Pisano in 1330. The originals of the Ghiberti doors were removed to protect them from the effects of pollution and acid rain and have been beautifully restored; some of the panels are now on display in the Cathedral Museum (☞ Museo dell'Opera del Duomo, *below*).

Ghiberti's north doors depict scenes from the life of Christ; his later east doors, facing the Duomo facade, depict scenes from the Old Testament. They are worth a close examination, for they are very different in style and illustrate with great clarity the artistic changes that marked the beginning of the Renaissance. Look at the far right panel of the middle row on the earlier north doors (*Jesus Calming the Waters*). Ghiberti here captured the chaos of a storm at sea with great skill and economy, but the artistic conventions he used are basically pre-Renaissance: Jesus is the most important figure, so he is the largest; the disciples are next in size, being next in importance; the ship on which they founder is a mere toy.

The panels on the east doors are larger, more expansive, more sweeping, and more convincing. Look at the middle panel on the left-hand door. It tells the story of Jacob and Esau, and the various episodes of the story (the selling of the birthright, Isaac ordering Esau to go hunting, the blessing of Jacob, and so forth) have been merged into a single beautifully realized street scene. A perspective grid is employed to suggest depth, the background architecture looks far more convincing than on the north door panels, the figures in the foreground are grouped realistically, and the naturalism and grace of the poses (look at Esau's left leg) have nothing to do with the sacred message being conveyed. Although the religious content remains, man and his place in the natural world are given new prominence and are portrayed with a realism not seen in art since the fall of the Roman Empire, more than a thousand years before.

As a footnote to Ghiberti's panels, one small detail of the east doors is worth a special look. Just to the lower left of the Jacob and Esau panel, Ghiberti placed a tiny self-portrait bust. From either side, the portrait is extremely appealing—Ghiberti looks like everyone's favorite uncle—but the bust is carefully placed so that there is a single spot in front of the doors from which you can make direct eye contact with the tiny head. When that contact is made, the impression of intelligent life—of *modern* intelligent life—is astonishing. It is no wonder that when these doors were completed, they received one of the most famous compliments in the history of art, from a competitor known to be notoriously stingy with praise: Michelangelo himself declared them so beautiful that they could serve as the Gates to Paradise. 🖾 *3,000 lire.* ☉ *Mon.–Sat. 1:30–6:30, Sun. 8:30–12:30.*

❸ **Campanile.** Giotto's bell tower is a shaft of multicolor marble decorated with reliefs now in the Museo dell'Opera del Duomo. A climb of 414 steps rewards you with a close-up of Brunelleschi's dome and a sweeping view of the city. 🖾 *8,000 lire.* ☉ *Apr.–Oct., Mon.–Sat. 9–6:30; Nov.–Mar., Mon.–Sat. 9–4:20.*

★ ❶ **Duomo** (Cattedrale di Santa Maria del Fiore). The historical heart of Florence is Piazza Duomo, the square surrounding the city's majestic Cathedral of Santa Maria del Fiore, more familiarly known as the

102

Florence

V. Panicale

Piazza
Mercato
Centrale

V. Guelfa

V. S. Gallo

Chiostro
dello
Scalzo ■

⑭

Cenacolo
di Sant
Apollonia

⑮

Via C. Battisti

⑰

Piazza
SS. Annunziata

⑱ Sinagoga/
Museo Ebraico

⑯

V. Laura

V. Colonna

Santa Maria
Maddalena
dei Pazzi ■

Perugino
Crucifixion ■

V. Cavour

V. Ricasoli

V. dell Ariento

V. S. Antonio

V. Faenza

V. Canto de Nelli

⑬

Piazza
S. Lorenzo

⑫

del Giglio

V. Conti

V. dei
Panzani

V. Martelli

V. Pucci

V. dei Servi

V. degli Alfani

V. della Pergola

Borgo Pinti

V. Cerretani

①

②

③

Piazza di
S. Giovanni

Piazza
del Duomo

④

V. Bufalini

V. S. Egidio

V. Fiesolana

V. Pecori

V. dei Tosinghi

V. d. Proconsolo

V. dei Pepi

V. Vecchietti

Piazza
della
Repubblica

V. degli
Speziali

V. dei Calzaiuoli

V. d. Studio

Borgo degli Albizi

Piazza
Salvemini

V. Strozzi

V. Anselmi

⑤

V. dei
Tavolini

V. Dante Alighieri

AE

V. dei Pandolfini

V. dell' Agnolo

V. Porta Rossa

⑩

V. Condotta

V. Magazzini

Piazza
S. Firenze

⑥

V. Ghibellina

V. Ghibellina

V. Verazzano

V. delle Terme

Borgo
SS. Apostoli

⑦

V. Vaccherreccia

⑧

V. d.
Gondi

V. Leoni

Borgo dei Greci

Via Torta

V. Benci

Piazza
Santa
Croce

V. di S. Giuse

Acciaioli

⑪

Ponte Vecchio

Via Por S. Maria

⑨

Lung. Archibusieri

Museo di Storia
■ della Scienza

V. dei Neri

Borgo S. Croce

Corso Tintori

㉘

Lung. Diaz

Piazza
S. Maria
Sopr' Arno

Arno

Costa dei Magnoli

Lung. Torrigiani

V. dei Bardi

Ponte alle Grazie

Lung. d. Grazie

Lung

Piazza
dei Mozzi

V. dei Renai

Via V. di S. Niccolò

KEY

i Tourist Information

AE American Express Office

0   440 yards

0   400 meters

S. Giorgio

㉕

❿

Duomo. In 1296 Arnolfo di Cambio was commissioned to build "the loftiest, most sumptuous edifice human invention could devise" in the newest Romanesque style on the site of the old church of Santa Reparata. The immense Duomo was not completed until 1436, the year when it was consecrated. The imposing facade dates only from the 19th century; it was added in the neo-Gothic style to complement Giotto's genuine Gothic (14th-century) campanile. The real glory of the Duomo, however, is Filippo Brunelleschi's dome, herald of the new Renaissance in architecture, which hovers over the cathedral (and the entire city, when seen from afar) with a dignity and grace that few domes, even to this day, can match. It was the first of its kind in the world, and for many people it is still the best.

Brunelleschi's **cupola** was epoch-making as an engineering feat. The space to be enclosed by the dome was so large and so high above the ground that traditional methods of dome construction—wooden centering and scaffolding—were of no use whatever. So Brunelleschi developed entirely new building methods, which he implemented with equipment of his own devising (including the modern crane). Beginning work in 1420, he built not one dome but two, one inside the other, and connected them with common ribbing that stretched across the intervening empty space, thereby considerably lessening the crushing weight of the structure. He also employed a new method of bricklaying, based on an ancient Roman herringbone pattern, interlocking each new course of bricks with the course below in a way that made the growing structure self-supporting. The result was one of the great engineering breakthroughs of all time: most of Europe's great domes, including St. Peter's in Rome, were built employing Brunelleschi's methods, and today the Duomo has come to symbolize Florence in the same way that the Eiffel Tower symbolizes Paris. The Florentines are justly proud, and to this day the Florentine phrase for "homesick" is *nostalgia del cupolone* (homesick for the dome).

The interior is a fine example of Italian Gothic. Much of the cathedral's best-known art has been moved to the nearby **Cathedral Museum** (☞ *below*). Notable among the works that remain, however, are two equestrian frescoes honoring famous soldiers: Andrea del Castagno's *Niccolò da Tolentino,* painted in 1456, and Paolo Uccello's *Sir John Hawkwood,* painted 20 years earlier; both are on the left-hand wall of the nave. *Niccolò da Tolentino* is particularly impressive: he rides his fine horse with military pride and wears his even finer hat—surely the best in town—with panache. It took restorers more than a decade from 1983 to 1995 to restore the structure of Brunelleschi's dome and clean the vast and crowded fresco of the *Last Judgment*—painted by Vasari and Zuccaro—on its interior. Originally, Brunelleschi wanted mosaics to cover the interior of the great ribbed cupola, but by the time the Florentines got around to commissioning the decoration, 150 years later, tastes had changed.

If time permits, you may want to explore the upper and lower reaches of the cathedral. Ancient remains have been excavated beneath the nave; the stairway down is near the first pier on the right. The climb to the top of the dome (463 steps) is not for the fainthearted, but once there the view is superb; the entrance is on the left wall just before the crossing. ✉ *Piazza del Duomo,* ☎ *055/2302885.* ◷ *Weekdays 10–5, 1st Sat. of month 10–3:30, Sun. 1–5. Excavation:* 🎫 *3,000 lire.* ◷ *Mon.– Sat. 10–5. Ascent to dome:* 🎫 *8,000 lire.* ◷ *Weekdays 8:30–6:20, Sat. 9:30–5 (1st Sat. of month 9:30–3:20).*

Mercato Nuovo (New Market). This open-air loggia was new in 1551. ⌐oday it harbors mostly souvenir stands; its main attraction is Pietro

Tacca's bronze *Porcellino* (Piglet) fountain on the south side, dating from around 1612 and copied from an earlier Roman work now in the Uffizi. Rubbing its drooling snout is a Florentine tradition—it is said to bring good luck. ⊠ *Corner of Via Por San Maria and Via Porta Rossa.*

★ ❹ **Museo dell'Opera del Duomo** (Cathedral Museum). The major attractions here—other than the originals of the Ghiberti door panels mentioned earlier and the *cantorie* (choir loft) reliefs by Donatello and Luca della Robbia—are two: Donatello's *Mary Magdalen* and Michelangelo's *Pietà* (not to be confused with his more famous *Pietà* in St. Peter's, in Rome). The High Renaissance in sculpture is in part defined by its revolutionary realism, but Donatello's *Magdalen* goes beyond realism: it is suffering incarnate. Michelangelo's heart-wrenching *Pietà* was unfinished at his death; the female figure supporting the body of Christ on the left was added by one Tiberio Calcagni, and never has the difference between competence and genius been manifested so clearly. ⊠ *Piazza del Duomo 9,* ☎ *055/2302885.* 🎟 *8,000 lire.* ⊙ *Mar.–Oct., Mon.–Sat. 9–6:20; Nov.–Feb., Mon.–Sat. 9–5:20.*

❺ **Orsanmichele.** This church, containing a beautifully detailed 14th-century Gothic tabernacle by Andrea Orcagna, was originally a granary. The building was transformed in 1336 into a church with 14 exterior niches. Each of the major Florentine trade guilds was assigned its own niche and paid for the sculpture the niche was to contain. The niches soon held works by Florence's most talented sculptors. Unfortunately, the best have been removed and replaced with copies. The originals will eventually be placed in a museum, perhaps even in Orsanmichele. Even so, all the statues are worth examining. One of those removed—Andrea del Verrocchio's *Doubting Thomas* (circa 1470)—was particularly deserving of scrutiny. Were the niche not empty, you would see Christ, like the building's other figures, entirely framed within the niche, and St. Thomas standing on its bottom ledge, with his right foot outside the niche frame. This one detail, the positioning of a single foot, brought the whole composition to life. It is particularly appropriate that this is the only niche to be topped with a Renaissance pediment, for it is the revolutionary vitality of sculpture like this that gave the Renaissance its name. ⊠ *Via dei Calzaiuoli.* 🎟 *Free.* ⊙ *Daily 9–noon and 4–6.*

★ ❾ **Palazzo degli Uffizi** (Uffizi Palace). The **Galleria degli Uffizi** (Uffizi Gallery) occupies the top floor of this U-shape building fronting on the Arno, designed by Vasari in 1559 to hold the administrative offices of Medici Grand Duke Cosimo I—*uffizi* means *offices* in Italian. And here later Medicis installed their art collections, creating what was Europe's first modern museum, open to the public (at first only by request, of course) since 1591. Today the palazzo houses the finest collection of paintings in Italy. Hard-core museum aficionados will want to pick up a complete guide to the collections, sold in bookshops and on newsstands, before they go.

The collection's highlights include Paolo Uccello's *Battle of San Romano* (its brutal chaos of lances is one of the finest visual metaphors for warfare ever committed to paint); Fra Filippino Lippi's *Madonna and Child with Two Angels* (the foreground angel's bold, impudent eye contact would have been unthinkable prior to the Renaissance); Sandro Botticelli's *Primavera* (its nonrealistic fairy-tale charm exhibits the painter's idiosyncratic genius at its zenith); Leonardo da Vinci's *Adoration of the Magi* (unfinished and perhaps the best opportunity in Europe to investigate the methods of a great artist at work); Raphael's *Madonna of the Goldfinch* (darkened by time, but the tenderness with which the figures in the painting touch each other is undimmed); Michelangelo's *Holy Family* (one of the very few easel works in oil he ever painted, clearly reflecting his stated belief that draftsmanship is a necessary ingredient of great painting); Rembrandt's *Self-Portrait as an Old Man* (which proves that even Michelangelo could, on occasion, be wrong); Titian's *Venus of Urbino* and Caravaggio's *Bacchus* (two very great paintings whose attitudes toward myth and sexuality are— to put it mildly—diametrically opposed); and many, many more. If panic sets in at the prospect of absorbing all this art at one go, bear in mind that the Uffizi is, except on Sunday, open late and isn't usually crowded in the late afternoon. The coffee bar inside the Uffizi has a terrace with a fine close-up view of Palazzo Vecchio. Advance tickets—with which you do not have to wait on line at the ticket office—can now be purchased from Consorzio ITA. ⊠ *Piazzale degli Uffizi 6,* ☎ *055/23885. Advance tickets:* ⊠ *Consorzio ITA, Viale Gramsca 9a, 50121,* ☎ *055/ 2347941.* ▨ *12,000 lire.* ☉ *Tues.–Sat. 8:30–6:50, Sun. 8:30–1:50.*

Museo della Storia della Scienza (Museum of Science History). Though it tends to be obscured by the glamour of the neighboring Uffizi, this science museum has a wealth of interest: Galileo's own instruments, a collection of antique armillary spheres, some of them real works of art, and a host of other reminders that the Renaissance made not only artistic but also scientific history. ⊠ *Piazza dei Guidici 1,* ☎ *055/293493.* ▨ *10,000 lire.* ☉ *Tues., Thurs., Sat. 9:30–1; Mon., Wed., Fri. 9:30– 1 and 2–5.*

❽ Palazzo Vecchio (Old Palace). Looming over Piazza della Signoria is Florence's forbidding, fortresslike city hall. The palazzo was begun in 1299 and designed (probably) by Arnolfo di Cambio, and its massive bulk and towering campanile dominate the piazza. It was built as a meeting place for the heads of the seven major guilds that governed the city at the time; over the centuries it has served lesser purposes, but today it is once again the City Hall of Florence. The interior courtyard is a good deal less severe, having been remodeled by Michelozzo in 1453; the copy of Verrocchio's bronze *puttino* (little putto), topping the central fountain, softens the effect considerably.

Although most of the interior public rooms are well worth exploring, the main attraction is on the second floor: two adjoining rooms that supply one of the most startling contrasts in Florence. The first is the vast **Sala dei Cinquecento** (Room of the Five Hundred), named for the 500-member Great Council, the people's assembly established by Savonarola, which met here. The Sala was decorated by Giorgio Vasari, around 1570, with huge frescoes celebrating Florentine history; depictions of battles with neighboring cities predominate. Continuing the martial theme, the Sala also contains Michelangelo's *Victory* group, intended for the never-completed tomb of Pope Julius II, plus other miscellaneous sculptures of decidedly lesser quality.

The second room is the little **Studiolo,** entered to the right of the Sala's entrance. The study of Cosimo de' Medici's son, the melancholy Francesco I, it was designed by Vasari and decorated by Vasari and Agnolo Bronzino. It is intimate, civilized, and filled with complex, questioning, allegorical art. It makes the vainglorious proclamations next door ring more than a little hollow. ⊠ *Piazza della Signoria,* ☎ *055/2768465.* ▨ *10,000 lire.* ☉ *Mon.–Wed. and Fri.–Sat. 9–7, Sun. 8–1.*

Piazza della Repubblica. This square marks the site of the ancient forum that was the core of the original Roman settlement The street plan in the area around the piazza still reflects the carefully plotted orthogonal grid of the Roman military encampment. The Mercato Vecchio (Old Market), located here since the Middle Ages, was demolished at the end of the last century, and the current piazza was constructed between

1890 and 1917 as a neoclassical showpiece. Nominally the center of town, it has yet to earn the love of most Florentines.

★ ❼ **Piazza della Signoria.** This is by far the most striking square in Florence. It was here, in 1497, that the famous "bonfire of the vanities" took place, when the fanatical monk Savonarola induced his followers to hurl their worldly goods into the flames; it was also here, a year later, that he was hanged as a heretic and, ironically, burned. A bronze plaque in the piazza pavement marks the exact spot of his execution.

The statues in the square and in the 14th-century **Loggia dei Lanzi** on the south side vary in quality. Cellini's famous bronze *Perseus Holding the Head of Medusa* is his masterpiece; even the pedestal is superbly executed. Other works in the loggia include *The Rape of the Sabine Women* and *Hercules and the Centaur,* both late 16th-century works by Giambologna, and, in the back, a row of sober matrons that date from Roman times.

In the square, Bartolomeo Ammannati's Neptune Fountain, dating from 1565, takes something of a booby prize. Even Ammannati himself considered it a failure, and the Florentines call it *Il Biancone,* which may be translated as "the big white man" or "the big white lump," depending on your point of view. Giambologna's equestrian statue, to the left of the fountain, pays tribute to the Medici Grand Duke Cosimo I. Occupying the steps of the Palazzo Vecchio are a copy of Donatello's proud heraldic lion of Florence, known as the *Marzocco* (the original is now in the Bargello); a copy of Donatello's *Judith and Holofernes* (the original is inside the Palazzo Vecchio); a copy of Michelangelo's *David* (the original is now in the Galleria dell'Accademia); and Baccio Bandinelli's *Hercules* (1534).

NEED A BREAK? Facing the statuary on the steps of the Palazzo Vecchio, is **Rivoire** (✉ West end of Piazza della Signoria) a café famous for its chocolate (both packaged and hot). Its outdoor tables and somewhat less expensive indoor counter are stylish, if pricey, places from which to observe the busy piazza.

★ ⓫ **Ponte Vecchio** (Old Bridge). This elegant bridge is to Florence what Tower Bridge is to London. It was built in 1345 to replace an earlier bridge that was swept away by flood, and its shops housed first butchers, then grocers, blacksmiths, and other merchants. But in 1593 the Medici Grand Duke Ferdinando I, whose private corridor linking the Medici palace (Palazzo Pitti) with the Medici offices (the Uffizi) crossed the bridge atop the shops, decided that all this plebeian commerce under his feet was unseemly. So he threw out all the butchers and blacksmiths and installed 41 goldsmiths and eight jewelers. The bridge has been devoted solely to these two trades ever since.

In the middle of the bridge, take a moment to study the **Ponte Santa Trinita,** the next bridge downriver. It was designed by Bartolomeo Ammannati in 1567 (possibly from sketches by Michelangelo), blown up by the retreating Germans during World War II, and painstakingly reconstructed after the war ended. By virtue of its graceful arc and delicate curves, Florentines like to claim it is the most beautiful bridge in the world. Given its simplicity, this may sound like idle Tuscan boasting.

Michelangelo Country: From San Lorenzo to the Accademia

Poet, painter, sculptor, and architect, Michelangelo was a consummate genius. His prodigious energy and virtuoso technique overcame the political and artistic vicissitudes of almost a century to produce some of the greatest sculpture of his—or any—age. This itinerary takes us to some of his most important creations, from the Biblioteca Laurenziana, perhaps his most intuitive work of architecture; to the Cappelle Medicee (Medici Chapels), whose magnificent sculptures are a key to understanding Michelangelo's genius; and to the Galleria dell'Accademia (Accademia Gallery), home to his most recognized work (including even the Sistine Chapel), the towering and beautiful *David*.

A Good Walk

Start at the church of **San Lorenzo** ⑫, visiting the **Biblioteca Laurenziana** and its famous anteroom, before circling the church to the northwest and making your way through the San Lorenzo outdoor market on Via del Canto de' Nelli to the entrance of the **Cappelle Medicee.** Retrace your steps through the market and take Via dei Gori east to Via Cavour and the **Palazzo Medici-Riccardi** ⑬, home to Florence's most important family throughout the Renaissance. Follow Via Cavour two blocks north to Piazza San Marco and the church of the same name, attached to which is the **Museo San Marco** ⑭, a memorial to the pious and exceptionally talented painter-monk, Fra Angelico. If you have time, detour northwest from Piazza San Marco to the Cenacolo di Sant'Apollonia and then north to the Chiostro dello Scalzo. From Piazza San Marco, take a short detour a half-block south down Via Ricasoli (which runs back toward the Duomo) to the **Galleria dell'Accademia** ⑮, where Michelangelo's most recognizable masterpiece, *David*, looks down on the admiring crowds. If you have time to make a detour, return to the east side of Piazza San Marco and take Via Cesare Battisti east into Piazza della Santissima Annunziata, one of Florence's prettiest squares, site of the **Ospedale degli Innocenti** ⑯ and, at the north end of the square, the church of **Santissima Annunziata** ⑰. One block southeast of the entrance to Santissima Annunziata, through the arch and on the left side of Via della Colonna, is the **Museo Archeologico** ⑱.

TIMING

The walk alone takes about one hour, plus 45 minutes for the Cappelle Medicee, 20 minutes for the Palazzo Medici-Riccardi, 40 minutes for the Museo di San Marco, 30 minutes for the Galleria dell'Accademia (*David*), and 40 minutes for the Museo Archeologico. Note that Cappelle Medicee and the Museo di San Marco close at 2. After visiting San Lorenzo, resist the temptation to explore the clothes' market that surrounds the church before going to the Palazzo Medici-Riccardi; you can always come back later, when the churches and museums have closed; the market is open until 7 PM.

Sights to See

Biblioteca Laurenziana (Laurentian Library). Michelangelo the architect was every bit as original as Michelangelo the sculptor. Unlike Brunelleschi (the architect of San Lorenzo), however, he was not bent on ordered harmony of the spheres in his architecture. He was interested in experimentation and invention and in expressing a personal vision at times highly idiosyncratic.

It was never more idiosyncratic than in the Laurentian Library and its famous **anteroom.** This strangely shaped anteroom has had scholars scratching their heads for centuries. In a space more than two stories high, why did Michelangelo limit his use of columns and pilasters to the upper two-thirds of the wall? Why didn't he rest them on strong pedestals instead of on huge, decorative curlicue scrolls, which rob them of all visual support? Why did he recess them into the wall, which makes them look weaker still? The architectural elements here do not stand firm and strong and tall, as inside the church next door; instead, they seem to be pressed into the wall as if into putty, giving the room a soft, rubbery look that is one of the strangest effects ever achieved by classical architecture. It is almost as if Michelangelo purposely set out to defy his predecessors—intentionally to flout the conventions of the High Renaissance in order to see what kind of bizarre, mannered effect might result. His innovations were tremendously influential and produced a period of architectural experimentation—the Mannerist era in architecture—that eventually evolved into the Baroque. As his contemporary Giorgio Vasari—the first art historian—put it, "Artisans have been infinitely and perpetually indebted to him because he broke the bonds and chains of a way of working that had become habitual by common usage."

Nobody has ever complained about the anteroom's staircase (best viewed head-on), which emerges from the library with the visual force of an unstoppable lava flow. In its highly sculptural conception and execution, it is quite simply one of the most original and elegant staircases in the world. ⊠ *Piazza San Lorenzo 9, entrance to the left of San Lorenzo.* 🕾 *Free.* ☉ *Mon.–Sat. 9–1.*

★ **Cappelle Medicee** (Medici Chapels). This magnificent complex includes the **Cappella dei Principi,** the Medici chapel and mausoleum that was begun in 1605 and kept marble workers busy for several hundred years, and the **New Sacristy,** designed by Michelangelo, so called to distinguish it from Brunelleschi's Old Sacristy. Both are part of the San Lorenzo complex.

Michelangelo received the commission for the New Sacristy in 1520 from Cardinal Giulio de' Medici, who later became Pope Clement VII and who wanted a new burial chapel for his father, Giuliano, his uncle Lorenzo the Magnificent, and two recently deceased cousins. The result was a tour de force of architecture and sculpture. Architecturally, Michelangelo was as original and inventive here as ever, but it is—quite properly—the powerful sculptural compositions of the side wall tombs that dominate the room. The scheme is allegorical: on the wall tomb to the right are figures representing day and night, and on the wall tomb to the left are figures representing dawn and dusk; above them are idealized portraits of the two cousins, usually interpreted to represent the active life and the contemplative life. But the allegorical meanings are secondary; what is most important is the intense presence of the sculptural figures, the force with which they hit the viewer. Michelangelo's contemporaries were so awed by the impact of this force (in his sculpture here and elsewhere) that they invented an entirely new word to describe the phenomenon: *terribilità* (dreadfulness). To this day it is used only when describing his work, and it is in evidence here at the peak of its power. During his stormy relations with the Medicis, Michelangelo once hid out in a tiny subterranean room that is accessed from the left of the altar. Ever the artist, he drew some charcoal sketches on the wall. If you want to see them, tell the ticket vendor and pay 1,000 lire extra; guided visit only. ⊠ *Piazza di Madonna degli Aldobrandini,* 🕾 *055/213206.* 🕾 *10,000 lire.* ☉ *Daily 8:30–1:50. Closed 2nd, 4th Sun. and 1st, 3rd, 5th Mon. of month.*

★ **⑮** **Galleria dell'Accademia** (Accademia Gallery). The collection of Florentine paintings, dating from the 13th to the 18th centuries, is notable, but the collection of statues by Michelangelo is famous; it includes the unfinished *Slaves*—which were meant for the tomb of Michelangelo's patron and nemesis Pope Julius II (and which seem to be fighting their way out of the marble)—and the original *David*, moved here from Piazza della Signoria in 1873. The *David* was commissioned in 1501 by the Opera del Duomo (Cathedral Works Committee), which gave the 26-year-old sculptor a leftover block of marble that had been ruined by another artist. Michelangelo's success with the defective block was so dramatic that the city showered him with honors, and the Opera del Duomo voted to build him a house and a studio in which to live and work.

Today the *David* is beset not by Goliath but by tourists, and seeing the statue at all—much less really studying it—can be a trial. After a 1991 attack upon it by a hammer-wielding frustrated artist who, luckily, inflicted only a few minor nicks on the toes, the sculpture is surrounded by a Plexiglas barrier. The statue is not quite what it seems. It is so poised and graceful and alert—so miraculously alive—that it is often considered the definitive embodiment of the ideals of the High Renaissance in sculpture. But its true place in the history of art is a bit more complicated.

As Michelangelo well knew, the Renaissance painting and sculpture that preceded his work were deeply concerned with ideal form. Perfection of proportion was the ever-sought Holy Grail; during the Renaissance, ideal proportion was equated with ideal beauty, and ideal beauty was equated with spiritual perfection.

But Michelangelo's *David*, despite its supremely calm and dignified pose, departs from these ideals. Michelangelo did not give the statue ideal proportions. The head is slightly too large for the body, the arms are slightly too large for the torso, and the hands are dramatically large for the arms. By High Renaissance standards these are defects, but the impact and beauty of the *David* are such that it is the *standards* that must be called into question, not the statue. Michelangelo, a revolutionary artist (and the first Mannerist) because he brought a new expressiveness to art, created the "defects" of the *David*. He knew exactly what he was doing, calculating that the perspective of the viewer would be such that, in order for the statue to appear proportioned, the upper body, head, and arms would have to be bigger as they are further away from the viewer's line of vision. But he also did it in order to express and embody, as powerfully as possible in a single figure, an entire biblical story. David's hands *are* too big, but so was Goliath, and these are the hands that slew him. ⊠ *Via Ricasoli 60*, ☎ *055/214375.* ▣ *12,000 lire.* ⊙ *Tues.–Sat. 8:30–6:50, Sun. 8:30–1:50.*

OFF THE BEATEN PATH   **MUSEO DELL'OPIFICIO DELLE PIETRE DURE –** This fascinating small museum is attached to an Opificio, or workshop, established in 1588 by Ferdinando I de' Medici to train craftsmen in the art of working with precious and semiprecious stones and marble. It is internationally renowned as a center for the restoration of mosaics and inlays in semiprecious stones. Informative exhibits include some magnificent antique examples of this highly specialized craft. ⊠ *Via degli Alfani 78.* ▣ *4,000 lire.* ⊙ *Tues.–Sat. 9–5:30.*

⑱ **Museo Archeologico** (Archaeological Museum). Of the Etruscan, Egyptian, and Greco-Roman antiquities here, the Etruscan collection is particularly notable—the largest in northern Italy. The famous bronze *Chimera* was discovered (without the tail, a reconstruction) in the 16th century. ⊠ *Via della Colonna 36*, ☎ *055/2478641.* ▣ *8,000 lire.* ⊙ *Tues.–Sat. 9–2, Sun. 9–1.*

OFF THE BEATEN PATH   **SANTA MARIA MADDALENA DEI PAZZI –** One of Florence's hidden treasures, Perugino's cool and composed *Crucifixion*, is in the chapter hall of the monastery adjacent to this church. ⊠ *Borgo Pinti 58.* ▣ *Donation requested.* ⊙ *Daily 9–noon and 5–7.*

CHIOSTRO DELLO SCALZO – Often overlooked by tourists, this small, peaceful 16th-century cloister was frescoed in monochrome by Andrea del Sarto with scenes from the life of St. John the Baptist, Florence's patron saint. ⊠ *Via Cavour 69.* ⊠ *Free.* ⊙ *Mon.–Thurs. 9–1.*

TORRE DEI CORBIZI – The tower at the south end of the small Piazza San Pier Maggiore dates from the Middle Ages, when, during the Guelph–Ghibelline conflict of the 13th and 14th centuries, Florence was awash with such towers—more than 200 of them. Today only a handful survive. From the Museo Archeologico, follow Via della Colonna east to Borgo Pinti and turn right, following Borgo Pinti through the arch of San Piero into the piazza. ⊠ *Piazza San Pier Maggiore.*

⑭ Museo San Marco. A former Dominican monastery adjacent to the church of San Marco now houses this museum, which—in fact, the entire monastery—is a memorial to Fra Angelico, the Dominican monk who, when he was alive, was as famous for his piety as for his painting. When the monastery was built in 1437, he decorated it with his frescoes, which were meant to spur religious contemplation; when the building was turned into a museum, other works of his from all over the city were brought here for display. His paintings are simple and direct and furnish a compelling contrast to the Palazzo Medici-Riccardi chapel (☞ *below*). Fra Angelico probably would have considered the glitter of Gozzoli's work there worldly and blasphemous. The entire monastery is worth exploring, for Fra Angelico's paintings are everywhere, including the Chapter House, at the top of the stairs leading to the upper floor (the famous *Annunciation*), in the upper-floor monks' cells (each monk was given a different religious subject for contemplation), and in the gallery just off the cloister as you enter. The latter room contains, among many other works, his beautiful *Last Judgment;* as usual, the tortures of the damned are far more inventive than the pleasures of the redeemed. ⊠ *Piazza San Marco 1,* ☎ *055/2388608.* ⊠ *8,000 lire.* ⊙ *Daily 8:30–2. Closed 1st, 3rd, 5th Sun. and 2nd, 4th Mon. of month.*

OFF THE BEATEN PATH **CENACOLO DI SANT'APOLLONIA –** The frescoes of this refectory of a former Benedictine monastery were painted in sinewy style by Andrea del Castagno, a follower of Masaccio. The *Last Supper* is a powerful version of this typical refectory theme. From the Cenacolo entrance, walk around the corner to Via San Gallo 25 and take a peek at the lovely 15th-century cloister that belonged to the same monastery but is now part of the University of Florence. ⊠ *Via XXVII Aprile 1.* ⊠ *Free.* ⊙ *Daily 8:30–2. Closed 1st, 3rd, 5th Sun. and 2nd, 4th Mon. of month.*

⑯ Ospedale degli Innocenti (Hospital of the Innocents). Built by Brunelleschi in 1419 to serve as a foundling hospital, it takes the historical prize as the very first Renaissance building. Brunelleschi designed the building's portico with his usual rigor, building it out of the two shapes he considered mathematically (and therefore philosophically and aesthetically) perfect: the square and the circle. Below the level of the arches, the portico encloses a row of perfect cubes; above the level of the arches, the portico encloses a row of intersecting hemispheres. The whole geometric scheme is articulated with Corinthian columns, capitals, and arches borrowed directly from antiquity. At the time he designed the portico, Brunelleschi was also designing the interior of San Lorenzo, using the same basic ideas. But since the portico was finished before San Lorenzo, the Ospedale degli Innocenti can claim the honor of ushering in Renaissance architecture. The 10 ceramic medallions depicting swaddled infants that decorate the portico are by Andrea della Robbia, done approximately in 1487. ⊠ *Piazza di Santissima Annunziata 1.*

★ ⓭ **Palazzo Medici-Riccardi.** The main attraction of this palace, begun in
1444 by Michelozzo for Cosimo de' Medici, is the interior chapel, the
so-called **Cappella dei Magi** on the upper floor. Painted on its walls is
Benozzo Gozzoli's famous *Procession of the Magi,* finished in 1460
and celebrating both the birth of Christ and the greatness of the Medici
family, whose portraits it contains. Like his contemporary Ghirlandaio,
Gozzoli was not a revolutionary painter and is today considered less
than first rate because of his technique, old-fashioned even for his day.
Gozzoli's gift, however, was for entrancing the eye, not challenging the
mind, and on those terms his success here is beyond question. The paintings are full of activity yet somehow frozen in time in a way that fails
utterly as realism, but succeeds triumphantly as soon as the demand
for realism is set aside. Entering the chapel is like walking into the middle of a magnificently illustrated child's storybook, and the beauty of
the illustrations makes this one of the most unpretentiously enjoyable
rooms in the entire city. ⊠ *Via Cavour 1,* ☎ *055/2760340.* ☞ *6,000
lire.* ☉ *Mon.–Tues. and Thurs.–Sat. 9–1 and 3–6, Sun. 9–1.*

⓬ **San Lorenzo.** The facade of this church was never finished. Like Santo
Spirito on the other side of the Arno, the interior of San Lorenzo was
designed by Filippo Brunelleschi in the early 15th century. The two church
interiors are similar in design and effect and proclaim with ringing clarity the beginning of the Renaissance in architecture. You may want to
read the entry on Santo Spirito now; it describes the nature of
Brunelleschi's architectural breakthrough, and its main points apply
equally well here (☞ Palazzo Pitti, Giardini Boboli, and Oltrarno, *below*).
San Lorenzo possesses one feature that Santo Spirito lacks, however,
which considerably heightens the dramatic effect of the interior: the
grid of dark, inlaid marble lines on the floor. The grid makes the rigorous regularity with which the interior was designed immediately visible and offers an illuminating lesson on the laws of perspective. If you
stand in the middle of the nave at the church entrance, on the line that
stretches to the high altar, every element in the church—the grid, the
nave columns, the side aisles, the coffered nave ceiling—seems to
march inexorably toward a hypothetical vanishing point beyond the
high altar, exactly as in a single-point-perspective painting. Brunelleschi's
Old Sacristy has stucco decorations by Donatello; the entrance is at
the end of the left transept. ⊠ *Piazza San Lorenzo.*

OFF THE   **MERCATO CENTRALE –** In this huge, two-story market hall, food is every-
BEATEN PATH where, some of it remarkably exotic, and many of the displays verge on
             the magnificent. At the Mercato Nuovo (☞ *above*), near the Ponte Vec-
             chio, you will see tourists petting the snout of the bronze piglet for good
             luck; here you will see Florentines petting the snout of a very real one.
             The Mercato Centrale has a number of small coffee bars scattered
             about; there is even one upstairs among the mountains of vegetables.
             ⊠ *Piazza del Mercato Centrale.*

⓱ **Santissima Annunziata.** This church was designed in 1447 by Michelozzo, who gave it an uncommon (and lovely) entrance cloister. The
interior is an extreme rarity for Florence: a sumptuous example of the
Baroque. But it is not really a fair example, since it is merely 17th-cen-
tury Baroque decoration applied willy-nilly to an earlier structure—
exactly the sort of violent remodeling exercise that has given the
Baroque a bad name ever since. The **Tabernacle of the Annunziata,** immediately inside the entrance to the left, illustrates the point. The
lower half, with its stately Corinthian columns and carved frieze bearing the Medici arms, was built at the same time as the church; the upper
half, with its erupting curves and impish sculpted cherubs, was added

200 years later. Each is effective in its own way, but together they serve only to prove that dignity is rarely comfortable wearing a party hat. ⊠ *Piazza di Santissima Annunziata.*

Around Santa Maria Novella

Piazza Santa Maria Novella is near the train station, and like the train stations of most other European cities, it is an area pervaded by a certain squalor, especially at night. Nevertheless, the streets in and around the piazza are an architectural treasure trove, lined with some of Florence's most elegant palazzi. This walk ends at Santa Trinita, home of Ghirlandaio's fresco cycle.

A Good Walk

Start in the Piazza Santa Maria Novella, dominated by the church of **Santa Maria Novella** ⑲ on the north side, then take Via delle Belle Donne, which leads from the east side of Piazza Santa Maria Novella to a minuscule square, at the center of which a curious shrine, known as the Croce al Trebbio, stands. Take Via del Trebbio east and turn right onto **Via Tornabuoni,** Florence's finest shopping street. At the intersection of Via Tornabuoni and Via Strozzi is the classical **Palazzo Strozzi** ⑳. One block west, down Via della Vigna Nuova, is Alberti's High Renaissance-style **Palazzo Rucellai** ㉑. Follow the narrow street opposite the palazzo (Via del Purgatorio) east almost to its end, then zigzag right and left, turning east on Via Parione to reach Piazza di Santa Trinita, where, in the middle, stands the **Colonna della Giustizia,** erected by Cosimo de' Medici in 1537. Halfway down the block to the south (toward the Arno) is the church of **Santa Trinita** ㉒, home to Ghirlandaio's glowing frescoes. Then go east on Borgo Santi Apostoli, a typical medieval street flanked by tower-houses, to Via Por Santa Maria. Alternatively, from Piazza Santa Trinita you can cross Ponte Santa Trinita and head into the Oltrarno neighborhood.

TIMING

The walk takes about 30 minutes, plus 30 minutes for Santa Maria Novella and 15 minutes for Santa Trinita. A visit to the Santa Maria Novella museum and cloister takes about 30 minutes.

Sights to See

Croce al Trebbio. This little street shrine was erected in 1308 by the Dominican friars (nearby Santa Maria Novella is a Dominican church) to commemorate a victory famous locally: it was here that they defeated their avowed enemies, the Patarene heretics, in a bloody street brawl. ⊠ *Via del Trebbio.*

㉑ **Palazzo Rucellai.** Architect Leon Battista Alberti designed perhaps the very first private residence done in High Renaissance style—which goes a step further than the Palazzo Strozzi. A comparison between the two is illuminating. Evident on the facade of the Palazzo Rucellai is the ordered arrangement of windows and rusticated stonework seen on the Palazzo Strozzi, but Alberti's facade is far less forbidding. Alberti devoted a far larger proportion of his wall space to windows, which soften the facade's appearance, and filled in the remainder with rigorously ordered classical elements borrowed from antiquity. The end result, though still severe, is less fortresslike, and Alberti strove for this effect purposely (he is on record as stating that only tyrants need fortresses). Ironically, the Palazzo Rucellai was built some 30 years *before* the Palazzo Strozzi. Alberti's civilizing ideas here, it turned out, had little influence on the Florentine palazzi that followed. To the Renaissance Florentines, power—in architecture, as in life—was just as impressive as beauty. ⊠ *Via della Vigna Nuova.*

⓴ Palazzo Strozzi. This is the most imposing palazzo on Via Tornabuoni. Designed (probably) by Giuliano da Sangallo around 1489 and modeled after Michelozzo's earlier Palazzo Medici-Riccardi (☞ Michelangelo Country, *above*), the exterior of the palazzo is simple and severe; it is not the use of classical detail but the regularity of its features, the stately march of its windows, that marks it as a product of the early Renaissance. The interior courtyard (entered from the rear of the palazzo) is another matter altogether. It is here that the classical vocabulary—columns, capitals, pilasters, arches, and cornices—is given uninhibited and powerful expression. Unfortunately, the courtyard's effectiveness is all but destroyed by the addition of a brutal metal fire escape. Its introduction here is one of the most disgraceful acts of 20th-century vandalism in the entire city. ✉ *Via Tornabuoni*.

⓳ Santa Maria Novella. The facade of this church looks distinctly clumsy by later Renaissance standards, and with good reason: it is an architectural hybrid. The lower half of the facade was completed mostly in the 14th century; its pointed-arch niches and decorative marble patterns reflect the Gothic style of the day. About a hundred years later (around 1456), architect Leon Battista Alberti was called in to complete the job. The marble decoration of his upper story clearly defers to the already existing work below, but the architectural features he added evince an entirely different style. The central doorway, the four ground-floor half-columns with Corinthian capitals, the triangular pediment atop the second story, the inscribed frieze immediately below the pediment—these are classical features borrowed from antiquity, and they reflect the new Renaissance era in architecture, born some 35 years earlier at the Ospedale degli Innocenti (☞ Michelangelo Country, *above*). Alberti's most important addition, however, the S-curve scrolls that surmount the decorative circles on either side of the upper story, had no precedent whatever in antiquity. The problem was to soften the abrupt transition between wide ground floor and narrow upper story. Alberti's solution turned out to be definitive. Once you start to look for them, you will find scrolls such as these (or sculptural variations of them) on churches all over Italy, and every one of them derives from Alberti's example here.

The architecture of the interior is, like the Duomo, a dignified but somber example of Italian Gothic. Exploration is essential, however, because the church's store of art treasures is remarkable. Highlights include the 14th-century stained-glass rose window depicting *The Coronation of the Virgin* (above the central entrance door); the Filippo Strozzi Chapel (to the right of the altar), containing late 15th-century frescoes and stained glass by Filippino Lippi; the chancel (the area around the altar), containing frescoes by Domenico Ghirlandaio (1485); and the Gondi Chapel (to the left of the altar), containing Filippo Brunelleschi's famous wooden crucifix, carved around 1410 and said to have so stunned the great Donatello when he first saw it that he dropped a basket of eggs.

One other work in the church is worth special attention, for it possesses great historical importance and beauty. It is Masaccio's *Holy Trinity with Two Donors,* on the left-hand wall, almost halfway down the nave. Painted around 1425 (at the same time Masaccio was working on his frescoes in Santa Maria del Carmine; ☞ Palazzo Pitti, Giardini Boboli, and Oltrarno, *below*), it unequivocally announced the arrival of the Renaissance era. The realism of the figure of Christ was revolutionary in itself, but what was probably even more startling to contemporary Florentines was the coffered ceiling in the background. The mathematical rules for employing perspective in painting had just been discovered (probably by Brunelleschi), and this was one of the first paintings to employ them with utterly convincing success. ⊠ *Piazza Santa Maria Novella.* ⊘ *Mon.–Sat. 7–12:30, Sun. 1–5.*

The **Museo di Santa Maria Novella,** entered to the left of Santa Maria Novella, includes church's cloisters, interesting for the faded fresco cycle by Paolo Uccello depicting tales from Genesis, with a dramatic vision of the Deluge. There are more, earlier and better preserved frescoes, painted by Andrea di Firenze in the 1360s in the chapter hall, or Cappella degli Spagnoli, off the cloisters. ⊠ *Santa Maria Novella church.* 🎫 *5,000 lire.* ⊘ *Mon.–Thurs. and Sat. 9–2, Sun. 8–1.*

㉒ **Santa Trinita.** Originally built in the Romanesque style, the church underwent a Gothic remodeling during the 14th century (remains of the Romanesque construction are visible on the interior front wall). Its major artistic attraction is the cycle of frescoes and the altarpiece in the Sassetti Chapel, the second to the altar's right, painted by Domenico Ghirlandaio, around 1485. Ghirlandaio was a conservative painter for his day, and generally his paintings exhibit little interest in the investigations into the laws of perspective that had been going on in Florentine painting for more than 50 years. But his work here possesses such graceful decorative appeal that his lack of interest in rigorous perspective hardly seems to matter. The wall frescoes illustrate the life of St. Francis, and the altarpiece, *The Adoration of the Shepherds,* nearly glows. ⊠ *Piazza Santa Trinita.*

In the center of Piazza Santa Trinita is a **column from the Terme di Caracalla,** in Rome, given to the Medici Grand Duke Cosimo I by Pope Pius IV in 1560. The column was raised here by Cosimo in 1565, to mark the spot where he heard the news, in 1537, that his exiled Ghibelline enemies had been defeated at Montemurlo, near Prato; the victory made his power in Florence unchallengeable and all but absolute. The column is called, with typical Medici self-assurance, the **Colonna della Giustizia,** the Column of Justice.

Palazzo Pitti, Giardini Boboli, and Oltrarno

This walk takes in two very different aspects of Florence: the splendor of the Medicis, manifest in the riches of mammoth Palazzo Pitti (Pitti Palace) and the gracious Giardini Boboli; and the charm of the Oltrarno, literally "beyond the Arno," a now-gentrified neighborhood of artisans and antiques shops.

A Good Walk

If you start from Santa Trinita, cross the Arno over Ponte Santa Trinita and continue south down Via Maggio until you reach the crossroads of Sdrucciolo dei Pitti (on the left) and the short Via Michelozzi (on the right). Turn left onto the Sdrucciolo dei Pitti. **Palazzo Pitti** ㉓, Florence's largest architectural set piece, lies before you as you emerge onto Piazza Pitti. Behind the palace are the **Giardini Boboli** ㉔. If you have time, walk through the gardens. At the top, the adjacent **Fortezza Belvedere** ㉕, commands a wonderful view but is not always open to the public. Return to Via Maggio from Palazzo Pitti, take Via Michelozzi west to Piazza Santo Spirito, dominated at its north end by the unassuming facade of the church of **Santo Spirito** ㉖. After your visit to perhaps Italy's most important architectural interior, and perhaps to the Cenacolo di Santo Spirito, next door, take Via Sant'Agostino, diagonally across the square from the church entrance, and follow it west to Via dei Serragli. Cross and follow Via Santa Monaca west through the heart of Florence's working-class and fiercely proud Oltrarno neighborhood—the equivalent of Rome's Trastevere—to Piazza del

Carmine and the church of **Santa Maria del Carmine** ㉗, where, in the attached Brancacci Chapel, is the Masaccio cycle that is famous throughout the world. Go to the far end of Piazza del Carmine and turn right onto Borgo San Frediano, then follow Via di Santo Spirito and Borgo San Jacopo east to reach the Ponte Vecchio.

TIMING

The walk alone takes about 45 minutes; allow one hour to visit the Galleria Palatina in Palazzo Pitti, or more if you visit the other galleries. Spend at least 30 minutes to an hour savoring the graceful elegance of the Giardini Boboli. When you reach the crossroads of the Sdrucciolo dei Pitti and Via Michelozzi, you have a choice. If the noon hour approaches, you may want to postpone the next stop temporarily to see the churches of Santo Spirito and Santa Maria del Carmine before they close for the afternoon. Otherwise, proceed to Palazzo Pitti, where you should bank on spending at least 30 minutes visiting the palace. The churches of Santo Spirito and Santa Maria del Carmine can be visited in 15 minutes each, but we strongly recommend that if you have time, you linger a while in either church to soak up the sheer historical and artistic grandeur that is the essence of Florence's beauty.

㉕ **Fortezza Belvedere** (Belvedere Fortress). This imposing structure was built in 1429 to help defend the city against siege. But time has effected an ironic transformation, and what was once a first-rate fortification is now a first-rate exhibition venue. Buses carry view-seeking tourists farther up the hill to the Piazzale Michelangelo, but, as the natives know, the best views of Florence are right here. To the north, all the city's monuments are spread out in a breathtaking cinemascopic panorama, framed by the rolling Tuscan hills beyond: the squat dome of Santa Maria Novella, Giotto's proud campanile, the soaring dome of the Duomo, the forbidding medieval tower of the Palazzo Vecchio, the delicate Gothic spire of the Badia, and the crenellated tower of the Bargello. It is one of the best city views in Italy. To the south the nearby hills furnish a complementary rural view, in its way equally memorable. The fortress, occasionally used as a setting for art exhibitions, is adjacent to the top of the Giardini Boboli. When used for exhibitions, admission varies; at other times it may or may not be open to the public. Check locally, as the view is worth it. ✉ *Porta San Giorgio.*

㉔ **Giardini Boboli** (Boboli Gardens). The main entrance to these landscaped gardens is in the right wing of Palazzo Pitti. The gardens began to take shape in 1549, when the Pitti family sold the palazzo to Eleanor of Toledo, wife of the Medici Grand Duke Cosimo I. The initial landscaping plans were laid out by Niccolò Pericoli Tribolo. After his death in 1550 development was continued by Bernardo Buontalenti, Giulio, and Alfonso Parigi, and, over the years, many others, who produced the most spectacular backyard in Florence. The Italian gift for landscaping—less formal than the French but still full of sweeping drama—is displayed here at its best. A description of the gardens' beauties would fill a page but would be self-defeating, for the best way to enjoy a pleasure garden is to wander about, discovering its pleasures for yourself. One small fountain deserves special note, however: the famous *Bacchino,* near the main entrance. It is a copy of the original, showing Pietro Barbino, Cosimo's favorite dwarf, astride a particularly unhappy tortoise. It seems to be illustrating—very graphically, indeed—the perils of too much pasta. ✑ *4,000 lire.* ◷ *Daily, 9 AM–1 hr before sunset. Closed 1st and last Mon. of each month.*

㉓ **Palazzo Pitti** (Pitti Palace). This enormous palace is one of Florence's largest—if not one of its best—architectural set pieces. The original palazzo, built for the Pitti family around 1460, comprised only the middle cube (the width of the middle seven windows on the upper floors) of the present building. In 1549 the property was sold to the Medicis, and Bartolomeo Ammannati was called in to make substantial additions. Although he apparently operated on the principle that more is better, he succeeded only in producing proof that more is just that, more.

Today the immense building houses several museums: the former **Royal Apartments**, containing furnishings from a remodeling done in the 19th century; the **Museo degli Argenti**, containing a vast collection of Medici household treasures; the **Galleria del Costume**, a showcase of the fashions of the past 300 years; the **Galleria d'Arte Moderna**, containing a collection of 19th- and 20th-century paintings, mostly Tuscan; and, most famous of all, the **Galleria Palatina**, containing a broad collection of 16th- and 17th-century paintings. The rooms of the latter remain much as the Medici family left them, and many art lovers view the floor-to-ceiling painting displays here as Italy's most egregious exercise in conspicuous consumption, aesthetic overkill, and trumpery. Still, the collection possesses high points that are very high indeed, including a number of portraits by Titian and an unparalleled collection of paintings by Raphael, among them the famous *Madonna of the Chair.* ⊠ *Piazza Pitti,* ☎ *055/210323. Museo degli Argenti:* ▦ *8,000 lire (also valid for Galleria del Costume).* ◷ *Daily 8:30–1:50; closed 2nd, 4th Sun. and 1st, 3rd, 5th Mon. of month. Galleria del Costume:* ▦ *8,000 lire (☞ above).* ◷ *Tues.–Sun. 8:30–1:50. Galleria d'Arte Moderna:* ▦ *4,000 lire.* ◷ *Daily 8:30–1:50; closed 2nd, 4th Sun. and 1st, 3rd, 5th Mon. of month. Galleria Palatina:* ▦ *12,000 lire.* ◷ *Tues.–Sat. 8:30–6:50, Sun. 8:30–1:50.*

㉗ Santa Maria del Carmine. The **Brancacci Chapel**, at the end of the right transept of this church, houses a masterpiece of Renaissance painting: a fresco cycle that changed the course of art forever. Fire almost destroyed the church in the 18th century; miraculously, the Brancacci Chapel survived almost intact.

The cycle is the work of three artists: Masaccio and Masolino, who began it in 1423, and Filippino Lippi, who finished it, after a long interruption during which the sponsoring Brancacci family was exiled, some 50 years later. It was Masaccio's work that opened a new frontier for painting; tragically, he did not live to experience the revolution his innovations caused, as he died in 1428 at the age of 27.

Masaccio collaborated with Masolino on several of the paintings, but by himself he painted *The Tribute Money* on the upper-left wall; *Peter Baptizing the Neophytes* on the upper altar wall; *The Distribution of the Goods of the Church* on the lower altar wall; and, most famous, *The Expulsion of Adam and Eve* on the chapel's upper-left entrance pier. If you look closely at the latter painting and compare it with some of the chapel's other works, you will see a pronounced difference. The figures of Adam and Eve possess a startling presence, a presence primarily due to the dramatic way in which their bodies seem to reflect light. Masaccio here shaded his figures consistently, so as to suggest emphatically a single, strong source of light within the world of the painting but outside its frame. In so doing, he succeeded in imitating with paint the real-world effect of light on mass, and he thereby imparted to his figures a sculptural reality unprecedented in its day. To contemporary Florentines his Adam and Eve must have seemed surrounded by light and air in a way that was almost magical. All the painters of Florence came to look.

These matters have to do with technique, but with *The Expulsion of Adam and Eve,* his skill went beyond technical innovation, and if you look hard at the faces of Adam and Eve, you will see more than just finely modeled figures. You will see terrible shame and terrible suffering, and you will see them depicted with a humanity rarely achieved in art. ⊠ *Brancacci Chapel, Piazza del Carmine.* ⬚ *5,000 lire.* ☉ *Mon. and Wed.–Sat. 10–5, Sun. 1–5.*

NEED A
BREAK?
A popular spot for lunch is **Carmine** (⊠ Piazza del Carmine), a moderately priced restaurant with outdoor tables during the warmer months. It's closed Sunday.

㉖ **Santo Spirito.** The plain, unfinished facade gives nothing away, but the interior, although it appears chilly (cold, even) compared with later churches, is one of the most important pieces of architecture in all Italy. One of a pair of Florentine church interiors designed by Filippo Brunelleschi in the early 15th century (the other is San Lorenzo, ☞ Michelangelo Country, *above*) it was here that Brunelleschi supplied definitive solutions to the two main problems of interior Renaissance church design: how to build a cross-shaped interior using classical architectural elements borrowed from antiquity and how to reflect in that interior the order and regularity that Renaissance scientists (of which Brunelleschi was one) were at the time discovering in the natural world around them.

Brunelleschi's solution to the first problem was brilliantly simple: turn a Greek temple inside out. To see this clearly, look at one of the stately arch-topped arcades that separate the side aisles from the central nave. Whereas the ancient Greek temples were walled buildings surrounded by classical colonnades, Brunelleschi's churches were classical arcades surrounded by walled buildings. This was perhaps the single most brilliant architectural idea of the early Renaissance, and its brilliance overthrew the previous era's religious taboo against pagan architecture once and for all, triumphantly reclaiming that architecture for Christian use.

Brunelleschi's solution to the second problem—making the entire interior orderly and regular—was mathematically precise: he designed the ground plan of the church so that all its parts are proportionally related. The transepts and nave have exactly the same width; the side aisles are exactly half as wide as the nave; the little chapels off the side aisles are exactly half as deep as the side aisles; the chancel and transepts are exactly one-eighth the depth of the nave; and so on, with dizzying exactitude. For Brunelleschi, such a design technique would have been far more than a convenience; it would have been a matter of passionate conviction. Like most theoreticians of his day, he believed that mathematical regularity and aesthetic beauty were opposite sides of the same coin, that one was not possible without the other. The conviction stood unchallenged for a hundred years, until Michelangelo turned his hand to architecture and designed the Medici Chapel and the Biblioteca Laurenziana in San Lorenzo across town (☞ Michelangelo Country, *above*), and thereby unleashed a revolution of his own that spelled the end of the Renaissance in architecture and the beginning of the Baroque. ⊠ *Piazza Santo Spirito.* ☉ *Thurs.–Tues. 8–noon and 4–5:30, Wed. 8–noon.*

OFF THE
BEATEN PATH
CENACOLO DI SANTO SPIRITO – In the monastery adjacent to the church, you can see Andrea Orcagna's fresco of the Crucifixion. ⊠ *Piazza Santo Spirito 29,* ⬚ *4,000 lire.* ☉ *Tues.–Sat. 9–2, Sun. 8–1.*

From Santa Croce to San Miniato

The Santa Croce neighborhood, on the southwest fringe of the historic center of Florence, was built up in the Middle Ages just outside the medieval city walls. The centerpiece of the neighborhood was the church of Santa Croce, which could hold great numbers of worshipers and accommodate the overflow in the vast piazza, which also served as a fairground and playing field for traditional, no-holds-barred football games. A center of leather-working since the Middle Ages, the neighborhood is still packed with leather craftsmen and shops selling leather goods.

A Good Walk

Begin your walk at the church of **Santa Croce** ㉘, and at the southeast end of the piazza go south on Via de' Benci and cross the Arno over Ponte alle Grazie. Turn left onto Lungarno Serristori and continue to Piazza Poggi, where a series of ramps and stairs climbs to **Piazzale Michelangelo,** where the city lies before you like a painting. From Piazzale Michelangelo, climb the stairs behind La Loggia restaurant to the church of San Salvatore al Monte, and go south on the lane leading to the stairs that climb to **San Miniato al Monte** ㉙, cutting through the fortifications hurriedly built by Michelangelo in 1529 when Florence was threatened by Emperor Charles V's troops. If you prefer, you can avoid the long walk by taking Bus 12 or 13 at the west end of Ponte alle Grazie and get off at the stop after Piazzale Michelangelo. You still have to climb the monumental stairs to San Miniato, but then the rest of your itinerary will be downhill. From San Miniato descend to San Salvatore al Monte and then to Piazzale Michelangelo, where you can get a bus back to the center of town.

TIMING

The walk alone takes about 1½ hours one way, plus 30 minutes in Santa Croce, 30 minutes in the Museo di Santa Croce, and 30 minutes in San Miniato. Depending on the amount of time you have, you can limit your sightseeing to Santa Croce or continue on to Piazzale Michelangelo. The walk to Piazzale Michelangelo is a long uphill hike, with the prospect of another climb to San Miniato from there. If you decide to take a bus, remember to buy your ticket before you board. Finally, since you go to Piazzale Michelangelo for the view, skip that stop on the itinerary if it's a hazy day.

Sights to See

Piazzale Michelangelo. From this lookout, you have a marvelous view of Florence and the hills around it, rivaling the vista from the Belvedere Fortress (☞ Palazzo Pitti, Giardini Boboli, and Oltrarno, *above*). It has a copy of Michelangelo's *David* and outdoor cafés that are packed with tourists during the day and with Florentines in the evening. In May, the Iris Garden off the piazza is abloom with more than 2,500 varieties of the flower that has been Florence's symbol since 1251, and it is open to the public. The Rose Garden on the terraces below the piazza is also open in May and June.

NEED A BREAK?

After seeing the light of the setting sun cast a glow on Florence's domes and towers from a vantage point on Piazzale Michelangelo, have a snack at the **Antico Vineria** (⊠ Via San Nicolò 60/r, off Piazza Poggi), a busy wineshop-trattoria with atmosphere. It's closed Sunday.

㉙ **San Miniato al Monte.** This church, like the Baptistery (☞ The Historic Heart of Florence, *above*), is a fine example of Romanesque architecture and is one of the oldest churches in Florence, dating from the 11th century. The lively green and white marble facade has a 12th-century mosaic topped by a gilded bronze eagle, emblem of San Miniato's sponsors, the Calimala (Wool Merchant's Guild). Inside are a 13th-century inlaid marble floor and apse mosaic. Artist Spinello Aretino covered the walls of the Sacristy with frescoes of the life of St. Benedict. The adjacent Chapel of the Portuguese Cardinal is one of the richest Renaissance works in Florence. Built to hold the tomb of a Portuguese cardinal, Prince James of Lusitania, who died young in Florence in 1459, it has a glorious ceiling by Luca della Robbia, a sculptured tomb by Antonio Rossellini, and inlaid pavement in multicolored marble. ⊠ *Viale Galileo Galilei, Piazzale Michelangelo.*

<table>
<tr><td>NEED A
BREAK?</td><td>The Santa Croce neighborhood has some sweet surprises hidden among its byways: **Vivoli** (⊠ Via Isola delle Stinche 7/r, off Via dell'Anguillara, one of the streets opposite the facade of Santa Croce) is Florence's most famous *gelateria* (ice-cream parlor). If you're just desperate for brownies and chocolate-chip cookies, find your way to **Carlie's American Bakery** (⊠ Via della Brache, also known as Via dei Legnaioli 12/r, a narrow street off Via dei Neri between Via dei Benci and Via dei Rustici).</td></tr>
</table>

★ ㉘   **Santa Croce.** Like the Duomo, this church is Gothic, but (also like the Duomo) its facade dates only from the 19th century. The interior is most famous for its art and its tombs. As a burial place, the church is a Florentine pantheon and probably contains a larger number of important skeletons than any church in Italy. Among others, the tomb of Michelangelo is immediately to the right as you enter (he is said to have chosen this spot so that the first thing he would see on Judgment Day, when the graves of the dead fly open, would be Brunelleschi's Duomo dome through Santa Croce's open doors); the tomb of Galileo Galilei, who produced evidence that the earth is not the center of the universe (and who was not granted a Christian burial until 100 years after his death because of it), is on the left wall, opposite Michelangelo; the tomb of Niccolò Machiavelli, the Renaissance political theoretician whose brutally pragmatic philosophy so influenced the Medici, is halfway down the nave on the right; the grave of Lorenzo Ghiberti, creator of the Gates of Paradise doors to the Baptistery, is halfway down the nave on the left; the tomb of composer Gioacchino Rossini, of "William Tell Overture" fame, is at the end of the nave on the right. The monument to Dante Alighieri, the greatest Italian poet, is a memorial rather than a tomb (he is actually buried in Ravenna); it is on the right wall near the tomb of Michelangelo.

The collection of art within the church and church complex is by far the most important of that in any church in Florence. Historically, the most significant works are probably the Giotto frescoes in the two adjacent chapels immediately to the right of the altar. They illustrate scenes from the lives of St. John the Evangelist and St. John the Baptist (in the right-hand chapel) and scenes from the life of St. Francis (in the left-hand chapel). Time has not been kind to them; over the centuries, wall tombs were introduced into the middle of them, whitewash and plaster covered them, and in the 19th century they underwent a clumsy restoration. But the reality that Giotto introduced into painting can still be seen. He did not paint beautifully stylized symbols of religion, as the Byzantine style that preceded him prescribed; he instead painted drama—St. Francis surrounded by grieving monks at the very moment of his death. This was a radical shift in emphasis, and it changed the course of art. Before him, the role of painting was to symbolize the attributes of God; after him, it was to imitate life. The style of his work is indeed primitive, compared with later painting, but in the proto-Renaissance of the early 14th century, it caused a sensation that was not equalled for another 100 years. He was, for his time, the equal of both Masaccio and Michelangelo.

Among the church's other highlights are Donatello's *Annunciation*, one of the most tender and eloquent expressions of surprise ever sculpted (on the right wall two-thirds of the way down the nave); Taddeo Gaddi's 14th-century frescoes illustrating the life of the Virgin, clearly showing the influence of Giotto (in the chapel at the end of the right transept); and Donatello's *Crucifix*, criticized by Brunelleschi for making Christ look like a peasant (in the chapel at the end of the left transept). Outside the church proper, in the **Museo dell'Opera di Santa Croce** off the cloister, is Giovanni Cimabue's 13th-century *Triumphal Cross,* badly damaged by the flood of 1966. An epitome of architectural geometry, the **Pazzi Chapel,** end of the cloister, is attributed to Brunelleschi. ⊠ *Piazza Santa Croce 16,* ☎ *055/244619. Church:* ⊙ *Apr.–Sept., Mon.–Sat. 8–6:30, Sun. 8–12:30 and 3–6:30; Oct.–Mar., daily 8–12:30 and 3–6:30. Church cloister and museum:* ⊠ *3,000 lire.* ⊙ *Apr.–Sept., Thurs.–Tues. 10–12:30 and 2:30–6:30; Oct.–Mar., Thurs.–Tues. 10–12:30 and 3–5:30.*

OFF THE BEATEN PATH

SINAGOGA – The Synagogue was built around 1874–1882 in a style that could be defined as an eclectic interpretation of Byzantine-Moorish motifs. The adjacent Museo Ebraico charts the history of Florence's Jewish Community. ⊠ *Via Farini 4,* ☎ *055/245252.* ⊠ *5,000 lire.* ⊙ *Mar.–Oct., Sun.–Thurs. 10–1 and 2–5, Fri. 10–1; Nov.–Feb., Sun.–Thurs. 10–1 and 2–4, Fri. 10–1.*

DINING

A typical Tuscan repast starts with an antipasto of *crostini* (toasted bread spread with a chicken liver pâté) or cured meats such as prosciutto *crudo* (a salty prosciutto), *finocchiona* (salami seasoned with fennel), and *salsiccia di cinghiale* (sausage made from wild boar). This is the time to start right in on the local wine—Chianti, *naturalmente.* Don't be surprised if the waiter brings an entire flask to the table. Customers are charged only for what they consume (*al consumo,* the arrangement is called), but it's wise to ask for a flask or bottle to be opened then and there, since leftover wines are often mixed together.

Primi piatti (first courses) can consist of excellent local versions of risotto or pasta dishes available throughout Italy. Peculiar to Florence, however, are the vegetable-and-bread soups such as *pappa al pomodoro* (tomatoes, bread, olive oil, onions, and basil), ribollita, or, in the summer, a salad called *panzanella* (tomatoes, onions, vinegar, oil, and bread). Before they are eaten, these are often christened with *un "C" d'olio,* a generous C-shape drizzle of the excellent local olive oil from the ever-present tabletop cruet.

Second to none among the *secondi piatti* (main courses) is *bistecca alla fiorentina*—a thick slab of local Chianina beef, grilled over charcoal, seasoned with olive oil, salt, and pepper, and served rare. *Trippa alla fiorentina* (tripe stewed with tomatoes in a meat sauce) and *arista* (roast loin of pork seasoned with rosemary) are also regional specialties, as are many other roasted meats that go especially well with the Chianti. These are usually served with a *contorno* (side dish) of white beans, sautéed greens, or artichokes in season, all of which can be drizzled with more of that wonderful olive oil.

Tuscan desserts are typically spartan. The cheese is the hard pecorino, and locals like to go for the even tougher *biscottini di Prato,* hard almond cookies, which provide an excuse to dunk them in the potent, sweet dessert wine called *vin santo*, made of dried grapes, which they say will bring the dead back to life.

Remember that dining hours are earlier here than in Rome, starting at 12:30 for the midday meal and at 7:30 for dinner. Many of Florence's restaurants are small, so reservations are a must. Note that the *r* in some of the following addresses indicates the red numbering system used for Florentine businesses, which differs from the black numbers used for residences.

CATEGORY	COST*
$$$$	over 110,000 lire
$$$	80,000–110,000 lire
$$	35,000–80,000 lire
$	under 35,000 lire

Prices are per person, for a three-course meal, including house wine and taxes.

$$$$ ✕ **Enoteca Pinchiorri.** A sumptuous Renaissance palace with high, fres-
★ coed ceilings and bouquets in silver vases is the setting for this restau-
rant, one of the most expensive in Italy, and also considered one of the best (though it has been known to have its off days). The "enoteca" part of the name comes from its former incarnation as a wineshop under owner Giorgio Pinchiorri, who still keeps a stock of vintage bottles in the cellar. Wife Annie Feolde has added her refined interpretations of Tuscan cuisine—*triglie alla viareggina* (mullet with tomato sauce) and *arrosto di coniglio* (roast rabbit)—to a nouvelle menu that includes *cannelloni di astice* (pasta stuffed with lobster), *filetto d'agnello con melanzane e pomodori canditi* (filet of lamb with eggplant and candied tomatoes). ⊠ *Via Ghibellina 87,* ☎ *055/242777. Reservations essential. Jacket and tie. AE, MC, V. Closed Sun., Aug., and 1 wk in Dec. No lunch Mon. and Wed.*

$$$ ✕ **Harry's Bar.** Americans love it, and it *is* the only place in town to get a perfect martini or a hamburger or a club sandwich, but it offers two typical Tuscan dishes every day. The small menu also has well-pre-
pared international offerings, and the bar is open until midnight. ⊠ *Lungarno Vespucci 22/r,* ☎ *055/2396700. Reservations essential. AE, MC, V. Closed Sun. and Dec. 15–Jan. 8.*

$$$ ✕ **Il Cestello.** Across the Arno from the church of San Frediano in Ces-
tello, the restaurant is part of the Excelsior hotel. A huge Florentine hearth keynotes the Renaissance tone of the dining room decor. The Tuscan-based menu features delicious risotto and pasta dishes, in-
cluding an exemplary pasta *e fagioli* (with beans), a rare selection of seafood, and an ever-changing sampling of whatever is fresh from the market. ⊠ *Excelsior hotel, Piazza Ognissanti 3,* ☎ *055/264201. Jacket and tie. AE, DC, MC, V.*

$$$ ✕ **Il Verrocchio.** In an elegant 18th-century villa, now a deluxe hotel, the restaurant is about 20 minutes from downtown Florence by car or taxi, and well worth the ride. The dining room has a huge fireplace, columns, and a high, vaulted ceiling. Outdoors you dine on a terrace overlooking the Arno. The menu changes with the seasons but can be described as Tuscan-international, with such offerings as *tagliata di manzo al rosmarino* (sliced Tuscan steak with rosemary) and delicate, fresh pasta dishes. ⊠ *Villa La Massa, Via La Massa 24, Candeli,* ☎ *055/6510101. AE, DC, MC, V. Closed Mon. and mid-Nov.–mid-Dec.*

$$$ ✕ **La Capannina di Sante.** Florence's best fish restaurant is situated,
★ not surprisingly, along a quiet stretch of the Arno, with indoor tables in an ample, unpretentious trattoria setting and tables outdoors on the terrace during the warmer months. Risotto and various types of pasta

are combined with seafood, and the *grigliata mista di pesce* (mixed grill of fish) is among the standouts. ⊠ *Piazza Ravenna,* ☎ *055/688345. AE, DC, MC, V. Closed Sun. No lunch.*

$$$ ✕ **La Loggia.** The view of Florence from the glassed-in veranda or dining terrace of a century-old mansion on Piazzale Michelangelo is what you and all the other tourists come for, but the relatively new management wants you to remember the food, too. Along with Florentine classics, host Gaetano offers seafood and southern Italian dishes, using produce from his farm in Impruneta. ⊠ *Piazzale Michelangelo 1,* ☎ *055/2342832. Jacket and tie. AE, DC, MC, V. Closed Wed.*

$$$ ✕ **Relais le Jardin.** Another hotel restaurant, this one with a turn-of-the-century, stained-glass-and-wood-paneling setting, stands on its own. This is gourmet cooking at its most refined, including such dishes as *fagottino di vitello* (veal roulade), stuffed with eggplant and cheese in wine sauce, or *calamari farciti* (shrimp-stuffed cuttlefish) with seafood sauce. ⊠ *Hotel Regency, Piazza Massimo D'Azeglio 3,* ☎ *055/245247. Reservations essential. Jacket and tie. AE, DC, MC, V. Closed Sun.*

$$$ ✕ **Terrazza Brunelleschi.** The rooftop restaurant of the Hotel Baglioni
★ has the best view in town. The dining room, decorated in pale blue and creamy tones, has wraparound picture windows framing a close-up of Brunelleschi's dome. The summer terrace outside is charming, with tables placed under arbors and with turrets for guests to climb to get an even better view. The menu offers some traditional Tuscan dishes, such as pappa al pomodoro and *tagliata* (sliced Tuscan steak garnished with arugula and aromatic olive oil). If you order carefully, your check may be in the $$ category. ⊠ *Hotel Baglioni, Piazza Unità Italiana 6,* ☎ *055/215642. Jacket and tie. AE, DC, MC, V.*

$$ ✕ **Alle Murate.** Situated between the Duomo and Santa Croce, this is a sophisticated but informal restaurant. The menu features creative versions of classic Tuscan dishes—*anatra alle erbe* (duck with herb and orange sauce)—but also southern Italian specialties such as *cavatelli con broccoli* (homemade pasta with broccoli and cheese). The main dining room has an elegant, uncluttered look, with warm wood floors and paneling and soft lights. In a smaller adjacent room called the *vineria,* table settings are simpler and the menu more limited. Since the Murate is known for its wine list, this is the place to splurge on a good vintage. ⊠ *Via Ghibellina 52/r,* ☎ *055/240618. AE, DC, MC, V. Closed Mon. No lunch.*

$$ ✕ **Angiolino.** This bustling little trattoria in the Oltrarno district is pop-
★ ular with locals and visitors. It has a real charcoal grill and an old wood-burning stove to keep customers warm on nippy days. The menu offers Tuscan specialties such as ribollita and a classic bistecca alla fiorentina. The bistecca can push the check up, as you pay by weight (order one for two people). ⊠ *Via Santo Spirito 36/r,* ☎ *055/2398976. AE, DC, MC, V. Closed Mon. and last 3 wks in July. No dinner Sun.*

$$ ✕ **Buca dell'Orafo.** One of the best of the Florentine *buca,* meaning hole-in-the-wall, restaurants, Buca dell'Orafo is set in the cellar of a former goldsmith's shop near the Ponte Vecchio. It offers all the Florentine specialties and prides itself on its bistecca. ⊠ *Via dei Girolami 28,* ☎ *055/213619. No credit cards. Closed Sun.–Mon. and Aug.*

$$ ✕ **Caffè Concerto.** A short taxi ride from city center takes you to this veranda-style restaurant, all glass and polished wood alongside the Arno. The excellent, traditional Tuscan cuisine—and equally fine Tuscan wine list—attracts visiting celebrities and a steady Florentine clientele. ⊠ *Lungarno Colombo 7,* ☎ *055/677377. Reservations essential. AE, DC, MC, V. Closed Sun.*

$$ ✕ **Cantinetta Antinori.** Set on the ground floor of a Renaissance palace, this is an elegant place for lunch after shopping in nearby Via Tornabuoni. The Antinori family is best known as wine producers, and their wares

124

Florence Dining and Lodging

V. Panicale
V. Guelfa
V. Gallo
V. S. Gallo
V. Laura
V. Colonna

Piazza
Mercato
Centrale

Piazza
SS. Annunziata

V. dell' Ariento
V. d. Canto de Nelli
V. S. Antonino
V. S. Faenza
V. Cavour
V. Ricasoli
V. dei Servi
V. degli Alfani

V. dei Giglio
V. d. Conti

Piazza
S. Lorenzo

V. Martelli
V. Pucci
V. della Pergola

V. Cerretani

V. Bufalini

Borgo Pinti

V. Fiesolana

Piazza di
S. Giovanni

Piazza
del Duomo

V. Pecori
V. dei Tosinghi
V. Vecchietti

V. d. Studio

V. S. Egidio

V. dei Pepi

Piazza
della
Repubblica

V. degli Speziali

V. d. Proconsolo

Borgo degli Albizi

Piazza
Salvemini

V. Strozzi
V. Anselmi
V. dei Calzaiuoli

AE

V. dei Pandolfini
V. Ghibellina

V. dell' Agnolo

V. Porta Rossa

Piazza
S. Firenze

V. Ghibellina

V. delle Terme
Borgo SS. Apostoli

Piazza della
Signoria

V. d.
Gondi

Via Torta

V. Verrazzano

Acciaioli

V. Por S. Maria
V. Vacchereccia

V. Leoni

Borgo dei Greci

Piazza
Santa
Croce

V. di S. Giuseppe

Ponte Vecchio

Lung. Archibusieri

V. dei Neri

V. Benci

Borgo S. Croce

Lung. Diaz

Corso Tintori

Arno

Piazza
S. Maria
Sopr' Arno

Costa dei Magnoli

Lung. Torrigiani

V. dei Bardi

Ponte alle Grazie

Lung. d. Grazie

Arno

Lung. Serristori

Piazza
dei Mozzi

V. dei Renai

Via V. di S. Niccolò

Via S. Miniato

**Forte di
Belvedere**

S. Giorgio

KEY

i Tourist Information

AE American Express Office

0   440 yards

0   400 meters

V. di Belvedere

may be sampled with light salads, bread, sausage, and cheese snacks or more complete meals. ⊠ *Piazza Antinori 3,* ☎ *055/292234. AE, DC, MC, V. Closed weekends and Aug.*

$$ ✕ **Hosteria da Ganino.** On a side street between the Duomo and Palazzo Vecchio, this trattoria is informal, rustic, and cheerful. The menu features homemade pasta, and the fettuccine with porcini mushrooms is a specialty. Main courses uphold Florentine tradition, with grilled steak and chops and bean dishes. Get there early: it seats only about 35; double that number in good weather at outside tables. ⊠ *Piazza dei Cimatori 4/r,* ☎ *055/214125. AE, DC, V. Closed Sun. and Aug. 15–25.*

$$ ✕ **Il Cibreo.** Trendsetter that he is, chef Fabrio Picchi has made Cibreo
★ into Florence's newest pilgrimage spot for gourmands. His menu of Tuscan country dishes relies less on his memories than on his lively imagination, which has created updated versions of Florentine classics, such as pappa al pomodoro, presented as a thick red dollop on a sparkling white Ginori plate, and *anatra farcita di pinoli e uvetta* (duck stuffed with pine nuts and raisins). Don't miss the yellow-pepper soup—made, thanks to the restaurant's location near the Sant'-Ambrogio market, with the freshest ingredients available. You'll dine in an upscale trattoria-style dining room or, during warmer weather, in a piazza overlooking the market. A café annex across the street serves drinks and snacks all day. There is also a small, inconspicuous, and inexpensive tavern annex around the corner. ⊠ *Via dei Macci 118/r,* ☎ *055/2341100. Reservations essential. AE, DC, MC, V. Closed Sun.–Mon., July 25–Sept. 5, and Dec. 31–Jan. 7.*

$$ ✕ **La Giostra.** Only about five minutes from the cathedral or from Santa Croce, the Giostra has the typically unpretentious look of a trattoria, but with a difference: the gourmet touch of the courteous owner-chef. Try his fusilli *del Boboli* (with fresh vegetables and mozzarella cheese). Like the menu, the wine list offers good value. Service is informal, and the restaurant is open until midnight, a rarity in Florence. ⊠ *Borgo Pinti 10/r,* ☎ *055/241341. AE, DC, MC, V.*

$$ ✕ **Le Fonticine.** Owner Silvano Bruci is from Tuscany, wife Gianna from
★ Emilia-Romagna, and the restaurant combines the best of both worlds in a setting liberally hung with their extensive collection of paintings. Emilia-Romagna specialties such as tortellini ready the taste buds for Tuscan grilled porcini mushrooms so meaty they provide serious competition for the bistecca alla fiorentina. ⊠ *Via Nazionale 79/r,* ☎ *055/ 282106. AE, DC, MC, V. Closed Sun.–Mon, and July 25–Aug. 25.*

$$ ✕ **Pallottino.** Pallottino has the look of a typical Florentine trattoria, with dark chestnut tables and benches and copper utensils and old photos on the walls, but here the decor is somehow improved. The menu features traditional fare, from bread or bean soup to spaghetti *alla fiaccheraia* (with piquant fresh tomato sauce). Meat courses are varied; try *petto di pollo a modo nostro* (chicken breast with a creamy cheese and vegetable sauce). Prices are at the low end of this category. ⊠ *Via Isola delle Stinche 1/r,* ☎ *055/289573. AE, DC, MC, V. Closed Mon. and Aug. 1–20.*

$$ ✕ **Sostanza** (a.k.a. Il Troia). Il Troia is Florence's oldest restaurant,
★ founded in 1869. Travelers usually love it, in spite of, or perhaps because of, the no-frills decor and the brusque service. Why? Along with a quintessential bistecca alla fiorentina with a hefty price tag, within this small room you'll be sure to find an entire world of Florence aficionados. The waiters may be surly but the new friends you'll make at the communal tables—chances are you'll sit next to an art historian from Vassar or a bookstore owner from London—will more than make up for it. ⊠ *Via del Porcellana 25/r,* ☎ *055/212691. No credit cards. Closed Sun. and Aug. No dinner Sat.*

$$ ✕ **Toscano.** A small table attractively set in a show window identifies this restaurant, about five minutes from Palazzo Medici-Riccardi. It lives up to its name in ambience and cuisine. The cold-cuts counter at the entrance, terra-cotta tile floors, and beamed ceilings typify a Tuscan trattoria, but the pink tablecloths, arty photos on the walls, and a touch of creative cuisine take it out of the ordinary. The kitchen prides itself on top-quality meat; this is the place to try tagliata or *spezzatino peposo* (beef stew with lots of black pepper and a wine sauce). The fixed-price menu is a good value, at about 30,000 lire, including water and wine. ⊠ *Via Guelfa 70/r,* ☎ *055/215475. AE, DC, MC, V. Closed Tues. and Aug.*

$ ✕ **La Maremmana.** A display of garden-fresh vegetables and fruit catches your eye as you enter this popular trattoria near Santa Croce. Authentic Tuscan cuisine is offered in the dining room, which has the usual wood paneling and long tables that you will probably be asked to share. The fixed-price menu offers generous servings and good value, and it may include ribollita and *stracotto* (beef stew). ⊠ *Via dei Macci 77/r,* ☎ *055/241226. DC, MC, V. Closed Sun. and Aug.*

$ ✕ **Mario.** Clean and classic, this family-run trattoria on the corner of Piazza del Mercato near San Lorenzo offers genuine Florentine atmosphere and cooking, with no frills but under a wooden ceiling dated 1536. Open for lunch only, it's just around the corner from Za-Za (☞ *below*). ⊠ *Via Rosina 2/r (Piazza del Mercato Centrale),* ☎ *055/218550. Reservations not accepted. No credit cards. Closed Sun. No dinner.*

$ ✕ **Mossacce.** You share a heavy wooden trattoria table here and watch the cook in the glassed-in kitchen prepare your order, chosen from a menu of Florentine classics. ⊠ *Via del Proconsolo 55/r,* ☎ *055/294361. Reservations not accepted. AE, MC, V. Closed weekends and Aug.*

$ ✕ **Za-Za.** Slightly more upscale than neighboring trattorias, Za-Za attracts white-collar workers and theater people. Ranks of Chianti flasks are part of the decor, and you couldn't ask for a more typically Florentine dining experience, with traditional atmosphere and food. ⊠ *Piazza Mercato Centrale 26/r,* ☎ *055/215411. Reservations essential. AE, DC, MC, V. Closed Sun.*

Wine Bars

Don't have time for a trattoria? Head for one of Florence's wine bars for a fast focaccia, sandwich, or snack, and a glass of Chianti Classico. Of these, **Le Cantine** (⊠ Via dei Pucci) is stylish and popular. **Cantinone del Gallo Nero** (⊠ Via Santo Spirito 6) serves meals in a brick-vaulted wine cellar. **Le Volpi e l'Uva** (⊠ Piazza de' Rossi 1) is popular among Florentines. The city's best, **Fuori Porta** (⊠ Via dei Monte all Croci 10), is a 15-minute walk from city center.

More modest bets: **Borgioli** (⊠ Piazza dell'Olio). **Fiaschetteria** (⊠ Via dei Neri 2, corner of Via dei Benci). **Fratellini** (⊠ Via dei Cimatori). **Nicolino** (⊠ Volta dei Mercanti). **Piccolo Vinaio** (⊠ Via Castellani).

LODGING

Florence's importance not only as a tourist city but as a convention center and the site of the Pitti fashion collections throughout the year has guaranteed a variety of accommodations, many in former villas and palazzi. However, these very factors mean that, except during the winter, reservations are a must.

A few hotels can be found near the A1 autostrada exits: **Sheraton Firenze** (☎ 055/64901, ℻ 055/680747, $$$$). **Holiday Inn** (☎ 055/6531841, ℻ 055/6531806, $$$). **Forte Agip** (☎ 055/4205081, ℻ 055/4219015, $$$).

If you do find yourself in Florence with no reservations, go to the **Consorzio ITA** office (✉ Train station). It's open every day from 8:20 AM to 9 PM. Otherwise your best bet is to try some of the inexpensive (but clean) accommodations at a one- or two-star hotel; many are on **Via Nazionale** (✉ Leads east from Piazza Stazione) and on **Via Faenza** (✉ Second left off Via Nazionale).

CATEGORY	COST*
$$$$	over 450,000 lire
$$$	300,000–450,000 lire
$$	190,000–300,000 lire
$	under 190,000 lire

Prices are for a double room for two, including tax and service.

$$$$ ⊡ **Excelsior.** Traditional Old World charm finds a regal setting at the
★ Excelsior, a neo-Renaissance palace complete with painted wooden ceilings, stained glass, and acres of Oriental carpets strewn over marble floors in the public rooms. The rooms are furnished with the opulence of 19th-century Florentine antiques and sumptuous fabrics, set off by charming old prints of the city and long mirrors of the Empire style. Plush touches include wall-to-wall carpeting in the rooms and thick terry-cloth towels on heated racks in the bathrooms. ✉ *Piazza Ognissanti 3, 50123,* ☎ *055/264201,* FAX *055/210278. 163 rooms. Restaurant, piano bar. AE, DC, MC, V.*

$$$$ ⊡ **Grand Hotel.** Across the piazza from the Excelsior, this Florentine classic, also an ITT-Sheraton "Luxury Collection" hotel, provides all the luxurious amenities of its sister. Here most rooms and public areas are decorated in sumptuous Renaissance style with rich fabrics in distinctive Florentine style. Many rooms have frescoes or canopied beds. Baths are in marble. A few rooms have balconies overlooking the Arno. ✉ *Piazza Ognissanti 1, 50123,* ☎ *055/288781,* FAX *055/217400. 107 rooms. Restaurant, bar, parking (fee). AE, DC, MC, V.*

$$$$ ⊡ **Grand Hotel Villa Cora.** Built near the Boboli Gardens and Piazzale Michelangelo in 1750, the Villa Cora retains the opulence of the 18th and 19th centuries. The decor of its remarkable public and private rooms runs the gamut from neoclassical to rococo and even Moorish, and reflects the splendor of such former guests as the Empress Eugénie, wife of Napoléon III, and Madame Von Meck, Tchaikovsky's mysterious benefactress. ✉ *Viale Machiavelli 18, 50125,* ☎ *055/2298451,* FAX *055/229086. 48 rooms. Restaurant, piano bar, pool. AE, DC, MC, V.*

$$$$ ⊡ **Plaza Hotel Lucchesi.** Elegant without being ostentatious, this hotel
★ is right on the Arno near Santa Croce. Front bedrooms have views of the river and hills beyond; rear rooms on the top floor have balconies and knockout views of Santa Croce. Spacious, quiet bedrooms (double glazing throughout) are furnished comfortably in mahogany and pastel fabrics against creamy white walls. The roomy, welcoming lounges and piano bar are favorite meeting places for Florentines. ✉ *Lungarno della Zecca Vecchia 38, 50122,* ☎ *055/26236,* FAX *055/2480921. 97 rooms. Restaurant, piano bar, parking (fee). AE, DC, MC, V.*

$$$$ ⊡ **Regency.** In this stylish hotel in a respectable residential district near the synagogue, the noise and crowds of Florence seem far away, though you are less than 10 minutes away from the Accademia and Michelangelo's *David*. The rooms are decorated in richly colored and tasteful fabrics and antique-style furniture faithful to the hotel's 19th-century origins as a private mansion. It has one of Florence's best hotel restaurants (☞ *above*). ✉ *Piazza Massimo D'Azeglio 3, 50121,* ☎ *055/245247,* FAX *055/2346735. 34 rooms. Restaurant, parking (fee). AE, DC, MC, V.*

$$$$ ⊡ **Villa San Michele.** The setting for this hideaway is so romantic—nestled in the hills of nearby Fiesole—that it once attracted Brigitte Bar-

dot for her honeymoon. The villa was originally a monastery whose facade and loggia have been attributed to Michelangelo. Many of the rooms now contain sumptuous statuary, paintings, and whirlpool baths. Many have a panoramic view of Florence, while others look onto the former cloister. A luxuriant garden surrounds the whole affair. The restaurant is excellent. This is one of Italy's costliest hotels. ⊠ *Via Doccia 4, Fiesole, 59451,* ☎ *055/59451,* FAX *055/598734. 36 rooms. Restaurant, piano bar, pool. AE, DC, MC, V. Closed Dec.–mid-Mar.*

$$$ 🏨 **Baglioni.** This large turn-of-the-century building was conceived in the European tradition of grand hotels; it's between the train station and the cathedral. The charming roof terrace has the best view in Florence and is home to the Terrazza Brunelleschi restaurant. The hotel has well-proportioned rooms, some decorated in antique Florentine style, and many with leaded-glass windows. Most rooms have been done in pastel tones harmonizing with the carpeting or mellow parquet. There is a full range of conference facilities, which makes it a favorite of businesspeople. ⊠ *Piazza dell'Unità Italiana 6, 50123,* ☎ *055/23580,* FAX *055/2358895. 195 rooms. Restaurant. AE, DC, MC, V.*

$$$ 🏨 **Beacci Tornabuoni.** This is perhaps *the* classic Florentine pensione (although by law all lodgings have been reclassified as hotels of various categories). Set in a 14th-century palazzo, it has old-fashioned style and just enough modern comfort to keep today's guests happy. Half board is required, but the food is good and can also be served in the rooms, most of which have views of the red-tile roofs in the neighboring downtown area. ⊠ *Via Tornabuoni 3, 50123,* ☎ *055/212645,* FAX *055/283594. 30 rooms. Restaurant, bar. AE, DC, MC, V.*

$$$ 🏨 **Brunelleschi.** Architects united a Byzantine tower, a medieval church,
★ and a later building in a stunning structure in the very heart of Renaissance Florence to make this the city's most unique hotel. This remarkable place even has its own museum displaying the ancient Roman foundations and pottery shards found during restoration. Medieval stone walls and brick arches contrast pleasingly with the plush, contemporary decor. The comfortable, soundproof bedrooms, many with good views, are done in coordinated patterns and soft colors; the ample bathrooms feature beige travertine marble. Brunelleschi ranks high for atmosphere, interest, and comfort. ⊠ *Piazza Sant'Elisabetta (Via dei Calzaiuoli), 50122,* ☎ *055/562068,* FAX *055/219653. 96 rooms, 7 junior suites. Restaurant, bar, meeting rooms. AE, DC, MC, V.*

$$$ 🏨 **Hermitage.** Comfortable and charming are suitable adjectives for this hotel occupying the top two floors of a palazzo next to Ponte Vecchio and the Uffizi. Inviting living rooms overlooking the Arno, bright breakfast rooms, flowered roof terrace, and well-lighted bedrooms have the decor and atmosphere of a well-kept Florentine home. Double glazing, air-conditioning, and attentive maintenance sustain the relaxing ambience. (The hotel has an elevator at the top of a short flight of stairs from the street.) ⊠ *Vicolo Marzio 1 (Piazza del Pesce, Ponte Vecchio), 50122,* ☎ *055/287216,* FAX *055/212208. 29 rooms. MC, V.*

$$$ 🏨 **J&J.** Away from the crowds, on a quiet street within walking distance of the sights, this unusual hotel is a converted 16th-century monastery. Its large, suitelike rooms are ideal for honeymooners, families, and small groups of friends traveling together. Some rooms are on two levels, and all are imaginatively arranged around a central courtyard and decorated with flair. There are also smaller, more intimate rooms, some opening onto their own little courtyard. The gracious owners chat with guests in the elegant lounge; breakfast is served in a glassed-in Renaissance loggia or in the central courtyard. ⊠ *Via di Mezzo 20, 50121,* ☎ *055/2345005,* FAX *055/240282. 20 rooms. Bar. AE, DC, MC, V.*

$$$ 🏨 **Kraft.** The efficient and comfortable Kraft is modern, but it has many period-style rooms, some with balconies, and a rooftop terrace café.

Its location near the Teatro Comunale (it is also next to the U.S. consulate) gives it a clientele from the music world. ⊠ *Via Solferino 2, 50123,* ☎ *055/284273,* FAX *055/2398267. 77 rooms. Pool. AE, DC, MC, V.*

$$$ 🏨 **Monna Lisa.** Housed in a Renaissance palazzo, the hotel retains its
★   original marble staircase, terra-cotta floors, and painted ceilings. Its rooms still have a rather homey quality, and though on the small side, many have contemplative views of a lovely garden. The ground-floor lounges give you the feel of living in an aristocratic town house. ⊠ *Borgo Pinti 27, 50121,* ☎ *055/2479751,* FAX *055/2479755. 30 rooms. Bar. AE, DC, MC, V.*

$$ 🏨 **Bencistà.** Below the luxurious Villa San Michele in Fiesole, this hotel has the same tranquil setting and is even two centuries older. The rooms are furnished with antiques, and half board is required. ⊠ *Via Benedetto da Maiano 4, Fiesole, 50014,* ☎ *055/59163,* FAX *055/59163. 44 rooms, 32 with bath. No credit cards.*

$$ 🏨 **La Residenza.** On Florence's most elegant shopping street, on the upper floors of a restored 15th-century building, La Residenza has character and comfort. The roof garden and adjacent sitting room are added attractions. Paintings and etchings add interest to the room decor, while soundproofing and satellite TV help guests to relax. ⊠ *Via Tornabuoni 8, 50123,* ☎ *055/218684,* FAX *055/284197. 24 rooms, 20 with bath. Restaurant, parking (fee). AE, DC, MC, V.*

$$ 🏨 **Loggiato dei Serviti.** This hotel was not designed by Brunelleschi,
★   Florence's architectural genius, but it might as well have been. A mirror image of the architect's famous Ospedale degli Innocenti across the way, the Loggiato is tucked away on one of the city's quietest and loveliest squares. Occupying a 16th-century former monastery, the building was originally a refuge for traveling priests. Vaulted ceilings and tasteful furnishings, some of them antiques, make this a place for those who want to get the feel of Florence in a spare, Renaissance building while enjoying modern creature comforts. The hotel has no restaurant. ⊠ *Piazza Santissima Annunziata 3, 50122,* ☎ *055/289592,* FAX *055/ 289595. 29 rooms. Parking (fee). AE, DC, MC, V.*

$$ 🏨 **Morandi alla Crocetta.** Near Piazza Santissima Annunziata, this is
★   a charming and distinguished residence in which guests are made to feel like privileged friends of the family. It is close to the sights but very quiet, in a former monastery, and is furnished comfortably in the classic style of a gracious Florentine home. The Morandi is not only an exceptional hotel but also a good value. Very small, it is worth booking well in advance. ⊠ *Via Laura 50, 50121,* ☎ *055/2344747,* FAX *055/ 2480954. 10 rooms. AE, DC, MC, V.*

$$ 🏨 **Pendini.** The atmosphere of an old-fashioned Florentine pensione is intact here, though most bedrooms have been freshly renovated. Public rooms are delightful; furnishings throughout are early 19th-century antiques or reproductions. Most bedrooms have brass or walnut beds, pretty floral wallpaper, and pastel carpeting; baths are modern. Many rooms can accommodate extra beds. The location is central, and rates are low for the category. Off-season rates are a real bargain. ⊠ *Via Strozzi 2, 50123,* ☎ *055/211170,* FAX *055/281807. 42 rooms. AE, DC, MC, V.*

$ 🏨 **Alessandra.** The location, a block from the Ponte Vecchio, and clean, ample rooms make this a good choice. The English-speaking staff is friendly and helpful. ⊠ *Borgo Santi Apostoli 17, 50123,* ☎ *055/ 283438. 25 rooms, 16 with bath. AE, MC, V. Closed Dec. 15–26.*

$ 🏨 **Apollo.** A friendly Italian-Canadian couple owns and manages this conveniently located hotel near the station, offering good value in spacious rooms decorated in Florentine style. The gleaming new bathrooms, though compact, have such amenities as hair dryers. The staff is helpful and attentive to guests' needs. ✉ *Via Faenza 77, 50123,* ☎ *055/ 284119,* FAX *055/210101. 15 rooms. Parking (fee). AE, DC, MC, V.*

$ 🖭 **Bellettini.** You couldn't ask for anything more central; this small hotel
★ is on three floors (the top floor has two nice rooms with a view) of a
palazzo near the Duomo. The cordial family management takes good
care of guests, providing a relaxed atmosphere and attractive public
rooms with a scattering of antiques. Breakfast, with homemade cakes,
and air-conditioning are included in the low room rate. The good-size
rooms have Venetian or Tuscan provincial decor; bathrooms are bright
and modern. ✉ *Via dei Conti 7, 50123,* ☎ *055/213561,* FAX *055/ 283551. 28 rooms. Bar, parking (fee). AE, DC, MC, V.*

$ 🖭 **Liana.** This small hotel near the English Cemetery is in a quiet 19th-
century villa that formerly housed the British Embassy. Its clean and
pleasant rooms all face a stately garden. ✉ *Via Vittorio Alfieri 18, 50121,*
☎ *055/245303,* FAX *055/2344596. 17 rooms. AE, MC, V.*

$ 🖭 **Nuova Italia.** Near the train station and within walking distance of
the sights, this hotel is run by a genial English-speaking family. It has
a homey atmosphere; rooms are clean and simply furnished, Rooms
have air-conditioning and double-glazed windows to ensure restful nights.
Some rooms can accommodate extra beds. Low bargain rates include
breakfast. ✉ *Via Faenza 26, 50123,* ☎ *055/268430,* FAX *055/210941.
20 rooms. Parking (fee). AE, DC, MC, V.*

NIGHTLIFE AND THE ARTS

The Arts

Concerts

The **Maggio Musicale Fiorentina** series of internationally acclaimed con-
certs and recitals is held in the Teatro Comunale (✉ Corso Italia 16,
☎ 055/2779236) from late April through June. From December to early
June, there is a concert season of the **Orchestra Regionale Toscana** (✉
Santo Stefano al Ponte Vecchio church, ☎ 055/210804). **Amici della
Musica** organizes concerts at the Teatro della Pergola (✉ Box office,
Via della Pergola 10/r, ☎ 055/2479652).

Film

English-language films are shown at the **Cinema Astro** (✉ Piazza San
Simone near Santa Croce). There are two shows every evening, Tuesday through Sunday (closed in July). The **Festival del Popolo** is held
each December, is devoted to documentaries, and is held in the Fortezza
da Basso. An international panel of judges gathers in late spring at the
Forte di Belvedere for the **Florence Film Festival,** during which they pre-
side over a wide selection of new releases.

Opera

Operas are performed in the **Teatro Comunale** (✉ Corso Italia 16, ☎
055/2779236) from December through February.

Nightlife

Unlike the Romans and Milanese, the reserved Florentines do not have
a reputation for an active nightlife; however, the following places attract a mixed crowd of Florentines and visitors.

Nightclubs

Yab (✉ Via Sassetti 5r, ☎ 055/282018) is one of largest, with a young
clientele. **Space Electronic** (✉ Via Palazzuolo 37, ☎ 055/2393082),
though one of Florence's oldest extant discos, keeps on top of trends in
music and decor. A less frenetic alternative is **Jackie O'** (✉ Via Erta Can-
ina 24, ☎ 055/2344904). **Full Up** (✉ Via della Vigna Vecchia 21/r, ☎

055/293006) draws a very young clientele. **Meccanò** (✉ Viale degli Olmi 1, in Cascine Park, ☎ 055/331371) is a multimedia experience in a high-tech disco with a late-night restaurant (closed Mon.).

River Club (✉ Lungarno Corsini 8, ☎ 055/282465) has winter-garden decor and a large dance floor; it, too, closes Sunday. The accent is on Brazil at **Caffè Voltaire** (✉ Via della Scala 9/r, ☎ 055/218255), where there's Latin food and music.

Piano Bars

Many of the more expensive hotels have their own piano bars, where nonguests are welcome to come for an *aperitivo* or an after-dinner drink. The best view is from the bar at the **Excelsior** (✉ Piazza Ognissanti 3, ☎ 055/264201), on a roof garden overlooking the Arno. Music, though not live piano, can be heard at the **Champagneria** (✉ Via Lambruschini 15/r, ☎ 055/490804), a bistro-type watering hole; it's closed Sunday.

OUTDOOR ACTIVITIES AND SPORTS

Participant Sports

Bicycling

Bikes are a good way of getting out into the hills, but the scope for biking is limited in the center of town. *See* Getting Around *in* Florence A to Z, *below,* for information on where to rent bicycles.

Canoeing

Those who get the urge to paddle on the Arno can try **Società Canottieri Firenze** (✉ Lungarno dei Medici 8, ☎ 055/282130) near the Uffizi.

Golf

Golf Club Ugolino (✉ Via Chiantigiana 3, Impruneta, ☎ 055/2301009) is a hilly 18-hole course in the heart of Chianti country just outside town. It is open to the public.

Running

Don't even think of running on city streets, where tour buses and triple-parked Alfa Romeos leave precious little space for pedestrians. Instead, head for the **Cascine,** the park along the Arno at the western end of the city. You can run to the Cascine along the Lungarno (stay on the sidewalk), or take Bus 17 from the Duomo. A cinder track lies on the hillside just below **Piazzale Michelangelo,** across the Arno from the city center. The views of the Florence skyline are inspirational, but the locker rooms are reserved for members, so come ready to run.

Swimming

Bellariva (✉ Lungarno Colombo 6, ☎ 055/677521). **Circolo Tennis alle Cascine** (✉ Viale Visarno 1, ☎ 055/356651). **Costoli** (✉ Viale Paoli, ☎ 055/675744). **Le Pavoniere** (✉ Viale degli Olmi, ☎ 055/367506).

Tennis

Circolo Tennis alle Cascine (✉ Viale Visarno 1, ☎ 055/356651). **Tennis Club Rifredi** (✉ Via Facibeni, ☎ 055/432552). **Il Poggetto** (✉ Via Mercati 24/b, ☎ 055/460127).

Spectator Sports

Horse Racing

You can make your bets at the **Ippodromo Visarno** (✉ Piazzale delle Cascine, ☎ 055/360056). Check the local papers to see when they're running.

Soccer

Italians are passionate about *calcio* (soccer), and the Florentines are no exception; indeed, *tifosi* (fans) of the Fiorentina team are fervent supporters. The team plays its home games at the **Stadio Comunale** (Municipal Stadium; ✉ Top of Viale Manfredo Fanti). Tickets for all games except those against their biggest rivals—Juventus of Turin and A. C. Milan—are difficult but not impossible to come by. Try the ticket booth **Chiosco degli Sportivi** (✉ North side of Piazza della Repubblica). Games are usually played on Sunday afternoon, from about late August to May. A medieval version of the game is played in costume each year on or around June 24, feast day of St. John the Baptist.

SHOPPING

Shops in Florence are generally open 9–1 and 3:30–7:30 but closed Sunday and Monday mornings most of the year. Summer hours are usually 9–1 and 4–8, with closings on Saturday afternoon but not Monday morning. When locating the stores, remember that the addresses with *r* in them, which stands for *rosso* (red) and indicates a commercial address, follow a separate numbering system from the black-numbered residential addresses. A rule of thumb for shopping in Florence is that if it *looks* expensive, it will more than likely be *more* expensive than you had anticipated. Most shops take major credit cards and will ship purchases, though it's wiser to take your purchases with you.

Markets

Those with a tight budget or a sense of adventure may want to take a look at the souvenir stands under the loggia of the **Mercato Nuovo** (☞ The Historic Heart of Florence *in* Exploring Florence, *above*), the stalls that line the streets near San Lorenzo. The **Mercato Centrale** (☞ Michelangelo Country *in* Exploring Florence, *above*) is the huge indoor food market next to the Mercato Nuovo. You can find bargains at the **Flea Market** on Piazza dei Ciompi. An **open-air market** is held in Cascine park every Tuesday morning. A **crafts fair** is held in Piazza Santo Spirito on the first Sunday of the month.

Shopping Districts

Florence's most elegant shops are concentrated in the center of town, **Via Tornabuoni** the fanciest address. **Galleria Tornabuoni,** one of the world's choicest shopping malls, is also a designer mecca. **Borgo Ognissanti** has the city's largest concentration of antiques shops. **Via Maggio,** across the river in Oltrarno, is also packed with antique shops. **Ponte Vecchio** houses the city's jewelers, as it has since the 16th century. Leather boutiques abound on **Via della Vigna Nuova.** The area near **Santa Croce** is the heart of the leather merchants' district.

Specialty Shops

ANTIQUES

At **Alberto Pierini** (✉ Borgo Ognissanti 22/r) the rustic Tuscan furniture is all antique, and much of it dates back to the days of the Medici. **Specialties at Paolo Ventura** (✉ Borgo Ognissanti 16/r) are antique ceramics from all periods and places of origin. **Galleria Luigi Bellini** (✉ Lungarno Soderini 5m, Oltrarno) claims to be Italy's oldest antiques dealer, which may be true, since father Mario Bellini was responsible for instituting Florence's international antiques biennial. At any rate, what matters is that the merchandise is genuine. **Giovanni Pratesi** (✉ Via Maggio 13/r) specializes in Italian antiques, in this case furniture, with some fine paintings, sculpture, and decorative objects turning up from time to time. Vying with Luigi Bellini as one of Florence's oldest antiques dealers, **Guido Bartolozzi** (✉ Via Maggio 18/r) deals in predominately period Florentine objects; the high quality is commensurate with the prices. At **Paolo Paoletti** (⊠ Via Maggio 30/r), look for Florentine antiques with an emphasis on Medici-era objects from the 15th and 16th centuries.

BOOKS, STATIONERY, AND PHOTOGRAPHY

Pineider (⊠ Piazza della Signoria 14/r and Via Tornabuoni 76/r) now has shops throughout the world, but it began in Florence and still does all its printing here. Personalized stationery and business cards are the mainstay, but the stores also sell fine desk accessories. **Centro Di** (⊠ Piazza dei Mozzi 1, Oltrarno) stands for Centro di Documentazione Internazionale, and it publishes art books and exhibition catalogues for some of the most important organizations in Europe. Centro Di stocks its own publications along with many others. One of Florence's oldest paper-goods stores, **Giannini** (⊠ Piazza Pitti 37/r, Oltrarno) is *the* place to buy the marbleized versions, which come in a variety of forms, from flat sheets to boxes and even pencils. Long one of Florence's best art bookshops, **Salimbeni** (⊠ Via Matteo Palmieri 14/r) specializes in publications on Tuscany; it publishes many itself. **Alinari** (⊠ Via della Vigna Nuova 46/r) is one of Florence's oldest and most prestigious photographers, and in this store, next to its museum, prints of its historic photographs are sold along with books and posters.

CLOTHING

At **Casa dello Sport** (⊠ Via dei Tosinghi 8/r) you'll find casual wear for the entire family—sporty clothes by some of Italy's most famous manufacturers. The elegant boutique **Laurèl** (⊠ Via della Vigna Nuova 67/r) has a reputation for the quality and understatement that is the hallmark of Florentine women's fashions. The aristocratic Marchese di Barsento **Emilio Pucci** (⊠ Via dei Pucci 6/r) was a household name in Florence, and until his death in 1992, he presided over the opening of the Renaissance *Calcio in Costume* festivities each year. He became an international name during the early 1960s, when the stretch ski clothes he designed for himself caught on with the dolce vita crowd. His pseudo-psychedelic prints and "palazzo pajamas" then became the rage. The shop in the family palazzo still sells the celebrated Pucci prints, along with a line of wines from the family estate in Chianti.

EMBROIDERY AND FABRICS

Signora **Loretta Caponi** (⊠ Borgo Ognissanti 12/r) is synonymous with Florentine embroidery, and her luxury lace, linens, and lingerie have earned her a worldwide reputation. The fabric outlet **Antico Setificio Fiorentino** (⊠ Via della Vigna Nuova 97/r) really *is* antique, as it has produced antique fabrics for over half a millennium. Swaths of handmade material of every style and description are for sale, and the decorative tassels make lovely typically Florentine presents as well. **Filpucci** (⊠ Via della Vigna Nuova 14/r) is Italy's largest manufacturer of yarns. Nearby factories produce skeins of the stuff for Italy's top designers, and the extensive stock of its retail outlet in Florence encourages the talented to create their own designs. **Officina Farmaceutica di Santa Maria Novella** (⊠ Via della Scala 16/r) is redolent of the thousand perfumes in this Art Nouveau emporium of herbal cosmetics, soaps, and sachets based on centuries-old recipes devised by monks. The name **Pratesi** (⊠ Lungarno Amerigo Vespucci 8/r) is a byword for luxury, in this case linens that have lined the beds of the rich and famous, with an emphasis on the former.

HOUSEWARES

For housewares nothing beats **Bartolini** (⊠ Via dei Servi 30/r), with a wide selection of well-designed, practical items. **Sbigoli Terrecotte** (⊠ Via Sant'Egidio 4/r) carries a wide selection of terra-cotta and ceramic vases, pots, cups, and saucers.

Della Loggia (⊠ Via Por Santa Maria 29/r) combines precious and semi-precious stones in contemporary settings made of precious and non-precious metals, such as the gold and steel pieces usually on display in its windows. **Gherardi** (⊠ Ponte Vecchio 5), Florence's king of coral, has the city's largest selection of finely crafted and encased specimens, as well as other precious materials such as cultured pearls, jade, and turquoise. Antique jewelry is the specialty at **Melli** (⊠ Ponte Vecchio 44/r); it is displayed alongside period porcelains, clocks, and other museum-quality objects. The venerable **Piccini** (⊠ Ponte Vecchio 23/r) has literally been crowning the heads of Europe for almost a century, and combines its taste for the antique with contemporary jewelry. One of Florence's oldest jewelers, **Settepassi-Faraone** (⊠ Via Tornabuoni 25/r) has supplied Italian (and other) royalty with finely crafted gems for centuries. Its selection of antique-looking classics has been updated with a choice of contemporary silver.

Spurred on by the revival of Carnival in recent years, **I Maschereri** (⊠ Borgo Pinti 18/r) has begun to produce fanciful masks in commedia dell'arte and contemporary styles.

The **Gucci** (⊠ Via Tornabuoni 73/r) family is practically single-handedly responsible for making designers' initials (in this case the two interlocking Gs) a status symbol. This Florence store is the one that started it all, and prices on the clothing and leather goods are slightly better here than elsewhere. **Ugolini** (⊠ Via Tornabuoni 20/r) once made gloves for the Italian royal family, but now anyone can have the luxury of its exotic leathers, as well as silk and cashmere ties and scarves. Born near Naples, the late Salvatore Ferragamo made his fortune custom-making exotic shoes for famous feet, especially Hollywood stars, and so **Ferragamo** (⊠ Via Tornabuoni 16/r) knows about less-than-delicate shoe sizes. His palace at the end of the street has since passed on to his wife, Wanda, and displays designer clothing, but elegant footwear still underlies the Ferragamo success.

Giotti (⊠ Piazza Ognissanti 3/r) stocks the largest selection of Bottega Veneta's woven-leather bags, plus a full line of the firm's other leather goods and its own leather clothing. **Leather Guild** (⊠ Piazza Santa Croce 20/r) is one of many such shops throughout the area that produce inexpensive, antique-looking leather goods of mass appeal, but here you can see the craftspersons at work, a reassuring experience. **Il Bisonte** (⊠ Via del Parione 31/r, just off Via della Vigna Nuova) is known for its natural-looking leather goods, all stamped with the store's bison symbol. The ultimate fine leathers are crafted into classic shapes at **Casadei** (⊠ Via Tornabuoni 33/r), winding up as women's shoes and bags.

SIDE TRIPS

Fiesole

An half-day excursion to the ancient Roman town of Fiesole, set in the hills 8 km (5 mi) above Florence, gives you a pleasant respite from museums and a wonderful vantage point of the city. Fiesole began life as an ancient Etruscan and later Roman village that held some power until it succumbed to the barbarian invasions and eventually gave up its independence in exchange for Florence's protection. The medieval cathedral, some other old churches, the ancient Roman amphitheater, and lovely old villas behind garden walls are clustered on a series of hilltops.

The **Duomo** (⊠ Piazza Mino da Fiesole) has a stark medieval interior. In the raised presbytery, the **Salutati Chapel** was frescoed by 15th-century artist Cosimo Rosselli, but it was his contemporary, sculptor Mino da Fiesole, who put the town on the artistic map. The Madonna on the altarpiece and the tomb of Bishop Salutati are his work. The **Roman amphitheater** is about 30 yards away. Climb the hill to the church of **San Francesco** to get to the terrace for a good view of Florence and the plain below. The air is usually clearest early in the morning or late in the afternoon. If you really want to stretch your legs, walk along Via Vecchia Fiesolana, a narrow lane, to the church of **San Domenico** and the **Badia Fiesolana,** Fiesole's cathedral, 4 km (2½ mi) southwest of Fiesole.

Festival

From June through August, Estate Fiesolana is a festival of theater, music, dance, and film that takes place in the churches and the archaeological area of Fiesole (⊠ Teatro Romano, Fiesole, ☎ 055/599931).

Arriving and Departing

The trip from Florence by car or bus takes about 20 minutes. Take city Bus 7 from the Stazione di Santa Maria Novella (Santa Maria Novella Train Station), Piazza San Marco, or the Duomo to Fiesole. A walk around Fiesole can take from one to two or three hours, depending on how far you stroll from the main piazza.

Florentine Gardens and Villas

Like the Medicis you can get away from Florence's hustle and bustle by heading for the hills. Take a break from city sightseeing to enjoy the gardens and villas set like jewels in the hills around the city. Villa di Castello and Villa La Pietraia, both just northwest of Florence, can be explored in one trip. The Italian garden at Villa Gamberaia is a quick 5-mi jaunt from the city.

Villa di Castello

A fortified residence in the Middle Ages, Villa di Castello was rebuilt in the 15th century by the Medicis. The Accademia della Crusca, a 400-year-old institution that is official arbiter of the Italian language, now occupies the palace, which is not open to the public. The gardens are the main attraction. From the villa entrance walk uphill through the 19th-century park laid out in Romantic style, set above part of the formal garden. You'll reach the terrace, which affords a good view of the geometric layout of the Italian garden below; stairs on either side descend to the parterre.

Though the original garden design has been altered somewhat over the centuries, the allegorical theme of animals devised by Tribolo in the 1540s to the delight of the Medicis is still evident. The artificial cave, Grotta degli Animali (Animal Grotto), displays an imaginative menagerie of sculpted animals by Giambologna and his assistants. Two bronze sculptures by Ammanati, centerpieces of fountains studding the Italian garden, can now be seen indoors in Villa La Pietraia (☞ *below*). Another Ammanati sculpture, a figure of an old man representing the Appenines, is at the center of a pond on the terrace overlooking the Italian garden. Allow about 45 minutes to visit the gardens; you can easily visit Villa La Pietraia (☞ *below*) from here, making for a three- or four-hour trip in total. ⊠ *Via di Castello 47, Castello,* ☎ *0571/ 454791.* ▨ *4,000 lire (includes entrance to Villa La Pietraia).* ☯ *Tues.–Sun. 9–1 hr before sunset.*

Villa La Pietraia

Splendidly planted gardens of Villa La Pietraia sit high above the Arno plain on Castello Hill, allowing a sweeping view of Florence. The villa was built around a medieval tower and reconstructed after it was purchased by the Medicis in 1575. Virtually the only trace of the Medicis having lived here is the 17th-century courtyard frescoes depicting glorious episodes of the clan's history. In the 1800s the villa served as a country residence of King Victor Emmanuel II (who kept his mistress here) while Florence was the temporary capital of the newly united Kingdom of Italy.

An Italian-speaking guide will bring you through the 19th-century-style salons. The Italian garden—also altered in the 1800s—and the vast park behind the palace suggest a splendid contrast between formal and natural landscapes. Allow 60–90 minutes to explore the park and gardens, plus 30 minutes for the guided tour of the so-called museum, the villa interior. This property is best visited after the Villa di Castello (☞ *above*). ⊠ *Via della Pietraia 40, Castello,* ☎ *050/454791.* 🎟 *4,000 lire (includes entrance to Villa di Castello).* ⊘ *Tues.–Sun. 9–1 hr before sunset.*

Villa Gamberaia

Villa Gamberaia, near the village of Settignano on the eastern outskirts of Florence, was the rather modest country home of the Rossellino family, which fostered some great early Renaissance sculptors. In the early 1600s, the villa eventually passed into the hands of the wealthy Capponi family. They spared no expense in rebuilding it and, more importantly, creating the Italian garden, one of the finest near Florence. Festooned with statues and fountains, the garden suffered damage during World War II but has been restored according to the original 17th-century design. This excursion takes about 1½ hours, allowing 45 minutes to visit the garden. ⊠ *Via del Rossellino 72, near Settignano,* ☎ *055/697205.* 🎟 *12,000 lire.* ⊘ *Weekdays 9–noon and 1–6, weekends by appointment.*

Arriving and Departing

VILLA DI CASTELLO

By car, head northwest from Florence on Via Reginaldo Giuliani (also known as Via Sestese) to Castello, about 6 km (3¾ mi) northwest of city center in the direction of Sesto Fiorentino; follow signs to Villa di Castello. Or take Bus 28 from city center, and tell the driver you want to get off at Villa di Castello; from the stop, walk north about ¼ mi up the tree-lined allée from the main road to the villa.

VILLA LA PIETRAIA

By car, follow directions to Villa di Castello (☞ *above*), but take the right off Via Reginaldo Giuliani, following the sign for Villa La Pietraia. You can walk from Villa di Castello to Villa La Pietraia in about 15 minutes; turn left beyond the gate of Villa di Castello and continue straight along Via di Castello to the imposing Villa Corsini; take Via della Pietraia uphill to the entrance.

VILLA GAMBERAIA

To reach Villa Gamberaia from Florence by car, head east on Via Aretina, an extension of Via Gioberti, which is picked up at Piazza Beccaria; follow the sign to the turnoff to the north to Villa Gamberaia, about 8 km (5 mi) from Florence center. By bus, take Bus 10 to Settignano. From Settignano's main Piazza Tommaseo walk east on Via di San Romano; the second lane on the right is Via del Rossellino, which leads southeast to the entrance of Villa Gamberaia. The walk (☞ *above*) from the piazza takes about 10 minutes.

FLORENCE A TO Z

Arriving and Departing

By Bus

Long-distance buses offer inexpensive if somewhat claustrophobic service between Florence and other cities in Italy and Europe. One operator is **SITA** (✉ Via Santa Caterina da Siena 15/r, ☎ 055/483651 weekdays, 055/211487 weekends). Also try **Lazzi Eurolines** (✉ Via Mercadante 2, ☎ 055/215154).

By Car

Florence is connected to the north and south of Italy by the Autostrada del Sole (**A1**). It takes about an hour via scenic roads to get to Bologna (although heavy truck traffic over the Apennines often makes for slower going) and about three to Rome. The Tyrrhenian Coast is an hour away on **A11** West.

By Plane

Although the A. Vespucci Airport, called **Peretola** (✉ 10 km/6 mi northwest of Florence, ☎ 055/333498), accommodates flights from Milan, Rome, and some European cities, it is still a relatively minor airport. **Galileo Galilei Airport** (✉ Pisa, 80 km/50 mi west of Florence, ☎ 050/500707) is used by most international carriers; for flight information, call the **Florence Air Terminal** (✉ Santa Maria Novella Train Station, ☎ 055/216073) or Galilei airport information.

International travelers flying on Alitalia to Rome's **Leonardo da Vinci Airport** and headed directly for Florence can make connections at the airport for a flight to Florence, but if the layover is a long one, consider taking the FS airport train to Termini station in Rome, where fast trains for Florence are frequent during the day.

BETWEEN THE AIRPORTS AND DOWNTOWN

By Bus. There is no direct bus service from Pisa's airport to Florence. Buses do go to Pisa itself, but then you have to change to a slow train service. There is a local bus service from Peretola to Florence.

By Car. From Peretola take autostrada **A11** directly into the city. Driving from the airport in Pisa, take **S67**, a direct route to Florence.

By Train. A scheduled service connects the station at Pisa's Galileo Galilei Airport with Florence's Santa Maria Novella Train Station, roughly a one-hour trip. Trains start running about 7 AM from the airport, 6 AM from Florence, and continue service every hour until about 11:30 PM from the airport, 8 PM from Florence. You can check in for departing flights at the **air terminal** (✉ Track 5, Galileo Galilei Airport station, ☎ 055/216073).

By Train

Florence is on the principal Italian train route between most European capitals and Rome and within Italy is served quite frequently from Milan, Venice, and Rome by nonstop Intercity (IC) trains. **Santa Maria Novella Train Station** (✉ Near the downtown area, ☎ 055/288785 for information) is the most convenient city-center station; avoid trains that stop only at the Campo di Marte Station in an inconvenient location on the east side of the city.

Getting Around

By Bicycle

Brave souls (cycling in Florence is difficult, at best) may rent bicycles at easy-to-spot locations at Fortezza da Basso, the Santa Maria Novella

Train Station, and Piazza Pitti. **Alinari** (✉ Via San Zanobi 9/r, ☎ 055/490113). **Motorent** (✉ Via Guelfa 85/r, ☎ 055/280500). **Ciao e Basta** (✉ Lungarno Pecori Girardi 1, ☎ 055/2342726).

By Bus

Maps and timetables are available for a small fee at the **ATAF** booth next to the train station or at the office at Piazza del Duomo 57/r, or for free at visitor information offices (☞ Contacts and Resources, *below*). Tickets must be bought in advance and can be purchased at tobacco stores, newsstands, from automatic ticket machines near main stops, or at ATAF booths (next to the station and at strategic locations throughout the city). The ticket must be canceled in the small validation machine immediately upon boarding. Two types of tickets are available, both valid for one or more rides on all lines. One costs 1,400 lire and is valid for 60 minutes from the time it is first canceled; the other costs 1,900 lire and is valid for 120 minutes. A multiple ticket—four tickets each valid for 60 minutes—costs 5,400 lire. A 24-hour tourist ticket costs 5,000 lire. Long-term visitors or frequent users of the bus should consider a monthly pass, which is sold at the ATAF office.

By Car

In the city, abandon all hope of using a car, since most of the downtown area is a pedestrian zone. For **traffic information** in Florence, call ☎ 055/577777.

By Moped

Those who want to go native and rent a noisy Vespa (Italian for "wasp") or other make of motorcycle or moped may do so at Motorent or Alinari (☞ By Bicycle, *above*). Helmets are mandatory and can be rented at either place.

By Taxi

Taxis usually wait at stands throughout the city (such as in front of the train station and in Piazza della Repubblica), or you can call for one (☎ 055/4390 or 055/4798). The meter starts at 4,000 lire.

Contacts and Resources

Consulates

U.S. Consulate (✉ Lungarno Vespucci 38, ☎ 055/2398276. ⊘ Weekdays 8:30–noon and 2–4). **U.K. Consulate** (✉ Lungarno Corsini 2, ☎ 055/284133. **Canadians** should contact their consulate in Rome (☞ Contacts and Resources *in* Rome A to Z).

Doctors and Dentists

For English-speaking doctors and dentists, you can get a list from the U.S. consulate. Contact **Tourist Medical Service** (✉ Viale Lorenzo Il Magnifico, ☎ 055/475411).

Emergencies

Police (✉ Main station, Via Zara 2, near Piazza della Libertà, ☎ 113). **Ambulance** (☎ 118). **Misericordia** (✉ Piazza del Duomo 20, ☎ 055/212222). If you need hospital treatment—and an interpreter—you can call AVO, a group of volunteer interpreters who offer their services free (☎ 055/403126; Mon., Wed., Fri. 4–6 PM, ☎ 055/2344567).

English-Language Bookstores

Paperback Exchange (✉ Via Fiesolana 31/r, ☎ 055/2478154) will do just that, besides selling books outright. **BM Bookshop** (✉ Borgo Ognissanti 4/r, ☎ 055/294575) has a fine selection of books on Florence. **Seeber** (✉ Via Tornabuoni 68, ☎ 055/215697) has English-language books alongside the other titles.

Guided Tours

EXCURSIONS

Contact bus operators (☞ Arriving and Departing, *above*) a day in advance, if possible, because excursions are popular. Comfortable buses with English-speaking guides make full-day trips from Florence to Siena and San Gimignano (departure 9 AM, return 6 PM, lunch not included) and afternoon excursions to Pisa (departure 2 PM, return 7 PM), with pickup and return from the main hotels. The Siena excursion costs about 68,000 lire, the Pisa excursion about 48,000 lire. Good bus and train connections make it easy for you to do these on your own, however.

ORIENTATION

The major bus operators (☞ Arriving and Departing, *above*) offer half-day itineraries, all of which generally follow the same plan, using comfortable buses staffed with English-speaking guides. Morning tours begin at 9, when buses pick visitors up at the main hotels. Stops include the cathedral complex, the Accademia, Piazzale Michelangelo, and the Pitti Palace (or, on Monday, the Museo dell'Opera del Duomo). Afternoon tours stop at the main hotels at 2 PM and take in Piazza della Signoria, the Uffizi Gallery (or the Palazzo Vecchio on Monday, when the Uffizi is closed), the nearby town of Fiesole, and, on the return, the church of Santa Croce. A half-day tour costs about 48,000 lire, including museum admissions.

Late-Night Pharmacies

The following are open 24 hours a day, seven days a week. (For others, ☎ 055/110.) **Comunale No. 13** (⊠ Santa Maria Novella Train Station, ☎ 055/289435). **Molteni** (⊠ Via Calzaiuoli 7/r, ☎ 055/289490). **Taverna** (⊠ Piazza San Giovanni 20/r, ☎ 055/284013).

Travel Agencies

American Express (⊠ Via Guicciardini 49/r, near Piazza Pitti, ☎ 055/288751; ⊠ Via Dante Alighiere 20/r, ☎ 055/50981) is also represented by **Universalturismo** (⊠ Via Speziali 7/r, off Piazza della Repubblica, ☎ 055/217241). **CIT** (⊠ Via Cavour 56, ☎ 055/294306; ⊠ Piazza Stazione 51, ☎ 055/2396963). **Thomas Cook** is represented by **World Vision** (⊠ Via Cavour 154/r, ☎ 055/579294).

Visitor Information

Ufficio Informazione Turistiche Commune di Firenze (Florence Tourist Information Office; ⊠ Via Cavour 1/r, next to Palazzo Medici–Riccardi, ☎ 055/290832; ⊠ Next to train station, ☎ 055/212245; ⊠ Piazza della Signoria, Chiasso dei Baroncelli 17/r, ☎ 055/2302124). **APT** (tourist office; ⊠ Via Manzoni 16, just off Piazza Beccaria, ☎ 055/2346284).

4 Tuscany

Lucca, Siena, and the Hill Towns

Without a doubt, Nature outdid herself in Tuscany. Punctuated by thickly wooded hills, snowcapped peaks, sun-warmed vineyards, olive groves, and dramatic hill towns, Tuscany's milk-and-honey vistas have changed little since Renaissance artists first beheld them.

ROME MAY BE THE CAPITAL OF ITALY, but Tuscany is the heart. Stretching from the Apennines to the sea, midway between Milan and Rome, the region is quintessentially Italian, in both its appearance and its history. Its scenic variety is unmatched in Italy; its past has been ignoble (it produced the Guelph-Ghibelline conflict of the Middle Ages) and glorious (it gave birth to the Renaissance). Its towns are justly famous for their wealth of fine architecture and art, but visitors often go home even more enthusiastic about Tuscany's unspoiled hilly landscapes, about the delicious Chianti wines produced by vineyards on those hills, and about the robust and flavorful Tuscan cooking. Be sure to allot some portion of your time here for leisurely strolls, unhurried meals, and aimless wandering around this peerless countryside, where the true soul of Tuscany is to be found.

Updated by
Barbara Walsh
Angelillo

Tuscany also produced the Italian language. Thanks to the eminence of their writings, it was the Tuscan dialect of Dante, Petrarch, and Boccaccio, all native sons, that grew to be the national tongue, a fact of which the Tuscans are rightly proud. Today the purest Italian is said to be spoken in the area between Siena and Arezzo, and even visitors with limited textbook Italian can often hear the difference. As they enter the region, the language suddenly becomes much easier to understand and takes on a bell-like clarity and mellifluous beauty unequaled throughout the rest of Italy.

It also takes on a notorious wit. As a common proverb has it, "Tuscans have Paradise in their eyes and the Inferno in their mouths" (a wry reference to Dante), and the sting of their wit is as famous throughout Italy as is the beauty of their speech. Happily, the Tuscans usually reserve their wit for each other and treat visitors with complete and sincere courtesy.

For a long time, the Tuscan hill towns were notorious as well. Even their earliest civilized settlers, the Etruscans, chose their city-sites for defensive purposes (the fortress-town of Fiesole, above Florence, is a fine surviving example). With the end of the Roman Empire, the region fell into disunity, and by the 11th century, Tuscany had evolved into a collection of independent city-states, each city seeking to dominate, and sometimes forcibly overpower, its neighbors. The region then became embroiled in an apparently endless international quarrel between a long succession of popes and Holy Roman Emperors. By the 13th century, Tuscany had become a battleground: the infamous conflict between the Guelphs and the Ghibellines had begun.

The Guelphs and the Ghibellines are the bane of Italian schoolchildren; their infinitely complicated, bloody history is to Italy what the Wars of the Roses are to England. To oversimplify grossly, the Ghibellines were mostly allied with both the Holy Roman Emperor (headquartered over the Alps in Germany) and the local aristocracy (dominated by feudal lords); the Guelphs were mostly allied with both the pope (headquartered in Rome) and the emerging middle class (dominated by the new trade guilds). Florence, flourishing as a trade center, was (most of the time) Guelph; its neighboring city-states Pisa and Siena were (most of the time) Ghibelline. But the bitter struggles that resulted were so byzantine in their complexity, so full of factional disputes and treachery, that a dizzying series of conflicts within conflicts resulted. (Dante, for instance, was banished from Florence not for being a Ghibelline but for being the wrong brand of Guelph.)

Eventually the Florentine Guelphs emerged victorious, and in the 15th century the region was united to become the Grand Duchy of Tuscany, controlled from Florence by the Medici grand dukes. Today the hill towns are no longer fierce, although they retain a uniquely medieval air, and in most of them the citizens walk the same narrow streets and inhabit the same houses that their ancestors did 600 years ago.

Tuscan art, to most people, means Florence, and understandably so. The city is unique and incomparable, and an astonishing percentage of the great artists of the Renaissance lived and worked there. But there is art elsewhere in Tuscany, and too often it is overlooked in favor of another trip to the Uffizi. Siena, particularly, possesses its own style of architecture and art quite different from the Florentine variety; the contrast is both surprising and illuminating. And even the smallest of the hill towns can possess hidden treasures, for the artists of the Middle Ages and the Renaissance took their work where they could find it. Piero della Francesca's fresco cycle in the church of San Francesco in Arezzo is perhaps the preeminent hidden treasure. Tucked away in a small church in a small town, and, sadly, faded, the frescoes are artistically the equal of almost everything Florence has to offer and are all the more appealing for their uncrowded setting.

Pleasures and Pastimes

Dining

Though Florentine cuisine now predominates throughout Tuscany, the Etruscan influence on regional food still persists after more than three millennia. Just as the ancient Etruscans were responsible for the introduction of the cypress to the Tuscan landscape, so they are also credited with the use of herbs in cooking. Basic ingredients such as tarragon, sage, rosemary, and thyme appear frequently, happily coupled with game, Chianina beef, or even seafood. Each region has its own specialties, usually based on simple ingredients, and Tuscans are disparagingly called *mangiafagioli*, or bean eaters, by other Italians. However, Tuscan chefs have recently discovered the rest of the world, and for better or worse, an "international cuisine" has been gradually making its appearance throughout the region.

Fortunately, Tuscany's wines remain unaltered. Grapes have been cultivated here since Etruscan times, and Chianti still rules the roost (almost literally when selected by the Gallo Nero Black Rooster label, a symbol of one of the region's most powerful wine-growing consortiums; the other is a putto, or cherub). The robust red wine is still a staple on most tables, and the discerning can select from a multitude of other varieties, including such reds as Brunello di Montalcino and Vino Nobile di Montepulciano, and whites such as Valdinievole and Vergine della Valdichiana. The dessert wine *vin santo* is produced throughout the region and is often sipped with *biscottini di Prato,* (hard almond cookies), perfect for dunking.

CATEGORY	COST*
$$$$	over 110,000 lire
$$$	60,000 lire–110,000 lire
$$	35,000 lire–60,000 lire
$	under 35,000 lire

Prices are per person, for a three-course meal, including house wine and taxes.

Lodging

Tuscany is not an inexpensive place to stay, especially the main towns and tourist centers. But the selection of options includes some wonderful properties, including some fine Renaissance and even medieval palazzi where you'll feel more like Lorenzo de Medici than a 20th-century tourist. To keep costs down, stick to less-visited towns and farmhouse lodgings.

CATEGORY	COST*
$$$$	over 350,000 lire
$$$	220,000 lire–350,000 lire
$$	100,000 lire–220,000 lire
$	under 100,000 lire

Prices are for a double room for two, including tax and service.

Exploring Tuscany

Tuscany has two basic geographical regions—comprised of the famous Tuscan hill towns just south of Florence, and the area immediately to the west, a string of cities that were historically the enemies of Florence, which fought to control them in order to have access to the sea.

Numbers in the text correspond to numbers in the margin and on the Tuscany, Lucca, and Siena maps.

Great Itineraries

Although Tuscany is relatively small—no important destination is more than a few hours' drive from Florence—the desire to linger is strong: can you really get enough of sitting on a hillside *terrazza* (terrace) with a good espresso or a robust chianti and watching the evening settle over a landscape of soft-edged hills, proud medieval towns, quiet villages, and cypress-ringed villas?

It only takes a few days for the region to leave an indelible mark on the memory and, for many, the soul. Seven days would allow for leisurely explorations of the main towns and for meandering along country roads to rustic, elegant estates and wineries. In five days, you can see the most interesting towns, but you'll need to stick to the main sights and move briskly between destinations. If three days is the limit, you can take in all the highlights, if not the small corners.

IF YOU HAVE 3 DAYS

Florence is a practical starting point. See **Lucca** ④–⑪ and the Torre Pendente in **Pisa** ⑫, then head for ⚅ **San Gimignano** ⑭ to overnight. The next day, explore the tiny streets of **Siena** ⑮–⑳ for a few hours, then move on to ⚅ **Montepulciano** ㉔ for the night. The following day, see **Arezzo** ㉖ and head back to Florence, your starting point, via the A1.

IF YOU HAVE 5 DAYS

From Florence, head for industrial **Prato** ① to see its striking medieval core; historic **Pistoia** ②, site of bitter Guelph-Ghibelline feuding; and **Montecatini Terme** ③, one of Europe's most famous spas. Stay over in ⚅ **Lucca** ④–⑪ and spend part of the next day exploring this most elegant of cities, then head for **Pisa** ⑫; see the Leaning Tower and then move on to hilltop **Volterra** ⑬, a fortress town, and beautiful ⚅ **San Gimignano** ⑭, the archetypal Tuscan town and a good place to spend your second night. On the third day, while away the morning in **Siena** ⑮–⑳, perhaps Italy's loveliest medieval city, before heading for the **Abbey of Monte Oliveto Maggiore** ㉑, **Montalcino** ㉒ of wine-growing fame, the **Abbey of Sant'Antimo**, and then ⚅ **Montepulciano** ㉔, where you should overnight. Trace your road back on the morning of your fourth day for a tour of **Pienza** ㉓, designed for Pope Pius II to be the perfect Renaissance town. Move on to handsome but under-appreciated **Arezzo** ㉖ and ⚅ **Cortona** ㉕, where there are galleries and lodging, stopping at **Chiusi** and **Chianciano** along the way. Spend part of your fifth day in Cortona or Arezzo before returning to Florence.

IF YOU HAVE 7 DAYS

Be sure to rent a car if your goal is to soak up the essence of Tuscany—it's the only way to get to many of the vineyards and estates.

As you approach **Prato** ①, you'll have time to visit the Pecci Center of Contemporary Art. In **Montecatini Terme** ③ ride the funicular up to older Montecatini Alto. If you're an architecture buff, extend your **Pisa** ⑫ exploration beyond the main square to include the Renaissance buildings of the Piazza dei Cavalieri. To really savor the Tuscan countryside, forgo **Volterra** ⑬ when leaving Pisa; instead take the S67 east toward Florence, but before entering the city turn south to pick up the meandering S222—the Strada Chiantigiana that runs through the heart of the Chianti wine country. One of the most scenic sections starts in Strada in Chianti, 16 km (10 mi) south of Florence, and runs 10 km (6 mi) through rolling hillsides dotted with olive groves and vineyards. The S222 Strada Chiantigiana leads directly to ⊡ **Siena** ⑮–⑳ through **Castellina in Chianti.** If you want to see ⊡ **San Gimignano** ⑭, turn west at Castellina in Chianti toward Poggibonsi and San Gimignano. Pause at **Colle Val d'Elsa** and take time to make the lengthy detour around Colle Val d'Elsa's workaday lower town to reach the upper town on the ridge, where the medieval center remains practically intact. Between Colle Val d'Elsa and Siena, be sure to visit **Monteriggioni,** a hilltop hamlet encircled by formidable 13th-century walls.

From Siena head south toward ⊡ **Montepulciano** ⑭, ⊡ **Cortona** ㉕, and **Arezzo** ㉖. For a taste of a more rugged landscape, don't take the autostrada back to Florence, but detour through the **Casentino,** a mountainous region blanketed with a vast forest that is a far cry from the pastoral images associated with Tuscany. Return to Florence along the winding S70, the splendidly scenic **Consuma** road wrought with hairpin turns and blind corners that require that even the best driver be alert.

When to Tour Tuscany

In summer, try to arrive in towns early in the morning. Italians are early risers, and most shops and museums open by 8:30. If you get up at cockcrow, you can avoid both the crowds and the often oppressive heat. In any case, Tuscany is not about late nights; most bars close their shutters at midnight.

If you plan to visit the frescoes in the Palazzo Pubblico in Siena at midday, be prepared to wait in line and, once inside, to be shuffled along by iron-willed guardians eager to see you in and out in the fastest time possible. If you want to photograph the towers of San Gimignano from a distance, do it in early morning, when the light is good and lines of neon-colored, diesel-spewing tour buses snaking up the hill will not ruin a perfect picture.

WESTERN TUSCANY

Tuscan Gateway: Prato, Pistoia, Lucca, and Pisa

Set in the shadows of the rugged coastal Alpi Apuane, where Michelangelo quarried his marble, this area isn't as lush as the south and lacks its vineyards and olive groves. The population centers here are sprawling cities, with some rather unattractive suburbs in addition to their stunning medieval and Renaissance centers.

Arezzo
26

Cortona
25 S71

S73

Monte San Savino

Lucignano
Sinalunga
S326

Chianciano
Chiusi

A1

Montepulciano
24

S69

Pienza
23

S73

Abbey of
Monte Oliveto
Maggiore
21

Montalcino
22

S2

Siena
15 — 20

S223

S2

Colle di Val d'Elsa

Monteriggioni
S2

San Gimignano
14

S73

S68

Volterra
13

S439

S68

Grosseto

S223

S73

Bruna

S322

Ombrone

S1

(A12)

S1

Cornia

Follonica

Punta Ala

20 miles

30 km

S1

A12

Piombino

Porto Azzuro

TO GENOA

TO CORSICA

TO PALERMO

TO CORSICA
SARDINIA

Portoferraio

Isola d'Elba

ARCIPELAGO

TOSCANO

Pianosa

N

Prato

❶ *17 km (10½ mi) northwest of Florence, 60 km (37 mi) east of Lucca.*

The wool industry in this city, one of the world's largest manufacturers of cloth, was known throughout Europe as early as the 13th century. It was further stimulated in the 14th century by a local cloth merchant, Francesco di Marco Datini, who built his business, according to one of his surviving ledgers, "in the name of God and of profit."

Prato's main attraction is its 11th-century **Duomo.** Romanesque in style, it is famous for its Chapel of the Holy Girdle (to the left of the entrance), which enshrines the sash of the Virgin; it is said that the girdle was given to the apostle Thomas by the Virgin herself when she miraculously appeared after her Assumption. The Duomo also contains 15th-century frescoes by Prato's most famous son, the libertine monk Fra Filippo Lippi; the best known depict Herod's banquet and Salome's dance. ⊠ *Piazza del Duomo.* ☉ *May–Oct., daily 6:30–noon and 4–7; Nov.–Apr., daily 6:30–noon and 3:30–6:30.*

Sculpture by Donatello that originally adorned the Duomo's exterior pulpit is now on display in the **Museo dell'Opera del Duomo.** ⊠ *Piazza del Duomo 49,* ☎ *0574/29339.* 🎫 *5,000 lire (includes Galleria Comunale).* ☉ *Mon. and Wed.–Sat. 9:30–12:30 and 3–6:30, Sun. 9:30–12:30.*

The collection at the **Galleria Comunale** examines Tuscan and Sienese painting, mainly that from the 14th century. ⊠ *Palazzo Pretorio, Piazza del Comune,* ☎ *0574/452302.* 🎫 *5,000 lire (includes Museo dell'Opera del Duomo).* ☉ *Mon. and Wed.–Sat. 9:30–12:30 and 3–6:30, Sun. 9:30–12:30.*

Prato's **Pecci Center of Contemporary Art** is acquiring a burgeoning collection of works by Italian and other artists. ⊠ *Viale della Repubblica,* ☎ *0574/570620.* 🎫 *10,000 lire.* ☉ *Wed.–Sun. 10–7.*

For a look at gracious country living, Medici style, detour 7 km (4 mi) south of Prato to the elegant **Villa Medici in Poggio a Caiano.** Built by Giuliano da Sangallo for Lorenzo the Magnificent, the villa was lavished with frescoes by important masters such as Andrea del Sarto and Pontormo. 🎫 *4,000 lire.* ☉ *Apr.–May and Sept., Mon.–Sat. 9–5:30; June–Aug., Mon.–Sat. 9–6:30; Mar. and Oct., Mon.–Sat. 9–4:30; Nov.–Feb., Mon.–Sat. 9–3:30. Closed 2nd and 3rd Mon. of month. Ticket office closes 1 hr before closing.*

Dining

$$$ ✕ **Piraña.** Oddly named for the cannibalistic fish swimming in an aquarium with a full view of the diners, this sophisticated restaurant, decorated in shades of blue with steely accents, is a local favorite. Seafood is the specialty and may take the form of *raviolo di branzino in crema di scampi* (ravioli stuffed with sea bass with a creamy shrimp sauce) and *rombo al forno* (baked turbot). It's a bit out of the way for sightseers but handy if you have a car, as it's near the Prato Est autostrada exit. ⊠ *Via G. Valentini 110,* ☎ *0574/25746. AE, DC, MC, V. Closed Sun. and Aug. No lunch Sat.*

$$ ✕ **La Veranda.** A large antipasto buffet greets you just inside the door of this restaurant near Prato's 13th-century Castello dell'Imperatore. Although it's an elegant place with its pale pink walls, terra-cotta tiled floors, and Venetian glass chandeliers, the atmosphere is friendly and family oriented. The large menu offers several international dishes, including Spanish paella, but never ignores Tuscan specialties, such as *agnello alla cacciatora* (lamb with a tangy wine-vinegar sauce). ⊠ *Via* *dell'Arco 10,* ☎ *0574/38235. AE, DC, MC, V. Closed Sun. and Aug. No lunch Sat.*

Shopping

LOCAL SPECIALTY

Prato's toothsome biscottini (literally "bi-," or twice, and "cotti"— cooked) are baked twice for the extra-dense texture, lending itself to submersion in your caffè. The crunchy comestibles are sold in bakeries and food stores around town.

Pistoia

❷ *18 km (11 mi) northwest of Prato, 36 km (20 mi) northwest of Florence, 40 km (25 mi) east of Lucca, 108 km (67 mi) north of Siena.*

The town saw the beginning of the bitter Guelph-Ghibelline conflict of the Middle Ages. Reconstructed after heavy bombing during World War II, it has preserved some fine Romanesque architecture.

The **Cathedral of San Zeno** in the main square houses the *Dossale di San Jacopo,* a magnificent silver altarpiece. The two half-figures on its left side are by Filippo Brunelleschi (1377–1446), better known as the first Renaissance architect (and designer of Florence's magnificent Duomo dome). ⊠ *Piazza del Duomo.* ☎ *Illumination of altarpiece 2,000 lire.*

The 14th-century Palazzo del Comune houses the **Museo Civico,** containing medieval art. ⊠ *Museo Civico, Piazza del Duomo,* ☎ *0573/371275.* ☎ *5,000 lire; free Sat. 3–7.* ☉ *Tues.–Sat. 9–1 and 3–7, Sun. 9–12:30.*

The **Ospedale del Ceppo,** a hospital founded during the 14th century, has a superb early 16th-century terra-cotta frieze by Giovanni della Robbia. In the church of **Sant'Andrea** (⊠ Via Pappe to Via Sant'Andrea), the fine early 14th-century pulpit by Giovanni Pisano depicts the life of Christ. ⊠ *Piazza Ospedale, a short way down Via Pacini from Piazza del Duomo.*

☾ Just outside town is the **Giardino Zoologico,** a small zoo especially laid out to accommodate the wiles of both animals and children. ⊠ *Via Pieve a Celle 160, Pistoia,* ☎ *0573/939219.* ☎ *13,000.* ☉ *Apr.–Sept., daily 9–7; Oct.–Mar., daily 9–5.*

Dining

$$ ✕ **La Casa degli Amici.** Literally "the house of friends," the name of this restaurant is indicative of the owners' vision—or at least their gracious nature. The two industrious women take care in creating the homey specialties such as *ribollita* (a thick soup of white beans, bread, cabbage, and onions), *pasta e fagioli* (a thick soup of pasta and beans), and some creative dishes, too. In summer, you can dine outdoors on the terrace. ⊠ *Via Bonellina 111, just outside the old walls, on the road toward the exit of A11,* ☎ *0573/380305. DC, MC, V. Closed Tues. and Aug.*

$$ ✕ **Leon Rosso.** At this small and usually crowded restaurant, you'll repast on Tuscan cuisine, starting with appetizing crostini and *fusilli all'orto* (corkscrew pasta with seasonal vegetables). For dessert try *panna cotta* (milk custard) with caramel sauce. ⊠ *Via Panciatichi 4, down Via Roma off the Piazza del Duomo,* ☎ *0573/29230. AE, DC, MC, V. Closed Sun. and Aug.*

$$ ✕ **Rafanelli.** *Maccheroni all'anatra* (pasta with duck sauce) and other game dishes—the specialties here—have been prepared with attention to tradition and quality for more than half a century by the same family. The restaurant is just outside the old city walls in a garden setting

with alfresco dining in summer. ⊠ *Via Sant'Agostino 47,* ☎ *0573/532046. AE, DC, MC, V. Closed Mon. and Aug. No dinner Sun.*

Montecatini Terme

❸ *16 km (10 mi) west of Pistoia, 48 km (30 mi) west of Florence, 55 km (34 mi) northeast of Pisa.*

Immortalized in Fellini's 8½, Montecatini Terme is Italy's premier spa, both for its reputed curative powers and, at least once upon a time, for its great popularity among the wealthy. It is renowned for its mineral springs, which flow from five sources and are used to treat liver and skin disorders. Those "taking the cure" report each morning to one of the town's *stabilimenti termali* (thermal establishments) to drink their prescribed cupful of water, whose curative effects became known in the 1800s. The town's wealth of Art Nouveau buildings went up during its most active period of development, at the beginning of this century. Of these structures, the most attractive is the **Stabilimento Tettuccio,** a neoclassical edifice with colonnades. Here Montecatini's healthful tonic spouts from fountains set up on marble counters, the walls are decorated with bucolic scenes depicted on painted ceramic tiles, and an orchestra plays under a frescoed dome.

An older town of Montecatini, called **Montecatini Alto,** sits on top of a hill near the spa town and is reached by a funicular.

Lucca

★ ❹ *27 km (17 mi) west of Montecatini Terme, 74 km (46 mi) southeast of La Spezia.*

It was in this picturesque fortress town that Caesar, Pompey, and Crassus agreed to rule Rome as a triumvirate in 56 BC; it was later the first town in Tuscany to accept Christianity. Today it still has a mind of its own, and when most of Tuscany was voting communist as a matter of course, its citizens rarely followed suit. It is best explored on foot.

★ ❺ The round-arched facade of the **Duomo** (⊠ Piazza del Duomo) is a fine example of the rigorously ordered Pisan Romanesque style, in this case happily enlivened by an extremely disordered collection of carved columns. Take a closer look at the decoration of the facade and that of the porch below; they make this one of the most entertaining church exteriors in Tuscany. The Gothic interior contains a moving Byzantine crucifix (called the Volto Santo, or Holy Face), brought here in the 8th century, and the masterpiece of the Sienese sculptor Jacopo della Quercia, the marble *Tomb of Ilaria del Caretto* (1406).

❻ Slightly west of town center is the church of **San Michele** (⊠ Piazza San Michele), with a facade even more fanciful than the Duomo's; it was heavily restored in the 19th century, however, and somewhat jarringly displays busts of modern Italian patriots such as Garibaldi and Cavour.

❼ The church of **San Frediano** (⊠ Piazza San Frediano, just inside the middle of the north town wall) contains more works by Jacopo della Quercia, and, bizarrely, the lace-clad mummy of the patron saint of domestic servants, Santa Zita. Southeast of the north town wall is **Piazza del Mercato,** where the **Anfiteatro Romano,** or Roman Amphitheater, once stood. The piazza takes its oval shape from the theater, but the tiers disappeared when medieval houses were built on top of them.

❾ **Pinacoteca Nazionale** is worth a visit to see the Mannerist, Baroque, and Rococo works. ⊠ *Palazzo Mansi, Via Galli Tassi 43, near the west*

Lucca

Duomo, **5**
Museo Nazionale, **10**
Palazzo Guinigi, **11**
Piazza del Mercato, **8**
Pinacoteca
Nazionale, **9**
San Frediano, **7**
San Michele, **6**

walls of the old city, ☎ *0583/55570.* 🎟 *8,000 lire.* ⊘ *Tues.–Sat. 9–7, Sun. 9–2.*

⑩ On the eastern end of the historic center, the **Museo Nazionale** houses an extensive collection of local Romanesque and Renaissance art. ⊠ *Villa Guinigi, Via della Quarquonia,* ☎ *0583/46033.* 🎟 *4,000 lire.* ⊘ *May–Sept., Tues.–Sun. 9–7; Oct.–Apr., Tues.–Sun. 9–2.*

⑪ The tower of the medieval **Palazzo Guinigi** contains one of the city's most curious sights: a grove of ilex trees has grown at the top of the tower, and its roots have grown into the room below. From the top, you will have a magnificent view of the city and the surrounding countryside. ⊠ *Town center.* 🎟 *4,500 lire.* ⊘ *10–sunset, 9–sunset in summer.*

OFF THE
BEATEN PATH

MARLIA – The Villa Reale, 8 km (5 mi) north of Lucca in Marlia, was once the home of Napoléon's sister, Princess Elisa. Restored by the Counts Pecci-Blunt, this estate is celebrated for its spectacular gardens, laid out in the 18th and 19th centuries. Gardening buffs adore the legendary *teatro di verdura,* a theater carved out of hedges and topiaries; concerts are occasionally offered here. ⊠ *Villa Reale,* ☎ *0583/30108.* 🎟 *8,000 lire.* ⊘ *Guided tours July–Sept., Tues.–Sun. at 10, 11, 4, 5, 6; Oct.–Nov. and Mar.–June, Tues.–Sun. at 10, 11, 3, 4, 5. Closed Dec.–Feb.*

FESTIVAL DI MARLIA – Held in July and August, this is one of the most popular among Tuscany's many summer music events. Contact the Lucca Visitor Information office (⊠ Piazzale Verdi, ☎ 0583/419689).

Dining and Lodging

$$$ ✕ **Solferino.** About 6 km (4 mi) outside town along the road to Viareggio, this restaurant prepares elegant renditions of Tuscan country-style cooking. Amid fine silver, linens, and crystal, you'll be treated to ingredients from the family farm in such dishes as *stagliolini con pernice rossa* (fresh pasta with partridge sauce). Ask for a piece of *buccellato,* Lucca's celebrated dessert bread. ⊠ *San Macario in Piano,* ☎ *0583/59118. Reservations essential. AE, DC, MC, V. Closed Wed. and Jan. 7–15. No lunch Thurs.*

$$–$$$ ✕ **La Mora.** Detour to this former stagecoach station, now a gracious,
★ rustic country inn 9 km (6 mi) outside Lucca, for local specialties—from *minestra di farro* (wheat soup) with beans to *tacconi* (a particular shape of homemade pasta) with rabbit sauce and lamb from the nearby Garfagnana hills. You'll be tempted by the varied crostini and delicious desserts. ⊠ *Via Sesto di Ponte a Moriano 1748,* ☎ *0583/406402. AE, DC, MC, V. Closed Wed. and Oct. 10–30.*

$$ ✕ **Buca di Sant'Antonio.** Some of the local dishes served at this rustic former inn are nice surprises, such as ravioli *di ricotta alle zucchine* (cheese ravioli with zucchini) and roast *capretto* (kid) or agnello with savory herb seasoning. ⊠ *Via della Cervia 3, near the church of San Michele,* ☎ *0583/55881. AE, DC, MC, V. Closed Mon. and last 3 wks in July. No dinner Sun.*

$$ ✕ **Da Giulio in Pelleria.** A large trattoria that is quintessentially Tuscan in atmosphere, food, and clientele, this tavern is in one of Lucca's characteristic old neighborhoods near the ramparts and Porta San Donato, and handy to the Pinacoteca Nazionale. The menu features Lucca's specialties, including hearty barley or wheat soups and roasted meats—beware, the portions are generous. ⊠ *Via delle Conce 47,* ☎ *0583/55948. Closed Sun.–Mon., and Aug. AE, DC, MC, V.*

$$ ✕ **Il Giglio.** Just off Piazza Napoleone, this restaurant has quiet, turn-of-the-century charm and classic cuisine. It's a place for all seasons, with a big fireplace and an outdoor terrace in summer. Among the local specialties are *farro garfagnino* (a thick soup made with grain and beans), and *coniglio con olive* (rabbit stew with olives). ✉ *Piazza del Giglio 3,* ☎ *0583/494508. AE, DC, MC, V. Closed Wed. No dinner Tues.*

$$$$ 🏨 **Locanda l'Elisa.** An intimate Relais & Châteaux hotel in a neoclassical villa, this deluxe spin-off of the adjacent Villa La Principessa (☞ *below*) is a notch higher on the scale of style and comfort. ✉ *Massa Pisana, 55050,* ☎ *0583/379737,* FAX *0583/379019. 10 suites. Restaurant, bar, pool. AE, DC, MC, V.*

$$$$ 🏨 **Villa La Principessa.** Three kilometers (two miles) outside of Lucca, you'll stay in an exquisitely decorated 19th-century country mansion. Some rooms have handsome beamed ceilings, and doors are individually decorated; antique furniture and portraits impart an aura of gracious living. The grounds are well manicured, the pool large and inviting. The restaurant is closed Sunday. ✉ *Massa Pisana, 55050,* ☎ *0583/370037,* FAX *0583/379136. 40 rooms and suites. Restaurant, pool. AE, DC, MC, V. Closed Nov.–Mar.*

$$ 🏨 **La Luna.** On a quiet, airy courtyard close to historic Piazza del Mercato, this family-run hotel occupies two newly renovated wings of an old building. The bathrooms are modern, but some of the rooms still have the atmosphere of Old Lucca. A parking lot for guests is a bonus. ✉ *Corte Compagni 12 (corner of Via Fillungo), 55100,* ☎ *0583/493634,* FAX *0583/490021. 30 rooms. Free parking. AE, DC, MC, V. Closed last 3 wks in Jan.*

$ 🏨 **Ilaria.** Rooms are small but fresh and functional in this family-run hotel beside a minuscule canal within easy walking distance of the main sights. ✉ *Via del Fosso 20, 55100,* ☎ *0583/47558. 17 rooms, 12 with bath. AE, DC, MC, V.*

Nightlife and the Arts

The **Estate Musicale Lucchese,** one of many music festivals throughout Tuscany, runs throughout the summer in Lucca. Contact the Lucca Visitor Information office (✉ Piazzale Verdi, ☎ 0583/419689) for details.

Shopping

LOCAL SPECIALTIES

Lucca's **olive oil,** available throughout the city, is exported throughout the world; you'll find it at any food store. A particularly delicious version of **buccellato**—a sweet, anise-flavored bread with raisins that is a specialty of Lucca—is baked at **Pasticceria Taddeucci** (✉ Piazza San Michele 34).

MARKET

On the second Sunday of the month, there's a **flea market** in Piazza San Martino.

Pisa

⑫   *22 km (14 mi) southwest of Lucca, 75 km (46 mi) south of La Spezia, 22 km (14 mi) north of Livorno, 64 km (40 mi) northwest of Volterra, 77 km (48 mi) west of Florence.*

There is more to Pisa than its famous Leaning Tower—but not much more. The city offers surprisingly little beyond the tower and its companion works: the Duomo, the Battistero (Baptistry), and the Camposanto. Nearby Lucca (☞ *above*) is more deserving of your attention.

You'll want to focus your attention to the **Piazza del Duomo,** also known as the Campo dei Miracoli (Field of Miracles), at the northwestern edge of town. On it stand the Duomo, the Baptistery, and the famous Leaning Tower.

The **Torre Pendente** (Leaning Tower) was begun in 1174, the last of the three structures to be built, and the lopsided settling began when construction reached the third story. The tower's architects attempted to compensate by making the remaining floors slightly taller on the leaning side, but the extra weight only made the problem worse. The settling has continued, and a few years ago it accelerated to a point that led many to fear it would simply topple over, despite all efforts to prop the structure up. Now it has been firmly anchored to the earth. Legend holds that Galileo conducted an experiment on the nature of gravity by dropping metal balls from the top of the 187-ft-high tower; historians say this legend has no basis in fact (which is not quite to say that it is false). The tower is not open to the public, but you have a great view of its leanings from the outside. ⊠ *Campo dei Miracoli.*

The **Duomo** was the first building to use the horizontal marble stripe motif (borrowed from Moorish architecture in the 11th century) common to Tuscan cathedrals. It is famous for the Romanesque panels on the transept door facing the tower, which depict the life of Christ, and for its beautifully carved 14th-century pulpit, by Giovanni Pisano. The lovely Gothic **baptistery**, which stands across from the Duomo's facade, is best known for the pulpit carved by Giovanni's father, Nicola, in 1260. ⊠ *Campo dei Miracoli. Duomo:* ☞ *2,000 lire, free Nov.–Mar.* ☉ *Apr.–Oct., Mon.–Sat. 10–5, Sun. 1–5; Nov.–Mar. daily 10–12:30 and 3–5:30. Baptistery:* ☞ *10,000 lire allows admittance to 1 other attraction; 15,000 lire for baptistery and all 3 sites (☞ below).* ☉ *Apr.–Oct., daily 8–7:30; Nov.–Mar., daily 10–12:30 and 3–5:30.*

The walled area on the northern side of the Campo dei Miracoli is the **Camposanto** (cemetery), which is filled, according to legend, with earth brought back from the Holy Land during the Crusades. Its galleries contain numerous frescoes, notably *The Drunkenness of Noah,* by Renaissance artist Benozzo Gozzoli, and the disturbing *Triumph of Death* (14th century), whose authorship is disputed, but whose subject matter shows what was on people's minds in a century that saw the ravages of the Black Death. ⊠ *Camposanto,* ☎ *050/560547.* ☞ *10,000 lire.* ☉ *Apr.–Oct., daily 8–7:30; Nov.–Mar., daily 9–5:30.*

At the southeast corner of the sprawling Campo dei Miracoli, the **Museo dell'Opera del Duomo** holds a wealth of medieval sculptures and the ancient Roman sarcophagi that inspired Nicola Pisano's figures. The well-arranged **Museo delle Sinópie** across the street, on the south side of the square, holds the *sinopie,* or preparatory drawings, for the Camposanto frescoes and is of limited interest to most tourists. *Museo dell'Opera del Duomo:* ⊠ *Via Arcivescovado,* ☎ *050/560547.* ☞ *10,000 lire.* ☉ *Apr.–Oct., daily 9–7:30; Nov.–Mar., daily 9–5:30. Museo delle Sinopie:* ⊠ *Piazza del Duomo,* ☎ *050/560547.* ☞ *10,000 lire.* ☉ *Apr.–Oct., daily 8–7:30; Nov.–Mar., daily 9–5:30.* ☞ *Combined admission to baptistery, Camposanto, and museums: 10,000 lire for any 2 sites; 15,000 lire for all 4.*

In the center of town, **Piazza dei Cavalieri** is central to some fine Renaissance buildings: the **Palazzo dei Cavalieri,** the **Palazzo dell'Orologio,** and the church of **Santo Stefano dei Cavalieri.** The square was laid out by Giorgio Vasari in about 1560. Vasari was better known for the chronicles of the lives of Renaissance artists that made him the first art historian.

Along the northern side of the Arno, the **Museo di San Matteo** contains some incisive examples of local Romanesque and Gothic art. ⊠ *Lungarno Mediceo,* ☎ *050/541865.* ☞ *8,000 lire.* ☉ *Tues.–Sat. 9–7, Sun. 9–1.*

OFF THE
BEATEN PATH

FORTE DEI MARMI – Tuscany's most exclusive summer beach resort is a favorite of moneyed Tuscans and Milanese, whose villas are neatly laid out in an extensive pine wood. In summer, a beachcomber's bonanza takes place on Wednesday mornings, when everything from faux designer sunglasses to plastic sandals and terry-cloth towels goes on sale. It's 35 km (22 mi) northwest of Lucca and 65 km (30 mi) northwest of Florence, and also near the marble-producing towns of **Carrara** (where Michelangelo also quarried his stone), **Seravezza,** and **Pietrasanta.**

ELBA – The largest island in the Tuscan archipelago, Elba is an hour by ferry or a half hour by Hovercraft from Piombino, or a short hop by air from Pisa. Its main port is Portoferraio, fortified in the 16th century by the Medici Grand Duke Cosimo I. Victor Hugo spent his boyhood here, and Napoléon his famous exile in 1814–15, when he built (out of two windmills) the Palazzina Napoleonica dei Mulini and (a few miles outside town) the Villa San Martino. Rugged landscape and pristine beaches with an array of sports are the island's main highlights. Portoferraio, the liveliest town and a transportation hub, is the best base for exploring the island. Good beaches can be found at Biodola, Procchio, and Marina di Campo. From Elba, private visits can be arranged to the other islands in the archipelago, including Montecristo, which inspired Alexander Dumas's 19th-century best-seller *The Count of Monte Cristo* and is now a wildlife refuge. Elba's restaurants specialize in seafood, to be paired with the local Moscato and Aleatico wines. ⊠ *Palazzina Napoleonica and Villa San Martino,* ☎ *0565/915846.* ▱ *6,000 lire for both if visited on same day.* ◷ *Tues.–Sat. 9–1:30, Sun. 9–1.*

Dining and Lodging

$$ ✕ **Bruno.** A pleasant restaurant, with beamed ceilings and the look of a country inn, Bruno is just outside Pisa's old city walls, a short walk from the bell tower and cathedral. Dine on classic Tuscan dishes, from *zuppa alla pisana* (a thick vegetable soup) to *baccalà* (cod) with leeks. ⊠ *Via Luigi Bianchi 12,* ☎ *050/560818. AE, DC, MC, V. Closed Tues. No dinner Mon.*

$$ ✕ **La Pergoletta.** On an old town street named for its "beautiful towers," this restaurant in a medieval tower is small and simple, with a shady garden for outdoor dining. The signora who is the owner-cook offers traditional Tuscan minestra di farro and *grigliata* (grilled beef, veal, or lamb). ⊠ *Via delle Belle Torri 36,* ☎ *050/542458. MC, V. Closed Tues. and Aug.*

$$ ✕ **Osteria dei Cavalieri.** Just off the beautiful old Piazza dei Cavalieri, this tavern and wine cellar in a centuries-old tower attracts diners with its one-course lunch menus. Prix-fixe menus of either seafood, meat, or vegetarian dishes, such as freshly made *tagliolini* (noodles) and *tagliata di manzo* (sliced beefsteak, usually served with mushrooms) are also offered. ⊠ *Via San Frediano 16,* ☎ *050/580858. AE, DC, MC, V. Closed Sun. and Aug. No lunch Sat.*

$$$ ▥ **Cavalieri.** Opposite the railway station, in an unremarkable 1950s building, this Jolly Group hotel offers functional, modern comforts in completely soundproof and air-conditioned rooms, all with color TVs and minibars. The restaurant specializes in homemade pasta and seafood and is open every day. ⊠ *Piazza della Stazione 2, 56100,* ☎ *050/43290,* ⅢX *050/502242. 100 rooms. Bar. AE, DC, MC, V.*

$$ ▥ **Royal Victoria.** In a pleasant palazzo facing the Arno, a 10-minute walk from the Campo dei Miracoli, this hotel is about as close as Pisa comes to Old World ambience. It's comfortably furnished, with antiques and reproductions in the lobby and in some rooms, whose style ranges from the 1800s, complete with frescoes, to the 1920s. ⊠ *Lungarno*

Pacinotti 12, 56100, ☎ 050/940111, ℻ 050/940180. 48 rooms, 40 with bath. AE, DC, MC, V.

TUSCAN HILL TOWNS
The Quintessential Tuscany

This area of rustic small cities and towns south of Florence has three distinct subdivisions. The first, directly south of Florence, is the Chianti district, Italy's most famous wine-producing area; its hill towns, olive groves, and vineyards comprise the quintessential Tuscany. Many British and northern Europeans have relocated here, drawn by the unhurried life, balmy climate, and picturesque villages; there are so many Britons, in fact, that the area has been nicknamed Chiantishire. Still, it remains strongly Tuscan in character and is sparsely populated. Marking the southernmost extremity of the Chianti region is the second subregion—Siena, a force unto itself; there's nowhere else in Italy where medieval strength and the elegance of the Renaissance are in such perfect balance. Farther south is the third area, where soft green olive groves give way to a blanket of oak and rich dark green cypress forests and reddish brown earth; here and there throughout this area are the vineyards that produce Brunello di Montalcino. Here, the towns are the size of the roads—small—and as old as the hills.

From Florence, there are two basic routes to Siena. The speedy modern S2 is good if you're making a day trip from Florence; to really experience the countryside, take the narrower and more meandering S222, known as the Strada Chiantigiana because it runs through the heart of the wine-producing region. Its most scenic section connects Strada in Chianti, 16 km (10 mi) south of Florence, and Greve in Chianti, 11 km (7 mi) farther south, whose triangular central piazza is surrounded by restaurants and vintners offering *degustazioni* (wine tastings).

Volterra

⑬ *64 km (40 mi) southwest of Pisa, 50 km (31 mi) west of Siena.*

D. H. Lawrence, in his *Etruscan Places,* sang the praises of Volterra, "standing somber and chilly alone on her rock." The town has long been known for its alabaster, which has been mined since Etruscan times; today the Volterrans use it to make ornaments and souvenirs sold all over town. **Piazza dei Priori,** where the 13th-century **Palazzo dei Priori** is emblazoned with heraldic emblems, is one of Tuscany's quintessential medieval squares.

A magnificent collection of small alabaster funerary urns that once held the ashes of deceased Etruscans (along with many other Etruscan artifacts) may be seen at the **Museo Etrusco Guarnacci** (⊠ Via Don Minzoni). Later art can be found in the **Duomo,** at the **Pinacoteca** (⊠ Palazzo Minucci-Solaini, Via dei Sarti 1), and at the **Museo di Arte Sacra** (⊠ Via Roma). The town's best-known Renaissance works are the 15th-century frescoes in the Duomo by Benozzo Gozzoli and the 16th-century *Deposition* by Rosso Fiorentino in the Pinacoteca. ▣ *Combined admission to Museo Etrusco Guarnacci, Pinacoteca, and Museo di Arte Sacra: 10,000 lire.* ✆ *Mar. 16–Oct. 14, daily 9:30–7 (Museo di Arte Sacra closes 1– 3); Oct. 15–Mar. 15, daily 9:30–2 (Museo di Arte Sacra 9–1).*

The walls of Volterra also harbor one of the few pieces of Etruscan architecture that escaped Roman destruction: the **Arco Etrusco** (⊠ Porta all'Arco), with its weatherworn Etruscan heads.

Dining and Lodging

$$ ✕ **Etruria.** Turn-of-the-century frescoes on the walls and outdoor dining in the warm weather denote this restaurant on the town's main square. An array of local game is used in such specialties as *pappardelle alla lepre* (broad noodles in hare sauce) and *cinghiale alla maremmana* (roast boar). ✉ *Piazza dei Priori 8, ☎ 0588/86064. AE, DC, MC, V. Closed Thurs.*

$$ ⊞ **San Lino.** In a former convent, this hotel has modern comforts and its own regional restaurant. On top of that, it's within the town walls, 10 minutes' walk from the main piazza. ✉ *Via San Lino 26, 56048, ☎ 0588/85250, ℻ 0588/80620. 43 rooms. Restaurant, pool. AE, DC, MC, V. Closed Nov. 9–Mar. 1.*

Shopping

LOCAL CRAFTS

Volterra has a number of shops that sell boxes, jewelry, and other objects made of alabaster. The **Cooperativa Artieri Alabastro** (✉ Piazza dei Priori 5, ☎ 0588/87590) has two large showrooms in a medieval building with an array of alabaster objects. In a former medieval monastery, the **Galleria Agostiniane** showrooms (✉ Piazza XX Settembre 3, ☎ 0588/86868) craft alabaster objects of all kinds. Visitors can see a video on how the mineral is quarried and carved. At the **Rossi** (✉ Via Lungo Mura del Mandorlo, ☎ 0588/86133) you can actually see the craftsmen at work; there are objects for all tastes and budgets.

San Gimignano

★ ⑭ *27 km (17 mi) east of Volterra, 57 km (35 mi) southwest of Florence, 31 km (20 mi) northwest of Siena.*

Time seems to have stood still since the Middle Ages in this most remarkable of all Tuscan hill towns, and it still lives up to its original name, San Gimignano-of-the-Beautiful-Towers. Its high walls and narrow streets are typical of Tuscan hill towns, but it is the surviving medieval "skyscrapers" that set the town apart from its neighbors and give the town a uniquely photogenic silhouette. Today 14 towers remain, but at the height of the Guelph-Ghibelline conflict, a forest of more than 70 such towers dominated the city. The towers were built partly for defensive purposes—they were a safe refuge and useful for pouring boiling oil on attacking enemies—and partly to bolster the egos of their owners, who competed with deadly seriousness to build the highest tower in town.

Many of the town's most important medieval buildings are clustered around the central **Piazza del Duomo.** They include the **Palazzo del Podestà,** with its imposing tower, the **Torre Grossa;** the **Palazzo del Popolo,** now the Museo Civico (municipal museum), displaying Sienese and Renaissance paintings; and the Romanesque **Collegiata,** containing fine 15th-century frescoes by Domenico Ghirlandaio in the **Chapel of Santa Fina.** 🎟 *Combination ticket (16,000 lire) valid for all San Gimignano museums and the Chapel of Santa Fina. Museo Civico:* 🎟 *7,000 lire.* ◷ *Apr.–Sept., Tues.–Sun. 9:30–7:30; Oct. and Mar., Tues.–Sun. 9:30–6; Nov.–Feb., Tues.–Sun. 9:30–1:30 and 2:30–4:30. Torre Grossa:* 🎟 *7,000 lire.* ◷ *Same as Museo Civico (above);* 🎟 *12,000-lire combination ticket for museum and tower available only Apr.–Sept., Tues.–Sun. 12:30–3 and 6–7:30; Oct.–Mar., Tues.–Sun. 12:30–2:30. Chapel of Santa Fina:* 🎟 *3,000 lire.* ◷ *Apr.–Sept., Tues.–Sun. 9–12:30 and 3–6; Oct.–Mar., Tues.–Sun. 9:30–12:30 and 3–5:30.*

Before leaving San Gimignano, be sure to see its most revered work of art, at the northern end of town, in the church of **Sant'Agostino:** Benozzo Gozzoli's utterly stunning 15th-century fresco cycle depicting the life of St. Augustine. Also try a taste of **Vernaccia,** the local dry white wine.

Dining and Lodging

$$–$$$ ✕ **Bel Soggiorno.** On the top floor of a 100-year-old inn, this rustic restaurant has a wall of windows from which to view the landscape. Tuscan specialties include *zuppa del granduca* (a medieval soup recipe of mushrooms, grain, and potatoes) and *sorpresa in crosta* (spicy rabbit stew with a bread crust). ✉ *Via San Giovanni 91,* ☎ *0577/940375. AE, DC, MC, V. Closed Mon. and Jan. 7–Feb.*

$$–$$$ ✕ **Le Terrazze.** Seasonal Tuscan classics are prepared in this restaurant in a time-honored inn in the heart of San Gimignano. A charming view of rooftops and the countryside and specialties like homemade pasta, a variety of grilled mushrooms, and grilled meats are in store. ✉ *Piazza della Cisterna 23,* ☎ *0577/940328. AE, DC, MC, V. Closed Tues. and Nov.–Mar. 9. No lunch Wed.*

$$ ✕ **La Mangiatoia.** In this rustic trattoria, near the church of Sant Agostino, prices are more moderate than at places with a view, and the food is simple Tuscan country cooking. ✉ *Via Mainardi 5, off Via San Matteo,* ☎ *0577/941528. MC, V. Closed Mon. and Nov. 4–25.*

$$$ 🏨 **Santa Chiara.** In a low contemporary building with a plethora of
★ balconies and terraces on a panoramic hillside site just outside San Gimignano's walls, this hotel is an airy and spacious oasis, and an upscale base from which to explore the countryside and hill towns. The hotel has no restaurant but serves an ample buffet breakfast, and light meals in summer. ✉ *Via Matteotti 15, 53037,* ☎ *0577/940701,* FAX *0577/942096. 41 rooms. Pool. AE, DC, MC, V. Closed Jan. 10– Feb. 28.*

$$ 🏨 **Pescille.** This rambling farmhouse 4 km (2½ mi) outside San
★ Gimignano has been converted into a handsome hotel, in which restrained contemporary and country classic motifs blend well. ✉ *Località Pescille, Strada Castel San Gimignano, 53037,* ☎ *0577/940186,* FAX *0577/943165. 40 rooms. Pool, tennis court. AE, DC, MC, V. Closed Nov.–Feb.*

Monteriggioni

20 km (12 mi) southeast of San Gimignano, 93 km (58 mi) southeast of Pisa, 55 km (34 mi) south of Florence.

On your way north from Siena toward Colle Val d'Elsa, San Gimignano, and Volterra, be sure to visit this tiny hamlet, which sits on a rise within a circle of formidable 13th-century walls. Its 14 square towers, which Dante likened to giants, were Siena's northernmost defense against Florence. Take time to make the lengthy detour around Colle Val d'Elsa's workaday lower town up to the ridge, where the medieval center remains practically intact.

Dining

$$ ✕ **Il Pozzo.** On the village square, this rustic tavern serves hearty Tuscan country cooking and savory wines. The specialties are homemade fresh pasta, main courses of filet of Tuscan beef with *porcini* mushrooms and *piccione ripieno* (stuffed squab), and homey desserts. ✉ *Piazza Roma 2,* ☎ *0577/304127. AE, DC, MC, V. Closed Mon., Jan. 7–Feb. 7, and Aug. 1–7. No dinner Sun.*

Siena

⓯ *15 km (9 mi) southeast of Montereggioni, 106 km (66 mi) southeast of Pisa, 68 km (42 mi) south of Florence.*

Italy's most enchanting medieval city, Siena is the one trip you should make in Tuscany if you make no other. Florence's great historical rival was founded by Augustus around the time of the birth of Christ, although legend holds that it was founded much earlier by Remus, brother of Romulus, the legendary founder of Rome. During the late Middle Ages, the city was both wealthy and powerful (it saw the birth of the world's oldest bank, the Monte dei Paschi, still very much in business). It was bitterly envied by Florence, which in 1254 sent forces that besieged the city for over a year, reducing its population by half and laying waste to the countryside. The city was finally absorbed by the Grand Duchy of Tuscany, ruled by Florence, in 1559.

Unlike Renaissance Florence, Siena is a Gothic city, laid out over the slopes of three steep hills and practically unchanged since medieval times.
★ Its main square, the **Piazza del Campo,** is one of Italy's finest. Fan shaped, its nine sections of paving represent the 13th-century government of Nine Good Men, and, on the widest side, like an ornament, is the Fonte Gaia, so called because it was inaugurated to great jubilation. The bas-reliefs on it are reproductions of the originals by Jacopo della Quercia. Twice a year, on July 2 and August 16, the square explodes in a frenzy of rivaling local quarters as the site of the famous **Palio,** a horse race in which the city's 17 neighborhoods compete to possess the cloth banner that gives the contest its name. Unlike many other such competitions in Italy, the Palio has a mystique in which the townspeople are deeply involved, and the rivalries it generates are taken very seriously.

★ **⓰** Dominating the Piazza del Campo is the **Palazzo Pubblico,** which has served as Siena's Town Hall since the 1300s. It now also contains the **Museo Civico,** its walls covered with pre-Renaissance frescoes, including Simone Martini's early 14th-century *Maestà* and *Portrait of Guidoriccio da Fogliano,* and Ambrogio Lorenzetti's famous *Allegory of Good and Bad Government,* painted from 1327 to 1329 to demonstrate the dangers of tyranny. The original bas-reliefs of the Jacopo della Quercia fountain, moved to protect them from the elements, are also on display. The climb up the palazzo's bell tower is long and steep, but the superb view makes it worth every step. ⊠ *Piazza del Campo,* ☎ *0577/292263. Bell tower:* ▣ *6,000 lire, including Museo Civico.* ☉ *Daily 10–hr before sunset. Museo Civico:* ▣ *6,000 lire.* ☉ *Mar.–Apr., Mon.–Sat 9:30–6:30; Nov. 2–Dec. 24, Mon.–Sat. 9:30–1:30; Dec. 27– Jan. 5, Mon.–Sat. 9:30–1:30.*

★ **⓱** Siena's **Duomo,** perched on a lofty piazza several blocks west of Piazza del Campo, is beyond question one of the finest Gothic cathedrals in Italy. Its facade, with its multicolored marbles and painted decoration, is typical of the Italian approach to Gothic architecture, lighter and much less austere than the French. The cathedral, as it now stands, was completed in the 14th century, but at the time the Sienese had even bigger plans. They decided to enlarge the building, using the current church as the transept of the new church, which would have a new nave running toward the southeast. The beginnings of construction of this new nave still stand and may be seen from the steps outside the Duomo's right transept. But in 1348 the Black Death decimated Siena's population, the city fell into decline, funds dried up, and the plans were never carried out.

The Duomo's interior is one of the most striking in Italy and possesses a fine coffered and gilded dome. It is most famous for its unique and

Siena

magnificent inlaid marble floors, which took almost 200 years to complete (beginning around 1370); more than 40 artists contributed to the work, made up of 56 separate compositions depicting biblical scenes, allegories, religious symbols, and civic emblems. The Duomo's carousel pulpit, which is almost as famous as the floors, was carved by Nicola Pisano around 1265; the life of Christ is depicted on the rostrum frieze. In the **Biblioteca Piccolomini,** a room painted by Pinturicchio in 1509, frescoes depict events from the life of native son Aeneas Sylvius Piccolomini, who became Pope Pius II in 1458. The frescoes are in excellent condition and have a freshness rarely seen in work so old. ☒ *Biblioteca Piccolomini,* ☎ *0577/283048.* ☒ *2,000 lire; combination ticket for admission to the Biblioteca Piccolomini, Museo dell'Opera Metropolitana, and Battistero, 8,500 lire.* ☉ *Mar.–Oct., daily 9–7:30; Nov.–mid-Mar., daily 10–1 and 2:30–5.*

⑱ The **Museo dell'Opera Metropolitana** occupies part of the unfinished new cathedral's nave and contains a small collection of Sienese art and the cathedral treasury. Its masterpiece is unquestionably Duccio's *Maestà,* painted around 1310 and magnificently displayed in a room devoted entirely to Duccio's work. ☒ *Piazza del Duomo, next to the Duomo,* ☎ *0577/283048.* ☒ *6,000 lire; combination ticket available (☞ Duomo, above).* ☉ *Mar. 12–Sept., daily 9–7:30; Oct., daily 9–6:30; Nov.–Dec. and Jan. 2–Mar. 11, daily 9–1:30.*

Steps between the cathedral and its museum lead to the **Battistero** (baptistery), adorned with 15th-century frescoes. Its large bronze baptismal font (also 15th century) was designed by Jacopo della Quercia and is adorned with bas-reliefs by various artists, including two by Renaissance masters: Lorenzo Ghiberti (*The Baptism of Christ*) and Donatello (*Herod Presented with the Head of St. John*). ☒ *Piazza San Giovanni.* ☒ *3,000 lire, combination ticket available (☞ Duomo, above).*

In the former hospital of **Santa Maria della Scala,** now a museum and restoration center, you can see the ongoing refurbishment on a huge stained glass window by Duccio. ⊠ *Piazza del Duomo, opposite the front of the cathedral,* ✍ *5,000 lire.*

⑲ Chief among Siena's other gems is the **Pinacoteca Nazionale,** several blocks southeast of the entrance to the Duomo; it contains a superb collection of Sienese art, including Ambrogio Lorenzetti's 14th-century depiction of a castle that is generally considered the first nonreligious painting—the first pure landscape—of the Christian era. ⊠ *Via San Pietro 29,* ☎ *0577/281161.* ✍ *8,000 lire.* ☉ *Tues.–Sat. 9–7, Mon. 8:30–1:30, Sun. 8–1.*

⑳ The church of **San Domenico's Cappella di Santa Caterina** displays frescoes by Il Sodoma portraying scenes from the life of St. Catherine. ⊠ *Northwest of the Duomo.*

NEED A BREAK?

Not far from the church of San Domenico, the **Enoteca Italica** (⊠ Fortezza Medicea, Viale Maccari, ☎ 0577/288497) is a fantastically stocked wine cellar in the bastions of the Medici fortress. Here you can taste wines from all over Italy and have a snack, too. It's open from noon–1 AM.

Dining and Lodging

$$ ✕ **Al Marsili.** This 900-year-old wine cellar is a marvelous place to dine, under broad, brick-vaulted ceilings. Tuscan and Italian specialties, among them homemade pastas such as *tortelloni burro e salvia* (large cheese-filled ravioli with a butter and sage sauce) are a delight to the palate. Various meat dishes are cooked in wine, and the wine list features the finest Tuscan and Italian labels, including stars from the nearby Chianti country. ⊠ *Via del Castoro 3, between Piazza del Campo and the cathedral,* ☎ *0577/47154. AE, DC, MC, V. Closed Mon.*

$$ ✕ **Le Logge.** Near Piazza del Campo, this classic Sienese trattoria has
★ rustic dining rooms on two levels and tables outdoors from June to October. Tuscan dishes are the draw, such as *malfatti all'osteria* (ricotta and spinach dumplings in a cream sauce) and *anatra al finocchio* (roast duck with fennel). ⊠ *Via del Porrione 33,* ☎ *0577/48013. AE, DC, MC, V. Closed Sun. and 2 wks in June and Nov.*

$$ ✕ **Tullio Tre Cristi.** This is a typical and historic neighborhood trattoria, still reliable and trammeled by loyal customers. The paintings on the walls were executed by famous local artists of the 1920s, but the culinary tradition here goes back even further. Try spaghetti *alle briciole,* a poorman's dish of pasta with bread-crumbs, tomato, and garlic, or veal *escalopes* (cutlets) subtly flavored with *dragoncello* (tarragon). You can eat outdoors in summer. ⊠ *Vicolo di Provenzano 1, take Via dei Rossi from Via Banchi di Sopra,* ☎ *0577/280608. MC, V. Closed Tues.*

$$$$ 🏨 **Certosa di Maggiano.** A former 14th-century monastery converted
★ into an exquisite country hotel, this haven of gracious living is a little more than about 1½ km (1 mi) from the center of Siena. The atmosphere is that of an exclusive retreat in which a select number of guests enjoy the style and comfort of an aristocratic villa. This is also served by a helipad. ⊠ *Via Certosa 82, 53100,* ☎ *0577/288180,* FAX *0577/288189. 18 rooms. Restaurant, pool, tennis court, horseback riding. AE, DC, MC, V.*

$$$$ 🏨 **La Suvera.** This luxurious estate in the lovely valley of the River Elsa,
★ 28 km (17 mi) west of Siena and 56 km (35 mi) south of Florence, was once owned by Pope Julius II. The papal villa and adjacent building accommodate guests in magnificently furnished rooms and suites appointed with antiques and modern comforts. With excellent facilities such as drawing rooms, a library, Italian garden, park, the Oliviera restau-

rant (serving estate wines) and even a helipad to use, guests find it hard to tear themselves away, though there is plenty to see in the vicinity. ⊠ *Pievescola (Casola d'Elsa), off S541, 53030,* ☏ *0577/960300,* FAX *0577/960220. 19 rooms, 13 suites. Restaurant, bar, pool, sauna, tennis court, horseback riding, meeting rooms. AE, DC, MC, V. Closed Nov.–Easter.*

$$$$ 🏨 **Park.** Set among olive groves and gardens on a hillside just outside the city walls, this hotel offers solid comfort and spacious double rooms with views of the grounds and countryside, which also includes a nine-hole practice golf course. A historic 16th-century villa, it has the easy elegance and antique charm of patrician Tuscan country life. The Olivo restaurant is known for fine regional cuisine. ⊠ *Via Marciano 18, 53100,* ☏ *0577/44803,* FAX *0577/49020. 63 rooms. Restaurant, bar, pool, 2 tennis courts. AE, DC, MC, V.*

$$ 🏨 **Chiusarelli.** In a well-kept neoclassic villa, built in the early 1900s complete with caryatids, this hotel has functional rooms that are airy and reasonably quiet. A handy location—near the long-distance bus terminal and a parking area and only a 10-minute walk from the main sites—is the big plus here. The small garden invites reading; a downstairs restaurant caters to tour groups. ⊠ *Viale Curtatone 9, 53100,* ☏ *0577/280562,* FAX *0577/271177. 50 rooms. MC, V.*

$$ 🏨 **Duomo.** Occupying the top floor of a 300-year-old building near Piazza del Campo, this quiet hotel is furnished in a neat contemporary style, with traces of the past showing in the artfully exposed brickwork in the breakfast room. Many bedrooms have superb views of the city's towers and the hilly countryside. Two rooms have balconies. ⊠ *Via Stalloreggi 38, 53100,* ☏ *0577/289088,* FAX *0577/43043. 23 rooms. Breakfast room. AE, DC, MC, V.*

$$ 🏨 **Piccolo Hotel Oliveta.** This little hotel in a rejuvenated 18th-century brick farmhouse has lots of atmosphere. Just outside Porta Romana and only 10 minutes from Piazza del Campo on foot, it has simply furnished rooms and a garden overlooking olive groves and verdant hills. A Palio-time option includes tickets to the race. ⊠ *Via Piccolomini 35, 53100,* ☏ *0577/283930,* FAX *0577/870009. 16 rooms. Free parking. AE, MC, V.*

$–$$ 🏨 **Antica Torre.** A restored 17th-century tower within the town walls in the southeast corner of Siena, Antica Torre is a 10-minute walk from Piazza del Campo. It is the work of a cordial couple who have created the atmosphere of a private home, furnished simply but tastefully and with only eight guest rooms. The old stone staircase, wooden beams, and original brick vaults here and there are reminders of the building's august age. ⊠ *Via Fieravecchia 7, 53100,* ☏ FAX *0577/222255. 8 rooms. AE, MC, V.*

Nightlife and the Arts

MUSIC

In late July and August, Siena hosts the **Settimane Musicali Senesi,** a series of concerts held in churches and courtyards with performances of local and other music.

Shopping

LOCAL SPECIALTIES

The city is known for a variety of **cakes** and **cookies,** their recipes of medieval origin—*cavallucci* (sweet spice biscuits), *panforte* (traditional Sienese Christmas fruitcake with honey, hazelnuts, almonds, and spices), and *ricciarelli* (almond paste cookies)—as well as for its ceramics.

Abbey of Monte Oliveto Maggiore

㉑ *37 km (23 mi) southeast of Siena.*

This Benedictine abbey, Tuscany's most visited, is an oasis of olive and cypress trees amid the harsh landscape of a zone known as the *crete*, where erosion has sculpted the hills starkly, laying open gashes of barren rock in lush farmland. Secluded amid thick woodlands in the deep-cut hills south of Siena, it is accessible by car but not easily by bus.

Olivetans, or "White Benedectines," founded it in 1313; this breakaway group sought to return to the simple ideals of the early Benedictines. The monastery's mellow brick buildings, restored in the last century and set in one of Tuscany's most striking landscapes, protect a treasure or two. Only the **main cloister, church,** and portions of the **park** are open to the public. The wooden choir in the church, with exquisite inlay designs, is an understated work of art that dates from 1503.

In the main cloister of the abbey, the frescoes by Luca Signorelli and Il Sodoma on the walls of the portico relate the life of St. Benedict with earthy realism, a quality that came naturally to Il Sodoma, described by Vasari as "a merry and licentious man . . . of scant chastity." ▨ *Free.* ☉ *Daily 9:15–noon and 3:15–5:45.*

Dining

$–$$ ✕ **La Torre.** This pleasant restaurant and café in the massive tower at the abbey's entrance provide more than adequate sustenance to visitors. The local specialties—served in a cozy dining room in winter or on an attractive terrace under tall cypresses in good weather—include *pici ai funghi* (homemade pasta with mushroom sauce) or *zuppa di funghi* (mushroom soup). The wine list is remarkably good, and the tourist menu is a good value. ☎ *0577/707022. AE, DC, MC, V. Closed Tues.*

Montalcino

22 *25 km (15½ mi) south of the Abbey of Monte Oliveto Maggiore, 24 km (15 mi) west of Pienza, 41 km (25 mi) south of Siena.*

Another medieval hill town with a special claim to fame, Montalcino is home to **Brunello di Montalcino,** one of Italy's finest red wines. You can sample it in wine cellars in town or visit a nearby winery for a free guided tour and tasting; you must call ahead for reservations. One such winery is the Fattoria dei Barbi (☞ Taverna dei Barbi, *below*).

Dining

$$$ ✕ **Poggio Antico.** One of Italy's renowned gourmet chefs Roberto Minnetti abandoned his highly successful restaurant in Rome a few years ago and moved to the country just outside Montalcino. Now he and his wife, Patrizia—who is also Poggio Antico's hostess—serve fine Tuscan cuisine, masterfully interpreted by Roberto, in a relaxed but elegant dining room replete with arches and beamed ceilings. The seasonal menu might suggest *ravioli di castagne al burro e salvia* (ravioli with chestnut stuffing) or venison in a sweet-and-sour sauce. ⊠ *Località I Poggi, 4 km (2½ mi) outside Montalcino on road to Grosseto,* ☎ *0577/849200. V. Closed Mon. and 20 days in Jan. No dinner Sun.*

$$ ✕ **Taverna dei Barbi.** A meal at this tavern, set among vineyards and
★   mellow brick buildings on winery estate Fattoria dei Barbi, may well be a highlight of your journey through this part of Tuscany. The rustic dining room features a beamed ceiling, huge stone fireplace, and arched windows. The estate farm produces many of the ingredients used in such traditional specialties as *stracotto nel brunello* (braised veal cooked with beans, in Brunello wine) and a dessert called *ricotta montata* (farm-fresh ricotta whipped with vin santo, sugar, and vanilla). The estate-produced Brunello is excellent, and other wines with the Barbi label are available. ⊠ *Fattoria dei Barbi,* ☎ *0577/849357. Reservations essential. AE, DC, MC, V. Winery (English-speaking guides)*

weekdays 9–1 and 3–6, weekends 2:30–6. Closed Wed., Jan. 15–31, and July 1–15. No dinner Tues.

Abbey of Sant'Antimo

10 km (6 mi) south of Montalcino, 31 km (19 mi) south of Siena.

It's well worth your while to visit this abbey, a medieval gem of pale stone set in the silvery green of an olive grove. The exterior and interior sculpture is outstanding, particularly the nave capitals, a combination of French, Lombard, and even Spanish influences. The **sacristy** (rarely open) forms part of the primitive Carolingian church (founded in 781 AD), its entrance flanked by 9th-century pilasters. The small **vaulted crypt** dates from the same period. Above the nave runs a *matroneum* (women's gallery), an unusual feature once used to separate the congregation. Equally unusual is the ambulatory, whose three radiating chapels (rare in Italian churches) were probably copied from the French model. ◪ *Free.* ⊙ *Daily 9–noon and 2–7 (winter 10–noon and 2–4).*

Pienza

㉓ *10 km (6 mi) northeast of the Abbey of Sant'Antimo.*

Pienza owes its appearance to Pope Pius II, who had grand plans to transform his home village of **Corsignano**—the town's former name—into a model Renaissance town. The man entrusted with the transformation was Bernardo Rossellini, a protegé of the great Renaissance architectural theorist Leon Battista Alberti. His mandate was to create a cathedral, a papal palace, and a town hall (plus miscellaneous buildings) that adhered to the vainglorious pope's principles. Gothic and Renaissance styles were fused, and the buildings were decorated with Sienese and Florentine paintings. The net result was a project that expressed Renaissance ideals of art, architecture, and civilized good living in a single scheme: it stands as an exquisite example of the architectural canons that Alberti formulated in the early Renaissance and which were utilized by later architects, including Michelangelo, in designing many of Italy's finest buildings and piazzas. Today the cool grandeur of Pienza's center seems almost surreal in this otherwise unpretentious village, known locally for *pienzino,* also called *cacio,* a smooth sheep's-milk cheese.

Montepulciano

㉔ *12 km (7 mi) east of Pienza, 13 km (8 mi) west of the A1, 65 km (40 mi) south of Florence.*

Perched high on a hilltop, Montepulciano is made up of a pyramid of redbrick buildings set within a circle of cypress trees. At an altitude of almost 2,000 ft, it is cool in summer and chilled in winter by biting winds that sweep its spiraling streets. The town has an unusually harmonious look, the result of the work of three architects, Sangallo il Vecchio, Vignola, and Michelozzo, who endowed it with fine palaces and churches in an attempt to impose Renaissance architectural ideals on an ancient Tuscan hill-town—the pièce de résistance is the beautiful **Piazza Grande.** On the hillside below the town walls is the church of **San Biagio,** designed by Sangallo, a paragon of Renaissance architectural perfection considered his masterpiece.

Dining and Lodging

$$$$ ✕▦ **Locanda dell'Amorosa.** A medieval hamlet set in Tuscan farmland
★   has become a rustic retreat for city folk for a meal or weekend in the country, only a half hour by car from Siena or Arezzo and even less

from Montepulciano, Cortona, and Monte Oliveto Maggiore. The stone and brick buildings have been tastefully adapted to accommodate guests, and the restaurant serves regional dishes that seem to taste even better in such apt surroundings. You can take home estate-produced wines and preserves as a souvenir of your stay. There's a tavern (closed Monday–Tuesday and January 8–March 7, no lunch) and wine bar. ⊠ *Località Amorosa, Sinalunga, 10 km (6 mi) off the Valdichiana exit of A1, 53048,* ☎ *0577/679497,* FAX *0577/632001. 17 rooms. 2 restaurants. AE, DC, MC, V.*

$$ 🏨 **Il Marzocco.** A 16th-century building within the town walls, this hotel is furnished circa 19th century, complete with dignified, old-fashioned parlors and a billiard room. Furnished in heavy turn-of-the-century style or in spindly white wood, many bedrooms have large terraces overlooking the countryside. Many rooms are large enough to accommodate extra beds. ⊠ *Piazza Savonarola 18, 53045,* ☎ *0578/757262,* FAX *0578/757530. 16 rooms, 15 with bath or shower. Restaurant. AE, DC, MC, V. Closed Nov. 20–Dec. 5.*

$ 🏨 **La Bandita.** This attractive old farmhouse possesses great charm, with terra-cotta floors throughout, lace curtains and antiques in the bedrooms, and a fireplace and grandfather's 19th-century Tuscan provincial furniture in a large, brick-vaulted living room. Some rooms can accommodate an extra bed. A garden and meals are available to guests. The restaurant is closed Tuesday. ⊠ *Via Bandita 72, Bettolle, 1 km (⅔ mi) from Valdichiana exit of A1 autostrada, 53048,* ☎ *0577/624649,* FAX *0577/624649. 8 rooms. Restaurant. MC, V.*

Nightlife and the Arts

The **Cantiere Internazionale d'Arte,** held in July and August, is a multifaceted festival of figurative art, music, and theater, ending with a major theatrical production in Piazza Grande. Contact the Montepulciano Visitor Information office (⊠ Piazza Minzoni 2, ☎ 0578/757442) for info.

Shopping

In this sleepy town, mild retail therapy can be had at the many wine cellars, antiques dealers, and few trendy shops.

En Route The road leading to Chianciano climbs and dips, winding through woods of evergreens and oaks and affording glimpses of the vineyards that are the pride of this part of Tuscany. Two of Italy's best wines—Brunello di Montalcino and Vino Nobile di Montepulciano—are created here and bear the names of the towns where they are made.

Chianciano

9 km (5½ mi) south of Montepulciano.

This small medieval town, surrounded by walls, has billboards proclaiming that Chianciano's restorative waters are indispensable for a *fegato sano* (a healthy liver). Outside the old walls is a modern spa with neat parks and a host of hotels.

Chiusi

11 km (7 mi) east of Chianciano, 2½ km (1½ mi) east of the A1, 126 km (78 mi) south of Florence.

Known for the frescoed tombs that date from the 5th century BC in its necropolis, Chiusi was one of the most powerful of the 12 ancient cities in the Etruscan federation. It's a transportation hub accessible from either the main north–south rail line or by car or bus from the A1 autostrada.

Cortona

㉕ *46 km (28½ mi) northeast of Chiusi.*

Magnificently situated, with olives and vineyards creeping up to its walls, one of Tuscany's prettiest villages commands sweeping views over Lake Trasimeno and the plain of the Valdichiana. Its two fine galleries and scattering of churches are rarely visited; its delightful medieval streets are a pleasure to wander for their own sake.

Cortona may be one of Italy's oldest towns—"Mother of Troy and Grandmother of Rome," in popular speech. Tradition claims that it was founded by Dardanus, the founder of Troy (after whom the Dardanelles are named). He was fighting a local tribe, so the story goes, when he lost his helmet (*corythos* in Greek) on Cortona's hill. In time a town grew up that took its name (Corito) from the missing headgear. By the 4th century BC the Etruscans had built the first set of town walls, whose cyclopean traces can still be seen in the 2-mi sweep of the present fortifications. As a member of the Etruscans' 12-city Dodecapolis, it became one of the federation's leading northern cities. An important consular road, the Via Cassia, which passed the foot of its hill, maintained the town's importance under the Romans. Medieval fortunes waned, however, as the plain below reverted to marsh. After holding out against neighbors like Perugia, Arezzo, and Siena, the *comune* was captured by King Ladislas of Naples in 1409 and sold to the Florentines two years later.

The heart of Cortona is formed by **Piazza della Repubblica** and the adjacent **Piazza Signorelli.** Wander into the courtyard of the picturesque **Palazzo Pretorio,** and, if you want to see a representative collection of Etruscan bronzes, climb its centuries-old stone staircase to the **Museo dell'Accademia Etrusca** (Gallery of Etruscan Art). ⊠ *Piazza Signorelli 9,* ☎ *0575/630415.* ⊡ *5,000 lire.* ☉ *Apr.–Sept., Tues.–Sun. 10–1 and 4–7; Oct.–Mar., Tues.–Sun. 9–1 and 3–5.*

The **Museo Diocesano** (Diocesan Museum) houses an impressive number of large and splendid paintings by native son Luca Signorelli, as well as a beautiful *Annunciation* by Fra Angelico, a delightful surprise to find in this small, eclectic town. ⊠ *Piazza del Duomo 1,* ☎ *0575/62830.* ⊡ *5,000 lire.* ☉ *Apr.–Sept., Tues.–Sun. 9–1 and 3–6:30; Oct.–Mar., Tues.–Sun. 9–1 and 3–5.*

Dining and Lodging

$$ ✕ **La Loggetta.** Above Cortona's main medieval square, this attractive restaurant is housed in a 16th-century wine cellar. In good weather you can eat outdoors, overlooking the 13th-century town hall, dining on regional dishes and such specialties as *ravioli gnudi,* "naked ravioli," made with spinach and ricotta but without pasta, and tagliata. The owners pride themselves on their selection of Tuscan wines. ⊠ *Piazza Pescheria 3,* ☎ *0575/630575. AE, DC, MC, V. Closed Nov. 5–20 and Mon. Sept.–May.*

$$ ✕ **Tonino.** It must be host Tonino's own *antipastissimo*— an incredible variety of delectables—that make this large modern establishment noisy and crowded at times. But it is very satisfactory indeed when not, when you can enjoy the view of the Chiana valley and savor Chianina beefsteak. ⊠ *Piazza Garibaldi,* ☎ *0575/630500. AE, DC, MC, V. Closed Tues. No dinner Mon.*

$$$ ▦ **Il Falconiere.** A charming old villa less than 3½ km (2 mi) outside Cortona, this once belonged to an early 19th-century poet and has been lovingly restored and impeccably furnished in the local style as an upscale inn. The winter garden and terrace have been transformed into a restaurant that features Tuscan dishes and seasonal specialties. The restaurant is closed Monday from November to March; no lunch is served Tuesday. ⊠ *Località San Martino, 52044,* ☎ *0575/612679,* ℻ *0575/612927. 12 rooms. Restaurant, bar, pool. AE, DC, MC, V. Closed Nov.–Mar.*

Arezzo

㉖ *29 km (18 mi) north of Cortona, 81 km (50 mi) southeast of Florence.*

The birthplace of the poet Petrarch; of the Renaissance artist and art historian Giorgio Vasari; and of Guido d'Arezzo, the inventor of musical notation, Arezzo is today best known for the magnificent, but very
★ faint, Piero della Francesca frescoes in the church of **San Francesco** (⊠ Via Cavour in town center). Painted between 1452 and 1466, they depict *The Legend of the True Cross* on three walls of the choir. What Sir Kenneth Clark called "the most perfect morning light in all Renaissance painting" may be seen in the lowest section of the right wall, where the troops of the Emperor Maxentius flee before the sign of the cross. Unfortunately, part of the frescoes may be hidden from view while restoration work takes place.

With its irregular shape and sloping brick pavement, framed by buildings of assorted centuries, Arezzo's **Piazza Grande** echoes Siena's Piazza del Campo. Though not so grand, it is lively enough during the outdoor antiques fair every first Sunday of the month and when the **Joust of the Saracen,** featuring medieval costumes and competition, is held there on the first Sunday of September. The curving, tiered apse on Piazza Grande belongs to **Santa Maria della Pieve,** one of Tuscany's finest Romanesque churches. And Arezzo's medieval **Duomo** (⊠ At the top of the hill) harbors an eye-level fresco of a tender Magdalen by Piero della Francesca; look for it next to the large marble tomb near the organ. ⊠ *Piazza Grande.*

The church of **San Domenico** (⊠ Piazza Fossombroni, north of Piazza Grande) just inside the walls, houses a 13th-century crucifix by Cimabue. **Casa di Giorgio Vasari** (Giorgio Vasari house) was designed and decorated by the region's leading Mannerist artist in 1540 for his own use. ⊠ *Via XX Settembre 55,* ☎ *0575/300301.* ⊡ *Free.* ☼ *Tues.–Sat. 9–7, Sun. 9–1.*

The **Museo Archeologico** (Archaeological Museum) exhibits a fine collection of Etruscan bronzes. ⊠ *Via Margaritone 10,* ☎ *0575/20882.* ⊡ *8,000 lire.* ☼ *Tues.–Sat. 9–2, Sun. 9–1.*

Dining and Lodging

$$ ✕ **Buca di San Francesco.** A frescoed cellar restaurant in a historic building next to the church of San Francesco, this "buca" (literally "hole," figuratively "cellar") has a medieval atmosphere and serves straightforward local specialties, including *ribollita* (a thick soup of white beans, bread, cabbage, and onions). Meat eaters will find the lean Chianina beef and the *saporita di Bonconte* (a selection of several meats) succulent treats. ⊠ *Piazza San Francesco 1,* ☎ *0575/23271. AE, DC, MC, V. Closed Tues. and July. No dinner Mon.*

$$ ✕ **Tastevin.** Tastevin has introduced creative cooking—penne Tastevin (with cream of truffles) and seafood or meat carpaccio—to Arezzo, but also remains true to tradition. Two of the dining rooms are done out in a warm Tuscan provincial style, one in more sophisticated bistro style. At the small bar the talented owner plays and sings Sinatra and show tunes, for which a 15% cover charge will appear on the *conto* (bill). ⊠ *Via dei Cenci 9, close to San Francesco and the central Piazza Guido Monaco,* ☎ *0575/28304. AE, MC, V. Closed Mon. (Sun. in summer) and Aug. 1–25.*

$ ✕ **Spiedo d'Oro.** Cheery red-and-white tablecloths brighten up this large, reliable trattoria near the archaeological museum. This is your chance to try authentic homemade Tuscan specialties, such as *zuppa di pane* (bread soup), *pappardelle all'ocio* (noodles with duck sauce), and osso buco *all'aretina* (with herbs). ✉ *Via Crispi 12,* ☎ *0575/22873. No credit cards. Closed Thurs. and July 1–18.*

$$ ⊞ **Castello di Gargonza.** Enchantment reigns at this tiny 13th-century hamlet in the countryside near Monte San Savino, part of the fiefdom of the aristocratic Florentine Guicciardini family restored by the modern Count Roberto Guicciardini as a way to rescue a dying village. A castle, church, and the cobbled streets set the stage. Rooms can be had by the night. All houses—cottages and apartments, really—are for rent by the week; they have one to six rooms each, sleep two to seven people, and have as many as four baths. La Torre restaurant (closed Tuesday) serves local specialties. ✉ *52048 Monte San Savino, 52100,* ☎ *0575/847021, FAX 0575/847054. 25 houses with bath. Restaurant, pool. AE, DC, MC, V. Closed Jan. 10–Feb. 10.*

$$ ⊞ **Continental.** Centrally located near the train station and within walking distance of all major sights, the Continental has been a reliable and convenient place to stay since it opened in the 1950s. Bright white furnishings with yellow accents are throughout; gleaming new bathrooms complete with hair dryers and a pleasant roof garden are welcome pluses. The restaurant is closed Monday; no dinner is served Sunday. Rates are at the low end of the $$ category. ✉ *Piazza Guido Monaco 7, 52100,* ☎ *0575/20251, FAX 0575/350485. 74 rooms. Restaurant. AE, DC, MC, V.*

Outdoor Activities and Sports

HORSEBACK RIDING

A well-reputed outfit is **Rendola Riding** (✉ Rendola Valdarno, Arezzo, ☎ 0575/987045).

Shopping

FLEA MARKET

The first Sunday of each month, a colorful **flea market** selling antiques and not-so-antiques takes place in the **Piazza Grande.**

GOLD

Gold production here is on an industrial scale. **Uno-A-Erre** is the biggest of several factories. Bigtime baubles can be purchased on a small scale in town center. For gold jewelry set with precious or semiprecious stones, try **Il Diamante** (✉ Via Guido Monaco 69), **Borghini** (✉ Corso Italia 126), **Prosperi** (✉ Corso Italia 76), or **Aurea Monilia** (✉ Piazza San Francesco 15).

KNITWEAR

A cottage knitwear industry is burgeoning in Arezzo. For sweaters, try **Maglierie** (✉ Piazza Grande).

TUSCANY A TO Z

Arriving and Departing

By Car

The Autostrada del Sole (**A1**) connects Florence with Bologna, 105 km (65 mi) north, and Rome, 277 km (172 mi) south, and passes close to Arezzo.

By Plane

The largest airports in the region are Pisa's **Galileo Galilei Airport** (☎ 050/500707) and Florence's **Peretola Airport** (☎ 055/373498).

By Train

The coastal line from Rome to Genoa passes through Pisa and all the beach resorts. The main line from Rome to Bologna passes through Arezzo, Florence, and Prato.

Getting Around

By Boat

Boat services link the islands of Tuscany's archipelago with the mainland; passenger and car ferries leave from Piombino for Elba.

Navarma Line (⊠ Piazzale Premuda, ☎ 0565/225211). **Elba Ferries** (⊠ Viale Regina Margherita, ☎ 0565/220956). **Toremar** (⊠ Piazzale Premuda 13, ☎ 0565/31100); the ferry to Giglio leaves from Porto Santo Stefano on the Argentario peninsula (Toremar, ⊠ Piazzale Candi, ☎ 0564/818506).

By Bus

Tuscany is crisscrossed by bus lines that connect the smaller towns and cities on the autostrade and superhighways. They are a good choice for touring the hill towns around Siena, such as San Gimignano; you can then take a Tra-In or Lazzi bus from Siena to Arezzo and get back onto the main Rome–Florence train line. From Chiusi on the main train line you can get a bus to Montepulciano. Buses connect Florence and Siena with Volterra.

By Car

The best way to see Tuscany, making it possible to explore the tiny towns and country restaurants that are so much a part of the region's charm, is by car. Drivers should be prepared to navigate through bewildering suburban sprawls around Tuscan cities; to reach the historic sections where most of the sights are, look for the CENTRO STORICO signs. In many small towns you must park outside the walls.

A11 leads west from Florence and meets the coastal **A12** between Viareggio and Livorno. The **A1** autostrada links Florence with Arezzo and Chiusi (where you turn off for Montepulciano). A toll-free superstrada links Florence with Siena. For Chianti wine country scenery, take the **S222** south of Florence through the undulating hills between Strada in Chianti and Greve in Chianti (☞ Tuscan Hill Towns, *above*).

By Train

Italy's main rail line, which runs from Milan to Calabria, links Florence and Arezzo in Tuscany and runs past Chiusi and Cortona on its way south. Another main line connects Florence with Pisa by way of Prato, Pistoia, and Lucca. There are a few other local lines.

Contacts and Resources

Car Rental

Cars are for rent at the airports and in the larger cities in Tuscany; Alitalia may offer economical fly/drive packages with discounts on car rentals and hotels.

Avis has offices at Peretola Airport in Florence (☎ 055/372588). **Arezzo** (⊠ Piazza della Repubblica 1/a, ☎ 0575/354232). **Lucca** (⊠ Via Castracane 1217, ☎ 0583/490383). **Siena** (⊠ Via Simone Martini, 36 ☎ 0577/270305). **Hertz** has offices at Galileo Galilei Airport in Pisa (☎ 050/49187). **Prato** (⊠ c/o Autonoleggio Europa, Viale Vittorio Veneto 57, ☎ 0574/21055). **Siena** (✉ Viale XXIV Maggio 10, ☎ 0577/45085).

Emergencies

Police, fire (☎ 113). **Ambulance,** medical emergency (☎ 118).

Fishing

For a license, contact the **Federazione Italiana della Pesca Sportiva** (✉ Via dei Neri 6, Firenze) in Florence.

Guided Tours

From Florence, **American Express** (✉ Via Guicciardini 49/r, ☎ 055/288751) operates one-day excursions to Siena and San Gimignano and can arrange for cars, drivers, and guides for special-interest tours in Tuscany. **CIT** (✉ Via Cavour 56, ☎ 055/294306) has a three-day Carosello bus tour from Rome to Florence, Siena, and San Gimignano, as well as a five-day tour that also takes in Venice.

Horseback Riding

Rifugio Prategiano (✉ Montieri, Grosseto, ☎ 0566/997703). **Le Cannelle** (✉ Parco dell'Uccellina, Talamone, Grosseto, ☎ 0564/887020). For more information, contact the **Federazione Italiana Sport Equestre** (✉ Via Paoletti 54, Firenze, ☎ 055/480039).

Sailing

Charters in Tuscany are available through the **Centro Nautico Italiano** (✉ Piazza della Signoria 31/r, Firenze, ☎ 055/287045). **Mario Lorenzoni** (✉ Via degli Alfani 105/r, Firenze, ☎ 055/284790). **Renato Lessi** (✉ Località Porto, Castiglione della Pescaia, Grosseto, ☎ 0564/922793). For more information, contact the **Federazione Italiana Vela** (✉ CP 49, Marina di Carrara, ☎ 0585/57323) or the **Federazione Italiana Motonautica** (✉ Via Goldora 16, 55044 Marina di Pietrasanta, ☎ 0584/20963).

Skiing

For information, contact the **Federazione Italiana Sport Invernali** (✉ Viale Matteotti 15, Firenze, ☎ 055/576987).

Travel Agencies

In Florence: **American Express** (✉ Via Guicciardini 49/r, ☎ 055/288751). **CIT** (✉ Via Cavour 56, ☎ 055/294306). **Thomas Cook** (✉ c/o World Vision, Via Cavour 154/r, ☎ 055/579294).

Visitor Information

REGIONAL

Stop in **Florence** (✉ Via di Novoli, ☎ 055/439311).

LOCAL

There are tourist offices, generally open 9–12:30 and 3:30–7:30, in **Arezzo** (✉ Piazza della Repubblica 28, ☎ 0575/377678). **Cortona** (✉ Via Nazionale 72, ☎ 0575/630352). **Lucca** (✉ Piazzale Verdi, ☎ 0583/419689). **Montepulciano** (✉ Piazza Don Minzoni 2, ☎ 0578/757442). **Pisa** (✉ Piazza Duomo 8, ☎ 050/560464). **Pistoia** (✉ Palazzo dei Vescovi, ☎ 0573/21622). **Prato** (✉ Via Cairoli 48, ☎ 0574/24112). **San Gimignano** (✉ Piazza del Duomo, ☎ 0577/940008). **Siena** (✉ Via di Città 43, ☎ 0577/42209; ✉ Piazza del Campo 55, ☎ 0577/280551). **Volterra** (✉ Via Turazza 2, ☎ 0588/86150).

5 Venice

It's easy to forgive Venice—thanks to its myriad canals—for its eternal preoccupation with its own beauty. All the picture books in the world won't prepare you for the city's exotic landmarks, such as the Basilica di San Marco and the Palazzo Ducale, which rise from the lagoons like mirages. With sumptuous palaces and romantic waterways, Venice is straight out of an 18th-century Canaletto masterpiece.

Updated by
Giuliano
Davenport

I **T IS CALLED LA SERENISSIMA.** The literal translation of this name is ungainly: "the most serene." The term "Serene Republic" more successfully suggests the monstrous power and majesty of this city that was for centuries the unrivaled mistress of trade between Europe and the Orient and the staunch bulwark of Christendom against the tides of Turkish expansion. It suggests, too, the extraordinary beauty of the city—and surely Venice is the most beautiful city in the world (although the Florentines would surely disagree)—and its lavishness and fantasy, the result not just of its remarkable buildings but of the very fact that Venice is a city built on water, a city created more than 1,000 years ago by men who dared defy the sea, implanting their splendid palaces and churches on mud banks in a swampy and treacherous lagoon.

No matter how many times you have seen it in pictures or movies or TV commercials, the real thing is more surreal and dreamlike than you ever imagined. Its landmarks, the Basilica di San Marco and the Palazzo Ducale, seem hardly Italian: delightfully idiosyncratic, they are exotic mélanges of Byzantine, Gothic, and Renaissance styles. Piazza San Marco is a true public gathering space, full of jovial music and laughter, yet only a minute's walk away are streets so quiet that your footsteps echo on the stone pavements and shuttered, crumbling facades. Sunlight shimmers and silvery mist softens every perspective here, a city renowned in the Renaissance for its artists' rendering of color. It is a city full of secrets, ineffably romantic, and—at times—given over entirely to pleasure.

You must walk everywhere in Venice—Venezia in Italian—and where you cannot walk, you go by water. Occasionally, from fall to spring, you have to walk *in* water, when extraordinarily high tides known as *acque alte* invade the lower parts of the city, flooding Piazza San Marco for a few hours. Unless you're lucky to find some makeshift *passarelle* (plank bridges) that appear from nowhere to keep certain busy routes open, you'll have to take off your socks and shoes, roll up your pant legs, and wade in with everyone else, or sport big rubber boots to avoid contact with the notoriously filthy water. The problem of protecting Venice and its lagoon from dangerously high tides has generated extravagant plans and so many committee reports that the city may sink as much under the weight of paper as under water. Progress is being made, however. For centuries Venice's canals were regularly dredged to keep them clean and navigable. After nearly 30 years' neglect, the dredging of canals was finally resumed in 1993. It is hoped that waterless and malodorous canals (caused by *acque basse*—exceptionally low tides) will soon be a thing of the past. Today, Venetians are being encouraged by state subsidies to renovate their homes, rather than leave the city to live and work on the mainland—a trend that over the last three decades has drastically reduced Venice's resident population.

In spite of these problems, Venetians have mastered the art of living well in their singular city. You'll see them going about their daily affairs in *vaporetti* (ferries), crowded aboard the *traghetti* (traditional gondola ferries) that ply between the banks of the Grand Canal, in the *campi* (squares, also piazzi), and along the *calli* (narrow Venetian streets). They are nothing if not skilled—and remarkably tolerant—in dealing with the veritable armies of tourists from all over the world that at peak times flow through the city. Get away from Piazza San Marco when it's crowded; you'll be surprised to find many areas of Venice practically deserted. Explore the districts of Cannaregio or

Castello, quiet areas where you can find the time and space to sit and contemplate the watercolor pages of Venetian history.

Founded on the marshes by the Roman Veneti escaping from the barbarians, Venice rose from the waters to dominate the Adriatic and hold the gorgeous East in fee. Early in its history the city called in Byzantine artists to decorate its churches with brilliant mosaics, still glowing today. Then the influence of Lombard-Romanesque architecture from the 11th to 13th centuries gave rise to the characteristic type of palace for which Venice is famous the world over. Many of the sumptuous palaces along the Grand Canal were built at that time, strong reminders of Venice's control of the major trade routes to the East. Subsequently, Gothic styles from elsewhere in Europe were adapted to create a new kind of Venetian Gothic art and architecture.

Venice attained a peak of power and prosperity in the 15th and 16th centuries. It extended its domain inland to include all of what is now known as the Veneto region and even beyond. In the last half of the 15th century, the Renaissance arrived in Venice, and the city's greatest artists—Giovanni and Gentile Bellini and Carpaccio in the late 15th century; Giorgione, Titian, Veronese, and Tintoretto in the 16th century—played a decisive role in the development of Western art, and their work still covers walls and ceilings and altars all over the city today.

The decline of Venice came slowly. For 400 years the powerful maritime city-republic had held sway. After the 16th century the tide changed. The Ottoman Empire blocked Venice's Mediterranean trade routes, and newly emerging sea powers, such as Britain and the Netherlands, broke Venice's monopoly by opening oceanic trading routes. Like its steadily dwindling fortunes, Venice's art and culture began a prolonged decline, leaving only the splendid monuments to recall a fabled past, with the luminous paintings of Canaletto and the beautiful frescoes of Tiepolo striking a glorious swan song.

You can see the panoply of history by visiting only the major museums and churches, but if you want a fuller picture of the districts that keep this a living city, get off the beaten path as often as you can. You will almost certainly lose your way (everyone does), but Venetians are usually only too pleased to direct you if you ask; chances are, they will admire your initiative and put you back on the right track.

Pleasures and Pastimes

Carnival

" . . . All the world repaire to Venice to see the folly and madnesse of the Carnevall . . .'tis impossible to recount the universal madnesses of this place during this time of licence," commented traveler John Evelyn in 1646. Indeed, Carnevale (Carnival) was once a festival that was an excuse for all manner of carnal indulgence. In its 18th-century heyday, festivities began on December 26 and lasted two months; nowadays the festival has lost some of its more outlandish flavor and lasts only 10 days (the 10 days preceding Ash Wednesday), but the event has become so vast—and so commercialized—that Venice frequently has to be "shut" during this time owing to the sheer weight of numbers.

Dining

The general standard of Venetian restaurants has suffered from the onslaught of mass tourism, but it is still possible to eat well in Venice at moderate prices. Although seafood is a specialty here, the fact that the wholesale cost of fish is generally higher than meat is reflected in the prices, and you will find some fish dishes very expensive, especially those that are priced by weight (mainly baked or steamed fish).

Lodging

Most of Venice's hotels are in renovated palaces. The most exclusive of these are indeed palatial, although even they may have some small, dowdy "Cinderella"-type rooms. In lower categories, space is at a premium; some rooms may be cramped, and not all hotels have lounging areas. Because of preservation laws, some cannot install elevators. Air-conditioning can be essential for those who suffer in summer heat; some hotels charge a supplement for it. Although the city has no cars, it does have boats plying the canals and pedestrians chattering in the streets, even late at night, so ask for a quiet room if noise bothers you. And during the summer months, don't leave your room lights on at night *and* your window wide open: mosquitoes can descend en masse.

EXPLORING VENICE

The church of San Marco is unquestionably the heart of Venice, but venturing even 50 yards from it can sometimes lead to confusion. Although the smaller canals (a canal is called a *rio*) are spanned by frequent bridges, the Grand Canal can only be crossed on foot at three points—near the train station, at the Rialto Bridge, and at the Accademia Bridge—which decidedly complicates matters. It's supremely maddening to find yourself on the wrong bank of a canal with no bridge in sight.

A street is called a *calle,* but a street that runs alongside a canal is called either a *riva* or a *fondamenta.* The closed-in streetscapes of Venice make it hard to see any reference point, such as the spire of the Campanile, above the rooftops, and the narrow backstreets often take unpredictable turns that foul up your sense of direction. Streets and canals may look deceptively familiar, only to make sudden dead ends. To get around Venice, travelers often use the vaporetti, which circulate through the city on set routes. A map of vaporetto routes is always helpful.

A scheme called *Dal Museo alla Città* (From Museum to City) was begun in 1995 to encourage visitors to seek out art not only in museums but also throughout the city proper—primarily in the churches and *scuole* (charitable confraternity halls) for which it was originally commissioned. As part of this, more than a dozen places selected for their artistic merit now have fixed visiting hours when tourists can be sure of finding the place open and of not intruding on church services. At these times there should always be someone available to provide information, a free leaflet (available in English); also, postcards and booklets about these important sights are sold.

In many Venetian sites, new lighting systems have been installed, all of which take 500-lire coins. Regular store opening hours are usually 10–noon and 4–6 PM in winter or 5–7 PM in summer. Most churches are usually open from 8 or 9 until noon or 12:30, and from 3 or 4 until about 7. Major basilicas are open all day in season.

Numbers in the text correspond to numbers in the margin and on the Venice map.

Great Itineraries

IF YOU HAVE 2 DAYS

Begin the first day with a look at Piazza San Marco and the surrounding buildings. Follow this with a cruise down the Grand Canal to see the more important palazzi. The second day, visit some of the prominent churches of Venice in the Merceria district and finish with a trip to the islands of Murano and Torcello.

IF YOU HAVE 4 DAYS

Spend your first day visiting the sights in and around that most famous of piazze, Piazza San Marco, including the Basilica di San Marco and the Museo Correr. Dedicate the next day to cruising down the Grand Canal, stopping to visit the Accademia Gallery and the Ca' Rezzonico. Don't forget to walk over the Ponte Rialto to the surrounding markets. End your day with a visit to San Stae, a particularly characteristic neighborhood. On the third day, visit the Campo Santi Giovanni e Paolo and the Campo dell'Arsenale, only a short walk from your next stop, the Museo Storico Navale. Return to Piazza San Marco and take the 52 or 82 vaporetto line from San Zaccaria for a look at the impressive churches of San Giorgio Maggiore and Il Redentore, both of which are particularly beautiful sights at sunset. On your final day visit the islands of the lagoon: be sure not to miss Murano and its glass museums, along with the islands of Burano and Torcello.

IF YOU HAVE 6 DAYS

Start at Piazza San Marco, where you should visit the Basilica di San Marco, the Museo Correr, and the Palazzo Ducale, ending your day on the Ponte dei Sospiri. Dedicate the next day to cruising the Grand Canal, stopping at Santa Maria della Salute and the nearby Peggy Guggenheim Collection, before visiting the Galleria dell'Accademia. Next visit the Ca' Rezzonico and explore the Rialto Bridge area. Spend the late afternoon walking through the neighborhood of San Stae. On the third day, visit Santa Maria dei Miracoli, Campo Santi Giovanni e Paolo, the Campo dell'Arsenale, and finally the Naval History Museum. If you have time, try to visit the island of San Pietro di Castello before returning to Piazza San Marco via the Scuola di San Giorgio degli Schiavoni. On the fourth day, take the 52 or 82 vaporetto line from San Zaccaria for a look at the impressive churches of San Giorgio Maggiore and Il Redentore, as well as the island of the Giudecca. Head directly across from the Giudecca to the Zattere, a lively promenade in the Dorsoduro neighborhood where you will find a number of pizzerias. Spend the fifth day exploring Titian's works: Start in Campo Santo Stefano and then head for the Scuola dei Carmini and the church of San Sebastiano. A must is the Friari, home of some of Titian's best. Next, visit the Scuola di San Rocco, where you will find some delightful paintings by Tintoretto. Devote your final day to exploring the islands of the lagoon. If you can, squeeze in a visit to the cemetery island of San Michele.

Piazza San Marco, the Heart of Venice

The most evocative square in the world, Piazza San Marco (St. Mark's Square) is the heart of Venice, a vast open square enclosed by an orderly procession of arcades marching toward the fairy-tale cupolas and marble lacework of the Basilica di San Marco. Perpetually animated during the day when it's filled with people and crowds of fluttering pigeons, it can be magical at night, especially in the winter, when melancholy mists swirl around the lampposts and bell tower.

A Good Walk

Start your day in the **Piazza San Marco** ① with a morning visit to the **Basilica di San Marco** ②, home of the Pala d'Oro and the Museo di San Marco. Next, get a bird's-eye view of the piazza and city from the **Campanile** ③. Move on to the smaller **Piazzetta San Marco** for a visit to the glorious **Palazzo Ducale** ④ and a look at the Ponte dei Sospiri at the east wing of the palace. Return to Piazza San Marco where directly opposite the facade of the basilica you will find the **Museo Correr** ⑤ in the Ala Napoleonica.

TIMING

A full day is required to visit each sight thoroughly. If you have limited time, you will need to discipline yourself from straying too far from the Piazza San Marco; a half-day should be enough to see the essential sights, but do not miss the Pala d'Oro in the basilica, the Palazzo Ducale, and, of course, the piazza itself.

If you come during the most popular seasons, like the Venetians, you will have to adapt to the crowds, visiting at odd hours to avoid tour groups.

Sights to See

★ ❷ **Basilica di San Marco.** This is one of Europe's most beautiful churches. An opulent synthesis of Byzantine and Romanesque styles, it is laid out in a Greek cross topped off with five plump domes. The basilica did not actually become the cathedral of Venice until as late as 1807, but its role as the church of the doge (the elected head of the Venetian republic) gave it immense power and wealth. It was begun in 1063, and inaugurated in 1094, to house the remains of St. Mark the Evangelist, which were filched from Alexandria two centuries earlier by two agents of the doge. The story goes that they stole the saint's remains and hid them in a barrel under layers of pickled pork to get them past the Muslim guards.

That escapade is illustrated in a mosaic in the lunette (semicircular decoration) over the farthest left of the front doors. This 13th-century mosaic is the earliest one on this heavily decorated facade; look at it closely and you can see a picture of the church as it appeared in the 13th century.

Over the years this church stood as a symbol of Venetian wealth and power, and it was endowed with all the riches the Republic's admirals and merchants could carry off from the Orient, earning it the nickname Chiesa D'Oro (Golden Church). The four bronze horses that prance and snort over the central doorway (copies only, but the originals are on view indoors in the Museo di San Marco, ☞ *below*) were classical sculptures that victorious Venetians took away from Constantinople in 1204, along with a lot of other loot that you can see inside. Just inside the central front doors in the church porch, look for a medallion of red porphyry set in the floor to mark the spot of another of Venice's political coups: the reconciliation between Barbarossa, the Holy Roman Emperor, and Pope Alexander III, brought about by Doge Sebastiano Ziani in 1177.

One of the innovations of this church was a roof of brick vaulting, rather than wood, enabling the ceiling to be decorated with mosaics. As you enter the basilica, you'll find it surprisingly dark inside, compared to the soaring light-filled Gothic cathedrals of northern Europe. This is because many of the original windows were filled in and covered with even more mosaics. In the mysterious dusk, candles flicker and the gold tiles of mosaics glitter softly, sensuously. (The tiles were laid on at slight angles to achieve precisely this effect.) The earliest mosaics are from the 11th and 12th centuries; later ones were done as late as the 16th century, such as the *Last Judgment* on the arch between the porch and the nave, said to be based on drawings by Tintoretto. The dim light, the galleries high above the naves—they served as the *matroneum,* the women's gallery—the massive altar screen, or iconostasis, the single massive Byzantine chandelier, even the Greek cross ground plan, give San Marco an exotic aspect quite unlike that of most Christian churches. The effect is remarkable. Here the pomp and mystery of Oriental magnificence are wedded to Christian belief, creating an intensely awesome impression.

Go into the **Cappella Zen** (Zen Chapel) (to the right just off the porch, and named after a local cardinal rather than any form of Buddhism) to see some earlier (13th-century) mosaics, telling the story of the life of St. Mark. Next to it, the **battistero** (baptistery) contains a bronze font cover by Jacopo Sansovino and the tomb of Doge Andrea Dandolo (1307–54), a friend of Petrarch and a writer in his own right. Several of the earlier doges were buried here, while later ones were interred in the church of Santi Giovanni e Paolo (☞ *below*).

Two more chapels, both in the left transept, are worth a special look: the **Cappella della Madonna di Nicopeia** (Chapel of the Madonna of Nicopeia), which holds a precious icon (part of the loot from Constantinople) that many consider Venice's most powerful protector; and next to it, on the left, a small chapel dedicated to the Virgin Mary with fine 15th-century mosaics depicting her life, possibly based on drawings by Andrea Mantegna.

If you stand in the central aisle facing the main altar, notice the polygonal pulpit to the right, at the intersection of the nave and right transept. After the coronation ceremony, each new doge stood here for the people to behold him in the glory of his new office.

The **Sanctuary** in the Basilica of San Marco charges an admission fee, but it's well worth it. The main altar, with its green marble canopy lifted high on carved alabaster columns, covers the tomb of St. Mark. Behind this is the real attraction: the **Pala d'Oro** (Golden Altarpiece), a dazzling gilded silver screen encrusted with 1,927 precious gems and 255 enameled panels. It was originally made in Constantinople in the 11th century, but was continually embellished over the next few centuries by Byzantine and Venetian master craftsmen, reaching its present state of extraordinary sumptuousness in the mid-14th century. The excellently produced color booklet on the Pala (3,000 lire at the card shop to the left of the atrium) is a good investment, so as not to miss its incredible artistic and narrative detail. The bronze door leading from the sanctuary back into the sacristy is another Sansovino work; check out the top left corner, where the artist included a self-portrait and, above that, a picture of his friend and fellow artist Titian. Tickets for the Sanctuary also include admission into the **Tesoro** (Treasury), which is entered from the right transept. It contains some exquisite pieces, many of them exotic treasures borne away from Constantinople and other vanquished places.

From the atrium, climb the steep stairway to the **Galleria** and the **Museo di San Marco** (St. Mark's Museum) for a look at the interior of the church from the organ gallery and a sweeping view of Piazza San Marco and the Piazzetta dei Leoncini from the outdoor gallery. The highlight of the museum is the close-up of the four magnificent gilded bronze horses that once stood outside on the gallery. The originals were probably cast in Imperial Rome, and later transported to the New Rome, Constantinople. Napoléon hauled them off to Paris after he conquered Venice in 1797, but they were returned after the fall of the French Empire.

Be warned: Guards at the door turn away any visitors, male or female, wearing shorts or inappropriate attire. If you want to take a free guided tour in English in summer (with less certainty in winter, since the guides are volunteers), wait on the left in the porch for a group to form. ⊠ *Basilica of San Marco, 30122.* ☎ *Free.* ☉ *Mon.–Sat. 9:30–5, Sun. 2–5. Museum:* ☎ *041/5225205.* ☎ *3,000 lire.* ☉ *Apr.–Sept.,*

Venice

Sacca della Misericordia

Canale delle Navi

San Michele

33 36

440 yards
400 meters

C. Racchetta
Fondamente
Rio S. Caterina
32

Strada Nuova
Rio d. Santi Apostoli
R. d. Gesuiti Nuove
C. d. Testa
Ruga della Panada
C. d. Squero
dei Mendicanti

Campo d. Pescheria
Erberia
del Vin
9
16
Campo Santi Giovanni e Paolo
R. Barbaria delle Tole
17
18
19
R. d. S.
Francesco
R. d. S.

Campo Manin
del Carbon
Merceria
R. d. Fava
Sal. di S. Lio
Rio d. S. Marina
Rigo
Giuffa
R. d. S. Severo
R. d. S. Lorenzo
15
C. Lion
23
C. d. Furlani
R. d. Scudi
R. d. Gorne
Canale d. Galeazze

Campo Manin
C. d. Bande
Fond. Osmarin
R. d. Greci
R. d. Pietà
Darsena Grande

Fabbri
R. d. Palazzo
SAN ZACCARIA
1
2
3
4
5
Molo
Riva degli
Schiavoni
20
21
R. d. Arsenale
Rio della Tana
Rio d. Vergini
Pietro
Rio d. S. Daniele
S. IP.
22

Frezzaria
S. Moisè
R. d.
Piazza San Marco
22

Canale di S. Marco

V. Garibaldi
Riva dei Sette Martiri
R. d. S. Giuseppe
Rio d. S. Anna
Rio dei Giardini

37
Isola di S. Giorgio Maggiore

Fond. delle Zitelle
Calle Michelangelo

Riva dei Partigiani

KEY
i Tourist Information
▲ Boat stop

daily 10–5; Nov.–Mar., daily 10–4:30. Sanctuary: ☎ 041/5225697.
🎟 3,000 lire. ⊙ Apr.–Sept., Mon.–Sat. 9:30–5, Sun. 1–4:30; Oct.–Mar.,
Mon.–Sat. 10–4, Sun. 1–4:30 (hrs for Museum and Sanctuary may
vary slightly at different times of yr). Tours from left porch: ⊙ Apr.–Sept.,
Mon.–Sat. at 11 AM.

★ ❸ **Campanile.** The tall brick bell tower is a reconstruction of the original, which stood for 1,000 years before it collapsed one morning in
1912, practically without warning (miraculously none of the surrounding buildings suffered serious damage, and the only victim was
a cat). In the 15th century, clerics found guilty of immoral behavior
were suspended in wooden cages from the tower, sometimes to sub-
sist on bread and water for as long as a year, sometimes to starve to
death. The pretty marble loggia (covered gallery) at its base was built
in the early 16th century by Jacopo Sansovino. It, too, has been carefully restored. The view from the tower on a clear day—spanning the
city, the Lido, the lagoon, and the mainland as far as the distant Alps—
is worth the price of admission. Oddly, you can't see the myriad canals
that snake through the 117 islets on which Venice is built. ⊠ *Piazza
San Marco,* ☎ *041/5224064.* 🎟 *5,000 lire.* ⊙ *Daily 9:30–5:30; closed
for maintenance Dec.–Jan.*

❺ **Museo Correr.** Inside this museum you will find a fascinating, diverse
collection of historical items and old master paintings. These works
were once the private collection of the aristocrat Teodoro Correr, who
donated them to the city in 1830. Exhibits range from the absurdly
high-soled shoes worn by 16th-century Venetian ladies (who had to
be supported by a servant on each side in order to walk on these pre-
carious perches) to fine art by the talented Bellini family of Renaissance
painters. ⊠ *Piazza San Marco, Ala Napoleonica,* ☎ *041/5225625.* 🎟
14,000 lire includes entrance to Palazzo Ducale. ⊙ *Apr.–Oct., daily
9–5; Nov.–Mar., daily 10–4; last entry 1 hr before closing.*

★ ❹ **Palazzo Ducale** (Doge's Palace). This Gothic-Renaissance fantasia of
pink-and-white marble, a majestic expression of the prosperity and power
attained by Venice during its most glorious period, rises above Piazzetta
San Marco. Its top-heavy design (the dense upper floors rest on the
graceful ground-floor colonnade) has always confounded architectural purists, who insist that proper architecture be set out the other
way around. The building was much more than just a palace. Rather
it was a sort of combination White House, Senate, torture chamber,
and prison rolled into one. Venice's government, set up sometime in
the 7th century as a participatory democracy, provided for an elected
ruler, the doge, to serve for life, but in practice he was simply a fig-
urehead. Power really rested with the Great Council, originally an elected
body but, from the 13th century on, an aristocratic stronghold, with
members inheriting their seats from their noble ancestors. Laws were
passed by the Senate, a group of 200 elected from the Great Council
(which could have as many as 1,700 members). Executive powers belonged to the College, a committee of 25 leaders. In the 14th century,
the Council of Ten was formed to deal with emergency situations; this
group's meetings were not open to the public, and the Council of Ten
often proved more powerful than the Senate, though its members
could only serve for limited terms before new members were elected.

A fortress for the doge existed on this spot in the early 9th century;
the building you see today was a product of the 12th century, although, like the basilica next door, it was continually added to and transformed throughout the centuries. You enter the palace at the ornate
Gothic **Porta della Carta** (Gate of the Paper, where official decrees were
traditionally posted), which opens onto an immense courtyard. Ahead

is the **Scala dei Giganti** (Stairway of the Giants), guarded by huge statues of Mars and Neptune by Jacopo Sansovino. Ordinary mortals do not get to climb these stairs, however; after paying your fee, walk along the arcade to reach the central interior staircase. Its upper flight is called the **Scala d'Oro** (Golden Staircase), also designed by Sansovino, with its lavish gilded decoration. Although it may seem odd that the government's main council rooms and reception halls would be so far upstairs, imagine how effectively foreign emissaries must have been intimidated by this arduous climb.

Visitors must have also been overwhelmed by the sumptuous decoration of these apartments, their walls and ceilings covered with works by Venice's greatest artists. Among the grand rooms you can visit are the **Anticollegio** (a waiting room outside the College's chamber), which features two fine paintings, Tintoretto's *Bacchus and Ariadne Crowned by Venus* and Veronese's *Rape of Europa;* the **Sala del Collegio** (College Chamber), its ceiling magnificently painted by Veronese; and the **Sala del Senato** (Senate Chamber), with Tintoretto's *Triumph of Venice* on the ceiling. The huge *Paradise* on the end wall of the **Great Council Hall** is by Jacopo Tintoretto (1518–94): it is a dark, dynamic masterpiece. This is the world's largest oil painting (23 × 75 ft), a vast work commissioned for a vast hall. The massive carved and gilded ceiling is breathtaking, even dizzying, as you wheel around searching for the best vantage point from which to admire Veronese's majestic *Apotheosis of Venice* filling one of the center panels. Step onto the balcony of the Great Council Hall for a view of St. Mark's Basin, its waters churning with the wakes of countless boats. Look at the frieze of portraits of the first 76 doges around the upper part of the walls. One portrait is missing: a black painted curtain near the left-hand corner of the wall opposite Tintoretto's painting marks the spot where the portrait of doge Marin Falier should be. A Latin inscription bluntly explains that Falier was executed for treason in 1355. The Republic never forgave him.

At the ticket office of the Doge's Palace you can book a guided tour (unfortunately, only given in Italian) of the palace's secret rooms; it takes you to the doge's private apartments, up into the attic and Piombi prison, and through hidden passageways to the torture chambers, where prisoners were interrogated. The 18th-century writer and libertine, Casanova, a native of Venice, was imprisoned here in 1755, having somehow offended someone in power (the official accusation was of being a Freemason); he made a daring escape 15 months later and fled to France, where he continued his career of intrigue and scandal. From the east wing of the Doge's Palace, the enclosed marble **Ponte dei Sospiri** (Bridge of Sighs) arches over a narrow canal to the cramped, gloomy cell blocks of the so-called New Prison. During the age of Romanticism, the bridge's tragic and melancholic history made it one of the prize sights for 19th-century tourists. The bridge's name comes from the sighs of those being led to execution. Take a look out its windows to see the last earthly view many of these prisoners had. ✉ *Palazzo Ducale, Piazzetta San Marco,* ☎ *041/5224951.* 🎟 *14,000 lire includes entrance to Museo Correr.* ☉ *Apr.–Oct., daily 9–7 (ticket office closes at 6); Nov.–Mar., daily 9–5 (last entry 1 hr before closing). "Secret Itineraries" tour (in Italian only):* 🎟 *10,000 lire.* ☉ *Sept.–June, Thurs.–Tues. at 10 AM and noon; July–Aug., Thurs.–Tues. at 10 AM; reserve at least 1 day ahead.*

★ ❶ **Piazza San Marco.** Historically and geographically, St. Mark's Square is the logical place to start exploring the city. If you stand at the piazza's far end, facing the basilica, you'll notice that rather than being a strict rectangle it opens wider at the basilica end, enhancing the perspective and creating the illusion of being even larger than it is. On your left, the long arcaded building is the **Procuratie Vecchie,** built in the early 16th century as offices and residences for the powerful Procurators of San Marco, administrators of the basilica. Across the piazza, on your right hand, is the **Procuratie Nuove,** built half a century later in a more grandiose classical style. The Procuratie Nuove has impeccable architectural lineage: it was originally planned by perhaps Venice's greatest Renaissance architect, Jacopo Sansovino (1486–1570) of Florence, to carry on the look of his **Libreria Vecchia,** where the Marciana National Library is now housed (and where interesting special exhibitions are often held), though Sansovino died before the building was begun. The actual designer was Vincenzo Scamozzi (circa 1552–1616), a pupil of Andrea Palladio and a devout Neoclassicist; later sections were completed by Baldassare Longhena (1598–1682), Venice's other great architect, who belonged firmly to the Baroque tradition.

When Napoléon entered Venice with his troops in 1797, he called Piazza San Marco "the world's most beautiful drawing room"—and promptly gave orders to redecorate it. His architects demolished an old church that stood behind you, at the end of the square farthest from the basilica, and put up the **Ala Napoleonica** (Napoleonic Wing), or Fabbrica Nuova (New Building), to unite the two 16th-century buildings on either side.

Today the arcades of these three grand buildings shelter shops and cafés. Several of the cafés have their own small orchestras that play outdoors in fair weather; though patrons of the cafés must pay an additional charge for the entertainment, passersby in the piazza can enjoy it for free. On warm summer nights, the orchestras compete to see which can draw the biggest crowd, and the fun is infectious. To see the piazza at its most magical, however, get up at the crack of dawn. Only then is the piazza *senza popolo* (without people), when you can't help but feel that you're wandering through a Canaletto painting.

NEED A BREAK?   On the Procuratie Vecchie side of Piazza San Marco is the historic **Caffè Quadri** (closed Mon.), which was shunned by Venetians during the 19th century when the occupying Austrians made it their gathering place. **Caffè Florian** (closed Wed.), on the Procuratie Nuove side, is where Casanova, Wagner, and Proust regularly visited. Like a gondola ride, eating and drinking at cafés may be a splurge, but it's a treat you shouldn't miss.

Piazzetta San Marco. This square leads from Piazza San Marco down to the waters of St. Mark's Basin. This landing stage, now crowded with excursion boats, was once the grand entrance to the Republic. Two tall columns rise here on the waterfront: one is topped by the winged lion, a traditional emblem of St. Mark that became by extension the symbol of Venice itself; the other bears aloft a statue of St. Theodore (the first patron saint of Venice) and his dragon.

Torre dell'Orologio. The Clock Tower was erected in 1496 and is endowed with an enameled timepiece and animated figures of Moors that strike the hour (HORAS NON NUMERO NISI SERENAS says the inscription on the tower—"Only happy hours"). During Ascension Week (40 days after Easter) and on Epiphany (Jan. 6), an angel and three wise men go in and out of the doors and bow to the Virgin. Unfortunately, it is closed for restoration.

Along the Grand Canal

Venetians call it the Canalazzo, but to the rest of the world it's the Grand Canal, the city's main thoroughfare. A 3-km-long (2-mi-long) ribbon of water it was, and to some extent still is, the Fifth Avenue of Venice. It was here that the city's richest families lived, building for themselves a series of magnificent palaces, remarkable even by the city's standards. Here, the combination of being surrounded by water and the most opulent, luxurious, and fantastic efforts of a people obsessed with opulence, luxury, and fantasy has created a seemingly endless unfolding panorama of unique architectural richness. The sheer numbers of these buildings can produce a sort of cultural shell shock as you head up the canal. Accordingly, it makes sense to attempt little more at first than to sample, to breathe in, the unparalleled magnificence of the Grand Canal, letting it wash over you (only metaphorically, of course; it may not be deep but it's very dirty). To begin your exploration, catch vaporetto 1 at the San Marco landing stage. Don't forget to return for a gondola ride an hour or so before sunset; couples have long known that this is the most romantic way to see Venice. However, for an overall sightseeing tour of the canal, you get a better, more extensive view from a vaporetto—which is both higher in the water and much less expensive. Try to get one of the coveted seats in the prow, where you have a clear view. Once off the vaporetto, keep in mind the two-man traghetti that allow you, at many points along the Canalazzo, to ferry across from one bank to the other for only 500 lire.

The Grand Canal has an average depth of about 9 ft and varies from 40 to 76 yards in width. It winds like an inverted letter S through Venice, from the San Marco landing to the landing at the train station (Ferrovia), passing under three bridges and between 200 palaces dating from the 14th century to the 18th century, most of them in Venetian Gothic or Renaissance style.

A Good Boat Trip

As you leave Piazza San Marco on the vaporetto, **Santa Maria della Salute** ⑥, the huge, white, domed 17th-century Baroque church designed by Longhena, can be seen on the left. Not far from this stop is the small **Peggy Guggenheim Collection** ⑦, filled with engaging important 20th-century works. Across the canal you can see the imposing terraced front of the **Gritti Palace** hotel (☞ Lodging, *below*), which occupies the former Palazzo Pisani. A few minutes farther on, on the left bank at the Ca' Rezzonico stop, is Longhera's Baroque **Ca' Rezzonico** ⑧. Be sure to visit the Museo del Settecento Veneziano, housed here in gilded salons.

The canal narrows and boat traffic increases as you approach the **Ponte Rialto** ⑨, arched high over the canal. The Ca' d'Oro landing on the right, just beyond the Rialto, marks the lovely Venetian Gothic palace of **Ca' d'Oro** ⑩. Across from the Ca' d'Oro, you'll see the classical facade, with loggias on two stories, of the **Palazzo Corner della Regina** ⑪. Just beyond the Corner della Regina you can't miss the imposing bulk of the grand Baroque **Ca' Pesaro** ⑫, designed by Longhena, and unfortunately closed for restoration.

Not far beyond, on the left, another white church is adorned with Baroque statues; this is San Stae, and the landing here is a gateway to an untrammeled Venetian neighborhood of narrow canals and airy squares. Back on the right bank, the Renaissance **Palazzo Vendramin-Calergi** ⑬ is now the winter home of Venice's glamorous Casino (☞ Nightlife and the Arts, *below*). Continuing along the Grand canal in the direction of the railway station, you will see on your right the 16th-century bridge Ponte delle Guglie, famed for its spires and adjacent to the elegant facade of **Palazzo Labia** ⑭.

TIMING

All of these sights can be comfortably visited in one day. Jumping on and off the vaporetto is easy, although you may be tempted just to take the ride and view the sights from the canal.

Sights to See

⑩ Ca' d'Oro. This lovely Venetian Gothic palace is adorned with marble traceries and ornaments that were once embellished with pure gold. Today it houses the **Franchetti Gallery**, a fine collection of tapestries, sculptures, and paintings. ⊠ *Galleria Franchetti, Cannaregio,* ☎ *041/5238790.* 🎫 *4,000 lire.* 🕐 *Daily 9–2.*

⑫ Ca' Pesaro. Designed by Longhena, this palace is typical of the grand Baroque style. It's now home to two rather dull art collections, the **Museo Orientale** (Oriental Art Museum) and the **Galleria d'Arte Moderna** (Modern Art Gallery), containing mostly 19th-century and some 20th-century works, although the intention is also to display the gallery's large collection of contemporary works when restoration is completed. ⊠ *San Stae, S. Croce,* ☎ *041/721127.* 🕐 *Museo Orientale Tues.–Sun. 9–1:30; Galleria d'Arte Moderna closed for restoration until 1999.*

★ ⑧ Ca' Rezzonico. This huge Baroque mansion was begun by Longhena in the 1660s and completed by another architect, Giorgio Massari, in the 1740s. Here you'll find Venice's most magnificent ballroom—site of Venice's greatest costume balls (the last of which was held in the 1960s to honor Elizabeth Taylor and Richard Burton). This was the English poet Robert Browning's last home, where he died in 1889. Be sure to visit the **Museo del Settecento Veneziano** (Museum of 18th-Century Venice), housed in gilded salons here and newly completed after various stages of restoration. Pictures by the 18th-century Venetian painters Francesco and Gianantonio Guardi and Pietro Longhi, and a fine series of frescoes by their younger contemporary Giandomenico Tiepolo at the back of the palace, really open a window onto that charming and delightfully frivolous social era. ⊠ *Fondamenta Rezzonico, S. Barnaba,* ☎ *041/2410100.* 🎫 *12,000 lire.* 🕐 *Apr.–Mar., Mon.–Sun. 10–5 (last admission at 4).*

⑪ Palazzo Corner della Regina. Now housing the Biennale's library, this palace is among the most beautiful in Venice. It was built in 1724 and named after the *regina* (queen) of Cyprus, Caterina Cornaro, who was born in an older palace on this site. Head for the second floor *portego—* a hall running the length of a palace, a feature typical of Venetian palazzi. ⊠ *Calle della Regina, San Stae,* ☎ *041/5218701.* 🎫 *Free.* 🕐 *Mon.–Thurs. 9–5:30, Fri. 9–1.*

⑭ Palazzo Labia. Once the palatial stamping grounds of Venice's showiest 18th-century family, the palace today is the Venetian headquarters of RAI, the Italian radio and television giant. It is hard to imagine a broadcasting company in any other country establishing itself among such opulent splendor, however apt in Italy. The **Tiepolo Room,** a gorgeous ballroom in the palazzo, exhibits the final flowering of Venetian painting: Giambattista Tiepolo's illusionistic frescoes of Anthony and Cleopatra, teeming with dwarfs, Barbary pirates, and toy dogs. The artist's true sense of pleasure is evident. ⊠ *Campo San Geremia, Canal Cannaregio,* ☎ *041/5242812.* 🎫 *Ballroom free, Wed.–Fri. 3–4; guided tour of ballroom and other rooms (available in English): 12,000 lire.* 🕐 *Tour Wed.–Fri. 3–4, by prior arrangement.*

⑬ **Palazzo Vendramin-Calergi.** In 1883 the great German composer Wagner died in this Renaissance palazzo designed by Coducci in 1509 in white stone with red marble medallions and an imposing carved frieze. It is now the winter home of Venice's glamorous **Casino** (☞ Nightlife and the Arts, *below*).

❼ **Peggy Guggenheim Collection.** Visit and delight in this small but choice gallery of 20th-century painting and sculpture in the heiress's lavish former apartments in the Palazzo Venier dei Leoni. Through wealth and social connections, Guggenheim (1898–1979) became a serious patron of art—she was once married to the painter Max Ernst—and her holdings include several works by Picasso, Kandinsky, Ernst, Pollock, and Motherwell, among others. ✉ *Entrance on Calle San Cristoforo, Dorsoduro,* ☎ *041/5206288.* ☞ *10,000 lire.* ☉ *Apr.–Nov., Wed.–Mon. 11–6.*

★ ❾ **Ponte Rialto** (Rialto Bridge). The canal narrows and boat traffic increases as you approach this bridge arched high over the canal. The windows in the arch belong to the shops inside. This is a commercial hub of the city, with open-air vegetable, fruit, and fish markets on the left, and on the right, an upscale shopping district.

❻ **Santa Maria della Salute.** Longhena designed this huge, white, domed 17th-century Baroque church. ✉ *Punta della Dogana, Dorsoduro.* ☉ *Daily 10–noon and 4–6.*

The Arsenal and Beyond

The city's eastern districts and some of its most beautiful churches are along the path of the Mercerie, one of Venice's busiest streets. It's actually a five-part series of streets (Merceria dell'Orologio, Merceria di San Zulian, Merceria del Capitello, Merceria di San Salvador, and Merceria 2 Aprile) leading more or less directly from Piazza San Marco to the Rialto bridge.

A Good Walk

Head out of Piazza San Marco under the clock tower onto the Mercerie. At Campo San Zulian and the church of San Giuliano, turn right onto Calle Guerra and Calle delle Bande to reach the white marble church of **Santa Maria Formosa** ⑮. Follow Calle Borgoloco into Campo San Marina, where you turn right, cross the little canal, and take Calle Castelli to the church of **Santa Maria dei Miracoli** ⑯. Behind the church, bear right to Calle Larga Giacinto Gallina, which leads to **Campo Santi Giovanni e Paolo** ⑰, site of the massive Dominican church of Santi Giovanni e Paolo, or San Zanipolo. The powerful equestrian monument of Bartolomeo Colleoni, by Florentine sculptor Andrea del Verrocchio (1435–88), stands in the square.

Behind the east end of San Zanipolo, on Barbaria del le Tole, is the church of Santa Maria dei Derelitti, with its over-the-top Baroque facade by Longhena, and the attached **Ospedaletto** ⑱. Continue beyond the Ospedaletto to another large church, **San Francesco della Vigna** ⑲, with its stern classical Palladian facade.

Go left as you leave the church to begin the 500-yard walk to the **Campo dell'Arsenale** ⑳, the main entrance to the immense Arsenal dockyard. The **Museo Storico Navale** ㉑ on nearby Campo San Biagio has four floors of scale boat models. If you still have time and energy, go east to the island and church of **San Pietro di Castello** ㉒; two footbridges lead to this island. About midway between the Arsenal and Piazza San Marco, on your way back from the eastern district, is the **Scuola di San Giorgio degli Schiavoni** ㉓.

TIMING

An exploration of this neighborhood and as far east as the island of San Pietro should take four to five hours. Try to avoid walking around this mostly open neighborhood during the hottest hours of the day if you plan to travel in summer. Allow some time to browse through the Merceria district.

Sights to See

⑳ Campo dell'Arsenale. The immense **Arsenal** dockyard was founded in 1104 to build and equip the fleet of the Venetian republic. It was augmented continually through the 16th century. For a republic founded on sea might, having a huge state-of-the-art shipyard was of paramount importance, and this one was renowned for its size and its employees' skill. All subsequent dockyards were named after it (the name comes from the Arabic *d'arsina,* meaning workshop). No wonder it has such a grandiose entrance, with four stone lions from ancient Greece guarding the great Renaissance gateway. ⊠ *Arsenale, Castello.*

★ **⑰ Campo Santi Giovanni e Paolo.** This large square has the massive Dominican church of **Santi Giovanni e Paolo**—or San Zanipolo as it's known in the slurred Venetian dialect—on one side, and the powerful equestrian **monument of Bartolomeo Colleoni** by Florentine sculptor Andrea del Verrocchio (1435–88) on the other. Colleoni had served Venice well as a *condottiere,* or mercenary commander (the Venetians preferred to pay others to fight for them on land). When he died in 1475, he left his fortune to the city on the condition that a statue be erected in his honor "in the piazza before St. Mark's." The republic's shrewd administrators coveted Colleoni's ducats but had no intention of honoring anyone, no matter how valorous, with a statue in Piazza San Marco. So they commissioned the statue and put it up before the Scuola di San Marco, which is off to the side and the headquarters of a charitable confraternity, enabling them to collect the loot. San Zanipolo contains tombs of several doges, as well as a wealth of art. Don't miss the Rosary Chapel, off the left transept; with its Veronese ceiling paintings, it's a sumptuous study in decoration, built in the 16th century to commemorate the victory of Lepanto in western Greece in 1571, when Venice and a combined European fleet succeeded in destroying the Turkish navy. ⊘ *San Zanipolo Mon.–Sat. 9–noon and 3–6.*

㉑ Museo Storico Navale (Naval Museum). Four floors of scale boat models and an annex containing actual boats—from gondolas to doges' ceremonial boats—are guaranteed to fascinate children and boat lovers. ⊠ *Campo San Biagio, Arsenale, Castello,* ☎ *041/5200276.* ⊡ *2,000 lire.* ⊘ *Weekdays 9–1, Sat. 9–noon.*

⑱ Ospedaletto. Literally little hospital, this was founded in the 16th century and was one of Venice's four Foundling Hospitals. The church of **Santa Maria dei Derelitti** (of the Destitute) was also attached to the Ospedaletto. Each hospital had an orchestra and choir of little orphans (one of which was presided over by Antonio Vivaldi). Note the large gallery above the Derelitti's altar, built to accommodate the young musicians. The orphanage is now an old people's home, but the beautiful 18th-century **Sala della Musica** (Music Room), where rehearsals took place and patrons and honored guests were received—the only one of its kind to survive—has been magnificently restored and can be visited (enter through the church). On the Music Room's end wall is a lovely fresco by Jacopo Guarana, depicting Apollo, the God of Music, surrounded by the orphan musicians conducted by their music master, Pasquale Anfossi. ⊠ *Calle Barbaria de le Tole, Castello.* ⊡ *Free; donations appreciated.* ⊘ *Church and Music Room Apr.–Sept., Thurs.–Sat. 4–7; Oct.–Mar., Thurs.–Sat. 3–6.*

19 **San Francesco della Vigna.** This large classical church was built by Sansovino in 1534. A pretty cloister opens out from the severely simple gray-and-white interior. Not many tourists find their way here, and local youngsters play ball in the square shadowed by the church's austere classical Palladian facade. The interior is unadorned and it contains no major or particularly interesting works of art. ⊠ *Campo di Confraternita, Castello.* 🎟 *Free.* ☉ *Mon.–Sat. 9–12:30 and 3–6.*

22 **San Pietro di Castello.** This is an island church connected to the mainland by two footbridges. The church served as Venice's cathedral for centuries; now it presides over a picturesque workaday neighborhood, and its tipsy bell tower leans over a grassy square. ⊠ *Campo San Pietro Apostolo, Castello.* 🎟 *Free.* ☉ *Mon.–Sat. 8:30–noon and 3–6.*

NEED A BREAK? If you're this far afield, you may need sustenance to get you back to the center of town. There are several moderately priced snack bars and trattorias on Via Garibaldi, midway between the Arsenal and the island of San Pietro. **Sottoprova** (closed Tues.) has tables outdoors.

16 **Santa Maria dei Miracoli.** Perfectly proportioned and sheathed in marble, this church is an early Renaissance gem, decorated inside with exquisite marble reliefs. Notice how the architect, Pietro Lombardo, made the church look bigger with various optical illusions: varying the color of the exterior marble to create the effect of distance; using extra pilasters to make the building's canal side look longer; slightly offsetting the arcade windows to make the arches look deeper. The church was built in the 1480s to house an image of the Virgin that is said to perform miracles—look for this icon on the high altar. ⊠ *Calle delle Erbe, Castello.* 🎟 *Free.* ☉ *Daily 8–noon and 3–5.*

15 **Santa Maria Formosa.** This graceful white marble church was inspired by a vision of *una Madonna formosa* (a buxom Madonna) that appeared to Saint Magno in the 7th century. The matronly Madonna told him to follow a small white cloud and build a church wherever it settled. The present building, built by Mauro Coducci in 1492, was grafted on to the foundations of an earlier 11th-century church that replaced Magno's original. The church's interior is a unique architectural blend, merging a welter of Renaissance decoration with Coducci's ersatz collection of Byzantine cupolas, barrel vaults, and narrow-columned screens. Of interest are two fine paintings, Bartolomeo Vivarini's *Madonna of the Misericordia* and Palma Vecchio's *Santa Barbara.* Outside there is a lively square with a few sidewalk cafés and a small vegetable market on weekday mornings. ⊠ *Campo Santa Maria Formosa, Castello.* 🎟 *Free.* ☉ *Daily 8:30–12:30 and 5–7.*

23 **Scuola di San Giorgio degli Schiavoni.** This is one of numerous *scuole* built during the time of the Republic. These weren't schools, as the present-day Italian word would imply, but confraternities devoted to charitable works. Many scuole were decorated lavishly, both in the private chapels and in the meeting halls where work was discussed. The Scuola di San Giorgio degli Schiavoni features works by Vittore Carpaccio (circa 1465–1525), a local artist who often filled his otherwise devotional paintings with acutely observed details of Venetian life. Study the exuberance of his *St. George* as he slays the dragon or the vivid colors and details in *The Funeral of St. Jerome* and *St. Augustine in His Study.* ⊠ *Ponte dei Greci, Castello,* ☎ *041/5228828.* 🎟 *5,000 lire.* ☉ *Tues.–Sat. 10–12:30 and 3–6 (6:30 in summer); Sun. 10–12:30 (9:30–12:30 in summer).*

The Western and Northern Districts

If churches, further ramblings along dreamy canals, and masterpieces by great Venetian artists (such as Titian and Tintoretto) continue to interest you, head out of Piazza San Marco under the arcades of the Fabbrica Nuova at the far end of the square.

A Good Walk

Leave Piazza San Marco via the Calle Bocca di Piazza. (Here you can take the long-awaited detour for an expensive Bellini at the fabled Harry's Bar; just turn left down Calle Vallaresso, behind the Hotel Luna Baglioni.) Next take Calle Larga XXII Marzo (or "wide street"), to **Campo Santo Stefano** ㉔, which is dominated by the 14th-century church of Santo Stefano. Join the stream of pedestrians crossing the Grand Canal on the Accademia Bridge to the district called Dorsoduro (literally, "hard back") because of its strong clay foundation. The bridge leads you directly to the **Galleria dell'Accademia** ㉕, with its unparalleled collection of Venetian art.

Continue toward Campo Santa Margherita, passing Mondonovo, one of Venice's best mask shops (☞ Shopping, *below*). At Campo Santa Margherita, a busy neighborhood shopping square, stop in to see Giambattista Tiepolo's ceiling paintings in the **Scuola dei Carmini** ㉖. Tiepolo was strongly influenced by Paolo Veronese, some of whose finest works can be seen if you take a short and rewarding canal-side detour along Fondamenta del Soccorso, making a sharp left turn along Fondamenta de San Sebastiano, and crossing the second bridge on the right, which leads to the **Church of San Sebastiano** ㉗.

Retracing your steps, continue from Campo Santa Margherita to the Franciscan church of **I Frari** ㉘. Behind the Frari is the **Scuola di San Rocco** ㉙, filled with dark, dramatic canvases by Mannerist Tintoretto. In the area around San Rocco, narrow alleys and streets give way to small canals and lead to little squares, where posters advertising political parties and sports events seem to be the only signs of life. Head back past the Frari to **Campo San Polo** ㉚, one of Venice's largest squares. From here you take Calle della Madonetta, Calle dell'Olio, Rugheta del Ravano, and Ruga Vecchia San Giovanni to the Rialto shopping district, where you can cross the Grand Canal for the shortcut back to San Marco. Alternatively, you can go north from Campo San Polo by way of Calle Bernardo, Calle dello Scaleter, Rio Terrà Parrucchetta, and Calle del Tintor to **Campo San Giacomo dell'Orio** ㉛, where the 13th-century church of San Giacomo stands on an enchanting square. Here you're not far from the San Stae vaporetto landing, so you can take the boat back along the Grand Canal to the heart of the city.

TIMING

Not including time spent in the Galleria dell'Accademia, walking this route will take approximately three to four hours, not including time to get totally lost. There are fewer people out and about in the early afternoon, which makes it easier to get around, but keep in mind that many of the shops and some churches are also closed at that time. Also remember: only three bridges span the Grand Canal, so be sure to be near one of them when you're ready to call it a day. If you're not, you may have to backtrack.

Sights to See

㉛ **Campo San Giacomo dell'Orio.** The 13th-century church of San Giacomo stands on this square, which few visitors ever happen upon (and there are a number of reasonably priced pizzerias nearby).

③⓪ Campo San Polo. One of Venice's largest squares and a favorite playground for neighborhood children, this *campo* has a church of the same name open to the public.

②④ Campo Santo Stefano. One of the nicest campi in all of Venice, this neighborhood square, until 1802, was used for bullfights, during which bulls (or oxen) were tied to a stake and baited by dogs. For years the square was grassy, all except for a stone avenue known as the *liston.* This became such a popular place to stroll that it led to a Venetian expression, *andare al liston,* which means "go for a walk." Check out the 14th-century **Santo Stefano** and its bell tower—the tipsiest in all Venice—and stop in to see the ship's-keel roof, a type found in several of Venice's older churches and the work of its master shipbuilders. ⊠ *Campo Santo Stefano.* ⬚ *Free.* ⊙ *Mon.–Sat. 9–noon.*

NEED A BREAK?	**Caffè Paolin** (⊠ 4 Campo S. Angelo), with tables occupying most of one end of the square, makes some of the best *gelato* (ice cream) in Venice and is a pleasant place to sit and watch the passing parade. It's closed Mon.

★ ②⑤ Galleria dell'Accademia (Accademia Gallery). Housed in this magnificent museum is unquestionably the most extraordinary collection of Venetian art in the world. Highlights include Giovanni Bellini's altarpiece from the church of San Giobbe (notice how he carried the church's architectural details right into the frame of the painting) and his moving *Madonna with St. Catherine and the Magdalen;* a fine *St. George* by Andrea Mantegna, Bellini's brother-in-law from Padua; and Veronese's monumental canvas, *Feast in the House of Levi.* Here is the Venetian High Renaissance in all its richness, even glamour. The painting was commissioned as a Last Supper, but the Inquisition took issue with Veronese's inclusion of jesters and German soldiers in the painting. Veronese avoided the charge of profanity by changing the title, and the picture was then supposed to depict the bawdy, but still biblical, feast of Levi. A room preserved from the Scuola della Carità—which previously occupied the museum's site—holds on one wall its original masterpiece, Titian's *Presentation of the Virgin.*

Don't miss the room containing various views of 15th- and 16th-century Venice by Vittore Carpaccio and Giovanni Bellini's brother Gentile—study them to see how little the city has changed since then. Room V holds one of the gallery's most famous paintings, the *Tempest,* by Giorgione (1477–1510), a work that has consistently baffled art historians as to its meaning, while charming all with its magical painterly qualities and exquisite landscape. The work is nothing if not ambiguous—what exactly is going on between this impassive young soldier and naked woman suckling a child?—but possesses a haunting melancholy and a distinct sense of threat created by the gathering summer storm in the background. For the first time in art, the atmosphere of a painting became as important as the figures. In 1995, the top floor of the Accademia was reopened to show additional works previously in storage—including paintings by Cima di Conegliano, Veronese, and Mansueti—and to host special exhibitions. ⊠ *Campo della Carità, Accademia, Dorsoduro,* ☎ *041/5222247.* ⬚ *12,000 lire.* ⊙ *Fri.–Sat. 10:30–6:30, Tues.–Thurs. 9–7, Sun. 9–1.*

NEED A BREAK?	**Bar Belle Arti** (⊠ Accademia Gallery, Campo della Carità) is a coffee bar and sandwich shop with a variety of tasty *panini* (sandwiches), *frittate* (frittatas), and beer. It closes Sun.

★ **❷❽ I Frari.** This immense Gothic church, with its russet-color brick, was built in the 14th century for the Franciscans. The Frari (*frari* means friars) is deliberately austere and plain, befitting the simplicity of the Franciscans' lives, in which spirituality and poverty were key tenets. Paradoxically, however, the Frari also contains a number of the most sumptuous and brilliant pictures in any Venetian church. Chief among them are the magnificent **Titian altarpieces,** arguably the most dazzling works that the prolific artist produced. For its mellow luminosity, first check out Giovanni Bellini's *Madonna and Four Saints* in the sacristy, painted in 1488 for precisely this spot. The contrast with the heroic energy of Titian's large *Assumption* over the main altar—painted little more than 30 years later—is startling, and clearly illustrates the immense and rapid development of Venetian Renaissance painting. This altarpiece caused a sensation when it was unveiled in 1519 and was immediately acclaimed for its winning combination of Venetian color—especially the glowing reds—and Central Italian–classical Roman figure style.

The *Pesaro Madonna* over the first altar on the left nave near the main altar is also by Titian; his wife, who died shortly afterward in childbirth, posed for the figure of Mary. The Madonna was radical for its time because the main figure was not placed squarely in the center of the painting, creating a dynamic result. On the same side of the church, look at the spooky pyramid-shape monument to the sculptor Antonio Canova (1757–1822), containing his heart. Across the nave is a neoclassical 19th-century monument to Titian, executed by two of Canova's pupils. ✉ *Campo dei Frari, San Polo,* ☎ *041/5222637.* ☑ *2,000 lire.* ◷ *Mon.–Sat. 9–noon and 2:30–6, Sun. 3–6.*

❷❼ San Sebastiano. Veronese established his reputation with the paintings he did at this church when still in his twenties, after leaving his native Verona. He continued to embellish the interior for over a decade with amazing perspective and trompe l'oeil scenes. In 1588 he was finally buried here. ✉ *Campo San Sebastiano, Dorsoduro.* ◷ *Sun.–Fri. 2:30–5:30.*

❷❻ Scuola dei Carmini. This *scuola* is home to Giambattista Tiepolo's ceiling paintings. The paintings, now displayed on the second floor, were commissioned to honor the Carmelite order by depicting prominent Carmelites in conversation with saints and angels. Of the three great Venetian painters whose names start with *T* (Titian, Tintoretto, and Tiepolo), Tiepolo came last chronologically (he painted in the 18th century; the others were 16th-century artists) and achieved the greatest international fame in his own time. An underlying melancholy in his ethereal, brightly colored paintings betrays a man of sober piety. Tiepolo's vivid techniques transformed some unpromising religious themes into flamboyant displays of color and movement. Mirrors are available on the benches to make it easier to see the ceiling without getting a sore neck. ✉ *Campo dei Carmini, Dorsoduro,* ☎ *041/5289420.* ☑ *5,000 lire.* ◷ *Mon.–Sat. 9–noon and 3–6. Closed Sun.*

❷❾ Scuola Grande di San Rocco. This workshop is famed for its many dark, dramatic canvases by Tintoretto. Born some 30 years after Titian, Jacopo Robusti—called Tintoretto because his father was a dyer—was more mystical and devout than the sophisticated Titian. Though his colors are equally brilliant, he carried Titian's love of motion and odd composition to almost surreal effects, in the same Mannerist vein as El Greco (who was at one time a pupil of Titian's). In 1564, Tintoretto beat other painters competing for the commission to decorate this building by submitting not a sketch but a finished work, which he additionally offered gratis. The series of more than 50 paintings he ultimately created took a total of 23 years to complete. These works, depicting Old and New Testament themes, were restored in the 1970s, and Tintoretto's inventive use of light has once more been revealed. ✉ *Campo San Rocco, Frari,* ☎ *041/5234864.* ✇ *8,000 lire.* ☉ *Weekdays 10–4.*

Islands of the Lagoon

The perfect vacation from your Venetian vacation is an escape to the magical islands of the city's lagoon—Murano, Burano, and Torcello—which can provide a welcome relief after the brooding, enclosed charms of Venice itself. Far from the madding crowd, Torcello is the actual birthplace of Venice, today visited for its haunting melancholy, its great Byzantine-era church, and that famous outpost of elegance, the Locanda Cipriani. The island is also perfect for picnics, but bring food from Venice. Burano is a toy town of little houses all painted in a riotous explosion of color—blue, yellow, pink, ocher, and dark red; here, visitors love to shop for the best in Venetian lace. Murano is known the world over for its glass—but guided tours usually involve high-pressure attempts to make you buy, with little time left for anything else. It's more adventurous, and worth the extra effort, to make your own way around the islands, using the good vaporetto connections.

There are several options in getting to these islands: lines 12 and 14 to Murano, Burano, and Torcello from the landing stage at Fondamente Nove, almost due north of San Marco; and Line 52, which you can pick up in town (☞ Getting Around *in* Venice A to Z, *below*), to Fondamente Nuove, San Michele, and Murano, where you would then change to Line 14 to continue to Torcello and Santa Maria Elisabetta on the Lido.

Numbers in the text correspond to numbers in the margin and on the Venice and Venetian Lagoon maps.

A Good Boat Trip

Take Line 52 from Piazza San Marco to the Fondamente Nuove stop. There, in the Campo dei Gesuiti, is the church of **I Gesuiti** ㉜. It's only a five-minute ride from there to **San Michele** ㉝, the cemetery island that is home to the church of San Michele in Isola. Another five minutes on Line 52 takes you to **Murano** ㉞. Cross the Ponte Vivarini and turn right onto Fondamenta Cavour. Follow the Fondamenta Cavour around the corner to the Museo Vetrario, one of the most famous glass factories in the world.

Make your way back along the same route to the landing stage, and take Line 12 to **Burano** ㉟, where you can see traditional lace making at the Scuola di Merletti di Burano.

Line 12 continues from the Burano landing stage to the sleepy green island of **Torcello** ㊱, about 10 minutes farther. A brick-paved lane leads up from the landing stage and follows the curve of the canal toward the center of the island. You pass the Locanda Cipriani, renowned as one of Hemingway's haunts. Just beyond is the grassy square that holds the only surviving monuments of the island's past splendor. Next to it is the cathedral of Santa Maria Assunta, also built in the 11th century.

TIMING

Boats leave every hour and the trip takes about 50 minutes each way. Stopping on every island and visiting the various sights will take a full day. If, however, you limit yourself to Torcello, Burano, and Murano, a full morning or a full afternoon will suffice.

Sights to See

★ ③⑤ **Burano.** This small island is a fishing village with houses painted in cheerful colors and a raffishly raked bell tower on the main square, about 100 yards from the landing stage and clearly visible from there. Lace is to Burano what glass is to Murano, but be prepared to pay a lot for the real thing. Stalls line the way from the landing stage to Piazza Galuppi, the main square; the vendors, many of them fishermen's wives, are generally good-natured and unfamiliar with the techniques of the hard sell.

The **Scuola di Merletti di Burano** (Lace Museum) on Piazza Galuppi is the best place to learn the intricacies of the lace-making traditions of Burano. It is also useful for learning the nature of the skills involved in making the more expensive lace, in case you intend to buy some lace on your way back to the vaporetto. ✉ *Piazza Galuppi,* ☎ *041/730034.* ▥ *5,000 lire.* ⊙ *Tues.–Sat. 9–6, Sun. 10–4.*

③② **I Gesuiti.** This 18th-century church dominates the Campo dei Gesuiti. It is extravagantly baroque in style; the classical arches and straight lines of the Renaissance have been abandoned in favor of flowing, twisting forms. The marble of the gray-and-white interior is used like brocade, carved into swags and drapes. Titian's *Martyrdom of St. Lawrence,* over the first altar on the left, is a dramatic example of the great artist's feel for light and movement. ✉ *Campo dei Gesuiti.* ▥ *Free.* ⊙ *Mon.–Sat. 8:30–noon and 4–6.*

★ ③④ **Murano.** Like Venice, Murano is made up of a number of smaller islands linked by bridges. The island is known exclusively for its glassworks, which you can visit to see how glass is made. Many of these line the **Fondamenta dei Vetrai,** the canal-side walkway leading away from the Colonna landing stage. The houses along this walk are simpler than many of their Venetian counterparts; traditionally they were workmen's cottages. Just before the junction with Murano's Grand Canal—250 yards up from the landing stage—is the church of **San Pietro Martire.** This 16th-century reconstruction of an earlier Gothic church has several works by Venetian masters: notably, the *Madonna and Child* by Giovanni Bellini, and *St. Jerome* by Veronese.

The **Museo Vetrario** (Glass Museum) has a collection of Venetian glass that ranges from priceless antique to only slightly less expensive modern. The museum gives you a good idea of the history of Murano's glassworks, which were moved here from Venice in the 13th century because they were a fire risk. It's useful, too, to get a clear idea of authentic Venetian styles and patterns if you're planning to make some purchases later. ✉ *Murano,* ☎ *041/739586.* ▥ *8,000 lire.* ⊙ *Apr.–Oct., Thurs.–Tues. 10–5; Nov.–Mar., Thurs.–Tues. 10–4.*

③③ **San Michele.** Venice's cypress-lined cemetery island is home to the pretty Renaissance church of **San Michele in Isola,** designed by Coducci in 1478, and Venice's **cemetery.** It is a unique experience to walk among the gravestones with the sound of lapping water on all sides. The American poet Ezra Pound, the great Russian impresario and art critic Sergey Diaghilev, and the composer Igor Stravinsky are buried here. For most Venetians, however, the stay here is short-lived, as the cemetery has a policy of transferring those interred more than 10 years to another, less grandiose cemetery, making room for more recent burials.

★ ③⑥ **Torcello.** This is where the first Venetians landed in their flight from the barbarians 1,500 years ago. Even after many settlers left to found the city of Venice on the island of Rivo Alto (Rialto), Torcello continued to grow and prosper until its main source of income, wool man-

Venetian Lagoon

ufacturing, was priced out of the marketplace. It's hard to believe now, looking at this almost deserted island, that in the 16th century it had 20,000 inhabitants and 10 churches.

The island's cathedral, **Santa Maria Assunta,** dates from the 11th century. The ornate Byzantine mosaics are testimony to the importance and wealth of an island that could attract the best artists and craftsmen of its day. The vast mosaic on the inside of the facade depicts the Last Judgment as artists of the 11th and 12th centuries imagined it: figures writhe in vividly depicted contortions of pain. Facing it, as if in mitigation, is the calm mosaic figure of the Madonna, alone in a field of gold above the staunch array of Apostles. ⊠ *Torcello,* ☎ *041/730084.* ▦ *1,500 lire.* ⊙ *Daily 10–12:30 and 2–5 in winter, 2–6:30 in summer.*

NEED A BREAK?	**Locanda Cipriani** (⊠ Torcello, ☎ 041/730150) is an inn famous for its good food and the patronage of Ernest Hemingway, who often came to Torcello for the solitude. These days Locanda Cipriani is about the busiest spot on the island, as well-heeled customers arrive on high-speed powerboats for lunch. If you want to have lunch or dinner, count on at least 80,000 lire for a set menu. It's closed on Tuesday and from January to the beginning of Carnival.

San Giorgio Maggiore and the Giudecca

Beckoning all travelers across the Basin of San Marco like some sort of Venetian Bali Hai is the island of San Giorgio Maggiore, separated by a small channel from the Giudecca. A tall brick campanile on that distant bank perfectly complements the Campanile of San Marco. Behind it looms the stately dome of one of Venice's greatest churches, San Giorgio Maggiore. The island of Giudecca, a crescent cupped around the southern shore of Venice, is one of the most mysterious neighborhoods in all of Venice, with an obscure history and a somber feel.

Numbers in the text correspond to numbers in the margin and on the Venice map.

A Good Boat Trip

Take Line 82 from San Zaccaria near San Marco and head for the island of San Giorgio Maggiore, across the lagoon. Here you should visit Palladio's church of **San Giorgio Maggiore** ㊲. Return to the pier and proceed by vaporetto (still Line 82) to the island of **Giudecca** ㊳. Here, explore the neighborhood and visit the church of Il Redentore, also by Palladio. If you have the time, continue on the vaporetto to the next stop, Zattere, which is opposite the Giudecca Bank. The promenade here is enchanting; you can eat in one of the many pizzerias that line the promenade and enjoy the lively atmosphere. Otherwise, you can return directly to San Marco.

TIMING

The journey takes only an hour, which should give you plenty of time to enjoy the sights. Allow at least an hour to visit each of the churches, and another hour to two hours to visit the Giudecca neighborhood and the Zattere promenade.

Sights to See

㊳ **Giudecca.** The island of Giudecca has always been seen as a place apart. Its name is something of a mystery. According to some, it derives from the possible settlement of Jews here in the 14th century, and according to others it was so called because in the 9th century nobles condemned to exile (*giudicato* means judged or sentenced) were sent here. It became a pleasure garden for wealthy Venetians during the long and luxurious decline of the Republic. In one regard it is still the province of the wealthy: the exclusive Cipriani hotel (☞ Lodging, *below*) lies secluded on its eastern tip.

Palladio's church **Il Redentore** is a tranquil, stately facade, actually a series of superimposed temple fronts topped by a dome and a pair of slim, almost minaretlike, bell towers. The interior, like San Giorgio Maggiore's (☞ *below*), is perfectly proportioned and airy, in contrast to the dusky mystery of the Basilica di San Marco. Palladio's work is evident throughout the Venetian Arc (☞ Chapter 6). ⊠ *Fondamenta San Giacomo, Giudecca.* ☾ *Mon.–Sat. 3–6.*

㊲ **San Giorgio Maggiore.** A church has been on this island since the late 8th century, with a Benedictine monastery added in the 10th century. The present church of San Giorgio Maggiore was begun in 1566 by Palladio, the greatest architect of his time. Two of Palladio's hallmarks are mathematical harmony and architectural elements borrowed from classical antiquity, both of which are demonstrated in this superbly proportioned neoclassical church of red brick and white marble. Inside, the church is refreshingly airy and simply decorated. Two important late Tintoretto paintings hang on either side of the chancel: *The Last Supper* and *The Gathering of Manna*. Over the first altar on the right-hand side of the nave is an *Adoration of the Shepherds* by Jacopo Bassano (1517–92), a painter from Bassano del Grappa on the mainland who possessed considerable originality and was especially adept at portraying nature and country life. The campanile is so high—offering fine views of Venice and its harbor—that it was struck by a lightning bolt in 1993.

The monastery of San Giorgio Maggiore, where the conclave that elected Pope Pius VII took place in 1800, later a barracks for the occupying Austrians, now houses an artistic and cultural foundation where conferences are often held, and is usually closed to the public. Palladio designed the monastery's first cloister, and Longhena was the architect for the grand baroque library. ⊠ *Isola di San Giorgio Maggiore,* ☎ *041/5289900.* ☞ *Free.* ☉ *Mon.–Sat. 9–6.*

DINING

Venetian cuisine is based on seafood (which can be pricey; ask price in advance), with a few culinary excursions inland. Antipasto may take the form of a seafood salad, prosciutto *di San Daniele* (cured ham of the Veneto region), or pickled vegetables. As a first course Venetians favor risotto, a creamy rice dish that may be cooked with vegetables or shellfish. Pasta, too, is good with seafood sauces; Venice is *not* the place to order spaghetti with tomato sauce. *Pasticcio di pesce* is pasta baked with fish, usually *baccalà* (cod). A classic first course is *pasta e fagioli* (thick bean soup with pasta). *Bigoli* is strictly a local pasta, made of whole wheat, usually served with a salty *tonno* (tuna) sauce. Polenta, made of cornmeal, is another pillar of regional cooking. It's often served as an accompaniment to *fegato alla veneziana* (liver with onions). Local seafood includes *granseola* (crab), *moeche* (small, soft-shelled crabs), and *seppie* or *seppioline* (cuttlefish).

The dessert specialty in Venice is *tiramisù,* a heavenly concoction of mascarpone (a rich, soft double-cream cheese), espresso, chocolate, and *savoirdi* (ladyfingers). The recipe originated on the mainland, but the Venetians have adopted it enthusiastically. Local wines are the dry white Tocai and Pinot from the Friuli region and bubbly white Prosecco, a naturally fermented sparkling wine that is a shade less dry. The best Prosecco comes from the Valdobbiadene; Cartizze, which is similar, is considered superior by some but is expensive. Popular red wines include merlot, cabernet, Raboso, and Refosco. You can sample all of these and more in Venice's many *bacari* (old-style wine bars), where wine is served by the glass (known as an *ombra* in Venetian dialect) and accompanied by *cicchetti* (assorted tidbits), often substantial enough for a light meal.

Under the auspices of the restaurant association, most of the city's restaurants offer special *menù turistici* (tourist menus), moderately priced according to the level of the restaurant and generally representing good value. You may not find a *pane e coperto* (cover charge), but a service charge of 10%–15% will almost surely be on the check.

It's always a good idea to reserve your table or have your hotel *portiere* (concierge) do it for you. Dining hours are short, starting at 12:30 or 1 for lunch and ending at 2:30 or 3, when restaurants close for the afternoon, opening up again to start serving at about 8 and closing again at 11 or midnight. Most close one day a week and are also likely to close without notice for vacation or renovation. Few have signs on the outside, so when the metal blinds are shut tight, you can't tell a closed restaurant from a closed TV-repair shop. This makes them hard to spot as you explore the city.

CATEGORY	COST*
$$$$	over 120,000 lire
$$$	80,000–120,000 lire
$$	50,000–80,000 lire
$	under 50,000 lire

Prices are per person, including three courses, wine, and service.

$$$$ ✕ **Grand Canal.** The Grand Canal restaurant at the newly renamed
★   Hotel Monaco and Grand Canal is a favorite with Venetians, who enjoy
      eating in summer on the lovely canal-side terrace looking across the
      mouth of the Grand Canal to San Giorgio Maggiore, and in the cozy
      dining room in winter. All the pasta is made fresh daily on the premises,
      and the smoked and marinated salmon are also prepared on site. Chef
      Fulvio De Santa's traditional Venetian dishes are top flight; you'll mar-
      vel over savory meat and fish dishes such as scampi *alla Ca' d'Oro* (in
      a cognac sauce), served with rice. ✉ *Hotel Monaco and Grand Canal,
      Calle Vallaresso 1325, San Marco,* ☎ *041/5200211. Jacket required.
      AE, DC, MC, V.*

$$$$ ✕ **Harry's Bar.** The humble door of this very less-than-humble watering
      place leads to the legendary Venetian hangout of such notables as
      Hemingway, Maugham, and Onassis, not to mention Barbara Hutton,
      Peggy Guggenheim, and Orson Wells. Harry's is still known for the
      best and driest martinis in town, the most heavenly Bellinis (fresh
      peach juice and champagne), and for its kitchen's fine *cucina verita* (cook-
      ing style that employs seasonal produce, simple methods, and short cook-
      ing times to preserve ingredient freshness). The decor is boring
      beige-on-beige, but the "pictures" on the walls upstairs—windows
      that look out on spectacular Santa Maria della Salute—easily compete
      with the finest Canaletto *vedute* (scenic paintings). ✉ *Calle Vallaresso
      1323, San Marco,* ☎ *041/5285777. Reservations essential. AE, DC,
      MC, V.*

$$$$ ✕ **La Caravella.** Affixing your gaze on the choices of chateaubriand,
      bouillabaisse, and calves' kidneys' *au trois moutardes* (with three mus-
      tards), you might think you had wandered into a temple of French haute
      cuisine here. Continue reading the very extensive menu to discover some
      of the best Venetian specialties in town, such as *taglierini alla granse-
      ola* (delicate pasta with crab sauce), scampi in port sauce, and fillets
      of locally caught sea bass and sole. The front room of this old favorite—
      long admired for its fine wine list and cordial, gracious service—is like
      the dining saloon of an old Venetian sailing ship. Many prefer the pretty
      garden courtyard open from May to September. ✉ *Calle Larga XXII
      Marzo 2397, in Saturnia Internazionale hotel, San Marco,* ☎ *041/
      5208901. Reservations essential. AE, DC, MC, V.*

$$$$ ✕ **Quadri.** In the 19th century, princes, dukes, and countesses dined
      here, and you'll feel like one when you walk into the gilded salons of
      Venice's most beautiful restaurant. The decor is stunning—Quadri's
      second-floor aerie gives you a pigeon's-eye view of Piazza San Marco—
      and the four-star truffles-on-everything kitchen is also a major draw.
      Come September, when the Venice Film Festival is in session, the se-
      quins-and-sunglasses set takes over. ✉ *Piazza San Marco 120–124,*
      ☎ *041/5289299. Reservations essential. AE, DC, MC, V. Closed Aug.
      3–20.*

$$$ ✕ **Al Covo.** This small and charming *osteria* changes its menu ac-
      cording to the day's bounty—mostly local seafood caught just hours
      before and specialties from other European waters. Cesare Benelli and
      his American spouse, Diane, insist on only the freshest ingredients and
      claim to not use butter or animal fats. Try the *zuppa di pesce* (fish broth)
      followed by the fish of the day either grilled, baked, or steamed. Diane
      will guide you through some of her homemade desserts and the ex-
      tensive wine selection. ✉ *Campiello della Pescaria 3968, Castello,*
      ☎ *041/5223812. AE, MC, V. Closed Wed.–Thurs. and 1 wk in Aug.*

$$$ ✕ **Da Arturo.** On the Calle degli Assassini—a name common to sev-
      eral Venetian streets and a reminder of the centuries gone by when vi-
      olence and betrayal were everyday occurrences—this tiny restaurant
      can offer a most peaceful and enjoyable evening. It has the distinction
      (in Venice) of *not* serving seafood. Instead you'll choose from among

fresh vegetable and salad dishes; tasty, tender, and generous meat courses, including the delicately pungent *braciola alla veneziana* (pork chop schnitzel with vinegar); and an authentic creamy homemade tiramisù to finish. ⊠ *Calle degli Assassini 3656, San Marco,* ☎ *041/ 5286974. Reservations essential. No credit cards. Closed Sun. and 4 wks in Aug.*

$$$ ✕ **Fiaschetteria Toscana.** This warm restaurant in a former Tuscan wine and oil storehouse merits a jaunt from terra firma to Cannaregio for its cheerful, courteous service, fine cucina, and rose-hued walls. Gastronomic highlights include a delicate tagliolini, perhaps prepared *alla buranella* (with shrimp) today, and the zabaglione. The wine list is—predictably—something special. In warm weather, the best tables are in the arbor on the square. ⊠ *Campo San Giovanni Crisostomo 5719, Cannaregio,* ☎ *041/5285281. AE, DC, MC, V. Closed Tues. and July 1–15.*

$$$ ✕ **Osteria Da Fiore.** Tucked away in a little calle off the top of Campo
★ San Polo, Da Fiore is always packed. It's imperative to reserve for a superlative seafood lunch or dinner, which might include delicate hors d'oeuvres of moeche, scallops, and tiny octopus, followed by a succulent risotto or *tagliolini con scampi e zucchine* (noodles with shrimp and zucchini), and a perfectly cooked main course of *rombo* (turbot) or *branzino* (sea bass). ⊠ *Calle del Scaleter 2202/A, San Polo,* ☎ *041/ 721308. Reservations essential. AE, DC, MC, V. Closed Sun.–Mon., Aug. 10–early Sept., and Dec. 25–Jan. 15.*

$$ ✕ **Al Mondo Novo.** This restaurant is owned by a fish wholesaler in the Rialto market, who himself eats here every day, so you can be sure that everything is absolutely fresh. Star dishes prepared by Signora Trevisan, the owner's wife, include *cape sante* (scallops) and *cape longhe* (razor clams), risottos and pastas, and the best of the day's catch grilled on charcoal. Meat dishes are also available. ⊠ *Salizzada San Lio 5409, Castello,* ☎ *041/5200698. AE, MC, V. Closed Wed. and Feb.–Mar.*

$$ ✕ **Cantinone Storico.** On a quiet canal near the Accademia, this comfortable trattoria serves excellently prepared specialties such as risotto *terra mare* (with seafood, vegetables, and porcini mushrooms) and tagliolini alla granseola. The house wines are quaffable, even good. ⊠ *Fondamenta di Ca' Bragadin 660/1, Dorsoduro,* ☎ *041/5239577. AE, MC, V. Closed Sun., last wk July–1st wk Aug., and Jan. 19–26.*

$$ ✕ **Da Ignazio.** Smallish, pleasant, and near Campo San Polo, Ignazio is reliable for good food at reasonable prices, barring expensive fish dishes. The cuisine is classic Venetian, from seafood risotto to fegato alla veneziana, but there are standard Italian items as well. ⊠ *Calle dei Saoneri 2749, San Polo,* ☎ *041/5234852. AE, DC, MC, V. Closed Sat.*

$$ ✕ **Da Remigio.** This very popular local trattoria near the church of San Giorgio dei Greci offers reliable and tasty fish and meat dishes. ⊠ *Salizzada dei Greci 3416, Castello,* ☎ *041/5230089. Reservations essential. No credit cards. Closed Tues. No dinner Mon.*

$$ ✕ **Locanda Montin.** Peggy Guggenheim used to take many of the leading artists of the day—including Jackson Pollock and Mark Rothko—to this archetypal Venetian inn, not far from her Palazzo Venier dei Leoni, in Dorsoduro. The walls are still covered with modern art, but it's far from the haute bohemian hangout it used to be, except for when the Biennale crowd takes charge. Outside, you can dine under an elongated arbor and enjoy such specialties as rigatoni *ai quattro formaggi* (with four cheeses), spaghetti *Adriatica*, and antipasto *Montin* (seafood antipasto). You might let the waiter order for you, as regulars do. ⊠ *Fondamenta di Borgo 1147, Dorsoduro,* ☎ *041/5227151. AE, DC, MC, V. Closed Wed., Jan. 7–26, and 15 days in Aug.*

Venice Dining and Lodging

Dining ●

Al Covo, **34**
Al Mascaron, **28**
Al Mondo Novo, **25**
Cantinone Storico, **11**
Da Arturo, **12**
Da Ignazio, **4**
Da Remigio, **33**
Fiaschetteria
Toscana, **20**
Grand Canal, **23**

Harry's Bar, **24**
L'Incontro, **6**
La Caravella, **18**
Le Bistrot, **21**
Locanda Montin, **7**
Osteria Da Fiore, **3**
Quadri, **22**
San Trovaso, **8**
Vini da Gigio, **1**
Vino Vino, **14**

Lodging ○

Accademia, **9**
American, **10**
Bernardi
Semenzato, **2**
Bucintoro, **35**
Cipriani, **36**
Concordia, **27**
Danieli, **29**
Flora, **17**

Gritti Palace, **16**
Hotel Pausania, **5**
Locanda Fiorita, **13**
Londra Palace, **31**
Metropole, **32**
Paganelli, **30**
Riva, **26**
San Samuele, **15**
Saturnia
Internazionale, **19**

Sacca della Misericordia

Canale delle Navi

San Michele

0   440 yards
0   400 meters

Rocchetta

Fondamenta

Rio S. Caterina

C.

R.d. Cestiti Nuove

C.d. Squero

Rio d. della Panada

Rio d. Santi Apostoli

② roda ova

Campo d. escheria

Campo Santi Giovanni e Paolo

R. Barbaria delle Tole

dei Mendicanti

R. d. S.

Giustina

②⓪

Rio d. S. Marina

C.d. Testa

Campo di S. Maria Formosa

Sal. di S. Lio

R.d. S. Severo

R.d. S. Lorenzo

R. d. S. Francesco

②⑧

②⑤

C.d. Bande

C.d. Specchier

②⑥

②①

②⑦

R. d. Palazzo

Fond. Osmarin

C. Lion

C.d. Furlani

C.d. Pestrin

R. d. Scudi

R. d. Grecci

R. d. Pietà

Canale d. Galeazze

Darsena Grande

Rio d. Vergini

Rio d. S. Daniele

di S. Pietro

③③

③②

Riva degli Schiavoni

③④

R. d. Garpa

Molo

②②

Frezzaria

R. d. S. Moisè

②③ ②④

Piazza San Marco

②⑨ ③⓪ ③①

R. d. Arsenale

③⑤

Rio della Tana

V. Garibaldi

Rio d. S. Anna

Canale di S. Marco

Riva dei Sette Martiri

R. d. S. Giuseppe

Rio dei Giardini

Isola di S. Giorgio Maggiore

Fond. delle Zitelle

Calle Michelangelo

③⑥

Rio dei Partigiani

▲   Boat stop

$$ ✕ **Vini da Gigio.** A quaint, friendly, family-run trattoria on the quay
★ side of a canal just off the Strada Nuova, Da Gigio is very popular with
Venetians and visiting Italians, who appreciate the affable service; ex-
cellently cooked homemade pasta, fish, and meat dishes; and imagi-
native and varied cellar and good-quality draft wine. It's good, too,
for a cheap, simple lunch at tables in the barroom. ✉ *Fondamenta de
la Chiesa 3628/a, Cannaregio,* ☎ *041/5285140. AE, DC, MC, V.
Closed Mon., 2 wks in Jan., and 2 wks in Aug. No dinner Sun.*

$ ✕ **Al Mascaron.** The convivial, crowded Al Mascaron, with its paper
tablecloths and very informal atmosphere, is a regular stop for Vene-
tians who drop in to gossip, drink, play cards, and eat cicchetti at the
bar. You can bet on delicious seafood, pastas, risottos, and seafood sal-
ads. So popular has Mascaron become that the owners, Gigi and
Momi, have opened an offshoot called Mascareta a few doors down
the calle (at No. 5183), where you can enjoy a glass of wine and cold
snacks. ✉ *Calle Lunga Santa Maria Formosa 5225, Castello,* ☎ *041/
5225995. No credit cards. Closed Sun., end Dec.–mid-Jan., last 2 wks
in Aug.*

$ ✕ **Le Bistrot.** Live music, poetry readings, and art exhibits attract the
younger crowd to this café-brasserie. Centrally located, it's open all
day and offers a limited menu with the emphasis on pancakes and piz-
zas at lunchtime and in the evening until 1 AM. Service and cover are
included in the prices, and there are tables outside in the summer. ✉
Calle dei Fabbri 4685, San Marco, ☎ *041/5236651. MC, V. Closed
Tues. in winter.*

$ ✕ **L'Incontro.** This trattoria has a faithful clientele of Venetians and vis-
★ itors, attracted by flavorsome food, friendly service, and reasonable
prices. Menu choices include freshly made Sardinian pastas, juicy
steaks, wild duck, boar, and (with advance notice) roast suckling pig.
You'll find it between San Barnaba and Campo Santa Margherita. ✉
Rio Terrà Canal 3062/a, Dorsoduro, ☎ *041/5222404. MC, V. Closed
Mon.*

$ ✕ **San Trovaso.** A wide choice of Venetian dishes and pizzas, reliable
house wines, and economical fixed-price menus make this busy tav-
ern, conveniently near the Accademia Gallery, a good value. ✉ *Fon-
damenta Priuli 1016, Dorsoduro,* ☎ *041/5203703. AE, DC, MC, V.
Closed Mon.*

$ ✕ **Vino Vino.** The annex of the extremely expensive Antico Martini
restaurant, this is a highly informal wine bar where you can sample
Italian vintages and munch on a limited selection of (microwaved) dishes
from the kitchens of its upscale big sister, next door. It's open 10
AM–midnight. ✉ *Calle delle Veste 2007/a, near Campo San Fantin, San
Marco,* ☎ *041/5237027. Reservations not accepted. No credit cards.
Closed Tues.*

★ ✕ **Torcello Picnic.** No, this is not a restaurant, but one of the dreami-
est dining experiences in Venice. Stock up before you take your vaporetto
trip out to historic Torcello (☞ Islands of the Lagoon *in* Exploring Venice,
above): get a bottle of Teroldego Rotaliano from a *vinatteria* (wine shop),
chilled pâtés and a wedge of *taleggio* cheese from a *salumeria* (deli), a
hunk of bread from a *panneteria* (bakery), a *semifreddo di fragoline*
(liquor-drenched cake) from a *pasticerria* (pastry shop), and three gi-
gantic Venetian peaches from one of the open-air markets, such as that
on the Campo Santa Margherita. With the 11th-century campanile of
the church of Santa Maria Assunta as backdrop, couples will quickly
feel like reenacting the famous scene Katherine Hepburn and Rozzano
Brazzi filmed here for *Summertime.*

LODGING

Due to the city's great popularity, Venetian hotels can cater to all tastes and price ranges. Rates are a little higher than in Rome and Milan, but you can save considerably during off-season. Most hotel rates include breakfast. It is essential to know how to get to your hotel when you arrive in Venice, as it can range from arriving in a water taxi or gondola direct to the front door or wandering down curious alleys and side streets with recurring feelings of déjà vu.

The busiest times for hotels are spring and autumn; December 20–January 2; and the two-week Carnival period leading up to Ash Wednesday, usually in February. Book well in advance. If you don't have reservations, you can almost always get a room in any category by going upon arrival to the **AVA** (Venetian Hoteliers Association) booths at the train station, airport, and the municipal parking garage at Piazzale Roma (☞ Hotel Association *in* Venice A to Z, *below*).

CATEGORY	COST*
$$$$	over 500,000 lire
$$$	290,000–500,000 lire
$$	180,000–290,000 lire
$	120,000–180,000 lire

Prices are for a standard double room for two, including taxes and service.

$$$$ 🏨 **Cipriani.** It's impossible to feel stressed in this sybaritic oasis of stunning rooms and suites, some with garden patios. The hotel launch whisks you to Giudecca from San Marco and back at any hour of the day or night; those just dining at the exceptional Ristorante Harry Cipriani can use it as well. Cooking courses and fitness programs are offered. The newly restored and subtly integrated 17th-century style Palazzo Vendramin, an annex of seven suites and three double rooms, is open all year. ⊠ *Giudecca 10, 30133,* ☎ *041/5207744,* ℻ *041/5203930. 104 rooms and suites. Restaurant, bar, air-conditioning, pool, tennis courts. AE, DC, MC, V. Closed Dec.–mid-Mar.*

$$$$ 🏨 **Danieli.** Venice's largest luxury hotel, the Danieli is a collage of newer buildings around a 15th-century palazzo built for the Doge Dandolo. You'll feel like a doge in this palace, oozing with sumptuous Venetian decor and atmosphere. Some suites are positively palatial, but some of the less attractive rooms are overpriced. The four-story-high lobby is supreme, its chic salons and bar offering relaxation and celebrity sightings. The rooftop terrace restaurant is justly famous for top-notch cuisine and its heavenly view of San Giorgio Maggiore and St. Mark's Basin, which can also be seen from the best rooms. Guests have access to pool and tennis courts. ⊠ *Riva degli Schiavoni 4196, Castello, 30122,* ☎ *041/5226480,* ℻ *041/5200208. 231 rooms and suites. Restaurant, bar, air-conditioning. AE, DC, MC, V.*

$$$$ 🏨 **Gritti Palace.** Queen Elizabeth, Greta Garbo, and Winston Churchill
★   made this their Venetian address. The feeling of being in an aristocratic private home pervades this legendary hotel, replete with fresh flowers, fine antiques, sumptuous appointments, and Old World service. The dining terrace on the Grand Canal is best in the evening when the boat traffic dies down. Guests have access to pool and tennis courts. ⊠ *Campo Santa Maria del Giglio 2467, San Marco, 30124,* ☎ *041/794611,* ℻ *041/5200942. 93 rooms. Restaurant, bar, café, air-conditioning. AE, DC, MC, V.*

$$$ 🏨 **Concordia.** Twenty rooms in this centrally located, attractive, and well-run hotel overlook the basilica of San Marco, as does the spacious breakfast room-cum-bar (a welcome haven, where light meals and snacks are also available all day). The romantic *mansarda*—a rooftop room

with a panoramic view over the Piazza San Marco—is a nice dining spot. The management makes a special effort to offer good price deals at off-peak times, so check when booking. ⊠ *Calle Larga San Marco 367, San Marco, 30124,* ☎ *041/5206866,* FAX *041/5206775. 57 rooms. Breakfast room, air-conditioning. AE, DC, MC, V.*

$$$ 🏨 **Londra Palace.** This grand hotel commands a fine view of San Giorgio and St. Mark's Basin and has a distinguished ambience. A recent renovation has imparted a neoclassical touch to the rooms, with light pastel colors and plenty of marble. The Deux Lions restaurant offers fine Venetian and French cuisine, and the piano bar is open late. Perks include a complimentary Mercedes for one-day excursions, free entrance to the city casino (☞ Nightlife, *below*), and the therapeutic solarium. ⊠ *Riva degli Schiavoni 4171, Castello, 30122,* ☎ *041/5200533,* FAX *041/5225032. 36 rooms, 17 suites. Restaurant, piano bar, air-conditioning. AE, DC, MC, V.*

$$$ 🏨 **Metropole.** Only a few minutes' stroll from Piazza San Marco, the Metropole offers spacious rooms and sitting areas furnished with style and panache from the owner's impressive collection of antiques. Many rooms have a view of the lagoon, but the others overlooking a canal and peaceful gardens are also inviting. Special rates—including, in low season, the best rooms at the lowest price (if the hotel is not full)—are well worth checking out. You can step from your water taxi or gondola directly into the hotel lobby. ⊠ *Riva degli Schiavoni 4149, Castello, 30122,* ☎ *041/5205044,* FAX *041/5223679. 73 rooms. Restaurant, bar, air-conditioning. AE, DC, MC, V.*

$$$ 🏨 **Saturnia Internazionale.** There's lots of Old World charm in this historic palace, which is centrally located near Piazza San Marco but still manages to retain an air of peace and tranquility. Its beamed ceilings, damask-hung walls, and authentic Venetian decor impart real character to the solid comfort of its rooms and salons. Many rooms have been extensively redecorated and endowed with more glamorous—and larger—bathrooms. La Caravella restaurant (☞ Dining, *above*) is of special note. ⊠ *Calle Larga XXII Marzo 2398, San Marco, 30124,* ☎ *041/5208377,* FAX *041/5207131. 95 rooms. Restaurant, bar, air-conditioning. AE, MC, V.*

$$ 🏨 **Accademia.** Probably the most enchanting hotel in Venice, the Ac-
★ cademia is also one of its most popular, so early reservations are a must. Just beyond an iron gate, a secret garden awaits, complete with mini Palladian-style villa, canal parterre, and verdant trees (all rarities in Venice). Lounges, bar, and a wood-paneled breakfast room are cheery, and breakfast outside on the garden terrace is a special treat. ⊠ *Fondamenta Bollani 1058, Dorsoduro, 30123,* ☎ *041/5237846,* FAX *041/5239152. 27 rooms, 25 with bath or shower. Bar, breakfast room, air-conditioning. AE, DC, MC, V.*

$$ 🏨 **American.** One of the smartest hotels in its class, the American is on a quiet canal near the Accademia Bridge. Rooms and public areas are stylish but classic, with warm wood detail and period furniture. Beautiful terraces overlooking the canal teem with red geraniums. Breakfast on the main terrace is shaded by a lovely vine canopy. ⊠ *Rio San Vio, 628 Accademia, 30123,* ☎ *041/5204733,* FAX *041/5204048. 30 rooms. Bar, breakfast room, air-conditioning. AE, MC, V.*

$$ 🏨 **Bucintoro.** Whistler once stayed here and, today, the Bucintoro is still favored by artists who are drawn by the lagoon views outside each room. Off the tourist track, this friendly, family-run hotel on the waterfront by the Arsenal has clean, simple rooms and prices that are unbeatable for such a spectacular location. ⊠ *Riva San Biagio 2135, Castello, 30122,* ☎ *041/5223240,* FAX *041/5235224. 28 rooms, 18 with bath. No credit cards. Closed Dec.–mid-Jan.*

$$ 🖭 **Flora.** This hotel has what many in this category lack: plenty of sitting rooms and a pretty courtyard. It's in a quiet, though central, location near San Moisè and Piazza San Marco. Rooms have Venetian period decor, a bit dark for some; a handful are rather small, with tiny bathrooms. When booking, ask for a room with a view of the courtyard or the garden. ⊠ *Calle Bergamaschi 2283 (off Calle Larga XXII Marzo), San Marco, 30124,* ☎ *041/5205844,* 🖷 *041/5228217. 44 rooms. Bar, air-conditioning. AE, DC, MC, V.*

$$ 🖭 **Hotel Pausania.** One of the newer additions to the Venetian hotel scene, this 14th-century palazzo delivers all of the modern comforts with taste, from the moment you ascend the grand staircase graced with a fountain. Light-shaded rooms are spacious, with comfortable furniture and carpets with rugs thrown over them. Some rooms face the small and quiet canal in front of the hotel, while others look out over the large garden courtyard. ⊠ *Rio di San Barnaba 2824, Dorsoduro, 30123,* ☎ *041/5222083,* 🖷 *041/5222989. 25 rooms. Bar, breakfast room, air-conditioning. AE, DC, MC, V.*

$$ 🖭 **Paganelli.** The lagoon views here so impressed Henry James that he wrote the Paganelli up in the preface to his *Portrait of a Lady.* This enchanting, small hotel on the waterfront near Piazza San Marco, with an annex on the quiet square of Campo San Zaccaria (three rooms overlook the lagoon, six face the square), is tastefully decorated in the Venetian style. ⊠ *Riva degli Schiavoni 4687, Castello, 30122,* ☎ *041/5224324,* 🖷 *041/5239267. 20 rooms, 19 with bath or shower. Bar. AE, DC, MC, V.*

$ 🖭 **Bernardi Semenzato.** This is a particularly inviting little hotel just
★ off Strada Nuova, and near the Rialto. All the rooms in the main hotel maintain high standards, making the Bernardi better value than ever. Prices are even lower in the nearby annex (which includes a big room with a lovely canal view). ⊠ *Calle dell'Oca 4366, Cannaregio, 30121,* ☎ *041/5227857,* 🖷 *041/5222424. 18 rooms in main hotel, 11 with bath or shower; 7 rooms in annex, 2 with bath or shower. AE, MC, V. Closed 1st 2 wks Dec.*

$ 🖭 **Locanda Fiorita.** This welcoming, small hotel is tucked away in a
★ sunny little square (where breakfast is served in the summer), just off Campo Santo Stefano, near the Accademia Bridge, and is centrally located for sightseeing. The rooms have beamed ceilings and are simply furnished. ⊠ *Campiello Novo 3457, San Marco, 30124,* ☎ *041/ 5234754,* 🖷 *041/5228043. 10 rooms, 7 with shower. AE, MC, V. Closed 2 wks mid-Jan.*

$ 🖭 **Riva.** This small hotel, close to San Marco, is at the junction of three canals much used by all manner of Venetian watercraft. Although they are endlessly fascinating to watch, the boats can seem a little noisy early in the morning. ⊠ *Ponte dell'Angelo 5310, Castello, 30122,* ☎ *041/ 5227034. 12 rooms, 10 with bath. No credit cards. Closed mid-Nov.–Feb. 1, except 2 wks at Christmas.*

$ 🖭 **San Samuele.** Centrally located near the Grand Canal and Palazzo Grassi, this friendly hotel, run by Signor Veronese (whose namesake Paolo, the 16th-century painter, lived practically next door), has clean, sunny rooms. ⊠ *Salizzada San Samuele 3358, San Marco, 30124,* ☎ *041/5228045. 10 rooms, 2 with bath. No credit cards.*

NIGHTLIFE AND THE ARTS

The Arts

You'll find a list of current and upcoming events in the *Guest in Venice* booklet, free at your hotel, or available from the **Assessorato al Turismo** (⊠ Ca' Giustinia, 2nd floor) and **Calle del Ridoto** (⊠ Close to

Piazza San Marco). Keep an eye out for **posters** announcing concerts and other events.

Venice hosts important temporary exhibitions in the Doge's Palace, in Palazzo Grassi at San Samuele on the Grand Canal, and in other venues. The **Biennale,** a cultural institution, organizes many events throughout the year, including the film festival, which begins at the end of August. The big Biennale international art exhibition, usually held from mid-June to the end of September, has been held since 1993 on odd-numbered years at the **Giardini Castello** (Castello Gardens).

Concerts

There are regular concerts at the church of the Pietà (⊠ Riva degli Sciavoni, San Zaccaria, Castello), with an emphasis on Vivaldi, and also in San Stae and surrounding churches—though prices tend to be high and the performance quality uneven. Concerts—sometimes free—are also performed in other churches by visiting choirs and musicians. For information on these often impromptu events, ask at the APT office (☞ Visitor Information *in* Venice A to Z, *below*) and look for posters on walls and in restaurants and shops. **Kele e Teo Agency** (⊠ San Marco 4930, ☎ 041/5208722, FAX 041/5208913) and **Box Office** (⊠ Calle Loredan 4127, off Salizzada San Luca, ☎ 041/988369) handle tickets for many musical events.

Festivals

Carnevale (Carnival) takes place usually the 10 or more days leading up to Ash Wednesday (Feb. 1–21 in 1998). During the festivities, the crowds of revelers make the city almost impossible to visit, so unless you are intent on joining in, stay away until it is over. For information on Carnival, check with the main APT office (☞ Visitor Information *in* Venice A to Z, *below*). On the third Sunday of July, the **Feast of Il Redentore** (the Redeemer) is celebrated with the building of a pontoon bridge over the channel to the Giudecca, commemorating the doge's annual visit to this church to offer thanks for the end of a 16th-century plague. Traditionally, the Venetians take to the water in boats en masse, as midnight fireworks explode over the lagoon.

Opera and Ballet

Teatro La Fenice (⊠ On Campo San Fantin) is one of Italy's oldest opera houses, a pilgrimage shrine for opera lovers everywhere, and scene of many memorable operatic premieres, including, in 1853, the dismal first night flop of Verdi's *La Traviata*. Unfortunately this great opera house was very badly damaged by a fire in January 1996 and although plans are being made to restore the building, performances are not forecast to recommence until the year 2000.

Nightlife

Piazza San Marco in fair weather, when the cafés stay open late, is a meeting place, though young Venetians tend to gravitate toward Campo San Luca and Campo San Salvador and Bartolomeo, near Rialto. There is far more nightlife in Venice than meets the eye. The best up-to-date guide to live music venues, discos, and late bars is *Fuori Orario: di Notte a Venezia e Mestre* (*Out of Hours: By Night in Venice and Mestre*), published by the Assessorato alla Gioventù (City Youth Department) (⊠ Corte Contarina 1529, 4th Floor, near Piazza San Marco), and available free at APT information offices. At present, the guide is only available in Italian, but with its useful maps and easy-to-follow notes it should be decipherable to any serious nighthawk.

Bars, Discos, and Nightclubs

The **Martini Scala Club** (✉ Calle delle Veste ☎ 041/5224121) is an elegant piano bar with a restaurant. Tunes start at 9 and go until the wee hours; it's closed Tuesday. Young Venetians burn the midnight oil at **Ai Canottieri** (✉ Fondamenta San Giobbe 690, Cannaregio, ☎ 041/715408, closed Sun. and in summer), accompanied by live music on Thursday and Saturday nights. **Devil's Forest Pub** (✉ Calle del Stagneri 5185, off Campo San Bartolomeo, ☎ 041/5200623) is a favored hangout of many young Venetians; it's closed Monday. **Paradiso Perduto** (✉ Fondamenta della Misericordia 2540, Cannaregio, ☎ 041/720581) serves up good pizzas and other hot plates at low prices, plus live music usually on weekends; it closes Wednesday and the first two weeks of August. **Al Vapore** (✉ Via Fratelli Bandiera 8, Marghera, ☎ FAX 041/930796) draws young Venetians out of the city to the mainland. **Fiddler's Elbow** (✉ Strada Nuova, Cannaregio 3847, ☎ 041/5239930) offers all the typical trappings of an Irish pub: gab, grub, and frothy Guinness.

For dancing try the **Disco Club El Souk** (✉ Accademia 1056, Dorsoduro, ☎ 041/5200371), beside the Accademia Gallery; admission 5 PM–8 PM is free, and 18,000 lire 10 PM–4 AM. Outside Venice on nearby Lido is **Acropolis Disco Club** (✉ Lungomare Marconi 22, Lido, ☎ 041/5260466), one of the more trendy, hip spots. The prices are equally as fashionable, admission peaking at 20,000 lire. Expect disco Friday through Sunday and live music on other nights.

Casino

The city-run gambling casino operates June–September in a modern building on the Lido (✉ Lungomare Marconi 4, ☎ 041/5297111) and in the splendorous Palazzo Vendramin Calergi (✉ Grand Canal, ☎ 041/5297111) during the other months. Both are open daily 3 PM–about 4:30 AM.

OUTDOOR ACTIVITIES AND SPORTS

Golf

The **Golf Club Lido di Venezia** (✉ Via del Forte, Alberoni, Lido, ☎ 041/731333), with an 18-hole course, is on Lido island.

Horseback Riding

Circolo Ippico Veneziano (✉ Ca' Bianca, the Lido, ☎ 041/5265162), rents horses for riding trails on the Lido only, but it can refer you to terra firma clubs around the Venetian Arc.

Running

The best running route, heading east past the Giardini (public gardens) in the Castello district and over to the pine wood on Sant'Elena, allows a magnificent view of the city as you run back toward the center, when you may need some inspiration.

Swimming

Many Venetians and visitors are happy to swim from the seaward-facing side of the Lido. There is free public access to the beach (look for the signs SPIAGGIA LIBERA) at either end of the Lido (Bus C, leaving every 20 minutes from the Santa Maria Elisabetta landing, goes all the way to Alberoni at one end, where there are usually fewer people; Bus B goes to the beach at San Nicolò at the other end). The strand in between is sectioned off in the summer season into private beaches offering various facilities—changing rooms, bar, showers—for the use of guests of hotels on the Lido; nonguests are charged a fixed daily or weekly rate.

However, considering the reputedly polluted state of the Adriatic, you may opt for the cleanliness of a pool. Venice's only public pool is the **Piscina Comunale** (⌧ On the island of Sacca Fisola, at the far end of Giudecca, ☏ 041/5285430); take Line 82 to Sacca Fisola. The deluxe hotels **Excelsior** (☏ 041/5260201) and **Hotel des Bains** (☏ 041/5265921) are both on Lungomare Marconi on the Lido; their pools are open to nonguests for a fee.

Tennis

The **Hotel des Bains** (☞ Swimming, *above*) rents tennis courts to nonguests. The exclusive **Sea Gull Club** of the Cipriani hotel (☞ Lodging, *above*) will also let nonguests play for a fee. There are several tennis clubs on the Lido, including **Lido Tennis Club** (☏ 041/5260954). The Lido's **Club Ca' del Moro** (⌧ Via F. Parri, ☏ 041/770965) has tennis and an outdoor swimming pool in summer.

SHOPPING

You're sure to find plenty of pleasing shops and boutiques as you explore Venice. It's always a good idea to mark the location of a shop that interests you on your map; otherwise you may not be able to find it in the maze of tiny streets. Shops are usually open 9–12:30 or 1 and 3:30 or 4–7:30 and are closed Sunday and on Monday morning. However, many tourist-oriented shops are open all day, every day. Food shops are closed Wednesday afternoon, except over the Christmas and New Year period. Some shops close for both a summer and a winter vacation.

Food Markets

The morning open-air fruit and vegetable market at **Rialto** offers animated local commerce and color. On Tuesday through Saturday mornings, the adjacent **fish market** teaches an impressive lesson in ichthyology, presenting some species you've probably never seen before. In the Castello district is **Via Garibaldi,** the scene of another lively food market on weekday mornings.

Shopping Districts

The main shopping areas are the **Mercerie,** the succession of narrow and crowded streets winding from Piazza San Marco to the Rialto, and the area around Campo San Salvador, Calle del Teatro, Campo Manin, and Campo San Fantin. The **San Marco** area is full of shops and couture boutiques such as Armani, Missoni, Valentino, Fendi, and Versace.

Specialty Stores

EMBROIDERED FABRICS

Venice's top name is **Jesurum** (⌧ Piazza San Marco 60–61). It is one of the few stores in Venice whose lace *is* made in and around the city. Go to **Lorenzo Rubelli** (⌧ Campo San Gallo 1089, just off Piazza San Marco) for the same sumptuous brocades, damasks, and cut velvets used by the world's most prestigious decorators.

Much of the lace and embroidered linen sold in Venice and on Burano is really made in China or Taiwan. At **Norelene** (⌧ Calle de la Chiesa 727, near the Accademia) you'll find wonderful hand-printed fabrics. **Venetia Studium** (⌧ Calle Larga XXII Marzo 2403, San Marco) has beautiful Fortuny-inspired lamps, furnishings, clothes, and accessories.

GLASSWARE

Glass, most of it made in **Murano,** is Venice's number-one product, and you'll be confronted by mind-boggling displays of traditional and contemporary glassware, often kitsch. Take your time and be selective. You will probably find that prices in Venice's shops and the showrooms of Murano's factories are pretty much the same. However, because of competition, shops in Venice stocking wares from various glassworks may charge slightly lower prices.

Galleria San Nicolò (⊠ Calle del Traghetto 2793, Dorsoduro, by the Ca' Rezzonico vaporetto stop) is owned by the American glass expert Louise Berndt. Opened in 1994, this shop shows the best of contemporary glass, including superb work by Yoichi Ohira, a Japanese designer long resident in Venice. The **Domus** shop (⊠ Fondamenta dei Vetrai, Murano) has a selection of smaller objects and jewelry from the best glassworks. For chic, contemporary glassware designs, **Carlo Moretti** is a good choice; his signature designs are on display at **L'Isola** (⊠ Campo San Moisè 1468, near Piazza San Marco).

Marina Barovier has an excellent selection of collectors' 20th-century glass at her gallery (⊠ Calle delle Botteghe 3172, San Marco, just off Campo Santo Stefano). Go to Michel Paciello's **Paropàmiso** for stunning Venetian glass beads and traditional jewelry from all over the world (⊠ Frezzeria 1701, near Piazza San Marco). **Pauly** (⊠ Piazza San Marco 73–77) is a centrally located store with a wide array of glassware.

In a category all his own is **Gianfranco Penzo** (⊠ Campo del Ghetto Nuovo 2895), who decorates Jewish ritual vessels in glass, makes commemorative plates, and takes special orders. **Salviati** (⊠ Piazza San Marco 79B) is a reliable and respected firm. **Venini** (⊠ Piazzetta dei Leoncini 314) has been an institution since the 1930s, attracting some of the foremost names in glass design. **Vetri d'Arte** (⊠ Piazza San Marco 140) offers moderately priced glass jewelry.

MASKS

The prices of wholesaler **Emilio Massaro** (⊠ Calle Vitturi 2934, San Marco) tend to be cheaper than anywhere else; you can watch the masks being created. **Mondonovo** (⊠ Rio Terrà Canal) is a cut above most other mask stores in the city. **Laboratorio Artigiano Maschere** (⊠ Barbaria delle Tole, near Santi Giovanni e Paolo) is home to Giorgio Clanetti, the man credited with starting the current revival in mask-making.

PRINTS

Piazzesi (⊠ Campiello della Feltrina, near Santa Maria del Giglio), a shop named after the classic old print of Venice, makes a distinctive gift or souvenir. Hand-printed paper and desk accessories, memo pads, and address books abound at this well-known shop.

VENICE A TO Z

Arriving and Departing

By Bus
Buses connect the bus terminal (⊠ Piazzale Roma, near the vaporetto stop of that name) to Mestre, the Brenta Riviera, Padua, and other destinations in the region.

By Car
If you bring a car to Venice, you will have to pay for a garage or parking space during your stay. Warning: do not be waylaid by illegal touts—often wearing fake uniforms, and whose activities have in recent years become a scandal in a city generally remarkably free of con men and criminals—who may try to flag you down and offer to arrange parking and hotels, but continue on until you reach the automatic ticket machines.

Parking at **Piazzale Roma** (✉ Autorimessa Comunale, end of S11 road) costs between 15,000 and 25,000 lire. The private **Garage San Marco** (✉ Piazzale Roma, end of S11 road) costs between 30,000 and 45,000 lire per 24 hours, depending on the size of the car.

To reach the privately run **Tronchetto** parking area, follow the signs to turn right before Piazzale Roma. Parking here costs around 35,000 lire per 24 hours under cover and slightly less outside. (Do not leave valuables in the car. There is a left-luggage office, open daily 8 AM–8 PM, next to the Pullman Bar on the ground floor of the municipal garage at Piazzale Roma.) The Venetian Hoteliers Association (AVA; ☞ Hotel Association *in* Contacts and Resources, *below*) has arranged a discount of about 40% for hotel guests who use the official Tronchetto parking facility. Be sure to ask for a voucher on checking into your hotel; it will be issued when you settle the hotel bill. Present the voucher at Tronchetto when you pay the parking fee. Line 82 runs from Tronchetto to Piazzale Roma and Piazza San Marco and also goes on to the Lido in summer. (When there is thick fog or extreme tides, a bus runs to Piazzale Roma instead.) Avoid private boats—they are a rip-off. You can take your car to the Lido; the car ferry (Line 17) leaves about every 50 minutes from a landing at Tronchetto, but in summer there can be long queues. The cost is from 12,000 to 30,000 lire, depending on the size of the car.

By Plane

Marco Polo airport (✉ Tessera, about 10 km [6 mi] north of the city on the mainland, information ☎ 041/2609260) is served by domestic and international flights, including connections from London, Amsterdam, Brussels, Frankfurt, Munich, Paris, Vienna, and Zurich.

BETWEEN THE AIRPORT AND VENICE

By Boat. Depending on where your hotel is, this may be the best way to get to Venice from the airport. The most direct way is by the **Cooperativa San Marco** launch, with regular scheduled service throughout the day, until midnight; it takes about an hour to get to the **landing** (✉ Just off Piazza San Marco), stopping at the Lido on the way, and the fare is 20,000 lire per person, including bags. A **water taxi** (a sleek, modern motorboat known as a *motoscafo*) from the airport costs about 100,000 lire, but it is always essential to agree on a water-taxi fare before boarding, for information call ☎ 041/5415084.

By Bus. Blue **ATVO** buses make the 25-minute nonstop trip from the airport to Piazzale Roma, which is where the road ends at the entrance to Venice; from Piazzale Roma you can get a water bus to the landing nearest your hotel. The ATVO fare is 7,000 lire. There are local **ACTV** buses from the airport, but you need a ticket (fare 1,200 lire) before boarding the bus, and there is no ticket office at the airport. You can buy a ticket at the tobacconist-newsstand in the airport, but it is not always open. Also, luggage can be a hassle on the ACTV bus, which is usually crowded with local commuters.

By Taxi. A yellow taxi from the airport to Piazzale Roma costs about 60,000 lire.

By Train

Venice has rail connections with every major city in Italy and the rest of Europe. Some trains do not terminate at **Santa Lucia Station** (✉ On the Grand Canal in the northwest corner of the city). Instead, they stop only at the **Venezia-Mestre Station** (✉ On the mainland). All trains traveling to and from Santa Lucia stop at Mestre; to get from Venezia-Mestre to Santa Lucia, or vice versa (a 10-minute trip), take the first available train, remembering there is a *supplemento* (extra charge) for traveling on Intercity and Eurocity trains, and that if you do not pay it before boarding, you are liable for a hefty fine. For information call ☎ 041/ 715555 from 7:15 AM to 9:30 PM.

Getting Around

First-time visitors find that getting around Venice presents some unusual problems: The layout is complex; the waterborne transportation can be bewildering; the house-numbering system is baffling; many street names in the *sestieri* (six districts) of San Marco, Cannaregio, Castello, Dorsoduro, Santa Croce, and San Polo, are duplicated; and often you must walk, whether you want to or not. It's essential to have a good map showing all street names and vaporetto routes; buy one at a newsstand. In the areas where you're most likely to wander, signs are posted on many corners pointing you in the right direction for the nearest major landmark—San Marco, Rialto, Accademia, etc.—but don't count on finding such signs once you're deep into residential neighborhoods.

By Gondola

If you simply mustn't leave Venice without a gondola ride, the best time is in the late afternoon or early evening hours, when the Grand Canal isn't so heavily trafficked. Also, it's best to start from a station on the Grand Canal because the lagoon is usually choppy. Make it clear that you want to see the smaller canals, and come to terms on the cost and duration of the ride before you start. Gondoliers are supposed to charge a fixed minimum of about 80,000 lire for up to five passengers for 50 minutes. After 8 PM and up to 8 AM the rate increases to approximately 100,000. The official tariffs are quoted in the "Guest in Venice" booklet (☞ Visitor Information, *below*). Bargaining may get you a better price.

By Motoscafo

These stylish powerboat water taxis are extremely expensive, and the fare system is as complex as Venice's layout. A minimum fare of about 40,000 lire gets you nowhere, and you'll pay three times as much to get from one end of the Grand Canal to the other. Always agree on the fare before starting out, but usually a fixed rate for a maximum of seven minutes is 30,000 lire and then 500 lire for every 15 *seconds* thereafter. Beware of other additions such as hand luggage and late or early hours.

By Traghetto

Few tourists know about the two-man gondolas that ferry people across the Grand Canal at various fixed points. They are the cheapest and shortest gondola ride in Venice and can save a lot of walking. The fare is 1,000 lire, which you hand to the gondolier when you get on. Look for traghetto signs.

By Vaporetto

ACTV vaporetti run the length of the Grand Canal and circle the city. There are about 20 lines, some of which connect Venice with the major and minor islands in the lagoon. Line 1 is the Grand Canal local, calling at every stop and continuing via San Marco to the Lido. (It takes about 45 minutes from the station to San Marco.)

The fare is 3,500 lire on most lines. A 24-hour tourist ticket costs 15,000 lire; a 72-hour tourist ticket costs 30,000 lire; these are especially worthwhile if you are visiting the islands (☞ Islands of the Lagoon, *above*). The seven-day ticket (55,000 lire) is a good value if you plan a longer stay.

There have been many changes to other routes in recent years, and more changes may yet occur. There are also some routes that only run in the summer. At press time (spring 1997), there are two VapLine 52 routes, one running from the railway station (Ferrovia) to San Zaccaria (at San Marco) via Zattere and the Giudecca Canal, and on to the Lido and vice versa. The other goes in the opposite direction around Venice, from the railway station, skirting the north of the city, via Fondamente Nove (where some boats leave for the islands of the northern lagoon) and Murano (you can cut out the Murano loop by changing boats at Fondamente Nove, using the same ticket) and continuing via the Arsenal to San Zaccaria and Zitelle on the island of Giudecca.

There are also two Line 82 routes, one of which runs from the Tronchetto, via Piazzale Roma, the railway station (Ferrovia), and Rialto, and continues, during the day, down the Grand Canal, with fewer stops than Line 1, to San Marco and, in the summer, on to the Lido (some 82 boats on this route only go as far as Rialto—check before you board if you need to travel farther). The other route goes from Tronchetto to San Zaccaria via the Giudecca Canal.

Timetables are posted at every landing stage, and in the "Guest in Venice" booklet (☞ Visitor Information, *below*) but there is not always a ticket booth operating. You may get on a boat without a ticket, but you will have to pay a higher fare. For this reason, it may be useful to buy *un blochetto* (a book of tickets) in advance. Landing stages are clearly marked with name and line number, but check before boarding, particularly with the 52 and 82, to make sure the boat is going in your direction.

Contacts and Resources

Consulates
U.K. Consulate (☒ Campo della Carità 1051, Dorsoduro, ☎ 041/5227207). There is no U.S. or Canadian consular service.

Doctors and Dentists
The U.K. Consulate (☞ *above*) can recommend doctors and dentists. Your hotel or any pharmacy should also be able to offer advice.

Emergencies
General (☎ 167/355920 toll-free). **Carabinieri** ☎ 112. **Police** ☎ 113. **Ambulance** (Venice Hospital), ☎ 041/5230000. **Red Cross First Aid Station** (☒ 55 Piazza San Marco, near Caffè Florian, ☎ 041/5286346); open Monday–Saturday 8:30–1.

English-Language Bookstores
Fantoni (☒ On Salizzada San Luca) specializes in art books. A good general-interest bookstore is **Emiliana Editrice** (☒ Calle Goldoni, between Piazza San Marco and Campo San Luca). **Studium** (☒ Calle de la Canonica, off Piazzetta dei Leoncini, to the left of the San Marco Basilica) also stocks good general-interest books. **Libreria Editrici Filippi** (☒ On Casseleria, between Ponte de l'Anzolo, take the last left off Calle de la Canonica) has the best selection on Venice and its history. **Enrico Dori's** newspaper shop (☒ On the Frezzaria shopping street, to the right of San Marco post office) has the best stock of English-language periodicals; it's open early and closes late.

Guided Tours
EXCURSIONS
The **Cooperativa San Marco** (☒ Just off San Marco) organizes tours of the islands of Murano, Burano, and Torcello. The 3½-hour tours depart daily at 9:30 and 2:30 from the landing stage in front of the

Giardini Reali (⊠ Piazza San Marco); they cost about 25,000 lire. Tours tend to be annoyingly commercial and emphasize glass-factory showrooms, pressuring you to buy, sometimes at higher prices than normal.

American Express (⊠ Salizzada San Moisè 1471, San Marco, ☎ 041/ 5200844, ℻ 041/5229937) offers car trips to the Venetian villas, Padua and Asolo, available year round for about 160,000 lire. Bookings should be made the day before.

Excursions aboard the ***Burchiello*** motor launch, from Venice to Padua along the Brenta Canal, are expensive (about 170,000 lire) and not necessarily the best way to see the famous villas, since so much time is spent on the boat. Tours run from April through October on Tuesday, Thursday, and Saturday.

ORIENTATION TOURS

Two-hour walking tours of the San Marco area can be booked through **American Express** (⊠ Salizzada San Moisè 1471, San Marco, ☎ 041/ 5200844, ℻ 041/5229937) and other travel agencies. The American Express "Jewels of the Venetian Republic" tour (about 36,000 lire) ends with a glassblowing demonstration. From April 25 to November 15, American Express offers an afternoon walking tour that ends with a gondola ride (about 40,000 lire).

In recent years, Venice's municipal Youth Department has been running a special program to help young visitors: **"Rolling Venice,"** as it is somewhat oddly titled, is open to everyone aged 14–29, and costs 5,000 lire to join at Rolling Venice's offices behind the Piazza San Marco Post Office (⊠ Assessorato alla Gioventù, Corte Contarini 1529, ☎ 041/2707650), open weekdays 9:30–1, plus Tuesday and Thursday 3–5. Their other office (⊠ Santa Lucia railway station) is open July–September. Benefits include handy guidebooks to the city and (sometimes substantial) discounts in hotels, restaurants, shops, and on ACTV vaporetto tickets. The Youth Department has also produced two useful leaflets, "Dormire Giovani" ("Accommodations for Young People") and "Fuori Orario: di Notte a Venezia e Mestre" ("Out of Hours: By Night in Venice and Mestre"); *see* Visitor Information, *below*.

PERSONAL GUIDES

You can get a list of licensed guides and their rates from the main **APT tourist office** (⊠ Palazzetto Selva, off Piazza San Marco, ☎ 041/ 5236356). Or contact the **Guides' Association** (⊠ Calle San Antonio 5448/A, Castello, ☎ 041/5239902, ℻ 041/5232012). **American Express** (⊠ Salizzada San Moisè 1471, San Marco, ☎ 041/5200844, ℻ 041/5229937) provides guides for walking or gondola tours of Venice, or cars with driver and guide for tours of the mainland.

SPECIAL-INTEREST TOURS

American Express (⊠ Salizzada San Moisè 1471, San Marco, ☎ 041/ 5200844, ℻ 041/5229937) offers group gondola rides with serenades, daily from May through October in the evening (about 40,000 lire), and other tours that go on to include dinner, followed by cabaret entertainment of Venetian folk songs and a visit to the Casino (about 120,000 lire, drinks not included).

During the summer, free guided tours (some in English, including one at 11 AM) of the **Basilica di San Marco** are offered by the Patriarchate of Venice; information is available in the atrium of the church (☎ 041/ 5200333); no tours Sunday.

Hotel Association

AVA (Venetian Hoteliers Association) booths: (⊠ Train station; airport; and municipal parking garage at Piazzale Roma).

Late-Night Pharmacies

Venetian pharmacies take turns opening late or on Sunday; the weekly list of late-night pharmacies is posted on the front of every pharmacy. English-speaking staff: **Farmacia Italo-Inglese** (✉ Calle della Mandola 3717, in San Marco district, ☎ 041/5224837). **Farmacia Internazionale** (✉ Calle Larga XXII Marzo 2067, in San Marco district, ☎ 041/5222311).

Travel Agencies

American Express (✉ Salizzada San Moisè 1471, ☎ 041/5200844). **Sattis Viaggi** (✉ Calle Larga dell'Ascensione 1261, ☎ 041/5285101/2/3). **Wagons-Lits/Turismo** (✉ Piazzetta dei Leoncini 289, ☎ 041/5223405).

Visitor Information

The **main APT** (tourist office) is housed in an elegant 19th-century coffeehouse (✉ Palazzetto Selva, off Piazza San Marco, ☎ 041/5226356, FAX 041/5230399). **Information booths** (✉ Santa Lucia train station, ☎ 041/719078; Lido ✉ Gran Viale S. Maria Elisabetta 6A, ☎ 041/5265721, FAX 041/5298720).

The *Guest in Venice* booklet is free at your hotel and also available at the **Assessorato al Turismo** (✉ Ca' Giustinia, 2nd floor) and the **Calle del Ridoto** (✉ Close to Piazza San Marco). The Italian-language *Dormire Giovani* (*Accommodations for Young People*) and *Fuori Orario: di Notte a Venezia e Mestre* (*Out of Hours: By Night in Venice and Mestre*) are available for free at the **main APT** (☞ *above*) and the **Assessorato alla Gioventù** (City Youth Department: ✉ Corte Contarina 1529, 4th floor, near Piazza San Marco).

6 Venetian Arc

Verona, Padua, Vicenza, and Palladio Country

The art and architecture of every city in the Venetian Arc—Verona, Vicenza, Padua, Treviso—echo in some way the graces and refinements of Venice. Here you'll find Asolo—the City of a Hundred Horizons; Padua, ennobled by Giotto's frescoes; Verona's romantic Romeo and Juliet *settings; and the villas of Andrea Palladio, where 16th-century aristocrats led the privileged life.*

AS ROME PRESIDES OVER THE LAZIO REGION, all of Venetia falls under the historical and spiritual influence of its namesake city. Take any city in the Venetian Arc and travelers will quickly note that all repeat, in one way or another, the grace and refinement of Venice. No lagoons, perhaps, but the region's architecture, paintings, and way of life all bask in the reflected splendor of La Serenissima.

Updated by
Giuliano
Davenport

Much of the pleasure of exploring this area comes from discovering the individual variations on the overall Venetian theme that confer special charm on each of the towns you'll visit. Some, such as Verona, Treviso, and Udine, have a solid medieval look; Asolo has an idyllic setting; Bassano combines a bit of both. If you are a confirmed or fledgling oenophile, you'll enjoy tasting local wines within view of the vineyards that produce some of the best-known Italian vintages—among them, Soave, Valpolicella, Bardolino, and Prosecco. But most of all, you'll find artistic jewels everywhere, from the great Venetian masters in Verona to Veronese's lighthearted frescoes in Villa Barbaro at Maser.

Pleasures and Pastimes

Concerts and Opera
The love of Italian culture need not stop at Venice. Verona, Trieste, and Vicenza offer some of the most spectacular opportunities for indulging in the passions of open-air operas and concerts.

Dining
In the main cities of the Veneto region, restaurants are in the middle to upper ranges of each price category, but in smaller towns and in the countryside you can find some real bargains. At the eastern end of the Arc, in less trafficked Friuli–Venezia Giulia, prices are generally lower. Seafood is the specialty along the coast, of course, but inland the cuisine varies from the delicate risotto, radicchio, and asparagus of the Veneto to the more decisively flavored cooking of the Trieste area, heavily influenced by Austria. San Daniele del Friuli, near Udine, is famous for its delicious prosciutto *crudo* (cured). Polenta, made of cornmeal, is a staple throughout the area; it is served with thick, rich sauces or grilled as an accompaniment to meat dishes. Trieste's position near the Austrian and Slovenian borders has fostered a varied—and somewhat heavier—cuisine reflecting the tastes of those countries.

The best local wines are Soave, Tocai, Prosecco, Riesling, and pinot—all white; and Bardolino, Valpolicella, merlot, cabernet, and pinot nero—reds. The Collio designation indicates wines from vineyards in the eastern part of Friuli, up against the Slovenian border. One of the best known and rarest wines produced here is the sauternelike Picolit, made in very limited quantities. Grappa is a locally distilled aquavit.

CATEGORY	COST*
$$$$	over 100,000 lire
$$$	80,000–100,000 lire
$$	40,000–80,000 lire
$	under 40,000 lire

Prices are per person, including house wine, service, and tax.

Liqueurs
The Veneto and Friuli regions are renowned for their grappas (distilled wines). Justifiably popular are those made by the families Nardini, in Bassano, and Nonino, at Udine. Trieste is the home of the famous Stock liqueur.

Lodging

The area around Venice has been playing host to visitors for centuries, and the result is a range of comfortable accommodations at every price. As with dining, common sense should tell you that the slightly out-of-the-way small hotel will cost you less than its counterpart in a stylish Adriatic resort. Expect to pay more as you approach Venice, since many of the mainland towns absorb the overflow during the times when Venice becomes most crowded, such as Carnival (the two weeks preceding Lent) and throughout the summer.

CATEGORY	COST*
$$$$	over 250,000 lire
$$$	180,000–250,000 lire
$$	90,000–180,000 lire
$	under 90,000 lire

Prices are for a standard double room for two, including tax and service.

Shopping

Many of the goods normally associated with Venice are actually produced in the surrounding areas of the Venetian Arc—which means that with a bit of diligence or luck you can pick up a bargain from the source. Mountain towns and villages such as Bassano del Grappa have the strongest handicraft tradition, and you can find a wide range of goods in artisans' shops on the side streets. The main towns on the coastal plain are often associated with one or two specialties, either because of traditional skills or because of ancient trading rights that set a pattern of importing specific items from other parts of the Mediterranean.

Villas and Palazzi

Countless villas are sprinkled throughout the Venetian hinterland. These gracious country homes give insight into the way wealthy Venetians used to—and still do—vacation. Many of the villas are privately owned but are open to the public at certain times or by special request. Local tourist offices can be helpful in providing information on visiting these jewels.

Exploring the Venetian Arc

The area known as the Venetian Arc comprises principally the coastal crescent and the inland plain that stretches from the mouths of the Po and Adige rivers southwest of Venice. In addition the cities of Trieste and Udine lie east of Venice, and close to the Slovenian border. They bridge two Italian regions—the Veneto and Friuli–Venezia Giulia—a landscape of flat green farmland spotted with low hills that swells and rises steeply inland in a succession of plateaus and high meadows to the snow-tipped Alps.

Numbers in the text correspond to numbers in the margin and on the Venetian Arc and Verona maps.

Great Itineraries

Hard as it may seem to leave the unique beauty of Venice behind, the Venetian Arc is the perfect last course to round off your stay. The towns are all beautiful, mixing grandiose architecture and medieval aristocracy in a flawless manner. One of these towns, Verona, also unknowingly produced the most tragic of all storie d'amore (love stories)—*Romeo and Juliet*. The sorrow that this tale inspires can be drowned in the delights of some of the best-known Italian wines.

Many towns can be seen on one- or two-day excursions from Venice itself. A three-day itinerary will exclude Trieste and restrict you to the other principal sights, but you can make up for it at night either by taking in a show or simply eating out to get an impression of the region and its people. A five-day exploration will give you plenty to remember and even savor, but you will have to discipline yourself to keep up a swift pace. A seven-day trip will give you the time to savor the architecture, history, and culture of this beautiful region.

IF YOU HAVE 3 DAYS

Begin your drive at **Villa Pisani** ①, the most splendid of all Veneto villas. Move on to **Padua** ②, taking in the Cappella Scrovegni. Continue toward 🎭 **Verona** ③–⑯, the city of *Romeo and Juliet*. The following day see some of Palladio's works in **Vicenza** ⑰ and head for **Marostica** ⑱, 🎭 **Bassano del Grappa** ⑲, and **Asolo** ⑳. Save the last day for **Treviso** ㉒, **Conegliano** ㉓, and stop for a tour of **Udine** ㉔. Return to Venice along the A4, leaving out **Trieste** ㉗.

IF YOU HAVE 5 DAYS

Follow the itinerary described above until Asolo. Instead of moving on directly to Treviso, travel toward **Villa Barbaro** ㉑ in Maser and then on to **Treviso** ㉒. Visit **Conegliano** ㉓ and 🎭 **Udine** ㉔, where you can overnight. The next day head for **Cividale** ㉕ and down then to 🎭 **Trieste** ㉗. Spend a day in this border city and then move on to **Miramare Castle** ㉖ before taking the A4 back to Venice.

IF YOU HAVE 7 DAYS

Follow the itinerary described above, but in **Bassano del Grappa** ⑲ take in a visit to the famous Nardini distillery on the edge of town. From **Treviso** ㉒, head to Oderzo on the magnificent Red Wine Road, which winds through the cabernet and merlot country along the Piave River.

When to Tour the Venetian Arc

There is no particular good or bad time to see the sights around the Venetian Arc. Most of the year, the area is relatively free from very heavy traffic and congestion. If, however, you want to get the most out of your stay, come during the early summer months (May, June, July) or immediately after the end of August. Opera and theater buffs should come in the summer months, as most performances in this region are outdoors and are on only in spring and summer. It's a pleasure to walk in Verona, Vicenza, and Padua at the end of summer when temperatures aren't at their highest.

PADUA, VERONA, AND VICENZA

Great Cities of the Veneto

Foremost among the treasures of the Veneto region are the beautiful villas Andrea Palladio (1508–80) built to render la vita all the more dolce for 16th-century aristocrats. Other important sights include Giotto's 14th-century frescoes in Padua's Scrovegni Chapel and many of Donatello's greatest statues. Romeo and Juliet? In Verona, visitors are charged a small fee to see what is alleged to be the tomb of Juliet and not far away there is a 13th-century building in which the lovely Juliet Capuletti lived. Of Romeo, alas, the landmarks are vaguer.

Villa Pisani

❶   *10 km (6 mi) southeast of Padua.*

This extraordinary house in **Stra,** also called Villa Nazionale, is the most spectacular of all the Veneto villas. In the 16th to 18th centuries, wealthy Venetians sought to enjoy *villegiatura*—a vacation and escape from harried city life—by building stately residences on their country estates throughout Venetia. Many of them were constructed on the Brenta

Venetian Arc

Tolmin

Nova Goria

Monfalcone

SLOVENIA

CROATIA

Trieste **27**

26 Miramare Castle

Golfo di Trieste

Koper

Portoroz

Piran

Vizinada

Umag

N

20 miles

30 km

Gorizia

Isonzo

25 Cividale

S54 S56

Udine **24**

A23

S13

S464

S463

Tagliamento

Meduna

Pordenone

A28

Portogruaro

Caorle

Adriatic Sea

Lido di Jesolo

Livenza

Golfo di Venezia

TO SPLIT, DUBROVNIK
AND ISTANBUL

S251

Sella di
Fadalto

Vittorio Veneto

Feltre

S550

23 Conegliano

Oderzo

Piave

S53

A27

S13

Treviso **22**

S14

A4

Alberoni

Chioggia

Laguna Veneta

Venice

Valdobbiadene

Villa Barbaro

Montebelluna

21

20 Asolo

S307

S248

Padua **2**

1 Villa Pisani

Brenta

A4 (E70)

Piove
di Sacco

Adige

Po

S245

S307

Marostica **18**

19

S248

S47

S53

Abano Terme

Praglia

Monselice

Este

S10

Montagnana

Legnago

Montegrotto Terme

Bassano del Grappa

Schio

S46

Valdagno

Vicenza **17**

A4

S11

S. Bonifacio

Trento

Rovereto

S47

A22

S12

Valdagno

Adige

Verona **3** — **16**

S12

S4/B4

ITALY

River, the main waterway used by Venetians to go inland. Villa Pisani is an imposing 18th-century edifice that once belonged to Napoléon, who appreciated its similarities to Versailles. See the grandiose frescoes by Giambattista Tiepolo on the ceiling of the ballroom. If you have youngsters surfeited with the old masters in tow, explore the gorgeous **park** and the **maze** (open only in the summer). It is about 7 km (4¼ mi) east of Padua. ⊠ *Stra,* ☎ *0423/923004.* ✉ *8,000 lire.* ☉ *Villa: Apr.–Sept., Tues.–Sun. 9–6; Oct.–Mar., Tues.–Sun. 9–1. Grounds: Apr.–Sept., Tues.–Sun. 9–6; Oct.–Mar. Tues.–Sun. 9–4.*

Padua

❷ *37 km (23 mi) west of Venice and 92 km (57 mi) east of Verona.*

Bustling Padua (Padova), with a medieval nucleus, is the seat of a famous university founded in 1222. Formerly one of the major cultural centers in northern Italy, it has lost some of its splendor to modernization. Pick up a map and brochures at the tourist office in the train station and head straight down Corso del Popolo, which changes its name to Corso Garibaldi about 400 yards on, when it crosses the Bacchiglione River.

★ The **Cappella degli Scrovegni** (Scrovegni Chapel) was erected in the 13th century by a wealthy Paduan, Enrico Scrovegno, to honor his deceased father. Scrovegni called on Giotto to decorate its interior, a task that occupied the great artist and his helpers from 1303 to 1305. They created a magnificent fresco cycle, arranged in typical medieval comic-strip fashion, illustrating the lives of Mary and Christ. The realism in these frescoes—which include the first blue skies in Western painting—was revolutionary. ⊠ *Piazza Eremitani 8,* ☎ *049/8204550.* ✉ *10,000 lire; groups 7,000 per person (includes free guide).* ☉ *Daily 9–7.*

The 13th-century **Chiesa dei Eremitani** contains some fragments of frescoes by Andrea Mantegna (1431–1506), the brilliant locally born artist, some of whose masterpieces are in nearby Mantua: most of these frescoes, however, were destroyed in the Allied bombing of 1944. The **Museo Civico di Padova** (Civic Museum of Padua), housed in what used to be the monastery of the church, has its quota of works by Venetian masters. ⊠ *Piazza Eremitani 10,* ☎ *049/8204550.* ✉ *Church free; Museo Civico 10,000 lire; groups 7,000 per person (includes free guide).* ☉ *Tues.–Sun. 9–7.*

The medieval-era **Padua University,** familiarly known as Il Bo', reveals a 16th-century facade. In the 15th century, this structure was known as the Osteria del Bo' (Ox Inn), a favorite student hangout. This is worth a visit to see the exquisite and perfectly proportioned anatomy theater and a hall harboring a lectern used by Galileo. ⊠ *Via VIII Febbraio,* ☎ *049/8209711.* ✉ *7,000 lire.* ☉ *Guided visits only; call for tour times.*

Palazzo della Ragione (also called Il Salone) was built in the Middle Ages as the seat of Padua's parliament. Today its street-level arcades shelter shops and cafés. In the frescoed Great Hall on the upper level is an enormous wooden horse, a 15th-century replica of the bronze steed in Donatello's equestrian statue of Gattamelata. ⊠ *Piazza della Ragione.* ✉ *8,000 lire.* ☉ *Oct.–Mar. daily 9–6; Apr.–Sept. 9–7. During special exhibitions, hrs and admission price may vary.*

The huge basilica **Sant'Antonio** is a cluster of Byzantine domes and slender, minaret-like towers that gives the church an Oriental look, reminiscent of San Marco in Venice. The interior is sumptuous, too, with marble reliefs by Tullio Lombardo, the greatest in a talented family of marble carvers who decorated many churches in the area—among them, Santa Maria dei Miracoli in Venice. The artistic highlights here, however, all bear Donatello's name; the 15th-century Florentine master did the remarkable series of bronze reliefs illustrating the life of St. Anthony—whose feast day, June 13, draws pilgrims from all over Europe—as well as the bronze statues of the Madonna and saints on the high altar. ⊠ *Via del Santo Basilica.*

To mark the 800th anniversary of the birth of St. Anthony in 1195, a new museum, the **Museo Antoniano,** with 300 exhibits relating to the image of the saint and of the basilica, was opened in 1995 on the first floor of the church cloister building. Standing in front of the church is Donatello's powerful statue of the condottiere (mercenary general) Gattamelata, which was cast in bronze—a monumental technical achievement—in about 1450 and was to have an enormous influence on the development of Italian Renaissance sculpture. ⊠ *Via del Santo Basilica. Church:* ☎ *Free.* ⏲ *Apr.–Sept. 6:30 AM–7:45 PM; Oct.–Mar. 6:30 AM–7 PM. Museum:* ☎ *7,000 lire.* ⏲ *Daily 9–7.*

The **Orto Botanico** (Botanic Garden) was founded in 1545 by order of the Venetian Republic to supply the university with medicinal plants. The garden is in front of Sant'Antonio. ⊠ *Via Donatello.* ☎ *5,000 lire.* ⏲ *Apr.–Sept., daily 9–12:30 and 3–6; Oct.–Mar. Mon.–Sat. 9–1.*

Piazza dei Signori exhibits some fine examples of 15th- and 16th-century buildings. The cathedral **Santa Magdalena** is just a few steps from Piazza dei Signori.

Laid out in 1775, **Prato della Valle** is an unusual and attractive piazza with a wooded oval park at the center, surrounded by a canal. At the southeast end of this immense square is the church of **Santa Giustina,** with finely inlaid choir stalls and Veronese's colossal altarpiece, *The Martyrdom of St. Justine.* A market is featured here weekends (☞ Shopping, *below*). ⊠ *Prato della Valle.* ⏲ *Mon.–Sat. 7:30–noon and 3:30–7:30, Sun. 7–1 and 3:30–7:30.*

OFF THE BEATEN PATH

ABANO TERME AND MONTEGROTTO TERME – These two spas, about 12 km (7½ mi) south of Padua, are set in the dreamy landscape of the Euganean Hills. Colorful gardens and fresh summer breezes make them havens for those seeking a break from city life.

PRAGLIA – This Benedictine monastery, hidden in the hills, provides guided tours of its evocative 15th-century halls and cloisters. You can also buy wine and honey produced here by the monks. To get here head 12 km (7 mi) southwest of Padua, following signs for ABANO TERME on the south side of the city. ☎ *049/9900010.* ☎ *Offerings appreciated.* ⏲ *Tours Apr.–Oct., Tues.–Sun. (except major religious holidays) every ½ hr 3:30–5:30; Nov.–Mar., Tues.–Sun. every ½ hr 2:30–4:30.*

MONTAGNANA – This medieval city is 50 km (30 mi) southwest of Padua. Its surrounding walls are remarkably well preserved, and there are 24 towers, a moat, and four city gates. Its former rivals, Este and Monselice, are only 20 km (12 mi) east on the same road.

Dining and Lodging

Hotels in nearby Vicenza, in Bassano del Grappa, along the Brenta, and in Venice are better in terms of variety and quality than in Padua itself, which caters primarily to business travelers.

$$$ ✕ **Belle Parti.** Angelo Rasi's sophisticated Belle Parti remains the best restaurant in town. Adventurous, Venetian-accented seasonal specialties might include risotto *al fior d'arancio con gamberi di fiume* (with oranges and river prawns) and *quaglia tartufata in crosta* (truffled quails

in pastry). The wine list offers a fine selection of the area's best bottles. ⊠ *Via Belle Parti 11,* ☎ *049/8751822. AE, DC, MC, V. Closed Sun. and 1st 3 wks in Aug. No lunch Mon.*

$$ ✕ **Cavalca.** A family-run establishment with a long tradition, Cavalca is just off Piazza dei Signori in the heart of Padua. Classic decor and simple but courteous service are hallmarks here. The specialties are pasta *e fagioli* (pasta and bean soup), roast *capretto* (kid), or a platter of *arrosti misti* (assorted roast meats). ⊠ *Via Manin 8,* ☎ *049/8760061. Reservations essential. AE, DC, MC, V. Closed Wed., Jan. 12–22, and July 1–21. No dinner Tues.*

$ ✕ **Fagiano.** Near the Sant'Antonio, Fagiano is a popular trattoria with locals and tourists. The specialties are hearty standbys: pasta e fagioli and *fagiano farcito* (stuffed pheasant). ⊠ *Via Locatelli 45,* ☎ *049/ 8750073. MC, V. Closed Mon. and July 15–Aug. 15.*

$$$ ▦ **Donatello.** Directly opposite the basilica Sant'Antonio, Donatello has rooms with a view of the square and church, but it can be noisy. Rooms are contemporary, with color TVs. ⊠ *Via del Santo 102, 35137,* ☎ *049/8750634,* **FAX** *049/8750829. 49 rooms, 42 with bath or shower. Restaurant, minibars, parking (fee). AE, DC, MC, V. Closed mid-Dec.–mid-Jan.*

$$$ ▦ **Villa Ducale.** Set in its own statuesque gardens, one of the country residences built along the Brenta River by Venetian noblemen has been turned into a stylish hotel with stuccoed walls and ceilings, Murano glass chandeliers and mirrors, and Venetian-style marble flooring. This is not in Padua but in Dolo, halfway between Venice and Padua, and is connected to both by a regular local train service. ⊠ *Riviera Martiri della Libertà 75, Dolo, 35137,* ☎ *041/5608020,* **FAX** *041/420094. 11 rooms. Restaurant, air-conditioning. MC, V.*

Nightlife and the Arts

BARS

The ever-popular **Caffè Pedrocchi** (⊠ Corso Garibaldi, ☎ 149/8762576), in a monumental 19th-century neoclassical coffeehouse that looks like a cross between a museum and a stage set, serves up an impressive cappuccino. The upstairs rooms, with their frescoed ceilings, often feature art shows.

JAZZ

A university crowd flocks to the **Video Club Sisma** (⊠ Via Chiesanuova 106, Padua, ☎ 049/8716577) for its art and film exhibitions mixed with music.

NIGHTCLUBS

Big Club (⊠ Via Armistizio, ☎ 049/680934). **Wag** (⊠ Via Savonarola 149, ☎ 049/8721530). **Le Petit Palais** (⊠ Via Vecellio 1, ☎ 049/600134). Pool sharks head to **Limbo** (⊠ Via San Fermo 44, ☎ 049/656882), with a game room upstairs and live music downstairs.

Outdoor Activities and Sports

GOLF

The 18-hole **Golf Club Padova** (⊠ Via Noiera 57, Valsanzibio di Galzignano, ☎ 049/9130078, **FAX** 049/9131193) is 18 km (11 mi) south of Padua.

HORSEBACK RIDING

Scuola Padovana Equitazione (⊠ Via Libia 20, Padua, ☎ 049/8717244) offers riding and private lessons for beginners.

Shopping

Padua has a Saturday market featuring a wide range of goods in **Prato della Valle,** where an antiques market is held the third Sunday of every month.

Verona

❸ *89 km (53 mi) west of Padua, 60 km (37 mi) southwest of Vicenza.*

On the banks of the fast-flowing Adige River, Verona possesses classical and medieval monuments, a picturesque town center where bright geraniums bloom in window boxes, and a romantic reputation, thanks to being the setting of Shakespeare's *Romeo and Juliet*. It is one of Italy's most alluring cities, despite extensive industrialization and urban development in its newer sections. Inevitably, with its lively Venetian air, proximity to Lake Garda, and renowned summer opera season, it attracts hordes of tourists, especially vacationing Germans and Austrians, who drive through the Brenner Pass just to the north.

Verona grew to power and prosperity within the Roman Empire as a result of its key commercial and military position in northern Italy. After the fall of the Empire, the city continued to flourish under the guidance of Barbarian kings such as Theodoric, Alboin, Pepin, and Berenger I, reaching its cultural and artistic peak in the 13th and 14th centuries, under the Della Scala dynasty. (You'll see the *scala,* or ladder, emblem all over town.) In 1404, however, Verona traded its independence for security and placed itself under the control of Venice. (The other recurring architectural motif is the lion of St. Mark, symbol of Venetian rule.) Verona remained under Venetian protection until 1797, when Napoléon invaded. In 1814 the entire Veneto region was won by the Austrians, and it was finally united with the rest of Italy in 1866.

★ ☙ ❹ The obvious place to start is at the **Arena di Verona** in **Piazza Brà,** the vast and airy square at the center of the city. Built by the Romans in the 1st century AD, the arena is one of the largest and best-preserved Roman amphitheaters anywhere. Only four arches remain of the outer rings, but the main structure is so complete that it takes little imagination to picture it as the site of the cruel deaths of countless gladiators, wild beasts, and Christians. Today it hosts Verona's summer opera, famous for spectacular productions and audiences of as many as 22,000. The best operas to see here are the big splashy ones that demand huge choruses, Cinerama sets, lots of color and movement, and, if possible, camels, horses, and/or elephants. The music can be excellent, and the acoustics are fine, too. If you go, be sure to take or rent a cushion—four hours on 2,000-year-old marble can be an ordeal. ⊠ *Arena di Verona, Piazza Brà, 045/8003204.* ⊡ *8,000 lire; free 1st Sun. of month.* ☉ *Tues.–Sun. 8–6:30; (8–1:30 during opera season July–Aug.).*

❺ Piazza delle Erbe (Vegetable Market Square) is the site of an ancient Roman forum and today a colorful market in the morning, when huge rectangular umbrellas are raised to shade the neat ranks of fruits and vegetables.

❻ The 12th-century **Palazzo della Ragione** has a somber courtyard, Gothic staircase, and medieval tower; it overlooks **Piazza dei Signori,** just off Piazza Brà, and is enclosed on all sides by stately public build-**❼** ings. The graceful **Loggia del Consiglio** (⊠ Piazza dei Signori) was built **❽** in the 12th century to house city council meetings. The **Palazzo del Governo** (⊠ Piazza dei Signori) was the medieval stronghold from which the Della Scalas ruled Verona with an iron fist.

222

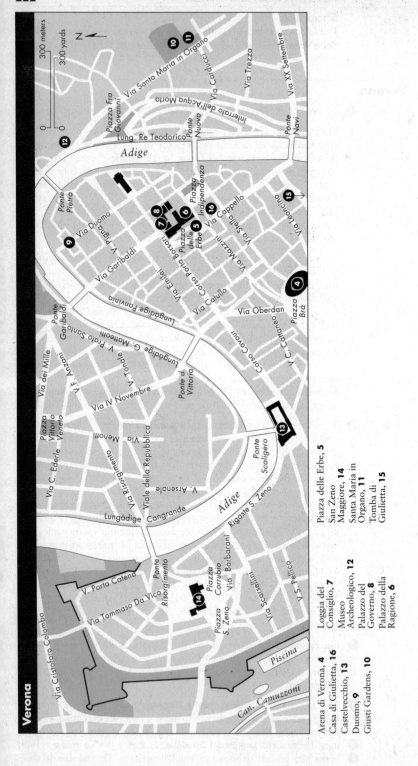

Verona

300 meters
300 yards

Arena di Verona, **4**
Casa di Giulietta, **16**
Castelvecchio, **13**
Duomo, **9**
Giusti Gardens, **10**

Loggia del
  Consiglio, **7**
Museo
  Archeologico, **12**
Palazzo del
  Governo, **8**
Palazzo della
  Ragione, **6**

Piazza delle Erbe, **5**
San Zeno
  Maggiore, **14**
Santa Maria in
  Organo, **11**
Tomba di
  Giulietta, **15**

⑨ The ornate Romanesque **Duomo** has not only some architectural characteristics typical of the Venetian style, but also some of those typical of the Byzantine style. ⊠ *Via Duomo.* ⊘ *Daily 7–noon and 4–7.*

⑩ The formal **Giusti Gardens,** laid out on several levels around a 16th-century villa, is a symbol of things long past. There's a fine view of the city from the terrace, from which the German poet and dramatist Johann von Goethe recorded his inspiration. At the southern end of the gardens is the Gothic church of **Sant'Anastasia.** ⊠ *Via Giardino Giusti,* ☎ *045/8034029.* ▭ *5,000 lire.* ⊘ *Gardens Apr.–Sept., daily 9–8; Oct.–Mar., daily 9–sunset. Sant'Anastasia daily 7–noon and 4–7.*

⑪ The choir and sacristy of medieval **Santa Maria in Organo** are covered in inlaid-wood masterpieces of the 15th-century monk Fra Giovanni. A series of panels depicts varied scenes—local buildings, an idealized Renaissance town, wildlife, and fruit—that radiate a love of life and reveal the artist's eye for detail. ⊠ *Via Giardino Giusti,* ☎ *045/591440.* ⊘ *Daily 7:30–11.*

⑫ The modest **Museo Archeologico** is in an old monastery above a Roman theater that was built in the same era as the Arena di Verona. The Roman theater is on the museum grounds and is sometimes used for dramatic productions. From here there are good views over the entire city. ⊠ *Rigaste del Redentore,* ☎ *045/8000360.* ▭ *5,000 lire; free 1st Sun. of month.* ⊘ *Tues.–Sun. 8–1.*

🖐 **⑬** The 14th-century **Castelvecchio** was built for Cangrande II Della Scala. A crenelated building in russet brick with massive walls, towers, turrets, and a vast courtyard, it looks like a fairy-tale castle that guards a bridge across the Adige. The whole street to which it belongs is lined with attractive old buildings and palaces of the old nobility. Inside, the **Museo di Castelvecchio** gives you a good look at the castle's vaulted halls and the treasures of Venetian painting and sculpture that they contain. ⊠ *Corso Cavour,* ☎ *045/594734.* ▭ *7,000 lire; free 1st Sun. of month.* ⊘ *Tues.–Sun. 8–6:30; hrs and admission may change during special exhibitions.*

⑭ **San Zeno Maggiore** is possibly one of Italy's finest examples of a Romanesque church. It's set between two medieval bell towers and has a 13th-century rose window and 12th-century portal. The brick color scheme is typical of most Romanesque churches in Italy, but especially impressive here. Inside, look for Mantegna's *Madonna* over the main altar; there's a peaceful cloister off the left nave. ⊠ *Piazza San Zeno,* ☎ *045/8006120.* ⊘ *Daily 8–noon and 4–6:30.*

Romantic souls may want to see what the astute tourist office says is **⑮** **Tomba di Giulietta** (Juliet's Tomb). It's a pretty spot, though hardly a major attraction. Authentic or not, it is still popular with lovesick Italian teenagers, who leave notes for the tragic lover. ⊠ *Via del Pontiere,* ☎ *045/8000361.* ▭ *5,000 lire; free 1st Sun. of month.* ⊘ *Tues.–Sun. 8–6:30.*

⑯ At **Casa di Giulietta** (Juliet's House), the balcony in the small courtyard will help to bring Shakespeare's play to life. Historians now believe that the couple had no real-life counterparts, but this hasn't discouraged anyone from imagining that they did. After all, historians are not as renowned for their storytelling as Shakespeare is. ⊠ *Via Cappello 23,* ▭ *8,000 lire.* ⊘ *Tues.–Sun. 8–6:30.*

Dining and Lodging

$$$$ ✕ **Dodici Apostoli.** Vaulted ceilings, frescoed walls, and a medieval ambience make this an exceptional place to enjoy classic local and regional dishes. Near Piazza delle Erbe, it stands on the foundations of a Roman temple. Specialties include *zuppa scaligera* (soup of meat stock with vegetables and bread) and *vitello Lessinia* (veal with mushrooms, cheese, and truffles). ⊠ *Corticella San Marco 3,* ☎ *045/596999. AE, DC, V. Closed Mon., Jan. 1–7, and June 15–July 7. No dinner Sun.*

$$$$ ✕ **Le Arche.** True to its name, this elegant restaurant is in a medieval building a step away from the Della Scala tombs. The dining room is furnished in art-nouveau style, featuring candlelight and flowers, and it has a turn-of-the-century air. Only seafood is served, absolutely fresh and superlatively prepared in the Venetian tradition. Zingers include ravioli *di branzino con vongole* (stuffed with sea bass with clam sauce) and *scorfano con olive nere* (baked sea scorpion with black olives). ⊠ *Via Arche Scaligere 6,* ☎ *045/8007415. AE, DC, MC, V. Closed Sun., 1st 2 wks of Jan., and July 1–21. No lunch Mon.*

$$–$$$ ✕ **Osteria All'Oste Scuro.** This trusty, family-run trattoria varies its selection of traditional Veronese dishes, such as pasta e fagioli, polenta *con lardo* (with bacon), and *pastisada de caval* (horse-meat stew). From September to May, once- or twice-weekly special fixed-price dinners feature an Italian regional menu paired with regional wines. These gastronomic treats are valuable; book in advance. ⊠ *Vicolo San Silvestro 10,* ☎ *045/592650. MC, V. Closed Sun. No dinner Sat.*

$$ ✕ **Al Calmiere.** This congenial trattoria on the lovely piazza in front of San Zeno Maggiore, one of the city's finest churches, is the ideal place to enjoy Veronese specialties of tagliatelle with *fegatini di pollo* (chicken-liver sauce), various types of pasta in *brodo* (broth), *bolito* (boiled) and roast meats, and local wines (there are some 20 different Valpolicellas alone available) at reasonable prices. The interior, with an enormous open fireplace used for cooking, is especially cozy in winter. ⊠ *Piazza San Zeno 10,* ☎ *045/8030765. AE, DC, MC, V. Closed Thurs. and July. No dinner Wed.*

$$ ✕ **Antico Caffè Dante.** This historic coffeehouse has been taken over by Guido Morari, the proprietor of the upmarket Nuovo Marconi restaurant next door, and its stuccoed interior with portraits of Italian national heroes has been restored. It is now a brasserie-style café-restaurant with a short but varied menu, including a delicious asparagus risotto (in season), fresh *papparedelle* (thick ribbons of pasta) with scampi, and *stinco di maiale* (roast pork shin) served with polenta. Tempting homemade cakes and pastries are served all day. ⊠ *Piazza dei Signori 2,* ☎ *045/595249. AE, DC, MC, V. Closed Sun. in winter.*

$$ ✕ **La Greppia.** The classic decor with vaulted ceilings sets the tone in this bustling restaurant off Via Mazzini between the Arena and Piazza delle Erbe. The kitchen produces fine versions of local and regional dishes, especially *tortelli di zucca* (pasta filled with squash) and *bolliti* (assorted boiled meats served with a choice of sauces). Service is courteous and efficient. ⊠ *Vicolo Samaritana 3,* ☎ *045/8004577. AE, DC, V. Closed Mon., 1st wk of Jan., June 15–30.*

$ ✕ **Pizzeria Vesuvio.** Between Castelvecchio and San Zeno Maggiore, this authentic Neapolitan pizzeria has tables on the riverbank in summer, with a lovely breezy view of the Adige. ⊠ *Via Rigaste 41,* ☎ *045/595634. MC, V. Closed Mon.*

$$$$ 🏨 **Colomba d'Oro.** This attractive four-star hotel right by the Arena occupies a building that dates from the 14th century. Repeatedly renovated over the past few years, it has retained a clubby atmosphere and European charm while providing up-to-date comfort. There is no restaurant. ⊠ *Via Cattaneo 10, 37122,* ☎ *045/595300,* 🖷 *045/594974. 49 rooms, 2 suites. Parking (fee). AE, DC, MC, V.*

$$$$ 🏨 **Gabbia d'Oro.** This historic building off Piazza delle Erbe in the ancient heart of Verona was fully and tastefully restored in 1990. Public rooms and individually furnished guest rooms have frescoes, beamed

ceilings, and antique prints and furnishings. Guests can relax outdoors in the medieval courtyard or on the roof terrace. ⊠ *Corso Porta Borsari 4/a, 37122,* ☎ *045/8003060,* FAX *045/590293. 27 rooms. Restaurant, bar. AE, DC, MC, V.*

$$$$ ⊡ **Villa del Quar.** This tranquil 16th-century villa surrounded by gar-
★ dens and vineyards in the Valpolicella country is only 7 km (4½ mi) from town center (and easily reached by taxi). Architect Leopoldo Montresor and his wife, Evelina, who live here with their young children, recently converted part of the villa into a stylish and sophisticated hotel. No expense has been spared: all rooms have marble bathrooms (some with Jacuzzi) and antique European furniture. ⊠ *Via del Quar 12, Pedemonte, 37122,* ☎ *045/6800681,* FAX *045/6800604. 18 rooms, 4 suites. Restaurant, bar, air-conditioning, pool. AE, DC, MC, V.*

$$ ⊡ **Torcolo.** The warm welcome extended by the owners, Signoras
★ Diana and Silvia, the pleasant rooms decorated unfussily, and the central location on a peaceful street close to Piazza Brà and the Arena make the Torcolo outstanding value in its class. Breakfast is served outside on the terrace in front of the hotel in summer. ⊠ *Vicolo Listone 3, 37122,* ☎ *045/8007512,* FAX *045/8004058. 19 rooms. MC, V.*

Nightlife and the Arts

DISCOS

Alter Ego (⊠ Via Torricelle 9, ☎ 045/915130) packs a 20-something crowd that might call itself alternative. **Berfi's** (⊠ Via Lussemborgo 1, ☎ 045/508024) is a popular but expensive spot. **Excalibur** (⊠ Via Provolo 24, ☎ 045/594295) attracts the youngest crowds.

OPERA

Of all the venues for enjoying opera in the region, pride of place must go to the summer opera season in the **Arena di Verona.** The season runs from July through August, and the 22,000 in the audience sit on the original stone terraces that date from the time when gladiators fought to the death. The opera stage is huge and best suited to grand operas such as *Aïda,* but the experience is memorable no matter what is being performed. Sometimes, while sipping a drink in a café at **Piazza Brà,** you can overhear the opera. A 15% advance-sale fee is added to price of ticket for bookings made more than 24 hrs before performance. ⊠ *Contact: Ente Lirico Arena di Verona, Piazza Brà 28, 37121 Verona,* ☎ *045/590109,* FAX *045/8011566. Box office:* ⊠ *Via Dietro Anfiteatro 6B,* ☎ *045/8005151,* FAX *045/8013287.* ☉ *Sept.–June. weekdays 8:40–12:20 and 3–5:50; Sat. 8:40–12:20; July–Aug. Closed Mon. Open days without performances 9:30–12:20 and 3–6:20; days of performances 10–12:20 and 3:30–9:30.*

Outdoor Activities and Sports

GOLF

The 18-hole **Golf Club Verona** (⊠ Ca' del Sale 15, Sommacampagna, ☎ 045/510060, FAX 045/510242) is 16 km (10 mi) west of Verona or 2 km (1¼ mi) from the Sommacampagna exit on the A4 autoroute.

TENNIS

There are public courts at **Via Col. Galliano** (☎ 045/592828).

Shopping

ANTIQUES

The area around the Gothic church of Sant'Anastasia is full of antiques shops, most of them catering to serious collectors. Picnic on the Piazza dei Signori in the cool breeze after a strenuous day of antiques hunting.

FLEA MARKETS

Verona's **Piazza delle Erbe** daily market has a selection of food, wine, clothing, some antiques, and even pets.

Vicenza

⑰ *60 km (37 mi) east of Verona, 32 km (20 mi) west of Padua.*

Vicenza bears the distinctive signature of the 16th-century architect Andrea Palladio and was designated by UNESCO in 1994 as a preeminent site of world cultural heritage. The architect, whose name is the basis of the term "Palladian," gracefully incorporated elements of classical architecture—columns, porticoes, and domes—into a style that reflected the Renaissance celebration of order and harmony. His elegant villas and palaces were influential in propagating classical architecture in Europe, especially Britain, and later in America—most notably, at Thomas Jefferson's Monticello.

In the mid-16th century Palladio was given the opportunity to rebuild much of Vicenza, which had suffered great damage during the bloody wars waged against Venice by the League of Cambrai, an alliance of the Papacy, France, the Holy Roman Empire, and several neighboring city-states. He imposed upon the city a number of his grand Roman-style buildings—rather an overstatement, considering the town's status. With the basilica, begun in 1549 in the very heart of Vicenza, he ensured his reputation and embarked on a series of lordly buildings, all of which proclaim the same rigorous classicism.

The Gothic **Duomo** contains a gleaming altarpiece by Lorenzo Veneziano, a 14th-century Venetian painter. The cathedral itself was partly destroyed in World War II, but nearly all the damaged areas have been restored. ✉ *Piazza Duomo.* 🎫 *Free.* ⊘ *Daily 7–noon and 3:30–7.*

Corso Palladio is a memorable avenue, lined with a succession of imposing palaces and churches that run the gamut from Venetian Gothic to Baroque. Many of these palaces were designed by Palladio. The church of **Santa Corona** holds an exceptionally fine *Baptism of Christ* (1500) by Giovanni Bellini over the altar on the left, just in front of the transept. ✉ *Contrà S. Corona.* ⊘ *Daily 8:30–noon and 2:30–6.*

The exquisite and unmistakably Palladian **Palazzo Chiericati** houses the city municipal art gallery, with a representative collection of Venetian paintings. ✉ *Piazza Matteotti,* ☎ *0444/321348.* 🎫 *5,000 lire.* ⊘ *Tues.–Sat. 9:30–noon and 2:30–5, Sun. 9:30–noon.*

★ The **Teatro Olimpico** is Palladio's last, and perhaps most exciting, work. Based closely on the model of the ancient Roman theater, it represents an important development in theater and stage design and is noteworthy for its acoustics and the cunningly devised false perspective of a classical street in the permanent backdrop. The anterooms are all frescoed with important figures in Venetian history. ✉ *Piazza Matteotti,* ☎ *0444/323781.* 🎫 *8,000 lire.* ⊘ *Mar. 16–Oct. 15, Mon.–Sat. 9:30–12:20 and 3–5:30, Sun. 9:30–12:20; Oct. 16–Mar. 15, Mon.–Sat. 9:30–12:20 and 2–4:30, Sun. 9:30–12:20.*

At the heart of Vicenza is **Piazza dei Signori,** also the site of Palladio's "basilica," a confusing name, since it is not a church but a courthouse and public meeting hall, the **Palazzo della Ragione.** An early Palladian masterpiece, it was actually a medieval building that the architect modernized, and the skill with which he wedded the graceful two-story exterior loggias to the existing Gothic structure is remarkable. Also note the **Loggia del Capitaniato,** opposite, which Palladio designed, but never completed. ✉ *Piazza dei Signori,* ☎ *0444/323681.* ⊘ *Tues.–Sat. 9:30–noon and 2:30–5, Sun. 9:30–noon.*

....

OFF THE
BEATEN PATH

VILLA VALMARANA DEI NANI – This is an 18th-century country house decorated with a series of marvelous frescoes by Giambattista Tiepolo:

these are fantastic visions of a mythological world, including one of his most stunning works, the *Sacrifice of Ighegenia*. The neighboring Foresteria, or guest house, holds more frescoes, showing vignettes of 18th-century Veneto life at its most charming, done by Tiepolo's son, Giandomenico. You can walk from Vicenza, but it is easier to take Bus 8 from Corso Palladio to the Via San Bastiano stop. From there you climb a gentle ⅓ km (¼ mi) until you reach the villa. ✉ *Via San Bastiano 8,* ☎ *0444/321803.* 🎟 *10,000 lire.* ☉ *Nov.–mid-Mar., Wed.–Thurs. and weekends 10–noon; Mar.–Apr., Tues.–Sat. 2:30–5:30; May–Sept., Tues.–Sat. 3–6; Oct.–Nov., Tues.–Sat. 2–5.*

VILLA LA ROTONDA – This is the most famous Palladian villa of all. In truth, it can hardly be called a villa, since Palladio was inspired by ancient Roman temples. Serene and symmetrical, it was the model for Jefferson's Monticello. Take the time to admire it from all sides, and you'll see that it was the inspiration not just for Monticello, but for nearly every state capitol in the United States. The interior is typical of Palladio's grand style, with a unique juxtaposition of solids and voids. It is within walking distance of the Villa Valmarani dei Nani. ✉ *Via della Rotonda 29,* ☎ *0444/321793.* 🎟 *Grounds 7,000 lire; interior and grounds 10,000 lire.* ☉ *Grounds Mar. 15–Nov. 4, Tues.–Thurs. 10–noon and 3–6. Interior Mar. 15–Nov. 4, Wed. only 10–noon and 3–6.*

Dining and Lodging

$$ ✕ **Da Remo.** About a mile outside town, Da Remo is worth the taxi ride simply because it is one of Vicenza's best restaurants. In an attractive country house setting, with light, airy dining rooms and a garden terrace, you can enjoy a relaxing meal of Venetian specialties, among them *faraona* (guinea hen) with radicchio, and risotto with seasonal vegetables. ✉ *Via Ca'Impenta 14,* ☎ *0444/911007. AE, DC, MC, V. Closed Mon., last wk in July, and 1st 3 wks in Aug. No dinner Sun.*

$$ ✕ **Scudo di Francia.** A Gothic palace in the heart of town houses the
★ white vaulted dining rooms of Scudo di Francia. The regional cuisine features specialties such as *bignè caldi al prosciutto e tartufo* (hot pastry puffs with ham and truffles), pasta e fagioli, and *baccalà alla vicentina* (creamy cod). ✉ *Contrà Piancoli 4,* ☎ *0444/323322. AE, DC, MC, V. Closed Mon. and Aug. No dinner Sun.*

$–$$ ✕ **Al Paradiso.** This pizzeria–trattoria just off the Piazza dei Signori is one of a pair right next door to each other, owned by two brothers; the other is Vecchia Guardia. It's particularly attractive in summer, when you can sit at tables outside. The pizzas and other dishes are tasty and very reasonably priced. ✉ *Via Pescherie Vecchie 5,* ☎ *0444/322320. Vecchia Garda,* ☎ *0444/321231. AE, DC, MC, V. Closed Mon. Vecchia Garda closed Thurs.*

$$ 🛏 **Due Mori.** In the heart of Vicenza just off Piazza dei Signori, this small hotel was recently refurbished and is a favorite with regular visitors. ✉ *Contra Do Rode 26, 36100,* ☎ *0444/321886,* ℻ *0444/326217. 27 rooms. MC, V.*

Nightlife and the Arts

MUSIC AND THEATER

Vicenza's Teatro Olimpico has a concert season in May and June, as well as a classical drama season in September. Even if your Italian is dismal, it's particularly thrilling to see a performance in Palladio's magnificent theater; this masterpiece was designed to be used, not just admired. For details, contact the Teatro Olimpico (☞ *above*).

Shopping

JEWELRY

Vicenza is one of Italy's leading centers for the production and sale of jewelry. Each year, in January and June, it plays host to an international trade fair for goldsmiths. For details inquire at the local tourist office (☞ Contacts and Resources *in* Venetian Arc A to Z, *below*).

VILLA BARBARO, TREVISO, AND THE HILLSIDE TOWNS

Northern Arc

In this area directly north of Venice, market towns cling to the steep foothills of the Alps and the Dolomites alongside streams that rage down from the mountains. Villa Barbaro, Palladio's most beautiful creation, is here, as are the arcaded streets of Treviso and the graceful Venetian Gothic styles of the smaller hill towns.

Marostica

⑱ *7 km (4¼ mi) west of Bassano del Grappa and 26 km (16 mi) northeast of Vicenza.*

The first and most evident feature of Marostica is its castle, perched on the hillside overlooking the surrounding countryside. But the town's most famous characteristic is its main square, paved in checkerboard fashion.

Outdoor Activity

MEDIEVAL CHESS

A game of chess is acted out here by people in medieval costume on the second weekend in September in even-numbered years; for information, call 0424/7212 or fax 0424/72800.

Bassano del Grappa

⑲ *7 km (4¼ mi) east of Marostica, 37 km (23 mi) north of Venice.*

Bassano del Grappa is a beautifully located town directly above the swift-flowing waters of the Brenta River at the foot of the Mt. Grappa massif (5,880 ft). Bassano's old streets are lined with low buildings sporting wooden balconies and eye-catching flowerpots. Bright ceramic wares produced here and in nearby Nove are displayed in shops along byways that curve uphill toward a centuries-old square, and, even higher, to a belvedere with a good view of Mt. Grappa and the beginning of the Valsugana Valley.

Bassano's most famous landmark is the **covered bridge** that has spanned the Brenta since the 13th century. Rebuilt countless times (floods are frequent), the present-day bridge is a postwar reconstruction using Andrea Palladio's 16th-century design. The great architect astutely chose to use wood as his medium, knowing that it could be replaced quickly and cheaply. Almost as famous is the **Nardini liquor shop** (⊠ At one end of the bridge), redolent of the grappa that has been distilled here for more than a century. Stop in for a sniff or a snifter.

Dining and Lodging

$$ ✕ **Al Ponte–Da Renzo.** An ample family-run establishment on the Brenta River, this popular restaurant has big picture windows with a vista of the old town and the famed covered bridge. The tree-shaded garden for outdoor dining has the same view. Seafood antipasto and grilled fish fresh from the Adriatic are featured. You'll also enjoy regional dishes with fresh seasonal ingredients. ✉ *Via Volpato 60,* ☎ *0424/503055. V. Closed Tues. and Jan. No dinner Mon.*

$–$$ ✕ **Birreria Ottone.** This Old World restaurant in town center is a favorite with the locals, who tout the excellent cuisine, draft wine and beer, and the friendly Wipflinger family, headed by Otto, whose Austrian forebear founded this beer hall about 100 years ago. Equally good for a simple lunch or a more elaborate dinner, Ottone's specialties include a delicious goulash cooked with cumin. ✉ *Via Matteoti 47/50,* ☎ *0424/522206. MC, V. Closed Tues. and 1st 3 wks in Aug. No dinner Mon.*

$$$–$$$$ ▥ **Villa Palma.** This gracefully refurbished 18th-century country villa, only a short drive from Asolo (10 km/6 mi) and Bassano (5 km/3 mi), combines modern comforts and conveniences—including Jacuzzi baths or sauna showers, and fax and computer facilities—with rural calm and Old World style and charm—wooden beams, vaulted brick ceilings, and tasteful furnishings. In summer meals are served on the terrace, overlooking the splendid garden. ✉ *Via Chemin Palma 30, Mussolente, 36061,* ☎ *0424/577407,* ℻ *0424/87687. 21 rooms and suites. Restaurant, air-conditioning. AE, DC, MC, V.*

$$$ ▥ **Belvedere.** This historic hotel has richly decorated public rooms with
★ period furnishings and Oriental rugs. A fireplace and piano music in the lounge and an excellent restaurant with a garden make for a very pleasant stay. The rooms are decorated in traditional Venetian or chic contemporary style. ✉ *Piazzale G. Giardino 14, 36061,* ☎ *0424/ 529845,* ℻ *0424/529849. 91 rooms. Restaurant, air-conditioning. AE, DC, MC, V.*

$$ ▥ **Al Castello.** In a restored town house at the foot of the medieval Civic Tower, the Cattapan family's Castello is a reasonable, attractive proposition. Rooms are well equipped and furnished simply. ✉ *Piazza Terraglio 19, 36061,* ☎ *0424/523462,* ℻ *0424/228665. 9 rooms. Café-bar, air-conditioning. AE, MC, V.*

Shopping

CERAMICS

Bassano del Grappa and nearby Nove are the best bets for ceramic items.

WROUGHT-IRON GOODS

A large number of shops in town feature wrought-iron and copper utensils, many of them made on the premises.

Asolo

★ ➋ *18 km (11 mi) east of Marostica, 11 km (7 mi) east of Bassano and 33 km (20½ mi) northwest of Treviso.*

The romantic, charming hillside hamlet of Asolo was the consolation prize of an exiled queen. At the end of the 15th century, Venetian-born Caterina Cornaro was sent here by Venice's doges to keep her from interfering with their administration of her former kingdom of Cyprus, which she had inherited. To soothe the pain of exile, she established a lively and brilliant court in Asolo. Over the centuries, Venetian aristocrats continued to build gracious villas on the hillside, and in the 19th century Asolo once again became the idyllic haunt of musicians, poets, and painters. From the outside, you can explore villas once inhabited by Robert Browning and the actress Eleanora Duse. Be warned that Asolo's dreamy Old World atmosphere disappears on holiday weekends when the crowds pour in.

In town center is **Piazza Maggiore,** with its Renaissance palaces and turn-of-the-century cafés. Uphill from the piazza, past Caterina's ruined castle and some Gothic-style houses, is the **Roman fortress** that stands on the summit.

Dining

$$ ✕ **Hosteria Ca'Derton.** The location is an attraction here: Ca'Derton is right on the main square. It has a pleasant, old-fashioned ambience, with early photos of Asolo on the walls and bouquets of dried flowers on each table. The friendly proprietor takes pride in the homemade pasta and desserts and offers a good selection of both local and international dishes. ⊠ *Piazza D'Annunzio 11,* ☎ *0423/952730. AE, DC, MC, V. Closed Tues., Feb. 15–28, and Aug. 17–31. No dinner Mon.*

Shopping

ANTIQUES MARKETS

There are **antiques markets** in the center of Asolo on the second Sunday of the month (except July and August).

Villa Barbaro

㉑ *7 km (4¼ mi) northeast of Asolo and 33 km (20½ mi) northwest of Treviso.*

Villa Barbaro is one of the most gracious Renaissance creations of Palladio. The fully furnished villa just outside the town of Maser is still inhabited by its owners, who make you slip heavy felt scuffs over your shoes to protect the highly polished floors. The elaborate stuccos and opulent frescoes by Paolo Veronese bring the 16th century to life. After La Rotonda, this is Palladio's greatest villa and is definitely worth going out of your way to see. ⊠ *Via Cornuda 2,* ☎ *0423/923004.* 🎟 *10,000 lire.* ☉ *Apr.–Sept., Tues. and weekends 3–6; Oct.–Mar., weekends 2:30–5.*

Dining and Lodging

$$ ✕ **Agnoletti.** In the town of Giavera del Montello near Maser, Agno-
★ letti is an 18th-century inn with Old World atmosphere and a lovely summer garden. The kitchen can produce an all-mushroom menu; but if you order something else, at least try the mushroom zuppa or *crostata* (tart). ⊠ *Giavera del Montello, Via della Vittoria 191,* ☎ *0422/776009. No credit cards. Closed Mon.–Tues., Jan. 1–20, and July 1–15.*

$$ ✕ **Da Bastian.** A good place to stop for lunch before visiting the Villa Barbaro, this contemporary spot has a pleasant garden for outdoor dining. Varied antipasto of pâtés, homemade vegetarian ravioli, and broiled meat with tasty sauces top the menu. ⊠ *Via Cornuda,* ☎ *0423/565400. No credit cards. Closed Thurs. and Aug. No dinner Wed.*

$$$$ 🏨 **Villa Cipriani.** This historic old villa is set in a romantic garden on the hillside and surrounded by other gracious country homes. Tastefully furnished with 19th-century antiques, it offers Old World atmosphere, all creature comforts, and attentive service. The excellent restaurant has a terrace overlooking the garden. ⊠ *Via Canova 298, 31011,* ☎ *0423/952166,* FAX *0423/952095. 31 rooms. Restaurant. AE, DC, MC, V.*

Treviso

㉒ *30 km (19 mi) north of Venice.*

The arcaded streets, frescoed houses, and channeled streams that run through the center of Treviso date mostly from the 15th century. The most important church in Treviso is **San Nicolò,** an impressive Gothic building with an ornate vaulted ceiling. San Nicolò has frescoes of the saints by 14th-century artist Tommaso da Modena on the columns. But the best is the remarkable series of 40 portraits of Dominican friars by the same artist in the seminary next door. They are astoundingly realistic, considering that some were painted as early as 1352, and include one of the earliest-known portraits of someone wearing glasses. ⊠ *Capitolo dei Domenicani, Seminario Vescovile, Via San Nicolò,* ☎ *0422/3247.* ☉ *Apr.–Sept., daily 8–12:30 and 3:30–7; Oct.–Mar., daily 8–12:30 and 3–5:30. To enter, ring at custodian's desk at seminary entrance.*

Inside the **Duomo,** on the altar of one of the chapels to the right, is an *Annunciation* by Titian. ⊠ *Piazza Duomo* ☉ *10:30–12:30.*

Piazza dei Signori is the heart of medieval Treviso and still the town's social center, with outdoor cafés and some impressive public buildings. One of these, the **Palazzo dei Trecento,** has a small alley leading behind it. Follow the alley for about 200 yards to the **Pescheria** (fish market), on an island in one of the small rivers that flow through town.

Dining and Lodging

$$$ ✕ **Da Alfredo.** Clones of this, from the original Toulà house, have
★   sprouted up in unlikely places—even Japan. This is your chance to enjoy the art nouveau decor and classic international cuisine for which it became famous. Among regional dishes are risotto *con funghi* (with mushrooms) or asparagus in season. For cooking, ambience, and service, it's one of the region's best. ⊠ *Via Collalto 26,* ☎ *0422/540275. AE, DC, MC, V. Closed Mon. and July 25–Aug. 25. No dinner Sun.*

$$ ✕ **Beccherie.** In a town known for good eating, this rustic inn is a fa-
★   vorite. It's in the heart of old Treviso, behind the main square, and there are tables outside for fair-weather dining under the portico. Specialties vary with the season. In winter, look for *crespelle al* radicchio (crepes with radicchio) and faraona in *salsa peverada* (a peppery sauce); spring heralds risotto with spring vegetables, stinco di *vitello* (veal), and *pasticcio di melanzane* (eggplant casserole). ⊠ *Piazza Ancilotto 10,* ☎ *0422/56601. AE, DC, MC, V. Closed Mon., and July 12–30. No dinner Sun.*

$$$$ 🏨 **Continental.** You'll find this hotel within the old city walls, between the train station and the sights. It is a traditional four-star hotel offering solid comfort. Rich fabrics and Oriental rugs lend an air of opulence. ⊠ *Via Roma 16, 31100,* ☎ *0422/411216,* FAX *0422/55054. 80 rooms. Air-conditioning, minibars, concierge. AE, DC, MC, V.*

$$ 🏨 **Al Fogher.** On the outskirts, Al Fogher is handy if you're traveling by car. This part of the Best Western chain has a bright contemporary look, with lots of modern art on the walls and room decor about equally divided between classic and modern. ⊠ *Viale della Repubblica 10, 31100,* ☎ *0422/432950,* FAX *0422/430391. 54 rooms. Restaurant, air-conditioning, minibars. AE, DC, MC, V.*

Outdoor Activities and Sports

HORSEBACK RIDING

Lancenigo (⊠ 6 km [3½ mi] north of Treviso, ☎ 0422/63357) provides riding and lessons for riding and jumping.

Shopping

LOCAL CRAFTS

Shops in Treviso feature wrought-iron and copper utensils.

Conegliano

③ *23 km (14 mi) north of Treviso and 71 km (44 mi) west of Udine.*

Conegliano is in the heart of wine-producing country. The town itself is attractive, with Venetian-style villas and frescoed houses, but the real attraction is the wine.

Lodging

$$ ☒ **Canon d'Oro.** The town's oldest inn, the Canon d'Oro is in a 15th-century building in a central location near the train station. The restaurant's tranquil decor lets you concentrate on the good food, mainly regional specialties such as risotto, Canon d'Oro gnocchi, baccalà alla vicentina, and *fegato alla veneziana* (liver with onions). ☒ *Via XX Settembre 129, 31015,* ☎ *0438/34246,* FAX *0438/34246. 19 rooms. Restaurant. AE, MC, V.*

En Route   Well marked and leading southeast from Conegliano, the **Strada del Vino Rosso** (Red Wine Road) winds its way through cabernet and merlot country along the Piave River, and there are dozens of places to stop, sample, and buy the red—and some rosé—wines. The road ends at Oderzo.

UDINE AND TRIESTE
Eastern Arc

Italy's northeastern corner is an ethnically jumbled cocktail of Italian, Slavic, and central European cultures. A potentially fascinating area, its peripheral position usually puts it beyond the range of most visitors. The old Hungarian port of Trieste—a symbol of Italian nationalist aspirations for so long—and the medieval city of Udine are perfect bases for local excursions.

Udine

㉔ *71 km (44 mi) east of Conegliano, 64 km (40 mi) north of Trieste and 100 km (62 mi) east of Venice.*

Udine, in Italy's Friuli–Venezia Giulia region, commands a view of the surrounding plain and the Alpine foothills; according to legend, it stands on a mound erected by Attila the Hun so he could watch the burning of the important Roman center of Aquileia to the south. Udine flourished in the Middle Ages, thanks to its good location for trade and the rights it gained from the local patriarch to hold regular markets. There is a distinct Venetian feel to the city, noticeable in the architecture of Piazza della Libertà, under the stern gaze of the lion of St. Mark, symbol of Venetian power.

The **Museo Archeologico Nazionale** is the best place to trace the history of the area and the importance of Cividale and Udine in the formative period following the collapse of the Roman Empire. Among the interesting exhibits is a large collection of Lombard artifacts, including weapons, jewelry, and domestic wares from this warrior race, which swept into what is now Italy in the 6th century. ☒ *Piazza del Duomo,* ☎ *0432/700700.* 🎫 *5,000 lire.* ☉ *Mon.–Sat. 9:30–2, Sun. 9:30–1.*

Dining and Lodging

$$ ✗ **Alla Buona Vite.** This classic restaurant in the center of town specializes in seafood. *Tagliolini dello chef* (noodles with a creamy scampi sauce) and *rombo al limone e capperi* (turbot with lemon and capers) are among the many choices here. ☒ *Via Treppo 10,* ☎ *0432/21053. AE, DC, MC, V. Closed Mon. and Aug. No dinner Sun.*

$$ ✗ **Antica Maddalena.** Just a few steps from Udine's pretty Piazza del-
★ l'Unità you'll find this elegant eating place, defined by its owner as a deluxe trattoria. Lots of warm wood tones, fresh flowers, and stained glass complement a menu of regional and Italian specialties, among them zuppa di funghi porcini, gnocchi *con zucca e ricotta* (with squash

and ricotta cheese), and carpaccio *di salmone con rucola* (with chopped salmon with lemon and arugula). ⊠ *Via Pelliccerie 4,* ☏ *0432/25111. AE, DC, MC, V. Closed Sun. and Mon., 2 wks in Feb., and 2 wks in Aug.*

$$ ✕ **Trattoria al Lepre.** A characteristic *focolare* (hearth) in one of the dining rooms is a symbol of traditional local cooking, and that's what you'll enjoy in this simple establishment. The specialties include tagliatelle con funghi and stinco di maiale. ⊠ *Via Poscolle 27,* ☏ *0432/ 295798. AE, DC, MC, V. Closed Sun. and 10 days in Aug.*

$$$ 🏨 **Astoria Hotel Italia.** Centrally located, the Italia offers soundproofed, air-conditioned rooms furnished in traditional style. Public rooms feature Venetian glass chandeliers and comfortable armchairs. ⊠ *Piazza XX Settembre 24, 33100,* ☏ *0432/505091,* FAX *0432/509070. 80 rooms. Restaurant, minibars. AE, DC, MC, V.*

En Route From Udine, the road eastward follows the coast under the shadow of the huge geological formation called the Carso, a large, barren expanse of limestone that forms a giant ledge, most of which is across the border in Slovenia. Italian territory goes only a few miles inland in this strip, and Italy's small Slovenian minority ekes out an agricultural existence in the region, which has changed hands countless times since the final days of Imperial Rome.

Cividale

㉕ *17 km (11 mi) east of Udine on S54.*

Cividale dates from the time of Julius Caesar. It is popularly supposed (particularly by locals) that it was built by Caesar when he was commander of Roman legions in the area. The city straddles the River Natisone and contains many examples of Venetian Gothic buildings, particularly the **Duomo** and the **Palazzo Comunale.** ⊠ *Piazza Duomo,* ☏ *0432/731144.* ⊘ *Apr.–Sept., Mon.–Sat. 9:30–noon and 3–7, Sun. 3–6:45; Oct.–Mar., Mon.–Sat. 9:30–noon and 3–6, Sun. 3–5:45.*

Miramare Castle

★ ㉖ *7 km (4¼ mi) north of Trieste, 78 km (48 mi) south of Udine and 156 km (97 mi) east of Venice.*

This seafront castle is a 19th-century extravaganza in white stone, built for the Archduke Maximilian of Hapsburg (brother of Emperor Franz Josef). Maximilian spent a brief, happy time here until Napoléon III of France took Trieste from the Hapsburgs and sent the poor archduke packing. He was given the title of Emperor of Mexico in 1864 as a compensation, but met his death before a Mexican firing squad in 1867. You can visit the lush grounds and admire the memorable views over the Adriatic. ☏ *040/224143.* 🎫 *Free; guided tour 10,000 lire.* ⊘ *Grounds daily, 9:30–hr before sunset; castle Mon.–Sat. 9:30–1, Sun. 9:30–12:30; call for afternoon hrs June–July.*

Trieste

㉗ *64 km (40 mi) southeast of Udine and 163 km (101 mi) east of Venice.*

Surrounded by rugged countryside and beautiful coastline, Trieste is built on a hillside above what was once the chief port of the Austro-Hungarian Hapsburg Empire. Typical of Trieste are its turn-of-the-century cafés, much like Vienna's coffeehouses; these are social and cultural centers of the city, and much-beloved refuges from the city's prevailing northeast wind, the "bora."

The sidewalk cafés on the vast seaside **Piazza dell'Unità d'Italia** are popular meeting places in the summer months. The square is similar to Piazzetta San Marco in Venice; both are focal points of architectural interest that command the best views of the sea. Behind **Palazzo Comunale** (Town Hall) (⊠ At the end of Piazza dell'Unità d'Italia), going away from the sea, steps lead uphill, following the city's pattern of upward expansion from its roots as a coastal fishing port in Roman times.

Civico Museo Revoltella e Galleria d'Arte Moderna was founded in 1872 when the Venetian Baron Revoltella left the city his palazzo, library, and art collection. The gallery has one of the most important collections of 19th- and 20th-century art in Italy, with Italian artists particularly well represented. ⊠ *Via Diaz,* ☎ *040/311361.* ▣ *5,000 lire.* ☉ *Mon. and Wed.–Sat. 10–1 and 3–8, Sun. 10–1.*

The solid Romanesque construction of **San Silvestro** church dates from the 11th century. Just beyond it is the Baroque extravagance of **Santa Maria Maggiore,** which backs onto a network of alleys closed to traffic. ⊠ *Via S. Silvestro.* ☉ *Mon.–Sat. 10–1.*

The 14th-century **Cattedrale di San Giusto** incorporates two much older churches, one dating from as far back as the 5th century. The exterior adds even more to the jumble of styles involved by using fragments of Roman tombs and temples: You can see these most clearly on the pillars of the main doorway. The highlights of the interior are the 13th-century mosaics and frescoes. ⊠ *Piazza Cattedrale.* ☉ *Weekdays 9:30–4:30, Sun. mass.*

From the hilltop **Castello di San Giusto** you get some of the best views of the area. In the 15th century this castle was built by the Venetians, who always had an eye for the best vantage point in the cities they conquered or controlled. The Hapsburgs, subsequent rulers of Trieste, enlarged it to its present size. Some of the best exhibits in the **Castle Museum** are the displays of weaponry and armor. ⊠ *Piazza Cattedrale 3,* ☎ *040/313636.* ▣ *Museum 2,000 lire.* ☉ *Grounds daily to sunset; museum Tues.–Sun. 9–1.*

Piazza della Borsa is the square containing Trieste's original stock exchange, the **Borsa Vecchia,** a neoclassical building now serving as the chamber of commerce. The **statue of Leopold I** is at one end of the square.

OFF THE
BEATEN PATH

GROTTA GIGANTE – This is the largest cave in the world open to tourists: it is more than 300 ft high, 900 ft long, and 200 ft wide, with spectacular stalactites and stalagmites. Reserve 45 minutes for the tour. It is not far from Trieste, about 15 km (9 mi) north of the city (take Tram 2 from Piazza Oberdan). ☎ 040/630464. ▣ 10,000 lire. ☉ Apr.–Sept., tours every ½ hr 9–noon and 2–7; Oct. and Mar., tours every ½ hr 9–noon and 2–5; Nov.–Feb., tours every hr 10–noon and 2:30–4:30. Closed Mon.

Dining and Lodging

$$ ✕ **Suban.** Though in the hills on the edge of town, this historic trattoria is worth the taxi ride. The rustic decor is rich in dark wood, stone, ★ and wrought iron, and you'll find typical regional fare with imaginative variations. Among the specialties are *jota carsolina* (typical local minestrone made of cabbage, potatoes, and beans) and duck breast in Tokay sauce. ⊠ *Via Emilio Comici 2,* ☎ *040/54368. AE, DC, MC, V. Closed Mon.–Tues. and Aug. 1–20.*

$$$–$$$$ ▥ **Duchi d'Aosta.** On the spacious Piazza dell'Unità d'Italia, this hotel is beautifully furnished in Venetian–Renaissance style and lavished with

Old World atmosphere. Its restaurant, Harry's Grill, is one of the city's most elegant. ⊠ *Piazza dell'Unità d'Italia 2, 34121,* ☎ *040/7600011,* FAX *040/366092. 52 rooms. Restaurant, bar. AE, DC, MC, V.*

$$–$$$ 🖫 **Colombia.** Unpretentious but adequate, this small hotel caters mainly to a business clientele. There is no restaurant, but there's a typical beer cellar restaurant close by. ⊠ *Via della Geppa 18, 34121,* ☎ *040/369333,* FAX *040/369644. 40 rooms. AE, DC, MC, V.*

Nightlife and the Arts

Contact the tourist information office (⊠ Stazione Centrale, ☎ 040/ 420182) for further details on events.

MUSIC

Trieste holds an open-air operetta festival each summer (July–August) and an opera season in winter (October–April).

Outdoor Activities and Sports

GOLF

At press time (spring 1997), the nine-hole **Golf Club Trieste** (⊠ Padriciano 80, 6 km [4 mi] from town center, ☎ 040/226159) was adding another nine holes to its course.

Shopping

Trieste's busy shopping street, **Corso Italia,** is reached from Piazza della Borsa.

ANTIQUES

There are antiques markets on the streets of the city's old center on the third Sunday of summer months until November. Trieste has some 60 antiques dealers, jewelers, and secondhand shops, and a large antiques fair is held in the city in early November.

VENETIAN ARC A TO Z

Arriving and Departing

By Car

The main access roads to the Venetian Arc from southern Italy are both linked to the **A1** (Autostrada del Sole), which connects Bologna, Florence, and Rome. They are the **A13**, which culminates in Padua, and the **A22**, which passes through Verona in a north–south direction. The road linking the region from east to west is the **A4**, which is the primary route from Milan to as far as Trieste.

By Plane

The main airport serving the Venetian Arc is **Marco Polo** (☎ 041/ 2609260) in Venice (☞ Venice A to Z *in* Chapter 5), which handles international and domestic flights to the region. A few European airlines schedule flights to **Villafranca Airport** (⊠ 11 km [7 mi] west of Verona, ☎ 045/8095666), also served by a number of charter flights. A regular bus service connects Villafranca with Verona's Porta Nuova railway station.

Treviso Airport (⊠ About 32 km [20 mi] north of Venice, ☎ 0422/22667) is also served by charter flights. Flights to Treviso usually include transportation from the airport to Venice or other destinations; otherwise there is a local bus service to Treviso every half hour during the day, or a taxi will come from Treviso, only 6 km (4 mi) away, to pick you up.

There are domestic flights to **Ronchi del Legionari Airport** (⊠ 35 km [22 mi] north of Trieste, ☎ 0481/773224), linked with Via Miramare in the center of town by a regular bus service.

By Train

The most important train routes arriving from the southern part of Italy will stop almost every hour in either Verona, Padua, or Venezia. From northern Italy and the rest of Europe, trains usually enter via Milan to the west or through Porta Nuova station in Verona.

Getting Around

By Bus

There are interurban and interregional connections throughout the Veneto and Friuli. Local tourist offices may be able to provide details of timetables and routes; otherwise contact the local bus station, or in some cases the individual bus companies operating from the station.

Bus stations: Bassano (✉ Piazzale Trento, ☎ 0424/30850). **Padua** (✉ Piazzale Boschetti, ☎ 049/8206811). **Treviso** (✉ Via Lungosile Mattei, ☎ 0422/412222). **Trieste** (✉ Piazza Liberta, ☎ 040/425001). **Venice** (✉ Piazzale Roma, ☎ 041/5287886 for buses to Brenta Riviera, Padova, and Treviso; ☎ 041/5205530 for buses to Conegliano and Udine and for buses covering the Conegliano–Vittorio Veneto–Cortina route). **Verona** (✉ Porta Nuova, ☎ 045/8004129). **Vicenza** (✉ Viale Milano 138, ☎ 0444/544333).

By Car

The main highway in the region is **A4,** which connects Verona, Padua, and Venice with Trieste. The distance from Verona, in the west, to Trieste is 263 km (163 mi). Branches link A4 with Treviso (**A27**), Pordenone (**A28**), and Udine (**A23**).

By Train

To the west of Venice, on the main line running across the north of Italy, are Padua (20 min), Vicenza (1 hr), and Verona (1½ hrs); to the east is Trieste (2 hrs). Local trains link Venice to Bassano del Grappa (1 hr), Padua to Bassano del Grappa (1 hr), Vicenza to Treviso (1 hr), and Udine to Trieste (1 hr). Treviso and Udine both lie on the main line from Venice to Treviso, on which Eurocity trains continue to Vienna and Prague.

Contacts and Resources

Car Rental

Avis: Padua (✉ Piazza Stazione 1, ☎ 049/664198). **Trieste** (✉ Piazza della Libertà, c/o Silos, ☎ 040/421521, and at the airport, ☎ 0481/777085). **Udine** (✉ Viale Leopardi 5/A, ☎ 0432/501149). **Verona** (✉ Stazione FS/train station, ☎ 045/26636). **Vicenza** (✉ Viale Milano 88, ☎ 0444/321622). **Hertz: Padua** (✉ Piazza Stazione 5, ☎ 049/657877). **Trieste** (✉ Piazza della Libertà, c/o Silos, ☎ 040/422122; ✉ Airport, ☎ 0481/777025). **Udine** (✉ Via Crispi 19, ☎ 0432/609160). **Verona** (✉ Stazione FS, ☎ 045/25832). **Vicenza** (✉ Viale Europa 50, ☎ 0444/321313).

Emergencies

Police, Ambulance, Fire (☎ 113). For first aid, ask for *"pronto soccorso,"* and be prepared to give your address. **Doctors and Dentists** (☎ 112). **Ospedale Civile e Policlinico dell'Università** (✉ Padua, ☎ 049/8211111). **Late-Night Pharmacies** take turns staying open late and on Sunday. For information on which is open, call ☎ 192.

Guided Tours

Many of the best tours begin and end in Venice because so much of the region is accessible from there (☞ Venice A to Z *in* Chapter 5). The **Burchiello excursion boat** makes an all-day villa tour along the Brenta

Canal, but the trip is expensive and not necessarily the best way to see the villas, since so much time is spent on the boat. For those who prefer to go it alone, **American Express** (☞ Travel Agencies, *below*) suggests itineraries that can be followed by rented car, with or without a hired driver, or it is possible to follow the Brenta quite easily by local train and bus. **Robe Vicentine** (☎ FAX 0444/585168) offers tours around the Vicenza area, with guided visits to local villas, Renaissance-style lunches and dinners, and other entertainments in Palladian villas. Local tourist offices will be able to put you in contact with the **Tourist Guides Association** or provide you with a list of authorized guides, for whom there is an official tariff rate.

Trieste and Vicenza offer special weekend package deals ("T for you" and "Vicenza Weekend") that include discounts in hotels and restaurants, free or reduced-price entrance to a selection of the cities' main tourist attractions, and some guided tours. Contact the Trieste Tourist office and/or the Conzorsio di Promozione Turistica "Vicenza è" (☞ *below*).

Travel Agencies

For agencies in Venice, *see* Venice A to Z *in* Chapter 5.

Padua (⊠ Tiarè Viaggi/American Express representative, Via Risorgimento 20, ☎ 049/666133). **Trieste** (⊠ Paterniti Viaggi/American Express representative, Corso Cavour 7, ☎ 040/366161, FAX 040/368888). **Verona** (⊠ Fabretto Viaggi, American Express representative, Corso Porta Nuova 11, ☎ 045/8009040, FAX 045/8009045).

Visitor Information

Veneto Regional Tourist Office (⊠ Palazzo Sceriman, 168 Lista di Spagna, Cannaregio, 30121 Venice, ☎ 041/2792644).

Padua (⊠ Stazione Ferroviaria train station, ☎ 049/8752077; ⊠ Museo Civico Eremitani, ☎ 049/875-1153; ⊠ Prato delle Valle, ☎ 049/8753087). **Treviso** (⊠ Via Toniolo 41, ☎ 0422/547632, FAX 0422/541397). **Trieste** (⊠ Stazione Centrale, ☎ 040/420182). **Udine** (⊠ Piazza Primo Maggio 7, ☎ 0432/295972). **Verona** (⊠ Via Leoncino 61, ☎ 045/592828; ⊠ Piazza delle Erbe 42, ☎ 045/8030086; ⊠ Railway station, ☎ 045/8000861). **Vicenza** (⊠ Piazza Matteotti 12, ☎ 0444/320854; ⊠ Conzorsio di Promozione Turistica "Vicenza è," ☎ 0444/327141).

7 Italian Riviera

Genoa, the Cinque Terre, and Portofino

It was the Italians who perfected il dolce far niente—the sweet art of idleness—and all signs indicate they did it here, in the region called Liguria, better known as the Italian Riviera. To the west and east of Genoa, an art-filled city of understated splendor, the twin rivieras bask in the sun, dotted with seaside resorts and quaint villages. Like pearls in a string, the coastal towns of Rapallo, the Cinque Terre, and Portovenere glisten and glow—but everyone agrees Portofino wins the beauty contest.

THE ITALIAN RIVIERA IS JUST PLAIN GLAMOROUS, an oxymoronic statement, but how else can one encapsulate the cosmopolitan flavor of the area, its blend of the provincial and smart set, primitive and old-fashioned, luxurious and up-to-date?

Updated by
Barbara Walsh
Angelillo

Here, the eye is caught by the contours of a coastline that follows a serpentine arc from Ventimiglia to La Spezia; by the Ligurian Alps, which plunge sheerly or slope gradually to the sea; by the style and color of the resorts, the busy ports, and the stately yachts outlined against the horizon. For centuries, the region's charm has inspired scenic-hungry poets and artists; here is where Shelley praised the "soft blue Spezian bay"; here is where Lord Byron dared to swim from Portovenere to Lerici. Today, still, travelers searching to escape from the conceits of civilization head for the Italian Riviera for a cure. Mellowed by the balmy breezes blowing off the sea, they bask in the sun, then explore the tiny coastal towns where many things that are splendiferous haven't made it into the guidebooks yet.

Liguria's narrow strip of mountain-protected coastline varies considerably between the two rivieras. The Riviera di Ponente (western Riviera), which runs from the French border to Genoa, has protected bays and wide sandy beaches and is generally more developed and commercialized than its counterpart to the east, the Riviera di Levante. There, starting at Genoa, the coastline becomes steeper, rocky, and it's punctuated by minuscule bays and inlets.

If this coastline is a necklace, hung with jewels, the most scintillating pendant is the Portofino promontory. The mere sight of the village—it is the most photographed village in the world—is a pleasure in itself. If you pull up to the wharf by boat, chances are you'll shoot all your film before you disembark. Pastel houses frame the square, lending an air of festivity that becomes sheer enchantment at sunset when the houses are reflected in the dancing waters of the harbor. Other than the village square, several picturesque churches, and a castle, there aren't that many things to see in Portofino. The people here are the real attractions—it was, after all, Bogie and Bacall and Taylor and Burton who put the place on the map.

Farther along the coast is a second peninsula; here the road weaves inland, leaving the visitor to hike or take a train or boat to explore the Cinque Terre, a collective community of five fishing villages perched on bluffs above the sea. This area is the Italian Riviera at its unbuttoned best.

Set in the heart of the region is Genoa, Italy's largest port, which every American schoolchild knows as the birthplace of Christopher Columbus. That famous explorer was neither the first nor the last in the long line of seafaring Genoans. Today, most visitors come to Liguria less to see the art treasures of Genoa than for the region's mild climate, fine seafood, and coastal villages. But then relaxed Liguria is the sort of place where knowing the difference between scrub pine and cypress means more than knowing the difference between Rococo and Renaissance.

Pleasures and Pastimes

Dining

Liguria's cooking holds some surprises. It employs all sorts of seafood—especially anchovies, sea bass, squid, and octopus—but it makes even wider use of vegetables and the aromatic herbs that grow wild on the hillsides, together with liberal amounts of olive oil and garlic. Pesto is Liguria's classic pasta sauce; it's made from pine nuts, garlic, oil, cheese, and a type of basil that grows only along the coastal hills. You will also find *pansoti* (ravioli) and *trofie* (a chewy short pasta) with *salsa di noci,* a delicate sauce made of garlic, walnuts, and cream that, like pesto, is pounded in a mortar. *Vitello* (veal) is the most popular meat; *cima alla genovese,* breast of veal stuffed with a mixture of eggs and vegetables, is served as a cold cut. You should also try the succulent *agnello* (lamb) and fresh wild mushrooms picked from the hills.

When not snacking on pizza sold by the slice or by weight, the Genoese and other Ligurians eat *torta pasqualina* (vegetable pie), or *focaccia,* a salty, pizzalike bread that goes well with a glass of wine. Local vineyards tend to produce mainly light and refreshing whites, such as Pigato, Vermentino Ligure, and Cinque Terre. Rossese and Dolceacqua are good reds. Desserts are less rich than those in other Italian regions; *panna cotta,* a milk custard, and *gelato* (ice cream) are favorites.

CATEGORY	COST*
$$$$	over 85,000 lire
$$$	65,000–85,000 lire
$$	35,000–65,000 lire
$	under 35,000 lire

Prices are per person, including house wine, service, and tax.

Hiking and Walking

The hilly terrain makes walking strenuous but rewarding, with stunning views of the sea and little villages dotting the coast. Portofino invites walking, whether you opt for the classic and relatively easy walk from Portofino to the Abbey of San Fruttuoso or the more challenging hike from Ruta to the top of Mount Portofino. You can walk from one to another of the five Cinque Terre fishing towns, thumbing your nose at the tourists on the sightseeing boats. Everywhere in Liguria roads, mule paths, or footpaths lead into the hills, where you can discover the region at its unspoiled best.

Lodging

If you want to delve into Genoa's artistic and historic treasures, stay in the city and make it your base for exploring the rest of the region on day-trips by train, bus, or car. If you want to take a more relaxed approach, settle into a resort and make your day trips from there, including one to Genoa. When choosing your lodgings in Genoa you should be aware that this is ranked as one of Italy's noisiest cities; make sure your windows are double-glazed (*doppi vetri*). Because visitors generally prefer to stay in the towns and resorts along the coast, Genoa has relatively few hotels, and they tend to be geared more to the needs of business travelers than to tourists. Resort hotels are obviously the places to go for sea views, recreation facilities, and a vacation atmosphere. Reserve ahead year-round for Genoa and during peak Easter and summer seasons for resorts. The best bargains and the warmest welcomes can be found in the less-visited inland areas: there are few hotels in this part of Liguria, but many of them are family-run and special because of it.

CATEGORY	COST*
$$$$	over 300,000 lire
$$$	170,000–300,000 lire
$$	110,000–170,000 lire
$	under 110,000 lire

Prices are for a standard double room for two, including service and tax.

Sailing

With so much coastline (350 km/217 mi) and so many pretty little harbors, it's no wonder that the Riviera attracts pleasure craft of all shapes and sizes, from rowboats to megayachts. San Remo, Rapallo, Santa Margherita Ligure, Chiavari, Finale Ligure, and Sestri Levante have large, well-equipped marinas. Every year in October, Genoa hosts a mammoth international boat show.

Exploring the Italian Riviera

All of Liguria's cities, towns, and resorts dot the elongated coastal strip and are connected by a highway stretching some 260 km (161 mi) from Ventimiglia on the French border to La Spezia and Sarzana. At the center, Genoa separates the western (Ponente) from the eastern (Levante) Riviera, forming two distinct geographic areas to explore (three, including Genoa itself). The hilly and mountainous hinterland, very different in scenery and character from the Riviera, can be explored conveniently from towns along the coast. From the sea, a series of narrow valleys extend inland, giving access to the sparsely settled interior.

Getting around the Riviera is an expedient affair, though the pace in the Riviera is leisurely. The freedom of a car is indispensable, but public transportation in the region is excellent, with every sight of interest reachable by train and/or bus. You could drive from one end of the Riviera to the other on the autostrada in less than three hours; a fast train takes less than two hours to cover the same route. The A10 and A12 autostrada on either side of Genoa skirt the coast, avoiding local traffic on the old Via Aurelia, laid out by the ancient Romans. The Via Aurelia, now known as national highway S1, connects practically all the towns along the coast. If you don't have a car, use local trains to get from one place to another along the coast and local buses to go inland.

Numbers in the text correspond to numbers in the margin and on the Italian Riviera and Genoa maps.

Great Itineraries

In seven days you can visit the prettiest resorts and fishing villages, spend a day or two in Genoa, and perhaps make an excursion inland. Five days would allow you to see the highlights, but you will probably want to see Genoa in a day so that you can visit more of the smaller towns. In three days you will be able to see Genoa and perhaps two major resorts and two or three of the smaller, more picturesque towns.

IF YOU HAVE 3 DAYS

Tour time is limited, and you should concentrate on select towns. On your first day begin on the eastern Riviera di Levante. Stop at the delightful fishing villages of **Portovenere** ④ and **Camogli** ③, detouring for a look at romantic **Portofino** ㉞, the jewel in the Riviera's crown. For a more casual resort atmosphere, opt instead for **Rapallo** ㉜ or 🏨 **Santa Margherita Ligure** ㉝. On the second day see 🏨 **Genoa** ⑧–㉙, exploring the historic center, the old harbor, and the **Acquario** ㉙, Europe's best. The western Riviera should be the focus of the third day; head for glitzy **San Remo** ④ or the more sedate resort of **Bordighera** ③, but allow about half a day along the way to visit the medieval centers of Albenga, Cervo, and Taggia. Naturally, you should follow this itinerary in the opposite direction if you are arriving in the region from the west.

IF YOU HAVE 5 DAYS

You can organize your itinerary to take you from one end of the Riviera to the other or you can start in Genoa and head east or west from there. If you make Genoa your base you can alternate excursions along the coast and into the interior with city sightseeing. On your first day explore ⌖ **Genoa** ⑧–㉙. If the day is a clear one, take the **Granarolo funicular** ⑨ to the top for an aerial view of the city. On the second day head west, making a detour to Spotorno, and proceed to Noli, one of the best-preserved medieval towns on the entire Riviera. Then see the medieval delights of Cervo before going on to sophisticated ⌖ **San Remo** ④ and palm-studded ⌖ **Bordighera** ③, staying over in either re-sort town. Basque in the sun on the third day or venture inland to the well-preserved medieval villages of Dolcedo and Valloria instead. On the fourth and fifth days explore the eastern Riviera, starting with stately **Nervi** ㉚, near Genoa. The Portofino promontory has multiple attrac-tions, from the fishing village of **Camogli** ㉛ to chichi **Portofino** ㉞; don't miss the remarkable sea views from the hamlets of San Rocco, San Niccolò, and Punta Chiappa, accessible by foot from Camogli. You can overnight in a stylish resort such as ⌖ **Santa Margherita Ligure** ㉝ or ⌖ **Rapallo** ㉜; alternatively, you can go for lower-key ⌖ **Sestri Lev-ante** ㊱, an industrial town with a charming medieval center, or the se-cluded town of ⌖ **Levanto** ㊳, closer to the Cinque Terre. If you have time on your fifth day, a daylong excursion by train or boat to the five rock-perched coastal villages of the **Cinque Terre** ㊴ is highly recom-mended. Proceed to ⌖ **Portovenere** ㊶. Then, bypass industrialized La Spezia and wind up in the pretty port village of **Lerici** ㊷.

IF YOU HAVE 7 DAYS

If you begin your visit of the region in ⌖ **Genoa** ⑧–㉙, spend two days there; do take the **Granarolo funicular** ⑨ and a boat tour of the port. You will have time for an excursion to **Nervi** ㉚, studded with palatial old mansions, gorgeous gardens, and a promenade cut into the rock overhanging the sea. On the third day head west from Genoa, either working your way gradually to Ventimiglia or going directly to Ven-timiglia and then heading back to Genoa. On the western Riviera, see the extraordinary cactus collection in the **Giardino Hanbury** ① near **Ven-timiglia** ②, then turn inland to the medieval town of Dolceacqua, only 10 km (6 mi) away. If it strikes your fancy, stop for tea in genteel **Bor-dighera** ③ before continuing on to the much busier and more commercial resort of ⌖ **San Remo** ④; stay overnight in San Remo or ⌖ **Finale Lig-ure** ⑤. On the fourth day, if you're driving, take the coast road (S1) from Finale Ligure to Noli and Spotorno. If you don't have a car, a bus from Spotorno takes you to Noli, where time has practically stood still since the Middle Ages. With the exception of Albisola Marina and Pegli, you can skip the industrialized coast between **Savona** ⑥ and Genoa.

On the fifth day, head east from Genoa on the A12 autostrada or on the slower S1 highway to the Riviera di Levante to see the offhand charm of **Camogli** ㉛. Take the turnoff for **Rapallo** ㉜ and **Santa Margherita Ligure** ㉝ and, if the traffic isn't heavy, head for ⌖ **Portofino** ㉞. At the height of the season an excursion boat to Portofino from Camogli, Santa Margherita Ligure, or Rapallo may avoid the traffic jams on the nar-row access road. You may want to consider staying in ⌖ **Chiavari** ㉟, a good hub for forays into the mountains on your sixth day, or even in ⌖ **Levanto** ㊳, where you can make a detour to the **Cinque Terre** ㊴. On the seventh day head east to **La Spezia** ㊵ and look for signs to **Por-tovenere** ㊶. Doubling back to La Spezia, take the coast road to charm-ing **Lerici** ㊷. The La Spezia turnoff on the A12 and S1 highways is only about 15 km (9 mi) from the border of Tuscany.

When to Tour the Italian Riviera

Though shops, cafés, clubs, and restaurants stay open late in resorts during high season (at Easter and during the summer), during the rest of the year they close early. Many hotels and restaurants in resort towns

close from November through March. Avoid driving through Ventimiglia
on Friday, the busy market day.

RIVIERA DI PONENTE

The Riviera di Ponente stretches from Ventimiglia on the French border to Genoa. For the most part it is an unbroken chain of popular
beach resorts sheltered from the north by the Ligurian and Maritime
Alps, mountain walls that guarantee mild winters and a long growing
season—resulting in its other nickname, the *Riviera dei Fiori* (Riviera
of Flowers). Actually the name is prettier than the sight of once-verdant hillsides now swathed in plastic to form immense greenhouses.
Many towns on the western Riviera have suffered from an epidemic
of overdevelopment, but most have preserved their historic cores, usually their most interesting features. In major resorts large new marinas cater to the pleasure-craft crowd. The Riviera di Ponente has both
sandy and pebbly beaches with some quiet bays. Varazze, with a wide,
sandy beach and many tall palm trees, is perhaps the last pleasant beach
resort on the Riviera di Ponente before greater Genoa's industrial influence takes over.

Giardino Hanbury

★ ❶ *6 km (4 mi) east of Ventimiglia, 165 km (102 mi) southwest of Genoa,
23 km (14 mi) west of San Remo.*

Mortola Inferiore, only 2 km (1¼ mi) from the French border, is site
of the world-famous Giardino Hanbury (Hanbury Garden), one of the
largest botanical gardens in Italy. Planned and planted by a wealthy
English merchant, Sir Thomas Hanbury, and his botanist brother,
Daniel, in 1867, the terraced gardens contain a variety of species from
five continents—including many palms and succulents (plants of the
cactus group). There are panoramic views of the sea from the gardens,
which descend right down to the beach. ⊠ *Giardino Hanbury, Mortola Inferiore,* ☎ *0184/229507.* 🎟 *10,000 lire.* ⊙ *June–Sept., daily
9–6; Oct.–May, Thurs.–Tues. 10–4.*

OFF THE
BEATEN PATH
BALZI ROSSI CAVES – At the French border, 7 km (4 mi) from Ventimiglia
and 2 km (1¼ mi) from the Giardino Hanbury, are the Balzi Rossi (Red
Rocks), caves in the sheer rock in which prehistoric humans left traces of
their lives and magic rites. You can visit the caves and a small museum
containing some of the objects found there. ☎ *0184/38113.* 🎟 *4,000
lire.* ⊙ *July–Aug., Tues.–Sun. 9–1 and 2:30–6:30; Sept.–June, 9–1 and
2:30–6.*

Ventimiglia

❷ *6 km (4 mi) east of Mortola Inferiore, 159 km (98 mi) southwest of
Genoa, 17 km (10 mi) west of San Remo, 40 km (25 mi) northeast of
Nice.*

Ventimiglia was once a pre-Roman settlement known as Albintimil-
ium and contains some important archaeological remains, such as a
2nd-century AD amphitheater. A vital trade center for hundreds of
years, Ventimiglia declined in prestige as Genoa grew and is now little more than a frontier town that lives on tourism and the cultivation
of flowers. The town is divided in two by the Roia River. The **Città Vecchia** (Old City), on the western side, is what you'll see first: it is a well-
preserved and typical medieval town. The 11th-century **Duomo**
(Cathedral) has a Gothic portal dating from 1222. Walk up **Via del**

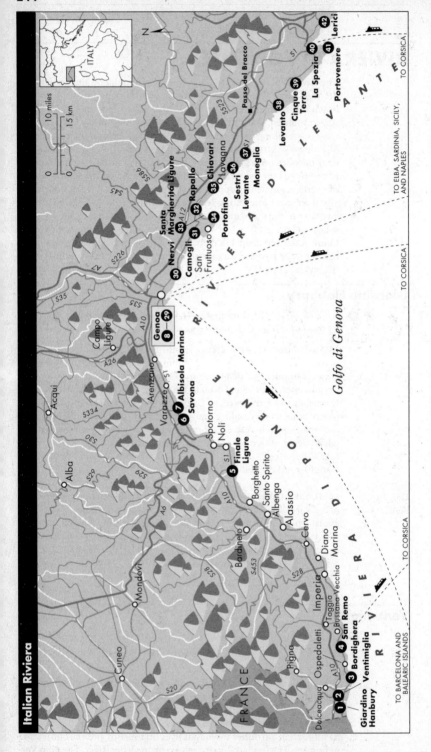

Italian Riviera

244

Capo to the ancient walls, which offer fine views of the coast. On Friday the large flower market, open to trade only, is chaotic with bargain hunters from France, creating traffic gridlock; it's best to avoid it on that day.

<table>
<tr><td>OFF THE
BEATEN PATH</td><td>**DOLCEACQUA** – From Ventimiglia, a provincial road swings up the Nervia River valley to this lovely sounding medieval town, whose name translates as Sweetwater, with its ruined castle. Beyond is **Pigna,** another medieval village built in concentric circles on a hilltop.</td></tr>
</table>

Lodging

$$ ★ **La Riserva.** Just 5 km (3 mi) west of Ventimiglia, but more than 1,100 ft above sea level, is the village of Castel d'Appio, where you'll find this innlike establishment. The staff is very helpful, providing, for example, regular lifts into town for those without cars. But there's no real need to leave La Riserva; apart from its excellent restaurant, it offers numerous activities and a lovely terrace for drinks or sunbathing or candlelight dinners. Full-board rates are a good value. Try for a room facing the sea. ⊠ *Castel d'Appio, 18039,* ☎ *0184/229533,* FAX *0184/229712. 29 rooms. Restaurant, bar, pool. AE, DC, MC, V. Closed Sept. 30–Easter (except Dec. 22–Jan. 6).*

Outdoor Activities and Sports

CYCLING

The Riviera's hilly terrain is a challenge for cyclists; to join them, contact the **Ventimiglia Cycling Club** (⊠ Corso Genoa 112, ☎ 00184/352879).

Bordighera

❸ *5 km (3 mi) east of Ventimiglia, 12 km (7½ mi) west of San Remo, 115 km (71 mi) southwest of Genoa.*

Bordighera, on a large promontory with lush vegetation, wears its genteel past as a famous winter resort with unstudied ease. A large English colony, still very much in evidence, settled here in the second half of the 19th century, attracted by the mild climate. Bordighera is an elegant town with a fin-de-siècle atmosphere; expect to find people taking afternoon tea in the cafés. This garden spot was the first town in Europe to grow date palms, and its citizens still have the exclusive right to provide the Vatican with palm fronds for Easter celebrations. Walk along the **Lungomare Argentina,** the magnificent mile-long seafront promenade, beginning at the western end of the town, for a good view westward to the French Côte d'Azur. Thanks partly to its year-round English residents, Bordighera does not close down entirely in the winter like many Riviera resorts. With plenty of fine hotels and restaurants, it makes a good base for excursions and is quieter and less commercial than San Remo.

Dining and Lodging

$$–$$$ ✕ **La Reserve Restaurant.** This traditional and informal trattoria has access to the beach and excellent views of the sea from the dining room. There are even changing rooms for anyone who wants a post-lunch dip. Concentrate on the seafood here: specialties are seafood ravioli *al finocchio selvatico* (with wild fennel) and a grilled seafood assortment. ⊠ *Via Arziglia 20,* ☎ *0184/261322. AE, DC, MC, V. Closed Mon. (except July–Aug.) and Nov.*

$$–$$$ ✕ **Le Chaudron.** The charming rustic interior, with ancient Roman arches, has the look of restaurants across the French border in Provence. Ligurian specialties are featured on the predominantly seafood menu of this centrally located restaurant: try the *pansoti* (cheese ravioli with

walnut sauce) and *branzino* (sea bass), served with artichokes or mushrooms. A café annex serves a daily lunch special. ✉ *Piazza Bengasi 2,* ☎ *0184/263592. Reservations essential. DC, MC, V. Closed Mon., Feb., and July 1–15.*

$$ ✕ **Piemontese.** Only a block from the seaside and five minutes from the train station, this simple restaurant features the typical cooking of the neighboring Piedmont region, including *risotto al Barolo* (rice with Barolo wine, sausage, and porcini mushrooms) and *bagna cauda* (raw vegetables with a garlic and oil sauce). Ligurian dishes and seafood are also on the menu. ✉ *Via Roseto 8, off Via Vittorio Veneto,* ☎ *0184/261651. AE, MC, V. Closed Tues. and Nov. 20–Dec. 20.*

$$$–$$$$ ▨ **Grand Hotel del Mare.** At the top of a steep hill rising from the beach, this elegant hotel lives up to its name; the service and facilities are impeccable. The large rooms have panoramic views of the coastline; ask for one facing the water. One floor features beautiful antique furnishings. The hotel restaurant enjoys a fine reputation. ✉ *Via Portico della Punta 34, 18012,* ☎ *0184/262201,* FAX *0184/262394. 115 rooms. Restaurant, piano bar, saltwater pool, tennis courts, exercise room, beach. AE, DC, MC, V. Closed Nov. 1–Dec. 20.*

$$$ ▨ **Grand Hotel Capo Ampelio.** This hotel occupies a converted villa on a hill overlooking the town and the coastline. Traditional architectural features in the reception rooms and staircases are enhanced by convenient modern features in the rooms, all with balconies. The hotel is somewhat outside the town center, so rooms are quiet. ✉ *Via Virgilio 5, 18012,* ☎ *0184/264333,* FAX *0184/264244. 104 rooms. Restaurant, bar, pool. AE, DC, MC, V. Closed Oct. 10–Dec. 22.*

San Remo

★ ❹ *12 km (7 mi) east of Bordighera, 146 km (90 mi) southwest of Genoa, 60 km (37 mi) east of Nice.*

The self-styled capital of the Riviera di Ponente is San Remo, also its largest resort. Renowned for its royal visitors, its famous casino (one of only four in Italy), and its romantic setting, San Remo still maintains some of the glamour of its heyday from the late 19th century to World War II. Among the rich and famous who flocked to San Remo, drawn by the mild climate and pleasant countryside, were Alfred Nobel, who built a summer house here, and Russian Empress Maria Alexandrovna, wife of Czar Alexander II. San Remo also has elegant world-class hotels, where you can stop to have a drink, and exotic gardens, in addition to its promenades.

The Russian Orthodox church of **San Basilio,** with its onion domes, stands at one end of the Corso dell'Imperatrice and, like that imposing seafront promenade, is a legacy of the Empress. San Remo is famous for the **Mercato dei Fiori,** Italy's most important wholesale flower market, held in a market hall between Piazza Colombo and Corso Garibaldi and open to dealers only. More than 20,000 tons of carnations, roses, mimosa, and innumerable other cut flowers are dispatched from here each year.

The old part of San Remo, **La Pigna,** or pinecone, is a warren of alleyways worth exploring, climbing upward to Piazza Castello, with a splendid view of the town. The newer parts of San Remo suffer from the same epidemic of overbuilding that transformed so many towns on the western Riviera for the worse. And as center of northern Italy's flower-growing industry, the resort is surrounded by hills where once-verdant terraces are now blanketed with plastic to form immense greenhouses.

The **San Remo Casino** is a sophisticated establishment reminiscent of the turn of the century, with a restaurant and nightclub. ⊠ *Corso Inglese, San Remo.* ⊘ *Daily 2 PM–2 AM.*

OFF THE
BEATEN PATH

BUSSANA VECCHIA – About 8 km (5 mi) by bus or car east of San Remo, in the hills where flowers are cultivated for export, is Bussana Vecchia, a self-consciously picturesque ghost town that was largely destroyed by an earthquake in 1877. The inhabitants packed up and left en masse after the quake, and for almost a century, the houses, church, and crumbling bell tower were empty shells, overgrown by weeds and wildflowers. Since the 1960s an artist's colony has grown up among the ruins. Painters, sculptors, artisans, and bric-a-brac dealers have restored dwellings for themselves and sell their wares to visitors.

Dining and Lodging

$
★

✕ **Nuovo Piccolo Mondo.** This small, centrally located trattoria has plenty of charm and a homey atmosphere—the old wooden chairs date from the 1920s, when the place opened. Family-run, it has a faithful clientele, so get there early to grab a table and order Ligurian specialties such as spaghetti with artichokes and *polpo e patate* (stewed octopus with potatoes). ⊠ *Via Piave 7,* ☎ *0184/509012. No credit cards. Closed Sun. and 1st 3 wks in July.*

$$$$

🏨 **Royal.** It would take a dedicated hedonist to determine whether this deluxe hotel or the Splendido in Portofino is the most luxurious in Liguria. One major difference is the location: only a few paces from the Casino and the train station, the Royal is definitely part of San Remo, unlike the Splendido, which is set above Portofino. The rooms have a mixture of modern equipment and antique furnishings, each with a unique feel. The heated seawater swimming pool (⊘ Apr.–Sept.) is set in a subtropical garden. On the terrace, there's candlelight dining and music each night under the stars in season. ⊠ *Corso Imperatrice 80, 18038,* ☎ *0184/5391,* FAX *0184/661445. 142 rooms and suites. Restaurant, bar, saltwater pool, miniature golf, tennis courts. AE, DC, MC, V. Closed Oct. 6–Dec. 21.*

$$

🏨 **Paradiso.** This small hotel is adjacent to a lush public park near the Royal, so it shares the advantages of its grander neighbor's central location. A quiet, palm-fringed garden gives it an air of seclusion, which is a plus in this sometimes hectic city. The rooms are modern and bright, and many have a little terrace. The hotel restaurant has a good fixed-price menu. ⊠ *Via Roccasterone 12, 18038,* ☎ *0184/571211,* FAX *0184/578176. 41 rooms. Restaurant, bar. AE, DC, MC, V.*

Outdoor Activities and Sports

GOLF

The 18-hole **San Remo Golf Club** (⊠ Via Campo Golf, ☎ 0184/557093) is 5 km (3 mi) north of the town. The Golf Club is closed Tues.

Taggia

10 km (6 mi) northeast of San Remo, 20 km (12 mi) west of Imperia.

The town of Taggia has a medieval core and one of the most imposing medieval stone bridges in the area. The church of **San Domenico,** on a rise south of Taggia, was part of a monastery that was founded in the 15th century and was a beacon of faith and learning in western Liguria for 300 years.

Shopping

An **antiques market** is held here on the fourth weekend of the month.

Imperia

23 km (14 mi) east of Taggia, 116 km (71 mi) southwest of Genoa.

Imperia actually consists of two towns: **Porto Maurizio,** a medieval town built on a promontory, and **Oneglia,** now an industrial center for oil refining and pharmaceuticals. Obviously, Oneglia can be skipped entirely. Porto Maurizio has a virtually intact medieval center, the Parasio quarter, an intricate spiral of narrow streets and stone portals, and some imposing 17th- and 18th-century palaces.

OFF THE
BEATEN PATH
    OLIVE MUSEUM – The story of the olive—its cultivation and the manufacture of olive oil—is the theme of this small museum in Imperia set up by the Carli olive oil company. Displays show farm implements, types of presses, and utensils used in making olive oil in many countries throughout history. ⊠ *Museo dell'Ulivo, Via Garessio 11, Imperia,* ☎ *0183/720000.* ✉ *Free.* ☉ *Mon. and Wed.–Sat. 9–noon and 3–6.*

Dining

$ ✕ **Candidollo.** This charming and good-value restaurant is worth a de-
★   tour to the village of Diano Borello, on the valley road a couple of miles north of Diano Marina, 6 km (4 mi) east of Imperia. It's a rustic country inn, with checked tablecloths and worn terra-cotta floors. Host Bruno Ardissone uses locally grown ingredients and seasonal traditional recipes. The menu usually includes *coniglio al timo* (rabbit with thyme and other herbs) and *lumache all'agliata* (grilled snails in piquant sauce). ⊠ *Diano Borello,* ☎ *0183/43025. No credit cards. Closed Tues. and Nov.–Mar. No lunch Mon.*

Cervo

10 km (6 mi) northeast of Imperia, 106 km (65 mi) southwest of Genoa, 35 km (22 mi) east of San Remo.

One of the most interesting towns on the entire western Riviera, Cervo is the quintessential Ligurian coastal village, nicely polished for the tourists who come to explore its narrow byways and street staircases. It is a remarkably well-preserved medieval town, crowned with a big Baroque church.

Nightlife and the Arts

In July and August the square in front of the church is the setting for **chamber music** concerts.

Albenga

23 km (14 mi) north of Cervo, 90 km (55 mi) southwest of Genoa, 57 km (35 mi) northeast of San Remo.

Albenga has a medieval core, with narrow streets laid out by the ancient Romans. They form a network of alleys punctuated by centuries-old towers, surrounding the **cathedral** and **baptistery** dating back to the 5th century AD.

OFF THE
BEATEN PATH
    BARDINETO – For a look at some of the Riviera's mountain scenery, make an excursion by car to Bardineto. From Borghetto Santo Spirito (between Albenga and Finale Ligure), drive 25 km (15 mi) inland to reach this attractive village in the middle of an area rich in mushrooms, chestnuts, and raspberries, as well as local cheese. A ruined castle stands high above the village.

Finale Ligure

⑤ *20 km (12 mi) northwest of Albenga, 72 km (44 mi) southwest of Genoa, 52 km (32 mi) northeast of Imperia.*

Finale Ligure is made up of three villages: **Finalborgo, Finalmarina,** and **Finalpia.** The latter two have fine sandy beaches and modern resort amenities. The most attractive village is Finalborgo, a medieval settlement planned to a rigid blueprint, with 15th-century walls. The village is crowned by the impressive ruins of the huge **Castel Gavone.** The Baroque church of **San Biagio** houses many works of art, and the 14th- to 15th-century Dominican convent of **Santa Caterina** can be visited for the shade of the courtyard or to see the museum of paleontology and natural history, which houses prehistoric remains found in the area. ⊠ *Museo Civico,* ☏ *019/690020.* ⊡ *Free.* ☉ *May–Sept., Tues.–Fri. 10–noon and 3–6, weekends 9–noon; Oct.–Apr., Tues.–Fri. 9–noon and 2:30–4:30.*

Dining

$$–$$$ ✕ **Ai Torchi.** Develop your taste for homemade pesto (pasta sauce made of basil and pine nuts) at this restaurant in the center of Finalborgo. ⊠ *Via dell'Annunziata 12,* ☏ *019/690531. AE, DC, MC, V. Closed Tues. (except in Aug.) and Mon. (Oct.–May), and Jan. 7–mid-Feb.*

OFF THE BEATEN PATH   **NOLI –** Just 9 km (5½ mi) northeast of Finale Ligure, the picturesque ruins of a castle loom benevolently over the tiny town of Noli, a medieval gem. It is hard to believe that this charming village was, like Genoa, Venice, Pisa, and Amalfi, a prosperous maritime republic in the Middle Ages. If you don't have a car, you can get a bus for Noli at Spotorno, where local trains stop.

En Route   The countryside around Finale Ligure is pierced by deep, narrow valleys and caves; the limestone outcroppings provide the warm pinkish stone found in many buildings in Genoa. Here there are rare reptiles and rare species of flora.

Savona

⑥ *11½ km (7 mi) east of Spotorno, 48 km (29 mi) southwest of Genoa.*

Savona is the fifth-largest seaport in Italy and handles vast oil and coal cargoes, as well as car and truck ferries. Much of the town is modern and not very interesting, although a small, austere older quarter near the harbor contains some fine homes of the town's merchant class. The large **Palazzo della Rovere** (⊠ Via Pia) was designed for Pope Julius II by the Florentine Giuliano da Sangallo in 1495. There is also the 14th-century **Palazzo degli Anziani,** as well as three 12th-century towers. Every other year (next in 1998) on Good Friday, antique wooden carvings depicting the Passion of Christ are carried in procession.

Shopping

LOCAL SPECIALTIES AND CRAFTS

Watch for shops selling **crystallized fruit,** which is a local specialty. In **Millesimo,** a town 4 km (2½ mi) west and 36 km (18 mi) inland of Savona, little rum chocolates known as *millesimi* are produced. Look for bargains, too, in wrought-iron work, relief work on copper plate, and pieces in local sandstone.

Albisola Marina

⑦ *4½ km (3 mi) northwest of Savona, 43 km (26 mi) east of Genoa.*

Albisola Marina preserves its centuries-old tradition of ceramic making. Numerous shops here sell these distinctive wares, and a whole sidewalk, **Lungomare degli Artisti,** has been transformed by the colorful ceramic works of well-known artists. It runs along the beachfront. The 18th-century **Villa Faraggiana** (⊠ Near the parish church on Via dell'Oratorio) has interesting antique ceramics and exhibits on the history of the craft. 🎫 *Free.* ☉ *Apr.–Sept., Wed.–Mon. 3–7.*

Shopping

CERAMICS

Ceramiche San Giorgio (⊠ Corso Matteotti 5, ☎ 019/482747) has been producing ceramics since the 17th century and is known for both classic and modern designs. **Mazzotti** (⊠ Corso Matteotti 25, ☎ 019/481626) has an exclusive selection and a small in-house museum. In Albisola Superiore, **Ernan** (⊠ Corso Mazzini 77, ☎ 019/489916) features the classic blue-and-white Old Savona patterns typical of the 18th century.

Varazze

7 km (4 mi) northeast of Albisola, 36 km (22 mi) west of Genoa.

Varazze, known for its fine sandy beach, is a good place to stop for some sea and sun. The town also has well-preserved ancient ramparts, with a 10th-century church facade built into one of the rampart walls.

Pegli

23 km (14 mi) northwest of Varazze, 13 km (8 mi) west of Genoa.

Once a popular summer home for many patrician Genoese families, Pegli still has museums, parks, and some elegant old villas with well-tended gardens. This residential suburb manages to maintain its dignity despite encroaching industry and the proximity of airport and port facilities. Two lovely villas make it worth an excursion (they're especially good for letting children work off steam while romping in the gardens). Pegli can be reached conveniently by commuter train from Principe Station in Genoa.

☺ **Villa Doria,** near the Pegli train station, has a large park. The villa itself, built in the 16th century by the Doria family, has been converted into a **naval museum.** ⊠ *Villa Doria, Piazza Bonavino 7, Pegli,* ☎ *010/6969885. Villa:* 🎫 *6,000 lire.* ☉ *Tues.–Thurs. 9–1, Fri.–Sat. 9–7, 1st and 3rd Sun. of month 9–1. Park:* 🎫 *Free.* ☉ *Daily 10–noon and 2–6.*

☺ **Villa Durazzo Pallavicini** is set in 19th-century gardens featuring temples and artificial lakes. The villa has an archaeological museum. ⊠ *Via Pallavicini 11, Pegli,* ☎ *010/6981048.* 🎫 *6,000 lire.* ☉ *Tues.–Thurs. 9–7, Fri.–Sat. 9–1, 2nd and 4th Sun. of month 9–1.*

GENOA

❽ *501 km (310 mi) northwest of Rome, 236 km (146 mi) northwest of Florence, 142 km (88 mi) south of Milan, 170 km (105 mi) southeast of Turin, and 194 km (120 mi) northeast of Nice.*

Busy, sprawling Genoa, which stretches for 20 km (12 mi) along the coast, can offer a fascinating, rich, and colorful experience. Known as *La Superba* (The Proud), Genoa was from the 13th century a great maritime center that rivaled Venice and Pisa in power and splendor. In fact, Genoa has a proud history of trade and navigation that predates Columbus. Modern container ships unload at docks that centuries before served galleons and vessels bound for the spice routes. By the 3rd century BC, when the Romans conquered Liguria, Genoa was already an important trading station. The Middle Ages and the Renaissance saw the rise of Genoa as a great seaport and city. As a jumping-off place for the Crusaders, a commercial center of tremendous wealth and prestige, and a strategic bone of international contention, it was of key importance to Europe. Its bankers, merchants, and princes adorned the city with palaces and churches and amassed impressive art collections. By the 18th century, however, Genoa had declined as a sea power. Although it brims with historical curiosities and buildings (its lively medieval center is Europe's largest), it is also a thoroughly modern city struggling with problems of traffic, noise, and air pollution as well as a growing immigrant population. Its port is being equipped to keep up with new technologies; the city is also advanced in communications, electronics, and general commerce.

Europe's biggest boat show takes place here, as does the Euroflora flower show (held every five years—next in 2001). Classical dance and music are richly represented; the new Teatro Carlo Felice is a showcase (☞ Nightlife and the Arts, *below*), and the annual Niccolò Paganini Violin Contest, internationally renowned, also takes place in Genoa.

The historic harbor area was given a face-lift for the Columbus celebrations in 1992, and some of the fair installations, such as the Bigo elevator ride with harbor view, have become a permanent part of the city scene. The Acquario (Aquarium), the largest in Europe and second largest in the world, is one of Genoa's more recent attractions.

Medieval and Renaissance Genoa

A Good Walk

The best way to start your exploration of Genoa is to see it from above. From Piazza Principe, behind the Principe Station, take the **Granarolo funicular** ⑨ and return to start your walk along Via Balbi, which runs southeast from Principe Station toward the medieval town. On Via Balbi you pass Palazzo Balbi Durazzo, also known as **Palazzo Reale** ⑩, and **Palazzo dell'Università** ⑪. Continue straight ahead, crossing Piazza Santissima Annunziata to Via Bensa and continuing southeast on Via Cairoli to reach Via Garibaldi, where you can pause to see the collections in the museums of **Palazzo Rosso** ⑫ and **Palazzo Bianco** ⑬. Stop in at **Palazzo Tursi** ⑭, Genoa's Town Hall, and ask the guard at the door if it happens to be open to visitors that day; if it is you can see Paganini's violin. At the end of Via Garibaldi go left and left again to Piazza del Portello, where you can take the **Castelletto** ⑮ elevator for another view of the city from above. Returning to Piazza Fontane Marose at the end of Via Garibaldi, turn southwest, taking Via Luccoli into the medieval *caruggi* district. Beyond Piazza Soziglia, detour to the left, taking Via Campetto to Piazza San Matteo, flanked by the well-preserved houses of the Dorias and the church of **San Matteo** ⑯. Head southwest to the cathedral of **San Lorenzo** ⑰, medieval Genoa's religious heart. To the northeast of the cathedral is Via Indoratori, on which you turn northwest. Follow it to Via degli Orefici, on which you turn left to reach the **Loggia dei Mercanti** ⑱. Head north on Via San Luca to the **National Gallery** ⑲. At the northern end of Via San Luca is the church of **San Siro** ⑳.

TIMING

Allow a full day. The National Gallery is open until 7 every day except Monday.

Sights to See

Caruggi District. The winding, picturesque alleys—known as caruggi—that zigzag through the medieval city contain many medieval build-

Genoa

Corso Dagali

Piazza E. Brignole

Corso Firenze

Corso Carbonara

Corso Firenze

Corso Paganini

Corso Paganini

V. Brig. de Ferrari

Parco Villa Gruber

11
Via Balbi

Piazza d. Annunziata

Via P. Bensa

Lomellini

Via Caroli

Via del Campo

V. delle Fontane

Via Caffaro

Gal. Garibaldi

Salita S. Maria di Sanità

Via G. Mameli

20

13 14

15

Piazza Portello

Battistine

Piazzale Mazzini

Via M. Piaggio

Via Palestro

12

Via de la Maddalena

Via Garibaldi

19

Via S. Luca

Piazza Fontane Marose

29

Piazza Caricamento

18

Via degli Orefici

Piazza Soziglia

Via Luccoli

Piazza Corvetta

Campetto

Vico Indoratori

V. David Chiassone

Via 25 Aprile

Via Roma

28

Via S. Lorenzo

16

Via Ceba

Viale IV Novembre

Via F. Turati

17

24

23

E. Vernazza

Via di Canneto il Curto

Via dei Giustiniani

Piazza G. Matteotti

Piazza De Ferrari

Via XII Ottobre

Via S. Bernardo

Salita Pollaiuoli

V. Pta. Soprana

Via Dante

Via XX Settembre

Piazza Embriaci

27

Via di Santa Croce

V. S. Donato

25

22

Via S.M. di Castello

Stradone di S. Agostino

Piazza Negri

26

21

Piazza Dante

Corso M. Quadrio

NUOVA METROPOLITANA LEGGERA

Piazza Sarzano

Gall. C. Colombo

S. Leonardo Mura S. Chiara

Via Corsica

Via Ravasco

Via Fieschi

Piazza Carignano

Via Alessi

N

ings (some decorated with typical Ligurian black-and-white facades); these buildings are on a more human scale than the grand, airy palaces of Via Garibaldi. But the caruggi district is also the city's most disreputable. Don't go there after dark, or on holidays, when shops are closed and the alleys deserted. Wealthy Genoese built their homes in this quarter, south of Piazza Soziglia, in the 16th century. Prosperous guilds, such as the goldsmiths, for whom Vico dei Indoratori and Via Orefici were named, also set up shop here.

⑮ Castelletto. One of Genoa's handy municipal elevators takes you here from Piazza Portello, at the end of Via Garibaldi, for a good view of the old city. ⧉ *600 lire one-way.* ☉ *Continuous service 6:40 AM–midnight.*

OFF THE   **MUSEO D'ARTE ORIENTALE CHIOSSONE –** In the Villetta di Negro park on
BEATEN PATH   the hillside above Piazza Portello, this museum has one of Europe's most extensive collections of Oriental art. The Japanese, Chinese, and Thai collections are noteworthy, and you can get a fine view of the city from the museum's terrace. ⊠ *Piazzale Mazzini (Piazza Corvetto),* ☎ *010/542285.* ⧉ *6,000 lire.* ☉ *Tues. and Thurs.–Sat. 9–1; 1st and 3rd Sun. of month, 9–1.*

⑨ Granarolo funicular. Actually a cog railway, this takes you up the steeply rising terrain from the downtown area to one of the fortified gates in the 17th-century city walls. Dotted around the circumference of the city are a number of huge fortresses, and this gate was part of the city's system of defenses. It takes 15 minutes to hoist you from Piazza del Principe, behind the Principe Station on Piazza Acquaverde, to **Porta Granarolo,** 1,000 ft above, where you can get a good sense of the size of Genoa. ⧉ *1,500 lire; bus tickets valid.* ☉ *Departs on the ¼ hr, 6 AM–11:45 PM.*

⑱ Loggia dei Mercanti (covered market). Here's the place to go for a wide array of handicrafts and tempting foods. ⊠ *Piazza Banchi.*

⑲ National Gallery. This collection, housed in the richly adorned **Palazzo Spinola** north of Piazza Soziglia, contains, among other fine works, masterpieces by Luca Giordano and Guido Reni. The *Ecce Homo,* by Antonello da Messina, is a hauntingly beautiful painting and is also of historical interest because it was the Sicilian da Messina who first brought Flemish oil paints and techniques to Italy from his voyages in the Low Countries. ⊠ *Piazza Pellicceria 1,* ☎ *010/294661.* ⧉ *8,000 lire.* ☉ *Mon. 9–1, Tues.–Sat. 9–7, Sun. 2–7.*

⑬ Palazzo Bianco. Originally white, as its name suggests, this palace has become considerably darkened from age and grime. It has a fine art collection, with the Spanish and Flemish schools well represented. ⊠ *Via Garibaldi 11,* ☎ *010/291803.* ⧉ *6,000 lire.* ☉ *Tues., Thurs.–Fri., and Sun. 9–1; Wed. and Sat. 9–7.*

⑪ Palazzo dell'Università. Built in the 1630s as a Jesuit college, this has been the site of Genoa's university since 1803. Climb the stairway flanked by lions to visit the elegant courtyard, with its portico of double Doric columns. ⊠ *Via Balbi 5.*

★ **⑩ Palazzo Reale.** This palace is most sumptuous in a city where conspicuous consumption was a game played by high society. Also known as Palazzo Balbi Durazzo, it was used as a royal palace by Italy's rulers. The palace, which dates from the 17th century, contains paintings, sculptures, tapestries, and Oriental ceramics. The building was bought by the Royal House of Savoy in the early 19th century and has some magnificent rooms decorated in the lavish and frivolous rococo style; the gallery of mirrors and the ballroom on the upper floor are particularly good examples. There are also works by Sir Anthony Van Dyck, who lived in Genoa for six years, from 1621, and painted many fine portraits of the Genoese nobility. ⊠ *Via Balbi 10*, ☎ *010/27101*. ⌨ *8,000 lire.* ☉ *Sun.–Tues. 9–1:30, Wed.–Sat. 9–7.*

⑫ Palazzo Rosso (Red Palace). The 17th-century Baroque palace was named after the red stone used in its construction. It now contains, apart from a number of lavishly frescoed suites, works by Titian, Veronese, Reni, Rubens, and Van Dyck. ⊠ *Via Garibaldi 18*, ☎ *010/282641*. ⌨ *6,000 lire.* ☉ *Tues., Thurs.–Fri., and Sun. 9–1; Wed. and Sat. 9–7.*

⑭ Palazzo Tursi. Wealthy Nicolò Grimaldi had this palace built in the 16th century of pink stone quarried in the region. It now houses the Town Hall, and is aptly known as Palazzo Municipale (Municipal Palace). Visitors are welcome to view the richly decorated rooms and the famous Guarnerius violin that belonged to Paganini and is played once a year on Columbus Day (October 12). However, when the rooms are in use by Genoa's officials, as is often the case, they are closed to the public. ⊠ *Via Garibaldi 9*, ☎ *010/20982223*. ⌨ *Free.* ☉ *Weekdays; call for hrs.*

⑰ San Lorenzo. This cathedral stands at the heart of medieval Genoa's political and religious center. The cathedral is embellished inside and out with the contrasting black slate and white marble so common in Liguria. It was consecrated in 1118 to St. Lawrence, who passed through the city on his way to Rome in the 3rd century; the last campanile dates from the early 16th century. For hundreds of years the building was used for state, as well as religious, purposes: civic elections, court rulings, and religious ceremonies and festivals all took place here. Note the lively 13th-century Gothic portal and the 15th- to 17th-century frescoes inside. The **Museo del Tesoro di San Lorenzo** (San Lorenzo Treasury Museum), in the cathedral, contains some stunning medieval pieces. The art of goldsmiths and silversmiths, for which medieval Genoa was renowned, is particularly well represented here. ⊠ *Cathedral of San Lorenzo*, ☎ *010/311269*. ⌨ *8,000 lire.* ☉ *Mon.–Sat. 9–noon and 3–8; guided visits every ½ hr (last visits at 11 and 5:30).*

⑯ San Matteo. This black-and-white church dates from the 12th century; its crypt contains the tomb of Andrea Doria, who framed a constitution for the city in 1529 and began his family's reign. Doria won his fame as an admiral, serving, in turn, the French and Spanish crowns, but managing to maintain the independence of his native city. ⊠ *Piazza San Matteo.*

⑳ San Siro. Genoa's oldest church served as the city's cathedral from the 4th to the 9th centuries. It was rebuilt in the 16th and 17th centuries. ⊠ *Via San Luca.*

Santissima Annunziata. The 16th- to 17th-century church has exuberantly frescoed vaults and is an excellent example of Genoese Baroque architecture. ⊠ *Piazza della Nunziata.*

★ Via Garibaldi. Thirteen palaces were built along what was once known as the Via Aurea (Golden Street) in just 10 years. Genoa's leading patrician families built their residences here from 1554 onward to escape the cramped conditions of the medieval section of town. It is one of the most impressive streets in Italy, and the palace-museums house some of the finest art collections in the country. Most of the other palaces without museums on Via Garibaldi can be visited only by special application, but many have courtyards that are open to the public.

The Southern Districts and the Aquarium

A Good Walk

Start at **Porta di Sant'Andrea** ㉑ and pay homage to the purported **child-hood home of Christopher Columbus** ㉒ on the square. Then follow Via Dante into Piazza de Ferrari where the **Teatro Carlo Felice** ㉓ stands. The west side of the piazza is flanked by the **Palazzo Ducale** ㉔, with its imposing neoclassic facade on Piazza Matteotti. Leading uphill from Piazza Matteotti, Salita Pollaiuoli takes you to **San Donato** ㉕. On the west side of the church is Stradone Sant'Agostino, which leads to Piazza Negri and **Sant'Agostino** ㉖. From the west end of elongated Piazza Sarzana, take Via Santa Croce and turn north onto Via Santa Maria di Castello, climbing up to the church of **Santa Maria di Castello** ㉗ atop the hill. From Piazza Embriaci turn west and follow the little streets downhill to Via Canneto il Curto, turning downhill on Via San Lorenzo to reach Piazza Caricamento and the Old Port, where you can take a ride in the panoramic **Bigo elevator** ㉘ and visit the **Acquario** ㉙.

TIMING

This walk will take from two to three hours, with stops at churches and the museum at Sant'Agostino, and not counting the Aquarium visit.

Sights to See

㉙ **Acquario** (Aquarium). Fifty tanks full of marine fauna and flora reproduce saltwater and freshwater habitats. This is a must for children. ✉ *Ponte Spinola,* ☎ *010/2481205.* ✇ *14,000 lire.* ☉ *Tues.–Fri. 9:30–6:30, weekends 9:30–8; ticket office Tues.–Fri. 9:30–5:30, weekends 9:30–7.*

㉘ **Bigo elevator.** The view from the top of this mast erected as a symbol of the 1992 Columbus Quincentennial events takes in the harbor, city, and sea. ✇ *4,000 lire.* ☉ *Mar.–Aug., Tues.–Sat. 11–1 and 3–6, Sun. 11–1 and 2:30–6:30; Sept.–Feb., Tues.–Sat. 11–12:30 and 2:30–4, Sun. 11–1 and 3–6.*

㉒ **Childhood home of Christopher Columbus.** The ivy-covered ruins of this fabled medieval house stand in the gardens adjacent to the Porta di Sant'Andrea.

Harbor. A boat tour gives you a good perspective on the layout of the harbor, which dates to Roman times. The Genoa inlet, the largest along the Italian Riviera, was also used by the Phoenicians and Greeks as a harbor and a vantage point from which they could penetrate inland to form settlements and to trade. The **Lanterna,** a lighthouse more than 360 ft high, was built in 1544 at the height of Andrea Doria's career; it is one of Italy's oldest lighthouses and a traditional emblem of Genoa.

㉔ **Palazzo Ducale.** This palace was built in the 16th century over a medieval hall, and its facade was rebuilt in the late 18th century. The building has been restored and houses temporary exhibitions. ✉ *Piazza Matteotti and Piazza de Ferrari.*

Piazza San Matteo. The excellently preserved medieval square was, for 500 years, the seat of the Doria family who ruled Genoa and much of Liguria from the 16th to the 18th century. The square is bounded by 13th- to 15th-century houses decorated with portals and loggias. ✉ *South of Piazza Soziglia.*

㉑ **Porta di Sant'Andrea.** The twin-towered, 12th-century edifice also known as Porta Soprana stands at the old gateway to the Roman road that led through Genoa.

㉕ **San Donato.** The 12th-century Romanesque church with its original portal and octagonal campanile is slightly north of Sant'Agostino. ✉ *Piazza San Donato.*

㉖ **Sant'Agostino.** This 13th-century Gothic church was damaged during World War II, but it still has a fine campanile and two well-preserved cloisters, which now house an excellent sculpture museum. ✉ *Piazza Sarzano 35/r,* ☎ *010/201661.* ▨ *6,000 lire.* ☾ *Tues.–Sat. 9–7, Sun. 9–12:30.*

㉗ **Santa Maria di Castello.** One of Genoa's greatest religious buildings was an early Christian church. It was rebuilt in the 12th century and finally completed in 1513. You can visit the adjacent cloisters and see the fine artwork contained in the museum. Call ahead to book a visit. ✉ *Salita di Santa Maria di Castello 15,* ☎ *010/2549511.* ▨ *Free.* ☾ *Mon.–Sat. 9–noon and 3:30–6, Sun. 3:30–6; call ahead.*

㉓ **Teatro Carlo Felice.** The World War II–ravaged opera house in Genoa's modern center, **Piazza de Ferrari,** has finally been rebuilt, reopening in 1991 with a massive, much-criticized tower. It stands next to the **Academy of Fine Arts,** which contains a collection of Ligurian paintings from the 13th to the 19th centuries. ✉ *Largo Pertini 4,* ☎ *010/581957.* ▨ *Free.* ☾ *Mon.–Sat. 9–1.*

Dining and Lodging

$$$–$$$$ ✕ **Gran Gotto.** Innovative classic regional dishes are served in this elegant, spacious restaurant punctuated with contemporary paintings. The service is quick and helpful. Try *filetti di triglia* (red mullet fillets with rosemary, celery, and balsamic vinegar) and the sumptuous *flan di cioccolato* (dark chocolate flan with white chocolate sauce), one of the many excellent homemade desserts. It's near Brignole Station in the modern part of town. ✉ *Via Viale Brigata Bisagno 69/r,* ☎ *010/564344. Jacket and tie. AE, DC, MC, V. Closed Sun. and Aug. 10–31. No lunch Sat.*

$$$–$$$$ ✕ **Zeffirino.** The five Belloni brothers share the chef's duties at this re-
★ markable restaurant, which is full of odd combinations. The decor is a mixture of styles and materials, ranging from rustic wood to modern metallic. Try the *passutelli* (ravioli stuffed with ricotta cheese and fruit) or any of the homemade pasta dishes. ✉ *Via XX Settembre 20,* ☎ *010/591990. Jacket and tie. AE, DC, MC, V. Closed Wed.*

$$–$$$ ✕ **Sette Nasi.** The historic Quarto dei Mille district is the setting for this large establishment, with accents of gray slate and pink marble. The chef, Fausto Nasi, specializes in a wide range of Ligurian seafood dishes and makes some mean homemade desserts. Summertime meals are served on the terrace, which has excellent sea views. Top off a lovely day spent at the annexed pool and beach club with a dinner of ravioli *di pesce* (seafood) or lasagna with pesto. ✉ *Via Quarto 16,* ☎ *010/3731344. AE, DC, MC, V. Closed Tues. and Nov.*

$$ ✕ **Da Genio.** On a byway in old Genoa, near Piazza Dante, this classic trattoria serves equally classic Genoese dishes, including *trenette al pesto* (pasta with pesto sauce) and minestrone, also laced with a dollop of pesto. ✉ *Salita San Leonardo 61/r,* ☎ *010/588463. MC, V. Closed Sun. and Aug.*

$$ ✕ **Marinella.** This restaurant is perched on seaside shoals in Nervi, 10 km (6 mi) east of the center of Genoa. Competing for attention are an impressive wrought-iron chandelier and great sea views from windows and terrace. (There's an inexpensive hotel annex, too.) Try *zuppa di pesce* (fish stew); main dishes change from day to day, according to the fishermen's catch. ✉ *Passeggiata Anita Garibaldi 18, Nervi,* ☎ *010/3728343. MC, V. Closed Mon. and Nov.*

$ ✕ **Trattoria Walter.** This casual family-run restaurant is in the city heart, with nice touches of vaulted ceilings and classical music. The owners pride themselves on courteous service and a menu featuring Genoese specialties such as *stoccafisso in umido con patate* (dried codfish stew with potatoes). ✉ *Vico Colalanza 2, corner of Via San Luca*, ☎ *010/290524. No credit cards. Closed Sun. and Thurs. evening, and Aug. 13–Sept. 3.*

$$$$ 🏨 **Bristol Palace.** This grand hotel, on a fashionable downtown shopping street, was built in the last century and maintains the old-fashioned traditions of courtesy and discretion. The rooms are large, with high ceilings; paintings decorate the large reception rooms. There's no restaurant, but you're in the heart of the downtown area. ✉ *Via XX Settembre 35, 16121*, ☎ *010/592541*, FAX *010/561756. 98 rooms. Bar, café, snack bar. AE, DC, MC, V.*

$$$ 🏨 **Novotel.** Opened in 1994, this is a good choice for tourists who value modern comfort over atmosphere. It is in a semicentral area just beyond one end of the harbor; you can take a bus or taxi to the heart of town. ✉ *Via Cantore 8/c, 16126*, ☎ *010/64841*, FAX *010/6484844. 223 rooms. Restaurant, bar, pool, free parking. AE, DC, MC, V.*

$$$ 🏨 **Villa Pagoda.** If you want to stay at a top-quality hotel outside the
★ center of Genoa, try this unusual establishment in Nervi, 10 km (6 mi) east of Genoa. It occupies a 19th-century building designed like a pagoda, built at a time when Europe was fascinated by the exotic Orient. Most of the spacious rooms have gorgeous views of the sea, and the hotel is adjacent to a large, shady park. ✉ *Via Capolungo 15, Nervi, 16167*, ☎ *010/3726161*, FAX *010/321218. 18 rooms. Restaurant, bar, beach. AE, DC, MC, V.*

$$ 🏨 **Agnello d'Oro.** The central location in Genoa's old quarter, about
★ 100 yards from Principe Station, makes this hotel a good choice for budget travelers who want to be in the heart of things. There are simple modern furnishings in renovated rooms, several of which have a balcony with a view. ✉ *Vico delle Monachette 6, 16126*, ☎ *010/2462084*, FAX *010/2462327. 30 rooms. Bar. AE, DC, MC, V.*

$$ 🏨 **Cairoli.** On a historic street near Principe Station and the Aquarium, this hotel's central location is a real plus. Happily, the rooms have been soundproofed so you'll get a good night's sleep—not always the easiest thing to do in this noisy city. Family-operated, it is neatly furnished and has a roof terrace. ✉ *Via Cairoli 14, 16124*, ☎ *010/206531*, FAX *010/280041. 14 rooms, 12 with bath. Free parking. AE, DC, MC, V.*

Nightlife and the Arts

Opera
The **opera** season (October–May) at **Teatro Carlo Felice** (✉ Passo al Teatro 4, ☎ 010/53811; box office ☎ 010/591697) attracts many lavish productions and occasionally sees the debut of a new work.

Shopping

Liguria is famous for its fine laces, its silver and gold filigree work, and its ceramics. Look also for bargains in velvet, macramé, olive wood, and marble. Genoa is the best spot to find all these specialties. In the heart of the medieval quarter, **Via Soziglia** is lined with shops selling handicrafts and tempting foods. **Via XX Settembre** is famous for its wide range of small, exclusive shops. Fine shops also line **Via Luccoli.**

Chocolates
Judge for yourself whether the handmade chocolates at **Pietro Romanengo fu Stefano** (✉ Via Soziglia 74, ☎ 010/297869) are the best in Genoa (the management says they are).

Jewelry, Perfumes, and Clothing

The well-established **Codevilla** (⊠ Via Orefici 53, ☎ 010/206567) is one of the best jewelers on a street devoted to goldsmiths. At **Pescetto** (⊠ Via Scurreria 8, ☎ 010/206633), you'll find designer clothes, perfumes, and gifts in this elegant shop near Codevilla.

Wines

Vinoteca Sola (⊠ Piazza Colombo 13, near Brignole station, ☎ 010/561329) maintains a good selection of Italian and Ligurian wines.

RIVIERA DI LEVANTE

On the Road to Portofino

Of the two Ligurian Rivieras, the Riviera di Levante, east of Genoa, is the wilder and more rugged, yet here you will also find towns world-famous for their panache and casual elegance, such as Portofino and Rapallo. Around every turn, the hills drop sharply to the sea and are pierced by compact bays and inlets. You may want to choose a base and take short day trips or explore the area by boat from the larger towns. You can anchor your boat in the relatively calm waters of small *ciazze* (coves) punctuating the coast.

Beaches on this coast are rocky, with many spectacular cliffs near the sea. Portofino Promontory has one sandy beach, on the east side, at Paraggi. From Chiavari to Cavi di Lavagna, the coast becomes a bit gentler, with a few sandy areas. Sailing conditions along the rugged coast from Sestri Levante down to Portovenere are good. Beyond sailing, waterskiing, tennis, and golf are popular activities.

Nervi

30 *11 km (7 mi) east of Genoa, 97 km (60 mi) west of La Spezia.*

Nervi is an elegant turn-of-the-century resort. It's famous for the mile-long Anita Garibaldi promenade, with its splendid sea views, and for palm-lined roads, and 300 acres of parks rich in orange trees and exotics.

The curious and eclectic collections in the **Museo di Villa Luxoro**, housed in a turn-of-the-century mansion, include 17th- and 18th-century Genoese furnishings, furniture, ceramics, and ornaments; Flemish and Genoese paintings and drawings; old silver and lace; and antique clocks. ⊠ *Via Aurelia 29,* ☎ *010/322673.* 🎟 *6,000 lire.* 🕐 *Tues.–Sat. 9–1.*

Nightlife and the Arts

An **International Festival of Ballet** is usually held in July in an amphitheater set up on the grounds of Villa Gropallo. The festival sometimes skips a year. For information contact City of Genoa Tourist Office (☎ 010/2467658).

Camogli

★ **31** *10 km (6 mi) southwest of Nervi, 23 km (14 mi) northwest of Chiavari.*

Camogli, at the edge of the large promontory and nature reserve known as the Portofino peninsula, has always been a town of sailors. By the 19th century this small village was leasing its ships throughout the Continent. The village is dotted with multicolored houses, a huge 17th-century sea wall in the harbor, and the Dragone Castle, built onto the sheer rock face by the harbor. Within the castle is the **Ac-**

quario (Aquarium), with displays of local marine life. The tanks are actually built into the ramparts. ⊠ *4,000 lire.* ⊙ *May–Sept., daily 10– noon and 3–7; Oct.–Apr., Fri.–Sun. 10–noon and 2:30–6, Tues.–Thurs. 10–noon.*

OFF THE
BEATEN PATH

SAN ROCCO, SAN NICOLÒ, AND PUNTA CHIAPPA – From Camogli you can reach, by foot or boat, these hamlets with their remarkable sea views. They lie along the western coast of the peninsula and are more natural and less fashionable than those facing south on the eastern coast. The small Romanesque church at San Nicolò was where sailors who survived dangerous voyages came to offer thanks.

SAN FRUTTUOSO – On the sea at the foot of Mt. Portofino, 30 minutes by boat from Camogli (20 minutes by boat from Portofino) the medieval abbey of San Fruttuoso—built by the Benedictines of Monte Cassino— protects a minuscule fishing village and can be reached only on foot or by boat from Camogli, Portofino, Santa Margherita Ligure, or Rapallo. The restored abbey is now property of a national conservation fund (FAI). The church holds the tombs of some illustrious members of the Doria family. The historic abbey and its grounds are a delightful place to spend a few hours, perhaps lunching at one of the modest beach trattorias nearby. But boatloads of visitors can make it very crowded very fast; it's best appreciated off-season. ☎ *0185/772703.* ⊠ *5,000 lire.* ⊙ *Mar.–Apr., Tues.–Sun. 10–1 and 2–4; May–Oct. Tues.–Sun. 10–1 and 2–6; Nov.–Jan., weekends 10–1 and 2–4. Closed Feb.*

Dining and Lodging

$$$ ✕ **Vento Ariel.** This tiny, friendly restaurant is right on the port, and it has informal but elegant decor and place settings. It serves seafood only and regularly runs out of items because it relies on the day's catch. Try the spaghetti *alle vongole* (with clams) or the grilled mixed fish, which differs according to the day's haul. ⊠ *Calata Porto,* ☎ *0185/771080. AE, DC, MC, V. Closed Wed. and Jan.*

$$$–$$$$ ▣ **Cenobio dei Dogi.** Although this hilltop villa perched over the town
★ was once the summer home of Genoa's doges (medieval elected rulers), it now has a modern look. Guests can relax in the well-kept park affording outstanding views of the Portofino peninsula, or they can enjoy numerous sporting activities. ⊠ *Via Cuneo 34, 16032,* ☎ *0185/7241,* 𝔽𝔸𝕏 *0185/772796. 107 rooms. Restaurant, bar, pool, tennis courts, private beach. AE, MC, V.*

Nightlife and the Arts

The festival of **San Fortunato,** held on the second Sunday of May each year, is noteworthy for the **Sagra del Pesce,** a public—and free—feast of freshly caught fish cooked in a frying pan 12 ft wide.

Ruta

4 km (2½ mi) east of Camogli.

This is a base for hikes on Mt. Portofino. The footpaths up to and around the mountain cover terrain with a wide variety of plant species, as well as excellent views of the Riviera di Levante.

Rapallo

㉜ *10 km (8 mi) east of Camogli, 37 km (23 mi) west of Genoa, 79 km (49 mi) east of La Spezia.*

Rapallo was once one of Europe's most fashionable resorts, but it passed its heyday before World War II and has suffered from the building boom brought on by tourism. Ezra Pound and D. H. Lawrence lived here, and many other writers, poets, and artists have been drawn to it. Today, the town's harbor is filled with yachts. A single-span bridge on the eastern side of the bay is named after Hannibal, who is said to have passed through the area after crossing the Alps. Two ancient buildings are highlights in the center of town: the cathedral of Santi Gervasio and Protasio, at the western end of Via Mazzini, was founded in the 6th century; across the road is the Leper House of San Lorenzo, which still retains parts of its original medieval frescoes on its exterior walls.

The **Museo del Pizzo a Tombolo,** in a 19th-century mansion, has a collection of antique lace. Rapallo was renowned for this type of handiwork. ⊠ *Villa Tigullio.* ☎ *Free.* ☉ *Oct.–Aug., Tues.–Wed., Fri.–Sat. 3–6, Thurs. 10–12:30.*

Dining and Lodging

$$ ✗ **Da Ardito.** This lively trattoria is in the village of San Pietro di Novella, which is just north of Rapallo. It's extremely popular with wine lovers, who appreciate the attention given to the wine list. For a change from seafood, try the *pansotti alla salsa di noci* (pasta served with creamy walnut sauce). ⊠ *Via Canale 9, San Pietro di Novella,* ☎ *0185/51551. Reservations essential. MC, V. Closed Mon. and Feb.*

$$$$ 🏨 **Grand Hotel Bristol.** This large Victorian showcase has undergone total renovation. It is in an elevated position overlooking road and sea outside Rapallo, and is set in lush gardens with a huge seawater pool. Spacious rooms, many with balcony and sea view, are decorated in soft colors in a smart, contemporary style and have extra-large beds. Dinner is served on the roof terrace. ⊠ *Via Aurelia Orientale 369, 16035,* ☎ *0185/273313,* 🅵🅰🆇 *0185/55800. 90 rooms and suites. Restaurant, bar, pool, 18-hole golf course, tennis court, horseback riding, meeting rooms. AE, MC, V. Closed Jan.–Feb.*

$$ 🏨 **Giulio Cesare.** Only a block from the sea, this old town house was transformed into a hotel that offers rooms with modern furnishings and sea views. Many rooms have balconies, but noise may be a problem, since the hotel is on a main street. ⊠ *Corso Colombo 52, 16035,* ☎ *0185/50685,* 🅵🅰🆇 *0185/60896. 33 rooms. AE, MC, V. Closed Nov.–mid-Dec.*

Outdoor Activities and Sports

GOLF
The **Rapallo Golf Club** (☎ 0185/261777) has a lush 18-hole course about 2 km (1¼ mi) northwest of the center of town.

HORSEBACK RIDING
The **Rapallo Riding Club** (⊠ Via Santa Maria del Campo 196, ☎ 0185/50462) is near the golf club, about 2 km (1¼ mi) northwest of town.

Shopping

LOCAL CRAFTS
The attractive coastal village of **Zoagli** (⊠ On S1, 4 km [2½ mi] east of Rapallo) has been famous for **silk, velvet,** and **damask** ever since the Middle Ages.

The traditional, light (they weigh only 3 pounds) *campanine* chairs made of olive wood or walnut are still produced in **Chiavari** (⊠ On S1, 12 km [7 mi] east of Rapallo) by a few craftsmen. **Macramé lace** can also be found here.

Santa Margherita Ligure

㉝ *3 km (2 mi) south of Rapallo, 40 km (25 mi) southeast of Genoa, 82 km (51 mi) northwest of La Spezia.*

A pretty resort favored by well-to-do Italians, Santa Margherita Ligure has everything a Riviera playground should have—plenty of palm trees and attractive hotels, cafés, and a marina packed with yachts. There are even some of the trompe l'oeil frescoes typical of the old buildings on this part of the Riviera. It's a pleasant and convenient base for excursions by land and by sea.

Dining and Lodging

$$ ✕ **Da Baicin.** A very friendly family runs this bright trattoria. Outdoor
★ tables afford a view of the seaside gardens in the center of Santa Margherita. The specialties of the house are *zuppa di pesce* (fish stew) and *pansoti alla salsa di noci* (cheese ravioli with walnut sauce). ⊠ *Via Algeria 5,* ☎ *0185/286763. AE, DC, MC, V. Closed Mon. and mid-Nov.–mid-Dec.*

$$ ✕ **Il Frantoio.** The large, hand-carved wooden screws that turned the olive press for which this rather elegant little restaurant is named stand at the entrance. And here you not only consult from the wine list, you can also choose from the olive oil list for just the right piquancy or mellowness. Quality is a keynote in the food, too, as in the specialties: spaghetti with shellfish cooked in a pastry crust, and either rabbit or seafood with pomegranate sauce. ⊠ *Via del Giunchetto 23/a,* ☎ *0185/286667. AE, DC, MC, V. Closed Tues. and Nov. 7–30.*

$$$$ 🏨 **Grand Hotel Miramare.** Take the shore road south from town to reach this palatial turn-of-the-century hotel overlooking the bay. It has a lush garden and swimming pool, and a private swimming area on the sea. The bright and airy rooms are decorated in contemporary or late 19th-century style. The best have sea views, as do the hotel terraces. ⊠ *Lungomare Milite Ignoto 30, 16038,* ☎ *0185/287013,* FAX *0185/284651. 84 rooms. Restaurant, bar, pool, beach, waterskiing. AE, DC, MC, V.*

$$$$ 🏨 **Imperial Palace.** Via Pagana climbs north out of Santa Margherita Ligure on its way toward Rapallo; just outside town it passes this Old World–style luxury hotel, which is set in an extensive park. The rooms are furnished with antiques; many overlook the shore drive to the sea. The reception rooms are elegantly decorated with tall windows, plush chairs, and potted plants. ⊠ *Via Pagana 19, 16038,* ☎ *0185/288991,* FAX *0185/284223. 102 rooms. Restaurant, bar, pool. AE, DC, MC, V. Closed Nov. 1–Mar. 27.*

$$$ 🏨 **Continental.** This stately seaside mansion with a columned portico was built in the early 1900s and set in a lush garden shaded by tall palms and pine trees. The decor is a blend of traditional furnishings, mostly in 19th-century style, with some more functional pieces. There is also a modern wing. The hotel's own cabanas and swimming area are at the bottom of the garden. Ask for a room with a sea view and balcony. ⊠ *Via Pagana 8, 16038,* ☎ *0185/286512,* FAX *0185/284463. 76 rooms. Restaurant, bar. AE, DC, MC, V. Closed Nov.*

$ 🏨 **Fasce.** An extremely good value, this small, modern hotel is on one
★ of the town's main thoroughfares, but from its pleasant roof garden you have views of the sea and surrounding hills. The Italian owner and his English wife take cordial interest in their guests' well-being and comfort, providing free bus passes and bicycles. Rooms are attractive, with satellite TVs. ⊠ *Via Bozzo 3, 16038,* ☎ *0185/286435,* FAX *0185/283580. 16 rooms. Restaurant. AE, DC, MC, V.*

Portofino

★ *5 km (3 mi) south of Santa Margherita Ligure, 38 km (23 mi) south-east of Genoa, 87 km (54 mi) northwest of La Spezia.*

Portofino is one of the most picturesque villages along the coast. It is also precious, in the true sense of the word. Unless you are traveling on a deluxe level and can keep up with the Agnellis and Berlusconis, you will probably choose a hotel in Rapallo or Santa Margherita Ligure rather than one of Portofino's few and very expensive establishments. Tiny Portofino has an aura of romance and affluence. Some of Europe's wealthiest lay anchor here, but they stay out of sight during the day in their secluded villas or on their gorgeous yachts, appearing only in the evening after buses and boats have carried off the day-trippers. There's little to do in Portofino, other than stroll around the wee harbor, walk to Punta del Capo, and a look at the pricey boutiques. Cafés and restaurants are pricey, too. If you have had to sit out a traffic jam to get there, you may wonder why you bothered. Trying to reach Portofino by bus or car on the single narrow road can be a nightmare in the summer and on holiday weekends. An alternative is to take a boat from Santa Margherita. If getting there was easy and you find the village relatively empty of tourists, you'll probably agree that it is a pretty place indeed.

From the harbor, follow the signs for the climb to the **Castello di San Giorgio,** with its medieval relics and excellent views. ☞ *4,000 lire.* ☉ *Apr.–Sept., Wed.–Mon. 10–6; Oct.–Mar., Wed.–Mon. 10–4.*

Sitting on a ridge above the harbor is the church of **San Giorgio,** which is supposed to contain the saint's relics, brought back from the Holy Land by the Crusaders. Not surprisingly, Portofino enthusiastically celebrates **St. George's Day** (April 23). Other excellent views can be seen from the lighthouse at Punta del Capo, a 15-minute walk along a marked path from the village.

Dining and Lodging

$$$$ ✕ **Il Pitosforo.** A chic, tan clientele, many with luxury yachts in the harbor, gives this waterfront restaurant a glamorous atmosphere that is augmented by prices only the wealthy can afford. Spaghetti *ai frutti di mare* (with seafood) is recommended; adventurous diners might want to try *lo stocco accomodou* (dried cod in a savory sauce of tomatoes, raisins, and pine nuts). ⊠ *Molo Umberto I, 9,* ☎ *0185/269020. Reservations essential. AE, DC, MC, V. Closed Mon.–Tues. and Jan.–mid-Feb.. No lunch June–Sept.*

$$$$ ⊞ **Splendido.** Most people resort to superlatives when trying to describe ★ this luxury hotel, built in the '20s on a hill overlooking the sea. The abiding impression is one of color, from the coordinated fabrics and furnishings of the rooms to the fresh flowers in the reception rooms and on the large terrace. It's like a Jazz Age film set, and you almost expect to see a Bugatti or Daimler roll up the winding drive from Portofino below. A network of footpaths leads away from the wooded grounds. The Splendido's relatively small size means you get even more personal attention than at other luxury hotels. ⊠ *Viale Baratta 13, 16034,* ☎ *0185/269551,* ℻ *0185/269614. 64 rooms. Restaurant, 2 bars, pool, tennis court. AE, DC, MC, V. Closed Jan.–mid-Mar.*

Outdoor Activities and Sports

HIKING

If you have the stamina, you can hike to the Abbey of San Fruttuoso (☞ Off the Beaten Path *in* Camogli, *above*) from Portofino. It's a steep climb at first, and the walk takes about 2½ hours one-way. By boat, the trip takes about 20 minutes.

Chiavari

35 *22 km (13 mi) southeast of Portofino, 38 km (23 mi) southeast of Genoa, 69 km (43 mi) northwest of La Spezia.*

Chiavari is a fishing town, rather than village, and it has considerable character, with narrow, twisting streets and a good harbor. Chiavari's citizens were energetic explorers, and many emigrated to South America in the 19th century. The town boomed, thanks to the wealth of the returning voyagers, but Chiavari still retains many medieval traces in its buildings.

There is an interesting **Museo Archeologico** (archaeological museum) in the center of town. Here you can see finds from an 8th-century BC necropolis, or ancient cemetery (literally, city of the dead), excavated nearby. ⊠ *Palazzo Rocca, Piazza Matteotti.* ☎ *Free.* ☉ *Tues.–Thurs. 9–1, Fri.–Sun. 2–7.*

Outdoor Activities and Sports

HORSEBACK RIDING

Riding is a rewarding way to explore the wooded hills framing Chiavari. **Rivarola Carasco** (⊠ Via Veneto 212, ☎ 0185/382204) provides mounts.

Sestri Levante

36 *8 km (5 mi) southeast of Chiavari, 50 km (31 mi) southeast of Genoa, 59 km (36 mi) northwest of La Spezia.*

Though industrialized, with steelworks and shipyards, Sestri Levante has good views and an interesting medieval district surrounding what is known as the Baia del Silenzio (Bay of Silence), the small harbor just behind Piazza Matteotti. Walk up one of the alleyways to see some of the worked slate doorways of the older houses.

En Route   From Sestri, S1 turns inland past the spectacular Passo del Bracco and does not reach the coast again until the large port of La Spezia, more than 60 km (37 mi) southeast. The Cinque Terre, five towns that lie on the less accessible coastal strip between Levanto and Portovenere (near La Spezia) could be reached only by boat or on foot until about 50 years ago.

Moneglia

37 *12 km (7 mi) southeast of Sestri Levante, 58 km (36 mi) northwest of La Spezia, 58 km (36 mi) southeast of Genoa.*

The town of Moneglia, sheltered by the wooded hills of a nature preserve, faces a little bay guarded by ruined castles. An out-of-the-way alternative to fussier resorts, it's a quiet base for walks and excursions by boat, car, or train to Portofino and the Cinque Terre towns.

Lodging

$$ ⊞ **Villa Edera.** Ingeniously merging an older building on a verdant hillside with a smart contemporary stone and glass wing, the family that owns this small hotel offers guests their personal and caring attention. Terraces, a garden, luminous bedrooms, and lounges with stylish wicker armchairs are among the comforts. Mamma Ida's cooking is special, too. ⊠ *Via Venino 12, 16030,* ☎ *0185/49291,* FAX *0185/49470. 11 rooms. Restaurant. AE, MC, V. Closed Nov. 6–Mar.*

Nightlife and the Arts

A **classical guitar** festival is held here in September.

Levante

38 *25 km (15 mi) southeast of Sestri Levante, 32 km (20 mi) northwest of La Spezia, 83 km (51 mi) southwest of Genoa.*

Levanto is a secluded town with good beaches and a few graceful buildings that date from the 13th century. Many of the buildings are adorned with clever trompe l'oeil paintings that give the impression that real town folk are looking at you from their windows.

Dining and Lodging

$$–$$$ ✕ **Araldo.** Arches and frescoes add to the atmosphere of this elegant
★ little restaurant. Ambience, food, and service are outstanding; the menu, featuring creative Mediterranean cuisine, changes with the seasons and offers more than 100 wines. Try *pesce con patate alla ligure* (fillets of fish baked with potatoes in wine with olives and fresh thyme). ⊠ *Via Jacopo 24,* ☎ *0187/807253. AE, DC, MC, V. Closed Tues. (except July–Aug.) and Nov.*

$$$ ⌂ **Stella Maris.** In Levanto center and only a 10-minute walk from the
★ beach, this is a real find. It takes up one floor of a 19th-century palazzo (the ground floor houses a palatial bank). Seven rooms are decorated with original frescoes and 19th-century furniture, and seven are modern; the couple who run the hotel have an infectious enthusiasm for the building's history and decoration. A half-board plan is included in the price, but that's no sacrifice because the home cooking features Ligurian seafood specialties; you can have your homemade gelato in the sunny garden. ⊠ *Via Marconi 4, 19015,* ☎ *0187/808258,* ⅛ *0187/807351. 15 rooms. Restaurant. AE, DC, MC, V. Closed Nov.*

Cinque Terre

★ **39** *Monterosso is 12 km (7 mi) east of Levanto; Vernazza is 3½ km (2 mi) east of Monterosso; Corniglia is 3 km (2 mi) east of Vernazza; Manarola is 3 km (2 mi) east of Corniglia; Riomaggiore is 1½ km (1 mi) east of Manarola and 10 km (6 mi) west of La Spezia.*

The aura of isolation that has surrounded five almost inaccessible coastal villages known as Cinque Terre, together with their dramatic coastal scenery, has made them one of the eastern Riviera's premier attractions, especially for those who visit them effortlessly, by excursion boat. Clinging haphazardly to steep cliffs, they are linked by footpaths, by train, and now by narrow, unasphalted and rather tortuous roads, a fairly recent development. The local train on the Genoa–La Spezia line stops at each town between Levanto and Riomaggiore. Built against steep cliffs and linked by trails, the villages have long been a favorite destination for hikers. The classic, lower coastal trail is the Blue Trail (Trail 2), and the walk takes about five hours. You can catch a train back to your base. If you walk all or part of the way, wear sturdy shoes and a hat and carry a water bottle, as there is little shade. The westernmost village is Monterosso, but the easiest to reach by car is Riomaggiore, easternmost of the villages and closest to La Spezia and the A12 autostrada.

The largest of the five fishing towns is **Monterosso,** with a 12th-century church in the Ligurian style, lively markets, and small beaches. To the east is **Vernazza,** a charming village of narrow streets, small squares and arcades, and the remains of forts dating from the Middle Ages. The buildings, narrow lanes, and stairways of **Corniglia,** the middle village, are strung together on a hillside amid vineyards; excellent views of the entire coastal strip can be seen on a clear day. The enchanting pastel houses in **Manarola** are nestled into a steep hill, hugging the rocky shoreline. At the eastern end of the Cinque Terre is **Riomaggiore,** huddled around a tiny harbor dotted with fishing boats and hemmed in by sheer cliffs.

Dining and Lodging

$$ ✕ **Il Gigante.** A good introduction to Ligurian seafood is the *zuppa di pesce* (fish soup) served at this traditional trattoria in Monterosso al Mare. This soup is usually served as a first course, but is filling enough to be an entrée. Daily specials might include risotto *di frutti di mare* (with shellfish) and spaghetti with an octopus sauce. ⊠ *Monterosso al Mare,* ☎ *0187/817401. AE, DC, MC, V. Closed Tues.*

$$$ 🏨 **Porto Roca.** In a panoramic position above the sea, Porta Roca is
★ set slightly apart, blessedly removed from the crowds who visit Monterosso, especially on weekends. It has the look of a well-kept villa; its interiors have authentic antique pieces and there are ample terraces. The rooms are bright and airy, with sea breezes. Porto Roca is on a network of not-too-demanding hill walks and has a faithful American clientele. ⊠ *Via Corone 1, 19016 Monterosso,* ☎ *0187/817502,* FAX *0187/817692. 43 rooms. Restaurant, bar. AE, MC, V. Closed Nov. 4– Mar. 23.*

La Spezia

④⓪ *8 km (5 mi) north of Portovenere, 103 km (64 mi) southeast of Genoa, 144 km (89 mi) northwest of Florence.*

La Spezia is a large industrialized naval port on routes to the Cinque Terre and to Portovenere. La Spezia lacks the charm of the smaller towns, but it does have the remains of the massive 13th-century Castel San Giorgio.

Outdoor Activities and Sports

WATERSKIING

La Spezia Motorboat Club (⊠ Via della Marina 224, ☎ 0187/50401) will get you up and skiing.

Portovenere

★ ④① *24 km (15 mi) east of Riomaggiore, 114 km (70 mi) southeast of Genoa.*

Portovenere's small colorful houses, some dating from the 12th century, were once all connected to the 12th- to 16th-century citadel, so that in times of attack the villagers could reach the safety of the battlements. The town has a strategic position at the end of a peninsula that extends southeast from the Cinque Terre and forms the western border of the Gulf of La Spezia. Lord Byron is said to have written *Childe Harold* here. The huge, strange grotto at the base of the seaswept cliff is named after the poet, whose strength and courage were much admired after he swam across the gulf to the village of San Terenzo, near Lerici, to visit his friend Shelley. Above the grotto, on a formidable solid mass of rock, is San Pietro, a 13th-century Gothic church built on the site of an ancient pagan shrine. With its black-and-white-stripe exterior, it is a landmark recognizable from far out at sea.

Dining and Lodging

$$ ✕ **Da Iseo.** Try to get one of the tables outside at this waterfront restaurant, with bistro accents and paintings of Portovenere. Seafood is the only choice: it's fresh and plentiful. Pasta courses are inventive;

try spaghetti *alla Giuseppe* (with shellfish and fresh tomato) or spaghetti *alla Iseo* (with a seafood curry sauce). ⊠ *Portovenere,* ☎ *0187/790610. AE, DC, MC, V. Closed Wed. and Jan. 2–Feb. 15.*

$ ✗ **Antica Osteria del Carrugio.** Near the castle built to defend the coast from Pisan incursions, this is a 100-year-old tavern with maritime decor. The menu features seafood, which varies with the catch of the day. Specialties include *mescina* (soup of beans, chick peas, and wheat) and *polpo in insalata* (octopus salad). ⊠ *Via Cappellini 66,* ☎ *0187/900617. Reservations not accepted. No credit cards. Closed Thurs. and mid-Nov.–mid-Dec.*

$$$ 🏨 **Royal Sporting.** Appearances are deceptive at this modern hotel, **★** which is on the beach about a 10-minute walk from the village. From the outside, the stone construction seems austere and unwelcoming, but the courtyards and interior are colorful and vibrant. There are fresh flowers and potted plants in the reception rooms and terraces, and the cool, airy rooms all have sea views. The sports facilities are among the best in the area. ⊠ *Via dell'Olivo 345, 19025,* ☎ *0187/790326,* FAX *0187/529060. 62 rooms. Restaurant, bar, pool, tennis court, beach. AE, DC, MC, V. Closed mid-Oct.–Apr. (except Easter wk).*

Lerici

㊷ *11 km (7 mi) east of La Spezia, 65 km (40 mi) northeast of Pisa.*

Lerici, near Liguria's border with Tuscany, is set on a magnificent coastline of gray cliffs and pine forests. The town once belonged to Tuscan Pisa, and the medieval castle that stands above the splendid bay, which has attracted lovers of nature for centuries, is 13th-century Pisan. Shelley was one of Lerici's best-known visitors and spent some of the happiest months of his life in the lovely white village of **San Terenzo,** 2 km (1¼ mi) away. The Villa Magni, where he lived, has a collection devoted to him. After Shelley drowned at sea here in 1822, the bay was renamed Golfo dei Poeti, in honor of him and Byron.

Dining and Lodging

$$$$ ✗ **Miranda.** Perched amid the clustered old houses in the seaside hamlet of Tellaro, 4 km (2 mi) southeast of Lerici, this small family-run inn has become a pricey gourmet's destination because of chef Angelo Cabani's imaginative way with Ligurian cooking. His unusual dishes include *insalata di gamberoni e aragosta con finocchio* (shrimp and lobster salad with fennel) and *involtino di branzino farcito di cozze* (fish roulade stuffed with mussels). ⊠ *Via Fiascherino 92,* ☎ *0187/964012. Reservations essential. AE, DC, MC, V. Closed Mon. and mid-Jan.–mid-Feb.*

$$ 🏨 **Florida.** A seafront hotel, this family-run establishment has bright rooms with all the extras you would expect in a higher category, including soundproofing and a balcony with a sea view. For an even better view, loll in one of the deck chairs on the roof terrace. The Florida overlooks a small beach area and is close to tennis courts and a golf course. ⊠ *Lungomare Biaggini 35, 19032,* ☎ *0187/967332,* FAX *0187/967344. 37 rooms. AE, DC, MC, V. Closed Jan. 7–Mar. 15.*

ITALIAN RIVIERA A TO Z

Arriving and Departing

By Boat

Genoa is Italy's largest port and can be reached from the United States as well as other parts of Liguria and Italy (Sardinia, La Spezia, and

Savona). Ships berth in the heart of Genoa, including cruise ships of the Genoa-based **Costa Cruise Line** (✉ Via Gabriele D'Annunzio 2, ☎ 010/54831). Ferries to various ports around the Mediterranean are operated by **Tirrenia Navigazione** (✉ Stazione Marittima, ☎ 010/2758041).

By Bus

The main bus station in Genoa is at Piazza Principe. Several bus lines, including **PESCI**, provide connections along the Ligurian coast and link Genoa with other parts of Italy, with the French Riviera, and with other cities in Europe. Bus tickets, reservations, and information in Genoa are handled by **PESCI** (✉ Piazza della Vittoria 94/r, Genoa, ☎ 010/564936), **Geotravels** (✉ Piazza della Vittoria 302/r, ☎ 010/587181), and **Guimar Tours** (✉ Via Balbi 192, ☎ 010/256337).

By Car

Autostrada **A12** south from Genoa links up with the autostrada network for all southern destinations; Rome is a six-hour drive from Genoa. The 150-km (93-mi) trip north to Milan on **A7** takes two hours. Nice is 2½ hours west on **A10**.

By Plane

Cristoforo Colombo International Airport (✉ Sestri Ponente, ☎ 010/2411), is only 6 km (4 mi) from the center of Genoa. It has regular service to all main European cities. The nearest airports for U.S. flights are Nice, in France, about 2½ hours west of Genoa, and Milan, about 2 hours northeast. **Volabus** services (☎ 010/5997414) from Cristoforo Colombo connect with Genoa's Brignole Station, stopping also at Piazza Acquaverde (Principe Station).

By Train

Frequent and fast train service connects Liguria with the rest of Italy. Genoa is 1½ hours from Milan and five hours from Rome. Many services from France (in particular, the French Riviera) pass along the Ligurian Coast on the way to all parts of Italy.

Getting Around

By Boat

This is the most pleasant—and, in some cases, the only—way to get from place to place within Liguria. A busy network of local services connects many of the resorts. For general information about availability of services in Liguria, contact **Servizio Marittimo del Tigullio** (✉ Calata Zingari, Genoa, ☎ 010/265712). Another source is **Alimar** (✉ Calata Zingari, Genoa, ☎ 010/255975). Or contact **Camogli–San Fruttuoso Maritime Services** (✉ Società Golfo Paradiso, Via Scalo 2, Camogli, ☎ 0185/772091), which runs between Camogli and San Fruttuoso (on the Portofino promontory), as well as between Recco and Punta Chiappa, two other towns close to Camogli. Summer excursions link both ports with the Cinque Terre and Portovenere.

By Bus

STIE and **PESCI** (☞ Arriving and Departing by Bus, *above*) buses run the length of the Ligurian Coast in both directions. Local buses serve the steep valleys that run to some of the towns along the western coast. Tickets may be bought at local bus stations, or at newsstands for local buses. Buy your ticket before you board the bus.

By Car

Two good roads run parallel to each other along the coast of Liguria. Closer to shore and passing through all the towns and villages is **S1**, which has excellent views at almost every turn but which gets crowded in July and August. More direct and higher up than S1 is the **autostrada**, known as **A10** west of Genoa and **A12** to the east. This route saves a lot of time on weekends, in summer, and on days when festivals slow traffic in some resorts to a standstill.

By Train
Regular service, connecting all parts of Liguria, operates from Genoa's two stations, **Stazione Principe** (points west) and **Stazione Brignole** (points east). All the coastal resorts are on this line, and many international trains stop along the coast west of Genoa on their way from Paris to Milan or Rome.

Contacts and Resources

Car Rental
Avis: Genoa (⊠ Piazza Acquaverde, ☎ 010/255598, for reservations, ☎ 06/4780150). **La Spezia** (⊠ Via Fratelli Rosselli 86/88, ☎ 0187/33345). **San Remo** (⊠ Corso Imperatrice 96, ☎ 0184/73897). **Budget: Genoa** (⊠ Airport, ☎ 010/6503822). **Hertz: Genoa** (⊠ Via delle Casacce 3, ☎ 010/564412). **La Spezia** (⊠ Via Casaregis 76/r, ☎ 010/592101). **San Remo** (⊠ Via XX Settembre 17, ☎ 0184/85618).

Emergencies
Police, Doctor (☎ 113). **Genoa municipal police** (☎ 010/53631). **Ambulance** (☎ 010/595951). **Ospedale Generale Regionale San Martino** (⊠ Viale Benedetto XV, Genoa, ☎ 010/516748).

Guided Tours
ORIENTATION TOURS
Informal **harbor cruise** or **excursion cruises** among coastal towns are scheduled and operated by the main ferry lines (☞ Getting Around by Boat, *above*), but you can have as much fun—if not more—negotiating a price with a boat owner at one of the smaller ports. You're likely to get a boat operator who commands rudimentary English at best.

A three-hour **bus tour** of Genoa with an English-speaking guide is the best way to see the city and its panoramic upper reaches. A coach with multilingual guide aboard leaves every day at 9 AM from the **AMT** (municipal bus company) office (⊠ Piazza della Vittoria, ☎ 010/5997414), stopping to pick up passengers at several points in the center of town; the last pick-up point is Piazza Acquaverde, at the Stazione Principe, at 9:25. Tickets (about 20,000 lire) can be purchased on the bus, but seats should be reserved at **Cooptur Liguria** (☎ 010/592658), or AMT. The tour includes an optional one-hour walking tour of the historic center and an optional 15-minute walk through the fishing enclave of Boccadasse.

You can also take a boat tour of Genoa harbor. The tour lasts about an hour and includes a visit to the breakwater outside the harbor, the Bacino delle Grazie, and the Molo Vecchio (Old Pier). You can see extensive views of the city throughout the tour. For information, contact the **Cooperativa Battellieri** (⊠ Stazione Marittima, Ponte dei Mille, Genoa, ☎ 010/265712).

Late-Night Pharmacies
Genoa: Europa (⊠ Corso Europa 676, ☎ 010/380239). **Ghersi** (⊠ Corte Lambruschini, Tower A, ☎ 010/541661).

Visitor Information
Genoa: Main **APT** (tourist board) (⊠ Palazzina Santa Maria, Old Port, ☎ 010/24871, FAX 010/2467658). Additional offices: (⊠ Principe Station, ☎ 010/2462633); (⊠ Airport, ☎ 010/2415247).

Local tourist offices are **IAT: Alassio** (⊠ Palazzo Hanbury, Via Gibb 26, ☎ 0182/640346, FAX 0182/644690). **Albenga** (⊠ Via B. Ricci, corner of Piazza San Michele, ☎ 0182/554752, FAX 0182/51325). **Bordighera** (⊠ Palazzo del Parco, ☎ 0184/262322, FAX 0184/264455). **Camogli** (⊠ Via XX Settembre 33r, ☎ 0185/771066). **Imperia** (⊠ Via Matteotti 54/a, ☎ 0183/24947, FAX 0183/24950). **La Spezia** (⊠ Via Mazzini 47, ☎ 0187/770900, FAX 0187/770908). **Lerici** (⊠ Via Gerini 40, ☎ 0187/967346). **Levanto** (⊠ Piazza Cavour 12, ☎ 0187/808125, FAX 0187/808125.). **Rapallo** (⊠ Via A. Diaz 9, ☎ 0185/230346, FAX 0185/63051). **San Remo** (⊠ Corso Nuvoloni, ☎ 0184/571571, FAX 0184/507649). **Varazze** (⊠ Viale Nazioni Unite, ☎ 019/934609, FAX 019/97298). **Ventimiglia** (⊠ Via Cavour 61, ☎ 0184/351183).

8 Piedmont/ Valle d'Aosta

From Turin to the Alps and Across the Po Plain

Italy's windows on France and Switzerland, Piedmont and the magnificent Valle d'Aosta come as delightful surprises in a land of many natural splendors. Monte Bianco (Mont Blanc) and Monte Cervino (the Matterhorn) offer stellar skiing. Nearby Alpine valleys cradle storybook castles. The "Italian Detroit"—Turin, home of the Fiat empire, marvels with splendid piazzas and museums and other well-known exports—Borsalino hats, vermouth, and Asti Spumante.

Updated by
Barbara Walsh
Angelillo

FROM ALPINE VALLEYS hemming the highest mountains in Europe to the mist-shrouded lowlands skirting the Po River, from pulsating industrial centers turning out the best of Italian design to tiny stone villages isolated above the clouds, and from hearty peasant cooking in farmhouse kitchens to French-accented delicacies washed down by some of Italy's finest wines, Piedmont and the spectacular Valle d'Aosta promise the traveler a store of historical, cultural, and natural riches.

Piedmont's Italian Alps afford excellent skiing and climbing at renowned resort towns such as Courmayeur and Breuil-Cervinia. In the lowlands, Turin, the regional capital, is a historical center that today also serves as the heart of Italy's booming auto industry. Nearby are Alba, home of delectable Italian white truffles, seasonal delicacies that sell for more than $1,000 per pound; Asti, Barolo, and Barbaresco, the famous wine centers; and the modern business hubs Ivrea, Novara, and Alessandria.

Tucked away at the foot of the Pennine, Graian, Cottian, and Maritime Alps (the name Piemonte, in Italian, means "foot of the mountains"), Piedmont and the autonomous region of Valle d'Aosta just north of it seem more akin to neighboring France and Switzerland. Well-dressed women in the refined cafés of Turin are addressed more often as *madama* than *signora,* and French is often used in the more remote mountain hamlets.

Piedmont was originally inhabited by Celtic tribes who were absorbed by the Romans. As allies of Rome, the Celts held off Hannibal when he came down through the Alpine passes with his elephants but were eventually defeated, and their capital—Taurasia, the present Turin—was destroyed. The Romans rebuilt the city, giving its streets the grid pattern that survives today. Roman ruins can be found throughout both regions and are particularly conspicuous in the town of Aosta.

With the fall of the Roman empire, Piedmont suffered the fate of the rest of Italy and was successively occupied and ravaged by barbarians from the east and the north. In the 11th century, a feudal French family named Savoy ruled Turin briefly; toward the end of the 13th century they returned to the area, where they would remain, almost continuously, for 500 years. In 1798 the French Republican armies invaded Italy, but when Napoléon's empire fell, the House of Savoy returned to power.

Beginning in 1848, Piedmont was one of the principal centers of the Risorgimento, the movement for Italian unity. In 1861 the Chamber of Deputies of Turin declared Italy a united kingdom. Rome became the capital in 1870, marking the end of Piedmont's importance in the political sphere. Nevertheless, the architectural splendors of Turin, together with some unheralded but excellent museums, continue to draw travelers.

Piedmont became one of the first industrialized regions in Italy, and the automotive giant FIAT—the Fabbrica Italiana Automobili Torino—was established here in 1899. Today the region is the center of Italy's automobile, metalworking, chemical, and candy industries, having attracted thousands of workers from Italy's impoverished south.

The Valle d'Aosta, to the north, is famous for its impressive fortified castles and splendid Alpine beauty. It was settled in the 3rd millennium BC by people from the Mediterranean and later by a Celtic tribe known as the Salassi, who eventually fell to the Romans. The Saracens were here in the 10th century; by the 12th century, the Savoy family had established itself, and the region's feudal nobles moved into the countryside, building the massive castles that still stand. Valle d'Aosta enjoyed relative autonomy as part of the Savoy kingdom and was briefly ruled by the French four separate times. The region is still officially bilingual, so you will hear both Italian and French.

Pleasures and Pastimes

Dining

These two regions offer rustic specialties, from farmhouse hearths and fine cuisine with a French accent—and everything in between. The favorite form of pasta is *agnolotti* (similar to ravioli), filled with meat, spinach, or cheese. Another regional specialty is *fonduta*—a local form of fondue, made with melted Fontina (a cheese from the Valle d'Aosta), eggs, and sometimes grated truffles. Alba is the home of *tartufi bianchi* (white truffles), much rarer and more expensive than black ones and considered the tastiest by connoisseurs. They sell for at least $1,000 a pound wholesale. Another local dish is *bagna cauda*, a hot sauce (*bagna cauda* means hot bath) made from butter, oil, anchovies, cream, and shredded garlic. It is served with *cardi* (edible thistles) or other raw vegetables.

Turin is renowned for its delicate pastries and fine chocolates, especially for the hazelnut *gianduiotti*. Valle d'Aosta is famous for a variety of schnappslike brandies made from fruits or herbs.

Piedmont is one of Italy's most important wine-producing regions. Most of the wines are full-bodied reds, such as Barolo, Nebbiolo, Freisa, Barbera, and Barbaresco. Asti Spumante, a sparkling wine, comes from the region, as does vermouth, which was developed in Piedmont by A. B. Carpano in 1786. Many prefer dry (brut) Spumante to the sweet Asti varietal.

CATEGORY	COST*
$$$$	over 90,000 lire
$$$	60,000–90,000 lire
$$	35,000–60,000 lire
$	under 35,000 lire

Prices are per person, including house wine, service, and tax.

Lodging

There is a high standard of Old World opulence in Turin's better hotels, and it is translated into the Alpine idiom in the top resort hotels in the mountains. Less-expensive hotels in cities and towns are generally geared to business travelers. You can usually count on a measure of charm at resorts and the Italian version of gemütlichkeit even in more modest resort hotels. Summer and winter occupancy rates and prices are usually quite high at resorts, with summer vacationers and skiers, respectively, monopolizing available accommodations. Hotels in mountain resorts may offer attractive half-board or off-season rates that can sometimes reduce the cost by a full price category. Many mountain resort hotels cater primarily to half- or full-board guests only, for stays of at least a week. It's better to take a package deal on a ski vacation; it may give you a break on the price of lift tickets.

CATEGORY	COST*
$$$$	over 300,000 lire
$$$	220,000–300,000 lire
$$	150,000–220,000 lire
$	under 150,000 lire

Prices are for a standard double room for two, including service and 9% tax (12% for luxury establishments).

Skiing

This is the major sport in both Piedmont and the Valle d'Aosta. Resorts with excellent facilities abound near the highest mountains in Europe—Monte Bianco (Mont Blanc), Monte Rosa, Monte Cervino (the Matterhorn), and the Gran Paradiso.

Exploring Piedmont/Valle d'Aosta

The vast Po Plain that stretches eastward in a wide swathe across the top of the Italian peninsula begins in Piedmont, where the River Po has its source in the Coolidge Glacier on 1,200-ft-high Monviso. But Piedmont is primarily a mountainous region. High Alpine crests rise to the north and west of the plain. The Maritime Alps lie to the south, and the rolling hills of the Monferrato and Langhe districts make folds in the landscape southeast of Turin. Nature has endowed Piedmont and the Valle d'Aosta with some striking scenery.

Numbers in the text correspond to numbers in the margin and on the Piedmont/Valle d'Aosta and Turin maps.

Great Itineraries

With the exception of the mountain resorts, which may be packed at the height of the season, much of Piedmont and Valle d'Aosta is off the beaten track for tourists. These regions of Italy offer the pleasures of discovery: uncrowded, unhurried samplings of scenery, art, food, and some of Italy's finest wines.

Turin, the regional capital and the area's largest city, and its environs are easily reached by car or public transportation from the city center. Don't be put off by Turin's industrial reputation; sure, it is the capital and headquarters of one of the world's major car manufacturers, but it is also home to beautiful churches, elegant piazzas, and interesting museums. Next, as you wind your way northeast into the Valle d'Aosta, you are in the Italian Loire, where solid, imposing castles sit in the shadow of Europe's most impressive peaks, Mont Blanc and the Matterhorn. The ancient Roman city of Aosta itself is of great interest to the visitor. One of Italy's most popular winter playgrounds, the Valle d'Aosta offers world-class skiing and accommodations. The third area of interest is the fertile Po Valley and its fortified cities, especially Asti, world-famous for its wine.

The amount of time you choose to spend here depends on your interests. If you want to admire the highest mountains in the Alps from the pistes or the deck of a chalet, sneak up on the chamois in the Gran Paradiso National Park, and still have time to devote to Turin and the wine country, a total of nine days should be sufficient. Five days would give you a chance to visit Turin's attractions, make an excursion into the mountains, and discover some of the smaller cities. In three days you can see Turin and then head to Aosta for a look at some impressive Roman ruins and a quick trip into the mountains. If you budget your time carefully, you can spend half a day in Asti.

IF YOU HAVE 3 DAYS

Visitors with limited time should concentrate first on ⚅ **Turin** ①–⑯ and its main sites, including the **Duomo** ②, where the famous shroud is housed; the 17th-century **Palazzo Reale** ③, former residence of the Savoy royal family; and the churches of **San Carlo** ⑥ and **Santa Cristina** ⑦, which flank the impressive **Piazza San Carlo** ⑧, considered by many to be Italy's finest square. Take time to enjoy one or more of the city's authentic Old World cafés and the view from the striking **Mole Antonelliana** ⑪, an odd structure that was once the world's tallest building. On the second day, head northeast along the A5 motorway to

Aosta ㉖ to see its large and well-preserved Roman ruins before continuing on to ☷ **Courmayeur** ㉗ for magnificent views of the **Monte Bianco** ㉘. You have several choices for the third day: You can stay in the mountains, heading for ☷ **Breuil-Cervinia** ㉔ for a look at the Matterhorn, or you can double back from Aosta to ☷ **Cogne** ㉙, where you can make a foray into the Gran Paradiso National Park. Another alternative is to return to Turin and head southeast into the vineyard-blanketed hills around medieval **Asti** ㉚.

IF YOU HAVE 5 DAYS

Spend two days in ☷ **Turin** ①–⑯, then head for the Roman city of **Aosta** ㉖, perhaps stopping on the way to see the fairy-tale castle of **Fénis** ㉕. On the third day, you can drink in the views of the **Monte Bianco** ㉘ from ☷ **Courmayeur** ㉗, see the Matterhorn from ☷ **Breuil-Cervinia** ㉔, or follow the trails from ☷ **Cogne** ㉙ into the Gran Paradiso National Park. On the fourth day double back to Turin and make an excursion to **Saluzzo** ㉒, an old town steeped in 15th-century atmosphere. On the fifth day continue southeast to **Asti** ㉚, exploring the rolling hills where great wines and good food make this a gourmet's paradise.

IF YOU HAVE 9 DAYS

Make ☷ **Turin** ①–⑯ your base for three days, from which you can explore the city and the outlying towns, including **Saluzzo** ㉒, with its picturesque hilltop center and castles. Another excursion from Turin takes you to the castle at **Rivoli** ⑱, a sanctuary of contemporary art, and then over a pilgrim's route to two medieval abbeys, **Sant'Antonio di Ranverso** ⑲ and the **Sacra di San Michele** ㉑. Travel westward to Piedmont's high mountains and see the resorts of **Sestriere** and ☷ **Bardonecchia**, close to the French border. On the fourth day head for the mountains of the Valle d'Aosta; visit the castle at **Fénis** ㉕ on the way to ☷ **Aosta** ㉖, a good base for excursions into the mountains that will keep you moving on the fifth and sixth days between ☷ **Courmayeur** ㉗, ☷ **Breuil-Cervinia** ㉔, and ☷ **Cogne** ㉙. Head south on the seventh day, doubling back to Turin and continuing southeast to **Asti** ㉚. Follow the provincial roads through the vineyards of the hilly Monferrato and Langhe districts of south-central Piedmont, delving into their culinary and enological delights. On the ninth day head east across the fertile Po Plain toward the rice-growing capital of **Vercelli** ㉜, making sure you see the Duomo, the final resting place of several Savoy rulers. The easternmost city of Piedmont is ☷ **Novara** ㉝, of little interest, but a rest stop on the way to Milan, only 32 km (20 mi) away.

When to Tour Piedmont/Valle d'Aosta

Unless you are dead set on skiing, the region can be visited in either summer or winter. In winter, road conditions can be treacherous, especially higher up in the mountains, requiring the use of snow tires or chains. The ski resorts of the Valle d'Aosta are popular with Italians and non-Italians alike, so book your accommodations in advance. If you intend to visit the region in summer, try to avoid the month of August, which is the holiday month for the vast majority of Italians, many of whom will come here for an Alpine holiday of walking, hiking, and relaxation.

TURIN

❶ *176 km (105 mi) northwest of Genoa, 97 km (59 mi) southeast of Milan.*

Turin—in Italian, Torino—is roughly in the center of Piedmont/Valle d'Aosta; it is on the Po River, on the edge of the Po plain that stretches eastward all the way to the Adriatic. Apart from its role as northwest Italy's major industrial, cultural, and administrative hub, Turin is a cen-

Piedmont/Valle d'Aosta

SWITZERLAND

Mte. Cervino
(Matterhorn)

24 Breuil-Cervinia

Monte Rosa

28 Monte Bianco

Great St. Bernard
Pass

S406 Valtournenche

27 Courmayeur

Gressoney-
la-Trinité

Dora

S26

S27

26 Aosta

Nus Châtillon

Saint
Vincent

S26

Little St. Bernard
Pass

Baltéa

S26

VALLE D'AOSTA

25

Fénis Castle

Verrès

S505

29 Cogne

**Forte di
Bard** **23**

Pont St. Martin

Gran Paradiso

S26

Ceresole Reale

Ivrea

FRANCE

Forno Alpi Gràie

S460

Orco

Dora Baltéa

Cuorgnè

Balme

Céres

A5

S26

Bardonecchia

S25

Chivasso

Susa

S24

A4

Sacra di San Michele **21** **20**

**Sant'Antonio
di Ranverso**

Avigliana

19 **18**

Rivoli

Sestriere

TO
CLAVIERE

S23

Stupinigi

17

Turin

1 — 16

S10

ITALY

N

S589

S20

A21

S23

Carignano

Pinerolo

A6

TO
BRÀ

S29

TO
ALBA

0   10 miles

0   15 km

22 **Saluzzo**

ter of education, science, and the arts. It also has a reputation as Italy's capital of black magic and the supernatural. This distinction is enhanced by the presence of Turin's most controversial, fascinating, and unsettling relic, the Sacra Sindone (Holy Shroud), still believed by many Catholics to be the cloth in which Christ's body was wrapped when he was taken down from the cross.

Many of Turin's major sights are clustered around Piazza Castello, and others are on or just off the porticoed Via Roma, one of the city's main thoroughfares, which leads 1 km (½ mi) from Piazza Castello south to Piazza Carlo Felice, a landscaped park with a fountain in front of the train station. First opened in 1615, Via Roma was largely rebuilt in the 1930s, during the time of Premier Benito Mussolini.

Downtown Turin

A Good Walk

Start on Piazza San Giovanni at the **Duomo** ②, hushed and shadowy repository of a controversial relic. Step into the **Palazzo Reale** ③, adjacent to the Duomo, to see the sumptuous interiors and, in a separate wing also on Piazza Castello, the **Armeria Reale.** The massive building occupying an entire block at the center of Piazza Castello is **Palazzo Madama** ④, but you can see it only from the outside. In the northwest corner of the same square, take time to observe Guarini's lively architectural vision in the church of **San Lorenzo** ⑤. Go southwest on Via Roma, a street rebuilt with arcades in the 1930s, during the time of Premier Benito Mussolini. Continuing a few blocks down Via Roma, you come to **Piazza San Carlo** ⑧, with its twin churches of **San Carlo** ⑥ and **Santa Cristina** ⑦. Just off the northeast end of Piazza San Carlo is the imposing **Palazzo dell'Accademia delle Scienze** ⑨, where you may devote upwards of an hour or two to the collections in the Museo Egizio and Galleria Sabauda. To the east, across the street is the graceful **Palazzo Carignano** ⑩, not only historic but also an example of Piedmontese Baroque. The east facade of the palace faces Piazza Carlo Alberto, where you turn into Via Po, heading east to Via Montebello, where you turn left to reach the **Mole Antonelliana** ⑪, Turin's oddest and most conspicuous building.

TIMING

This walk takes the better part of a day if you allow plenty of time for the museums. Since it includes the most important of Turin's sights, it can constitute a satisfactory, albeit sketchy, visit.

Sights to See

② **Duomo.** The most impressive piece in Turin's 15th-century cathedral is the shadowy, black marble–walled **Cappella della Sacra Sindone** (Chapel of the Holy Shroud), where the Holy Shroud was housed before a severe fire in 1997. The chapel was designed by the priest and architect Guarino Guarini (1604–83), a genius of the Baroque style who was official engineer and mathematician to the court of Duke Carlo Emanuele II of Savoy. The fire was major setback to ongoing restorations; at press time (spring 1997) the chapel was closed indefinitely due to the severe damage.

The **shroud** is a four-yard-long sheet of linen, unremarkable except for the fact that it contains an imprint of what the faithful claim is an image of the crucified Christ. It first made an appearance around the middle of the 15th century, when it was presented to Ludovico of Savoy in Chambéry. In 1578 it was brought to Turin by another member of the Savoy royal family, Duke Emanuele Filiberto. It is only in the last few years that the Catholic Church has allowed rigorous scientific study of the shroud. The results have been double edged. On the one hand, three separate university teams—in Italy, Britain, and the United States—have concluded, as a result of carbon 14 dating, that the cloth is a forgery dating from between 1260 and 1390. On the other hand, they are unable to explain how the shroud's image, which is like a photographic negative, could have been created, and the shroud continues to be revered as a holy relic. The shroud will still be displayed to the public—a rare occurrence—in celebration of the cathedral's 500th year, but not in the fire-damaged chapel; at press time a location had not been determined. The shroud will again be exhibited in 2000 to mark the beginning of the third millennium. ⊠ *Piazza San Giovanni.*

★ ⑪ **Mole Antonelliana.** You won't miss the unusual square dome and thin, elaborate spire tower of this Turin landmark above the city's rooftops. This odd structure, built between 1863 and 1897, was originally intended to be a synagogue, but costs escalated and eventually it was bought by the city of Turin. In its time it was the tallest building in the world. There is an excellent view of the city, the plain surrounding it, and the Alps beyond from a terrace at the top of the dome. Take the elevator to the top. ⊠ *Via Montebello 20,* ☎ *011/8170496.* ☐ *5,000 lire.* ☉ *Tues.–Fri. 10–4, weekends 9–7.*

⑩ **Palazzo Carignano.** One of Guarini's Baroque triumphs, this redbrick palace was built from 1679 to 1685 and is one of Turin's and Italy's most historic buildings. Kings of Savoy, Carlo Alberto (1798–1849) and Vittorio Emanuele II (1820–78), were born within its walls. Italy's first parliament met here from 1860 to 1865. This is unfortunately not open to the public. ⊠ *Piazza Carignano.*

⑨ **Palazzo dell'Accademia delle Scienze** (Palace of the Academy of Sciences). Guarini's large Baroque tour de force, prefiguring the 18th century's preoccupation with logic and science, houses two of Turin's most famous museums, the Museo Egizio and the Galleria Sabauda.

The **Museo Egizio** (Egyptian Museum) is considered by many to be one of the finest outside Cairo. Its superb collection includes statues of pharaohs and mummies, and entire frescoes taken from royal tombs. Equally fascinating are the papyrus, art objects, and day-to-day utensils taken from the tombs of less noble ancient Egyptians. Look for the papyrus *Book of the Dead* and the 13th-century BC statue of Ramses II, which still glistens in its original colors. ⊠ *Via Accademia delle Scienze 6,* ☎ *011/5617776.* ☐ *12,000 lire.* ☉ *Tues.–Sat. 9–7, Sun. 9–2.*

The **Galleria Sabauda** houses the collections of the house of Savoy. It is particularly rich in 16th- and 17th-century Dutch and Flemish paintings: note Jan Van Eyck's *St. Francis with Stigmata,* with the saint receiving the marks of Christ's wounds while a companion cringes beside him as if feeling it all himself. Other Dutch masterpieces include paintings by Anthony Van Dyck and Rembrandt. Piero del Pollaiuolo's *Tobias and the Angel* is showcased, and other Italian artists featured include Fra Angelico, Andrea Mantegna, and Paolo Veronese. ⊠ *Via Accademia delle Scienze 6,* ☎ *011/547440.* ☐ *8,000 lire.* ☉ *Tues.–Wed. and Fri.–Sat. 9–2, Thurs. 10–7, every other Sun. 9–2.*

④ **Palazzo Madama.** In the center of Piazza Castello, this castle was named for the French queen Maria Cristina, who made it her home in the 17th century. The castle incorporates the remains of a Roman gate, as well as medieval and Renaissance additions. The architect Filippo Juvarra (1678–1736) designed the castle's elaborate Baroque facade in the early 18th century: he was intent on dispelling the idea that Italy's importance as a producer of contemporary art and architecture

In case you want to be welcomed there.

We're here to see that you're always welcomed at establishments everywhere. That's why millions of people carry the American Express® Card – for peace of mind, confidence, and security, around the world or just around the corner.

do more

In case you're running low.

We're here to help with more than 118,000 Express Cash locations around the world. In order to enroll, just call American Express before you start your vacation.

do more

Express Cash

And just in case.

We're here with American Express® Travelers Cheques
and Cheques *for Two.*® They're the safest way to carry
money on your vacation and the surest way to get a
refund, practically anywhere, anytime.
Another way we help you...

do more ®

**Travelers
Cheques**

was in decline. Juvarra's bold use of the Baroque is also evident in the interior of the castle, where the huge marble staircase heralds his patron's wealth and prestige. The large assembly hall was the scene of the first Italian Senate meetings in the mid-19th century. Today the castle houses the **Museo Civico d'Arte Antica** (Civic Museum of Ancient Art), which has a rich collection of Gothic, Renaissance, and Rococo sculpture and paintings, as well as medieval illuminated manuscripts. This museum has been closed for some time for extensive restorations, and the building remains closed to the public. ⊠ *Piazza Castello.*

❸ **Palazzo Reale** (Royal Palace). This 17th-century palace is the former Savoy royal residence. It is an imposing work of brick, stone, and marble that stands on the site of Turin's ancient Roman city gates. In contrast to its austere exterior, the palace's interior is characterized by luxurious, mostly Rococo, decor, including tapestries, gilded ceilings, and sumptuous 17th- to 19th-century furniture. ⊠ *Piazza Castello,* ☎ *011/4361455.* 🎟 *8,000 lire.* ☉ *Tues.–Sun. 9–7.*

The **Armeria Reale** (Royal Armory), in a wing of the Royal Palace, holds one of Europe's most stunning collections of arms and armor. It is a must-see for connoisseurs. ⊠ *Entrance on Piazza Castello,* ☎ *011/543889.* 🎟 *8,000 lire.* ☉ *Tues. and Thurs. 2:30–7, Wed., Fri. (groups only), and weekends 9–1:30.*

❽ **Piazza San Carlo.** While standing in the stately, formal expanse, you too may proclaim this to be the grandest square in Italy. In the center stands a **statue of Duke Emanuele Filiberto of Savoy,** victor, in 1557, of the battle of San Quintino. The melee heralded the peaceful resurgence of Turin under the Savoys, after years of bloody dynastic fighting. The fine bronze statue, erected in the 19th century, is one of Turin's symbols.

NEED A
BREAK?

The historic **Café San Carlo** (⊠ Piazza San Carlo) is usually ebullient with the energy of locals, gathered at the marble-top tables under the huge crystal chandelier. On the opposite side of the square is **Stratta,** one of Turin's best-known, and sinful, chocolate shops.

❻ **San Carlo.** The ornate Baroque facade of this 17th-century church was enhanced in the latter part of the 19th century to harmonize with the facade of Santa Cristina. ⊠ *Piazza San Carlo, entrance to the southern end of the square.*

❺ **San Lorenzo.** The cupola and vividly painted interior of the church are standouts. Guarino Guarini was in his mid-sixties when he began work on the church in 1668, but the sprightly collection of domes, columns, and florid Baroque features seems more the work of a younger architect cutting his teeth with a daring display of mathematical invention. ⊠ *Piazza Castello.*

NEED A
BREAK?

Baratti e Milano (⊠ Just to the east of Piazza Castello), in the glass-roofed gallery between Via Lagrange and Via Po, is another one of Turin's charming Old World cafés. It's famous for its chocolates, so you can indulge your sweet tooth here or buy some *gianduiotti* (hazelnut-flavored chocolates) or candied chestnuts to take home to friends.

❼ **Santa Cristina.** Built in the mid-17th century, this church received a Baroque-style face-lift by Juvarra in 1715. ⊠ *Piazza San Carlo.*

Along the Po

The River Po is narrow and unprepossessing here in Turin, only a hint of the broad and mighty watercourse that it becomes as it flows eastward toward the Adriatic.

A Good Tour

Start at the east end of Piazza Vittorio Veneto, at the end of Via Po. Cross the river on Ponte Vittorio Emanuele I, the bridge leading to the church of **Gran Madre di Dio** ⑫, a replica of Rome's Pantheon. To reach the church of **Santa Maria del Monte** ⑬, follow Corso Moncalieri south and then wend your way upward to the top of the hill. Then return to Corso Moncalieri and cross the next bridge downstream, Ponte Umberto I, to the **Parco del Valentino,** opened in 1856. One of the city's many pretty pedestrian paths, **Viale Virgilio** runs parallel to the river and leads to the **Castello del Valentino** ⑭, reminiscent of the castles on the Loire. Go south on Viale Virgilio to the **Borgo Medioevale** ⑮, replica of a medieval hamlet and castle. From the park, catch a bus or taxi or just keep on walking south on Corso Massimo d'Azeglio to the **Museo dell'Automobile** ⑯, a low modern building that sweeps you into a world of nostalgia for the sleek, glamorous cars of yesteryear.

TIMING

Three hours should be enough to allow you to cover the ground with ease, but if you are an automobile buff, allow well over an hour for the Museo dell'Automobile.

Sights to See

⑮ **Borgo Medioevale** (Medieval Village). This was a veritable forerunner of today's theme parks. The village, a faithful reproduction of medieval Piedmontese buildings, was created for the Turin Exposition of 1884. A visit here is like stepping back into the Middle Ages, with craftsmen's shops, houses, churches, and stores clustered along narrow streets and lanes. ⊠ *By the riverside, southern edge of the Parco del Valentino.* ▨ *Free.* ☉ *Daily 9–7.*

⑭ **Castello del Valentino.** The design of this 17th-century castle, built more for appearance than for defense, is based on models of 16th-century French châteaux. It stands on the left bank of the Po, in the pretty **Parco del Valentino,** laid out in 1856. The interior is particularly elaborate, with frescoed walls and rich decoration, but the real attraction of the castle is its riverside setting amid the greenery of the park. The castle is closed for restoration. ⊠ *Parco del Valentino.*

⑫ **Gran Madre di Dio** (Great Mother of God). The 19th-century church was built in a neoclassical style based on the Pantheon in Rome. ⊠ *East bank of the Po, west of Piazza Castello.*

⑯ **Museo dell'Automobile** (Car Museum). No visit to car-manufacturing Turin would be complete without a pilgrimage to see perfectly conserved Bugattis, Ferraris, and Isotta Fraschinis. Here you'll get an idea of the importance of FIAT—and automobiles in general—to Turin's economy. There's a collection of antique cars dating from 1893, and displays show how the city has changed over the years as a result of its premier industry. ⊠ *Corso Unita d'Italia 40,* ☎ *011/677666.* ▨ *8,000 lire.* ☉ *Tues.–Sun. 10–6:30.*

⑬ **Santa Maria del Monte.** The church and convent standing on top of 150-ft Monte dei Cappuccini date from 1583. Don't be surprised if you find yourself in the middle of a wedding party: local couples often come here to have their pictures taken.

Dining and Lodging

$$$$ ✕ **Vecchia Lanterna.** Sumptuously decorated with brocades, old paintings, and rich carpets, this elegant, intimate restaurant in the center of town serves classic food, made from age-old regional recipes. For a first course, try *flan di tartufo nero con fonduta di groviera* (black truffle tart with fondue), and for a second course, *suprême di anatra allo scalogno* (glazed duck). A set menu of local fare is offered at a special price. ⊠ *Corso Re Umberto 21,* ☎ *011/537047. Reservations essential. Jacket and tie. DC, MC, V. Closed Sun. and Aug. No lunch Sat.*

$$$–$$$$ ✕ **Cambio.** The setting and atmosphere of this town center restaurant
★ in a palace dating from 1757 is nearly unmatched. It is probably one of Europe's most beautiful and historic restaurants, with decorative moldings, mirrors, and hanging lamps that look just as they did when Italian national hero Cavour dined here more than a century ago. The cuisine draws heavily on Piedmontese tradition and is paired with a wide array of fine Piedmontese wines. Great pastas might include agnolotti in an *arrosto* (roast veal) sauce; the veal carbonada is another savory treat. ⊠ *Piazza Carignano 2,* ☎ *011/546690. Reservations essential. Jacket and tie. AE, DC, MC, V. Closed Sun. and Aug.*

$$$ ✕ **Due Lampioni.** Join the stylish clientele of this elegant Baroque-style restaurant in a 17th-century palace in the heart of the city. It serves fine classic cuisine and an excellent selection of French and Italian wines. Try the artichoke flan *Vecchio Piemonte* (with meat sauce) and *agnello ai funghi con marsala* (boned leg of lamb with mushrooms in a Marsala wine sauce). ⊠ *Via Carlo Alberto 45,* ☎ *011/8179380. Jacket and tie. AE, DC, MC, V. Closed Sun. and Aug.*

$$$ ✕ **La Prima Smarrita.** Intimate and elegant, this restaurant is widely
★ recognized by critics as one of Turin's best. It is on the fringes of the Lingotto neighborhood, a short taxi ride from the city center. Host Moreno Grossi's light, innovative versions of Mediterranean dishes are a departure from the usual Piedmontese fare. Try *tortelli di borragine* (fresh pasta filled with borage and served with fresh tomato sauce) or sea bass with artichokes, potatoes, and olives. And for dessert try the *gianduia* (hazelnut chocolate) mousse. The wine cellar's bounty is excellent. ⊠ *Corso Unione Sovietica 244,* ☎ *011/3179657. Reservations essential. Jacket and tie. AE, DC, MC, V. Closed Mon. and Aug.*

$$–$$$ ✕ **Taverna delle Rose.** The cooking of the Piedmont and Veneto regions, with some creative touches, dominates in this character-filled restaurant near the train station. One dining room has walls covered with paintings; the other is done in old bricks and candlelight. Specialties include *faraona farcita di carciofi* (guinea fowl stuffed with artichokes) and roast venison with raspberry sauce. From the Veneto comes *bigoli con ragù d'anatra* (whole-wheat pasta with duck sauce). ⊠ *Via Massena 24,* ☎ *011/538345. AE, DC, MC, V. Closed Sun. and Aug. No lunch Sat.*

$$ ✕ **Da Mauro.** Try the Tuscan dishes in this lively, popular family-run trattoria. Specialties include cannelloni *alla Mirella* (baked with mozzarella cheese, prosciutto, and tomato), *involtini di Gorgonzola* (veal roulades with Gorgonzola cheese and a sauce of peppers and olives), and famous grilled Florentine beef. ⊠ *Via Maria Vittoria 21,* ☎ *011/8170604. Reservations not accepted. No credit cards. Closed Mon. and July.*

$$ ✕ **Ostu Bacu.** You'll find this small wood-paneled restaurant, in the same family for three generations, on the edge of town near the autostrada to Milan. Regional Piedmontese dishes are the draw, such as agnolotti and *fritto misto di carne* (a typical Piedmontese specialty of fried mixed meats, vegetables, and sweet morsels). ⊠ *Corso Vercelli 226,* ☎ *011/2464579. AE, DC, MC, V. Closed Sun. and Aug.*

$$ ✕ **Tre Galline.** Set in a portion of the ancient Roman wall only a few blocks northwest of Piazza Castello, this trattoria has a long history of serving good Piedmontese cooking. The *insalata di gallina* (chicken salad) has the tang of mustard, and the *stinco di vitello* (veal shin) is redolent of thyme. ⊠ *Via Bellezia 37,* ☎ *011/4366553. AE, DC, MC, V. Closed Sun. and Aug. No lunch Mon.*

$–$$ ✕ **Porto di Savona.** Look for this centuries-old tavern under the arcades of vast Piazza Vittorio Veneto, where it once served as a terminal for the Turin-Savona stagecoach line. The small street-level and upstairs dining rooms have a decidedly old-fashioned air; the marble stairs are well-worn and the walls don period photos of Old Turin. Customers sit at long wooden tables to eat home-style Piedmontese cooking, including gnocchi with the owner's handmade Gorgonzola and *bollito* (mixed boiled meats). The Barbera house wine is good. There are outdoor tables under the arcades. ⊠ *Piazza Vittorio Veneto 2,* ☎ *011/8173500. MC, V. Closed Mon. and 2 wks Aug. No lunch Tues.*

$$$$ ▦ **Principi di Piemonte.** Over a half century old, the Principi is one of the best hotels in town and often caters to a famous clientele. The rooms, elegantly furnished in antique style, are spacious and light, with high ceilings. It's in a convenient location. ⊠ *Via Gobetti 15, 10123,* ☎ *011/5629693,* ☎ *011/5620270. 107 rooms. Restaurant, bar. AE, DC, MC, V.*

$$$$ ▦ **Turin Palace.** You're right across from the train station at this century-old building in the center of town. Quiet, spacious, and well-furnished rooms have high ceilings and feature either leather-and-wood classic modern style or Imperial Louis XV furnishings. It's the classiest in town. ⊠ *Via Sacchi 8, 10128,* ☎ *011/5625511,* ☎ *011/5612187. 123 rooms. Restaurant, bar. AE, DC, MC, V.*

$$$ ▦ **Victoria.** Uncommon style and comfort are the hallmarks of this bou-
★ tique hotel, personally decorated and supervised by the caring management to create the atmosphere of a refined town house. The newer wing has a grand marble staircase and rooms individually decorated according to a theme, from romantic to clubby. The same attention to detail is given to the older rooms and to the attractive sitting room and breakfast room overlooking a small park. ⊠ *Via Nino Costa 4, 10123,* ☎ *011/5611909,* ☎ *011/5611806. 90 rooms. Bar. AE, DC, MC, V.*

$$ ▦ **Genio.** This 121-year-old building is done in a smart, modern style. The rooms are large and bright, with big, comfortable beds. There's no restaurant, but you're in the hub of town center. ⊠ *Corso Vittorio Emanuele 47, 10125,* ☎ *011/6505771,* ☎ *011/6508264. 90 rooms. Bar. AE, DC, MC, V.*

$$ ▦ **Liberty.** Liberty is the Italian term that refers to the Art Nouveau style, and this small, conveniently located hotel maintains that style in turn-of-the-century furnishings and an Old World atmosphere, enhanced by the Anfossi family's attentive courtesy. The hotel is a favorite of academics, artists, and others who appreciate its solid, old-fashioned comfort. ⊠ *Via Pietro Micca 15, 10121,* ☎ *011/5628801,* ☎ *011/5628163. 35 rooms. Restaurant. AE, DC, MC, V.*

Nightlife and the Arts

Music

Classical music concerts are held in the famous **Conservatorio Giuseppe Verdi** (⊠ Via Mazzini 11) throughout the year, but mainly in the winter months. The September music festival also highlights classical music. Sacred music and some modern religious pieces are performed in the **Duomo** on Sunday evening; these are usually advertised in the vestibule or in the local edition of Turin's nationally distributed daily, *La Stampa.*

Nightclubs

A plush after-hours venue for Turin's smart set, **Hennessy** (⊠ Strada Traforo del Pino 23, ☎ 011/8998522) is in the upscale Superga residential district; it's closed Monday. The aptly named **Big Club** (⊠ Corso Brescia 28, ☎ 011/2485656) is a large disco that also hosts rock concerts. Hot Latin music, often live, is dished up with gusto every day but Monday at **Sabor Latino** (⊠ Via Stradella 10, ☎ 011/852327). **Pick Up** (⊠ Via Barge 8, ☎ 011/4472204) caters to a mixed crowd of young Turinese, university students, and visitors; it, too, closes Monday.

Opera

The **Teatro Regio** (☎ 011/8815241, FAX 011/8815214), one of Italy's leading opera houses, begins its season in December. You can buy tickets for most performances (premieres are sold out well in advance) at the box office.

Outdoor Activities and Sports

Boating

Turin makes good use of the Po's recreational potential for boating. The **Lega Navale di Torino** (Turin Boating League) (⊠ Corso Unione Sovietica 316, ☎ 011/530979) organizes courses and special races throughout the summer.

Golf

There are several courses in the Turin area. Three 18-hole courses are northwest of the city, one at **La Mandria,** 18 km (11 mi) northwest (☎ 011/9235719), and two at **Fiano Torinese,** 20 km (12 mi) northwest (☎ 011/9235440).

Soccer

Turin's two professional soccer clubs, **Juventus** and **Torino,** play their games in the **Stadio delle Alpi** (⊠ Northwest city periphery, 6 km [3½ mi]), a new stadium that was used during the World Cup of 1990. Juventus is Italy's most successful club, and there is fierce rivalry among its supporters and those of visiting clubs. Home matches are usually played on Sunday afternoons during the season, which runs from late August to mid-May. The tourist office (☞ Piedmont/Valle d'Aosta A to Z, *below*) can provide information on where to find tickets, which are difficult to come by.

Shopping

Antiques

Piazza San Carlo, Via Po, and **Via Maria Vittoria** are lined with antiques shops, some—but not all—specializing in 18th-century furniture and domestic items.

Boutiques

Most people know that Turin produces more than 75% of Italy's cars, but they don't realize that it is also a clothing manufacturing city. Top-quality boutiques stocking local, national, and international lines are clustered along Via Roma and Via Garibaldi.

Food and Flea Markets

Go to the famous **Balon Flea Market** (⊠ Piazza Repubblica) on a Saturday morning for some excellent bargains in secondhand books and clothing and some stalls selling local specialties such as gianduiotti.

TURIN ENVIRONS

Stupinigi

⑰ *8 km (5 mi) southwest of Turin.*

The **Palazzina di Caccia** in the town of Stupinigi is an elaborate build-ing built by Juvarra in 1729 as a hunting lodge for the House of Savoy. It is more like a royal villa, with its many wings, landscaped gardens, and surrounding forests. This regal aspect was not lost on Napoléon, who lived here before claiming the crown of Italy. The castle interior is sumptuously decorated and today houses a collection of art and fur-niture in the appropriately named **Museo d'Arte e Ammobiliamento.** Take Bus 41 from Porta Nuova Station. ☎ *011/3581220.* ✆ *10,000 lire.* ⊙ *Tues.–Sun. 9–11:50 and 2–4:20.*

Rivoli

⑱ *13 km (8 mi) west of Turin.*

The Savoy court was based in Rivoli in the Middle Ages. The 14th- to 15th-century Casa del Conte Verde, right in the center of town, is a good example of medieval architecture of the transitional period, when its defensive function was giving way to the decorative. To get to Rivoli, take Tram 1 from downtown Turin, then Bus 36.

The 18th-century Savoy castle, built in the Baroque style under the di-rection of Juvarra, now houses the **Museo d'Arte Moderna** (Modern Art Museum), which contains many examples of 20th-century Italian art. The Futurist movement is particularly well represented. ⊠ *Piazza del Castello,* ☎ *011/9581547.* ✆ *10,000 lire.* ⊙ *Tues.–Fri. 10–5, week-ends 10–7, 1st and 3rd Thurs. of month 10–10.*

Abbey of Sant'Antonio di Ranverso

⑲ *23 km (14 mi) west of Turin, 10 km (6 mi) west of Rivoli.*

The Abbey of Sant'Antonio di Ranverso was originally an abbey hos-pital, founded in the 12th century by the Hospitalers of St. Anthony to care for victims of St. Anthony's Fire, a crippling disease contracted by eating contaminated grains. Pilgrims came here over the centuries for cures or, sometimes, to offer thanks for a miraculous recovery. The 15th-century fresco decorations, with their lifelike depictions of pil-grims and saints, retain their original colors. ☎ *011/9367450.* ✆ *5,000 lire.* ⊙ *Tues.–Sun. 9–12:30 and 2–5.*

Avigliana

⑳ *29 km (18 mi) west of Turin, 6 km (4 mi) west of the Abbey of Sant'Antonio di Ranverso.*

Perhaps due to its attractive setting, medieval Avigliana was a favorite of the Savoys up until the mid-15th century. Medieval houses still line the twisting and narrow streets. **Casa della Porta Ferrata,** on the street of the same name, is a well-preserved example of Piedmont Gothic do-mestic architecture: notice how the fascination with narrow, pointed arches is carried through even to private houses.

Outdoor Activities and Sports

GOLF

Avigliana has a well-laid-out 18-hole golf course, **Le Fronde** (☎ 011/ 935083); it is closed January and February.

Sacra di San Michele

★ **㉑** *43 km (27 mi) west of Turin, 14 km (8½ mi) west of Avigliana.*

A car is essential for an excursion to the Sacra di San Michele (Abbey of St. Michael). San Michele was built on Monte Pirchiriano in the 11th century to stand out: it is the most prominent location for miles around. When monks came to enlarge the abbey, they had to build part of the structure on supports more than 90 ft high—an engineering feat that was famous in medieval Europe. By the 12th century, this important abbey controlled 176 churches in Italy, France, and Spain, and one of the abbeys under its influence was Mont-Saint-Michel in France. Because of the abbey's strategic position, it came under numerous attacks over the next five centuries, and it was eventually abandoned in 1622. It was restored in the late 19th and early 20th centuries.

From Porta dello Zodiaco, a splendid Romanesque doorway decorated with the signs of the zodiac, you climb 150 steps, past 12th-century sculptures, to reach the church. The interior has 16th-century frescoes on the walls: on the left are religious subjects representing New Testament themes; on the right are stories depicting the founding of the church. Go down to the crypt to see the 9th- to 12th-century chapels. ▧ *Donation requested.* ☉ *Apr.–Sept., daily 9–noon and 3–7; Oct.–Mar., daily 9–noon and 2–dusk.*

Saluzzo

㉒ *58 km (36 mi) southwest of Turin.*

The older and more interesting part of Saluzzo hugs a hilltop in the Po Valley and is crowned by a castle. This town of time-worn russet brick was once a flourishing medieval center and was seat of a ducal court during the Renaissance. The narrow, winding streets and frescoed houses, the Gothic cathedral and the church of San Giovanni, and the 15th-century Casa Cavassa, a richly decorated palace that now houses a museum, take you back in time to the age of chivalry.

Knights and dames of old, heroes and heroines of an allegorical poem written by Marquis Tommaso III of Saluzzo, humanist lord of the castle, parade in full costume in the 15th-century frescoes in the **Baron's Hall** of the **Castle of Manta**, only 4 km (2½ mi) south of Saluzzo. The castle's exterior is austere, but the frescoes and other interior decorations, along with the surrounding park and good views, make it worth a visit. ⊠ *Via al Castello, Manta,* ☎ *0175/87822.* ▧ *5,000 lire.* ☉ *Tues.–Sun. 10–1 and 2–6. Closed last 2 wks in Dec. and Jan.*

Sestriere

93 km (58 mi) west of Turin, 32 km (20 mi) east of Briançon.

In the early 1930s, before skiing became a sport for everyone, the patriarch of the FIAT automobile dynasty had this resort built, with two distinctive tower hotels and ski facilities that have been developed into some of the best in the Alps. The resort lacks the charm of other, older Alpine centers, overdevelopment added some eyesores, and the mountains don't have the striking beauty of those in the Valle d'Aosta. But skiers have an excellent choice of trails, some of them crossing the border into France.

Lodging

$$$ ▦ **Principi di Piemonte.** Large and elegant, this luxurious hotel is on the slopes above the town, near the lifts and golf course. Its secluded location heightens the sense of exclusivity, a quality appreciated by a very stylish clientele. There is a restaurant and a cozy bar for après-ski relaxation. ⊠ *Via Sauze, 10058,* ☎ *0122/7941,* FAX *0122/755411. 94 rooms. Restaurant, bar. AE, DC, MC, V. Closed Easter–June, Sept.–Dec. 21.*

$$ ⊞ **Miramonti.** Nearly every room has a terrace at this pleasant, centrally located modern chalet. The ample, comfortable rooms are done in traditional mountain style, featuring lots of wood paneling and co-ordinated floral-print fabrics. ⊠ *Via Cesana 3, 10058,* ☎ *0122/755333,* FAX *0122/755375. 30 rooms. Restaurant, bar. DC, MC, V.*

Outdoor Activities and Sports

GOLF

Sestriere's 18-hole golf course (☎ 0122/755170) is open from mid-June to mid-September.

SKIING

At 6,670 ft, this resort was built in the late 1920s under the auspices of Turin's Agnelli clan. Although near the French border, it is just 93 km (58 mi) west of Turin. The slopes get good snow from November through May.

A quaint village with slate-roof houses, **Claviere** (17 km/11 mi west of Sestriere) is one of Italy's oldest ski resorts. Its slopes overlap with those of the French resort of Montgenevre.

Bardonecchia

36 km (22 mi) northwest of Sestriere, 89 km (55 mi) west of Turin, 20 km (12 mi) south of Modane.

This is one of Italy's oldest winter resorts, attracting hardy sports enthusiasts from Turin ever since the 1920s. It is near the entrance to the Fréjus train and automobile tunnels. The town gets plenty of sun and is at the center of a vast ski area.

Lodging

$$ ⊞ **Asplenia.** Skiers love this small, modern version of a mountain
★ chalet, near the center of town and the ski lifts. The ample rooms are comfortably furnished, with a small entryway and a balcony affording beautiful views. ⊠ *Viale della Vittoria 31, 10052,* ☎ *0122/999870,* FAX *0122/96192. 25 rooms. MC, V. Closed Easter–May and Sept.–Nov.*

$$ ⊞ **Des Geneys-Splendid.** One of the best hotels in the area, this establishment is in a private park near the center of town. Its 1930s style is evident in the arched windows on the ground floor, the stucco walls, and the long wrought-iron balconies. The public rooms are spacious and comfortable, and there's a playroom for children. ⊠ *Via Einaudi 21, 10052,* ☎ *0122/99001,* FAX *0122/999295. 57 rooms. Restaurant, bar. DC, MC, V. Closed mid-Apr.–mid-June and mid-Sept.–mid-Dec.*

$$ ⊞ **Riky.** This central, modern hotel has lots to offer: good service, comfy and spacious rooms, a good restaurant, and pleasant public rooms, including a children's playroom equipped with video games. There's a solarium and a piano bar with a cozy fireplace. Catering mainly to longer stays at half-board rates, it offers excellent low-season rates (nearly half price) for people staying at least a week. ⊠ *Via della Vittoria 22, 10052,* ☎ *0122/9353. 76 rooms. Restaurant, bar. AE, DC, V. Closed Apr.–June and Sept.–mid-Dec.*

VALLE D'AOSTA, THE MATTERHORN, AND MONT BLANC

Mountain Magic

The highest peaks in the Alps, the unspoiled beauty of Italy's oldest national park, magnificent scenery, bracing mountain air, and warm hospitality are the attractions of the Valle d'Aosta. The main Aosta Valley, largely on an east–west axis, is hemmed in by high mountains where glaciers have gouged out 14 tributary valleys, six to the north and eight to the south. Distances here are relative: short horizontally, as the crow flies, and much longer vertically, on steep slopes over tortuous roads.

Beyond Ivrea, the road takes you through countryside that becomes hillier and hillier, passing through steep ravines guarded by brooding, romantic castles. Another change that you may not notice from your car is the beginning of French-speaking territory, as you enter the Aosta region, about 18 km (11 mi) north of Ivrea. Pont St. Martin is the first village of the region.

Forte di Bard

㉓ *3 km (1½ mi) beyond Pont St. Martin.*

A few minutes beyond the French-speaking village of Pont St. Martin, you pass through the narrow Gorge de Bard and reach the Forte di Bard (closed to the public), a 19th-century reconstruction of a fort that stood for eight centuries, serving the Savoys for six of them. In 1800 Napoléon entered Italy through this valley and used the cover of darkness to get his artillery units past the castle unnoticed. Ten years later he remembered this inconvenience and had the fortress destroyed.

Saint Vincent

88 km (55 mi) north of Turin, 46 km (29 mi) north of Ivrea, 97 km (60 mi) northwest of Vercelli.

The town of Saint Vincent has been a popular spa resort since the late 18th century. Its main claim to fame these days is the **Casinò de la Vallée,** one of Europe's largest gambling casinos. Remember to pack your black tie—and plenty of lire.

Dining and Lodging

$$$$ ✕ **Batezar.** With only eight tables, this restaurant is considered one of
★ Italy's best. The ambience is rustic yet elegant, with arches and beamed ceilings enhanced by local antiques and fine crystal and silver place settings. There's an extensive à la carte menu, changing with the season, but also recommended are the set menus. For a starter, try the *tazzarella* (a small pizza with porcini mushrooms, mozzarella, and truffles) or fettuccine with herbs, artichokes, and filet of rabbit. Book well in advance. ✉ *Via Marconi 1, steps from casino,* ☎ *0166/513164. Reservations essential. Jacket and tie. AE, DC, MC, V. Closed Wed., June 10–30, Nov. 15–30. No lunch weekdays.*

$$$$ 🏨 **Billia.** A luxury belle-epoque hotel with pseudo-Gothic touches, the Billia is in a park in the middle of town and connected directly to the casino by a passageway. Half the rooms are done in modern and half in period decor, replete with all creature comforts. The hotel has extensive facilities, including a conference center and a private fishing reserve on a nearby mountain stream. ✉ *Viale Piemonte 72, 11027,* ☎

0166/5231, FAX 0166/523799. *250 rooms. 3 restaurants, bar, pool, sauna, tennis courts, health club, fishing, billiards, casino, nightclub. AE, DC, MC, V.*

$–$$ ⊞ **Elena.** The central location is the selling point of this hotel near the casino. The spacious rooms, some with balconies and/or king-size beds, are decorated with color-coordinated fabrics in a comfortable modern style and have air-conditioning. ⊠ *Via Biavaz 2 (Piazza Zerbion), 11027,* ☎ *0166/512140,* FAX *0166/537459. 48 rooms. Restaurant, bar, air-conditioning. AE, DC, MC, V. Closed Nov.–Feb.*

Breuil-Cervinia

㉔ *30 km (18 mi) north of Saint Vincent, 27 km (17 mi) north of Châtillon.*

Breuil-Cervinia is a village at the base of the Matterhorn (Monte Cervino, in Italian; Mont Cervin in French). Like the village, the famous peak straddles the border between Italy and Switzerland, and all sightseeing and skiing facilities are operated jointly. Splendid views of the peak can be seen from Plateau Rosa and the Cresta del Furggen, both of which can be reached by cable car from the center of Breuil-Cervinia. While many locals complain that the tourist facilities and the condominiums in the village have changed the face of their beloved Breuil, most would agree that the cable car has given them access to climbing and off-trail skiing in ridges that were once inaccessible.

Lodging

$$$$ ⊞ **Hermitage.** A marble relief of St. Theodolus at the entrance reminds
★ guests that this was the site of the saint's hermitage. But asceticism has given way to sybaritic comfort and elegance in what is now one of the most exclusive hotels in this Alpine region. A Relais & Châteaux property, it has the look and atmosphere of a relaxed but posh family chalet, with a fire always glowing in the enormous hearth and a romantic, candlelit dining room. The decor includes rustic antiques, petit-point upholstery, and the Neyroz family's collection of paintings of the Matterhorn. The bright bedrooms have balconies; suites have antique fireplaces and 18th-century furnishings. ⊠ *Strada Cristallo, 11021,* ☎ *0166/948998,* FAX *0166/949032. 36 rooms. Restaurant, bar, indoor pool, sauna, health club. AE, DC, MC, V. Closed May–June and Sept. 10–Nov.*

$$$–$$$$ ⊞ **Bucaneve.** This small, centrally located hotel is decorated in typical mountain style, with lots of wood paneling throughout, cheery floral upholstery in spacious lounges, and terraces dripping with geraniums. Après-ski, there's a restaurant and a cozy bar with a big fireplace and pianist in the evening. The hotel caters to longer stays at half-board rates. ⊠ *Piazza Jumeaux 10, 11021,* ☎ *0166/949119,* FAX *0166/948308. 26 rooms. Restaurant, bar, sauna, exercise room. AE, MC, V. Closed May–July and Sept.–Oct.*

$$$–$$$$ ⊞ **Cristallo.** An elegantly modern hotel high above town, the Cristallo has spectacular views. The two restaurants serve local specialties, such as fonduta and *bistecca alla valdostana* (chops cooked with cheese and ham). An overall feeling of pampering and comfort pervades. ⊠ *Via Piolet 6, 11021,* ☎ *0166/943411,* FAX *0166/948377. 103 rooms. 2 restaurants, bar, indoor and outdoor pools, tennis courts, exercise room. AE, DC, MC, V. Closed May–June, Sept.–Nov.*

$$–$$$ ⊞ **Neiges D'Antan.** In a pine wood at Perrères, just outside Cervinia,
★ this small, rustic family-run inn is quiet and cozy, with lots of wood decor, three big fireplaces, and a nice view of the Matterhorn. There are no TVs in the rooms: "It disturbs the atmosphere," says one of the proprietors. There's an excellent restaurant serving local specialties,

such as fonduta, *zuppa Valpellinentze* (a peasant soup of bread, cabbage, and Fontina cheese), and an opulent antipasto (local salami, country pâté, and tomino cheese). ✉ *Perrères, 3½ km (2 mi) outside Cervinia, 11021,* ☎ *0166/948775,* ℻ *0166/948852. 28 rooms. Restaurant, bar. AE, MC, V. Closed May 4–June 25, Sept. 15–Dec. 5.*

$$ 🏠 **Chalet Valdotain.** About a mile outside the town on the road from Châtillon, this Alpine chalet has wooden balconies and snug rooms with terrific views of the Matterhorn. It is known for good food and a friendly atmosphere. ✉ *Località Lago Bleu, 11021,* ☎ *0166/949428,* ℻ *0166/948874. 35 rooms. Restaurant, bar. AE, MC, V. Closed May and Oct.–Nov.*

Outdoor Activities and Sports

CLIMBING

Serious climbers can make the ascent of the Matterhorn from Breuil-Cervinia, having registered with the local mountaineering officials at the tourist office (☞ *Visitor Information in Piedmont/Valle d'Aosta A to Z, below),* but this climb is for serious and experienced climbers only.

SKIING

Because its slopes border the Cervino glacier, this resort at the foot of the Matterhorn offers year-round skiing.

Fénis Castle

★ ㉕   *17 km (10½ mi) west of Saint Vincent.*

The best-preserved fortress in the Valle d'Aosta, the many-turreted castle of Fénis was built in the mid-14th century by Aimone di Challant, a member of a prolific family that was related to the Savoys. This castle is the sort imagined by schoolchildren, with pointed turrets, portcullises, and spiral staircases. The 15th-century courtyard has a stairway leading to a loggia (open walkway) with wooden balconies. Inside you can see the medieval kitchen, with much of the original cooking equipment, and a collection of weapons in the armory. If you have time to visit only one castle in the Valle d'Aosta, this is it, even though parts of it may be closed for restoration. ☎ *0165/764263.* 🎫 *4,000 lire.* ☉ *Mar.–Oct., Wed.–Mon. 9–6:30 (group tour every ½ hr); Nov.–Feb., Wed.–Mon. 9:30–noon and 2–5 (group tour every hr).*

En Route   The highway continues climbing through the Valle d'Aosta to the town of Aosta itself. The road at this point is heading almost due west, with rivulets from the Parco Nazionale del Gran Paradiso (a wilderness reserve) streaming down from the left to join the Dora Baltea River, one of the major tributaries of the Po. Be careful driving here in late spring, when melting snow can turn some of these streams into torrents.

Aosta

㉖   *12 km (7 mi) west of Fénis Castle, 30 km (18 mi) west of Saint Vincent.*

Aosta stands at the junction of two important trade routes from France to Italy—from the valleys of the Rhône and the Isère. Its significance as a trading post was recognized by the Romans, who built a garrison here in the 1st century BC. The present-day layout of streets in this small city, which is tucked away in the Alps more than 644 km (400 mi) from Rome, is the clearest example of Roman street planning in Italy. Well-preserved Roman walls form a perfect rectangle around the center of Aosta, and the regular pattern of streets reflects its role as a military stronghold. St. Anselm was born in Aosta, and later became archbishop of Canterbury in England.

At the eastern entrance to town, in a square that commands a fine view over Aosta and the mountains, is the **Arco di Augusto** (Arch of Augustus), built in 25 BC to mark Rome's victory over the Celtic Salassi tribe.

The **Collegiata di Sant'Orso** (Collegiate Church of St. Orso) is the sort of church that has layers of history in its architecture. Originally there was a 6th-century chapel on this site, founded by the Archdeacon Orso, a local saint. Most of this structure was destroyed or hidden when an 11th-century church was erected over it. This church, in turn, was encrusted with Gothic, and later Baroque, features, leaving the church a jigsaw puzzle of styles, but—surprisingly—not a chaotic jumble. The 11th-century features are almost untouched in the crypt, and if you go up the stairs on the left from the main church you can see the 11th-century frescoes (ask the sacristan for entrance). These restored frescoes depict the life of Christ and the Apostles: although only the tops are visible, you can see the expressions on the faces of the disciples. Take the doorway by the entrance to the crypt to see the crowning glory of Sant'Orso—the 12th-century **cloister.** Beside the church, it is enclosed by some 40 stone columns with masterfully carved capitals representing Old and New Testament themes and scenes from the life of St. Orso. ☒ *Via Sant'Orso.*

The huge **Roman Porta Pretoria** is a remarkable relic of the Roman era. The area between the inner and outer gates was used as a mini–parade ground for the changing of the guard. ☒ *Western end of Via Sant' Anselmo.*

The 72-ft-high ruin of the facade of the **Teatro Romano** (Roman Theater) guards the ruins of the 1st-century BC amphitheater, which once held 20,000 spectators. Only seven of its original 60 arches remain, and these are built onto the facade of the adjacent convent of Santa Caterina. The convent usually allows visitors in to see these arches (ask at the entrance). ☒ *Via de Baillage.*

Aosta's **cathedral** dates from the 10th century, but all that remains from that period are the campaniles. The decoration inside is mainly Gothic, but the main attraction of the cathedral predates that era by 1,000 years: a carved ivory diptych (devotional work with two images) showing the Roman Emperor Honorius and dating from AD 406. For admission to **treasury,** contact the sacristan at Piccolo Seminario (☒ 2 Piazza Giovanni XXIII, behind cathedral). ☒ *Via Monsignor de Sales.*

Dining and Lodging

$$ ✕ **Piemonte.** A small restaurant in the center of town, the Piemonte
★   has a welcoming atmosphere and rustic decor. Heartwarming dishes might include *crespelle alla valdostana* (crepes with cheese) and *camoscio* (chamois) with polenta. ☒ *Via Porta Pretoria 13,* ☎ *0165/40111. MC, V. Closed Fri.*

$$ ✕ **Vecchio Ristoro.** The chef-proprietor of this centrally located, converted mill furnished with antiques and a large ceramic stove takes pride in creative versions of regional favorites. Among them may be *petto di faraona in crosta* (breast of guinea hen in a crisp potato crust) and *pizzoccheri* (buckwheat pasta), a specialty of his native Lombardy. ☒ *Via Tourneuve 4,* ☎ *0165/33238. AE, DC, MC, V. Closed Sun. No lunch Mon.*

$ ✕ **La Brasserie du Commerce.** Small, lively, and informal, this place is in the heart of Aosta, near central Piazza Chanoux. On a sunny summer day try to get a table on the terrace. Typical valley dishes, such as fonduta, are on the menu, together with a wide range of vegetable dishes and salads. ☒ *Via de Tillier 10,* ☎ *0165/35613. Reservations not accepted. MC, V. Closed Sun.*

$ ✕ **Taverna Nando.** A wine cellar with wooden floors and vaulted ceilings, this family-run tavern is in the center of Aosta, and it has a terrace for outdoor dining. The menu features regional specialties such as fonduta, *carbonada* (veal stew), and *cervo* (venison) with mushrooms. The wine list is impressive. ✉ *Via de Tillier 41,* ☎ *0165/44455. AE, DC, MC, V. Closed Thurs. and June.*

$$$ ▥ **Holiday Inn Aosta.** This modern, comfortable, and highly regarded hotel has the advantages of a central location and rooms with the chain's predictable amenities. There's local color, however, in the attractive Provençal fabrics and the views of the mountains. There are rooms equipped for people with disabilities. ✉ *Corso Battaglione Aosta 30, 11100,* ☎ *0165/236356,* ℻ *0165/236337. 50 rooms. Restaurant, bar. AE, DC, MC, V.*

$$ ▥ **Milleluci.** A small, cozy, family-run hotel, Milleluci is set in its own garden on a hillside overlooking Aosta, next to Jocteau Castle and with good views of the city and mountains. A huge brick hearth and rustic wooden beams highlight the lounge. Bedrooms are bright, with prints *de Provence* and attractive wood fittings. The hotel provides breakfast only. Rates are at the lower end of the $$ category. ✉ *Località Roppoz, 11100,* ☎ *0165/235278,* ℻ *0165/235284. 12 rooms. Bar, tennis court. AE, MC, V.*

$–$$ ▥ **Rayon du Soleil.** Saraillon, a residential district in the hills above Aosta, is the setting for this traditional redbrick mountain hotel in a park. There are excellent views from the rooms, which are large, bright, and quiet. Furnishings in mellow oak are solid and comfortable. There are rooms equipped for guests with disabilities. ✉ *Saraillon 16, 11100,* ☎ *0165/262247,* ℻ *0165/236085. 45 rooms. Restaurant, pool. AE, DC, MC, V. Closed Nov. and Jan.*

Nightlife and the Arts

Each summer there is a series of **concerts** held in different venues around the city. Organ recitals in July and August attract performers of world renown.

Shopping

LOCAL CRAFTS

Aosta and the surrounding countryside are famous for wood carvings and wrought-iron work. There is a permanent **crafts exhibition** in the arcades of Piazza Chanoux, in the heart of Aosta; it's a good place to pick up a bargain. Each year, on the last two days of January, the whole town turns out for the **Sant'Orso Fair,** when all sorts of handicrafts are on sale, including handmade lace from nearby Cogne, carved wood and stonework, and brightly colored woolens.

Courmayeur

★ ㉗ *35 km (21 mi) northwest of Aosta, 24 km (15 mi) from Chamonix.*

The main attraction of Courmayeur is a knock-'em-dead view of Europe's tallest peak, Mont Blanc. The jet-set celebrities who flock here are following a tradition that dates from the late 17th century, when Courmayeur's natural springs first began to draw visitors. The scenic spectacle of the Alps gradually surpassed the springs as the biggest drawing point (the Alpine letters of the English poet Shelley were almost advertisements for the region), but the biggest change in the history of Courmayeur came in 1965, when the Mont Blanc tunnel opened. Now Courmayeur stands on one of the main routes from France into Italy, although the planners have managed to maintain some restrictions on wholesale development within the town.

Dining and Lodging

$$ ✕ **Cadran Solaire.** This charming restaurant in town center, in what was the oldest tavern in Courmayeur, has been renovated by the Garin family, owners of the Maison de Filippo (☞ Monte Bianco, *below*), to highlight the 17th-century stone vault, old wooden floor, and huge fireplace. The menu offers seasonal specialties and innovative interpretations of regional dishes, such as *gnocchi gratinati* (potato and ricotta dumplings) and *filetto di trota alle nocciole* (fillet of trout with hazelnuts). ⊠ *Via Roma 122,* ☎ *0165/844609. AE, MC, V. Closed Tues., May, and Oct.*

$$$$ ▨ **Royal.** A classic mountain hotel in the center of town, the Royal is decorated with terraces, flowers, and wood paneling. Informal but elegant, it has modern rooms, a restaurant, and an evening piano bar. The hotel caters to longer stays with half- or full-board service. ⊠ *Via Roma 87, 11013,* ☎ *0165/846787,* FAX *0165/842093. 94 rooms. Restaurant, bar, grill, pool, sauna, health club. AE, DC, MC, V. Closed wk after Easter–mid-June and mid-Sept.–Dec. 1.*

$$$–$$$$ ▨ **Pavillon.** This is an elegant modern version of rustic chalet architecture, complete with warm golden-toned wood paneling, stylish furnishings, a clubby bar, and some stunning contemporary stained glass in the public areas and in the well-equipped health center. Full-board rates are good value. ⊠ *Strada Regionale 62, 11013,* ☎ *0165/846120,* FAX *0165/846122. 50 rooms. Restaurant, bar, indoor pool, sauna, health club. AE, DC, MC, V. Closed May–June 15 and Oct. 8–Nov.*

$$$ ▨ **Palace Bron.** A posh, comfortable hotel, Palace Bron is set in a pinewood at Plan Gorret, above the town itself. There are beautiful views, and it's ideal for relaxing. The rooms are comfortably furnished with period pieces. The restaurant has a fireplace. ⊠ *Plan Gorret, 11013,* ☎ *0165/846742,* FAX *0165/844015. 27 rooms. Restaurant, bar. AE, DC, MC, V. Closed May–June and Oct.–Nov.*

$$ ▨ **Cresta et Duc.** A bright, modern Alpine hotel in town center, the Cresta features plenty of wooden terraces, flowers, and wooden furnishings. For fun and relaxation there's a billiards room and lounges. The rooms are large and warm, and the hotel offers good full- and half-board rates. ⊠ *Via Circonvallazione 7, 11013,* ☎ *0165/842585,* FAX *0165/842591. 39 rooms (no singles). Restaurant, bar, billiards. AE, DC, MC, V. Closed Easter–June, mid-Sept.–mid-Dec.*

$$ ▨ **Croux.** This bright, comfortable hotel is near the town center on the road leading to Mont Blanc. Half the rooms have balconies, the other half have great views of Mont Blanc. There is no restaurant. ⊠ *Via Circonvallazione 94, 11013,* ☎ *0165/846735,* FAX *0165/845180. 33 rooms. Bar. AE, DC, MC, V. Closed mid-Apr.–June and Sept. 20–Dec. 20.*

Monte Bianco (Mont Blanc)

28 *3 km (2 mi) north of Courmayeur.*

At La Palud you can catch the cable car up to the Monte Bianco. The cable car crosses into France, so have your passport ready. Remember, too, that the cable car depends on the weather, and you may end up stuck on the French side overnight: have French money with you, in case.

You ride up to the viewing platform at **Punta Helbronner** (more than 11,000 ft), which is also the border post with France. Mont Blanc's attraction is not so much its shape (much less distinctive than the Matterhorn) as its expanse and the vistas from the top. The next stage, as you pass into French territory, is particularly impressive: you dangle over a huge glacial snowfield (more than 2,000 ft below) and make your way slowly to the viewing station above Chamonix. From this point you're looking down into France, and if you change cable cars, you can make your way down to Chamonix itself. The return trip covers the same route, and the total time should be 90 minutes, weather permitting. ✉ *Funivie La Palud*, ☎ *0165/89925.* ✆ *36,000 lire round-trip to Punta Helbronner; 43,000 lire from Punta Helbronner to Chamonix.*

Dining

$$ ✕ **Maison de Filippo.** Here you'll find country-style home cooking in a character-filled mountain house furnished with antiques. Reserve in advance, for it's one of the most popular restaurants in the Valle d'Aosta. There is a set menu only, featuring a daily selection of specialties including a wide choice of *antipasti* (starters) and pasta dishes, such as agnolotti in various sauces and spaghetti *affumicata* (with salami and bacon). The inn provides ample parking. ✉ *Entreves*, ☎ *0165/869797*, ℻ *0165/869719. Reservations essential. V. Closed Tues., June–July 6, and Nov.–mid-Dec.*

Outdoor Activities and Sports

SKIING

The famous **Courmayeur,** for the well-heeled, is well equipped and easy to reach, just outside the Italian end of the Mont Blanc tunnel. The skiing around Mont Blanc is particularly good, and the off-piste options are among the best in Europe.

Cogne

㉙ *52 km (32 mi) southeast of Courmayeur, 27 km (17 mi) south of Aosta.*

Cogne is the gateway to the **Parco Nazionale del Gran Paradiso.** This huge park, once the domain of King Vittorio Emanuele II and bequeathed to the nation after World War I, is one of Europe's most rugged and unspoiled wilderness areas, with wildlife and many plant species protected by law. Try to visit in May, when spring flowers are in bloom and most of the meadows are clear of snow. This is one of the few places in Europe where you can see the ibex (a mountain goat with horns up to 3 ft long) or the chamois (a small antelope whose soft skin nearly drove it to extinction).

FORTIFIED CITIES OF THE PO PLAIN

Southeast of Turin, in the hilly wooded area around Asti known as the Monferrato and another, similar area around Alba known as the Langhe, farther south, the rolling landscape is a patchwork of vineyards spotted with dark woods and dotted with little hill towns and castles. This is wine country, producing Italy's most famous reds and sparkling whites. And hidden away in the woods are the secret places where hunters and their dogs unearth the precious, aromatic truffles that are worth their weight in gold at Alba's truffle fair. To the north of these hills, across the Po, are the cities of the plain. Beyond them lies Lake Maggiore and eastward, across the Ticino River, is Milan.

Asti

㉚ *60 km (37 mi) southeast of Turin, 116 km (72 mi) northwest of Genoa, 127 km (78 mi) southwest of Milan.*

Asti is one of the main cities of the Monferrato. It is known to Americans mainly because of its wines (there are excellent reds as well as the famous sparkling white spumante), but its strategic position on trade routes between Turin, Milan, and Genoa has given it a broad economic base. In the 12th century, Asti began to develop as a republic, at a time when other Italian cities were also flexing their economic and military muscles. It flourished in the following century, when the inhabitants began erecting lofty towers for its defense. Some of these towers remain, giving the city a medieval look.

The center of Asti is studded with medieval towers, among them the 13th-century **Torre Comentini** and the well-preserved **Torre Troyana,** a tall, slender tower attached to the **Palazzo Troya** (✉ Piazza Medici).

Corso Vittorio Alfieri is Asti's main thoroughfare, running west–east across the city. This road, known in medieval times as Contrada Maestra, was built by the Romans. The 18th-century church of **Santa Caterina** has incorporated one of the medieval towers, the **Torre Romana** (itself built on an ancient Roman base), as its bell tower. ✉ *Western end of Corso Vittorio Alfieri.*

The **Duomo** is an object lesson in the evolution of the Gothic architectural style. The cathedral, built in the early 14th century, is decorated mainly in a Gothic style that emphasizes geometry and verticality: pointed arches and narrow vaults are counterbalanced by the earlier, Romanesque attention to balance and symmetry. The porch, on the south side of the cathedral facing the square, was built in 1470 and represents Gothic at its most florid and excessive.

The Gothic church of **San Secondo** (✉ South of Corso Alfieri) is dedicated to Asti's patron saint, who is also patron of the city's favorite folklore and sporting event, the annual *Palio,* the colorful medieval-style horse race held each year on the third Sunday of September in the vast Campo del Palio to the south of the church.

OFF THE
BEATEN PATH

ALBA – Thirty km (18 mi) southwest of Asti, this small town has a compact core studded with medieval towers and Gothic buildings, and a gracious Old World atmosphere. The town is the wine and truffle capital of the area. Visit in October for the National Truffle Fair, the Cento Torri Joust, and the Palio degli Asini (donkey races).

BAROLO – Some of Italy's finest wines are made within a radius of about 16 km (10 mi) of Alba. The zone is dotted with castles, and every town has a wineshop where you can sample the local vintage. The Castle of Barolo houses a wineshop and a museum of wine making. ✉ *Barolo.* ☉ *Fri.–Wed. 10–12:30 and 3–6:30. Closed Jan. and part of Feb.*

Dining and Lodging

$$$$ ✕ **Gener Neuv.** Family-run and one of Italy's top restaurants, the
★ Gener Neuv offers a sumptuous menu of regional specialties in a warm, welcoming atmosphere of rustic-style elegance, highlighted by excellent service, fine linen, silver, and crystal. The location in a park on the bank of the Tanaro River is splendid, although it resulted in severe flood damage in 1994; the restaurant had to be rebuilt. Your choices may include agnolotti *ai tre stufati* (with a filling of ground rabbit, veal, and pork) and faraona farcita *alle erbe* (with herbs). The prix-fixe menu is good value ($$$) but does not include beverages. ✉ *Lungo Tanaro 4,* ☎ *0141/557270,* FAX *0141/436723. AE, MC, V. Closed Mon. and Aug. No dinner Sun.*

$$$ ✕ **Falcon Vecchio.** There's been a restaurant in this ancient house in the historic center of Asti since the year 1670. Today, in intimate surroundings, the Falcon Vecchio serves rich local dishes that vary with the season. In fall and winter there are mushroom, truffle, and game dishes. Otherwise, there's a big selection of antipasti; grilled vegetables; and *bollito misto* (a steaming tray heaped with seven types of boiled

meat, served with various sauces). ⊠ *Via San Secondo 8,* ☎ *0141/ 593106. Reservations essential. AE, DC, MC, V. Closed Mon., 20 days in Aug., 10 days in Jan. No dinner Sun.*

$$$ 🏨 **Palio.** The hotel has the advantage of a central location in the historic heart of Asti and, though in an ultramodern building, it also has considerable character in individually decorated rooms featuring authentic antiques. Bathrooms in the minisuites are equipped with whirlpool baths. ⊠ *Via Cavour 106, 14100,* ☎ *0141/34371,* FAX *0141/34373. 29 rooms. AE, MC, V. Closed Aug. 10–25 and Dec. 23–Jan. 3.*

$–$$ 🏨 **Rainero.** An older hotel in the town center, near the station, Rainero has been under the same family management for three generations. It's been remodeled many times and is fitted with cheerful modern furnishings. There is no restaurant. ⊠ *Via Cavour 85, 14100,* ☎ *0141/353866,* FAX *0141/594985. 55 rooms. AE, DC, MC, V. Closed Jan. 1–8.*

Nightlife and the Arts

September is a month of fairs and celebrations in this famous wine city, and the **Asti Competition** in the middle of the month brings musicians, who perform in churches and concert halls.

Shopping

WINES

The **Enoteca** on Piazza Alfieri, a square adjacent to Campo del Palio, is a wine center and shop (🕐 Mon.–Sat. 9–4:30) where you can try the range of Asti vintages, buy some as souvenirs or picnic ingredients, and even have a light snack.

En Route From Alba double back to Asti to pick up the A21 autostrada. The road east from Asti to Alessandria is straight, skirting the southern edge of the Po plain, but for the first half of the drive you see to the south the green hillsides covered with vineyards. If you find yourself driving along this road during a thunderstorm (quite common on late summer afternoons) don't be surprised by the sound of explosions. Wine growers will often let off cannons loaded with blanks to force heavy clouds to rain, rather than build up and develop destructive hailstones.

Casale Monferrato

③ *42 km (26 mi) northeast of Asti, 31 km (19 mi) north of Alessandria, 75 km (46½ mi) southwest of Milan.*

Casale Monferrato, strategically situated on the southern banks of the Po, was held by the Gonzagas, rulers of Mantua, before falling into the hands of the Savoys: the 16th-century **Torre Civica,** marking the heart of Casale Monferrato in Piazza Mazzini, commanded extensive views up and down the Po.

Casale's most enlightening sight is the **Museo Israelitico** (Jewish Museum) in the women's section of the synagogue. Inside is a collection of documents and sacred art of a community that was vital to the prosperity of this mercantile city. The synagogue dates from the late 16th century, and neighboring buildings on the same street formed the Jewish ghetto of that period. ⊠ *Vicolo Olper 44, south of the Torre Civica,* ☎ *0142/71807.* 🎫 *5,000 lire.* 🕐 *Aug.–June, Sun. 10–noon and 3:30–5:30; at other times by appointment only (with extra charge of 10,000 lire per person). Closed Sat.*

Vercelli

㉜ *23 km (14 mi) north of Casale Monferrato, 80 km (50 mi) northeast of Turin, 74 km (46 mi) southwest of Milan.*

Vercelli is the rice capital of Italy and of Europe itself: Northern Italy's mainstay, risotto, owes its existence to the crop that was introduced to this fertile area in the late Middle Ages. **Piazza Cavour** is the heart of the medieval city and former market square. It was to this small square that merchants across northern Italy came in the 15th century to buy bags of the novelty grain from the East—rice. Rising above the low rooftops around the square is the **Torre dell'Angelo** (Tower of the Angel), whose forbidding military appearance reflects its origins as a watchtower. ⊠ *Piazza Cavour.*

The **Duomo,** a mainly late 16th-century construction on the site of what was a 5th-century church, contains tombs of several Savoy rulers in an octagonal chapel along the south (right) wall. The cathedral's *biblioteca* (chapter library—for entrance, see cathedral office) contains the "Gospel of St. Eusebius," a 4th-century document, and the *Codex Vercellensis,* an 11th-century book of Anglo-Saxon poetry. ⊠ *Piazza Sant'Eusebio.*

The **Basilica di Sant'Andrea,** a Cistercian abbey church built in the early 13th century with funds from another Abbey of St. Andrew (in England), witnessed the growing influence of northern Europe on Italy. Sant'Andrea is one of Italy's earliest examples of Gothic architecture, which spread from the north but ran out of steam before getting much farther south than the Po plain. The church interior is a soaring flight of Gothic imagination, with slender columns rising up to the ribbed vaults of the high ceiling. Tombs along the side aisle continue the preoccupation with stylized decoration and relief work. The gardens on the north side (Corso de Gasperi side) of the basilica hold the remains of the abbey itself and some of the secondary buildings. It is only here that the unadulterated Gothic style is interrupted. The buildings surround a cloister in which you can see the pointed Gothic arches resting on the severe and more solid 12th-century Romanesque column bases. ⊠ *Piazza G. Bicheri.*

The **Città Vecchia** is a collection of narrow streets and alleys. Many of the houses are five centuries old, and you can see partly hidden gardens and courtyards beyond the wrought-iron gates.

OFF THE BEATEN PATH | **BORSA MERCI –** You can take an unusual guided tour of the commodities market (⊠ Via Zumaglini 4, ☎ 0161/5981), where rice has been traded for centuries. Call first to check on tour times.

Novara

㉝ *23 km (14 mi) northeast of Vercelli, 95 km (59 mi) northeast of Turin, 51 km (31 mi) west of Milan.*

Novara is the easternmost city in Piedmont, only about 10 km (6 mi) west of the Ticino River, which forms the border with Lombardy. Milan is only 32 km (20 mi) beyond the border, and over the centuries the opposing attractions of this neighboring giant and of the regional capital, Turin, have made Novara a bit schizophrenic. In the Middle Ages, Novara's pivotal position actually made it a battlefield. A major engagement took place as recently as 1849, when the Austrian forces from the east defeated the Piedmontese armies.

Much of the present city dates from the late 19th and early 20th centuries, although there are interesting buildings from earlier periods scattered around Novara. Novara's most famous landmark is the tall, slender cupola of **San Gaudenzio.** The church itself, built between 1577 and 1690, conforms to a Baroque design, with twisted columns and sumptuous statues. The main attraction for most people, though, is the cupola, which was built from 1840 to 1888 and soars to a height of just under 400 ft. This spire is visible from everywhere in the city and the surrounding countryside, and has become as much a symbol of Novara as the Mole Antonelliana is of Turin.

The **Broletto,** a cluster of well-preserved late-medieval buildings, is next to the **Duomo,** of medieval origins but reconstructed in neoclassical style. The **Battistero** (baptistery), which is just outside the entrance to the cathedral, shows its august age in a much more evident manner. This rotunda-shaped building dates from the 5th century, although it was substantially enlarged in the 10th and 11th centuries. Recent restoration work has uncovered pre-Romanesque frescoes, more than 1,000 years old, decorating the inside walls. Their flat, two-dimensional style reflects the influence of Byzantine icons, and their restored colors add a frightening feel to the apocalyptic scenes depicted.

Lodging

$$ ⊞ **Italia.** This modern hotel in the center of the city offers comfortable rooms and efficient service; the facilities cater mainly to businesspeople. There is a restaurant, and some rooms have extensive views of the town. ⊠ *Via Solaroli 8, 28100,* ☎ *0321/399316,* ℻ *0321/399310. 55 rooms. Restaurant, bar. AE, DC, MC, V.*

PIEDMONT/VALLE D'AOSTA A TO Z

Arriving and Departing

By Bus

The main **bus station** is on the corner of Corso Inghilterra and Corso Vittorio Emanuele. The Turin-based **SADEM** line (⊠ Via della Repubblica 14, 10095 Grugliasco, Turin, ☎ 011/3111616) services the autostrada network to Genoa, Milan, and more distant destinations in Italy. The Turin-based **SAPAV** line (⊠ Corso Torino 396, 10064 Pinerolo, Turin, ☎ 011/322032) services the same area. **SITA** buses, part of the nationwide system, also connect Turin with the rest of Italy.

By Car

Italy's autostrada network links the region with the rest of Italy and neighboring France. Aosta, Turin, and Alessandria all have autostrada connections, with the **A4** heading east to Milan and the **A6** heading south to the Ligurian coast and Genoa. If you drive in from France or Switzerland, you pass through either the Mt. Blanc or Grand St. Bernard tunnels: these are two of the most scenically dramatic entrances to Italy.

By Plane

The region's only international airport, **Aeroporto Caselle** (information ☎ 011/5676361), is 18 km (11 mi) north of Turin. The airport is notoriously foggy in winter, and many flights are diverted to Genoa, on the coast, with bus connections provided to Turin. From Caselle Airport, **buses to Turin** arrive at the bus station on Corso Inghilterra in the center of the city.

By Train

Turin is on the main Paris–Rome express line and is also connected with Milan, only 90 minutes away on the fast train. The fastest trains cover the 667-km (400-mi) trip to Rome in about six hours, but most take about nine.

Getting Around

By Bus

SADEM and SAPAV (☞ Arriving and Departing by Bus, *above*) are the specialists in bus transportation in Piedmont and the Valle d'Aosta. **SAVDA** (✉ Strada Ponte Suaz 6, 11100 Aosta, ☎ 0165/361244) specializes in mountain service, providing frequent links between Aosta, Turin, and Courmayeur.

By Car

Turin is the hub of all the transportation systems in Piedmont, with autostrada connections to the north, south, and east. Well-paved secondary roads run through the rest of the region, following the course of mountain valleys in many places. Sudden winter storms can close off some of the mountain stretches: for information on road conditions, call ☎ 011/5711.

By Train

Services to the larger cities east of Turin are part of the extensive and reliable train network serving the Lombard Plain. West of the region's capital, however, the train services soon peter out in the steep mountain valleys. Continuing connections by bus serve these valleys, and information about train/bus mountain services can be obtained from train stations and tourist information offices.

Contacts and Resources

Car Rental

Avis Turin (✉ Corso Turati 15, ☎ 011/500852; ✉ Caselle Airport, ☎ 011/4701528). **Hertz** Turin (✉ Corso Marconi 19, ☎ 011/6504504; ✉ Caselle Airport, ☎ 011/4701103).

Emergencies

Emergencies (☎ 113). **Police** (☎ 112).

Guided Tours

Turin's group and personally guided tours are organized by the city's tourist office (☞ Visitor Information, *below*). **Alpine guides** are not only recommended, they're essential if you're planning to traverse some of the dramatic ranges outside Saint Vincent, Courmayeur, or Breuil-Cervinia. Before embarking on an excursion (however short) into the mountains in these areas, contact the representative of the **CAI** (Club Alpinisti Italiani; ✉ Piazza Chanoux 8, Aosta, ☎ 0165/40194) about the risks involved and the availability of an experienced guide. The main regional office listed above is open Tuesday and Friday. CAI information is also available at each tourist information office (☞ Visitor Information, *below*).

Late-Night Pharmacies

Pharmacies throughout the region take turns staying open late and on Sunday. Call (☎ 192) for the latest information, in Italian, on which are open.

Aosta Farmacia Centrale (✉ Piazza E. Chanoux 35, ☎ 0165/262205). **Turin Farmacia Internazionale** (✉ Via Carlo Alberto 24, ☎ 011/535144).

Visitor Information

Alba (✉ Piazza Medford, ☎ 0173/35833). **Aosta** (✉ Piazza E. Chanoux 8, ☎ 0165/236627, FAX 0165/34657). **Asti** (✉ Piazza Alfieri 34, ☎ 0141/530357, FAX 0141/538200). **Bardonecchia** (✉ Viale Vittoria 44, ☎ 0122/99032, FAX 0122/980612). **Breuil-Cervinia** (✉ Via Carrel 29, ☎ 0166/949136, FAX 0166/949731). **Courmayeur** (✉ Piazzale Monte Bianco, ☎ 0165/842060, FAX 0165/842072). **Novara** (✉ Via Dominioni 4, ☎ 0321/623398, FAX 0321/393291). **Saluzzo** (✉ Via Griselda 6, ☎ 0175/46710, FAX 0175/46718). **Turin** (✉ Via Roma 226, ☎ 011/535901, FAX 011/530070; ✉ Porta Nuova train station, ☎ 011/531327). **Vercelli** (✉ Viale Garibaldi 90, ☎ 0161/58002, FAX 0161/64632).

9 Milan, Lombardy, and the Lakes

From Ancient to Modern, from Nature to Renaissance

Old and new are often unexpectedly linked in Italy, and in Lombardy, they are married magnificently: modern Milan is just a few hours from the 19th-century resort towns of Lake Como, Maggiore, and Garda. The lakes remain the perfect escape from Milan, a metropolis that is Italy's business center and crucible of chic. With their opulent villas, exotic gardens, and Alpine vistas, the Italian lakes are among the most achingly beautiful places in Europe.

Updated by
Giuliano
Davenport

ONE IS TEMPTED TO DESCRIBE LOMBARDY as a place with something for everyone—Milan, capital of all that is new in Italy; the great Renaissance cities of the plain, Pavia, Cremona, and Mantua, where even the height of summer can be comparatively peaceful; and the lakes, where glacial waters framed by the Alps have been praised as the closest thing to Paradise by writers as varied as Virgil, Tennyson, and Hemingway.

The truth, of course, is more complicated. Milan can be disappointingly modern—rather too like the place you have come here to escape—but it is also the perfect blend of old and new, with historic buildings and art collections rivaling those in Florence and Rome. The lakes, home to dozens of fashionable resorts, have preserved an astonishingly unspoiled beauty, often enhanced by sumptuous summer palaces and exotic formal gardens. Still, one cannot imagine Catullus returning to his "jewel" Sirmione, on Lake Garda, without being a little daunted by its development as a lively resort town. The great towns of the Lombardy plain are rich in history, but their art and architecture pale before the staggering wealth of Rome, Florence, and Venice.

More than 3,000 years ago—the date and the details are lost in the mysteries of Etruscan inscriptions—explorers from the highly civilized realm of Etruria in central Italy wandered northward beyond the River Po. The Etruscans extended their dominance into this region for hundreds of years but left little of their culture. They were succeeded by the Cenomanic Gauls, who, in turn, were conquered by the legions of Rome in the latter days of the Republic.

The region became known as Cisalpine Gaul, and under the rule of Augustus it became a Roman province. Its warlike, independent people became citizens of Rome. Virgil, Catullus, and both the Plinys were born in the region during this relatively tranquil era.

The decline of the Roman Empire was followed by the invasions of the Huns and the Goths. Attila and Theodoric, in turn, gave way to the Lombards, who ceded their iron crown to Charlemagne as the emblem of his vast but unstable empire.

Even before the fragile bonds that held this empire together had begun to snap, the cities of Lombardy were erecting walls in defense against the Hungarians and against each other. These communes did, however, form the Lombard League, which, in the 12th century, finally defeated Frederick Barbarossa.

Once the invaders had been defeated, new and even bloodier strife began. In each city the Guelphs (bourgeois supporters of the popes) and the Ghibellines (noble adherents to the so-called emperors) clashed with each other. The communes declined, and each fell under the yoke of powerful local rulers. The Republic of Venice dominated Brescia and Bergamo. Mantua was ruled by the Gonzaga, and the Visconti and Sforza families took over Como, Cremona, Milan, and Pavia.

The Battle of Pavia in 1525, when the generals of Charles V defeated the French (and gave Francis I the chance to coin the famous phrase "All is lost save honor"), brought on 200 years of Spanish occupation. The Spaniards were, on the whole, less cruel than the local tyrants and were hardly resisted by the Lombards.

The War of the Spanish Succession, in the early years of the 18th century, threw out the Spaniards and brought in the Austrians instead, whose dominion was "neither liked nor loathed" during the nearly 100 years of its existence.

Napoléon and his generals routed the Austrians. The Treaty of Campoformio resulted in the proclamation of the Cisalpine Republic, which quickly became the Republic of Italy and, just as rapidly, the Kingdom of Italy, which lasted only until Napoléon's defeat brought back the Austrians. But Milan, as the capital of Napoléon's republic and of the Kingdom of Italy, had a taste of glory, and the city's inherently independent citizens, along with those of the other Lombardian cities, were not slow to resent and combat the loss of "national" pride.

From 1820 on, the Lombards joined the Piedmontese and the House of Savoy in a long struggle against the Hapsburgs and, in 1859, finally defeated Austria and brought about the re-creation of the Kingdom of Italy two years later.

Milan and other cities of Lombardy have not lost their independence and their hatred of domination. Nowhere in Italy was the partisan insurrection against Mussolini (to whom they first gave power) and the German regime better organized or more successful. Milan was liberated from the Germans by its own partisan organization before the entrance of Allied troops; escaping Allied prisoners could find sanctuary there when fighting was still going on far to the south.

Lombards are a forthright people. They are as much inclined to taciturnity as any Italian is ever apt to be, and, when they do talk, they mean exactly what they say. When they quote a price, there is little use haggling about it. A Milanese is inclined to be courteous, but probably has little time for pleasantries; his or her compatriot on the rice farm or in the mountains may be less talkative, but may take more interest in you as an individual.

Pleasures and Pastimes

Auto Racing

Though the fortunes of Italy's beloved Ferrari have waned in recent years, passion for the sport is undiminished here. A Formula 1 race is held in Monza, 15 km (9 mi) from Milan, every September. The track was built in 1922 in the Parco di Monza, where there is also a hippodrome, golf course, and other facilities.

Dining

Unlike most Italian regions, Lombardy exhibits a northern European preference for butter rather than oil as its cooking medium, which imparts a rich and distinctive flavor to the cuisine. Lombardy is the home of *alla milanese*–style cooking, for which means the food is usually dipped in egg and bread crumbs mixed with grated Parmesan, then sautéed in clarified butter. Among the most popular specialties is osso buco alla milanese with risotto. Risotto alla milanese contains chicken broth and saffron, imparting a rich flavor and yellow color. The lakes are a good source of fish, particularly trout and pike.

Gorgonzola, a piquant, creamy veined cheese, and panettone, a sweet yeast bread with raisins, citron, and anise, both hail from the Milan area and can be enjoyed throughout Lombardy. Although most of the wines in Lombardy can be paired well with the cuisine, try in particular to have the red Grumello or Sangue di Giuda (blood of Judas) wines or the delicious light sparkling whites from the Franciacorta area.

CATEGORY	MILAN*	OTHER AREAS*
$$$$	over 120,000 lire	over 90,000 lire
$$$	80,000–120,000 lire	60,000–90,000 lire
$$	45,000–80,000 lire	35,000–60,000 lire
$	under 45,000 lire	under 35,000 lire

Prices are per person, including first course, main course, dessert or fruit, house wine, service, and tax.

Golf

There are five courses near Milan and seven courses near Lake Como. To find courses in the area, contact local tourist offices, or the regional tourist offices.

Lodging

Lombardy is one of Italy's most prosperous regions, and hotels cater to a clientele that demands high standards and is willing to pay for extra comfort. Most of the famous lake resorts are expensive, although more basic—and reasonably priced—accommodations can be found in the smaller towns and villages. Milan may seem to have fewer tourists than other large Italian cities, but there is always competition for rooms, generated by the nearly year-round trade fairs and other business-related bookings. It is best—and almost essential in spring and summer—to make reservations.

Many Lombardy hotels are converted from beautiful old villas and have well-landscaped grounds. Try to visit one or two, even if they are out of your price range as accommodations.

CATEGORY	COST*
$$$$	over 400,000 lire
$$$	200,000–400,000 lire
$$	125,000–200,000 lire
$	under 125,000 lire

Prices are for standard double room for two, including tax and service.

Soccer

Like the rest of Italy, the region is soccer-mad, with fervent attention given to Milan's soccer teams, AC Milan and Inter Milan, which are two of the most successful in Europe. Matches are played on Sunday, with both teams sharing the San Siro soccer stadium in Milan for home matches. On match day, close to 85,000 fans fill the San Siro to watch, cheer, and boo the performances of each team. For the rest of the week, Sunday's performance is debated and scrutinized in bars, cafés, and restaurants (not to mention the home, workplace, barber shop . . .). Match tickets are difficult but not impossible to get; information is available from the city tourist offices.

Water Sports

Schools for sailing, scuba diving, waterskiing, and windsurfing are in Riva del Garda, on Lake Garda. Torbole, 5 km (3 mi) east of Riva del Garda on S240, is a prime spot for windsurfing. At Lake Como, there are well-equipped sailing and windsurfing schools as well as waterskiing.

Exploring Milan, Lombardy, and the Lakes

This area of northern Italy is dominated by the region of Lombardy and especially by Milan, which lies at its heart. From the north to the east of Milan lie all of the region's lakes. Some border Switzerland; others are at the foot of the Dolomites, Italy's foremost mountain range. Many of the region's most important cities are to the south and southeast of Milan. These cities all have in common a flat geographical surrounding bordered by the Po River, hence they are categorized here as cities of the plain.

"Nothing in the world," wrote Stendhal in 1817, "can be compared to the fascination of those burning summer days passed on the Milanese lakes, in the middle of those chestnut groves so green that they immerse their branches in the waves . . ." Millions of travelers have since agreed that, for sheer beauty, the lakes of Northern Italy—Como, Maggiore, Garda, and Orta—have few equals. Where else can you find magnificent 18th- and 19th-century villas on the shores of lakes bordered by toy villages and nestled under the foothills of mountains of almost Scandinavian grandeur? From Pliny to d'Annunzio, visitors have found this region—to quote Stendhal—"elegant, picturesque, and voluptuous."

"The lakes" actually denotes a vast region spread over the middle third of the northern border region. Though our tour is limited to the main four lakes, the best way to see the lake country is to rent a car in fall or spring and thread a path, at as leisurely a pace as possible, along the small mountain roads that link the lakes' least-spoiled northern tips. This is splendid mountain-driving country, with some of the most beautiful and challenging roads in the world. Without a car, however, it is still possible to see many of the region's sights, thanks to extensive bus routes and the many vaporetti that ferry the lakes.

The lakes are extremely popular seasonal resort areas. If your wish is not only to see the lakes but also to stay at them, the throngs that descend in July and August (particularly on weekends) make reservations absolutely necessary—especially so at Lake Como, the quintessential Italian lake resort.

Numbers in the text correspond to numbers in the margin and on the Milan and Lombardy and the Lakes maps.

Great Itineraries

The roads that connect major cities in the region are excellent and are supported by several major highways (Autostrada) as well as by secondary routes. Roads around the lakes, in particular Lake Garda and Lake Maggiore, are scenic but winding. Give yourself time to travel them at leisure. Traveling by car is usually the best way to get around and fully appreciate the beauty of the landscape. There are plenty of places to pull off for photographs or just a breath of fresh air.

A week is enough to see the area thoroughly, and although five days will not exclude any sights, you have to keep on the move. Three days will give you a taste of the major sights in the area, but time will be precious and morning starts will have to be early. All itineraries begin and end in Milan.

IF YOU HAVE 3 DAYS

Begin in **Milan** ①–⑩, taking in the city's major sights, before heading south on the A7 autostrada to the cities of **Pavia** ⑪ and **Cremona** ⑫, home to Stradivari, violin-maker extraordinaire. End your day in ⊠ **Mantua** ⑭. The next day head north on the A22 as far as **Riva del Garda** ⑰ and make your way back through **Gargnano** ⑱, **Gardone Riviera** ⑲, and down into the jewel of Lake Garda's crown, **Sirmione** ⑳. Overnight in ⊠ **Bergamo** ㉒. The next day go as far as **Madonna del Ghisallo** ㉓ and **Bellagio** ㉔ on Lake Como. Finally, move on to the Lake Maggiore via **Cernobbio** ㉗, taking time out to cruise the lake on one of the steamers. Return to Milan.

IF YOU HAVE 5 DAYS

Travel south along the A7 to **Pavia** ⑪ and **Cremona** ⑫, and then move on to the elegant, star-shaped fortress-city of **Sabbioneta** ⑬, ending your day in ⌘ **Mantua** ⑭, where you can enjoy Mantegna's masterpieces. The next day head north to Lake Garda through the lakefront towns of **Punta di San Vigilio** ⑮, **Malcesine** ⑯, and, at the top of the lake, the pretty town of **Riva del Garda** ⑰. Head down the western side of the lake through **Gargnano** ⑱ and **Gardone Riviera** ⑲, where you should visit Gabriele d'Annunzio's former home, Il Vittoriale, before reaching ⌘ **Sirmione** ⑳. The next day pass through the wealthy city of **Brescia** ㉑ and on to **Bergamo** ㉒. From here head via **Madonna del Ghisallo** ㉓ to ⌘ **Bellagio** ㉔ on Lake Como, said to be the prettiest town in Europe. Take time in the afternoon to explore the lake towns of **Varenna** ㉕ and **Tremezzo** ㉖, where you will find the magnificent **Villa Carlotta**. If you can manage an early start the following morning, head for **Cernobbio** ㉗ and then west to **Orto San Giulio** ㉙ on Lake Orto. It's only a short hop to the Lake Maggiore. You can explore the area from here by steamer, traveling north to ⌘ **Stresa** ㉚ on the western side of the lake. From here it's a short excursion to the town of **Verbania Pallanza** ㉛, across the bay of the same name. The following day head for **Milan** ①–⑩ to see the main sights. Alternatively, you could visit Milan before setting off on your tour of the rest of the region.

IF YOU HAVE 7 DAYS

If you have the luxury of seven days to tour the area, make sure to linger in some of the lake towns, especially **Riva del Garda** ⑰ and **Sirmione** ⑳ on Lake Garda, **Bellagio** ㉔ on Lake Como, and **Verbania Pallanza** ㉛ on Lake Maggiore, where you can explore the magnificent botanical gardens of Villa Taranto. Take an extra day to visit **Milan** ①–⑩, which may appear to be yet another industrialized city at first glance but which has a plethora of artistic and architectural treasures.

When to Tour Milan, Lombardy, and the Lakes

In summer months, particularly July and August, lake roads can become congested, especially on evenings and weekends. Fewer people visit in fall, winter, and spring, so many of the lakeside towns are deserted and some restaurants as well as hotels close during these months. Note that many of the ferry and steamer boat services stop running in October and recommence in May. Early summer, late summer, and early fall are the best times to see the area, but October can be a tad chilly for swimming.

MILAN

93 km (60 mi) northwest of Cremona, 38 km (24 mi) north of Pavia.

Milan's history as a capital city goes back at least 2,500 years. Its fortunes ever since, both as a great commercial trading center and as the object of regular conquest and occupation, are readily explained by its strategic position at the center of the Lombard plain. Directly south of the central passes across the Alps, Milan is bordered by three highly navigable rivers—the Po, the Ticino, and the Adda—which for centuries were the main arteries of an ingenious network of canals crisscrossing all Lombardy (and ultimately reaching most of northern Italy).

Virtually every invader in European history—Gaul, Roman, Goth, Longobard, and Frank—as well as every ruler of France, Spain, and Austria, has taken a turn at ruling the city and the region. Milan's glorious heyday of self-rule proved comparatively brief, from 1277 until 1500, when it was ruled by its two great family dynasties, the Visconti and subsequently the Sforza. These families were known, justly or not, for a peculiarly aristocratic mixture of refinement, classical learning, and cruelty, and much of the surviving grandeur of Gothic and Renaissance art and architecture is their doing. Be on the lookout in your

Lombardy and the Lakes

SWITZERLAND

Locarno
Ascona
Brissago
Cannobio
Cannero Riv.
Verbania Pallanza
31
Stresa
30
Lago di Orta
29 Orta San Giulio
Arona
Belgirate
Angera
Laveno
Lago Maggiore
S34
S33
S299
S32
S229
Lugano
Lago di Lugano
Menaggio
Tremezzo
26
Lago di Como
Bellano
Varenna **25**
Bellagio
24
23 Madonna del Ghisallo
Lecco
S38
S470
Varese
Lago Varese
Cernobbio
27
28 Como
S394
S342
S233
A8
A9
S35
S340
S342
S36
S36
S342
Bergamo **22**

TO TURIN
Novara
Abbiategrasso
Vigevano
Milan
1 — 10
Cassano d'Adda
Treviglio
S11
S11
S11
S271
S494
A7
Ticino
S415
Adda
A4
Crem
Certosa di Pavia
Pavia
11
Lodi
S235
S234
A1
Po
A7
S35
A21
S10
A26

N

ITALY
A21
A7
A21

0   20 miles
0   30 km

wanderings for the Visconti family emblem—a viper, its jaws straining wide, devouring a child.

If you are wondering why so little seems to have survived from Milan's antiquity, the answer is simple—war. Three times in the city's history, partial or total destruction has followed conflict—in AD 539, 1157, and 1944.

Exploring Milan

The subway system, known as the Metropolitana, is a good way to get around if long walks are out of the question, but staying above ground in the trolley cars or buses gives a better view.

A Good Walk

Start at the **Duomo** ① and visit its roof and **museum,** then move on to **Galleria Vittorio Emanuele** ②, just beyond the northern tip of the cathedral's facade. Continue across the transepts of the Galleria and head north to **La Scala** ③, where Verdi attained his fame. Head northeast on Via Manzoni, which leads to the **Giardini Pubblici** (great for kids); on the eastern side of the park is the **Civico Museo di Storia Naturale** ④. Via Manzoni and the southwestern corner of the park lead to Via Fatebenefratelli; follow it west to Via Pontaccio and then to Via Brera to the **Pinacoteca di Brera** ⑤, home to stellar masterpieces. Next, a brisk walk west along Via Pontaccio will bring you to the imposing **Castello Sforzesco** ⑥. A few blocks southwest of the Castello, on Corso Magenta is **Santa Maria delle Grazie,** home to the renowned *Last Supper* ⑦. Go east on Corso Magenta, across Via Carducci, to visit the city's **Civico Museo Archeologico** ⑧. Next to the Civico Museo Archeologico, Via Sant'Agnese leads to the church of **Sant'Ambrogio.** Across from the church's main doors, turn left on Via San Vittore to see the **Museo Nazionale della Scienza e della Tecnica** ⑨. After returning to your hotel for a well-earned rest, you may spend the night in one of the many restaurants that clutter the bohemian **Navigli district** ⑩.

TIMING

To visit each sight in Milan thoroughly will take a couple of days, but the most important sights can be seen in one day. Note that some sites are closed Monday: the Baptistery, Castello Sforzesco, Civico Museo Archeologico, Civico Museo di Storia Naturale, Museo Nazionale della Scienza e della Tecnica, Pinacoteca di Brera, Santa Maria delle Grazie (*Last Supper*). Expect long lines waiting to see the *Last Supper,* even in the early morning.

Sights to See

Baptistery. This subterranean ruin dating from the 4th century is beneath the Duomo's piazza. Although opinion remains divided, it is widely believed that this may have been where Ambrose (Milan's first bishop and patron saint) baptized Augustine. ⊠ *Battistero Paleocristiano, enter through cathedral, Piazza Duomo.* ⊡ *Free.* ☉ *Tues.–Sun. 10–noon and 3–5.*

❻ **Castello Sforzesco.** For the serious student of Renaissance military engineering, the imposing Castello must be something of a travesty, so often has it been remodeled or rebuilt since it was begun in 1450 by the condottiere (hired mercenary) who founded the city's second dynastic family, Francesco Sforza, fourth duke of Milan.

Though today the word "mercenary" has a strongly pejorative ring, during the Renaissance all Italy's great soldier-heroes were professionals hired by the cities and principalities that they served. Of them—and there were thousands—Francesco Sforza is considered to have been

Milan

0 ___ 440 yards
0 ___ 400 meters

V. Melzi d'Eril
V. Bertani
V. Niccolini
V. Bramante
V. Montello
V. Volta
Vle. Crispi
Bast. di Pta. Nuova
Pta. Nuova
Stazione Centrale
V. S. Gregorio
Vle. e. Tunisia
Vle. Vittoria Veneto
V. Lazzaretto
Pza. d. Repubblica
Bastioni di Pta. Venezia
V. Solferino
V. Statuto
C. Garibaldi
C. V. Palermo
V. Legnano
V. Moscova
C. Pta. Nuova
V. Filippo Turati
V. Manin
Giardini Pubblici
Parco Sempione
V. San Marco
V. Montebello
Fatebenefratelli
V. Borgonuovo
V. D. Giardini
V. D. Marchi
V. Senato
V. S. Spirito
V. S. Andrea
Spiga
C. Venezia
V. Mozart
Stazione Nord
V. Leopardi
V. Monti
V. Boccaccio
Pza. Castello
Foro Buonaparte
V. Pontaccio
V. Fiori Chiari
Brera
Mercato
Cusani dell'Orso
Monte di Pietà
V. Verdi
V. Manzoni
V. Monte Napoleone
Monforte
Pza. S. Maria delle Grazie
C. Magenta
V. Carducci
V. G.
V. Meravigli
V. Dante
V. Broletto
Pza. della Scala
C. Matteotti
C. V. Emanuele
V. d/ Modrone
V. Passione
V. S. Agnese
V. Luini
V. S. M. Fulcorina
V. S. Orsola
Bocheto
Orefici
Pza. del Duomo
V. Fil. Corridoni
V. San Vittore
V. Olona
Cappuccio
V. Circo
V. Torino
V. Mazzini
V. Velasca
V. Larga
C. Porta Vittoria
Freguglia
V. Manara
V. Edmondo de Amicis
Ariberto Ausonio
C. Pta. Genova
V. M. d'Oggioni
Naviglio
V. Stampa
V. S. Vito
C. Pta. Ticinese
S. Croce
V. Mulino d. Armi
Corso Italia
C. Porta Romana
V. S. Sofia
V. Francesco Sforza
V. S. D. Barnaba
V. S. D. Commenda
Vle. G. d'Annunzio
V. Gorizia
Pta. Genova
V. G. Mercalli
Bianca di Savoia
V. Quadronno
V. Lamarmora
V. Orti
Vle. Caldara
KEY
Vle. Galeazzo
Pta. Ticinese
Vle. Col di Lana
V. S. Martino
V. Carlo Crivelli
Vle. Beatrice d'Este
Pta. Vigentina
Pta. Romana

KEY
- *i* Tourist Information
- AE American Express Office

Castello Sforzesco, **6**
Civico Museo Archeologico, **8**
Civico Museo di Storia Naturale, **4**
Duomo, **1**
Galleria Vittorio Emanuele, **2**
La Scala, **3**
Last Supper, **7**
Museo Nazionale della Scienza e della Tecnica, **9**
Navigli district, **10**
Pinacoteca di Brera, **5**

one of the greatest and most honest. It is said he could remember not only the names of all his men, but of their horses, as well. And it is with his era, and the building of the Castello, that we know we have entered the enlightened age of the Renaissance. It took barely half a century before it and the city were under foreign rule.

Today, the Castello houses municipal museums devoted variously to Egyptian and other antiquities, musical instruments, paintings, and sculpture. Highlights are the **Salle delle Asse,** a frescoed room still sometimes attributed to Leonardo da Vinci, and Michelangelo's unfinished *Rondanini Pietà,* believed to be his last work—an astounding achievement for a man nearly 90 and a moving coda to his life. ⊠ *Piazza Castello,* ☎ *02/62083191.* 🎫 *Free.* 🕐 *Tues.–Sun. 9:30–5:30.*

NEED A BREAK? **Viel** (⊠ Largo Cairoli) just across the road from Castello Sforzesco, is said to be the best *gelateria* (ice-cream shop) in northern Italy.

----

❽ Civico Museo Archeologico. Housed in a former monastery, this museum has some enlightening relics from Milan's Roman past—from everyday utensils and jewelry to several fine examples of mosaic pavement. ⊠ *Corso Magenta 15,* ☎ *02/86450011.* 🎫 *Free.* 🕐 *Tues.–Sun. 9:30–5:30.*

❹ Civico Museo di Storia Naturale. Exhibits here appeal to animal and nature lovers. Just behind the museum is the **Giardini Pubblici** (Public Gardens), a refuge for active young children. ⊠ *Corso Venezia 55,* ☎ *02/62085405.* 🎫 *Free.* 🕐 *Tues.–Fri. 9:30–5:30, weekends 9:30–6:30.*

★ **❶ Duomo.** This intricate Gothic structure—Italy's largest—has been fascinating and exasperating visitors and conquerors alike since it was begun by Galeazzo Visconti III, first duke of Milan, in 1386. Consecrated in 1577, it was not wholly completed until 1897.

Whether you concur with travel writer H. V. Morton, writing 25 years ago, that the cathedral is "one of the mightiest Gothic buildings ever created," or regard it as a spiny pastiche of centuries, there is no denying that for sheer size and complexity it is unequaled. Its capacity—though it is hard to imagine the church filled—is reckoned to be 40,000. Usually it is empty, a perfect sanctuary from the frenetic pace of life outside and the perfect place for solitary contemplation. The poet Shelley swore by it—claiming it was the only place to read Dante.

The building is adorned with 135 marble spires and 2,245 marble statues. The oldest part is the **apse** (the end of the cruciform opposite the portals). Its three colossal bays of curving and counter-curved tracery, especially the bay adorning the exterior of the stained-glass windows, should not be missed.

Step inside and walk down the right aisle to the southern transept, to the **tomb of Gian Giacomo** Medici. The tomb owes something to Michelangelo, but is generally considered its sculptor's (Leone Leoni's) masterpiece; it dates from the 1560s.

Directly ahead is the Duomo's most famous sculpture, the rather gruesome but anatomically instructive figure of **St. Bartholomew,** whose glorious martyrdom consisted of being flayed alive. It is usually said the saint stands "holding" his skin, but this is not quite accurate. It would appear more that he is luxuriating in it, much as a 1950s matron might have shown off a new fur stole.

As you enter the apse to admire those splendid windows, glance at the sacristy doors to the right and left of the altar. The lunette on the right

We'll give you a $20 tip for driving.

See the real Europe with Hertz.

It's time to see Europe from a new perspective. From behind the wheel of a Hertz car. And we'd like to save you $20 on your prepaid Affordable Europe Weekly Rental. Our low rates are guaranteed in U.S. dollars and English is spoken at all of our European locations. Computerized driving directions are available at many locations, and Free Unlimited Mileage and 24-Hour Emergency Roadside Assistance are standard in our European packages. For complete details call 1-800-654-3001. Mention PC #95384 So, discover Europe with Hertz.

Offer is valid at participating airport locations in Europe from Jan.1 – Dec.15, 1998, on Economy through Full size cars. Reservations must be made at least 8 hours prior to departure. $20 will be deducted at time of booking. Standard rental qualifications, significant restrictions and blackout periods apply.

Pick up the phone.

Pick up the miles.

Use your MCI Card® to make an international call from virtually anywhere in the world and earn frequent flyer miles on one of seven major airlines.

Enroll in an MCI Airline Partner Program today. In the U.S., call **1-800-FLY-FREE.** Overseas, call MCI collect at **1-916-567-5151.**

1. To use your MCI Card, just dial the WorldPhone access number of the country you're calling from.
   (For a complete listing of codes, visit www.mci.com.)
2. Dial or give the operator your MCI Card number.
3. Dial or give the number you're calling.

# Austria (CC) ♦	022-903-012		# Netherlands (CC) ♦	0800-022-91-22
# Belarus (CC)			# Norway (CC) ♦	800-19912
From Brest, Vitebsk, Grodno, Minsk	8-800-103		# Poland (CC) ÷	00-800-111-21-22
From Gomel and Mogilev regions	8-10-800-103		# Portugal (CC) ÷	05-017-1234
# Belgium (CC) ♦	0800-10012		Romania (CC) ÷	01-800-1800
# Bulgaria	00800-0001		# Russia (CC) ÷ ♦	
# Croatia (CC) ★	99-385-0112		To call using ROSTELCOM ■	747-3322
# Czech Republic (CC) ♦	00-42-000112		For a Russian-speaking operator	747-3320
# Denmark (CC) ♦	8001-0022		To call using SOVINTEL ■	960-2222
# Finland (CC) ♦	08001-102-80		# San Marino (CC) ♦	172-1022
# France (CC) ♦	0-800-99-0019		# Slovak Republic (CC)	00-421-00112
# Germany (CC)	0130-0012		# Slovenia	080-8808
# Greece (CC) ♦	00-800-1211		# Spain (CC)	900-99-0014
# Hungary (CC) ♦	00▼800-01411		# Sweden (CC) ♦	020-795-922
# Iceland (CC) ♦	800-9002		# Switzerland (CC) ♦	0800-89-0222
# Ireland (CC)	1-800-55-1001		# Turkey (CC) ♦	00-8001-1177
# Italy (CC) ♦	172-1022		# Ukraine (CC) ÷	8▼10-013
# Kazakhstan (CC)	8-800-131-4321		# United Kingdom (CC)	
# Liechtenstein (CC) ♦	0800-89-0222		To call using BT ■	0800-89-0222
# Luxembourg	0800-0112		To call using MERCURY ■	0500-89-0222
# Monaco (CC) ♦	800-90-019		# Vatican City (CC)	172-1022

Is this a great time, or what? :-)

dates from 1393 and was decorated by Hans von Fernach. That on the left also dates from the 14th century and is ascribed jointly to Giacomo da Campione and Giovanni dei Grassi.

Don't miss the view from the Duomo's **roof:** walk outside the left (north) transept to the stairs and elevator. Sad to say, late 20th-century air pollution has, on all but the rarest days, drastically reduced the view. But even in fog, the roof itself creates a fairy-tale-like atmosphere. As you stand among the forest of marble pinnacles, remember that virtually every inch of this gargantuan edifice, including the roof itself, is decorated with precious white marble. ⊠ *Piazza del Duomo.* ⊠ *Stairs 5,000 lire, elevator 8,000 lire.* ⊙ *Mar.–Oct., daily 9–5:45; Nov.–Feb., daily 9–4:30.*

Duomo Museum. Exhibits here shed more light on the cathedral's history and include some of the treasures removed for safety from the exterior. ⊠ *Museo del Duomo, Piazza del Duomo 14B,* ☎ *02/860358.* ⊠ *8,000 lire.* ⊙ *Tues.–Sun. 9:30–12:30 and 3–6.*

NEED A BREAK?	The best alternative to a conventional restaurant is **Peck** (⊠ Via Spadari 9, ☎ 02/860842), one of Italy's, if not the world's, most irresistible food emporiums. In the Duomo area, it is something better than a shop—it's six shops. Best for a quick stand-up lunch is **Bottega del Vino** (⊠ Via Victor Hugo 4, ☎ 02/861040), which pours almost 200 wines by the glass. **Peck Rosticceria** (⊠ Via Cantù 3, ☎ 02/8693017) offers grilled takeout; it's closed Monday. For a relaxed lunch, try **Il Restaurant** (⊠ Via Victor Hugo 4, ☎ 02/876774); it's closed Sunday and two weeks in January. For do-it-yourself, try the **Delicatessen** (⊠ Via Spadari 11, ☎ 02/86461158).

★ ❷ **Galleria Vittorio Emanuele.** Anyone who has grown up on the periphery of a contemporary American city should recognize this spectacularly extravagant late 19th-century glass-topped, barrel-vaulted tunnel for what it is—one of the planet's earliest and most elegant shopping malls. It may be rivaled perhaps only by GUM, off Red Square in Moscow, for sheer belle epoque splendor. Its architect, Giuseppe Mengoni, accidently lost his footing while on the roof and tumbled to his death on the floor of his own creation, just days before its opening.

Like its suburban American cousins, the Galleria fulfills a variety of social functions vastly more important than its ostensible commercial purpose. This is the city's heart, midway between the cathedral and La Scala opera house, and it is sometimes called *Il Salotto* (the Living Room). It teems with life, inviting people-watching from the tables that spill from the Galleria's bars and restaurants, where you can enjoy a monstrously overpriced coffee.

Like the cathedral, the Galleria is a cruciform. The space at the crossing, however, forms an octagon. If this is where you're standing, don't be afraid to look up and gawk. Even in poor weather, the great glass dome makes for a splendid sight. And the mosaics, usually unnoticed, are a vastly underrated source of pleasure, even if they are not to be taken too seriously. They represent Europe, Asia, Africa, and America; those at the entrance arch are devoted to science, industry, art, and agriculture.

Books, clothing, food, wine, pens, jewelry, and myriad other goods are all for sale in the Galleria, and one of Milan's most traditional restaurants, Savini, is here (☞ Dining and Lodging, *below*). There is, in addition, one of those curious Italian institutions, an *albergo diurno* (daytime hotel), where you can take an hour's nap or a bath, get a haircut or a pedicure, and have your suit pressed or a button replaced. Most of its patrons are Italian, but it is hard to think of a better oasis for a vacationer worn out from sightseeing. ✉ *Piazza del Duomo, beyond northern tip of cathedral's facade.*

❸ La Scala (Teatro alla Scala). In this world-famous institution, Verdi established his reputation and Maria Callas sang her way into opera lore. The opera house was completely renovated after its destruction by Allied bombs in 1943 and reopened at a performance led by the great Arturo Toscanini in 1946.

You need know nothing of opera to sense that, like Carnegie Hall, La Scala is something rather more than an auditorium. It looms as a symbol—both for the performer who dreams one day of singing here and for the buff who knows every note of *Rigoletto* by heart. For some, a visit to La Scala will be—even more than to the Duomo—a solemn but pleasurable act of pilgrimage.

If you are lucky enough to be here during the opera season, which runs for approximately six months beginning each December 7, St. Ambrose Day, do whatever is necessary to attend—even if it requires perching among the rafters in one of the dreaded gallery seats. Hearing a Verdi or Puccini opera sung in Italian by Italians in Italy is a magical experience. For now, whet your appetite with a quick stroll through the theater's small museum, **Museo Teatrale alla Scala.** You will get a peek at the gilded grandeur of the boxes. ✉ *Piazza della Scala,* ☎ *02/8053418.* 🎟 *7,000 lire.* ☉ *Mon.–Sat. 9–noon and 2–6; plus May–Oct., Sun. 9:30–noon and 2:30–6; closed occasionally during rehearsals.*

★ ❼ Last Supper. H. V. Morton once noted that Milan might well be the only city on earth where you could give a taxi driver the title of a painting as your destination. If this appeals to you, flag one down and say, *"L'Ultima Cena,"* since this is how the *Last Supper* is known here.

The *Last Supper,* housed in the church and former Dominican monastery of **Santa Maria delle Grazie,** has had an almost unbelievable history of bad luck and neglect—its near destruction in an American bombing raid in August 1943 was only the latest chapter in a series of misadventures, including, if one 19th-century source is to be believed, being whitewashed by the monks. Well-meant but disastrous attempts at restoration have done little to rectify the problem of the work's placement: it is situated on a wall unusually vulnerable to climatic dampness. Yet the artist chose to work slowly and patiently in oil pigments—which demand dry plaster—instead of proceeding hastily on wet plaster according to the conventional fresco technique. Aldous Huxley called it "the saddest work of art in the world." After years beneath a scaffold, with restorers patiently shifting from one square centimeter to another, Leonardo's famous masterpiece still is in a sad state, and studies in further methods to preserve this great fresco continue.

Despite Leonardo's carefully preserved preparatory sketches in which the apostles are clearly labeled by name, there still remains some small debate about a few identities in the final arrangement. But there can be no mistaking Judas, small and dark, his hand calmly reaching forward toward the bread, isolated from the terrible confusion that has taken the hearts of the others. One critic, Professor Frederick Hartt, offers an elegantly terse explanation for why the composition works: it combines "dramatic confusion" with "mathematical order." Certainly, the amazingly skillful and unobtrusive repetition of threes, when first you see it—in the windows, in the grouping of the figures, and in their placement—adds a mystical aspect to what at first seems simply the perfect observation of spontaneous human gesture.

Santa Maria delle Grazie is the **Cenacolo Vinciano,** which used to be the order's refectory. Take at least a moment to visit Santa Maria delle Grazie itself. It's a handsome church, with a fine dome by Bramante, which was added along with a cloister about the time that Leonardo was commissioned to paint the *Last Supper.* If you're wondering how two such giants came to be employed decorating and remodeling the refectory and church of a comparatively modest religious order, and not, say, the Duomo, the answer lies in the ambitious but largely unrealized plan to turn Santa Maria delle Grazie into a magnificent Sforza family mausoleum. Though Ludovico il Moro Sforza, seventh duke of Milan, was but one generation away from the founding of the Sforza dynasty, he was its last ruler. Two years after Leonardo finished the *Last Supper,* Ludovico was defeated and was imprisoned in a French dungeon for the remaining eight years of his life. ⊠ *Corso Magenta, Cenacolo Vinciano,* ☎ *02/4987588.* 🎟 *12,000 lire.* ☉ *Tues.–Sun. 8–1:45, hrs may vary.*

NEED A BREAK?	For those who don't scream for ice cream, a venerable neighborhood institution, the **Bar Magenta** (⊠ Via Carducci 13 at Corso Magenta) provides an excellent alternative en route. Luncheon, beer, or coffee provides only an excuse for coming here; the real attraction is its casual but civilized, quintessentially Milanese ambience.

🖐 ❾ **Museo Nazionale della Scienza e della Tecnica.** Models based on technical projects by Leonardo da Vinci and collections of locomotives, planes, and cars—a diversion for children—are among the collection. ⊠ *Via San Vittore 21, near Sant'Ambrogio,* ☎ *02/485551.* 🎟 *10,000 lire.* ☉ *Tues.–Sun. 9:30–5.*

❿ **Navigli district.** This picturesque suburb in the southern part of the city was, in medieval times, a network of navigable canals, called *navigli,* which crisscrossed Milan. Almost all have been covered over, except for two long canals, Naviglio Grande and Naviglio Pavese, and part of a third, Darsena. The canals are lined with quaint shops, art galleries, cafés, pubs, restaurants, and clubs. Much of Milan's nightlife is centered here, and the neighborhood has a romantic, bohemian atmosphere. ⊠ *Corso Porta Ticinese.*

★ ❺ **Pinacoteca di Brera.** The picture collection in this art gallery is star studded, even by Italian standards. As everyone knows, the only way to "do" a large collection is to start with the best, while you're still fresh, and leave the charming minor masterpieces for afterward. We suggest you forgo the 20th-century work displayed along the long entrance corridor and begin in the larger, well-patrolled rooms.

In Room 22, note that Raphael painted *Betrothal of the Virgin* when he was 22. The other painting, Piero della Francesca's *Madonna with Saints and Angels,* is just as lovely, much aided by its skillful restoration and cleaning.

The gallery's best-known painting is probably the somber, beautiful, and moving *Dead Christ* by Mantegna, in Room 6. Though it is by far the smallest painting in the room, it dominates, with its sparse palette of gray and terra-cotta, and especially for its original perspective. Mantegna's shocking, almost surgical, precision—in the rendering of Christ's wounds, the face propped up on a pillow, the day's growth of beard—tells of an all-too-human agony. It is one of Renaissance painting's most quietly wondrous achievements, finding an unsuspected middle ground between the excesses of conventional gore and beauty in representing the Passion's saddest moment.

On your way out, pause a moment to view the fine paintings by Carlo Carrà (especially *La Musa Metafisica*, or *Metaphysical Muse*), suggesting Italy's confident and stylish response to the likes of Picasso and Max Ernst and to the schools of Cubism and Surrealism. ⊠ *Via Brera 28,* ☎ *02/862634.* ⊡ *10,000 lire.* ⊙ *Tues.–Sat. 9–5:30, Sun. 9–12:45.*

OFF THE
BEATEN PATH

THE LATIN QUARTER – Take time to wander around the lively quarter surrounding the Pinacoteca di Brera. The narrow streets, lined with boutiques, crafts shops, cafés, restaurants, and music clubs, comprise what is often referred to as Milan's Greenwich Village. A longtime haunt of artists and musicians, it has a number of clubs and cafés offering live music until late at night.

MINITALIA PARK – Between Milan and Bergamo, this theme park has a 1:500-scale relief model of Italy, with about 200 replicas of the country's most important monuments. ⊠ *A4 autostrada to Bergamo, 35 km (22 mi) from Milan, Capriate San Gervasio,* ☎ *02/9091341.* ⊡ *17,000 lire.* ⊙ *Mar.–Oct., daily 9–dusk.*

PARCO DELLA PREISTORIA – Kids of all ages marvel at the 70-ft-long brontosaurus, the fierce tyrannosaurus, and the 4-km (2½-mi) path with 20 more full-size replicas of prehistoric animals. There is a picnic area and, for the adults, two bars. It's 25 km (16 mi) east of Milan on the road to Brescia. ⊠ *SS11 near Cassano d'Adda,* ☎ *0363/78184.* ⊡ *11,000 lire.* ⊙ *Mar.–Nov., daily 9–dusk; ticket office closes at 6.*

Dining and Lodging

$$$$ ✕ **L'Antica Osteria del Ponte.** Rich, imaginative seasonal cuisine at the
★ whim of chef Ezio Santin is reason enough to make your way 20 km (12 mi) southwest of Milan to one of Italy's finest (and most expensive) restaurants. It is set in a traditional country inn, its interior a cozy combination of wooden ceiling beams with a blazing fire in chilly weather. The Naviglio Grande (Grand Canal) flows nearby: it was built to carry the area's produce to Milan. Inventive recipes include ravioli *di aragosta* (filled with lobster meat) in summer and, in the fall, a range of heartwarming specialties, many using the prized wild porcini mushrooms. ⊠ *Cassinetta di Lugagnano, 3 km (1¾ mi) north of Abbiategrasso,* ☎ *02/9420034. Reservations essential. Jacket and tie. AE, DC, MC, V. Closed Sun.–Mon., Dec. 25–Jan. 15, and Aug.*

$$$$ ✕ **Savini.** Red carpets and glass chandeliers characterize the classy Savini, in the Galleria Vittorio Emanuele. It's a typical old-fashioned Milanese restaurant, with dining rooms on three floors, including a "winter garden," with views of the Galleria. This is a good place to try the Milanese specialty risotto *al salto* (cooked as a sort of pancake, flipped in the pan) or *costoletta di vitello* (veal cutlets). ⊠ *Galleria Vittorio Emanuele,* ☎ *02/72003433. Jacket and tie. AE, DC, MC, V. Closed Aug. 10–20, Dec. 23–Jan. 3, and Sun.*

$$$$ ✕ **Scaletta.** The restaurant's name means "little stairway" in Italian, perhaps inspired by its own stairway ascending to culinary paradise. This tiny restaurant could be the dining room of a gracious home, with cool pastel colors, book-lined walls, and a superb collection of blown glass. Host-sommelier Aldo Bellini and genius cook Mamma Pina in the kitchen treat their guests with cordiality and take time to discuss wines and menus with you, if you like. Pina's cooking is a light, personalized version of traditional Italian cuisine; menus change frequently. Reserve two weeks ahead. ⊠ *Piazzale Stazione Porta Genova*

3, ☎ 02/58100290. *Reservations essential. No credit cards. Closed Sun.–Mon. and Aug.*

$$$–$$$$ ✕ **Boeucc.** Milan's oldest restaurant (pronounced "birch") is in the same
★ square as novelist Alessandro Manzoni's house, not far from La Scala. Subtly lit, with cream-color fluted columns, chandeliers, thick carpets, and a garden for warm-weather dining, it has come a long way from the time when it was simply a basement "hole" (*boeucc* is old Milanese for *buco*, or hole). It serves not only typical Milanese food, but also a wide range of other dishes, including penne *al branzino e zucchine* (with sea bass and zucchini sauce) and gelato *di castagne con zabaglione caldo* (chestnut ice cream with hot zabaglione). ⊠ *Piazza Belgioioso 2,* ☎ *02/76020224. Reservations essential. AE. Closed Sat. and Aug. No lunch Sun.*

$$–$$$ ✕ **Antica Trattoria della Pesa.** Turn-of-the-century decor, dark wood paneling, and old-fashioned lamps re-create the atmosphere of this restaurant at its opening more than 100 years ago. This is authentic Old Milan, as the menu confirms, offering risotto, minestrone, and osso buco. ⊠ *Viale Pasubio 10,* ☎ *02/6555741. AE, DC, MC, V. Closed Sun., 2 wks in Aug, and Dec. 23–Jan. 2.*

$$ ✕ **Al Cantinone.** Opera enthusiasts still come here for an after-theater drink, just as they did a century ago. The decor is classic Milanese trattoria, the service is fast, and the food is homey and reliable. A bonus: homemade pasta. Try the *pappardelle* (noodles) or ravioli with meat sauce, Tuscan style. There's a wide selection of grilled meats and a staggering choice of wines. ⊠ *Via Agnello 19, entrance on Via Ragazzi del 99,* ☎ *02/86461338. AE, DC, MC, V. Closed Sun., Aug., and Dec. 24–Jan. 2. No lunch Sat.*

$$ ✕ **La Capanna.** Signora cooks and her husband pours wine and sees that everything goes smoothly in this popular trattoria near the Piola Metro stop (and the university). The food is predominantly Tuscan—Tuscan salami, pappardelle, and steak—but some Milanese specialties are also on the menu. ⊠ *Via Donatello 9,* ☎ *02/29400884. AE, DC, MC, V. Closed Sat. and Aug. No dinner Mon.*

$$ ✕ **La Libera.** Although this establishment in the heart of Brera bills itself as a *birreria con cucina* (beer cellar with kitchen), its young clientele comes here as much for the excellent food and convivial atmosphere as for the draft beer. A soft current of jazz soothes the gentle ripple of conversation, amid restful dark green decor. Sample the creative cooking, including the insalata *esotica* (with avocado, chicken, rice, and papaya) or *rognone di vitello con broccoletti e ginepro* (veal kidneys with broccoli and juniper berries). ⊠ *Via Palermo 21,* ☎ *02/8053603. Reservations not accepted. No credit cards. Closed Sat., Aug., and Dec. 22–Jan. 1. No lunch Sun.*

$$ ✕ **Nabucco.** This smart, tastefully decorated restaurant in the Brera district offers such delights as risotto con porcini, an excellent range of salads, and homemade pastries and desserts. Although moderately priced, the good fixed-price lunches take it into the lower category. ⊠ *Via Fiori Chiari 10,* ☎ *02/860663. AE, DC, MC, V. Closed Sun. No lunch Mon.*

$$ ✕ **Trattoria Milanese.** Between the Duomo and the Basilica of Sant'Ambrogio, this small, popular trattoria has been run by the same family for more than 80 years and is crowded with businesspeople at lunch and with regulars at dinner, when lingering is allowed. Food is authentic regional, with risotto and *costoletta alla milanese* (breaded veal cutlet) good choices. ⊠ *Via Santa Marta 11,* ☎ *02/86451991. AE, D, MC, V. Closed Tues. and Aug.*

$–$$ ✕ **Bistrot di Gualtiero Marchese/Brunch.** Atop the Rinascente department store off Piazza del Duomo, this brunch eatery, bar, and bistro is supervised by the well-known chef Gualtiero Marchese and offers a variety of menus with a full range of prices. A bonus is a great view of the Duomo's spires. ⊠ *La Rinascente, Piazza Duomo,* ☎ *02/877120. AE, DC, MC, V. Closed Sun. No lunch Mon.*

$–$$ ✕ **La Bruschetta.** You'll find this tiny, busy pizzeria off Corso Vittorio Emanuele, behind the Duomo; it is run by a partnership of Tuscans and Neapolitans. The woodstove is in full view, so you can see your pizza cooking in front of you, although there are plenty of nonpizza dishes available, too, such as spaghetti *alle cozze e vongole* (with clam and mussel sauce). ⊠ *Piazza Beccaria 12,* ☎ *02/8692494. No credit cards. Closed Mon., Aug. 1–21, Dec. 24–28, and Good Fri.–Easter Mon.*

$ ✕ **La Giara.** The quality of the food from the limited menu in this simple Pugliese restaurant is a revelation. Here you eat tavern style, at wooden tables and benches, often sharing a table with other diners. Start with the antipasto *sott'olio* (eggplant, artichoke, mushroom, and tomato preserved in olive oil), and try one of the grilled-meat courses, cooked on a range at the front of the restaurant and eaten with nothing but the excellent Pugliese bread and olive oil. ⊠ *Viale Monza 10,* ☎ *02/26143835. No credit cards. Closed Wed.*

$ ✕ **San Tomaso.** The informality of a beer hall, a trendy young clientele, and a self-service counter here add up to pleasant, easy eating. Very busy at lunch, it's usually quieter at night. ⊠ *Via San Tomaso 5,* ☎ *02/874510. No credit cards. Closed Sun.*

$ ✕ **Taverna Moriggi.** Near the stock exchange, this is a dusky, wood-paneled wine bar serving a fixed-price lunch for about 30,000 lire, or cold cuts and cheeses in the evening. ⊠ *Via Moriggi 8,* ☎ *02/86450880. D, MC, V. Closed Sun. No lunch Sat.*

$$$$ ▥ **Duomo.** Guests' comfort is the important thing at this spacious, modern hotel: celebrities have been turned away when it was thought they would attract noisy fans and paparazzi. This is the obvious choice if a central location is also your priority: you're only 20 yards from the cathedral itself, yet within a quiet pedestrian-only zone. Air-conditioned rooms and duplex suites are swankly done in golds, creams, and browns. If in a room on the second, fourth, or fifth floor, you'll be eye to eye with the Gothic gargoyles and pinnacles of the Duomo. ⊠ *Via San Raffaele 1, 20121,* ☎ *02/8833,* ℻ *02/86462027. 153 rooms. Restaurant, bar, parking (fee). AE, DC, MC, V.*

$$$$ ▥ **Four Seasons.** The renaissance of a 14th-century monastery on an exclusive shopping street in the center of Milan and has produced a precious gem, for which you'll pay dearly. The hotel blends European sophistication with American comfort. Individually decorated rooms have opulent marble bathrooms; most rooms face the quiet courtyard. Downstairs is the hotel's well-regarded Il Teatro restaurant. ⊠ *Via Gesù 8, 20121,* ☎ *02/77088,* ℻ *02/7708500. 98 rooms. 2 restaurants, bar, business services, meeting rooms. AE, DC, MC, V.*

$$$$ ▥ **Pierre.** No expense was spared to furnish each room of this luxury hotel in a different style with the most elegant color-coordinated fabrics and a variety of modern and antique furniture. Everything is electronic: you can open the curtains, turn off the lights, have personal messages from the front desk appear on your TV screen—all with the touch of a button. The Pierre is on the inner beltway, near the medieval church of Sant'Ambrogio. ⊠ *Via De Amicis 32, 20123,* ☎ *02/72000581,* ℻ *02/8052157. 49 rooms. Restaurant, bar, parking (fee). AE, DC, MC, V.*

$$$$ ▥ **Principe di Savoia.** Of the three deluxe ITT-Sheraton Luxury Collection hotels in Milan, this is the most sumptuously posh. Behind the neoclassical facade, the decor is in 19th-century Lombard style, with lavish mirrors, drapes, and carpets. Bedrooms have been enlarged and are more comfortable than ever. ⊠ *Piazza della Repubblica 17, 20124,*

☎ 02/62301, FAX 02/6595838. *287 rooms. Restaurant, bar, health club. AE, DC, MC, V.*

$$$ 🏨 **Canada.** This friendly small hotel is close to Piazza del Duomo on the edge of a district full of shops and restaurants. It offers good value in rooms that are furnished in a nondescript fashion but have the usual modern trappings. ✉ *Via Santa Sofia 16, 20122,* ☎ *02/58304844,* FAX *02/58300282. 35 rooms. Bar. AE, DC, MC, V.*

$$$ 🏨 **Carlton-Senato.** This is the ideal choice for visitors who intend to spend time shopping—or window shopping—in the nearby high-fashion streets, Via della Spiga, Via Sant'Andrea, and Via Monte Napoleone. The hotel is very light and airy, with double-thick windows, a garage with direct access to the hotel, and lots of little touches (such as gratis chocolates and liqueurs) to make up for the rather functional rooms. Some have terraces large enough for a table, chair, and potted shrubs. At press time (spring 1997), the hotel was closed for restoration and scheduled to reopen September 1997. ✉ *Via Senato 5, 20124,* ☎ *02/76015535,* FAX *02/783300. 79 rooms. Restaurant, bar, air-conditioning, parking (fee). AE, MC, V. Closed Aug.*

$$$ 🏨 **Casa Svizzera.** A faithful clientele considers this one of Milan's best small hotels in its price category, so it's advisable to make reservations early. Adjacent to the Duomo and a few yards from the Galleria, it's central and handy to Metro and bus lines. The hotel is soundproofed; air-conditioned rooms sport TVs, refrigerator-bars, and cheery floral-print fabric. ✉ *Via San Raffaele 3, 20121,* ☎ *02/8692246,* FAX *02/72004690. 45 rooms. Bar. AE, DC, MC, V. Closed Aug. and Dec. 24–Jan. 6.*

$$–$$$ 🏨 **Gritti.** The Picassos, Matisses, and Van Goghs in the lobby here are originals—so the manager will tell you—except that they were painted quite recently "in the spirit." The Gritti is a bright hotel with a cheerful atmosphere, adequate rooms, and good views (from the inside upper floors) of tiled roofs and the gold Madonnina statue on top of the Duomo, only a few hundred yards away. ✉ *Piazza Santa Maria Beltrade 4, north end of Via Torino, 20123,* ☎ *02/801056,* FAX *02/89010999. 48 rooms. Restaurant, bar. AE, DC, MC, V.*

$$ 🏨 **Hotel Garda.** This modern hotel can claim the best location in Milan: it's a 2-minute walk from the main train station, 3 subway lines, and a multistory parking lot. Although the lobby looks spartan, rooms beyond are well furnished, comfortable, and clean. Most rooms overlook the busy center streets, thankfully quieter at night. ✉ *Via Napo Torriani 21, 20124,* ☎ *02/66982626,* FAX *02/66982576. 55 rooms. Bar, breakfast room. AE, MC, V.*

$–$$ 🏨 **London.** Close to the Duomo, the London has clean, spacious rooms
★ and an English-speaking staff. It has an arrangement with the Opera Prima restaurant in the same building, if you want to take your meals there at a discount (AE, DC, MC are accepted). ✉ *Via Rovello 3, 20121,* ☎ *02/72020166,* FAX *02/8057037. 29 rooms. Bar. MC, V. Closed Dec. 23–Jan. 3 and Aug.*

$–$$ 🏨 **San Francisco.** Near Metro stations on two lines (Loreto, Piola, or Pasteur stops) and not far from the Central Station, this modern hotel has a functional, flag-bedecked lobby, simply furnished rooms, and a small garden where guests can relax in fair weather. ✉ *Viale Lombardia 55, 20131,* ☎ *02/2361009,* FAX *02/26680377. 31 rooms. AE, DC, MC, V.*

Nightlife and the Arts

Bars

El Brellin (✉ Vicolo Lavandai at Alzaia Naviglio Grande, ☎ 02/58101351) is one of the many bars in the Navigli district. It is closed

Sunday. In the Brera quarter, **Momus** (⊠ Via Fiori Chiari 8, ☎ 02/8056227) is upscale and intimate.

Concerts

La Scala opera house (☞ Exploring Milan, *above*) features a two-month season of **classical concerts** in October and November.

Discos

Lizard (⊠ Largo La Foppa, ☎ 02/6590890) is trendy, loud, and expensive—a formula that doesn't deter the young Milanese crowd. It's closed Sunday evening, Monday, and Tuesday. **Nepentha** (⊠ Piazza Diaz 1, ☎ 02/804837) is also a popular spot; it's closed Sunday.

Gay Clubs

Milan's gay-friendly street, with restaurants, bars, bookshops, etc., is Via Sammartini, just behind the Stazione Centrale. **After Dark** (⊠ Via Certosa 134, ☎ 02/305585) is strictly men; it's closed Tuesday.

Jazz

Head to the hot spot of late, **Le Scimmie** (⊠ Via Ascanio Sforza 49, ☎ 02/89402874), for cool jazz and relaxed atmosphere. It's closed Tuesday.

Nightclubs

Milan clubs are good bets for an evening of dinner and dancing, but don't expect to get them for a song. Youngsters with plenty of money crowd **Stage** (⊠ Galleria Manzoni off Via Monte Napoleone, ☎ 02/76021071); it's closed Sunday. **Hollywood** (⊠ Via Como 15/c, ☎ 02/6598996) is the in place for the fashion set.

Opera

The season at Milan's famous **La Scala** opera house runs from December 7 (St. Ambrose Day) through May or later. Seats are usually sold out well in advance, but if you are prepared to pay the desk clerk at your hotel, you will probably be able to get hold of a pair of tickets. For information on schedules, ticket availability, and how to buy tickets, there is an **Infotel Scala Service** (with English-speaking staff) at the ticket office (⊠ Teatro alla Scala, Ufficio Biglietteria, Via Filodrammatici 2, ☎ 02/72003744), which is open daily 10–7. Telephone bookings are not accepted. From abroad you can book in advance, within a short specified period for each presentation (the dates are published at the beginning of the season; these tickets are allocated on a first-come, first-served basis), by applying for a reservation by mail or fax (transmitted 9–6 local time, with time and date of transmission, and sender's fax number indicated on the fax, to FAX 02/877996 or 02/8051625), or at CIT or other travel agencies (at agencies, no more than 10 days before performance). Consult the listings in the informative monthly *Milano Mese*, free at APT (tourist board) offices, or the weekly *Viva Milano*.

Theater

Milan's **Piccolo Teatro** (⊠ Via Rovello 2, ☎ 02/877663) is noted for its excellent productions, given in Italian, of course. **Teatro Manzoni** (⊠ Via Manzoni 40, ☎ 02/790543) is equally renowned.

Outdoor Activities and Sports

Golf

The **Parco di Monza** (⊠ 15 km/9 mi from Milan) has 18- and nine-hole courses. Contact the **Golf Club Milano** (☎ 039/303081).

Sports Center

The best-equipped of Milan's many sport centers is the **Centro Saini** (✉ Via Corelli 136, ☎ 02/7380841), in the vast Parco Forlanini. Much like a municipal gym, it offers squash and volleyball facilities and weight rooms. It's outside the city center; take Bus 38.

Shopping

At the northern end of Piazza della Scala, Via Manzoni leads straight into the heart of Milan's most luxurious shopping district, perhaps the most luxurious shopping district in all of Italy. Right here, in a few small streets laid out like a game of hopscotch—**Via Monte Napoleone, Via Sant'Andrea, Via della Spiga**—exist the shops of the great Italian designers, such as Armani, Versace, and Gianfranco Ferre (☞ Shopping Districts, *below*). Don't come here looking for affordable fashion—that has been relegated to the other side of the Duomo. Shops are usually open 9–1 (except Monday morning) and 4–7:30; many are closed in August.

Milan's fortissimo occurs twice a year, in March and October (for women) and June and January (for men), when the world's fashion elite descend upon the city for the famous ready-to-wear designer shows that invariably set next season's international styles.

Clothing

For the constant redefinition of cut, design, and style, **Giorgio Armani** (✉ Via Sant'Andrea) is the fashion temple. Hip, sleek, less formal Armani wear is sold at **Emporio Armani** (✉ Via Durini), at more informal prices. Head to **Prada** (✉ Galleria Vittorio Emanuele, ☎ 02/876979) for Miucca's bewitching, chic spartan design on everything from celebrities to runways these days, smart leather goods, and a look at the famous series of turn-of-the-century murals with a travel theme. **Gianfranco Ferre** (✉ Via Sant'Andrea) concentrates on swank, ready-to-wear apparel. Daring design and color on the cutting edge is the fashion at **Gianni Versace** (✉ Via Monte Napoleone). **Moschino** (✉ Via Sant'Andrea) counters the conventional. **La Rinascente** (✉ Piazza del Duomo) is one of the bigger department stores in Milan. **Coin** (✉ Piazza Loreto) is a smaller but stylish department store.

Flea Markets

Flea markets are popular in Milan. Food and a vast array of items, new and old, are displayed in open-air stalls. In many markets, bargaining is no longer the custom. You can try to haggle, but if you fear getting ripped off, go to the stalls where prices are clearly marked. On Saturday there is the huge **Mercato Papiniano** (✉ Viale Papiniano, and the Fiera di Senigallia, on Via Calatafimi) with old and new bargains. If you collect coins or stamps, go on Sunday morning to the specialized market at **Via Armorari** (✉ Near Piazza Cordusio). The best antiques markets are held on the last Sunday of each month along the Navigli and the third Saturday of each month on **Via Fiori Chiari** (✉ Near Via Brera).

Housewares

L'Utile e il Dilettevole (✉ Via della Spiga) sells enchanting Italian country-style items for the home.

Shoes

Beltrami (✉ Piazza San Babila 4/a) *scarpe* presently enjoy the fashion limelight, with assurance of good quality. For top-quality, classic design in the finest of hides choose **Ferragamo** (✉ Via Monte Napoleone 3). For a taste of the audacious mixed with tradition head to **Fratelli Rossetti** (✉ Corso Matteotti). Shoe addicts would be hard pressed not to find a gorgeous pair from **Lario 1898** (⊠ Via Monte Napoleone 21) in their closets.

Shopping Districts

Brera is a Milanese neighborhood with many unique shops. Walk along Via Brera, Via Solferino, Corso Garibaldi, and Via Paolo Sarpi. **Corso Buenos Aires** is a wide avenue with a variety of shops, several offering moderately priced items. **Corso Vittorio Emanuele** has clothing, leather goods, and shoe shops, some with items at reasonable prices. **Via Monte Napoleone** has 10 top-notch jewelers and a profusion of antiques stores and designer fashion boutiques, as well.

PAVIA, CREMONA, AND MANTUA

Cities of the Plain

Great Lombard cities of the Po River plain south of Milan are worthy of discovery: Pavia, celebrated for its Certosa, or charter house; Cremona, where history's great violin makers lived and worked; Sabbioneta, a diminutive utopian Renaissance city, the fruit of one man's lifelong obsession; and Mantua, home for almost 300 years of the fantastically wealthy Gonzaga dynasty.

Pavia

⑪ *38 km (24 mi) south of Milan (on E62), 57 km (35 mi) west of Cremona.*

Pavia was once Milan's chief local rival. The city dates at least from the Roman era and was the capital of the Lombard kings for two centuries (572–774). Pavia came to be known as "the city of a hundred towers" (of which only a handful have survived). Its prestigious university was founded in 1361 on the site of a 10th-century law school but has claims dating to antiquity.

The 14th-century **Castello Visconteo** now houses the local **Museo Civico** (Civic Museum), with an interesting archaeological collection and a picture gallery featuring works by Correggio. ⊠ *Piazza Castello,* ☎ *0382/33853.* ▣ *5,000 lire.* ⊙ *Tues.–Sat. 9–1:30, Sun. 9–1.*

In the Romanesque church of **San Pietro in Ciel d'Oro,** you can visit the tomb of Christianity's most celebrated convert, St. Augustine, housed in a Gothic marble ark on the high altar. ⊠ *Via Matteotti.* ▣ *Free.* ⊙ *Mon.–Sat. 9–5, Sun. mass.*

The main reason for stopping in Pavia is **Certosa** (the Carthusian monastery) 8 km (5 mi) north of Pavia city center. Its facade is stupendous, with much the same relish as the Duomo in Milan, the delightful first commandment of Victorian architecture: always decorate the decoration.

The Certosa's extravagant grandeur was due, in part, to the plan to have it house the tombs of the family of the first duke of Milan, Galeazzo Visconti III (he died during a plague, at age 49, in 1402). And extravagant it was—almost unimaginably so in an age before modern roads and transport. Only the very best marble was used in construction, transported, undoubtedly by barge, from the legendary quarries of Carrara, roughly 240 km (150 mi) away. Though the ground plan may be Gothic—a cruciform planned in a series of squares—the gorgeous fabric that rises above it is triumphantly Renaissance. On the facade, in the lower frieze, are medallions of Roman emperors and Eastern monarchs; above them are low reliefs of the life of Christ, as well as that of Galeazzo Visconti III.

The first duke was the only Visconti to be interred here, and then only some 75 years after his death, in a tomb designed by Gian Cristoforo Romano. Look for it in the right transept. In the left transept is a tomb of greater human appeal—that of a rather stern middle-aged man and a beautiful young woman. The man is Ludovico il Moro Sforza, seventh duke of Milan, who commissioned Leonardo da Vinci to paint the *Last Supper*. The woman is his wife, one of the most celebrated women of her day, Beatrice d'Este, the embodiment of brains, culture, birth, and beauty. Married when he was 40 and she was 16, they had enjoyed six happy years of marriage when she died suddenly, giving birth to a stillborn child. Ludovico commissioned the sculptor Cristoforo Solari to design a joint tomb for the high altar of Santa Maria delle Grazie in Milan. Originally much larger, the tomb for some years occupied the honored place in Santa Maria delle Grazie as planned. Then, for reasons that are still mysterious, the Dominican monks, who seemed to care no more for their former patron than they did for their faded Leonardo fresco, sold the tomb to their Carthusian brothers to the south. Sadly, part of the tomb, and its remains, were lost. ✉ *Certosa, 8 km (5 mi) north of Pavia city center,* ☎ *0382/925613.* ✉ *Free; donation requested.* ☉ *Nov.–Feb., Tues.–Sun. 9–11:30 and 2:30–5; Mar.–Apr. and Sept.–Oct., Tues.–Sun. 9–11:30 and 2:30–5:30; May–Aug., Tues.–Sun. 9:30–11:30 and 2:30–6.*

Dining

$$$ ✕ **Locanda Vecchia Pavia.** At this sophisticated, art-nouveau style
★ restaurant, you'll find creative versions of traditional regional cuisine, including *rane* (frogs), the local specialty, in risotto or on a spit. *Casoncelli* (stuffed pasta) and costoletta di vitello alla milanese are done with style, as are more imaginative seafood dishes. It's next to the duomo. ✉ *Via Cardinale Riboldi 2,* ☎ *0382/304132. Reservations essential. AE, DC, MC, V. No lunch Wed. Closed Mon., Jan. 1–9, and Aug.*

Nightlife and the Arts

During the first half of September, Pavia's **Settembre Pavese** festival presents street processions, displays, and concerts.

Cremona

⑫ *86 km (53 mi) east of Pavia, 67 km (42 mi) west of Mantua, 93 km (60 mi) southeast of Milan.*

If there is only one place in Italy to buy a violin, it's Cremona—as true today as when Andrea Amati (1510–80) opened up shop here in the middle of the 16th century. Though cognoscenti continue to revere the Amati name, it was the apprentice of Amati's nephew, Nicolo (1596–1684), for whom the fates had reserved a wide and lasting international fame. In a career that spanned an incredible 68 years, Antonio Stradivari (1644–1737) made more than 1,200 instruments—including violas, cellos, harps, guitars, and mandolins, in addition to his fabled violins. Labeled simply with a small printed slip, "Antonius Stradivarius Cremonensis. Faciebat anno. . . ." (the date added in a neat italic hand), they remain the best, most coveted, and most expensive stringed instruments in the world.

If you would like to see the original Stradivarius instruments, go to the second floor of **Palazzo del Comune** (City Hall), where five masterpieces by Cremonese *liutai* (violin makers), dating from the 16th to the 18th centuries, are on view. ✉ *Piazza del Comune,* ☎ *0372/4071.* ✉ *7,000 lire, valid for all other Cremona museums, including Museo*

Stradivariano (☞ *below*). ☉ *Tues.–Sat. 8:30–6, Sun. 9:15–12:15 and 3–5:30.*

Piazza del Comune, with its cathedral, campanile, baptistery, and City Hall, is particularly distinctive and harmonious. The combination of old brick, rose- and cream-colored marble, terra-cotta and old copper roofs brings Romanesque, Gothic, and Renaissance together with unusual success.

Don't miss **Torrazzo** (Big Tower), perhaps the tallest campanile in the country, visible for a considerable distance across the Po plain. ☒ *Piazza del Comune.* ☎ *6,000 lire.* ☉ *Apr.–Oct., Mon.–Sat. 10:30–noon and 3–6, Sun. 10:30–12:30 and 3–6:30.*

At No. 1 **Piazza Roma,** Antonio Stradivari lived, worked, and died. It's a lovely square of gardens, trees, and lawns. It is said that in addition to knowing all there was to know about woods, varnish, and the subtleties of assembling the 70-odd component parts that make up a violin, Stradivari liked to keep each new instrument in his bedroom for a month before varnishing it. This way, he claimed, by virtue of some mysterious somnolent transmigration, he gave a soul to each of his creations. In the center of the park is **Stradivari's grave,** marked by a simple tombstone.

The small **Museo Stradivariano** (Stradivarius Museum) has an informative display of Stradivari's plans and models, as well as violins made by Cremona's more modern masters. ☒ *Via Palestro 17,* ☎ *0372/461886.* ☎ *7,000 lire* (☞ *Palazzo del Comune, above).* ☉ *Tues.–Sat. 8:30–6, Sun. 9:15–12:15 and 3–6.*

Strolling about town, you may notice that violin making continues to flourish here. There are, in fact, more than 50 *liutai* (violin makers), many of them graduates of the **Scuola Internazionale di Liuteria** (International School of Violin Making) who continue to work by traditional methods in small shops scattered throughout Cremona. Visitors are usually welcome to these ateliers, especially if contemplating the acquisition of their own ready-made or custom-built Cremonese violin. You can always drop in on any shop you may be passing, otherwise the local tourist office has a list of workshops and will arrange appointments.

Dining

$$$$　✕ **Ceresole.** This is Cremona's best—and most expensive—establish-
★　　ment. It offers a variety of international dishes but concentrates on local delights: *cotecchino* (a rich boiled sausage) and risotto, for example. ☒ *Via Ceresole 4,* ☎ *0372/30099. No credit cards. Closed Mon. No dinner Sun.*

$$–$$$　✕ **Centrale.** Close to the cathedral, the Centrale is a favorite among
★　　the locals for traditional Cremonese fare, such as cotecchino with *mostarda* (mustard-hot crystallized fruit), at moderate prices. ☒ *Vicolo Petrusio 4,* ☎ *0372/28701. No credit cards. Closed Thurs. and July.*

Sabbioneta

⑬ *53 km (33 mi) southeast of Cremona, 34 km (21 mi) southwest of Mantua on S420.*

Vespasiano Gonzaga (1531–91), Sabbioneta's lord, founder, and chief architect, was not a particularly sympathetic man. The glory of his attainments in a life of public service is said to have been excelled only by the ignominy of his treatment of three wives and his only son. Upon retiring from military life at 47, he resolved to turn an old castle and a few squalid cottages into the Perfect City—a tiny, urbane metropolis where the most gifted artists and greatest writers would live in perfect harmony with a perfect patron. After some five years of planning and another five of work, the village was transformed into an elegant, star-shaped, walled fortress, with a rational grid of streets, two palaces, two squares, two churches, an exquisite theater (said to be the first in Europe with a roof) by Vincenzo Scamozzi, and a noble Gallery of Antiquities (a forerunner of today's art galleries). Gonzaga died four years later, survived only by the last of his wives.

When Aldous Huxley and his wife visited Sabbioneta in 1924, the town had reached an appalling state of neglect and decay. The Huxleys were given a tour (still the only way of seeing the interiors of most of Sabbioneta's buildings) much like the tour you take today.

In the majestic **Palazzo Ducale** are four fine equestrian figures of Vespasiano and his Gonzaga forebears. They were led through what had once been the Cabinet of Diana, the ducal saloon, and other rooms, only to discover that the rooms had been converted to serve the structure's new function as the town hall. They were shown the little **theater** (an adaption of Palladio's, at Vicenza, by the man who helped him build it), but it lacked its stage, and its frescoes were covered with whitewash. Today you will find the theater restored and its frescoes uncovered. The third building on the tour, the **Palazzo del Giardino,** has a dusty but impressive gallery of antique sculptures. Tours begin whenever enough interested people have assembled. Apply at the Ufficio Turistico (Tourist Office; ☞ Visitor Information *in* Milan, Lombardy, and the Lakes A to Z, *below*). ✉ Piazza Ducale. 🎟 *Tour 10,000 lire.* ☺ *Apr.–Sept., Tues.–Sun. 9–noon and 2:30–7; Oct.–Mar., Tues.–Sat. 9–noon and 2:30–5, Sun. 9–noon and 2:30–5:30.*

The **synagogue** is now a shuttered and derelict building, the sole surviving trace of Sabbioneta's prosperous 16th-century Jewish community. You'll have to ask someone to point out the synagogue, as it no longer has an address. ✉ *Town center.*

Mantua

 67 km (42 mi) east of Cremona, 64 km (40 mi) south of Bardolino.

Mantua (in Italian, Mantova) is known as the seat of the Gonzagas, who, like the Viscontis and Sforzas of Milan (with whom they intermarried), lived with the regal pomp and circumstance befitting one of Italy's richest family dynasties. Their reign, first as marquesses, and later as dukes, was a long one—stretching from the first half of the 14th century into the beginning of the 18th.

Even if you've had enough of old palaces, you may still wish to come to Mantua. First, Virgil was born near here. Second, Mantegna (painter of the poignant *Dead Christ* in Milan's Brera) was the Gonzaga court painter for 50 years, and his best-known and only large surviving fresco cycle can be seen here. In addition, there are two fine churches by Leon Battista Alberti (1404–72). Both (much like Mantegna's work here) proved highly influential and were widely emulated by lesser architectural lights later in the Renaissance.

A home to the Gonzagas for centuries, the 500-room **Palazzo Ducale** (Ducal Palace) gives one the sense that the palace took centuries to build. From a distance, the group of buildings dominates the skyline, and the effect is fascinating.

The **Appartamento dei Nani** (Dwarfs' Apartments) were literally that, dwarf collecting being one of the more amusing occupations of Renaissance princes. According to historians, the dwarfs were not mistreated but were considered to be something between members of the family and celebrity comics. The apartments were built both for the dwarfs' enjoyment and for that of the court.

The **Appartamento del Paradiso** is usually praised for its view but is somewhat more interesting for its decorator and first resident, Isabella d'Este. Not only was she married at 16, like her younger sister Beatrice (the beautiful young woman of the tomb in the Certosa at Pavia; ☞ Pavia, *above*), she was apparently also Ludovico il Moro Sforza's first choice for a wife—until he learned she was already affianced to a Gonzaga rival. Isabella, too, is regarded as one of the great patrons of the Renaissance. She survived her sister by more than 40 years, and the archives of her correspondence, totaling more than 2,000 letters, are regarded as some of the most valuable records of the era.

The high point of all 500 rooms, if not of the city, is the **Camera degli Sposi** (literally, "Chamber of the Wedded Couple," because Duke Ludovico and his wife are the focus of attention; it was actually an audience chamber). It was painted by Mantegna over a nine-year period, when he was at the height of his power, and finished when he was 44. Here, Mantegna made a startling advance in painting by organizing the picture's plane of representation in a way that systematically mimics the experience of human vision. Even now, more than five centuries later, you can almost sense the excitement of a mature artist, fully aware of his painting's great importance, expressing his vision with a masterly, joyous confidence. The interiors of Mantua's Palazzo Ducale may be seen today only on a rigorous guided tour conducted in Italian by the municipality. ⊠ *Piazza Sordello,* ☎ *0376/320283.* ☎ *12,000 lire.* ⊗ *Tues.–Sat. 9–1 and 2:30–6, Sun.–Mon. 9–1.*

The most serious Mantegna aficionado will want to visit the **Casa di Andrea Mantegna,** designed by the artist himself and built around an intriguing circular courtyard, which is usually open to view (the interior can only be seen by appointment or when open for occasional art exhibitions). The artist's tomb is in the first chapel on the left in another church, **Sant'Andrea,** (1471, some sections earlier or later) a masterwork of the architect Alberti, which itself is considered Mantua's most important Renaissance creation. *Casa di Andrea Mantegna:* ⊠ *Via Acerbi 47,* ☎ *0376/360506.* ☎ *Free.* ⊗ *Daily 9–12:30 and 3–6. Sant'Andrea:* ⊠ *Piazza delle Erbe, south of Piazza Sordello.* ⊗ *Daily 8–12:30 and 3–6.*

Palazzo Te is one of the greatest of all Renaissance palaces, built by Isabella d'Este's son, Federico II Gonzaga, between 1525 and 1535, for his mistress. Reopened in 1989 after restoration, it is the singular Mannerist creation of artist/architect Giulio Romano, decorated with mythological trompe l'oeil paintings that are not to every visitor's taste. Nevertheless, as the magnificently frescoed **Room of the Giants** proves, the palace does not skimp on pictorial drama. ⊠ *South of town walls,* ☎ *0376/365886.* ☎ *12,000 lire.* ⊗ *Mon. 3–6, Tues.–Sun. 10–6.*

Dining and Lodging

$$$$
★ ✕ **Al Bersagliere.** One of Lombardy's best restaurants can be found in this rustic four-room inn, located in the tiny riverside hamlet of Goito, some 16 km (10 mi) northwest of Mantua on Route 236 (the main Mantua–Brescia road). It has been run by a single family for more than 150 years. The fish in particular is excellent, as is a Mantuan classic, frog soup. ⊠ *Via Goitese 258, Goito,* ☎ *0376/60007. Reservations essential. AE, DC, MC, V. Closed Mon., 15 days in Jan., and 15 days in Aug. No lunch Tues.*

$$$ ✕ **L'Aquila Nigra.** Down a small side street opposite the Palazzo Ducale, this popular restaurant is set in a former medieval convent. Frescoes look down from the walls on diners making their way through local dishes, such as frittata di zucchine and *faraona al pepe verde* (guinea fowl with green pepper). ✉ *Vicolo Bonacolsi 4,* ☎ *0376/327180. Reservations essential. AE, DC, MC, V. Closed Sun.–Mon., 3 wks in Aug., and Dec. 24–Jan. 5.*

$$–$$$ ✕ **Trattoria dei Martini–Il Cigno.** In a romantic 16th-century palazzo featuring some period frescoes, this restaurant scores well with atmosphere. The menu features local specialties such as *tortelli di zucca* (pasta stuffed with pumpkin), *insalata di cappone* (capon salad), and local variations on the Lombard favorite, risotto. ✉ *Piazza Carlo d'Arco 1,* ☎ *0376/327101. Reservations essential. AE, DC, MC, V. Closed Mon.–Tues., 1 wk in Jan., 2 wks in Aug.*

$–$$ ✕ **Cento Rampini.** In a square in the heart of medieval Mantua, this friendly, family-run trattoria is a favorite with the locals themselves. Among the tasty traditional dishes are risottos, *agnoli* (meat-filled pasta dumplings), *luccio in salsa verde* (pike with herb sauce), and *cotoletta d'agnello al timo* (lamb cutlets with thyme). ✉ *Piazza Erbe 11,* ☎ *0376/366349. AE, DC, MC, V. Closed Mon., 1 wk in late Jan., and Aug. 1–15. No dinner Sun.*

$$$ 🏨 **San Lorenzo.** Rooms in this center city hotel are large, with authentic early 19th-century decor. Although there is no restaurant, you're within easy walking distance of many (☞ *above*). Some people may find the rooms in the front a little noisy at night, when locals perform their ritualistic *passeggiata,* or fashion-conscious stroll. The San Lorenzo has a rooftop terrace and exudes comfort and individual attention. ✉ *Piazza Concordia 14, 46100,* ☎ *0376/220500,* 🖷 *0376/327194. 41 rooms. Air-conditioning, minibars, parking (fee). AE, DC, MC, V.*

Nightlife and the Arts

Each year on the feast of the Assumption (August 15), a **contest** is held in Mantua to determine who is the best *madonnaro* (street artist). Some of the painters can re-create masterpieces in a matter of minutes.

LAKE GARDA, BRESCIA, AND BERGAMO

Of all the curious things to be noted about Lake Garda, one is its perennial attraction for writers. Even the 16th-century essayist Michel de Montaigne, whose 15 months of travel journals contain not a single other reference to nature, paused to admire the view down the lake from Torbole, which he called "boundless."

Lake Garda is 50 km (31 mi) long, ranges from roughly 1–16 km (½–10 mi) wide, and is as much as 1,135 ft deep. The terrain is flat at the lake's southern base, and mountainous at its northern tip. As a consequence, the standard descriptions of it vary from stormy inland sea to crystalline Nordic fjord. It is the biggest lake in the region and by most accounts the cleanest.

Punta di San Vigilio

⓯ *70 km (44 mi) north of Mantua, 6 km (4 mi) north of Bardolino, 28 km (17 mi) south of Malcesine.*

Punta di San Vigilio, which just about everyone agrees is the prettiest spot on Garda's eastern shore, is full of cypresses from the gardens of the 15th-century **Villa Guarienti di Brenzone.** Expect more fine views of the lake.

Bardolino

64 km (40 mi) north of Mantua, 6 km (4 mi) south of Punta di San Vigilio, 34 km (21 mi) south of Malcesine.

Bardolino, which makes unremarkable but famous red wine, is one of the biggest summer resorts on the lake. It stands on the eastern shore at the widest end of the lake. Here there are two handsome Romanesque churches: **San Severo,** from the 11th century, and **San Zeno,** from the 9th. Both are in the center of the small town. Bardolino is a very lively spot at night, especially in relation to other towns on the lake.

Nightlife and the Arts

Bardolino is host to several festivals, but the best one is the **Grape Cure Festival,** a great excuse to indulge in some of the local tonic, since the idea is that the more you drink the better the cure will be. Hold onto the aspirin, just in case.

Malcesine

🔟 *34 km (21 mi) north of Bardolino, 21 km (13 mi) south of Riva del Garda.*

Malcesine is one of the loveliest areas along the upper eastern shore of Lake Garda. It is principally known as a summer resort with sailing and windsurfing schools. The 13 campsites and tourist villages do tend to make the town a little crowded in summer. There are however, some nice walks from the town toward the mountains behind. Visit the 13th- to 14th-century **Castello Scaligero,** built by the Della Scalas.

OFF THE BEATEN PATH **MONTE BALDO –** You're in the Veneto now, and if you are fond of cable cars, take the 15-minute *funivia* (funicular) ride to the top of Monte Baldo (5,791 ft) for a great view of the whole lake in summer, or possibly a short ski run in winter.

Outdoor Activities and Sports

SKIING

Malcesine (☎ 045/7400044) is a well-equipped resort with six lifts and more than 11 km (7 mi) of runs of varying degrees of difficulty.

Riva del Garda

🔟 *21 km (13 mi) north of Malcesine, 29 km (18 mi) north of Gargnano.*

One of the biggest towns on the northern tip of the lake, Riva del Garda is large and prosperous, and if you're there in summer, you may want to lodge there if the towns farther south seem too crowded. Many of the town's public buildings date from the 15th century, when it was a strategic outpost of the Venetian Republic. The heart of town, the lakeside **Piazza 3 Novembre,** is surrounded by medieval *palazzi* (palaces). The **Torre Apponale,** predating the Venetian period by three centuries, looms above these houses: its crenelations recall its defensive purpose. Standing in the piazza and looking out onto the lake, you can understand Riva del Garda's importance as a windsurfing center. Mountain air currents ensure good breezes on even the sultriest midsummer days.

OFF THE BEATEN PATH **CASCATA DEL VARONE –** This attractive waterfall, some 295 ft high, is 4 km (2½ mi) north of town on the road to Tenno.

Outdoor Activities and Sports

WINDSURFING

Contact **Circolo Surf Torbole** (✉ Colonia Pavese, ☎ 0464/505385) for news on windsurfing in the area.

En Route After passing the town of Limone (where it is said the first lemon trees in Europe were planted) take the fork to the right about 5 km (3 mi) north of Gargnano and head to Tignale. The view from the **Madonna di Monte Castello** church, some 2,000 ft above the lake, is spectacular. Adventurous travelers will want to follow this pretty inland mountain road to Tremosine.

Gargnano

⓲ *29 km (18 mi) south of Riva del Garda, 12 km (7 mi) north of Gardone Riviera.*

This small port town was an important Franciscan center in the 13th century. One of the two houses owned and lived in by Mussolini is now a language school; the other, Villa Feltrinelli, has not yet been opened to the public, but plans are being made for a museum to open some time in 1999. An Austrian flotilla bombarded the town in 1866 and some of the houses still bear signs of cannon fire. The town comes alive in the summer months when mostly German tourists, many of whom have villas here, invade the small pebble beach.

Dining

$$$–$$$$ ✕ **La Tortuga.** La Tortuga is the best restaurant in this scenic village,
★ and one of the best on the lake itself. Specializing in local cuisine, it features soufflé *di verdure* (of greens) and the excellent *trota allo scalogno e tartufo* (trout with scallions and truffles). From the excellent—and extensive—wine list, try the local white Lugana, often served chilled, or a local grappa. ✉ *Gargnano,* ☎ *0365/71251. AE, MC, V. Closed Tues. and Jan.–Feb. No dinner Mon. Oct.–May.*

Outdoor Activities and Sports

HIKING

Tremosine, some 17 km (11 mi) north of Gargnano, is known as the "Garda Terrace," and is a mountain forest area that is an ideal place for nature hikes. For more information, write or call the **Ufficio Comunale** (✉ Via Papa Giovanni XXIII, ☎ 0365/953185).

En Route On the road from Gargnano to Gardone you pass the small town of **Toscolano-Maderno,** which has one of the oldest and biggest paper recycling factories in Italy. The town itself hails from Etruscan times but there are also remnants of Roman influence.

Gardone Riviera

⓳ *12 km (7 mi) south of Gargnano, 32 km (19 mi) north of Sirmione.*

Gardone Riviera is a once-fashionable turn-of-the-century resort, now delightfully faded, and the former home of the flamboyant Gabriele d'Annunzio (1863–1938), one of Italy's greatest modern poets. D'Annunzio's estate, **Il Vittoriale,** is an elaborate memorial to himself, clogged with the trappings of conquests in art, love, and war (of which the largest is a ship's prow in the garden), and complete with a mausoleum. ✉ *Gardone Riviera,* ☎ *0365/20130.* ▱ *18,000 lire, including tour of house.* ☉ *Oct.–Mar., Tues.–Sun. 9–12:30 and 2–5:30; open later Apr.–Sept.*

Dining and Lodging

$$$–$$$$ ✕🏨 **Villa Fiordaliso.** The pink-and-white lakeside Villa Fiordaliso—
★ once home to Claretta Petacci, given to her by her lover Benito Mussolini—is known as a high-quality restaurant, but it also has seven tastefully furnished rooms, some with their own balconies overlooking the lake. The art-nouveau style restaurant features seasonal ingredients like zucchini flowers or porcini mushrooms, paramount in salads and soups. ✉ *Via Zanardelli 132, 25083,* ☎ *0365/20158,* FAX *0365/290011. 7 rooms. AE, DC, MC, V. Closed Mon. and Jan.–Feb.*

$$$–$$$$ 🏨 **Villa del Sogno.** A small, winding road takes you from the village
★ to this imposing villa, which surveys the valley and the lake below it. The large hotel terrace and the quiet surrounding grounds add to the feeling of getting away from it all, and you'll probably think twice about a busy sightseeing itinerary once you've settled into position in the sun, with a cool drink in hand. ✉ *Corso Zanardelli 107, 25083,* ☎ *0365/290181,* FAX *0365/290230. 34 rooms. Restaurant, pool, tennis court. AE, DC, MC, V. Closed mid-Oct.–Easter.*

$$$ 🏨 **Grand Hotel Fasano.** A former 19th-century hunting lodge on the lakefront, the Fasano has matured into a seasonal hotel of a high standard. The staff is friendly, as are most of the guests, who seem to be keen on making the most use of the water sports at their disposal. It's worth paying a bit extra to get one of the larger rooms with a lake view and balcony. ✉ *Corso Zanardelli 160, 25083,* ☎ *0365/290220,* FAX *0365/290221. 75 rooms. Restaurant, bar, pool, beach, windsurfing, waterskiing. MC, V. Closed Nov.–mid-May.*

Nightlife and the Arts

MUSIC

Il Vittoriale (☎ 0365/20347) holds a series of concerts in its outdoor theater during July and August.

Sirmione

★ ⑳ *32 km (20 mi) south of Gardone Riviera, 41 km (25 mi) east of Brescia.*

The ruins at this enchanting town on the southwestern shore of Lake Garda are a reminder that Garda has been a holiday resort for the leisurely well-to-do since the height of the Roman era. The locals will almost certainly tell you that the so-called **Grotte di Catullo** (Grottoes of Catullus) were once the site of the villa of Catullus, one of the greatest pleasure-seeking poets of all time. Present archaeological wisdom, however, does not concur, and there is some consensus that this was the site of two villas of slightly different periods, dating from about the 1st century AD. But never mind—the view through the cypresses and olive trees is lovely, and even if Catullus didn't have a villa here, he is closely associated with the area and undoubtedly did have a villa somewhere nearby. ✉ *Grotte di Catullo, Sirmione,* ☎ *030/916157.* 🎫 *8,000 lire.* ☉ *Apr.–Sept., Tues.–Sun. 9–6; Oct.–Mar., Tues.–Sun. 9–4.*

☾ The **Rocca Scaligera** castle was built, along with almost all the other castles on the lake, by the Della Scala family. As hereditary rulers of Verona for more than a century before control of the city was seized by the Visconti in 1402, they counted Garda among their possessions. You may wish to go inside (particularly if you have children with you), since there is a nice view of the lake from the tower. Or you may want to go for a swim at the nearby beach before continuing on. Entry to the old part of town, still redolent of medieval times, is gained through the castle's gates, over what was originally a drawbridge. ✉ *Rocca Scali-*

gera, Sirmione. ☎ *030/916468.* 🎫 *7,000 lire.* ☉ *Sun. 9–1; June–Sept., Tues.–Sat. 9–6; Oct.–May, Tues.–Sat. 9–1.*

OFF THE BEATEN PATH	**GARDALAND AMUSEMENT PARK –** This park has more than 40 different rides and water slides and is one of Italy's biggest amusement parks to thrill your children. It is 16 km (10 mi) east of Sirmione. ✉ *Castelnuovo del Garda,* ☎ *045/6449777.* 🎫 *27,000 lire.* ☉ *July–mid-Sept., daily 9 AM–midnight; Apr.–June, daily 9–6 (some days until 7 or 8); mid- to late Mar. and Oct., weekends 9–6.*

Dining and Lodging

$$$ ✗ **Vecchia Lugana.** At the base of the peninsula and outside the town,
★ this restaurant is considered one of Italy's best. Fish from the lake, grilled trout, and fillet of perch with artichokes are especially good. There's also an elegant garden. ✉ *Piazzale Vecchia Lugana 1, Lugana di Sirmione,* ☎ *030/919012. AE, DC, MC, V. No dinner Mon. Closed Tues. and Jan.*

$$ ✗ **Ristorante del Pescatore.** The specialty of this simple rustic looking, but very popular restaurant is lake fish. Try grilled trout with a bottle of local white wine and finish your meal with a walk in the nearby public park. ✉ *Via Piana 20,* ☎ *030/916216. DC, MC, V. Closed Jan.–Feb. and Wed. Oct.–May.*

$$$$ 🏨 **Villa Cortine Palace.** A formidably decorative former private villa in a secluded park, Villa Cortine is in danger of being just plain ostentatious. It dominates a low hill, and the grounds—a colorful mixture of lawns, trees, statues, and fountains—go down to the lake. The villa itself dates from the early part of the 19th century, although a new wing (1952) has been added: the trade-off is between the more charming Old World decor in the older rooms and the better lake views from the newer ones. ✉ *Via Grotte 6, 25019,* ☎ *030/9905890,* FAX *030/916390. 57 rooms. Restaurant, bar, air-conditioning, pool, tennis court, beach. AE, DC, MC, V. Closed Oct.–Apr. 10.*

$$–$$$ 🏨 **Continental.** Conveniently located on the lakefront, right next to a spa, the Continental operates on a half-pension basis only. This works to keep the cost in check, and the hotel has the amenities and feel of a much more expensive establishment. Most rooms have balconies, but ask specifically for a lake view. ✉ *Via Punta Staffalo 7, 25019,* ☎ *030/9905711,* FAX *030/916278. 51 rooms. Air-conditioning, pool, beach. AE, DC, MC, V. Closed Dec.–Mar.*

$$ 🏨 **Hotel Sirmione.** Just inside the city walls, near the Castello, this hotel
★ and spa sits amid lakeside gardens and terraces. Some rooms display superb execution, with comfortable Scandinavian slat beds, matching floral draperies and wall coverings, and built-in white furniture. Many guests have been returning for years, largely due to the homespun feel and the attentiveness of its staff. Full and half pension are offered. ✉ *Piazza Castello 19, 25019,* ☎ *030/916331,* FAX *030/916558. 76 rooms. Restaurant, bar, air-conditioning, pool, spa, meeting rooms. AE, DC, MC, V.*

Brescia

㉑ *19 km (12 mi) west of Lake Garda, 49 km (30 mi) east of Bergamo.*

The ruins of the **Capitolino,** Capitoline temple built by the Emperor Vespasian in AD 73, testify to Brescia's Roman origin. Outstanding among the sculptures in the adjoining **Museo Romano** is the famed 1st-century bronze *Winged Victory.* ✉ *Via dei Musei 57/a,* ☎ *030/46031.* 🎫 *8,000 lire.* ☉ *Tues.–Fri. 9–12:30 and 3–5, weekends 9–12:30 and 3–6.*

In addition to the Brescia School, the **Pinacoteca Civica Tosio-Martinengo** accommodates paintings by Raphael, Tintoretto, Tiepolo, and Clouet. ⊠ *Piazza Moretto,* ☎ *030/3774999.* ▣ *6,000 lire.* ⊙ *Tues.–Fri. 9– 12:30 and 3–5, weekends 9–12:30 and 3–6.*

Palladio and Sansovino contributed to the splendid **Palazzo della Loggia,** the Lombard-Venetian palace of marble overlooking the Piazza della Loggia. The **Torre dell'Orologio** (Clock Tower; ⊠ Piazza della Loggia) dates from the 16th century and is modeled on the campanile in Venice's Piazza San Marco. In the church of **Madonna del Carmine** are a flight of stairs that climb to the ramparts of the Venetian **Castello,** high enough to give a panoramic view over the town and across the plain to the distant Alps. ⊠ *Piazza del Duomo. Closed Mon. and Wed.*

Dining and Lodging

$$$$ ✕ **Gualtiero Marchesi.** Never afraid to try something new, owner-chef ★   Gualtiero Marchesi is celebrated as the founder of *la cucina nuova* (nouvelle cuisine Italian-style). He first made his mark with impressive cookbooks, private-label products, and two restaurants in Milan. Since 1993 the kitchen in this deluxe hotel villa has been revered for its spectacular flights of fantasy grounded with classic Lombardian finesse. Tiny lake fish are served within white paper folded origami fashion, soups are garnished with caviar, and ravioli are served *aperto* (open and unsealed at the edges) or *fazzoletto,* handkerchief-style. You can easily become Romeo to Marchesi's dazzling Juliet—*a rombo in crosta di sale* (turbot in salt crust). The desserts—and prices—are heavenly. ⊠ *Via Vittorio Emanuele 11, Erbusco, part of the Albereta Hotel,* ☎ *030/7760562,* ℻ *030/7760379. Reservations essential. Jacket and tie. AE, DC, MC, V. Closed Mon. and Jan. 12–Feb. 12. No dinner Sun.*

$$$ ✕ **La Sosta.** Just south of Brescia's cathedral, La Sosta occupies a 17th-century building. The cuisine and service suggest a more expensive establishment, and the ambience is refined. A Brescian specialty is *casonsei* (large meat-filled ravioli). *Capretto alla bresciana* (roast kid with polenta) is an outstanding main course, but make sure you have room for it. ⊠ *Via San Martino della Battaglia 20,* ☎ *030/295603,* ℻ *030/292589. AE, DC, MC, V. Closed Mon., Dec. 24–Jan. 7, and 3 wks in Aug. No dinner Sun.*

$$$ ▥ **Vittoria.** Centrally located among 16th-century buildings, Vittoria has more than its share of atmosphere. Erected in 1933, the hotel is in the Venetian style, with a hint of Byzantium and the Spice Routes in its pointed arches and windows. Many of the rooms are adorned with antiques. ⊠ *Via delle X Giornate 20, 25019,* ☎ *030/280061,* ℻ *030/280065. 65 rooms. Restaurant, bar, air-conditioning, meeting rooms. AE, DC, MC, V.*

Nightlife and the Arts

Brescia's **Teatro Grande** (☎ 030/3750459) has a series of classical music concerts from November to May.

Bergamo

❷ *49 km (30 mi) west of Brescia, 58 km (36 mi) southeast of Bellagio.*

Bergamo is two cities—Bergamo Bassa (Lower Bergamo) and Bergamo Alta (Upper Bergamo), connected by a funicular railway. High up on the hillside, walled in by the ruins of ancient Venetian fortifications, surmounted by a fortress, is Bergamo Alta. The old city of Bergamo lies at the foot of the Bergamese Alps. It is one of northern Italy's most charming medieval centers.

The massive **Torre del Comune** offers a great view of the two cities, the lower and upper. Recent restoration has made the whole structure secure, and it is now open to the public. ⊠ *Piazza Vecchia*, ☎ *035/262566.* ⊙ *Apr.–Sept, daily 10–noon and 2–6; Mar. and Oct., weekends 10–noon and 2–6; Nov.–Feb., weekends 10–noon and 2–4.*

The **Duomo** of Bergamo and **baptistery** are the most notable buildings in Piazza Vecchia. But the most impressive is the **Colleoni Chapel,** which has been cleaned, and its elaborate marble decoration is resplendent. ⊠ *Piazza Vecchia*, ☎ *035/217317.* ⊙ *Colleoni Chapel Mar.–Oct., daily 9–noon and 2–6:30; Nov.–Mar., Tues.–Sat. 9–noon and 2:30–4:30. Baptistery visits by arrangement with Duomo parish priest.*

★ In the **Accademia Carrara** you will find one of Italy's greatest and most important art collections. Many of the Venetian masters are represented—Mantegna, Carpaccio, Tiepolo, Guardi, Canaletto—and there are some magnificent Bellinis and Botticellis as well. ⊠ *Bergamo Bassa, Piazza Carrara*, ☎ *035/399426.* ◪ *5,000 lire; Sun. free.* ⊙ *Wed.–Mon. 9:30–noon and 2:30–5:30.*

Dining and Lodging

$$$$ ✕ **Dell'Angelo–Taverna del Colleoni.** Angelo Cornaro has closed the
★ celebrated Antico Ristorante Dell'Angelo to concentrate all his attention on the Taverna del Colleoni, on the 15th-century Piazza Vecchia, right behind the Duomo, where he continues to serve a wide and imaginative range of fish and meat dishes, all expertly prepared. Tables outside in the summer are delightful. ⊠ *Piazza Vecchia 7*, ☎ *035/232596. AE, DC, MC, V. Closed Mon., 1 wk in Jan., and 2 wks in Aug.*

$$ ✕ **Agnello d'Oro.** A 17th-century tavern on a main street in Upper Bergamo, with wooden booths and walls hung with copper utensils and ceramic plates, Agnello d'Oro is a good place to imbibe the atmosphere as well as the good local wine. Specialties are typical Bergamasque risotto and varieties of polenta served with game and mushrooms. The same establishment also has 20 modestly priced rooms. ⊠ *Via Gombito 22*, ☎ *035/249883. AE, DC, MC, V. Closed Mon. and mid-Jan.–mid-Feb.*

$$ ✕ **Da Ornella.** On the main street in the Upper Town, this trattoria is well attended, so reservations are a must. Vaulted ceilings, wooden beams, and antique ceramic ware on the walls enhance the Old Worldliness. Ornella herself is in the kitchen, turning out casonsei in butter and sage and platters of assorted roast meats. ⊠ *Via Gombito 15*, ☎ *035/232736. Reservations essential. AE, DC, MC, V. Closed Thurs. and July. No lunch Fri.*

$$ ✕ **La Trattoria del Teatro.** Traditional regional food tops the bill at this good-value restaurant in the Upper Town. The polenta is heart rendering, and game is recommended in season. Fettuccine *con funghi* (with mushrooms) is a deceptively simple but rich and memorable specialty. ⊠ *Piazza Mascheroni 3*, ☎ *035/238862. No credit cards. Closed Mon. and July 15–30.*

$–$$ ✕ **Bernabò.** From the funicular it's worth heading straight ahead, past Piazza Vecchia to the old military fortress and this corner trattoria. It has two simple rooms with vaulted ceilings, wrought-iron lamps, and wood-paneled walls. The clientele is a mix of locals and economy-minded tourists. All are treated cordially. Specialties are casonsei served with butter and sage, and veal scallopini or game with polenta. Pizza is also served. ⊠ *Via Colleoni 31*, ☎ *035/237692. MC, V. Closed Thurs. and July 15–Aug. 15.*

$$$ ▦ **Cristallo Palace.** On the periphery of town, the Cristallo Palace offers the amenities of a modern, efficient hotel, plus the bonus of being on the *tangenziale* (the road that bypasses the center). The rooms are large and well equipped, and the service is polished and prompt. The hotel's restaurant, L'Antica Perosa, is very good, and its prices are at the lower range of this category. A shuttle runs into town in the mornings and late afternoon. ⊠ *Via Betty Ambiveri 35, 24126,* ☎ *035/311211,* FAX *035/312031. 90 rooms. Bar, air-conditioning. AE, DC, MC, V.*

$$$ 🏨 **Excelsior San Marco.** The most comfortable hotel in the lower part of Bergamo, the Excelsior San Marco is only a short walk from the walls of the Upper Town. The rooms are surprisingly quiet, considering the central location of the hotel. Its restaurant, Tino Fontana, has a rooftop terrace. ⊠ *Piazza della Repubblica 6, 24126,* ☎ *035/366111,* FAX *035/223201. 162 rooms. Bar, air-conditioning. MC, V.*

Nightlife and the Arts

An **International Piano Festival,** an event of more than 30 years' standing, is held in Bergamo's **Teatro Donizetti** (⊠ Piazza Cavour 14, ☎ 035/249631) in summer.

LAKE COMO

For those whose idea of heaven is palatial villas, rose-laden belvederes, operetta towns, hanging gardens of wisteria and bougainvillea, flickering lanterns casting a glow over lakeshore restaurants, and dreamy alpine vistas, heaven exists at Lake Como. Virgil liked Como at least as much as Garda, calling it simply our "greatest" lake. Stendhal described it as an "enchanting spot, unequaled on earth for loveliness," in his *Charterhouse of Parma.* Though summer crowds do their best to vanquish the lake's dreamy mystery and civilized, slightly faded, millionaire's-row gentility, they fail. Como remains a place of consummate partnership between the beauties of nature and those of humanity. Accordingly, our tour of the lake is of gardens and villas (of which a couple of the finest are now hotels). Like so many of Italy's most beautiful villa gardens, those of Como owe their beauty to the landscape architecture of two eras: Renaissance Italian, with its taste for order; and 19th-century English, with its fondness for illusions of natural wildness. The two are often framed by vast areas of the most picturesque farmland—notably olive groves, fruit trees, and vineyards.

Lake Como is some 47 km (30 mi) long north to south, and it is also Europe's deepest lake (almost 1,350 ft). Rarely out of sight to visitors, it looks like a burnished mirror—until a breeze ruffles its incandescence. Here, in the *centro di lago* (center region of the lake), travelers have long headed for Bellagio. This alluring town is known as the "punta di Bellagio" because it's at the point that divides Lake Como into three branches. It's an enchanting location, one that inspired Gabriel Faure to call Bellagio "a diamond contrasting brilliantly with the sapphires of the three lakes in which it is set." After just a few days on Lake Como, you'll understand why Verdi choose to compose *La Traviata* in Cadenabbia (across the lake from Bellagio). Today, for Milanese weekend-trippers, countless honeymooners, and visitors from around the world, going to Lake Como is not so much escape, as return; not so much getting away from it all, but returning to that *douceur de vie,* that sweetness of life rarely encountered today.

If you're not going by car, you arrive at the lake by pulling into the railway station at Como, a leading textile center, famous for its silks. Most visitors hasten to the *vaporetti* (water taxis) waiting to take them to the centro di lago, the most beautiful part of the lake. Art lovers, however, should note that 15 or so blocks south of the station is one of the greatest Italian Romanesque churches, Sant'Abbondio—a detour they will consider well worth making once they've seen its awe-inspiring, gigantic nave interior. Although you can take a bus up either shoreline, most people take a ferry to Bellagio, the key town of the centro di lago; be sure to take an express ferry as the local vaporetti can turn a half-hour ride into a three-hour ordeal. Once at Bellagio, vaporetti and car-ferries traverse the lake, making it easy for travelers to get to the other main towns, Cernobbio, Cadenabbia, and Varenna.

Madonna del Ghisallo

㉓ *48 km (30 mi) northwest of Bergamo, 18 km (11 mi) north of Cernobbio.*

The church of the Madonna del Ghisallo (the patroness of bicyclists) is not far from the shores of Lake Como arriving from Bergamo and offers a fine view of the surrounding area. You will often see cyclists parked outside taking a breather after their uphill struggle, but many come just as a homage to this unique Madonna. From Bergamo you pass it on the road to Bellagio. ⊠ *Magreglio.* ▦ *Free.* ☉ *Mar.–Nov.*

Bellagio

★ **㉔** *58 km (36 mi) northwest of Bergamo, 28 km (17 mi) north of Cernobbio.*

Sometimes called the prettiest town in Europe, Bellagio also has ferry services to most towns on the lake. Here, buildings always seem to be flag bedecked, geraniums rustle from every window, and bougainvillea veils the staircases, or *montées,* that thread through the town. At dusk, Bellagio's nightspots—including the wharf where an orchestra serenades dancers under the stars—beckon vacationers to come and make merry.

★ **Villa Serbelloni,** a property of the Rockefeller Foundation, can also be visited for its celebrated gardens, on the site of Pliny the Elder's villa, overlooking Bellagio. As there are only two guided visits per day restricted to 30 people, and these tend to be commandeered by group bookings especially during May, you'd do well to book far in advance with the Bellagio tourist office (☞ *Visitor Information in* Milan, Lombardy, and the Lakes A to Z, *below*), which organizes the tours. ▦ *5,000 lire.* ☉ *Guided visits mid-Apr.–mid-Oct., Tues.–Sun. at 10:30 and 4.*

The famous gardens of the **Villa Melzi** are open to the public and were once a favorite picnic spot for Franz Lizst. Although you can't get into the 19th-century villa, don't miss the lavish Empire-style family chapel. The Melzi were Napoléon's greatest allies in Italy (the family has passed down the name of Josephine to the present); directly across the lake is the Villa Carlotta, once residence of Count Sommariva, Napoléon's worst Italian enemy. ⊠ *3 km (2 mi) outside Bellagio,* ☎ *031/950318.* ▦ *5,000 lire.* ☉ *Late Mar.–early Nov., daily 9–6:30.*

OFF THE BEATEN PATH

VILLA BALBIANELLO – This may be the most magical house in all of Italy. It sits on its own little promontory, Il Dosso d'Avedo—separating the bays of Venus and Diana—around the bend from the tiny fishing village of Ossuccio. Relentlessly picturesque, the villa is comprised of loggias, terraces, and *palazzetini* (tiny palaces), all of which spill down verdant slopes to the lakeshore where an old Franciscan church, magnificent stone staircase, and statue of San Carlo Borromeo blessing the waters welcome visitors (the only access to the villa is by launch, which leaves Ossuccio three times a week). Designed in 1596 by Pellegrino Pelligrini, it was enlarged by Count Lambertenghi (who insisted on calling all his guests "Count," but refused the title himself). In 1974 it was sold to Count Monzino, who graciously willed it to the Fondo Ambiente Italiano, which has opened it to the public. Check with Bellagio tourist office (☞ Visitor Information *in* Milan, Lombardy, and the Lakes A to Z, *below*) for the hours of launch tours. ☒ *Il Dosso d'Avedo.* 🖃 *5,500 lire.* ☉ *Tues. and weekends 10–12:30 and 4–6:30.*

Varenna

㉕ *10 km (6 mi) north of Bellagio.*

Using the ferry boat services in Bellagio, make your way to the town of Varenna. The principal sight here is the spellbindingly beautiful garden of the **Villa Monastero,** which, as its name suggests, was a monastery before it was a villa. Now it's an international science center. ☒ *Varenna.* 🖃 *4,000 lire.* ☉ *Apr.–Oct., daily 9–noon and 2–5.*

Tremezzo

㉖ *34 km (21 mi) north of Cernobbio.*

If you are lucky enough to visit this small lakeside town late spring or very early summer, you will find the magnificent **Villa Carlotta** a riotous blaze of color, with more than 14 acres of azaleas and dozens of varieties of rhododendron in full bloom. The villa itself was built between 1690 and 1743 for the luxury-loving Marquis Giorgio Clerici. The range of the garden's collection is remarkable, particularly when you consider the difficulties of transporting delicate, exotic vegetation before the age of aircraft. Palms, banana trees, cactus, eucalyptus, a sequoia, orchids, and camellias are only the beginning of a list that includes more than 500 species.

According to local lore, one motive for the Villa Carlotta's magnificence was a keeping-up-with-the-Joneses sort of rivalry between the marquis's ambitious, self-made son-in-law, who inherited the estate, and the son-in-law's arch rival, who built *his* summer palace directly across the lake. Whenever either added to his villa and garden, it was tantamount to taunting the other in public. Eventually the son-in-law's insatiable taste for self-aggrandizement prevailed. The villa's last (and final) owners were Prussian royalty (including the "Carlotta" of the villa's name), and the property was confiscated during World War I.

The villa's interior is worth a visit, particularly if you have a taste for Antonio Canova's most romantic sculptures. The best known is his *Cupid and Psyche,* which depicts the lovers locked in an odd but graceful and passionate embrace, with the young god above and behind, his wings extended, while Psyche, her lips willing, waits for a kiss that will never come. Check with Bellagio tourist office (☞ Visitor Information *in* Milan, Lombardy, and the Lakes A to Z, *below*) for the hours of launch tours. ☒ *Tremezzo,* ☎ *0344/40405.* 🖃 *Villa and gardens 8,000 lire.* ☉ *Apr.–Sept., daily 9–6; mid- to late Mar. and Oct.–early Nov., daily 9–11:30 and 2–4:30.*

Dining and Lodging

$$ ✕ **Silvio.** At the edge of town, this family-owned trattoria with a terrace on the lakeshore is for those who love fresh lake fish. Served cooked or marinated, with risotto or as a ravioli stuffing, the fish is caught by Silvio's family. This is local cooking at its best. There are also 17 modestly priced rooms. ☒ *Lòppia di Bellagio, Via Carcano 12,* ☎ *031/950322. MC, V. Closed Jan.*

$–$$ ✕ La Pergola. In Pescallo, about a km (½ mi) from Bellagio, on the other side of the peninsula, La Pergola is a popular lakeside restaurant. Of course, try to reserve a table on the lakeside terrace and order the daily special of freshly caught lake fish. You can also stay in one of the inn's 13 rooms, all of which have baths. ⊠ *Pescallo,* ☎ *031/950263. AE, DC, MC, V. Closed Tues. and Nov.–Feb.*

$$$$ ▥ Grand Hotel Villa Serbelloni. They used to say that those who drove ★ Rolls-Royces stayed at the Villa d'Este hotel in Cernobbio and those who drove Bentleys came here. Once designed to cradle dukes and duchesses in high luxury, this hotel is now a refined haven for the discreetly wealthy. Just down the road from the punta di Bellagio, the hotel is set within a pretty park. Inside, the atmosphere is one of 19th-century luxury that has not so much faded as mellowed: the rooms are immaculate and plush. The public rooms are a riot of gilt, marble, and thick, colorful carpets. Service is unobtrusive, and the staff is particularly good about arranging transportation across and around the lake. The best rooms—in which Churchill and Kennedy have stayed—face the lake and the Tremezzina, a group of towns on the shores opposite Bellagio. ⊠ *Lungolago Bellagio, Via Roma 1, 22021,* ☎ *031/950216,* ℻ *031/951529. 95 rooms. Restaurant, air-conditioning, pool, beauty salon, tennis court, health club. AE, DC, MC, V. Closed end Oct.–early Apr.*

$$ ▥ Du Lac. In the center of Bellagio, by the Lake Como landing dock, Du Lac is a comfortable medium-size hotel owned by an Anglo-Italian family who set a relaxed and congenial tone. Most rooms have views of the lake and mountains, and there is a rooftop terrace garden for drinks or just unwinding. ⊠ *Piazza Mazzini 32, 22021,* ☎ *031/950320,* ℻ *031/951624. 48 rooms. Restaurant, bar, air-conditioning. MC, V. Closed late Oct.–late Mar.*

$$ ▥ Excelsior-Splendide. Chances are you'll be lulled to sleep at night here by the lilting sounds of an orchestra directly under your window—this hotel is opposite Bellagio's enchanting quay, where live music beckons one and all on summer nights. It's in town center, handy to restaurants, and just a five-minute walk from the stunning gardens of Villa Melzi. ⊠ *Lungo Lalio Mazzoni, 22021,* ☎ *031/950225,* ℻ *031/951224. 47 rooms. Restaurant, pool. AE, DC, MC, V. Closed Oct. 21–May 1.*

Cernobbio

㉗ *28 km (17 mi) south of Bellagio, 34 km (21 mi) south of Tremezzo, 50 km (31 mi) east of Lake Maggiore.*

Cernobbio is the first town you come to as you head north from the town of Como. Although many of the villas of the southwest branch (the lake's most overbuilt district) remain private and closed to the public, they can be enjoyed from a boat.

If you're planning to say "budget be damned" in only one place, the **Villa d'Este** could be it. If you can't stay at this legendary lakeside resort hotel, call ahead and ask to see the grounds or enjoy a wonderful meal in the hotel's restaurant (☞ Lodging, *below*).

Originally built for Cardinal Tolomeo Gallio (who began life humbly as a fisherman) over the course of approximately 45 years (it was completed in 1615), the Villa d'Este has had a colorful and somewhat checkered history, swinging wildly between extremes of grandeur and dereliction. Its tenants have included the Jesuits, two generals, a ballerina, the disgraced and estranged wife of a future king of England (Caroline of Brunswick and George IV, respectively), a family of ordinary Italian nobles, and, finally, a czarina of Russia. Its life as a private summer residence ended in 1873, when it was turned into the fashionable hotel it has remained ever since.

Though the gardens are not as grand as they are reputed to have been during the villa's best days as a private residence and though they have suffered some modification in the course of the hotel's building of tennis courts and swimming pools, they still possess an aura of stately, monumental dignity. The alley of cypresses is a fine example of a proudly repeated Italian garden theme. The fanciful pavilions, temples, miniature forts, and mock ruins make for an afternoon's walk of quietly whimsical surprises.

Lodging

$$$$ 🏨 **Villa d'Este.** From Napoléon to the Duchess of Windsor, this grand
★ establishment has welcomed the rich and famous of several centuries. One of the most luxurious hotels in Italy, the 16th-century Villa d'Este provides just about every conceivable comfort, even a nightclub. A broad veranda sweeps out to the lakefront, where a large swimming pool juts out above the water. Across the lake blue, snowcapped mountains gradually blend into the deep green of the slopes that lead down to the shore. Inside, sparkling chandeliers cast their light on broad marble staircases, and the rooms are furnished in the manner of wealthy Italians. The restaurant may possibly be the sole imperfection in an otherwise perfect Villa d'Este. ⊠ *Via Regina 40,* ☎ *031/3481,* 𝔽𝔸𝕏 *031/348844. 158 rooms. 2 restaurants, bar, indoor and outdoor pools, sauna, 8 tennis courts, squash. AE, DC, MC, V. Closed Nov.–Mar.*

Como

28 *34 km (20 mi) south of Bellagio, 40 km (25 mi) south of Tremezzo, 56 km (33 mi) east of Lake Maggiore.*

Como, on the shores of Lake Como, is part elegant resort, part industrial town. Parks and bustling cafés line its lakefront promenade, all a stone's throw from the splendid 15th-century Renaissance–Gothic **Duomo.** Other fragments of old Como include **San Fedele** (once the town's cathedral), at the heart of the medieval quarter, and the **Porta Vittoria,** the late 12th-century gate. Brave the industrial quarter to see **Sant'Abbondio,** a beautiful 11th-century church. If you're traveling by car leave it outside town center, as traffic can be mayhem and streets are often closed.

OFF THE   **CASTIGLIONE OLANA –** Just 18 km (12 mi) west of Como is a Gothic
BEATEN PATH   Collegiata and baptistery, with superlative frescos by Giotto's pupil
                Masolino da Panicale.

Dining and Lodging

$$$ ✕ **Da Angela.** Reservations are perfunctory at this small and intimate restaurant serving Piedmontese specialties. The female owner Angela and her staff are attentive, and the waiters will help you select from a menu that includes various homemade pasta dishes and tasty *coniglio alle olive e alloro* (rabbit with olives and bay leaves). ⊠ *Via Ugo Foscolo 16,* ☎ *031/304656. Reservations essential. AE, DC, MC, V. Closed Mon. and Aug.*

$$$ ✕ **La Locanda dell'Isola.** Isola Comacina, Lake Como's only island, five minutes by regular boat from Sala Comacina, is rustic and restful, but at times crowded. The same could be said for the Locanda, but in each case the visit is worth it. Forget any notions of choosing from a menu, because here the deal is a set price for a set meal, with drinks included in the price. The good news is that the food is delicious, the service

friendly, and the setting (eating outdoors on a shady terrace) magnificent. You'll have to pace yourself through a mixed antipasto, salmon, trout, chicken, salad, cheese, coffee, and dessert. ⊠ *Isola Comacina, Sala Comacina,* ☎ *0344/55083. No credit cards. Closed Nov.–Feb. and Tues. Sept.–May.*

$$$ 🏨 **Barchetta Excelsior.** Despite its rather unprepossessing exterior, this
★ centrally located, modern hotel is comfortable, with many rooms looking directly across Piazza Cavour over to Lake Como. The rooms are airy and spacious, with those on the upper floors commanding the best views. Ask for a lake view because not all rooms have one. ⊠ *Piazza Cavour 1, 22021,* ☎ *031/3221,* FAX *031/302622. 85 rooms. Restaurant, bar, air-conditioning. AE, DC, MC, V.*

$$$ 🏨 **Palace.** This well-run, refurbished grand 19th-century hotel on the waterfront has fine lake views and the advantage of being set back in its own gardens, where there is an outside bar in summer. ⊠ *16 Lungo Lago Trieste, 22021,* ☎ *031/303303,* FAX *031/303170. 99 rooms. Restaurant, bar, air-conditioning. AE, DC, MC, V.*

$$ 🏨 **Tre Re.** This clean, spacious, and welcoming hotel is just a few steps west of the cathedral and convenient to the lake. Although the exterior gives away the age of this 16th-century former convent, the rooms inside are airy, comfortable, and modern. The moderately priced restaurant shares an ample terrace with the hotel; it's popular with locals for Sunday lunch. ⊠ *Via Boldoni 20, 22021,* ☎ *031/265374,* FAX *031/241349. 34 rooms, 30 with bath or shower. Restaurant, bar. MC, V. Closed Dec. 10–Jan. 15.*

Outdoor Activities and Sports

SEAPLANES

The school at the **Seaplane Club Como** (⊠ Viale Masia 44, ☎ 031/574495) gives lessons to would-be pilots.

SKIING

In the province of Como, fine snow skiing facilities abound: Valsassina, Val Lesina, Valvarrone, Valcavargna, and Val d'Intelvi (⊠ Provincial Tourist Board, Como, Via Borgovico 148, ☎ 031/230329 or 031/230111).

WATERSKIING

Myriad facilities for waterskiing and all water sports can be found on the lake (⊠ Provincial Tourist Board, Como, Via Borgovico 148, ☎ 031/230329 or 031/230111).

LAKE MAGGIORE AND LAKE ORTA

Magnificently scenic, Lake Maggiore has its less mountainous eastern shore in Lombardy, its higher western shore in Piedmont, and its northern tip in Switzerland. Never more than 5 km (3 mi) wide, the lake is almost 50 km (30 mi) long. The better-known resorts are on the Piedmontese shore, particularly Stresa, a well-established tourist town that partly provided the setting for Hemingway's *A Farewell to Arms.*

A mountainous strip of land separates Lake Maggiore from Lake Orta, its smaller neighbor to the west, in Piedmont. Orta attracts fewer visitors than the three larger lakes, and consequently a tour around this lake can be a pleasant alternative in the summer.

Stresa is the main town on Lake Maggiore, and Orta San Giulio is the largest center on Lake Orta; all points of interest on the two lakes are reached from these towns, respectively.

Orta San Giulio

㉙ *15 km (9 mi) west of Stresa, 76 km (47 mi) northwest of Milan.*

Orta San Giulio is at the end of a small peninsula that juts out into Lake Orta about a third of the way up its eastern shore. Intricate wrought-iron balustrades and balconies adorn the 18th-century buildings of this small and charming town. Small cafés and shops line the shady main square, which looks out across the lake to the small island of San Giulio. There are few more relaxing experiences than sipping a drink at one of these cafés and looking out at the languid waters being stirred by a mountain breeze, with sailboats busily making their way nowhere in particular.

OFF THE
BEATEN PATH
SACRO MONTE (SACRED MOUNTAIN) – Rising up behind Orta and looking down on the lake, this hill offers an enjoyable and interesting hike up from Orta. Pass the church of the Assumption, and just ahead you see a gateway marked SACRO MONTE. This leads to the path up the hill, a comfortable climb that takes about 40 minutes for the round-trip. As you approach the top, you pass no fewer than 20 17th-century chapels, all devoted to St. Francis of Assisi. They are decorated with frescoes and striking, life-size terra-cotta statue groups (a total of almost 400 figures) that illustrate incidents in the saint's life. You can climb the campanile of the last chapel for a panoramic view over the whole lake and the town, about 350 ft below.

The island of **San Giulio,** just offshore, is accessible by hiring a boatman. The lake is no more than 2 km (1¼ mi) wide, and most charge about 10,000 lire for up to four people to make the round-trip. The island takes its name from the 4th-century St. Julius, who—like St. Patrick in Ireland—is said to have banished snakes from the island. Julius is also said to have founded the **Basilica** in AD 390, although the present building shows more signs of its renovations in the 10th and 15th centuries. Inside, there is a black marble pulpit (12th century) with elaborate carvings, and downstairs you'll find the crypt containing relics of the saint. In the sacristy of the church is a large bone said to be from one of the beasts destroyed by the saint, but on closer examination it seems to be a whalebone.

It only takes a few minutes to walk around the parts of the island that are open to the public: much of the area is taken up by the grounds of private villas. The view back across the lake to Orta, with Sacro Monte behind it, is memorable, particularly in the late afternoon, when the light picks up the glint of the wrought-iron traceries.

Lodging

$$$ 🏨 **Hotel San Rocco.** Half of the rooms in this converted 17th-century convent in a lakeside garden on the edge of town have views of the lake, garden, and surrounding mountains. Many have balconies and are furnished in modern style. The restaurant features international cuisine and beautiful views of the lake. Among the specialties is *pesce persico* (perch). ⊠ *Via Gippini da Verona 11, 28016,* ☎ *0322/905632,* FAX *0322/905635. 74 rooms. Restaurant, bar, pool, health club. AE, DC, MC, V.*

En Route   Follow the shore drive from Orta San Giulio north to Omegna, at the head of Lake Orta. A couple of kilometers west of Omegna, in the village of Quarna Sotto, there's a musical instrument factory that's worth a stop. The shore drive continues around the rest of the lake, and at the southern end you can pick up S229, which will take you back to the A4 autostrada.

Stresa

 70 km (43 mi) west of Cernobbio, 16 km (10 mi) east of Orta San Giulio.

Stresa, which has capitalized on its central lakeside position and its good connections to the Borromean Islands in Lake Maggiore, has to some extent become a victim of its own success. The luxurious elegance that distinguished it in its heyday has grown somewhat faded; the grand hotels are still grand but their surrounding parks and gardens are now encroached by traffic. Even the undeniable loveliness of the lakeshore drive has been threatened by the roar of diesel trucks and BMW traffic. One way to escape is to head for the Borromean Islands just off Stresa (☞ *below*).

As you wander around the grounds of **Villa Pallavicino,** with their palms and semitropical shrubs, don't be surprised if you're followed by a peacock or even an ostrich: they're part of the zoological garden, and they are allowed to roam almost at will. From the top of the hill on which the villa stands, you can see the gentle hills of the Lombardy shore of Lake Maggiore and, nearer and to the left, the jewel-like Borromean Islands. As well as a bar and restaurant in the grounds, there are also picnicking spots. ⊠ *Off Corso Umberto I,* ☎ *0323/31533.* ▨ *10,000 lire.* ☉ *Mid-Mar.–Oct. 30, daily 9–6.*

Boats to the **Borromean Islands** leave every 15 minutes from Stresa. Although you can hire a boatman to take you, it's cheaper and just as convenient to use the regular service. Make sure to buy a ticket allowing you to visit all the islands—Bella, Dei Pescatori, and Madre.

The islands take their name from the Borromeo family, which has owned them since the 12th century. **Isola Bella** (Beautiful Island) is the most famous of the three, and the first that you'll visit. Its name is actually a shortened form of Isabella, wife of the 16th-century Count Carlo III Borromeo who built the palace and terraced gardens for her. Few wedding presents anywhere have been more romantic. Wander up the 10 terraces of the gardens, where peacocks roam among the scented shrubs, statues, and fountains. The view of the lake is splendid from the top terrace. Before Count Carlo began his project, the island was rocky and almost devoid of vegetation, and the soil for the garden had to be transported from the mainland. Visit the **palazzo** to see the rooms where famous guests—including Napoléon and Mussolini—stayed in 18th-century splendor. ☎ *0323/30556.* ▨ *Garden and palazzo 10,000 lire.* ☉ *Apr.–Oct., daily 9–noon and 1:30–5:30.*

Stop for a while at the tiny **Isola dei Pescatori** (Island of the Fishermen), which is less than 100 yards wide and only about ½ km (¼ mi) long. Of the three islands, this is the one that has remained closest to the way they all were before the Borromeos began their building projects. The island's little lanes, strung with fishing nets and dotted with shrines to the Madonna, are so picturesque they practically drip off the canvas. Little wonder that this tiny fishing village is crowded with postcard stands in high season.

Isola Madre (Mother Island) is the largest of the three and, like Isola Bella, has a large botanical garden. Even dedicated nongardeners should stop to appreciate the profusion of exotic trees and shrubs running down to the shore in every direction. Two special times to visit are April (for the camellias) and May (when azaleas and rhododendrons are in bloom). Also on the island is a 16th-century palazzo, where an antique puppet theater is on display, complete with string puppets, prompt books, and elaborate scenery designed by Alessandro Sanquirico, who was a scenographer at La Scala in Milan. ☜ *12,000 lire.* ☉ *Apr.–Oct., daily 8:30–noon and 2–5:30.*

For more information about the islands and how to get there, contact the local tourist office (☞ Visitor Information *in* Milan, Lombardy, and the Lakes A to Z, *below*) or ask at the landing stages. ⊠ *Landing stage in Piazza Matteotti, look for* NAVIGAZIONE LAGO MAGGIORE *signs.* ☉ *Mid-Mar.–Oct.*

Verbania Pallanza

㉛ *16 km (10 mi) north of Stresa.*

Verbania Pallanza lies across the Gulf of Pallanza from Stresa. It's known for the **Villa Taranto,** which has magnificent botanical gardens containing some 20,000 species. Created by an enthusiastic Scotsman, Captain Neil McEachern, these gardens rank among Europe's finest. ⊠ *Verbania Pallanza,* ☏ 𝖥𝖠𝖷 *0323/56667.* ☜ *8,000 lire.* ☉ *Apr.–Oct., daily 8:30–7:30.*

Dining and Lodging

$$$–$$$$
★
✕ **Ristorante del Sole.** Chef Carlo Brovelli presides over this lakeside inn with a cheerfulness that is infectious. The lake figures into the menu, in the form of carpaccio made of fine slices of trout and perch. The seasonal menu suggests various interpretations of artichokes in spring, eggplant in summer. Squab caramelized in honey might also top the menu. There are also nine sizeable apartments. ⊠ *Piazza Venezia 5, Ranco, near Angera,* ☏ *0331/976507,* 𝖥𝖠𝖷 *0331/976620. Reservations essential. AE, DC, MC, V. Closed Tues. and Jan.–mid-Feb. No dinner Mon. Oct.–May.*

$$
✕ **Monferrato.** Off Piazza Cadorna and close to the embarcadero, this hotel restaurant serves risotto *con filetti di persico* (with perch fillets) and typical Piedmontese meat dishes, such as beef braised in Barolo wine. ⊠ *Via Mazzini 14,* ☏ *0323/31386. AE, DC, MC, V. Closed Tues. and Nov.–late Feb.*

$$$$
🏨 **Grand Hotel des Iles Borromees.** A palatial Old World hotel, this princely establishment has catered to a demanding European clientele since 1863. And though it still has the spacious salons and lavish decor of the turn of the century, it has also been discreetly modernized; rooms have luxurious bathrooms, and there is a fitness center, as well as convention facilities. ⊠ *Lungolago Umberto I 67, 28049,* ☏ *0323/30431,* 𝖥𝖠𝖷 *0323/32405. 172 rooms. Restaurant, bar, air-conditioning, spa, pool, golf privileges, tennis courts, exercise room. AE, DC, MC, V.*

$–$$
🏨 **Primavera.** In a plain 1950s building in the heart of Stresa, Primavera has balconies embellished with flower boxes. It has the advantage of a location in a quiet pedestrian zone only three minutes from the lake and embarcadero. Rooms are compact and simply furnished. ⊠ *Via Cavour 39, 28049,* ☏ *0323/31286,* 𝖥𝖠𝖷 *0323/33458. 32 rooms. AE, MC, V. Closed Jan.–Feb., and mid-Nov.–mid-Dec.*

En Route
If you're going to Stresa from Lake Orta, take the twisting mountain road past Mottarone, the tallest peak between the lakes, to Gignese, where you'll be about 2,300 ft above sea level and can take in a last dramatic view of Maggiore. Follow the road up to Lake Orta, through the town of Armeno, shaded first by forests of evergreens, then oaks. In the late summer and early fall, you're likely to see whole families out in these woods, crouched down in their hunt for wild mushrooms, or—if they're particularly lucky—truffles.

MILAN, LOMBARDY, AND THE LAKES A TO Z

Arriving and Departing

By Bus

Italian bus service is best avoided on intercity routes, since it is neither faster, cheaper, nor more convenient than the railways. Most bus companies use Piazza Castello as a terminus, because Milan has no central bus terminal. For bus information, call **Autostradale** (☎ 166/845010). You can also try **Zani Viaggi** (☎ 02/867131).

By Car

Two major autostrada routes cross at Milan: the **A1,** which leads south to Bologna, Florence, and Rome, and the **A4,** which runs west–east from Turin to Venice. **A7** angles southwest down to Genoa from Milan. The city is ringed by a bypass road (the Tangenziale).

By Plane

Malpensa (⊠ About 50 km/31 mi northwest of Milan, ☎ 02/38011172) handles all intercontinental air traffic. **Linate** (⊠ Less than 10 km/6 mi east of Milan) handles international and domestic air traffic. For air-traffic information for both airports and information on connections with Milan, call ☎ 02/74852200. Air **Pullman** (coaches) run twice daily in the morning between Malpensa and Linate airports. The fare is 22,000 lire, and the trip takes about 75 minutes.

BETWEEN THE AIRPORT AND DOWNTOWN

By Bus. There is bus service from **Malpensa** to Milan's Central Station. Buses usually leave every half hour in the morning and every hour in the evening. The trip costs 13,000 lire and takes about one hour. Buy your ticket inside before embarking. Buses leave **Linate** every 20 minutes for Milan's Central Station. The trip takes about 20 minutes; the cost is 5,000 lire. You can also take ATM municipal Bus 73 to Piazza San Babila (every 15 minutes); the cost is 1,500 lire. Alternatively, there is a bus-service link between the airport and an airport terminal at **Lumpagnano** (information ☎ 02/38011172). The trip costs 10,000 lire. Lumpagnano is on the subway route to the city center.

By Car. From **Malpensa** take Route S336 east to the A8 autostrada southeast toward Milan. The drive takes about 40 minutes, depending on traffic and destination. From **Linate,** take what was once the Old Brescia Road west into the central downtown area.

By Taxi. A taxi stand is directly outside the arrivals building doors at **Malpensa.** Approximate fare is 130,000 lire. From **Linate,** the approximate fare is 30,000 lire. The duration of the journey is less than 20 minutes.

By Train

Although Milan claims a bewildering number of railway stations, only one is of concern, **Milano Centrale** (⊠ About 5 km/3 mi northwest of the Duomo and Galleria, ☎ 02/147888088 for information, 02/72524370 for APT office), unless you travel on local routes at peculiar hours—in which case service can begin or terminate in suburban stations (most notably **Milano Lambrate** for Bergamo, and **Stazione Nord** for Como). Premium international (EC) service and premium (IC) domestic service connect Milano Centrale with major European cities. Metro line 3 links Milano Centrale with Piazza de Duomo.

Getting Around

By Bicycle

As part of its campaign to ban cars from Milan's center, the city government has begun to set up a network of one-way bicycle rental stations. At first, rentals were free; now there is a small charge. Though the bicycles are clearly intended for residents who would otherwise use cars, current opinion is that tourists may use them, too (although individual proprietors of stands may arbitrarily decide to disagree, especially if you are unable to explain your rights in Italian). Look for yellow stands filled with yellow bicycles.

By Boat

There is frequent daily ferry and hydrofoil service between towns on the lakes, and a range of round-trip excursions, with a dining service (optional) aboard. For all lakes call **Navigazione Laghi** (⊠ Via Ariosto 21, Milan, ☎ 02/4812086). Call locally: **Navigazione Lago di Garda** (⊠ Lake Garda, ☎ 030/9141321). **Navigazione Lago di Como** (⊠ Lake Como, ☎ 031/273324). **Navigazione Lago Maggiore** (⊠ Lake Maggiore, ☎ 0322/46651).

Lake tours can often be arranged by private launches at lakeside hotels.

By Bus

Trains are generally better than buses for getting around the cities of the plain. There is regular bus service between the small towns on the lakes, and it tends to be a cheaper way of getting around than ferry or hydrofoil service. The bus service around Lake Garda serves mostly towns on the western coast.

IN MILAN

Milan has an excellent system of public transport (for information, call ATM, ☎ 02/875495) consisting of trolley cars, buses, and a subway system, the **Metropolitana,** which runs on three lines. Tickets for each must be purchased before you board and must be canceled by machines at underground station entrances and mounted on poles inside trolleys and buses. Tickets cost 1,500 lire and can be purchased from news vendors, tobacconists, and machines at larger stops. Buy several at once—they remain valid until canceled. One ticket is valid for 75 minutes on all surface lines, or for one subway trip. A 24-hour ticket valid on all public transport lines costs 5,000 lire, and one ticket valid for 48 hours costs 9,000 lire; they are sold at **Duomo Metro** and **Stazione Centrale Metro** stations.

By Car

The A4 autostrada is the main east–west highway for this region. The A22 is a major north–south highway running just east of Lake Garda. Although these major highways will allow you to make good time between the cities of the plain, you'll have to follow secondary roads—often of great beauty—around the lakes. S572 goes along the southern and western shores of Lake Garda, S45b is along the northernmost section of the western shore, and S249 along the eastern shore. Around Lake Como, follow S340 along the western shore, S36 on the eastern coast, and S583 on the lower arms. S33 and S34 trace the western shore of Lake Maggiore.

IN MILAN

Serious pollution is responsible for a rigorously enforced effort to control excessive traffic in and out of the city's center. Cars lacking a special resident's permit will be stopped and ticketed. Parking in city center is possible 7AM–8PM for a fee. For **taxi service,** call ☎ 02/6767, 02/8585, or 02/8388. For **limousine service,** call Autonoleggio Pini, (☎

02/29400555, FAX 02/204748). If age or infirmity entitle you to special dispensation, ask your rental agency or hotel concierge about car permits for special cases.

By Taxi

Taxi fares in Milan seem expensive compared with those in American cities, but drivers are honest (to an extreme, compared with those in some cities). A short downtown hop averages 15,000 lire. Taxis wait at stands or can be called (☎ 02/6767, 02/8585, or 02/8388). It is not unknown to travel by taxi throughout the region, but the prices are prohibitive, making train or bus travel the better option.

By Train

From Milan, there is frequent direct service to Cremona, Bergamo, Pavia, Brescia, Mantua, Desenzano del Garda–Sirmione, and Como.

Contacts and Resources

Car Rental

Milan: **Avis** (⊠ Via Carlo Da'Ada 19, ☎ 02/58101748; ⊠ Linate Airport, ☎ 02/717214). **Hertz** (⊠ Via Novegro 49, ☎ 02/70200258; ⊠ Linate Airport, ☎ 02/70200256). **Europcar** (⊠ Via Galbani 12, ☎ 02/66710491; ⊠ Linate Airport, ☎ 02/76110277).

Consulates

Most nations maintain consulates in Milan. **Australia** (⊠ Via Borgogna 2, ☎ 02/76013330). **Canada** (⊠ Via Pisani 19, ☎ 02/6697451). **United Kingdom** (⊠ Via San Paolo 7, ☎ 02/723001) **United States** (⊠ Via Principe Amedeo 2, ☎ 02/290351).

Emergencies

There is now a nationwide network for all emergency calls. **Carabinieri** (☎ 112). English-speaking officers are available 24 hours a day to deal with every kind of emergency. **Police, Ambulance** (☎ 113). You can dial this number wherever you are and it will connect you to the nearest local police emergency service. For first aid, ask for *"pronto soccorso,"* and be prepared to give your address.

English-Language Bookstores

Milan: **American Bookshop** (⊠ Largo Cairoli at Via Camperio, ☎ 02/72020030). **English Bookshop** (⊠ Via Mascheroni 12, ☎ 02/4694468). **Feltrinelli Bookstore** (⊠ Via Manzoni 12, ☎ 02/76000386).

Late-Night Pharmacies

There are a number of pharmacies open 24 hours a day, including one on the upper level of **Milan Central Station** (☎ 02/6690735). The **Cooperativa Farmaceutica** (⊠ Piazza Duomo, ☎ 02/86460408) is also open 24 hours. Others take turns staying open late and on weekends; for the location of the nearest one, check the roster outside any chemist, or the list published in the *Corriere della Sera*.

Travel Agencies

Milan: **Compagnia Italiana Turismo** (⊠ CIT, Galleria Vittorio Emanuele, ☎ 02/863701). **American Express Travel Agency** (⊠ Via Brera 3, ☎ 02/809645). **Chiariva** (⊠ Largo Domodossola 1, ☎ 02/4818366).

Visitor Information

Ufficio Turistico: **Bellagio** (⊠ Piazza della Chiesa 14, ☎ 031/950204). **Bergamo** (⊠ Vicolo Aquila Nera at Piazza Vecchia, Upper Bergamo, ☎ 035/232730; ⊠ Viale Papa Giovanni 106, Lower Bergamo, ☎ 035/242226). **Brescia** (⊠ Corso Zanardelli 34, ☎ 030/43418). **Como** (⊠ Piazza Cavour 16, ☎ 031/290318; ⊠ Train station, ☎ 031/267214;

⊠ Provincial Tourist Board, Via Borgovico 148, ☎ 031/230111). **Cremona** (⊠ Piazza del Comune 8, ☎ 0372/23233). **Desenzano del Garda** (⊠ Piazza Mattetotti 27, ☎ 030/9141510). **Malcesine** (⊠ Via Capitanato del Porto 6, ☎ 045/7400055). **Mantua** (⊠ Piazza A. Mantegna 6, ☎ 0376/328253). **Milan** (⊠ Via Marconi 1, ☎ 02/72524301; ⊠ Stazione Centrale, ☎ 02/6690432; ⊠ Municipal Information Office, Galleria Vittorio Emanuele, Piazza della Scala, ☎ 02/62083101 or 02/878363). **Pavia** (⊠ Via Fabio Filzi 2, ☎ 0382/22156). **Riva del Garda** (⊠ Giardini di Porta Orientale 8, ☎ 0464/554444). **Sabbioneta** (⊠ Via Vespasiano Gonzaga 31, ☎ 0375/52039). **Sirmione** (⊠ Viale Marconi 2, ☎ 030/916245 or 030/916114). **Stresa** (⊠ Via Principe Tomaso 70, ☎ 0323/30150).

10 The Dolomites

Bolzano, Trento, and Cortina d'Ampezzo

Little wonder Leonardo da Vinci depicted the Dolomites in the background of his Mona Lisa. Nature's skyscrapers, they are among the most extraordinary mountain ranges in Italy. Scenery-hungry tourists explore their meadows, crystal clear lakes, and stupefying cliffs. In summer, they marvel at the dramatic rose-color peaks that take on a purple hue near sunset, in winter, the lure is the charming town of Cortina d'Ampezzo—where skiing is almost as important as being seen.

Updated by
Giuliano
Davenport

UNLIKE OTHER FAMOUS ALPINE RANGES, this vast mountainous domain in northeast Italy has remained relatively undeveloped. The virginal landscape is the ultimate playground for the family or traveler on a quest for an original adventure. Ski fanatics travel across the world to dare some of the steep slopes that test Olympic champions. Mountaineers risk the climb up sheer rock faces. For calmer souls the seduction of a landscape painted from a palette of extreme colors prevails. The lowland valleys are laced with rivers spanned by awkward bridges and are dotted with secluded villages, picture-book castles, and unexpected historic sites.

The Dolomites, sprawling over the Trentino–Alto Adige region and into parts of Lombardy by the Swiss border and the Veneto along the Austrian border, became known to Americans as a winter sports center after Cortina d'Ampezzo catapulted to fame by hosting the Winter Olympics of 1956. Today, scores of funiculars, chairlifts, and ski lifts provide access to 1,200 km (750 mi) of ski runs, as well as ski jumps and bobsled runs.

Then there are the "untouchable" zones—inaccessible by means of chairlift or ski lift. These are the famous plateaus topping some of the highest mountains, from which you can see Italy on one side and Austria or Switzerland on the other. To enjoy such a rare spectacle, you must spend arduous hours climbing beyond where the lifts leave you, and when you reach the top, you will probably see cows casually grazing on the grass. It can make you dizzy just thinking of how they got there, but contradictions are common in the Dolomites.

This expansive land of rocks and valleys has long attracted Italians and other Europeans seeking a diverse natural environment. What they—and you—find is a profusion of brilliant colors, architectural styles, and languages. A meander through the valleys becomes a botanical escapade, with rare plant species abounding; high above you on the cliffs are castles, protected by their size and position. The serious climber will get a closer view of these remote fortresses. There, on the higher levels, are some rarely seen animals: bears, deer, mountain goats, and birds of prey. It's perhaps not surprising that Reinhold Messer, the first man to climb Everest without oxygen, lives in the Dolomites.

Straddling the Brenner Pass—the main access point to Italy from central Europe—the Dolomites play host to a mixture of cultures and languages. The people of the Alto Adige are predominantly German speaking, and their crafts and food have an Austrian accent (until World War I, the area was Austria's South Tyrol). The Trentino, on the other hand, is Italian speaking. Reflecting this diversity, the area, since 1948, has enjoyed special status as the Autonomous Region of Trentino–Alto Adige, made up of the independent provinces of Trento and Bolzano. But there is still another language to be heard in the area: Ladin, an offshoot of Latin still spoken by a small Ladin community, can credit centuries of isolation in mountain strongholds for its survival.

Signs throughout much of the Dolomites are bilingual. Place-names are given in Italian with German equivalents, where useful, in parentheses below.

Pleasures and Pastimes

Cross-Country Skiing

The Dolomites are an ideal place to learn or improve your *sci di fondo* (cross-country skiing). The major Alpine resorts, and even many out-of-the-way villages, have prepared trails (usually loops marked off by kilometers) appropriate for differing degrees of ability. Two of the best are at Ortisei and Dobbiaco. You can have a lot of fun blazing new trails across virgin snowfields; you can usually get permission by asking at the nearest farmhouse or by inquiring at local tourist offices.

Dining

Encompassing the Germanic Alto Adige province and the Italian Trentino province, the Dolomites region combines Italian cuisine with local Tyrolean specialties, which are much like the dishes of Austria and central Europe. Local delicatessens teem with regional cheeses, pickles, salami, and smoked meats, while local bakeries present a wide selection of crusty dark rolls, caraway rye bread, and the like—perfect for picnics. Local dishes vary from one isolated mountain valley to the next. Don't miss speck, the local smoked ham. Other specialties include *canederli,* or *knoedel,* a type of dumpling with many variations, served either in broth or with a sauce; hot sauerkraut; ravioli made from rye flour, stuffed with spinach, and fried; and apple or pear strudel. And—as befits a wine-producing region—the local vintages (and fruit brandies) are delicious. In the fall in the South Tyrol, when autumn colors beautify the mountains, it's a tradition to make a tour of the cozy country wine taverns to drink the new wine and eat hot roast chestnuts.

CATEGORY	COST*
$$$$	over 85,000 lire
$$$	60,000 lire–85,000 lire
$$	30,000 lire–60,000 lire
$	under 30,000 lire

Prices are per person, including house wine, service, and tax.

Downhill Skiing

The Dolomites command some of the best downhill skiing environments and facilities in Europe, with some centers equipped for summer skiing. Generally the ski season runs from late November to April, by which time some people prefer to ski in shirtsleeves. The most comprehensive centers are Cortina d'Ampezzo, in the heart of the Dolomites to the east of Bolzano, and Madonna di Campiglio, west of Trento. These resorts are unabashedly upscale, but you get the extras you expect from world-class centers: miles of interconnecting runs linked by cable cars and lifts, plus skating rinks, heated indoor pools, and lively après-ski. Less-expensive adventures can be had at Badia Valley, south from Brunico, and Ortesei, a modern, popular resort.

Folk Festivals

Essentially rural in character, the Dolomites offer a rich selection of folk festivals, harvest fairs, and religious celebrations. Chief among these is Trento's weeklong festival of San Vigilio (the last week of June), when marching bands and costumed choirs perform in the streets and squares of the heart of the city. The other major towns have similar festivals, but equally enjoyable are the more informal and low-key celebrations in the villages of the many valleys, sometimes amounting to nothing more than excuses for hardworking mountain farmers to get together for some local wine and song.

Hiking and Walking

The Dolomites have a well-maintained network of trails for hiking and rock climbing, with *rifugi* (huts) on the most difficult ascents. It is important to follow safety procedures and have all the latest information on trails and conditions.

Lodging

Accommodations in the Dolomites range from restored castles to spick-and-span chalet guest houses, from stately 19th-century hotels to chic modern ski resorts. Even a small village may have scores of lodging places, many of them very inexpensive. Hotel information offices at train stations and tourist offices can help you avoid the language problem if you arrive without reservations: Bolzano train station has a 24-hour hotel service, and tourist offices will give you a list of all the hotels in the area, arranged by location and price. We've tried to mention here a few hotels in towns that make good bases for travel, as well as some notable hotels found along the road. Remember that many hotels in ski resorts cater primarily to longer stays at full or half board: it's wiser to book ski vacations as a package in advance. And a word of warning: although spring and fall are wonderful times to travel in the region, many mountain hotels are closed for a month or two after Easter and for about six weeks before Christmas.

CATEGORY	COST*
$$$$	over 300,000 lire
$$$	200,000 lire–300,000 lire
$$	80,000 lire–200,000 lire
$	under 80,000 lire

Prices are for a standard double room for two, including tax and service.

Shopping

Shopping is an event in the Dolomites, where larger towns, such as Bolzano, Bressanone, and Brunico, have shops clustered in arcaded shopping streets designed to keep shoppers dry on rainy or snowy days. The ethnic mixture, with its strong Tyrolean influence, makes for local products and crafts that are quite different from those elsewhere in Italy. Tyrolean clothing—loden goods, lederhosen, dirndls, and linen suits with horn buttons—is a good buy and costs less than in neighboring Austria. Local crafts, such as embroidered goods, wood carvings, figures for nativity scenes, pottery, and handcrafted copper and iron objects, make good gifts.

Exploring the Dolomites

The best—and only—way to get around in this mountainous region is by following the course of the valleys that find their way to the heart of the massifs that compose the Dolomites. Two of the most important valleys are those formed by the Isarco and Adige rivers. The Isarco River begins at the Brenner Pass and runs due south to Bolzano where it joins the Adige River. The Adige itself originates near the Swiss border and also runs south through Bolzano. Italy's main road and rail connections to north central Europe follow the same rivers northward en route to the Brenner Pass.

Numbers in the text correspond to numbers in the margin and on the Dolomites and Bolzano maps.

Great Itineraries

The area of the Dolomites is a vast expanse of valleys, mountain roads and hillside towns. Unfortunately most roads, although of excellent quality, can be hazardous, especially during the winter months. Instead of rushing to get all the sights into your travels, try to be discerning and stick to the areas you would most like to see. A further note of caution involves the closure of some roads during the winter season, which can begin as early as November and continue until May, in particular the high mountain passes such as Passo di Gavia and Passo dello Stelvio in the east.

IF YOU HAVE 3 DAYS
Start in **Trento** ① and head south to **Rovereto** ② and **Riva** on the tip of Lake Garda, then on to the quaint towns of **Pinzolo** ③ and **Madonna di Campiglio** ④ for a bird's-eye view of the Dolomites, ending your day via Dimaro in ⊞ **Bolzano** ⑨–⑯. The next day head for the lovely town of **Bressanone** ⑲ and on via **Brunico** ⑳ to the exclusive resort of ⊞ **Cortina d'Ampezzo** ㉒. The last day take the Great Dolomites road passing **Lake Carezza** ㉗ and return to Trento.

IF YOU HAVE 5 DAYS
Follow the three-day itinerary above as far as Dimaro, but instead of going directly to Bolzano, swing east and head for the dizzily high Passo di Gavia and down then to the small town of ⊞ **Bormio** ⑤. The next day proceed to the breathtaking **Passo dello Stelvio** ⑥ and on down to **Naturno** ⑦ before stopping in one of the pearls of the Alto Adige region, **Merano** ⑧. Continue on to ⊞ **Bolzano** ⑨–⑯, the principal city in this region. The next day head for **Cornedo** ⑰, **Chiusa** ⑱, and **Bressanone** ⑲. Move on to Brunico and ⊞ **Cortina d'Ampezzo** ㉒. The next day head to **Canazei** ㉓ via the breathtaking Passo di Sella and on down into **Ortisei** ㉔ in the heart of the Val Gardena. Return to Trento via **Fie** ㉕ and **Caldaro** ㉖.

IF YOU HAVE 8 DAYS
Follow the five-day itinerary as far as Brunico. The following day stroll through **Dobbiaco** ㉑ before moving on to ⊞ **Cortina d'Ampezzo** ㉒. From here follow the Great Dolomites Road through the Passo di Falzarego and slightly north through the Passo di Sella and into the Val Gardena and ⊞ **Ortisei** ㉔. On the last day, drive to **Fie** ㉕ and south on the A22. Just south of Cornedo, turn left onto the S241 to get to **Lake Carezza** ㉗. Continue along the road until you reach Vigo di Fassa, veering south onto the S48, passing through the small towns of Predazzo, Cavalese, and Ora, until you rejoin the A22 and continue south back to Trento.

When to Tour the Dolomites

If you are here for the skiing, most resorts open from mid-December to April. With the exception of the main bargain period known to Italians as *settimane bianche* (white weeks), usually running from January to February, the slopes are relatively crowd free. Booking well in advance of your ski holiday is highly recommended, as lack of snow in the early part of the season can sometimes cause overcrowding later on. During the rest of the year accommodations are easier to find, but booking is still recommended. Note that nearly all hotels and guest houses outside the main urban centers close from early November to mid- or late December.

WESTERN TRENTINO

The areas east and west of Trento are collectively known as the Trentino. The west side includes the peaks of the Brenta Massif, the Stelvio Pass, and the Venosta Valley. Some of the passes in this region close during the winter months so if you are traveling during this period you will not be able to follow the entire itinerary. Towns are given in order as you come upon them by road.

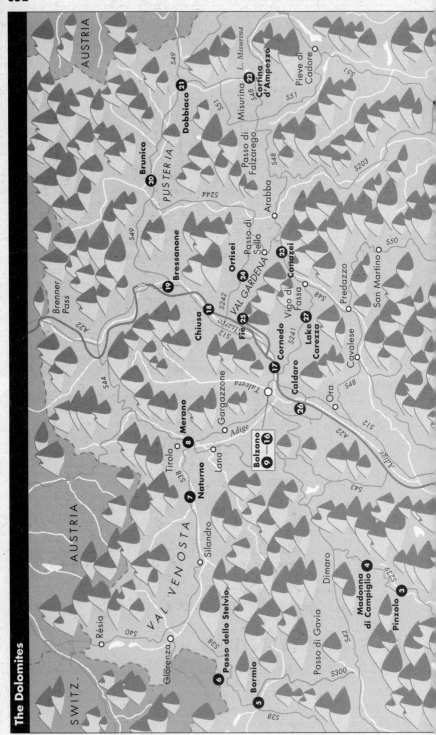

The Dolomites

AUSTRIA

SWITZ.

Brenner
Pass

AUSTRIA

PUSTERIA

VAL VENOSTA

VAL GARDENA

Résia

Glorenza

Silandro

Tirolo

Merano **8**

Naturno **7**

Lana

Gargazzone

Adige

Passo dello Stelvio

Bormio **6**

5

Bolzano
9 — 16

Talvera

Caldaro

Cornedo **17**

26

Ora

Fiè **25**

Chiusa **18**

Bressanone

Ortisei

Canazei **23**

24

Vigo di
Fassa

Lake
Carezza **27**

Predazzo

Cavalese

San Martino

19

Brunico **20**

Dobbiaco **21**

Passo di
Falzarego

Arabba

Passo di
Sella

L. Misurina

Misurina **22**

Cortina
d'Ampezzo

Pieve di
Cadore

Dimaro

Madonna
di Campiglio **4**

Pinzolo **3**

Passo di Gavia

Isarco

Brenner
Pass

S38

S40

S44

S38

S38

S42

S300

S239

S43

S42

S12

S48

S42

S241

S242

S12

S12

A22

A22

Adige

S44

S49

S49

S244

S51

S51

S48

S48

S48

S50

S203

S51

Trento

❶ *51 km (32 mi) south of Bolzano, 24 km (15 mi) north of Rovereto.*

Capital of the autonomous Trentino province, Trento has somehow escaped the ravages of commercialization and retains its architectural charm, artistic attractions, and historic importance.

It was here, from 1545 to 1563, that the structure of the Catholic Church was redefined, at the famous Council of Trent. This was the starting point of the Counter-Reformation, which brought half of Europe back to Catholicism. Until 1803, Trento itself was ruled by prince-bishops. You'll see the word *consiglio* (council) everywhere in Trento—in hotel, restaurant, and street names, and even on wine labels.

In Piazza del Duomo is a Baroque fountain of Neptune; the massive, low, Romanesque **Duomo** forms the southern edge of the square. Before entering the cathedral, pause to savor the view of the mountaintops ranged majestically around the city in every direction when skies are clear.

Step inside to see the unusual arcaded stone stairways on either side of the austere nave. Ahead of you is the *baldacchino* (altar canopy), a clear copy of Bernini's masterpiece in St. Peter's in Rome. In a small chapel to the right is a mournful 15th-century Crucifixion, with Mary and the Apostle John. This crucifix was a focal point of the Council of Trent: each decree agreed on during the two decades of deliberations was solemnly read out in front of it. Outside, walk around to the back of the cathedral to see an exquisite display of 14th-century stonemasons' art, from the small porch to the intriguing knotted columns on the graceful apse. Within the Duomo grounds is an **archaeological area,** displaying ancient ruins including a gate dating from the 9th century. ✉ *Piazza del Duomo.* 🎟 *Archaeological area 2,000 lire.* ⊙ *Weekdays 10–noon and 2–6, Sat. 10–noon.*

The crenelated **Palazzo Pretorio,** which seems to be a wing of the cathedral, was built in the 13th century as the prudently fortified residence of the prince-bishops. Endowed with considerable power and autonomy, these clerics enjoyed a unique position in the medieval hierarchy. The Palazzo Pretorio now houses the **Museo Diocesano Tridentino,** where you can see paintings showing the seating plan of the prelates during the Council of Trent; early 16th-century tapestries by Pieter van Aelst, the Belgian artist who carried out Raphael's designs for the Vatican tapestries; carved wood altars and statues; and an 11th-century sacramentary, or book of services. These and other precious objects all come from the cathedral's treasury. ✉ *Piazza Duomo 18,* ☎ *0461/234419.* 🎟 *6,000 lire includes Duomo archaeological area.* ⊙ *Mid-Feb.–mid-Nov., Mon.–Sat. 9:30–12:30 and 2:30–6.*

On the northwest side of the Piazza del Duomo is the Renaissance church of **Santa Maria Maggiore,** where many sessions of the Council of Trent were held. ✉ *Via Cavour.* ⊙ *Closed Sat.*

Locals refer to **Via Belenzani** as Trento's outdoor gallery because of the frescoed facades of the hallmark Renaissance palazzi. It's an easy 50-yard walk up the lane behind the church of Santa Maria Maggiore. The climb up **Via Manci** is pleasant, past 200 yards of souvenir shops and glassware outlets.

Castello del Buonconsiglio (Castle of Good Counsel), at the end of Via Manci, was once the stronghold of the prince-bishops; its position and size made it easier to defend than the Palazzo Pretorio. As you stand facing it, you can see the evolution of architectural styles, starting with the medieval fortifications of the Castelvecchio section on the far left, down to the more decorative Renaissance Magno Palazzo, built three centuries later in 1530. The Castello now houses the **Museo Provinciale d'Arte** (Provincial Art Museum), where exhibits of art and archaeology are displayed in medieval halls or under Renaissance coffered ceilings. The 13th-century **Torre dell'Aquila** (Eagle's Tower) holds the highlight of the museum, a fresco cycle of the months of the year. It is full of charming and informatively detailed scenes of 15th-century life in both court and countryside. ⊠ *Via B. Clesio 5,* ☎ *0461/233770.* ▥ *10,000 lire July–Oct., 5,000 lire Nov.–June.* ☉ *Apr.–Sept., Tues.–Sun. 9–noon and 2–5:30; Oct.–Mar., Tues.–Sun. 9–noon and 2–5. Admission and hrs vary when exhibitions are held.*

The **Torre Verde,** or Green Tower (⊠ Piazza Raffaello Sanzio), is part of Trento's 13th-century fortifications standing alongside other fragments of the city walls. **Torre Vanga** (⊠ Via Torre Vanga) is another 13th-century fortification, this time guarding the medieval bridge across the Adige, Ponte San Lorenzo.

OFF THE
BEATEN PATH

BELVEDERE DI SARDAGNA – Take the cable car from the station at the Ponte San Lorenzo bridge to this scenic spot, a vantage point 1,200 ft above Trento.

Dining and Lodging

$$$ ✕ **Chiesa.** Near the castle in a building that dates from about 1400,
★ this restaurant employs antiques of the decorative and recipe variety. One centuries-old recipe is the *taglieri di Bernardo Cles,* coin-shape pasta in a sauce of veal and lettuce—but no tomatoes: when the recipe was devised, tomatoes were not yet eaten in Italy. Other specialties include risotto *alle mele* with rice, vegetables, and barley, and the *tonco de Pontesel*—a stew of mixed meat served with polenta, made according to a 15th-century recipe. ⊠ *Via San Marco 64,* ☎ *0461/238766. Jacket and tie. DC, MC, V. Closed Sun. and Aug. 15–31. No dinner Wed.*

$$–$$$ ✕ **Le Due Spade.** Near the Duomo, small and cozy, with wood paneling and a beautiful antique stove providing warmth on chilly days, this typical Tyrolean tavern has plenty of atmosphere. Given its popularity with locals, reservations are a must. The cuisine is local, too, and you can sample traditional *gnocchetti di* ricotta (ricotta cheese dumplings) and polenta *con funghi* (with mushroom sauce). ⊠ *Via Don Rizzi 11,* ☎ *0461/234343. Reservations essential. AE, DC, MC, V. Closed Sun. No lunch Mon.*

$$$ ▦ **Accademia.** This friendly character-filled hotel occupies an ancient house in the historic center of Trento, close to Piazza del Duomo. The public rooms retain the ancient vaulting, but the bedrooms are modern and comfortably equipped. There's a good but expensive restaurant and a courtyard garden. ⊠ *Vicolo Colico 4/6, 38100,* ☎ *0461/233600,* 𝖥𝖠𝖷 *0461/230174. 43 rooms. Restaurant, bar. AE, DC, MC, V.*

$$$ ▦ **Grand Hotel Trento.** The spot on Piazza Dante and the sleek, dynamic façade make this hotel an anomaly amid ancient palaces. It is modern with impeccable appointments, from the woodwork in the lobby and lounges to the Clesio restaurant's lush drapery. Rooms are ample and have thick carpets in blues and creams with matching decor. During warmer months people avail of the cocktail terrace for a relaxing *aperitivo.* ⊠ *Via Alfieri 1/3 38100,* ☎ *0461/271000,* 𝖥𝖠𝖷 *0461/271001. 136 rooms. Restaurant, bar, health club, business center, parking (fee). AE, DC, MC, V.*

$$ ⊡ **Aquila d'Oro.** This small hotel offers comfort, efficiency, and a prime location in the historic town center. Most rooms have modern furniture in somber colors. The hotel serves breakfast, and the owner is more then willing to pitch in names of places for lunch and dinner. ⊠ *Via Belenzani 76, 38100,* FAX *0461/986282. 20 rooms. Breakfast room, bar. AE, DC, MC, V.*

Nightlife and the Arts

FESTIVALS

From late June to late September a regional **Superfestival** spotlights historic castles as venues for performances and evocations of fact and legend. Trains taking passengers on excursions to the castles are part of it, as are music, costumes, and banquets. The **Festivale di Musica Sacra** (Sacred Music Festival)—a monthlong series of concerts held in the churches of Trento and the Trentino—is held in May and June; for information call 0462/231044.

A summer bonus is the weeklong **San Vigilio Fair,** culminating on June 26, when townspeople don medieval clothing in honor of their patron saint. For more than 60 years the May wine festival **Mostra dei Vini** has attracted every Bacchus, from farmers of surrounding hillside towns to sommeliers from all over Italy. The weeklong festival includes tastings, sommelier tours, and prizes; for information call ☎ 0461/235858.

Shopping

ANTIQUES

Antichità Gasperetti (⊠ Via Torre Verde 52) mainly deals in furniture and paintings. **Antichità** (⊠ Piazza Santa Maria Maggiore 27) sells more specialized collectors' objects such as coins and stamps.

MARKETS

Piazza Lodron hosts a small morning market in the center of town. **Piazza d'Arogno** has a flea market the third Sunday of every month; there is also a crafts market every Friday and Saturday, but the big shopping day is Thursday, when the weekly market spreads out around this piazza.

WOODEN CRAFTS AND CERAMICS

Il Pozzo (⊠ Piazza Pasi 14/L) sells excellent handcrafted wooden objects. **Il Laboratorio** (⊠ Via Roma 12) specializes in terra-cotta pieces molded by local artists.

Rovereto

❷ *24 km (15 mi) south of Trento and 75 km (47 mi) south of Bolzano.*

A 15th-century castle looks down on the medieval town of Rovereto, on the main north–south valley of the Adige. But this district harbors more recent memories of warfare. Some of the fiercest fighting of World War I took place in the wooded hills around Rovereto, with Italian and Austrian troops bogged down in prolonged and costly conflict. Every night you're reminded of the thousands who fell: at nightfall the bells of the **Campana dei Caduti** (Bell of the Fallen) toll to commemorate war victims throughout the world.

En Route Traveling south from Rovereto, head west on S240, passing the lovely lakeside town of Riva del Garda, and then north on S45bis to Comano, a small but locally renowned spa. The road continues to Tione, a small farming community. From here head north on S239 to reach Pinzolo.

Pinzolo

❸ *75 km (47 mi) northwest of Rovereto, 14 km (9 mi) south of Madonna di Campiglio.*

In this quaint mountain village you can see a remarkable 16th-century fresco on the side of a small church. Follow the signs for the church of **San Vigilio,** which you'll come to after a short walk through the pines. On an exterior wall, a vivid fresco painted in 1539 by the artist Simone Baschenis describes the Dance of Death, with 40 ghoulish figures offering a stern rebuke to potential sinners. Unfortunately, the church is usually closed to the public.

Madonna di Campiglio

★ **❹** *14 km (9 mi) north of Pinzolo, 92 km (57 mi) southeast of Bormio, 88 km (55 mi) southwest of Bolzano.*

The chichi winter resort Madonna di Campiglio grooms more than 130 km (80 mi) of ski runs and operates some 39 lifts. The resort itself is at a 5,000-ft altitude, and some of the ski runs, summer hiking paths, and mountain biking routes venture onto the surrounding peaks, including Pietra Grande, more than 9,700 ft up. An excursion to the Spinale Peak on the year-round chairlift affords magnificent views of the Brenta Dolomites.

Lodging

$$$$ ⊞ **Golf.** You'll have to make your way up to Campo Carlo Magno, ★ the famous pass just north of town, to reach this grand hotel, the former summer residence of Hapsburg Emperor Franz Joseph. A modern wing has been added to the more-than-a-century-old structure, but Old World charm remains: rooms 114 and 214 are still lavished in the old imperial style. Replete with verandas, Persian rugs, and bay windows, it's practically on the fairway of a golf course that draws a tony summer crowd. A shuttle bus makes runs into town. ⊠ *Campo Carlo Magno, 38084,* ☎ *0465/441003,* ℻ *0465/440294. 120 rooms, 4 suites. Restaurant, bar, golf course. AE, DC, MC, V. Closed mid-Apr.–June, mid-Sept.–Nov.*

$$$$ ⊞ **Savoia Palace.** One of the more traditional hotels at the resort, this hotel is full of mountain-style furnishings with lots of carved wood and an intimate atmosphere. Two fireplaces blaze away in the bar, where guests recall the day's exploits on the ski slopes. The elegant restaurant serves a mixture of local specialties and hearty dishes drawing on Italian and Austrian influences. Guests stay on full- or half-board terms only. ⊠ *Via Dolomiti di Brenta, 38084,* ☎ *0465/441004,* ℻ *0465/440549. 55 rooms. Restaurant, bar. AE, DC. Closed mid-Apr.– June, mid-Sept.–Nov.*

$$$ ⊞ **Grifone.** A comfortable hotel that catches the sun, the Grifone has distinctive wood paneling on the outside, flower-decorated balconies, and rooms with views of the forested slopes. The restaurant serves home cooking as well as international dishes. ⊠ *Via Vallesinella 7, 38084,* ☎ *0465/442002,* ℻ *0465/440540. 40 rooms. Restaurant, bar. AE, MC, V. Closed mid-Apr.–June, Sept.–Nov.*

Nightlife and the Arts

In winter the town becomes a lively hub of activity with impromptu fairs and exhibitions. All nightclubs and discos here are part of the many chic hotel complexes.

Outdoor Activities and Sports

GOLF

Campo Carlo Magno (☎ 0465/41003) is also the name for a nine-hole course set in the mountains near Madonna di Campiglio, open from July through mid-September.

HIKING

The local tourist office (✉ Via Pradalago 4, ☎ 0465/442000, FAX 0465/440404) supplies maps of the dozen or so treks for walking amid waterfalls, lakes, and stupendous views.

SKIING

This quaint resort is one of the better-skied resorts in the Dolomites, with miles of interconnecting runs linked by cable cars and lifts. The popularity of this town is due to the well organized lodging, skiing, and trekking facilities it provides.

En Route Just a few kilometers north of Madonna di Campiglio is one of the highest points in the Dolomites, the **Campo Carlo Magno** pass. This is where Charlemagne is said to have stopped in AD 800 on his way to Rome to be crowned emperor. Stop here to glance over the whole of northern Italy. Resume your descent with caution (in the space of a couple of kilometers, you descend more than 2,000 ft) via hairpin turns and switchbacks. The strange, rocky pinnacles of the Dolomites, which jut straight up like chimneys and look at times more like Utah's Monument Valley than any European ranges, loom over scattered mountain lakes. Turn left at Dimaro, and continue 37 km (23 mi) east to Ponte di Legno through another high pass, **Passo del Tonale** (5,600 ft). Here turn right on S300 and, passing the so-called Black Lake on your left, head for Bormio, the famous Lombard skiing center, through the **Passo di Gavia,** which also must be approached carefully and attentively when open to traffic.

Bormio

⑤ *20 km (12 mi) south of Passo dello Stelvio, 100 km (60 mi) southwest of Merano.*

At the foot of the Stelvio Pass, in the Valtellina Valley, Bormio is one of the most famous ski resorts on the western side of the Dolomites, with 38 km (22 mi) of pistes. It differs greatly from Madonna di Campiglio in that it is both a town and a summer resort. With an altitude of close to 4,000 ft, Bormio is surrounded by clean, fresh air. Even Italians come here in the summer months to escape the humid conditions. There are plenty of shops, restaurants, and hotels throughout the town. Bormio has also been known for the therapeutic qualities of its waters since the Roman era. You'll find spas throughout the town.

Lodging

$$$ 🏨 **Posta.** Ostelli della Posta hotels, staging inns of days gone by, are a time-honored tradition in northern Italy. The warm reception and atmosphere of this town center hotel will temper the cold, with its warm wood detail in the low-vaulted areas. The rooms are cozy and comfortable, with heavy drapery and bed linens. Perks include a small health center with a pool, sauna, gym, and Turkish bath and a slopes shuttle bus. ✉ *Via Roma 66, 23032,* ☎ *0342/904753,* FAX *0342/904484. 50 rooms. Restaurant, pub, indoor pool, sauna, health club. AE, MC, V. Closed Oct.–Dec.*

$$ 🏨 **Larice Bianco.** This modern hotel in a quiet part of town, a five-minute walk from the center, is two minutes from hiking trails, ski lifts, and other activities. The rooms are comfortable and adequately sized and all have private balconies. There is a piano bar for guests to show off their après-ski glow and if the sun fails to impress there is even a solarium. The hotel restaurant serves typical Valdisotto cuisine. ⊠ *Via Funivia 10, 23032,* ☎ *0342/904693,* ℻ *0342/904614. 45 rooms. Restaurant, piano bar. AE, MC, V. Closed mid-Sept.–Dec.*

$$ 🏨 **Nazionale.** Bordering the Stelvio National Park, this central hotel caters to the winter and summer crowd. Rooms are small but well equipped, with TVs and safes. The exterior is, for the most part, wood, with balconies on nearly all floors except the top. The hotel operates a shuttle bus to and from the cable cars. ⊠ *Via al Forte 28, 23032,* ☎ *0342/ 903361,* ℻ *0342/905294. 48 rooms. 2 restaurants, bar, sauna, shops, recreation room. AE, MC, V. Closed Oct.–Dec.*

Outdoor Activities and Sports
Popular activities in the region include hill walking, mountain climbing, and snow and grass skiing.

Passo dello Stelvio

★ ❻ *20 km (12 mi) north of Bormio, 61 km (38 mi) west of Naturno, 80 km (48 mi) west of Merano.*

At just over 9,000 ft, Passo dello Stelvio (Stelvio Pass) is the second-highest pass in Europe. The view from the top is worth the effort because the pass connects the Venosta Valley with the Valtellina in neighboring Lombardy. Just to the left as you enter the pass is Switzerland.

Outdoor Activities and Sports
SKIING
Stelvio is a year-round skiing center, with summer skiing on many of its runs.

En Route Between the Stelvio Pass and Spondigna is 30 km (19 mi) of picturesque, winding road, with 48 hairpin turns. This section of road can be a bit hair raising for anyone who doesn't like mountain driving. In Spondigna keep to the right for the road to Naturno.

ALTO ADIGE AND CORTINA

Alto Adige (Sudtirol), the northern half of the region, was ceded to Italy at the end of World War I, hitherto having been part of the Austro-Hungarian Empire. As a result, everything here has more than a tinge of the Teutonic, which is none more apparent than in the fact that the majority of the inhabitants speak German. Ethnic differences have led to inevitable tensions (including, alas, acts of terrorism), though a large measure of autonomy has, for the most part, kept the lid on nationalist ambitions. Towns are listed in order as you come upon them by road.

Naturno

❼ *61 km (38 mi) east of Passo dello Stelvio, 14 km (9 mi) west of Merano, 44 km (27 mi) northwest of Bolzano.*

Naturno is a large horticultural center, with streets lined with colorful houses that display painted murals on their walls. Art lovers will appreciate the church of **San Procolo**, which is frescoed inside and out, and has wall paintings that are the oldest in the German-speaking world, dating from the 8th century. It is usually open only on Sunday.

Above the town, a short distance away, is the 13th-century Juval Castle, since 1983 the home of the South Tyrolese climber and polar adventurer Reinhold Messner—the first man to conquer Everest solo, and the first to scale all 14 of the world's highest peaks without oxygen. Since 1995, part of the castle has been a museum, showing Messner's collection of Tibetan art, mountaineering illustrations, and masks from around the world. ☏ 0473/221852. 🎫 12,000 lire. 🕓 Mid-Apr.– June and Sept.–mid-Nov., daily 10–5.

Dining

$$ ✕ **Juval Inn.** Just below Juval Castle, Reinhold Messner has opened the Juval Inn, an old-style hostelry in a restored farmhouse, serving traditional local dishes and wines provisioned from his own farm. ✉ Schlosswirt-Juval, ☏ 0473/668238. No credit cards. Closed Wed. and Easter–Oct.

Merano

★ ⑧ 24 km (15 mi) north of Bolzano, 100 km (62 mi) northeast of Bormio.

The second-largest town in the Alto Adige, Merano has been famous as a spa town for 150 years due to its therapeutic thermal waters with natural radioactivity. It is also renowned for its grape cure. Sheltered by mountains, Merano has an unusually mild climate, with summer temperatures rarely exceeding 80°F and winters that usually stay above freezing, despite the skiing that is within easy reach. Chairlifts and cable cars connect Merano with the high Alpine slopes of Avelengo and San Vigilio.

Along the narrow streets of Merano's old town, houses sport little towers and huge wooden doors, and the pointed arches of the Gothic cathedral sit with harmony next to neoclassical and art nouveau–style buildings.

In the heart of the old town **Piazza del Duomo** is the 14th-century Gothic **cathedral,** with a crenellated facade and an ornate campanile. The **Cappella di Santa Barbara,** just behind the cathedral, is an octagonal church containing a 15th-century pietà.

The **Terme** (Thermal Baths) is a huge complex and nerve center for spa facilities; although some hotels have their own, these are unique. Technicians are trained to treat you with mud packs, massages, and inhalation and sauna routines, or just with the thermal waters, which are said to be especially good for coronary and circulatory problems. Other cures include the famous grape cure at harvest time in the fall, when a two-week diet of fresh grapes has, since Roman times, been seen as a successful way to tone up digestive, liver, and urinary tract functions. For further information contact the local tourist office (☞ Visitor Information *in* The Dolomites A to Z, *below*). ✉ Close to the Ponte del Teatro.

Dining and Lodging

$$$$ ✕ **Andrea.** This relaxed but elegant showcase for fine cuisine and service is just off Via dei Portici and right by a cable-car station. Surrounded by wood paneling and lots of green plants, you can dine on local and international cuisine, such as risotto *alle erbe* (with herbs) and *filetto di vitello con salsa di alloro* (veal fillet with bay leaf sauce). A set menu (about 100,000 lire) offers a complete five-course dinner, including superb wine. ✉ Via Galilei 44, ☏ 0473/237400. Reservations essential. Jacket and tie. AE, DC, MC, V. Closed Mon. and 2 wks in Feb. No dinner Sun. Nov.–Mar.

$$$ ✕ **Flora.** There's room for only about 20 diners in this intimate candlelit restaurant under the historic arched arcades of Merano's ancient center. Chef Louis Oberstolz describes his cooking as "fresh, sponta-

neous, and natural, using only the finest ingredients." He offers a seven-course set menu. Among the specialties are *quaglia ripiena con fegato d'oca grasso* (boned quail stuffed with foie gras), and *schlutzkrapfen* (fresh pasta ravioli with various fillings). ✉ *Via dei Portici 75,* ☎ *0473/231484. Reservations essential. AE, DC, MC, V. Closed Sun. and mid-Jan.–mid-Feb. No lunch Mon.*

$$$ ✕ **Grill Stube/Schloss Maur.** Stained-glass lamps and wood paneling
★ create a warm art nouveau effect in these two restaurants of the Hotel Palace (☞ *below*). Schloss Maur is the height of elegance, with huge marble columns, high ceilings, and crystal chandeliers. Italian and international dishes include the signature spaghetti with a sauce of zucchini, sage, and green pepper or roast saddle of lamb and lobster. Grill Stube offers gourmet menus, and is open only in the evening and closed Sunday. ✉ *Hotel Palace, Via Cavour 2/4,* ☎ *0473/211300. Reservations essential. AE, DC, V.*

$–$$ ✕ **Terlaner Weinstübe Putz.** This local favorite is an old rustic stübe in Merano's old town. The seasonal menu focuses on Tyrolean specialties. Try zuppa *al vino bianco* (with white wine) and the various risottos, including one with asparagus in the spring, and with Barolo in chillier months. ✉ *Via dei Portici 231,* ☎ *0473/235571. No credit cards. Closed Wed. Feb.–Mar., and July.*

$$$–$$$$ 🏨 **Hotel Palace.** Merano's grandest hotel, formerly the Palace Kurho-
★ tel, is an opulent turn-of-the-century institution set in an extensive garden. Rooms are spacious, decorated in a stately modern classic design. The public rooms are attractive and comfortable with art-nouveau touches, Tiffany glass, marble pillars, and high ceilings. The impressive spa features all sorts of baths, massages, mud treatments, and other cures. A lovely fountain serves thermal Merano water. ✉ *Via Cavour 2/4, 39012,* ☎ *0473/211300,* 🖷 *0473/234181. 124 rooms. Restaurant, bar, indoor-outdoor pool, spa. AE, DC, MC, V. Closed Jan.–Feb. and mid-Nov.–mid-Dec.*

$$$ 🏨 **Castel Labers.** On a hilltop amid forested slopes about 3 km (2 mi) east of Merano's center, this castle hotel with red-tile gables, towers, and turrets is unmistakably Tyrolean in style. Ceiling beams, painted fresco decorations, and crossed halberds on the walls complete the look. The hospitable Stapf-Neubert family owns the hotel and takes an active part in its management. ✉ *Via Labers 25, 39012,* ☎ *0473/234484,* 🖷 *0473/234146. 32 rooms. Restaurant, pool, tennis court. AE, DC, MC, V. Closed Nov.–Mar.*

$$$ 🏨 **Schloss Rundegg.** A romantic, converted 12th-century castle with an original tower, Schloss Rundegg is furnished with antiques and rich fittings, such as Persian carpets. It's set in a park and functions as a fully equipped thermal spa. The restaurant even provides for special weight-loss and curative diets. Room 32, in the tower, has an interior staircase and 360-degree views. ✉ *Via Scena 2, 39012,* ☎ *0473/ 234100,* 🖷 *0473/237200. 30 rooms. Restaurant, bar, pool, sauna, spa. AE, DC, MC, V. Closed Jan. 6–31.*

$$–$$$ 🏨 **Minerva.** This 1909 hotel furnished in traditional period style is recommended by locals as a good budget hotel. Set in a garden, it's about 10 minutes by foot from the town center. Almost all rooms have balconies with views of the mountains. Full-board rates are economical. ✉ *Via Cavour 95, 39012,* ☎ *0473/236712,* 🖷 *0473/230460. 45 rooms. Restaurant, pool. AE, DC. Closed Nov.–Mar., except for Dec. 24–Jan. 1.*

Nightlife and the Arts

DISCO

The **Bristol** hotel has a disco that's popular with locals as well as with visitors.

WINE FESTIVAL

The **Grape Festival** on the second Sunday of October has parades and wine tastings in Piazza del Duomo.

Outdoor Activities and Sports

HORSE RACE

Farmers test their horses in the highly charged **horse race** that is the highlight of Easter Monday.

TENNIS

Tennis Merano (✉ Tennis Club Merano, Via Piave 46, ☎ 0473/236550) maintains 9 clay courts (4 indoor) and 2 hard courts, which are open to the public. Lessons are given at the tennis university.

Shopping

LOCAL CRAFTS AND SPECIALTIES

Merano's main shopping street, the narrow, arcaded **Via dei Portici** (Laubengasse) runs west from the cathedral. It features most of the best regional products: wood carvings, Tyrolean-style clothing, embroidery, cheeses, salami, and fruit schnapps.

MARKET

From the end of November until Christmas Eve, Merano holds a traditional *Christkindlmarkt* (Christmas market) in the main square.

Bolzano

❾ *24 km (15 mi) south of Merano, 110 km (68 mi) west of Cortina d'Ampezzo, 70 km (43 mi) north of Trento.*

Bolzano (Bozen) is the capital of the autonomous province of Alto Adige. It is protected by the mountains to the north and the east and is on the main north–south artery between northern Europe and Italy. This quiet city at the confluence of the Isarco (Eisack) and Talvera rivers has retained a provincial appeal, but it is juxtaposed with commercial features acquired to cater to the needs of tourists. There are no high-rises, but McDonald's can be seen—housed, of course, in a more archaic building.

❿ Bolzano's heart is pedestrians-only **Piazza Walther,** named after the 12th-century German wandering minstrel Walther von der Vogelweide, whose songs lampooned the papacy and praised the Holy Roman Emperor. The square serves as an open-air living room where locals and tourists alike can be found at all hours sipping a drink (perhaps a glass of chilled Riesling) at the café tables.

⓫ The city's Gothic **Duomo** was built between the 12th and 14th centuries; its lacy spire looks down on the mosaiclike tiles covering its pitched roof. Inside the church are 14th- and 15th-century frescoes and an intricately carved stone pulpit dating from 1514. ✉ *Piazza Walther.* ☉ *Weekdays 9:30–6, Sat. 9:30–noon.*

⓬ **Piazza Domenicani,** with its 13th-century **Dominican church,** is renowned as Bolzano's main repository for paintings, especially frescoes. In the adjoining **Cappella di San Giovanni** you can see frescoes of the Giotto school, one of which is the *Triumph of Death* (circa 1340). Despite its macabre title, this fresco shows the birth of a pre-Renaissance sense of depth and individuality. ☉ *Church and chapel Mon.–Sat. 9–6:30, Sun. mass.*

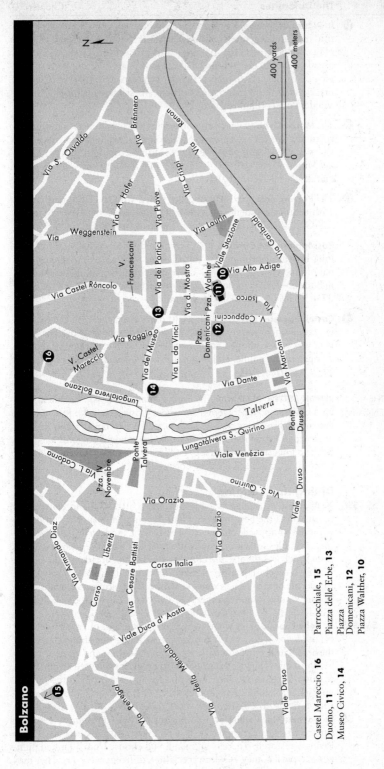

Bolzano

N

400 yards
400 meters

Via S. Osvaldo
Via Brénnero
Via Rénon
Via A. Hofer
Via Crispi
Via Weggenstein
Via
Via Piave
Via Laurin
Via Garibaldi
V. Franciscani
Viale Stazione
Via dei Portici
Via d. Mostra
Via Alto Adige
Via Castel Róncolo
Pza. Walther
Via Isarco
V. Cappuccini
Pza. Domenicani
Via Roggia
Via del Museo
V. Castel Mareccio
Via L. da Vinci
Via Dante
Via Marconi
Lungotálvera Bolzano
Talvera
Ponte Druso
Lungotálvera S. Quirino
Ponte Talvera
Viale Venézia
Via L. Cadorna
Pza. IV Novembre
Via S. Quirino
Viale Druso
Via Orazio
Via Orazio
Via Armando Diaz
Libertà
Corso Italia
Corso
Via Cesare Battisti
Viale Duca d' Aosta
Via delle Mendola
Via Penegal

Castel Mareccio, **16**
Duomo, **11**
Museo Civico, **14**
Parrocchiale, **15**
Piazza delle Erbe, **13**
Piazza Domenicani, **12**
Piazza Walther, **10**

⑬ In **Piazza delle Erbe,** a bronze statue of Neptune presides over a bountiful fruit and vegetable market. The stalls spill over with colorful displays of local produce; bakeries and grocery stores showcase hot breads, pastries, cheeses, and delicatessen meats—a complete range of picnic supplies. Try the speck and the Tyrolean-style apple strudel. The market is at the beginning of Bolzano's best-known shopping street, **Via dei Portici** (Laubengasse).

⑭ The **Museo Civico** (Civic Museum) houses a rich collection of traditional costumes, wood carvings, and archaeological exhibits. The mixture of styles is a reflection of the region's cultural cross-fertilization. ⊠ *Via del Museo 45,* ☎ *0471/974625.* ⊞ *3,000 lire.* ⊗ *Tues.–Sat. 9–12:30 and 2:30–5:30, Sun. 10–1.*

⑮ The **Parrocchiale** (parish church) of Gries, with its elaborately carved 15th-century wooden altar, is worth a visit. ⊠ *Corso Libertà,* ⊗ *Apr. 21–Oct. 30, weekdays 10–noon and 2–4, Sun. mass.*

Passeggiata del Guncina (⊠ Quartiere di Gries) is an 8-km- (5-mi-) long botanical promenade, dating from 1892, that culminates in a panoramic view of Bolzano. There are two other scenic promenades in Bolzano—ask in the local tourist office (⊠ Piazza Walther 8, ☎ 0471/ 975656, ⅢⅩ 0471/980300) for details.

⑯ **Castel Mareccio** (Schloss Maretsch) dates from the 13th century and is nestled under mountains and surrounded by vineyards. The castle is now a well-equipped conference center with a restaurant and bar, all open to the public. ⊠ *Lungotalvera Promenade,* ☎ *0471/976615.* ⊗ *Closed Tues.*

OFF THE **RENON (RITTEN) PLATEAU –** The Earth Pyramids of Renon Plateau make
BEATEN PATH up a bizarre geological formation where erosion has left a forest of tall, thin, needlelike spires of rock, each topped with a boulder. The Soprabolzano funicular leaves from Via Renon, about 300 yards left of Bolzano train station. At the top, an electric train takes you to the site, which is at Collalbo, just above Bolzano.

Dining and Lodging

$$–$$$ ✕ **Abramo.** Although outside Bolzano's attractive old center, this restaurant is the best in town. Chef Abramo Pantezi offers an Italian variation of nouvelle cuisine in an attractive, modern Renaissance setting. At tables set with crystal and silver, you'll choose among seafood dishes such as *salmone allo* champagne (salmon in champagne sauce). There's a vegetarian antipasto selection and a daily diet menu selected for calorie control. The extensive wine cellar features top-quality California vintages, among others. ⊠ *Piazza Gries 16,* ☎ *0471/280141. AE, DC, MC, V. Closed Sun. and Aug. 1–25.*

$$–$$$ ✕ **Belle Epoque.** This is the fashionable restaurant of Park Hotel Laurin (☞ *below*). During the summer months, a grill restaurant opens in the hotel's lush, extensive park. International cuisine and local specialties are the focus. The kitchen prides itself on dishes oriented around fresh seasonal ingredients, such as asparagus in spring and in the fall, savory game, including hare and venison. ⊠ *Park Hotel Laurin. Via Laurino 4,* ☎ *0471/980500. Jacket and tie. AE, DC, MC, V. Closed Sun.*

$$ ✕ **Gostner Flora's Bistrot.** In a medieval tower on Bolzano's market square, this tiny tavern has been around for centuries, and it has been lovingly restored. There is no menu; you choose from a limited number of typical homey Tyrolean specialties, different every day. They may include canederli or *schlutzkrapfen* (ravioli). The desserts are homemade, too. The young owner takes pride in a selection of good wines.

⊠ *Piazza delle Erbe 17,* ☎ *0471/974086. No credit cards. Closed Sun. No dinner Sat.*

$ ✕ **Batzenhausl.** A medieval building in the center of town houses this crowded *stübli* (Tyrolean-style drinking hall). It's a popular hangout for the local intellectual set, who hold long, animated conversations over glasses of local wine and tasty local South Tyrolean specialties, such as herrngröstl and apple pancakes with ice cream. Try the fried Camembert. ⊠ *Via Andreas Hofer 30,* ☎ *0471/976183. No credit cards. Closed Tues. and 2 wks in July. No lunch.*

$$$ ▥ **Park Hotel Laurin.** This big turn-of-the-century hotel, decorated in opulent art-nouveau style, is set in a large, shady park, in the middle of town. Most rooms have stunning views of the park and the mountains beyond. Some rooms carry through the Belle Epoque decor; others are furnished in a classic modern hotel style. The Belle Epoque restaurant (☞ *above*), with an outdoor buffet in the summer, serves local specialties. ⊠ *Via Laurino 4, 39100,* ☎ *0471/980500,* ℻ *0471/970953. 96 rooms. Restaurant, pool. AE, DC, MC, V.*

$$$ ▥ **Schloss Korb.** It's worth the 5-km (3-mi) drive west from Bolzano ★ to reach this hotel. It's set in a romantic 13th-century castle with a crenellated roof and a massive central tower, perched in a park amid vine-covered hills. Much of the ancient decor is preserved, and the public rooms are filled with Tyrolean antiques, elaborate wood carvings, old paintings, and attractive plants. The rooms are comfortably furnished—some tower rooms have the old Romanesque arched windows. ⊠ *Missiano, Strada Castel d'Appiano 5, 39056,* ☎ *0471/636000,* ℻ *0471/636033. 56 rooms. Indoor pool, sauna, tennis courts. No credit cards. Closed Nov.–Easter.*

$$–$$$ ▥ **Luna/Mondschein.** This central yet secluded hotel was built in 1798. Set in a lovely garden, it awashes a tranquil, friendly calm over its guests. The rooms are comfortable, with classic style using wood paneling throughout. Some rooms overlooking the garden have balconies, but even the rooms overlooking the garage have good views of the mountains. The two restaurants include a typical Tyrolean weinstübe that serves inexpensive local specialties in a cozy, convivial setting. ⊠ *Via Piave 15, 39100,* ☎ *0471/975642,* ℻ *0471/975577. 85 rooms. Restaurant, weinstübe. DC, MC, V.*

$$ ▥ **Città.** This palazzo hotel in town center occupies an entire corner of the square, with seating outside. The decor is modern but in keeping with the original style of the edifice. Rooms are well appointed, often with spacious bathrooms and excellent views out over the piazza. The restaurant serves local dishes at decent prices. An underground parking garage means you don't have to worry about parking fines: a common complaint in a mainly pedestrian city. ⊠ *Piazza Walter 21, 39100,* ☎ *0471/975221,* ℻ *0471/976688. 98 rooms. Restaurant, bar, parking. AE, MC, V.*

Nightlife and the Arts

Spring is heralded each May with large flower markets and events, including concerts and folklore and art exhibits.

FAIR

On August 24 is the **Bartolomeo Horse Fair,** on Renon Mountain just northeast of the town. Hundreds of farmers converge for a day of serious trading and frivolous merriment.

MUSIC

For the **International Busoni Piano Competition** in late August, concerts and recitals are held in halls and churches. Internationally acclaimed performers usually head the panel of judges.

Outdoor Activities and Sports

HIKING

Club Alpino Italiano (⊠ Piazza delle Erbe 46, Bolzano, ☎ 0471/978172) is a helpful organization that provides information for hiking and rock climbing. It is important to follow safety procedures and to have all the latest information on trails and conditions.

TENNIS

Courts can be found in Bolzano at **Circolo Tennis Bolzano** (⊠ Via M. Koller 8, ☎ 0471/280587).

Shopping

LOCAL CRAFTS

The long, narrow arcades of **Via dei Portici** house shops that specialize in Tyrolean crafts and clothing—lederhosen, loden goods, linen suits, and dirndls. The best store for locally made handcrafted goods is **Artigiani Atesini** (⊠ Via Portici 39).

MARKETS

From the end of November until Christmas Eve there are traditional **Christkindlmarkt** in the main square of Bolzano with stalls selling all kinds of Christmas decorations and local handcrafted goods. The outdoor fruit and vegetable market is held in the central **Piazza delle Erbe** (☞ *above*) Monday through Saturday 8–1. The big weekly flea market takes place Saturday morning in **Piazza della Vittoria.**

Cornedo

⑰ *6 km (4 mi) east of Bolzano and 24 km (15 mi) southwest of Chiusa.*

At the mouth of the Ega Valley (Eggental), Cornedo is a place to savor the view of the Catinaccio Mountains. Craggy peaks seem to be props for a lighting display, as pink and purple reflections dance over huge rocks. Their creation is the subject of a local German legend that tells of King Laurin, who lived in a vast palace on the Catinaccio, at a time when the mountain was covered with roses. King Laurin became infatuated with the daughter of a neighboring king, Similde, and kidnapped her, but Similde, searching for his daughter, recognized her place of imprisonment by the red roses that grew there. Laurin freed the girl and was made Similde's prisoner. When Laurin finally escaped he decreed that the betraying roses should be turned to rocks, so that they could be seen neither by day nor by night. Today, the spectacular pinkish-red display is at its best at dawn and at sunset.

Chiusa

⑱ *30 km (19 mi) northeast of Bolzano, 14 km (9 mi) south of Bressanone.*

Beautiful narrow streets lined with houses built in the 15th and 16th centuries best characterize Chiusa (Klausen). Geraniums and begonias fill window boxes beneath the carved wooden shutters.

Above the town of Chiusa is the Benedictine monastery of **Saviona** (Saeben), built as a castle in the 10th century but occupying a site that was fortified in Roman times. The monastery buildings date from the late Middle Ages and are a mixture of Romanesque and Gothic architecture, surrounded by walls and turrets. Guided visits are organized by the Tourist Association in Chiusa; contact the local tourist office (⊠ Piazza Tinne 40, ☎ 0472/847424, ℻ 0472/847244). Churches are open daily 9–5.

Bressanone

⑲ *14 km (9 mi) north of Chiusa, 40 km (25 mi) northeast of Bolzano, 100 km (62 mi) northwest of Cortina d'Ampezzo.*

Bressanone (Brixen) is an important artistic center of the Alto Adige and for centuries was the seat of prince-bishops. Like their counterparts in Trento, these medieval administrators had the delicate task of serving two opposing masters—the pope (the ultimate spiritual supervisor) and the Holy Roman Emperor (the civil and military leader). Since the papacy and the Holy Roman Empire were virtually at war throughout the Middle Ages, Bressanone's prince-bishops became experts at tact and diplomacy in order to survive. As you arrive from Brunico, you enter the town on Via Mercato Vecchio, a broad road leading to the imposing **Duomo.** It was built in the 13th century but acquired a Baroque facade 500 years later, and its 14th-century cloister is decorated with medieval frescoes.

The Bishop's Palace, which now houses the **Museo Diocesano** (Diocesan Museum), is a treasure trove of local medieval art, particularly Gothic wood carving. The wooden statues and liturgical objects were all collected from the cathedral treasury. During the Christmas season, the curators highlight displays of the museum's large collection of antique Nativity scenes: look for the shepherds wearing Tyrolean hats. The palazzo is beside the Duomo. ⊠ *Palazzo Vescovile,* ☎ *0472/836401.* ☞ *5,000 lire (2,000 lire for nativity scenes exhibition only).* ⊙ *Mid-Mar.–Oct., Mon.–Sat. 10–5; nativity scenes Dec. 15–Feb. 10, Mon.–Sat. 2–5.*

Dining and Lodging

$$ ✕ **Fink.** This restaurant under the arcades in the pedestrians-only town
★ center has a friendly staff and offers an affordable daily set menu. It has a rustic ambience upstairs with lots of wood paneling, and serves international as well as hearty Tyrolean specialties. Try the *carré di maiale gratinato* (pork roasted with cheese and served with cabbage and potatoes) or the *castrato alla paesana* (a kind of lamb stew). ⊠ *Via Portici Minori 4,* ☎ *0472/834883. AE, DC, MC, V. Closed Wed. and July. No dinner Tues. Oct.–June.*

$$$ ▨ **Dominik.** Well equipped and modern, this hotel is centrally located but has a quiet garden and dining terrace. Most doubles are spacious and modern, with comfortable armchairs, ample baths, and balconies. The superior restaurant features local trout (in season). ⊠ *Via Terzo di Sotto 13, 39042,* ☎ *0472/830144,* ℻ *0472/836554. 29 rooms. Indoor pool, sauna. AE, MC, V. Closed Nov. 4–Easter.*

$$–$$$ ▨ **Elefante.** One of the best and most famous hotels in the region, this
★ cozy inn is in a historic 15th-century building: there's been a hotel on the site for more than 500 years. The hotel takes its name from an incident in 1550, when King John of Portugal stopped here for a few days while leading an elephant over the Alps as a present for Austria's Emperor Ferdinand. Each room is different, many with antiques and paintings. Housed on the park property is the separate Villa Marzari, with 14 rooms. The hotel restaurant (closed Mon.) is known as one of the region's best. ⊠ *Via Rio Bianco 4, 39042,* ☎ *0472/832750,* ℻ *0472/836579. 44 rooms. Restaurant, pool. DC, MC, V. Closed Nov. 15–Dec. 20 and Jan. 10–Feb. 28.*

$$ ▨ **Croce d'Oro** (Goldenes Kreuz). A 5-centuries-old tradition of hospitality is still practiced by staff at this centrally placed hotel. Shops line the ground floor of the pink building, with styles inside ranging from the more modern, tasteful reception area to the tavern-style bar. The rooms are spacious with sturdy wood appointments. ⊠ *Bastioni*

Minori 8. 30042, ☎ *0472/836155,* FAX *0472/834255. 72 rooms. Restaurant, bar. AE, MC, V.*

Outdoor Activities and Sports

TENNIS

Tennis can be played at **Club Bressanone** (✉ Lungoisarco Sinistro, ☎ 0472/834792).

Shopping

From the end of November until Christmas Eve there are traditional **Christkindlmarkt** (Christmas markets) in the main square of Bressanone, with stalls selling all kinds of Christmas decorations and local handcrafted goods.

Brunico

★ ⑳ *33 km (20 mi) east of Bressanone, 65 km (40 mi) north of Cortina d'Ampezzo.*

With its medieval quarter nestling below the 13th-century bishop's castle, Brunico (Bruneck) is within the heart of the Pusteria Valley. This picturesque little town, often noted for its quiet and relaxing qualities, is divided by the Rienza River with the old quarter on one side and the modern quarter on the other.

The **Museo degli Usi e Costumi della Provincia di Bolzano** (Bolzano Province Customs and Costumes Museum, or Ethnographic Museum) re-creates a typical local village, and is built around an authentic 300-year-old mansion. It examines the functions and significance of traditional architecture. The wood-carving displays are particularly interesting. It's in the district of Teodone, just outside the town. ✉ *Via Duca, Teodone 24, 39031,* ☎ *0474/32087,* FAX *0474/31764.* ✉ *6,000 lire.* ☉ *Mid-Apr.– Oct., Tues.–Sat. 9:30–5:30, Sun. 2–6.*

Lodging

$–$$ ☷ **Andreas Hofer.** There's a Tyrolean feel to this comfortable hotel set in a large garden outside the center of town. Traditional chalet-style balconies overlook the Pusteria Valley. The rooms have modern furnishings, and there are several rooms with special features for people with disabilities. The hotel restaurant is recommended. ✉ *Via Campo Tures 1, 39031,* ☎ *0474/31469,* FAX *0474/31283. 54 rooms. Restaurant, sauna. MC, V. Closed Apr.–May and mid-Nov.–mid-Dec.*

$–$$ ☷ **Post.** Locals recommend this traditional, homey hotel for its friendly rates and restaurant, café, and pastry shop. It has its own parking, which is important because of the pedestrians-only rules in effect throughout much of the central area. ✉ *Via Bastioni 9, 39031,* ☎ *0474/ 555127,* FAX *0474/31603. 60 rooms, 55 with bath. Restaurant, café, free parking. MC, V. Closed Nov.–mid-Dec.*

Outdoor Activities and Sports

DOGSLED RACE

On January 22 locals turn up for the **dogsled race,** and there seems nary a soul without a flask of hot mulled wine to back their favorites.

SKIING

A comparatively inexpensive ski area is at **Badia Valley,** reached by heading south on S244 from Brunico.

Dobbiaco

㉑ *25 km (16 mi) east of Brunico, 34 km (21 mi) north of Cortina d'Ampezzo.*

In Dobbiaco (Toblach), just 12 km (7 mi) to the east along the Drau Valley, Austria's influence intensifies. Italian is spoken grudgingly here, Austrian money is accepted at most shops and restaurants, and the locals appear more blond and blue-eyed than the average Italian. It is not surprising that Gustav Mahler (1860–1911), the great Austrian composer, would have come here often for inspiration.

Lodging

$–$$ ☒ **Alpino Monte Rota/Alpengasthof Ratsberg.** To reach this hotel,
★ you take the 10-minute cable-car ride to Monte Rota. It is in traditional style, with the timeless look of local chalets. Front rooms have stunning mountain views from balconies, while those in the back look out over the dense mountain forest. You needn't take the cable car back down for sustenance: the Alpino has a good restaurant (which even serves some low-calorie dishes), a bar, and a Tyrolean-style stübe. ☒ *Monte Rota 10, 39034,* ☎ *0474/72213,* ℻ *0474/72916. 25 rooms. Restaurant, bar, pool, sauna. MC, V. Closed mid-Apr.–May and mid-Oct.–mid-Dec.*

$–$$ ☒ **Cristallo.** Wood beams and paneling lend an Old Tyrolean tone to this small hotel set in a garden just outside town. The architecture and furnishings reflect the local preference for combining traditional chalet design with functional, but comfortable, modern furniture. Most rooms enjoy a panoramic view of the valley; some of the best rooms have balconies. Guests relax in the cozy and informal stübe. ☒ *Viale S. Giovanni 37, 39034,* ☎ *0474/72138,* ℻ *0474/72755. 30 rooms. Restaurant, bar, indoor pool. AE, MC, V. Closed mid-Apr.–mid-May and mid-Oct.–mid-Dec.*

Outdoor Activities and Sports

SKIING

Prepared trails for cross-country skiing (usually loops marked off by kilometers) accommodate differing degrees of ability. One of the best of this kind can be found at **Dobbiaco.** Inquire at the local tourist office. Downhill skiing can be found at **Monte Rota** slopes, accessible from Dobbiaco. These offer considerably lower rates than in many of the more exclusive resorts.

Cortina d'Ampezzo

★ **㉒** *65 km (40 mi) south of Brunico, 140 km (87 mi) east of Bolzano.*

"The Pearl of the Dolomites" is set in a lush meadow 4,000 ft above sea level. Dense forests adjoin the town, and mountains encircle the whole valley. The town sprawls on the slopes along a fast-moving stream; a public park extends along one bank. Luxury hotels and the villas of the rich are conspicuously scattered over the slopes above the town— identifiable by their attempts to hide behind stands of firs and spruces.

The bustling center of Cortina d'Ampezzo has little nostalgia for old-time atmosphere, despite its Alpine appearance. The tone is set by elegant shops and stylish cafés, as opulent as their well-dressed patrons, whose corduroy knickerbockers may well have been tailored by Armani. Cortina is the place to go for a whiff of the heady aroma of wealth and sophistication; if you want authentic Tyrolean gemütlichkeit, pass through Cortina and stop at one of the resorts later on the tour.

Dining and Lodging

$$$ ✕ **De la Poste.** The exclusive restaurants of the hotel on Cortina's main square have a casually chic clientele and a lively atmosphere. There's an elegant, high-ceilinged main dining room with three big chandeliers where you can dine on soufflés and nouvelle cuisine dishes (every Friday fresh fish is served). There's also a more informal grill room with wood paneling and the family pewter collection. In ski season it's always crowded. ✉ *Piazza Roma 14,* ☎ *0436/4271. Reservations essential. Jacket and tie. AE, DC.*

$$–$$$ ✕ **Tana della Volpe.** Near the Olympic ice skating rink, this popular restaurant has a bona fide Tyrolean ambience, with wood-paneled dining rooms and a local clientele. Here you can try Cortina specialties such as *zuppa di* porcini (wild mushroom soup), ravioli *di cervo* (stuffed with venison), and game. ✉ *Via dello Stadio 27/a,* ☎ *0436/ 867494. AE, DC, MC, V. Closed mid-June–mid-July, Nov., and Wed. No lunch Thurs. May and Sept.*

$$ ✕ **Fanes.** This restaurant in the Hotel Fanes outside town serves homey food in rustic elegance. Game is a specialty, with dishes including *camoscio* (chamois) and *capriolo in salmì con* polenta (roe deer stewed in red wine and served with polenta). ✉ *Hotel Fanes, Via Roma 136,* ☎ *0436/3427. AE, DC, MC, V. Closed Mon.*

$$$$ 🏨 **Miramonti Majestic.** This imposing and luxurious hotel, nearly a century old, has a magnificent mountain valley location about a km (½ mi) south of town. A touch of Old World formality accompanies the imperial Austrian design, and the interior reflects the period style throughout. Most of the rooms have balconies and have been entirely redecorated. There's a restaurant, and in the cozy bar there's always a roaring fire in the hearth. ✉ *Località Peziè 103, 32043,* ☎ *0436/ 4201,* FAX *0436/867019. 116 rooms, 7 suites, 5 junior suites. Pool, sauna, golf course, tennis courts, exercise room. AE, DC, MC, V. Closed Easter–June and Sept. 15–Dec. 20.*

$$$ 🏨 **De la Poste.** Skiers who want to be seen keep returning to this lively hotel on the main square in a pedestrian zone. It's been under the same family management since 1826, and the furnishings feature antiques in characteristic Dolomite style. Almost all rooms have wooden balconies. The hotel's main terrace bar, on the square, is always crowded and is one of Cortina's social centers. ✉ *Piazza Roma 62, 32043,* ☎ *0436/4271,* FAX *0436/868435. 83 rooms. Restaurant, bar. AE, DC. Closed mid-Apr.–mid-June and mid-Oct.–mid-Dec.*

Nightlife and the Arts

DISCO

At **Europa** hotel (✉ Corso Italia 207, ☎ 0436/3221) you can expect to mingle with the couture set at the VIP disco; nonguests are welcome, but don't expect to spend less than 50,000 lire.

Outdoor Activities and Sports

SKIING

In Cortina d'Ampezzo, you will be challenged by plenty of slopes with the access to several mountain ranges in the vicinity.

TENNIS

Public courts can be used at **Via Sopiazes** (☎ 0436/2937).

En Route As you enter the Crepa Tunnel along the S48 from Cortina d' Ampezzo, the ascent for the Passo di Falzarego begins. The **Passo Pordoi** will lead to the so-called heart of the Dolomites. The roads around this region of the Sella mountains are deemed to be among the most spectacular in Europe and many consider their rugged beauty to be unparalleled.

A fork in the road farther ahead will lead left to Canazei and right into Val Gardena.

HEART OF THE DOLOMITES

The area between Cortina d'Ampezzo and east to Bolzano is dominated by two major valleys, the Val di Fassa and the famous Val Gardena. Both share the spectacular panorama of the Sella mountain range, known because of its circular shape as the Heart of the Dolomites. Val di Fassa is made up primarily of the Grande Strada delle Dolomiti (Great Dolomites Road), which runs from the mountain resort of Cortina d'Ampezzo as far as Bolzano. The route, opened in 1909, now comprises 110 km (68 mi) of easy grades and smooth driving between the two cities.

With some of the best views of the Dolomites, Val Gardena is famous as a ski resort, dotted with well-equipped picturesque towns overlooked by the oblong Sasso Lungo (Long Rock), which is more than 10,000 ft above sea level. It is also home of the Ladins, descendants of soldiers sent by the Roman Emperor Tiberius to conquer the Celtic population of the area in the 1st century AD. Forgotten in the narrow cul-de-sacs of isolated mountain valleys, the Ladins have developed their own folk traditions and speak an ancient dialect that is derived from Latin and is similar to Romansch, which is spoken in some high valleys in Switzerland.

Canazei

㉓ *60 km (37 mi) west of Cortina d'Ampezzo, 23 km (14 mi) east of Lake Carezza, 52 km (32 mi) east of Bolzano.*

Of the towns in the Fassa Valley, Canazei is the most popular ski resort as well as a summer haven. The area around this small town is full of mountain trails and ski slopes, surrounded by large pockets of conifers.

OFF THE BEATEN PATH **COL RODELLA –** An excursion from Campitello di Fassa to the vantage point at Col Rodella is a must. The cable car rises some 3,000 ft up the mountain to this most panoramic of vistas. From the balcony at the top you can see full circle around the region, including the Sasso Lungo and the rest of the Sella range.

En Route **Passo di Sella** is one of the most famous mountain passes in the Dolomites. It can be approached from the S48 and continues into Val Gardena among the most panoramic mountain scenery in Europe. The road descends to Ortisei, passing the small ski resort of Santa Cristina.

Lodging

$$$ 🏨 **Alla Rosa.** This recently renovated hotel offers all modern facilities and a big family welcome. Centrally located, the hotel has a modest restaurant with a choice of either local or international cuisine, and a cozy bar. The three-story building has balconies in half of all rooms, and large reception areas. The bedrooms are well laid out with a pleasant rustic and modern mix, but the real attraction is the view over the imposing Dolomites. ⊠ *Via Dolomite 142, 39046,* ☎ *0462/601107. 37 rooms. Restaurant, bar, recreation room. MC, V. Closed Oct.*

Ortisei

② *80 km (50 mi) west of Cortina d'Ampezzo, 28 km (17 mi) north of Canazei, 35 km (22 mi) northeast of Bolzano.*

Ortisei (St. Ulrich), the jewel in the crown of Val Gardena's ski resorts, is a hub of activity both in summer and, especially, in winter. There are hundreds of miles of hiking trails as well as several hundred miles of accessible ski slopes, including the Siusi slopes to the south. Hotels are everywhere and facilities are excellent, with swimming pools, ice rinks, health spas, tennis courts, and bowling. Most impressive of all is the location, a valley surrounded by formidable views in all directions. For further information on activities in Val Gardena contact the main tourist office (⊠ Ortisei, Str. Rezia 1, ☎ 0471/796328, ⅁AX 0471/796749).

For centuries Ortisei has also been famous for the expertise of its wood-carvers and there are still numerous workshops here. Apart from making religious sculptures—particularly the wayside Calvaries you come upon everywhere in the Dolomites—Ortisei's carvers were long famous for producing wooden dolls, horses, and other toys. As itinerant peddlers, every spring they traveled by foot with their loaded packs as far as Paris, London, and St. Petersburg to sell their wares. Fine historic and contemporary examples of all kinds of locally carved wooden sculptures and artifacts can be seen at the **Museo della Val Gardena** at Cesa di Ladins. ⊠ *Via Rezia 83, Ortisei,* ☎ *0471/797554.* ⅁ *5,000 lire.* ⊘ *July–Aug., daily 10–noon and 3–7; June, Sept., Dec. 28–30, Jan. 4–7, and Feb. 8–Apr. 1, Tues.–Fri. 3–6:30.*

Lodging

$$$ ⅁ **Aquila/Adler.** Since 1810, this hotel has been under the same family management. Today it is regarded as one of the best in the valley. Set in a large park, the original building has been enlarged and renovated several times in the intervening years, but it retains a lot of the old turreted-castle appeal. The Tyrolean character is carried through in special Tyrolean parties held once a week for guests. The rooms are spacious; some are suitable for guests with disabilities. ⊠ *Via Rezia 7, 39046,* ☎ *0471/796203,* ⅁AX *0471/796210. 94 rooms, most with bath. Restaurant, bar, pool, beauty salon, sauna, tennis courts, health club. AE, DC, MC, V. Closed mid-Apr.–mid-May and mid-Oct.–mid-Dec.*

$$–$$$ ⅁ **Posta Cavallino Bianco.** In town center and a five-minute walk from the main ski facilities, this hotel looks more like a gigantic doll house, with delicate wooden balconies and an eye-catching wooden gable. Inside, the decor is full of deep colors and ornate carpets and drapery. Wood is incorporated throughout the interior, most notable in the cozy hotel bar with a large handcrafted fireplace. The rooms are a good size with all utilities, but not all have balconies. The hotel also has a sun terrace and even a small disco. ⊠ *Via Rezia 22, 39046,* ☎ *0471/796392,* ⅁AX *0471/797517. 99 rooms. Restaurant, bar, coffee shop. MC, V. Closed mid-Apr.–mid-May and mid-Oct.–mid-Dec.*

Outdoor Activities and Sports

The Val Gardena comes alive with a parade of horse-drawn sleighs on January 1.

SKIING

With almost 600 km (370 mi) of accessible downhill slopes, Ortisei is one of the most popular resorts in the Dolomites. Prices are good and facilities are among the most modern. There are more than 90 km (56 mi) of cross-country skiing lanes.

TENNIS

Courts can be found in **Roncadizza** (☎ 0471/797275).

Fiè

㉕ *26 km (16 mi) southwest of Ortisei, 18 km (11 mi) east of Bolzano.*

Fiè (Voels) is set in a valley with the Renon mountains on one side and the Siusi on the other. The town is surrounded by acres of green coniferous forests. In the town is the parish church of **Santa Maria Assunta** in the late Gothic style, built in the 16th century. The church, due to restoration, is not open to the public.

Lodging

$$$ 🏨 **Turm.** The *turm* (tower) that houses this welcoming hotel on the edge
★ of the Sciliar National Park dates from the 13th century and has been used as a courthouse, prison, and tavern. Now owned and run by the Pramstrahler family, it's furnished with their charming collection of paintings and antiques. In addition, this picturesque hostelry also has an excellent restaurant. ⊠ *Piazza della Chiesa 9, Fiè allo Sciliar (Voels am Schlern), 39040,* ☎ *0471/725014,* ℻ *0471/725474. 23 rooms. Restaurant, indoor and outdoor pools, sauna. AE, DC, MC, V. Closed early Nov.–Dec. 20.*

Outdoor Activities and Sports

The **Oswald von Wolkenstein Cavalcade,** named after the medieval South Tyrolese knight and troubadour, is held every year over the first or second weekend of June. After a colorful procession, teams of local horsemen and women compete in fast-paced events.

Caldaro

㉖ *35 km (22 mi) west of Lake Carezza, 15 km (9 mi) south of Bolzano.*

Caldaro is a vineyard village with clear views of castles high up on the surrounding mountains, a backdrop that reflects the centuries of division that forged the unique character of the area. Caldaro architecture is famous for the way it blends Italian Renaissance elements of balance and harmony with the soaring windows and peaked arches of the local Gothic tradition. The church of **Santa Caterina,** on the main square, is a good example.

Close to the main square is the **South Tyrolean Museum of Wine,** illustrating the history of wine production in this region. ⊠ *Via dell'Oro 1,* ☎ *0471/963168.* 🎟 *3,000 lire.* ☉ *Easter–Oct., Tues.–Sat. 9:30–noon and 2–6, Sun. 10–noon.*

Lake Carezza

㉗ *23 km (14 mi) west of Canazei, 29 km (18 mi) east of Bolzano.*

A lake of icy cold glacial waters, **Lake Carezza** is some 5,000 ft above sea level. The azure blue of the waters can at times change to magical greens and purples, reflections of the surrounding forest and rosy peaks of the Dolomites.

THE DOLOMITES A TO Z

Arriving and Departing

By Car

The most important route in the region, **A22,** is the main north–south autostrada linking Italy with northern Europe via the Brenner Pass. It

links Bressanone, Bolzano, Trento, and Rovereto, and at Verona joins
the A4, running east–west across northern Italy from Trieste to Turin.

By Plane

The nearest airports are Verona's **Villafranca Airport** in Italy and **Munich Airport** in Germany, both well connected by road and rail with
the Dolomite area (☞ *below*).

By Train

The express train line that links the towns of Bolzano, Trento, and
Rovereto connects with other main lines at Verona, just south of the
region. Eurocity trains on the Dortmund–Venice and Munich–Rome
routes also stop at these stations.

Getting Around

By Bus

Local buses connect the train stations at Trento, Bolzano, and Merano with the mountain resorts. The service is fairly frequent between
most main towns during the day. Though some parts of the region remain out of the reach of public transportation, it is possible to visit
even the remotest villages without a car if you are equipped with the
local bus timetables, available from regional and local tourist offices
(☞ Visitor Information, *in* Contacts and Resources, *below*).

By Car

Autostrada **A22** connects Bressanone, Bolzano, Trento, and Rovereto.
Roads in the broad mountain valleys are usually wide two-lane routes,
but the roads up into the highest passes can be narrow and subject to
sudden closure, even in the months when they are open to drivers. A
Bolzano number (☎ 0471/993810 or 0471/978577) provides information on weather-related closures.

By Train

An express train line follows the course of the Adige Valley from the
Brenner Pass southward past Bolzano, Trento, and Rovereto. Branch
lines from Trento and Bolzano go to some of the smaller valleys, but
most of the mountain attractions described above are beyond the reach
of trains.

Contacts and Resources

Car Rental

Avis (✉ Piazza Verdi 18, Bolzano, ☎ 0471/971467).

Emergencies

Carabinieri (☎ 112). English-speaking officers are available 24 hours
a day to deal with any kind of emergency.

Police, Ambulance (☎ 113). For first aid, ask for "Pronto Soccorso,"
and be prepared to give your address.

Guided Tours

If you are without a car or if you don't care to drive over mountain
roads, guided tours from Bolzano or Trento can show you the Dolomites
the easy way. However, the sudden and frequent snowfalls mean that
tours are offered in summer only.

In Bolzano, city sightseeing and local excursions are organized by the
SAD bus company (✉ Via Conciapelli 60, near the train station, ☎ 0471/971259). In July and August, full-day mountain tours include a **Great Dolomites Tour** from Bolzano to Cortina and a tour of the **Venosta Valley** that climbs over the Stelvio Pass into Switzerland. A tour of the **Val Gardena** and the Siusi Alps is available from April to October.

In Trento, city sightseeing can be arranged through the city **APT** office (⊠ Via Alfieri 4, ☎ 0461/983880). From June through September, the **Calderari e Moggioli** travel agency (⊠ Via Manci 46, ☎ 0461/980275) offers a full-day guided bus tour of the **Brenta Dolomites** and the **Great Dolomites Tour,** a full-day drive over the Pordoi and Falzarego passes to Cortina d'Ampezzo and Lake Misurina.

The Trentino regional **APT** (⊠ Via Sighele 3, ☎ 0461/914444) organizes guided tours and excursions by train to castles in the region.

Hiking and Hill Walking
A helpful organization is the **Società degli Alpinisti Tridentini** (⊠ Via Manci 57, Trento, ☎ 0461/986462). **Club Alpino Italiano** (⊠ Piazza delle Erbe 46, Bolzano, ☎ 0471/978172) can also assist you. Local tourist offices can provide information on less-demanding trails (☞ Visitor Information, *below*).

Late-Night Pharmacies
Pharmacies take turns staying open late or on Sunday; for the latest information, consult the current list posted on the front door of each pharmacy or ask at the local tourist office (☞ Visitor Information, *below*).

Visitor Information
Alto Adige province (⊠ Piazza Parrocchia 11–12, Bolzano, ☎ 0471/993808, ℻ 0471/975448). **Trentino Tourist Board** (⊠ Via Sighele 3, Trento, ☎ 0461/914444, ℻ 0461/915978).

Bolzano (⊠ Piazza Walther 8, ☎ 0471/975656, ℻ 0471/980300). **Bormio** (⊠ Via Stelvio, ☎ 0342/903300, ℻ 0342/904696). **Bressanone** (⊠ Via Stazione 9, ☎ 0472/36401, ℻ 0472/36067). **Chiusa** (⊠ Piazza Tinne 40, ☎ 0472/847424, ℻ 0472/847244). **Cortina d'Ampezzo** (⊠ Piazzetta San Francesco 8, ☎ 0436/3231, ℻ 0436/3235). **Dobbiaco** (⊠ Via Dolomiti 3, ☎ 0474/972132). **Madonna di Campiglio** (⊠ Via Pradalago 4, ☎ 0465/442000, ℻ 0465/440404). **Merano** (⊠ Corso della Libertà 45, ☎ 0473/35223, ℻ 0473/35524). **Ortisei** (⊠ Str. Rezia 1, ☎ 0471/796328, ℻ 0471/796749).

11 Emilia-Romagna

Parma, Bologna, Rimini, and Ravenna

Gourmets the world over claim that Emilia-Romagna's greatest contribution to humankind has been gastronomic. Birthplace of fettuccine, tortellini, and lasagna, Bologna offers a bevy of great restaurants. But there are also many cultural riches here: Parma's Correggio paintings, Verdi's villa at Sant'Agata, the Renaissance splendors of Ferrara, and the Byzantine beauty of mosaic-rich Ravenna—glittering today as brightly as it did 1,500 years ago.

Updated by
Robert
Andrews

EMILIA-ROMAGNA OWES ITS BEGINNINGS to a road. In 187 BC the Romans laid out the Via Aemelia, a long highway running straight from the Adriatic port of Rimini to the central garrison town of Piacenza, and it was along this central spine that the primary towns of the region developed. The old Roman road still exists (S9), and a modern superhighway (A1 and A14) runs parallel to it. Most of the exploring in this chapter will be along either the old road or its modern counterpart.

Despite the unifying factor of the Via Emilia, as the highway is now called, the region has had a fragmented history. The eastern portion of the region, roughly the area from the city of Faenza to the coast, known as Romagna, has looked first to the east and then to Rome for art, political power, and, some say, national character. The western portion, Emilia, from Bologna to Piacenza, had a more northern, rather dour sense of self-government and dissent. Italians say that in Romagna a stranger will be offered a glass of wine; in Emilia, a glass of water—if anything at all.

The principal city of the region is Bologna. It was founded by the Etruscans but eventually came under the influence of the Roman Empire. The Romans established a garrison there, renaming the old Etruscan settlement Bononia, the Bologna of today.

It was after the fall of Rome that the region began its fragmentation. Romagna, centered in Ravenna, was ruled from Constantinople. Ravenna eventually became capital of the empire in the West in the 5th century, passing to papal rule in the 8th century. The city today, however, is still filled with reminders of two centuries of Byzantine rule.

The other cities of the region, from the Middle Ages on, became the fiefs of important noble families—the Este in Ferrara and Modena, the Pallavicini in Piacenza, the Bentivoglio in Bologna, and the Malatesta in Rimini. Today all these cities bear the marks of their noble patrons. When in the 16th century the papacy managed to exert its power over the entire region, some of these cities were divided among the families of the reigning popes—hence the stamp of the Farnese family on Parma, Piacenza, and Ferrara.

The region was one of the first to join the quest for a unified Italy in the 19th century, pledging itself to the king of Italy and the forces of Garibaldi in the 1840s. Loyalty to the crown did not last long, however. The Italian socialist movement was born in the region, and throughout Italy Emilia-Romagna has been known for rebellion and dissent. Benito Mussolini was born here, although in keeping with the political atmosphere of his home state, he was a firebrand socialist during the early part of his career. Despite being the birthplace of Il Duce, Emilia-Romagna did not take to fascism: it was in this region that the antifascist resistance was born, and during World War II the region suffered terribly at the hands of the Fascists and the Nazis.

Despite a long history of bloodletting, turmoil, and rebellion, the arts—both decorative and culinary—have always flourished in Emilia-Romagna. The great families financed painters, sculptors, and writers (Dante found a haven in Ravenna after being expelled from his native Florence). In modern times, Emilia-Romagna has given to the arts such famous sons as painter Giorgio Morandi, author Giorgio Bassani (author of *Garden of the Finzi-Continis*), filmmaker Federico Fellini, and tenor Luciano Pavarotti.

Bologna is the acknowledged leading city of Italian cuisine. It is home to two of the most famous Italian delicacies—foods that, sadly, have been poorly treated outside their native city. What the world calls "baloney" the Bolognese call *mortadella,* a robust pork sausage spiced with whole peppercorns (if there aren't peppercorns in it, then it isn't mortadella), which bears no resemblance to the stuff sliced at the typical U.S. deli counter. The other famous dish is spaghetti *al ragù,* known to the world as spaghetti *bolognese.* The spaghetti with meat sauce dished around the world is a far cry from the real thing. In Bologna a ragù sauce is made with onions, carrots, minced pork and veal, butter, and fresh tomatoes and is cooked for five or six hours in a special earthen pot. It is, in a word, exquisite. Few dining experiences in Italy can match the satisfaction of a properly cooked ragù.

Bologna is also the home of tortellini, lasagna, and *vitello* alla bolognese, a veal cutlet smothered with prosciutto and Parmesan cheese. The rest of the province has made substantial contributions to the kitchen. Parma is the home of Parma ham and the most famous of all Italian cheeses, Parmigiano (Parmesan). Modena is the birthplace of *zampone* (stuffed pigs' feet, which tastes much better than it sounds) and *aceto balsamico,* the jet-black, fragrant herb vinegar that is now a must on the shelves of any self-respecting gourmet.

Pleasures and Pastimes

Dining

Bologna's reputation as the culinary capital of Italy is well deserved, but there is much fine dining to be had in the other cities of Emilia-Romagna as well. The inland part of the region takes its cue from Bologna, but each city has a traditional dish of its own. In Piacenza rice dishes predominate, particularly risotto in *padella* (with fresh herbs and tomatoes). Parma is most famous for its ham; Modena, for meat products and the delicious balsamic vinegar; Rimini, reflecting its position on the sea, is home to an elaborate fish stew called *brodetto;* Ferrara is famous for simple foods: pears, peaches, asparagus, and zucchini. Crumbly, fresh Parmesan cheese is produced throughout the region and can be picked up at bargain prices from the farms along the Via Emilia and other outlets.

The two most important pastas of the region are pasta al ragù, usually narrow egg noodles served with bolognese sauce, and the stuffed pasta called tortellini, which can be served with the ragù, in a cream sauce, or even in soups. Ravioli stuffed with ricotta cheese and spinach is a specialty of the area, as are the larger versions of the same thing: *agnolotti,* which can be stuffed with cheese but more frequently are filled with minced pork or beef, and *tortelli,* stuffed with squash.

The best-known wine of the region is Lambrusco, a sparkling red that has some admirers and many detractors. Some praise it for its tartness; others condemn it for the same quality. A lesser-known wine is Vino del Bosco, also a sparkling red, which comes from the region around Ferrara.

CATEGORY	COST*
$$$$	over 90,000 lire
$$$	60,000–90,000 lire
$$	30,000–60,000 lire
$	under 30,000 lire

Prices are per person, including first course, main course, dessert or fruit, and house wine.

Lodging

In Italy, the region of Emilia-Romagna has a reputation for an efficiency that outstrips that in most of the rest of the country. Consequently, even the smallest hotels are well run, with high levels of service and quality. Bologna is very much a businessperson's city, and most of the hotels cater to travelers of this type. There are, of course, smaller, more intimate hotels that cater to the tourist.

The business of Rimini is tourism. There are hundreds of hotels, grand ones with all sorts of luxury facilities and modest boardinghouses with only a few rooms. Many offer full- or half-board plans—an economical alternative to eating in Rimini's many, but not particularly distinguished, restaurants. You should not go to Rimini during tourist season without confirmed hotel reservations: in July and August the city is filled to overflowing.

CATEGORY	COST*
$$$$	over 300,000 lire
$$$	160,000–300,000 lire
$$	100,000–160,000 lire
$	under 100,000 lire

Prices are for a standard double room for two, including service and tax.

Exploring Emilia-Romagna

A tour through Emilia-Romagna has something for everyone: great art, stirring history, fabulous food—even a day at the beach at the seaside resort of Rimini. The best way to see the region is to begin your tour in the west, in Piacenza, and to proceed east along the Via Emilia to the sea. The major towns are either on that route or just off it, the longest detours being no more than 48–65 km (30–40 mi) off the main road.

Numbers in the text correspond to numbers in the margin and on the Emilia-Romagna and Bologna maps.

Great Itineraries

Although the region of Emilia-Romagna has a geographical logic—following the Via Emilia through the Po Valley and Romagna plain—it is not a compact area, making it hard to cover much of in a short time. If you are traveling straight through, then you will have to confine your stops to places along the main north–west artery. Alternatively, you could base yourself in the regional capital, Bologna, and make forays from this hub. From Bologna there are two choices of itineraries: head north to Ferrara and then east to Ravenna, or continue along the Via Emilia, stopping for short visits at some of the smaller towns en route to Rimini and the sea. More time will permit you to acquaint yourself on a deeper level with the varying moods of the places you visit on your travels. Bologna, in particular, has the most to offer and repays as much time as you can give it.

We have divided the region into two areas of discovery. The first, which extends along the main north–west artery from Piacenza to Savignano, near the Adriatic coastal resort of Rimini, includes the famed opera country between Piacenza and Parma. Birthplace and home of the great Romantic composer Giuseppe Verdi, this area is awash with memorials to the composer, including villas, palazzi, and a theater. Also not to be missed are the beautiful cities of Bologna, one of the most important historical, culinary, and cultural cities in Italy; Modena, famous as the birthplace of Ferrari sports cars and "the world's greatest tenor," Luciano Pavarotti; and Parma, a delightful, dignified town that has been ruled by most of the European powers throughout its history. The second area extends along the Adriatic coast from Rimini, the Italian equivalent of southern Spain's holiday resorts, to Ravenna, once the last capital of the Roman Empire, later part of the Byzantine Empire, and home to the finest mosaics in Western art. The Adriatic coast is also where you'll find Ferrara, a city of towers and turrets, historical palaces, and a mighty castle protected by a moat.

IF YOU HAVE 3 DAYS

Given three days, you should set aside two nights to see ☒ **Bologna** ⑤–⑮ and its environs, including **Dozza** ⑯. The city itself has enough to fill much more than this, but while you are there, make a point of seeing the sights in and around Piazza Maggiore, including the **Basilica di San Petronio** ⑥, the **Palazzo Comunale** ⑦, with its art galleries, and the nearby two towers. On your second day here, buy a train ticket or drive the short distance to ☒ **Ferrara** ⑳, an unspoiled Renaissance city whose calm pace will provide a pleasant contrast to the regional capital. Where you spend your third day will depend on your route out of Emilia-Romagna. If you are going to Milan or Turin, make a stop after less than 100 km (62 mi) from Bologna at **Parma** ③, where you could cover the major sights in two or three hours. If you are heading toward the Adriatic coast, ☒ **Ravenna** ⑲ should be your priority stop. Of course, if you are heading north toward Venice, you should see Ferrara on this leg of the journey and take in Parma and Ravenna on the other days.

IF YOU HAVE 5 DAYS

Your itinerary will again depend on your route to and from Emilia-Romagna. Your extra freedom will allow you to spend longer in both ☒ **Parma** ③ and ☒ **Ravenna** ⑲, two essentials of any trip through the region. In Ravenna, make a point of seeing **Sant'Apollinare in Classe,** outside the city proper but well worth the excursion. More time in Parma will allow you to take full advantage of the outstanding cuisine and hotels here. Fine food and wine should also be evaluated at every opportunity in **Modena** ④ and Bologna, two centers of the culinary culture in this region famed both for its produce and its flair for putting it to good effect. Consider a day and a night for Parma and Modena together. Leave two days for ☒ **Bologna** ⑤–⑮ itself and one each for ☒ **Ferrara** ⑳ and Ravenna.

IF YOU HAVE 7 DAYS

A week in the region will allow you to explore all of its splendor. If you desire a beach resort scene, spend a couple of days in ☒ **Rimini** ⑱ and see its cathedral and sample some of its fish restaurants. If the resort scene doesn't appeal, skip it altogether and extend your stay in ☒ **Ravenna** ⑲ or ☒ **Bologna** ⑤–⑮. On your way to (or from) Bologna, drop in on a factory in the ceramic center of **Faenza** ⑰, famed for its faience pottery. The pleasures of ambling the streets of ☒ **Ferrara** ⑳ might tempt you to spend more than one night. Likewise, you might be tempted to while away a quiet couple of days in ☒ **Parma** ③. Northwest of Parma, make a slight detour from the autostrada or Via Emilia to see the cluster of places associated with the composer Verdi, centered on the village of **Busseto** ②. Still heading northwest, you could spend a pleasant morning or afternoon in the city of **Piacenza** ①, its elegance and harmony typical of Emilia-Romagna's centers of culture, and a fitting exit or entrance to the region. From here, it's a mere 66 km (40 mi) to Milan.

When to Tour Emilia-Romagna

The climate of Emilia-Romagna has never been its most popular aspect. In this predominantly flat landscape, the winters are gray and cold, and summers are airless and hot, though the heat is subdued on the coast by sea breezes. If you are here in summer, get up early and do as much as you can in the morning. The afternoon should be left unplanned; the hours after five are best for sightseeing and traveling. In winter, make sure you are equipped for the humid, penetrating cold. Fog is common throughout the low-lying areas of the region and can be beautiful, though it can also be very hazardous when driving and restricting to say the least on the panoramic views. At all times, make sure you reserve ahead for your accommodation requirements: the cities are usually awash with commercial conventions and business conferences.

ON THE ROAD TO PARMA AND BOLOGNA

Three of Italy's most interesting cities lie along the main north–west artery: Piacenza, Parma, and Bologna. The area between Piacenza and Parma is opera country: In the quiet backwater towns north of the Via Emilia, the Italian opera composer Giuseppe Verdi lived and worked. The composer of *Aïda, Rigoletto, La Traviata,* and *Otello* was born in a very simple farmhouse in the hamlet of Roncole and built the grand villa of Sant'Agata in the town of Busseto after he became world famous.

Piacenza

❶ *66 km (41 mi) southeast of Milan, 182 km (114 mi) east of Turin, 40 km (25 mi) west of Cremona, 62 km (39 mi) northwest of Parma, 150 km (94 mi) northwest of Bologna.*

The city of Piacenza has always been associated with industry and commerce. Its position on the River Po has made it an important inland port since the earliest times—the Etruscans, then the Romans, had thriving settlements on this site. As you approach the city today, you could be forgiven for thinking that it holds little of interest. Piacenza is surrounded by ugly industrial suburbs (with particularly unlovely cement factories and a power station), but these enclose a delightfully preserved medieval downtown.

The heart of the city is **Piazza dei Cavalli** (Square of Horses), dominated by the massive Palazzo del Comune, a severe turreted and crenellated Gothic building of the 13th century. It was the seat of town government during those times when Piacenza was not under the iron fist of a ruling family. The flamboyant equestrian statues from which the piazza takes its name are **statues** of members of the last and greatest of the rulers of Piacenza. On the right is Ranuccio Farnese; on the left is his father, Alessandro Farnese. Alessandro was a beloved ruler, enlightened and fair; Ranuccio, his successor, was less successful. Both statues are the work of Francesco Mochi, a master sculptor of the Baroque period.

Piacenza's impressive **Duomo** is from the mid-12th century. Attached to the massive bell tower is a *gabbia* (iron cage), where evildoers were exposed naked to the scorn (and missiles) of the crowd in the marketplace below. The interior of the cathedral is an odd mixture of Gothic and Baroque. Fine medieval stonework decorates the pillars and the crypt, and there are extravagant frescoes by 17th-century artist Guercino in the dome of the cupola. The Duomo can be reached by following Via XX Settembre down from Piazza dei Cavalli. ⊠ *Piazza Duomo.* ⊙ *Daily 7–noon and 4–7.*

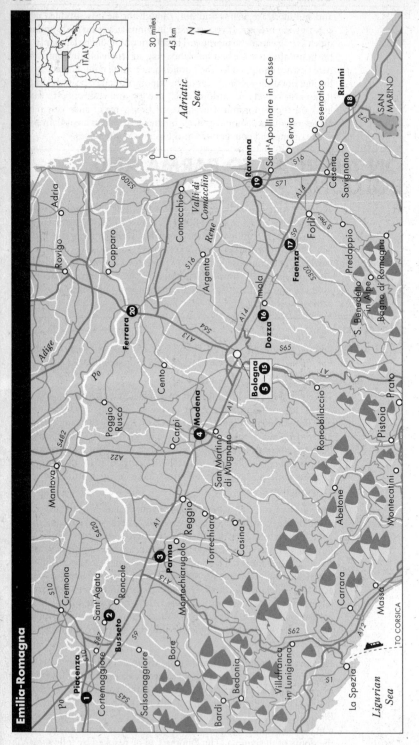

Emilia-Romagna

The **Museo Civico** (Civic Museum), the city-owned collection of Pia-
cenzan art and antiquities, is housed in the vast Palazzo Farnese, which
was started by the ruling family in 1558 but never completed. The museum was closed for many years for restoration and the reordering of
the collection, but it is again open to the public. The highlight of this
rather eclectic exhibit is the *Etruscan Fegato di Piacenza*, a bronze tablet
in the shape of a *fegato* (liver), with the symbols of the gods of good
and ill fortune marked on it. By comparing this master "liver" with
one taken from the body of a freshly slaughtered sacrifice, the priests
could predict the future. On a more humanistic note, the collection also
contains a painting by Botticelli, the *Madonna with St. John the Baptist,* and a series of Roman bronzes and mosaics. There is also a collection of carriages, arms and armor, and other paraphernalia owned
by the Farnese, giving a good idea of the splendor of that powerful family. ⊠ *Piazza Cittadella.* ☒ *4,500 lire.* ☉ *Tues.–Wed. and Fri. 9–12:30,
Thurs. 9–12:30 and 3:30–5:30, Sat. 9–12:30 and 3–6, Sun. 9:30–
noon and 3:30–6:30.*

Dining

$$$ ✕ **Antica Osteria del Teatro.** Set on a lovely piazza in the center of town,
★ this restaurant is generally touted to be the best in Piacenza. Try the
tortelli stuffed with ricotta, the roast duck, or the steamed sea bass.
⊠ *Via Verdi 16,* ☏ *0523/323777. Reservations essential. AE, DC, MC,
V. Closed Mon. and Aug. 1–25 and Jan. 1–10. No dinner Sun.*

$ ✕ **Agnello.** Central (on the corner of Piazza Cavalli), simple, and
cheap, Agnello is an excellent place to sit down and enjoy a lunchtime
snack. Try the tortelli *alla Piacentina* (with ricotta and spinach in a but-
ter and cheese sauce) or, for a meat dish, *coniglio alla Cacciatora* (rab-
bit in tomato sauce). ⊠ *Via Calzolai 2,* ☏ *0523/320874. Reservations
not accepted. No credit cards. Closed Mon.*

En Route   If you are driving from Piacenza, take S10 northeast for Cremona, but
turn off it just a few miles out of Piacenza and follow the signs for S587
to the town of Cortemaggiore. From Cortemaggiore, turn right onto
a smaller rural road (not numbered) and follow the signs for Busseto,
some 10 km (6 mi) away. If you plan to visit all the area's Verdi sights,
invest in an 8,000-lire ticket valid for Villa Pallavicino, Palazzo Or-
landi, Teatro Verdi, and Verdi's birthplace (but not Villa Sant'Agata).

Busseto

❷ *30 km (19 mi) southeast of Picenza, 15 km (9½ mi) south of Cremona,
40 km (25 mi) northwest of Parma.*

Busseto's main claim to fame is the **Villa Pallavicino,** where Verdi
worked and lived with his mistress (later wife), Giuseppina Strepponi.
There is a small **Verdi museum** here that displays such relics of the mae-
stro as his piano, scores, composition books, walking sticks, and other
bits of memorabilia. ☒ *4,000 lire.* ☉ *Apr.–Sept., Tues.–Sun. 9:30–12:30
and 3–7; Oct.–Nov., Tues.–Sun. 9:30–noon and 2:30–5.*

Palazzo Orlandi, owned for the past century by the Orlandi family, was
Verdi's home for a few years from 1845. Only a few of its stately rooms
are open to the public. ☒ *4,000 lire.* ☉ *Apr.–Sept., Tues.–Sun. 9:30–
12:30 and 3–7; Oct.–Nov., Tues.–Sun. 9:30–noon and 2:30–5.*

In the center of Busseto is the lovely **Teatro Verdi,** dedicated, as one
may expect, to the works of the hamlet's famous son. It is a well-pre-
served 19th-century-style theater, and it's worth a look to get a feel for
a place where Verdi worked. At press time (spring 1997), the theater
was planning to open later in the year after lengthy restorations; check

first. 🎫 *4,000 lire.* 🕐 *Apr.–Sept., Tues.–Sun. 9:30–12:30 and 3–7; Oct.–Mar., Tues.–Sun. 9:30–noon and 2:30–5.*

OFF THE
BEATEN PATH
VILLA SANT'AGATA – Five km (3 mi) north of Busseto, Villa Sant'Agata is the grand country home Verdi built for himself in 1849, where some of his greatest works were composed. For Verdi lovers, Sant'Agata is a veritable shrine. 🎫 *8,000 lire.* 🕐 *Apr.–Oct., Tues.–Sun. 9–11:40 and 3–6:40.*

RONCOLE – Giuseppe Verdi was born in a simple farmhouse on the edge of the town of **Roncole**, 3½ km (2 mi) southeast of Busseto. Equally modest is the church in which he took some of his earliest steps in a musical career; he was the church organist here when still in his teens. 🎫 *Verdi's birthplace 4,000 lire.* 🕐 *Apr.–Sept., Tues.–Sun. 9:30–12:30 and 3–7; Oct.–Nov., Tues.–Sun. 9:30–noon and 2:30–5.*

Parma

❸ *28 km (17½ mi) southeast of Roncole along S588 and A1 or Via Emilia, 62 km (39 mi) southeast of Piacenza, 97 km (61 mi) northwest of Bologna.*

Dignified, delightful Parma stands on the banks of a tributary of the River Po. Much of the historic center has been untouched by modern times, despite heavy damage during World War II, and thanks to the efforts being made by the city fathers to control traffic, strolling Parma's cobbled streets is a charming experience. The traffic regulations, although a boon to pedestrians, are a nightmare for motorists. Every obstacle is put in the way of motor traffic—one-way streets, no-turning zones, and the like—so it is best to leave your car outside the center and see the town on foot.

Almost every major European power has had a hand in ruling Parma at one time or another. The Romans founded the city—it was little more than a garrison on the Via Emilia—and then a succession of feudal lords held sway here. In the 16th century came the ever-avaricious Farnese family (who are still the dukes of Parma) and then, in fast succession, the Spanish, French, and Austrians, with the Austrians taking over following the upheavals in central Europe after the fall of Napoléon. The French influence is strong. The French novelist Stendhal lived in the city for several years and set his classic novel *The Charterhouse of Parma* here.

★ The **Piazza del Duomo**—site of the cathedral, the baptistery, the church of San Giovanni, and the palaces of the bishop and other notables—is the heart of the city. This square and its buildings make up one of the most harmonious, tranquil city centers in Italy.

The focal point of the piazza is the magnificent 12th-century **Duomo,** with its two vigilant stone lions standing guard beside the main door. The arch of the entrance is decorated with a delicate frieze of figures representing the months of the year, a motif repeated inside the baptistery on the right-hand side of the square.

Some of the original artwork still exists in the church, notably the simple yet evocative *Descent from the Cross,* a carving in the right transept, by Benedetto Antelami (1150–1230), a sculptor and architect whose masterwork is this cathedral's Baptistery (☞ *below*).

It is odd to turn from this austere work of the 12th century to the exuberant fresco in the dome, the *Assumption of the Virgin,* by the 16th-century painter Antonio Correggio. The fresco was not well received when it was unveiled in 1530. "A mess of frogs' legs," the bishop of Parma is said to have called it. In contrast to the rather dark, somber interior of the cathedral, though, the beauty and light of the painting in the dome are a welcome relief. Today, of course, Correggio is acclaimed as one of the leading masters of Baroque painting; his many works on view in Parma now constitute one of the greatest draws of the city. ⊠ *Piazza del Duomo.* ⊙ *Daily 9–12:30 and 3–7.*

The **Baptistery** is a solemn, simple Romanesque building on the exterior and an uplifting Gothic building within. The doors of the Baptistery are richly decorated with figures, animals, and flowers, and the interior is adorned with figures carved by Antelami, showing the months and seasons. It is to the side of the Duomo. ⊠ *Piazza del Duomo.* 🎟 *4,000 lire.* ⊙ *Daily 9–12:30 and 3–6.*

Once beyond the elaborate Baroque facade of **San Giovanni Evangelista,** the Renaissance interior reveals several works by Correggio; his *St. John the Evangelist* (left transept) is considered the finest of them. Also in this church (in the second and fourth chapels on the left) are works by Girolamo Parmigianino—a contemporary of Correggio's and the spearhead of the astonishing Mannerist art movement. Once seen, Parmigianino's anorexic and swan-necked Madonnas are never forgotten: they pose with all the precious élan of today's high-fashion models. ⊠ *Piazzale San Giovanni.* ⊙ *Daily 6:30–noon and 3:30–8.*

Next door to the church, in the adjoining monastery, is the **Spezieria di San Giovanni**—once a pharmacy where Benedictine monks used to mix medicines and herbals. The 16th-century decorations still survive, although the potions, which people of Parma swore would cure almost every malady, are, alas, gone—the pharmacy stopped production in 1881. ⊠ *Borgo Pipa 1, off of Piazzale San Giovanni.* 🎟 *4,000 lire.* ⊙ *Daily 9–1:45.*

★ Examples of Parma's own Correggio and Parmigianino, Leonardo da Vinci, El Greco, and Il Bronzino can be seen at the large **Galleria Nazionale,** housed in the vast but rather grim-looking **Palazzo della Pilotta,** on the banks of the river. The palace was built about 1600 and is so big that from the air it is Parma's most recognizable sight—hence, the destruction done to it when it was bombed by Allied forces in 1944. Much of the building has been restored, but not all. The palazzo takes its name from the ball game *pilotta,* a sort of handball played within the palace precincts in the 17th century.

To enter the art museum, which is on the ground floor of the palace, you pass through the magnificent and elaborately Baroque **Teatro Farnese,** built in 1628 and based on Palladio's theater in the northern Italian town of Vicenza. Built entirely of wood, the theater was burned badly during Allied bombing but has been flawlessly restored. ⊠ *Palazzo della Pilotta, Piazza Pilotta,* ☎ *0521/233309.* 🎟 *12,000 lire.* ⊙ *Daily 9–1:45.*

The **Camera di San Paolo** is the former dining room of the abbess of the Convent of St. Paul. It was extensively frescoed by Correggio, and despite the religious character of the building, the decorations are entirely secular, with ravishingly beautiful (and very worldly) depictions of mythological scenes—the *Triumphs of the Goddess Diana,* the *Three Graces,* and the *Three Fates.* It is near the Palazzo della Pilotta, off Strada Garibaldi. ⊠ *Via Melloni.* 🎟 *4,000 lire.* ⊙ *Daily 9–1:45.*

Near the central Piazza Garibaldi is **Madonna della Steccata,** a delightful 16th-century domed church famous for a wonderful fresco cycle by Parmigianino. The painter took so long to complete it that his exasperated patrons imprisoned him briefly for breach of contract before releasing him to complete the work. ⊠ *Via Dante.* ⏲ *Daily 9–noon and 3–6.*

Dining and Lodging

$$ ✕ **Croce di Malta.** The premises of this appealing turn-of-the-century style restaurant once housed a convent, then an inn. Traditional local fare includes light, delicate homemade pasta—try the tortelli with squash filling or tagliatelle in any fashion. Second courses are well-prepared, filling versions of classic veal and cheese dishes. ⊠ *Borgo Palmia 8,* ☎ *0521/235643. Reservations essential. AE, MC, V. Closed Sun. and 2 wks in Aug.*

$$ ✕ **La Greppia.** Here, at the best and most elegant restaurant in the city,
★ *padella alla Greppia* (green tagliatelle in mushroom sauce) is excellent, as are the pâté in Marsala wine, the *torta di melanzane* (eggplant pie), and the fried porcini mushrooms. ⊠ *Via Garibaldi 39/b,* ☎ *0521/233686. Reservations essential. AE, DC, MC, V. Closed Mon.–Tues. and July.*

$$ ✕ **Parma Rotta.** An old inn about 2 km (1¼ mi) from downtown
★ Parma, the Parma Rotta remains an informal neighborhood trattoria serving hearty dishes like *pasta e fagioli* (bean and pasta soup), roast pork, and spit-roasted lamb. Take advantage of the garden here to eat outside in summer. ⊠ *Via Langhirano 158,* ☎ *0521/966738. AE, DC, MC, V. Closed Sun. June–Aug., Mon. Sept.–May.*

$$ ✕ **Sant'Ambrogio.** This is an ideal spot if you seek informal dining in
★ the center of town. Duck and quail are the best bets, but try the *crauti spinaci* (boiled pork sausage with pickled cabbage or spinach). ⊠ *Vicolo Cinque Piaghe 1/a,* ☎ *0521/234482. AE, DC, MC, V. Closed Mon.*

$$$$ ⊟ **Palace Hotel Maria Luigia.** A top-quality hotel convenient to old Parma and the train station, the Maria Luigia has large, well-furnished rooms and is popular with business travelers. ⊠ *Viale Mentana 140, 43100,* ☎ *0521/231126. 105 rooms. Restaurant, bar, meeting rooms. AE, DC, MC, V.*

$$$ ⊟ **Park Hotel Stendhal.** The Stendhal is again one of the best hotels in Parma. It is on the edge of the historic center of town and convenient for the tourist and business traveler alike. Rooms are thickly carpeted and spacious, some with chandeliers and period furniture. Some rooms have views of the Palazzo della Pilotta. ⊠ *Via Bodoni 3, 43100,* ☎ *0521/208057,* 🗗 *0521/285655. 60 rooms. Restaurant, bar, meeting rooms. AE, DC, MC, V.*

$$ ⊟ **Torino.** A warm reception and pleasant, relaxed surroundings are the best reasons for staying in this former convent, tucked away in a quiet pedestrian zone in the heart of town. It has modern, smallish rooms with Correggio reproductions on the walls. ⊠ *Via Mazza 7, 43100,* ☎ *0521/281046,* 🗗 *0521/230725. 33 rooms. Bar, air-conditioning. AE, DC, MC, V. Closed Aug. 1–20.*

Nightlife and the Arts

Parma is the region's opera center, with performances held at the **Teatro Regio** (⊠ Via Garibaldi, ☎ 0521/218910). Opera here is taken just as seriously as in Milan, although tickets are a little easier to come by. Playwright Dario Fo helped found the **Teatro Due** (⊠ Viale Basetti 12, ☎ 0521/230242), a theater whose productions still maintain a mixture of comedy and politics—though your understanding of the themes will be limited without a knowledge of Italian.

Modena

❹ *56 km (35 mi) southeast of Parma along Route A1, 38 km (23 mi) northwest of Bologna.*

Old town Modena has today gained recognition for being home to three very contemporary names. The luxury high-performance cars Maserati and Ferrari come from Modena, and so does the world-famous opera star Luciano Pavarotti. The modern town that encircles the historic center is extensive, and although the old quarter is small, it is filled with an Old World atmosphere, narrow medieval streets, and pleasant piazzas.

The 12th-century **Duomo** is one of the finest examples of Romanesque architecture in the country. As in Parma, the exterior is decorated with medieval sculptures depicting scenes from the life of San Geminiano (patron saint of Modena) and fantastic beasts, as well as a realistic-looking scene of the sacking of a city by barbarian hordes, a reminder to the faithful to be ever vigilant in defense of the church. The bell tower is made of white marble and is known as *La Ghirlandina* (The Little Garland) because of its distinctive garland-shape weather vane on the summit.

The somber church interior is divided by an elaborately decorated gallery carved with scenes of the Passion of Christ. The carvings took 50 years to complete and are by an anonymous Modenese master of the 12th century. The tomb of San Geminiano is in the crypt. ✉ *Piazza Grande.* ⊙ *Daily 6:30–12:30 (closes noon July–Aug.) and 3:30–7.*

The principal museum of the town is housed in the **Palazzo dei Musei,** a short walk from the Duomo. (Follow Via Emilia, the old Roman road runs through the heart of the town, to Via di Sant'Agostino. The museum is in the piazza on the left). The collection was assembled in the mid-17th century by Francesco d'Este, Duke of Modena, and the gallery **Galleria Estense** is named in his honor. In the first room, there is a portrait bust of him by Bernini.

The duke was a man of many interests, as you can see from the collection of objets d'art—ivories, coins, medals, and bronzes, as well as fine art dating from the Renaissance to the Baroque. There are works here by Correggio, as well as by masters from other parts of Italy, such as the Venetians Tintoretto and Veronese, the Bolognese Reni and the Carracci brothers, and the Neapolitan Salvator Rosa.

The gallery also houses the duke's **library,** a huge collection of illuminated books, of which the best known is the beautifully illustrated bible of the 15th century, the *Bible of Borso d'Este.* A map, dated 1501, was one of the first in the world to show Columbus's discovery of America. ✉ *Piazza Sant'Agostino,* ☎ *059/222145.* ✇ *8,000 lire.* ⊙ *Tues. and Fri.–Sat. 9–7, Wed.–Thurs. 9–2, Sun. 9–1.*

The huge Baroque **palace** of the dukes of Modena now houses a military academy; once the province of the dukes only, it is still off-limits, except to flocks of cadets in elaborate uniforms. Behind the academy are Modena's large **public gardens.** ✉ *Piazza degli Estensi.*

Dining and Lodging

$$$ ✕ **Borso d'Este.** One of the city's most highly regarded restaurants—
★ particularly with the *crema* of the region's monied set—offers some delicious variations on old themes, like ravioli stuffed with game and Parmesan. Other specialties include *gnocchetti* (little dumplings) with melted cheese and radicchio, and a mushroom tart with truffle sauce.

✉ *Piazza degli Estensi 5,* ☎ *059/214114. Reservations essential. AE, DC, MC, V. Closed Sun. and Aug. No lunch Sat.*

$$$ ✕ **Fini.** A Modena institution, elegant, modern Fini is widely held to be the best restaurant the city has to offer. It's Pavarotti's favorite—and you could easily gain a Pavarottiesque figure by making a habit of the excellent local wines, *gran bollito misto,* a groaning board of boiled meats accented in a sauce *verde* (vegetable sauce), and homemade desserts. ✉ *Piazzale San Francesco,* ☎ *059/223314. Reservations essential. Jacket and tie. AE, DC, MC, V. Closed Mon.–Tues., July 20–Aug. 20, and last wk in Dec.*

$$ ✕ **Da Enzo.** This cheerful, well-patronized trattoria is in the old town's pedestrian zone, close by the synagogue and a few steps from Piazza Mazzini. All the classic Modenese specialties are here, including *zampone* (pig's trotters stuffed with minced meat) and *cotechino* (animal bladders stuffed with pork). For starters, try the *tortelloni di ricotta e spinaci* (pasta squares stuffed with ricotta and spinach). ✉ *Via Coltellini 17,* ☎ *059/225177. Weekend reservations essential. AE, DC, MC, V. Closed Mon.*

$$$ ⊡ **Canal Grande.** Once a ducal palace, the Canal Grande offers large, airy, well-equipped rooms with minibars. The hotel's restaurant, La Secchia Rapita, gets rave reviews. The restaurant is closed Wednesday and August. ✉ *Corso Canalgrande 6, 41100,* ☎ *059/217160,* FAX *059/221674. 75 rooms. Restaurant, bar, minibars. AE, DC, MC, V.*

$ ⊡ **La Torre.** Not particularly exciting, La Torre is nonetheless the best hotel choice in this price category, thanks to its location in the center of town just off the Via Emilia. The somewhat stuffy rooms are functional, comfortable, and well equipped. ✉ *Via Cervetta 5, 41100,* ☎ *059/222615,* FAX *059/216316. 26 rooms, 19 with shower. Bar. AE, DC, MC, V.*

Bologna

❺ *38 km (23 mi) southeast of Modena, 106 km (66 mi) north of Florence, 210 km (131 mi) southeast of Milan, 154 km (96 mi) southwest of Venice.*

Through its long history, first as an Etruscan city, then a Roman one, then as an independent city-state in the Middle Ages, Bologna has always been a power in the north of Italy. Through the centuries, the city has acquired a number of nicknames: Bologna the Learned, in honor of its ancient (the oldest in the world) university; Bologna the Turreted, recalling the forest of medieval towers that once rose from the city center (two remarkable examples still exist); and Bologna the Fat, a tribute to its preeminent position in the world of cuisine.

Wars, sackings, rebellions, and aerial bombing do not seem to have made much of an impression on the old center of the city: the narrow cobblestone streets are still there, as are the ancient churches, massive palaces, medieval towers, and famous arcades lining many of the main thoroughfares.

The streets are always bustling with students. The university was founded in the year 1050 and by the 13th century already had more than 10,000 students. It was a center for the teaching of law and theology, and it was ahead of its time in that many of the professors were women. Today the university has one of the most prominent business schools in Italy and has the finest faculty of medicine in the country. Marconi, the inventor of wireless telegraphy, first formulated his groundbreaking theories in the physics labs of the university.

The heart of the city is Piazza Maggiore and the adjacent Piazza del Nettuno. Arranged around these two squares are the imposing Basilica of San Petronio, the huge Palazzo Comunale, the Palazzo del Podestà, the Palazzo di Re Enzo, and the fountain of Neptune—one of the most harmonious groupings of public buildings in the entire country.

6 The **Basilica di San Petronio** was started in the 14th century, and work was still in progress on this vast building some 300 years later. It is still not finished, as you can see: the facade is only partially decorated, lacking most of the marble facing that the architects planned on several hundred years ago. The main doorway was carved by the great Sienese master of the Renaissance, Jacopo della Quercia. Above the center of the door is a Madonna and Child, flanked by Saints Ambrose and Petronius, patrons of the city.

The interior of the basilica is huge and echoing, 432 ft long and 185 ft wide. It is so vast that it's sobering to note that originally the Bolognans had planned an even bigger church (you can still see the columns erected to support the larger church outside the east end) but decided on this "toned-down" version in the interest of economy. The church museum contains models to show how the original church would have looked. The most important artworks in the church are in the left aisle, frescoes by Giovanni di Modena dating from the first years of the 1400s. Also in the left aisle, laid out in the pavement of the church, is a huge sundial, placed there in 1655, showing the time, date, and month. ⊠ *Piazza Maggiore.* ☉ *Basilica summer, daily 7:15–1:30 and 2:30–6:45; winter, daily 7:15–1 and 2:30–6:30. Museo di San Petronio (inside church) Mon., Wed., Fri.–Sun. 10–12:30.*

7 A mélange of styles and buildings, **Palazzo Comunale,** dates from the 13th to 15th centuries. When Bologna was an independent commune, this huge palace was the seat of government, a function it serves today. Over the door is a giant statue of Pope Gregory XIII, Bologna-born and most famous for his reorganization of the calendar—the system in use today.

The Palazzo Comunale's picture gallery, the **Collezioni Comunali d'Arte,** exhibits paintings from the Middle Ages as well as some Renaissance works by Luca Signorelli and Tintoretto. On the same floor, a separate **Giorgio Morandi museum** is dedicated to the 20th-century still-life artist; in addition to his paintings, you'll see a re-creation of his studio and living space. An equally good reason to come is to get a look at the views of the piazza from the upper stories of the palace. ⊠ *Piazza Maggiore (on the right as you face the Basilica di San Petronio).* ☷ *Collezioni Comunali and the Morandi museum 8,000 lire each; both 10,000 lire.* ☉ *Tues.–Sun. 10–6.*

8 The **Palazzo del Podestà,** which faces the Basilica di San Petronio, was erected in 1484, and attached to it is the soaring **Torre dell'Arengo.** The bells in this tower have rung since 1453, whenever the city has celebrated, mourned, or called its citizens to arms. ⊠ *Piazza Nettuno.*

9 The medieval **Palazzo di Re Enzo** is the building in which King Enzo of Sardinia was imprisoned for 23 years until his death in 1272. He had been unwise enough to wage war on Bologna and was captured after the fierce battle of Fossalta in 1249. The palace has other macabre associations: common criminals received the last rites of the church in the tiny chapel in the courtyard before being taken out to be executed in Piazza Maggiore. ⊠ *Piazza Nettuno, next to the Palazzo del Podestà.*

Sculptor Giambologna's elaborate 1566 Baroque **fountain** in Piazza Nettuno has been aptly nicknamed Il Gigante (The Giant). Given Bologna's

Bologna

landlocked position, the choice of subject—the God of the Sea, Neptune, and his attendant dolphins and mermaids, the water spurting jauntily from their breasts—seems rather odd. ⊠ *Piazza Nettuno, next to the Palazzo di Re Enzo.*

The busy, chic Via Rizzoli runs from Piazza Nettuno directly into the medieval section of the city, passing Piazza di Porta Ravegnana. Here are two of Bologna's famous towers: the taller **Torre degli Asinelli** is 320 ft high and leans an alarming 7½ ft out of the perpendicular; the other tower, the **Torre Garisenda,** was shortened for safety in the 1500s. It is now 165 ft high and tilts 10 ft. The towers were built at the same time (1488) and are mentioned by Dante in *The Inferno.* They are the only two that remain of the more than 200 that once graced the city—every family of any importance had a tower as a symbol of its prestige and power. For a fine view of the city climb up the 500 steep stairs of Torre degli Asinelli. ⊠ *Piazza di Porta Ravegnana.* 🎫 *3,000 lire.* ☉ *Summer, daily 9–6; winter, daily 9–5.*

The church of **Santo Stefano** is a remarkable building in that it is actually several churches contained in one building. The oldest, the church of Santi Vitale e Agricola, dates from the 8th century and contains a 14th-century nativity scene much loved by Bologna's children, who come at Christmastime to pay their respects to the baby Jesus. The church of San Sepolcro (12th century) contains the **Courtyard of Pontius Pilate,** so named for the basin in the center of the court that's said to be the basin Pilate washed his hands in after condemning Christ. Also in the building is a **museum** displaying various medieval religious works where you can buy sundry items made by the monks, such as honey, shampoo, and jam. ⊠ *Piazza Santo Stefano.* 🎫 *Free.* ☉ *Daily 9–noon and 3:30–6:30.*

⑫ The church of **San Domenico** contains the tomb of Saint Dominic, who died here in 1221. The tomb of the saint, called the Arca di San Domenico, is in the sixth chapel on the right. Many artists contributed to the decoration, notably Niccolò di Bari, who was so proud of his work here that he changed his name to Niccolò dell'Arca to recall this famous work. The young Michelangelo carved the angel on the right. In the right transept of the church is a tablet marking the last resting place of the hapless King Enzo, whose prison you saw in Piazza Maggiore (☞ Palazzo di Re Enzo, *above*). In the square in front of San Domenico are two curious tombs raised above the ground on pillars, commemorating two famous 14th-century lawyers. ⊠ *Piazza San Domenico, a few blocks south of Via Farini, off Via Garibaldi.* ⊙ *Daily 7–1 and 2–7 (winter 3–7).*

⑬ Inside the church of **San Giacomo Maggiore** is the burial chamber of the Bentivoglio family, the leading family in Bologna in the Middle Ages. The crypt is connected by underground passage to the Teatro Comunale, across the street—a rather odd feature, until you realize that the family palazzo of the Bentivoglio used to stand on that spot. The most notable tomb is that of Antonio Bentivoglio, carved by Jacopo della Quercia in 1435. You can tell his profession—lecturer in law—from the group of students carved on the base, all listening intently to their professor. ⊠ *Piazza Rossini, a few blocks up from Piazza di Porta Ravegnana, off Via Zamboni.* ⊙ *Daily 6–noon and 3:30–6.*

⑭ The collection in Bologna's principal art gallery—also one of the most important in Italy—the **Pinacoteca Nazionale,** contains many works by the immortals of Italian painting, including Raphael's famous *Ecstasy of St. Cecilia*. There is also a beautiful multipaneled painting by Giotto and a Parmigianino *Madonna and Saints*. The centerpieces of the collection, however, are the many rooms devoted to the two most important late 16th-century Bolognese masters, painters Guido Reni and Annibale Carracci. Some of the most interesting paintings, from a historical point of view, are by Giuseppe Crespi, a Bolognese painter of the 18th century who avoided grand religious or historical themes, preferring instead to paint scenes of daily life in his native city. These small canvases give you an excellent idea of the boisterous, earthy life of Old Bologna. ⊠ *Via delle Belle Arti 56,* ☎ *051/243222.* ☞ *8,000 lire.* ⊙ *Tues.–Sat. 9–2, Sun. 9–1.*

⑮ Take a stroll through the adjoining streets in the district of the **university,** a jumble of buildings, some dating as far back as the 15th century and most to the 17th and 18th centuries. This neighborhood, like neighborhoods in most college towns, has lots of bookshops, coffee shops, and cheap snack bars and restaurants. None of them are particularly distinguished, but they all give a good idea of student life in the city. Political slogans and sentiments are scrawled on walls all around the university and tend, for the most part, to be ferociously leftist.

Dining and Lodging

$$$$ ✕ **I Carracci.** For those who feel a tasty meal can taste even better if the decor is delicious, this restaurant—Bologna's most *bellissimo*—is a must. Frescoed with scenes of the four seasons, the place is named after the family of 17th-century artists who made Europe go for Baroque. Critics are hoping the kitchen will come up to par with the decor. ⊠ *Grand Hotel Baglioni, Via dell'Indipendenza 8 (hotel guests) or Via Manzoni 2,* ☎ *051/225445. Reservations essential. AE, DC, MC, V.*

$$$ ✕ **Al Pappagallo.** Almost directly beneath Bologna's famous Asinelli and Garisenda towers, the Pappagallo was once synonymous with gourmet eating. Though competition has shifted the spotlight from it

in recent years, it retains enough of its reputation and quality cuisine to merit at least one feast, served in a stylish, semiformal atmosphere. Try the first-course specialty, lasagna *del Pappagallo*, made with veal, sirloin of pork, and wood mushrooms. For a main course, go for the *filetto di tacchino* (turkey stuffed with truffles, ham, and Parmesan). ✉ *Piazza della Mercanzia 3/c*, ☎ *051/232807. Reservations essential. AE, DC, MC, V. Closed Sun.*

$$$
★ ✕ **Notai.** Bologna's best—so say many residents of the gastronomic capital of Italy. You'll hear the Angelus ring from the cathedral at this spot, just off beautiful Piazza Maggiore. The building is 14th-century, the decor is 19th-century, and the food can be sublime. For a true *boccadivino*—heavenly mouthful, that is—try the *piccoli* (small) chateaubriand in béarnaise sauce. ✉ *Via de' Pignattari 1*, ☎ *051/228694. Reservations essential. AE, DC, MC, V. Closed Sun.*

$$$ ✕ **Rosteria Luciano.** A changing list of daily specials at this art-deco style restaurant augments what is already one of Bologna's most varied menus. Some of the best offerings are grilled lamb and beef, breast of duck, and excellent guinea fowl. Among the desserts, the *ricottina al forno* (charcoal-flavored oven-baked ricotta) is worth the splurge. ✉ *Via Nazario Sauro 19*, ☎ *051/231249. Reservations essential. AE, DC, MC, V. Closed Wed., Aug., Dec. 23–Jan. 2.*

$$ ✕ **Bertino.** Happy, gregarious diners don't seem to mind the crammed quarters in the large, bustling room here. Maybe it is because popularity has not spoiled this traditional neighborhood trattoria, with simple, cared-for dishes. Tried-and-true highlights are the *paglia e fieno* (yellow and green pasta) with sausage, or choose from the steaming tray of bollito misto. ✉ *Via delle Lame 55*, ☎ *051/522230. AE, DC, MC, V. Closed Sun. and Aug. No dinner Mon.*

$$ ✕ **Da Carlo.** Dining on the medieval terrace in summer is a treat in this attractive restaurant, so be sure to reserve a table outside. The delicate game dishes, such as braised pigeon with artichokes, are favorites. ✉ *Via Marchesana 6*, ☎ *051/233227. Reservations essential. AE, DC, MC, V. Closed Sun., Tues., Jan. 1–22, Aug. 23–Sept. 3.*

$$ ✕ **Da Cesari.** Wine made by the owner's family, famous Bolognese dishes such as *gramigna alla salsiccia* (pasta with a sauce of sausage and tomato), and entrées such as duck with rosemary make this one of the best restaurants in Bologna in its price category. ✉ *Via de Carbonesi 8*, ☎ *051/237710. Reservations essential. AE, DC, MC, V. Closed Sun. and Aug.*

$$ ✕ **Osteria Du Madon.** American graduate students from the nearby Johns Hopkins institute and members of Bologna's championship basketball team are regulars at this informal restaurant under the porticoes not far from the city's famous towers. Among the specialties on a menu of classic local dishes are freshly made pastas and gnocchi, and lamb chops glazed with balsamic vinegar. ✉ *Via San Vitale 75*, ☎ *051/226221. AE, DC, MC, V. Closed Sun. and 1st 3 wks in Aug. No lunch Sat.*

$$ ✕ **Rostaria Antico Brunetti.** Housed in a Romanesque tower steps away from Piazza Maggiore, this wood-paneled restaurant was founded in 1873 and is known as Bologna's oldest. Specialties here range from "Mama's tortellini" to veal smothered in white-wine sauce, but most diners opt for the pizzas or fabulous pastas with seafood sauces. Dining is on two floors, but even then the restaurant fills quickly. ✉ *Via Caduti di Cefalonia 5*, ☎ *051/234441. AE, DC, MC, V. Closed Wed.*

$$ ✕ **Victoria.** It is not unusual for this unpretentious but tastefully decorated trattoria-pizzeria off Via dell'Indipendenza to have lines, so reserve ahead. Even if you can't, however, it's worth the wait. Although most people come for the wide choice of cheap pizzas, the pasta, fish, and meat dishes are also good bets. Draft or bottled beer and wine are available. Try for a place in the room with the lovely 17th-century

wooden ceiling. ⊠ *Via Augusto Righi 9c,* ☎ *051/233548. Reservations essential. AE, DC, MC, V. Closed Thurs.*

$$$$ 🏨 **Corona d'Oro.** Once a medieval printing house, this hotel has been
★ in business for more than a century. The public space is a delight, with a lyrical art-nouveau decor, an atrium, and enough flowers for a wedding. Guest rooms are grand and the prevailing tone is opulent if rather formal. ⊠ *Via Oberdan 12, 40126,* ☎ *051/236456,* FAX *051/262679. 35 rooms. Bar, meeting room. AE, DC, MC, V. Closed 2 wks in Aug.*

$$$$ 🏨 **Grand Hotel Baglioni.** Sixteenth-century frescoes by the Bolognese
★ Carracci brothers are rarely seen outside a museum or church, but here they provide the stunning backdrop for the public rooms and restaurant (☞ I Carracci, *above*) of one of Italy's most glamorous hotels. The rooms are warm and enchanting, and the staff is extremely attentive. It's just a few steps from the central Piazza Maggiore. ⊠ *Via dell'Indipendenza 8, 40121,* ☎ *051/225445,* FAX *051/234840. 131 rooms. Bar, meeting rooms, free parking. AE, DC, MC, V.*

$$$ 🏨 **Dei Commercianti.** Right next to San Petronio, Dei Commercianti provides comfort in a good area at reasonable prices. Some of the rooms can be dim and rather cramped: the best are on the top floor, which have a view, some with a terrace. ⊠ *Via dei Pignattari 11, 40124,* ☎ *051/233052,* FAX *051/224733. 35 rooms. Bar. AE, DC, MC, V.*

$$$ 🏨 **Orologio.** Under the same management as the Dei Commercianti (☞ *above*), the Orologio is in a quiet pedestrian zone off Piazza Grande and has been recently renovated. Top-floor rooms have good views of Bologna's skyline. ⊠ *Via IV Novembre 10, 40123,* ☎ *051/231253,* FAX *051/260552. 32 rooms. Bar. AE, DC, MC, V.*

$$ 🏨 **Accademia.** This small hotel is right in the middle of the university quarter, a comfortable base for exploring the area. The rooms are adequate, the staff friendly. ⊠ *Via delle Belle Arti 6, 40126,* ☎ *051/232318,* FAX *051/263590. 28 rooms, 24 with shower. No credit cards. Closed 10 days in Aug.*

$$ 🏨 **San Vitale.** Modern furnishings and a garden distinguish this modest hostelry, which is a five-minute walk from the center of town. The service is courteous, and rooms are clean and bright. Rates come into the bottom end of the price category. ⊠ *Via San Vitale 94, 40125,* ☎ *051/225966,* FAX *051/239396. 17 rooms. No credit cards.*

Nightlife and the Arts

The city hosts a wide selection of orchestral and chamber music concerts as well as an acclaimed opera season. The 18th-century **Teatro Comunale** (⊠ Largo Respighi 1, ☎ 051/529999) presents concerts by Italian and international orchestras throughout the year, but opera dominates the theater's winter season. All events sell out quickly, so be sure to reserve seats well in advance. Operetta and musicals abound during the winter season at the modern **Teatro Sala Europa** (⊠ Piazza Costituzione, ☎ 051/372540).

A wide range of theatrical productions are staged throughout the winter at the **Teatro Duse** (⊠ Via Cartoleria 42, ☎ 051/231836). Theater and ballet can be enjoyed at the historic **Arena del Sole** (⊠ Via Indipendenza 44, ☎ 051/270790). **Teatro delle Moline** (⊠ Via delle Moline 1, ☎ 051/235288) is just one of the many small venues where contemporary drama, dance, and comedy productions are performed. Children learning Italian may enjoy the kids' productions at the **Teatro Testoni** (⊠ Via Matteotti 16, ☎ 051/377968). Check concert schedules for the **Sala Bossi** (⊠ Piazza Rossini 2, ☎ 051/221483) and the **Sala Mozart** in the Accademia Filarmonica, the principal music school of the city (⊠ Via Guerazzi 13, ☎ 051/222997).

Outdoor Activities and Sports

SWIMMING

There is a public indoor swimming pool (⊠ Via Costa 174, ☎ 051/6152520) open May–September, daily 9:30–7, and October–April, weekdays noon–3, Saturday 10:30–1, and Sunday 9–12:30.

Dozza

16 *31 km (19 mi) southeast of Bologna, 15 km (9 mi) west of Imola.*

As you head southeast out of Bologna, the first port of call is the little hamlet of Dozza, just off the Via Emilia (S9). It is a small village on a hill crowned with a splendid restored medieval castle. Artists from all over Italy flock to the town in September of odd years to take part in the mural competition—it seems that every square foot of the town has been painted with colorful scenes done with varying degrees of skill. The **castle** is home to the **Enoteca Regionale,** the wine "library" for the region. Here you can sample the different vintages that come from the surrounding countryside, particularly Dozza's own Albana, a white wine that comes dry or sweet. ☎ *0542/678089.* ⚏ *5,000 lire.* ۩ *Apr.–Sept., Tues.–Sat. 10–noon and 3–6, Sun. 10–noon and 3–7; Oct.–Mar., Tues.–Sat. 10–noon and 2–5, Sun. 10–noon and 2–6.*

Dining

$$$$ ✕ **San Domenico.** Many gourmands venture out from Bologna—about
★ 33 km (20 mi) away—and even farther afield to this prize restaurant in the town of Imola. Ever since leading food critics discovered San Domenico, it has been counted among the top 10 Italian restaurants—and some say numero uno. The hefty prices are well spent among its tented ceilings, leather banquettes, and Bucellattesque silver. Specialties of the house are the homemade pâté with white truffles, a delicious breast of duck in a sauce of black olives, and hand-stuffed—and, yes, therefore, more expensive—tortellini. Make reservations well in advance. ⊠ *Imola, Via Sacchi 1,* ☎ *054/229000. Reservations essential. AE, DC, MC, V. Closed Sun., Mon. June–Aug. 20.*

Faenza

17 *49 km (30 mi) southeast of Bologna, 23 km (14 mi) southeast of Dozza, 14 km (9 mi) northwest of Forlì.*

Renowned faience pottery has been produced in Faenza, on the Via Emilia, since the 12th century. In the central **Piazza del Popolo** are dozens of shops selling the native wares. Faenza is unsurprisingly home to the **Museo delle Ceramiche** (Museum of Ceramics), one of the largest of its kind in the world, covering the potter's art in all phases of history and in all parts of the world. ⊠ *Viale Baccarini 19.* ⚏ *8,000 lire.* ۩ *Apr.–Oct., Tues.–Sat. 9–7, Sun. 9:30–1; Nov.–Mar., Tues.–Fri. 9–1:30, Sat. 9–1:30 and 3–6, Sun. 9:30–1. Closed national holidays.*

OFF THE   **PREDAPPIO –** From Faenza continue on S9 to the town of Forlì, 14 km
BEATEN PATH   (9 mi) away, and turn off onto the rural Route 9ter (in Italian travel parlance, the abbreviation "ter" means a third, variant highway). This leads you through hilly country to the small town of Predappio, the birthplace of Benito Mussolini and Il Duce's final resting place. The cemetery on the outskirts of town contains the crypt of the Mussolini family, with the former dictator himself in the place of honor. A spotlighted bust glowers at visitors, and glass cases contain some of his decorations and medals. It is a chilling place and has become the object of pilgrimage for followers of fascism (young and old), who write repugnant political slogans in the visitors' book. ⊠ *Cimitero Municipale.* ۩ *Daily 8 AM–sunset.*

SAVIGNANO – On S9 beyond Forlì, you pass through the modern towns of Forlimpopoli, Cesena, and Savignano. At this last town, there is a reminder that no matter how new the towns might look, you are still traveling in a place of great history—just outside the town is a small stream, the Rubicone. Cross it and you, too, have crossed the Rubicon, the river made famous by Julius Caesar when, in 49 BC, he defied the Senate of Rome by bringing his army across the river and plunging the country into civil war.

RIMINI, RAVENNA, AND FERRARA
Byzantine Splendors and Simple Pleasures

From Savignano, the road leads on to the next three important destinations: Rimini, Ravenna, and Ferrara.

Rimini

18 *121 km (76 mi) southeast of Bologna, 54 km (34 mi) southeast of Forlì, 52 km (32½ mi) southeast of Ravenna.*

Rimini is the principal summer resort on the Adriatic Coast and one of the most popular holiday destinations in Italy. Every summer, beginning in June, the city is flooded with vacationers, not just from Italy but from France, Austria, Germany, Scandinavia, and Great Britain, as well. The city is given over almost exclusively to tourism, with hundreds of hotels, grand and modest, and restaurants catering to virtually every national palate: you are just as likely to find a *bierkeller* (beer cellar) or an English tea shop as you are an Italian restaurant. The waterfront is lined with beach clubs that rent a patch of sand, a deck chair, and an umbrella by the day, week, month, or the entire season. Hotels along the beachfront have staked out their own private turf, so the chance of swimming (or even seeing the sea close up) without paying for the privilege is slim.

In the off-season, Rimini, in common with resorts the world over, is a ghost town. Some hotels and restaurants are open, but the majority are closed tight, hibernating until the return of the spendthrifty tourists. Summers are so crowded here that it is most unwise to go to Rimini without confirmed hotel reservations. For those who like sun by day, disco by night, and hordes of frolicking teenagers, Rimini is the town for you; those who prefer more sedate vacations are advised to stay away.

The **new town** has just about swallowed the **old town**, but there are signs here and there that tell of Rimini's long and turbulent history. Rimini stands at the junction of two great Roman consular roads: the Via Aemilia, or Emilia as it is known now, and the Via Flaminia. In addition, in Roman times, it was an important port, making it a strategic and commercial center. From the 13th century onward, the city was controlled by the Malatesta family, an unpredictable group capable of grand gestures and savage deeds. The famous lovers in Dante's *Inferno*, Paolo and Francesca, were Malatestas. Paolo was the brother of Gianciotto Malatesta; Francesca, Gianciotto's wife. Gianciotto murdered them both for having betrayed him. Sigismondo Malatesta, lord of the city in the middle of the 15th century, was considered a learned man of great wit and culture. He also banished his first wife, strangled his second, and poisoned his third. He lived with his beautiful mistress, Isotta, until her death. He was so grief-stricken that he raised a mag-

★ nificent monument in her honor, the **Tempio Malatestiano** (⊠ Via IV Novembre) It is the principal sight in the town.

Despite the irregular—from the church's point of view—nature of Sigismondo's relationship with Isotta, Sigismondo's memorial to his great love is today the **cathedral** of Rimini. The building was in fact originally a Franciscan church before Sigismondo took it over to make it into a monument to his beloved. The facade is a beautiful piece of Renaissance architecture by Leon Battista Alberti. It is in the shape of a Roman triumphal arch and is considered to be one of Alberti's masterpieces.

The interior is light and spacious and contains the tombs of both the lovers. The intertwined *I*, for Isotta, and *S*, for Sigismondo, are dotted about everywhere and look rather like "$" signs. The carvings of elephants and roses recall the coat of arms of the Malatesta family. Sigismondo's tomb, on the right of the entrance door, is some distance from Isotta's in the second chapel. (Her tomb is on the left wall of the chapel; the original inscription in marble had a pagan twist and was covered with another in bronze.) On the right, in what is now the Tempio's book and gift shop, is a wonderful but badly damaged fresco by Piero della Francesca showing Sigismondo paying homage to his patron saint. When the shop is closed, one of the cathedral's staff will be glad to unlock the room containing the fresco. Also on the right side of the church, look out for a crucifix attributed to Giotto, formerly over the main altar of the church. ⊠ *Via Quattro Novembre.* ☉ *Daily 7–noon and 3:30–7.*

Rimini's oldest monument is the **Arco d'Augusto** (Arch of Augustus), now stranded in the middle of a square just inside the city ramparts. It was erected in 27 BC, making it the oldest Roman arch in existence, and it marks the meeting of the Via Aemilia and the Via Flaminia. To reach the Arch of Augustus from the Tempio Malatestiano, walk up Via Quattro Novembre to Piazza Tre Martiri (where, legend says, the mule carrying Saint Anthony suddenly stopped and knelt in honor of the Holy Sacrament that was being carried past at the time) and turn left onto Corso d'Augusto. The arch lies at the end of the street. ⊠ *Largo Giulio Cesare.*

Dining and Lodging

$$ ✕ **Picnic.** This restaurant, near Tempio Malatestiano, is a good lunchtime spot to savor some simple, well-cooked dishes in a modern setting. You can order—indoors or in a leafy garden—a selection from a daily-changing menu that might include such choices as *pappardelle al sugo di carciofi* (pasta with artichoke sauce), *faraona ripiena alla castagne* (guinea hen with chestnut stuffing), or just have a pizza (evenings only). ⊠ *Via Tempio Malatestiano 30,* ☏ *0541/21916. MC, V. Closed Mon.*

$$ ✕ **Zio.** Nothing but seafood is served here, and all of it is good value
★ for the money. Two small rooms are unpretentiously furnished, one with antiques. Recommended treats are the *brodetto dell'Adriatica* (deliciously tangy shellfish broth), tortellini *al salmone* (in a salmon sauce), and simple grilled sole. ⊠ *Vicolo Santa Chiara 16,* ☏ *0541/786160. Reservations essential weekends and July–Aug. AE, DC, MC, V. Closed Wed. and mid-July–mid-Aug.*

$ ✕ **Rock Island.** Formerly a seafood restaurant, now a busy pub and *panineria* (sandwich bar), the Rock Island is at the end of a pier right on the sea. You can drink and snack here and take part in Rimini's raucous nightlife. Steamy, loud, and full of young people, it's not for the fainthearted. ⊠ *Porto Canale,* ☏ *0541/50178. Reservations not accepted. No credit cards. Closed weekdays in winter.*

$$$$ 🏨 **Grand Hotel.** Fellini paid homage to this grande dame of a hotel in
★   his *Amarcord*. The Grand is a turn-of-the-century extravaganza set in
a quiet park, within easy reach of its own private beach. The rooms
are large and airy, air-conditioned, and equipped with color TVs. ✉
Via Ramusio 1, 47037, ☎ *0541/56000,* FAX *0541/56866. 113 rooms,
6 suites. 2 restaurants, 2 bars, minibars, 2 pools, beauty salon, sauna,
4 tennis courts, private beach, nightclub. AE, DC, MC, V.*

$$$ 🏨 **Club House Hotel.** Ultramodern and right on the sea, the Club
House is a good hotel for summer vacations and is one of the few open
during the off-season (when rates are much lower). All rooms have bal-
conies and color TVs. ✉ *Viale Vespucci 52, 47037,* ☎ *0541/391460,*
FAX *0541/391442. 28 rooms. Restaurant, bar, minibars, private beach.
AE, DC, MC, V.*

$ 🏨 **Annarita.** Set back on a residential road leading off the main Viale
Vespucci, this is small but comfortable, with a loyal clientele (avail-
ability may consequently be limited). Facilities are rudimentary, rooms
are basic (though all have TVs), but the main benefits here are its close-
ness to the beach promenade and the friendly price. ✉ *Viale Misurata
24, 47037,* ☎ *0541/391044. 14 rooms. Restaurant, bar. No credit cards.*

En Route   There are two routes from Rimini to Ravenna. The coast road, S16,
hugs the shoreline as far as Cervia before edging inland. Although its
distance, 52 km (31 mi), is not great, the scenic route is slower by na-
ture. The coast north of Rimini is lined with dozens of small resort towns,
only one having any charm, the seaport of Cesenatico; the others are
mini-Riminis, and during summer the narrow road is hopelessly clogged
with traffic. A faster route is to head inland on A14 and then turn off
onto the inland S71, which leads directly into Ravenna; the distance
is 64 km (39 mi).

Ravenna

⑲   *76 km (47½ mi) east of Bologna, 52 km (32½ mi) northwest of Rim-
ini, 74 km (46 mi) southeast of Ferrara.*

Ravenna is a stately old city, still living on the dreams of its faded glory.
The high point in Ravenna's long history was 1,500 years ago, when
the city became the capital of the Roman Empire, but by then the em-
pire was in its period of irreversible decline. The city was taken by the
barbarian Ostrogoths in the 5th century; then, in the 6th, it was con-
quered by the Byzantines, who ruled the city from Constantinople.

Because Ravenna spent much of its history looking to the East, its
greatest art treasures show much Byzantine influence: above all, Ravenna
is a city of mosaics, the finest in Western art. A single 9,000-lire ticket
will admit you to six of Ravenna's most important monuments: the Tomb
of Galla Placidia, the church of San Vitale, the Neonian baptistery, and
the church of Sant'Apollinare Nuovo (☞ *below*), as well as the church
of Spirito Santo and the Museo Arcivescovile e Cappella Sant'Andrea.

★   The **Tomb of Galla Placidia** and the church of **San Vitale** have the best-
known, and most elaborate, mosaics in the city. The little tomb and
the great church stand side by side, but the tomb predates the church
by at least a hundred years. Galla Placidia was the sister of the last em-
peror of Rome, Honorius, the man who moved the imperial capital to
Ravenna in AD 402. She is said to have been beautiful and strong-willed,
taking an active part in the governing of the crumbling empire. She
was also one of the most active Christians of her day, endowing
churches and supporting priests and their congregations throughout
the realm. This tomb, built for her in the mid-5th century, is her mon-
ument.

Outside, the tomb is a rather uninspired building of red brick; within, however, the color and clarity of the mosaics that decorate the ceiling are startling. The deep blue and gold catch the light and seem to glitter. The central dome has symbols of Christ and the evangelists, and over the door is a depiction of the Good Shepherd. The Apostles, in groups of two (there are only eight of them, for some reason), ring the inner part of the dome. Notice the small doves at their feet, drinking from the water of faith. In the tiny transepts are some delightful pairs of deer (which represent souls), drinking from the fountain of resurrection. There are three sarcophagi in the tomb, and, it is thought, not one contains the remains of Galla Placidia. She died in Rome in AD 450, and there is no record of her body having been transported back to the place where she wished to lie.

The mosaics of the Galla Placidia tomb are simple works that have not yet received the full impact of Byzantine influence. Quite the opposite is the case of the mosaics in the church of San Vitale, next door. The church was built in AD 547, after the Byzantines conquered the city, and it is decorated in an exclusively Byzantine style. In the area behind the altar are the most famous works in the church. These show accurate portraits of the emperor of the East, Justinian, attended by his court, and the bishop of Ravenna, Maximian. Facing him, across the chancel, is the emperor's wife, Theodora, with her entourage, holding a chalice containing the communion wine. From the elaborate headdresses and heavy cloaks of the emperor and empress, you can get a marvelous sense of the grandeur of the imperial court.

On the ceiling above the royal couple, ruling over all, is a mosaic of Christ the King. With him is the saint for whom the church is named, Vitale, and the founder of the church, Bishop Ecclesio, who holds a model of the building. ⊠ *Via San Vitale off Via Salara, near Piazza del Popolo.* ☎ *6,000 lire for both, 5,000 lire for adjacent Museo Nazionale.* ☉ *Summer, daily 9–5:30; winter, daily 9–4:30.*

Next to the Church of San Vitale, the **Museo Nazionale** of Ravenna contains artifacts of ancient Rome, Byzantine fabrics and carvings, and other pieces of early Christian art. The collection is housed in a former monastery but is well displayed and artfully lit. ⊠ *Via Fiandrini.* ☎ *8,000 lire.* ☉ *Tues.–Sun. 8:30–7:30.*

Next door to Ravenna's 18th-century cathedral, the **Neonian baptistery** is one of the town's most important mosaic sites. In keeping with the purpose of the building, the great mosaic in the dome shows the baptism of Christ, and beneath that scene are the apostles. The lowest band of mosaics contains Christian symbols, the Throne of God and the Cross. ⊠ *Via Battistero.* ☎ *5,000 lire (includes Museo Arcivescovile and Cappella Sant'Andrea).* ☉ *Summer, daily 9–5:30; winter, daily 9:30–4:30.*

The **tomb of Dante** is in a small neoclassical building next door to the large church of St. Francis. Exiled from his native Florence, the great poet, author of *The Divine Comedy,* died here in 1321. The Florentines have been trying to reclaim their famous son for hundreds of years, but the Ravennans refuse to give him up, arguing that Florence did not welcome Dante in life, so it doesn't deserve him in death. A small **museum** is on the site. ⊠ *Via Ricci. Tomb:* ☎ *Free.* ☉ *Summer, daily 9–7; winter, daily 9–noon and 2–5. Museum:* ☎ *3,000 lire; free on Sun. and holidays.* ☉ *Daily 9–noon.*

The last great mosaic site in the city proper is the church of **Sant'-Apollinare Nuovo.** Since the left side of the church was reserved for women, it is only fitting that the mosaic decoration on that side is a scene of 22 virgins offering crowns to the Virgin Mary. On the right wall are 26 men carrying the crowns of martyrdom. They are approaching Christ, who is surrounded by angels. The mosaics in Sant'-Apollinare Nuovo date from the early 6th century and are slightly older than the works in San Vitale. ⊠ *Via Roma, at intersection of Via Guaccimanni.* 🎫 *5,000 lire (includes church of Spirito Santo).* ⊙ *Summer, daily 9–7; winter, daily 9:30–4:30.*

OFF THE BEATEN PATH	**SANT'APOLLINARE IN CLASSE** – This church, about 5 km (3 mi) southeast of Ravenna, is landlocked now, but when it was built, it stood in the center of the busy shipping port of Classis. The arch above and the area around the high altar are rich in mosaics. Those on the arch, older than those behind it, are considered superior to the rest. They show Christ in judgment and the 12 lambs of Christianity leaving the cities of Jerusalem and Bethlehem. In the apse is the figure of Sant'Apollinare himself, a bishop of Ravenna, and above him is a magnificent Transfiguration decorated with flowers, trees, and little birds. ⊠ *Classe.* ⊙ *Summer, daily 8:30–noon and 2–6; winter, daily 8:30–noon and 2–5:30.*

Dining and Lodging

$$–$$$ ✕ **Bella Venezia.** A refined classical decor sets the tone in this elegant
★   restaurant. Dishes are carefully prepared and concentrate on local specialties. Try the risotto *Bazzani* (a buttery, cheesy concoction with ham, mushrooms, and peas) and, for the entrée, *bistecca all'ortolana* (veal with a slice of ham and zucchini bathed in a toothsome creamy sauce). A good-value tourist menu is available. ⊠ *Via IV Novembre 16,* ☎ *0544/212746. Reservations essential weekends. AE, DC, MC, V. Closed Sun.*

$ ✕ **Ca' de Ven.** A vaulted wine cellar in the heart of the old city, the Ca' de Ven is a wonderful place for a hearty lunch or dinner. You sit at long tables with the other diners and feast on platters of delicious cold cuts; *piadine* (flat Romagna bread); and cold, heady white wine. If you're here in chilly weather, try the wholesome pasta e fagioli. ⊠ *Via C. Ricci 24,* ☎ *0544/30163. Reservations not accepted. MC, V. Closed Mon.*

$ ✕ **Ristorante Scai.** Roast meat and game are what this restaurant does best, and a changing menu provides diners with pasta stuffed with roe deer, as well as main courses of lamb, veal, guinea fowl, or bollito misto. Many locals just come for the pizzas. ⊠ *Piazza Baracca 22, near church of San Vitale, at end of Via Cavour,* ☎ *0544/212520. Reservations not accepted. AE, DC, MC, V. Closed Mon.*

$$ 🏨 **Hotel Centrale Byron.** In the heart of Ravenna's old town, this is an old-fashioned, well-managed hotel, its rooms spacious and comfortably furnished. Because its location is in a pedestrian zone, tranquillity is assured, though you will have to leave your car in one of the nearby garages. ⊠ *Via IV Novembre 14, 48100,* ☎ *0544/33479,* FAX *0544/34114. 54 rooms. Bar. AE, DC, MC, V. Closed Dec. 20–Jan. 5.*

$ 🏨 **Ravenna.** A functional stopover near the train station but still only a few minutes' walk from the center of town, this modern hotel offers smallish rooms with TVs and telephones, and there are wheelchair facilities. ⊠ *Viale Maroncelli 12, 48100,* ☎ *0544/212204,* FAX *0544/212077. 25 rooms, 16 with shower. Bar. MC, V.*

Ferrara

20   *47 km (29 mi) northeast of Bologna, 74 km (46 mi) northwest of Ravenna along S16.*

Ferrara is a city of turrets and towers, a mighty castle protected by a deep moat, and grandiose historic sites. Although the site has been inhabited since before Christ and was once the possession of Ravenna, the history of Ferrara begins in the 13th century, with the coming of the Este family. From 1259 until 1598 the city was ruled by the dukes of the Este family, and in those 3½ centuries the city was stamped indelibly with their mark.

It was during the Renaissance that the court of the Este came into full flower. In keeping with their time, the dukes could be politically ruthless—brother killed brother, son fought father—but they were avid scholars and enthusiastic patrons of the arts. Duke Niccolò III murdered his wife and her lover but was a man of cultivation. The greatest of all the dukes, Ercole I, tried to poison his nephew, who laid claim to the duchy (and when that didn't work, Ercole I beheaded him), but it is to this pitiless man that Ferrara owes its great beauty. One of the most celebrated names in Italian history, Lucrezia Borgia, married into the Este family—and it seems that her infamous reputation is not at all deserved. She was beloved by the Ferrarese people and was mourned greatly when she died. She is buried in the church of Corpus Domini in the city.

★ Naturally enough, the building that was the seat of Este power dominates the town: it is the massive **Castello Estense,** placed square in the center of the city in Piazza della Repubblica. It is a suitable symbol for the Este family: cold and menacing on the outside, lavishly decorated within. The public rooms are grand, but deep in the bowels of the fortress are chilling dungeons where enemies of the state were held in wretched conditions—a function these quarters served as recently as 1943, when antifascist prisoners were detained there.

The castle was begun in 1385, but work was going on as late as the 16th century. The Sala dei Giochi (the Games Room) is extravagantly decorated with walls painted to show pagan athletic scenes, and the Sala dell'Aurora to show the times of the day. Oddly enough, the one chapel that is on view is not Catholic, but Protestant (one of the few to survive the Counter Reformation), placed here for the use of the Protestant princess Renée of France, who married into the Este family in the 16th century. From the terraces of the castle and from the hanging garden, reserved for the private use of the duchesses, are fine views of the town and surrounding countryside. ⊠ *Piazza Castello.* 🖾 *6,000 lire.* ☉ *Tues.–Sun. 9:30–5:30.*

A few steps from the castle is the magnificent Gothic **Duomo,** with its facade of three tiers of arches and beautiful carvings over the central door. It was begun in 1135 and took more than a hundred years to complete. The interior does not live up to the expectations fostered by the facade. It was completely remodeled in the 17th century, and none of the original decoration remains in place. ⊠ *Corso dei Martiri della Libertà.* ☉ *Mon.–Sat. 7:30–noon and 3–6:30, Sun. 7:30–1 and 4–7:30.*

The treasures of Duomo's old interior are preserved in the **cathedral museum** above the church (entrance inside the church). Here are some of the lifelike carvings taken from one of the doors of the Duomo, dating from the 13th century and showing the months of the year. Also in the museum are a statue of the Madonna by the Sienese master Jacopo della Quercia and two masterpieces by the Ferrarese painter Cosimo Tura, an *Annunciation* and *St. George Slaying the Dragon.* ⊠ *Corso dei Martiri della Libertà.* 🖾 *Free, but donation appreciated.* ☉

Summer, Mon.–Sat. 10–noon and 3:30–6; winter, Mon.–Sat. 10–noon and 4–6.

The area behind the Duomo, the southern part of the city stretching between the Corso della Giovecca and the ramparts of the city above the river, is the oldest and most characteristic part of Ferrara. In this part of the old town various members of the Este family built themselves pleasure palaces, the most famous of which is the **Palazzo Schifanoia** (*schifanoia* means carefree, or literally, "fleeing boredom"). Begun in the 14th century, the palace was remodeled in 1466 and is the first Renaissance palazzo in the city. The interior is lavishly decorated, particularly the **Salone dei Mesi,** with an extravagant series of frescoes showing the months of the year. The recently opened **Sala degli Stucchi** boasts a beautifully carved wooden ceiling from 1467, by Domenico di Paris, and an array of stuccos. The palazzo now houses the **Museo Civico** (City Museum), with its collection of coins, statuary, and paintings. ⊠ *Via Scandiana 23.* ▣ *6,000 lire; free 2nd Sun. of each month.* ⊘ *Daily 9–7.*

The grand but unfinished courtyard is the most interesting part of the luxurious **Palazzo di Ludovico il Moro,** a magnificent 15th-century palace built for Ludovico Sforza, husband of Beatrice d'Este. It also houses the region's **Museo Archeologico,** a repository of the relics of early man, the Etruscans, and Romans, found in the country surrounding the city. Unfortunately, the museum is closed indefinitely. ⊠ *Near the Palazzo Schifanoia, on Via XX Settembre.*

The courtyard of the peaceful palace called the **Palazzo del Paradiso** contains the tomb of the great writer Ariosto, author of the most popular work of literature of the Renaissance, the poem "Orlando Furioso." The building now houses the **city library.** ⊠ *Via Scienze.* ▣ *Free.* ⊘ *Weekdays 9–7:30, Sat. 9–1.*

The Estes were patrons of the poet Ariosto, and he passed a good deal of his life in Ferrara. The interior of **Ariosto's house** has been converted into an office building and is not open to the public. ⊠ *Via Ariosto 67.*

One of the best-preserved of the Renaissance palaces scattered along Ferrara's old streets is the charming **Casa Romei.** Downstairs there are rooms with 15th-century frescoes and several sculptures collected from churches that have been destroyed. The house lies not far from the **Palazzo del Paradiso,** in the area behind Ferrara's castello. ⊠ *Via Savonarola 30.* ▣ *4,000 lire.* ⊘ *Weekdays 8:30–2, weekends 8:30–7:30.*

On the busy Corso della Giovecca is the **Palazzina di Marfisa d'Este,** an elegant 16th-century home that belonged to Marfisa d'Este, a great patron of the arts. The house has painted ceilings, fine 16th-century furniture, and a garden containing a grotto and an outdoor theater. ⊠ *Corso della Giovecca 170.* ▣ *3,000 lire; free 2nd Sun. of month.* ⊘ *Summer, daily 9–12:30 and 3–6; winter, daily 9–12:30 and 2–5.*

The **Palazzo dei Diamanti** (Palace of Diamonds) is so called for the 12,600 blocks of diamond-shape stone that stud the facade. The palace was built in the 15th and 16th centuries and today contains an extensive art gallery devoted primarily to the painters of Ferrara. ⊠ *Corso Ercole d'Este 21.* ▣ *8,000 lire.* ⊘ *Tues.–Sat. 9–2, Sun. 9–1.*

Dining and Lodging

$$–$$$ ✕ **La Provvidenza.** One of the best-known restaurants in Ferrara,
★ Provvidenza is a pleasant country-style inn with a lovely garden for summertime dining alfresco. The local specialties—fish grilled over charcoal (Thursday and Friday) and the bollito misto (weekends in winter)—are the best. ⊠ *Corso Ercole d'Este 92,* ☎ *0532/205187.*

Reservations essential. AE, DC, MC, V. Closed Mon. and 10 days in mid-Aug.

$–$$ ✕ **Le Grazie.** In an atmospheric part of the old town, down a long cobbled street, this restaurant is a leading choice of pasta lovers. Try the tagliatelle *con cuori di carciofo e noci* (with artichoke hearts and nuts). Other dishes are local, as is the wine list. ⊠ *Via Vignatagliata 61,* ☎ *0532/761052. Reservations essential. MC, V. Closed Tues.*

$$$$ ⊡ **Duchessa Isabella.** On a quiet street near Piazza Ariostea, this converted 16th-century mansion is the place for those who relish period atmosphere—from the painted wooden ceiling in the elegant dining room to the sumptuously draped and individually named bedrooms and suites. Some may find the formality wearying and the tone somewhat bogus; others will find a stay here marvelous. ⊠ *Via Palestro 70, 44100,* ☎ *0532/202121,* ƒ*AX 0532/202638. 28 rooms. Restaurant, bar, meeting rooms. AE, MC, V.*

$$$ ⊡ **Ripagrande.** This hotel is in a meticulously restored 14th-century
★ palace in the heart of old Ferrara. The public rooms are in authentic period style, with antique furnishings, brick walls, and a wide marble staircase. Guest rooms are more modern; the best are on the top floor, with beamed ceilings, terraces, and views over the city. There are also suites on two or three levels, and a recommended restaurant with outdoor dining in summer. ⊠ *Via Ripagrande 21, 44100,* ☎ *0532/765250,* ƒ*AX 0532/764377. 40 rooms. Restaurant, bar, meeting rooms. AE, DC, MC, V.*

$$ ⊡ **Locanda Borgonuovo.** It calls itself a bed-and-breakfast, and its atmosphere is strongly reminiscent of the best kind of B&B, with individually named rooms of a comfortable size, all tastefully furnished with good-quality antiques. What really sets this place apart, though, is the attention to detail and the smiling, courteous attention of the hostess, who also puts on a fine breakfast. The locanda is in a quiet lane in the center of town. ⊠ *Via Cairoli 29, 44100,* ☎ *0532/211100,* ƒ*AX 0532/248000. 4 rooms. AE, MC, V.*

$–$$ ⊡ **San Paolo.** On the edge of the old city, San Paolo is the best inexpensive choice in town. The 10-minute walk from the heart of Ferrara's medieval quarter is effortless in a town so amenable to strolling, and there are some good restaurants in the vicinity. The rooms are modern, with TVs and telephones. ⊠ *Via Baluardi 9, 44100,* ☎ *0532/ 762040,* ƒ*AX 0532/762040. 20 rooms, 15 with shower. No credit cards.*

EMILIA-ROMAGNA A TO Z

Arriving and Departing

By Plane
Bologna is an important business and convention center and is therefore served by air routes that link it with other Italian cities, as well as by direct flights to European capitals. The airport, **Guglielmo Marconi** (⊠ Borgo Panigale, ☎ 051/6479615) is 7 km (4 mi) from town. Bus service connects it with a downtown air terminal at the central train station in Bologna proper.

By Train
Bologna is an important rail hub for the entire northern part of Italy and has frequent, fast train service to Rome, Milan, Florence, and Venice. For information about train departures call 1478/88088 (toll free).

Getting Around

By Bus

Private bus service links all the cities of Emilia-Romagna, with Bologna being the central hub. The *autostazione* (bus terminal) is at the top of Via dell'Indipendenza (✉ In Piazza XX Settembre, ☎ 051/350172, information). City-run bus routes connect major towns with smaller villages and hamlets in the district, but routes are roundabout, and schedules vary from place to place.

By Car

The Via Emilia (S9) runs through the heart of the region. It is a straight, low-lying modern road, the length of which can be traveled in a few hours. Ferrara and Ravenna are joined to it by good modern highways.

By Train

The railway follows the Via Emilia (S9), and all the cities covered can be reached by train.

Contacts and Resources

Emergencies

Police (☎ 112). **Ambulance** (☎ 113). **Doctors and Dentists** (☎ 113). **Late-Night Pharmacies** (☎ 051/192 information).

Travel Agencies

Bologna Marconi Tours (✉ Via Marconi 47, ☎ 051/235783). **Rimini** Urbinati (✉ Viale Vespucci 127, ☎ 0541/391660 or 390720).

Visitor Information

Bologna (✉ Gugliemo Marconi airport, ☎ 051/6472036; ✉ train station, ☎ 051/246541; ✉ Piazza Maggiore 6, ☎ 051/239660). **Ferrara** (✉ Corso Giovecca 21, ☎ 0532/209370). **Modena** (✉ Piazza Grande 17, ☎ 059/206660). **Parma** (✉ Via Melloni 16, ☎ 0521/234735). **Piacenza** (✉ Piazzetta Mercanti 7, ☎ 0523/329324). **Ravenna** (✉ Via Salara 8, ☎ 0544/35404). **Rimini** (✉ Via Dante 86, in front of the train station, ☎ 0541/51331 or 0541/51480; ✉ Piazzale Fellini 3, waterfront, ☎ 0541/56902).

12 Umbria and the Marches

Perugia, Assisi, Urbino, Spoleto, and Orvieto

Legends linger in this mystical, ethereal birthplace of the saints, a region where medieval enclaves wear their ancient histories lightly. Here, you'll find Gothic treasures—Giotto's frescoes at Assisi's Basilica di San Francesco and Orvieto's awe-inspiring cathedral— while more urbane pleasures await at Spoleto's Festival dei Due Mondi. To the east lies the timeless city of Urbino. A visit there reveals more about the artistic energy of the Renaissance than dozens of history books.

Updated by
Robert
Andrews

BIRTHPLACE OF SAINTS AND CONDOTTIERI, Umbria has remained true to its name: "land of shadows." The hills, olive groves, and terraced vineyards of this mystic province are often wrapped in a bluish haze that gives its landscape an ethereal painted look—a landscape often recognized in the frescoes of its celebrated local artists, even when they were decorating churches far from their native soil. Blessed with steep, austere hills, deep valleys, and fast-flowing rivers, the region—roughly halfway between Florence and Rome—has not yet been swamped by tourism and has escaped the unplanned industrial expansion that afflicts much of central Italy. No town in Umbria boasts the extravagant wealth of art and architecture of Florence, Rome, or Venice, but this works in your favor. Cities can be experienced whole, rather than as a series of museums and churches, forced marches through 2,000 years of Western culture; in Umbria the visitor comes to know the towns as people live in them today.

This is not to suggest that the cultural cupboard is bare—far from it. Perugia, the capital of the region, and Assisi, Umbria's most famous city, are rich in art and architecture, as are Orvieto, Todi, and Spoleto. Virtually every small town in the region has a castle, church, or museum worth a stop.

The earliest inhabitants of Umbria, the Umbri, were thought by the Romans to be the most ancient inhabitants of Italy. Little is known about them, since with the coming of Etruscan culture, the tribe fled into the mountains in the eastern portion of the region. The Etruscans, who founded some of the great cities of Umbria, were in turn supplanted by the Romans. Unlike Tuscany and other regions of central Italy, Umbria had few powerful medieval families to exert control over the cities in the Middle Ages—its proximity to Rome ensured that Umbria would always be more or less under papal domination.

The relative political stability of the region did not mean that Umbria was left in peace. Located in the center of the country, it has for much of its history been a battlefield where armies from north and south clashed. Hannibal destroyed a Roman army on the shores of Lake Trasimeno, and the full and bloody course of the interminable Guelph-Ghibelline conflict of the Middle Ages was played out in Umbria. Dante considered it the most violent place in Italy. Trophies of war still decorate the facade of the Palazzo dei Priori in Perugia, and the little town of Gubbio continues a warlike rivalry begun in the Middle Ages—every year it challenges the Tuscan town of Sansepolcro to a crossbow tournament. Today, of course, the bowmen shoot at targets, but neither side has forgotten that 500 years ago its ancestors shot at each other.

In spite of—or perhaps because of—this bloodshed, Umbria has produced more than its share of Christian saints. The most famous is Saint Francis, the decidedly unmartial saint whose life shaped the Church and the history of his time. His great shrine at Assisi is visited by hundreds of thousands of pilgrims each year. Saint Clare, his devoted follower, was Umbria-born, as were Saint Benedict, Saint Rita of Cascia, and, ironically, the shadowy patron saint of lovers, Saint Valentine.

East of Umbria, the Marches—or Le Marche, in Italian—stretch between the hills of the southern Apennines down to the Adriatic sea. It is a scenic region of mountains and valleys, with great turreted castles standing on high peaks defending passes and roads—silent testament to the region's warlike past. The Marches have passed through numerous hands. First the Romans supplanted the native civilizations; then

Charlemagne supplanted the Romans (and gave the region its name—
it was divided into "marks," or provinces, under the rule of the Holy
Roman Emperor); then began the seemingly never-ending struggle between popes and local lords. Cesare Borgia succeeded in wresting control of the Marches from the local suzerains, annexing the region to
the papacy of his father, Alexander VI.

Despite all this martial tussling, it was in the lonely mountain town of
Urbino that the Renaissance came to its fullest flower; that small town
became a haven of culture and learning that rivaled the greater, richer,
and more powerful city of Florence, and even Rome itself.

Pleasures and Pastimes

Dining

Umbria is mountainous, and the cuisine of the region is typical of mountain people everywhere. The food is hearty and straightforward, with
a stick-to-the-ribs quality that sees hard-working farmers and artisans
through a long day's work and helps them make the steep climb home
at night. Italians are generally thought not to eat much meat, but this
is untrue of Italy in general and of Umbria in particular. Novelist Anthony Burgess once observed that a beefsteak in Italy is never "*una bistecca*" but always "*una bella bistecca*"—a beautiful steak—and a
simple steak in Umbria is almost always *bella*.

The region has made several important contributions to Italian cuisine.
Particularly prized are black truffles from the area around Spoleto (signs
warning against unlicensed truffle hunting are posted at the base of
the grand Ponte delle Torri) and from the hills around the tiny town
of Norcia. Norcia, in fact, exports truffles to France and hosts a truffle festival every November. Many regional dishes are given a shaving
of truffle before serving; unless the truffle is a really good one, however, its subtle taste may not come through. The local pasta specialty—
thick, handmade spaghetti called *ciriole* or *strangozzi*—is good *al
tartufo*, with a dressing of excellent local olive oil and truffles.

In addition, Norcia's pork products—especially sausages, salami, and
arista (bone marrow of pig)—are so famous that pork butchers throughout Italy are called *norcini*, no matter where they hail from, and pork
butcher shops are called *norcinerie*.

In the Marches, fish in various forms is the thing to look for. One of
the characteristic dishes in Ancona is *brodetto*, a rich fish chowder containing as many as nine types of Adriatic saltwater fish. Ascoli Piceno,
inland, is famous for two dishes: olives *ascolane* (stuffed, rolled in batter, and deep fried) and *vincisgrassi* (a local version of lasagna, far richer
than you're likely to find elsewhere in Italy). Ascoli Piceno is also the
home of the licorice-flavored liqueur anisette.

CATEGORY	COST*
$$$	60,000–85,000 lire
$$	25,000–60,000 lire
$	under 25,000 lire

*Prices are per person, including first course, main course, dessert or fruit,
and house wine.*

Hiking

Magnificent scenery makes Umbria excellent hiking and mountaineering
country. The area around Spoleto is particularly good, and the tourist
office supplies itineraries of walks and climbs to suit all ages and levels of ability.

Lodging

Virtually every historic town in Umbria has some kind of hotel, no matter how small the place may be. In most cases a small city boasts one or two hotels in a high price category and a few smaller, basic hotels in the inexpensive-to-moderate ($–$$) range. The cheaper the hotel, the fewer the services. Most basic hotels offer breakfast, but few have restaurants or bars.

A recent and popular trend is the conversion of old villas and monasteries into first-class hotels. These tend to be outside the towns, in the countryside, and the splendor of the settings often outweighs the problem of getting into town. In all cases, these country hotels are comfortable, often luxurious, and offer a mixture of Old World charm and modern convenience.

Reservations at any hotel are recommended, and traveling in high season to Perugia, Assisi, Spoleto, or Orvieto without advance bookings is a chancy proposition.

CATEGORY	COST*
$$$$	over 300,000 lire
$$$	160,000–300,000 lire
$$	100,000–160,000 lire
$	under 100,000 lire

Prices are for a standard double room for two, including tax, service, and breakfast.

Shopping

Pottery and wine are the two most famous Umbrian exports, and examples of both commodities are excellent and unique to the region. Torgiano, south of Perugia, is one of the best-known centers of wine making, where you can watch the process and buy the product; you can find some of the best ceramics at Gubbio, Perugia, and Assisi. Those with the most flair are found in Deruta, south of Torgiano on S3bis. The red glazes of Gubbio pottery have been famous since medieval times. The secret of the original glaze died with its inventor some 500 years ago, but there are contemporary potters who produce a fair facsimile.

Swimming

Lakes Trasimeno and Piediluco offer safe and clean bathing facilities. Castiglione del Lago, on Lake Trasimeno, has a public beach, with no strong undercurrents or hidden depths.

Exploring Umbria and the Marches

The steep hills and deep valleys that make Umbria and the Marches so picturesque also make them difficult to explore. Driving routes must be chosen carefully to avoid tortuous mountain roads; major towns are not necessarily linked to each other by train, bus, or highway. A convenient base for exploring the region might be Perugia, the largest city in Umbria, but to see the region properly you would still need to stay overnight in other towns along the way. Next we head east across the Apennines to the Marches region; we begin exploring it in the hilltop city of Urbino, travel down to the Adriatic coast to visit Ancona, and then climb back west into the hills to Loreto and Ascoli Piceno. Back in Umbria, we concentrate on two memorable towns: Spoleto, site of the famous arts festival, south of Perugia; and Assisi, St. Francis's hometown, just east of Perugia. The final tour centers on Orvieto, built on a huge rock outcropping in western Umbria, southwest of Perugia.

Numbers in the text correspond to numbers in the margin and on the Umbria and the Marches, Perugia, and Assisi maps.

Great Itineraries

The region of Umbria is particularly suited to touring in a limited time. Basing yourself in Perugia, you can see all the major sights in the regional capital in the equivalent of a day, making easy excursions to the hill villages on your other days without feeling stressed out by constant travel. East of Perugia, the Marches invite leisurely exploring, though also some lengthy rides in between the main points of interest.

IF YOU HAVE 3 DAYS

In ⊞ **Perugia** ①–⑤, your main stops will be the refurbished Galleria Nazionale and the Collegio del Cambio, both contained in the atmospheric **Palazzo dei Priori** ③; much of the rest of your time will be spent alternately ambling along Corso Vannucci and toiling up and down the steep lanes on either side. Devote your second day to ⊞ **Assisi** ⑬–⑳, where the spiritual and the material are fused in a place that remains in essence a small medieval Umbrian town. The choice for a third excursion is a tough one, and you won't be disappointed by whichever place you opt for. Consider **Spoleto** ⑫: a tight-knit hill town whose narrow streets abound with evocative views and delightful surprises.

IF YOU HAVE 5 DAYS

Given five days, you will be able to spend a couple of them exploring the neighboring region of Marche. How you enter these rather inaccessible parts will depend on your mode of transport. In any case, start your tour in **Perugia** ①–⑤, and follow the schedule outlined above for your first two days. If you are traveling by public transport, spend your third night in ⊞ **Spoleto** ⑫, from which you can jump on a train bound for ⊞ **Ancona** ⑨, where you can board a bus or a train for Pésaro and **Urbino** ⑧. This hilltop gem retains its proud, self-contained character, almost untouched by ugly 20th-century construction. Calculate at least half a day for reaching Urbino from Spoleto, and it's not much shorter by car, crossing the Marches border from ⊞ **Gubbio** ⑦, where you might spend your third day appreciating the views, shops, and choice hotels and restaurants.

IF YOU HAVE 7 DAYS

Reserve four days for Umbria and three for the Marches. With greater flexibility you can choose how many nights you want to spend in Umbria's capital, **Perugia** ①–⑤, and how many in the region's smaller centers. More time in Perugia will allow you to explore the city thoroughly, including the archaeological museum, and you might take in the easy excursion to the wine village of **Torgiano** ⑥. ⊞ **Spoleto** ⑫ and ⊞ **Assisi** ⑬–⑳ are essential stops farther afield, where you might stay for a night in each. ⊞ **Gubbio** ⑦, is also worth overnighting in, whereas the primary sites of **Orvieto** ㉑—the cathedral and a couple of good museums—can be seen on your way to or from Rome, only about 90 minutes away. ⊞ **Urbino** ⑧ is the premier destination in the Marches. The region's biggest city, ⊞ **Ancona** ⑨ has little of interest, but good facilities—sleep here if you must; otherwise head south for the infinitely preferable inland town of ⊞ **Ascoli Piceno** ⑪. There is little in the way of hotels, galleries, or sophisticated shops here, but the atmosphere is marvelously quaint. On the way, or en route back, drop in at the holy sanctuary of **Loreto** ⑩, nestled in the mountains 24 km (15 mi) south of Ancona.

When to Tour Umbria and the Marches

The forested hills of Umbria and the Marches ensure beguiling colors in the fall and an explosion of greenery in spring—and less crowds.

From a culinary standpoint, winter is best: January–April heralds the Norcia and Spoleto truffle season; October–December brings a bounty of fresh local mushrooms.

Book accommodations far in advance if you are planning to visit in June and July, when the Spoleto Festival dei Due Mondi and the Jazz Festival of Perugia take place. Sightseers and pilgrims throng the streets of Assisi year round; the religious festivals of Christmas, Easter, the feast of Saint Francis (October 4), and the Calendimaggio Festival (May 1) draw even more visitors.

PERUGIA TO GUBBIO
Umbrian Heights

Perugia

❶ *180 km (112 mi) north of Rome, 153 km (96 mi) southeast of Florence, 455 km (284 mi) southeast of Milan.*

Perugia, the largest and richest of Umbria's cities, is an old and elegant place of great character. Despite a rather grim crust of modern suburbs, Perugia's location on a series of hills high above the suburban plain has ensured that the medieval city remains almost completely intact. Perugia is the best well-preserved hill town of its size, and few other places in Italy illustrate better the concept of the self-contained city-state that so shaped the course of Italian history.

The best approach to the city is by train—the station is in the unlovely suburbs, but there are frequent buses running directly to Piazza d'Italia, the heart of the old town. If you are driving to Perugia, it is best to leave your car in one of the parking lots near the station and then take the bus or the escalator (which passes through fascinating subterranean excavations of the Roman foundations of the city) to the center of town.

The nerve center of the city is the broad, stately **Corso Vannucci,** a pedestrian street that runs from Piazza d'Italia to Piazza IV Novembre. As evening falls, Corso Vannucci is filled with Perugians out for their evening *passeggiata,* a pleasant predinner stroll that may include a pause for an aperitif at one of the many bars that line the street.

❷ The **Duomo** is a large and rather plain building dating from the Middle Ages but with many additions from the 15th and 16th centuries. The interior is vast and echoing, with little in the way of decoration. There are some elaborately carved choir stalls, executed by Giovanni Battista Bastone in 1520. The great relic of the church—the wedding ring of the Virgin Mary that the Perugians stole from the nearby town of Chiusi—is kept in a chapel in the left aisle. The ring is the size of a large bangle and is kept under lock (15 locks, actually) and key every day of the year except July 30, when it is exposed to view. ⊠ *Piazza IV Novembre.* ☉ *Daily 8–noon and 4–7:30.*

There is a large array of precious objects associated with the cathedral in the **Museum of the Duomo,** including vestments, vessels, manuscripts, and gold work, as well as one outstanding piece of artwork, an early masterpiece by Luca Signorelli, the altarpiece showing the Madonna with Saint John the Baptist, Saint Onophrius, and Saint Lawrence (1484). ⊠ *Piazza IV Novembre.* ▥ *2,000 lire.* ☉ *Wed.–Fri. 9–noon, Sat. 9–noon and 3:30–5:30, Sun. 3:30–5:30.*

Umbria and the Marches

Adriatic Sea

ITALY

Numana

Ancona **9**

Loreto **10**

Recanati

Macerata

Potenza

Senigallia

Marotta

Jesi

S76

Misa

Fano

A14

S424

Metauro

Cesano

Pesaro

S78

S3

Pergola

Fabriano

S3b

S16

S423

Fossombrone

S3

Urbino **8**

E78/S73bis

SAN MARINO

S72

Gubbio **7**

S298

S258

S73

Città di Castello

S3bis

Tevere

Umbertide

S71

Sansepolcro

S73

S75

Lago

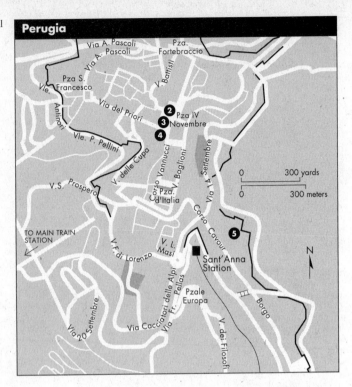

★ ❸ The **Palazzo dei Priori** is an imposing building, begun in the 13th century, with an unusual staircase that fans out into the square. The facade is decorated with symbols of Perugia's pride and past power: the griffin is the city's symbol; the lion denotes Perugia's allegiance to the Guelph (or papal) cause. Both figures support the heavy chains of the gates of Siena, which fell to Perugian forces in 1358.

The fourth floor of the Palazzo dei Priori contains the region's most comprehensive art gallery, the **Galleria Nazionale d'Umbria.** Enhanced by skillfully lit displays and computers allowing you to focus on details of the works and background information on them, the collection in 33 rooms includes work by native artists—most outstandingly Pinturicchio and Perugino—and others of the Umbrian and Tuscan schools, including Gentile da Fabriano, Duccio, Fra Angelico, Fiorenzo di Lorenzo, and Piero della Francesca. In addition to paintings, the gallery has frescoes, sculptures, and some superb examples of crucifixes from the 13th and 14th centuries; other rooms are dedicated to the city of Perugia itself, showing how the medieval city evolved. ⊠ *Corso Vannucci 19, Piazza IV Novembre.* 🎫 *8,000 lire.* ☉ *Mon.–Sat. 9–7, Sun. 9–1. Closed 1st Mon. of each month.*

★ ❹ The series of elaborate rooms of **Collegio del Cambio** housed the meeting hall and chapel of the guild of bankers and money changers. The walls were frescoed from 1496 to 1500 by the most important Perugian painter of the Renaissance, Pietro Vannucci, better known as Perugino. The iconography prevalent in the works includes common religious themes, like the Nativity and the Transfiguration (on the end walls), but also figures intended to inspire the businessmen who congregated here. On the left wall are female figures representing the virtues, beneath them the heroes and sages of antiquity. On the right wall are the prophets and sibyls—said to have been painted in part by

Perugino's most famous pupil, Raphael, whose hand, the experts say, is most apparent in the figure of Fortitude. On one of the pilasters is a remarkably honest self-portrait of Perugino, surmounted by a Latin inscription and contained in a faux frame. The Collegio is attached to Pallazzo dei Priori, but entered via Corso Vannucci. ⊠ *Corso Vannucci 25.* ☎ *5,000 lire.* ☉ *Mar.–Oct., Mon.–Sat. 9–12:30 and 2:30–5:30, Sun. 9–12:30; Nov.–Feb., Tues.–Sat. 8–2, Sun. 9–12:30. During Christmas season (Dec. 20–Jan. 6) museum follows summer timetable.*

⑤ A 10-minute walk south of the center along Corso Cavour leads to the **Archaeological Museum of Umbria,** which contains an excellent collection of Etruscan artifacts from throughout the region. Perugia was a flourishing Etruscan site long before it fell under Roman domination in 310 BC. (Other than this collection, little remains of Perugia's mysterious ancestors, although the Gate of Augustus, in Piazza Fortebraccio, the northern entrance to the city, is of Etruscan origin.) ⊠ *Piazza Giordano Bruno.* ☎ *4,000 lire.* ☉ *Mon.–Sat. 9–1:30 and 2:30–7, Sun. 9–1.*

☾ Umbria's only attraction aimed directly at the younger set is **La Città della Domenica,** a Disney-style playground in the town of Montepulito, 8 km (5 mi) west of Perugia on the secondary road that leads to Corciano. The 500 acres of parkland contain a variety of buildings based on familiar fairy-tale themes—Snow White's House, the Witches' Wood—as well as a reptile house, a medieval museum, an exhibit of shells from all over the world, game rooms, and a choice of restaurants. ⊠ *Località Montepulito.* ☎ *075/5054941.* ☎ *15,900 lire (16,900 lire Sun. and holidays).* ☉ *Mid-Mar.–late-Sept., daily 9–7; late Sept.–Oct., weekends, and holidays 9–7; Nov.–mid-Mar. (aquarium and reptile house only), Sat. 2–7, Sun. 10–7.*

Dining and Lodging

$$ ✕ **Il Falchetto.** Here you'll find exceptional food at reasonable prices, making this Perugia's best restaurant bargain. The service is smart but relaxed in the two medieval dining rooms, with the kitchen and chef on view. The house specialty is *falchetti* (homemade gnocchi with spinach and ricotta cheese). ⊠ *Via Bartolo 20,* ☎ *075/5731775. Reservations essential. AE, DC, MC, V. Closed Mon.*

$$ ✕ **La Rosetta.** This restaurant, in the hotel of the same name, is a peaceful, elegant spot. In the winter you dine inside under medieval vaults; in summer, in the cool courtyard. The cuisine is simple but reliable and flawlessly served. ⊠ *Piazza d'Italia 19,* ☎ *075/5720841. Reservations essential. AE, DC, MC, V.*

$$ ✕ **La Taverna.** Medieval steps lead to this rustic restaurant on two levels, where lots of wine bottles and artful clutter heighten the tavern atmosphere. The menu features regional specialties and better-known Italian dishes. Good choices include *chitarrini* (pasta), with either *funghi* (mushrooms) or *tartufi* (pricier truffles), and grilled meats. ⊠ *Via delle Streghe 8, next to the Teatro Pavone, off Corso Vannucci,* ☎ *075/5724128. Dinner reservations essential. AE, DC, MC, V. Closed Mon.*

$$$$ 🛏 **Brufani Hotel.** The two hotels (this one and the Palace Hotel Bellavista; ☞ *below*) in this 19th-century palazzo were once one. The Brufani's public rooms and first-floor guest rooms have high ceilings and are done in the grand belle epoque style. The second-floor rooms are more modern, and many on both floors have a marvelous view of the Umbrian countryside or the city. ⊠ *Piazza d'Italia 12, 06121,* ☎ *075/5732541,* FAX *075/5720210. 24 rooms. Restaurant, bar, air-conditioning, meeting rooms. AE, DC, MC, V.*

$$$ 🏨 **Locanda della Posta.** This luxuriously decorated small hotel in the
★ center of Perugia's historic district is a delight to behold, from its faux-
marble moldings, paneled doors, and tile bouquets in the baths to the
suede-upholstered elevator and fabric-covered walls. Architectural de-
tails of the 18th-century palazzo are beautiful, and views of city
rooftops from windows and balconies are soothing. Breakfast is included
here. ⊠ *Corso Vannucci 97, 06121,* ☎ *075/5728925,* ℻ *075/5722413.*
39 rooms. Breakfast room, lobby lounge. AE, DC, MC, V.

$$$ 🏨 **Palace Hotel Bellavista.** Though the hotel's entrance is unimpres-
sive, the public rooms are palatial, with antiques imparting a discreet
tone of belle epoque grandeur. Guest rooms are spacious, unfussy, and
mostly with stupendous views. Prices are at the lower end of this category, and weekly rates are available. ⊠ *Piazza d'Italia 12, 06121,* ☎
075/5720741, ℻ *075/5729092. 74 rooms. Bar, meeting rooms. AE,*
DC, MC, V.

$$ 🏨 **Priori.** On an alley leading off the main Corso Vannucci, this un-
pretentious but elegant hotel has spacious and cheerful rooms with mod-
ern furnishings. There is a panoramic terrace where breakfast (included
in the price) is served in summer. The hotel is difficult to find if you're
driving, and a car is an encumbrance wherever you are in Perugia's
historic center. ⊠ *Via Vermiglioli 3, 06123,* ☎ *075/5723378,* ℻
075/5723213. 49 rooms. Bar. No credit cards.

$ 🏨 **Rosalba.** This is a bright and friendly choice on the fringes of Pe-
rugia's historic center. Rooms—each equipped with telephones and
TVs—are scrupulously clean, and the ones at the back enjoy a view.
Although somewhat out of the way, the hotel is only a matter of min-
utes from Corso Vannucci by virtue of the nearby escalator stop, sav-
ing a good deal of legwork. Parking is easy, too. ⊠ *Via del Circo 7,*
06121, ☎ *075/5728285. 11 rooms. No credit cards.*

Nightlife and the Arts

Summer sees two music festivals in Perugia: the **Jazz Festival of Um-
bria** (July) and the **Festival of Sacred Music** (September). Event and ticket
information for both festivals can be obtained, year-round, from the
Perugia Tourist Office (⊠ Piazza IV Novembre 3, ☎ 075/5723327).

A true devotee of Umbrian music should consider the lengthy trek to
the **Chamber Music Festival of Umbria,** which is held every August and
September in the town of Città di Castello, about 80 km (49½ mi) north
of Perugia on the S3bis. For information, contact the tourist office (⊠
Via R. di Cesare 2/b, ☎ 075/8554817).

Shopping

Perugia is a well-to-do town, and judging by the array of expensive
shops on **Corso Vannucci,** the Perugians are not afraid to part with their
money. The main streets of the town are lined with clothing shops sell-
ing the best-known Italian designers, either in luxurious boutiques or
shops—such as Gucci, Ferragamo, Armani, and Fendi—run by the de-
sign firms themselves.

The best and most typical thing to buy in Perugia is, of course, some
of the famous and delicious **Perugina chocolate.** *Cioccolato al latte*
(milk chocolate) and *fondente* (dark chocolate) are available in tiny
jewel-like boxes or in giant gift boxes the size of serving trays. The
most famous chocolates made by Perugina are the round chocolate-
and hazelnut-filled candies called Baci (kisses), which come wrapped
in silver paper and, like fortune cookies, contain romantic sentiments
or sayings.

Torgiano

❻ *15 km (9 mi) southeast of Perugia.*

Wine aficionados are certain to want to visit this home to the famous **Lungarotti winery,** best known for delicious Rubesco Lungarotti, San Giorgio, and chardonnay. The town is also home to a fascinating wine museum, which has a large collection of ancient wine vessels, presses, documents, and tools that tell the story of viticulture in Umbria and beyond. The museum traces the history of wine in all its uses—for drinking at the table, as medicine, and in mythology. You can also pick up one of the winery's award-winning reds or whites to take home. ✉ *Corso Vittorio Emanuele 11.* 🎫 *5,000 lire.* ⊘ *Apr.–Sept., daily 9–1 and 3–7; Oct.–Mar., daily 9–1 and 3–6.*

Gubbio

❼ *40 km (25 mi) northeast of Perugia.*

The trip from Perugia to Gubbio follows S298 through rugged, mountainous terrain. There is something otherworldly about this small jewel of a medieval town tucked away in a mountainous corner of Umbria. Even at the height of summer, the cool serenity and silence of Gubbio's streets remain intact. The town is perched on the slopes of Mt. Ingino, and the streets are dramatically steep.

Gubbio's relatively isolated position has kept it free of hordes of high-season visitors, but even during the busiest times of year the city lives up to its Italian nickname, the City of Silence. Parking in the central Piazza dei Quaranta Martiri (named for 40 hostages murdered by the Nazis in 1944) is easy and secure, and it is wise to leave your car there and explore the narrow streets on foot.

★ The striking Piazza Grande is dominated by **Palazzo dei Consoli,** a medieval building attributed to a local architect known as Gattapone—a man still much admired by today's residents (every other hotel, restaurant, and bar has been named after him), though recent studies have suggested that the palazzo was in fact the work of another architect, Angelo da Orvieto.

The Palazzo dei Consoli houses a small museum, famous chiefly for the **Tavole Eugubine,** seven bronze tablets written in the ancient Umbrian language, employing Etruscan and Latin characters, and providing the best key to understanding this obscure tongue. Also in the museum are a fascinating miscellany of coins, medieval arms, paintings, and majolica and earthenware pots, not to mention the exhilarating views over Gubbio's roofscape and beyond from the lofty loggia. For a few days at the beginning of May, the palace also displays the famous *ceri,* the ceremonial pillars at the center of Gubbio's annual festivities (☞ Festivals, *below*). ✉ *Piazza Grande.* 🎫 *4,000 lire.* ⊘ *Mid-Mar.–June, daily 9–12:30 and 3:30–6; July and Sept., daily 10–1:30 and 3–6; Aug., daily 10–1:30 and 3–7; Oct.–mid-Mar., daily 10–1 and 2–5.*

The **Duomo,** on a narrow street on the highest tier of the town, dates from the 13th century, with some Baroque additions—in particular, a lavishly decorated bishop's chapel. ✉ *Via Ducale.* ⊘ *Daily 8–12:45 and 3–7:30.*

The **Palazzo Ducale** is a scaled-down copy of the Palazzo Ducale in Urbino (Gubbio was once the possession of that city's ruling family, the Montefeltro). Gubbio's palazzo contains a small **museum** and a **courtyard.** There are magnificent views from some of the public rooms. ✉

Via Ducale. ▨ 4,000 lire. ⊙ Mon.–Sat. 9–1:30 and 2:30–7, Sun. 9–1:30; hrs change, so check with tourist office.

Just outside the city walls at the eastern end of town (follow Corso Garibaldi or Via XX Settembre to the end), is a **funicular** that provides a bracing ride to the top of Mt. Ingino. Aside from the spectacular views, the mountain commands the basilica of **Sant'Ubaldo,** repository of Gubbio's famous **ceri,** three 16-ft-high poles crowned with statues of Saints Ubaldo, George, and Anthony. The pillars are transported to the Palazzo dei Consoli on the first Sunday of May to honor the Festival of Ceri (☞ Festivals, below). ▨ Top of Mt. Ingino.

Dining and Lodging

$$ ✕ **Grotta dell'Angelo.** This rustic trattoria is in the lower part of the Old Town, near the main square and tourist information office. The menu features simple local specialties, including capocollo (a type of salami), strangozzi pasta, and lasagna tartufate (with truffles). There are a few tables for outdoor dining. Inexpensive guest rooms are available here as well. ▨ Via Gioia 47, ☎ 075/9273438. Reservations essential. AE, DC, MC, V. Closed Tues. and Jan. 7–Feb. 7.

$$ ✕ **Porta Tessenaca.** This atmospheric restaurant occupies what used to be the stables of the ducal palace. The brick vaulted setting is perfect, if somewhat touristy, and the food is excellent Umbrian fare; there are three fixed-price menus. If possible, opt for the strangozzi ai porcini (with porcini mushrooms) for starters, and the duck for the next course. There is a good selection of wine. ▨ Via Piccardi 21, ☎ 075/9272765. AE, DC, MC, V.

$$ ✕ **Taverna del Lupo.** It's one of the best restaurants in the city, as well as one of the largest—it seats 200 people and can get a bit hectic during the high season. Lasagna made in the Gubbian fashion, with ham and truffles, is the best pasta. You'll also find excellent desserts and an extensive wine cellar here. ▨ Via G. Ansidei 21, ☎ 075/9274368. Reservations essential. AE, DC, MC, V. Closed Mon. Oct.–July.

$$ 🏨 **Hotel Bosone.** Occupying the old central Palazzo Raffaelli, the Hotel Bosone has many rooms decorated with frescoes from the former palace. The suites furnished with period detail are particularly lavish. ▨ Via XX Settembre 22, 06024, ☎ 075/9220688, ℻ 075/9220552. 30 rooms. Bar. AE, DC, MC, V. Closed Jan.

$ 🏨 **Hotel Gattapone.** Right in the center of town is this recently renovated hotel with wonderful views of the sea of rooftops. It is casual and family run, with good-size, modern, comfortable rooms, some with well-preserved timber-raftered ceilings. ▨ Via Ansidei 6, 06024, ☎ 075/9272489, ℻ 075/9271269. 13 rooms. AE, DC, MC, V. Closed Jan.

Festivals

Every May 15th teams of Gubbio's young men, dressed in medieval costumes, race up the steep slopes to the basilica of Sant'Ubaldo carrying its heavy, cherished pillars to celebrate **Festival of the Ceri** (Candles). This festival, enacted faithfully every year since 1151, is to thank the town's patron saints for their assistance in a miraculous Gubbian victory over a league of 11 other towns.

Among the region's other historical pageants, Gubbio's costumed **crossbow tournament** is particularly exciting for young and old alike. The Palio della Balestra usually takes place on the last Sunday in May; contact the Gubbio tourist agency (▨ Piazza Oderisi 6, ☎ 075/9220693) for details.

THE MARCHES
Mirror to the Renaissance

An excursion from Umbria into the region of the Marches is recommended for those who want to get off the beaten track and see a part of Italy rarely visited by foreigners. It must be admitted that traveling in the Marches is not as easy as in Umbria or Tuscany. Beyond the narrow coastal plain and away from major towns, the roads are steep and twisting. Train travel in the region is slow, and destinations are limited, although one can reach Ascoli Piceno by rail, and there's an efficient bus service from the coastal town of Pesaro to Urbino, the other principal tourist city of the region.

Urbino

8 *170 km (106 mi) northeast of Perugia, 190 km (119 mi) east of Florence, 30 km (19 mi) southwest of Pésaro.*

Urbino is a majestic city, sitting atop a steep hill, with a skyline of towers and domes. It is something of a surprise to come upon it—the location is remote—and it is even stranger to reflect that this quiet country town was once a center of learning and culture almost without rival in western Europe. The town looks much as it did in the glory days of the 15th century, a cluster of warm brick and pale stone buildings, all topped with russet-colored tiled roofs. The focal point is the immense and beautiful Ducal Palace.

The tradition of learning in Urbino continues to this day. The city is the home of a small but prestigious Italian state university—one of the oldest in the world—and during term time the streets are filled with hordes of noisy students. It is very much a college town, with the usual array of bookshops, record stores, bars, and coffeehouses. During the summer, the Italian student population is replaced by foreigners who come to study Italian language and arts at several prestigious private fine-arts academies.

Urbino's fame rests on the reputation of three of its native sons: Duke Federico da Montefeltro, the enlightened warrior-patron who built the Ducal Palace; Raphael, one of the most influential painters in history and an embodiment of the spirit of the Renaissance; and the architect Donato Bramante, who translated the philosophy of the Renaissance into buildings of grace and beauty. Why three of the greatest men of the age should have been born within a generation of one another in this remote town has never been explained. Oddly enough, there is little work by either Bramante or Raphael in the city, but the duke's influence can still be felt strongly, even now, some 500 years after his death.

★ The **Ducal Palace** holds the place of honor in the city, and in no other palace of its era are the principles of the Renaissance stated quite so clearly. If the Renaissance was, in ideal form, a celebration of the nobility of man and his works, of the light and purity of the soul, then there is no place in Italy, the birthplace of the Renaissance, where these tenets are better illustrated. From the moment you enter the peaceful courtyard, you know that you are in a place of grace and beauty, the harmony of the building reflecting the high ideals of the men who built it.

Today the palace houses the **National Museum of the Marches**, with a superb collection of paintings, sculpture, and other objets d'art, well arranged and properly lit. It would be hard to mention all the great works in this collection—some originally the possessions of the Montefeltro family, others brought to the museum from churches and palaces throughout the region—but there are a few that must be singled out. Of these, perhaps the most famous is Piero della Francesca's enigmatic work, long known as *The Flagellation of Christ*. Much has been written about this painting, and few experts agree on its meaning. Legend had it that the three figures in the foreground represented a murdered member of the Montefeltro family (the barefoot young man) and his two murderers. Others claimed the painting was a heavily veiled criticism of certain parts of Christian Europe—the iconography is obscure and the history extremely complicated. Recently, however, Sir John Pope-Hennessy—the preeminent scholar of Italian Renaissance art—has proved that it represents the arcane subject of the Vision of Saint Lawrence. All the experts have always agreed that the painting is one of Piero della Francesca's masterpieces. Piero himself thought so. It is one of the few works he signed (on the lowest step supporting the throne).

Other masterworks in the collection are Paolo Uccello's *Profanation of the Host,* Piero della Francesca's *Madonna of Senigallia,* and Titian's *Resurrection* and *Last Supper.* Duke Federico's study is an astonishingly elaborate but tiny room decorated with inlaid wood, said to be the work of Botticelli. ⊠ *Piazza Duca Federico,* ☎ *0722/2760.* ≈ *8,000 lire.* ☉ *Mon.–Sat. 9–7, Sun. 9–1.*

The **house of Raphael** really is the house in which he was born and where he took his first steps in painting (under the direction of his artist father). There is some debate about the fresco of the Madonna that adorns the house. Some say it is by Raphael, whereas others attribute it to the father—with Raphael's mother and the young painter himself standing in as models for the Madonna and Child. Either way, it's an interesting picture. ⊠ *Via Raffaello.* ≈ *5,000 lire.* ☉ *Apr.–Sept., Mon.–Sat. 9–1 and 3–7, Sun. 9–1; Oct.–Jan. and Mar., Thurs.–Sat. and Mon.–Tues. 9–2, Sun. 9–1.*

Dining and Lodging

$$ × **La Vecchia Fornarina.** These two small rooms just down from Urbino's central Piazza della Repubblica are often filled to capacity. The trattoria specializes in meaty country fare, such as rabbit and *vitello alle noci* (veal cooked with nuts) or *ai porcini* (with mushrooms). There is also a good range of pasta dishes. ⊠ *Via Mazzini 14,* ☎ *0722/320007. Reservations essential. AE, DC, MC, V.*

$ 🏨 **Hotel San Giovanni.** This hotel is in the Old Town and is housed in a renovated medieval building. The rooms are basic, clean, and comfortable—with a wonderful view from Nos. 18–21 and 24–31—and there is a handy restaurant–pizzeria below. ⊠ *Via Barocci 13, 61029,* ☎ *0722/2827. 33 rooms, 21 with shower. No credit cards. Closed July and Christmas wk.*

En Route   To reach Ancona, on the Adriatic coast, from Urbino, take the E78 or S3 to the superhighway A14, which runs along the coast but inland by a km (⅔ mi) or so. The coast road, S16, is a congested two-lane highway with little to recommend it.

Ancona

❾ *87 km (54 mi) southeast of Urbino, 60 km (37½ mi) southeast of Pésaro, 139 km (87 mi) northeast of Perugia, 262 km (164 mi) east of Florence, 286 km (179 mi) northeast of Rome.*

Ancona was probably once a lovely city. It is set on an elbow-shape bluff (hence its name; *ankon* is Greek for "elbow") that juts out into the Adriatic. But Ancona was the object of serious aerial bombing during World War II—it was, and is, an important port city—and was reduced to rubble. The city has been rebuilt in the unfortunate postwar poured-concrete style, practical and inexpensive but certainly not aesthetically pleasing. Unless you are taking a ferry to Venice, there is little reason to visit the city—with a few exceptions. Once in a while, glimpses of old architectural detail are redeeming, as seen in the Duomo San Ciriaco and the Loggia dei Mercanti. In addition, Ancona can be the base for an excursion to Loreto or to Ascoli Piceno, farther south along the Adriatic coast.

Dining and Lodging

$$ ✕ **La Moretta.** This family-run trattoria is on the central Piazza del Plebiscito. In summer there is dining outside in the square, which has a fine view of the Baroque church of San Domenico. Among the specialties of La Moretta are tagliatelle *in salsa di ostriche* (in an oyster sauce) and the famous brodetto fish stew. ⊠ *Piazza del Plebiscito 52,* ☏ *071/202317. Reservations essential. AE, DC, MC, V. Closed Sun.*

$$$ 🏨 **Grand Hotel Palace.** In the center of town, near the entrance to the port of Ancona, and widely held to be the best in town, this is an old-fashioned place well run by a courteous staff. ⊠ *Lungomare Vanvitelli 24, 60100,* ☏ *071/201813,* 🖷 *071/2074832. 41 rooms. Bar, free parking. AE, DC, MC, V.*

$$–$$$ 🏨 **Hotel Roma e Pace.** The only two reasons to stay in this hotel are the location and price. The rooms are ugly and cramped, and those facing the street are noisy (choose inward-facing ones). A historical note: in 1907 a Russian named Josef Dzhugashvili applied for a job here and was refused. He later found better-paying employment as supreme head of the Soviet Union under the name Stalin. ⊠ *Via Leopardi 1, 60100,* ☏ *071/202007,* 🖷 *071/2074736. 73 rooms. Restaurant, bar. AE, DC, MC, V.*

Loreto

🔟 *24 km (24 mi) south of Ancona on A14.*

★ Loreto is famous for one of the best-loved shrines in the world, that of the **house of the Virgin Mary.** The legend is that angels moved the house from Nazareth, where the Virgin was living at the time of the Annunciation, to this hilltop in 1295. The reason for this sudden and divinely inspired move was that Nazareth had fallen into the hands of Muslim invaders, not suitable landlords, the angelic hosts felt. More recently, following archaeological excavations made at the behest of the Church, evidence has come to light proving that the house did once stand elsewhere and was brought to the hilltop by human means around the time the angels are said to have done the job.

The house itself consists of three rough stone walls contained within an elaborate marble tabernacle; built around this centerpiece is the giant basilica of the Holy House, which dominates the town. Millions of visitors come to the site every year (particularly at Easter and on the Feast of the Holy House, December 10), and the little town of Loreto can become uncomfortably crowded with pilgrims. Many great Italian architects, including Bramante, Sangallo, and Sansovino, contributed to the design of the basilica. Inside are a great many mediocre 19th- and 20th-century paintings but also some fine works by Renaissance masters such as Luca Signorelli and Melozzo da Forlì. ⊠ *In church.* ☉ *June–Sept., daily 8–8; Oct.–May, daily 6 AM–7 PM.*

Nervous air travelers may take comfort in the fact that the Holy Virgin of Loreto is the patroness of air travelers and that Pope John Paul

II has composed a prayer for a safe flight—available in the church in a half-dozen languages.

Ascoli Piceno

⑪ *105 km (65 mi) south of Ancona.*

Ascoli Piceno is not a hill town; rather, it sits in a valley ringed by steep hills and cut by the fast-racing Tronto River. The town is almost unique in Italy, in that it seems to have its traffic problems—in the historic center, at any rate—pretty much under control; you can drive *around* the picturesque part of the city, but driving *through* it is most difficult. This feature makes Ascoli Piceno one of the most pleasant large towns in the country for exploring on foot. True, there is traffic, but you are not constantly assaulted by jams, noise, and exhaust fumes the way you are in other Italian cities.

★ The heart of the town is the majestic **Piazza del Popolo,** dominated by the Gothic church of San Francesco and the Palazzo del Popolo, a 13th-century town hall that contains a graceful Renaissance courtyard. The square itself functions as the living room of the entire city. At dusk each evening the piazza is packed with people standing in small groups, exchanging news and gossip as if at a cocktail party.

☾ Ascoli Piceno's **Giostra della Quintana** takes place on the first Sunday in August. Children should love this medieval-style joust and the richly caparisoned processions that wind through the streets of the old town. Contact Ascoli's tourist office (⊠ Piazza del Popolo, ☎ 0736/257288) for details.

Dining and Lodging

$$ ✕ **Ristorante Tornasacco.** In this family-run restaurant with modern
★ decor, you can sample Ascoli's specialties, like olives ascolane (here, stuffed with minced meat), as well as *maccheroncini alla contadina* (a homemade pasta in a thick meat sauce). ⊠ *Piazza del Popolo 36,* ☎ *0736/254151. AE, DC, MC, V. Closed Fri. and July 1–15.*

$ ▦ **Piceno.** This modest hostelry is one of the few lodgings in the historic center of town. It offers clean, basic amenities—no frills at all here. The staff is helpful and courteous, and the location is perfect. ⊠ *Via Minucia 10,* ☎ *0736/252553. 32 rooms, 18 with shower. No credit cards.*

En Route The 175-km (108-mi) drive to Spoleto takes you out of the Marches and back into Umbria. The route—S4 southwest to Rieti, then S79 north to Terni, then S3 into Spoleto—is roundabout but vastly preferable to a series of winding mountain roads that connect Ascoli Piceno with Umbria.

SPOLETO AND ASSISI

Spoleto and Assisi are two of the most popular towns in all of Italy, but for very different reasons. The medieval town of Spoleto hosts Italy's most prestigious international arts festival, the Festival of Two Worlds, while Assisi is the birthplace of one of Christianity's most beloved saints, St. Francis.

Spoleto

★ **⑫** *50 km (30 mi) south of Perugia, 35 km (20 mi) south of Assisi.*

"Quaint" may be an overused term, but it is the most appropriate word to describe this city, still enclosed by stout medieval walls. There is no traipsing through museums and churches in store for you here; rather, charming mazes of twisting streets and cobbled stairways, and wonderful peace and quiet.

Quiet, that is, except when Spoleto is hosting the **Festival dei Due Mondi** (Festival of Two Worlds) (☞ Nightlife and the Arts, *below*), an arts festival held every year from mid-June to mid-July. During that month the sleepy town is swamped with visitors who come to see world-class plays and operas, to hear concerts, and to see extensive exhibitions of paintings and sculpture. It is unwise to arrive during this period without confirmed hotel reservations. Parking in Spoleto is always difficult; park outside the walls in Piazza della Vittoria.

Spoleto is dominated by a huge **castle** that was built in 1359–63 by the Gubbio-born architect Gattapone. It was until recently a high-security prison but has been undergoing restoration and is to become a museum. The castle was built to protect the town's most famous monument, the massive bridge known as the **Ponte delle Torri** (Bridge of the Towers), built by Gattapone on Roman foundations. This massive structure stands 262 ft above the gorge it spans and was built originally as an aqueduct. The bridge is open to pedestrians, and a walk over it affords marvelous views—looking down to the river below is the best way to appreciate the colossal dimensions of the bridge. The central span is actually higher than that of the dome of St. Peter's in Rome.

Spoleto's **Duomo** is set in a lovely sloping square at the bottom of a flight of steps below the castle. The church facade is dourly Romanesque but with the pleasant light addition of a Renaissance loggia and eight rose windows. The contrast between the heavy medieval work and the graceful later embellishments graphically demonstrates the difference, not only in style, but in philosophy, of the two eras. The earlier was strong but ungiving; the later, human and open-minded.

The Duomo's interior boasts the best of the city's art, notably the immaculately restored frescoes in the apse by the great Fra Filippo Lippi, showing the Annuciation, the Nativity, and the Death of Mary, with a marvelous Coronation of the Virgin adorning the dome; be ready with a 500-lire coin to illuminate the masterpiece. The Florentine artist died shortly after completing the work, and his tomb—designed by his son, Filippino Lippi—lies in the church's right transept. Another fresco cycle, including work by Pinturicchio, can be seen in the Eroli chapel off the right aisle. ⊠ *Piazza Duomo.* ⊙ *Daily 8–1 and 3–6:30 (3–5:30 in winter).*

From Piazza del Duomo make your way to **Piazza del Mercato,** site of the old Roman forum and today the main square of the Old Town.

The **Arch of Drusus** was built by the Senate of Spoleto to honor the Roman general Drusus, son of the emperor Tiberius. ⊠ *Off the southern end of Piazza del Mercato.*

On an extension of the picturesque Via Fontesecca, with its tempting shops selling local pottery and other handicrafts, is the church of **Sant'Eufemia** (in the courtyard of the archbishop's palace), an ancient, austere church built in the 11th century. Its most interesting feature is the gallery above the nave where female worshippers were required to sit—a holdover from the Eastern Church—one of the few such galleries in this part of Italy. There is also a **museum** attached to the church containing some good paintings, including a Madonna by Fra Filippo Lippi. ⊠ *Via Saffi, between Piazza del Duomo and Piazza del Mercato.* 🏛 *Church 3,000 lire; museum 4,000 lire; both 5,000 lire.* ⊙ *Daily 10–12:30 and 3:30–7 (winter, 2:30–6).*

The small but well-preserved **Roman theater** is used in summer for performances of Spoleto's arts festival. The theater was the site of one of the town's most macabre incidents. During the Middle Ages, Spoleto took the side of the Holy Roman Emperor in the interminable struggle between Guelph (papal) and Ghibelline (imperial) factions over the question of who would control central and northern Italy. Four hundred of the pope's supporters were massacred in the theater, and their bodies were burned in an enormous pyre. It is not an episode of which Spoleto is proud, and, furthermore, the Guelphs were triumphant in the end. Spoleto was incorporated into the states of the Church in 1354. ⊠ *At the southern end of Corso Mazzini.* ✎ *4,000 lire.* ☉ *Mon.–Sat. 9–1:30 and 2:30–7 (winter, 2:30–5), Sun. 9–1.*

On the outskirts of the city, just off Via Flaminia (S3), is the lovely church of **San Salvatore.** You may already have seen a lot of old churches in Italy, but few are as old as this one. It needed renovation in the 9th century—by that time it was already 500 years old. It is nestled under cypresses and surrounded by Spoleto's cemetery and is quiet, cool, and peaceful. The church was built by Eastern monks in the 4th century, and little has been added (or removed) since its renovation. San Salvatore has an air of timelessness and antiquity rarely found in churches so close to major towns. ⊠ *Via della Basilica di San Salvatore.* ☉ *Nov.–Feb., daily 7–5; Mar.–Apr. and Sept.–Oct., daily 7–6; May–Aug., daily 7–7.*

Dining and Lodging

$$ ✕ **Il Pentagramma.** Just off the central Piazza della Libertà, this modern restaurant features such local dishes as *coda di bue alla spoletina* (oxtail) and lamb in a truffle sauce. ⊠ *Via Martani 4,* ☎ *0743/223141. Reservations essential during the festival and on weekends. DC, MC, V. Closed Mon.*

$$ ✕ **Il Tartufo.** Spoleto's most famous restaurant has a smart modern dining room on the second floor and a rustic dining room downstairs—both of which incorporate the ruins of a Roman villa. The traditional cooking is spiced up in summer to appeal to the cosmopolitan crowd that is attending (or performing in) the Festival of Two Worlds. As its name indicates, the restaurant specializes in dishes prepared with truffles, though there is a second menu from which you can choose items not containing this expensive delicacy. ⊠ *Piazza Garibaldi 24,* ☎ *0743/40236. Reservations essential. AE, DC, MC, V. Closed Wed. and mid-July–1st wk in Aug.*

$$ ✕ **Trattoria Panciolle.** In the heart of Spoleto's medieval quarter, this restaurant has one of the most romantic settings you could wish for. Dining outside in summer is a welcome respite, in a small piazza filled with lime trees. Specialties include strangozzi pasta with mushroom sauce and *agnello scottadito* (grilled lamb chops). Seven guest rooms are also available here. ⊠ *Via del Duomo 3,* ☎ *0743/45598. Reservations essential. AE, MC, V. Closed Wed.*

$$$ 🏨 **Dei Duchi.** This excellent, well-run hotel is a favorite among performers in the Festival of Two Worlds. It's in center of the town, near the Roman amphitheater. Some rooms have fine views of the city. ⊠ *Viale Matteotti 4, 06049,* ☎ *0743/44541,* 𝔽𝔸𝕏 *0743/44543. 49 rooms. Restaurant, bar, meeting rooms, free parking. AE, DC, MC, V.*

$$$ 🏨 **Hotel Gattapone.** The tiny four-star Hotel Gattapone at the top of the Old Town, near the Ponte delle Torri, has wonderful views of the ancient bridge and the wooded slopes of Monteluco. The rooms are modern and tastefully decorated. ⊠ *Via del Ponte 6, 06049,* ☎ *0743/223447,* 𝔽𝔸𝕏 *0743/223448. 16 rooms. Bar. AE, DC, MC, V.*

$$ 🏨 **Nuovo Clitunno.** A renovated 18th-century building houses this pleasant hotel, a five-minute walk from the town center. Bedrooms and public rooms, some with lovely timber-beamed ceilings, have a mixture of period as well as less characterful modern furniture. ✉ *Piazza Sordini 6, 06049,* ☎ *0743/223340,* FAX *0743/222663. 38 rooms. Restaurant, bar. AE, DC, MC, V.*

Nightlife and the Arts

The **Festival dei Due Mondi** (Festival of Two Worlds) in Spoleto (mid-June–mid-July) features star names in all branches of the arts—particularly music, opera, and theater—and draws thousands of visitors from all over the world. Tickets for all performances should be ordered in advance from the festival's box office, which has full program information starting in April (✉ Piazza Duomo 9, ☎ 0743/44325).

OFF THE
BEATEN PATH

VALNERINA – This is the name of the area east of Umbria, and it is the most beautiful of central Italy's many well-kept secrets. The roads that serve the rugged landscape are poor, but a drive through the region, even with all those time-consuming twists and turns, will be worth it to see forgotten medieval villages and dramatic mountain scenery. The first stop should be the **waterfalls at Marmore,** the highest falls in Europe. You'll find them a few miles east of Terni, on the road to Lake Piediluco and Rieti. The waters are diverted on weekdays to provide hydroelectric power for the town of Terni, so check with the tourist office (✉ Viale C. Battisti 7/a, ☎ 0744/423047) in Terni before heading there. On summer evenings, when the falls are in full spate, the cascading water is floodlit—and a welcome sight.

Close to the picturesque town of Ferentillo (northeast of Terni on S209) is the outstanding 8th-century abbey of **San Pietro in Valle.** There are fine frescoes in the nave of the church, and the cloister is graceful and peaceful. As a bonus, one of the abbey outbuildings houses a fine restaurant with moderate prices. Farther east are the towns of Norcia and Cascia; **Norcia** is the most famous town for Umbrian food specialties. It is also the birthplace of Saint Benedict. **Cascia** is the birthplace of the uncrowned patron saint of Italian women, Saint Rita.

Assisi

🔟 *47 km (30 mi) north and west of Spoleto on S3 and S75, 25 km (16 mi) east of Perugia.*

The first sight of Assisi is memorable. The hill on which Assisi sits rises dramatically from the flat plain, and the town is dominated at the top of the mount by a medieval castle; on the lower slopes of the hill is the massive Basilica di San Francesco, rising majestically on graceful arched supports. From a distance, Saint Francis's birthplace looks—to use an evocative phrase of travel essayist James Reynolds—"calm, white, pure as the fresh-washed wool from the Pascal Lamb."

Except in the depths of the off-season, Assisi, the most famous and most visited city in Umbria, is always thronged with sightseers and pilgrims. Somehow, though, despite the press of visitors, there is an unspoiled quality to the city—Assisi seems to be actually redolent of the sweet personality of its greatest citizen, Saint Francis, who is buried here in the huge 13th-century Basilica on the Hill of Paradise.

Saint Francis was born here in 1181, the son of a well-to-do merchant. He had, by his own account, a riotous youth but forsook the pleasures of the flesh quite early in life, adopting a life of austerity. His mystical approach to poverty, asceticism, and the beauty of man and nature struck a responsive chord in the medieval mind, and he quickly attracted a vast number of followers. He was a humble and unassuming man, and his compassion and humility brought him great love and veneration in his own lifetime. Without actively seeking power, as did many clerics of his day, he amassed great influence and political power, changing the history of the Catholic Church. He was the first person to receive the stigmata (wounds in his hands, feet, and side corresponding to the torments of Christ on the cross), injuries that caused him great pain and suffering, which he bore with characteristic patience. Nonetheless, Saint Francis welcomed the coming of "Sister Death," in 1226. Today the Franciscans are the largest of all the Catholic orders. And among the mass of clergy at Assisi, you can identify the saint's followers by their simple, coarse brown habits bound by sashes of knotted rope.

★ ⓮ The **Basilica di San Francesco** is one of Italy's foremost monuments and was begun shortly after the saint's death. What Saint Francis would have made of a church of such size, wealth, and grandeur—the opposite of all he preached and believed—is hard to imagine. His coffin, unearthed from its secret hiding place in 1818, is on display in the crypt below the lower church and is a place of piety. The basilica is not one church but two huge structures built one over the other. The lower church is dim and full of candlelit shadows, whereas the upper is bright and airy. Both are magnificently decorated artistic treasure houses, however, especially the upper church, where a fresco cycle by Giotto is a milestone in the history of Western art.

Visit the **lower church** first. The first chapel on the left of the nave was decorated by the Sienese master Simone Martini. Frescoed in 1322–26, the paintings show the life of Saint Martin—the sharing of his cloak with the poor man, the saint's knighthood, and his death.

There is some dispute about the paintings in the third chapel on the right. Experts have argued for years as to their authorship, with many saying that they were done by Giotto. The paintings depict the life of Saint Mary Magdalen. There is a similar dispute about the works above the high altar—some say they are by Giotto; others claim them for an anonymous pupil. They depict the marriage of Saint Francis to poverty, chastity, and obedience.

In the right transept are frescoes by Cimabue, a Madonna and saints, one of them Saint Francis himself. In the left transept are some of the best-known works of the Sienese painter Pietro Lorenzetti. They depict the Madonna with Saints John and Francis, a crucifixion, and a descent from the cross.

It is quite a contrast to climb the steps next to the altar and emerge into the bright sunlight and airy grace of the double-arched Renaissance cloister called the **Cloister of the Dead.** A door to the right leads to the treasury of the church and contains relics of Saint Francis and other holy objects associated with the order.

The **upper church** is dominated by Giotto's 28 frescoes, each portraying incidents in the life of Saint Francis. Although the artist was only in his twenties when he painted this cycle, the frescoes show that Giotto was the pivotal artist in the development of Western painting, breaking away from the stiff, unnatural styles of earlier generations and moving toward a realism and grace that reached their peak in the Renaissance. The paintings are viewed left to right, starting in the transept. The most beloved of all the scenes is probably *Saint Francis Preaching to the Birds,* a touching painting that seems to sum up the gentle spirit of the saint. It stands in marked contrast to the scene of the dream of Innocent III. The pope dreams of a humble monk who will steady the church. Sure

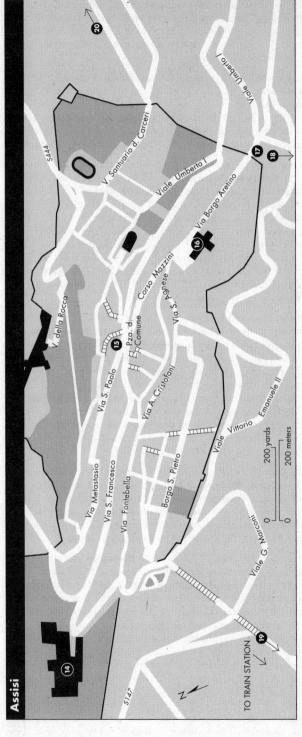

Assisi

Basilica di
San Francesco, **14**
Hermitage of the
Carceri, **20**
Porta Nuova, **17**
San Damiano, **18**
Santa Chiara, **16**

Santa Maria degli
Angeli, **19**
Temple of
Minerva, **15**

TO TRAIN STATION

enough, in the panel next to the sleeping pope, you see a strong Francis supporting a church that seems to be on the verge of tumbling down. ⊠ *Piazza di San Francesco.* ☉ *Upper and lower churches: summer, Mon.–Sat. 7 AM–sunset, Sun. 1–sunset; winter, Mon.–Sat. 7–noon and 2–sunset, Sun. 2–sunset.*

⑮ In the long, central square of the town, Piazza del Comune, is the **Temple of Minerva.** It is made up of bits and pieces of a Roman temple that dates from the time of Augustus and was later converted into a church. The expectations raised by the perfect classical facade are not met by the interior, subjected to a thorough Baroque assault in the 17th century. ⊠ *Piazza del Comune.* ☉ *Daily 7–noon and 2:30–sunset.*

⑯ In the southeastern part of Assisi, near the Porta Nuova, the 13th-century church of **Santa Chiara** is dedicated to Saint Clare, one of the earliest and most fervent of Saint Francis's followers and the founder of the order of the Poor Ladies, or Poor Clares, in imitation of the Franciscans. The church contains the body of the saint, and in the **Chapel of the Crucifix** (on the right) is the cross that spoke to Saint Francis and led him to a life of piety. A heavily veiled member of Saint Clare's order is stationed before the cross in perpetual adoration of the image. To get here from Piazza del Comune, walk down Corso Mazzini past the Pinacoteca. ⊠ *Piazza Santa Chiara.* ☉ *Daily 8–noon and 2:30–sunset.*

⑰ A little way beyond the church of Santa Chiara, along Via Borgo Aretino, the walls of Assisi are cut through by the **Porta Nuova** gate.

⑱ It was in the church of **San Damiano** that the crucifix spoke to Saint Francis, saying *"Vade, Francisce, et repara domum meam"* ("Go, Francis, and repair my house"). It was also in this church, pleasantly situated in an olive grove, that Saint Francis brought Saint Clare into the religious life. The church became the first home of her order, and it and its convent, simple and austere, give a far better idea of Saint Francis and his movement than the great basilica. The church is a 1-km (⅗-mi) walk from the Porta Nuova gate. ⊠ *Località San Damiano.* ☉ *Daily 10–noon and 2–6 (winter 2–5).*

⑲ On the outskirts of the town, on the plain near the train station, is the church of **Santa Maria degli Angeli.** It is a Baroque building constructed over the **Porziuncola,** a little chapel restored by Saint Francis. The shrine is much venerated because it was here, in the **Transito chapel,** then a humble cell, that Saint Francis died. ⊠ *Località Santa Maria degli Angeli.* ☉ *Daily 9–12:30 and 2:30–sunset.*

⑳ Just 4 km (2½ mi) east of Assisi is the **Hermitage of the Carceri,** a monastery set in dense woodlands on the side of Mt. Subasio. In the caves on the slope of the mountain, Francis and his followers established their first home, to which he returned often during his lifetime to pray and meditate. The church and monastery retain the tranquil contemplative air Saint Francis so prized. From a vantage point within the monastery visitors can take in one of the most beautiful vistas over the Umbrian countryside. True to their Franciscan heritage, the friars here are entirely dependent on alms from visitors. ⊠ *Eremo degli Carceri.* ⌨ *Donation accepted.* ☉ *Summer, daily 6:30 AM–7:30 PM; winter, daily 6:30 AM–5 PM.*

OFF THE
BEATEN PATH   **CANNARA** – A pleasant excursion from Assisi leads to this tiny town; a half-hour walk outside the town are the fields of Pian d'Arca, which legend identifies as the site of Saint Francis's sermon to the birds.

Dining and Lodging

$$ ✕ **Buca di San Francesco.** This central restaurant is Assisi's busiest and most patronized—it's no wonder the setting is lovely no matter what the season. In summer you dine outside in a cool green garden; in winter, in the cozy cellars of the restaurant. The food is first-rate, and the *filetto al rubesco* (fillet steak cooked in a heady red wine) is the specialty of the house. ✉ *Via Brizi 1,* ☎ *075/812204. Reservations essential. AE, DC, MC, V. Closed Mon. and July.*

$$ ✕ **La Fortezza.** Parts of the walls of this modern, family-run restaurant were built by the Romans. The service is personable and kitchen reliable. A particular standout is *anatra al finocchio selvatico* (duck cooked with wild fennel). La Fortezza also has seven simple but clean guest rooms available. ✉ *Vicolo della Fortezza 19/b,* ☎ *075/812418. Reservations essential. AE, DC, MC, V. Closed Thurs. Oct.–July, Feb.*

$ ✕ **La Stalla.** A km or two outside the town proper, this onetime stable has been turned into a simple and rustic restaurant. In summer, lunch and dinner are served outside under a trellis shaded with vines and flowers. In keeping with the decor, the kitchen turns out hearty country fare. ✉ *Via Eremo delle Carceri 8,* ☎ *075/812317. No credit cards. Closed Mon. Oct.–June.*

$$$ ⊞ **Hotel Subasio.** This hotel, close to the basilica of Saint Francis, has counted Marlene Dietrich and Charlie Chaplin among its guests. It is housed in a converted monastery and has plenty of atmosphere. Some of the rooms remain a little monastic, but the views, comfortable old-fashioned sitting rooms, flowered terraces, and a lovely garden more than make up for the simplicity. Ask for a room with a view of the valley. ✉ *Via Frate Elia 2, 06081,* ☎ *075/812206,* 𝔽𝔸𝕏 *075/816691. 61 rooms. Restaurant, bar. AE, DC, MC, V.*

$$ ⊞ **Hotel Umbra.** A 16th-century town house is home to this hotel, which
★ is in a tranquil part of the city, an area closed to traffic, near Piazza del Comune. The rooms are arranged as small apartments, each with a tiny living room and terrace. The restaurant does not serve lunch Tuesday and Wednesday. ✉ *Via degli Archi 6, 06081,* ☎ *075/812240,* 𝔽𝔸𝕏 *075/813653. 25 rooms. Restaurant, bar. AE, DC, MC, V. Closed mid-Jan.–mid-Mar. and Dec. 1–20.*

$$ ⊞ **San Francesco.** This is a centrally located hotel in a renovated 16th-century building. Some of the rooms have a view of the basilica or the valley. ✉ *Via di San Francesco 48, 06082,* ☎ *075/812281,* 𝔽𝔸𝕏 *075/816237. 44 rooms. Restaurant, bar. AE, DC, MC, V.*

En Route The drive to Orvieto on S3bis ("bis" means alternative highway) is a pleasant one that cuts south through the center of the region and takes you through Todi, a lovely hill town. Todi has an extraordinary grouping of Gothic palaces and a medieval cathedral in its central Piazza del Popolo. At Todi, change to S448, which connects with the main north–south autostrada (A1).

Orvieto

㉑ *112 km (70 mi) southwest of Assisi, 86 km (53 mi) south of Perugia, 96 km (60 mi) northwest of Rome, 37 km (23 mi) west of Todi, off A1.*

Commanding a dramatic position on a great square rock, Orvieto, one of Umbria's greatest cities, is an amazing sight, dominating the countryside for miles in every direction. This natural fort was first settled by the Etruscans, but not even Orvieto's defenses could withstand the might of the Romans, who attacked, sacked, and destroyed the city in 283 BC. From that time, Orvieto has had close ties with Rome. It was solidly Guelph in the Middle Ages, and for several hundred years popes sought refuge in the city, at some times needing protection from their enemies, at times fleeing from the summer heat of Rome.

★ Orvieto's position on its rock has meant that little new building has ever been done here, giving the town an almost perfect medieval character. The jewel, the centerpiece of Orvieto, is its **Duomo,** set in the wide and airy Piazza del Duomo. The church, built to commemorate the Miracle of Bolsena, was started in 1290 and received the attention of some of the greatest architects and sculptors of the time. It was further embellished inside by great Renaissance artists. The facade is a prodigious work, covered with carvings and mosaics, the latter intricately ornamenting practically every pillar and post and also used in large representations of religious scenes (many of these were restored or redone in the 18th and 19th centuries). The bas-reliefs on the lower parts of the pillars were carved by Maitani, one of the original architects of the building, and show scenes from the Old Testament and some particularly gruesome renderings of the Last Judgment and Hell, as well as a more tranquil Paradise. (They have been covered with Plexiglas following some vandalizing in the 1960s.)

The vast interior of the cathedral is famous chiefly for the frescoes in the **Cappella Nuova** (the last chapel on the right, nearest the high altar). The earliest works here are above the altar and are by Fra Angelico. They show Christ in Glory and the prophets. The major works in the chapel, however, are by Luca Signorelli and show a very graphic Last Judgment. The walls seem to be filled with muscular, writhing figures, and most critics draw a direct connection between these figures and the later Last Judgment of Michelangelo on the wall of the Sistine Chapel. Leonardo da Vinci, however, was less than impressed. He said that the figures, with their rippling muscles, reminded him of sacks "stuffed full of nuts."

Across the nave of the cathedral from the Cappella Nuova is the **Cappella del Corporale.** It houses the relics of the Miracle of Bolsena, the raison d'être for the Duomo. A priest in the nearby town of Bolsena suddenly found himself assailed by doubts about the transubstantiation—he could not bring himself to believe that the body of Christ was contained in the consecrated communion host. His doubts were put to rest, however, when a wafer he had just blessed suddenly started to drip blood. Drops of blood fell onto the linen covering the altar, and this cloth and the host itself are the principal relics of the miracle. They are contained in a sumptuous gold-and-enamel reliquary on the altar of this chapel and are displayed on the Feast of Corpus Christi and at Easter. ⊠ *Piazza Duomo.* ☉ *Daily 7–1 and 2:30–sunset.*

The medieval **Palazzo dei Papi,** once the summer residence of popes, contains the **Archaeological Museum.** ⊠ *Piazza Duomo.* ☜ *4,000 lire.* ☉ *Mon.–Sat. 9–1:30 and 2:30–7, Sun. 9–1.*

Orvieto is known for its **wines,** particularly the whites. Some of the finest wines in Umbria are produced here (Signorelli, when painting the Duomo, asked that part of his contract be paid in wine), and the rock on which the town sits is honeycombed with caves used to ferment the Trebbiano grapes that are used in making Orvieto vintages.

Dining and Lodging

$$ ★ ✕ **Le Grotte del Funaro.** This restaurant has an extraordinary spot, deep in a series of caves within the volcanic rock beneath Orvieto. Once you have negotiated the steep steps, typical Umbrian specialties, like tagliatelle *al vino rosso* (with red wine sauce) and grilled beef with truffles, await. Sample the fine Orvieto wines, either the whites or the lesser-known reds. ⊠ *Via Ripa Serancia 41,* ☎ *0763/343276. Reservations essential. Sept.–May. AE, DC, MC, V. Closed Mon.*

$$ ✕ **Maurizio.** In the heart of Orvieto, just opposite the cathedral, this ★ warm and welcoming restaurant gets its share of tourists and has a local clientele as well. The decor is unusual, with wood sculptures by Orvieto craftsman Michelangeli. The menu offers hearty soups and homemade pastas such as *tronchetti* (a pasta roll with spinach and ricotta filling). ⊠ *Via del Duomo 78,* ☎ *0763/341114. Reservations essential in summer. AE, MC, V. Closed Tues.*

$$$ ◫ **Hotel La Badia.** This is one of the best-known country hotels in Umbria. The 700-year-old building, a former monastery, is set in rolling parkland that provides wonderful views of the valley and the town of Orvieto in the distance. The rooms are well appointed. ⊠ *Località La Badia, 4 km (2½ mi) south of Orvieto, 05018,* ☎ *0763/90359,* FAX *0763/92796. 26 rooms. Restaurant, bar, pool, tennis courts, meeting rooms. AE, MC, V. Closed Jan.–Feb.*

$$$ ◫ **Hotel Maitani.** In a 17th-century Baroque palazzo, this hotel has rather ugly public rooms and no restaurant. On a better note, parquet and marble grace the floors and there's a deluxe roof terrace. The rooms are old-fashioned but comfortable. ⊠ *Via Maitani 5, 05018,* ☎ *0763/342011,* FAX *0763/342012. 39 rooms. Bar, air-conditioning. AE, DC, MC, V.*

$$–$$$ ◫ **Grand Hotel Reale.** The best feature of this hotel is its locale in the center of Orvieto, across a square that hosts a lively market. Facing the impressive Gothic-Romanesque Palazzo del Popolo, rooms are spacious and adequately furnished, with a traditional accent. ⊠ *Piazza del Popolo 25, 05018,* ☎ *0763/341247,* FAX *0763/341247. 32 rooms. Bar. MC, V.*

$$–$$$ ◫ **Villa Bellago.** Outside Orvieto, in a tranquil setting on a spit of land overlooking Lake Corbara, three farmhouses have been completely overhauled. The result is welcome: the hotel now includes well-lighted and spacious guest rooms, generous facilities, and a fine restaurant (closed Tuesday) specializing in imaginatively prepared Umbrian and Tuscan dishes. Fresh fish is always on the menu. ⊠ *Outside the village of Baschi, 7½ km (4½ mi) south of Orvieto on S448,* ☎ *0744/950521,* FAX *0744/950524. 12 rooms. Restaurant, bar, pool, tennis court, exercise room. AE, DC, MC, V. Closed 4 wks between Jan. and Feb.*

$$ ◫ **Virgilio.** The modest Hotel Virgilio is right in Piazza del Duomo, and the rooms with views of the cathedral are wonderful. The rooms are small but nicely furnished. ⊠ *Piazza del Duomo 5, 05018,* ☎ *0763/341882,* FAX *0763/343797. 13 rooms. Bar. MC, V. Closed Feb.*

Shopping

EMBROIDERY AND LACE

Minor arts, such as embroidery and lace making, flourish in Orvieto. One of the best shops for *merletto* (lace) is **Duranti** (⊠ Corso Cavour 107).

WINES

Excellent Orvieto wines are justly prized throughout Italy and in foreign countries. The whites pressed from the region's Trebbiano grapes are fruity, with a tart finish. Orvieto also produces its own version of the Tuscan dessert wine *vin santo*. It is darker than its Tuscan cousin and is aged five years before bottling. You may stop for a glass of *vino* (wine) at the **wine cellar** (⊠ No. 2, Piazza del Duomo), where there's also a good selection of sandwiches and snacks and vin santo is on sale.

WOODWORKING

Orvieto is a center of woodworking, particularly fine inlays and veneers. The Corso Cavour has a number of artisan shops specializing in woodwork, the best known being the **Michelangeli family studio** (⊠ Corso Cavour), crammed with a variety of imaginatively designed objects ranging in size from a giant *armadio* (wardrobe) to a simple wooden spoon.

OFF THE
BEATEN PATH **COUNTRYSIDE SOUTHEAST OF ORVIETO** – The countryside covered as you head southeast toward the town of Narni is rarely included in most travel itineraries—a pity, since the scenery and rustic charm of the small towns on the route make this one of the most pleasant parts of Umbria. It is also a manageable chunk of country that can be seen in a half day's touring by car.

UMBRIA AND THE MARCHES A TO Z

Arriving and Departing

By Bus
Perugia and Orvieto are served by the **Sulga Line** (☎ 075/5009641) with daily departures from Rome's Stazione Tiburtina and Fiumicino airport, and from Piazza Adua in Florence.

By Car
On the western edge of the region is the Umbrian section of the Autostrada del Sole (**A1**), the principal north–south highway in Italy. It links Florence and Rome with the important Umbrian town of Orvieto and passes near Todi and Terni. The **S3** intersects with A1 and leads on to Assisi and Urbino. The Adriatica superhighway (**A14**) runs north–south along the coast, linking the Marches to Bologna and Venice.

By Train
The main rail line from Rome to Ancona passes through Narni, Terni, Spoleto, and Foligno. Travel time from Rome to Spoleto is a little less than 90 minutes on intercity trains. The main Rome–Florence line stops at Orvieto. With a change of trains at the small town of Terontola, one can travel by rail from Rome or Florence to Perugia and Assisi.

Getting Around

By Bus
There is good local bus service between all the major and minor towns of Umbria. Some of the routes in rural areas, especially in the Marches, are designed to serve as many destinations as possible and are, therefore, quite roundabout and slow. Schedules often change, so consult with local tourist offices before setting out.

By Car
Umbria has an excellent and modern road network. Central Umbria is served by a major highway, **S75bis**, which passes along the shore of Lake Trasimeno and ends in Perugia. Assisi is well served by the modern highway **S75**, which connects to S3 and **3bis**, which cover the heart of the region. Major inland routes connect coastal **A14** to large towns in the Marches, including Urbino, Jesi, Macerata, and Ascoli Piceno, but inland secondary roads in mountain areas can be tortuous and narrow.

By Train
Branch lines link the central rail hub, Ancona, with the inland towns of Fabriano and Ascoli Piceno. In Umbria, a small, privately owned railway runs from Città di Castello in the north to Terni in the south via Perugia. The private line is run by Ferrovia Centrale Umbra (FCU) (☎ 075/29121).

Contacts and Resources

Emergencies

Police: Perugia (✉ Piazza dei Partigiani, ☎ 113). **Assisi** (✉ Piazza Matteotti 3, ☎ 075/812239). **Spoleto** (✉ Viale Trento e Trieste, ☎ 0743/40324). **Orvieto** (✉ Piazza Cahen, ☎ 0763/342476).

Visitor Information

Ancona (✉ Via Thaon De Revel 4, ☎ 071/33249; railway station, Piazza Fratelli Rosselli, ☎ 071/41703). **Ascoli Piceno** (✉ Piazza del Popolo, ☎ 0736/257288). **Assisi** (✉ Piazza del Comune 12, ☎ 075/812534). **Gubbio** (✉ Piazza Oderisi 6, ☎ 075/9220693). **Loreto** (✉ Via Solari 3, ☎ 071/977139). **Orvieto** (✉ Piazza Duomo, ☎ 0763/341772). **Perugia** (✉ Piazza IV Novembre 3, ☎ 075/5723327). **Spoleto** (✉ Piazza della Libertà 7, ☎ 0743/220311). **Urbino** (✉ Piazza Rinascimento 1, ☎ 0722/2613).

13 Campania

Naples, Pompeii, and the Amalfi Drive

Emperors, kings, and artists have all made Campania's sea-wreathed resorts and starlit isles their abodes for more than 2,000 years. And well they might, for this region is a compressed realm of undiluted beauty. Naples—the most operatic of cities—rules over its breathtaking bay. Nearby, ancient Romans once led carefree lives at Pompeii just as today's travelers now soak up the 24-karat sun on Capri. Beyond lie Sorrento, Positano, Amalfi, and Ravello. The locals dare you to find lovelier towns, even in your imagination.

CAMPANIA IS A REGION OF NAMES to conjure with—Capri, Sorrento, Pompeii, Paestum—names evoking visions of cliff-shaded coves, sun-dappled waters, and mighty ruins. And Naples, a tumultuous, animated city, the very heart of Campania, stands guard over these treasures.

Updated by
Robert
Andrews

Campania stretches south in flat coastal plains and low mountains from Baia Domizia, Capua, and Caserta to Naples and Pompeii on the magnificent bay; past Capri and Ischia; along the rocky coast to Sorrento, Amalfi, and Salerno; and farther still past the Cilento promontory to Sapri and the Calabria border. Inland lie the bleak fringes of the Apennines and the rolling countryside around Benevento.

On each side of Naples the earth fumes and grumbles, reminding us that all this beauty was born of cataclysm. Toward Sorrento, Vesuvius smolders sleepily over the ruins of Herculaneum and Pompeii, while north of Naples, beyond Posillipo, the craters of the Solfatara spew steaming gases. And nearby are the dark, deep waters of Lake Averno, legendary entrance to Hades.

With these reminiscences of death and destruction so close at hand, it's no wonder that the southerner in general, and the Neapolitan in particular, chooses to take no chances, plunging enthusiastically into the task of living each moment to its fullest.

Campania was probably settled by the ancient Phoenicians, Cretans, and Greeks. Traces of their presence here date from approximately 1000 BC, some 300 years before the legendary founding of Rome. Herculaneum is said to have been established by Hercules himself, and as excavation of this once-great city—Greek and later Roman—progresses, further light will be thrown on the history of the whole Campania region.

The origin of Naples, once called Parthenope and later Neapolis, presumably can be traced to what are now the ruins of Cumae nearby, which legend tells us was already in existence in 800 BC. Here, in a dark vaulted chamber, the Cumaean Sybil rendered her oracles. Greek civilization flourished for hundreds of years all along this coastline, but there was nothing in the way of centralized government until centuries later, when the Roman Empire, uniting all Italy for the first time, surged southward and, with little opposition, absorbed the Greek colonies. The Romans were quick to appreciate the sybaritic possibilities of such a lovely land, and it was in this region that the wealthy of the empire built their palatial country residences. Generally, the peace of Campania was undisturbed during these centuries of Roman rule.

Naples and Campania, with the rest of Italy, decayed with the Roman Empire and collapsed into the abyss of the Middle Ages. Naples itself regained some importance under the rule of the Angevins in the latter part of the 13th century and continued its progress in the 1440s under Aragonese rule. The nobles who served under the Spanish viceroys in the 16th and 17th centuries, when their harsh rule made all Italy quail, enjoyed their pleasures, and taverns and gaming houses thrived, even as Spain milked the area with its taxes.

After a short-lived Austrian occupation, Naples—Napoli in Italian—became the capital of the Kingdom of the Two Sicilies, which the Bourbon kings established in 1738. Their rule was generally benevolent, as far as Campania was concerned, and their support of the papal authority in Rome was an important factor in the development of the rest of Italy. Their rule was important artistically, too, for not only did it contribute greatly to the architectural beauty of the region, but it attracted great musicians, artists, and writers, who were only too willing to enjoy the easy life of court in such magnificent natural surroundings.

Finally, Giuseppe Garibaldi launched his famous expedition, and in 1860 Naples was united with the rest of Italy.

Times were relatively tranquil through the years that followed—with visitors of one nation or another thronging to Capri, to Sorrento, to Amalfi, and, of course, to Naples—until World War II. Allied bombings did considerable damage in Naples and the bay area. At the fall of the fascist government, the sorely tried Neapolitans rose up against Nazi occupation troops and in four days of street fighting drove them out of the city. A monument was raised to the *scugnizzo* (the typical Neapolitan street urchin) celebrating the youngsters who participated in the battle.

The war ended. Artists, tourists, writers, and ordinary lovers of beauty began to flow again into the Campania region that one ancient writer called "most blest by the Gods, most beloved by man." As the years have gone by, some parts gained increased attention from knowing visitors, while others lost the cachet they once had. The balance is maintained, with a steady trend toward more and more tourist development.

Pleasures and Pastimes

Beaches
The waters of the Bay of Naples are notoriously polluted. The waters around Capri and some, but not all, of Ischia's beaches offer clean swimming. Pollution is intermittent along the Amalfi Coast, where the deep waters are generally clean. Beaches in the Salerno area are best avoided; the water gets cleaner the farther south you go.

Dining
Campania's simple cuisine relies heavily on the bounty of the region's fertile farmland. Its tomatoes are exported all over the world, but to try them here is a new experience. Even during the winter you can find tomato sauce made with small sun-dried tomatoes plucked from bright red strands that you can see hanging outdoors on kitchen balconies. Pasta is a staple here, and spaghetti *al pomodoro* (with tomato sauce) and spaghetti *alle vongole* (with clam sauce, either white or red, depending on the cook's whims) appear on most menus.

Naples—the homeland of pizza—produces a simple pizza: *alla napoletana* (with anchovies); *alla margherita* (with tomato and mozzarella); and marinara (with tomato, garlic, and oregano). Locally produced mozzarella is used in many dishes; one of the most gratifying on a hot day is *insalata caprese* (with mozzarella, tomatoes, and basil). *Melanzane* (eggplant) and even zucchini are served parmigiana (fried and layered with tomato sauce and mozzarella). Meat may be served *alla pizzaiola* (cooked in a tomato-and-garlic sauce). Fish and seafood in general can be expensive, though fried calamari and *totani* (cuttlefish) are usually reasonably priced. Among the region's wines, Gragnano, Falerno, Lacrima Cristi, and Greco di Tufo are fine whites. Ischia and Ravello also produce good white wine. Campania's best-known reds are Aglianico, Taurasi, and the red version of Falerno.

Restaurant prices in the region are generally a little lower than in Rome and northern Italy, though Capri restaurants can be very expensive. On the islands, Sorrento peninsula, and Amalfi Coast, restaurants may be open every day of the week during the season, but may close for long periods in the winter.

CATEGORY	COST*
$$$$	over 85,000 lire
$$$	60,000–85,000 lire
$$	25,000–60,000 lire
$	under 25,000 lire

Prices are per person, including house wine, service, and tax.

Lodging

Although Capri, Ischia, Sorrento, and the Amalfi Coast offer generally fine accommodations in all categories, good establishments in Naples are scarce, so reserve well in advance. High-season rates apply at all coastal resorts in July and August. These rates extend from April or May through September at Sorrento and Amalfi Coast resorts, where Christmas and Easter also draw crowds and command top rates. Whereas coastal resorts elsewhere close up tight from fall to spring, at least some hotels and restaurants are open in Sorrento and on the Amalfi Coast year-round. It's always a good idea to book ahead, and it's imperative in high season. Campania hotel rates are generally lower than those in major tourist cities to the north, but rates in Capri's top hotels are at premium levels for Italy. On the other hand, even in Capri and especially along the Amalfi Coast, you can find charming little hotels with attractive rooms and wonderful views at very reasonable rates; just don't expect to find vacancies in August. During the summer, hotels on the coast almost always require that you take half board if they serve meals. Local tourist information offices will help you find accommodations.

CATEGORY	COST*
$$$$	over 300,000 lire
$$$	160,000–300,000 lire
$$	100,000–160,000 lire
$	under 100,000 lire

Prices are for a standard double room for two, including service and 9% tax (12% for luxury establishments).

Nightlife

In these parts, as elsewhere in southern Italy, nightlife usually takes the form of outdoor living in cafés and restaurants with views of the passing parade. Piazzas are lively until late in good weather, especially in resort towns on the islands and on the Sorrento peninsula. Capri's Piazzetta is a classic example. Entertainment in the coastal resorts is mainly seasonal.

Most of the best bars have the attraction of a good location (overlooking the Bay of Naples, for example) or comfortable setting; there is sometimes music and dancing, but these establishments cannot truly be called nightclubs.

Exploring Campania

Many of Campania's allurements hug the Bay of Naples—including the city itself and its satellite islands, Capri and Ischia, and the archaeological sites of Pompeii, Herculaneum, and the Phlegrean Fields at the northern end of the Bay. At the southern end, Sorrento also lies within this charmed circle, and itself lies within easy distance of Positano, Amalfi, and the pleasures of the Amalfi coast. Further distant, Paestum offers more classical marvels, while inland, Caserta and Benevento offer in turn a Bourbon palace and more majestic Roman remains.

Campania provides enough of both cultural stimulation and more basic relaxation to allow you a good deal of flexibility on choosing how to spend your time. Pace yourself, spend a little time planning, especially with only a limited number of days at your disposal, and even the brisk tempo of Naples is manageable, with peace and tranquillity only a hydrofoil ride away on Ischia and Capri.

Numbers in the text correspond to numbers in the margin and on the Campania, Naples, and Pompeii maps.

Great Itineraries

If art and antiquity are high on your list, and if you have only a few days to spend in the area, make Naples your base. Few fall in love with Naples at first sight, and many complain about its obvious flaws: urban decay and delinquency. But practically everyone who takes the time and trouble to discover its artistic riches and appreciate its vivacious atmosphere considers it worth the effort. Naples is near the most famous classical ruins, and you should dedicate at least a morning or afternoon to Pompeii or Herculaneum. And as the regional capital, it is connected by direct rail, road, and sea routes to nearly all the sights mentioned in this chapter.

With more time, or if you're looking for dramatic scenery and want to enjoy it at a relaxed pace, plan to spend time either in touristy Sorrento, on the islands of Capri and Ischia, or on the beautiful Amalfi Coast. Be warned, though: these areas become quite crowded in July and August, when throngs of vacationing Italians arrive.

IF YOU HAVE 3 DAYS

In ⌘ **Naples** ①–⑯ itself, a visit to the **Museo Archeologico Nazionale** ⑮ is an essential preparation (or follow-up) for an expedition to **Herculaneum** ⑳ and **Pompeii** ㉒–㊳, either of which is an indispensable sight for anyone visiting Campania. The islands of ⌘ **Ischia** ㊶ and ⌘ **Capri** ㊷ can also be approached from Naples, and make an ideal antidote to the city's noise. If you decide not to stay here, aim to spend a quiet day on one of the islands before returning to Naples. It is worth spending at least one night out of Naples, and a good alternative to the islands would be ⌘ **Sorrento** ㊸ an easy hydrofoil ride away, and a good base from which to tour the nearby **Amalfi Coast** ㊸–㊽, where you could visit three of the small towns—**Positano** ㊹, **Amalfi** ㊺, and **Vietri sul Mare** ㊼, for instance—on a third day's excursion.

IF YOU HAVE 5 DAYS

You could take in more than just one of the classical sights with more time, and a visit to the Greek temples of **Paestum** ㊾ is highly recommended for a glimpse at some of Magna Graecia's most stunning relics. You might also venture north to **Caserta** ㊴ to wander about the Royal Palace. Back in the Bay of Naples, spend your fourth and fifth days exploring ⌘ **Ischia** ㊶ and ⌘ **Sorrento** ㊸, both undemanding holiday resorts with plenty of natural beauty.

IF YOU HAVE 7 DAYS

A week in Campania will allow you to discover some of the more esoteric pleasures that Naples has to offer. Apart from the sheer vibrancy of its shopping streets and alleys, and the glorious views over the waterfront, **Naples** ①–⑯ has plenty of diversions within its tight mesh of streets, and you should make time for visiting some of its many famous churches—the **Duomo** ⑬, of course, but also **Santa Chiara** ⑪, **Santa Maria Donnaregina** ⑭, and the Cappella Sansevero, with its 18th-century sculptures. Don't forget, either, some of the capital's secondary museums, the **Museo Capodimonte** ⑯, for example, housed in another Bourbon royal palace with truly inspiring views. Outside town, head west to the volcanic region of the **Phlegrean Fields** ⑰–⑱, where Roman remains lie within a smoking, smoldering area rich with classical associations. Spend three nights on the Amalfi Coast, making sure to visit inland ⊞ **Ravello** ㊻ and pass some time in pretty **Pòsitano** ㊹, which defies any attempt to experience it on an overtight timetable. ⊞ **Capri** ㊷, too, deserves a couple of nights to appreciate fully its beauty—of secluded coves and beaches, not to mention the famous Blue Grotto—easily eclipsing the island's more lurid tourist trappings. You might pass a last day, perhaps en route out of Campania, in **Benevento** ㊵, which holds a well-preserved Roman theater and the renowned Arch of Trajan.

When to Tour Campania

Campania is not at its best in high summer: Naples is a sweltering inferno, the archaeological sites swarm, and the islands and Amalfi Coast resorts are similarly overrun with coaches and bad tempers. Any other time of year would be preferable, including winter, when the temperature rarely falls below the comfort threshold and rain is relatively rare. Swimming is possible year-round, though you will only see the hardiest bathers out between October and May.

Summer is also the worst time for ascents to Vesuvius: the best visibility occurs around spring and fall. Watch the clock, however, as the days get shorter: excursions to Vesuvius, Pompeii, Ercolano, and the islands all require some traveling, and it's easy to get caught out by the dark. At most archaeological sites visitors are rounded up two hours before sunset, so the earlier you arrive the better. Remember, too, that the majority of hotels, restaurants, and other tourist facilities in Sorrento, the Amalfi Coast, and the islands close down from November until around Easter, drastically reducing choice.

NAPLES

"Built like a great amphitheater around her beautiful bay, Naples is an eternally unfolding play acted by a million of the best actors in the world," Herbert Kubly observes in his *American in Italy.* "The comedy is broad, the tragedy violent. The curtain never rings down." Is it a sense of doom, living in the shadow of Vesuvius, that makes many Neapolitans so volatile, perhaps so seemingly blind to everything but the pain or pleasure of the moment? Poverty and overcrowding are the more likely causes, but whatever the reason, Naples is a difficult place for the casual tourist to quickly like. The Committee of Ninety-Nine, formed to counter Naples's negative image, has its work cut out. If you have the time and if you're willing to work at it, you'll come to love Naples as a mother loves her reprobate son; but if you're only passing through and hoping to enjoy a hassle-free vacation, spend as little time here as you can.

Why visit Naples at all? First, Naples is the most sensible base—particularly if you're traveling by public transportation—from which to explore Pompeii, Herculaneum, Vesuvius, and the Phlegrean Fields. Second, it's the home of the Museo Archeologico Nazionale (National Archaeological Museum). The most important finds from Pompeii and Herculaneum are on display here—everything from sculpture to carbonized fruit—and seeing them will add to the pleasure of your trip to Pompeii and Herculaneum.

Exploring Naples

In Naples you need a good sense of humor and a firm grip on your pocketbook and camera. Better still, leave all your valuables, including your passport, in the hotel safe. You'll probably be doing a lot of walking, for buses are crowded and taxis get stalled in traffic. If you come to Naples by car, park it in a garage as fast as you can, agree on

Campania

Formia

Sessa
Aurunca

Teano

Dragoni

S372

Carinola

A2

S7

Caiazzo

S87

Capua

Mondragone

Grazzanise

Caserta

39

Volturno

S264

Maddaloni

S7

Castel Volturno

S74

A2

S30

Villa Literno

Aversa

Caivano

Acerra

Giugliano in C.

Pomigliano

Casoria

A16

Naples

1 — **16**

S268

Vesuvius

Cumae

19

Ercolano

21

Pozzuoli

18 **17**

20

Scafati

Baia

Solfatara

Herculaneum

Casamicciola
Terme

41

Porto
d'Ischia

Pompeii

22 — **38**

S18

A3

Forio

Ischia

Golfo di Napoli

Castellammare

G

S145

Sorrento

43

44

Positano

*Tyrrhenian
Sea*

Capri

42

N

ITALY

KEY

Ferry

0   10 miles

0   15 km

the cost in advance, and then forget it for the duration of your stay (otherwise, window smashing and theft are constant risks). Take the Metropoltana (the city's subway system) to distant destinations and use the funiculars to get up and down the hills. Bus or funicular fares are 1,200 lire, valid for 90 minutes; 4,000 lire buys a ticket for the whole day. Subway tickets cost 1,500 lire each.

The tourist information office at **Piazza del Gesù** (☞ Contacts and Resources *in* Campania A to Z, *below*) can provide pamphlets with itineraries tracing the city's development in ancient, medieval, and modern times.

The sights outside the city limits are easy to reach from Naples; they can be treated as outings on their own.

A Good Tour

Start at the **Castel Nuovo** ①, facing the harbor on Piazza Municipio, housing a museum of mainly religious art. Pass the **Teatro San Carlo** ② on your way to the imposing **Palazzo Reale** ③, a royal palace redolent of Naples's past rulers. Next, turn back to the seafront where another royal fortress, the **Castel dell'Ovo** ④, sits overlooking the Santa Lucia waterfront. Walking further along the seafront, you might drop into the extensive **Acquario** ⑤ before visiting the **Villa Pignatelli** ⑥, a small museum holding a low-key collection of aristocratic knick-knacks. Walk up Via Ascensione, turn right onto Via Santa Teresa a Chiaia, left onto Via Bausan, and a left onto Via Colonna, leading to the funicular stop at Piazza Amedeo; take a ride up to the **Museo Duca di Martina** ⑦, another museum—though you might be content to take in the extraordinary views from the slopes of the Vómero hill. Also on the Vómero hill are the **Castel Sant'Elmo** ⑧ and the **Certosa di San Martino** ⑨, again, set in the same parkland and commanding magnificent vistas over city and sea to Vesuvius. Take a funicular ride down—this time to Piazza Montesanto—from which you are well placed to stroll northeast along Spaccanapoli, a straight line through the heart of Old Naples, taking in the churches of **Gesù Nuovo** ⑩ and **Santa Chiara** ⑪ en route. Farther up, you need only detour a few steps off this ancient artery to see some other art-rich religious monuments: **San Lorenzo Maggiore** ⑫, the **Duomo** ⑬, and **Santa Maria Donnaregina** ⑭. Continuing north on Via Duomo, take a left onto Via Foria, and you will end up at one of Italy's most important museums, the **Museo Archeologico Nazionale** ⑮, packed with archaeological relics of the classical era, and a must before venturing out of town to see Pompeii and Herculaneum. From here, footsore and weary, you deserve a taxi or bus to reach **Museo Capodimonte** ⑯, the greatest of the Bourbon palaces, where you can siesta in the park and admire the wonderful views over the Bay of Naples.

TIMING

You should start early to fit all these sights into just one day: the best option would be to split it between two days, ending one at the Certosa di San Martino, then tackling Spaccanapoli, the Archaeological Museum (where you really need half of a day), and Museo Capodimonte the next. Make sure you do not end up at any churches you wish to see at lunchtime, when they close for two or three hours. The views over the bay are good at any time, but especially at sunset. Since the museum may be closed in the afternoon, depending on the time of year, spend the morning here and the afternoon visiting either the Phlegrean Fields or Herculaneum and Vesuvius. Spend the evening back in Naples—perhaps at the world-famous San Carlo Opera House—and the following morning, set out for Pompeii.

Sights to See

☾ ❺ **Acquario** (Aquarium). Children and art-exhausted adults adore the aquarium in the public gardens on Via Caracciolo. Founded by a German
naturalist in the late 19th century, it's the oldest in Europe. About 200
species of fish and marine plants thrive in large tanks, undoubtedly better off here than in the highly polluted Bay of Naples, their natural habi-
tat. ✉ *Viale A. Dohrn,* ☎ *081/5833111.* ▣ *3,000 lire.* ☉ *May–Sept.,*
Mon.–Sat. 9–6, Sun. 10–6; Oct.–Apr., Mon.–Sat. 9–5, Sun. 9–2.

OFF THE
BEATEN PATH

EDENLANDIA – This is the largest amusement park in Campania. It's in
the Mostra d'Oltremare area of Naples, near San Paolo Stadium. ✉
Viale Kennedy, ☎ *081/2391182.* ▣ *Free; individual fares for rides.* ☉
Oct.-Mar., weekdays noon–8, weekends 11 AM–midnight; Apr.-Sept.,
Wed.-Fri. 3–10, weekends 11 AM–midnight.

MUSEO NAZIONALE FERROVIARIO – Children love to see the old-fashioned engines, cars, and railroad equipment on display in the restored
railway works, founded by the Bourbon rulers of Naples in the last century. ✉ *Corso San Giovanni a Teduccio,* ☎ *081/472003.* ▣ *Free.* ☉
Mon.-Sat. 9–2.

❹ **Castel dell'Ovo.** Dangling over Naples harbor on a thin promontory,
this 12th-century fortress built over the ruins of an ancient Roman villa
commands a view of the whole harbor—proof, if you need it, that the
Romans knew a premium location when they saw one. For the same
reason, some of the city's top hotels share the same site. ✉ *Santa Lucia*
waterfront. ☉ *Closed to the public.*

❶ **Castel Nuovo.** Also known as the Maschio Angioino, this massive
fortress was built by the Angevins (related to the French monarchy) in
the 13th century and completely rebuilt by the Aragonese rulers (descendants of an illegitimate branch of Spain's ruling line) who succeeded
them. The decorative marble triumphal arch that forms the entrance
was erected during the Renaissance in honor of King Alfonso I of Aragón,
and its rich bas-reliefs are credited to Francesco Laurana. Set incon-
gruously into the castle's heavy stone walls, the arch is one of the finest
works of its kind. Some rooms in the castle have recently been opened
to the public and contain sculptures and frescoes from the 14th and
15th centuries. ✉ *Castel Nuovo, Piazza Municipio.* ▣ *7,000 lire.* ☉
Mon.–Sat. 9–7, Sun. 9–1.

❽ **Castel Sant'Elmo.** Perched on the Vómero hill, the castle was built by
the Spanish to dominate the port and the old city. The Spanish garrison was quartered in now-decaying tenements aligned in a tight-knit
grid along incredibly narrow alleys; this notorious slum district is still
known as the Quartieri. The area can be reached by way of the funicular
from Piazza Montesanto up the Vómero hill. ✉ *Largo San Martino.*
▣ *4,000 lire.* ☉ *Tues.–Sun. 9–2.*

☾ ❾ **Certosa di San Martino.** A Carthusian monastery restored in the 17th
century in exuberant Neapolitan Baroque style, it now houses the
Museo Nazionale di San Martino, an eclectic collection of ships' models, antique *presepi* (Christmas crèches), and Neapolitan landscape paintings. The main reason to come, however, is to see the splendidly
decorated church and annexes, the pretty garden, and the view from
the balcony off Room 25. There's another fine view from the square
in front of the Certosa. The Certosa can be reached by way of the funicular from Piazza Montesanto up the Vómero hill, upon which it is
magnificently placed. ✉ *Museo Nazionale di San Martino,* ☎ *081/*
5781769. ▣ *8,000 lire.* ☉ *Tues.–Sun. 9–2.*

Golfo di Nápoli

Acquario, **5**
Castel dell'Ovo, **4**
Castel Nuovo, **1**
Castel Sant'Elmo, **8**
Certosa di San
Martina, **9**
Duomo, **13**
Gesù Nuovo, **10**

Museo Archeologico
Nazionale, **15**
Museo
Capodimonte, **16**
Museo Duca di
Martina, **7**
Palazzo Reale, **3**

San Lorenzo
Maggiore, **12**
Santa Chiara, **11**
Santa Maria
Donnaregina, **14**
Teatro San Carlo, **2**
Villa Pignatelli, **6**

KEY

Rail Lines
Metro

0   300 yards
0   300 meters

⑬ Duomo. Though established in the 1200s, the building you see was erected a century later and has since undergone radical changes, especially during the Baroque age. Inside the cathedral, 110 ancient columns salvaged from pagan buildings are set into the piers that support the 350-year-old wooden ceiling. Off the left aisle, you step down into the 4th-century church of Santa Restituta, which was incorporated into the cathedral; though it was redecorated in the late 1600s in the prevalent Baroque style, a few very old mosaics remain in the **baptistery.** The **chapel** also gives access to a series of paleochristian rooms dating from the Roman era.

On the right aisle of the cathedral, in the **chapel of San Gennaro,** are multicolored marbles and frescoes honoring St. Januarius, miracle-working patron saint of Naples, whose altar and relics are encased in silver. Twice a year—on September 19, his feast day, and on the first Sunday in May, which commemorates the transference of his relics to Naples—his dried blood, contained in two sealed vials, is believed to liquefy during rites in his honor. On these dates large numbers of devout Neapolitans offer up prayers in his memory. ⊠ *Via del Duomo.* ☎ *Baptistery 1,500 lire, chapel 5,000 lire, chapel of San Gennaro free.* ☉ *Baptistery and archaeological zone Mon.–Sat. 9–noon and 4:30–7, Sun. 9–noon; chapel of San Gennaro daily 7–noon and 4–7.*

OFF THE
BEATEN PATH

MUSEO FILANGIERI – This Neapolitan museum contains a private collection of arms, armor, furniture, paintings, and fascinating memorabilia. It's housed in the Florentine-style Renaissance Palazzo Cuomo. ⊠ *Via Duomo 288,* ☎ *081/203175.* ☎ *5,000 lire.* ☉ *Mon.–Sat. 9–7, Sun. 9–2.*

⑩ Gesù Nuovo. The oddly faceted stone facade of the church was designed as part of a palace, but plans were changed as construction progressed, and it became the front of an elaborately decorated Baroque church. ⊠ *Piazza Gesù Nuovo.* ☎ *Free.* ☉ *Daily 7–noon and 4–7 (until 6 Oct.–Mar.).*

Molo Beverello. This pier is a hive of activity from which boats and hydrofoils leave for Sorrento and the islands. ⊠ *On the harbor behind the Castel Nuovo.*

OFF THE
BEATEN PATH

SEAFRONT TOURS – Evening boat tours take in the waterfront of Naples, from the port at Mergellina to Cape Posillipo, with a view of Castel dell'Ovo (☞ *above*) on the way back. ⊠ *Naples waterfront,* ☎ *081/661434.* ☎ *10,000 lire.* ☉ *July–Sept., daily at 6, 7, and 8 PM.*

★ ✋ **⑮ Museo Archeologico Nazionale** (National Archaeological Museum). The huge red building, a cavalry barracks in the 16th century, is dusty and unkempt, but it holds one of the world's great collections of Greek and Roman antiquities, including such extraordinary sculptures as the *Hercules Farnese,* an exquisite Aphrodite attributed to the 4th-century BC Greek sculptor Praxiteles, and an equestrian statue of Roman Emperor Nerva. Vividly colored mosaics and countless artistic and household objects from Pompeii and Herculaneum provide insight into the life and art of ancient Rome. The most recent addition to the treasures on permanent display is an entire fresco sequence—more than 300 ft wide—discovered in 1765 in perfect condition at the Temple of Isis in Pompeii. Invest in an up-to-date printed museum guide, because exhibits are poorly labeled. ⊠ *Piazza Museo,* ☎ *081/440166.* ☎ *12,000 lire.* ☉ *Aug.–Sept., Mon.–Sat. 9–7, Sun. 9–1; Oct.–July, Wed.–Mon. 9–2.*

★ **⑯ Museo Capodimonte.** The 18th-century Bourbon royal palace, in a vast park that served as the royal hunting preserve and later as the site of the Capodimonte porcelain works, houses an impressive collection of fine and decorative art. Capodimonte's greatest treasure is the excellent collection of paintings well displayed in the **Galleria Nazionale** on the palace's top floor. Included are works from the 13th to the 18th centuries, including many familiar masterpieces by Dutch and Spanish masters, as well as by the great Italians. At the coffee bar halfway through, be sure to climb the stairs to the **roof terrace** for a sweeping view of the bay. Then continue through halls hung with dramatic Mannerist works of the 17th and 18th centuries, among them some stunning paintings by Caravaggio (1573–1610), originally hung in the city's churches. Downstairs are 19th-century Italian paintings and the **royal apartments**, where numerous portraits provide a close-up of the unmistakable Bourbon features, a challenge to any court painter. You'll also find beautiful antique furniture, most of it on the splashy scale so dear to the Bourbons, and a staggering collection of porcelain and majolica from the various royal residences. ⊠ *Parco di Capodimonte*, ☎ *081/7441307.* ⌨ *8,000 lire.* ☉ *Apr.–Oct., Tues.–Sun. 9–7:30; Nov.–Mar., Tues.–Sat. 9–6, Sun. 9–2.*

OFF THE BEATEN PATH

CATACOMBS OF SAN GENNARO – Many of these catacombs in Naples predate the Christian era by two centuries. The church was inspired by St. Peter's in Rome. The niches and corridors of the catacombs are hung with early Christian paintings. ⊠ *Via Capodimonte, next to Madre di Buon Consiglio church on Via Capodimonte.* ⌨ *5,000 lire.* ☉ *Guided tours daily every 45 min 9:30–11:45 AM.*

⑦ Museo Duca di Martina. The lushly shaded park and the view over Naples are two reasons to venture up the Chiaia funicular from Via del Parco Margherita. Set on the slopes of the Vómero hill in a park known as Villa Floridiana, it houses a fine collection of European and Oriental porcelain and other objets d'art in a neoclassical residence built in the early 19th century by King Ferdinand I for his wife; their portraits greet you as you enter. Enjoy the view from the terrace behind the museum. ⊠ *Via Cimarosa 77*, ☎ *081/5788418.* ⌨ *4,000 lire.* ☉ *Tues.–Sat. 9–2, Sun. 9–1.*

❸ Palazzo Reale (Royal Palace). Dominating Piazza del Plebiscito, the huge palace dates from the early 1600s. It was renovated and redecorated by successive rulers, including Napoléon's sister Caroline and her ill-fated husband, Joachim Murat, who reigned briefly in Naples after the French emperor had sent the Bourbons packing and before they returned to reclaim their kingdom. Don't miss seeing the **royal apartments**, sumptuously furnished and full of precious paintings, tapestries, porcelains, and other objets d'art. The monumental marble staircase gives you an idea of the scale on which Neapolitan rulers lived. ⊠ *Piazza del Plebiscito*, ☎ *081/5808111.* ⌨ *8,000 lire.* ☉ *Apr.–Oct., Tues.–Sun. 9–7:30; Nov.–Mar., Tues.–Sun. 9–1:30.*

Piazza Dante. Students from the nearby music conservatory hang out in this semicircular hub in an area rich in inexpensive trattorias and pizzerias, though presently fenced off for long-term work on the subway system.

Piazza del Plebiscito. The vast square next to the Palazzo Reale was laid out by order of Murat, whose architect was clearly inspired by the colonnades of St. Peter's in Rome. The large church of San Francesco di Paola in the middle of the colonnades was added as a thanks offering for the Bourbon restoration by Ferdinand I, whose titles reflect the somewhat garbled history of the Kingdom of the Two Sicilies—made up of Naples (which included most of the southern Italian mainland)

and Sicily, which were united in the Middle Ages, then separated and unofficially reunited under Spanish domination during the 16th and 17th centuries. In 1816, with Napoléon out of the way on St. Helena, Ferdinand IV of Naples, who also happened to be Ferdinand III of Sicily, officially merged the two kingdoms, proclaiming himself Ferdinand I of the Kingdom of Two Sicilies. His reactionary and repressive rule earned him a few more colorful titles among his rebellious subjects.

NEED A
BREAK?

Walking up the fashionable Via Chiaia, behind Piazza del Plebiscito, you'll come upon **Caflisch** (⊠ Via Chiaia 144), a historic café serving snacks and high-quality chocolates and pastries to nibble over a cappuccino or espresso.

⑫ San Lorenzo Maggiore. It is unusual to find the Gothic style in Naples, but it has survived to great effect in this church. Built in the Middle Ages and decorated with 14th-century frescoes, it is supposed to be where the poet Boccaccio first saw the model for his *Fiammetta*. ⊠ *Via Tribunali.*

⑪ Santa Chiara. The monastery church is a Neapolitan landmark and the subject of a famous old song. It was built in the 1300s in Provençal Gothic style, and it's best known for the quiet charm of its cloister garden, with columns and benches sheathed in 18th-century ceramic tiles painted with delicate floral motifs and vivid landscapes. The entrance is off the courtyard at the left of the church. ⊠ *Piazza Gesù Nuovo.* ⊠ *Free.* ⊙ *Daily 7–noon and 4–7 (until 6 Oct.–Mar.).*

⑭ Santa Maria Donnaregina. The towering Gothic funeral monument of Mary of Hungary, wife of Charles II of Anjou, who is said to have commissioned the frescoes in the church at a cost of 33 ounces of gold, is contained within this church. ⊠ *Largo Donnaregina.*

Spaccanapoli. Nowhere embodies the spirit of backstreet Naples better than the arrow-straight street divided into tracts bearing several names. It runs through the heart of the old city (*spacca* means "cut through") from west to east, retracing one of the main arteries of the Greek, and later Roman, settlement. ⊠ *Beginning with Via Scura just west of Via Toledo and ending with Via Vicaria Vecchia just east of Via del Duomo.*

❷ Teatro San Carlo. In 1737, forty years earlier than Milan's La Scala, this large 18th-century theater was first built—though it was destroyed by fire and rebuilt in 1816. You can visit the impressive interior, decorated in the white-and-gilt stucco of the neoclassical era, as part of a guided group, and visitors are sometimes allowed in during morning rehearsals. ⊠ *Via San Carlo, between Piazza Municipio and Piazza Plebiscito.*

NEED A
BREAK?

Across from the Teatro San Carlo towers the imposing entrance to the glass-roofed turn-of-the-century **Galleria Umberto,** a shopping arcade where you can sit at one of several cafés and watch the vivacious Neapolitans as they go about their business.

Via Benedetto Croce. This section of Spaccanapoli was named in honor of the illustrious philosopher born here in 1866, in the building at No. 12. Continue past peeling palaces, dark workshops where artisans ply their trades, and many churches and street shrines. Where the street changes to **Via San Biagio dei Librai,** the shops stage a special fair of hand-carved crèche figures during the weeks before Christmas.

Via Toledo. Sooner or later you'll wind up at one of the busiest commercial arteries in this perennially congested city (also known as Via

Roma). However, don't avoid dipping into this parade of shops and coffee bars where plump pastries are temptingly arranged.

❻ Villa Pignatelli. A small dignified museum on the grounds are of limited interest to anyone who doesn't like 19th-century furniture. But the collection of antique coaches and carriages in a pavilion on the grounds is worth a look. And a stroll in the park is a pleasant respite from the noisy city streets. ⊠ *Riviera di Chiaia 200; museum near the lower station of the Chiaia funicular,* ☎ *081/669675.* 🎫 *4,000 lire, park free.* ⏰ *Tues.–Sun. 9–2.*

Dining and Lodging

$$$ ✕ **Casanova Grill.** Soft lights and a trendy art-deco look set the tone at Hotel Excelsior's restaurant. The seasonal specialties and antipasti arranged on the buffet will whet your appetite for such traditional Neapolitan dishes as the simple spaghetti al pomodoro and the classic *carne* (meat) alla pizzaiola. ⊠ *Hotel Excelsior, Via Partenope 48,* ☎ *081/7640111. Jacket and tie. AE, DC, MC, V.*

$$$ ✕ **La Fazenda.** Overlooking the sea at Marechiaro, in one of the city's most picturesque spots, this restaurant is a favorite for leisurely dining and an invitingly informal atmosphere. The pastas, many with vegetable sauces, are particularly good. The specialty is seafood, but you can also find a good, honest *bistecca* (beefsteak) here. Desserts are homemade. Note that you must take a taxi. ⊠ *Discesa Marechiaro 58,* ☎ *081/5757420. AE, MC, V. Closed Mon. and Aug. 13–29.*

$$$ ✕ **La Sacrestia.** Neapolitans flock to this upscale patrician villa for the
★ restaurant's location—on the slopes of the Posillipo hill—and standards of food quality. The specialties range from tasty antipasti to linguine in *salsa di scorfano* (scorpion-fish sauce). The real thrust is seafood and there are interesting meat dishes as well. ⊠ *Via Orazio 116,* ☎ *081/ 7611051. AE, DC, MC, V. Closed Mon. Sept.–June, Sun. (July only), and Aug.*

$$ ✕ **Ciro a Santa Brigida.** Centrally located off Via Toledo near the Castel Nuovo, Ciro is a straightforward restaurant popular with business travelers, artists, and journalists who prefer food over frills. In dining rooms on two levels, customers enjoy classic Neapolitan cuisine. The *scaloppe alla* Ciro (veal with prosciutto and mozzarella) is heart rendering. There's pizza, too. ⊠ *Via Santa Brigida 71,* ☎ *081/5524072. AE, DC, MC, V. Closed Sun. and 2 wks in Aug.*

$$ ✕ **Don Salvatore.** Head to this unpretentious-looking place just west in the little port of Mergellina for good local dishes and seafood. Linguine *cosa nostra* (with shellfish) and other pastas with seafood sauces are specialties, and the *fritto misto* (mixed fried fish) is as light as a feather. ⊠ *Via Mergellina 5,* ☎ *081/681817. AE, DC, MC, V. Closed Wed.*

$$ ✕ **La Bersagliera.** You'll inevitably be drawn to eating at the Santa Lucia waterfront, in the shadow of the looming medieval Castel dell'Ovo—and this is one of the best places to do so. It's touristy but fun, with an irresistible combination of spaghetti and mandolins. The menu suggests uncomplicated timeworn classics, such as spaghetti *alla pescatora* (with seafood sauce) and melanzane alla parmigiana. ⊠ *Borgo Marinaro 10,* ☎ *081/7646016. AE, DC, MC, V. Closed Tues.*

$$ ✕ **Mimì alla Ferrovia.** Near the central station, this bustling fish restaurant has scooped plenty of plaudits in recent years. The service is polite without being obsequious, the atmosphere relaxed, sometimes noisy. Try the *céfalo* (mullet) when it's in season, or the lobster at just about any time. Other sure bets are *peperoni ripieni* (stuffed peppers) and grilled mushrooms. ⊠ *Via Alfonso D'Aragona 21,* ☎ *081/5538525. AE, DC, MC, V. Closed Sun. and Aug. 10–21.*

$$$$ ⊞ **Excelsior.** The lobby and lounges of this ITT-Sheraton Luxury Collection hotel are lavishly imbued with Oriental carpets and gilt or glass chandeliers. Rooms are of an Empire-style—with neoclassic furniture and brocades—or Neapolitan floral-print persuasion. Off the large semicircular lounge are a chic little bar and the Casanova restaurant. Request a front room for views of the bay. ⊠ *Via Partenope 48, 80121,* ☎ *081/7640111,* FAX *081/7649743. 136 rooms. Restaurant, bar, free parking. AE, DC, MC, V.*

$$$ ⊞ **Cavour.** Right on Piazza Garibaldi in the run-down Stazione Centrale area, the Cavour is the best choice for those who don't want to stray too far from the transport hub of the city. Comfortably furnished and air-conditioned guest rooms are surprisingly quiet, and the suites offer exceptional value. The lobby is a continual buzz of activity, and the street-level restaurant serves a formidable range of local dishes such as marjoram-accented *ravioli alla Caprese.* ⊠ *Piazza Garibaldi 32, 80133,* ☎ *081/283122,* FAX *081/287488. 96 rooms. Bar. AE, DC, MC, V.*

$$$ ⊞ **Jolly Ambassador.** The bedrooms and roof garden–restaurant of this uninspired but functional Jolly hotel command sweeping views of the sea—thanks to being on the top 14 floors of one of downtown's only skyscrapers. Dark brown and white predominate, but beyond decor it promises comfort and efficiency in a city where these are scarce commodities. ⊠ *Via Medina 70, 80133,* ☎ *081/416000,* FAX *081/5518010. 251 rooms. Restaurant, bar, free parking. AE, DC, MC, V.*

$$$ ⊞ **Paradiso.** This is something special off the beaten track. You can
★ take a taxi or funicular from downtown to the modern air-conditioned building perched on a hill above the port of Mergellina. Huge window walls in the lobby and front rooms reveal gorgeous views. The decor, in tones of blue and beige, is restful and attractive. Smallish rooms are smart, with built-in furnishings of rosy wood with marble surfaces. Ask for a room with a view; there's no extra charge. A roof terrace invites sitting, dining, and contemplating the entire bay and beyond Vesuvius. ⊠ *Via Catullo 11, 80122,* ☎ *081/7614161,* FAX *081/7613449. 74 rooms. Restaurant, bar, minibars, free parking. AE, DC, MC, V.*

$$ ⊞ **Rex.** This hotel, which falls in the higher end of its price category, has a fairly quiet location near the Santa Lucia waterfront. On the first two floors of an art-nouveau building, the decor ranges from 1950s modern to fake period pieces and even some folk art, haphazardly combined. It has no restaurant or elevator. ⊠ *Via Palepoli 12, 80132,* ☎ *081/7649389,* FAX *081/7649227. 38 rooms. Bar, free parking. AE, DC, MC, V.*

Nightlife and the Arts

The Arts

MUSIC

A classical music festival known as **International Music Weeks** takes place throughout May in Naples. Concerts are held at the Teatro San Carlo, the Teatro Mercadante, and in the neoclassic Villa Pignatelli. For information, contact the Teatro San Carlo box office (⊠ Via San Carlo 93/f, ☎ 081/7972111).

OPERA

Naples has a full opera season from fall through spring. The **Teatro San Carlo** (⊠ Via San Carlo 93/f, ☎ 081/7972111), where the season runs from December to May, is one of Italy's top opera houses.

Nightlife

NIGHTCLUBS

A sophisticated crowd heads to the fashionable **Gabbiano** (⊠ Via Partenope 26, ☎ 081/7645717) watering hole. Live music is usually on tap. **Papillon** (✉ Via Manzoni 207, ☎ 081/7690800) caters to a young crowd. **Rosolino** (✉ Via Nazario Sauro 5–7, ☎ 081/7640513) has a quiet piano bar and a restaurant with some moderately priced meals. For disco classics, locals and tourists head to **Shaker** (✉ Via Nazario Sauro 24, ☎ 081/416775).

Outdoor Activities and Sports

Bowling
Neapolitans strike out at **Bowling Oltremare** (✉ Viale Kennedy, ☎ 081/624444).

Fishing
For information on licenses and water quality, contact **Federazione Italiana Pesca Sportiva** (✉ Piazza Santa Maria degli Angeli, ☎ 081/7644921).

Golf
Minigolf Kennedy (✉ Via Camillo Guerra 60, ☎ 081/5871386), in the suburb of Chiaiano, west of Naples, has 18 holes of minigolf.

Horseback Riding
For riding in Campania, contact the **Centro Ippico Agnano** (✉ Via Circumvallazione, Agnano, between Naples and Pozzuoli, ☎ 081/5702695).

Sailing
Try **Nantic Coop** (✉ Piazza Amedeo 15, ☎ 081/415371) in summer. **Canotiri Savoia** (✉ Banchina Santa Lucia, ☎ 081/7646162) offers courses for sailors or would-be sailors in winter months only (October–June).

Waterskiing
Sci Nautico Partenopeo (✉ Lake Averno, Pozzuoli, ☎ 081/8662214) offers sessions and courses on what was once believed the mouth of hell, at Lake Avernus, west of Naples.

Shopping

Leather goods, coral, jewelry, and cameos are some of the best items to buy in Campania. In Naples, where many of the top leather and fashion houses have their factories, you'll find good buys in handbags, shoes, and clothing, but it's often wise to make purchases in shops rather than from street vendors.

Shopping Districts
The **Galleria Umberto** (☞ Need a Break? *above*) is a good introduction to shopping in Naples; a wide variety of retail outlets trade in the four glass-roofed arcades. Other areas and streets are more specialized: the area immediately around **Piazza dei Martiri** is the heart of luxury shopping, with perfume shops, fashion outlets, and antiques on display. **Via Toledo** is a better bet for bargains. Also try **Via Chiaia** for good deals.

THE PHLEGREAN FIELDS

The name—the fields of fire—was once given to the entire region west of Naples, including the island of Ischia. The whole area floats freely on a mass of molten lava very close to the surface. The fires are still smoldering. Greek and Roman notions of the Underworld were not the blind imaginings of a primitive people; they were the creations of poets and writers who stood on this very ground and wrote down what they saw. Today, it should take about a half of a day to assess it yourself.

Solfatara

⑰ *8 km (5 mi) west of Naples, 2 km (1¼ mi) east of Pozzuoli.*

Here at the sunken volcanic crater Solfatara you can experience first hand the volcanic nature of this other-worldly terrain. In fact, the only eruption of this semiextinct volcano was in 1198, though according to one legend, every crater in the Phlegrean Fields is one of the mouths of a hundred-headed dragon named Typhon that Zeus hurled down the crater of Epomeo on the island of Ischia. According to another, the sulfurous springs of the Solfatara are poisonous discharges from the wounds the Titans received in their war with Zeus. Both legends, of course, are efforts to dramatize man's struggle to overcome the mysterious and dangerous forces of nature. The stark, scorched area exerts a strange fascination, slightly marred by the modern apartment blocks peering over the rim. The area is safe if you stick to the path. 🎫 *6,000 lire. ☉ Daily 8:30–1 hr before sunset.*

Pozzuoli

⑱ *8 km (5 mi) west of Naples, 2 km (1¼ mi) west of Solfatara.*

The **Anfiteatro Flavio** (Amphitheater) here is the third-largest arena in Italy, after the Colosseum and Santa Maria Capua Vetere, and once accommodated 40,000 spectators, who were sometimes treated to mock naval battles when the arena was filled with water. The well-preserved underground passages and chambers are fascinating, and give a good sense of how the wild animals were hoisted up into the arena. 🎫 *4,000 lire. ☉ Daily 9–1 hr before sunset.*

You may want to make a short side trip to the town's harbor and imagine St. Paul landing here in AD 61 en route to Rome. His own ship had been wrecked off Malta, and he was brought here on the *Castor and Pollux,* a grain ship from Alexandria that was carrying corn from Egypt to Italy only 18 years before the eruption at Vesuvius.

Baia

12 km (8 mi) west of Naples.

Now largely under the sea, this was once the most opulent and fashionable resort area of the Roman Empire, the place where Sulla, Pompey, Julius Caesar, Tiberius, Nero, and Cicero built their holiday villas. Petronius's *Satyricon* is a satire on the corruption and intrigue, the wonderful licentiousness of Roman life at Baia. (Petronius was hired to arrange parties and entertainments for Nero, so he was in a position to know.) It was here at Baia that Emperor Claudius built a great villa for his wife Messalina (who spent her nights indulging herself at public brothels); here that Agrippina poisoned her husband and was, in turn, murdered by her son Nero; here that Cleopatra was staying when Julius Caesar was murdered on the Ides of March. You can visit the **excavations** of the famous **baths.** The site lies 6 km (4 mi) south of Pozzuoli. ✉ *Via Fusaro 35,* ☎ *081/8687592.* 🎫 *4,000 lire. ☉ Daily 9–1 hr before sunset.*

En Route   Follow the southern loop around Lake Miseno (a volcanic crater believed by the ancients to be the Styx, across which Charon ferried the souls of the dead) and Lake Fusaro. You'll take in some fine views of Pozzuoli Bay.

Cumae

 16 km (10 mi) west of Naples.

Perhaps the oldest Greek colony in Italy, Cumae overshadowed the Phlegrean Fields, including Naples, in the 6th and 7th centuries BC. The **Antro della Sibilla** (Sibyl's Cave) is here—one of the most venerated sites in antiquity. In the 5th or 6th century BC, the Greeks hollowed the cave from the rock beneath the present ruins of Cumae's acropolis. Visitors walk through a dark, massive stone tunnel that opens into a vaulted chamber where the Sibyl rendered her oracles. Standing here, the sense of mystery, of communication with the invisible, is overwhelming. "This is the most romantic classical site in Italy," wrote H. V. Morton. "I would rather come here than to Pompeii."

Virgil wrote the epic *The Aeneid,* the story of the Trojan prince Aeneas's wanderings, partly to give Rome the historical legitimacy that Homer had given the Greeks. On his journey, Aeneas had to descend to the Underworld to speak to his father, and to find his way in, he needed the guidance of the Cumaean Sibyl.

Virgil did not dream up the Sibyl's cave or the entrance to Hades—he must have stood both in her chamber and along the rim of Lake Avernus, as you yourself will stand. When he wrote, *"Facilis descensus Averno"*—"The way to hell is easy"—it was because he knew the way. In Book VI of *The Aeneid,* Virgil described how Aeneas, arriving at Cumae, sought Apollo's throne (remains of the **Temple of Apollo** can still be seen) and "the deep hidden abode of the dread Sibyl / An enormous cave . . . ."

The Sibyl was not necessarily a charlatan; she was a medium, a prophetess, an old woman whom the ancients believed could communicate with the Other World. The three most famous Sibyls were at Erythrae, Delphi, and Cumae. Foreign governments consulted the Sibyls before mounting campaigns. Wealthy aristocrats came to consult with their dead relatives. Businessmen came to get their dreams interpreted or to seek favorable omens before entering into financial agreements or setting off on journeys. Farmers came to remove curses on their cows. Love potions were a profitable source of revenue; women from Baia lined up for potions to slip into the wine of handsome charioteers who drove up and down the street in their gold-plated four-horsepower chariots.

With the coming of the Olympian gods, the earlier gods of the soil were discredited or given new roles and names. Ancient rites, such as those surrounding the Cumaean Sibyl, were now carried out in secret and known as the Mysteries. The Romans—like the later Soviets—tried in vain to replace these Mysteries by deifying the state in the person of its rulers. Yet even the Caesars appealed to forces of the Other World. And until the 4th century AD, the Sibyl was consulted by the Christian bishop of Rome. ⊠ *Via Acropoli.* ☎ *081/8543060.* ⌸ *4,000 lire.* ☉ *Daily 9–1 hr before sunset.*

Lago d'Averno

11 km (7 mi) west of Naples.

The best time to visit the fabled Lago d'Averno (Lake Avernus) is at sunset or when the moon is rising. There's a restaurant on the west side, where you can dine on the terrace. Forested hills rise on three sides; the menacing cone of Monte Nuovo rises on the fourth. The smell of sulfur hangs over this sad, lonely landscape seemingly at the very gates of hell. No place evokes Homer, Virgil, and the cult of the Other World better than this silent, mysterious setting. *To reach the lake, drive*

*west from Pozzuoli on S7 toward Cumae and then turn left (south) on
the road to Baia. About a km (½ mi) along, turn right and follow signs
to Lake Avernus.*

HERCULANEUM, VESUVIUS, POMPEII

Ancient Inspirations

Volcanic ash and mud preserved the Roman towns of Herculaneum
and Pompeii almost exactly as they were on the day Mt. Vesuvius erupted
in AD 79, leaving them not just archaeological ruins but testimonies of
daily life in the ancient world. All three sights can be visited from either Naples or Sorrento, thanks to the Circumvesuviana (☞ Getting
Around *in* Campania A to Z, *below*), the suburban railway that provides fast, frequent, and economical service.

Herculaneum

★ ⑳ *10 km (6 mi) south of Naples.*

Lying more than 60 ft below the town of Ercolano, the ruins of Herculaneum are set among the acres of greenhouses that make this area
one of Europe's principal flower-growing centers. Hercules himself is
said to have founded the town, which became a famous weekend retreat for the Roman elite. It had about 5,000 inhabitants when it was
destroyed; many of them were fishermen, craftsmen, and artists. A lucky
few patricians owned villas overlooking the sea. Herculaneum was damaged by an earthquake in AD 63, and repairs were still being made 16
years later when the gigantic eruption of Vesuvius (which also destroyed
Pompeii) sent a fiery cloud of gas and pumice hurtling onto the town,
which was completely buried under a tide of volcanic mud. This
semiliquid mass seeped into the crevices and niches of every building,
covering household objects and enveloping textiles and wood—seal-
ing all in a compact, airtight tomb.

Casual excavation—and haphazard looting—began in the 18th century, but systematic digs were not initiated until the 1920s. Today less
than half of Herculaneum has been excavated; with present-day Ercolano and the unlovely Resina Quarter (famous among bargain
hunters as the area's largest secondhand clothing market) sitting on
top of the site, progress is limited. From the ramp leading down to Herculaneum's neatly laid out streets and well-preserved edifices, you get
a good overall view of the site, as well as an idea of the amount of rock
that had to be removed to bring it to light.

If you feel closer to the past at Herculaneum than at Pompeii, it's in
part because there are fewer hawkers here. Also, though Herculaneum
had only one-fourth the population of Pompeii and has only been partially excavated, what has been found is generally better preserved. In
some cases, you can even see the original wooden beams, staircases,
and furniture.

At the entrance you should pick up a map showing the gridlike layout
of the dig. Decorations are especially delicate in the **House of the Mosaic Atrium,** with a pavement in a black-and-white checkerboard pattern, and in the **House of Neptune and Amphitrite,** named for the subjects
of a still-bright mosaic on the wall of the nymphaeum (a recessed
grotto with a fountain). Annexed to the latter house is a remarkably
preserved wineshop, where amphorae still rest on carbonized wooden
shelves. And in the **House of the Wooden Partition,** one of the best-
preserved of all, there is a carbonized wooden partition with three doors.

In the **baths,** where there were separate sections for men and women, you can see benches; basins; and the hot, warm, and cold rooms, embellished with mosaics. The **House of the Bicentenary** was a patrician residence with smaller rooms on the upper floor, which may have been rented out to artisan-tenants who were probably Christians because they left an emblem of the cross embedded in the wall. The palaestra and 2,500-seat theater, the sumptuously decorated suburban baths, and the House of the Stags, with an elegant garden open to the sea breezes, are all evocative relics of a lively and luxurious way of life.

Until a few years ago it was believed that most of Herculaneum's inhabitants had managed to escape by sea, since few skeletons were found in the city. Excavations at Porta Marina, the gate in the sea wall leading to the beach, have revealed instead that many perished there, a few steps from the only escape route open to them. Most important buildings can be seen in about two hours. The site entrance is a short walk south from the Circumvesuviana station. ⊠ *Corso Ercolano,* ☎ *081/ 7390963.* ☎ *12,000 lire.* ☉ *Daily 9–1 hr before sunset (ticket office closes 2 hrs before sunset).*

Vesuvius

㉑ *16 km (10 mi) east of Naples, 8 km (5 mi) northeast of Herculaneum.*

The profile of Vesuvius is so inseparable from the Bay of Naples area, and the ferocious power it can unleash so vivid as you tour the sites of the cities that it destroyed, you may be overwhelmed by the urge to explore the crater itself. In summer especially, the prospect of rising above the sticky heat of the city and sites below is a heady one.

The view when clear is magnificent, with the curve of the coast and the tiny white houses among the orange and lemon blossoms. If the summit is lost in mist, you'll be lucky to see your hand in front of your face. When you see the summit clearing—it tends to be clearer in the afternoon—head for it. If possible, see Vesuvius after you've toured the ruins of buried Herculaneum to appreciate the magnitude of the volcano's awesome power.

Reaching the crater takes some effort. From the Ercolano stop of the Circumvesuviana, take scheduled buses (journey-time one hour; departures currently at 8:40, 9:40, 10:40, 12:45, and 2—check locally for the latest times) or your own car to the Seggovia station, the lower terminal of the defunct chairlift. (Though there's talk of putting it back in working order, no one is optimistic about the possibility.) From here you must climb the soft, slippery cinder track on foot, a 30-minute ascent, and you must pay about 5,000 lire for compulsory guide service, though the guides don't do much more than tell you to stay away from the edge of the crater. If you're not in shape, you'll probably find the climb tiring. Wear nonskid shoes (not sandals). ☎ *Guide service 5,000 lire.*

Pompeii

★ *24 km (15 mi) southeast of Naples, 11 km (7 mi) northeast of Herculaneum.*

Ancient Pompeii was much larger than Herculaneum; a busy commercial center with a population of 10,000–20,000, it covered about 160 acres on the seaward end of the fertile Sarno Plain.

In 80 BC the Roman General Sulla turned Pompeii into a Roman colony, where wealthy patricians came to escape the turmoil of city life. The town was laid out in a grid pattern, with two main intersecting streets. The wealthiest took a whole block for themselves; those less fortunate built a house and rented out the front rooms, facing the street, as shops. The facades of these houses were relatively plain and seldom hinted at the care and attention lavished on the private rooms within.

When a visitor entered, he passed the shops and entered an open area (atrium). In the back was a receiving room. Behind was another open area, called the peristyle, with rows of columns and perhaps a garden with a fountain. Only good friends ever saw this private part of the house, which was surrounded by the bedrooms and the dining area.

Pompeiian houses were designed around an inner garden so that families could turn their backs on the world outside. Today we install picture windows that break down visual barriers between ourselves and our neighbors; the people in these Roman towns had few windows, preferring to get their light from the central courtyard—the light within. How pleasant it must have been to come home from the forum or the baths to one's own secluded kingdom, with no visual reminders of a life outside one's own.

Not that public life was so intolerable. There were wineshops on almost every corner, and frequent shows at the amphitheater. The public fountains and toilets were fed by huge cisterns, connected by lead pipes beneath the sidewalks. Since garbage and rainwater collected in the streets of Pompeii, the sidewalks were raised, and huge stepping stones were placed at crossings so pedestrians could keep their feet dry. Herculaneum had better drainage, with an underground sewer that led to the sea.

The ratio of freemen to slaves was about three to two. A small, prosperous family had two or three slaves. Since all manual labor was considered degrading, the slaves did all housework and cooking, including the cutting of meat, which the family ate with spoons or with their hands. Everyone loved grapes, and figs were popular, too. Venison, chicken, and pork were the main dishes. Oranges weren't known, but people ate quinces (a good source of vitamin C) to guard against scurvy. Bread was made from wheat and barley (rye and oats were unknown) and washed down with wine made from the grapes of the slopes of Vesuvius.

The government was considered a democracy, but women, children, gladiators, and Jews couldn't vote. They did, however, express their opinions on election day, as you'll see in campaign graffiti left on public walls.

Some 15,000 graffiti were found in Pompeii and Herculaneum. Many were political announcements—one person recommending another for office, for example, and spelling out his qualifications. Some were bills announcing upcoming events—a play at the theater, a fight among gladiators at the amphitheater. Others were public notices—that wine was on sale, that an apartment would be vacant on the Ides of March. A good many were personal, and give a human dimension to the disaster that not even the sights can equal. Here are a few:

At the baths: "What is the use of having a Venus if she's made of marble?"

At a hotel: "I've wet my bed. My sin I bare. But why? you ask. No pot was anywhere."

At the entrance to the front lavatory at a private house: "May I always and everywhere be as potent with women as I was here."

㉒ Enter through **Porta Marina,** so called because it faces the sea. It is near
the Pompeii–Villa Misteri Circumvesuviana Station. Past the **Temple**
㉓ of **Venus** is the **Basilica,** the law court and the economic center of the
city. These oblong buildings ending in a semicircular projection (apse)
were the model for early Christian churches, which had a nave (central aisle) and two side aisles separated by rows of columns. Standing
in the Basilica, you can recognize the continuity between Roman and
Christian architecture.

㉔ The Basilica opens onto the **Forum** (Foro), the public meeting place,
surrounded by temples and public buildings. It was here that elections
were held and speeches and official announcements made. At the far
㉕ (northern) end of the forum is the **Temple of Jupiter** (Tempio di Giove).

㉖ The renowned **House of the Faun** (Casa del Fauno) displays wonderful mosaics, though the originals are in the National Archaeological
Museum in Naples.

㉗ The **Forum Baths,** on Via delle Terme, is smaller than the Stabian Baths
㉘ (☞ *below*) but with more delicate decoration. The **House of the Tragic**
Poet (Casa del Poeta Tragico) is a typical middle-class house from the
last days of Pompeii. On the floor is a mosaic of a chained dog and
the inscription CAVE CANEM ("Beware of the dog").

㉙ The beautiful **Porta Ercolano** (Gate of Herculaneum) was a main gate
㉚ that led to Herculaneum and Naples. The **Casa dei Vettii** (House of the
Vetti) is the best example of a rich middle-class merchant's house, faithfully restored with vivid murals.

㉛ The **Villa of the Mysteries** (Villa dei Misteri), outside Pompeii's walls,
contains what some consider the greatest surviving group of paintings
from the ancient world, telling the story of a young bride (Ariadne)
being initiated into the mysteries of the cult of Dionysus. Bacchus
(Dionysus), the god of wine, was popular in a town so devoted to the
pleasures of the flesh. But he also represented the triumph of the irra-
tional—of all those mysterious forces that no official state religion could
fully suppress. The cult of Dionysus, like the cult of the Cumaean Sibyl,
gave people a sense of control over fate, and in its focus on the Other
World, helped pave the way for Christianity.

㉜ The **House of the Gilded Cupids** is an elegant, well-preserved home with
㉝ original marble decorations in the garden. On the walls of **Lupanare**
(brothel) are scenes of erotic games in which clients could engage.

㉞ The **Stabian Baths** were heated by underground furnaces whose heat cir-
culated among the stone pillars supporting the floor, rose through flues
in the walls, and escaped through chimneys. The water temperature could
be set for cold, lukewarm, or hot. Bathers took a lukewarm bath to prepare themselves for the hot room. A tepid bath came next, and then a
plunge into cold water to tone up the skin. A vigorous massage with oil
was followed by rest, reading, horseplay, and conversation.

㉟ The required Roman dress—togas—was washed at **Fullonica Stephani.**
The cloth was dunked in a tub full of water and chalk and stomped
upon like so many grapes. Once clean, the material was stretched
across a wicker cage and exposed to sulfur fumes. The fuller (cleaner)
carded it with a long brush, then placed it under a press. The harder
the pressing, the whiter and brighter it became. Many paintings and
㊱ mosaics were executed at **Casa di Menandro,** a patrician's villa. The
㊲ **Villa di Giulia Felice** (House of Julia Felix) has a large garden with a
lovely portico. The wealthy woman living here ran a public bathhouse
annex and rented out ground-floor rooms as shops.

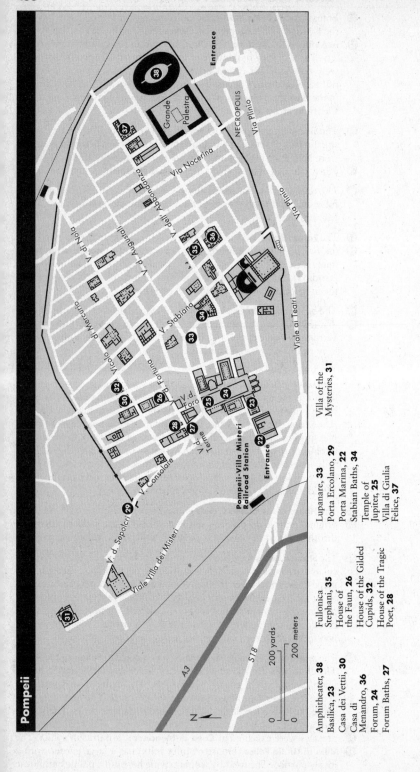

Pompeii

Amphitheater, **38**
Basilica, **23**
Casa dei Vettii, **30**
Casa di
Menandro, **36**
Forum, **24**
Forum Baths, **27**

Fullonica
Stephani, **35**
House of
the Faun, **26**
House of the Gilded
Cupids, **32**
House of the Tragic
Poet, **28**

Lupanare, **33**
Porta Ercolano, **29**
Porta Marina, **22**
Stabian Baths, **34**
Temple of
Jupiter, **25**
Villa di Giulia
Felice, **37**

Villa of the
Mysteries, **31**

38 The **Amphitheater** (Anfiteatro) was the stage for Olympic games, chariot races, and games between animals and gladiators. When an important person such as the Emperor was in attendance, exotic animals—lions and tigers, panthers, elephants, and rhinos—were released. Teams of gladiators worked for impresarios, who hired them out to wealthy citizens, many of whom were running for office and hoping that the gory entertainment would buy them some votes. Most gladiators were slaves or prisoners, but a few were Germans or Syrians who enjoyed fighting. When a gladiator found himself at another's mercy, he extended a pleading hand to the president of the games. If the president turned his thumb up, the gladiator lived; if he turned his thumb down, the gladiator's throat was cut. The arena got pretty bloody after a night's entertainment and was sprinkled with red powder to camouflage the carnage. The victorious gladiator got money or a ribbon exempting him from further fights. If he was a slave, he was often set free. If the people of Pompeii had trading cards—today's version being old *carta telefonica* (prepaid telephone cards)—they would have collected portraits of gladiators; everyone had his favorite. Says one piece of graffiti: "Petronius Octavus fought thirty-four fights and then died, but Severus, a freedman, was victor in fifty-five fights and still lived; Nasica celebrates sixty victories." Pompeii had a gladiator school (Caserma dei Gladiatori), which you can visit on your way back to Porta Marina.

To get the most out of Pompeii, buy a detailed printed guide and map and allow plenty of time—at least three or four hours. You should have a pocketful of small change (500 lire coins) for tipping the guards who are on duty at the most important villas. They will unlock the gates for you, insist on explaining the attractions, show you some soft Pompeiian pornography if you ask for it, and expect a tip for their services. Make sure the guide is registered and standing inside the gate; agree beforehand on the length of the tour and the price. Pompeii has its own stop (Pompeii–Villa Misteri) on the Circumvesuviana, close to the main entrance at the Porta Marina (there are other entrances to the excavations at the far end of the site, near the amphitheater). ✉ *Pompeii Scavi,* ☎ *081/8610744.* ✆ *12,000 lire.* ☉ *Daily 9–1 hr before sunset (ticket office closes 2 hrs before sunset).*

Nightlife and the Arts

Pompeii's late-summer festival of the performing arts, known as the **Panatenee Pompeiane,** hosts a series of classical plays in July and August. For information, contact one of the information offices in Naples or Pompeii (☞ Contacts and Resources *in* Campania A to Z, *below*).

CASERTA AND BENEVENTO

From Caserta, the Italian version of Versailles, if you proceed to Benevento you'll view an almost perfectly preserved Roman arch. Benevento was badly damaged by World War II bombings, and you will have to content yourself here with picking out the medieval and even older relics that have survived in the oldest part of the city. If you go by car, make a brief detour to the medieval hamlet of Caserta Vecchia on the hillside, where there is a very old cathedral and one or two good restaurants.

Caserta

★ **39** *25 km (16 mi) southeast of Naples, 11 km (7 mi) northeast of Herculaneum.*

The **royal palace,** known as the Reggia, is exemplary of mid-18th-century Bourbon royalty living. Architect Luigi Vanvitelli devoted 20 years to its construction under Bourbon ruler Charles II, whose son,

Charles III, moved in when it was completed in 1774. Both king and architect were inspired by Versailles, and the rectangular palace was conceived on a massive scale, with four interconnecting courtyards, 1,200 rooms, and a vast park. Though not as well maintained as its French counterpart, the main staircase puts the one at Versailles to shame, and the **royal apartments** are sumptuous. It was here, in what Eisenhower called "a castle near Naples," that the Allied High Command had its headquarters in World War II, and here German forces in Italy surrendered in April 1945. Most enjoyable are the gardens and parks, particularly the Cascades, where a life-size Diana and her maidens stand. ⊠ *Piazza Carlo III,* ☎ *0823/321400.* ⌧ *Royal apartments 8,000 lire, park 4,000 lire, minibus 1,500 lire.* ☉ *Royal apartments Apr.–Sept., daily 9–6; Oct.–Mar., Mon.–Sat. 9–1:30, Sun. 9–1; closed 2nd and 4th Mon. of each month. Park daily 9–1 hr before sunset.*

Capua

11 km (7 mi) northwest of Caserta, 33 km (20 mi) north of Naples.

The nondescript town of Capua is home to the **Museo Campano,** a provincial museum collection that includes Le Madri (the Mothers), 200 eerily impressive stone votive statues representing highly stylized mother figures. They were found on the site of a sanctuary devoted to Matuta, the ancient goddess of childbirth, and date from the 7th to the 1st century BC. ⊠ *Via Roma,* ☎ *0823/961402.* ⌧ *8,000.* ☉ *Tues.– Sat. 9–1:30, Sun. 9–1.*

Benevento

40 *60 km (37 mi) east of Naples, 35 km (22 mi) east of Caserta.*

Benevento owes its importance to its establishment as the capital of the Lombards, a northern tribe that invaded and settled what is now Lombardy when they were ousted by Charlemagne in the 8th century. Tough and resourceful, the Lombards moved south and set up a new duchy in Benevento, later moving its seat south to Salerno, where they saw the potential of the natural harbor. Under papal rule in the 13th century, Benevento built a fine cathedral and endowed it with bronze doors that were a pinnacle of Romanesque art. The cathedral, doors, and a large part of the town were blasted by World War II bombs. The **Duomo** has been rebuilt, with the remaining panels of the original bronze doors in the chapter library. Fortunately, the majestic 2nd-century AD **Arch of Trajan** survived unscathed. Roman emperor Trajan, who sorted out Rome's finances, brought parts of the Middle East into the empire, and extended the Appian Way through Benevento to the Adriatic. The ruins of the Teatro Romano (Roman Theater), with a seating capacity of 20,000, is still in good enough shape to host a summer opera and theater season. ⊠ *Take Via Carlo from the Duomo.* ⌧ *4,000 lire.* ☉ *Daily 9–1 hr before sunset.*

ISCHIA AND CAPRI

Swept Away

History's hedonists have long luxuriated on Campania's famous islands. The Roman emperor Tiberius built a dozen villas on Capri to indulge his sexual whims. Later residents have included dancer Rudolf Nureyev and droves of artists and writers. These days day-trippers make up the bulk of the visitors, diminishing the islands' social cachet but unable to tarnish their incomparable beauty. Ischia, less pretty and less chic than Capri, is still a popular landing point on account of spas, beaches, and hot springs.

Ischia

❹ *31 km (19 mi) west of Naples; 45 min by hydrofoil and 90 min by car ferry from Naples; 60 min by boat from Pozzuoli.*

While Capri wows you with its charm and beauty, Ischia takes time to cast its spell. In fact, an overnight stay is probably not long enough for the island to get into your blood. It does have its share of wine-growing villages beneath the lush volcanic slopes of Monte Epomeo and, unlike Capri, it enjoys a life of its own that survives when the tourists head home. But there are few signs of antiquity here, the architecture is unremarkable, the beaches are small and pebbly, there's little shopping beyond the high-trash gift shops, and most visitors are either German (off-season) or Italian (in-season). On the other hand, some of you will delight in discovering an island not yet discovered by Americans. Ischia also has some lovely hotel-resorts high in the mountains, offering therapeutic programs and rooms with breathtaking views. Should you want to plunk down in the sun for a few days and tune out the world, this is an ideal place to go; the mistake you shouldn't make is expecting Ischia to be an unspoiled, undiscovered Capri. When Augustus gave the Neapolitans Ischia for Capri, he knew what he was doing.

Unlike Capri, Ischia is volcanic in origin. From its hidden reservoir of seething molten matter come the thermal springs said to cure whatever ails you. As early as 1580, a doctor named Iasolino published a book about the mineral wells at Ischia. "If your eyebrows fall off," he wrote, "go and try the baths at Piaggia Romano. Are you unhappy about your complexion? You will find the cure in the waters of Santa Maria del Popolo. Are you deaf? Then go to Bagno d'Ulmitello. If you know anyone who is getting bald, anyone who suffers from elephantiasis, or another whose wife yearns for a child, take the three of them immediately to the Bagno di Vitara; they will bless you." Today the island is covered with thermal baths surrounded by tropical gardens.

Ischia Porto is the largest town on the island and the usual point of debarkation. It's no workaday port, however, but a pretty resort with plenty of hotels and low flat-roofed houses on terraced hillsides above the water. Its narrow streets often become flights of steps that scale the hill, and its villas and gardens are framed by pines.

Most of the hotels are along the beach in the part of town called **Ischia Ponte,** which gets its name from the *ponte* (bridge) built by Alfonso of Aragón in 1438 to link the picturesque castle on a small islet offshore with the town and port. For a while, the castle was the home of Vittoria Colonna, poetess and platonic soul mate of Michelangelo, with whom she carried on a lengthy correspondence, and granddaughter of Renaissance Duke Federico da Montefeltro. You'll find a typical resort atmosphere: countless cafés, shops, and restaurants, and a ½-mi stretch of fine sandy beach.

Another popular beach resort, just 5 km (3 mi) west of Ischia Porto, is **Casamicciola.** Next is chic and upscale **Lacco Ameno,** distinguished by a mushroom-shaped rock offshore and some of the island's best hotels. Here, too, you can enjoy the benefits of Ischia's therapeutic waters.

The far western and southern coasts of the island are more rugged and attractive. **Forio,** at the extreme west, is an ideal stop for lunch or dinner. The sybaritic hot pools of the **Poseidon Gardens** spa establishment are on the Citara beach, south of Forio. You can sit like a Roman senator on a stone chair recessed in the rock and let the hot water cascade over you—all very campy, and fun. **Sant'Angelo,** on the southern coast, is a charming village; the road doesn't reach all the way into town, so it's free of traffic, and it's a five-minute boat ride from the beach of Maronti, at the foot of cliffs. The inland towns of **Serrara, Fontana,** and **Barano** are all high above the sea; Fontana, most elevated of the three, is the base for excursions to the top of **Mt. Epomeo,** the long-dormant volcano that dominates the island landscape. You can reach its 2,585-ft peak in less than 1½ hours of relatively easy walking.

A good 35-km (22-mi) road makes a circuit of the island; the ride takes most of a day at a leisurely pace, if you're stopping along the way to enjoy the views and perhaps have lunch. You can book a **boat tour** (20,000 and 27,000 lire) around the island at the booths in various ports along the coast; there's a one-hour stop at Sant'Angelo. The **information office** is at the harbor. Remember that Ischia is off limits to visitors' cars from April through September; there's fairly good bus service, and you'll find plenty of taxis.

Dining and Lodging

$$ ✕ **Gennaro.** This small family restaurant on the seafront at Ischia Porto serves excellent fish in a convivial atmosphere. Specialties include spaghetti alle vongole and linguine all'aragosta. ⊠ *Via Porto 66,* ☎ *081/992917. AE, DC, MC, V. Closed Nov.–mid-Mar. and Tues. Mar.–Apr. and Oct.*

$$$$ 🏨 **Grand Hotel Punta Molino.** Right in the town of Ischia Porto, but set in a quiet zone near the sea and framed with pine trees and gardens, is one of the best hotels on the island. The decor is bright and contemporary, with some luxurious touches, and many rooms have sea views. There's a heated pool on one of the terraces. Half board is required. ⊠ *Lungomare Colombo, 80077,* ☎ *081/991544,* FAX *081/991562. 82 rooms. Restaurant, bar, spa, beach. AE, MC, DC, V. Closed Nov.–Mar.*

$$$$ 🏨 **Regina Isabella.** Tucked away in an exclusive corner of the beach
★ in Lacco Ameno, Ischia's top luxury hotel has full resort facilities and pampers guests with spa treatments as well. The rooms are ample and decorated in warm Mediterranean colors, and most have terraces or balconies. Don't miss the fun of socializing with chic vacationers in the elegant bar or restaurant or at poolside. ⊠ *Piazza Santa Restituta, Lacco Ameno, 80076,* ☎ *081/994322,* FAX *081/986043. 134 rooms. Restaurant, bar, indoor and outdoor pools, tennis court, beach. AE, DC, MC, V. Closed Oct. 16–Apr. 14.*

$$$–$$$$ 🏨 **Hotel San Montano.** Modern San Montano, replete with nautical motifs and ceramic-tile floors, overlooks the sea in a quiet spot. The rooms have compact English-navy furnishings, color TVs, and mini-bars. The San Montano has all resort facilities and provides spa treatments, too. ⊠ *Via Montevico 1, Lacco Ameno, 80076,* ☎ *081/994033,* FAX *081/980242. 67 rooms. Restaurant, pool, tennis court. AE, DC, MC, V. Closed Nov.–Mar.*

$$$ 🏨 **Villarosa.** A highlight at this gracious family-run hotel, in a villa with
★ bright and airy rooms, is the thermally heated pool in the villa garden. In high season, half board is required, and you must reserve well in advance. Prices fall into the lower end of this category. It's in the heart of Ischia Porto and only a short walk from the beach. ⊠ *Via Giacinto Gigante 3, 80077,* ☎ *081/991316,* FAX *081/992425. 37 rooms. Restaurant. AE, MC, V. Closed Nov.–Easter.*

$ 🏨 **Del Postiglione.** This attractive, pink, Mediterranean-style edifice is smaller than it appears, with only 11 guest rooms. Its aura of understated luxury is created by marble floors, tropical plants adorning the outside, and generous balconies overlooking one of Ischia Porto's quiet back streets, a couple of minutes from the seafront. Half board only is accepted in August. ⊠ *Via Giacinto Gigante 19, 80077,* ☎ FAX *081/991579. 11 rooms. Restaurant, bar, baby-sitting.* No *credit cards.*

Capri

42 *31 km (19 mi) south of Naples; 74 min by boat and 40 min by hydrofoil from Naples, direct helicopter service from Capodichino Airport.*

Erstwhile pleasure dome to Roman emperors, and now Italy's most glamorous seaside getaway, Capri (pronounced with an accent on the first syllable) is a craggy island at the southern approach to the Bay of Naples.

The summer scene on Capri calls to mind the stampeding of bulls through the narrow streets of Pamplona: If you can visit in the spring or fall, do so. Yet even the crowds are not enough to destroy Capri's very special charm. The town is a Moorish opera set of shiny white houses, tiny squares, and narrow medieval alleyways hung with flowers. You can take a bus or the funicular to reach the town, which rests on top of rugged limestone cliffs, hundreds of feet above the sea, and on which huge herds of *capra* (goats) once used to roam (giving the name to the island). Unlike the other islands in the Bay of Naples, Capri is not of volcanic origin but is an integral part of the limestone chain of the Apennines, left above water when some subterranean cataclysm sank its connecting link with the mainland.

The Phoenicians were the earliest settlers of Capri. The Greeks arrived in the 4th century BC and were followed by the Romans, who made it their playground. Emperor Augustus vacationed here; Tiberius built 12 villas, scattered over the island, and here he spent the later years of his life, refusing to return to Rome even when he was near death. Capri was one of the strongholds of the 16th-century pirate Barbarossa, who first sacked it and then made a fortress of it. Moors and Greeks had previously established their citadels on its heights, and pirates from all corners of the world periodically raided it. In 1806 the British wanted to turn it into another Gibraltar and were beginning to build fortifications when the French took it away from them in 1808. However, the Roman influence has remained the strongest, reflecting a sybaritic way of life inherited from the Greek colonists on the mainland.

Thousands of legends concerning the lives and loves of mythological creatures, Roman emperors, Saracen invaders, and modern eccentrics combine to give Capri a voluptuous allure—sensuous and intoxicating—like the island's rare and delicious white wine. (Most of the wine passed off as "local" on Capri comes from the much more extensive vineyards of Ischia.) Certainly, there are fewer pleasures more gratifying than gazing out at the sea from the quiet of a sun-dappled arbor while enjoying a glass of chilled wine and flavorful insalata caprese.

You may have to wait in line for the cog railway (3,000 lire round-trip) to **Capri town.** If it's not operating, there's bus and taxi service. From the upper station, walk out into Piazza Umberto I, much better known as the **Piazzetta,** the island's social hub. You can window-shop in expensive boutiques and browse in souvenir shops along Via Vittorio Emanuele, which leads south toward the many-domed **Certosa di San Giacomo.** The church and cloister of this much-restored monastery can be visited, and you should also pause long enough to enjoy the breathtaking view of Punta Tragara and the Faraglioni, three towering shoals, from the viewing stand at the edge of the cliff. ⊠ *Via Certosa.* ▣ *Free.* ☉ *Tues.–Sun. 9–2.*

All boats for Capri town dock at Marina Grande, where you can also board an excursion boat for the 90-minute tour to the **Blue Grotto.** If you're pressed for time, however, skip this sometimes frustrating and disappointing excursion. You board one boat to get to the grotto, and you have to transfer to another, smaller, one in order to get inside the grotto. If there's a backup of boats waiting to get in, you'll be given precious little time to enjoy the gorgeous color of the water and its silvery reflections. ⊠ *Marina Grande.* ▣ *About 22,000 lire, including 8,000-lire admission to grotto.* ☉ *Apr.–Sept., daily 9:30–2 hrs before sunset; Oct.–Mar., 10–noon.*

OFF THE
BEATEN PATH

BELVEDERE AND NATURAL ARCH – A short walk along Via Tragara leads to a belvedere overlooking the Faraglioni; another takes you out of town of on Via Matermania to the so-called Natural Arch, an unusual rock formation near a natural grotto that the Romans transformed into a shrine. The 20-minute walk from the Piazzetta along picturesque Via Madre Serafina and Via Castello to the belvedere at Punta Cannone gives you a panoramic view of the island.

From the terraces of **Giardini di Augusto** (Gardens of Augustus), a beautifully planted public garden with excellent views, you can see the village of **Marina Piccola** below—restaurants, cabanas, and swimming platforms huddle among the shoals. This is the best place on the island for swimming; you can reach it by bus or by following the steep and winding Via Krupp, actually a staircase cut into the rock, all the way down. (Friedrich Krupp, the German arms manufacturer, loved Capri and became one of the island's most generous benefactors.) Otherwise you swim off boats or take a hint from the family groups from Naples and Sorrento who swim off the unkempt but sandy beach at the end of Marina Grande past the cog railway station. ⊠ *Via Matteotti, beyond the monastery of San Giacomo.*

OFF THE
BEATEN PATH

VILLA JOVIS – From Capri town, the 45-minute hike east to Villa Jovis, the grandest of those built by Tiberius, is strenuous but rewarding. Follow the signs for Villa Jovis, taking Via Le Botteghe from the Piazzetta, then continuing along Via Croce and Via Tiberio. At the end of a lane that climbs the steep hill, with pretty views all the way, you come to the precipice over which the emperor reputedly disposed of the victims of his perverse attentions. From a natural terrace above, near a chapel, are spectacular views of the entire Bay of Naples and (on clear days) part of the Gulf of Salerno. Below are the ruins of Tiberius's palace. Allow 45 minutes each way for the walk alone. ⊠ *Via Tiberio.* ▣ *4,000 lire.* ☉ *Daily 9–1 hr before sunset.*

A tortuous road up leads to **Anacapri,** the island's only other town. Crowds are thickest around the square that is the starting point of the chairlift (6,000 lire) to the top of **Mt. Solaro.** Elsewhere, Anacapri is quiet and appealing. Look for the church of **San Michele,** where a climb to the choir loft rewards you with a perspective of the magnificent 18th-century majolica tile floor showing the Garden of Eden. To get to Anacapri, you can take a bus from Marina Grande (1,500 lire) or a taxi (about 15,000 lire one way; agree on the fare before starting out).

Anacapri is good for walks: Try the 40-minute walk (each way) to the **Migliara Belvedere** and the one-hour walk to the ruins of the Roman **Villa of Damecuta.** From Piazza della Vittoria, picturesque Via Capodimonte leads to **Villa San Michele,** charming former home of Swedish scientist Axel Munthe, now a museum of his antiques and furniture. ⊠ *Via Axel Munthe.* 🎫 *6,000 lire.* 🕐 *Nov.–Feb., daily 10:30–3:30; Mar., daily 9:30–4:30; Apr. and Oct., daily 9:30–5; May–Sept., daily 9–6.*

Dining and Lodging

$$$ ✕ **La Pigna.** Ensconced in a glassed-in veranda and offering outdoor dining in a garden shaded by lemon trees, the Pigna is one of Capri's favorite restaurants. The specialties are a house-produced wine, *farfalle impazzite* (bow-tie pasta with seafood and tomato), and *aragosta alla luna caprese* (lobster with mozzarella, tomato, and basil). The cordial host organizes party evenings with feasts of seasonal specialties and seafood. ⊠ *Via Lo Palazzo 30, Capri,* 🕾 *081/8370280. Reservations essential. AE, DC, MC, V. Closed Tues. and Nov.–Easter.*

$$–$$$ ✕ **La Capannina.** Known as one of Capri's best restaurants, La Capannina is only a few steps from the busy social hub of the Piazzetta.
★ It has a vine-draped veranda for dining outdoors by candlelight in a garden setting. The specialties, aside from an authentic Capri wine with the house label, are homemade ravioli alla caprese and regional dishes. ⊠ *Via Le Botteghe 14, Capri,* 🕾 *081/8370732. Reservations essential. AE, MC, V. Closed Nov. 10–Mar. 15 and Wed. Sept.–July.*

$$ ✕ **Al Grottino.** This small and friendly family-run restaurant, which is handy to the Piazzetta, has arched ceilings and lots of atmosphere; autographed photos of celebrity customers cover the walls. House specialties are gnocchi with tomato sauce and mozzarella, and linguine *ai gamberetti* (with shrimp and tomato sauce). ⊠ *Via Longano 27, Capri,* 🕾 *081/8370584. Reservations essential. AE, MC, V. Closed Tues. and Nov. 3–Mar. 20.*

$$$$ 🏨 **Europa Palace Hotel.** A modern resort atmosphere pervades this large Mediterranean-style hotel set in lovely gardens. Each of four junior suites has a private swimming pool and terrace. The bedrooms are tastefully decorated in contemporary style, with white predominating; marble is featured in the bathrooms, and many rooms have balconies. The only minus is being in Anacapri, a bus or cab ride from the restaurants and shops in the town of Capri. ⊠ *Via Capodimonte, Anacapri, 80071,* 🕾 *081/8373800,* 🖷 *081/8373191. 93 rooms. Restaurant, bar, air-conditioning, pool. AE, DC, MC, V. Closed Nov.–Mar.*

$$$$ 🏨 **Quisisana.** Catering largely to Americans, this is the most luxurious and traditional hotel in the center of town. Spacious rooms are done in traditional or modern decor with some antique accents; many have arcaded balconies with views of the sea or the charming enclosed garden, in which there's a swimming pool. The bar and restaurant are casually elegant. ⊠ *Via Camerelle 2, Capri, 80073,* 🕾 *081/8370788,* 🖷 *081/8376080. 143 rooms. Restaurant, bar, pool, sauna, tennis court. AE, DC, MC, V. Closed Nov.–mid-Mar.*

$$$$ 🏨 **Scalinatella.** The name means "little stairway," and that's how this
★ charming but modern small hotel is built, on terraces following the slope of the hill, overlooking the gardens, pool, and sea. The bedrooms are intimate, with alcoves and fresh, bright colors; the bathrooms feature Jacuzzis. The hotel has a small bar but no restaurant. ⊠ *Via Tragara 8, Capri, 80073,* 🕾 *081/8370633,* 🖷 *081/8378291. 30 rooms. Bar, air-conditioning, pool, tennis court. AE, MC, V. Closed Nov.–Mar. 14.*

$$$$ 🏨 **Villa Brunella.** This quiet family-run gem nestles in a garden setting just below the lane leading to the Faraglioni. Comfortable and tastefully furnished, the hotel also has spectacular views, a swimming pool, and a terrace restaurant known for good food. ⊠ *Via Tragara 24, Capri, 80073,* 🕾 *081/8370122,* 🖷 *081/8370430. 18 rooms. Restaurant, bar, pool. AE, DC, MC, V. Closed Nov.–Mar.*

$$$ 🏨 **San Michele.** You'll find this large white villa-hotel next to Axel Munthe's Capri home. Surrounded by luxuriant gardens, the San Michele offers solid comfort and good value, along with spectacular views. It's modern, with some Neapolitan period pieces adding atmosphere. Most rooms have a terrace or balcony overlooking either the sea or island landscapes. ✉ *Via G. Orlandi 5, Anacapri, 80071,* ☎ *081/8371442,* ℻ *081/8371420. 56 rooms. 2 restaurants, pool. AE, DC, MC, V. Closed Nov.–Mar.*

$$$ 🏨 **Villa Krupp.** Occupying a quiet location overlooking the Gardens of Augustus, this historic hostelry was the onetime home of Maxim Gorky, whose guests included Lenin. Rooms are plain but spacious, and some have a balcony. ✉ *Viale Matteotti 12, Capri, 80073,* ☎ *081/8370362,* ℻ *081/8376489. 12 rooms. MC, V. Closed Nov.–Feb.*

$$$ 🏨 **Villa Sarah.** This whitewashed Mediterranean building has a homey look and bright, simply furnished rooms. It's close enough to the Piazzetta (a 10-minute walk) to give easy access to the goings-on there, yet far enough away to ensure restful nights. There's a garden and a small bar, but no restaurant. ✉ *Via Tiberio 3/a, Capri, 80073,* ☎ *081/8377817,* ℻ *081/8377215. 20 rooms. AE, MC, V. Closed Nov.–Mar.*

$$ 🏨 **Aida.** A 10-minute walk from the center of town in a tiny lane that borders the Gardens of Augustus, the Aida offers a tranquil haven from Capri's bustle and hard sell. The staff is sociable, and the rooms, which look onto a small garden, are spacious, comfortably furnished, and immaculately clean. The beach, at Marina Piccola, is only 20 minutes away. ✉ *Via Birago, Capri, 80073,* ☎ *081/8370366. 9 rooms, 5 with shower. No credit cards. Closed mid-Oct.–Apr.*

Nightlife and the Arts

Capri's **New Year's Eve** celebrations last all evening with dancing and music culminating in a magnificent fireworks display. On **New Year's Day** there are marching bands, pageants, and all the revelry you would expect on this exuberant island.

THE AMALFI DRIVE

Sorrento to Salerno

As travelers journey down the fabled Amalfi Drive, their route takes them past rocky cliffs plunging into the sea and small boats lying in sandy coves like brightly colored fish. Erosion has contorted the rocks into mythological shapes and hollowed out fairy grottoes where the air is turquoise and the water an icy blue. White villages, dripping with flowers, nestle in coves or climb like vines up the steep, terraced hills. The road must have a thousand turns, each with a different view, on its dizzying 69-km (43-mi) journey from Sorrento to Salerno.

Sorrento

🔟 *50 km (31 mi) south of Naples.*

Sorrento is across the Bay of Naples, on autostrada A3 and S145; the Circumvesuviana railway, which stops at Herculaneum and Pompeii, provides another connection. The coast between Naples and Castellammare, where road and railway turn off onto the Sorrento peninsula, seems at times depressingly overbuilt and industrialized. Yet Vesuvius looms to the left, you can make out the 3,000-ft-high mass of Mt. Faito ahead, and on a clear day you can see Capri off the tip of the peninsula. The scenery improves considerably as you near Sorrento, where the coastal plain is carved into russet cliffs rising perpendicularly from the sea. This is the Sorrento (north) side of the peninsula; on the other side is the Amalfi Coast, more dramatically scenic and somewhat less overcome by tourists in summer. Many prefer the charming towns on the Amalfi Coast to the tourist haven of Sorrento, but Sorrento has at least two advantages: the Circumvesuviana railway terminal and a fairly flat terrain. (Positano, and to a lesser extent Amalfi and Ravello, clings to hillsides and requires some strenuous walking.)

Until the mid-20th century Sorrento was a small, genteel resort favored by central European princes, English aristocrats, and American literati. Now the town has grown and spread out along the crest of its famous cliffs, and apartments stand where citrus groves once bloomed.

Tour groups arrive by the busload, and their ranks are swollen by Italian vacationers in the peak summer season. Like most resorts, Sorrento is best off-season, either in spring and early autumn or in winter, when Campania's mild climate can make a stay pleasant anywhere along the coast. Another reason to avoid the peninsula during peak season is the heavy traffic on the single coast road, where cars and buses may be backed up for miles.

Highlights include a stroll around town, with views of the Bay of Naples from the **Villa Comunale** or from the terrace behind the **Museo Correale.** The museum features a collection of decorative antiques, from precious porcelain to furniture to landscape paintings of the Neapolitan school. ⊠ *Via Correale.* ⌺ *Museum and garden 8,000 lire, garden 2,000 lire.* ⊗ *Apr.–Sept., Mon. and Wed.–Sat. 9–12:30 and 5–7, Sun. 9–12:30; Oct.–Mar., Mon. and Wed.–Sat. 9–11:30 and 3–5, Sun. 9–11:30.*

Explore the town's churches and narrow alleys and follow **Via Marina Grande,** which turns into a pedestrian lane and stairway, to Sorrento's only real **beach,** where the fishermen pull up their boats. You can take a bus or walk a mile or so to Capo Sorrento, then follow the signs to the **Villa of Pollio Felice,** the scattered seaside remains of an ancient Roman villa, where you can swim off the rocks or simply admire the setting.

Before you leave Sorrento, consider a side trip west along the road that skirts the tip of the peninsula; if you enjoy dramatic seascapes, this will be worth the extra time.

Dining and Lodging

$$ ✕ **Antica Trattoria.** An Old World dining room inside and garden tables in fair weather make this a pleasant place to enjoy the local cooking. The atmosphere is homey and hospitable. The menu is voluminous and your choice will be difficult, but the specialties include spaghetti alle vongole and gamberetti Antica Trattoria (in tomato sauce). You can also opt for one of the four fixed-price menus. ⊠ *Via Giuliani 33,* ☎ *081/8071082. AE, MC, V. Closed Mon. and Jan. 10–Feb. 10.*

$$ ✕ **Parrucchiano.** Centrally located and popular, this is one of Sorrento's oldest and best restaurants. You walk up a few steps to glassed-in veranda dining rooms filled, like greenhouses, with vines and plants. The menu offers classic local specialties, among them *panzerotti* (pastry shells filled with tomato and mozzarella) and scaloppe *alla sorrentina* (with tomato and mozzarella). ⊠ *Corso Italia 71,* ☎ *081/8781321. MC, V. Closed Wed. Nov.–May.*

$$$$ ▥ **Cocumella.** This hotel is set in a cliff-top garden in a quiet residential area on the edge of Sorrento (it's really in the adjacent town of Sant'Agnello). Occupying a historic old villa that was a monastery in the 17th century, it features a tasteful blend of antique and contemporary appointments, with vaulted ceilings and archways, a din-

ing veranda, and stunning tiled floors. It's exclusive and elegant without being stuffy. ⊠ *Via Cocumella 7, Sant'Agnello, 80065,* ☎ *081/8782933,* FAX *081/8783712. 61 rooms and suites. Restaurant, bar, pool, tennis court. AE, DC, MC, V. Closed Jan.–Feb.*

$$$$ ⭐ 🏨 **Excelsior Vittorio.** Magnificently set overlooking the Bay of Naples, this is a belle-epoque dream come true. Gilded salons worthy of a Proust heroine, stunning gardens, and an impossibly romantic terrace where orchestras lull guests with equal doses of Cole Porter and Puccini: in all, a truly intoxicating experience. Caruso stayed here, and now so does Pavarotti and Princess Margaret. Save your pennies, splurge—but come! ⊠ *Piazza Tasso 34, 80067,* ☎ *081/8071044,* FAX *081/8771206. 109 rooms and suites. Restaurant, bar, pool. AE, DC, MC, V.*

$$$$ 🏨 **Imperial Hotel Tramontano.** The birthplace of the poet Torquato Tasso—the first of an impressive list of literary credentials—this palatial villa lies within a semitropical garden in the center of Sorrento. The sumptuous furnishings and belle-epoque tone are set off by the spectacular views out to sea. ⊠ *Via Veneto 1, 80067,* ☎ *081/8782588,* FAX *081/8072344. 120 rooms. Restaurant, bar, beach, meeting rooms. AE, MC, V. Closed Jan.–Feb.*

$$$ 🏨 **Eden.** In a quiet but central location, the Eden has a garden and bright, though undistinguished, guest rooms. The lounge and lobby have more character. Undergoing renovation work in 1997, the hotel may yet present a more inspiring aspect to its guests. ⊠ *Via Correale 25, 80067,* ☎ *081/8781909,* FAX *081/8072016. 60 rooms. Restaurant, bar, pool. AE, DC, MC, V. Closed Nov.–Feb.*

$ 🏨 **City.** The convenient location and excellent value for the money are the best reasons to stay in this modest establishment, close to the bus and train stations. Bedrooms are small and functional. The atmosphere is relaxed, and the management is always ready with information and advice. ⊠ *Corso Italia 221, 80067,* ☎ FAX *081/8772210. 13 rooms. MC, V.*

Nightlife and the Arts

BARS AND CAFÉS

At **Circolo dei Forestieri** (⊠ Via de Maio 35, Sorrento, ☎ 081/8074033) you'll get a memorable view of the Bay of Naples from the terrace. Drinks are moderately priced, and there is live music nightly in summer and every weekend the rest of the year. The bar **Villa Pompeiana** (⊠ Via Marina Grande 6, Sorrento, ☎ 081/8772428) in the Bellevue Syrene Hotel has a garden terrace and an indoor tavern with an ancient-Roman setting. There's music in summer. It's closed December–February.

FILM

Every November and December, the **International Cinema Convention** in Sorrento draws an elite collection of producers, directors, and stars in a less frantic atmosphere than that of the festival in Cannes. While much of the activity revolves around deal making, a number of previews are screened. For details contact the Sorrento tourist office (☞ Contacts and Resources *in Campania A to Z, below*).

Shopping

LOCAL CRAFTS

Around **Piazza Tasso** are a number of shops selling **embroidered goods** and **intarsia** (wood inlay) work, a centuries-old tradition here. Along narrow **Via San Cesareo,** where the air is pungent with the perfumes of fruit and vegetable stands, there are more shops selling local and Italian crafts—everything from jewelry boxes to trays and coffee tables with intarsia decorations. **Ferdinando Corcione,** in his shop on Via San Francesco, gives demonstrations of his intarsia work, producing decorative plaques with classic or contemporary motifs.

Positano

★ ㊹ *14 km (9 mi) east of Sorrento, 40 km (25 mi) west of Salerno.*

When John Steinbeck lived here in 1953, he wrote that it was difficult to consider tourism an industry because "there are not enough [tourists]." Alas, Positano, a village of white Moorish-type houses clinging dramatically to slopes around a small sheltered bay, has since been discovered. The artists came first, and, as happens wherever artists go, the wealthy followed and the artists fled. What Steinbeck wrote, however, still applies: "Positano bites deep. It is a dream place that isn't quite real when you are there and becomes beckoningly real after you have gone. Its houses climb a hill so steep it would be a cliff except that stairs are cut in it. I believe that whereas most house foundations are vertical, in Positano they are horizontal. The small curving bay of unbelievably blue and green water laps gently on a beach of small pebbles. There is only one narrow street and it does not come down to the water. Everything else is stairs, some of them as steep as ladders. You do not walk to visit a friend, you either climb or slide."

In the 10th century Positano was part of Amalfi's Maritime Republic, which rivaled Venice as an important mercantile power. Its heyday was in the 16th and 17th centuries, when its ships traded in the Near and Middle East, carrying spices, silks, and precious woods. The coming of the steamship in the mid-19th century led to the town's decline, and some three-fourths of the town's 8,000 citizens emigrated to America, mostly to New York. One major task of Positano's mayor has been to find space in the overcrowded cemetery for New York Positanesi who want to spend eternity here.

What had been reduced to a forgotten fishing village is now the number-one attraction on the coast, with hotels for every budget, charming restaurants, and dozens of boutiques. From here, you can take hydrofoils to Capri during the summer, escorted bus rides to Ravello, and tours of the Grotta dello Smeraldo.

If you're staying in Positano, check whether your hotel has a parking area. If not, you will have to pay for space in a parking lot, which is almost impossible to find during the high season, from Easter to September. The best bet for day-trippers is to get to Positano early enough so that space is still available. No matter how much time you spend in Positano, make sure you have some comfortable walking shoes—no heels, please!—and that your back and legs are strong enough to negotiate steps.

Dining and Lodging

$$ ✕ **Buca di Bacco.** After an aperitif at the town's most famous and fashionable café downstairs, you dine on a veranda overlooking the beach. The specialties include spaghetti alle vongole and *grigliata* mista (mixed grilled seafood). ⊠ *Via Rampa Teglia 8,* ☎ *089/875699. AE, DC, MC, V. Closed Nov. 6–Mar.*

$$ ✕ **'O Capurale.** Among the popular restaurants on the beach promenade, this one just around the corner has the best food and lowest prices. Tables are set under vines on a breezy sidewalk in the summer, indoors and upstairs in winter. Spaghetti con melanzane and crepes *al formaggio* (with cheese) are among the specialties. ⊠ *Via Regina Giovanna 12,* ☎ *089/875374. AE, DC, MC, V. Closed Nov.–mid-Feb.*

$$$$ ▥ **Le Sirenuse.** A handsome 18th-century palazzo in the center of ★ town is the setting for this luxury hotel in which bright tiled floors, precious antiques, and tasteful furnishings are featured in ample and luminous salons. The bedrooms have the same sense of spaciousness

and comfort; most have splendid views from balconies and terraces. The top-floor suites have huge bathrooms and Jacuzzis. One side of a large terrace has an inviting swimming pool; on the other is an excellent restaurant—both share the hotel's view of the town, beach, and sea. ☒ *Via Cristoforo Colombo 30, 84017,* ☎ *089/875066,* FAX *089/ 811798. 60 rooms. Bar, sauna. AE, DC, MC, V.*

$$$$ 🏨 **San Pietro.** Extraordinary is the word for this luxurious oasis for the
★ affluent international set. Outside the town and set high above the sea with garden terraces, the San Pietro has sumptuous Neapolitan baroque decor and masses of flowers in the lounges, elegantly understated rooms (most with terraces), and marvelous views. There's a pool on an upper level, and an elevator whisks guests to the private beach and beach bar. The proprietors organize boating excursions and parties and provide car and minibus service into town. ☒ *Via Laurito, 84017,* ☎ *089/875455,* FAX *089/811449. 60 rooms. Restaurant, 2 bars, pool, tennis court, beach, dock. AE, DC, MC, V. Closed Nov.–Mar.*

$$$ 🏨 **Palazzo Murat.** The location is perfect—in the heart of town, near the beachside promenade, but set in a quiet, walled garden. The old wing is a historic palazzo with tall windows and wrought-iron balconies; the new wing is a whitewashed Mediterranean building with arches and terraces. You can relax in antiques-accented lounges or in the charming vine-draped patio, and since there's no restaurant, you will avoid the half-board requirement applied in most hotels here in high season. ☒ *Via dei Mulini 23, 84017,* ☎ *089/875177,* FAX *089/811419. 28 rooms. Bar. AE, DC, MC, V. Closed Nov. 5–Mar.*

$$ 🏨 **La Fenice.** Paradise found. This tiny and unpretentious hotel beck-
★ ons with bougainvillea-laden vistas, castaway cottages, and a turquoise pool, all perched over a private beach. Guest rooms—accented with coved ceilings, whitewashed walls, and native folk art—are simple havens of tranquility (book the best, those closest to the sea, only if you can handle *very* steep walkways). Situated on the peaceful outskirts of town, this is happily open year-round. ☒ *Via G. Marconi, 4, 84017,* ☎ *089/ 875513,* FAX *089/811309. 10 rooms. Pool. AE, MC, V.*

$$ 🏨 **Santa Caterina.** There is more to this hotel than meets the eye: Rooms descend on three levels down the steep slope. The owners have made the most of the exquisite view of the town and seashore, which can be relished from each of the rooms. On street level (the top floor), there is also a good fish restaurant. It's quite a hike to the beach—a good 15 minutes down the steps—but that's nothing new in Positano. ☒ *Via Pasitea 113, 84017,* ☎ *089/811513,* FAX *089/875019. 12 rooms. Restaurant, bar. AE, DC, MC, V. Closed Jan. 10–Feb. 20.*

Nightlife

L'Africana (☒ Vettica Maggiore, Praiano, 10 km (6 mi) east of Positano on the coast road, ☎ 089/874042) is the premier nightclub on the Amalfi Coast and is built into a fantastic grotto above the sea.

Shopping

The picturesque streets of this coastal resort are lined with **boutiques** selling **casual fashions** and **beachwear** in splashy colors and extravagant fabrics.

Grotta dello Smeraldo

13 km (8 mi) along the coast road from Positano, 4 km (2½ mi) west of Amalfi.

A peculiar green light that casts an eerie emerald glow over impressive formations of stalagmites and stalactites, many of them underwater, inspired the name for Grotta dello Smeraldo (Emerald Grotto). You can park at the signposts for the grotto along the coast road and take an elevator down, or you can drive on to Amalfi and return to the grotto by the more romantic route: via boat (boat tours leave from the Amalfi seafront approximately every two hours, according to demand; the charge is 10,000 lire per person). ✉ *5,000 lire.* ☉ *Apr.–Sept., daily 9–5; Oct.– Mar., daily 10–3 (hrs vary).*

Amalfi

㊺   *17 km. (11 mi) east of Positano, 25 km (16 mi) west of Salerno.*

"The sun—the moon—the stars and—Amalfi," Amalfitans used to say. Although Amalfi would seem to be a leading choice for a town to stay in along the drive, it would have to be a distant third—after Ravello and Positano—because of the congestion caused by tour buses, which make Amalfi the main stopping point on their excursions. The town is romantically situated at the mouth of a deep gorge and has some good-quality hotels and restaurants. It's also a convenient base for excursions to Capri and the Emerald Grotto.

During the Middle Ages, Amalfi was an independent maritime state— a little Republic of Venice—with a population of 50,000. The ship compass, trivia fans will be pleased to know, was invented here in 1302.

Amalfi's main historical site is its **Duomo** (Cathedral of St. Andrew), which shows an interesting mix of Moorish and early-Gothic influences. The interior is a 10th-century Romanesque skeleton in an 18th-century Baroque dress. The transept and the choir are 13th century. The handsome 12th-century campanile has identical Gothic domes at each corner. Don't miss the beautiful late 13th-century Moorish cloister, with its slender double columns. At least one critic has called the cathedral's facade the ugliest piece of serious architecture in Italy—decide for yourself. The same critic snickers at the tourists who fail to note the cathedral's greatest treasure, the 11th-century bronze doors from Constantinople. Turn right out of the doors for the **cloisters,** with whitewashed arches and palms, and a small museum in the adjoining crypt. ✉ *Duomo free, cloisters and crypt 3,000 lire.* ☉ *Duomo Apr.– Sept., daily 7:30 AM–9 PM; Oct.–Mar., daily 7:30–noon and 4–6:30. Cloisters and crypt Apr.–Sept., daily 9–9; Oct.–Mar., daily 10–1 and 2:30–5:30.*

The **parking problem** here is as bad as that in Positano. The small lot in the center of town fills quickly; if you can afford the steep prices, make a luncheon reservation at one of the hotel restaurants and have your car parked for you.

The main street leads back through town from the cathedral to the mountains, and passes a ceramic workshop and some water-driven paper mills where handcrafted paper is made and sold. Though it's not always open, there's a **paper museum** where you can see exactly how the mills work.

NEED A BREAK?	Stop in at the **Pansa** pastry shop (✉ Piazza del Duomo) for a giant *sfogliatella* (a multilayered pastry shaped like a scallop with a ricotta filling) or any of the other oven-fresh goodies.

Dining and Lodging

$$ ✗ **La Caravella.** You'll find this welcoming establishment tucked away
★   under some arches lining the coast road, next to the medieval Arsenal, where Amalfi's mighty fleet once was provisioned. La Caravella has a nondescript entrance but a pleasant interior decorated in a medley of colors and paintings of Old Amalfi. It's small and intimate; specialties include *scialatielli* (homemade pasta with shellfish sauce) and *pesce al*

limone (fish with lemon sauce). ⊠ *Via M. Camera 12,* ☎ *089/871029. AE, DC, MC, V. Closed Nov. 10–30 and Tues. Oct–June.*

$$$$ 🏨 **Santa Caterina.** A large mansion perched above terraced and flow-
★ ered hillsides on the coast road just outside Amalfi proper, the Santa
Caterina is one of the best hotels on the entire coast, offering gracious
living in a wonderfully scenic setting. The rooms are tastefully decorated; most have small terraces or balconies with great views. There
are lovely lounges and terraces for relaxing, and an elevator whisks
guests to the seaside saltwater pool, bar, and swimming area. On
grounds lush with lemon and orange groves, there are two romantic
villa annexes. ⊠ *Strada Amalfitana 9, 84011,* ☎ *089/871012,* 🕿
089/871351. 70 rooms. Restaurant, bar, pool. AE, DC, MC, V.

$$$ 🏨 **Hotel Dei Cavalieri.** This terraced, white, Mediterranean-style hotel
on the main road outside Amalfi has three villa annexes on grounds
just across the road that extend all the way to a beach below. The bed-
rooms are air-conditioned and functionally furnished, with splashy ma-
jolica tile floors contributing a bright note throughout. An ample
buffet breakfast is served, and, though half board is mandatory dur-
ing high season, you can dine either at the hotel or at several restau-
rants in Amalfi by special arrangement. ⊠ *Via M. Comite 32, 84011,*
☎ *089/831333,* 🕿 *089/831354. 60 rooms. Restaurant, bar. AE, DC,
MC, V.*

$$$ 🏨 **Miramalfi.** A modern building perched above the sea, the Miramalfi
has wonderful views, simple but attractive decor, terraces, swimming
pool, and a sunning/swimming area on the sea, as well as a quiet location just below the coast road, only 1 km (½ mi) from the center of
town. Almost all rooms have balconies with sea views. ⊠ *Via Quasi-
modo 3, 84011,* ☎🕿 *089/871588. 48 rooms. Restaurant, pool, beach.
AE, DC, MC, V.*

Ravello

★ ㊻ *5 km (3 mi) northeast of Amalfi, 25 km (16 mi) west of Salerno.*

Perched on a ridge high above Amalfi and the neighboring town of
Atrani, the enchanting village of Ravello has stupendous views, quiet
lanes, and two irresistibly romantic gardens—that of **Villa Rufolo,** where
medieval ruins frame spectacular vistas, and **Villa Cimbrone,** a private
estate with lush gardens open to the public (the villa is now a hotel).
The villa's famous lookout point, the Belvedere of Infinity, overlooks
the impossibly blue Bay of Salerno, a panorama Gore Vidal has called
"the most beautiful in the world."

Dining and Lodging

$$ ✕ **Cumpa Cosimo.** This family-run restaurant a few steps from the cathe-
★ dral square offers a cordial welcome in two simple but attractive din-
ing rooms. There's no view, but the food is excellent. Among the
specialties are cheese crepes and roast lamb or kid. ⊠ *Via Roma 44,*
☎ *089/857156. AE, DC, MC, V. Closed Mon. Nov.–Mar.*

$$$$ 🏨 **Hotel Palumbo.** Occupying a 12th-century patrician palace fur-
nished with antiques and endowed with modern comforts, this hotel
has an elegant, warm atmosphere that gives you the feeling of being a
guest in a lovely private home, under the personal care of courtly host
Signor Vuilleumier. With lovely garden terraces, breathtaking views,
and a sumptuous upstairs dining room, the hotel is a memorable one.
⊠ *Palazzo Confalone, 84010,* ☎ *089/857244,* 🕿 *089/858133. 23
rooms. Restaurant, bar. AE, DC, MC, V.*

$$$–$$$$ ⊞ **Villa Cimbrone.** This magical place takes the breath away: sus-
★ pended over the azure sea and set amid rose-laden gardens, it was once
the home of Lord Grimthorpe and the holiday hideaway of Greta
Garbo. Now exquisitely transformed into a hotel, the Gothic-style *castello*
has guest rooms ranging from palatial to cozy (opt for the Peony
Room, which has its own terrace). The villa is a strenuous hike from
the town center and cannot be reached by car—two reasons why it re-
mains the most peaceful place in Italy. ⊠ *Via S. Chiara 26, 84010,* ☏
089/857459, FAX *089/857777. 9 rooms. Breakfast room, minibars, li-
brary. AE, MC, V. Closed Nov.—Mar.*

$$$ ⊞ **Caruso Belvedere.** Charmingly old-fashioned, spacious, and com-
★ fortable, this rambling villa hotel has plenty of character and a full share
of Ravello's spectacular views from its terraces and balconied rooms.
Relax in the garden belvedere with its memorable vistas. The restaurant is known for fine food and locally produced house wine. ⊠ *Via
Toro 52, 84010,* ☏ *089/857111,* FAX *089/857372. 24 rooms. Restaurant, room service, baby-sitting, laundry service, free parking. AE, DC,
MC, V.*

$$ ⊞ **Villa Amore.** A 10-minute walk from the main Piazza Duomo, this
hotel is family-run, with a garden and an exhilarating view from most
of its bedrooms. If you're looking for tranquillity, this is the place to
find it, especially at dusk, when the valley is tinged with a glorious pur-
ple light. Rooms are small, with modest if modern furnishings, and break-
fast features delicious homemade jam. Full board is available here and
may be required in the summer. Reserve ahead. ⊠ *Via Santa Chiara,
84010,* ☏FAX *089/857135. 12 rooms. Restaurant, bar. MC, V.*

Vietri sul Mare

㊼ *6 km (4 mi) west of Salerno, 15 km (8 mi) east of Amalfi.*

This Amalfi Coast town is a major ceramics center, and its distinctive
pottery, with sunny motifs and bright colors, is sold in towns along
the coast.

Shopping

CERAMICS
Many small shops in Vietri sul Mare offer goods from local pottery
workshops. You can pick over all kinds of dusty wares at the **Solimene
works** (⊠ Vietri sul Mare).

Salerno

㊽ *42 km (26 mi) northwest of Paestum.*

Spread out along its bay, Salerno is a sad testimony to years of neglect
and overdevelopment. An imposing **Romanesque cathedral,** built in 1085
and remodeled in the 18th century, has Byzantine doors (1099) from
Constantinople and an outstanding 12th-century pulpit. In the **Dioce-
san Museum** behind it is a collection of astounding medieval carved
tablets. Occupying two floors of the **monastery of San Benedetto,** the
Provincial Museum holds a handsome bronze head of Apollo fished
out of the bay in the 1930s. ⊠ *Via San Benedetto.* ☉ *Daily 9–1.*

Paestum

★ ㊾ *42 km (26 mi) southeast of Salerno.*

One of Italy's most majestic sights lies on the edge of a flat coastal plain:
the remarkably well-preserved **Greek temples** of Paestum. S18 from
the north passes the train station (Stazione di Paestum), which is about
800 yards from the ruins, through the perfectly preserved **Porta Sirena**

archway. The ruins stand on the site of the ancient city of Poseidonia, founded by Greek colonists in the 7th century BC. When the Romans took over the colony in 273 BC and called it Paestum, they enlarged the settlement, adding an amphitheater and a forum. Much of the archaeological material found on the site is displayed in the **museum,** and several rooms are devoted to the unique tomb paintings discovered in the area, rare examples of Greek and pre-Roman pictorial art. About 200 yards from the museum (in front of the main entrance), framed by banks of roses and oleanders, is the **Temple of Poseidon** (or Neptune), a magnificent Doric edifice, with 36 fluted columns and an extraordinarily well-preserved entablature (area above the capitals). Not even Greece itself possesses such a fine monument of Hellenic architecture. On the left of the temple is the so-called **Basilica,** the earliest of Paestum's standing edifices; it dates from very early in the 6th century BC. The name is an 18th-century misnomer, for the structure was in fact a temple sacred to Hera, the wife of Zeus. Behind it an ancient road leads to the **Forum** of the Roman era and the single column of the **Temple of Peace.** Beyond is the **Temple of Ceres.** Try to see the temples in the late afternoon, when the light enhances the deep gold of the stone and the air is pierced with the cries of the crows that nest high on the temples. ☞ *Museum and temple area 8,000 lire.* ☉ *Excavations daily 9–2 hrs before sunset; museum daily 9–7 (9 AM–10 PM July–Aug.); closed 1st and 3rd Mon. of each month.*

Lodging

$$ ☒ **Helios.** Directly across the road from the Porta della Giustizia and only a few steps from the temples, the Helios has cottage-type rooms, each with a minibar, in a garden setting. Suites are also available. A pleasant restaurant serves local specialties and seafood. The home-produced ricotta and mozzarella are especially recommended. ⊠ *Via Principe di Piemonte 1, Zona Archeologica, 84063,* ☎ *0828/811451,* FAX *0828/811600. 29 rooms. Restaurant. AE, DC, MC, V.*

CAMPANIA A TO Z

Arriving and Departing

By Bus
Marozzi (☎ 06/44249519), a Rome-based line, runs direct, air-conditioned buses from Rome to Pompeii, Salerno, Sorrento, and Amalfi. Buses leave Rome's Stazione Tiburtina 7 AM on Friday, Saturday, and Sunday; tickets are 15,000 lire.

By Car
Italy's main north–south route, **A2** (also known as the Autostrada del Sole), connects the capital with Naples and Campania. In good traffic the ride takes less than three hours.

By Plane and Helicopter
Capodichino Airport (☎ 081/7896111), 8 km (5 mi) north of Naples, serves the Campania region. It handles domestic and international flights, including several flights daily between Naples and Rome (flight time 45 minutes). From May to September there is direct helicopter service (☎ 081/7896273 or 081/5844355) between Capodichino Airport and Capri or Ischia.

International travelers flying Alitalia to Rome's **Leonardo da Vinci Airport** can go directly from the airport to Naples's Mergellina train station via Alitalia's twice-daily airport train. Luggage is checked through to Naples, and meals are available on the train. Airport-train arrangements must be made when you buy your plane ticket. The service also operates in the other direction, returning from Naples to the Leonardo da Vinci Airport.

By Train

There are trains every hour between Rome and Naples. Intercity trains make the trip in less than two hours. Trains take either the inland route (through Cassino) or go along the coast (via Formia). Intercity and express trains to Naples stop at **Stazione Centrale** (Central Station; ✉ Piazza Garibaldi, ☎ 1478/88088 toll-free).

Getting Around

By Boat

Hydrofoil and passenger and car ferries connect the islands of Capri and Ischia with Naples and Pozzuoli year-round. In summer, Capri and Ischia are serviced by boats from the Amalfi Coast. Boats and hydrofoils for these islands and for Sorrento leave from Naples's **Molo Beverello** (✉ Piazza Garibaldi). They also leave from **Mergellina** (✉ About 1½ km, or 1 mi, to the west of Piazza Municipio).

Caremar (☎ 081/5513882). **Lauro** (☎ 081/5513236). **Navigazione Libera del Golfo** (☎ 081/5527209). **Alilauro** (☎ 081/5522838). **SNAV** (☎ 081/7612348).

By Bus

There is an extensive network of local buses in Naples and throughout Campania. **ACTP** buses (☎ 081/7005091) connect Naples with Caserta in one hour, leaving every 20 minutes from Piazza Garibaldi in Naples, every 40 minutes on Sunday. There are about six buses a day Monday–Saturday from Piazza Garibaldi to Benevento. The trip takes 90 minutes. **SITA** buses (☎ 081/5522176) for Salerno leave every 30 minutes Monday–Saturday and every two hours on Sunday from the SITA terminal (✉ Via Pisanelli, near Piazza Municipio). SITA buses also serve the Amalfi Coast, connecting Sorrento with Salerno.

By Car

Autostrada **A3**, a southern continuation of A2 from Rome, runs through Campania and into Calabria, to the south. It also connects with autostrada **A16** to Bari, which passes Avellino and is linked with Benevento by expressway. Take **S18** south from Naples for Ercolano (Herculaneum), Pompeii, and the Sorrento peninsula; for the Sorrento peninsula and the Amalfi Coast, exit at Castellammare di Stabia. To get to Paestum, take **A3** to the Battipaglia exit and take the road to Capaccio Scalo/Paestum. All roads on the Sorrento peninsula and Amalfi Coast are narrow, serpentine, and tortuous, although they have outstanding views. In summer hydrofoil and ferry lines have a residents-only policy for cars going on Ischia and Capri. Cars are not allowed on Ischia and Capri during high season, from about April through October.

By Train

Frequent local trains connect Naples with Caserta and Salerno. Travel time between Naples and Sorrento on the Circumvesuviana line (☞ *below*) is one hour. Benevento is on the main line between Naples and Foggia.

A network of suburban trains connects Naples with several points of interest. The line used most by visitors is the **Circumvesuviana** (☎ 081/7792444), which runs from Corso Garibaldi Station and stops at Stazione Centrale before continuing to Ercolano (Herculaneum), Pompeii, and Sorrento. The **Circumflegrea** (☎ 081/5513328) runs from Piazza Montesanto Station in Naples to the archaeological zone of Cumae, with three departures in the morning. The **Ferrovia Cumana**

(☎ 081/5513328) runs from Piazza Montesanto Station to Pozzuoli and Baia.

Naples has a **Metropolitana** (subway system). Although rather old, it provides frequent service and can be the fastest way to get around the traffic-clogged city.

Contacts and Resources

Car Rental
Avis: Caserta (✉ Stazione FS, ☎ 0823/443756). **Naples** (✉ Stazione Centrale, ☎ 081/5537171; ✉ Via Partenope 23, ☎ 081/7645600). **Sorrento** (✉ Viale Nizza 53, ☎ 081/8782459).

Hertz: Caserta (✉ Reggia Palace Hotel, Viale Carlo III ☎ 0823/424090). **Naples** (✉ Piazza Garibaldi 93, ☎ 081/5548657). **Sorrento** (✉ Garage Di Leva, Via degli Aranci 9, ☎ 081/8071646).

Emergencies
Police (☎ 112). **Naples: Ambulance** (☎ 081/7520696). **Doctors and Dentists** (☎ 081/7513177).

Guided Tours
Appian Line (☎ 06/4884151). **Carrani Tours** (☎ 06/4880510 or 06/4742501). **Tourcar** (✉ Piazza Matteotti 1, ☎ 081/5523310). **STS** (✉ Piazza Medaglie d'Oro 41, ☎ 081/5789292).

Late-Night Pharmacies
Farmacia Helvethia (✉ Piazza Garibaldi 11, opposite Stazione Centrale, Naples, ☎ 081/5548894).

Visitor Information
EPT: Naples (✉ Piazza dei Martiri 58, ☎ 081/405311; ✉ Stazione Centrale, ☎ 081/268779; ✉ Stazione Mergellina, ☎ 081/7612102; ✉ Capodichino Airport, ☎ 081/7805761).

Amalfi (✉ Corso Roma 19, ☎ 089/871107). **Benevento** (✉ Piazza Roma, ☎ 0824/319938). **Capri** (✉ Marina Grande pier, ☎ 081/8370634; ✉ Capri town, Piazza Umberto I, ☎ 081/8370686). **Caserta** (✉ Piazza Dante, ☎ 0823/321137). **Naples** (✉ Piazza del Gesù, ☎ 081/5523328). **Porto d'Ischia** (✉ Via Iasolino, Porto Salvo, ☎ 081/991146). **Ravello** (✉ Piazza Duomo, ☎ 089/857096). **Salerno** (✉ Via Roma 258, ☎ 089/224744). **Sorrento** (✉ Circolo Forestieri, Via de Maio 35, ☎ 081/8074033).

14 Apulia

Bari, Brindisi, and the Gargano Peninsula

The gateway to Italy's south, Apulia is steeped in relics from antiquity that are only now coming to the surface. The region invites intrepid exploration of its whitewashed ports, imposing castles, and trulli, *strange igloo-shape dwellings. The cities of Brindisi, Bari, and Lecce possess many fascinations, and the coastline is full of seductions— unspoiled coves, bougainvillea-draped vistas, and seas that shimmer under a blazing sun.*

Updated by
Robert
Andrews

IT'S A PITY THAT MOST TOURISTS see Apulia (called Puglia by the Italians—English-speakers are really using the Latin term) as merely a blur outside their car or train windows as they hurtle toward Bari or Brindisi for ferry connections to Greece.

This ancient land, the heel and spur of Italy's boot, possesses some of the country's most unspoiled scenery, interesting artistic and historical sites, and finest beaches. What's more, beyond the increasingly popular seaside resorts and the few major sites lay sunbaked countryside where expanses of silvery olive trees and giant prickly-pear cacti fight their way through the rocky soil, as if in defiance of the relentless summer heat. Local buildings, too, do their best to dispel the effects of the sun: whitewashed ports stand coolly over the turquoise Mediterranean; the landscape is studded with the odd stone trulli, used as farmhouses and storage bins.

The trulli date to the Middle Ages, but Apulia had long before then been inhabited, conquered, and visited. The Greeks and later the Romans were quick to recognize the importance of this strategic peninsula, and among the nations later to raid or colonize Apulia were the Normans, Moors, and Spaniards, each leaving a mark. Romanesque churches and the powerful castles built by 13th-century Holy Roman Emperor Frederick II of Swabia (part of present-day Bavaria), king of Sicily and Jerusalem, are among the most impressive of buildings in the region. Frederick II was an outstanding personality in the Middle Ages, dubbed Wonder of the World for his wide-ranging interests in literature, science, mathematics, and nature.

All these schools can still be pursued in present-day Apulia, but less intellectual attractions include the inexpensive, hearty cuisine, which employs local seafood and produce and has evolved from more than 2,000 years of foreign influences. Colorful local markets provide the chance to purchase local crafts, ranging from lace, wood carvings, and baskets to ceramic pots and painted clay whistles. As for terrain, hundreds of miles of beaches and an extensive cave complex let you explore, exercise, or just stay cool.

Pleasures and Pastimes

The Arts
In keeping with the provincial nature of Apulia, the arts take on a folk flavor, with processions on religious occasions more prevalent than performing arts in theaters or opera houses. Still, there are some good festivals and pageants to help broaden your experience of life in Italy's deep south. The best newspaper for listings is the daily *Gazzetta del Mezzogiorno,* which covers the entire region.

Beaches
For the Italians and other tourists who return each summer, the sea is one of the major attractions of Apulia. Though no longer "undiscovered," the beaches along the Gargano Peninsula offer safe swimming and sandy beaches. The whole coastline between Bari and Brindisi is well served with beach facilities. In even the smallest villages you'll find beaches where there are changing rooms and—essential in the blazing Apulian sun—beach umbrellas. If you don't mind venturing farther afield, Gallipoli, on the south coast of the heel, is exceptional.

Dining
Anyone who likes to eat will love Apulia. Southern cuisine is hearty and healthy, based around homemade pastas and cheeses, fresh veg-

etables, seafood, and local olive oil. Open-air markets and delicatessens burst with local fruits, vegetables, pastries, sausages, smoked meats, and cheeses.

Here you will find dishes unavailable elsewhere in Italy, such as *'ncapriata,* also called *favi e fogghi* (a first course fava-bean puree with bitter chicory or other cooked vegetables). Focaccia *barese* (stuffed with fried onions, black olives, anchovies, and ricotta) makes a great snack or lunch.

Apulia's pasta specialties include *orecchiette* (ear-shaped pasta), *troccoli* (homemade noodles cut with a special ridged rolling pin), and *strascenate* (rectangles of pasta with one rough side and one smooth side). Among the many typical sauces is *salsa alla Sangiovanniello* (sauce of olive oil, capers, anchovies, parsley, and hot peppers) from Brindisi.

Don't miss the dairy products, such as ricotta and buttery *burrata* cheese, and sample Apulia's wealth of excellent local wines, ranging from the strong white wine of Martina Franca to the sweet white Moscato di Trani and the rich, dry red Castel del Monte to the sweet red Aleatico di Puglia.

CATEGORY	COST*
$$$$	over 85,000 lire
$$$	60,000–85,000 lire
$$	25,000–60,000 lire
$	Under 25,000 lire

Prices are per person, including house wine, service, and tax.

Lodging

There has been a rapid development of tourist facilities in some areas of Apulia, particularly along the miles of sandy beaches on the Gargano spur. Here, and elsewhere on the coast, big white Mediterranean-style beach hotels have sprung in profusion. Most are similar in design, price, and quality. In summer, many cater only to guests paying full board (lodging plus three meals per day) or half board (lodging plus breakfast and one other meal) for longer stays; if you are traveling at this time, make your reservations through a travel agent. During Easter, rooms in the Alberobello area may be at a premium.

In some cases, such as visiting Bari during the annual Trade Fair in September, you must make reservations. Outside the big cities, hotel accommodations are limited and modest—both in amenities and price—though this may be more than compensated for by friendly service. Throughout the region, hotels are often booked up with commercial travelers, so reserve well in advance.

Many establishments, particularly the beach resorts, close during the winter months, so check for this also when choosing accommodations. And remember that in a region like this—blazing hot in summer and bitter cold in winter—air-conditioning and central heating are important.

CATEGORY	COST*
$$$$	over 300,000 lire
$$$	160,000–300,000 lire
$$	100,000–160,000 lire
$	under 100,000 lire

Prices are for a standard double room for two, including service and tax.

Shopping

Apulia is rich in folk art, reflecting the influences of the many nations that have passed through the region or ruled it. Don't expect boutiques;

instead, snatch up handmade goods, such as pottery with traditional designs, and baskets, textiles, and carved wood figures. These are on sale in shops and in open markets, where some bargaining can enter into the purchase.

Exploring Apulia

If you are mainly interested in spending time at the beach, the promontory of Gargano in the north harbors some of Apulia's best coastline, although there are pleasant beach resorts within easy reach of most of the region's attractions. Convenient travel bases include Alberobello or Martina Franca in the trulli country; Lecce, near the tip of the heel; and the small ports of Barletta, Molfetta, and Trani, up the coast from Bari.

Bari and Brindisi are notorious for purse-snatchings, car thefts, and break-ins. If you are driving in these cities, try not to leave valuables in the car or lock everything inside the trunk, and find a guarded parking space if possible.

Numbers in the text correspond to numbers in the margin and on the Apulia and Bari maps.

Great Itineraries

Apulia's attractions are so varied and scattered that you may want to take a full week or more to explore it at a leisurely pace, selecting two or three bases in different parts of the region and taking day trips to nearby sights.

IF YOU HAVE 3 DAYS
With three days in Apulia, you will need to focus on one stop per day, starting in **Bari** ①–④. Here, a stroll around the old town will occupy a morning. After lunch, head south as far as ▓ **Lecce** ㉓; spend the next day in this Baroque town. On the morning of the third day, retrace your steps northwest to **Brindisi** ㉒, stopping at the famous column marking the end of the Via Appia. Veer west along the Via Appia (the S7) and carry on to ▓ **Taranto** ㉑ for your last night to take in the Museo Nazionale. If you are heading back to Bari, drive through the **trulli district** ⑯–⑳ to get an impression of the dwellings.

IF YOU HAVE 5 DAYS
Spend a couple of days exploring the forested promontory ▓ **Gargano Peninsula** ⑨–⑮, northwest of **Bari** ①–④, where you'll need about two hours to absorb the flavor of this old center. Take the coastal road (S16) from the city northwest toward **Molfetta** ⑤, **Trani** ⑥, and **Barletta** ⑦, with old ports reminiscent of Venetian ports such as Dubrovnik, across the Adriatic Sea in Croatia. The seaside fishing villages–cum–resorts of ▓ **Vieste,** ▓ **Peschici** ⑪, and ▓ **Rodi Garganico** ⑫ offer the best choice of accommodations, although ▓ **Foggia** ⑨ or ▓ **Manfredonia** ⑩ make good bases. Aim to spend your fourth night in ▓ **Alberobello** ⑯, the capital of trulli country—touristy but engaging—or in whitewashed ▓ **Ostuni** ⑲. From Alberobello, it's a short run to **Taranto** ㉑ to whip around the archaeological museum. Break your journey for an hour or two in **Brindisi** ㉒, but save your last night for ▓ **Lecce** ㉓, a treat that will generate some of your most abiding memories of Apulia.

IF YOU HAVE 7 DAYS
If your base is **Bari** ①–④, devote about a half-day to the city before venturing to the **Gargano Peninsula** ⑨–⑮. A car is indispensable since transport connections are tortuous and slow, but be prepared to abandon it for a half-day ramble through the **Foresta Umbra** ⑬ and **Monte Sant'Angelo** ⑭, dominated by a large Norman castle that was once host

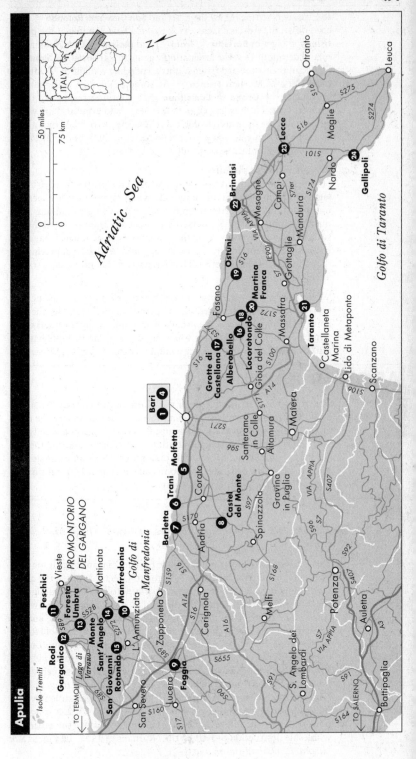

479

Apulia

to Crusaders setting off for the East, and **San Giovanni Rotondo** ⑮. Proceed down the Adriatic Coast back toward Bari, landing at the pretty fishing villages of **Barletta** ⑦, **Trani** ⑥, and **Molfetta** ⑤, and making an inland detour to view the fascinatingly geometrical **Castel del Monte** ⑧. Head southeast toward trulli country, spending a night in 🔆 **Alberobello** ⑯ or 🔆 **Martina Franca** ⑳. At some point take a trip underground at the **Grotte di Castellana** ⑰, a soothing respite from the summer heat. The bustling cities of **Taranto** ㉑ and **Brindisi** ㉒ are worth stopping in for their archaeological relics. Spend your last two nights in the heel of Italy, dividing your time between the Baroque pleasures of 🔆 **Lecce** ㉓ and the seaside village of 🔆 **Gallipoli** ㉔.

When to Tour Apulia

Summers are torrid this far south, and even the otherwise perfect villages of the interior are too dazzlingly white for comfort between the months of July and early September. So unless you are planning to be thoroughly idle—always a seductive prospect in Apulia—avoid the hot season. Of course, if you're on the Gargano Peninsula, which has Apulia's only elevation of any significance, you'll be able to appreciate all the more the forested interior. The Gargano littoral, however, is strictly a summer-holiday zone.

Wintertime in Apulia can see heavy bursts of rain, often lasting several days at a time. However, the temperatures rarely fall into the chill zone. In spring, the days are usually warm and the light crystal clear; you can generally find water warm enough for comfortable bathing into October. Note that lodging availability can be limited off-season.

AROUND BARI

The coast has a strong flavor of the Norman presence in the south, embodied in the distinctive Apulian-Romanesque churches, the most graceful contribution of the Normans. Bari is a busy, commercial port, with charm in its compact, labyrinthine old quarter abutting the sea. Molfetta and Barletta are small fishing ports. Make an excursion inland to the imposing Castel del Monte, an enigmatic, 13th-century octagonal structure of unknown origin.

Bari

❶ *260 km (162 mi) southeast of Naples, 450 km (281 mi) southeast of Rome.*

Bari is a big, hectic, rough-and-tumble port and a transit point for travelers catching ferries across the Adriatic to Greece. Most of the city is set out in a logical 19th-century grid pattern, following the designs of Joachim Murat, Napoléon's brother-in-law and "King of the Two Sicilies." The heart of the modern town is Piazza della Libertà, but just beyond it, across Corso Vittorio Emanuele, is the *città vecchia* (old town), a maze of narrow, crooked streets on the promontory that juts out between Bari's old and new ports. Here, overlooking the sea and just off

❷ Via Venezia, is the **Basilica di San Nicola,** built in the 11th century to house the bones of Saint Nicholas, who is better known to us as Saint Nick, or Santa Claus. His remains are said to have been stolen by Bari sailors from Myra, in what is now Turkey. The basilica, a solid and powerful construction, was the only building to survive the otherwise wholesale destruction of Bari by the Normans in 1152. ✉ *Piazza San Nicola.* ☉ *Daily 9–noon and 5–7.*

❸ A century younger than the basilica, the **Cattedrale** (cathedral) is the seat of the local bishop and was the scene of many significant politi-

Basilica di
San Nicola, **2**
Castello, **4**
Cattedrale, **3**

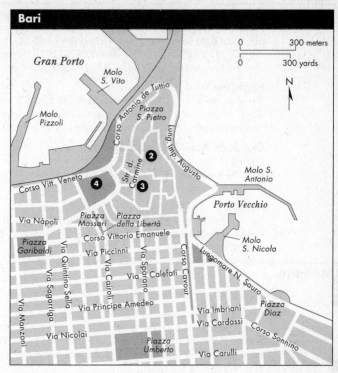

Bari

cal marriages between important families in the Middle Ages. Its solid architecture reflects the Romanesque style favored by the Normans of that period. ⊠ *Piazza dell'Odegitria.* ☉ *Daily 9–noon and 5–7.*

❹ The huge **Castello** (castle) looms behind the cathedral. The current building dates from the time of Holy Roman Emperor Frederick II, who rebuilt an existing Norman-Byzantine castle to his own exacting specifications. Designed more for power than beauty, it looks out beyond the cathedral to the small Porto Vecchio (Old Port). Inside is a collection of medieval Apulian art. ⊠ *Piazza Federico II di Svevia.* 🖾 *4,000 lire.* ☉ *Tues.–Sat. 8:30–1 and 3:30–7, Sun. 8:30–1, Mon. 3:30–7 (times may change).*

Dining and Lodging

$$ ✕ **Ristorante al Pescatore.** This is one of Bari's best fish restaurants, in the old town opposite the castle and just around the corner from the cathedral. The cooking is done outside, where (in summer) you can sit amid a cheerful clamor of quaffing and dining. Try the *céfalo* (mullet) if it is available, accompanied by crisp salad and a carafe of invigorating local wine. ⊠ *Piazza Federico II di Svevia,* ☎ *080/5237039. Reservations essential in high season. AE, DC, MC, V. Closed Mon.*

$$$$ 🏨 **Sheraton Nicolaus.** This large, modern hotel on the edge of the city is easily reached by car from Highway S16, which skirts the congested center of town. It caters mainly to businesspeople and is well equipped for meetings, conferences, and banquets. Rooms are spacious and comfortable, with the usual Sheraton amenities. There's even an indoor pool and a sauna. ⊠ *Via Agostino Ciasca 9, 70124,* ☎ *080/ 5042626,* ᴀᴀ *080/5042058. 175 rooms. Restaurant, bar, indoor pool, sauna, meeting rooms. AE, DC, MC, V.*

$$ 🏨 **Adria.** In a city sadly short of inexpensive hotels, this two-star's main virtue is its convenience for the train station. Facilities are adequate if undistinguished, but this is primarily a one-night stopover. Guest rooms are comfortable enough—avoid those facing inward, if you can. Turn right out of the station to find this hotel. ⊠ *Via L. Zuppetta 10, 70121,* ☎ *080/5246699,* FAX *080/5213207. 35 rooms, 20 with shower. Restaurant, bar, garage. AE, DC, MC, V.*

Nightlife and the Arts

Bari has the famous **Teatro Petruzzelli** (⊠ Corso Cavour, ☎ 080/5241761), which features performances of drama, opera, and ballet. The theater was restored after a devastating fire in 1991.

Outdoor Activities and Sports

BIKING

G. S. De Bendictus (⊠ Via Nitti 23, ☎ 080/5744345) rents bikes and mountain bikes.

FISHING

For information on approved spots and license applications, contact **Federazione Italiana Pesca Sportiva** (⊠ Molo Pizzoli, Bari, ☎ 080/5247070).

Molfetta

❺ *25 km (16 mi) northwest of Bari.*

Molfetta has an unusual 12th-century cathedral with distinct Byzantine features, such as the pyramid-shape covers to the three main domes. If you are in the area around Easter, don't miss Molfetta's colorful Holy Week processions, a surefire hit for young and old alike if you're traveling with kids.

Trani

❻ *18 km (11 mi) northwest of Molfetta, 43 km (27 mi) northwest of Bari.*

Smaller than the other ports along this coast, Trani has a quaint old town with polished stone streets and buildings, medieval churches, and a harbor filled with fishing boats. The 11th-century **Duomo,** considered one of the finest in Apulia, is built on a spit of land jutting into the sea. The Jewish community flourished here in medieval times, and on Via Sinagoga (Synagogue Street) two of the four **synagogues** still exist: the 13th-century **Santa Maria Scolanova** and **Santa Anna,** which still bears a Hebrew inscription.

Dining and Lodging

$$ ✕ **La Regia.** Just in front of the cathedral, on a spit of land jutting out
★ into the sea, La Regia has an antique feel, with stonework, vaulted ceilings, and terra-cotta tile floors. Regional specialties are presented imaginatively: try the baked crepes (similar to cannelloni); risotto made with salmon, crab, and cream; lobster; or grilled fish. ⊠ *Piazza Archivio 2,* ☎ *0883/586568. Reservations essential for Sun. lunch and dinner on summer weekends. MC, V. Closed Mon.*

$$$ 🏨 **Royal.** This is an unpretentious and modern four-star hotel near the train station. Furnishings are comfortable, and there is a piano bar by the restaurant. Rates include breakfast. ⊠ *Via De Robertis 29, 70059,* ☎ *0883/588777,* FAX *0883/582224. 40 rooms. Restaurant. AE, DC, MC, V.*

$ 🏨 **La Regia.** This small hotel occupies a 17th-century palazzo; it's above the restaurant of the same name (☞ *above*) and under the same ownership. The rooms are comfortable and well proportioned, but the best feature is the superb location opposite Trani's cathedral. ⊠ *Pi-*

azza Duomo 2, 70059, ☎ 0883/584527, FAX 0883/553798. 9 rooms.
Restaurant, bar. MC, V. Closed Nov. 1–17.

Barletta

❼ *13 km (8 mi) northwest of Trani, 56 km (35 mi) northwest of Bari.*

☾ In Barletta, kids love the **Colossus,** a bronze statue more than 15 ft tall,
thought to be of the Byzantine emperor Valentinian and dating from
the 5th century AD. Part of Venice's booty after the sack of Byzantium's
capital, Constantinople, in the 1200s, the Colossus was abandoned on
the beach near Barletta when the ship carrying it to Venice foundered
in a storm. ⊠ *Next to the church of San Sepolcro, Corso Vittorio
Emanuele.*

Dining

$$ ✕ **La Casaccia.** Near a picturesque castle, this simple restaurant serves
such local dishes as homemade orecchiette and penne *piccanti* (spicy).
⊠ *Corso Cavour 40, ☎ 0883/533719. Reservations not accepted. No
credit cards. Closed Mon.*

Nightlife and the Arts

The **Disfida a Barletta,** held on the last Sunday in August, is a reen-
actment of an event of the same name, which took place in 1503. The
disfida (challenge) was issued by 13 Italian officers to 13 French offi-
cers, after one of the French insulted the Italians by stating that Italy
would always be under foreign domination. The Italians taught the rash
Frenchman and his compatriots a lesson. Every Italian child learns this
story at school.

Outdoor Activities and Sports

SAILING

The local **sailing club** (⊠ Via Cristoforo Colombo, ☎ 0883/33354)
offers lessons and rentals.

Castel del Monte

★ ☾ ❽ *30 km (19 mi) south of Barletta, 56 km (35 mi) west of Bari.*

Built on an isolated hill in the first half of the 13th century by Fred-
erick II, Castel del Monte is a huge, bare, octagonal castle with eight
towers. Very little is known about the structure, since virtually no records
exist. It has none of the usual defense features associated with medieval
castles, so it probably had little military significance. Some theories sug-
gest it might have been built as a hunting lodge or may have served as
an astronomical observatory or a stop for pilgrims on their quest for
the Holy Grail. ⊠ *On signposted minor road 18 km (11 mi) south of
Andria.* ▨ *4,000 lire.* ⊙ *Apr.–Sept., Mon.–Sat. 8:30–7, Sun. 9–1; Oct.–
Mar., Mon.–Sat. 8:30–1 and 2–sunset, Sun. 9–1.*

Dining

$$ ✕ **Ostello di Federico.** This large, beautifully positioned restaurant, at
the foot of the hill on which the celebrated Castel del Monte rises, has
a terrace overlooking splendid scenery, plus a bar, and a pizzeria with
a wood oven. The restaurant serves local dishes, including orecchiette
a rape (with bitter greens), and local cheeses, such as ricotta and
creamy burrata. ⊠ *Castel del Monte, ☎ 0883/569877. Reservations
essential. AE, DC, MC, V. Closed Mon., 1st 2 wks in Nov., last wk in
Jan.*

Shopping

In Andria, **copper** objects and containers are made and sold.

THE GARGANO PENINSULA

The spur of Italy's boot is where the region's most beautiful and popular beaches are found. Until a few years ago, this rocky peninsula of whitewashed coastal towns, wide sandy beaches, and craggy limestone cliffs topped by deep-green scrub pine was practically unknown: some parts of the interior are still well off the usual tourist track. The resort business here has boomed in the past decade, though, and beaches can become crowded in midsummer. For the kids, the beaches and forests of the Gargano Promontory are great places for letting off steam, and many towns stage puppet shows in their public gardens.

Foggia

⑨ *95 km (60 mi) west of Bari, 39 km (24 mi) southwest of Manfredonia.*

Foggia, the chief city in Apulia's northernmost province is not the most inspiring destination, though it makes a useful overnight stop for visitors to the Gargano. On the main line from Rome and Naples, and easily accessible from the autostrada, Foggia has all the amenities one might expect from a major commercial center, the venue for numerous fairs and conventions throughout the year. This means that while it enjoys a decent selection of lodgings and restaurants, you'll need to reserve to make sure of accommodations. This is the place to attend to money matters or rent a car for excursions to the Gargano.

Dining and Lodging

$$ **✕ Mangiatoia.** In an old farmhouse, this rustic restaurant has lovely
★ arches, white walls, and wood-beamed ceilings. There's air-conditioning, but you can dine outdoors in a large garden, where tables made from wagon wheels surround an old well. Seafood is the specialty; fish and shellfish are displayed live in tanks. The chef will supply recipes for dishes, such as spaghetti *ai datteri di mare al cartoccio* (with razor clams in bags), and fettuccine in a creamy scampi sauce. It's on the main road to Bari, near the Foggia Agricultural Fairgrounds. ⊠ *Via Virgilio 2,* ☎ *0881/634457. Reservations essential. MC, V. Closed Mon.*

$$$ **⊡ Cicolella.** Near the station, this 1920s hotel has modern amenities and tastefully decorated rooms, a few of which have balconies. There are also some suites that are particularly recommended, though these fall into the $$$$ category. The restaurant (closed weekends) specializes in international dishes and well-prepared local dishes. ⊠ *Via Ventiquattro Maggio 60, 71100,* ☎ *0881/688890,* 🆊 *0881/678984. 106 rooms. Restaurant, meeting rooms. AE, DC, MC, V.*

Manfredonia

⑩ *60 km (37 mi) northwest of Barletta, 39 km (24 mi) northeast of Foggia.*

This lazy resort town on the southern lip of the promontory was once a flourishing port ferrying crusaders across the Adriatic to Greece and beyond. It now makes an excellent starting point for expeditions into the peninsula. There is a small **museum** in the Angevin castle located on the seafront, containing relics of the Daunian people who once inhabited the Gargano. Apart from some adequate hotels and a buzz of the evening *passeggiata*—the most Mediterranean of pageants when locals dress in their most stylish clothing and stroll through the streets—there is little else.

Lodging

$$ ⊞ **Gargano.** The functional, rather boxy rooms in this typical, white beach hotel are decorated in blue and white and have terraces. The public rooms are open-plan, the dining area overlooks the pool and the sea, and the dance club–bar keeps it lively on summer evenings. ⊠ *Viale Beccarini 2, 71043,* ☎ *0884/587621,* ℻ *0884/586021. 46 rooms. Restaurant. MC, V.*

Outdoor Activities and Sports

BIKING

Bicycles can be serviced at **G. S. Cicli Castriotta** (⊠ Viale Beccarini 7, ☎ 0884/583424).

En Route From Manfredonia, take the winding coastal road (S89), which threads through miles of silvery olive groves interspersed with almond trees and prickly-pear cacti. Along the way you'll come across many local craftsmen's stalls, selling homemade preserves, baskets, and carved olive-wood bowls and utensils.

Mattinata

15 km (9 mi) northeast of Manfredonia.

Just inland of a fine sandy beach, where most of the campsites and hotels are located, this is a generally quiet village that comes into its own in the summer season.

Lodging

$$–$$$ ⊞ **Baia delle Zagare.** On the shore road around the Gargano Peninsula, north of Mattinata, Baia delle Zagare is a secluded, modern group of cottages overlooking an inlet. An elevator takes you down to a private beach, and the hotel restaurant is good enough to warrant staying on the premises all day. (You're expected to take full board in August.) ⊠ *Strada Litoranea (17 km/10 mi northeast), 71030,* ☎ *0884/ 4155,* ℻ *0884/4884. 144 rooms. Restaurant, pool, tennis court, beach. MC, V. Closed Oct.–May.*

$–$$ ⊞ **Alba del Gargano.** Although in the town center, the modern Alba provides a restful atmosphere. Large balconies overlook a quiet courtyard garden, and a frequent (and free) bus service connects with a private beach, where you can use the hotel's beach chairs and umbrellas. Rooms are comfortably furnished, and there is a good restaurant. ⊠ *Corso Matino 102, 71030,* ☎ *0884/4771,* ℻ *0884/4772. 40 rooms, 3 suites. Restaurant, bar, beach. MC, V.*

Vieste

50 km (30 mi) northeast of Manfredonia.

This large town on the tip of the spur is the Gargano's main commercial center and an attractive place to wander around. Make for the **castle,** not open to the public but offering good views from its high position overlooking the beaches and town. The resort attracts legions of tourists in summer, some of them bound for the **Tremiti Islands,** connected to Vieste by regular ferries.

Lodging

$$$$ ⊞ **Pizzomunno.** Probably the most luxurious resort on the Gargano,
★ Pizzomunno is right on the beach and is surrounded by a large park. It is large, white, modern, air-conditioned, and well equipped. The rooms are ample and comfortable, all with terraces. Here you can unwind, or try your hand at tennis or archery. ⊠ *Via Litoranea, 71019,* ☎ *0884/ 708741,* ℻ *0884/707325. 183 rooms. Restaurant, air-conditioning,*

pool, sauna, health club, cinema, dance club, children's programs. AE, DC, MC, V. Closed Oct.–Mar.

<table>
<tr><td>OFF THE
BEATEN PATH</td><td>**TREMITI ISLANDS –** A ferry service from Termoli, north of the Gargano (1 hr, 40 min), and a hydrofoil service from Vieste, Peschici, Rodi Garganico, and Manfredonia (40 min to 1 hr, 40 min) connect the mainland with these three small islands north of the Gargano. Although somewhat crowded with Italian tourists in summer, they are famed for their sea caves, pine forests, and craggy limestone formations. There are also interesting medieval churches and fortifications on the islands.</td></tr>
</table>

Peschici

⑪ *22 km (14 mi) northwest of Vieste.*

You may want to make this pleasant resort on Gargano's north shore your base for spending a few days exploring the surrounding beaches and coast. Development has not wreaked too much damage on this whitewashed town, and the mazelike center retains its characteristic low houses topped with little domes.

Rodi Garganico

⑫ *20 km (12 mi) west of Peschici, 40 km (25 mi) west of Vieste.*

This fishing village squeezed between the hills and the sea takes its name from the island of Rhodes, recalling its former Greek population. Ringed by pine woods and citrus groves, Rodi is linked by hydrofoils with the Tremiti Islands, and things can get pretty hectic in high summer.

Dining

$$ ✕ **Gabbiano.** Admire the view facing the sea in Rodi Garganico at this cheerful restaurant while savoring freshly caught seafood. ✉ *Via Trieste 14,* ☎ *0884/965283. MC, V. Closed Thurs.*

Foresta Umbra

★ **⑬** *30 km (19 mi) southwest of Vieste, 25 km (16 mi) south of Rodi Garganico.*

In the middle of the peninsula is the majestic Foresta Umbra (Shady Forest), a dense growth of beech, maple, sycamore, and oak generally found in more northerly climates, thriving here because of the altitude—3,200 ft above sea level. Between the trees are occasional dramatic vistas opening out over the Gulf of Manfredonia. From the north coast, take S528 (midway between Peschici and Rodi Garganico) south to head through the interior of the Gargano, where you'll discover a different world.

Monte Sant'Angelo

★ **⑭** *60 km (19 mi) southwest of Vieste, 16 km (10 mi) north of Manfredonia.*

Perched amid olive groves on the rugged white limestone cliffs overlooking the gulf is the town of Monte Sant'Angelo. Pilgrims have flocked here for nearly 1,500 years—among them, Saint Francis of Assisi and the Crusaders setting off for the Holy Land from the then-flourishing port of Manfredonia. The town is centered on the **Sanctuary of San Michele,** built over the grotto where the archangel Michael is believed to have appeared before shepherds in the year 490. If you're here with kids, the supposed angelic visitation is guaranteed to capture young imaginations. Walk down a long series of steps to get to the grotto itself—on the walls you can see the hand tracings left by pilgrims as votive symbols.

Steps lead left from the sanctuary down to the **Tomb of Rotari,** which is believed to have been a medieval baptistery, with some remarkable 12th-century reliefs. More steep steps lead up to the large, ruined **Norman castle** that dominates the town with a view of the intricate pattern of the streets and steps winding their way up the side of the valley. The town's medieval quarter, the **Rione Junno,** is a maze of little white houses squeezed into a corner of the narrow valley.

Lodging

$ ⊞ **Hotel Rotary.** This simple but welcoming modern hotel is set amid olive and almond groves just outside town. Most rooms have terraces with a good view of the Gulf of Manfredonia. ⊠ *Via per Pulsano, 71037,* ☎ FAX *0884/562146. 22 rooms. Restaurant. AE, MC, V.*

Shopping

Shoemaker Domenico Palena displays his unique **leather sculptures** at his tiny shop in the Junno quarter. Most shops in the Junno sell a local specialty called **ostia piena** (filled host), a pastry made with candied almonds and wafers of the type similar to communion hosts. The best place to get—or munch—them is at the southern end of the Junno, by the Villa Comunale. Local **wood** craftsmen make and sell wooden utensils, furniture, and wrought-iron goods.

San Giovanni Rotondo

⑮ *25 km (16 mi) west of Monte Sant'Angelo.*

The ancient village of San Giovanni Rotondo, on the winding S272, has gained importance in recent years as a center of religious pilgrimage. Devotees have flocked here to pay their respects to the shrine and tomb of Padre Pio (1887–1968), a monk revered for his pious life, for miraculous intercessions, and for his having received the stigmata, the signs of Christ's wounds. The **Casa Sollievo della Sofferenza** (Foundation for the Mitigation of Suffering), supported through contributions from around the world, is a testament to the enduring appeal of this holy man.

En Route   A short ride south on S273, and then east (left) at L'Annunziata, will take you back to Manfredonia, where you can link up with the coastal road to return to Bari.

ALBEROBELLO, LOCOROTONDO, OSTUNI, AND MARTINA FRANCA

The Trulli District

The inland area to the southeast of Bari is one of Italy's oddest enclaves, a flat land devoted to olive cultivation and dotted with the idiosyncratic habitations that have lent their name to the district. The origins of the igloo-shape trulli go back to the 13th century and maybe further: the trulli are built of local limestone, without mortar, and with a hole in the top for escaping smoke. Some are painted with mystical or religious symbols; some are isolated, and others are joined together with roofs on various levels. The center of trulli country is Alberobello, holding the greatest concentration of the buildings, though you will spot scores of them all over this region, some in states of disrepair but always adding a quirky charm to the landscape. If you're traveling *en famille*, the igloolike dwellings are sure to intrigue children.

Alberobello

★ ☝ ⑯ *59 km (37 mi) southeast of Bari on S100 south and east on S172, 45 km (28 mi) north of Taranto.*

The **trulli** zone of Alberobello, where more than 1,000 trulli crowd together along steep, narrow streets, is a national monument. It is also one of the most popular tourist destinations in Apulia and a gold mine for people who enjoy shopping for souvenirs (☞ Shopping, *below*).

Dining and Lodging

$$–$$$ ✕ **Il Poeta Contadino.** Proprietor Marco Leonardo serves "creative regional cooking" in this rustic-style restaurant. In the heart of the attractive trulli zone, it features candlelit tables and a refined, understated ambience. Specialties to look for are fish platters and antipasti. ⊠ *Via Indipendenza 21,* ☎ *080/721917. Reservations essential. AE, DC, MC, V. Closed Sun. evening and Mon. (Oct.–June), Jan. 7–22, and 10 days June–July.*

$$ ✕ **Trullo d'Oro.** This welcoming restaurant occupies five trulli houses
★   and is decorated in the rustic style, with dark wood beams, whitewashed walls, and an open hearth. Local country cooking includes dishes using lamb and veal, vegetable and cheese antipasti, pasta dishes with crisp raw vegetables on the side, and almond pastries. Among the specialties are roast lamb with *lampasciuni* (a type of wild onion) and spaghetti *al trullo*, made with tomatoes, garlic, olive oil, *rughetta* (arugula), and four cheeses. ⊠ *Via F. Cavallotti 29,* ☎ *080/721820. Reservations essential. AE, DC, MC, V. Closed Mon. and Jan. 6–Feb. 2.*

$$$ ▥ **Dei Trulli.** Trulli-style cottages in a pine wood near the trulli zone make this a pleasant hotel, decorated with rustic furnishings, including folk art rugs. There is a modestly priced restaurant serving local specialties. Guests are expected to take half or full board in high season. ⊠ *Via Cadore 28, 70011,* ☎ *080/9323555,* **FAX** *080/9323560. 33 rooms. Restaurant, pool. AE, MC, V.*

Shopping

In the trulli zone, you'll find small shops selling hand-painted **clay figurines. Rugs** and **fabrics** are the best bets here, but there is also a good deal of shoddy material.

Grotte di Castellana

☝ ⑰ *20 km (12 mi) northwest of Alberobello.*

The Grotte di Castellana is a huge network of caves discovered in 1938. You can take one of the hourly guided tours through the grottoes, which are filled with fantastically shaped stalagmites and stalactites: the grottoes constitute the largest network of caves on the Italian mainland. Children will love it. ☎ *080/4965511.* ▤ *15,000 lire (1-hr tour).* ☻ *Apr.–Oct., daily 8:30–12:30 and 2:30–6:30; Nov.–Mar., daily 8:30–12:30.*

Dining

$$ ✕ **Al Parco Chiancafredda.** The refined ambience and cuisine of this restaurant, set apart from the tourist haunts, make it pricier than its neighbors. But the food and service are worth it: try such regional dishes as *sformato di verdura* (vegetable stew) and *agnello alla castellanese* (local lamb). ⊠ *Via Chiancafredda 12,* ☎ *080/4968710. Reservations essential. MC, V. Closed Tues. and Nov.*

$$ ✕ **Taverna degli Artisti.** Near the caves, this rustic tavern-style restaurant with a big garden specializes in local home cooking, such as roast lamb, homemade orecchiette, and dishes with fanciful names like *timballo fine del mondo* (end-of-the-world timbale) and *involtini al purgatorio* (purgatory roulades). ⊠ *Via Vito Matarrese 27,* ☎ *080/4968234. AE, MC, V. Closed Dec. and Thurs. Oct.–June.*

Locorotondo

⑱ *9 km (5 mi) southeast of Alberobello on S172, 40 km (25 mi) north of Taranto.*

Still inside the trulli district, Locorotondo is an attractive hillside town in the Itria Valley. The *rotondo* in the town's name refers to the circular pattern of the houses, which is apparent from any vantage point at the top of the town.

Ostuni

⑲ *50 km (30 mi) west of Brindisi, 40 km (25 mi) northeast of Locorotondo.*

This sun-bleached, picturesque medieval town lies on three hills a short distance from the coast. The old center, on the highest of the hills, has steep cobbled lanes and stupendous views out over the coast and the surrounding plain.

Dining and Lodging

$$ ✕ **Chez Elio.** Enjoy local dishes and a memorable view of the coastline
★ from the terrace of this modern restaurant, set amid green hills outside town. White walls and table linens contrast with plants and bright flowers, creating a light, fresh atmosphere. Specialties include orecchiette with tomato sauce and tagliatelle with blueberries. ⊠ *Via dei Colli Selva 67,* ☎ *0831/302030. Reservations essential. AE, MC, V. Closed Mon.*

$$ ▦ **Incanto.** At this modest yet modern hotel outside the old town, you can admire the countryside and the sea in the distance from many of its rooms, which are basic. It's adequate as an overnight base for seeing the area, and prices fall at the very bottom of this category. ⊠ *Via dei Colli, 72017,* ☎ *0831/301781,* ﬀ *0831/338302. 70 rooms. Restaurant, bar. AE, DC, MC, V.*

Martina Franca

⑳ *6 km (4 mi) south of Locorotondo, 36 km (22 mi) north of Taranto.*

Martina Franca is an appealing town with a dazzling mixture of medieval and Baroque architecture in the light-colored local stone. Ornate balconies hang above the twisting, narrow streets, with little alleys leading off into the surrounding hills. Martina Franca was developed as a military stronghold in the 14th century, when a surrounding wall with 24 towers was built, but now all that remains of that role are the four gates that had been the only entrances to the town. Each July and August Martina Franca holds a music festival.

Dining and Lodging

$$ ✕ **La Tavernetta.** This small restaurant with a vaulted ceiling in the old town center serves large portions of good home cooking, starting with a pottery bowl full of local olives, and excellent house wine. Specialties include favi e fogghi and, in summer, orecchiette with cocomero (a vegetable that looks like a miniature round watermelon but tastes like a cross between a cucumber and a honeydew melon). Main-courses

include mixed grilled lamb, liver, and spicy local sausage. ⊠ *Corso Vittorio Emanuele 30,* ☎ *080/4306323. MC, V. Closed Mon. (except Aug.).*

$$$ ⌂ **Park Hotel San Michele.** This garden hotel makes a pleasant base in the warm months, thanks to the pool. The two categories of rooms have a small price difference: opt for the higher-priced ones. All are spacious, some embellished with handsome furniture and bowls of fruit. It's favored by local businesspeople. ⊠ *Viale Carella 9, 74015,* ☎ *080/ 8807053,* ☒ *080/4808895. 86 rooms. Restaurant, bar, pool. AE, DC, MC, V.*

Nightlife and the Arts

Martina Franca concentrates on music in its annual **Festival of the Itria Valley** each July and August.

TARANTO, BRINDISI, LECCE, GALLIPOLI

Across the Heel and South

This far south, the mountains run out of steam and the land is uniformly flat although agriculturally quite important. The monotonous landscape, however, is redeemed by some of the region's best sandy coastline and a handful of alluring small towns. Not that the first two stops on this tour, Taranto and Brindisi, fit this description: both are big ports where historical importance is obscured by unsightly heavy industry. Nonetheless, Taranto has its special attractions, not the least its archaeological museum; Brindisi's marks the end of the Appian Way. Farther south, in the Salentine peninsula, Lecce is an unexpected oasis of grace and sophistication, and its swirling architecture will melt even the most uncompromising critic of the Baroque.

Taranto

㉑   *100 km (62 mi) southeast of Bari on the A14 and A7, 40 km (25 mi) south of Martina Franca on S172.*

Taranto—the stress is on the first syllable—was an important port even in Roman times. It lies toward the back of the instep of the boot on the broad Mare Grande bay, which is connected to a small internal Mare Piccolo basin by two narrow channels, one artificial and one natural. The old town is on an island between the larger and smaller bodies of water; the modern city stretches inward along the mainland. Little remains of Taranto's past except the 14th-century church of San Domenico, at one end of the island, and the city's maritime heritage: Taranto is the home of a famous naval academy. The archaeological museum remains closed for restoration.

★   A shining beacon to shed light on the millennia of local history is the **Museo Nazionale,** whose large collection of prehistoric, Greek, and Roman artifacts came mainly from the immediate vicinity. The museum is just over the bridge from the old town on the promontory. Some of the prehistoric items from Apulian tombs date to before 1000 BC, but more plentiful are the examples of intricate craftsmanship in the Grecian jewelry dating from around 500 BC. The museum is a testament to the importance of this ancient port, which has always taken full advantage of its unique trading position at the end of the Italian peninsula. ⊠ *Corso Umberto 41,* ☎ *099/4532112.* ☒ *8,000 lire.* ☉ *Mon.– Sat. 9–2, Sun. 9–1.*

Dining and Lodging

$$ ✕ **L'Approdo.** Overlooking the channel separating the old and new towns and just next to the bridge itself, this restaurant serves good seafood, pizza (lunch only), and pasta. ⊠ *Via Matteotti 4,* ☎ *099/4533524. MC, V. Closed Fri.*

$$$ ⌂ **Golf Hotel.** Less than an hour's drive along the coast from Taranto, this hotel, as its name implies, caters to golf enthusiasts, but its modern amenities and proximity to the sea (300 meters) make it a good refuge for beach fans, too. ⊠ *Località Riva dei Tessali, Castellaneta Marina, 74011,* ☎ *099/8439251,* FAX *099/8439255. 70 rooms. Bar, pool, tennis courts. AE, DC, MC, V. Closed Oct.–Mar.*

$$$ ⌂ **Grand Hotel Delfino.** This big, modern, well-equipped hotel downtown caters to business clients. Airy rooms have balconies. The restaurant features regional seafood. ⊠ *Viale Virgilio 66, 74100,* ☎ *099/7323232,* FAX *099/7324654. 198 rooms. Restaurant, minibars, pool. AE, DC, MC, V.*

Nightlife and the Arts

Taranto has Easter processions (Holy Thursday and Good Friday), called the **Procession of the Madonna Addolorata and of the Mysteries.**

Outdoor Activities and Sports

GOLF

Apulia's only 18-hole golf course is the **Riva dei Tessali** (⊠ Marina di Castellaneta, 40 km/25 mi west of Taranto along the coast road, ☎ 099/8439007).

SAILING

Sailors should contact the **Lega Navale** (⊠ Lungomare Vittorio Emanuele II, ☎ 0883/533354); you can also rent boats and take lessons here.

Brindisi

㉒ *114 km (71 mi) southeast of Bari, 72 km (45 mi) east of Taranto.*

Occupying the head of a deep inlet on the eastern (Adriatic) coast, Brindisi (stress placed on first syllable) has long been one of Italy's most important ports, and today most people think of the town only as a terminus for the ferry crossing that links Italy with Greece. Although this impression fails to give credit to the broader importance of the city (it has a population of nearly 100,000), it is a present-day reminder of the role Brindisi has always played as gateway to the eastern Mediterranean and beyond. Brindisi has seen a constant flow of naval and mercantile traffic over the centuries, and in the Middle Ages it was an important departure point for several Crusades to the Holy Land.

The core of the city is at the head of a deep channel, which branches into two harbors with the city between them. Look for the steeple of the cathedral to get your bearings, but go beyond it and down the steps to the water's edge. Just to the left is a tall **Roman column** and the base of another one next to it. These were built in the 2nd century AD and marked **the end of the Via Appia** (Appian Way), the Imperial Roman road that led from the capital to this important southern seaport. ⊠ *Viale Regina Margherita.*

A short walk from the column, the mosaic floor in the apse of the **Duomo** is worth stopping to have a look at; the floor dates from the 12th century, although much of the rest of the cathedral was rebuilt in the 18th. ⊠ *Piazza Duomo.*

The **Castello Svevo,** another of the defense fortifications built by the illustrious Frederick II in the 13th century, guards the larger of Brindisi's two inner harbors, though it is inaccessible by the public. ⊠ *Piazza Castello.*

Lodging

$$$ 🏨 **Majestic.** A modern hotel across from the train station and near the port, the Majestic is fully air-conditioned and furnished in comfortable, though uninspired, style. The hotel is somewhat overpriced for what it offers, but breakfast is included. ⊠ *Corso Umberto 151, 72100,* ☎ *0831/222941,* FAX *0831/524071. 68 rooms. Restaurant. AE, DC, MC, V.*

$$$ 🏨 **Mediterraneo.** Comfort and a convenient central location are the advantages of this modern, air-conditioned hotel—though it is less accessible from the port than the Majestic. Most rooms have balconies. ⊠ *Viale Aldo Moro 70, 72100,* ☎ *0831/582811,* FAX *0831/587858. 65 rooms. Restaurant. AE, DC, MC, V.*

Nightlife and the Arts

The **City of Brindisi Festival** (July–September) is a citywide display of art and folklore; contact the tourist office (☞ Visitor Information *in* Apulia A to Z, *below*).

Outdoor Activities and Sports

SAILING

Contact Brindisi's **Lega Navale** (⊠ Via Vespucci, ☎ 0831/418824).

Lecce

❷❸   *40 km (25 mi) southeast of Brindisi on S16, 87 km (54 mi) east of Taranto.*

Although Lecce, the crowning jewel on the tour of Apulia, was founded before the time of the ancient Greeks, it is almost always associated with the term Lecce Baroque. This is because of a citywide impulse in the 17th century to redo the town in the Baroque fashion. But this was Baroque with a difference. Although Baroque architecture is often heavy and monumental, here it took on a lighter, more fanciful tone.

★   Just look at the **Basilica di Santa Croce,** with the **Palazzo della Prefettura** abutting it. Although every column, window, pediment, and balcony is given a curling Baroque touch—and then an extra one for good measure—the overall effect is lighthearted. The scale of the buildings is unintimidating and the local stone is a glowing honey color: it couldn't look menacing if it tried. ⊠ *Via Umberto I.*

In the middle of **Piazza Sant'Oronzo** is a **Roman column** of the same era and style as the one in Brindisi. Next to the column the shallow rows of seats in the **Roman amphitheater** suggest a small-scale Roman Colosseum or Verona's arena.

Dining and Lodging

$$ ✕ **Plaza.** Tucked away behind Lecce's castle, this high-quality restaurant has been keeping the city's gourmets happy for 30 years. Regional dishes reveal a personal touch. Try the *tubettini alle cozze* (pasta with clams) and the antipasti, worth dipping into. ⊠ *Via 140 Fanteria 12,* ☎ *0832/305093. AE, MC, V. Closed Sun. and Aug.*

$$ 🏨 **Risorgimento.** An old-fashioned hotel in a converted palace in the heart of the Baroque old town, the Risorgimento combines historic charm with modern comfort. The roof garden has great town views. ⊠ *Via Augusto Imperatore 19, 73100,* ☎ *0832/242125,* FAX *0832/245571. 57 rooms. Restaurant, lounge, meeting rooms. AE, DC, MC, V.*

$ ⊡ **Cappello.** This popular hotel is close to the train station but outside the old city walls, about a 10-minute walk from the town center. Rooms are small but clean and comfortable. Reservations are advised. ⊠ *Via Montegrappa 4, 73100,* ☎ *0832/308881,* ℻ *0832/301535. 32 rooms. Bar. AE, DC, MC, V.*

Nightlife and the Arts

In July, the public gardens are venues for productions of **drama** and, sometimes, **opera**. A **Baroque music festival** in September is held in churches throughout the city.

Shopping

Wrought-iron work is the local specialty. Also look for works in **papier-mâché,** particularly nativity scenes.

Gallipoli

㉔   *37 km (23 mi) south of Lecce on S101.*

The modern section of the town of Gallipoli, on the Gulf of Taranto, lies on the mainland; turn right on the main street at the end of the central square and cross a 17th-century bridge to the old town, crowded onto its own small island in the gulf. The Greeks called it Kallipolis, the Romans Anxa. Like the famous Turkish town of the same name on the Dardanelles, the Italian Gallipoli occupies a strategic location and thus was repeatedly attacked through the centuries—by the Normans in 1071, the Venetians in 1484, the British in 1809. The historic quarter, a mesh of narrow alleys and squares, is guarded by a formidable Aragonese **castello,** a massive fortification that grew out of an earlier Byzantine fortress that you can still see at the southeast corner. Notable sanctuaries in town are the Baroque **Duomo** and the **church of La Purissima**, with a stuccoed interior as elaborate as a wedding cake (note especially the tiled floor).

Dining and Lodging

$$ ✕ **Marechiaro.** You have to cross a little bridge to this simple port-side
★   restaurant, actually not far from the town's historic center. It's built out onto the sea, replete with wood paneling, flowers, and terraces with panoramic coastal views. Try the renowned *zuppa di pesce alla gallipolina* (fish stew made without tomatoes), succulent shellfish, and linguine with seafood. ⊠ *Lungomare Marconi,* ☎ *0833/266143. Reservations essential weekends. AE, DC, MC, V. Closed Tues. Oct.–May.*

$$$ ⊡ **Costa Brada.** The rooms all have terraces with sea views at this mod-
★   ern white beach hotel of classic Mediterranean design. The interiors are comfortable and tasteful; Rooms 110–114 are particularly spacious and overlook the beach. The hotel accepts only half-board or full-board guests in the high season. ⊠ *At Baia Verde beach, Litoranea Santa Maria di Leuca, 73014,* ☎ *0833/202551,* ℻ *0833/202555. 87 rooms. Restaurant, snack bar, indoor and outdoor pools, sauna, tennis court, exercise room. AE, DC, MC, V.*

$$–$$$ ⊡ **Le Sirenuse.** There is a private beach and pine forest at this gleaming white Mediterranean-style beach hotel complex. Its comfortable rooms are air-conditioned with terraces. Half- or full-board is required in high season. ⊠ *At Baia Verde beach, 73014,* ☎ *0833/202536,* ℻ *0833/202539. 125 rooms. Pool, tennis court, beach. MC, V. Closed Nov.–Apr.*

Outdoor Activities and Sports

BEACHES

Ample swimming, clean, fine sand, and water sports make **Gallipoli** a good choice for families.

APULIA A TO Z

Arriving and Departing

By Plane

Alitalia flies regularly from other Italian cities to Bari and Brindisi. **Palese Airport** is 8 km (5 mi) west of Bari. **Papola Casale Airport** is 5 km (3 mi) north of Brindisi. Regular bus service connects the two airports with the cities.

By Train

Bari is a transit point for train connections with northern Italy.

Getting Around

By Bus

Direct, if not always frequent, connections operate between most destinations in Apulia. In many cases the bus service is actually the backup to the train service (☞ *below*).

By Car

Driving is probably the best way to get around Apulia and the only way to see remote sights. Apulia is linked with the Italian autostrada system, making it just a four- or five-hour drive from Rome to the Gargano Peninsula or Bari. Roads are good, and major cities are linked by fast autostrade. Secondary roads connect the whole region; more direct—but sometimes less scenic—routes provide a convenient link between Bari, Brindisi, and Lecce. Don't plan on any night driving in the countryside, because the roads can become confusing without the aid of landmarks or large towns.

By Train

Good train service, operated by **FS** (Italian State Railways), links Bari to Brindisi, Lecce, and Taranto, but smaller destinations can often be reached only by completing the trip on a connecting bus operated by the railroad. The private **Ferrovie Sud-Est** (FSE) line connects the trulli area and Martina Franca with Bari and Taranto, and the fishing port of Gallipoli with Lecce.

Contacts and Resources

Car Rental

Bari: Avis (✉ Via Zuppetta 5/a, ☎ 080/5247154). **Hertz** (✉ Piazza Moro 47, ☎ 080/5242250). **Brindisi: Avis** (✉ Via del Mare 50, ☎ 0831/526407). **Hertz** (✉ c/o Silver Travel, Corso Garibaldi 95, ☎ 0831/528333). **Foggia: Avis** (✉ Train station, ☎ 0881/678912). **Hertz** (✉ Via Trinitapoli 2, ☎ 0881/608400). **Taranto: Avis** (✉ Corso Umberto 61, ☎ 099/4532278). **Hertz** (✉ Corso Umberto 49 (☎ 099/4533763).

Emergencies

Police, Ambulance, Fire, First-Aid (Pronto Soccoroso) (☎ 113).

Guided Tours

The **CIT** office in Bari (☞ *below*) is the best connection for guided tours in Apulia, otherwise poorly served by tour operators. The CIT office can put you in touch with one of a number of local operators that offer everything from chauffeur-driven cars to inclusion in part of a longer excursion.

Late-Night Pharmacies

Pharmacies take turns remaining open late and on Sunday. A list of hours is posted on each *farmacia* (pharmacy).

Travel Agencies

Bari: CIT (⊠ Via Abate Gimma 150, ☎ 080/5213552). **Wagon-Lits** (⊠ Thomas Cook, Via Cardassi 85, ☎ 080/5540580).

Visitor Information

Bari (⊠ Piazza Moro 32a, ☎ 080/5242244). **Brindisi** (⊠ Piazza Dionisi, ☎ 0831/521944). **Foggia** (⊠ Via Perrone 17, ☎ 0881/723141). **Lecce** (⊠ Piazza Sant'Oronzo, ☎ 0832/304443). **Taranto** (⊠ Corso Umberto 113, ☎ 099/4532392). **Trani** (⊠ Via Cavour 140, ☎ 0883/588830; ⊠ Kiosk in Piazza della Repubblica, summer only, ☎ 0883/43295). **Vieste (Gargano)** (⊠ Piazza Kennedy, ☎ 0884/708806).

15 Sicily

On this fabled island, you may ski down a snow-muffled volcano, walk through palm and orange groves, and swim within sight of majestic ruins—all in the same day. Sicily's subtleties make it seem more like an offshoot of far-off kingdoms than of Italy. It has a stubborn personality: cynical yet passionate, languorous yet industrious. Marvels abound, including the panoramic perfection of Taormina, the Valley of the Temples, and the unforgettable sight of a rose-tinted moon rising over Mt. Etna.

Updated by
Robert
Andrews

EN ROUTE SOUTH TO SICILY, you realize you are entering a world apart from the north. Ample, succulent lemons whirl by the hurtling train's windows, while cacti wave their prickly appendages and balmy air wafts gently about. Women look up from clotheslines, a sunglassed *ragazzo* (teenager) on a Vespa pauses at a stoplight just below. Once arrived, you may be surprised to see a profusion of blond hair and blue eyes and to learn that two of the most popular man's names are Ruggero (Roger) and Guglielmo (William).

Lying in a strategic position between Europe and Africa, Sicily at one time hosted two of the most advanced and enlightened capitals of Europe—a Greek one in Siracusa and an Arab-Norman one in Palermo. (The Normans are responsible for the blond-haired Rogers and blue-eyed Williams.) Sicily was one of the great melting pots of the ancient world and home to every great civilization that existed in the Mediterranean: Greek and Roman; then Arab and Norman; and, finally, French, Spanish, and Italian. Something of all of these peoples was absorbed into the island's artistic heritage, a rich tapestry of art and architecture that includes massive Romanesque cathedrals, two of the best-preserved Greek temples in the world, Roman amphitheaters, and delightful Baroque palaces and churches.

Modern Sicily is still a land of surprising contrasts. The traditional graciousness and nobility of the Sicilian people exist side by side with the atrocities and destructive influences of the Mafia, although recent events suggest that the Mafia's grip on the island is being slowly loosened. Alongside some of the most exquisite architecture in the world are the shabby products of some of the worst speculation imaginable. In recent years, Sicily, like much of the Mediterranean coast, has experienced a boom in tourism and a surge in condominium development that has only now begun to be checked. The chic boutiques purveying lace and linen in jet-set resort towns like Taormina give no clue to the poverty in which their wares are produced.

In Homer's *Odyssey,* Sicily represented the unknown end of the world, yet the region eventually became the center of the known world under the Normans, who recognized a paradise in its deep blue skies and temperate climate, its lush vegetation, and rich marine life. Much of this paradise does still exist today. Add to it Sicily's unique cuisine—another harmony of elements—which mingles Arab and Greek spices with Spanish and French dishes, using some of the world's tastiest seafood, and you can understand why those who arrived here were often reluctant to leave.

You do not have to be paranoid about safety in Sicily, but you do have to be careful: do not flaunt jewelry, and keep your handbag securely strapped across your chest. Leaving valuables visible in your car while you go sightseeing is inviting trouble. Be careful; then enjoy the company of the Sicilians. You will find them to be friendly and often willing to go out of their way to help tourists. It is not uncommon in small towns for visitors to receive invitations to a local's house for dinner. It doesn't matter if you don't speak Italian or speak only a little: they aren't usually offended if your pronunciation isn't perfect. One of the reasons for this, no doubt, is the fact that many Sicilians or their close relatives have themselves been strangers in foreign lands, and empathy goes a long way.

Pleasures and Pastimes

Beaches

There is a surfeit of beaches in Sicily, but many of them are too rocky, too crowded, or too dirty to be enjoyed for long. Among the exceptions are Mondello, near Palermo, a popular sandy beach on a tiny peninsula jutting out into the Mediterranean; Sant'Alessio and Santa Teresa, north of Taormina (the beaches just below Taormina itself are disappointing); and Capo San Vito, on the northern coast, near Erice, a sandy beach on a promontory overlooking a bay in the Gulf of Castellammare.

Camping

Sicily has excellent camping facilities on both the main island and its satellite islands. The two best are El Bahira, in San Vito Lo Capo, and Bazia, in Furnari Marina, west of Milazzo. Both have restaurants and showers, as well as swimming pools, tennis courts, and discos.

Dining

Sicilian cooking reflects the different Mediterranean influences that have left their mark on the island. Fish, vegetables, and grains are used in imaginative combinations, sometimes served with Italian pastas or Arab or North African ingredients, such as couscous. Sweet and sour tastes are deftly mingled, and cooks have distinctive touches, so that *caponata* (an antipasto of eggplant, capers, olives, and, in eastern Sicily, peppers) is different at every restaurant.

Sicily has always been one of Italy's poorest areas, so meat is seen rarely on menus. When it is featured, it is usually prepared *alla brace* (skewered) or in *falso magro* (a thin slice of meat rolled around sausage, onion, bacon, bits of egg, and cheese).

Seafood from Sicilian waters is the best and most varied in all Italy. *Tonno* (tuna) is a staple in many coastal areas, and *pesce spada* (swordfish) is equally common, if more expensive. Try *ricci* (sea urchins), a specialty of Mondello, near Palermo. Fish sauces for pasta are also noteworthy: pasta *con le sarde* is made with fresh sardines, olive oil, anchovies, raisins, and pine nuts, and has the distinctive flavor of wild fennel. In Catania, spaghetti *alla Norma,* named for the heroine in the opera by local composer Vincenzo Bellini, is prepared with a sauce of tomatoes and fried eggplant.

Desserts from Sicily are famous. *Cassata siciliana* is a traditional Easter cake, a rich sponge cake with candied fruit, marzipan, and icing. Gelato is excellent and is usually homemade, as are brilliant *granite* (granitas) in flavors such as lemon. Gooey cakes and very sweet desserts—like chestnut ice cream covered with hot zabaglione—satiate your cravings for a sugar fix. The sweet dessert wine, Marsala, is Sicily's most famous, but there is a range of other local wines, from the dark red Faro to the sparkling dry Regaleali, which is excellent with fish.

CATEGORY	COST*
$$$	60,000–85,000 lire
$$	25,000–60,000 lire
$	under 25,000 lire

Prices are per person, including house wine, service, and tax.

Kids' Stuff

Almost every major city in Sicily has a theater giving performances of the world-famous Sicilian *pupi* (marionettes). The most popular are in Palermo, Acireale, and Taormina. Stories center on heroes from the Norman fables, distressed damsels, and Saracen invaders. Even if you can't understand Italian, the action is fast and furious, so it's easy to figure out what's going on. Palermo has an International Museum dedicated to these and other types of marionettes. If you are in Sicily at Carnival time (about 45 days before Easter), Acireale, near Catania, has one of the best carnivals in Italy, with dozens of colorful torch-lit floats with papier-mâché characters aboard that are pulled through the streets by costumed revelers.

Lodging

Though Sicily is Italy's largest region, it has some of the most remote countryside and only a limited number of good-quality hotels. The major cities and resorts of Palermo, Taormina, and Agrigento are the only spots with a real range of accommodations. There are, of course, some superb establishments, such as converted villas with views over the sea or well-equipped modern hotels, but it is best not to expect to come across some charming spot in the middle of nowhere. If you want to get away from the major centers, make reservations well in advance.

Hotels in the $$$$ bracket provide comfort and services to match those in other Italian regions; they are usually the older, more established hotels. In the $$–$$$ range, you'll find newer hotels built to cater to the increased tourist trade of the past 20 years. Chains, such as Jolly Hotels, are predictable but reliable. Inexpensive establishments are usually family-run and offer a basic level of comfort: although the bathroom will be clean, it will probably also be down the hall.

CATEGORY	COST*
$$$$	over 300,000 lire
$$$	160,000–300,000 lire
$$	100,000–160,000 lire
$	under 100,000 lire

Prices are for a standard double room for two, including service and tax.

Scuba Diving

The island of Ustica, north of Palermo, is an international center for scuba diving and snorkeling. Its rugged coast is dotted with grottoes that are washed by crystal-clear waters and filled with an incredible variety of interesting marine life. In July Ustica hosts an International Meeting of Marine Fishing that attracts sportsmen as well as marine biologists from all over the world.

Shopping

Sicily is one of the leaders in the Italian ceramics industry, with important factories at Caltagirone, in the interior, and Santo Stefano di Camastra, along the northern coast between Messina and Cefalù. Colorful Sicilian folk pottery can still be bought at bargain prices.

Place mats, tablecloths, napkins, and clothing decorated with fine petit point are good buys in Cefalù, Taormina, and Erice, but they are not cheap. Make sure that any linen you buy is produced in Sicily and not on another continent.

Collectors have been combing Sicily for years for pieces of the colorful *carretti siciliani* (Sicilian carts). Before the automobile, these were the major form of transportation in Sicily, and they were decorated in bright primary colors and in primitive styles, with scenes from the Norman troubadour tales. The axles of these carts were ornamented with open filigree work, which was also brightly painted.

Skiing

Skiing is fast becoming a popular sport in Sicily. Ski areas can be found on the slopes on the north side of Mt. Etna. The most popular is at Linguaglossa, in a magnificent pine forest about 45 km (27 mi) from Catania. The other area for skiing in Sicily is in the Le Madonie mountains, south of Cefalù.

Exploring Sicily

Sicily is about 180 km (112 mi) north to south and 270 km (168 mi) across. For exploration purposes, the country can be divided into four distinct areas of interest: historic Palermo and its environs; the western coast to Agrigento—the Greek temple belt; Eastern Sicily, of untrammeled inland villages and coastal towns such as Siracusa; and the northeastern Aeolian Islands, an archipelago of seven volcanic islands.

Sicily is so dense with places of interest that not even a week is sufficient to explore the island in depth, though with a car at your disposal you will be able to cover all the most important sites. The best way to visit it is to travel counterclockwise along the coast by car, bus, or train, making occasional detours inland.

You needn't visit all seven of the Aeolian Islands individually. In summer, boats connect all seven, so you can stick to admiring most of them from the sea, getting off at Lipari, which is the most well developed for tourism, though all of the islands except Stromboli offer some kind of accommodation, from small, family-run guesthouses to beds in private homes.

Numbers in the text correspond to numbers in the margin and on the Sicily, Palermo, and Agrigento maps.

Great Itineraries

In nine days, you can do a thorough loop around the island, which starts in Palermo, moves west and south to the stunning Greek cities of Selinunte and Agrigento, then dips inland and continues southeast to Siracusa, and finally heads north to picturesque Taormina and the Aeolian Islands. Smaller explorations concentrated around Palermo and environs can be done in three or five days.

IF YOU HAVE 3 DAYS

A three-day sojourn on the island should not necessitate the use of a car if you base yourself in Sicily's capital, ⊞ **Palermo** ①–⑪. In this hub of Norman Sicily, the highlights include the **Palazzo dei Normanni** ② and the **Regional Archaeological Museum** ⑪, as well as a handful of characteristic churches. Head out to **Monreale** ⑫ to admire the splendid cathedral, and compare it with the slightly earlier mosaic-laden monument at **Cefalù** ⑬. Spend your last day exploring this seaside resort.

IF YOU HAVE 5 DAYS

A longer time on the island will allow you to add choice excursions to the three-day itinerary. From **Cefalù** ⑬ proceed westward along the northwestern coast to panoramic ⊞ **Erice** ⑮, a good spot to overnight. Just up the road is **Trapani** ⑯, a port-city that has little to offer the visitor. Heading east through the interior, drop in on the imposing half-finished temple of **Segesta** ⑭, then swing south to the ruins of **Selinunte** ⑲, whose remarkable metopes you will have seen in Palermo's archaeological museum. Following the coast down, aim for the Greek temple site at ⊞ **Agrigento** ⑳–㉗. Allow a full day to explore before heading north on the S189, back to Palermo.

IF YOU HAVE 9 DAYS

This itinerary is an extension of the five-day itinerary, *above*. Head inland toward **Enna** ㉘, worth a quick whirl around, then make a lunch-stop at **Piazza Armerina** ㉙ before viewing the exuberant mosaics of the Roman villa at **Casale** ㉚, for many the highlight of any Sicilian tour. If you have time, stop off to see the Ceramics Museum at **Caltagirone** ㉛ before continuing on the S124 to ⊞ **Siracusa** ㉝. You'll need a full day to absorb this venerable city and its extensive archaeological park. Head north up the coast—a visit to **Catania** ㉞ is of limited interest—and carry straight on until you can see the silhouette of **Mt. Etna** ㉟ (a view best admired in the morning), an essential stop on any Sicilian tour. Spend the night in 🔝 **Taormina** ㊱. A couple of hours are enough for a drive up to the village of **Castelmola**, above Taormina; otherwise, go directly to **Messina** ㊲, which you should reach in time for lunch. If you can, see the Regional Museum here for your last blast of Sicilian art, before crossing the Straits to the seven islands of the Aeolian archipelago: **Lipari** ㊳ (the largest and best developed for tourism), **Vulcano** ㊴, **Salina** ㊵, **Panarea** ㊶, **Stromboli** ㊷, **Alicudi** ㊸, and **Filicudi** ㊹. Then, it's back to the mainland.

When to Tour Sicily

Sicily comes into its own in the spring, but you're not alone in knowing this. Taormina and Erice attract a flood of visitors around Easter, and any visit scheduled for this time should be backed up by solid advance bookings. Many sites, such as inland Segesta, are at their best in the clear spring light, and are far enough off the beaten track to ensure a fairly hassle-free time. August, on the other hand, is hellish wherever you choose to roam not just for the presence of fellow travelers, but for the extreme, uncomfortably hot temperatures. Cities should be avoided. Beaches don't necessarily offer refuge from the sizzling temperatures; they can get pretty clogged with Italian and foreign vacationers. Come in September or October, and you'll find acres of beach space. Cefalù, like Taormina, sees year-round tourism, though some of the luxury hotels close down for the winter. As with Easter, Christmas and New Year's see a lot of movement on the island, and reservations should always be made as early as possible. Other festivals, such as Agrigento's almond festival in February, can also mean a dearth of available accommodation.

PALERMO AND ENVIRONS

The Sicilian capital is a multilayered, vigorous metropolis, packed with interest, but also exhausting. As long as you approach the city in the right frame of mind, you'll find it an enriching and enjoyable place to explore, with a strong historical profile. Regulate your pace, don't attempt to see too much too quickly, and keep your head. If you have a car, install it in a garage as soon as you can, and don't take it out until you are ready to depart.

The heritage of the past encompasses all ages, but Palermo's most unique aspect is its Arab-Norman identity, an improbable marriage that, mixed in with Byzantine and Jewish elements, created some unforgettable and resplendent works of art. These are most notable in the churches, small jewels such as San Giovanni degli Eremiti or larger-scale works such as the cathedral. The Arab-Norman theme is continued in the cathedral at nearby Monreale and in Cefalù, a viable alternative to staying in the capital itself.

Palermo

❶ *717 km (448 mi) south of Naples, 928 km (580 mi) south of Rome.*

Once the intellectual capital of southern Europe, Palermo has always been at the crossroads of civilization. Favorably situated on a crescent-shaped bay at the foot of Monte Pellegrino, it has attracted almost every people and culture touching the Mediterranean world. To Palermo's credit, it has absorbed these diverse cultures into a unique personality that is at once Arab and Christian, Byzantine and Roman, Norman and Italian.

Sicily

Palermo was first colonized by Phoenician traders in the 6th century BC, but it was their descendants, the Carthaginians, who built the important fortress here that caught the covetous eye of the Romans. After the First Punic War, the Romans took control of the city, in the 3rd century BC. After several invasions by the Vandals, Sicily was settled by Arabs, who made the country an emirate and made Palermo a showpiece capital that rivaled both Cordoba and Cairo in Asian splendor. Nestled in the fertile Conca d'Oro (Golden Conch) plain; full of orange, lemon, and carob groves; and enclosed by limestone hills, Palermo became a magical world of palaces and mosques, minarets and palm trees.

It was so attractive and sophisticated a city that the Norman ruler Roger de Hauteville decided to conquer it and make it his capital (1061). The Norman occupation of Sicily resulted in the Golden Age of Palermo (from 1072 to 1194), a remarkable period of enlightenment and learning in which the arts flourished. The city of Palermo, which in the 11th century counted more than 300,000 inhabitants, became the center of the Norman court in all Europe and one of the most important ports of trade between East and West.

Eventually the Normans were replaced by the Swabian ruler Frederick II, the Holy Roman Emperor, and incorporated into the Kingdom of the Two Sicilies. You will also see evidence in Palermo of the Baroque art and architecture of the Spanish viceroys, who came to power after the bloody Sicilian Vespers uprising of 1282, in which the French Angevin dynasty was overthrown. The Aragonese viceroys also brought the Inquisition to Palermo, which some historians believe helped foster the protective secret societies that eventually evolved into today's Mafia.

Palermo's main attractions are easily reached on foot, though you may choose to spend a morning taking a city bus tour to help you get oriented. The tourist attractions are scattered along three major streets: Corso Vittorio Emanuele, Via Maqueda, and Via Roma. The tourist information office in Piazza Castelnuovo will give you a map and a valuable handout that lists opening and closing times, which sometimes change with the seasons.

★ ❷ The **Palazzo dei Normanni** (Norman Royal Palace), at the far end of the Corso, away from the harbor, is now the seat of the Sicilian Parliament. The palace was, unfortunately, closed to the public for security reasons in 1992, but the **Cappella Palatina** (Palatine Chapel) inside, one of Italy's greatest art treasures, remains open. Built by Roger II in 1132, this is a dazzling example of the unique harmony of artistic elements that came together under the Normans. In it, the skill of French and Sicilian masons was brought to bear on the decorative purity of Arab ornamentation and the splendor of Greek Byzantine mosaics. The interior is covered with glittering mosaics and capped by a splendid Arab honeycomb stalactite wooden ceiling. Biblical stories blend happily with scenes of Arab life—look for one showing a picnic in a harem—and Norman court pageantry. Stylized Moorish palm branches run along the walls below the mosaics and recall the battlements on Norman castles—each one a different mosaic composition.

Upstairs are the royal apartments, including the **Sala di Ruggero** (King Roger's Hall), decorated with medieval murals of hunting scenes. Tour guides escort you around these halls, which once hosted one of the most splendid courts in Europe. French, Latin, and Arabic were spoken here, and Arab astronomers and poets exchanged ideas with Latin and Greek scholars in what must have been one of the most unique mar-

Palermo

Porto

Villa Giulia

Orto Botanico

Foro Italico

KEY

i Tourist Information

Villa Giardini Garibaldi

Pza. Marina

V. F. Crispi

Cala

Via

Via Alloro

Via Garibaldi

Corso Via Lincoln

Corso dei Mille

Train Station

Via Roma

Corso Vittorio Emanuele

Via Roma

Pza. Pretoria

Via Maqueda

Corso Tukory

Via Maqueda

Via Candelai

Teatro Massimo

Pza. Verdi

Via Albergheria

Via Mongitore

Via Papireto

Pza. Vitt. Emanuele Orlando

Via Voltruno

Corso Alberto Amadeo

Villa Bonanno

Pza. d. Parlamento

V. Benedettini

C. Re Ruggero

Corso Finocchiaro Aprile

Via C. Lascaria

Via d'Ossuna

Via G. Mosca

Colonna Rotta

Via Pisani

Pza. Indipendenza

V. G. il Buono

Via Zisa

Via Cipressi

Piazza Danisinni

Via Cappuccini

Corso Vittorio Emanuele

N

0   300 yards
0   300 meters

Duomo, **4**

International Museum of Marionettes, **10**

Martorana, **8**

Palazzo Abatellis, **9**

Palazzo dei Normanni, **2**

Quattro Canti, **5**

Regional Archaeological Museum, **11**

San Cataldo, **7**

San Giovanni degli Eremiti, **3**

Santa Caterina, **6**

riages of culture in the Western world. ☒ *Piazza Indipendenza. Palatine Chapel.* ☎ *001/7054317.* ☞ *Free.* ☉ *Weekdays 9–noon and 3–5, Sat. 9–noon, Sun. 9–10 and noon–1. Tours must be arranged in advance. Closed during religious services and for weddings.*

❸ Distinguished by its five pink domes, **San Giovanni degli Eremiti** is one of the most picturesque of Palermo's churches. The 12th-century church was built by the Normans on the site of an earlier mosque—one of 200 that once stood in Palermo. The emirs ruled Palermo for almost two centuries and brought to it their passion for lush gardens and fountains. One is reminded of this while sitting in San Giovanni's delightful cloister of twin half-columns, surrounded by palm trees, jasmine, oleander, and citrus trees. You'll find the church to the left of the front of Palazzo dei Normanni. ☒ *Via dei Benedettini.* ☉ *Daily 9–12:30, Mon. and Thurs. also 3–6.*

❹ The **Duomo** is a prime example of Palermitan eclecticism. Its turrets, towers, dome, and arches come together in the kind of meeting of diverse elements that King Roger, whose tomb is inside along with that of Frederick II, fostered during his reign. Be sure to walk outside and look at the back of the apse, which is gracefully decorated with interlacing Arab arches, inlaid with limestone and black volcanic tufa. ☒ *Corso Vittorio Emanuele.* ☉ *Daily 7–noon and 4–6.*

❺ Bisecting Corso Vittorio Emanuele is **Quattro Canti** (Four Corners), actually the intersection with Via Maqueda. Here four rather traffic-blackened Baroque palaces from the Spanish rule meet at concave corners, each with its own fountain and representations of a Spanish ruler, patron saint, or one of the four seasons.

Just off the Quattro Canti, **Piazza Pretoria** has as its centerpiece a lavishly decorated fountain, originally intended for a Florentine villa. Its abundance of nude figures so shocked some Palermitans when it was unveiled in 1575 that it got the nickname the "Fountain of Shame." It is even more of a sight at night, when illuminated.

Piazza Bellini holds a trio of eminent churches, among them the splendid Baroque church of **Santa Caterina** (1596). Its walls are covered in ❻ decorative 17th-century inlays of precious marble. ☒ *Piazza Bellini.*

Two churches, accessible by a staircase from Piazza Bellini, stand next to each other forming a delightful Norman complex. The orange-red ❼ domes belong to **San Cataldo** (1160), whose spare but intense interior, punctuated by antique Greek columns, retains much of its original medieval simplicity. If the church is closed, the custodian at La Martorana (☞ *below*) will let you in during public hours. ☒ *Piazza Bellini.* ☉ *Apr.–Sept., Mon.–Sat. 8–1 and 3:30–6:30, Sun. 8–1; Oct.–Mar., Mon.–Sat. 9:30–1 and 3:30–5:30, Sun. 9:30–1.*

❽ Distinguished by an elegant campanile, the **Martorana** was erected in 1143 but had its interior altered considerably during the Baroque period. High along the western wall, however, is some of the oldest mosaic artwork of the Norman period. Near the entrance is an interesting mosaic of Roger being crowned by Christ. In it, Roger is dressed in a bejeweled Byzantine stole, reflecting the Norman court's penchant for all things Byzantine. Archangels along the ceiling wear the same stole, wrapped around their shoulders and arms. Like the archangels, the Norman monarchs liked to think of themselves as emissaries from heaven, engaged in defending Christianity by ridding the island of infidel invaders. ☒ *Piazza Bellini.* ☉ *Apr.–Sept., Mon.–Sat. 9:30–1 and 3:30–6:30; Oct.–Mar., Mon–Sat. 9:30–1 and 3:30–5:30.*

❾ Near the port, the **Palazzo Abatellis** houses the Regional Gallery of Sicily. Among its treasures is an Annunciation (1474) by Sicily's prominent Renaissance master, Antonello da Messina, and an arresting fresco by an unknown painter, titled *The Triumph of Death*, a macabre depiction of the plague years. ✉ *Via Alloro 4,* ☎ *091/6164317.* 🎫 *2,000 lire.* 🕐 *Mon.–Sat. 9–1:30 (Tues. and Thurs. also 3–5:30), Sun. 9–12:30.*

❿ The **International Museum of Marionettes** contains an impressive display of Sicilian and European puppets. The traditional Sicilian *pupi,* with their glittering armor and fierce expressions, have become a symbol of Norman Sicily. Plots center on the chivalric legends of the troubadours, who, before the puppet theater, kept alive tales of Norman heroes in Sicily, such as Orlando Furioso and William the Bad. ✉ *Via Butera 1,* ☎ *091/328060.* 🎫 *5,000 lire.* 🕐 *Mon.–Sat. 9–1; weekdays Apr.–Sept. also 4–7.*

The outdoor market **Vucciria** spreads out into a maze of side streets around Piazza Domenico. Its name is a dialect word that means "voices" or "hubbub," and it's easy to see why. Hawkers everywhere deliver their unceasing chants from behind stands brimming with mounds of olives, blood oranges, wild fennel, and long-stemmed artichokes. One of them goes at the trunk of a swordfish with a cleaver, while across the way another holds up a giant squid or dangles an octopus. It may be Palermo, but this is really the Casbah. ✉ *Between Via Maqueda and Via Roma, and accessible from Corso Vittorio Emanuele.*

NEED A BREAK?	The **Vucciria** is full of stalls selling street food. Everything from *calzoni* (deep-fried meat- or cheese-filled pockets of dough) to *panelle* (chickpea-flour fritters). If you're feeling adventurous for something typically Palermitan, look for a stall with a big cast-iron pot selling delicious *guasteddi* (fresh buns filled with thin strips of calf's spleen, ricotta cheese, and a delicious hot sauce).

⓫ On Via Roma, the **Regional Archaeological Museum** has a small but excellent collection. Especially interesting are the examples of prehistoric cave drawings and a marvelously reconstructed Doric frieze from the Greek Temple at Selinunte that gives you a good idea of the high level of artistic culture attained by the Greek colonists in Sicily some 2,500 years ago. ✉ *Piazza Olivella 4,* ☎ *091/6620220.* 🎫 *2,000 lire.* 🕐 *Mon.–Sat. 9–2, Sun. 9–1; Tues. and Fri. also 3–7.*

In Piazza Verdi, west of Via Roma at the top of Via Maqueda, take a glance at the formidable neoclassic **Teatro Massimo** (☞ Nightlife and the Arts, *below*), newly opened after long-term renovations.

OFF THE BEATEN PATH	**FLEA MARKET** – Antique marionettes of the Norman cavaliers or brilliantly colored pieces from the *carretti siciliani* would be supreme finds here. This is also the antiques-store neighborhood, which spreads to the next street, Corso Amedeo. ✉ *Market behind Palermo's Duomo, on Via Papireto.*

Dining and Lodging

$$$ ✕ **Charleston.** You'll feel pampered by the discreet service and elegant
★ surroundings in this famous Palermo restaurant. Impeccably outfitted waiters coast effortlessly through the high-ceiling rooms, offering help with the extensive menu and wine list. Specialties run the gamut of Sicilian and international dishes, with an emphasis on seafood, in keeping with the cuisine of the island. Try the spaghetti *all'aragosta,* with its delicious lobster sauce, or the pesce spada *arrosto* (roasted), but leave

room for the house dessert, *semifreddo alle mandorle*, a soft ice cream made with almonds. The whole restaurant operation moves 8 km (5 mi) north to Mondello during the summer, where it sets up shop in a pavilion on the sea. ✉ *Piazza Ungheria 30*, ☎ *091/321366. Mondello:* ✉ *Charleston le Terrazze, Viale Regina Elena,* ☎ *091/450171. Reservations essential. Jacket and tie. AE, DC, MC, V. Closed Sun.*

$$$ ✕ **Da Renato.** The view from this top-quality restaurant on the sea road
★ toward Cefalù is enough out of the way to make it the insider's choice. And the clientele consists mainly of well-heeled locals who know their way around a good seafood menu. *Frutti di mare* (mixed seafood) makes a good antipasto, and the *zuppa di mare* (fish soup) is hearty enough to be a meal in itself. Grills are also recommended. ✉ *Via Messina Marina 224,* ☎ *091/6302881. AE, DC, MC, V. Closed Mon. and Aug. 10–25.*

$$$ ✕ **Gourmand's.** A chic clientele frequents this modern restaurant, with its high-tech decor (lots of metal and primary colors) and nouvelle cuisine–influenced menu. *Pesce spada affumicato* (smoked) goes well with a bottle of local Regaleali. It's in the northern end of Palermo, near Piazza Castelnuovo. ✉ *Via della Libertà 37/e,* ☎ *091/323431. AE, DC, MC, V. Closed Sun. Jan.–Oct. and Aug. 10–25.*

$$ ✕ **Lo Scudiero.** Despite being on the busy Piazza Ruggero Settimo, Lo Scudiero has a subdued atmosphere, appreciated in this noisy city. The antipasti give you a delicious introduction to Sicilian cuisine, and the *carpaccio di pesce* (swordfish steak) is fab. Alternatively, try some of the non-seafood items on the menu—the meat dishes are excellent, especially the bistecca. ✉ *Via Turati 7,* ☎ *091/581628. Reservations essential. AE, DC, MC, V. Closed 1 wk in Aug. No dinner Sun. No lunch Mon.*

$$ ✕ **Strascinu.** The specialty in this informal and busy restaurant is pasta con le sarde, the famous Arab-Sicilian blend of fresh sardines, wild fennel fronds, sultanas, and pine nuts. ✉ *Viale Regione Siciliana 2286,* ☎ *091/401292. AE, DC, MC, V. Closed 2 wks in Aug.*

$ ✕ **Antica Focacceria San Francesco.** This place in Palermo's heart is an institution, as you can see from the turn-of-the-century wooden cabinets and fixtures of what is still a neighborhood bakery. It bakes and fries the snacks that locals love—and from which you can well make an inexpensive meal. You can sit at marble-topped tables while you eat or take food out. Beverages, including wine and beer, are sold. There is a good gelateria under the same management in the piazza. ✉ *Via Paternostro 58,* ☎ *091/320264. Reservations not accepted. No credit cards.*

$ ✕ **Pizzeria Bellini.** The pizzas are good, the pastas are better, but the best reason to eat in this former theater is the location, overlooking the churches of San Cataldo and La Martorana in the heart of old Palermo. Get here early to make sure of a seat next to the window— or better still, in summer, eat alfresco. Trade is brisk, and so is the service, which can be offhand. ✉ *Piazza Bellini 6,* ☎ *091/6165691. AE, MC, V. Closed Wed.*

$ ✕ **Shangai.** There is nothing Chinese about this Palermo institution in the busy Vucciria market. It's on a terrace above the market (the source of all the ingredients): look down and order your fish from the displays below, and it will be hoisted up in a wicker basket. The atmosphere is jovial and frantic, with lots of teasing and shouting. Calamari *al forno* (baked in the oven) is always a good bet. ✉ *Vicolo Mezzani 34,* ☎ *091/589702. No credit cards. Closed Sun.*

$$$$ ⌂ **Villa Igea.** A short taxi ride through some rough-looking districts
★ of Palermo takes you to this oasis of luxury and comfort, in its own tropical garden at the edge of the bay. A meander through the grounds reveals such relics as an ancient Greek temple at the water's edge. The large rooms (many with terraces overlooking the gardens and the sea) are furnished individually, the nicest with an Italian art-nouveau fla-

vor. Spacious lobbies and public rooms unfold onto a terrace with its own restaurant. Sports facilities help make this elegant villa a self-contained enclave in frenetic Palermo. ⊠ *Salita Belmonte 43, 90142,* ☎ *091/543744,* FAX *091/547654. 111 rooms, 6 suites. Restaurant, bar, pool, tennis court. AE, DC, MC, V.*

$$$ 🏨 **Grande Albergo e delle Palme.** There is a faded charm about this grande dame, whose public rooms suggest the elegant life of Palermo society before World War I, when tea dances and balls were held here. Guest rooms are uneven—some are charming period pieces stuffed with antiques and heavy fabrics, others are dark and cramped. There is an American-style cocktail bar and a rooftop terrace. ⊠ *Via Roma 396, 90139,* ☎ *091/583933,* FAX *091/331545. 187 rooms, 5 suites. Restaurant, parking (fee). AE, DC, MC, V.*

$$$ 🏨 **Mediterraneo.** Though uninspiring, this hotel is nonetheless a useful, convenient base for exploring Palermo's sights. From the large air-conditioned 1970s-style lobby, elevators ascend five stories to rather boxy rooms without much of a view, though equipped with TVs and telephones. The bill includes breakfast. ⊠ *Via Rosolino Pilo 43, 90037,* ☎ *091/581133,* FAX *091/586974. 106 rooms. Restaurant, bar, parking (fee). AE, DC, MC, V.*

$$$ 🏨 **Mondello Palace.** This is the leading hotel at the Mondello resort,
★ making the best use of its location near the beach. The private beach has cabins and changing rooms for the use of Mondello Palace guests, as well as sailing and windsurfing facilities and an exercise room. The rooms are well equipped and large, and most have balconies. In summer you can choose between the hotel's own restaurant or the beachside venue of Palermo's excellent Charleston (☞ *above*)—just across the road. ⊠ *Viale Principe di Scalea, Mondello Lido, just north of Palermo, 90139,* ☎ *091/450001,* FAX *091/450657. 82 rooms, 9 suites. Restaurant, bar, pool, exercise room, beach, windsurfing, boating. AE, DC, MC, V.*

$$ 🏨 **Grande Albergo Sole.** The main attraction of this hotel is the location, just steps away from the Quattro Canti and Piazza Pretoria. The downside is the rumble of traffic in some rooms, though they are comfortable enough, with old-fashioned charm and period furnishings. Public rooms are right out of the 1950s. ⊠ *Corso Vittorio Emanuele 291, 90139,* ☎ *091/581811,* FAX *091/6110182. 154 rooms. Restaurant, bar. AE, DC, MC, V.*

$ 🏨 **Principe di Belmonte.** This is a tasteful choice among Palermo's cheaper hotels. It is family-run and friendly and centrally located—a convenient walk both from the port and Piazza Castelnuovo—but is on a relatively quiet street. Rooms are smallish. Advance reservations are advised. ⊠ *Via Principe di Belmonte 25, 90139,* ☎ *091/331065,* FAX *091/6113424. 17 rooms, 14 with bath. Bar. AE, DC, MC, V.*

Nightlife and the Arts

FESTIVALS

July 11–15, Palermo stages a **street fair** in honor of its patron saint, Santa Rosalia. There are fireworks displays in the evenings. **Epiphany** (January 6) is celebrated with Byzantine rites and a procession of townspeople in local costume through the streets of **Piana degli Albanesi**, near Palermo. The village, 24 km (15 mi) south of the island's capital, is named for the Albanian immigrants who first settled there, bringing with them the Byzantine Catholic rites.

MUSIC AND OPERA

The monumental neoclassic **Teatro Massimo** (⊠ Piazza Verdi, at the top of Maqueda, ☎ 091/6053315) finally reopened in May 1997, after undergoing years of restoration. Construction of the theater was started in 1875 by Giovanni Battista Basile and completed by his son, Ernesto, in 1897. Claimed to be Italy's largest, the theater was featured in scenes in *The Godfather Part III,* directed by Francis Ford Coppola. A program of concerts and operas is presented throughout the year. The grandiose **Politeama Garibaldi** auditorium stages a winter season of opera and orchestral works (✉ Piazza Ruggero Settimo, ☎ 091/6053315). Choral and chamber recitals are performed at the **Teatro Golden** (✉ Via Terrasanta, ☎ 091/300745).

PUPPET SHOW

Bring children to the **Opera dei Pupi** (✉ Via Bara all'Olivella 95, ☎ 091/323400). Check with the tourist office for details.

THEATER

Palermo's **Teatro Biondo** (✉ Via Roma, ☎ 091/582364) is Sicily's foremost theater, featuring a winter season of plays from November to May.

Shopping

ANTIQUES

Modern "adaptations" of the **carretti siciliani,** an early version of the automobile, are available at the **flea market** (✉ Via Papireto, behind the Duomo).

CERAMICS

De Simone has a wide selection of ceramics decorated in a modern style that remind many of Picasso. You can browse through the **workshop** (✉ Piazza Leoni 2) or get a glimpse of what's on offer at a more central **retail outlet** (✉ Via Daita 136, near Piazza Ruggero Settimo).

Monreale

⑫ *10 km (6 mi) southwest of Palermo.*

Don't miss the splendid **Duomo** of Monreale, lavishly executed with mosaics depicting events from the old and new testaments. There are 130 pictures, covering 6,000 square yards. Be sure to see the rear exterior and the graceful Romanesque **cloister** to the left, laced with intricate arches, mosaic-inlaid twin columns, and capitals that represent one of the richest collections of Sicilian medieval sculpture. In a corner by the stylized palm-tree fountain, look for a capital showing William II offering the cathedral to the Virgin. Bring 500-lire coins to illuminate the mosaics. ✉ *Piazza Duomo,* ☎ *091/6404413.* ⊙ *Daily 8:30–noon and 3:30–6:30. Cloister:* ☎ *091/6404403.* 💷 *2,000 lire.* ⊙ *Mon.–Sat. 9–1, Sun. 9–12:30; Mon.–Tues. and Thurs. also 3–6.*

Dining

$$ ✕ **La Botte.** It's worth the short drive or inexpensive taxi fare to reach this good-value restaurant, which features local specialties. Dine alfresco on daily specials, such as *pennette agli odori* (with chopped tomato, garlic, and fresh herbs, including parsley, basil, mint, and oregano), or regular favorites, such as *involtini* (meat or fish roulades). Local wines are a good bet. ✉ *Contrada Lenzitti 20, S186,* ☎ *091/414051. AE, DC, MC, V. Closed Mon.–Thurs. and June 20–Aug. 20.*

Cefalù

★ **⑬** *70 km (42 mi) east of Palermo.*

Cefalù is a charming town built on a spur jutting out into the sea and dominated by a massive 12th-century Romanesque **Duomo,** one of the finest Norman cathedrals in Italy. King Roger began it in 1131 as a thanks offering for having been saved here from a shipwreck. Its mosaics rival those of Monreale. Both cathedrals are dominated by colossal mosaic figures of the Byzantine Pantocratic Christ, high in the bowl of their apses. The Monreale figure is an austere and powerful image, emphasizing the divinity of Christ, while the Cefalù Christ, softer and more compassionate, seems to stress his humanity. The traffic going in and out of Cefalù town can be heavy in summer; you may want to take the 50-minute train ride or 40-minute bus ride from Palermo instead of driving. ⊠ *Piazza Duomo,* ☎ *0921/722021.* ☉ *Daily 8–noon and 3–7. No shorts or beachwear.*

Dining and Lodging

$$ ✕ **Gabbiano.** "Seagull" is an appropriate name for a harborside seafood restaurant with a nautical theme. House specialties are involtini di pesce spada and spaghetti marinara. ⊠ *Via Lungomare Giardina 17,* ☎ *0921/421495. AE, DC, MC, V. Closed Wed.*

$$ ✕ **La Brace.** There is a lively atmosphere in this bistro-style restaurant near the cathedral in town center. Graceful ceiling arches and rustic walls lend an informal air that tourists like. Stick to the excellent grills, and save room for the homemade cassata siciliana. ⊠ *Via Venticinque Novembre 10,* ☎ *0921/423570. AE, DC, MC, V. Closed Mon. and mid-Dec.–mid-Jan.*

$$$ 🏠 **Baia del Capitano.** The peaceful district of Mazzaforno, about 5 km
★ (3 mi) outside town, sets the stage for this handsome hotel with great amenities. The building is less than 30 years old, but it blends in with the traditional homes nearby. The colorful gardens, extending to the surrounding olive groves, are ideal for quiet reading or an afternoon siesta in the shade. A good sandy beach is an easy walk away, but many guests stay by the pool and have drinks on the terrace. The rooms are large and quiet. ⊠ *Contrada Mazzaforno, Mazzaforno, 90015,* ☎ *0921/ 420005,* 🅵🅰🅇 *0921/420163. 39 rooms. Restaurant, bar, pool, tennis court. AE, MC, V. Closed Jan.–Mar.*

$$$ 🏠 **Kalura.** Caldura is the setting for this modern hotel on a small
★ promontory is hard to reach without a car. Taxis from Cefalù take only a few minutes, though. Sports facilities keep you from getting too sedentary, and the private beach is ideal for swimming. Most rooms have views of the sea, and the decor is bright and cheerful. ⊠ *Contrada Caldura,* ☎ *0921/421354,* 🅵🅰🅇 *0921/423122. 65 rooms. Restaurant, bar, pool, tennis court, beach. AE, DC, MC, V.*

WESTERN COAST TO AGRIGENTO

Land of Temples

Western Sicily has a remote air, less developed than the eastern coast, and redolent of the North African culture that for centuries exerted a strong influence on this end of the island. This quality is most tangible in the coastal towns of Trapani and Marsala, and the outlying island of Pantelleria, itself nearer to the Tunisian coast than the Sicilian. In contrast, the cobbled streets of the hilltop town of Erice, outside Trapani, retain a strong medieval complexion, giving the town the air of a last outpost gazing out over the Mediterranean. The Greek presence is still strong, however, in the splendidly isolated site of Segesta, and the cluster of ruined temples at Selinunte. But the crowning glory of this tour is the concentration of Greek temples at Agrigento, occupying a fabulous position on a height between the modern city and the sea.

Segesta

🄬 *85 km (53 mi) southwest of Palermo, 30 km (19 mi) east of Trapani.*

Segesta is where one of the most impressive **Greek temples** in the world is located—on the side of a windswept barren hill overlooking a valley of wild fennel. Virtually intact, the temple is considered by some to be finer, in its proportions and setting, than any other Doric temple left standing. The Greeks started the temple in the 5th century BC but never finished it. The walls and roof are missing, and the columns were never fluted. Just over 1 km (½ mi) away, near the top of the hill, are the remains of a fine Greek theater, with impressive views, especially at sunset, of nearby Monte Erice and the sea.

Erice

15   *35 km (22 mi) west of Segesta, 112 km (70 mi) west of Palermo.*

Erice perches 2,450 ft above sea level, an enchanting medieval mountaintop aerie of castles and palaces, fountains and cobblestone streets. Erice was the ancient Eryx and was dedicated to a fertility goddess, whom the Phoenicians called Astarte; the Greeks, Aphrodite; and the Romans, Venus. According to Virgil, Aeneas built a temple to the goddess here, but it was destroyed when the Arabs took over and renamed the place Mohammed's Mountain. When the Normans arrived, they built a castle where today there is a public park with benches and belvederes, from which there are striking views of Trapani, the Egadi Islands, and, on a *very* clear day, Cape Bon and the Tunisian coast.

Dining and Lodging

$$ ✕ **La Taverna di Re Aceste.** This popular restaurant is named for Aces-
★ tus, the first king of Erice, and the house specialty, couscous Aceste (a spicy Arab-influenced couscous-and-seafood mixture) is in his honor, as are the murals along the walls. The chef also has a special pesto dish made with wild herbs. Try the grilled fish, but ask for the price, since you'll be paying by weight, not per order. The helpful waiters will guide you through the daily specials and the wine list. ⊠ *Viale Conte Pepoli,* ☎ *0923/869084. AE, DC, MC, V. Closed Nov. and Wed. Oct.– May. No dinner Tues.*

$$$ 🏨 **Moderno.** Local craft work and some antiques decorate the gracious
★ rooms of this intimate and well-run hotel on the cobblestone streets of the medieval town. Some rooms are in the modern annex. The main building has a fire blazing in the lounge in winter. The restaurant serves seafood pasta and homemade desserts. Ask for a room with a sea view. ⊠ *Via Vittorio Emanuele 63, 91016,* ☎ *0923/869300,* FAX *0923/869139. 40 rooms. Bar. AE, DC, MC, V.*

$$ 🏨 **Ermione.** Spectacular views and cool breezes are the rewards of a visit to Erice, and this 1960s hotel overlooking the Tyrrhenian Sea is in a position to offer both. Nearly every room has a good view, although some would say that the terrace bar has the most panoramic vista. The hotel restaurant is popular locally, with fish couscous a standout. ⊠ *Via Pineta Comunale 43, 91016,* ☎ *0923/869138,* FAX *0923/869587. 46 rooms. Restaurant, bar, pool. AE, DC, MC, V.*

Trapani

16   *30 km (18 mi) west of Segesta, 107 km (67 mi) west of Palermo.*

The modern town of Trapani, below Erice, is the departure point for ferries to the Egadi Islands and the island of Pantelleria, near the African coast. This rugged western end of Sicily is reminiscent of the terrain in American westerns—as it well should be, for many "spaghetti westerns" were filmed here. If you fancy North African couscous, Trapani is the place to try the Sicilian version, made with fish instead of meat. The result is a kind of fish stew with semolina, spiced with cinnamon, saffron, and black pepper.

Dining

$$ ✕ **P&G.** Couscous is a specialty of this small, popular restaurant on a
★ quiet street between the train station and the Villa Margherita public gardens. The couscous features fish in summer (Friday only) and meat in winter. A mixed grill of meats in a zesty orange sauce will revive any appetite suffering from fish fatigue. Wash it all down with a bottle of Donnafugata, a good white from the Rallo vineyards at Marsala. ✉ *Via Spalti 1,* ☎ *0923/547701. Reservations essential. AE, MC, DC, V. Closed Sun. and Aug.*

Pantelleria

⓱ *100 km (62 mi) southwest of Sicily.*

Pantelleria, near the Tunisian coast, is one of Sicily's most evocative islands, although many find its starkness unappealing. Its volcanic formations, scant patches of forest, prehistoric tombs, and dramatic seascapes constitute an otherworldly landscape. From its grapes—the *zibibbo*—the locals make an amber-colored dessert wine and a strong, sweet wine called Tanit. Daily ferries and hydrofoils connect the island with Trapani.

Marsala

⓲ *30 km (18 mi) south of Trapani, 140 km (87 mi) southwest of Palermo.*

The quiet seaside town of Marsala is world famous for its rich-colored, sweet-tasting wine. In 1773 a British merchant named John Woodhouse happened upon Marsala and discovered that the wine there was as good as the port the British had long imported from Portugal. Two other wine merchants, Whitaker and Ingram, rushed in, and by 1800 Marsala was exporting its wine all over the British Empire.

Selinunte

⓳ *88 km (55 mi) southeast of Marsala, 15 km (9 mi) south of Castel-vetrano.*

Near the town of Castelvetrano, an overwhelming array of ruined Greek temples is perched on a plateau overlooking the Mediterranean at Selinunte. The city was one of the most superb colonies of ancient Greece. The original complex held seven temples scattered over two sites separated by a harbor. Of the seven, only one—reconstructed in 1958—still stands. Founded in the 7th century BC, Selinunte became the rich and prosperous rival of Segesta, which in 409 BC turned to the Carthaginians for help. The Carthaginians sent an army commanded by Hannibal to raze the city. The temples were demolished, the city was razed, and 16,000 of Selinunte's inhabitants were slaughtered. The beautiful metopes preserved in Palermo's Regional Archaeological Museum (☞ Palermo, *above*) come from the frieze of Temple E here. There is also a small museum at the site that contains other excavated pieces. Selinunte is named after a local variety of wild celery that in spring still grows profusely among the ruined columns and overturned capitals. ⊞ *Site and museum: 2,000 lire.* ☉ *Daily 9–1 hr before sunset.*

Agrigento

⓴ *100 km (60 mi) southeast of Selinunte, 126 km (79 mi) south of Palermo.*

Look out for the golden temples of Agrigento on a rise above the highway, a short distance inland from the sea. Agrigento, or Akragas as the Greeks called it, was settled by the Greeks in 580 BC and grew wealthy through trade with Carthage, just across the Mediterranean. Despite attacks from the Carthaginians at the end of the 5th century BC, the city survived through the Roman era, the Middle Ages (when it came under Arab and Norman rule), and into the modern age, and structures from all these eras sit side by side in Agrigento today. The birthplace of both the ancient Greek philosopher Empedocles and the modern Italian playwright Luigi Pirandello, Agrigento is a study in contrasts, but its chief attraction, the Valley of the Temples, remains one of the most impressive classical sites in all of Italy.

★ Coming upon the **Valley of the Temples** for the first time is a memorable moment—whether in the sunshine of spring, when they are surrounded by blossoming almond trees, or at night, when they are floodlit. Even in winter, when the vegetation is limited—perfectly limited—to agaves and gnarled gray olive trees, it is easy to understand why Pindar called Agrigento "the most beautiful city built by mortal men." Exiting from the highway, walk down from the parking lot on Via dei Templi and turn left.

㉑ The first temple you encounter as you enter the complex is the **Temple of Hercules**—eight pillars of the oldest temple in Agrigento, built during the 5th century BC. Up the hill from the Temple of Hercules, is
㉒ the **Temple of Concord,** one of the best-preserved Doric temples in the world and certainly the most impressive in Sicily. In the late afternoon, as the sun descends below the horizon, the temple's sandstone begins to change from honey-gold to pink russet, and the vertical lines of the fluted columns and their triangular pediment sharpen against the fading skyline. The columns were probably once covered by brightly painted stucco.

㉓ Follow up the Via Sacra to reach the **Temple of Juno,** which commands an exquisite view of the valley, especially at sunset. If you look carefully, you can see red fire marks on some of the columns—the result of the Carthaginian attack in 406 BC that destroyed the city. From the parking lot in the Piazzale dei Templi (where there is a bar selling drinks and ice cream), cross to the opposite side of the road, where some of the most
㉔ impressive ruins lie. The **Temple of Jupiter** is the largest temple ever planned in Sicily. Though never completed, it was considered the eighth wonder of the world. The nearby sleeping giant is a copy of one of the 38 colossal Atlas figures, or telamones, that supported the temple's immense roof. Note that the Temple of Jupiter is generally closed at 5.

The four columns supporting part of an entablature of the much-
㉕ photographed **Temple of Castor and Pollux,** have become a symbol of Agrigento, even though they were reconstructed in 1836, and probably from diverse buildings. At the end of Via dei Templi, where it turns
★ ㉖ left and becomes Via Petrarca, stands the **National Archaeological Museum,** which contains one of the original telamones, an impressive collection of Greek vases dating from the 7th century BC, and models of what the temples once looked like. ⊠ *Contrada San Nicola,* ☎ *0922/ 401565.* ☜ *Free.* ☉ *Daily 8–1 (hrs may vary; check for afternoon times).*

On the opposite side of the road from the archaeological museum is
㉗ the **Hellenistic and Roman Quarter,** which consists of four parallel streets, running north and south, that have been uncovered, along with the foundations of some houses from the Roman settlement (2nd century BC). Some of these streets still have their original mosaic pavements.

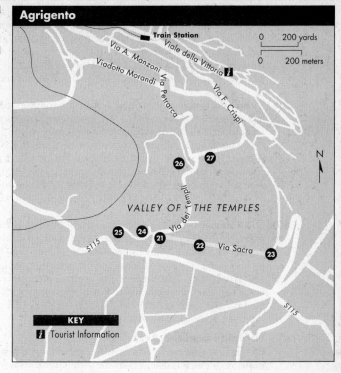

There is little reason to go up the hill to the rather dreary modern city of Agrigento, where industrial speculation keeps threatening to encroach upon the Valley of the Temples below—except to ring the doorbell at the **Convent of Santo Spirito** on the Salita di Santo Spirito off Via Porcello and try the *kus-kus* (sweet cake) made of pistachio nuts and chocolate, that the nuns there prepare.

OFF THE
BEATEN PATH

PIRANDELLO HOUSE – One of Agrigento's native sons was the distinguished dramatist Luigi Pirandello (1867–1936), whose plays, such as *Six Characters in Search of an Author,* express the fundamental ambiguity of life. Pirandello is buried under a pine tree behind the house where he was born, in Piazzale Caos, a few kilometers west of town. His house has been made into a museum of Pirandello memorabilia. Every year a festival of Pirandello's plays is held in Agrigento from late July to early August. ☎ 0922/511102. 🎟 *Free.* ⊙ *Weekdays 9–1:30 and 3–5:45, Sat. 9–1:30.*

Dining and Lodging

$$ ✕ **Caprice.** The specialty of this popular restaurant in the temple area is meat prepared alla brace, although there is also a good selection of seafood, particularly pesce spada. The waiters—when they are not rushed—are proud to explain some of the less-familiar entries on the wine list, which is relatively extensive. ⊠ *Via Panoramica dei Templi 51,* ☎ *0922/26469. AE, DC, MC, V. Closed Fri. and July 1–15.*

$$ ✕ **Taverna Mosè.** This restaurant can get busy in the early evening, when it becomes too dark for temple exploring. The atmosphere bustles with waiters shouting orders at each other and at the kitchen. The house specialties are homemade sausages and grilled fish, and the wine list is varietal, so to speak. ⊠ *Contrada San Biagio,* ☎ *0922/26778. AE. Closed Mon. and Aug.*

$$ ✕ **Vigneto.** Unless you make reservations at this popular restaurant, it's best to arrive early to snag one of the good tables on the terrace, which has a memorable view of the temples. Seasonal daily specials and the fish market's freshest top the changing menu. *Arrosti* (roast meats) are always a good bet. ⊠ *Via Cavaleri Magazzeni 11,* ☎ *0922/ 414319. Reservations essential. AE, MC, V. Closed Tues. and Nov.*

$$$ 🏨 **Jolly dei Templi.** Guests travel 8 km (5 mi) southeast of town to Villagio Mosè to stay in this Jolly hotel. Rooms are large, bright, and airy, and if there's a sense of having seen it all before, you probably have—in one of the other Jolly hotels or in any well-equipped U.S. motel. That is the price to pay for what are always comfortable, hassle-free accommodations. The Pirandello restaurant here is excellent, so you won't have to head into Agrigento to dine. ⊠ *Parco Angeli, Villagio Mosè, 92100,* ☎ *0922/606144,* 𝐅𝐀𝐗 *0922/606685. 144 rooms. Restaurant, bar, pool. AE, DC, MC, V.*

$$$ 🏨 **Villa Athena.** There is much demand for this well-furnished former
★ villa right in the midst of the archaeological zone, so make reservations as early as possible. Many rooms—they're all different—have terraces looking out on the large gardens and the swimming pool. The temples are an easy walk from the hotel, and there is a convivial atmosphere in the bar, where a multinational crowd swaps stories. ⊠ *Via dei Templi 33, 92100,* ☎ *0922/596288,* 𝐅𝐀𝐗 *0922/402180. 40 rooms. Restaurant, bar, pool. AE, DC, MC, V.*

Nightlife and the Arts

On the first weekend in February, Agrigento hosts a **Festa delle Mandorle,** or Almond Blossom Festival, with international folk dances, a costumed parade, and the sale of marzipan and other sweets made from almonds.

EASTERN SICILY

On the Road to Taormina

Sicily's interior is for the most part underpopulated and untrammeled, though the Imperial Roman Villa at Casale, outside Piazza Armerina, gives precious evidence from an epoch gone by. Don't miss Caltagirone, a ceramics center of renown. On the coast, Siracusa offers a fascinating mix of ancient Greek, Renaissance, and Baroque architecture with some excellent museums. To the north, Catania packs the vivacity of Palermo, if not the artistic wealth; the city makes a good base for exploring lofty Mt. Etna, as does Taormina. Messina's scant attractions include unparalleled position opposite the mountains of Calabria, one of the island's best museum collections.

Enna

28 *105 km (63 mi) northeast of Agrigento, 136 km (85 mi) southeast of Palermo, 85 km (53 mi) west of Catania.*

Deep in Sicily's interior, the fortress city of Enna commands exceptional views of the rolling plains surrounding it, and, in the distance, Mt. Etna. The narrow winding streets are dominated at one end by the impressive castle built by Frederick II, easily visible as you approach the town.

Piazza Armerina

29 *40 km (25 mi) south of Enna, 110 km (69 mi) west of Catania.*

Reached through pine and eucalyptus woods and low farmland, Piazza Armerina is a tiny Baroque town noted mainly for the sumptuous emperor's Imperial Roman Villa country house nearby (☞ *below*).

Dining

$$ ✕ **Centrale da Totò.** At this reliable trattoria, the emphasis is on a family clientele, rather than intimate or expense-account dining, and the portions reflect this *mangia, mangia* outlook. Try the *pappardelle alla Centrale* (wide pasta with a rich tomato sauce and fresh vegetables). ⊠ *Via Mazzini 29*, ☎ *0935/680153. AE, DC, MC, V. Closed Mon. Oct.–Mar.*

Nightlife and the Arts

The **Palio dei Normanni,** a medieval tournament with participants dressed in 14th-century fashion, takes place on August 13.

Casale

30 *6 km (4 mi) southwest of Piazza Armerina.*

The exceptionally well-preserved **Imperial Roman Villa** here is thought to have been a hunting lodge of the Emperor Maximianus Heraclius (4th century AD). The excavations were not begun until 1950, and all the wall decorations and vaulting have been lost. However, some of the best mosaics of the Roman world cover more than 12,000 square ft under a shelter shaped to give an idea of the layout of the original buildings. The mosaics were probably made by Carthaginian artisans, because they are similar to those in the Tunis Bardo Museum. The entrance was through a triumphal arch that led into an atrium surrounded by a portico of columns. Through this, the *thermae,* or bathhouse, is reached. It is colorfully decorated with mosaic nymphs, a Neptune, and slaves massaging bathers. The peristyle leads to the main villa, where in the Salone del Circo you look down on mosaics that illustrate Roman circus sports. Another apartment shows hunting scenes of tigers, elephants, and ostriches; the gym shows girls exercising; the private apartments are covered with scenes from Greek and Roman mythology; and Room 38 even reveals a touch of eroticism. ⊠ *Imperial Roman Villa, Casale,* ☎ *0935/680036.* ⌨ *2,000 lire.* ☺ *Daily 9– 1 hr before sunset.*

Caltagirone

31 *30 km (18 mi) southeast of Piazza Armerina, 60 km (37 mi) southwest of Catania.*

Built over three hills, the charming Baroque town of Caltagirone is a leader in the Sicilian ceramics industry. Here you will find majolica balustrades, tile-decorated windowsills, and a monumental **tile staircase** of 142 steps—each decorated with a different pattern. On the feast of San Giacomo (July 24), the staircase is illuminated with candles that form a tapestry design over the steps. It is the result of months of work preparing the 4,000 *coppi*, or cylinders of colored paper that hold oil lamps. At 9:30 PM on July 24, a squad of hundreds of boys springs into action to light the lamps, so that the staircase flares up all at once. There is an interesting **Ceramics Museum** in the public gardens, which were designed by Basile, the master of Sicilian Art Nouveau. The exhibits in the museum trace the history of the craft from specimens excavated from the earliest settlements, through the influential Arab period, to the present. ⊠ *Museo Regionale della Ceramica, Giardino Pubblico,* ☎ *0933/21680.* ⌨ *Free.* ☺ *Daily 9–6.*

Shopping

CERAMICS

The ceramic creations of **De Simone**, whose Picasso-like faces on plates and pitchers are popular abroad, can be seen at the shop, **Akatos** (⊠ Via Romeo 14).

Palazzolo Acreide

③② *60 km (40 mi) east of Caltagirone, 40 km (25 mi) west of Trapani.*

This small inland town is best known for its archaeological zone, the old Greek *Akrai,* containing the foundations of a temple dedicated to Aphrodite, and a well-preserved theater.

Dining

$ ✕ **Da Alfredo.** This one-man show (Alfredo is the owner-chef) is on one of the most attractive streets of this Baroque town between Caltagirone and Siracusa. Specialties depend on the season and the whims of Alfredo himself. Homemade pasta, such as tubular penne and cheese-filled ravioli, are specialties, and the sauces are hearty and spicy. During the summer, Alfredo transfers to Fontane Bianche, a seaside resort south of Siracusa. ⊠ *Via Duca d'Aosta 27,* ☎ *0931/883266. AE. Closed Wed. and June–Sept. 10.*

Siracusa

③③ *100 km (60 mi) east of Caltagirone, 60 km (37 mi) south of Catania.*

Greek Sicily began along the Ionian coast, and some of the finest examples of Baroque art and architecture were also created here, particularly in Siracusa. The city was founded in 734 BC by Greek colonists from Corinth and soon grew to rival, and even surpass, Athens in splendor and power. Siracusa became the largest, wealthiest city-state in Magna Graecia and the bulwark of Greek civilization. Although it suffered from tyrannical rule, kings such as Dionysius filled their courts in the 5th century BC with Greeks of the highest artistic stature—among them, Pindar, Aeschylus, and Archimedes. The Athenians did not welcome the rise of Siracusa and sent a fleet to destroy the rival city, but the natives outsmarted them in what was one of the greatest naval battles of ancient history (413 BC). Siracusa continued to prosper until it was conquered two centuries later by the Romans.

There are essentially two areas to explore in Siracusa—the Archaeological Park, on the mainland, and the island of Ortygia, the ancient city first inhabited by the Greeks, which juts out into the Ionian sea and is connected to the mainland by two small bridges.

The **Archaeological Park,** at the western edge of town, contains the ruins of a fine **Roman amphitheater** and the most complete **Greek theater** existing from antiquity. A comparison of these two structures reveals much about the differences between the Greek and Roman personalities. The Greek theater, in which the plays of Aeschylus premiered, was hewn out of the hillside rock in the 5th century BC. All the seats converge upon a single point—the stage—which had the natural scenery and the sky as its background. Drama as a kind of religious ritual was the intention here. In the Roman amphitheater, however, the emphasis was on the spectacle of combative sports and the circus. The arena is one of the largest of its kind and was built around the 2nd century AD. The corridor where gladiators and beasts entered the ring is still intact, and the seats, some of which still bear the occupants' names, were hauled in and constructed on the site from huge slabs of limestone. A crowd-pleasing show, and not the elevation of men's minds, was the intention here. Climb to the top of the seating area in the Greek theater, which could accommodate 15,000, for a fine view. In May and June of even-numbered years, performances of Greek tragedies are held here. If the Archaeological Park is closed, go up Viale G. Rizzo from Viale Teracati, to the belvedere overlooking the ruins, which are flood-lit at night.

Near the entrance to the park is the gigantic **altar of Hieron,** which was once used by the Greeks for spectacular sacrifices involving hun-dreds of animals. Just beyond the ticket office you will come upon a lush tropical garden full of palm and citrus trees. This is the **Latomie del Paradiso,** a series of quarries that served as prisons for the defeated Athenians, who were enslaved; the quarries once rang with the sound of their chisels and hammers. At one end is the Orecchio di Dionisio, with an ear-shape entrance and unusual acoustics inside, as you'll dis-cover if you clap your hands. The legend is that Dionysius used to lis-ten in at the top of the quarry to hear what the slaves were plotting below. ✉ *Viale Augusto,* ☎ *0931/66206.* 🎟 *2,000 lire.* ⊘ *Daily 9–1 hr before sunset (last tickets sold 2 hrs before sunset).*

Not far from the Archaeological Park, off Viale Teocrito, are the **cat-acombs** of San Giovanni, one of the earliest-known Christian sites in the city. Inside the crypt of San Marciano is an altar where St. Paul preached on his way through Sicily to Rome. The frescoes in this small chapel are still bright and fresh, though some date from the 4th cen-tury AD. ✉ *Piazza San Giovanni.* 🎟 *4,000 lire.* ⊘ *Mid-Mar.–mid-Nov., daily 9–6; mid-Nov.–mid-Mar., daily 9–1 and 3–6.*

The impressive collection contained in Siracusa's splendid **Archaeological Museum** is arranged by region around a central atrium and ranges from neolithic pottery to fine Greek statues and vases. You will want to com-pare the Landolina Venus—a headless, stout goddess of love who rises out of the sea in measured modesty (she is a 1st-century-AD Roman copy of the Greek original)—with the much earlier (300 BC) elegant Greek statue of Hercules in Section C. Of a completely different type is a marvelous fanged Gorgon, its tongue sticking out, that once adorned the cornice of the temple of Athena in order to ward off evil-doers. The pieces are generally well lit, and there are also several in-teresting, instructive exhibits. One depicts the Temple of Apollo, the oldest Doric temple in Sicily, on the island of Ortygia. ✉ *Viale Teocrito,* ☎ *0931/464022.* 🎟 *2,000 lire.* ⊘ *Tues.–Sat. 9–1, Sun. 9–1:30. Closed 1st and 3rd Sun. of the month.*

Close to Siracusa's Archaeological Museum, the **Papyrus Museum** demonstrates how papyruses are prepared from reeds and then painted—an ancient tradition in the city. Siracusa, it seems, has the only climate outside the Nile Valley in which the papyrus plant—from which we get our word "paper"—thrives. ✉ *Viale Teocrito 66,* ☎ *0931/61616.* 🎟 *Free.* ⊘ *Tues.–Sun. 9–2.*

The central part of Siracusa is a modern city, with Corso Gelone its main shopping street. At its southern end, Corso Umberto leads to the **Ortygia Island** bridge, which crosses a pretty harbor lined with fish restau-rants. In the piazza on the other side of the bridge, you'll find the ruins of the **Temple of Apollo** depicted in the Archaeological Museum. In fact, little of this noble Doric temple still remains today, except for some crumbled walls and shattered columns, along with a fragment (the win-dow in the south wall) of a Norman church that was built much later on the same spot. ✉ *Piazza Pancali.*

Apart from the Temple of Apollo, Ortygia is composed almost entirely of warm, restrained Baroque buildings. This uniformity is the result of an earthquake in 1693 that necessitated major rebuilding at a time when the Baroque was very popular. Wander into the backstreets—especially along Via della Maestranza or Via Veneto—and notice the bulbous wrought-iron balconies (said to have been invented to accommodate ladies' billowing skirts), the window surrounds and cornices of buildings decorated with mermaids and gargoyles, and the stucco decoration on Palazzo Lantieri on Via Roma.

Ortygia's main piazzas are **Piazza Archimede**, with its Baroque fountain festooned with fainting sea nymphs and dancing jets of water, and ★ **Piazza del Duomo,** one of Italy's most beautiful piazzas. The **Duomo** is an archive of island history, beginning with the bottommost excavations that have unearthed remnants of Sicily's distant past, when the Siculi inhabitants worshiped their deities here. During the 5th century BC, the Greeks built a temple to Athena over it, and in the 7th century, Siracusa's first Christian cathedral was built on top of the Greek structure. The elegant columns of the original temple were incorporated into the present structure and are clearly visible, embedded in the exterior wall along Via Minerva. The Greek columns were also used to dramatic advantage inside, where on one side they form chapels connected by elegant wrought-iron gates. The Baroque facade, added in 1700, displays a harmonious rhythm of concaves and convexes. In front, the piazza is encircled by pink and white oleanders and elegant buildings ornamented with filigree grillwork. ⊠ *Piazza del Duomo.*

In the right corner of Piazza del Duomo is the elegant **Palazzo Beneventano del Bosco,** with an impressive interior courtyard ending in a grand winding staircase. At one end of Piazza del Duomo stands the Baroque church of **Santa Lucia alla Badia,** with an engaging wrought-iron balcony and pleasing facade. Siracusa's **Regional Museum** is housed inside Palazzo Bellomo, a lovely Catalan-Gothic building with mullioned windows and an elegant exterior staircase. Among the select group of paintings and sculptures inside is a Santa Lucia by Caravaggio and a damaged, but still brilliant, *Annunciation* by Antonello da Messina. ⊠ *Via Capodieci 14,* ☎ *0931/69617.* ▱ *2,000 lire.* ☾ *Mon.–Sat. 9–1:30, Sun. 9–12:30.*

Just off the promenade along the harbor, you'll find the **Fountain of Arethusa,** a freshwater spring next to the sea. This anomaly is explained by a Greek legend that tells how the nymph Arethusa was changed into a fountain by the goddess Artemis (Diana) when she tried to escape the advances of the river god Alpheus. She fled from Greece, into the sea, with Alpheus in close pursuit, and emerged in Sicily at this spring. Supposedly even today, if you throw a cup into the River Alpheus in Greece, it will emerge here at this fountain, which at present is home to a few tired ducks and some dull-colored carp—but no cups. Steps lead to the tree-lined promenade along the harbor front, where you can buy a drink and watch the ships come in. The southern tip of Ortygia island is occupied by the **Castello Maniace,** now an army barracks but once a castle of Frederick II, from which there are fine views of the sea.

North of the city, on the highlands that overlook the sea, the fortress of **Euryalus** was created by Dionysius, with the help of Archimedes, for protection against the Carthaginians. This astonishing boat-shape structure once covered 15,000 square yards. The intricate maze of tunnels is fascinating, and the view from the heights is superb. ⊠ *Belvedere, 8 km (5 mi) northwest of Siracusa.* ☾ *Daily 9–1 hr before sunset.*

Dining and Lodging

$$–$$$ ✕ **Ionico.** Enjoy seaside dining in the coastal Santa Lucia district. The
★ Ionico boasts a terrace and veranda for alfresco meals, and the inte-

rior is plastered with diverse historical relics and has a cheerful open hearth for the winter. Chef-proprietor Roberto Giudice cooks meals to order or will suggest a specialty from a selection of market-fresh ingredients. Try the pasta *con acciughe e il pan grattato* (in an anchovy sauce). ⊠ *Riviera Dionisio il Grande 194,* ☎ *0931/65540. AE, DC, MC, V. Closed Tues.*

$$ ✕ **Archimede.** The antipasto misto should whet your appetite for the predominantly seafood menu of this small establishment in the Old Town. Risotto di mare and pesce spada are specialties, but the menu veers away from seafood when game is in season. Otherwise, sample the involtini *all'Archimede* (stuffed with cheese and ham, baked in bread crumbs). ⊠ *Via Gemmellaro 8,* ☎ *0931/69701. AE, DC, MC, V. No dinner Sun.*

$$ ✕ **Arlecchino.** A bustling bohemian atmosphere pervades this restaurant, found midway between the archaeological zone and the Old Town. It's popular with artists and students, always a sign of good value. The Palermo-born proprietor serves specialties from his hometown, such as risotto *ai ricci* (with sea urchins) and homemade cassata for dessert. ⊠ *Via dei Tolomei 5,* ☎ *0931/66386. AE, DC, MC, V. Closed Mon. and (sometimes) Aug.*

$$ ✕ **Minosse.** You'll find this small, old-fashioned restaurant in the heart of Siracusa's Città Vecchia. Fish is the specialty, and it comes broiled, baked, stuffed, and skewered. For an introduction to the local seafood, try the antipasto misto di frutti di mare. Ask for the daily special as your main course, or try the pesce spada alla brace. The zuppa di pesce is a local favorite. ⊠ *Via Mirabella 6,* ☎ *0931/66366. AE, MC, V. Closed Mon. (may remain open daily in Apr.–Sept.).*

$$$ ☷ **Forte Agip.** This standard motel, with modern comforts is across the street from the archaeological zone. The rooms are bright and clean, and the restaurant serves some local specialties as well as classic hotel food. ⊠ *Viale Teracati 30, 96100,* ☎ *0931/463232,* ℻ *0931/67115. 87 rooms. Restaurant, bar, minibars. AE, DC, MC, V.*

$$$ ☷ **Jolly Hotel.** The rooms are uniformly comfortable in this member of the Jolly hotel chain, Italy's answer to Holiday Inns. The big advantage, apart from knowing that the plugs work and the rooms are soundproofed, is the location. The hotel is ½ km (¼ mi) from the train station and within easy walking distance of the archaeological zone. ⊠ *Corso Gelone 45, 96100,* ☎ *0931/461111,* ℻ *0931/461126. 100 rooms. Restaurant, bar. AE, DC, MC, V.*

Nightlife and the Arts

The feast of the city's patroness, Santa Lucia (St. Lucy), is held on December 13 at **Santa Lucia alla Badia** (⊠ Piazza del Duomo). A splendid silver statue of the saint is carried from the cathedral to the church on the site of her martyrdom, near the Catacombs of San Giovanni. A torchlight procession and band music accompany the bearers. In May and June 1998, Siracusa's impressive **Greek Theater** (⊠ Archaeological Park, ☎ 0931/67710) will be the setting for performances of classical drama and comedy; the festival is held in even-numbered years only.

Noto

32 km (20 mi) southwest of Siracusa.

Modeled on a hierarchical plan following the destruction of the old town during the great earthquake of 1693, Noto presents a pleasing ensemble of honey-colored Baroque architecture, strikingly uniform in style, but never dull. Its centerpiece is the majestic Duomo, completed in 1776, atop a broad flight of steps.

Dining

$ X **Il Giglio.** Seafood dishes with a Spanish touch are the specialty at
this pleasant trattoria in the center of town run by Maria Luz Corruchaga
and her husband, Corrado. Particularly recommended are pasta *al nero
di seppia* (with cuttlefish) and *zuppa di vongole e cozze* (clam and mus-
sel soup), though you won't find these on the good-value tourist menu.
Paella is a pleasant surprise. ⊠ *Piazza Municipio,* ☎ *0931/838640.
AE, MC, V. No lunch Sat.*

Catania

③④ *60 km (37 mi) north of Siracusa, 94 km (59 mi) south of Messina.*

The chief wonder of Catania, Sicily's second city, is that it is there at all.
Its successive populations were deported by one Greek tyrant, sold into
slavery by another, and driven out by the Carthaginians. Every time the
city got back on its feet, it was struck by a new calamity: plague decimated the population in the Middle Ages, a mile-wide stream of lava
from Mt. Etna swallowed most of the city in 1669, and 25 years later a
disastrous earthquake forced the Catanese to begin again. Today the city
needs considerable renovation. Traffic flows in ever-increasing volume
and adds to the smog from the industrial zone between Catania and Siracusa, but the views of Mt. Etna from Catania are superb. To Mt. Etna,
Catania also owes a fertile surrounding plain and its site on nine successive layers of lava. Many of Catania's buildings are constructed from
solidified lava, and the black lava stone has given the city a singular appearance. As a result, Catania is known as the city of lava and oranges.
Catania's greatest native son is the composer Vincenzo Bellini, whose
operas have thrilled audiences since their premieres about 170 years ago.
His home, now the **Bellini Museum,** in Piazza San Francesco, preserves
memorabilia of the man and his work. ⊠ *Piazza San Francesco 3,* ☎
095/7150535. ▧ *Free.* ☉ *Mon.–Sat. 9–1:30, Sun. 9–12:30.*

The **Villa Bellini** (⊠ To the north, just off Via Etnea), Catania's public gardens, on clear days has lovely views of snowcapped Mt. Etna.
The **Duomo** (⊠ At the bottom end of Via Etnea), is a fine work by Vac-
carini (1736), as is the obelisk-balancing elephant carved out of lava
stone in the piazza in front. Bellini is buried inside the cathedral. Also
inside is the sumptuous chapel of St. Agatha, Catania's patron saint,
who is credited with having held off, more than once, the fiery flows
of lava that threatened the city. During her feast (February 3–5), huge
16-ft-tall, highly ornate carved wooden *cannelore* (large bundles of candles) are paraded through the streets at night.

NEED A   If you haven't had cannoli yet in Sicily, the pastry shops along Via Etnea
BREAK?   are good places to try one of these wafer tubes filled with silky smooth
              ricotta cheese. If you're in need of something more substantial, duck into
              one of the trattorias along this street and order a dish of pasta *alla
              Norma.* It's named after one of Bellini's most famous operas and con-
              sists of short pasta with a rich eggplant-and-tomato sauce, garnished
              with basil leaves and grated ricotta cheese.

Dining and Lodging

$$$ X **Costa Azzurra.** As this seafood restaurant is in the Ognina district,
 ★   reserve a table on the veranda by the edge of the sea. There are good
views of the harbor. The fritto misto can be ordered as an antipasto
or a main course, and the pesce spada steak is a simple classic—served
grilled with a large slice of lemon. ⊠ *Via De Cristofaro 4 in Ognina,
just north of the center, on the way to the Taormina road,* ☎ *095/494920.
Jacket and tie. AE, DC, MC, V. Closed Mon.*

$$ ✕ **Pagano.** This restaurant, behind the Hotel Excelsior, has been around since the 1950s and remains a favorite with locals for genuine Catanese cooking. Seafood is the specialty, but it's the unpretentious kind that won't jettison the check into the stratosphere. Try *insalata di polipo* (octopus salad) as a starter and then sarde or *acciughe* (anchovies) in a variety of sauces. Like the sober, rather dated decor, the service is formal. ⊠ *Via De Roberto 37,* ☎ *095/537045. AE, DC, MC, V. Closed Aug. 15. No lunch Sat.*

$$$ ⊞ **Excelsior.** Ask for a room facing Piazza Verga, a neat tree-lined square in this quiet but central district of Catania. The Excelsior has air-conditioning and sound-insulated windows in all rooms. The rooftop garden is one of Catania's most chic meeting places, and the American Bar should provide solace to anyone waxing nostalgic for a Manhattan. ⊠ *Piazza Verga 39, 95129,* ☎ *095/537071,* FAX *095/537015. 158 rooms. Restaurant, bar. AE, DC, MC, V.*

$$ ⊞ **Savona.** The Savona is an efficiently run and well-maintained hotel a stone's throw from Piazza del Duomo. The rooms are spacious and comfortable, solidly furnished, and equipped with TV and telephones. Prices include Continental breakfast. Parking may be a problem. ⊠ *Via Vittorio Emanuele 210, 95124,* ☎ *095/326982,* FAX *095/7158169. 25 rooms, 15 with shower. Bar. No credit cards.*

Nightlife and the Arts

Teatro Bellini (⊠ Piazza Bellini, Catania, ☎ 095/7306111) hosts an opera season from October to mid-June, attracting top singers and productions to the birthplace of the great operatic composer Vincenzo Bellini.

Mt. Etna

★ ③⑤ *30 km (19 mi) north of Catania, 60 km (37 mi) south of Messina.*

Catania is the departure point for excursions around—but not always to the top of—Mt. Etna. Buses leave from in front of the train station in early morning, or you can take the Circumetnea railroad around the volcano's base. Mt. Etna is one of the world's major active volcanoes and is the largest and highest in Europe. The cone of the crater rises to 10,958 ft above sea level. It has erupted 10 times in the past three decades, most spectacularly in 1971 and 1983, when rivers of molten lava destroyed the two highest stations of the cable car that rises from the town of Sapienza. Travel in the proximity of the crater depends on Mt. Etna's temperament, but you can walk up and down the enormous lava dunes and wander over its moonlike surface of dead craters. The rings of vegetation change markedly as you rise, with vineyards and pine trees gradually giving way to growths of broom and lichen.

Taormina

★ ③⑥ *43 km (27 mi) southwest of Messina, 50 km (31 mi) north of Catania.*

The natural beauty of the medieval mountaintop town of Taormina is so great that even the considerable overdevelopment that it has suffered in the past 50 years has not spoiled its grandeur. The view of the sea and Mt. Etna from its jagged cactus-covered cliffs is as close to perfection as a panorama can get, especially on clear days when the snow-capped volcano's white puffs of smoke are etched against the blue sky. Writers have extolled Taormina's beauty almost since its founding in the 6th century BC by Greeks from Naples. Goethe and D. H. Lawrence were among its enthusiasts. The Greeks put a lofty premium on finding impressive locations to stage their dramas, and Taormina's **Greek**

Theater occupies one of the finest sites of any such theater. It was built during the 3rd century BC and rebuilt by the Romans during the 2nd century AD. Its acoustics are exceptional: even today a stage whisper can be heard in the last rows. In summer, Taormina hosts an arts festival of music, film, and dance events, many of which are held in the Greek Theater (☞ *below*) ✉ *Via Teatro Greco*. 🎫 *2,000 lire*. ⊙ *Daily 9–2 hrs before sunset*.

The main street in town is **Corso Umberto,** which is lined with boutiques and antiques shops. There are also the inevitable, and all too numerous, shops selling cheap pottery and jewelry made from Mt. Etna's black lava stone, but **Piazza 9 Aprile,** along the Corso, commands wonderful views and is the perfect place to sit and have a cappuccino.

Taormina's many 14th- and 15th-century palaces have been carefully preserved. Especially beautiful is the **Palazzo Corvaja** (✉ Palazzo Corvaja, Largo Santa Caterina, ☎ 0942/23243), with characteristic black-lava and white-limestone inlays. Today it houses the tourist office. The medieval **Castello Saraceno** (✉ Monte Tauro), enticingly perched on an adjoining cliff above the town, can be reached by footpath or car.

NEED A BREAK?   If a marzipan devotee, you should not leave Taormina without trying it at **Bar Mocambo** (✉ Piazza 9 Aprile). It's shaped and colored into various fruits, including the ubiquitous *fico d'India* (prickly pear).

Dining and Lodging

$$-$$$ ✕ **Delfino.** This seaside restaurant is across the road from the cable-★ car station in Mazzarò, to the east of Taormina proper. Seafood takes pride of place here, from hearty starters, such as the zuppa di pesce or risotto marinara, to main courses like *gamberetti* (shrimp) alla brace. Arrive early or reserve one of the best tables overlooking the sea. ✉ *Via Nazionale, Mazzarò,* ☎ 0942/23004. *AE, DC, MC, V. Closed Nov.– Easter.*

$$ ✕ **Luraleo.** You can dine indoors by candlelight or in the vine-covered garden in summer. It's touristy, but the food is of a high standard, with the accent on fish—delight in the different risotto with salmon and pistachios, a house specialty. There is a rich selection of antipasti. Service can be slow. ✉ *Via Bagnoli Croci 27,* ☎ *0942/24279. DC, MC, V. Closed Wed. Oct.–June.*

$$$$ 🏨 **San Domenico Palace.** Sweeping views from this converted 15th-★ century convent will linger in your mind long after you're gone. Luxury and comfort are bywords in this deluxe hotel, which has managed to sneak a number of unobtrusive 20th-century comforts in (such as wheelchair access and climate control). The essential Renaissance flavor is preserved, however, with the cloisters and the chapel, now a bar. Rooms are brimming with antiques and fresh flowers. ✉ *Piazza San Domenico 5, 98039,* ☎ *0942/23701,* 𝖥𝖠𝖷 *0942/625506. 111 rooms. 2 restaurants, 2 bars, pool. AE, DC, MC, V.*

$$$ 🏨 **Jolly Diodoro.** High on a cliff near the Greek amphitheater, this hotel commands superlative views. A departure from the sometimes functional Jolly mold is the relaxing, sprightly garden, where you can have a drink and watch the play of light over the sea. ✉ *Via Bagnoli Croce 75, 98039,* ☎ *0942/23312,* 𝖥𝖠𝖷 *0942/23391. 103 rooms. Restaurant, bar, pool. AE, DC, MC, V.*

$$-$$$ 🏨 **Villa Fiorita.** This converted private home near the Greek amphitheater has excellent northerly coastal views from nearly every room. Rooms vary in size and furnishings, but most are bright, breezy, and colorful, with large windows and balconies (do ask). Prices are reasonable considering the compact swimming pool and garden. Note that

the elevator is at the top of 65 steps. ⌧ *Via Pirandello 39, 98039,* ☎ *0942/24122,* F̄A̅X̄ *0942/625967. 24 rooms. Pool, sauna. AE, MC, V.*

Nightlife and the Arts

CONCERTS

The Palazzo dei Congressi, near the entrance to the Greek theater, is the venue for the summer festival of **classical music,** held each year from May to September. For information, call 0942/21142, or check with the tourist office.

FILM FESTIVAL

Taormina hosts an international **film festival** each July and August in the grand setting of the Roman amphitheater. For information, call 0942/23220.

THEATER

Taormina's **Greek Theater** is the setting for regular theatrical performances from July to September. For information, call 0942/23220.

Shopping

ANTIQUES

Pieces of carretti siciliani sometimes surface at **Chez le Français** (⌧ Piazza San Domenico 6).

Castelmola

5 km (3 mi) west of Taormina.

If your passion for heights hasn't been quelled, visit Castelmola, the tiny town above Taormina, where the Bar Turrisi makes its own refreshing almond wine—the perfect complement to the spectacular 360-degree panorama.

Dining

$$ ✕ **Il Faro.** As you sit under a grape arbor in this family-run country
★ restaurant, the wild cliffs and sea unfurl in views below. Meat dishes are recommended alla brace, particularly *pollo* (chicken) and *coniglio* (rabbit). Owners Piera and Francesco make the antipasto with home-grown vegetables. Start your meal with *bruschetta all'ortolana* (country bread toasted with olive oil, topped with tomatoes and onions). ⌧ *Via Rotabile, Contrada Petralia,* ☎ *0942/28193. No credit cards. Closed Wed. (may close Oct.–Mar.).*

En Route The 50-km (30-mi) stretch of road between Taormina and Messina is flanked by lush vegetation and seascapes. Inlets punctuated by gigantic oddly shaped rocks distract from the road. It was along this coast, legend says, that the giant one-eyed cyclopes hurled their boulders down on Ulysses and his terrified men as they fled to the sea and on to their next adventure in Homer's *Odyssey.*

Messina

㊲ *43 km (27 mi) northeast of Taormina, 94 km (59 mi) northeast of Catania.*

Messina's ancient history tells of series of disasters, but the city nevertheless managed to develop a fine university and a thriving cultural environment. But at 5 o'clock in the morning on December 28, 1908, Messina changed from a flourishing metropolis of 120,000 to a heap of rubble, shaken to pieces by an earthquake that turned into a tidal wave and left 80,000 dead and the city almost completely leveled. As you approach the sickle-shape bay, through which ferries connect Sicily to the mainland, you see nothing of relatively recent disaster, except for the modern countenance of a 3,000-year-old city. The somewhat flat look is a precaution of seismic planning: tall buildings are not permitted.

The reconstruction of Messina's **Duomo** (originally constructed by the Norman King Roger II in 1197) has retained much of the original plan, including a handsome crown of Norman battlements, an enormous apse, and a splendid wood-beam ceiling. The adjoining **bell tower**—of a much later date—is one of the city's principal attractions. It contains one of the largest and most complex mechanical clocks in the world, constructed in 1933 with a host of gilded automatons—a roaring lion, a crowing rooster, and numerous biblical figures—that spring into action every day at the stroke of noon. ⊠ *Piazza del Duomo.*

NEED A BREAK?	**Billé** (⊠ Corner of Piazza Cairoli and Via Cannizzaro) proffers good lunchtime snacks, if you don't mind standing up. You can sample (or take away) such typical Sicilian snacks as *arancini* (deep-fried, breaded rice balls stuffed with cheese or meat sauce), mozzarella in *carrozza* (deep-fried bread pockets), and *piddoni* (savory parcels of mozzarella or vegetables).

Messina is the birthplace of the great Renaissance painter Antonello da Messina, whose *Polyptych of the Rosary* (1473) can be viewed along with two large Caravaggios in the **Regional Museum,** along the sea in the northern outskirts of the city. ⊠ *Viale della Libertà,* ☎ *090/ 361292.* ⊡ *2,000 lire.* ☉ *Mon., Wed., Fri. 9–1:30; Tues., Thurs., Sat. 9–1:30 and 3–5:30; Sun. 9–12:30.*

OFF THE BEATEN PATH	**REGGIO DI CALABRIA** – From Messina, a hydrofoil will speed you across the strait to this city on the toe of the boot, where two larger-than-life-size 5th-century Greek bronze statues are exhibited in the excellent **National Museum of Magna Graecia.** The statues—known as the Riace bronzes—were found by accident by an amateur deep-sea diver off the coast of Calabria in 1972 and are worth going out of your way to see. ⊠ *Piazza de Nava, Corso Garibaldi,* ☎ *0965/812255.* ⊡ *8,000 lire.* ☉ *Daily 9–6:30. Closed 1st and 3rd Sun. of the month Oct.–Mar.*

Dining

$$$ ✕ **Alberto.** Transferred from the center of town to Mortelle, Messina's
★   seaside satellite 10 km (6 mi) up the coast, this deluxe restaurant still brings in plenty of business. If you're adventurous and feeling flush, have the waiter order for you: you'll get a succession of seafood courses. À la carte items are also delicious, particularly the spaghetti con frutti di mare *al cartoccio* (cooked in silver foil) and the involtini di pesce spada. Vintage Marsala sipped with one of the rich homemade desserts makes for a grand finale. ⊠ *Via Nazionale, Mortelle,* ☎ *090/ 321009. AE, DC, MC, V. Closed Mon. and Jan.*

$$ ✕ **Pran Pron.** A change of ownership does not seem to have significantly altered the tone or standards of this bastion of traditional Sicilian cooking. The kitchen still turns out favorite appetizers of smoked salmon and pesce spada; you can also have the risotto di mare that changes with each day's catch of fish. The *bistecca* (steak) here is charcoal grilled and renowned locally. There are now two fixed-price menus, so let's hope that the standards are maintained, along with the antiques and refined decor. ⊠ *Via Ugo Bassi 157,* ☎ *090/2938584. AE, MC, V. Closed Wed. and 2–3 wks in July–Aug. No dinner Sun.*

Nightlife and the Arts

Messina stages a **folklore parade** of huge traditional effigies, called Giganti, each year on August 13 and 14.

THE AEOLIAN ISLANDS

Just off Sicily's northeast coast lies an archipelago of seven spectacular islands of volcanic origin. The Aeolian Islands were named after Aeolus, the Greek god of the winds, who is said to keep all the Earth's winds stuffed in a bag in his cave here. The Aeolians are a fascinating world of grottoes and clear-water caves carved by the waves through the centuries. Superb snorkeling or scuba diving abounds. All Sicily's islands—and these seven in particular—are extremely popular in summer, and some of them are unpleasantly overcrowded in July and August. Access is gained via ferry and hydrofoil from Sicily only (☞ Getting Around *in* Sicily A to Z, *below*). Lipari provides the best range of accommodations and is a good jumping-off point for day trips to the other islands.

The bars in the Aeolian Islands, and especially those on Lipari, are known for their granite of fresh strawberries, melon, peaches, and other fruits. Many Sicilians, especially Aeolians and in Messina, Taormina, and Catania, begin the hot summer days with a granita *di caffè* (a coffee ice topped with whipped cream), into which they dunk their breakfast rolls. You can have one any time of day.

Lipari

38 *37 km (23 mi) north of Milazzo.*

The largest and most developed of the Aeolians, Lipari welcomes you with distinctive pastel-colored houses. Fields of spiky agaves dot the northernmost tip of the island, **Aquacalda,** indented with pumice and obsidian quarries. In the west is **San Calogero,** where you can explore hot springs and mud baths. From the red lava base of the island rises a plateau crowned with a 16th-century castle and a 17th-century **cathedral.** Next door is the **Archaeological Museum,** one of the best in Europe, with an intelligently arranged collection of prehistoric finds—some dating as far back as 4000 BC—from various sites in the archipelago. ⊠ *Via Castello,* ☎ *090/9880174.* ☞ *Free.* ☉ *Daily 9–2.*

Local buses circle the island and provide wondrous views of the other islands. Renting a moped is a fun way to cover the island, but test your machine out first. You may be greeted at the dock by people offering hotels and rooms in private homes.

Vulcano

39 *55 km (34 mi) northwest of Milazzo, 18 km (10 mi) northwest of Lipari.*

True to its name, Vulcano has a profusion of fumaroles sending up jets of hot vapor, but the volcano here has long been dormant. You can ascend to the crater (1,266 ft above sea level) on muleback for a wonderful view, or take boat rides into the grottoes around the base. From Capo Grillo there is a view of all the Aeolians. You'll find relatively higher-priced lodging and restaurants here.

Salina

40 *15 km (10 mi) north of Lipari, 52 km (38 mi) northwest of Milazzo.*

The second-largest island, Salina is also the most fertile—which accounts for its good wine, the golden Malvasia. Excursions go up Mt. Fossa delle Felci, which rises to over 3,000 ft. It is also the highest of the islands, and the vineyards and fishing villages along its slopes add to its allure. Malvasia wine here is locally produced, unlike that found on other islands. Salina has a good range of reasonably priced accommodations and restaurants—and fewer crowds.

Panarea

④ *55 km (34 mi) north of Milazzo, 18 km (10 mi) north of Lipari.*

Panarea has some of the most dramatic scenery of the islands: wild caves carved out of the rock and dazzling flora. The exceptionally clear water and the richness of life on the seabed make Panarea especially suitable for underwater exploration. There is a small Bronze Age village at Capo Milazzese. There is scant lodging beyond exclusive establishments here.

Stromboli

④ *63 km (40 mi) north of Milazzo, 40 km (25 mi) north of Lipari.*

The island consists entirely of the cone of an active volcano. The view from the sea—especially at night, as an endless stream of glowing red-hot lava flows into the water—is unforgettable. Stromboli is in a constant state of mild dissatisfaction, and every now and then its anger flares up, so authorities insist that you climb to the top (about 3,031 ft above sea level) only with a guide. The climb takes about four hours. You will find a small selection of reasonably priced hotels and restaurants.

Alicudi

④ *65 km (40 mi) west of Lipari, 102 km (68 mi) northwest of Milazzo.*

The farthest outpost of the Aeolians remains sparsely inhabited (although it does have a hotel), wild, and at peace. Here and on Filicudi (☞ *below*) there is a tiny selection of accommodations, but you can rent rooms cheaply. There is about one eatery on both islands.

Filicudi

④ *30 km (16 mi) west of Salina, 82 km (54 mi) northwest of Milazzo.*

Just a dot in the sea, Filicudi is famous for its unusual volcanic rock formations and the enchanting **Grotta del Bue Marino** (Grotto of the Sea Ox). At Capo Graziano there is a prehistoric village. The island has a hotel, and some local families put up guests.

SICILY A TO Z

Arriving and Departing

By Car and Ferry
Frequent **car ferries** cross the strait between Villa San Giovanni in Calabria and Messina on the island. The crossing usually takes about half an hour, but during the summer months there can be considerable delays. From Naples, overnight car ferries operate daily to Palermo and once a week to Catania and Siracusa; there is also an overnight ferry from Genoa to Palermo.

By Passenger Boat
Besides the ferries mentioned above (☞ *above*), passenger-only **aliscafi** (hydrofoils) also cross the strait from Reggio di Calabria in about 15 minutes.

By Plane
Sicily can be reached from all major cities via Rome, Milan, or Naples. Planes land at **Punta Raisi Airport** (✉ 32 km/20 mi west of Palermo,

☎ 091/591698). Catania's **Fontanarossa Airport** (✉ 5 km/3 mi south of city center, ☎ 095/7306266) also services flights. At both, there is bus service into the center of town. During the high season, there are also direct charter flights to Sicily from New York, London, and Paris.

By Train

There are direct **express trains** from Milan and Rome to Palermo, Catania, and Siracusa. The Rome–Palermo journey takes at least 11 hours. After Naples, the run is mostly along the coast, so try to book a window seat on the right. At Villa San Giovanni, in Calabria, the train is separated and loaded onto a ferryboat to cross the strait to Messina.

Getting Around

Renting a car is definitely the best way to travel in Sicily. The trains are unreliable and slow, and the buses, though faster and air-conditioned in summer, can be subject to delays and strikes.

By Bus and Train

Air-conditioned coaches connect major and minor cities and are often faster and more convenient than local trains but slightly more expensive.

By Car

This is the ideal mode of Sicilian exploration. Modern highways circle and bisect the island, making all main cities easily reachable. Cars can be rented at airports and downtown locations in every major city.

By Ferry and Hydrofoil

The Aeolian Islands are reachable by hydrofoil from Messina, Palermo, and Milazzo. The latter also has a ferryboat service to the islands, as do Palermo and Naples, but on a less frequent schedule. In summer there are numerous boats and hydrofoil excursions connecting the individual islands.

By Train

Main lines connect Messina, Taormina, Siracusa, and Palermo. Secondary lines are generally very slow and unreliable. The Messina–Palermo run, along the northern coast, is especially scenic.

Contacts and Resources

Car Rental

Cars can be rented at airports and downtown locations in every major city.

Avis: Palermo (✉ Punta Raisi airport, ☎ 091/591684; ✉ Via Principe Scordia 28, ☎ 091/586940). **Catania** (✉ Fontanarossa airport, ☎ 095/340500; ✉ Via Federico De Roberto 10, ☎ 095/536470). **Hertz: Palermo** (✉ Punta Raisi airport, ☎ 091/591682; ✉ Via Messina 7/e, ☎ 091/331668). **Catania** (✉ Fontanarossa airport, ☎ 095/341595; ✉ Via Toselli 16/c, ☎ 095/322560). **Maggiore: Palermo** (✉ Punta Raisi airport, ☎ 091/591681; ✉ Via De Gasperi 179, ☎ 091/513172). **Catania** (✉ Fontanarossa airport, ☎ 095/340594; ✉ Piazza Verga 48, ☎ 095/538109).

Emergencies

Police, Ambulance, Fire (☎ 113). **Hospital:** Palermo (☎ 091/6662207). Catania (☎ 095/322216).

Guided Tours

Saturday-morning tours of Palermo and Monreale are provided by the Italian tour operator **CST** (✉ Via E. Amari 124, Palermo, ☎ 091/582294; ✉ Corso Umberto 101, Taormina, ☎ 0942/23301), leaving at 9 AM from outside the Politeama Hotel. CST also arranges complete seven-day tours of Sicily's major sights in a comfortable air-conditioned coach with an English-speaking guide. Departures are once a week from either Palermo and Catania, and the cost includes all meals and accommodations in three- or four-star hotels.

Visitor Information

Aeolian Islands (✉ Corso Vittorio Emanuele 202, Lipari, ☎ 090/9880095). **Agrigento** (✉ Viale della Vittoria 255, ☎ 0922/401352; ✉ Via Cesare Battisti 15, ☎ 0922/20454). **Caltagirone** (✉ Palazzo Libertini, ☎ 0933/53809). **Caltanisetta** (✉ Corso Vittorio Emanuele 109, ☎ 0934/530411). **Catania** (✉ Largo Paisiello 5, ☎ 095/7306233; ✉ Rail station, ☎ 095/7306255; ✉ Airport, ☎ 095/7306266). **Cefalù** (✉ Corso Ruggero 77, ☎ 0921/21050 and 0921/21458). **Enna** (✉ Via Roma 413, ☎ 0935/528228; ✉ Piazza Napoleone Colajanni 6, ☎ 0935/26119). **Erice** (✉ Via Conte Pepoli 11, ☎ 0923/869388). **Marsala** (✉ Via XI Maggio 100, ☎ 0923/714097). **Messina** (✉ Piazza della Repubblica, ☎ 090/672944; ✉ Via Calabria 301/b, ☎ 090/674236; ✉ Piazza Cairoli 45, ☎ 090/2936294). **Monreale** (✉ Piazza Duomo, ☎ 091/6564570). **Palermo** (✉ Piazza Castelnuovo 35, ☎ 091/583847; ✉ Punta Raisi airport, ☎ 091/591698). **Piazza Armerina** (✉ Via Cavour 1, ☎ 0935/680201). **Siracusa** (✉ Via San Sebastiano 43, ☎ 0931/67710; ✉ Via Maestranza 33, ☎ 0931/464255. **Taormina** (✉ Palazzo Corvaja, Largo Santa Caterina, ☎ 0942/23243). **Trapani** (✉ Piazza Saturno, ☎ 0923/29000; ✉ Via Vito Sorba 15, ☎ 0923/27077).

16 Sardinia

An uncut jewel of an island, Sardinia remains unique and enigmatic. Too distant from Rome to be influenced by the character of the mainland, this island is as fascinating as its prehistoric stone structures, the nuraghi. *Modern luxury can also be found here: just follow the high-fliers who sail their yachts to the Costa Smeralda. Severely beautiful, Sardinia is a prime destination for anyone seeking a getaway.*

Updated by
Robert
Andrews

THE SECOND-LARGEST ISLAND in the Mediterranean—just smaller than Sicily—Sardinia is about 180 km (112 mi) from mainland Italy and very much off the beaten track. A Phoenician stronghold in ancient times and later a Spanish dominion, Sardinia doesn't seem typically "Italian" in its color and flavor. It lies just a bit too far from the mainland—from imperial and papal Rome and from the palaces of the Savoy dynasty—to have been transformed by the events that forged a national character. Yet Giuseppe Garibaldi, the charismatic national hero who led his troops in fervid campaigns to unify Italy in the mid-19th century, chose to spend his last years in relative isolation on the small island of Caprera, just off the coast of Sardinia.

Although Sardinia (Sardegna) is now less than an hour by air and only several hours by boat from mainland Italy, it is removed from the mainstream of tourism except for July and August, when Italians take its beautiful coasts and clean waters by storm. The interior is *never* crowded; Italian tourists in Sardinia come for the sea, not for the rugged and deserted mountain scenery.

Sardinia closely resembles Corsica, the French island across the 16-km-wide (10-mi-wide) windswept Strait of Bonifacio to the north. A dense bush, or *macchia*, barely penetrable in some districts, covers large areas. The terrain is rough, like the short, sturdy shepherds you see in the highlands—impassive figures engaged in one of the few gainful occupations that the stony land allows. Shaggy flocks of sheep and goats are familiar features in the Sardinian landscape, just as their meat and cheese are staples of the island's cuisine. The main highway linking Cagliari with Sassari was begun in 1820 by the Savoy ruler Carlo Felice; designated Highway 131, but still referred to as the Carlo Felice Highway by the islanders, it heads northwest through the fertile Campidano Plain for 216 km (134 mi) to Sassari.

Aside from the chic opulence of the Costa Smeralda, there's little sophistication in Sardinia, but the cost of living on the island is typically higher than on the mainland. The sprawling cities of Cagliari and Sassari have a distinctly provincial air. Newer hotels may seem a little old-fashioned, and hotels—of any vintage—are hard to find inland. There's little traffic on the roads, and trains, buses, and people in general move at a gentle pace. In hamlets, women swathed in black shawls and long, full skirts look with suspicion upon strangers passing through. Sardinians are courteous but remote, perhaps because of their innate dignity.

Like mainland Italians, the Sardinians are of varied origin. On the northwest coast, fine traceries of ironwork around a balcony underscore the Spanish influence. In the northeast, the inhabitants boast Genoese or Pisan ancestry, and the headlands display the ruined fortresses of the ancient duchy of Malaspina on the Italian mainland. As you explore the southern coast, you'll come upon the physiognomies, customs, dialects, place-names, and holy buildings of the Turks, the Moors, the Phoenicians, the Austrians, and the mainland Italians. If there are any pure Sardinians—or Sards—left, perhaps they can be found in the south-central mountains, south of Nuoro, under the 6,000-ft crests of the Gennargentu Massif, in the rugged country still ironically called Barbagia, "Land of Strangers."

Pleasures and Pastimes

The Arts

As one of Italy's most—perhaps *the* most—remote regions, Sardinia is not really a prime spot for sophisticated visual or performing arts. This same remoteness, however, can prove fruitful for sampling some of the culture here, sometimes natively inspired, sometimes drawing on the influences of the traders and invaders who have left their mark on the islands over the millennia. Sardinia's own brand of Catholicism—occasionally bordering on the grotesque—can be witnessed in the local *feste,* or festivals. Ostensibly, the festivals celebrate a saintly or religious occasion, but often they are imbued with an almost pagan feel.

Beaches

Sardinia's beaches are among the best in the Mediterranean; its waters are among the cleanest, with the exception of those in the immediate vicinity of Cagliari, Arbatax, and Porto Torres. The beach resorts of the Costa Smeralda are exclusive and expensive, but elsewhere on the island you can find a wide range of beaches.

Many agree that the most beautiful beaches on the island are those of Cala Luna and Cala Sisina, hidden among the rocky cliffs near Baunei and Dorgali, on the eastern coast; they can be reached only by boat from Cala Gonone or Arbatax, and can definitely be considered remote. For more accessible beaches with more amenities, go to Santa Margherita di Pula, near Cagliari, where there are several hotels; to Villasimius and the Costa Rei, on the southeastern coast; or to the sandy coves sheltered by wind-carved granite boulders on the northern coast in the Gallura district and the archipelago of La Maddalena. There are also beaches around Olbia, Alghero, and on the Costa Paradiso, near Castelsardo.

Dining

In the island's restaurants you'll find that Sardinian regional cuisine is basically Italian, with interesting local variations. Meat dishes are usually veal, lamb, or *porcheddu* (roast suckling pig). On the coast, seafood is king and is served in great variety. Langouste or *aragosta* (lobster) is a specialty of the northern coast; it can be expensive. Foreign conquerors left legacies of bouillabaisse (known here as *zimino*), couscous, and paella, but there are native pastas: *malloreddus* (small shells of bran pasta sometimes flavored with saffron) and *culingiones* (the Sardinian version of ravioli). Sharp cheese made of pecorino (sheep's milk), and thin crispy bread called *carta di musica* are typical island fare. Try the *sebadas* (fried cheese-filled ravioli doused with honey) for dessert. The red wines are sturdy and strong, the whites tend toward a light and delicate quality. Amber-colored Vernaccia is dry and heady.

CATEGORY	COST*
$$$$	over 85,000 lire
$$$	60,000–85,000 lire
$$	35,000–60,000 lire
$	under 35,000 lire

Prices are per person, including house wine, service, and tax.

Fishing

Check locally for regulations on deep-sea fishing. Underwater fishing is restricted to the daylight hours, and no more than 5 kilos (11 pounds) of fish and shellfish may be taken. No oxygen tanks or nets may be used for underwater fishing. Freshwater fishing is good along the Flumendosa, Tirso, Rio Mannu, and other rivers rising in the mountainous interior and in the artificial basins of Flumendosa and Omodeo.

Golf

Sardinia has two world-class golf courses, including the Pevero Golf Club on the Costa Smeralda, which was designed by Robert Trent Jones; and the Is Molas 18-hole course at Santa Margherita di Pula. Four more courses are planned for the Costa Smeralda.

Horseback Riding

Spaghetti westerns were once filmed in Sardinia, and it's easy to imagine why: the rugged, mountainous terrain of the inland is the perfect frontier setting for an adventure on horseback. On the barren hilltops of the Barbagio you may even catch a glimpse of the wild dwarf horse that is native to these parts, though numbers have dwindled over the years. If you prefer a more sedate way of seeing the island on horseback, you can stick to the coast, where the riding is easier but the scenery is still magnificent. Group itineraries and horse rentals can be arranged (☞ Contacts and Resources *in* Sardinia A to Z, *below*).

Kids' Stuff

Sardinia is a vast playground where children can explore and swim in season. There's nothing like a long hike along deserted beaches or through herb-perfumed hills to send them to bed early. Let them clamber over the nuraghi and poke into the countless *domus de janas* (witches' houses) and *tombe di giganti* (giants' tombs), fancifully named grottoes hewn in the rock by the island's prehistoric inhabitants. Near Sassari, at Anghelu Ruhu, and near Dorgali, they served as burial places, but with a little imagination you can make up some fanciful fairy tales.

Lodging

The island's most luxurious hotels are on the Costa Smeralda. They have magnificent facilities but close from fall to spring; many are too out of the way to be good touring bases. Other, equally attractive coastal areas have seen a spate of resort hotels and villa colonies sprouting up, but they, too, close from October through April, which narrows the choice of hotels considerably during the other months. In the cities suggested as touring bases, you can expect to find standards of comfort slightly below those of the mainland. The best accommodations may be available at commercial hotels, which means little atmosphere. In smaller towns throughout the island, you'll find modest hotels offering basic accommodations, restrained but genuine hospitality, and low rates.

CATEGORY	COST*
$$$$	over 300,000 lire
$$$	160,000–300,000 lire
$$	100,000–160,000 lire
$	under 100,000 lire

Prices are for a standard double room for two, including service and 9% tax (12% for luxury hotels).

Nightlife

Nightlife in much of Sardinia means a quiet drink before turning in early, tired out from the day's outdoor activity. But as if to make up for the sleepy atmosphere of most of the island, the Costa Smeralda sparkles most nights in the summer. Be prepared to part with a cool sum if you visit the Costa, but if that doesn't deter you, go to the complex at the Cervo for a selection of high-class bars, restaurants, and discos.

Sailing

Sailing enthusiasts tack for Sardinia in droves by virtue of its craggy coast, full of inlets only accessible by sea. You can also witness the very rich engage in one of their favorite sports—yachting—at the posh resorts of Costa Smeralda each August, when a number of regattas are held.

Shopping

Sardinia is crafts heaven. Locally produced goods include bright woolen shawls and rugs, hand-carved wooden objects, gold filigree jewelry in traditional forms, coral jewelry, and, above all, handwoven baskets in all shapes and sizes. The best places to go for crafts are the various ISOLA centers in Cagliari, Olbia, Castelsardo, and Sant'Antioco. This government-sponsored exhibition of island crafts displays items that are also for sale.

Exploring Sardinia

The entire island is about 260 km (162 mi) from north to south, and roughly 120 km (75 mi) across. Driving is the best way to travel to and through the island's most interesting sights. Sardinia's mountainous terrain can make driving rigorous and long. Local transportation is not geared to the needs of visitors, so you can see more in less time if you have a car. If you don't, your best bet is to establish yourself in one of the larger towns and make excursions to as many attractions as time and schedules allow. There are bus and train connections to most places, except some of the Costa Smeralda and Su Nuraxi nuraghe.

Numbers in the text correspond to numbers in the margin and on the Sardinia and Cagliari maps.

Great Itineraries

Three days in Sardinia will only give you enough time to see one corner of the island. With five days to spend here, you will be able to venture out to some of the attractions in the north of the island. A fairly comprehensive tour taking in the coastline and interior can be accomplished in seven days.

IF YOU HAVE 3 DAYS

You would do well to confine your visit to ⊞ **Cagliari** ①–⑦ and its environs, if you can arrange your own transport or a taxi. In Sardinia's capital, you'll find Italianate architecture, churches of all styles, and the Museo Archeologico, with the countries best antiquity collection. You can make easy day-excursions from Cagliari, and your priority should be the **Su Nuraxi** ⑫, the island's best preserved nuraghic monument. On your third day, head out to the small village of **Pula** ⑨; great beaches are here and just outside is Nora, a Carthaginian and Roman archaeological site.

IF YOU HAVE 5 DAYS

Cut down your visit to ⊞ **Cagliari** ①–⑦ to two days, still leaving enough time for a visit to **Pula** ⑨. Spend your third night in ⊞ **Alghero** ⑰, an appealing walled town on the northwest coast with a distinctly Spanish flavor, perhaps stopping for lunch en route at **Oristano** ⑭. For your last two nights, you have a choice. You could spend them in the lap of luxury by checking into one of the top-class hotels in and outside of ⊞ **Porto Cervo** ㉒, amid the international jet set on the Costa Smeralda. If you are on a limited budget or prefer adventure, make ⊞ **Nuoro** ⑮ your base from which to explore the rugged interior of the island. Spend as little time as possible exploring the provincial capital before veering south into the mountainous **Barbagio** region, the island's most primitive district.

Spend your first two days exploring ⊞ **Cagliari** ①–⑦. On the third day, you could hit the beaches at **Villasimius** ⑧ on the southeastern tip of the island. Alternatively, go southwest from Cagliari, taking in the remains of antiquity outside of **Pula** ⑨, before moving up along the western coast on the Carlo Felice highway as far as the sleepy village of **Sant'Antioco** ⑩. Here, you can catch a ferry over to the small island of **San Pietro** ⑪, a favorite weekend retreat of wealthy Cagliarans, with delightful picnic and swimming spots. Continue up toward Oristano, making an inland detour to the fascinating nuraghe of **Su Nuraxi** ⑫, off the main road outside the quiet town of Barumini. Wildlife enthusiasts may want to take another jaunt north of Barumini to the **Giara di Gesturi** ⑬, a basalt plateau with the island's more exotic wildlife. ⊞ **Oristano** ⑭ saw its heyday in the Middle Ages, but it now merits a cursory walk through town and glimpse of the Carthiginian ruins at Tharros, just outside the city. Head northeast for **Nuoro** ⑮, a town of little interest, and strike south into the **Barbagia** region: tortuous roads wind and loop their way over a wild and primitive terrain that seems impervious to the 20th century. If you prefer coastal attractions to the inland ones, spend no more than half a day exploring the region and then head west from Nuoro on road 129 to Bosa, where you turn right into hilly and arid scrub country that eventually brings you to ⊞ **Alghero** ⑰, on the northwest coast, where you should consider overnighting. While heading northeast across an area fringed with low cliffs, inlets, and small bays, don't be distracted by **Sassari** ⑱, but stop to appreciate the exquisite nature of the seaside resorts, including **Castelsardo** ⑲, a walled citadel that is a delight for basket lovers, and to the relaxed fishing village of **Santa Teresa di Gallura** ⑳. Forge on to pamper yourself on the sun-kissed beaches of one of Europe's premier summer holiday meccas, the **Costa Smeralda,** its most exclusive address ⊞ **Porto Cervo** ㉒.

When to Tour Sardinia

If you can help it, avoid Sardinia in steamy August, when not only is the island swamped by tourists from the mainland, but the Sards, too, take their annual break. A combination of unbearable heat, crowded beaches, accommodation shortage, and shuttered shops and offices can be a hair-splitting experience. May and September, on the other hand, are much quieter and still temperate. Sudden storms can be a hazard, but these quickly blow over. The sea remains good for swimming well into October. In winter, rain and clouds are common over high ground—and most of Sardinia is mountainous—and it snows most years in the Barbagia region. In the south, the weather rarely turns cold, but winter is not beach weather. The mountainous interior is probably at its best in the spring, when the woods and valleys are alive with color and burgeoning growth. For the gradations of color, the fall is also a good time.

Try to coincide your visit to Sardinia with one of the famous annual festivals. The main ones are at Cagliari (beginning of May), Sassari (Ascension Day—the 40th day after Easter—and August 14), and Nuoro (penultimate Sunday in August). These are mega affairs, with accommodation and restaurant space at a premium, so plan well ahead. There are smaller festivals throughout the year, some of the best in the scattered mountain villages of the interior, such as the celebrations in local costume during the Feast of St. John, June 24, at Fonni, in the heart of the Barbagio; these festivities are not just expressions of religious devotion but also an explicit statement of community identity.

CAGLIARI AND ENVIRONS

Cagliari

❶ *30 km (19 mi) northeast of Pula, 50 km (31 mi) west of Villasimius, 212 km (132 mi) south of Sassari.*

The island's capital reveals impressive Italianate architecture and churches in a variety of styles; it's clear that medieval Spanish conquerors from Aragon were here, as well as Austrians and Italians. Sardinia's largest city, Cagliari (the stress is on the first syllable) is characterized by its busy commercial center and waterfront with broad avenues, as well as by the typically narrow streets of the old town on a hill. Explorations from town can include the ancient site of Nora and the popular picnic islands of Sant'Antioco and San Pietro.

❷ Begin your visit at the **Museo Archeologico,** within the walls of the castle that the Pisans erected in the early 1300s to ward off attacks by the Aragonese and Catalans, from what is now Spain. Among the intriguing artifacts from Nuraghic, Carthaginian, and Roman times are bronze statuettes from the tombs and dwellings of Sardinia's earliest inhabitants, who remain a prehistorical enigma. These aboriginal people left scant clues to their origins. Ancient writers called them the nuraghic people, from the name of their stone dwellings, the nuraghi. The structures' features are unique to Sardinia, just as the Aztec pyramids' are to Mexico. Archaeologists date the nuraghi from about 1300–1200 BC, a time when the ancient Israelites were establishing themselves in Canaan; when the Greeks were besieging Troy; when the Minoan civilization collapsed in Crete; when the Ramses pharaohs reigned in Egypt; and when many migrations were taking place along the shores and water routes of the Mediterranean. During the next 1,000 years, the nuraghic people gradually withdrew to the island's highland fastnesses to avoid more disciplined and better-armed invaders. (Their only weapons, say the chroniclers, were stones and boulders hurled down from the hilltops.) They eventually succumbed when the Romans, following on the heels of Carthaginian invaders, conquered the island in the 3rd century BC. ⊠ *Cittadella dei Musei, Piazza Arsenale,* ☎ *070/655911.* ⊠ *4,000 lire.* ⊙ *Apr.–Sept., Tues.–Sun. 9–2 and 3–8; Oct.–Mar., Tues.–Sun. 9–7.*

❸
❹ The medieval **Tower of San Pancrazio,** part of the imposing Pisan defenses, is just outside the archaeological museum. The **Tower of the Elephant,** twin to that of San Pancrazio, is at the seaward end of the bastions. **Piazza Palazzo,** at the top of Via Martini, is where you'll find the
❺ **cathedral,** which has been extensively rebuilt and restored. The tiers of columns on the facade echo those of medieval Pisan churches, but only the center portal is an authentic relic of that era. All around the church are the narrow streets of the **Spanish quarter,** where humble dwellings still open directly onto the sidewalk and the wash is hung out to dry on elaborate wrought-iron balconies.

❻ The Bastion of St. Remy, better known as the **Terrazza Umberto I,** is a monumental neoclassic staircase and arcade. It was added in the 19th century to the bastion built by the Spaniards 400 years earlier. From here, take in the magnificent view over the city and port, the sandy beaches, and the lagoons shimmering in the sun. If here at sunset, look south.

❼ Cagliari also has a **Roman amphitheater** (below the Museo Archeologico), some very old churches, and a few good restaurants near the waterfront.

Sardinia

CORSICA
(FRANCE)

TO TOULON
TO GENOA
TO LIVORNO

Bonifacio

Santa Teresa
di Gallura

La Maddalena

21

20

Palau

TO GENOA,
LIVORNO,
CIVITAVECCHIA

Isola
Asinara

Golfo dell'
Asinara

Costa
Paradiso

S200

S133

Costa
Smeralda

Baia Sardinia

22 Porto Cervo

Porto Rotondo

Golfo Aranci

24

Stintino

Castelsardo

19

S127

23 Olbia

Porto Torres

Sassari 18

S199

S125

Oschiri

Capo Caccia
Grotto of Neptune

Alghero

17

ITALY

S131

Ozieri

Siniscola

Bosa Macomer

S129

Nuoro 15

Mt. Ortobene

Cala
Gonone

Oliena Dorgali

Golfo
di
Orosei

Orgosolo

Fonni

16

Mt. Spada

Sorgono

Baunei

Tonara

Bruncu Spina

San Salvatore

Aritzo

Monti del
Gennargentu

San Giovanni
in Sinis

Cabras

Oristano 14

Giara di
Gesturi

Arbatax

Tharros

Arborea

13

Su Nuraxi

Isili

12

Barumini

S131 Carlo Felice
Hwy.

N

S126

S125

Iglesias Domusnovas

S130

San Sperate

Portoscusa

Cagliari

1   7

San Pietro

Carbonia

S195

Costa
Rei

11

Villasimius

10

S195

Golfo
di
Cagliari

8

Sant'Antioco

Pula

Capo
Boi

Capo
Carbonara

9

Nora

TO CIVITAVECCHIA

Santa
Margherita
di Pula

TO NAPLES

Mediterranean   Sea

TO PALERMO

TO MALTA

TO TUNIS

KEY

0   30 miles

0   45 km

Ferry Line

Dining and Lodging

$$$ ✕ **Dal Corsaro.** This formal restaurant near the port is one of the island's most commended eating places, so make reservations. The decor is refined, the welcome cordial. The menu features seafood and meat specialties, such as seafood antipasto and porcheddu, and the wine list is exceptional. ⊠ *Viale Regina Margherita 28,* ☎ *070/664318. Reservations essential. AE, DC, MC, V. Closed Sun., Aug., and 1 wk at Christmas.*

$$ ✕ **Il Gatto.** "The Cat," near the train station and the central Piazza del Carmine, is popular with locals. Follow their lead and make sure you have reservations because the restaurant can fill up quickly. It serves some of the best Sardinian seafood, such as the risotto with shellfish, but for a change of pace try the savory gnocchi alla Gorgonzola. ⊠ *Viale Trieste 15,* ☎ *070/663596. Reservations essential. AE, DC, MC, V. Closed Sun. No lunch Sat.*

$$$ ▥ **Panorama.** With its unprepossessing exterior, this useful hotel in downtown Cagliari is geared toward the business class. Rooms are functional, spacious, and comfortable: try to reserve one on the upper of the nine floors and enjoy the view over the harbor and bay. Rates are low in the category. ⊠ *Viale Armando Diaz 231, 09100,* ☎ *070/307691,* ⅎ *070/305413. 97 rooms. Restaurant, bar, pool, meeting rooms. AE, DC, MC, V.*

$$ ▥ **Quattro Mori.** A sure bet, this hotel is convenient to the train station and town center. Rooms are clean and homey, with wood and wicker. The name—"four moors"—refers to Sardinia's emblem of four blindfolded Moorish heads in profile. ⊠ *Via G.M. Angioj 27, 09124,* ☎ *070/668535,* ⅎ *070/666087. 21 rooms. Bar. AE, DC, MC, V.*

Nightlife and the Arts

FESTIVAL

Sardinia's greatest annual festival, the **Festa di Sant'Efisio** on May 1 involves a procession between Cagliari and Pula (☞ *below*), a good chance to take part in the centuries-old folklore.

MUSIC

Cagliari's **university** (⊠ Via Università) holds concerts throughout the academic year.

Outdoor Activities and Sports

FISHING

For information on obtaining a fishing license, write to **Assessorato Regionale alla Difesa dell'Ambiente** (⊠ Via Biasi 7/9, 09100, Cagliari, ☎ 070/6066620).

SAILING

The **Lega Navale Italiana** at Marina Piccola in Cagliari (☎ 070/303794) will furnish information on the island's facilities.

Shopping

The best place for crafts is **ISOLA** (⊠ Via Bacaredda 176, ☎ 070/400707), a government-sponsored exhibition of artisanal crafts where most of the work is for sale.

OFF THE
BEATEN PATH

SAN SPERATE – Practically every wall in this town outside of Cagliari has been brightened with *murales* (mural paintings) by local artists and some well-known Italian painters, transforming the entire town into an open-air art gallery.

Villasimius

❽ *50 km (31 mi) east of Cagliari.*

The eastern route takes you through some dismal industrial suburbs on the road that leads to the scenic coast and beaches of Capo Boi and Capo Carbonara; Villasimius ranks as the chief resort here.

Pula

❾ *30 km (19 mi) south of Cagliari.*

The area southwest of the capital has its share of fine scenery and good beaches—resort villages sprawl along the coast, and the Is Molas championship golf course near Pula has won tributes from Tom Watson, Jack Nicklaus, and other professionals of the sport. On the marshy shoreline between Cagliari Airport and Pula, huge flocks of flamingos are a common sight.

Visit the small **archaeological museum,** with finds from the Nora site (☞ *below*). ⊠ *Corso Vittorio Emanuele 67,* ☎ *070/9209610.* 💴 *4,000 lire.* ☉ *Daily 9–8 (9–6 in Oct.–Mar.).*

★ For the real thing, head to the narrow promontory less than 3 km (2 mi) outside the town of Pula called **Nora,** the site of a Phoenician, then Carthaginian and, later, Roman settlement. Extensive excavations here have shed light on life in this ancient city from the 8th century BC onward. Many of the exhibits in Cagliari's archaeological museum were found here. An old Roman road passes the moss-covered ruins of temples, an amphitheater, and a small Roman theater. You can make out the channels through which hot air rose to warm the Roman baths; watch for the difference between the simple mosaic pavements laid by the Carthaginians and the more elaborate designs of the Romans. Taking in the views from Nora, you can see why the Phoenicians chose the site for settlement. They always scouted for locations with good harbors, cliffs to shelter their craft from the wind, and a position such as a promontory, from which they could defend themselves from attack. If the sea is calm, look under the clear waters along the shore for more ruins of the ancient city, submerged by earthquakes, rough seas, and erosion. ⌑ *Free.* ⊙ *Excavations Apr.–Sept., daily 9–8; Oct.–Mar., daily 9–5.*

OFF THE BEATEN PATH

SANT'EFISIO – The little Romanesque church at the base of the Nora promontory plays a part in one of the island's most colorful annual events. Efisio, the patron saint of Sardinia, was a 3rd-century Roman soldier who converted to Christianity. A procession in early May accompanies a statue of the saint all the way from Cagliari and back again. The processional round-trip takes four days, with festive stops along the way, and culminates in a huge parade down Cagliari's main avenue. If you're in Sardinia from May 1 to May 4, don't miss it.

Lodging

The hotels and beaches that cater to the summer hotel trade around Nora are concentrated a couple of miles south of the town, in a conglomeration of hotels that is the town of Santa Margherita di Pula.

$$$$
★

🏨 **Is Morus.** A luxurious enclave, the Is Morus is on a sandy cove and offers all the amenities of a fine beach resort, with low, attractive buildings shaded by pinewoods, plus the option (for guests taking half- or full-board) of golfing at the fine Is Molas course, about 11 km (7 mi) away. ⌧ *Santa Margherita, 09019,* ☎ *070/921171,* FAX *070/ 921596. 85 rooms. Restaurant, bar, pool, miniature golf, tennis court, beach. AE, DC, MC, V. Closed Nov.–Easter.*

$$$

🏨 **Flamingo.** Also directly on the beach and in a shady setting, this resort hotel features a main building and several two-story cottages nestled among the eucalyptus trees. ⌧ *Santa Margherita, 09010,* ☎ *070/ 9208361,* FAX *070/9208359. 134 rooms. Restaurant, piano bar, pool, tennis court, miniature golf, dance club. AE, DC, MC, V. Closed Oct. 10–May.*

Outdoor Activities and Sports

GOLF

Guests at any of the hotels in Santa Margherita di Pula can avail of the international-standard 18-hole **Is Molas** course (☎ 070/9209165); the adjacent **Is Molas Golf Hotel** (☎ 070/9241006) offers special golfing vacations.

Sant'Antioco

⑩ *92 km (57 mi) west of Cagliari.*

Off the southwest coast is Sant'Antioco, one of two islands that is a popular picnic spot with good beaches. You can drive over a causeway to get on the island, where the most hectic activity seems to be the silent repairing of nets by local fishermen who have already handled their daily catch.

Shopping

Visitors can stock up on local crafts at **ISOLA** (⌧ Lungomare Vespucci).

OFF THE BEATEN PATH

CARBONIA AND IGLESIAS – If your curiosity prods you to explore more esoteric places, you could go just inland of Sant'Antioco to explore the rugged, once-booming mining country around Carbonia, a town built by Mussolini in 1938 to serve as an administrative center for the coal

miners and their families. With its overpowering fascist architecture, it
has been called an urban UFO set down in the Sardinian landscape.
Nearby Iglesias is an authentic Sardinian town, with a medieval cathedral; traveling east past Domusnovas on the Cagliari–Iglesias highway,
you can detour and drive right through an immense cave, the Grotta di
San Giovanni.

San Pietro

⑪ *5 km (3 mi) northwest of Sant'Antioco.*

A ferry at the small northern port of Calasetta connects Sant'Antioco
with the smaller island of San Pietro. This is a favorite of wealthy Cagliar-
ians, many of whom have built weekend cottages here.

FROM BARUMINI TO THE COSTA SMERALDA
The Bare and the Beautiful

A more traditional—and wild—Sardinia awaits the traveler who ven-
tures into the mountainous inland of the island. The Italian film di-
rectors, the Taviani brothers, made the hinterland of the Barbagia
region, where traditional Sardinian customs are maintained in remote
hilltop villages, the subject of an extraordinary portrait of rural life among
the sheepherders of the area, *Padre Padrone*. Inland Sardinians are a
hardy people, used to living in a climate that is as unforgiving in winter as it is intolerable in summer. Old traditions, including the vendetta,
are firmly rooted in the social fabric of this mountainous land that is
both barren and beautiful. Here, rare species of wildlife share the
rocky uplands with sturdy medieval churches and mysterious nuraghi—
ancient stone citadels left by prehistoric people. You may want to
make your base Oristano, on the west coast and the medieval center
of Sardinian nationalism.

As you move northward the timeless beauty of the landscape begins
to show greater sign of 20th-century development. The sunny resort
of Alghero, the Spanish-influenced port on the west coast, is de rigueur
among wealthy Sardinians. In the '60s and '70s, the Costa Smeralda,
the luxury resort complex developed by the Aga Khan on the northeast corner of Sardinia, was *the* place to summer, along with the Côte
d'Azur.

Su Nuraxi

★ **⑫** *60 km (37 mi) north of Cagliari.*

It is worth making a detour to the fascinating nuraghe of Su Nuraxi,
off the main road outside the quiet little town of Barumini. You could
spend hours clambering over this extraordinary structure of concen-
tric rings of stone walls, chambers, passages, wells, and beehive tower.
This nuraghe is probably about half its original height, and some of
the smaller towers around the main one have been reduced by pillag-
ing and erosion to mere circles of stones on the ground. The nuraghi
were fortified villages, prehistoric versions of medieval walled towns
and the forts of the American West. Though this particular type of construction is unique to Sardinia, similar buildings dating from the same
era are found in other parts of the Mediterranean, such as Cyprus and
the Balearic islands off Spain. Of the 7,000 nuraghi on Sardinia, Su
Nuraxi is the most impressive, with those of Sant'Antine and Losa, both

near Macomer, close runners-up. It's a good idea to take a flashlight along. ⊠ *1 km (½ mi) west of Barumini.* ⌷ *Free.* ⊙ *Daily 9–1 and 4–sunset.*

Giara di Gesturi

⑬ *8 km north of Barumini, 68 km (42 mi) north of Cagliari.*

On the basalt plateau of Giara di Gesturi roam some of the island's more exotic wildlife, including a species of wild dwarf horse. Another rare species in the Giara is the mouflon, a wild sheep distinguishable from its domesticated counterpart by its long curving horns and skittishness, however well intentioned. Long hunted for their decorative horns, the mouflon are now an endangered species, with only a few surviving on Sardinia and Corsica.

Oristano

⑭ *93 km (58 mi) northwest of Cagliari, 89 km (56 mi) southwest of Nuoro, 120 km (75 mi) south of Sassari.*

Oristano, on the west coast, shone in the Middle Ages when it was capital of the Giudicato of Arborea, an independent duchy led by Sardinia's own Joan-of-Arc-type heroine, Eleanora di Arborea. In the 14th century, Eleanora inherited the difficult task of defending the duchy's freedom, constantly undermined by the superior military might of the Spanish troops from Aragon. Although the duchy eventually reverted to Aragonese rule, Eleanora made a lasting contribution to Sardinia by implementing a code of law that was adopted throughout the island and remained in effect until Sardinia's unification with Italy in 1847. Now an important but slow-paced agricultural center, Oristano is the scene of livestock fairs and a rousing series of horse races, called Sa Sartiglia, marking the end of the February's Carnival.

OFF THE BEATEN PATH

CABRAS – Ten kilometers (6 mi) west of Oristano, you can see the extensive marshlands where fishermen pole round-bottomed rush boats through shallow ponds teeming with eel and crayfish.

THARROS – The ruins of this Carthaginian city are along the road marked San Giovanni di Sinis; its position afforded it a strategic view over scenic Sinis peninsula. Like Nora to the south (☞ *above*), the site was chosen because it commanded the best views of the harbor and could provide an easy escape route if inland tribes threatened. It is 10 km (6 mi) west of Cabras and 20 km (12 mi) west of Oristano.

Dining and Lodging

$$$ ★ ✕ **Il Faro.** Locals and visiting foodies consider this elegant restaurant to be one of the best in the area, as it offers authentic and well-prepared seasonal dishes. There's *capretto allo spiedo* (spit-roasted goat) in the winter and an aromatic *zuppa di fave* (fava bean soup) with bacon and fennel in the spring. Seafood is featured throughout the year. ⊠ *Via Bellini 25,* ☎ *0783/70002. AE, DC, MC, V. Closed Jan. 1–15 and July 1–15. No dinner Sun.*

$$ ✕ **Salvatore.** In this classic seafood restaurant near the church of Santa Giusta, just outside Oristano, you can sample seafood from the tidal ponds of Cabras and Santa Giusta. Specialties are spaghetti *alla bottarga* (with smoked fish roe) and grilled *anguilla* (eel). ⊠ *Via Carbonia 1,* ☎ *0783/357134. MC, V. No dinner Sun.*

$ 🏨 **Cama.** Near the train station, this hotel is also within walking distance of Oristano's interesting old town center. Rooms are air-conditioned, but otherwise undistinguished. A parking lot and garage make it convenient for drivers. ⊠ *Via Vittorio Veneto 119, 09170,* ☎ *0783/74374,* FAX *0783/74375. 54 rooms. Restaurant, bar, parking (fee). MC, V.*

Nightlife and the Arts

The **Sartiglia** festival, on the last Sunday of Carnival season, includes rich costumes and a ritual joust. Each summer, the town holds an **arts and crafts exhibition,** with local foods and wines given prominence. Contact the tourist office (⊠ Via Cagliari 278, ☎ 0783/74191) for information.

Shopping

Interesting **ceramic** items can be found in the small crafts shops in Oristano.

En Route   On your way to Tharros, you'll pass the ghost town of **San Salvatore,** revived briefly in the 1960s as a location for spaghetti westerns and since abandoned. The saloon of the movie set still stands, a marvel for kids. Farther along, among the dunes, are large **rush huts** formerly used by fishermen and now much in demand as back-to-nature vacation homes. The 5th-century church of **San Giovanni di Sinis,** also on the peninsula, is the oldest Christian church in Sardinia.

Nuoro

⓯ *89 km (56 mi) northeast of Oristano, 181 km (113 mi) north of Cagliari.*

The provincial capital of Nuoro presents a somewhat shabby air, on the edge of a gorge in the harsh mountainous area that culminates in **Gennargentu,** the island's highest massif (6,000 ft). The only things likely to interest you in Nuoro are the views from the park on Sant'-Onofrio hill and the exhibits in the **Museo della Vita e delle Tradizioni Popolari Sarde** (Museum of Sardinian Life and Folklore), where you can see local costumes, domestic and agricultural implements, and traditional jewelry. ⊠ *Via Mereu 56,* ☎ *0784/31426.* ⊡ *3,000 lire.* ☉ *Tues.–Sat. 9–1 and 3–7, Sun. 3–7.*

Make an excursion about 3 km (2 mi) east to **Mt. Ortobene** (2,900 ft) for some dizzying views over the gulch below Nuoro. Here you can also see up close the imposing statue of Christ the Redeemer that overlooks the city. Picnic tables make this a handy spot for an alfresco lunch stop.

OFF THE BEATEN PATH   **ORGOSOLO** – This old center of banditry halfway between Nuoro and Fonni is still a poor and largely depopulated village, but the houses have been daubed with *murales* (mural paintings) by local artists and some well-known Italian painters, transforming the town into an open-air art gallery.

Dining and Lodging

$$$ ✕⊡ **Su Gologone.** Despite attracting tourists in droves, this bustling
★   country inn still manages a friendly atmosphere. The restaurant alone is worth a detour for an authentic Sardinian meal. Island specialties include *maccarones de busa* (thick homemade pasta), culingiones, porcheddu, and sebadas. Wash it all down with the local Vernaccia. The hotel organizes riding and trekking expeditions. ⊠ *Località Su Gologone, 08025,* ☎ *0784/287512,* FAX *0784/287668. 65 rooms. Restaurant, bar, pool, miniature golf, tennis court. AE, MC, V. Closed Nov.–Mar.*

Nightlife and the Arts

The **Festa del Redentore** (Feast of the Redeemer) is held on the next-to-last Sunday in August.

Shopping

WOODEN MASKS

Crafted for local festivals, these disguises available at local shops make unusual and festive souvenirs.

Fonni

16 *30 km (19 mi) south of Nuoro.*

In the heart of the **Barbagia** region, Fonni is the highest town on the island and a good base for excursions by car to all sites of interest in this mountainous district that is Sardinia's most primitive, as well as the Monte Spada and the Bruncu Spina refuge on the Gennargentu Massif. Life in some villages seems not to have changed much since the Middle Ages. Here a rigidly patriarchal society perpetuates the unrelenting practice of vendetta, and strangers are advised to mind their own business. Tortuous roads wind and loop their way through the landscape; towns are small and undistinguished, their social fabric seemingly impervious to the 20th century. On feast days elaborate regional costumes are taken out of mothballs and worn as an explicit statement of community identity.

OFF THE BEATEN PATH

ARBATAX – If you have the stamina, take the rickety old train that runs on a single-gauge track between Cagliari and Arbatax, midway up the east coast. If all goes well, it takes about nine hours to cover the approximately 250 km (155 mi) of track, guaranteeing you a look at a Sardinia few tourists ever see. With daily, early-morning departures, the train rattles up into the Barbagia district through some breathtaking mountain scenery, then eases down into the desert landscape inland of Arbatax, where the trip ends on the dock next to the fishing boats. The train is run by the Ferrovie Complementari (☎ 070/491304), and the ticket costs less than 12,000 lire.

Nightlife and the Arts

You can see one of the most characteristic of the Barbagia's celebrations in local costume in Fonni on the **Feast of St. John,** June 24.

Shopping

Special **candies** are made from honey and nougat and sold in hilltop **Tonara,** southwest of Fonni. In the mountain village of **Aritzo,** about 3½ km (2 mi) south of Fonni, high up in the Barbagia, you'll find handcrafted **wooden utensils** and **furniture.**

En Route Head west on road 129 from Nuoro to Bosa, where you turn right into hilly and arid scrub country, with its abundance of cactus and juniper. Pines and olive trees shelter low buildings from the steady winds that make these parts ideal for sailing. About the only cash crop here is cork from the cork trees dotting the landscape. Yet in the low valleys and along the riverbeds, masses of oleander bloom in the summer, creating avenues of color.

Alghero

17 *34 km (21 mi) southwest of Sassari.*

Among the larger centers on the northwest coast is Alghero, an appealing walled resort town with a distinctly Spanish flavor. It was built and inhabited in the 14th century by the Aragonese and Catalans, who constructed seaside ramparts and sturdy towers encompassing an inviting nucleus of narrow, winding streets. Rich, wrought-iron scrollwork decorates balconies and screened windows; Spanish motifs appear in stone portals and in bell towers. The dialect spoken here is a version of Catalan, not Italian: locals would find it easier to converse in Barcelona than in Rome.

Nearby are broad sandy beaches and the spectacular heights of **Capo Caccia,** an imposing limestone headland to the west. At the base of the sheer cliff, the pounding sea has carved an entrance to the vast **Grotto of Neptune,** a fantastic cavern, which you must visit with a guide. By land, you reach the entrance at the base of the cliff by descending the more than 600 steps of the aptly named *escala del cabirol* (mountain goat's stairway), a dizzying enterprise—and the ascent is just as daunting. The excursion by sea is much less fatiguing, but is not possible when seas are rough. Boats leave the port of Alghero four times daily, or every hour or so in peak season, and the trip takes 2½ hours. *Grotto:* 12,000 *lire (includes mandatory tour).* Apr.–Sept., *daily 9–7; Oct., daily 10–5; Nov.–Mar., daily 8–2; tours on the hr. Boat tour:* ✉ *Navisarda,* ☎ *079/975599.* 15,000 *lire excluding ticket for grotto.* Apr.–Oct., *daily.*

Dining and Lodging

$$ ✕ **La Lepanto.** A covered veranda by the seafront marks out Alghero's top seafood restaurant, usually thronged with locals. The specialty is aragosta cooked in a variety of ways, including *alla catalana* (with tomato and onions). For starters, try risotto *nero di seppia* (with cuttlefish sauce). ✉ *Via Carlo Alberto 133,* ☎ *079/979116. AE, DC, MC, V. Closed Mon. Oct.–May.*

$ ✕ **Da Pietro.** On a narrow street in the picturesque old town near Largo San Francesco, this seafood restaurant has vaulted ceilings and a bustling atmosphere. The menu features *bucatini all'algherese* (pasta with a sauce of clams, capers, and tomatoes) and baked fish with white wine sauce. ✉ *Via Ambrogio Machin 18,* ☎ *079/979645. AE, DC, MC, V. Closed Wed. Oct.–May and 3 wks at Christmas.*

$$$–$$$$ 🏨 **Villa Las Tronas.** The villa is a former royal mansion on a rocky bluff
★ above the sea but still near the center of town. The gardens sheltering the hotel from the road impart a regal sense of seclusion, and there are great views across the water to the old town. Inside, the turn-of-the-century atmosphere is complemented by modern comforts and good en-suite facilities. The restaurant is open in summer only. ✉ *Lungomare Valencia 1, 07041,* ☎ *079/981818,* FAX *079/981044. 29 rooms. Restaurant, pool, exercise room, beach. AE, DC, MC, V.*

$$$ 🏨 **Carlos V (Carlos Quinto).** On the shore boulevard about 1 km (½ mi) from the center of town, this hillside hotel is modern but attractive, with porticoes and terraces, one of which has a swimming pool. Smallish but bright rooms all have a balcony, many with a sea view. Low season rates are a bargain. ✉ *Lungomare Valencia 24, 07041,* ☎ *079/979501,* FAX *079/980298. 110 rooms. Restaurant, pool, tennis courts. AE, MC, V.*

$ 🏨 **San Francesco.** Centrally located in Alghero's Spanish quarter, this hotel occupies the convent that was once attached to the church of San Francesco. The rooms are grouped around the 14th-century cloister and, though somewhat cramped, are modern and quiet. Breakfast is included in the price. ✉ *Via Machin 2, 07041,* ☎FAX *079/980330. 21 rooms. Bar, meeting rooms. MC, V. Closed Nov.*

Shopping

JEWELRY AND CORAL

Coral, still harvested in the bay, and gold jewelry are displayed in many specialist shops as well as more touristy outlets throughout Alghero's old quarter.

Sassari

⑱ *34 km (21 mi) northeast of Alghero, 212 km (132 mi) north of Cagliari.*

Inland Sassari is important as a university town and administrative center, notable for its historic, ornate cathedral and an archaeological museum. Sassari is the hub of several highways and secondary roads leading to various scenic coastal resorts, among them Stintino and Castelsardo (☞ *below*).

Castelsardo

⑲ *32 km (20 mi) northeast of Sassari.*

The walled seaside citadel of Castelsardo is a delight for basket lovers. Roadside stands and shops in the old town sell tons of island crafts: rugs, wrought iron, and baskets—in myriad shapes and colors.

☽ Take the children to see the **Elephant Rock** on the road into Castelsardo; hollowed out by primitive man to become a domus de janas, it resembles an elephant, trunk and all.

Shopping

There is an **ISOLA** workshop on Lungomare Colombo, where local handicrafts can be bought. The local specialty is a brightly colored basket made of dwarf palms.

Santa Teresa di Gallura

⑳ *68 km (42 mi) northeast of Castelsardo, 65 km (41 mi) northwest of Olbia.*

At the northern tip of Sardinia, Santa Teresa di Gallura retains the relaxed, carefree air of an authentic fishing village turned resort.

Dining and Lodging

$$ ✕🏠 **Canne al Vento.** This cheerful, family-run hotel and restaurant on
★ the edge of town is a popular choice. The restaurant specializes in authentic island cuisine, for example zuppa *cuata* (bread, cheese, and tomato soup), porcheddu, or seafood. The guest rooms fall into the inexpensive ($) category. ⊠ *Via Nazionale 23, 07028,* ☎ *0789/754219,* ⅜ *0789/754948. 22 rooms. MC, V. Closed Mon. and Oct.–Apr.*

$$$–$$$$ 🏠 **Grand Hotel Corallaro.** This hotel offers luxury accommodations in a panoramic spot overlooking the sea, not far from town center. ⊠ *Via Nazionale 85, 07028,* ☎ *0789/755475,* ⅜ *0789/755431. 82 rooms. Restaurant, pool, Turkish bath, exercise room. AE, DC, MC, V.*

La Maddalena

㉑ *30 km (19 mi) east of Santa Teresa di Gallura, 45 km (20 mi) northwest of Olbia.*

From the port of Palau you can visit the archipelago of La Maddalena, seven granite islands embellished with lush green scrub and wind-bent pines. Pilgrims pay homage to Garibaldi's tomb on the grounds of his hideaway on Caprera, one of the islands.

Porto Cervo

★ ㉒ *30 km (19 mi) north of Olbia.*

Sardinia's northeastern coast is fringed with low cliffs, inlets, and small bays. This has become an upscale vacationland, with glossy resorts, such as Baia Sardinia and Porto Rotondo, just outside the confines of the famed Costa Smeralda, developed by the Aga Khan, who accidentally discovered its charms—and potential—in 1965, when his yacht took shelter here from a storm. The Costa Smeralda is still dominated by his personality; its attractions remain geared to those who can measure themselves by the yardstick of his fabled riches. Sardinia's most expensive hotels are here, and the world's most magnificent yachts anchor in the waters of Porto Cervo. The trend has been to keep this enclave of the really rich an exclusive haven by encouraging more multimillionaires to build discreetly luxurious villas, and planning four more golf courses for their leisure.

All along the coast, carefully tended lush vegetation surrounds vacation villages and elaborate villa colonies that have sprung up over the past decade in a range of spurious architectural styles best described as bogus Mediterranean.

Lodging

$$$$ 🏨 **Cala di Volpe.** Long a magnet for the beautiful people, this establishment was built to resemble an ancient Sardinian village. The hotel's decor is rustic-elegant, with beamed ceilings, Sardinian arts and crafts, and porticoes overlooking the sea. The presidential suite in the highest tower has a private pool. ⊠ *Cala di Volpe, 07020,* ☎ *0789/96083,* FAX *0789/96442. 123 rooms and suites. Restaurant, bar, air-conditioning, pool, 3 tennis courts, beach. AE, DC, MC, V. Closed Oct.– mid-May.*

$$$$ 🏨 **Cervo.** Low Mediterranean buildings surround a large pool and garden in the heart of the Costa Smeralda's Porto Cervo. This complex is next to the marina and piazzetta (small piazza), a popular spot to see and be seen. The rooms are large and most have a terrace. ⊠ *Porto Cervo, 07020,* ☎ *0789/92003,* FAX *0789/92593. 88 rooms. Restaurant, piano bar, air-conditioning, pool, beach. AE, DC, MC, V. Closed Oct.–Easter.*

$$$ 🏨 **Nibaru.** Pinkish-red brick buildings with tiled roofs stand in a secluded inlet set in lush gardens—not bad for a hotel that enjoys all the best features of the Costa Smeralda at comparatively low rates. Guests are just a few yards from the sea and some superb swimming spots and also within easy access to the Pevero Golf Club and the tennis courts of Porto Cervo. ⊠ *Cala di Volpe, 07020,* ☎ *0789/96038,* FAX *0789/ 96474. 45 rooms. Restaurant, bar, pool. AE, DC, MC, V. Closed Oct.–May.*

Outdoor Activities and Sports

GOLFING

An 18-hole, world-class **Pevero Golf Course,** designed by Robert Trent Jones, is on the Bay of Pevero, near Porto Cervo (☎ 0789/96210).

SAILING

The **Yacht Club Costa Smeralda** at Porto Cervo (☎ 0789/91332) offers temporary memberships.

Shopping

Contemporary **pottery** displaying traditional motifs is a hot item, snatched up at whim along the Costa Smeralda.

Olbia

㉓ *30 km (19 mi) south of Costa Smeralda, 106 km (66 mi) north of Nuoro.*

Set amid the resorts of Sardinia's northeastern coast, Olbia is a lively little seaport, not heavily industrialized, at the head of a long, wide bay.

Lodging

$$ ▣ De Plam. Though aesthetically unimpressive, this seafront hotel can at least claim the best views in Olbia. The rooms are furnished in a motel style that is functional if not particularly memorable. It's convenient to the port (though still a taxi ride away), and the town center is a short walk away. ⊠ *Via de Filippi 33, 07026,* ☎ *0789/25777,* ℻ *0789/22648. 60 rooms. Restaurant, bar, air-conditioning, meeting rooms. AE, DC, MC, V.*

Shopping

The local **ISOLA** (⊠ Corso Umberto 28) has works for sale.

Golfo Aranci

㉔ *19 km (12 mi) northeast of Oristano.*

At the mouth of the Gulf of Olbia, Golfo Aranci is a blossoming resort and debarkation point for FS ferries from the mainland.

SARDINIA A TO Z

Arriving and Departing

By Boat

Large modern ferries run by Tirrenia Lines, Navarma Lines, and the FS (Italian State Railways) connect the island with the mainland. **Tirrenia** (☎ 06/4742041 or 06/4742242 in Rome, 010/258041 in Genoa, 081/7613688 in Naples) sails to several ports in Sardinia from Genoa, Civitavecchia, Naples, Palermo, and Trapani. **Navarma** (☎ 0565/9361) transports passengers and cars between Livorno and Olbia. **FS** ferries (☎ 0766/23273 on the mainland, 0789/46800 in Golfo Aranci) carry trains as well as passengers and cars; they sail from Civitavecchia to Golfo Aranci, near Olbia. The Civitavecchia–Olbia/Golfo Aranci run takes about eight hours and there are overnight sailings. Depending on the season, the service is scheduled two or three times a week; reservations are essential in the summer.

By Plane

Alitalia and Meridiana connect Rome, Milan, Pisa, and other cities on the mainland and in southern Europe with Sardinia. Flying is by far the fastest and easiest way to get to the island. The Rome–Cagliari flight takes about an hour. Sardinia's major airports are at Cagliari and Alghero, with another, smaller one, at Olbia, providing access to the Costa Smeralda.

Cagliari airport (☎ 070/240079) at Elmas is about 6 km (4 mi) from the center of town, and there is a regular bus service from the airport to Piazza Matteotti, in front of the train station. Alghero's **Fertilia Airport** (☎ 079/935035) is 13 km (8 mi) from the city. A bus links the airport with the air terminal on Corso Vittorio Emanuele II. **Costa Smeralda Airport** (☎ 0789/52600) is 4 km (2½ mi) outside Olbia.

Getting Around

By Bus

Cagliari is linked with the other towns of Sardinia by a network of buses. Local destinations are served by **ARST** (☎ 070/4098324). Major cities, excluding Olbia, are served by **PANI** (☎ 070/652326). The heart of the Sardinian bus system is the **Stazione Autolinee** (✉ Piazza Matteotti, across the square from the main tourist office) in Cagliari. You can pick up a schedule and route map from either of these sources; if you can't find a convenient bus service, you can go to the west side of the square to the main train station. City buses in Cagliari and Sassari operate on the same system as those on the mainland: buy your ticket first, at a tobacco shop or machine, and cancel it by punching it in the machine on the bus. Fares are low: about 1,100 lire per ride or 3,100 lire all day.

By Car

The best way to get around Sardinia is to drive. The roads are generally in good condition, but bear in mind that such roadside conveniences as gas stations and refreshment stands are infrequent on some routes, especially in the east. Cars may be taken on board most of the ferry lines connecting Sardinia with the mainland.

By Train

There are fairly good connections between Olbia, Cagliari, Sassari, and Oristano. You can reach Nuoro via Macomer; Alghero is reached via Sassari. Service on the few other local lines is infrequent and slow. The fastest train between Olbia and Cagliari takes more than four hours. A local train connects Golfo Aranci, the FS port for the train ferry, with Olbia and takes 20 minutes.

Contacts and Resources

Car Rental

Avis: Cagliari (✉ Train station, ☎ 070/668128; ✉ Airport, ☎ 070/240081). Olbia (✉ Via Genova 67, ☎ 0789/22420; ✉ Airport, ☎ 0789/69540). Sassari (✉ Via Mazzini 2, ☎ 079/235547). **Hertz:** Cagliari (✉ Piazza Matteotti 1, ☎ 070/668105; ✉ Airport, ☎ 070/240037). Olbia (✉ Via Regina Elena 34, ☎ 0789/21733; ✉ Airport, ☎ 0789/66024). Sassari (✉ Corso Francesco Vico, ☎ 079/232184). **Maggiore:** Sassari (✉ Viale Italia 3, ☎ 079/235507).

Emergencies

Police (☎ 112 or 113). **Hospital** (✉ Via Peretti, Cagliari, ☎ 070/543266). **Ambulance** (✉ Cagliari, ☎ 070/4092901).

Late-night pharmacies are open on a rotating basis; information on current schedules is pinned up on any pharmacy door or can be obtained by calling (☎ 192).

Guided Tours

HORSEBACK RIDING

The **Associazione Nazionale di Turismo Equestre** (✉ Via Carso 35a, Sassari, ☎ 079/299889) can provide information on renting mounts and joining riding parties with itineraries along the coast or into the heart of the island. The **Centro Vacanze Alabirdi** (✉ Arborea, near Oristano, ☎ 0783/800512) organizes horseback riding vacations. The **Centro Vacanze Su Gologone** (✉ Oliena, (☎ 0784/287512) also offers riding vacations.

ORIENTATION

Guided tours are good introductions to Sardinia. Travel from the Italian mainland is included, as are travel and accommodations on Sardinia. They should be booked through a travel agent.

Chiariva offers two group tours of Sardinia by bus with guide. A nine-day tour leaves from Genoa; an eight-day tour departs from Rome. Both operate from April–September. **Aviatour** has a similar eight-day tour leaving from either Milan or Rome. The tour also runs from April–September only. **Appian Line** can arrange a fly-drive package on the Costa Smeralda; transportation is by air, the rental car is picked up at the airport at Olbia. Accommodations are in good, but not outlandishly expensive, hotels on this famous coastline for the rich.

Travel Agency
Cagliari (✉ Viaggi Orru; ✉ Via Roma 95; ☎ 070/659858).

Visitor Information
Alghero (✉ Piazza Porta Terra 9, ☎ 079/979054). **Cagliari** (✉ Piazza Matteotti, ☎ 070/669255; ✉ Piazza Deffenu 9, ☎ 070/654811 or 167/013153 toll-free; ✉ Elmas Airport, ☎ 070/240200). **Nuoro** (✉ Piazza Italia 19, ☎ 0784/30083). **Olbia** (✉ Via Catello Piro, ☎ 0789/21453; ✉ City Hall, Golfo Aranci, ☎ 0789/21672 June–Aug. only); ✉ Costa Smeralda Airport, ☎ 0789/21453). **Oristano** (✉ Via Cagliari 278, ☎ 0783/74191). **Sassari** (✉ Viale Umberto 72, ☎ 079/233534).

17 Portraits of Italy

ITALY AT A GLANCE: A CHRONOLOGY

ca. 1000 BC   Etruscans arrive in central Italy.

ca. 800   Rise of Etruscan city-states.

753   Traditional date for the founding of Rome.

750   Greek city-states begin to colonize Sicily and southern Italy.

600   Latin language becomes dominant in Etruscan League; Rome becomes established urban center.

510   Foundation of the Roman republic; expulsion of Etruscans from Roman territory.

410   Rome adopts the 12 Tables of Law, based on Greek models.

343   Roman conquest of Greek colonies in Campania.

312   Completion of Appian Way to the south of Rome; an extensive Roman road system begins to develop.

264–241   First Punic War (with Carthage): increased naval power helps Rome gain control of southern Italy and then Sicily.

218–200   Second Punic War: Hannibal's attempted conquest of Italy, using elephants, is eventually crushed.

176   Roman Forum begins to take shape as the principal civic center in Italy.

146   Third Punic War: Rome razes city of Carthage and emerges as the dominant Mediterranean force.

133   Rome rules entire Mediterranean Basin except Egypt.

49   Julius Caesar conquers Gaul.

45   Civil War leaves Julius Caesar as sole ruler; Caesar's Forum is established.

44   Julius Caesar is assassinated.

31   The Battle of Actium resolves the power struggle that continued after Caesar's death; Octavian becomes sole ruler.

27   Rome's Imperial Age begins; Octavian (now named Augustus) becomes the first emperor and is later deified. The Augustan Age is celebrated in the works of Virgil (70 BC–AD 19), Ovid (43 BC–AD 17), Livy (59 BC–AD 17), and Horace (65 BC–AD 27).

14 AD   Augustus dies.

29   Jesus is crucified in the Roman colony of Judea.

43   Rome invades Britain.

50   Rome is the largest city in the world, with a population of a million.

65   Emperor Nero begins the persecution of Christians in the empire; Saints Peter and Paul are executed.

70–80   Vespasian builds the Colosseum.

98–117   Trajan's military successes are celebrated with his Baths (98), Forum (110), and Column (113); the Roman Empire reaches its apogee.

165   A smallpox epidemic ravages the Empire.

ca. 150–200   Christianity gains a foothold within the Empire, with the theological writings of Clement, Tertullian, and Origen.

212   Roman citizenship is conferred on all nonslaves in the Empire.

238   The first wave of Germanic invasions penetrates Italy.

293   Diocletian reorganizes the Empire into West and East.

313   The Edict of Milan grants toleration of Christianity within the Empire.

330   Constantine founds a new Imperial capital (Constantinople) in the East.

410   Rome is sacked by Visigoths.

476   The last Roman Emperor, Romulus Augustus, is deposed.

552   Eastern Emperor Justinian (527–565) recovers control of Italy.

570   Lombards gain control of much of Italy, including Rome.

590   Papal power expands under Gregory the Great.

610   Heraldius revives the Eastern Empire, thereafter known as the Byzantine Empire.

774   Frankish ruler Charlemagne invades Italy under papal authority and is crowned Holy Roman Emperor by Pope Leo III (800).

ca. 800–900   The breakup of Charlemagne's (Carolingian) realm leads to the rise of Italian city-states.

811   Venice is founded by mainlanders escaping Barbarian invasions.

1054   The Schism develops between Greek (Orthodox) and Latin churches.

ca. 1060   Europe's first university is founded in Bologna.

1077   Pope Gregory VII leads the Holy See into conflict with the Germanic Holy Roman Empire.

1152–90   Frederick I (Barbarossa) is crowned Holy Roman Emperor (1155); punitive expeditions by his forces (Ghibellines) are countered by the Guelphs, creators of the powerful Papal States in central Italy. Guelph–Ghibelline conflict becomes a feature of medieval life.

1204   Crusaders, led by Venetian doge Dandolo, capture Constantinople.

1257   The first of four wars is declared between Genoa and Venice; at stake is the maritime control of the eastern Mediterranean.

1262   Florentine bankers issue Europe's first bills of exchange.

1264   Charles I of Anjou invades Italy, intervening in the continuing Guelph–Ghibelline conflict.

1275   Marco Polo reaches the Orient.

1290–1375   Tuscan literary giants Dante Alighieri (1265–1321), Francesco Petrarch (1304–74), and Giovanni Boccaccio (1313–75) give written imprimatur to modern Italian language.

1309   The pope moves to Avignon in France, under the protection of French kings.

1355   Venetian doge Marino Falier is executed for treason.

1376   The pope returns to Rome, but rival Avignonese popes stand in opposition, creating the Great Schism until 1417.

1380   Venice finally disposes of the Genoese threat in the Battle of Chioggia.

1402 The last German intervention into Italy is repulsed by the Lombards.

1443 Brunelleschi's cupola is completed on Florence's Duomo.

1447 Nicholas V founds the Vatican Library. This begins an era of nepotistic popes who devalue the status of the papacy but greatly enrich the artistic and architectural patronage of the Holy City.

1469-92 Lorenzo "Il Magnifico," the Medici patron of the arts, rules in Florence.

1498 Girolamo Savonarola, the austere Dominican friar, is executed for heresy after leading Florence into a drive for moral purification, typified by his burning of books and decorations in the "Bonfire of Vanities."

1499 Leonardo da Vinci's *Last Supper* is completed in Milan.

1508 Michelangelo begins work on the Cappella Sistina.

1509 Raphael begins work on his *Stanze* in the Vatican.

1513 Machiavelli's *The Prince* is published.

1521 The Pope excommunicates Martin Luther of Germany, precipitating the Protestant Reformation.

1545-63 The Council of Trent formulates the Catholic response to the Reformation.

1546 Andrea del Palladio, architectural genius, wins his first commission in Vicenza.

1571 The combined navies of Venice, Spain, and the Papacy defeat the Turks in the Battle of Lepanto.

1626 The Basilica di San Pietro is completed in Rome.

1633 Galileo Galilei faces the Inquisition.

1652 Sant'Agnese in Agone church, Borromini's Baroque masterpiece, is completed in Rome.

1667 The Piazza di San Pietro, designed by Bernini, is completed.

ca. 1700 Opera develops as an art form in Italy.

1720-90 The Great Age of the Grand Tour: Northern Europeans visit Italy and start the vogue for classical studies. Among the famous visitors are Edward Gibbon (1758), Jacques-Louis David (1775), and Johann Wolfgang von Goethe (1786).

1778 Teatro alla Scala is completed in Milan.

1796 Napoléon begins his Italian campaigns, annexing Rome and imprisoning Pope Pius VI four years later.

1815 Austria controls much of Italy after Napoléon's downfall.

1848 Revolutionary troops under Risorgimento (Unification) leaders Giuseppe Mazzini (1805-72) and Giuseppe Garibaldi (1807-82) establish a republic in Rome.

1849 French troops crush rebellion and restore Pope Pius IX.

1860 Garibaldi and his "Thousand" defeat the Bourbon rulers in Sicily and Naples.

1870 Rome is finally captured by Risorgimento troops and is declared capital of Italy by King Vittorio Emanuele II.

1900 King Umberto I is assassinated by an anarchist; he is succeeded by King Vittorio Emanuele III.

1915 Italy enters World War I on the side of the Allies.

1922 Fascist "black shirts" under Benito Mussolini march on Rome; Mussolini becomes prime minister and later "Duce" (head of Italy).

1929 The Lateran Treaty: Mussolini recognizes Vatican City as a sovereign state, and the Church recognizes Rome as the capital of Italy.

1940–44 In World War II, Italy fights with the Axis powers until its capitulation (1943), when Mussolini flees Rome. Italian partisans and Allied troops from the landings at Anzio (January 1944) win victory at Cassino (March 1944) and force the eventual withdrawal of German troops from Italy.

1957 The Treaty of Rome is signed, and Italy becomes a founding member of the European Economic Community.

1966 November flood damages many of Florence's artistic treasures.

1968–79 The growth of left-wing activities leads to the formation of the Red Brigades and provokes right-wing reactions. Bombings and kidnappings culminate in the abduction and murder of Prime Minister Aldo Moro in 1980.

1980 Southern Italy is hit by a severe earthquake.

1991 Waves of refugees from neighboring Albania flood southern ports on the Adriatic. Mt. Etna erupts, spewing forth a lava stream that threatens the Sicilian town of Zafferana.

1992 The Christian Democrat Party, in power throughout the postwar period, loses its hold on a relative majority in Parliament.

1993 Italians vote for sweeping reforms after the Tangentopoli (Bribe City) scandal exposes widespread political corruption, including politicians' collusion with organized crime. A bomb outside the Galleria degli Uffizi in Florence kills five, but spares the museum's most precious artworks; authorities blame the Cosa Nostra, flexing its muscles in the face of a crackdown.

1994 A center-right coalition wins in spring elections, and media magnate Silvio Berlusconi becomes premier—only to be deposed within a year. Italian politics seem to be evolving into the equivalent of a two-party system.

1995 Newly appointed Lamberto Dini takes hold of the government's rudder and, as president of the Council of Ministers, institutes major reforms and replaces old-line politicians.

1996 A league of center-left parties wins national elections and puts together a government coalition that sees the Democratic Party of the Left (PDS), the former Communist party, into power for the first time ever in Italy. Thousands of Romans gathered in Piazza del Campidoglio to bid farewell to the late beloved actor Marcello Mastroianni, revered for his portraits of the consummate Italian charmer in films such as *La Dolce Vita, 8½*—both Federico Fellini films—and *Divorce Italian Style.*

1997 An austerity program designed to meet the European Union's economic standards for adoption of the Euro currency reinforces Italy's economic stability but fuels political controversy. Romans welcome the return of the bronze equestrian statue of Roman emperor Marcus Aurelius to its pedestal in Piazza del Campidoglio as a symbol of Rome's historic grandeur. Pope John Paul II makes a long-postponed trip to war-torn Sarajevo.

THE ARTLESS ART OF ITALIAN COOKING

You are staying with friends in their villa in a windswept olive orchard above Florence. After a day in town—a morning at the Palazzo Pitti, afternoon in the Brancacci Chapel—you have returned to rest. In the garden, you find your hostess lifting heavy tomatoes into a basket, the acrid smell of their skins wafting up in the gentle September heat. You pick basil and tug figs from a tree that warms its back against the 14th-century kitchen wall. Inside, you watch while your hostess rinses the greens in the quarried stone sink. The tomatoes are still sun-warm when she scoops them, chopped, into a blender with the basil and a stream of olive oil; she pours the mixture into a faience bowl over steaming pasta. You eat at the kitchen table, pour wine from a crockery pitcher, and wipe your bowl with torn chunks of flour-flecked bread. Over the greens your hostess drizzles more olive oil and a bit of rock salt pinched from an open bowl. The figs melt in your mouth like chocolate. A scalding syrup of Arabic coffee streams from the *macchinetta*, and you're ready for a midnight survey of the olive groves.

SIMPLE, EARTHY, at once wholesome and sensual, as sophisticated in its purity as the most complex cuisine, as inspired in its aesthetics as the art and architecture of its culture, Italian cooking strikes a chord that resonates today as it did in the Medici courts. Its enduring appeal can be traced to an ancient principle: respect for the essence of the thing itself—nothing more, nothing less. Like Michelangelo freeing the prisoners that dwelt within the stone—innate, organic—an Italian chef seems to intuitively seek out the crux of the thing he is about to cook and flatter it, subtly, with the purest of compliments. To lay a translucent sheet of prosciutto—earthy, gamey, faintly redolent of brine—across the juicy pulchritude of a melon wedge is a stroke of insight into the nature of two ingredients as profound as the imaginings of Galileo.

Considering the pizzas, lasagnas, and red-drenched spaghetti that still pass for Italian food abroad (despite a wave of enlightenment that revived "Northern" techniques in the 1980s), it's no surprise that visitors to Italy are often struck by the austerity of the true Italian dishes put before them. The pasta is only lightly accented, not drowning in an industrial ladle-full of strong, soupy sauce. And while there may have been a parade of vegetable *antipasti,* the salad itself bears no resemblance to the smorgasbord of Anglo-American salad bars—it's a simple mix of greens, a drizzle of oil, a spritz, perhaps, of red-wine vinegar. If you've just come from Germanic countries, you'll notice a lack of Maggi, the bottled brown "flavor enhancer" that singes the tongue with monosodium glutamate, on the table. If you've come from Belgium, you'll miss the sauceboat of Hollandaise. And if you've come from France, you may shrug dismissively at the isolated ingredients you're served, saying as other Frenchmen before you, "But this is not really a true *cuisine . . .*"

Ah, but it is. Shunning the complexities of heavy French sauces and avoiding the elaborate farce, Italian cuisine—having unloaded the aspirations of *alta cucina* onto its northern neighbors when Catherine de' Medici moved (chefs and all) to Paris—stands alone, proud, purist, unaffected.

The Italians' pride comes in part from a confidence in their raw ingredients, an earthiness that informs the appreciation of every citizen-connoisseur, from the roughest peasant in workers' blue to the vintner in shoulder-tied cashmere: they are in touch with land and sea. In the country, your host can tell you the source of every ingredient on the table, from the neighbor's potted goose to the porcini gathered in the beech grove yesterday. In the city, the market replaces the country network, and aggressive shopping will trace the genealogy of every mushroom, every artichoke, every wooden scoop of olives. And in balconies overhanging the seashore, the squid floating in their rich, blue-black ink were bought from a fisherman on the beach at dawn.

The spectrum of Italian regional cooking is as broadly varied as Italy's terrain, and cuisine and countryside are intimately allied. Emerging into sunlight from the Great St. Bernard pass into the Valle d'Aosta, the Piedmont, the hills of Lombardy, you'll find wood-lined alpine trattorias offering rib-sticking gnocchi and air-dried beef, bubbling pots of *bagna cauda*, slabs of polenta, hearty walnut *torta*. The pearl-spotted rice of Arborio, in the Po Valley, fuels an extraordinary array of risottos in Milan, where chefs shun olive oil in favor of the region's rich butter. Descend to Alba and savor the earthy perfume of truffles, the muscular Barolo wines. Cross over into Liguria and the cuisine changes as abruptly as the landscape: wild herbs, greens, and ground nuts flavor a panoply of sauces (consider the famous pesto, flavored with a "riviera" basil rarely found elsewhere), served as condiments to meat as often as over pasta. The succulent pink pork of a Parma ham, the golden butterfat in a Reggiano cheese were nurtured on the same fertile soil of Emilia-Romagna, both the culinary and agricultural heart of Italy, while the *bistecca* of Tuscany comes from Chianina beef, pampered on local prairie grass and slaughtered at a tender age. Head south for sun-plumped eggplant, and quasi-tropical artichokes—in Rome, fried in delicate batter; in Calabria, stuffed with meat and sharp Pecorino from its hillside sheep herds. The chickpeas in Sicilian dishes remind you you're nearly in North Africa. And, of course, on this slender leg of land you are never far from the sea, and the harvest of its *frutti di mare* graces nearly every region—but none more than the islands and tide-washed shores of the south. Careening in your rental car down the western coast, clinging to the waterfront through sea-shanty villages that cantilever over the roaring surf, you feel a morning lag: your breakfast of *latte macchiato* and sugary *cornetto* has worn away. A real espresso would hit the spot; you hurtle down a web of switchbacks and pull into a seaside inn. You sip aromatic coffee and watch the waves. An hour passes in reverie—an aperitif, perhaps? Another hour over the Martini rosso, and you give in to the impulse, adjourning to the dining room. The odor of wood smoke drifts from the kitchen. A nutty risotto with a blush of tomato precedes a vast platter—austere, unembellished—of smoke-grilled fish, still sizzling, lightly brushed with oil, and glittering with rock salt. At the table beside yours, when the platter arrives, the woman rises and fillets the fish dextrously, serving her husband and sons.

THERE'S A WHOLESOMENESS in the way Italians eat that is charming and contagious. If American foodies pick and kvetch and French gastronomes worship, Italians plunge into their meal with frank joy, earnest appreciation, and ebullient conversation. Yet they do not overindulge: portions are light, the drinking gentle, late suppers spartan with concern for digestion uppermost. It's as if the voice of Mamma still whispers moderation in their ear. They may, on the other hand, take disproportionate pleasure in watching guests eat, in surrounding them with congenial company, in pouncing on the bill. (This wholesome spirit even carries into the very bars: unlike the dark, louche atmosphere of Anglo lounges and pubs, in Italy you'll drink your *amaro* in a fluorescent-lit coffee bar without a whiff of sin in the air.)

Yet for all their straightforwardness, Italians are utterly at ease with their heritage, steeped from birth in the art and architecture that surrounds them. Without a hint of the grandiose, they'll construct a still life of figs and Bosc pears worthy of Caravaggio; a butcher will drape iridescent pheasants and quail, heads dangling, with the panache of a couturier. Consider the artless beauty of ruby-raw beef on an emerald bed of arugula, named for the preferred colors of the Venetian painter Carpaccio; pure white porcelain on damask; a mosaic of olives and pimientos in blown glass; a flash of folkloric pottery on a polished plank of oak. In fact, it must be said: a large part of the pleasure of Italian dining is dining in Italy. We have all eaten in Italian restaurants elsewhere. The food can be superb, the ingredients authentic, the pottery and linens imported by hand. Yet who can conjure the blood-red ocher crumbling to gold on a Roman wall, the indigo and pastel hues of fishing boats rocking in a marina, the snow flurry of sugar papers on a café floor? These impart the essence that—as much as the basil on your *bruschetta*—flavors your Italian dining experience.

Inside the great walls of Lucca, you are lunching—slowly, copiously, and at length—in the shade of a vaulted portico. Strips of roasted eggplant and pepper steeped in garlic and oil; tortelloni stuffed with squab in a pool of butter and sage; roasted veal laced with green peppercorns; blackberries in thick cream. The bottle of Brunello di Montalcino, alas, is drained. It has been a perfect morning, walking the ramparts, and you have found the perfect restaurant: a Raphaelesque perspective of arcades and archways, pillars, porches, and loges spreads before you. The shadows and lines are strong in the afternoon sun; you admire from your seat in the cross breeze. It's only slowly that you realize that this Merchant/Ivory moment has a sound-track, so organic to the scene you hadn't noticed—but now you feel goosebumps rising on your neck. It is Puccini: a young woman is singing, beautifully, from a groined arcade across the square, accompanied by a portable tape player.

". . . Ma quando vien lo sgelo . . . il primo sole è mio . . ."

Your coffee goes cold, untouched until the song, the moment, are over—and, in all its multifaceted magnificence, your Italian meal as well.

—Nancy Coons

THE PASSIONATE EYE: ITALIAN ART THROUGH THE AGES

ITALIAN ART FLOWS as naturally as its wine, its sunshine, and its amore, and it has been springing from the Italian spirit for nearly as long. Perhaps nowhere in the world has such a vital creative impulse flourished so bountifully within the noble sweep of the classical tradition. Perhaps no other country's cultural life has been so inextricably interwoven with its history.

And yet, Italy lives comfortably in the midst of all her accumulated treasures. She accepts them casually and affectionately, as she does her children and her flowers. True, some of her precious store has been gathered into world-famous museums, but Italians know best and love most intimately the art that surrounds their daily activity. They go to church among thousand-year-old mosaics, buy their groceries in a shop open since the time of Columbus, picnic on the steps of a temple that was old when Christ was born, and attend the opera in the same theaters where Rossini and Verdi saw their works premiered. Italy wears the raiment of her heritage with a light and touching grace. She must: It is the very fabric of her life. For travelers from other countries, however, Italian art remains unique, extraordinary, worthy of worship. Here we offer a short history, focusing on Italy's greatest artistic achievement, the Renaissance—often called the nursery of Western art. The discoveries of 14th- and 15th-century Italian artists making it possible to render a realistic image of a person or an object determined the course of Western art right up until the late 19th century. Following the essay is a glossary of art and architectural terms that will prove useful in understanding the artistic treasures of Italy.

Art in the Middle Ages

The eastern half of the Roman Empire, based in Constantinople (Byzantium) was powerful long after the fall of Rome in AD 476: Italy remained influenced—and at times ruled—by the Byzantines. The artistic revolution began when artists started to rebel against the Byzantine ethic, which dictated that art be exclusively Christian and that its aim be to arouse a sensation of mystical awe and reverence in the onlooker. This ethic forbade frivolous pagan portraits, bacchanalian orgy scenes, or delicate landscapes with maidens gathering flowers, as painted and sculpted by the Romans. Instead, biblical stories were depicted in richly colored mosaics—rows of figures against a gold background. (You can see some of the finest examples of this art at Ravenna, once the Western capital of the Empire, on the Adriatic coast.) Even altarpieces, painted on wood, followed the same model—stiff figures surrounded by gold, with no attempt made at an illusion of reality.

In the 13th century, the era of St. Francis and of a new humanitarian approach to Christianity, artists in Tuscany began to portray real people in real settings. Cimabue was the first to feel his way in this direction, but it was Giotto who broke decisively with the Byzantine style. Even if his sense of perspective is nowhere near correct and his figures still had typically Byzantine slanting eyes, he painted palpably solid people who, presumably, experienced real emotions.

By the end of the 14th century, the International Gothic Style (which had arrived in Italy from France) had made further progress toward realism, but more with depictions of plants, animals, and clothes than with the human figure. And, as you can see from Gentile da Fabriano's *Adoration of the Magi*, housed in the Uffizi Gallery in Florence, it was mainly a decorative art, still very much like a Byzantine mosaic.

Italian architecture during the Middle Ages followed a number of different trends. In the south, the solid Norman Romanesque style was dominant; towns such as Siena and Pisa in central Italy had their own Romanesque style, more graceful than its northern European counterparts. Like northern Romanesque, it was dominated by simple geometric forms, but buildings were covered with decorative toylike patterns done in multicolored marble. In northern Italy, building was in a more solemn red brick.

In Tuscany, the region around Florence, the 13th century was a time of great political and economic growth, and there was a desire to celebrate the new wealth and power in the region's buildings. This is why such civic centers as the Palazzo Vecchio in Florence are so big and fortresslike. Florence's cathedral, the Duomo, was built on a colossal scale mainly in order to outdo the Pisans and the Sienese, Florence's rivals. All these Tuscan cathedrals are in the Italian version of Gothic, a style that originated in France and found its expression there in tall, soaring, light-and-airy verticality, intended to elevate the soul. The spiritual aspect of Gothic never really caught on in Italy, where the top priority for a church (as representative of a city) was to be grander and more imposing than the neighboring cities' churches.

Art in the Renaissance

The Renaissance, or "rebirth," did not evolve simply from a set of newfound artistic skills; the movement represented a revolution in attitudes whereby each individual was thought to play a specific role in the divine scheme of things. By fulfilling this role, it was believed the individual gained a new dignity. It was no coincidence that this revolution took place in Florence, which in the 15th century was an influential, wealthy, highly evolved city-state. Artists here had the leisure, prestige, and self-confidence to develop their talent and produce works that would reflect this new dignity and strength as well as their own prowess.

The sculptor Donatello, for example, wanted to astound, rather than please, the spectator with his defiant warts-and-all likenesses and their intense, heroic gazes. In painting, Masaccio's figures have a similarly assured air.

Art had changed gears in the early Renaissance: the Classical Age was now the model for a noble, moving, and realistic art. Artists studied ancient Roman ruins for what they could learn about proportion and balance. They evolved the new science of perspective and took it to its limits with sometimes bizarre results, as in Uccello's dizzily receding *Deluge* (in Florence's church of Santa Maria Novella) or his carousel-like *Battle of San Romano* (in the Uffizi in Florence). One of the most frequently used perspective techniques was that of foreshortening, or making an object seem smaller and more contracted, to create the illusion of distance. From this technique emerged the *sotto in su* effect—literally, "from below upwards," meaning that the action in the picture takes place above you, with figures, buildings, and landscapes correspondingly foreshortened. It's a clever visual trick that must have delighted visitors who walked into, for example, Mantegna's Camera degli Sposi in Mantua and saw what appeared to be people curiously looking down at them through a gap in the ceiling.

The concept of the universal man was epitomized by the artist who was at home with an array of disciplines, including the science of perspective, Greek, Latin, anatomy, sculpture, poetry, architecture, philosophy—even engineering, as in the case of Leonardo da Vinci, the universal man par excellence. Not surprisingly, there was a change in attitude toward artists: whereas previously they had been considered merely anonymous workmen trained to carry out commissions, now they were seen as giant personalities, immensely skillful and with highly individual styles.

The new skills and realistic effects of Florentine painting rapidly found a sympathetic response among Venetian painters. Gentile Bellini and Antonio Carpaccio, just two of the many whose work fills the Accademia, took to covering their canvases with crowd scenes, buildings, canals, processions, dogs, ships, parrots, and chimneys. These were generally narrative paintings, telling the story of a saint's life or simply depicting everyday scenes.

It was the emphasis on color, though, that made Venetian art Venetian, and it was the 15th-century masters of color, preeminently Giovanni Bellini and Giorgione, who began to use it no longer as decoration but as a means to create a particular atmosphere. How different the effect of Giorgione's *Tempest* (in the Accademia) would be with a sunny blue sky instead of the ominous grays and dark greens that fill the background! For the first time, the atmosphere not the figures became the central focus of painting.

In architecture the Gothic excesses of the 13th century were toned down in the 14th, while the 15th ushered in a completely new approach. The humanist ideal was expressed through classical Roman design.

In Florence, Brunelleschi used Roman columns for the basilica of San Lorenzo; Roman-style rustication (massive exterior blocks) for the Pitti Palace; and Roman round arches—as opposed to pointed Gothic ones—for his Spedale degli Innocenti (Foundling Hospital), which is generally considered the first truly classical building of the Renaissance. Leon Battista Alberti's treatise on ideal proportion was even more influential as a manifesto of the Renaissance movement. Suddenly, architects had become erudite scholars and architecture far more earnest.

High Renaissance and Mannerism

Florence in the late 15th century and Rome in the early 16th (following its sacking in 1527) underwent a traumatic political and religious upheaval that naturally came to be reflected in art. Classical proportion and realism no longer seemed enough. The heroic style suddenly looked hollow and outdated. Tuscan artists such as Pontormo and Rosso Fiorentino found expression for their unease in discordant colors, elongated forms, tortured looks in staring eyes. Giambologna carved his *Hercules and the Centaur* (in Florence's Museo del Bargello) at the most agonizing moment of their battle, when Hercules bends the entaur's back to the point where it is about to snap. This is Mannerism, a style in which optimism and self-confidence are gone. What remains is a self-conscious, stylized show of virtuosity, the effect of which is neither to please (like Gothic) nor to impress (like Renaissance art), but to disquiet. Even Bronzino's portraits are cold, unsmiling, and far removed from the relaxed mood of the Renaissance portrait. By the 1530s an artistic exodus from Florence had taken place; Michelangelo had left for Rome, and Florence's golden age was over.

Venice, meanwhile, was following its own path. Titian's painting was a more virtuoso version of Bellini's and Giorgione's poetic style, but Titian later shifted the emphasis back to figures, rather than atmosphere, as the central focus of his paintings. Titian's younger contemporaries in Venice—Veronese, Tintoretto, and Bassano—wanted to make names for themselves. They started working on huge canvases—which gave them more freedom of movement—playing all sorts of visual games: juggling with viewpoints and perspective and using dazzlingly bright colors. This visual trickery suggests a natural parallel with the self-conscious artifice of Florentine painting of the same period, but the exuberance of these Venetian painters, and the increasingly emotional quality of their work remained significantly more vital than the arid and ever more sterile works of central Italy toward the end of the 16th century.

Mannerism found a fairly precise equivalent in architecture. In Florence the rebellious younger generation (Michelangelo, Ammanati, Vasari) used the same architectural vocabulary as the Renaissance architects, but distorted it deliberately and bizarrely in a way that would have made Alberti's hair stand on end. Michelangelo's staircase at the Biblioteca Laurenziana in Florence, for example, spreads out like a stone fan, filling almost the entire floor space of the vestibule. Likewise, the inside walls are treated as if they were facades, though with columns and niches disproportionately large for the size of the room.

Andrea del Palladio, whose theories and elegant palaces were to be immensely influential on architecture elsewhere in Europe and as far north as England, was one of the greatest architects of the period.

The 17th and 18th Centuries

In the second half of the 16th century, Italy was caught up in the Counter-Reformation. This movement was a reaction against the Protestant Reformation of the Christian church that was sweeping through Europe. The Counter-Reformation enlisted art as a weapon, an instrument for the diffusion of the Catholic faith. Artists were discouraged from expressing themselves as freely as they had been before and from creating anything that was not of a religious nature. But within this religious framework they were able to evolve a style that appealed to the senses. The Baroque—an emotional and heroic style that lasted through most of the 17th century—was propaganda art, designed to overwhelm the masses through its visual illusion, dramatic lighting, strong colors, and violent movement. There was an element of seduction in this propaganda: the repressive religiosity of the Counter-Reformation went hand in hand with a barely disguised eroticism. The best-known example of this ambiguity is Bernini's sculpture of the *Ecstasy of Santa Teresa* in Rome, in which the saint sinks back in what could be a swoon of either pain or pleasure, while a smiling angel stands over her holding an arrow. Both the painting and architecture of this period make extensive use of sensuous curves.

The cradle of the Baroque was Rome, where Pietro da Cortona and Bernini channeled their genius into spectacular theatrical frescoes, sculptures, palaces, and churches. Rome had become the artistic center of Italy. Florence was politically and artistically dead by this time, and Venice was producing only hack imitations of Titian's and Tintoretto's paintings. In the 18th century, Venice came back into its own and Rome was practically finished as an artistic center. Venetian artists adopted the soft, overripe version of Baroque—known as Rococo—that had originated in France. Free from the spiritual ideals that motivated the Baroque style, Rococo celebrated sensuousness (and sensuality) for its own sake. Although Venice was nearing the last stages of its political decline, there was still immense wealth in the city, mostly in the hands of families who wished to make the world know about it—and what better way than through vast, dazzling Rococo canvases, reassuringly stylized and removed from reality? The revival began with Sebastiano Ricci and was expertly elaborated on by Tiepolo. But it could never have taken place had there not been a return to the city's great artistic traditions. Late 16th-century color technique and expertise were drawn on and fused with what had been learned from the Baroque to create the breathtaking, magical, decadent world of the Venetian Rococo.

This was the final flowering of Venetian painting. The death of Francesco Guardi in 1793, compounded by the fall of the Republic of Venice in 1797, marked the effective end of the city's artistic life. Neoclassicism found no champion here, except for the sculptor Canova, who, in any case, did his finest work after he left Venice.

Today, the great tradition of Italian art is widely diffused, perhaps diluted, but it is certainly too early to write its obituary. That has been done periodically over the past 20 centuries, inevitably to the chagrin of the mistaken commentator. In the midst of the burgeoning vitality, which charms and occasionally maddens the visitor, the arts are not long to be neglected. Italians live the tradition too deeply.

—Sheila Brownlee

ARTISTICALLY SPEAKING: A GLOSSARY

THE ELOQUENCE of the world's greatest masterpieces can be deafening, and Italy's treasures—their message made manifest in marble, pigment, and precious metals—instill a spirit of awe. The privilege of enjoying this bounty of the ages can be greatly deepened and enhanced by a familiarity with the language and terms of art-speak. Here is a limited glossary for the interested layman. Many of these Italian words are now part of the basic art history vocabulary.

Acanthus: Sculptural ornamentation from antiquity; it's based on the foliage of the acanthus plant.

Apse: A semicircular terminus found behind the altar in a church.

Atrium: The inner courtyard of an ancient Roman villa or an early church.

Badia: From *abbazia*; an abbey church.

Baldachino: A columned canopy—often made of stone—above a church altar.

Baptistery: A separate structure or area in a church where rites of baptism are held.

Baroque: A 17th-century European art movement in which dramatic, elaborate ornamentation was used to stir viewers' emotions. The most famous Italian Baroque artists were Carracci, Bernini, and Caravaggio.

Basilica: A rectangular church structure, usually divided into three or five aisles by rows of columns.

Belvedere: Usually a lookout point for vistas; the word means "beautiful view."

Campanile: A bell tower of a church.

Capital: The crowning section of a column, usually decorated with Doric, Ionic, or Corinthian ornament.

Chiaroscuro: Meaning "light/dark"; refers to the distribution of light and shade in a painting, either with a marked contrast or a muted tonal gradation.

Cinquecento: The 16th century; used in reference to Italian art or literature.

Contrapposto: A dramatic pose of a sculpted figure in which the upper portion of the body is placed in opposition to the lower portion.

Cortile: A courtyard, often with a second-story gallery.

Cupola: Dome.

Duomo: Cathedral.

Fresco: A wall-painting technique—favored by the Renaissance greats—in which pigment was applied to wet lime plaster. Such painting was usually done to one small section at a time so that the plaster wouldn't dry before the pigment was applied.

Gothic: Delicate medieval architectural and ornamental style using pointed arches, high interior vaulting, and flying buttresses to emphasize height and, via symbolism, an ascension to heaven. The term is also used to describe the painting style made famous by Giotto and Simone Martini.

Grotesques: Wall decoration of fantasy animal/human forms embellished with flowers; first used in the Golden House of Nero and rediscovered during the Renaissance.

Loggia: Roofed balcony or gallery.

Maestà: Majestic image of the Virgin Mary enthroned and surrounded by angels.

Mannerism: Style of the mid-16th century, in which artists—such as Bronzino and Il Rosso—sought to replace the warm, humanizing ideals of Leonardo and Raphael with super-elegant, coldly emotional forms. Portraits in the Mannerist style feature florid colors, high-fashion anatomies, and frosty demeanors.

Nave: A church's main aisle, often flanked by columns.

Palazzo: A palace or other important building.

Pentimento: A visible correction in a painting or drawing.

Perspective: The illusion of three-dimensional space that was obtained in the early 15th-century with the discovery that all parallel lines running in one direction meet at a single point on the horizon known as the vanishing point. Leonardo da Vinci later perfected aerial perspective, in which gradations of *sfumato* (haze) and color can be used to create the illusion of distance.

Piano Nobile: The main floor of a palace (sometimes the second floor).

Pietà: A hallowed image of the Virgin Mary holding the crucified body of Christ on her lap.

Polyptych: A painting—often an altarpiece—on multiple wooden panels that are joined. A three-paneled painting is a tryptych.

Predella: A series of small paintings found below the main section of an altarpiece.

Putti: Cherubs.

Quattrocento: The 15th century; used in reference to Italian art and literature.

Renaissance: Major school of Italian art, literature, and philosophy (14th century–16th century) that fused innovations in realism with the rediscovery of the great heritage of classical antiquity. After Giotto introduced a new naturalism into painting in the 14th century, Florentine artists of the 1430s, such as Masaccio and Fra Fillipo Lippi, paved the way for the later 15th-century realism of Botticelli and Signorelli. While reaching first flower in Florence, the movement culminated in Rome with the High Renaissance (circa 1490–1520) and the masterpieces of Leonardo, Raphael, and Michelangelo.

Rococo: Light, dainty 18th-century art and architectural style created in reaction to heavy Baroque. Tiepolo is the leading painter of the Rococo style.

Romanesque: Architectural style of the 11th and 12th centuries that reworked ancient Roman forms, particularly barrel and groin vaults. Stark, severe, and magisterial, Romanesque basilicas are among Italy's most awe-inspiring churches.

Sacra Conversazione: The motif of the "holy conversation," showing the Madonna and Child in the midst of and/or interacting with saints.

Tondo: Circular painting or sculpture.

Trompe l'Oeil: Illusionary tricks of perspective used to dissolve painted space into the real space of the spectator.

Veduta: A scene or vista painting, favored in the 18th century.

BOOKS AND VIDEOS

Books

The Italians, by Luigi Barzini, is a comprehensive, lively analysis of the Italian national character, still worthy reading although published in 1964 (Atheneum). More recent musings on Italian life include *Italian Days,* by Barbara Grizzuti Harrison (Ticknor & Fields), and *That Fine Italian Hand,* by Paul Hofmann (Henry Holt), for many years *New York Times* bureau chief in Rome. Matthew Spender's *Within Tuscany* (Viking) and Tim Parks's *Italian Neighbors* (Grove) are accounts of life in rural Tuscany and Verona by British expatriates.

Classics of the travel essay genre include James Morris's *World of Venice* (Harcourt Brace Jovanovich), Mary McCarthy's *Venice Observed* and *The Stones of Florence* (both HBJ also), Lawrence Durrell's *Sicilian Carousel* (out of print), Elizabeth Bowen's *A Time in Rome* (Penguin), and James Lees-Milne's *Roman Mornings* and *Venetian Mornings* (New Amsterdam). To some observers, the most beautiful book about the most beautiful city in the world is Richard de Combray's *Venice, Frail Barrier* (Doubleday). Historic musings about Italy are offered in Henry James's perceptive *Italian Hours* (offered in many editions, including *Traveling in Italy with Henry James: Essays,* William Morrow), Edith Wharton's *Italian Backgrounds* and *Italian Villas and their Gardens* (Ecco Press), and Axel Munthe's *Story of San Michele* (Carroll and Graf) about his celebrated villa on Capri.

For historical background, Edward Gibbon's *Decline and Fall of the Roman Empire* is available in three volumes (Modern Library). Consult Giorgio Vasari's *Lives of the Artists* and *The Autobiography of Benvenuto Cellini,* and Machiavelli's *The Prince* (all available in Penguin Classics) for eyewitness accounts of the 16th century. Otherwise, *The Civilization of the Renaissance in Italy,* by 19th-century Swiss historian Jacob Burckhardt (Modern Library), offers a classic foundation. Christopher Hibbert's *House of Medici* (Quill/William Morrow) details the family's rise and fall.

A comprehensive introduction to Italian art is Frederick Hartt's *History of Italian Renaissance Art* (Abrams). For aficionados of Rome's artistic treasures, Georgina Masson's *Companion Guide to Rome* (Penguin) is a must. Eloquent writing as well as important scholarship is found in the works of such celebrated art historians as Richard Krautheimer, John Pope-Hennessy, John Shearman, Irving Lavin, Charles de Tolnay, and André Chastel. Palladio's architecture is beautifully distilled in James Ackerman's *Palladio* (Penguin).

For lively historical fiction, pick up Irving Stone's *Agony and the Ecstasy* (NAL) based on the life of Michelangelo. Susan Sontag's *Volcano Lover* (Farrar Straus Giroux), set in 18th-century Naples, is about Sir William Hamilton, his wife Emma, and Lord Nelson. *The Leopard,* by Giuseppe di Lampedusa (Pantheon), is a compelling portrait of Sicily during the political upheavals of the 1860s. Historical fiction set in World War II includes *History: A Novel,* by Elsa Morante (Vintage Aventura), about the fate of inhabitants of wartime Rome, and *Bread and Wine* by Ignazio Silone (Signet Classics), about Italian peasants under the control of the Fascists. Anne Cornelison's nonfiction *Women of the Shadows* portrays the life of peasant women in early–World War I southern Italy (Vintage). More recently, mysteries set in Italy have found great popularity, including the Urbino Macintyre series of Edward Sklepowich and the Lovejoy series of Jonathan Gash. Florence is the setting for two of Magdalen Nabb's entertaining thrillers: *Death in Autumn* and *Death of a Dutchman.*

To catch glimpses of the Tuscan landscape pick up Harold Acton's *Great Houses of Tuscany: The Tuscan Villas* (Viking) or Carey More's *Views from a Tuscan Vineyard* (Pavillion). From a recent look at Umbrian life, try Lisa St. Aubin de Terán's *A Valley in Italy: The Many Seasons of a Villa in Umbria* (HarperCollins). The glories of historic Italian gardens are caught in the ravishing photographs of three recent volumes: Judith Chatfield's *Gardens of the Italian Lakes* (Rizzoli), Ethne Clark's *Gardens of Tuscany* (Weidenfeld & Nicolson), and Nicolas Saphiena's *Gardens of Naples* (Scala Books). Waverley Root's *Food of Italy* (Vintage), published in 1977, is not a cookbook but an unsurpassed region-by-region exploration of the subject. Marcella Hazan's *Essentials of Classic Italian Cooking* (Knopf)—with modern sensibilities and lowfat diets in mind—is an update of her earlier cookbooks. It goes well with *Italian Wine* (Knopf), by her husband, Victor Hazan, or with *Vino*, by Burton Anderson (Little Brown). *Made in Italy,* a shopper's guide by Annie Brody and Patricia Schultz (Workman) is unrevised but still valuable for its knowledge of Italian products and producers.

Magazines

A magazine for Italophiles, *Italy Italy,* published in Italy in English, is available in the United States (Italian American Multimedia Corporation: ✉ 138 Wooster St., New York, NY 10012, ☎ 212/674–4132, 𝖥𝖠𝖷 212/674–4933; $30 for 6 yearly issues). Italian travel magazines, such as *Bell'Italia, Dove,* and *Gulliver,* often give pointers to new, exotic, and overlooked destinations.

Videos

The delightful *Roman Holiday* (1953), in which a young princess plays hooky from her royal entourage to go "slumming" with Gregory Peck, won Audrey Hepburn an Oscar. In *Summertime* (1955), a visiting American (Katharine Hepburn) falls in love with Venice and a handsome Venetian shopkeeper (Rossano Brazzi). Federico Fellini's *La Dolce Vita* (1961), with Marcello Mastroianni discovering the decadence of high society in Rome, gave its name to an era. *Fellini's Roma* (1972) is the director's paean to the city; *Amarcord* (1974), his paean to the small Adriatic town of his childhood. Merchant/Ivory's *Room with a View* (1986), a period piece based on the E. M. Forster novel of the same name, is good cinema with good views of Florence.

ITALIAN VOCABULARY

	English	Italian	Pronunciation
Basics			
	Yes/no	Sí/No	see/no
	Please	Per favore	pear fa-**vo**-ray
	Yes, please	Sí grazie	see **grah**-tsee-ay
	Thank you	Grazie	**grah**-tsee-ay
	You're welcome	Prego	**pray**-go
	Excuse me, sorry	Scusi	**skoo**-zee
	Sorry!	Mi dispiace!	mee dis-spee-**ah**-chay
	Good morning/ afternoon	Buon giorno	bwohn **jor**-no
	Good evening	Buona sera	**bwoh**-na **say**-ra
	Good bye	Arrivederci	a-ree-vah-**dare**-chee
	Mr. (Sir)	Signore	see-**nyo**-ray
	Mrs. (Ma'am)	Signora	see-**nyo**-ra
	Miss	Signorina	see-nyo-**ree**-na
	Pleased to meet you	Piacere	pee-ah-**chair**-ray
	How are you?	Come sta?	**ko**-may **stah**
	Very well, thanks	Bene, grazie	**ben**-ay **grah**-tsee-ay
	And you?	E lei?	ay **lay**-ee
	Hello (phone)	Pronto?	**proan**-to
Numbers			
	one	uno	**oo**-no
	two	due	**doo**-ay
	three	tre	tray
	four	quattro	**kwah**-tro
	five	cinque	**cheen**-kway
	six	sei	say
	seven	sette	**set**-ay
	eight	otto	**oh**-to
	nine	nove	**no**-vay
	ten	dieci	dee-**eh**-chee
	eleven	undici	**oon**-dee-chee
	twelve	dodici	**doe**-dee-chee
	thirteen	tredici	**tray**-dee-chee
	fourteen	quattordici	kwa-**tore**-dee-chee
	fifteen	quindici	**kwin**-dee-chee
	sixteen	sedici	**say**-dee-chee
	seventeen	diciassette	dee-cha-**set**-ay
	eighteen	diciotto	dee-**cho**-to
	nineteen	diciannove	dee-cha-**no**-vay
	twenty	venti	**vain**-tee
	twenty-one	ventuno	vain-**too**-no
	twenty-two	ventidue	vayn-tee-**doo**-ay
	thirty	trenta	**train**-ta

forty	quaranta	kwa-**rahn**-ta
fifty	cinquanta	cheen-**kwahn**-ta
sixty	sessanta	seh-**sahn**-ta
seventy	settanta	seh-**tahn**-ta
eighty	ottanta	o-**tahn**-ta
ninety	novanta	no-**vahn**-ta
one hundred	cento	**chen**-to
ten thousand	diecimila	dee-eh-chee-**mee**-la
one hundred thousand	centomila	chen-to-**mee**-la

Useful Phrases

Do you speak English?	Parla inglese?	**par**-la een-**glay**-zay
I don't speak Italian	Non parlo italiano	non **par**-lo ee-tal-**yah**-no
I don't understand	Non capisco	non ka-**peess**-ko
Can you please repeat?	Può ripetere?	pwo ree-**pet**-ay-ray
Slowly!	Lentamente!	**len**-ta-men-tay
I don't know	Non lo so	noan lo **so**
I'm American/ British	Sono americano(a)	**so**-no a-may-ree-**kah**-no(a)
	Sono inglese	**so**-no een-**glay**-zay
What's your name?	Come si chiama?	**ko**-may see kee-**ah**-ma
My name is . . .	Mi chiamo . . .	mee kee-**ah**-mo
What time is it?	Che ore sono?	kay **o**-ray **so**-no
How?	Come?	**ko**-may
When?	Quando?	**kwan**-doe
Yesterday/today/ tomorrow	Ieri/oggi/domani	**yer**-ee/**o**-jee/do-**mah**-nee
This morning/ afternoon	Stamattina/Oggi pomeriggio	sta-ma-**tee**-na/**o**-jee po-mer-**ee**-jo
Tonight	Stasera	sta-**ser**-a
What?	Che cosa?	kay **ko**-za
What is it?	Che cos'è?	kay ko-**zay**
Why?	Perché?	pear-**kay**
Who?	Chi?	kee
Where is . . .	Dov'è . . .	doe-**veh**
the bus stop?	la fermata dell'autobus?	la fer-**mah**-ta del ow-toe-**booss**
the train station?	la stazione?	la sta-tsee-**oh**-nay
the subway station?	la metropolitana?	la may-tro-po-lee-**tah**-na
the terminal?	il terminal?	eel ter-mee-**nahl**
the post office?	l'ufficio postale?	loo-**fee**-cho po-**stah**-lay
the bank?	la banca?	la **bahn**-ka
the . . . hotel?	l'hotel . . .?	lo-**tel**
the store?	il negozio?	ell nay-**go**-tsee-o
the cashier?	la cassa?	la **kah**-sa
the . . . museum?	il museo . . .?	eel moo-**zay**-o

the hospital?	l'ospedale?	lo-spay-**dah**-lay
the first aid station?	il pronto soccorso?	eel **pron**-to so-**kor**-so
the elevator?	l'ascensore?	la-shen-**so**-ray
a telephone?	un telefono?	oon tay-**lay**-fo-no
Where are the restrooms?	Dov'è il bagno?	doe-**vay** eel **bahn**-yo
Here/there	Qui/là	kwee/la
Left/right	A sinistra/a destra	a see-**neess**-tra/ a **des**-tra
Straight ahead	Avanti dritto	a-**vahn**-tee **dree**-to
Is it near/far?	È vicino/lontano?	ay vee-**chee**-no/ lon-**tah**-no
I'd like . . .	Vorrei . . .	vo-**ray**
a room	una camera	**oo**-na **kah**-may-ra
the key	la chiave	la kee-**ah**-vay
a newspaper	un giornale	oon jor-**nah**-lay
a stamp	un francobollo	oon frahn-ko-**bo**-lo
I'd like to buy . . .	Vorrei comprare . . .	vo-**ray** kom-**prah**-ray
a cigar	un sigaro	oon see-**gah**-ro
cigarettes	delle sigarette	day-lay see-ga-**ret**-ay
some matches	dei fiammiferi	day-ee fee-ah-**mee**-fer-ee
some soap	una saponetta	**oo**-na sa-po-**net**-a
a city plan	una pianta della città	**oo**-na **pyahn**-ta day-la chee-**tah**
a road map of . . .	una carta stradale di . . .	**oo**-na **cart**-a stra-**dah**-lay dee
a country map	una carta geografica	**oo**-na **cart**-a jay-o-**grah**-fee-ka
a magazine	una rivista	**oo**-na ree-**veess**-ta
envelopes	delle buste	day-lay **booss**-tay
writing paper	della carta da lettere	**day**-la **cart**-a da **let**-air-ay
a postcard	una cartolina	**oo**-na car-toe-**lee**-na
a guidebook	una guida turistica	**oo**-na **gwee**-da too-**reess**-tee-ka
How much is it?	Quanto costa?	**kwahn**-toe **coast**-a
It's expensive/ cheap	È caro/economico	ay **car**-o/ay-ko-no-mee-ko
A little/a lot	Poco/tanto	**po**-ko/**tahn**-to
More/less	Più/meno	pee-**oo**/**may**-no
Enough/too (much)	Abbastanza/troppo	a-bas-**tahn**-sa/**tro**-po
I am sick	Sto male	sto **mah**-lay
Please call a doctor	Chiami un dottore	kee-**ah**-mee oon doe-**toe**-ray
Help!	Aiuto!	a-**yoo**-toe
Stop!	Alt!	ahlt
Fire!	Al fuoco!	ahl **fwo**-ko
Caution/Look out!	Attenzione!	a-ten-**syon**-ay

Dining Out

A bottle of . . .	Una bottiglia di . . .	**oo**-na bo-**tee**-lee-ah dee
A cup of . . .	Una tazza di . . .	**oo**-na **tah**-tsa dee
A glass of . . .	Un bicchiere di . . .	oon bee-key-**air**-ay dee
Bill/check	Il conto	eel **cone**-toe
Bread	Il pane	eel **pah**-nay
Breakfast	La prima colazione	la **pree**-ma ko-la-**tsee**-oh-nay
Cocktail/aperitif	L'aperitivo	la-pay-ree-**tee**-vo
Dinner	La cena	la **chen**-a
Fixed-price menu	Menù a prezzo fisso	may-**noo** a **pret**-so **fee**-so
Fork	La forchetta	la for-**ket**-a
I am diabetic	Ho il diabete	o eel dee-a-**bay**-tay
I am vegetarian	Sono vegetariano/a	**so**-no vay-jay-ta-ree-**ah**-no/a
I'd like . . .	Vorrei . . .	vo-**ray**
I'd like to order	Vorrei ordinare	vo-**ray** or-dee-**nah**-ray
Is service included?	Il servizio è incluso?	eel ser-**vee**-tzee-o ay een-**kloo**-zo
It's good/bad	È buono/cattivo	ay **bwo**-no/ka-tee-vo
It's hot/cold	È caldo/freddo	ay **kahl**-doe/**fred**-o
Knife	Il coltello	eel kol-**tel**-o
Lunch	Il pranzo	eel **prahnt**-so
Menu	Il menù	eel may-**noo**
Napkin	Il tovagliolo	eel toe-va-lee-**oh**-lo
Please give me . . .	Mi dia . . .	mee **dee**-a
Salt	Il sale	eel **sah**-lay
Spoon	Il cucchiaio	eel koo-kee-**ah**-yo
Sugar	Lo zucchero	lo **tsoo**-ker-o
Waiter/Waitress	Cameriere/cameriera	ka-mare-**yer**-ay/ka-mare-**yer**-a
Wine list	La lista dei vini	la **lee**-sta **day**-ee **vee**-nee

INDEX